P9-BZQ-484

## Praise for *The War of the World*

"A hugely ambitious panorama and moral analysis of the military-industrial slaughter of the twentieth century. . . . A heartbreaking, serious and thoughtful survey of human evil that is utterly fascinating and dramatic, and always has something new to tell us. . . . Superb narrative history . . . a sumptuous treasure trove of fresh facts and . . . interpretations."
—Simon Sebag Montefiore, *The New York Times Book Review*

"In *The War of the World*, British historian Niall Ferguson offers a novel analysis of the causes of twentieth-century violence. . . . It is . . . a fascinating read, thanks to Ferguson's gifts as a writer of clear, energetic narrative history."
—*The Washington Post*

"In *The War of the World* [Niall Ferguson] has produced a sweeping and handsomely controlled narrative in which he balances wide-screen storytelling and close-focus anecdote, character sketch, and psychological insight with analysis and counterfactual speculation. Even those who have read widely in twentieth-century history will find fresh, surprising details."
—*The Boston Globe*

"Blends together economic, financial and political analysis in a manner that far too few historians are equipped to do. He is a fine debunker."
—*The Economist*

"With such a theme, Mr. Ferguson has set himself an enormous undertaking, but he is more than up to the task. Again he shows himself to be a writer of extraordinary energy and versatility." —*The Wall Street Journal*

"Ferguson is a skilled storyteller, and he offers many striking reflections on the bloodiest years of the past century, including a compelling analysis of appeasement."
—*The New Yorker*

"Fascinating . . . supremely readable and thought-provoking."
—*Financial Times* (London)

"*The War of the World* sounds abstract and academic, but it's neither. Ferguson tells his tale of evil in human terms. . . . His prose has a most unacademic zip to it. . . . Even readers who disagree with much of Ferguson's dour conclusions will come away from this book informed, impressed."
—Harry Levins, *St. Louis Post-Dispatch*

"A sweeping, big-picture view of the bloodiest century in human history. . . . Ferguson writes with an eye for telling detail. . . . A lucid, blood-soaked study."   —*Kirkus Reviews*

"In this thought-provoking, highly engaging and nearly impossible to put down book, [Ferguson] challenges readers to think outside the box—even if they disagree."   —*Library Journal*

"Compelling . . . [Ferguson's] richly informed analysis overturns many basic assumptions."   —*Publishers Weekly*

"An icon-busting British historian asks why the twentieth century was the bloodiest in history and questions whether Asia, rather than the West, emerged on top at its end."   —*STL Today*

"Clearly Ferguson is not cowed by the size of any topic, including, here, man's inhumanity to man. . . . [*The War of the World*] is . . . a deeply disturbing chronicle of the last century's descent into hell, with World War II the black heart of the epoch's seamless shame."   —*The American Scholar*

"Here is a work of originality and depth, history at its most challenging and controversial. . . . No one . . . can afford to overlook it."   —*The Times* (London)

"Big, bold and brilliantly belligerent."   —*The Sunday Telegraph* (London)

"Deftly paced, continent-crossing account of the last century's 'age of hatred.' . . . It is gripping stuff."   —*The Guardian* (London)

PENGUIN BOOKS

# THE WAR OF THE WORLD

Niall Ferguson is Laurence A. Tisch Professor of History at Harvard University, a Senior Research Fellow of Jesus College, Oxford University, and a Senior Fellow of the Hoover Institution, Stanford University. The bestselling author of *Paper and Iron*, *The House of Rothschild*, *The Pity of War*, *The Cash Nexus*, *Empire*, and *Colossus*, he also writes regularly for newspapers and magazines all over the world. Since 2003 he has written and presented three highly successful television documentary series for British television: *Empire*, *American Colossus*, and, most recently, *The War of the World*. He, his wife, and their three children divide their time between the United States and the United Kingdom.

# NIALL FERGUSON

# The War of the World

## Twentieth-Century Conflict and the Descent of the West

PENGUIN BOOKS

PENGUIN BOOKS

Published by the Penguin Group

Penguin Group (USA) Inc., 375 Hudson Street, New York, New York 10014, U.S.A.
Penguin Group (Canada), 90 Eglinton Avenue East, Suite 700, Toronto,
Ontario, Canada M4P 2Y3 (a division of Pearson Penguin Canada Inc.)
Penguin Books Ltd, 80 Strand, London WC2R 0RL, England
Penguin Ireland, 25 St Stephen's Green, Dublin 2, Ireland (a division of Penguin Books Ltd)
Penguin Group (Australia), 250 Camberwell Road, Camberwell,
Victoria 3124, Australia (a division of Pearson Australia Group Pty Ltd)
Penguin Books India Pvt Ltd, 11 Community Centre, Panchsheel Park, New Delhi – 110 017, India
Penguin Group (NZ), 67 Apollo Drive, Rosedale, North Shore 0632,
New Zealand (a division of Pearson New Zealand Ltd)
Penguin Books (South Africa) (Pty) Ltd, 24 Sturdee Avenue,
Rosebank, Johannesburg 2196, South Africa

Penguin Books Ltd, Registered Offices:
80 Strand, London WC2R 0RL, England

First published in Great Britain by Allen Lane, Penguin Books Ltd 2006
First published in the United States of America by The Penguin Press,
a member of Penguin Group (USA) Inc. 2006
Published in Penguin Books (UK) 2007
Published in Penguin Books (USA) 2007

7   9   10   8

Excerpt from "The Waste Land" from *Collected Poems 1909–1962* by T. S. Eliot.
By permission of Faber and Faber and the T. S. Eliot Estate.

Illustration credits appear on page xi.

THE LIBRARY OF CONGRESS HAS CATALOGED
THE HARDCOVER EDITION AS FOLLOWS:
Ferguson, Niall.
The war of the world : twentieth-century conflict and the descent of the West / Niall Ferguson.
p.   cm.
Includes bibliographical references and index.
ISBN 1-59420-100-5 (hc.)
ISBN 978-0-14-311239-6 (pbk.)
1. War.   2. War—Causes.   3. World politics—20th century.   I. Title.
JZ6385.F47   2006
303.6'6—dc22       2006050304

Printed in the United States of America

*for
Felix,
Freya,
Lachlan
and
Susan*

*Where be these enemies? Capulet, Montague,*
*See what a scourge is laid upon your hate,*
*That heaven finds means to kill your joys with love.*

*Romeo and Juliet, V.iii*

*What is that sound high in the air*
*Murmur of maternal lamentation*
*Who are those hooded hordes swarming*
*Over endless plains, stumbling in cracked earth*
*Ringed by the flat horizon only*
*What is the city over the mountains*
*Cracks and reforms and bursts in the violet air*
*Falling towers*
*Jerusalem Athens Alexandria*
*Vienna London*
*Unreal*

*The Waste Land, V*

# Contents

# CONTENTS

## PART III
## Killing Space

## PART IV
## A Tainted Triumph

# List of Illustrations

*Picture Acknowledgements*

Picture 1; taken from *Source Records of the Great War*, Vol. VII (1928)

Pictures 2–6, 10, 12, 14, 37, 48: AKG images, London

Pictures 7, 13, 15, 40, 43, 44, 46, 47: Hulton Archive/Getty Images

Picture 16: © DACS 2006 (supplied by Bridgeman Art Library)

Picture 21: The David King Collection

Pictures 25, 30: Mary Evans Picture Library

Pictures 26, 38, 49: Empics

Picture 27: Reproduced with permission of Curtis Brown Group Ltd, London, on behalf of the Isaiah Berlin Literary Trust. Copyright © Isaiah Berlin Literary Trust

Picture 28: Ty Rogers

Picture 29: Mrs H. Lappo

Picture 33: Hulton-Deutsch Collection/Corbis

Pictures 34, 35: Auschwitz-Birkenau Museum and Memorial

Picture 42: Time Life Pictures/Getty Images

Picture 45: Ullstein Bild

# List of Maps

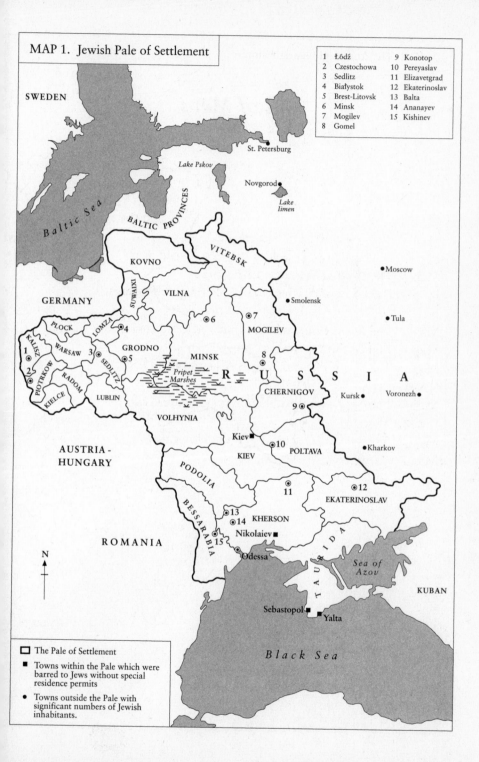

MAP 1. Jewish Pale of Settlement

| 1 Łódź | 9 Konotop |
| 2 Czestochowa | 10 Pereyaslav |
| 3 Sedlitz | 11 Elizavetgrad |
| 4 Białystok | 12 Ekaterinoslav |
| 5 Brest-Litovsk | 13 Balta |
| 6 Minsk | 14 Ananayev |
| 7 Mogilev | 15 Kishinev |
| 8 Gomel | |

SWEDEN

St. Petersburg

Lake Pskov

Novgorod

Lake Ilmen

Baltic Sea

BALTIC PROVINCES

KOVNO

VITEBSK

Moscow

GERMANY

SUWAŁKI

VILNA

Smolensk

Tula

PLOCK

LOMZA

●6

●7

KALISZ

WARSAW

3

GRODNO

MOGILEV

●4

●5

MINSK

R U S S I A

PIOTRKOW

SEDLITZ

RADOM

KIELCE

LUBLIN

Pripet
Marshes

●8

CHERNIGOV

Kursk

Voronezh

AUSTRIA-
HUNGARY

VOLHYNIA

●9

PODOLIA

Kiev

KIEV

●10

POLTAVA

Kharkov

BESSARABIA

●11

●12

EKATERINOSLAV

●13

●14

KHERSON

ROMANIA

●15

Nikolaiev

Odessa

T A U R I D A

Sea of
Azov

KUBAN

Sebastopol

Yalta

Black Sea

N

☐ The Pale of Settlement

■ Towns within the Pale which were
barred to Jews without special
residence permits

● Towns outside the Pale with
significant numbers of Jewish
inhabitants.

MAP 2. The Austro-Hungarian Empire

N

PRUSSIA

SAXONY

*Elbe*

BOHEMIA

Prague •

Iglau •

MORAV

Brünn •

BAVARIA

*Danube*

*Inn*

Linz •

UPPER AUSTRIA

LOWER AUSTRIA

Vienna

Pressb

VORARLBERG

SWITZ.

Innsbruck •

SALZBURG

S T Y R I A

Graz •

TYROL

CARINTHIA

Klagenfurt •

Laibach •

GORZ

CARNIOLA

Agram •

*Save*

• Milan

Venice •

Trieste •

ISTRIA

RIJERA

C R O A T I A

HER

DA

I T A L Y

A D R I A T I C

MAP 3. The German diaspora in the 1920s

NORWAY

NORTH

SEA

SWEDEN

DENMARK

Baltic Sea

UNITED
KINGDOM

Tallin

Ri

L A

LITHUA.

Memel

FREE CITY OF
DANZIG

Königsberg

Białys

Hamburg

R. Weser

NETHERLANDS

Berlin

Posen

Warsaw

Brest–Lit

GERMANY

Cologne

R. Rhine

R. Elbe

Łódź

POLAND

Lu

BELGIUM

Dresden

LUXEMBOURG

Frankfurt

Breslau

Lemberg

Prague

CZECHOSLOVAKIA

Krakow

FRANCE

R. Danube

Munich

Vienna

Pressburg

SWITZERLAND

AUSTRIA

Budapest

Czerno

HUNGARY

ITALY

Trieste

YUGOSLAVIA

R

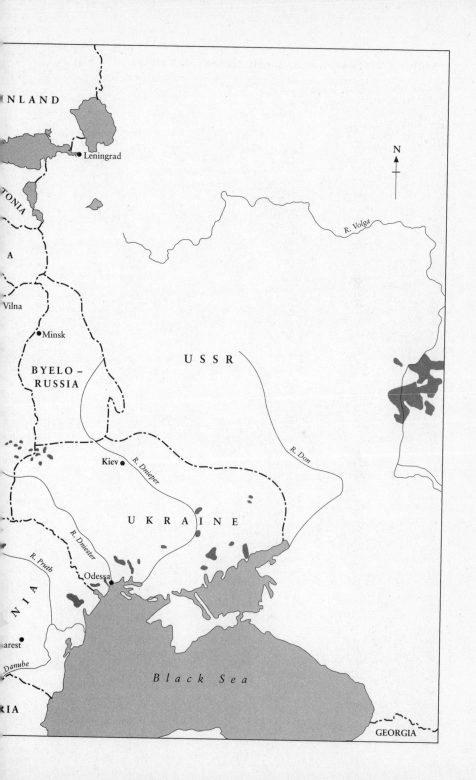

MAP 4. Political boundaries after the Paris peace treaties, c. 1924

ICELAND

*N*

SWEDEN

NORWAY

NORTHERN IRELAND

IRISH FREE STATE

DENMARK

GREAT BRITAIN

NETH.

GERMANY

BELGIUM

Demilitarized Rhineland

CZECH

LUX.

*Atlantic Ocean*

SWITZ.

AUSTRIA

FRANCE

YU

*Adriatic S*

ITALY

PORTUGAL

Corsica

SPAIN

Sardinia

*Mediterranean Sea*

Sicily

Gibraltar (GB)

MOROCCO

ALGERIA

TUNIS

Malta

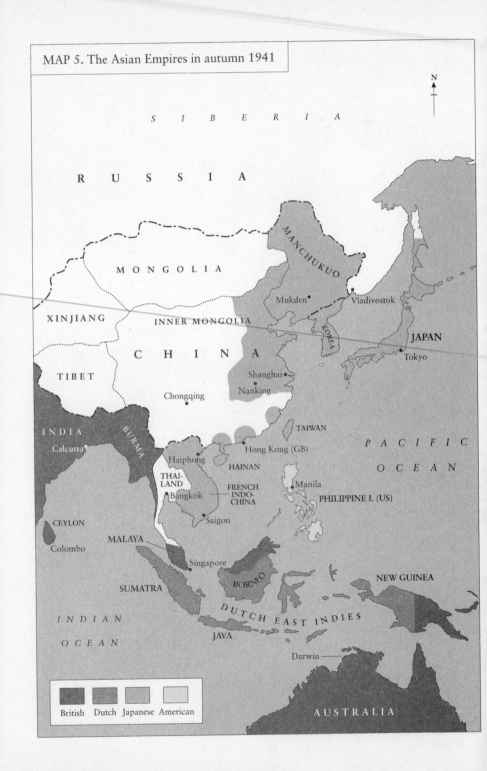

MAP 5. The Asian Empires in autumn 1941

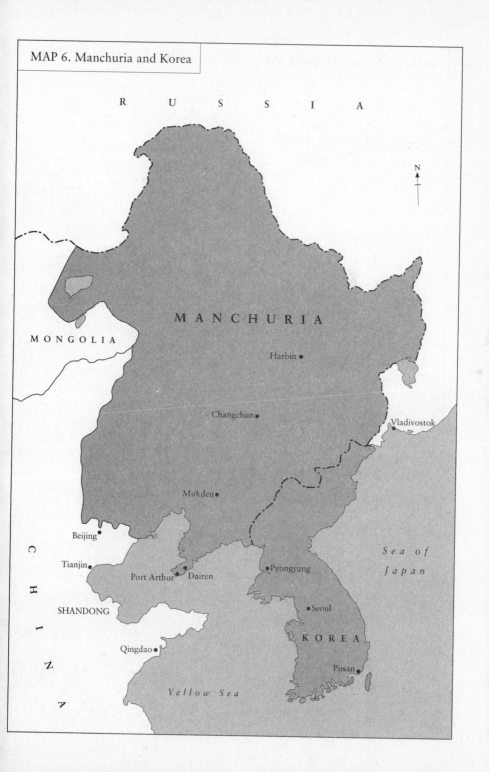

MAP 6. Manchuria and Korea

RUSSIA

N

MONGOLIA

MANCHURIA

Harbin

Changchun

Vladivostok

Mukden

Beijing

Sea of
Japan

CHINA

Tianjin

Port Arthur  Dairen

Pyongyang

SHANDONG

Seoul

KOREA

Qingdao

Pusan

Yellow Sea

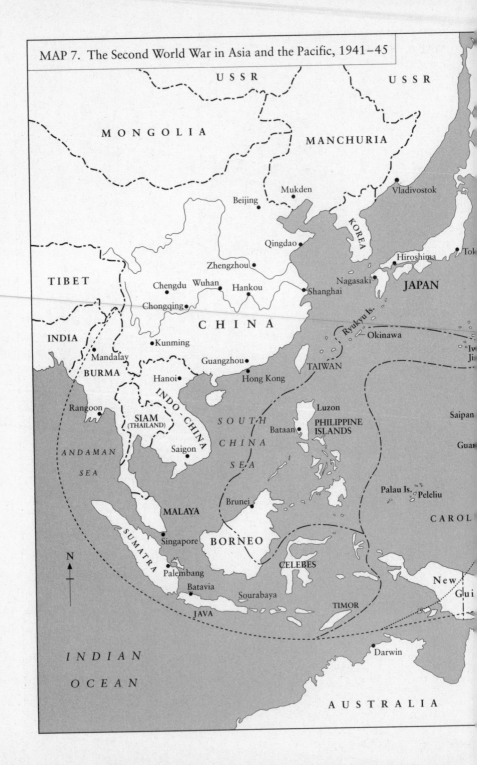

MAP 7. The Second World War in Asia and the Pacific, 1941–45

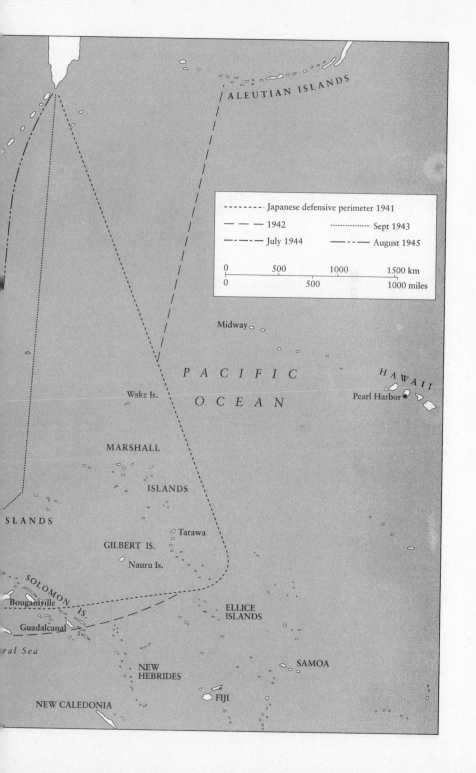

ALEUTIAN ISLANDS

- - - - - - Japanese defensive perimeter 1941
— — — 1942                  ·············· Sept 1943
—·—·— July 1944              —··—··— August 1945

| 0 | 500 | 1000 | 1500 km |

| 0 | 500 | 1000 miles |

Midway

P A C I F I C

HAWAII

Wake Is.

O C E A N

Pearl Harbor

MARSHALL

ISLANDS

SLANDS

Tarawa

GILBERT IS.

Nauru Is.

SOLOMON IS.

Bougainville

ELLICE
ISLANDS

Guadalcanal

ral Sea

NEW
HEBRIDES

SAMOA

NEW CALEDONIA

FIJI

MAP 8. The Nazi Empire at its maximum extent, autumn 1942

ICELAND

*Norwegian Sea*

N

NORWAY

SWEDEN

*Atlantic Ocean*

Northern Ireland

DENMARK

Danz

EIRE

GREAT BRITAIN

Hamburg ● Berlin

NETH.

BELGIUM

GREATER GERMANY

Prague

REICHSPROTECTORATE BOHEMIA–MORAVIA

FRANCE

SWITZ.

Vienna

CRO

PORTUGAL

*Adriatic*

I T A L Y

Corsica

SPAIN

*Sardinia*

*Mediterranean Sea*

*Sicily*

MOROCCO

ALGERIA

TUNISIA

Malta

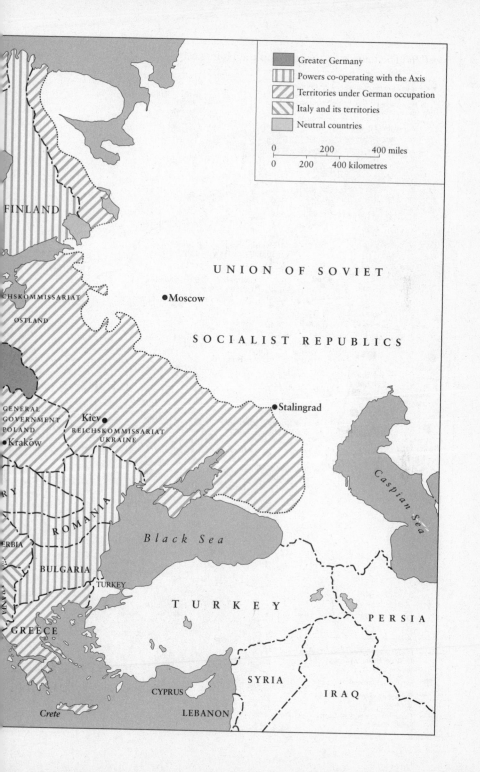

Greater Germany
Powers co-operating with the Axis
Territories under German occupation
Italy and its territories
Neutral countries

0          200          400 miles
0     200     400 kilometres

FINLAND

UNION OF SOVIET

●Moscow

CHSKOMMISSARIAT

OSTLAND

SOCIALIST REPUBLICS

GENERAL
GOVERNMENT    Kiev●                          ●Stalingrad
POLAND        REICHSKOMMISSARIAT
●Kraków       UKRAINE

RY                                                        Caspian Sea

ROMANIA

ERBIA                              Black Sea

BULGARIA
          TURKEY

TURKEY                    PERSIA

GREECE

CYPRUS                    SYRIA

Crete         LEBANON                    IRAQ

# MAP 9. The Pale of Settlement and the Holocaust

• Cities and towns conquered by the Germans between June and December 1941, in which the majority of the Jewish inhabitants were at once murdered. This map shows only a portion of such towns, with the approximate number of Jews killed.

*Baltic Sea*

N

*The Front Line in January 1942*

Riga 27,000

Dvinsk 30,000

Braslav 1,800

• Moscow

Kovno 3,800

Glubokoye 2,500

Vitebsk 16,000

Troki 550

Vileika 4,000

Rudnya 1,200

Smolensk 3,000

Vilna 70,000

Lida 6,000

Mir 1,200

Borisov 7,620

Treblinka 800,000

Białystok 5,000

Slonim 10,000

Nesvizh 4,000

Mogilev 4,844

Chelmno 350,000

Bobruisk 179

Gomel 4,000

Sobibor 250,000

Kovel 27,000

Pinsk 30,000

**UNDER GERMAN**

Majdanek 250,000

Sarny 3,000

Auschwitz-Birkenau

Rovno 22,000

Zhitomir 7,000

Kiev 33,711

**OCCUPATION**

Bełżec 650,000

Babi Yar 100,000

Kharkov 20,000

Lutsk 21,000

*R*

Berdichev 35,000

Poltava 12,000

Vinnitsa 15,000

*U*

*S*

*S*

*I*

*A*

Uman 30,000

Dnepropetrovsk 37,000

Taganrog 2,000

Mariupol 90,000

Nikolaev 94,000

Melitopol 2,000

Rostov -on-Don 18,000

Odessa 60,000

Simferopol 10,000

Kerch 7,000

*Black Sea*

The boundary between Nazi Germany and the Soviet Union, 28 September 1939– 26 June 1941

■ Extermination camps

–·– The eastern boundary of the Pale of Settlement, 1835–1914

– · – The western frontier of Tsarist Russia, 1815–1914

MAP 10. Germany partitioned, 1945

Kiel

Hamburg

Bremen

Hanover

Dusseldorf

Cologne

Bonn

Frankfurt

Nuremberg

Stuttgart

Munich

Salzburg

Vienna

Berlin

Leipzig

Dresden

Prague

NETHERLANDS

FRANCE

SWITZERLAND

POLAND

Gdánsk

CZECHOSLOVAKIA

AUSTRIA

N

- - - German borders 1937

——— Division between East and West
Germany after 1949

*Post war administrative regions*

British

American

French

Soviet

The division of Berlin

Tegel

Charlottenburg

Gatow

Pankow

Tempelhof
Zehlendorf

Treptow

# A note on transliteration and other linguistic conventions

There are at least seven different systems for the transliteration of Mandarin Chinese into Roman characters. Broadly speaking, the English-speaking world switched from one system (Wade-Giles) to another (Hanyu Pinyin) towards the end of the period covered by this book, partly in response to its official adoption by the People's Republic of China and the International Organization for Standardization. Thus, to take perhaps the most obvious example, Peking became Beijing.

On the advice of colleagues who specialize in Asian history, I have adopted the Pinyin system, despite the obvious risk of anachronism. The exceptions are those earlier Wade-Giles romanizations (notably Yangtze, Chiang Kai-shek and Nanking) which have become too familiar to readers of English for it to be anything but confusing to replace them. Similar problems arise with the romanization of Russian names. I have tried as far as possible to use the Anglo-American BGN/PCGN system.

In this context, the significance of the name 'Manchuria' is worth a brief comment. It was the contemporary Japanese and European designation for China's three north-eastern provinces, Liaoning, Jilin, and Heilongjiang, and was intended to emphasize the region's history as the ancestral home of the last imperial dynasty, the Qing. It was not an integral part of pre-Qing China, a point of some importance to Russian and Japanese would-be colonizers.

Finally, Japanese names are rendered in the way usual in Japan, with the given name second, as in 'Ferguson Niall'.

# Introduction

*The houses caved in as they dissolved at its touch, and darted out flames; the trees changed to fire with a roar ... So you understand the roaring wave of fear that swept through the greatest city in the world just as Monday was dawning – the stream of flight rising swiftly to a torrent, lashing in a foaming tumult round the railway stations ... Did they dream they might exterminate us?*

H. G. Wells, *The War of the Worlds*

## THE LETHAL CENTURY

Published on the eve of the twentieth century, H. G. Wells's *The War of the Worlds* (1898) is much more than just a seminal work of science fiction. It is also a kind of Darwinian morality tale, and at the same time a work of singular prescience. In the century after the publication of his book, scenes like the ones Wells imagined became a reality in cities all over the world – not just in London, where Wells set his tale, but in Brest-Litovsk, Belgrade and Berlin; in Smyrna, Shanghai and Seoul.

Invaders approach the outskirts of a city. The inhabitants are slow to grasp their vulnerability. But the invaders possess lethal weapons: armoured vehicles, flame throwers, poison gas, aircraft. They use these indiscriminately and mercilessly against soldiers and civilians alike. The city's defences are overrun. As the invaders near the city, panic reigns. People flee their homes in confusion; swarms of refugees clog the roads and railways. The task of massacring them is made easy. People are slaughtered like beasts. Finally, all that remains are smouldering ruins and piles of desiccated corpses.

All of this destruction and death Wells imagined while pedalling around peaceful Woking and Chertsey on his newly acquired bicycle. Of course (and here was the stroke of genius), he cast Martians as the perpetrators. When such scenes subsequently became a reality, however, those responsible were not Martians but other human beings – even if they often justified the slaughter by labelling their victims as 'aliens' or 'subhumans'. It was not a war between worlds that the twentieth century witnessed, but rather a war of the world.

The hundred years after 1900 were without question the bloodiest century in modern history, far more violent in relative as well as absolute terms than any previous era. Significantly larger percentages of the world's population were killed in the two world wars that dominated the century than had been killed in any previous conflict of comparable geopolitical magnitude (see Figure I.1). Although wars between 'great powers' were more frequent in earlier centuries, the world wars were unparalleled in their severity (battle deaths per year) and concentration (battle deaths per nation-year). By any measure, the Second World War was the greatest man-made catastrophe of all time. And yet, for all the attention they have attracted from historians, the world wars were only two of many twentieth-century conflicts. Death tolls quite probably passed the million mark in more than a dozen others.* Comparable fatalities were caused by the genocidal or 'politicidal' wars waged against civilian populations by the Young Turk regime during the First World War, the Soviet regime from the 1920s until the 1950s and the National Socialist regime in Germany between 1933 and 1945, to say nothing of the tyranny of Pol Pot in Cambodia. There was not a single year before, between or after the

* The Mexican Revolutionary War (1910–20), the Russian civil war (1917–21), the civil war in China (1926–37), the Korean War (1950–53), the intermittent civil wars in Rwanda and Burundi (1963–95), the post-colonial wars in Indo-China (1960–75), the Ethiopian civil war (1962–92), the Nigerian civil war (1966–70), the Bangladeshi war of independence (1971), the civil war in Mozambique (1975–93), the war in Afghanistan (1979–2001), the Iran–Iraq War (1980–88) and the on-going civil wars in Sudan (since 1983) and Congo (since 1998). Before 1900 only the rebellions of nineteenth-century China, in particular the Taiping Rebellion, caused comparable amounts of lethal violence: see Appendix.

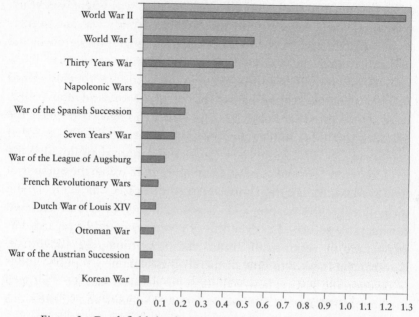

*Figure I.1* **Battlefield deaths as percentages of world population**

world wars that did not see large-scale organized violence in one part of the world or another.

Why? What made the twentieth century, and particularly the fifty years from 1904 until 1953, so bloody? That this era was exceptionally violent may seem paradoxical. After all, the hundred years after 1900 were a time of unparalleled progress. In real terms, it has been estimated, average per capita global domestic product – an approximate measure of the average individual's income, allowing for fluctuations in the value of money – increased by little more than 50 per cent between 1500 and 1870. Between 1870 and 1998, however, it increased by a factor of more than six and a half. Expressed differently, the compound annual growth rate was nearly thirteen times higher between 1870 and 1998 than it was between 1500 and 1870. By the end of the twentieth century, thanks to myriad technological advances and improvements in knowledge, human beings on average lived longer and better lives than at any time in history. In a substantial proportion of the world, men succeeded in avoiding premature death, thanks to improved nutrition and the conquest of infectious diseases.

Life expectancy in the United Kingdom in 1990 was seventy-six years, compared with forty-eight in 1900. Infant mortality was one twenty-fifth of what it had been. Men not only lived longer; they grew bigger and taller. Old age was less miserable; the rate of chronic illness among American men in their sixties in the 1990s was roughly a third of what it had been at the start of the century. More and more people were able to flee what Karl Marx and Friedrich Engels had called 'the idiocy of rural life', so that between 1900 and 1980 the percentage of the world's population living in large cities more than doubled. By working more efficiently, people had more than treble the amount of time available for leisure. Those who spent their free time campaigning for political representation and the redistribution of income achieved considerable success. Barely a fifth of countries could be regarded as democratic in 1900; in the 1990s the proportion rose above half. Governments ceased to provide merely the fundamental public goods of defence and justice; new welfare states evolved that were pledged to eliminate 'Want . . . Disease, Ignorance, Squalor and Idleness', as the 1944 Beveridge Report put it.

To explain, in the context of all these advances, the extraordinary violence of the twentieth century, it is not enough simply to say that there were more people living closer together, or more destructive weapons. No doubt it was easier to perpetrate mass murder by dropping high explosives on crowded cities than it had once been to put dispersed rural populations to the sword. But if those were sufficient explanations, the end of the century would have been more violent than the beginning and the middle. In the 1990s the world's population for the first time exceeded six billion, more than three times what it had been when the First World War broke out. But there was actually a marked decline in the amount of armed conflict in the last decade of the century. The highest recorded rates of military mobilization and mortality in relation to total population were clearly in the first half of the century, during and immediately after the world wars. Moreover, weaponry today is clearly much more destructive than it was in 1900. But some of the worst violence of the century was perpetrated with the crudest of weapons: rifles, axes, knives and machetes (most obviously in Central Africa in the 1990s, but also in Cambodia in the 1970s). Elias Canetti once tried to imagine a world in which 'all weapons [were] abolished and in the next war only biting [was] allowed'. Can we be sure there would be no genocides in such a radically disarmed world? To understand why the last hundred years were so destructive of human life, we therefore need to look for the motives behind the murders.

When I was a schoolboy, the history textbooks offered a variety of explanations for twentieth-century violence. Sometimes they related it to economic crisis, as if depressions and recessions could explain political conflict. A favourite device was to relate the rise of unemployment in Weimar Germany to the rise of the Nazi vote and Adolf Hitler's 'seizure' of power, which in turn was supposed to explain the Second World War. But, I came to wonder, might not rapid economic growth sometimes have been just as destabilizing as economic crisis? Then there was the theory that the century was all about class conflict – that revolutions were one of the main causes of violence. But were not ethnic divisions actually more important than the supposed struggle between proletariat and bourgeoisie? Another argument was that the twentieth century's problems were the consequences of extreme versions of political ideologies, notably communism (extreme socialism) and fascism (extreme nationalism), as well as earlier evil 'isms', notably imperialism. But what about the role of traditional systems like religions, or of other apparently non-political ideas and assumptions that nevertheless had violent implications? And just who was fighting the twentieth century's wars? In the books I read as a boy, the leading roles were always played by nation states: Britain, Germany, France, Russia, the United States and so on. But was it not the case that some or all of these polities were in some measure multinational rather than national – were, indeed, empires rather than states? Above all, the old history books told the story of the twentieth century as a kind of protracted, painful but ultimately pleasing triumph of the West. The heroes (Western democracies) were confronted by a succession of villains (the Germans, the Japanese, the Russians) but ultimately good always triumphed over evil. The world wars and the Cold War were thus morality plays on a global stage. But were they? And did the West really win the hundred years war that was the twentieth century?

Let me now reformulate those preliminary schoolboy thoughts in rather more rigorous terms. In what follows, I shall argue that historians' traditional explanations for the violence of the twentieth century are necessary but not sufficient. Changes in technology, in particular the increased destructiveness of modern weaponry, were important, no doubt, but they were merely responses to more deep-seated desires to kill more efficiently. There is in fact no correlation over the century between the destructiveness of weaponry and the incidence of violence.

Nor can economic crises explain all the violent upheavals of the century. As noted already, perhaps the most familiar causal chain in modern historiography leads from the Great Depression to the rise of fascism and the outbreak of war. Yet on closer inspection this pleasing story falls apart. Not all the countries affected by the Great Depression became fascist regimes; nor did all the fascist regimes engage in wars of aggression. Nazi Germany started the war in Europe, but only after its economy had recovered from the Depression. The Soviet Union, which started the war on Hitler's side, was cut off from the world economic crisis, yet ended up mobilizing and losing more soldiers than any other combatant. For the century as a whole, no general rule is discernible. Some wars came after periods of growth; others were the causes rather than the consequences of economic crises. And some severe economic crises did not lead to wars. Certainly, it is now impossible to argue (though Marxists long tried to) that the First World War was the result of a crisis of capitalism; on the contrary, it abruptly terminated a period of extraordinary global economic integration with relatively high growth and low inflation.

It can of course be argued that wars happen for reasons that have nothing to do with economics. Eric Hobsbawm called 'the Short Twentieth Century' (1914–91) 'an era of religious wars, though the most militant and bloodthirsty religions were secular ideologies of nineteenth-century vintage'. At the other end of the ideological spectrum, Paul Johnson blamed the century's violence on 'the rise of moral relativism, the decline of personal responsibility [and] the repudiation of Judaeo-Christian values'. Yet the rise of new ideologies or the decline of old values cannot be regarded as causes of violence in their own right, important though it is to understand the intellectual origins of totalitarianism. There have been extreme belief-systems on offer for most of modern history, but only at certain times and in certain places have they been widely embraced and acted upon. Anti-Semitism is a good example in this regard. Likewise, to attribute responsibility for wars to a few mad or bad men is to repeat the error upon which Tolstoy heaped scorn in *War and Peace*. Megalomaniacs may order men to invade Russia, but why do the men obey?

Nor is it convincing to attribute the violence of the century primarily to the emergence of the modern nation state. Although twentieth-century polities developed unprecedented capabilities for mobilizing masses of people, these could be, and were, as easily harnessed to peaceful as to violent ends. States could certainly wield more 'social control' in the 1930s than ever before. They employed legions of civil servants, tax collectors and policemen. They provided education, pensions and in some cases subsidized insurance against ill health and unemployment. They regulated if they did not actually own the railways and roads. If they wanted to conscript every able-bodied adult male citizen, they could. Yet all of these capabilities developed even further in the decades after 1945, while the frequency of large-scale war declined. Indeed, it was generally the states with the most all-embracing welfare states that were the least likely to be involved in war in the 1950s, 1960s and 1970s. Just as it was an earlier revolution in warfare that had transformed the early modern state, it may well have been total war that made the welfare state, creating that capacity for planning, direction and regulation without which the Beveridge Report or Johnson's Great Society would have been inconceivable. It was surely not the welfare state that made total war.

Did it matter how states were governed? It has become fashionable among political scientists to posit a correlation between democracy and peace, on the ground that democracies tend not to go to war with one another. On that basis, of course, the long-run rise of democracy during the twentieth century should have reduced the incidence of war. It may have reduced the incidence of war between states; there is, however, at least some evidence that waves of democratization in the 1920s, 1960s and 1980s were followed by increases in the number of civil wars and wars of secession. This brings us to a central point. To consider twentieth-century conflict purely in terms of warfare between states is to overlook the importance of organized violence within states. The most notorious example is, of course, the war waged by the Nazis and their collaborators against the Jews, nearly six million of whom perished. The Nazis simultaneously sought to annihilate a variety of other social groups deemed to be 'unworthy of life', notably mentally ill and homosexual Germans, the social elite of occupied Poland and the Sinti and Roma peoples. In all, more than three million people from these other groups were murdered. Prior to these events, Stalin had perpetrated comparable acts of violence against national minorities within the Soviet Union as well as executing or incarcerating millions of Russians guilty or merely suspected of political dissidence. Of around four million non-Russians who were deported to Siberia and Central Asia, at least 1.6 million are estimated to have died as a result of the hardships inflicted on them. A minimum estimate for the total victims of all political violence in the Soviet Union between 1928 and 1953 is twenty-one million. Yet genocide* predated totalitarianism. As we shall see, the policies of forced resettlement and deliberate murder directed against Christian minorities in the last years of the Ottoman Empire amounted to genocide according to the 1948 definition of the term.

In short, the extreme violence of the twentieth century was highly variegated. It was not all a matter of armed men clashing. Of the total deaths attributed to the Second World War, half at least were of civilians. Sometimes they were the victims of discrimination, as when

---

* The United Nations Convention on the Prevention and Punishment of the Crime of Genocide of 1948 is a widely misunderstood document. Its second Article sets out a clear definition of the word which Raphael Lemkin had coined four years before in his book *Axis Rule in Occupied Europe*. It covers 'any of the following acts committed with intent to destroy, in whole or in part, a national, ethnical, racial or religious group, as such:

    a) Killing members of the group;

    b) Causing serious bodily or mental harm to members of the group;

    c) Deliberately inflicting on the group conditions of life calculated to bring about its physical destruction in whole or in part;

    d) Imposing measures intended to prevent births within the group;

    e) Forcibly transferring children of the group to another group.'

It is not only genocide that is declared a punishable offence by the Convention, but also conspiracy to commit genocide, direct and public incitement to commit genocide, the attempt to commit genocide and complicity in genocide.

people were selected for murder on the basis of their race or class. Sometimes they were the victims of indiscriminate violence, as when the British and American air forces bombed whole cities to rubble. Sometimes they were murdered by foreign invaders; sometimes by their own neighbours. Clearly, then, any explanation for the sheer scale of the carnage needs to go beyond the realm of conventional military analysis.

Three things seem to me necessary to explain the extreme violence of the twentieth century, and in particular why so much of it happened at certain times, notably the early 1940s, and in certain places, specifically Central and Eastern Europe, Manchuria and Korea. These may be summarized as ethnic conflict, economic volatility and empires in decline. By ethnic conflict, I mean major discontinuities in the social relations between certain ethnic groups, specifically the breakdown of sometimes quite far-advanced processes of assimilation. This process was greatly stimulated in the twentieth century by the dissemination of the hereditary principle in theories of racial difference (even as that principle was waning in the realm of politics) and by the political fragmentation of 'borderland' regions of ethnically mixed settlement. By economic volatility I mean the frequency and amplitude of changes in the rate of economic growth, prices, interest rates and employment, with all the associated social stresses and strains. And by empires in decline I mean the decomposition of the multinational European empires that had dominated the world at the beginning of the century and the challenge posed to them by the emergence of new 'empire-states' in Turkey, Russia, Japan and Germany. This is also what I have in mind when I identify 'the descent of the West' as the most important development of the twentieth century. Powerful though the United States was at the end of the Second World War – the apogee of its unspoken empire – it was still much less powerful than the European empires had been forty-five years before.

# GENE POOLS

Not without reason, Hermann Göring explicitly called the Second World War 'the great racial war'. That was indeed how many contemporaries experienced it. The importance then attached to notions of racial difference now seems rather strange. The science of modern genetics has revealed that human beings are remarkably alike. In terms of our DNA we are, without a shadow of a doubt, one species, whose origins can be traced back to Africa between 100,000 and 200,000 years ago, and who began to spread into new continents only as recently as 60,000 years ago – in evolutionary terms, the proverbial blink of an eye. The differences we associate with racial identities are superficial: pigmentation (which is darker in the melanocytes of peoples whose ancestors lived close to the equator), physiognomy (which makes eyes narrower and noses shorter at the eastern end of the great Eurasian landmass) and hair type. Beneath the skin, we are all quite similar. That is a reflection of our shared origins.* To be sure, geographical dispersion meant that humans formed groups which became physically quite distinct over time. That explains why the Chinese look quite different from, say, the Scots. However, outright 'speciation' – to be precise, the development of 'isolating barriers' that would have made interbreeding impossible – did not have time to subdivide the species *Homo sapiens*. Indeed, the genetic record makes it clear that, despite their outward differences and despite the obstacles of distance and mutual incomprehension, the different 'races' have been interbreeding since the very earliest times. Luigi Luca Cavalli-Sforza and his collaborators have shown that most Europeans are descended from farmers who migrated northwards and westwards from the Middle East. The DNA record suggests that there were successive waves of such migration, attended always by some mingling of the incomers with indigenous nomads. The great *Völkerwanderung* ('wandering of the peoples') of the late Roman Empire left a similar

* All the human mitochondrial DNA sequences that exist today are descended from that of one African woman, just as all the Y chromosomes can be traced back to that of one man. Indeed, it has been estimated that all the human DNA in existence today originated with as few as 86,000 individuals.

genetic legacy. Most striking of all have been the consequences of the modern migrations associated with the European discovery of the New World in the late fifteenth century and the subsequent era of conquest, colonization and concubinage. Biologists today call the process 'demic diffusion'. Nineteenth-century racists spoke of 'miscegenation'; Noël Coward simply called it 'the urge to merge'. But the phenomenon was already a familiar one when Shakespeare wrote *Othello* (whose mixed marriage is doomed more by his credulity than his colour) and *The Merchant of Venice* (which also touches on the issue, notably when Portia tests her suitors).

The results are plainly legible to those who study the human genome today. Between a fifth and a quarter of the DNA of most African-Americans can be traced back to Europeans. At least half of the inhabitants of Hawaii are of 'mixed' ancestry. Likewise, the DNA of today's Japanese population indicates that there was intermarriage between early settlers from Korea and the indigenous Jomonese people. Most of the Y chromosomes found in Jewish males are the same as those found among other Middle Eastern men; for all their bitter enmity, Palestinians and Israelis are genetically not so very different. The evolutionist Richard Lewontin famously calculated that around 85 per cent of the total amount of genetic variation in humans occurs among individuals in an average population; only 6 per cent occurs among races. The genetic variants that affect skin colour, hair type and facial features involve an insignificant amount of the billions of nucleotides in an individual's DNA. To some biologists, this means that, strictly speaking, human races do not exist.

Others might prefer to say that they are in the process of ceasing to exist. A generation of American social scientists working during and after the 1960s documented the rise of interracial marriage in the post-war United States, portraying it as the most important measure of assimilation in American life. Though 'multi-culturalism' has done much to challenge the idea that assimilation should always and everywhere be the goal of ethnic minorities, a rising rate of intermarriage is still widely regarded as a key indicator of diminishing racial prejudice or conflict. In the words of two leading American sociologists, 'rates of intermarriage ... are particularly good indications of the acceptability of different groups and of social integration'. The US census currently distinguishes between four 'racial' categories: 'black', 'white', 'Native American' and 'Asian or Pacific Islander'. On this basis, one in twenty children in the United States is of mixed origin, in that their parents do not both belong to the same racial category. The number of such mixed-race couples quadrupled between 1990 and 2000, to roughly 1.5 million.

And yet throughout the twentieth century men repeatedly thought and acted as if the physically distinctive 'races' *were* separate species, categorizing this group or that group as somehow 'subhuman'. While 'demic diffusion' has occurred peacefully and even imperceptibly in some settings, in others interracial relationships have been viewed as deeply dangerous. How, then, are we to explain this central puzzle: the willingness of groups of men to identify one another as aliens when they are all biologically so very similar? For it was this willingness that lay at the root of much of the twentieth century's worst violence. How could Göring's 'great racial war' happen if there were no races?

Two evolutionary constraints help to explain the shallowness but also the persistence of racial differences. The first is that when men were few and far between – when life was 'solitary, poor, nasty, brutish and short', as it was for 99 per cent of the time our species has existed – the overriding imperatives were to hunt or gather sufficient food and to reproduce. Men formed small groups because cooperation improved the individual's chances of doing both. However, tribes that came into contact with one another were inevitably in competition for scarce resources. Hence, conflict could take the form of plunder – the seizure by violence of another tribe's means of subsistence – and downright murder of unrelated strangers to get rid of potential sexual rivals. Man, so some neo-Darwinians argue, is programmed by his genes to protect his kin and to fight 'the Other'. To be sure, a warrior tribe that succeeded in defeating a rival tribe would not necessarily act rationally if it killed all its members. Given the importance of reproduction, it would make more sense to appropriate the rival tribe's fertile females as well as its food. In that sense, even the evolutionary logic that produces tribal violence also promotes interbreeding, as captured womenfolk become the victors' sexual partners.

Nevertheless, there may be a biological check on this impulse to rape alien females. For there is evidence from the behaviour of both humans and other species that nature does not necessarily favour breeding between genetically very different members of the same species. No doubt there are sound biological reasons for the more or less universal taboos on incest in human societies, since inbreeding with siblings increases the risk that a genetic abnormality may manifest itself in offspring. On the other hand, a preference for distant relatives or complete strangers as mates would have been a handicap in prehistoric times. A species of hunter-gatherers that could only reproduce successfully with genetically (and geographically) distant individuals would not have lasted long. Sure enough, there is strong empirical evidence to suggest that 'optimal outbreeding' is achieved with a surprisingly small degree of genealogical separation. A first cousin may actually be biologically preferable as a mate to a wholly unrelated stranger. The very high levels of cousin-marriage that used to be common among Jews and still prevail among the highly endogamous Samaritans have resulted in remarkably few genetic abnormalities. Conversely, when a Chinese woman marries a European man, the chances are relatively high that their blood groups may be incompatible, so that only the first child they conceive will be viable. Finally, it must be significant in its own right that separate human populations so quickly developed such distinctive facial characteristics. Some evolutionary biologists argue that this was a result not just of 'genetic drift' but of 'sexual selection' – in other words, a culturally triggered and somewhat arbitrary preference for eye-folds in Asia or long noses in Europe quite rapidly accentuated precisely those characteristics in populations that were isolated from one another. Like attracted and continues to attract like; those who are drawn to 'the Other' may in fact be atypical in their sexual predilections.

A further possible barrier to interbreeding is that races may have a 'sociobiological' function as extended kinship groups, practising a diffuse kind of nepotism that stems from our innate desire to reproduce our genes not only directly through sex but also indirectly by protecting our cousins and other relatives. Human beings do seem predisposed to trust members of their own race as traditionally defined (in terms of skin colour, hair type and physiognomy) more than members of other races – though how far this can be explained in

evolutionary terms and how far in terms of inculcated cultural prejudice is clearly open to question. Taken together, these factors may
help to explain why races seem to be dissolving rather slowly, despite
the unprecedented mobility and interaction of the modern era. Recent
work on 'microsatellite markers' has challenged the view that in
strictly biological terms races do not really exist, showing that American ethnic groups identifying themselves as, variously, white, African-
American, East Asian and Hispanic *are* in some respects genetically
distinguishable. The key point to grasp is the fundamental tension
between our inherent capacity for interbreeding and the persistence
of discernible genetic differences. Racial differences may be genetically
few, but human beings seem to be designed to attach importance to
them.

It may be objected that the historian, especially the modern historian, has no business dabbling in evolutionary biology. Is not his
proper concern the activity of civilized man, not primitive man? 'Civilization' is, of course, the name we give to forms of human organization
superior to the hunter-gathering tribe. With the advent of systematic
agriculture between 4,000 and 10,000 years ago, people became less
mobile; at the same time, more reliable supplies of food meant that
their tribes could become much larger. Divisions of labour developed
between cultivators, warriors, priests and rulers. Yet civilized settlements were always vulnerable to raids by unreconstructed tribes, who
were hardly likely to leave undisturbed such concentrations of the
nutritious and the nubile. And even when – as happened gradually
over time – most human beings opted for the pleasures of the settled
life, there was no guarantee that settled societies would coexist peacefully. Civilizations geographically distant from one another might
trade amicably with one another, allowing the gradual emergence of
an international division of labour. But it was just as possible for one
civilization to make war on another, for the same base motives that
had actuated man in prehistoric times: to expropriate nutritional and
reproductive resources. Historians, it is true, can study only those
human organizations sophisticated enough to keep enduring records.
But no matter how complex the administrative structure we study, we
should not lose sight of the basic instincts buried within even the most
civilized men. These instincts were to be unleashed time and again

after 1900. They were a large part of what made the Second World War so ferocious.

## DIASPORAS AND PALES

'Two peoples never meet,' the American anthropologist Melville J. Herskovits once wrote, 'but they mingle their blood.' Mingling, however, is only one of a range of options when two diverse human populations meet. The minority group may remain distinct for breeding purposes but become integrated into the majority group in all or some other respects (language, religious belief, dress, lifestyle). Alternatively, interbreeding can go on, at least for a time, but one or both of the two groups may nevertheless preserve or even adopt distinct cultural or ethnic identities. Here is an important distinction. Whereas 'race' is a matter of inherited physical characteristics, transmitted from parents to children in DNA, 'ethnicity' is a combination of language, custom and ritual, inculcated in the home, the school and the temple. It is perfectly possible for a genetically intermixed population to split into two or more biologically indistinguishable but culturally differentiated ethnic groups. The process may be voluntary, but it may also be based on coercion – notably where major changes of religious belief are concerned. One or both groups may even opt for residential and other forms of segregation; the majority may insist that the minority lives in a clearly delineated space, or the minority may choose to do so for its own reasons. The two groups may cordially ignore one another, or there may be friction, perhaps leading to civil strife or one-sided massacres. The groups may fight one another or one group may submit to expulsion by the other. Genocide is the extreme case, in which one group attempts to annihilate the other.

Why, if minorities face such risks by not assimilating, do ethnic identities persist, even in cases where no biological distinction exists? There are, to be sure, fewer ethnic groups in the world today than there were a century ago; witness the decline in the number of living languages. Yet despite the best efforts of the global market and the nation state to impose cultural uniformity, many minority cultures have proved remarkably resilient. Indeed, persecution has sometimes tended to strengthen the self-consciousness of the persecuted. Passing on an inherited culture may simply be gratifying in its own right; we enjoy hearing our children singing the songs our parents taught us. A more functional interpretation is that ethnic groups can provide valuable networks of trust in nascent markets. The obvious cost of such networks is, of course, that their very success may arouse the antagonism of other ethnic groups. Some 'market-dominant minorities' are especially vulnerable to discrimination and even expropriation; their tightly knit communities are economically strong but politically weak. While this may be true of the Chinese diaspora* in parts of Asia today, it also has applicability to the Armenians in the Ottoman Empire before the First World War or the Jews in Central and Eastern Europe before the Second. However, because exceptions suggest themselves (the Scots were unquestionably a 'market-dominant minority' throughout the British Empire, but aroused minimal hostility), two qualifications need to be added. The first is that the economic dominance of a vulnerable minority may matter less than its political lack of dominance. It is not only wealthy minorities that are persecuted; by no means all the European Jews were rich, and the Sinti and Roma were among Europe's poorest people when the Nazis condemned them to annihilation. The crucial factor may have been their lack of formal and informal political representation. The second qualification is that, if an ethnic group is to be deprived of its rights, property or existence, it cannot be too well armed. Where there are two ethnic groups, both of which have weapons, civil war is more likely than genocide.

Of considerably less importance is the relative size of an ethnic minority. There are, indeed, cases when a majority population was the victim of violent persecution by a minority, counter-intuitive though that may be. As the people of predominantly Jewish cities in the Pale of Settlement† discovered repeatedly in the first half of the

---

* The term 'diaspora' was originally used to refer to all the Jews living dispersed among the Gentiles after the Captivity. It is also a useful term for other emigrant communities that have nevertheless retained their original ethnicity.
† The term 'Pale', in the sense of a territory with clearly determined boundaries and/or subject to a distinct jurisdiction, was also used to refer to the area of eastern Ireland under English jurisdiction between the late 12th and the 16th centuries and to territory

twentieth century, numbers do not always mean safety. Also relatively insignificant as a predictor of ethnic conflict is the degree of assimilation between two populations. It might be thought that a high level of social integration would discourage conflict, if only because of the difficulty of identifying and isolating a highly assimilated minority. Paradoxically, however, a sharp rise in assimilation (measured, for example, by rates of intermarriage) may actually be the prelude to ethnic conflict.

Assimilation, to give perhaps the most important of all examples, was in fact quite far advanced in Central and Eastern Europe by the 1920s. In many places of mixed settlement, rates of intermarriage across ethnic barriers rose to unprecedented heights. By the later 1920s, nearly one in every three marriages involving a German Jew was to a Gentile. The rate rose as high as one in two in some big cities. The trend was similar, with only minor degrees of variation, in Austria, Czechoslovakia, Estonia, Hungary, parts of Poland, Romania and Russia (see Table I.1). This could, of course, be interpreted as an indicator of successful assimilation and integration. Yet it was in precisely these places that some of the worst ethnic violence occurred in the 1940s. One hypothesis explored below is that there was some kind of backlash against assimilation, and particularly against miscegenation, in the mid-twentieth century.

This possibility should disturb but not surprise us. We have, after all, seen instances of such backlashes in our own time. Horrific violence between Tutsis and Hutus occurred in Rwanda in the 1990s, even though intermarriage between Tutsi men and Hutu women used to be quite common. Ethnic conflict also exploded in Bosnia, despite high rates of inter-ethnic marriage in previous decades. These episodes also serve to remind us that there is no linear spectrum of inter-ethnic behaviour, with peaceful mingling at one end and bloody genocide at the other. The most murderous racial violence can have a sexual dimension to it, as in 1992, when Serbian forces were accused of a

---

in northern France under English jurisdiction between the mid-14th and mid-16th centuries. The Russian *cherta osedlosti* (literally 'boundary of settlement'), to which the Jews of the Tsarist empire were confined after 1791, had a somewhat different character. As in the case of the term 'diaspora', the word has a more general applicability to any territory associated with settlement by a particular ethnic group.

Table I.1. Mixed marriages as a percentage of all marriages involving one or two Jewish partners, selected European countries, regions and cities in the 1920s

| | Percentage of mixed marriages per 100 couples | | Percentage of mixed marriages per 100 couples |
|---|---|---|---|
| **Luxembourg** | 15.5 | Slovakia | 7.9 |
| Basel | 16.1 | Carpatho-Russia | 1.3 |
| Strasbourg | 21.2 | **Hungary** | 20.5 |
| **Germany** | 35.1 | Budapest | 28.5 |
| Prussia | 35.9 | Trieste | 59.2 |
| Bavaria | 35.9 | **Poland** | 0.2 |
| Hessen | 19.9 | Posen/Poznań | 39.2 |
| Württemberg | 38.1 | Breslau/Wrocław | 23.8 |
| Baden | 26.4 | Lemberg/Lwów | 0.5 |
| Saxony | 43.5 | Bucharest | 10.9 |
| Berlin | 42.7 | **Soviet Union (European)** | 12.7 |
| Magdeburg | 58.4 | Russia (European) | 34.7 |
| Munich | 47.3 | Leningrad | 32.1 |
| Frankfurt am Main | 30.4 | Kirovograd | 8.8 |
| Hamburg | 49.1 | Ukraine | 9.6 |
| **Austria** | 20.9 | Byelorussia | 6.1 |
| Vienna | 19.8 | **Latvia** | 3.3 |
| **Czechoslovakia** | 17.2 | **Lithuania** | 0.2 |
| Bohemia | 36.3 | **Estonia** | 13.5 |
| Moravia-Silesia | 27.6 | Vilna | 1.2 |

Note: All data are for the period 1926 to 1929 or 1930 except Trieste (1921–1927), Poland (1927), Lemberg/Lwów (1922–1925), Soviet Union (1924–1926), Russia (1926), Leningrad (1919–1920), Kirovograd (1921–1924), Ukraine (1926), Byelorussia (1926), Lithuania (1928–1930), Estonia (1923) and Vilna (1929–1931).

systematic campaign of rape directed against Bosnian Muslim women, with the aim of forcing them to conceive and give birth to 'Little Četniks'. Was this merely one of many forms of violence designed to terrorize Muslim families into fleeing from their homes? Or was it perhaps a manifestation of the primitive impulse described above – to eradicate 'the Other' by impregnating females as well as murdering males? It would certainly be simplistic to regard raping women as a form of violence indistinguishable in its intent from shooting men. Sexual violence directed against members of ethnic minorities has often been inspired by erotic, albeit sadistic, fantasies as much as by 'eliminationist' racism. The key point to grasp from the outset is that

1

the 'hatred' so often blamed for ethnic conflict is not a straightforward emotion. Rather, we encounter time and again that volatile ambivalence, that mixture of aversion and attraction, which has for so long characterized relations between white Americans and African-Americans. In calling the period from 1904 to 1953 the Age of Hatred, I hope to draw attention to the very complexity of that most dangerous of human emotions.

## THE RACE MEME

If it can plausibly be argued that 'race' is not a genetically meaningful concept, the question the historian must address is why it has nevertheless been such a powerful and violent preoccupation of modern times. An answer that suggests itself – also, as it happens, from the literature on evolutionary biology – is that racism, in the sense of a strongly articulated sense of racial differentiation, is one of those 'memes' characterized by Richard Dawkins as behaving in the realm of ideas the way genes behave in the natural world. The *idea* of biologically distinct races, ironically, has been able to reproduce itself and retain its integrity far more successfully than the races it claims to identify.

In the ancient and medieval worlds, no identity was wholly indelible. It was possible to become a Roman citizen, even if one had been born a Gaul. It was possible to become a Christian, even – at first especially – if one had been born a Jew. At the same time, blood feuds could run for years, even centuries, between ethnically indistinguishable but irreconcilably hostile clans. The notion of immutable racial identity came late to human history. The Spanish expulsion of the Jews in 1492 was very unusual in defining Jewishness according to blood rather than belief. Even in the eighteenth-century Portuguese Empire, it was possible for a mulatto to acquire the legal rights and privileges of a white through the payment of a standard fee to the crown. As is well known, the first ostensibly scientific attempt to subdivide the human species into biologically distinct races was by the Swedish botanist Carolus Linnaeus (Carl von Linné). In his *Systema Naturae* (1758), he identified four races: *Homo sapiens americanus*, *Homo sapiens asiaticus*, *Homo sapiens afer* and *Homo sapiens europ-*

*aeus*. Linnaeus, like all his many imitators, ranked the various races according to their appearance, temperament and intelligence, putting European man at the top of the evolutionary tree, followed (in Linnaeus's case) by American man ('ill-tempered . . . obstinate, contented, free'), Asian man ('severe, haughty, desirous') and – invariably at the bottom – African man ('crafty, slow, foolish'). Whereas European man was 'ruled by customs', Linnaeus argued, African man was ruled by 'caprice'. Already by the time of the American Revolution, this way of thinking was astonishingly widespread; the only real debate was whether racial differences reflected gradual divergence from a common origin or, as polygenists insisted, the lack of such a common origin. By the end of the nineteenth century, racial theorists had devised more elaborate methods of categorization, most commonly based on skull size and shape, but the basic ranking never changed. In his *Hereditary Genius* (1869), the English polymath Francis Galton devised a sixteen-point scale of racial intelligence, which put ancient Athenians at the top and the Australian aborigines at the bottom.

This was a profound transformation in the way people thought. Previously, men had tended to believe that it was power, privilege and property that were inheritable, as well, no doubt, as the social obligations that went with them. The royal dynasties who still ruled so much of the world in 1900 were the embodiments of this principle. Even the republics that occasionally arose in the modern period – in the Netherlands, North America and France – tended to retain the hereditary principle with respect to wealth, if not to office and status. In the eighteenth and nineteenth centuries new political doctrines arose. One theory asserted that power should not be a hereditary attribute, and that leaders should be selected by popular acclamation. Another called for the demolition of the edifice of inherited privilege; all men should instead be equal before the law. A third argued that property should not be monopolized by an elite of wealthy families, but should be redistributed according to individual needs. Yet even as democrats, liberals and socialists advanced these arguments, racists asserted that the hereditary principle should nevertheless apply in every other field of human activity. Racial theorists claimed that not only colour and physiognomy but also intelligence, aptitude, character and even morals and criminality were passed on in the blood from generation to generation. This was another central paradox of the modern era. Even as the hereditary principle ceased to govern the allocation of office and ownership, so it gained ground as a presumed determinant of capability and conduct. Men ceased to be able to inherit their father's jobs; in some countries during the twentieth century they even ceased to be able to inherit their estates. But they could inherit their traits, as legacies of their parents' racial origins.

The crucial normative question, however, was how far the manifest ability of the different races to interbreed ought to be tolerated. To some, 'miscegenation' seemed simply to be inevitable. A number of thinkers even came to regard it as desirable – that, at any rate, was a strong implication of early anthropological theories about 'exogamy', as well as the developing understanding of hereditary illness and the somewhat exaggerated perils of cousin-marriage. However, an increasingly frequent reaction to the phenomenon was condemnation. In his *History of Jamaica* (1774), for example, Edward Long found 'the Europeans [there] . . . too easily led aside to give a loose to every kind of sensual delight: on this account some black or yellow *quasheba* is sought for, by whom a tawney [*sic*] breed is produced'. Arthur, comte de Gobineau, in his *Essay on the Inequality of Human Races* (1853–55), echoed Linnaeus in identifying three archetypal races, of which the Aryan (white) was supreme and, as usual, responsible for all the great achievements of history. But Gobineau introduced a new idea: that the decline of a civilization tended to come when its Aryan blood had been diluted by intermarriage. He, too, regarded the fusion of the intellectually superior white race and more emotional dark and yellow races as inevitable, since the former was essentially masculine, the latter essentially feminine. Yet that did not make miscegenation any less repellent to him: 'The more this product reproduces itself and crosses its blood, the more the confusion increases. It reaches infinity, when the people is too numerous for any equilibrium to have a chance of being established . . . Such a people is merely an awful example of racial anarchy.'

In its most extreme forms, hostility to 'racial anarchy' produced discrimination, segregation, persecution, expulsion and, ultimately, attempted annihilation. For many years it seemed to be incumbent on historians to deny the existence of such a continuum of racial discrimination and to treat one particular event – the National Socialist 'Final Solution' to the 'Jewish Question' – as *sui generis*, a unique 'Holocaust', without precedent or parallel. A central hypothesis of this present book, however, is that German anti-Semitism in the mid-twentieth century was an extreme case of a general (though by no means universal) phenomenon. In claiming that Jews were systematically trying to 'pollute the blood' of the German *Volk*, Hitler and the other National Socialist ideologues were, as we shall see, saying nothing novel. Nor was it unique that such ideas became the basis not just for segregation and expulsion but ultimately for systematic genocide. The principal distinguishing feature of what became known as the Holocaust was not its goal of racial annihilation but the fact that it was carried out by a regime which had at its disposal all the resources of an industrialized economy and an educated society.

This is not to say that all the perpetrators of the Holocaust were actuated by fears of miscegenation, though there is compelling evidence that this was indeed a strong motivation among many leading Nazis. Many of those who actively contributed towards genocide were motivated by crude material greed. Others were little more than morally blinkered cogs in a bureaucratic machine whose 'cumulative radicalization' they did not individually will. Some perpetrators were merely ordinary men acting under peer-group pressure or systematic military brutalization; others were amoral technocrats obsessed with their own pseudo-scientific theories; still others were brainwashed youths in the grip of an immoral secular religion. Nevertheless, we need to recognize that the racial world view was fundamental to the Third Reich and that this was rooted in a particular conception of human biology – a singularly successful 'meme' that had already replicated itself all over the world by the start of the twentieth century. It could be transmitted even to quite remote and seemingly unpropitious locations. In the late nineteenth century, Argentina was widely regarded as an ideal destination for Jewish emigrants from Europe precisely because of the absence of anti-Semitism. Yet by the early 1900s writers like Juan Alsina and Arturo Reynal O'Connor were warning that the Jews posed a mortal threat to Argentine culture.

'Only a few years ago,' lamented the Labour Zionist journal *Brot und Ehre* in 1910,

we could speak about Argentina as a new *Eretz Israel*, a land that opened generously its door for us, where we enjoyed the same freedom the Republic gives all its inhabitants, without distinction of nationalities or beliefs. And now? The whole atmosphere around us is filled with hatred of Jews, eyes hostile to Jews are staring from all corners; they lie in wait in all directions, awaiting an opportunity to attack ... All are against us ... And this is not simply a hatred of Jews; it is a sign of a future movement, which is long known [elsewhere] under the name of anti-Semitism.

## BLOOD BORDERS

Why did large-scale ethnic conflict occur in some places and not in others? Why in Central and Eastern Europe more than in South America? One answer to that question is that in certain parts of the world there was an exceptional mismatch between ethnic identities and political structures. The ethnic map of Central and Eastern Europe, to take the most obvious example, was a true patchwork (Figure I.2). In the north – to name only the largest groups – there were Lithuanians, Latvians, Byelorussians and Russians, all linguistically distinct; in the middle, Czechs, Slovaks and Poles; in the south, Italians, Slovenes, Magyars, Romanians and, in the Balkans, Slovenes, Serbs, Croats, Bosniaks, Albanians, Greeks and Turks. Scattered all over the region were German-speaking communities. Language was only one of the ways the different ethnic groups could be distinguished. Some of those who spoke German dialects were Protestants, some Catholics and some Jews. Some of those who spoke Serbo-Croat were Catholics (Croats), some Orthodox (Serbs and Macedonians) and some Muslims (Bosniaks). Some Bulgarians were Orthodox; others (the Pomaks) were Muslim. Most Turkic-speakers were Muslims; a few (the Gagauz) were Orthodox.

The political geography of Central and Eastern Europe before the nineteenth century had been consistent with this exceptionally hetero-geneous pattern of settlement. The region had been divided between

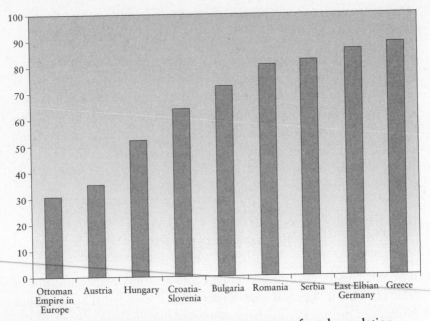

*Figure I.*2 **Majority population as a percentage of total population**

large dynastic empires. Most people had primarily local loyalties while at the same time owing allegiance to a remote imperial sovereign. Many had identities that defied rigid categorization, speaking more than one language; typically, Austrian demographers drew a distinction between 'mother tongue' and 'language of everyday use'. Most Slavs continued to work the land, as they had as serfs before the emancipations of the nineteenth century. The towns of Central and Eastern Europe, by contrast, were often quite ethnically distinct from the surrounding countryside. In the north, Germans and Jews predominated in urban areas, as they also did in the basin of the Danube; further east the towns were inhabited by Russians, Jews and Poles. The towns of the Adriatic coast were often Italian; some Balkan towns were distinctly Greek or Turkish. Most striking of all were those cosmopolitan trading centres where no one ethnic group predominated. One of many examples that might be cited was Salonika, present-day Thessaloniki, an Ottoman port of Greek provenance where Jews slightly outnumbered Christians and Muslims. Each religious community could, in turn, be subdivided into sects and linguistic sub-groups: there were Judesmo-speaking Sephardic Jews as well as Ashkenzim, Christian Greeks, Bulgarians and Macedonians – some speaking Greek, some Vlach, some a Slavic language – and myriad kinds of Muslim: Sufis, Bektashis and Mevlevis as well as Naqshbandis and Ma'min, who were converts from Judaism.

However, with the emergence after 1800 of the nation state as an ideal for political organization, these heterogeneous arrangements began to break down. A number of ethnic groups were sufficiently large and well organized that by the early twentieth century they had already established their own nation states – Greece, Italy, Germany, Serbia, Romania, Bulgaria, Albania – though in each case there were ethnic minorities within their borders and diaspora groups beyond their borders.* The Magyars enjoyed nearly all the privileges of independence as the junior partners within the Austro-Hungarian Dual Monarchy. The Czechs could aspire to some measure of political autonomy within Bohemia and Moravia. The Poles could dream of restoring their lost sovereignty at the expense of the three empires that had snuffed it out. But many other ethnic groups could not credibly aspire to statehood. Some were simply too few in number: Sorbs, Wends, Kashubes, Vlachs, Székelys, Carpatho-Rusyns and Ladins. Others were too scattered: the Sinti and Roma (often known, misleadingly, as Gypsies). Still others could aspire to build states only on the Ottoman periphery: the Jews and the Armenians.

The more the model of the nation state was applied to Central and Eastern Europe, then, the greater the potential for conflict. The discrepancy between the reality of mixed settlement – a complex patchwork of pales and diasporas – and the ideal of homogeneous

---

* In the eastern regions of the German Reich, for example, there were more than 3 million Poles, more than 100,000 Czechs, around the same number of Lithuanians and around 90,000 Sorbs, to say nothing of significant Danish populations in the north and French-speaking Alsatians in the west. One in every four inhabitants of Bulgaria was not an ethnic Bulgarian. Minorities accounted for 18 per cent of the population of Romania, 16 per cent of the population of Serbia and 10 per cent of the population of Greece. At the same time, just over 13 million Germans lived outside the Reich; 4 million Romanians lived outside Romania (compared with a total population of Romania of 5.5 million); just under 2 million Serbs lived outside Serbia (compared with a total population of Serbia of 2.3 million); and 2 million Greeks lived outside Greece (compared with a total Greek population of 2.2 million).

political units was simply too great. The stakes, as national borders took on increasing importance, were too high, and diverging birth rates only served to heighten the anxieties of those who feared minority status. It was, in theory, conceivable that all the different ethnic groups in a new state would agree to subsume their differences in a new collective identity, or to share power in a federation of equals. But it turned out to be just as likely that a majority group would set itself up as sole, or at least senior, proprietor of the state and its assets. The more functions the state was expected to perform (and the number of these functions grew by leaps and bounds after 1900) the more tempting it became to exclude this or that minority from some or all of the benefits of citizenship, while at the same time ratcheting up the costs of residence in the form of taxation and other burdens.

It is therefore no coincidence that so many of the locations where mass murder was perpetrated in the 1940s lay in precisely these regions of mixed settlement – in such many-named towns as Vilna/Wilna/Vilne/Vilnius, Lemberg/Lwów/L'viv and Czernowitz/Cernăuți/Chernovtsy/Chernivtsi. Nor is it a coincidence that a significant number of leading Nazis came from beyond the eastern frontier of the German Reich of 1871. To give just a few examples: Alfred Rosenberg, author of *The Myth of the Twentieth Century* and a key figure in Nazi racial policy, was born in Reval/Tallinn, Estonia. The son of a German emigrant to Argentina, Walther Darré, Hitler's Minister for Agriculture, developed his version of racial theory while breeding horses in East Prussia. The Nazi Secretary of State Herbert Backe was born in Batumi, Georgia, where his mother's peasant family had settled in the nineteenth century. Rudolf Jung, who grew up in the German enclave of Iglau/Jihlava in Bohemia, was only one of many Germans from the borderlands to attain high rank in the SS. Significantly, Breslau/Wrocław in Upper Silesia was one of those places where local Nazis campaigned most overtly for legislation against miscegenation in 1935. Austrians and Sudeten Germans supplied a disproportionate number of anti-Semitic contributions to the newspaper *Der Stürmer*. At least two of the small group of SS officers who ran the Bełżec death camp were so-called 'ethnic Germans' from the Baltic and Bohemia.

Yet Central and Eastern Europe was only the most lethal of the 'killing spaces' of the twentieth century. As will become clear, there were other parts of the world that shared some of its key characteristics: a multi-ethnic population, shifting demographic balances and political fragmentation. Considered as a single region, the nearest equivalent at the other end of the Eurasian landmass was Manchuria and the Korean peninsula. In the later part of the twentieth century, for reasons explored in the epilogue to this book, the zones of intense conflict shifted – to Indo-China, Central America, the Middle East and Central Africa. But it is on the first two regions that we must focus our attention if we are fully to grasp the peculiarly explosive character of the fifty-year war of the world.

## VOLATILITY AND ITS DISCONTENTS

Why has extreme violence occurred only at certain times? The answer is that ethnic conflict is correlated with economic *volatility*. It is not enough simply to look for times of economic crisis when trying to explain social and political instability. A rapid growth in output and incomes can be just as destabilizing as a rapid contraction. A useful measure of economic conditions, too seldom referred to by historians, is volatility, by which is meant the standard deviation of the change in a given indicator over a particular period of time. Reliable estimates of gross domestic product are unfortunately available for only a few countries for the entire century. However, figures for prices and interest rates are easier to come by, and these make it possible to measure economic volatility with some degree of precision for a substantial number of countries.

A straightforward and testable proposition is that times of high volatility were associated with socio-political stresses and strains. It is certainly suggestive that, for the seven major industrialized economies (Canada, France, Germany, Italy, Japan, the United Kingdom and the United States) the volatility of both growth and prices reached its highest point between 1919 and 1939 and declined steadily in the post-Second World War period (see Figure I.3). Economic historians were preoccupied for a long time with the identification of economic cycles and waves of various amplitudes. They tended to overlook

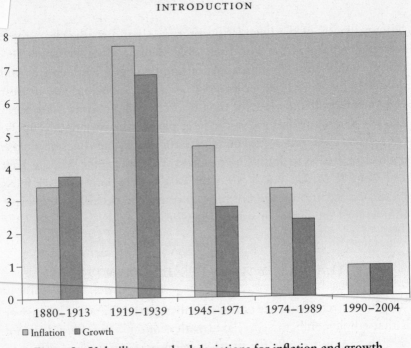

*Figure I.3* Volatility: standard deviations for inflation and growth,
G7 economies, 1880–2004

changes in the frequency and amplitude of booms and busts. Yet
precisely these were and remain crucial. If economic activity were as
regular as the seasons, the expectations of economic actors would
adjust accordingly and we would be no more surprised by spurt of
growth or a crash than we are by the advent of summer and winter.
But it was precisely the unpredictability of twentieth-century economic
life that produced such strong shifts in what John Maynard Keynes
called the 'animal spirits' of employers, lenders, investors, consumers
and indeed government officials.

Over the past hundred years, there have been profound changes in
the structure of economic institutions and the philosophies of those who
run them. Prior to 1914, the degree of freedom in the international
mobility of goods, capital and labour was unprecedented and has only
recently and partially been equalled. Governments were only just beginning to extend the scope of their operations beyond the provision of
security, justice and other elementary public goods. Central banks were
at least to some extent constrained in their operations by self-imposed

rules fixing the values of national currencies in terms of gold; this made for long-run price stability, though also higher volatility in growth than we are now accustomed to. These things changed radically during and after the First World War, which saw a significant expansion of the role of government and a breakdown of the system of fixed exchange rates known as the gold standard. It seemed to many contemporaries that there was a conflict between what international market forces could do in allocating goods, workers and capital optimally, and what governments ought to strive for – for example, maintaining or raising levels of industrial employment, stabilizing the prices of primary products or altering the distribution of income and wealth. Yet the inter-war experiments with protective tariffs, deficit finance, confiscatory taxation and floating exchange rates generally had the unintended consequence of magnifying economic fluctuations. Planned economies did better, but at a considerable cost in both efficiency and freedom. Though the records of both the welfare state and the planned economy were markedly better in the two decades after the end of the Second World War, it was only by moving back in the direction of the free market after 1979 that governments were able to achieve relative stability in prices and growth. Only since 1990 has it been possible for some commentators to speak tentatively of the 'death of volatility' – though it remains to be seen how far this represents the improvement of international economic institutions, how far the success of fiscal and monetary pragmatism at the national level and how far simply a fortunate and quite possibly ephemeral conjuncture between Western profligacy and Asian parsimony.

This stylized narrative, it should be stressed, applies to a limited sample of countries and to somewhat arbitrarily defined sub-periods. As will become clear, it would be a mistake to regard the performance of the major industrial economies as a proxy for the performance of the world economy as a whole. The severity of the inter-war extremes of inflation and deflation, growth and contraction, varied greatly between different European countries. And there were quite different trends in volatility in African, Asian and Latin American economies from the 1950s onwards.

Economic volatility matters because it tends to exacerbate social conflict. It seems intuitively obvious that periods of economic crisis create incentives for politically dominant groups to pass the burdens of adjustment on to others. With the growth of state intervention in economic life, the opportunities for such discriminatory redistribution clearly proliferated. What could be easier in a time of general hardship than to exclude a particular group from the system of public benefits? What is perhaps less obvious is that social dislocation may also follow periods of rapid growth, since the benefits of growth are very seldom evenly distributed. Indeed, it may be precisely the minority of winners in an upswing who are targeted for retribution in a subsequent downswing.

Once again it is possible to illustrate this point with reference to the best-known of cases, that of the Jews of Europe. Traditionally, historians have sought to explain the electoral success of anti-Semitic parties in Germany and elsewhere – as well as that of the occasionally anti-Semitic Populists in the United States – with reference to the Great Depression of the late 1870s and 1880s. However, the decline in agricultural prices that characterized that period provides only part of the explanation. Economic growth was not depressed; nor did stock markets fail to recover from the setbacks of the 1870s. What was galling to those trapped in relatively stagnant economic sectors like traditional handcrafts and small-scale agriculture was the evident prosperity of those better placed to profit from international economic integration and increased financial intermediation. As a rule, sudden and violent punctuations like stock market bubbles and busts had a bigger impact than long-run structural trends in prices and output. The polarizing social and political effects of economic volatility proved to be a recurrent feature of the twentieth century.

## EMPIRE-STATES

Twentieth-century violence is unintelligible if it is not seen in its imperial context. For it was in large measure a consequence of the decline and fall of the large multi-ethnic empires that had dominated the world in 1900. What nearly all the principal combatants in the world wars had in common was that they either were empires or sought to become empires. Moreover, many large polities of the period that claimed to be nation states or federations turn out, on close inspection, to have been empires too. That was certainly true of the Union of Soviet Socialist Republics; it remains true of today's Russian Federation. The United Kingdom of Great Britain and Ireland (after 1922 only Northern Ireland) was and is to all intents and purposes an English empire; for brevity's sake, it is still commonly referred to as England.* The Italy created in the 1850s and 1860s was a Piedmontese empire, the German Reich of 1871 in large measure a Prussian one. The two most populous nation states in the world today are both the results of imperial integration. Modern India is the heir of the Mughal Empire and the British Raj. The borders of the People's Republic of China are essentially those established by the Qing emperors. Arguably, even the United States is an 'imperial republic'; some would say it always has been.

Empires matter, firstly, because of the economies of scale that they make possible. There is a demographic limit to the number of men most nation states can put under arms. An empire, however, is far less constrained; among its core functions are to mobilize and equip large military forces recruited from multiple peoples and to levy the taxes or raise the loans to pay for them, again drawing on the resources of more than one nationality. Thus, as we shall see, many of the greatest battles of the twentieth century were fought by multi-ethnic forces under imperial banners; Stalingrad and El Alamein are only two of many examples. Secondly, the points of contact between empires – the borderlands and buffer zones between them, or the zones of strategic rivalry they compete to control – are likely to witness more violence than the imperial heartlands. The fatal triangle of territory between the Baltic, the Balkans and the Black Sea was a zone of conflict not just because it was ethnically mixed, but also because it was the junction where the realms of the Hohenzollerns, Habsburgs, Romanovs and Ottomans met, the fault line between the tectonic plates of four great empires. Manchuria and Korea occupied a similar position in the Far East. With the rise of oil as the twentieth century's principal fuel, so too did the Persian Gulf

---

* To the chagrin of Scotsmen and Welshmen afflicted with inferiority complexes. When this author was an undergraduate at Oxford, all modern history fell into two categories: 'English History' and 'General History'. In a concession to Celtic sentiment, the former category was later renamed 'British History' and then 'The History of the British Isles'.

in the Near East. Thirdly, because empires are often associated with the creation of economic order, the flows and ebbs of international commercial integration are closely associated with their rise and fall. Economic constraints and opportunities may also determine the timing and direction of imperial expansion, as well as the duration of an empire's existence and the nature of post-colonial development. Finally, the widely varying life expectancies of empires may offer a clue as to the timing of violence, since warfare would appear to be more prevalent at the beginning and especially at the end of an empire's existence.

It is an error not unlike the old economic historians' search for perfectly regular cycles of business activity to suppose that the rise and fall of empires or great powers has a predictable regularity to it. On the contrary, the most striking thing about the seventy or so empires historians have identified is the extraordinary variability in the chronological as well as the spatial extent of their dominion. The longest-lived empire of the second millennium was the Holy Roman Empire, which may be dated from the coronation of Charlemagne in 800 until its dissolution by Napoleon in 1806. The Ming dynasty in China (1368–1644) and its immediate successor, the Manchu or Qing dynasty, lasted together more than five hundred years, as did the Abbasid caliphate (750–1258). The Ottoman Empire (1453–1922) lasted just under five hundred years, showing signs of dissolution only in the last half century of its existence. The continental empires of the Habsburgs and the Romanovs each existed for more than three centuries, expiring in rapid succession at the end of the First World War. The Mughals ruled a substantial part of what is now India for around two hundred years. Of similar duration were the realms of the Mamluks in Egypt (1250–1517) and the Safavids in Persia (1501–1736). It is more difficult to give exact dates to the maritime empires of the West European states, since these had multiple points of origin and duration, but the Spanish, Dutch, French and British empires may all be said to have endured in the region of three hundred years. The lifespan of the Portuguese empire was closer to five hundred. Nor, it should be noted, do the histories of all these empires exhibit a uniform trajectory of rise, apogee, decline and fall. Empires could rise, decline and then rise again, only to collapse in response to some extreme shock.

The empires created in the twentieth century, by contrast, were all

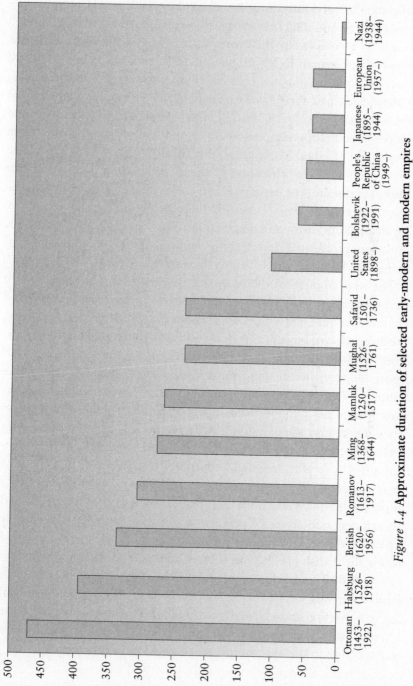

*Figure I.4* Approximate duration of selected early-modern and modern empires

of comparatively short duration. The Bolsheviks' Soviet Union (1922–1991) lasted less than seventy years, a meagre record indeed, though one not yet equalled by the People's Republic of China, established in 1949. The German Reich founded by Bismarck (1871–1918) lasted forty-seven years. Japan's colonial empire, which can be dated from 1905, lasted just forty. Most ephemeral of all modern empires was the so-called Third Reich of Adolf Hitler, which did not extend beyond its predecessor's borders before 1938 and had retreated within them by the end of 1944. Technically, the Third Reich lasted twelve years; as an empire in the true sense of the word it lasted barely half that time. Yet despite – or perhaps because of – their lack of longevity, the twentieth-century empires proved to be exceptional in their capacity for dealing out death and destruction. Why was this? The answer lies in the unprecedented degrees of centralized power, economic control and social homogeneity to which they aspired.

The new empires of the twentieth century were not content with the somewhat haphazard administrative arrangements that had characterized the old – the messy mixtures of imperial and local law, the delegation of powers as well as status to certain indigenous groups. They inherited from the nineteenth-century nation-builders an insatiable appetite for uniformity; in that sense, they were more like 'empire-states' than empires in the old sense. The new empires repudiated traditional religious and legal constraints on the use of force. They insisted on the creation of new hierarchies in place of existing social structures. They delighted in sweeping away old political institutions. Above all, they made a virtue of ruthlessness. In pursuit of their objectives, they were willing to make war on whole categories of people, at home and abroad, rather than on merely the armed and trained representatives of an identified enemy state. It was entirely typical of the new generation of would-be emperors that Hitler could accuse the British of excessive softness in their treatment of the Indian nationalists. This helps to explain why the epicentres of the century's great upheavals were so often located precisely on the peripheries of the new empire-states. It may also have been the reason that these empire-states, with their extreme aspirations, proved so much more ephemeral than the old empires they sought to supplant.

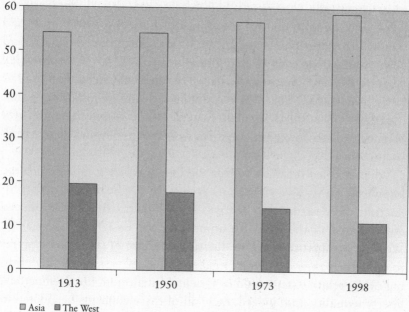

*Figure I.5* **The West and Asia: shares of world population**

## THE DESCENT OF THE WEST

The story of the twentieth century has sometimes been presented as a triumph of the West; the greater part of it has been called the 'American Century'. The Second World War is often represented as the apogee of American power and virtue; the victory of the 'Greatest Generation'. In the last years of the century, the end of the Cold War led Francis Fukuyama famously to proclaim 'the end of history' and the victory of the Western (if not Anglo-American) model of liberal democratic capitalism. Yet this seems fundamentally to misread the trajectory of the past hundred years, which has seen something more like a reorientation of the world towards the East.

In 1900 the West really did rule the world. From the Bosphorus to the Bering Straits, nearly all of what was then known as the Orient was under some form or another of Western imperial rule. The British had long ruled India, the Dutch the East Indies, the French

Indo-China; the Americans had just seized the Philippines; the Russians aspired to control Manchuria. All the imperial powers had established parasitical outposts in China. The East, in short, had been subjugated, even if that process involved far more complex negotiations and compromises between rulers and ruled than used to be acknowledged. This Western dominance was remarkable in that over half the world's population were Asians, while barely a fifth belonged to the dominant countries we have in mind when we speak of 'the West' (see Figure I.5).

What enabled the West to rule the East was not so much scientific knowledge in its own right as its systematic application to both production and destruction. That was why, in 1900, the West produced more than half the world's output, and the East barely a quarter. Western dominance was also due to the failure of the Asian empires to modernize their economic, legal and military systems, to say nothing of the relative stagnation of Oriental intellectual life. Democracy, liberty, equality and, indeed, race: all of these concepts originated in the West. So did nearly all of the significant scientific breakthroughs from Newton to Einstein. Historians influenced by Asian nationalism have very often made the mistake of assuming that the backwardness of Eastern societies in around 1900 was the consequence of imperial 'exploitation'. This is in large measure an illusion; rather, it was the decadence of Eastern empires that made European domination possible.

It is only when the extent of Western dominance in 1900 is appreciated that the true narrative arc of the twentieth century reveals itself. This was not 'the triumph of the West', but rather the crisis of the European empires, the ultimate result of which was the inexorable revival of Asian power and the descent of the West. Gradually, beginning in Japan, Asian societies modernized themselves or were modernized by European rule. As this happened, the gap between European and Asian incomes began to narrow. And with that narrowing, the relative decline of the West became unstoppable. This was nothing less than the reorientation of the world, redressing a balance between West and East that had been lost in the four centuries after 1500. No historian of the twentieth century can afford to overlook this huge – and ongoing – secular shift.

If the Orient had simply 'occidentalized' itself, of course, we might still salvage the idea of an ultimate Western triumph. Yet no Asian country – not even Japan in the Meiji era – transformed itself into a replica of a European nation state. On the contrary, most Asian nationalists insisted that their countries must modernize à la carte, embracing only those aspects of the Western model that suited their purposes, and retaining important components of their traditional cultures. This was hardly surprising. Much of what they saw of Western culture – in its imperialist incarnation – did not invite imitation. The crucial point, of course, is that the reorientation of the world could not have been, and was not, achieved without conflict. For the Western powers had no desire to relinquish their mastery over Asia's peoples and resources. Even when they were comprehensively beaten by Japanese forces in 1942, the Europeans and Americans alike fought back with the aim of restoring the old Western dominance, though with distinctly mixed results. In many ways, it was not until the collapse of the Soviet Union in 1991 that the last European empire in Asia could be said to have fallen. In that sense it seems justifiable to interpret the twentieth century not as the triumph but as the descent of the West, with the Second World War as the decisive turning point. For the death throes of the Occident's empire in the Orient were as bloody as anything that happened in Central and Eastern Europe, not least because of the extreme reactions against Western models of development that they inspired in countries such as Japan, China, North Korea, Vietnam and Cambodia. It was a descent, in the sense that the West could never again wield the power it had enjoyed in 1900. It was also a descent, however, in that much of what arose in the East to challenge that power was recognizably descended from Western ideas and institutions, albeit through a process of cultural miscegenation.

## THE FIFTY YEARS WAR

The potential instability of assimilation and integration; the insidious spread of the meme that identifies some human beings as aliens; the combustible character of ethnically mixed borderlands; the chronic volatility of mid-twentieth-century economic life; the bitter struggles between old multi-ethnic empires and short-lived empire-states; the convulsions that marked the decline of Western dominance – these, then, are the principal themes that will be explored and elaborated on below.

At the centre of the story, as may already be clear, are the events we know as the Second World War. But only as I tried to write an adequate sequel to my earlier book about the First World War did I come to appreciate just how un-illuminating it would be to write yet another book within the chronological straitjacket of 1939 to 1945 – yet another book focused on the now familiar collisions of armies, navies and air forces. Was there, I began to ask myself, really such a thing as the Second World War? Might it not be more correct to speak of multiple regional conflicts? After all, what began in 1939 was only a European war between Poland and, on the other side, Nazi Germany and the Soviet Union, with Britain and France siding with the under-dog more in word than deed. Poland's Western allies did not really enter the fray until 1940, whereupon Germany won a short continental war in Western Europe. In 1941, even as the war between Germany and Britain was in its infancy, Hitler began a quite different war against his former ally Stalin. Meanwhile, Mussolini pursued his vain dreams of an Italian empire in East and North Africa and the Balkans. All of this was more or less entirely unrelated to the wars that were launched by Japan in Asia: the one against China, which had begun in 1937, if not in 1931; the one against the British, Dutch and French empires, which had been won by the middle of 1942; and the one against the United States, which was unwinnable. Meanwhile, civil wars raged before, during and after these interstate wars, notably in China, Spain, the Balkans, the Ukraine and Poland. And no sooner had this supposedly homogeneous Second World War ended, than a new wave of violence swept the Middle East and Asia, which histori-ans refer to somewhat euphemistically as decolonization. Civil wars and partitions scarred India, Indo-China, China and Korea; in the last case, internecine war escalated into interstate war with the inter-ventions of an American-led coalition and Communist China. There-after the two superpowers made war by proxy. The theatres of global conflict changed, from Central and Eastern Europe and Manchuria-Korea to Latin America, Indo-China and sub-Saharan Africa.

It might therefore be said that the late 1930s and early 1940s witnessed the crescendo of an entire century of organized violence – a global Hundred Years War. Even to speak of 'a second Thirty Years War' is to understate the scale of the upheaval, for in truth the era of truly global conflict began ten years before 1914 and ended eight years after 1945. Nor will Hobsbawm's attractive idea of a 'short twentieth century' from 1914 to 1991 quite do. There were discontinuities just as important as that of 1989 – perhaps more so – in 1979. On the other hand, the collapse of the Soviet empire saw the revival of ethnic conflicts that had been dormant during the Cold War, not least in the Balkans – a resumption rather than the end of history. In the end, I have elected to locate the war of the world between two dates: 1904, when the Japanese struck the first effective blow against European dominance of the Orient; and 1953, when the end of the Korean War drew a line through the Korean peninsula, matching the Iron Curtain that had already been drawn through Central Europe. But what followed this Fifty Years War was not a 'long peace' but what I have called the Third World's War.

Historians always yearn for closure, for a date when their narratives can end. But in writing this book I have begun to doubt whether the war of the world described here can genuinely be regarded as over even now. Rather like Wells's science-fiction *War of the Worlds*, which has been reincarnated as an artefact of popular culture at more or less regular intervals,* the War of the World chronicled here stubbornly refuses to die. As long, it seems, as men plot the destruction of their fellow-men – as long as we dread and yet also somehow yearn to see our great metropolises laid waste – this war will recur, defying the frontiers of chronology.

---

* Forty years after its first publication, at a time when the devastating power of aerial bombardment was being demonstrated in China and Spain, the story reached a mass audience in the United States as a result of Orson Welles's radio dramatization, the verisimilitude of which alarmed many American listeners. In 1953 a film version, starring Gene Barry and Ann Robinson, became an Oscar-winning metaphor for the Cold War, 'fought with the terrible weapons of super-science'. Twenty-five years later, it was the turn of Jeff Wayne to produce a musical version of the Martian invasion for the strife-torn seventies. In their most recent incarnation, under the direction of Steven Spielberg, the Martians devastate the North-Eastern United States in ways that Islamist terrorists must yearn to replicate.

# PART I

# The Great Train Crash

# I

# Empires and Races

*What an extraordinary episode in the economic progress of man that age was which came to an end in August 1914!*

John Maynard Keynes

*Out of the oil-smooth spirit of the two last decades of the nineteenth century, suddenly, throughout Europe, there rose a kindling fever . . . people were enthusiastic hero-worshippers and enthusiastic adherents of the social creed of the Man in the Street; one had faith and was sceptical . . . one dreamt of ancient castles and shady avenues . . . but also of prairies, vast horizons, forges and rolling-mills . . . Some [people] hurl[ed] themselves . . . upon the new, as yet untrodden century, while others were having a last fling in the old one.*

Robert Musil

## 9/11/01

The world on September 11, 1901, was not a bad place for a healthy white man with a decent education and some money in the bank. Writing eighteen years later, the economist John Maynard Keynes could look back, with a mixture of nostalgia and irony, to the days when the class to which he belonged had enjoyed 'at a low cost and with the least trouble, conveniences, comforts, and amenities beyond the compass of the richest and most powerful monarchs of other ages':

The inhabitant of London could order by telephone, sipping his morning tea in bed, the various products of the whole earth, in such quantity as he might see fit, and reasonably expect their early delivery upon his doorstep; he could at the same moment and by the same means adventure his wealth in the natural resources and new enterprises of any quarter of the world, and share, without exertion or even trouble, in their prospective fruits and advantages; or he could decide to couple the security of his fortunes with the good faith of the townspeople of any substantial municipality in any continent that fancy or information might recommend.

Not only could Keynes's inhabitant of London buy the world's wares and invest his capital in a wide range of global securities; he could also travel the earth's surface with unprecedented freedom and ease:

He could secure forthwith, if he wished it, cheap and comfortable means of transit to any country or climate without passport or other formality, could despatch his servant to the neighbouring office of a bank for such supply of the precious metals as might seem convenient, and could then proceed abroad to foreign quarters, without knowledge of their religion, language, or customs, bearing coined wealth upon his person, and would consider himself greatly aggrieved and much surprised at the least interference.

But the crucial point, as Keynes saw it, was that the man of 1901 'regarded this state of affairs as normal, certain, and permanent, except in the direction of further improvement, and any deviation from it as aberrant, scandalous, and avoidable.' This first age of globalization was an idyll, indeed:

The projects and politics of militarism and imperialism, of racial and cultural rivalries, of monopolies, restrictions, and exclusion, which were to play the serpent to this paradise, were little more than the amusements of his daily newspaper, and appeared to exercise almost no influence at all on the ordinary course of social and economic life, the internationalisation of which was nearly complete in practice.

It is worth turning back to *The Times* of that golden age to verify Keynes's justly famous recollection. Exactly a century before two hijacked planes slammed into the twin towers of the World Trade

Center, 'globalization' was indeed a reality, even if that clumsy word was as yet unknown. On that day – which was a sunny Wednesday – Keynes's inhabitant of London could, as he sipped his breakfast tea, have ordered a sack of coal from Cardiff, a pair of kid gloves from Paris or a box of cigars from Havana. He might also, if anticipating a visit to the grouse moors of Scotland, have purchased a 'Breadalbane Waterproof and self-ventilating Shooting Costume (cape and kilt)'; or he might, if his interests lay in a different direction, have ordered a copy of Maurice C. Hime's book entitled *Schoolboy's Special Immorality*. He could have invested his money in any one of nearly fifty US companies quoted in London – most of them railroads like the Denver and Rio Grande (whose latest results were reported that day) – or, if he preferred, in one of the seven other stock markets also covered regularly by *The Times*. He might, if he felt the urge to travel, have booked himself passage on the P&O liner *Peninsular*, which was due to sail for Bombay and Karachi the next day, or on one of the twenty-three other P&O ships scheduled to sail for Eastern destinations over the next ten weeks – to say nothing of the thirty-six other shipping lines offering services from England to all the corners of the globe. Did New York seem to beckon? The *Manitou* sailed tomorrow, or he could wait for the Hamburg-America Line's more luxurious *Fürst Bismarck*, which sailed from Southampton on the 13th. Did Buenos Aires appeal to him more? Did he perhaps wish to see for himself how the city's Grand National Tramway Company was using – or rather, losing – his money? Very well; the *Danube*, departing for Argentina on Friday, still had some cabins free.

The world, in short, was his oyster. And yet, as Keynes understood, this oyster was not without its toxic impurities. The lead story in *The Times* that September 11 was a 'hopeful' report – vainly hopeful, as it turned out – that the American President William McKinley was showing signs of recovering from the attempt on his life five days earlier by the anarchist Leon Czolgosz. ('The President is in great order,' his physician was quoted as saying. In fact, McKinley died on September 14.) This attack had awakened the American public to a hitherto neglected threat from within. The paper's New York correspondent reported that the police were engaged in rounding up all the known anarchists in the city, though the plot to kill the President was believed to have been hatched in Chicago, where two anarchist leaders, Emma Goldman and Abraham Isaak, had already been arrested. 'I only done my duty,' Czolgosz explained, by which he meant the anarchist's duty to kill rulers and wage war on established governments. 'I thought', he added as he was led to the electric chair, 'it would help the working people.' The news that the President's condition was improving and that the perpetrator's associates were being rounded up might have reassured our breakfasting reader, as it had reassured the stock market the previous day. He would nevertheless have been aware that assassinations of heads of state were becoming disturbingly frequent.* The ideology of anarchism and the practice of terrorism were just two of the 'serpents' in the garden of globalization that Keynes had forgotten about by 1919.

What of the 'projects and politics of militarism and imperialism, of racial and cultural rivalries'? There was ample evidence of these on September 11, 1901. In South Africa the bitterly contested war between the British and the Boers was approaching the end of its second year. The official communiqués from the British commander, Lord Kitchener, were sanguine. In the preceding week, according to his latest report, sixty-seven Boers had been killed, sixty-seven wounded and 384 taken prisoner. A further 163 had surrendered. By contrast, *The Times* listed the deaths of eighteen British soldiers, of whom just seven had been victims of enemy action. Here was a very British measure of military success, a profit and loss account from the battlefield. However, the methods the British had by this time adopted to defeat their foes were harsh in the extreme, though *The Times* made no mention of these. To deprive the Boers of supplies from their farms, their wives and children had been driven from their homes and herded into concentration camps, where conditions were atrocious; at this stage, roughly one in three inmates was dying because of poor sanitation and disease. In addition, Kitchener had ordered the construction of a network of barbed wire and blockhouses to disrupt the Boers' lines of communication. Even these measures did not strike *The Times*'s editorial writers as sufficient to end the war:

---

* The King of Italy had been murdered the year before, the Empress of Austria-Hungary two years before that. In 1903 it would be the turn of the King of Serbia.

To permit [the Boers] to protract the struggle and to exacerbate it by resort to deeds of barbarous cruelty . . . would not raise the character of the mother country in the eyes of her daughter nations, her partners in the Empire . . . The whole nation is agreed that we must carry through the task we have undertaken in South Africa. There should be no hesitation in adopting the policy and the means necessary to attain the end in view with the utmost rapidity and completeness.

Only the newspaper's man in Cape Town, who evidently felt some unease at the harshness of British policy, sounded a note of warning:

The rod of iron should remain the rod of iron, and there is no need – indeed, it would be a mistake – to clothe it in velvet. He who wields it, however, should remember that the exercise of power is never incompatible with the manner of an English gentleman . . . The political views of the Dutch . . . will never be changed by individual Englishmen giving them occasion to doubt our inherited ability to rule.

The Englishman's 'inherited ability to rule' was being put to the test in other parts of Africa too. That same day's *Times* reported punitive expeditions against the Wa-Nandi tribe in Uganda and against the 'spirit of lawlessness' in the Gambia, which nebulous entity was held responsible for the deaths of two British officials. That the editors shared the widely held conservative view of the Empire as militarily overstretched (or, rather, undermanned) seems clear; how else to explain their call for a revival of the eighteenth-century militia as 'the embodiment of the principle that it is the duty of every man to assist in the defence of his country'?

A further reason for disquiet was the apparently fraught state of relations between the continental great powers. *The Times*'s Paris correspondent reported the imminent visit of the Russian Tsar, Nicholas II, to France, and offered two theories as to the purpose of his visit. The first was that he was coming to pave the way for the latest of many Russian bond issues on the Paris market; the second, that his intention was to reassure the French of his government's commitment to the Franco-Russian military alliance. Whichever explanation was correct, the newspaper's reporter saw dangers in this manifestation of harmony between Paris and St Petersburg. Since the

German annexation of Alsace-Lorraine in 1871, he noted, France was 'to-day the only nation in Europe which has some claims to put forward, and the only one which neither can nor should admit that the era of European peace is definitive ... What she might do if circumstances impelled her and patriotism as well, were it a question of filling the breach made in her territory ... no one knows or can know.' Yet the most likely consequence of the Tsar's visit would be to strengthen Germany's rival alliance with Austria and Italy, recently under some strain because of disagreements over German import tariffs. Too strong an affirmation of the Franco-Russian 'Alliance of the Two' would tend to increase the risks of a war with this 'Alliance of the Three':

I make no allusion [the paper's correspondent concluded darkly] to the elements which at any moment may combine with those of the existing alliances, because the hour for action has not yet struck and is not near striking. Those who at present belong to neither of the alliances have time to wait and to continue their meditations before making a decision.

To be sure, our imaginary reader might have taken some comfort from the news that the Tsar was also paying a visit to his cousin the German Kaiser on his way to France, an event solemnly described by the semi-official *Norddeutsche Zeitung* as symbolizing the shared commitment of the Russian and German governments to the maintenance of peace in Europe. Less reassuring, however, was the news of a deterioration in relations between the French and Ottoman governments, which prompted *The Times* to speculate that the Sultan was considering 'the growing Pan-Islamic movement' as a possible weapon against both the French and the British empires. In the Balkans, too, there were grounds for concern. The paper reported signs of a slight improvement in Austro-Hungarian relations, but noted:

The respective influence of the two Powers in the Balkans are [*sic*] based upon different factors. Russian influence is founded upon community of race, common historic memories, religion, and proximity; while that of Austria-Hungary is chiefly manifest in the economic ... sphere. Nothing has happened during recent years to diminish either Russian or Austrian influence. Both Powers have maintained their old positions ...

In the eyes of pacifists, certainly, the world of 1901 was not quite the Eden of Keynes's recollection. At the 10th meeting of the Universal Peace Congress, then sitting in Glasgow, Dr R. Spence Watson prompted cries of 'Hear, hear' when he called 'the present . . . as dark a time as they had ever known'. Warming to his theme, Watson denounced not only 'that terrible war in South Africa, which they could not think of without humiliation' but also 'the swooping down of the Christian nations upon China, the most detestable bit of greed which history has recorded' – an allusion to the recent international expedition to suppress the Boxer Rebellion in China. An advertisement on the front page of that same edition of *The Times* lends some credibility to his impugning of the expedition's motive:

> CHINESE WAR LOOT. – Before disposing of Loot, it is advisable to have it valued by an expert. Mr Larkin, 104, New Bond-street, VALUES and BUYS ORIENTAL ART-SPECIALITIES.

Socialists might also have questioned Keynes's complacent claim that 'the greater part of the population . . . were, to all appearances, reasonably contented with [their] lot' and that 'escape was possible, for any man of capacity or character at all exceeding the average, into the middle and upper classes'. In the week preceding September 11, *The Times* reported, there had been 1,471 deaths in London, corresponding to an annual rate of 16.9 per thousand, including '7 from smallpox, 13 from measles, 14 from scarlet fever, 20 from diphtheria, 27 from whooping cough, 17 from enteric fever, 271 from diarrhoea and dysentery [and] 4 from cholera . . .' In Wales, meanwhile, twenty miners were feared dead after an explosion at the Llanbradach colliery near Caerphilly. Across the sea in Ireland seven members of the Amalgamated Society of Carpenters and Joiners had been arrested and charged with 'conspiracy, assault and intimidation', having led a carpenters' strike for higher wages. The number of registered paupers in London, according to the paper, was just under 100,000. There was as yet no 'old age pension scheme . . . of giving State aid to those who had already in the past made some provision for the future'. The best escape from poverty in the United Kingdom was, in reality, geographical rather than social mobility. Between 1891 and 1900, *The Times* recorded, no fewer than 726,000 people had emigrated from the United Kingdom. Would so many have left if, in truth, they had been 'reasonably contented'?

## EMPIRES

The world of 1901 was a world of empires, but the problem was their weakness, not their strength.

The oldest, the Qing and the Ottoman, were relatively decentralized entities; indeed to some observers they seemed on the verge of dissolution. Their fiscal systems had for too long been based primarily on quasi-feudal transfers from the rural periphery to the metropolitan centre. Other sources of revenue were becoming more important – notably the duties levied on overseas trade – but by the end of the nineteenth century these had largely been frittered away. The process was further advanced in China. Beginning in the 1840s with Xiamen, Guangzhou, Fuzhou, Ningbo and Shanghai, numerous Chinese ports had come under European control, initially as bridgeheads for hard-faced Scots intent on building a mass market for Indian opium. Eventually there were more than a hundred such 'treaty ports', where European citizens enjoyed the privileges of 'extraterritoriality' – living in 'concessions' or 'settlements' with complete immunity from Chinese law. The Imperial Maritime Customs Administration, though nominally a branch of the Chinese Government, was staffed by foreign officials and run by an Ulsterman, Sir Robert Hart. In much the same way, numerous Turkish taxes were collected by a European Council of the Public Debt, which had been established in 1881 and was controlled by foreign bondholders.* These strikingly visible limitations of sovereignty – the magnificent offices of the Hong Kong and Shanghai Bank on the Shanghai Bund (embankment), the building of

---

* The Council had seven members: two from France, one each from Germany, Austria, Italy and the Ottoman Empire itself, and one from Britain and Holland together. Until the debt was liquidated, the Decree of Muharrem ceded to the Council all the revenues from the salt and tobacco monopolies, the stamp and spirits tax, the fish tax and the silk tithe in certain districts, as well as some potential increases from customs duties and the tax on shops. Revenues from certain Ottoman possessions – Bulgaria, Cyprus and Eastern Rumelia – also flowed to it.

the Public Debt Administration in Istanbul – reflected both financial and military weakness. To pay for modern armaments and infrastructure that they could not make for themselves, the Chinese and the Turkish governments had borrowed substantial sums by floating loans in Europe; domestic intermediaries simply could not compete with the sums and the terms offered by the European banking houses, which were able to tap much wider and deeper pools of savings through the bond markets of London, Paris and Berlin. But the mortgaging or hypothecation of specific revenue streams like customs duties meant that these passed into foreign control in the event of a default. And defaults tended to happen in the wake of military setbacks like those suffered by Turkey in the 1870s and China in the 1890s; it turned out that simply buying Western hardware did not suffice to win wars.

It is therefore not surprising that by 1901 so many Westerners expected both these venerable empires to go the way of the Safavid and Mughal empires, which had disintegrated in the eighteenth century, with European economic influence as the fatal solvent. Yet this was not what happened. Instead, both in China and in Turkey, a new generation of political modernizers came to power, inspired by nationalism and intent on avoiding the fate that had befallen earlier Eastern empires. The challenge for the Young Turks who came to power in Istanbul in 1908 was the same as that which faced the Chinese republicans who overthrew the last Qing Emperor three years later: how to transform sprawling, enfeebled empires into strong nation states.

Somewhat similar processes were already at work in the Austrian and Russian empires, though this was much less obvious in 1901. Although similar to their Asian counterparts in their social foundations, both empires had modernized their revenue-gathering and war-making capabilities in the eighteenth century. Yet both were already struggling to cope with the technological and political challenges of industrialized warfare. The smaller Central European realm of the Habsburgs was primarily weakened by its ethnic diversity. There were at least eighteen nationalities dispersed across five distinct kingdoms, two grand duchies, one principality, six duchies and six other miscellaneous territorial units. German-speakers accounted for less than a quarter of the population. Because of its institutional decentralization, Austria-Hungary struggled to match the military expenditures of the other great powers. It was stable, but weak. The Carinthian-born novelist Robert Musil nicely captured the contemporary sense of retarded imperial development:

There was no ambition to have world markets or have world power. Here one was in the centre of Europe, at the focal point of the world's old axes; the words 'colony' and 'overseas' had the ring of something as yet utterly untried and remote . . . One spent enormous sums on the army; but only just enough to assure one of remaining the second weakest among the great powers.

There were, to be sure, periodic debates about internal reform. The 'dualism' that since 1867 had divided most power between a pluralistic Austria and a Magyar-dominated Hungary produced endless anomalies, like the arcane distinction between *kaiserlich-königlich* (imperial-royal) (k.k.) and *kaiserlich und königlich* (k.u.k.), which inspired Musil to nickname the country 'Kakania':

On paper it called itself the Austro-Hungarian monarchy; in speaking, however, one referred to it as Austria; that is to say, it was known by a name that it had, as a State, solemnly renounced by oath, while preserving it in all matters of sentiment, as a sign that feelings are just as important as constitutional law and that regulations are not the really serious thing in life. By its constitution it was liberal, but its system of government was clerical. The system of government was clerical, but the general attitude to life was liberal. Before the law all citizens were equal, but not everyone, of course, was a citizen. There was a parliament, which made such vigorous use of its liberty that it was usually kept shut; but there was also an emergency powers act by means of which it was possible to manage without parliament, and every time everyone was just beginning to rejoice in absolutism, the Crown decreed that there must now again be a return to parliamentary government. [N]ational struggles . . . were so violent that they several times a year caused the machinery of State to jam and come to a dead stop. But between whiles, in the breathing-spaces between government and government, everyone got on excellently with everyone else and behaved as though nothing had been the matter.

Czechs in particular chafed at their second-class status in Bohemia, and were able to give more forthright political expression to their grievances after the introduction of universal male suffrage in 1907. But schemes for some kind of Habsburg federalism never got off the ground. The alternative of Germanization was not an option for the fragile linguistic patchwork that was Austria; the most that could be achieved was to maintain German as the language of command for the army, though with results lampooned hilariously by the Czech writer Jaroslav Hašek in *The Good Soldier Švejk*. By contrast, the sustained Hungarian campaign to 'Magyarize' their kingdom's non-Hungarians, who accounted for nearly half the population, merely inflamed nationalist sentiment. If the trend of the age had been towards multi-culturalism, then Vienna would have been the envy of the world; from psychoanalysis to the Secession, its cultural scene at the turn of the century was a wonderful advertisement for the benefits of ethnic cross-fertilization. But if the trend of the age was towards the homogeneous nation state, the future prospects of the Dual Monarchy were bleak indeed. When the satirist Karl Kraus called Austria-Hungary a 'laboratory of world destruction' (*Versuchsstation des Weltuntergangs*), he had in mind precisely the mounting tension between a multi-tiered polity – summed up by Kraus as an '*aristodemoplutobürokratischen Mischmasch*' – and a multi-ethnic society. This was what Musil was getting at when he described Austria-Hungary as 'nothing but a particularly clear-cut case of the modern world': for 'in that country . . . every human being's dislike of every other human being's attempts to get on . . . [had] crystallized earlier'. Reverence for the aged Emperor Francis Joseph was not enough to hold this delicate edifice together. It might even end up blowing it apart.

If Austria-Hungary was stable but weak, Russia was strong but unstable. 'There's an invisible thread, like a spider's web, and it comes right out of his Imperial Majesty Alexander the Third's heart. And there's another which goes through all the ministers, through His Exellency the Governor and down through the ranks until it reaches me and even the lowest soldier,' the policeman Nikiforych explained to the young Maxim Gorky. 'Everything is linked and bound together by this thread . . . with its invisible power.' As centralized as Austria-Hungary was decentralized, Russia seemed equal to the task of maintaining military parity with the West European powers. More-over, Russia exercised the option of 'Russification', aggressively imposing the Russian language on the other ethnic minorities in its vast imperium. This was an ambitious strategy given the numerical predominance of non-Russians, who accounted for around 56 per cent of the total population of the empire. It was Russia's economy that nevertheless seemed to pose the biggest challenge to the Tsar and his ministers. Despite the abolition of serfdom in the 1860s, the country's agricultural system remained communal in its organization – closer, it might be said, to India than to Prussia. But the bid to build up a new class of thrifty peasant proprietors – sometimes known as *kulaks*, after their supposedly tight fists – achieved only limited success. From a narrowly economic perspective, the strategy of financing industrialization by boosting agricultural production and exports was a success. Between 1870 and 1913 the Russian economy grew at an average annual rate of around 2.4 per cent, faster than the British, French and Italian and only a little behind the German (2.8 per cent). Between 1898 and 1913, pig iron production more than doubled, raw cotton consumption rose by 80 per cent and the railway network grew by more than 50 per cent. Militarily, too, state-led industrialization seemed to be working; Russia was more than matching the expenditures of the other European empires on their armies and navies. Small wonder the German Chancellor Theobald von Bethmann Hollweg worried that 'Russia's growing claims and enormous power to advance in a few years, will simply be impossible to fend off'. Nevertheless, the prioritization of grain exports (to service Russia's rapidly growing external debt) and rapid population growth limited the material benefits felt by ordinary Russians, four-fifths of whom lived in the countryside. The hope that they would gain land as well as freedom aroused among peasants by the abolition of serfdom had been disappointed. Though living standards were almost certainly rising (if the revenues from excise duties are any guide), this was no cure for a pervasive sense of grievance, as any student of the French *ancien régime* could have explained. A disgruntled peasantry, a sclerotic aristocracy, a radicalized but impotent intelligentsia and a capital city with a large and volatile populace: these were precisely the combustible ingredients the historian Alexis de Tocqueville had identified in 1780s France. A Russian revolution of rising expectations was in the making – a revolution Nikiforych vainly warned Gorky to keep out of.

The West European overseas empires were altogether different in character. The products of three centuries of commerce, conquest and colonization, they were the beneficiaries of a remarkable global division of labour. At the heart of this 'imperialism' – the word became a term of abuse as early as the late 1850s* – were a few great cities, which generally combined political, commercial and industrial functions. In their own right, these teeming metropolises were monuments to the material progress of mankind, even if the slums of their East Ends revealed how unequally the fruits of that progress were distributed. Outwards from London, Glasgow, Amsterdam and Hamburg there radiated the lines – shipping lines, railway lines, telegraph lines – that were the sinews of Western imperial power. Regular steamships connected the great commercial centres to every corner of the globe. They criss-crossed the oceans; they plied its great lakes; they chugged up and down its navigable rivers. At the ports where they loaded and unloaded their passengers and cargoes, there were railway stations, and from these emanated the second great network of the Victorian age: the iron rails, along which ran rhythmically, in accordance with scrupulously detailed timetables, a clunking cavalcade of steam trains. A third network, of copper and rubber rather than iron, enabled the rapid telegraphic communication of orders of all kinds: orders to be obeyed by imperial functionaries, orders to be filled by overseas merchants – even holy orders could use the telegraph to communicate with the thousands of missionaries earnestly disseminating West European creeds and ancillary beneficial knowledge to the heathen. These networks bound the world together as never before, seeming to 'annihilate distance' and thereby creating truly global markets for commodities, manufactures, labour and capital. In turn, it was these markets that peopled the prairies of the American Mid-West and the steppe of Siberia, grew rubber in Malaya and tea in Ceylon,

---

* From the *Westminster Review*, October 1858: 'To lower the intellectual vigour of the nation . . . to exhibit to the world how the waywardness of mind will yield beneath the compression of a stern resolution – these are the tasks set itself by Imperialism.'

bred sheep in Queensland and cattle in the pampas, dug diamonds from the pipes of Kimberley and gold from the rich seams of the Rand.

Globalization is sometimes discussed as if it were a spontaneous process brought about by private agents – firms and non-governmental organizations. Economic historians chart with fascination the giddy growth of cross-border flows of goods, people and capital. Trade, migration and international lending all reached levels in relation to global output not seen again until the 1990s. A single monetary system – the gold standard – came to be adopted by nearly every major economy, encouraging later generations to look back on the pre-1914 decades as a literally 'golden' age. In economic terms it doubtless was. The world economy grew faster between 1870 and 1913 than in any previous period. It is inconceivable, however, that such high levels of international economic integration would have come about in the absence of empires. We should bear in mind that, taken together, the possessions of all the European empires – the Austrian, Belgian, British, Dutch, French, German, Italian, Portuguese, Spanish and Russian – covered more than half of the world's land surface and governed roughly the same proportion of its population. This was a political globalization unseen before or since. When these empires acted in concert, as they did in Africa from the 1870s and in China from the 1890s, they brooked no opposition.

The *ultima ratio* of the Western empires was, of course, force. But they would not have lasted as long as they did if they had relied primarily on coercion. Their strongest foundation was their ability to create multiple scale-models of themselves through colonial settlement and collaboration with indigenous peoples, giving rise to a kind of 'fractal geometry of empire'. It meant that a respectable English traveller could anticipate with some confidence the availability of afternoon tea or a stiff gin at the local gentleman's club whether he was in Durban, Darwin or Darjeeling. It meant that a late Victorian British official could be relied on to have a working knowledge of the local languages and law whether he was in St Kitts, Sierra Leone or Singapore. To be sure, each territory struck its own distinctive balance between Europeans and local elites, depending first and foremost on the attractiveness of the local climate and resources to European

## Table 1.1: Empires in 1913

| | Territory (sq. miles) | Population |
|---|---|---|
| Austria | 115,882 | 28,571,934 |
| Hungary | 125,395 | 20,886,487 |
| Belgium | 11,373 | 7,490,411 |
| Africa | 909,654 | 15,000,000 |
| France | 207,054 | 39,601,509 |
| Asia | 310,176 | 16,594,000 |
| Africa | 4,421,934 | 24,576,850 |
| America | 35,222 | 397,000 |
| Oceania | 8,744 | 85,800 |
| Germany | 208,780 | 64,925,993 |
| Africa | 931,460 | 13,419,500 |
| Asia | 200 | 168,900 |
| Pacific | 96,160 | 357,800 |
| Italy | 110,550 | 34,671,377 |
| Africa | 591,230 | 1,198,120 |
| Netherlands | 12,648 | 6,022,452 |
| Asia | 736,400 | 38,000,000 |
| Portugal | 35,490 | 5,957,985 |
| Asia | 8,972 | 895,789 |
| Africa | 793,980 | 8,243,655 |
| Spain | 194,783 | 19,588,688 |
| Africa | 85,814 | 235,844 |
| Russia (European) | 1,862,524 | 120,588,000 |
| Asian Russia | 6,294,119 | 25,664,500 |
| United Kingdom | 121,391 | 45,652,741 |
| India | 1,773,088 | 315,086,372 |
| Europe | 119 | 234,972 |
| Asia | 166,835 | 8,478,700 |
| Australia & Pacific | 3,192,677 | 6,229,252 |
| Africa | 2,233,478 | 35,980,913 |
| Other | 4,011,037 | 9,516,015 |
| United States | 2,973,890 | 91,972,266 |
| Non-contiguous terr. | 597,333 | 1,429,885 |
| Philippines | 127,853 | 8,600,000 |
| Turkey (Asian) | 429,272 | 21,000,000 |
| European Turkey | 104,984 | 8,000,000 |
| Japan | 87,426 | 52,200,679 |
| Asia | 88,114 | 3,975,041 |
| China | 1,532,420 | 407,253,080 |
| Asia | 2,744,750 | 26,299,950 |
| TOTAL WORLD | 57,268,900 | 1,791,000,000 |
| European empires | 29,607,169 | 914,000,000 |
| European empires (%) | 52% | 51% |

Note: Population totals rounded as some figures for colonial populations were clearly estimates.

immigrants. But by 1901 a kind of ornate uniformity had emerged, modelled on that elaborate system of social hierarchy which foreigners mistook for a class system, but which the British themselves understood as an elaborate and partially unwritten taxonomy of inherited status and royally conferred rank.

All the established empires of 1901 sought to make virtues out of their necessities. From the Delhi Durbars of 1877 and 1903 to the parades through Vienna that marked the Emperor Francis Joseph's birthday, they staged colourful festivities that celebrated their ethnic diversity. British theorists of empire like Frederick Lugard began to argue that 'indirect rule', which effectively delegated substantial power to local chiefs and maharajas, was preferable to hands-on 'direct rule'. Even so, the Western empires were, like their Eastern counterparts, manifestly nearing their ends, as Rudyard Kipling divined in 'Recessional' (1897), his finest poem. By the end of the nineteenth century, the costs to the British of maintaining control over their distant possessions were perceptibly rising relative to the benefits, which in any case flowed to a relatively few wealthy investors. Guy de Maupassant's *Bel-Ami* (1885) gives a good flavour of the unedifying nexus that had developed between political elites, financial markets and imperial expansion:

She was saying:

'Oh, they've done something very clever. Very clever ... It really is a wonderful operation ... An expedition against Tangier had been agreed upon between the two of them the day Laroche became Foreign Secretary and gradually they've been buying up the whole of the Moroccan loan which had dropped to sixty-four or sixty-five francs. They did their buying very cleverly, using ... shady dealers who wouldn't arouse any suspicion. They even succeeded in fooling the Rothschilds, who were surprised at seeing such a steady demand for Moroccan stock. Their reply was to mention the names of all the dealers involved, all unreliable and on their beam ends. That calmed the big banks' suspicions. And so now we're going to send an expedition and as soon as we've succeeded, the French government will guarantee the Moroccan debt. Our friends will have made about fifty or sixty million francs. You see how it works?' ...

He said: 'It really is very clever. As for that louse Laroche, I'll get even with him for this. The blackguard! He'd better look out . . . I'll have his ministerial blood for this!'

Then he began to think. He said more quietly:

'But we ought to take advantage of it.'

'You can still buy the loan,' she said. 'It's only at seventy-two.'

To be sure, widening franchises at home and in some settler colonies did not necessarily portend decolonization – if anything, the British Empire became truly popular only in the last half-century of its existence. But democratization did make it harder to justify major peacetime expenditures on imperial security when metropolitan electorates were manifestly more interested in social security. Only in time of war, as the British discovered in their painful struggle to subjugate the Boers, could the public be relied on to rally to the flag; and even that emotion could quickly turn to disenchantment when the price of victory became clear. This was something of which even the most enthusiastic imperialists were acutely aware. Of the 726,000 people who had left the United Kingdom in the last decade of the nineteenth century, 72 per cent had gone not to other parts of the British Empire but to the United States. 'The great problem of the coming years', conceded *The Times* uneasily,

will be to consolidate the Empire, to bring its several parts into organic and vital relation with each other and with the old country, their common origin and home, to convert the noble impulse which has led the sons of all the colonies to help the Empire in its need [in South Africa] into a working bond of indissoluble union.

As the newspaper admitted, however, 'the solution of this problem is not to be propounded off-hand'.

## MISCEGENATION

This imperial world had once been a racial melting pot. Whether in the Caribbean, America or India, British businessmen and soldiers had felt no compunction about sleeping with and in many cases marrying indigenous women. To take a native concubine had been the norm for employees of the Hudson's Bay Company; it had been positively encouraged by its East Indian counterpart, which in 1778 offered five rupees as a christening present for every child born to a soldier and his (invariably) Indian wife. The founders of the British colony for freed slaves at Sierra Leone had also made no objection to mixed marriages. The situation was, of course, somewhat different for those Africans and their descendants who remained as slaves in the New World, but there too interbreeding had gone on. Thomas Jefferson was by no means the only master to take advantage of his power for the sake of sexual gratification: there were at least 60,000 'mulattos' in North America by the end of the colonial period.

'Demic diffusion' had gone even further in other empires, where settlers tended to be single men rather than whole families. In Brazil sexual relations between early Portuguese settlers, natives and African slaves were relatively uninhibited, even if largely confined to concubinage. The story was broadly the same in Spanish America. By 1605, when the Hispanic-Peruvian historian Garcilaso de la Vega sought to give a precise definition of the term 'Creole', he had to coin such terms as 'Quarteron' or 'Quartratuo' to convey the difference between Creoles proper (the offspring of Spanish and Indian parents) and the children produced by a Spaniard and a Creole. The Dutch too had little hesitation in taking native concubines when they settled in Asia (though the practice was less common among the Boers in South Africa). From Canada to Senegal to Madagascar, the *métis* were an almost universal by-product of French colonial settlement. One French colonial writer, Médéric-Louis-Elie Moreau de Saint-Méry, identified thirteen different hues of skin colour in his account of the island of Saint-Domingue, published in 1797.

Yet by 1901 there had been a worldwide revulsion against 'miscegenation'. As early as 1808, all 'Eurasians' had been excluded from the East India Company's forces, and in 1835 intermarriage was formally banned in British India. In the aftermath of the 1857 Mutiny, attitudes towards interracial sex hardened as part of a general process of segregation, a phenomenon usually, though not quite justly, attributed to the increasing presence and influence of white women in India. As numerous stories by Kipling, Somerset Maugham and others testify,* interracial unions continued, but their progeny were viewed with undisguised disdain. In 1888 the official brothels that served the British army in India were abolished, while in 1919 the Crewe Circular expressly banned officials throughout the Empire from taking native mistresses. By this time, the idea that miscegenation implied degeneration, and that criminality was correlated to the ratio of native to white blood, had been generally accepted in expatriate circles. Throughout the Empire, there was also a growing (and largely fantastic) obsession with the sexual threat supposedly posed to white women by native men. The theme can be found in two of the most popular works of fiction produced by the British rule in India, E. M. Forster's *A Passage to India* and Paul Scott's *The Jewel in the Crown*, and also gave rise to a bitter campaign to prevent Indian judges hearing cases involving white women. By 1901 racial segregation was the norm in most of the British Empire. It was most explicit in South Africa, however, where Dutch settlers had from an early stage banned marriage between *burghers* and blacks. Their descendants were the driving force behind subsequent legislation. In 1897 the Boer republic of the Transvaal prohibited white women from having extramarital intercourse with black men, and this became the template for legislation in the Cape Colony (1902), Natal and the Orange Free State (1903), as well as in neighbouring Rhodesia.

In many ways, pseudo-science merely provided sophisticated rationales for such measures. Ideas like 'Social Darwinism', which erroneously inferred from Darwin's theories a struggle for survival between the races, or 'racial hygiene', which argued that physical and mental degeneration would result from miscegenation, came some time after prohibitions had been enacted. This was especially obvious in Britain's North American colonies and the United States. From the earliest phase of British settlement in North America there had been laws designed to discourage miscegenation and to circumscribe the rights of mulattos. Interracial marriage may have been a punishable offence in Virginia from as early as 1630 and was formally prohibited

---

* A fine example of the genre is W. Somerset Maugham's 'The Pool', in which a hapless Aberdonian businessman tries in vain to Westernize his half-Samoan bride. In British India, apparently European ladies were scrutinized for traces of the 'tar brush', such as a distinctive tinge of colour beneath their fingernails.

by legislation in 1662; the colony of Maryland had passed similar legislation a year earlier. Such laws were passed by five other North American colonies. In the century after the foundation of the United States, no fewer than thirty-eight states banned interracial marriages. In 1915, twenty-eight states retained such statutes; ten of them had gone so far as to make the prohibition on miscegenation constitutional. There was even an attempt, in December 1912, to amend the federal constitution so as to prohibit 'forever ... intermarriage between negros or persons of color and Caucasians ... within the United States'. The language of the various statutes and constitutional articles certainly changed over time, as rationalizations for the ban on interracial sex evolved, and as new threats to racial purity emerged. Definitions of whiteness and blackness became more precise: in Virginia, for example, anyone with one or more 'Negro' grandparents was defined as a 'Negro', but it was possible to have one 'Indian' great-grandparent and still be white in the eyes of the law. Depending on patterns of immigration, a number of states extended their prohibitions to include 'Mongolians', 'Asiatic Indians', Chinese, Japanese, Koreans, Filipinos and Malays. Penalties also varied widely. Some laws simply declared interracial unions null and void, depriving couples of the legal privileges of marriage; others specified penalties of up to ten years in prison. Nevertheless, the underlying motivation seems remarkably consistent and enduring.

Legal prohibitions could not prevent the emergence of a substantial mixed-race population in North America. Yet precisely this social reality appears to have heightened, if it did not actually create, anxieties about miscegenation, giving rise to a large body of more or less lurid literature on the subject. In *The Races of Men*, published in Philadelphia in 1850, Robert Knox emphatically repudiated the idea that any good could come of the 'amalgamation of races'; the 'mullato' was 'a monstrosity of nature'. Among the most influential opponents of miscegenation was the Swiss-American polygenist and Harvard professor Jean Louis Rodolphe Agassiz. In August 1863 he was asked by Samuel Gridley Howe, the head of Lincoln's American Freedman's Inquiry Commission, whether 'the African race ... will be a *persistent* race in this country; or, will it be absorbed, diluted, & finally effaced by the white race'. The government, Agassiz replied, should 'put every possible obstacle to the crossing of the races, and the increase of the half-breeds':

The production of half-breeds is as much a sin against nature, as incest in a civilized community is a sin against purity of character . . . Far from presenting to me a natural solution of our difficulties, the idea of amalgamation is most repugnant to my feelings, I hold it to be a perversion of every natural sentiment . . . No efforts should be spared to check that which is abhorrent to our better nature, and to the progress of the higher civilization and a purer morality . . . Conceive for a moment the difference it would make in future ages, for the prospect of republican institutions and our civilization generally, if instead of the manly population descended from cognate nations the United States should hereafter be inhabited by the effeminate progeny of mixed races, half indian, half negro, sprinkled with white blood . . . I shudder from the consequences . . . How shall we eradicate the stigma of a lower race when its blood has once been allowed to flow freely into that of our children?

Within the broader debate over the abolition of slavery, argument raged as to the relative strength, morals and fecundity of mulattos, with some authorities asserting their 'hybrid vigour', while others – notably the physician and 'niggerologist' Josiah Nott – insisted on their degeneracy. In 1864 two anti-abolition journalists caused an outcry by publishing a satirical tract entitled *Miscegenation: The Theory of the Blending of the Races, Applied to the American White Man and Negro*, which argued facetiously that interbreeding made the races more fertile, and that this was the key to the success of Southern arms in the Civil War. What most opponents of emancipation actually believed was that (in the words of the eminent palaeontologist and evolutionary biologist E. D. Cope) 'the hybrid is not as good a race as the white, and in some respects it often falls below the black especially in the sturdy qualities that accompany vigorous physique.' According to Nott, miscegenation would lead ultimately to extinction because the children of mixed marriages would be sterile themselves or would produce sterile progeny. The 'half-caste' was also suspected of posing a threat to social order. The sociologist Edward Byron Reuter argued that it was mulattos, a 'discontented and psychologically unstable group', who were responsible for 'the acute phases of the so-called race problem'. It is striking, too, that precursors of the story later told in Arthur Dinter's notorious novel *The Sin Against the Blood* (see Chapter 7) can already be found in American novels like Robert Lee Durham's *Call of the South* (1908), in which it is the daughter of the president himself who gives birth to a dark-skinned child.

Thus, although slavery was abolished after the Civil War, the Southern states lost little time in erecting a system of segregation, in which prohibitions on intermarriage and intercourse played a central role. That said, the absence of formal prohibitions in the North by no means implied a toleration of interracial relationships. Franz Boas, Professor of Anthropology at Columbia University, was highly unusual in recommending intermarriage (albeit only 'between white men and negro women') as a way of reducing racial tensions. Few shared his vision. Indeed, as Gunnar Myrdal noted in *An American Dilemma* (1944), racial anxieties appeared to increase when formal barriers between the races were removed. Mixed-race couples were generally ostracized by white society and, as long as the Supreme Court upheld the legality of state bans on mixed marriages, such couples remained a very small minority. American anxieties about racial mingling were only increased by the new waves of immigration from Eastern and Southern Europe in the late nineteenth and early twentieth centuries, despite the fact that, at least in the first generation, the new immigrants practised quite strict endogamy. Yet it was not in the United States that the reaction against interracial marriage took its most extreme form. It was in Europe; most surprisingly, in Germany.

## THE JEWISH 'QUESTION'

It is at first sight odd that hostility to miscegenation should also have manifested itself as anti-Semitism. Of all ethnic groups, few exceeded the Jews in their commitment – in principle, at least – to endogamy. The Torah is quite explicit on this score:

When the Lord thy God shall bring thee into the land whither thou goest to possess it, and hath cast out many nations before thee . . . thou shalt smite them, and utterly destroy them; thou shalt make no covenant with them, nor shew mercy unto them: Neither shalt thou make marriages with them; thy daughter thou shalt not give unto his son, nor his daughter shalt thou take unto thy son.

Divine retribution would be swift and severe in cases of transgression. Daughters who dared to marry out of the faith were formally pronounced dead. Some, though not all, Jewish communities followed this injunction quite strictly. In Britain, for example, the small Jewish community that had re-established itself in the late seventeenth century saw very few marriages out before the 1830s, when the apostasy of Nathan Rothschild's daughter and her marriage to Henry Fitzroy caused intense family distress and communal dismay. Indeed, the rate of intermarriage between Jews and Gentiles remained very low in Britain before 1901, despite the relatively small size of the Jewish community. It is not too much to say that in Victorian times opposition to mixed marriages was probably stronger among Jews than among non-Jews. Yet this did not prevent anxieties about the sexual appetites of Jews from surfacing in British literature. An early example is Farquhar's play of 1702 *The Twin Rivals*, in which the licentious Mr Moabite, a rich Jew of Lombard Street, secretly conveys to his house a young lady about to give birth to his bastard child, whom he wishes to raise as a Jew. Hogarth's *The Harlot's Progress*, dramatized by Theophilus Cibber in 1733, further develops the theme of Jewish lasciviousness, and still more Jewish fornicators and lechers can be found in Fielding's play *Miss Lucy in Town*, or in Smollett's *Roderick Random* and *Peregrine Pickle*. Where the eighteenth century satirized, the early nineteenth century romanticized. The 'wandering Jew' with his beautiful (and perhaps convertible) daughter were familiar figures in novels like Scott's *Ivanhoe* and John Galt's *The Wandering Jew*, not to mention George Eliot's relatively benign *Daniel Deronda*. By the end of the nineteenth century, by contrast, Jews in English literature had become more closely associated with 'white slavery', a euphemism for prostitution.

The German experience was different. Because they came so much later to overseas empire, Germans adopted 'scientific' racism at a relatively late date. There was no German translation of Gobineau's *Essay on the Inequality of Human Races* (1853–5) until 1898. And, since so few Germans emigrated to tropical colonies, they were more likely to apply imported theories of Social Darwinism and 'racial hygiene' to Jews – the nearest identifiable 'alien' race – than to Africans or Asians. The composer Richard Wagner provides a good example of the way the race 'meme' spread to Germany. Wagner read Gobineau in the original French in 1880 and immediately adopted the idea of the declining racial purity of the German people, which he somewhat eccentrically dated back to the rape of German women by invading armies during the Thirty Years War of 1618–48. Especially detrimental, in Wagner's view, was any mingling of German and Jewish blood. As early as 1873 – in other words, even before he had read Gobineau – Wagner had rejected the idea that mixed marriages were a 'solution to the [Jewish] problem', arguing that 'then there would no longer be any Germans, since the blonde German blood is not strong enough to resist this leech. We can see how the Normans and Franks became French, and Jewish blood is much more corrosive than Roman.' Others followed similar lines of reasoning. In *The Jewish Question as a Question of Races, Customs and Culture* (1881), the Berlin philosopher and economist Eugen Dühring, another follower of Gobineau, lamented the 'implanting of the character traits of the Jewish race' and called for a prohibition on mixed marriages to preserve the purity of German blood. Theodor Fritsch's *Anti-Semitic Catechism* (1887) warned Germans to keep their blood 'pure' by avoiding contact of all kinds with Jews. His new version of the Ten Commandments included: 'Regard it as a crime to contaminate the noble stuff of your people with Jewish matter. Know that Jewish blood is indestructible and forms body and soul in the Jewish way for all future generations.' 'Guard against the Jew within you,' warned another, for no German could be certain that all his ancestors had resisted Jewish contamination. One of the defining works of German racial thought – *The Foundations of the Nineteenth Century* (1899) – was in fact written by an Englishman, Houston Stewart Chamberlain, who had emigrated to Germany in his twenties and married one of Wagner's daughters. Chamberlain too argued that Germany faced a choice between racial homogeneity or 'chaos'. The leader of the Pan-German League, Heinrich Class, was another who regarded 'half-bloods' as playing a malign role in German society.

Some German anti-Semitic literature was crudely sensationalist. As in England, there were lurid allegations that Jews played a leading part in the organization of prostitution. In a tract entitled *Brothel Jews*, it was alleged that Jews considered 'the corruption of our virgins, the trade in girls, the seduction of women as no sin, but a sacrifice that they make to their Jehovah; the same applies to the spread of degenerative diseases and plagues that they thereby facilitate'. In vain did German-Jewish feminists like Bertha Pappenheim point out that many of the victims of the 'white slave trade' were themselves Jewish girls from Eastern Europe. The stereotype of the lecherous Jew seducing or raping non-Jewish females also made its first appearances in German caricatures at around this time. Sensational in a rather different way were those works that sought to expose the Jewish ancestry of supposedly blue-blooded families. The authors of the volume known as the *Semi-Gotha*, a parody of the aristocratic handbook the *Almanach de Gotha*, alleged that there were more than a thousand old aristocratic and recently ennobled Gentile families now partly or wholly Jewish through marriage. Yet interwoven with such muck-raking were more sinister intimations of radical 'solutions' to the so-called 'Jewish question'. In *Jews and Indo-Germans* (1887), the Orientalist Paul de Lagarde characterized Jews as 'bearers of decay', comparing them with 'trichinae and bacilli'. The best remedy in such cases was 'annihilation' by means of 'surgical intervention and medication'. In a Reichstag debate in 1895, the anti-Semitic deputy Hermann Ahlwardt referred to Jews as 'cholera bacilli' and called for the authorities to 'exterminate' them as the British had exterminated the 'Thugs' in India. As early as 1899 the anti-Semitic German Social Reform Party called for a 'final solution' of the 'Jewish question' to take the form of 'complete separation and (if self-defence requires it) ultimately the annihilation of the Jewish people'. The racial hygienist Alfred Ploetz's German League also called for the 'extermination of less valuable elements from the population'.

From such declarations it is all too tempting to draw a more or less straight line to Hitler's death camps. It should nevertheless be stressed that there were also strong countervailing tendencies at the turn of the century. As has often been remarked, someone in 1901 trying to predict a future Holocaust would have been unlikely to pick Germany as the country responsible. Jews accounted for less than 1 per cent of the German population, and that proportion had been declining for two decades. In absolute and relative terms, there were far larger Jewish communities in the Western provinces of Russia (see Chapter 2) and the eastern parts of Austria-Hungary – notably Galicia, Bukovina and Hungary itself – to say nothing of Romania and, it should be noted, the United States, which already had the biggest Jewish population in the world. Of the fifty-eight European cities with Jewish populations in excess of 10,000 in around 1900, just three – Berlin, Posen and Breslau – were in Germany, and only in Posen did the Jewish community account for more than 5 per cent of the population. Moreover, the process of assimilation was much further advanced in Germany than in Russia and Austria. Legal obstacles to marriage between Jews and non-Jews were removed in 1875, bringing the Reich into line with Belgium, Britain, Denmark, France, Holland, Switzerland and the United States. (Hungary followed only in 1895, while in Austria one party or the other was obliged to change religion, or both were obliged to register as 'confessionless'. In the Russian Empire it remained illegal.) The results were striking. In 1876 around 5 per cent of Prussian Jews who married took non-Jews as their spouses. By 1900 the proportion had risen to 8.5 per cent. For the Reich as a whole, the percentage rose from 7.8 per cent in 1901 to 20.4 per cent in 1914. Such statistics must be used with caution, since the inherent probability of a mixed marriage must be a function of the relative sizes of the two populations concerned; other things being equal, such marriages were and are more likely to occur where Jewish communities are relatively small. However, contemporary researchers were struck by the fact that the intermarriage rates were highest in Germany in those places where the Jewish communities were largest, namely the big cities of Berlin, Hamburg and Munich. By the early 1900s, around one in five Hamburg Jews who married took a non-Jew as his or her spouse; Berlin was not far behind (18 per cent), followed by Munich (15 per cent) and Frankfurt (11 per cent). There was also a discernible rise in intermarriage in Breslau. The figures were markedly lower in Austria-Hungary – even in Vienna, Prague and Budapest – while in Galicia and Bukovina there were virtually no mixed marriages. In the United States, too, there was much less intermarriage than in Germany at this time, reflecting the large proportion of Jews in the US who had migrated from less assimilationist Eastern Europe; indeed, it was not until the 1950s that American Jews began to marry out the way German Jews had done in the 1900s. Switzerland and the United Kingdom also lagged behind; only the Danish and Italian Jewish communities evinced comparable intermarriage rates. In the eyes of the Posen-born sociologist Arthur Ruppin, this trend 'constitute[d] a serious menace to the continued existence' of the Jewish communities of Berlin and Hamburg. On the other hand, he could not resist observing, the spread of intermarriage gave the lie to the claims of anti-Semites 'that Jewish blood destroys the pure "Aryan" race and that physiological antipathy is such that marriage between the two races is unnatural . . . The parties who contract the marriage are surely the best judges as to whether there exists any physical antipathy!'

When anti-Semites called for legal discrimination against the Jews, they therefore had to define what they meant by a Jew with considerable care since the progeny of mixed marriages were already quite numerous – even if, contrary to the fears of some anti-Semites, the average number of children produced by mixed marriages was significantly fewer than the number produced by 'pure' Jewish or Christian marriages. By 1905 there were already more than 5,000 mixed couples in Prussia alone and by 1930 between 30,000 and 40,000. Estimates for the number of children produced by such mixed marriages in the first three decades of the twentieth century range from 60,000 to 125,000. In fact, only a minority of the children born to such couples were raised as Jews, though that was irrelevant from a racialist viewpoint. The criteria devised by the Pan-German leader Heinrich Class in 1912 were that everyone who had belonged to a Jewish religious community on the date of the Reich's foundation in 1871 was a Jew and so, too, were all their descendants: 'Thus for example the grandson of a Jew who had converted to Protestantism in 1875, whose daughter had married a non-Jew, for example an officer, would be treated as a Jew.' The fact that he felt the need to write such a sentence was in itself significant.

Nor was German political culture especially receptive to anti-Semitism, though anti-Semitic parties enjoyed a brief flurry of success in the 1880s and 1890s. Nowhere in the world were the egalitarian and secular teachings of Karl Marx (himself an apostate married to a Gentile) more widely accepted than in Germany; by 1912 the German Social Democrats were the biggest party in the country's far from impotent parliament, the Reichstag. Admittedly, some German socialists were not wholly immune to anti-Semitism, having inherited from the generation of 1848 a tendency to elide the categories of capitalist and Jew. Yet the leadership of the German Social Democratic Party was consistent in its opposition to notions of racial discrimination. While one American state after another introduced legal and even constitutional bans on interracial marriages, the Reichstag rejected a proposal to introduce similar legislation for the German colonies. Indeed, Jews suffered no form of legal discrimination under the *Kaiserreich*. Moreover, their access to higher education and thence to the professions was as good as it was anywhere else in Europe, if not better. Jews were far more likely to be the victims of discrimination and, indeed, violence in Tsarist Russia, as we shall see. That was precisely why so many Jews at the turn of the century left the Russian Empire for Germany, Austria-Hungary and destinations further west. Indeed, it is impossible to understand what befell the Jews in the twentieth century other than in the context of this westward exodus, which was often accompanied by a weakening of traditional Jewish practices, most obviously endogamy.

To some German Jews – not only Arthur Ruppin but also Felix Theilhaber and others – the increase in mixed marriages was just one symptom of a general 'downfall of the Jewish religion', which also manifested itself in apostasy, suicide, low fertility and physical or mental degeneracy. Indeed, it was Ruppin's growing conviction that assimilation spelt the death of Judaism that converted him to Zionism. But in the eyes of others, interracial marriage was in fact the best answer to the Jewish 'question'. In his 1874 story *Between the Ruins*, the Pressburg-born Jew Leopold Kompert had portrayed the love between a Jewish boy and a Christian girl as a symbol of assimilation and an antidote to superstition and prejudice. As the Austrian Social Democrat Otto Bauer put it, 'This last of all Jewish problems' would be resolved by 'young men's inclinations and young women's choice in love'. Other German proponents of intermarriage included the

Zionist Adolf Brüll, who believed that an infusion of soldierly 'Aryan' genes would strengthen the character of East European Jews. In the words of Otto Weininger, himself a convert to Christianity, 'the pairing instinct is the great remover of the limits between individuals, and the Jew, *par excellence*, is the breaker down of such limits'. Even some anti-Semites succumbed to this very instinct. The late nineteenth-century German publicist Wilhelm Marr, author of *The Victory of Jewry over Germandom* (1879), is usually credited with coining the term 'anti-Semitism'. Echoing Friedrich Nietzsche, Marr feared that 'The future and life itself belonged to Jewry; to Germandom, the past and death.' Yet in his revealing autobiographical essay entitled 'Within Philo-Semitism', Marr admitted to having had Jewish girlfriends while still at school and later as a young man in Poland. He also recalled flirting with two young Jewish women on a transatlantic steamer. Marr married three times in all: one wife was the daughter of an apostate Jew, one was a 'half Jewess' and the third a 'full Jewess'. As Rudolph Loewenstein once observed, 'the sexual factor is one of the most powerful unacknowledged motivations underlying anti-Semitism'. In short, between Germans and Jews there was what deserves to be called a 'love-hate' relationship. Those who projected trends in inter-marriage, fertility and apostasy were not unreasonable in thinking that the Jewish 'question', in Germany at least, was answering itself – through a willing dissolution.

## THE ECONOMICS OF ANTI-SEMITISM

Anti-Semitism in 1901 was, it is almost superfluous to say, about more than just fears of miscegenation. Economic grievances were just as important. It was the extraordinary social and geographical mobility of *Ashkenazim* in the aftermath of their eighteenth- and early nineteenth-century emancipation that created core constituencies for anti-Jewish policies. Those who felt the Rothschilds and their ilk had made illicit profits by manipulating the stock exchange were not especially interested in racial hygiene. Authors like the Frenchman Alphonse Toussenel, writer of *The Jews, Kings of the Epoch* (1847), were radicals – men of the Left, indignant at the leading role played by Jewish bankers in what Toussenel called a new 'financial feudal-ism'. Marx himself wrote a review article 'On the Jewish Question', which identified the capitalist, regardless of his religion, as 'the real Jew'. Similar hostility to the Jews as 'parasites' was expressed by both the French socialist Pierre-Joseph Proudhon and the Russian anarchist Mikhail Bakunin. The unscrupulous Jewish financier is a figure who crops up in the literatures of most European countries in the nineteenth century; not only in Gustav Freytag's *Soll und Haben* but also in Balzac's *La maison Nucingen*, Zola's *L'Argent* and Trollope's *The Way We Live Now*. Zola's Gundermann, for example, is the quintes-sential 'banker king, the master of the bourse and of the world . . . the man who knew [all] secrets, who made the markets rise and fall at his pleasure as God makes the thunder . . . the king of gold'. The inspiration behind Edouard Drumont's *Jewish France* (1886) was the collapse of the Union Générale bank four years before, which Dru-mont and others sought to blame on the Rothschilds. To Auguste Chirac and numerous others, the Third Republic was wholly in the grip of 'Jewish finance'.

In Germany, too, the most politically successful anti-Semites of the late nineteenth century were those like Otto Böckel, the self-styled 'Peasant King', who directed their fire at the economic role of the Jews. His pamphlet *The Jews: Kings of Our Time* (1886), which had sold 1.5 million copies by 1909, adapted earlier French arguments to the tastes of the Hessian peasants who were the principal constituents for his Anti-Semitic People's Party. Böckel himself was a Reichstag deputy from 1887 to 1903; at the movement's zenith in 1893, he was one of seventeen self-styled Anti-Semites sitting in the Reichstag. By this time, it was not only as financiers that Jews were coming under attack, though it is noteworthy that 31 per cent of the richest families in Germany were Jewish and 22 per cent of all Prussian millionaires. German Jews were also strikingly better represented among pro-fessionals than among entrepreneurs or business executives. Jews might account for fewer than one in every hundred Germans; but by the second quarter of the twentieth century one in nine German doctors was a Jew, and one in six lawyers. There were also above-average numbers of Jews working as newspaper editors, journalists, theatre directors and academics. Indeed, they were under-represented in only one of Germany's elite occupational groups, and that was the officer corps of the army. Anti-Semitism, then, was sometimes nothing more than the envy of under-achievers. There was, nevertheless, a countervailing influence on the way Jews were perceived in Germany, and that was the growing number of them who migrated from Eastern Europe to Germany in the late nineteenth and early twentieth centuries. By 1914 around a quarter of the Jews in Germany were defined as foreign or Eastern (which included those who originated in the borderland provinces of Upper Silesia and Posen). Relatively poor, Orthodox in their faith, Yiddish in their speech, the so-called *Ostjuden* elicited much the same response among German Jews as among German Gentiles: disquiet, bordering on revulsion.

Jewish professional success was even more conspicuous in Austria-Hungary, where they in any case accounted for a larger share of the urban population. They were more than merely prominent in the Viennese intelligentsia and played a leading role in the Prague business community. The numbers of immigrant *Ostjuden* were also much larger in Vienna than in Berlin. Perhaps not surprisingly, it was therefore primarily on the basis of economic grievances that anti-Semites like the Pan-German Georg Ritter von Schönerer and the Christian Socialist Karl Lueger achieved political success in pre-war Austria-Hungary. It was Lueger who, as mayor of Vienna from 1897 until 1910, most perfectly encapsulated the challenge of practising anti-Semitism in the context of very rapid social assimilation when he declared: 'I decide who is a Jew.' When Neville Laski, president of the Board of Deputies of British Jews, visited Vienna twenty years later, the Minister for Commerce cheerfully explained that Lueger's anti-Semitism 'had been scientific because [when] Lueger said "He is a Jew whom I say is a Jew" . . . he thereby avoided any anti-Semitism against a useful Jew'.

As this suggests, economic anti-Semitism inspired quite different policy responses from racial anti-Semitism. The slogan *Kauft nicht von Juden!* – 'Don't buy from Jews!' – was used by the German Catholic magazine *Germania* as early as 1876. Three years later the clergyman turned anti-Semitic demagogue Adolf Stoecker called for Jews to be excluded from the teaching profession and the judiciary. Such proposals were especially attractive to Gentile small

businessmen, professionals and white-collar employees who felt themselves unable to match the performance of their Jewish contemporaries. The German National Clerical Workers' Association was among
the first German associations expressly to exclude Jews from membership by inserting a so-called 'Aryan paragraph' in their rules and
regulations. So too did many student fraternities, including some
traditionally liberal *Burschenschaften*. When Bernhard Förster and
Max Liebermann von Sonnenberg circulated a petition calling for
Jews to be excluded from certain branches of the German civil service,
4,000 signatures out of the 225,000 they collected were from university students. Significantly, it was an academic – the historian Heinrich
von Treitschke – who in 1879 coined the phrase: 'The Jews Are Our
Misfortune!'

Academics were especially strongly represented among the members
of the Pan-German League, whose leader after 1908, Heinrich Class,
was one of the most extreme anti-Semites of the Wilhelmine era. In
his pseudonymously written book, *If I Were the Kaiser* (1912), Class
published a remarkable and ominous list of recommendations to
restrict the economic opportunities of Jews:

1 Germany's borders should be closed to further Jewish immigration.
2 Jews resident in Germany who did not have German citizenship
   should be 'immediately and ruthlessly' (*schnellstens und rück-
   sichtslos*) expelled.
3 Jews with German citizenship, including converts to Christianity
   and the offspring of mixed marriages, should be given the legal
   status of foreigners.
4 Jews should be excluded from all public office.
5 Jews should not be permitted to serve in the army or navy.
6 Jews should be disenfranchised.
7 Jews should be excluded from the teaching and legal professions
   and from the direction of theatres.
8 Jewish journalists should be permitted to work only for newspapers explicitly identified as 'Jewish'.
9 Jews should not be permitted to run banks.
10 Jews should not be allowed to own agricultural land or mortgages
   on agricultural land.

11  Jews should pay double the taxes levied on Germans 'as compensation for the protection they enjoy as ethnic aliens (*Volksfremde*)'.

Significantly, Class regarded these 'coldly cruel' measures as a remedy for the consequences not of economic crisis but of economic growth. It was the creation of a German Customs Union in 1834 that had made the ascent of the Jews in Germany possible, because Jews – 'a people born to trade in money and goods' – knew better than Germans how to take advantage of the enlarged free market:

As a result of all these factors and a host of other economic circumstances, the opportunities for business rose in an unprecedented way. The generality of Germans adjusted slowly to the new conditions . . . indeed, one might say that whole classes to this day have not yet come to terms with them – one thinks in particular of the small-town *Mittelstand* and almost the whole of agriculture. The Jews were quite different . . . [since] their instinct and spiritual orientation is towards business. Their halcyon day had dawned; now they could make the most of their abilities.

Apart from anything else, Class's account illustrates perfectly that fluctuations in racial prejudice could be caused as much by economic upswings as by crises.

## THE GERMAN DIASPORA

In 1901 the Jewish diaspora was still in the early stages of what promised to be a profound transformation. Over 70 per cent of the world's 10.6 million Jews were Ashkenazim living in Central and Eastern Europe, of whom more than three million lived in Russian territory. As we shall see, these people had strong incentives to move westwards and, in their hundreds of thousands, they were doing precisely that, forming vibrant new Jewish communities in New York, in the East End of London, in Berlin, Budapest and Vienna. That did not signify the decline of the established Jewish communities in Eastern Europe, however. Demographically, if not in other ways, they continued to thrive. It would be more accurate to say that the Jews, like so much else at the start of the twentieth century, were being globalized. At the same time, similar processes were transforming another diaspora. In their millions – perhaps as many as five million in all – Germans had migrated across the Atlantic in the course of the nineteenth century, establishing large and proudly Germanic communities in the American Mid-West. Yet an earlier German diaspora was meanwhile struggling to come to terms with the experience of relative decline.

In 1901 there were more than thirteen million Germans living beyond the Reich's eastern frontier. Around nine million lived in Austria, but around four million lived further east, principally in Hungary, Romania and Russia. There were substantial German communities along the Baltic coast, in Poland, Galicia and Bukovina, as well as in Bohemia and Moravia. There were also Germans to be found in Slovakia, Hungary, Transylvania and Slovenia. Nor were these settlements confined to the Habsburg lands. There were German populations in Russian territory, too, in Volhynia, in Bessarabia and Dobrudja, around the mouths of the rivers Prut and Dniester, and along the southern reaches of the Volga. It is not at all easy to rescue the history of these mostly vanished communities from the exaggerated claims made for them in the 1930s and 1940s by Nazi propagandists. Nevertheless, there is no question that many German settlements could trace their roots back centuries. It had been in the late tenth century, at the behest of King Stephan I, that German settlers had first come to western Hungary. In the twelfth century this process was repeated when the Siebenbürger 'Saxons'* were encouraged to settle in Transylvania, where they founded towns like Klausenberg, Hermannstadt and Bistritz. At around the same time German communities also sprang up in Slovakia, notably Pressburg (now Bratislava), Kaschau (Kosice) and Zips (Spisská), as well as in Slovenia, notably Laibach (now Ljubljana). Often these settlements had a strategic character; their intention was to create fortified settlements along the Eastern Marches of Christendom. This was most clearly the case along the Baltic coast. By 1405 the Teutonic Knights' realm extended from the River Elbe all the way up to Narva Bay. Thorn (Toruń), Marienburg (Malbork), Mümmelburg (Memel) and Königsberg (now

---

* They were in fact from Franconia, not Saxony.

Kaliningrad) were all founded by the Order. Yet the Germans also put down civilian as well as military roots in Eastern Europe. Numerous towns in Poland, such as Lublin and Lemberg (Lwów), were established in the thirteenth and fourteenth centuries on the basis of German legal models. Though often obliterated by the ravages of twentieth-century war (most completely in Königsberg), the German architectural legacy is still visible today in Toruń – to say nothing of Prague, where the oldest of all German universities was founded by the Emperor Charles IV in 1348.

Despite the storms and stresses of the intervening centuries, the position of the Germans in Central and Eastern Europe had often remained privileged, if not dominant. Not only did German dynasties, German soldiers and German officials run two of the great empires of the region. They were also among the principal landowners of the Baltic. They were the officials and professors of Prague and Czernowitz. They farmed some of the best land in Transylvania and worked the mines of Resita and Anina. Yet the migrations that had produced these various communities had not been sustained on a sufficiently large scale to supplant entirely the indigenous peoples. The numbers of German migrants were in any case small, perhaps 2,000 people a year in the twelfth and thirteenth centuries. Already by the fifteenth and sixteenth centuries the German influence in Polish towns had been discernibly diluted. In the seventeenth and eighteenth centuries, first Sweden and then Russia checked German colonization of the eastern Baltic. The Habsburgs' efforts to resettle Germans ('Swabians') in the Banat, Bukovina and the Balkans during the eighteenth century could only partly compensate for these tendencies. The German colonists attracted to the banks of the Volga and the coast of the Black Sea by the Empress Catherine the Great were as effectively cut off from the culture of their fatherland as if they had crossed the Atlantic. In the second half of the nineteenth century, somewhat higher non-German birth rates further reduced the relative size of this German diaspora. More importantly, large-scale migration of Slav peasants from the countryside into traditionally German towns created an acute sense of 'population pressure'. The inner city of Prague, for example, went from being 21 per cent German-speaking to just 8 per cent between 1880 and 1900 as a result of an influx of Czechs. The lignite mining town of Brüx (Most) went from 89 per cent German to 73 per cent. More isolated German communities in places like Trautenau (Trutnov) in north-eastern Bohemia, or Iglau (Jihlava) in Moravia, began to think of themselves as inhabitants of 'language islands' (*Sprachinseln*). Such demographic and social shifts help to explain why the Germans outside Germany felt a sense of cultural and political vulnerability. It was German workers in Trautenau who, in 1904, founded the German Workers' Party. Their principal goal, declared its leader in 1913, was 'the maintenance and increase of [German] living space' (*Lebensraum*) against the threat posed by Czech *Halbmenschen* ('half-humans'). This was in fact a response to the creation of a *Czech* National Socialist Party in 1898.

The easternmost territories of Germany were subject to similar demographic trends. Germans who lived in the Prussian provinces of East Prussia, West Prussia, Posen and Upper Silesia also felt a sense of unease at, for example, the way the non-German population of the Reich's periphery was seasonally if not permanently swollen by Polish migrant workers. (It was on this subject that the young Max Weber conducted his first sociological research.) The experience of Memel (East Prussia), Danzig (West Prussia), Bromberg (Posen) and Breslau (Lower Silesia) was not wholly different from that of German communities in the easternmost parts of Austria-Hungary. The crucial point is that many of the eastern regions inhabited by German minorities were also areas of relatively dense Jewish settlement. Ironically, in view of later events, the relationships between Germans and Jews in these borderlands were sometimes close to symbiotic. Both groups were more likely than Slavs to live in towns; they also spoke variations of the German language, since the Yiddish of the East European *shtetl* (literally, 'wee town', identical to the German *Städtl*) was essentially a German dialect, no further removed from High German than the language of the Transylvanian Saxons, even if in Galicia Yiddish signs were often written in Hebrew characters. The so-called *Mauscheldeutsch* spoken by Jews in Bohemia and the other western Habsburg lands was closer still to German. In Breslau, Jews were the backbone of the German liberal intelligentsia; fewer than half were observant and many in fact converted to Christianity, ceasing to regard themselves as Jews. In Prague roughly half of all Jews were German-speakers and considered themselves a part of the German community; indeed, they were in some sense the German community, since German-speaking Jews accounted for just under half of all the Germans in Prague. As one Prague Jew from a notable professional family put it, 'We would have thought crazy anyone who would have said to us that we were not German.' In Galicia, too, assimilation often meant Germanization, despite the fact that Germans accounted for only a tiny fraction (0.5 per cent) of the population. Though born in Vienna, the religious philosopher Martin Buber was raised by his grandparents in Galicia and studied first in Lemberg, then in Vienna, Leipzig, Berlin and Zurich – a Germanophone intellectual itinerary that led him ultimately to embrace Hassidic Orthodoxy and Zionism. The author Karl Emil Franzos, the son of a Sephardic Jew who had himself studied medicine in Erlangen, was raised in the Galician village of Czortków and studied in Czernowitz, which he eulogized as 'the courtyard of the German paradise' and where he was a member of the 'Teutonia' student fraternity. To a thoroughly Germanized Jew like Franzos, Galicia and Bukovina could seem like 'Half-Asia', the title of his most famous series of stories and sketches. Like so many others, his literary road led him westwards – to Vienna, Graz, Strasbourg and finally Berlin.

Traditionally, it was Czechs, not German Gentiles, whom assimi-lated German-speaking Jews viewed with mistrust. It was Poles, not Germans, who ritually hanged effigies of Judas during their Holy Week parades. It was Byelorussians, not Germans, who roared with laughter when the drunken Cossack beat the skinflint Jew in the puppet theatre. It was only at the turn of the nineteenth century that this German-Jewish affinity began to break down. From the mid-1890s, however, Germans in Vienna and then in Prague began to adopt the principle of racial exclusion for membership of voluntary associations like gymnastics clubs and student fraternities. Typically, it was in Lemberg that one of the most notorious trials of Jewish brothel-keepers took place, furnishing the more salacious anti-Semites with plentiful raw material. Likewise, calls for a restriction of Jewish immigration, if not their outright expulsion, were more likely to garner applause in Königsberg than in Cologne. It was in the Danzig periodical the *Anti-Semite's Mirror* that Karl Paasch proposed either extermination or expulsion of the Jews as the simplest solution to the Jewish 'question'. It was in Prague that Albert Einstein's appointment to a professorship was delayed because of his 'semitic origin' – some six years after the publication of his epoch-making special theory of relativity. It was in Czernowitz, where immigration had increased the proportion of Jews in the population to more than 30 per cent, that Karl Franzos's stories of doomed love between Jews and Gentiles seemed to make most sense. Here, in what seemed to have become once again the Eastern Marches of a beleaguered 'Germandom', the idea that the solution might lie in assimilation, and particularly in intermarriage, was countenanced by few. For here it was the Germans, not the Jews, who had begun to fear dissolution.

## A GLISTERING WORLD

The world in 1901 was economically integrated as never before. Here Keynes was clearly right, just as he was right to see how hard that integration would be to restore once it had been interrupted. He was right, too, that economic interdependence was associated with unprecedented economic growth, though we can now see that there were marked disparities in performance between regions and countries (see Figure 1.1). Gross domestic product per capita was growing nineteen times faster in the United States than in China, and twice as fast in Britain as in India. Perhaps more alarming, from a *Times* reader's point of view, the economies of nearly all Britain's imperial rivals were growing roughly one a half times faster than her own.

Yet it was not the economic future that would have worried our prosperous and healthy white man as he leafed through his morning paper. It was, above all, the enormous potential for conflict in this world of empires and races. Was it a coincidence that the anarchists arrested in Chicago for being behind the assassination attempt on President McKinley were, to judge by their surnames, both Jews? Was there a way of bringing the war in South Africa to a swift conclusion that would not leave the Boers permanently embittered? Were the French and Germans, to say nothing of the Russians and Austrians, bound sooner or later to go to war with one another once again? And

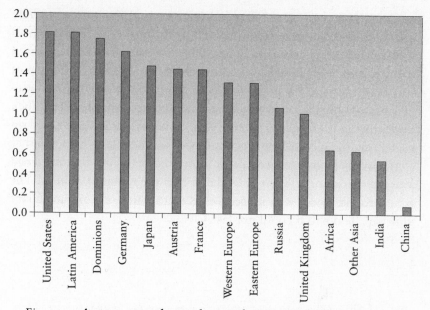

*Figure 1.1* Average annual growth rate of per capita GDP, 1870–1913

what of the social problems that were driving so many young Britons to seek their fortunes overseas? Was the country's moral fibre being eaten away by 'secularism', 'indifferentism' and 'irreverence', as the Methodist Ecumenical Conference feared? Was 'degeneration . . . the prime cause of criminality', as the Congress of Criminal Anthropology in Amsterdam had been informed? All these items of news amounted, surely, to more than 'mere amusements'. They were compelling evidence that, though it glistered, this was no golden age.

Who understood this best at the time? Perhaps it is not wholly surprising that a disproportionate number of the principal contributors to that 'kindling fever' recalled by Musil – the extraordinary ferment of new ideas which ushered in the new century – were Jews or the children of Jews from Central and Eastern Europe. The physics of Albert Einstein, the psychoanalysis of Sigmund Freud, the poetry of Hugo von Hofmannsthal, the novels of Franz Kafka, the satire of Karl Kraus, the symphonies of Gustav Mahler, the short stories of Joseph Roth, the plays of Arthur Schnitzler, even the philosophy of Ludwig Wittgenstein – all owed a debt, not so much to Judaism as a faith, as to the specific milieu of a highly numerate and literate but rapidly assimilating ethnic minority permitted by the times and circumstances to give free rein to their thoughts, but also aware of the fragility of their own individual and collective predicament. Each in his different way was a beneficiary of the *fin-de-siècle* combination of global integration and the dissolution of traditional confessional barriers. Each flourished in the 'mishmash' that was 'Kakania', an empire based on such a multiplicity of languages, cultures and peoples – held together so tenuously by its ageing emperor's gravitational pull – that it seemed like the theory of relativity translated into the realm of politics. The time around 1901 was indeed, as Keynes said, 'an extraordinary episode'. Too bad it could not last.

# 2

# Orient Express

*What we need to hold Russia back from revolution is a small victorious war.*                    Vyacheslav Pleve (*attributed*)

## YELLOW AND WHITE PERILS

In September 1895 Tsar Nicholas II received an unusual gift: an oil painting by the German artist Herman Knackfuss, based on a sketch by his sovereign, the Emperor William II. Entitled 'The Yellow Peril', it depicted seven women in martial attire gazing anxiously from a mountaintop towards an approaching storm. The iconography bears the unmistakable stamp of the Kaiser's unsubtle mind. Each of the women symbolizes one of the principal European nations; Britannia is instantly identifiable by the Union Jack on her shield. A large white cross hovers in the sky above them. Gesturing grimly towards the storm clouds, within which lurks a cross-legged Buddha, is a winged angel, a fiery sword in his hand. Already, lightning from the storm has struck the many-spired city on the plain below; fire is raging. Lest anyone fail to grasp the meaning of the allegory, the Kaiser himself explained it in an accompanying letter. It depicted, he wrote,

The powers of Europe represented by their respective Genii called together by the Arch-Angel Michael – sent from Heaven – to *unite* in resisting the inroad of Buddhism, heathenism and barbarism for the Defence of the Cross. Stress is especially laid on the *united* resistance of *all* European powers . . .

On the border of his original sketch, William had inscribed a passionate plea: 'Nations of Europe, defend your holiest possessions.'

The possession he had in mind was their common Christian heritage. The 'Yellow Peril' was plainly the 'heathenism and barbarism' of Asia. The implication was that the European empires and the United States would need to unite if the subjugation of Asia were to be maintained. For months before the painting of 'The Yellow Peril', the Kaiser had been urging the Tsar to act in concert with him 'to cultivate the Asian Continent and to defend Europe from the inroads of the Great Yellow race'.

The Kaiser's fantasy was soon realized. Just five years later, Germany did indeed join forces with Austria-Hungary, Britain, France, Italy, Russia and the United States – as well as, it should be noted, Japan – to suppress the Boxer Rebellion, an inchoate, anti-Christian movement that had arisen in the impoverished province of Shandong in 1898. The Boxers ('The Righteous and Harmonious Fists') initially directed their ire at European missionaries, dozens of whom were murdered; then, with the encouragement of the Empress Dowager Cixi, they proceeded to besiege the Western embassies in the heart of the imperial capital, Beijing, killing the German Minister. 'It may be', William declared as the German expeditionary force set sail, 'the beginning of a great war between the Occident and Orient.' Evoking the memory of fifth-century Huns, he urged his troops to 'make the name German remembered in China for a thousand years so that no Chinaman will ever again dare even to squint at a German':

You have to remedy the serious wrong which has been done . . . Live up to Prussia's traditional steadfastness! Show yourselves Christians . . . Give the world an example of virility and discipline! . . . No pardon will be given, and prisoners will not be made. Anyone who falls into your hands falls to your sword!

Nothing could have better symbolized the dominance the West had established over the East by the end of the nineteenth century than the destruction of the Boxers, whose faith in martial arts and animistic magic availed them naught against the well-armed eight-power expedition.* Having raised the siege of the Beijing legations, the inter-

* The Boxers believed that after one hundred days of training in martial arts they would be impervious to bullets. After three hundred days they would be able to fly.

national force staged a 'grand march' through the Forbidden City, pausing only to 'acquire' some ancestral Manchu tablets for the British Museum before holding a memorial service for the recently deceased Queen Victoria at the Meridian Gate. They then undertook punitive raids deep into Shanxi province, Inner Mongolia and Manchuria. In Baoding, for example, local officials suspected of involvement in the deaths of missionaries were tried by military courts and publicly beheaded; temples and sections of the city wall were symbolically blown up. In Taiyuan, the capital of Shanxi, the governor was executed for his support of the Boxers; a public memorial to the 'martyred' missionaries was also erected. There was political as well as symbolic retribution. Under the so-called 'Boxer Protocol' signed in 1901, the European powers were granted the right to maintain their own military forces in the imperial capital; a heavy indemnity (£67.5 million) was also imposed on the Chinese government, and arms imports suspended. If, as the journalist George Lynch wrote, this was a war of civilizations, there seemed little doubt as to which one was winning. Yet this victory was to prove deceptive. In reality, the first cracks in the edifice of a united Western hegemony were just about to appear.

Though his mistaken allusion to Attila's sack of Rome somewhat spoilt the effect, the Kaiser's depiction of the 'Yellow Peril' implicitly alluded to previous invasions of Europe from the East: the Moorish conquest of Spain in the seventh century, the depredations of Genghis's and Timur's Mongol hordes in the thirteenth and fourteenth, the Ottoman siege of Vienna in the seventeenth. It was a common *fin-de-siècle* nightmare that this process could be repeated in the twentieth. The Russian anarchist Mikhail Bakunin warned the European empires against their 'great game' in Asia: 'Since Asiatics number in the hundreds of millions, the most likely outcome of these intrigues ... will be to awaken this hitherto immobile Asian world, which will overrun Europe once again.' The philosopher and poet Vladimir Solovev discerned 'a dark cloud approaching from the Far East', as well as a 'locust swarm uncountable / and insatiable like it too'. In his 'Short Tale of the Antichrist', he prophesied that the Japanese and Chinese would join forces to invade and conquer all of Europe as far as the English Channel. Dmitri Mamin-Sibiriak's short story 'The Last

Glimmerings' warned of 'a real flood of . . . yellow-faced barbarians . . . surging over the continent'. Such anxieties were present in Britain too. The Oxford historian Charles Pearson warned: 'We shall wake to find ourselves . . . thrust aside by peoples whom we looked down upon as servile, and thought of as bound to minister to our needs.' Though it might be 'lower', Pearson warned, Asian civilization was more 'vigorous' and 'resilient'. 'That the future will have a "Yellow" question – perhaps a "yellow peril" – to deal with,' wrote Sir Robert Hart, who ran the Imperial Chinese Maritime Customs, 'is as certain as that the sun will shine tomorrow.'

In reality, however, it was a 'white peril' that menaced Asia – and indeed the rest of the world. In all history, there had never been a mass movement of peoples to compare with the exodus from Europe between 1850 and 1914. Total European emigration in that period exceeded 34 million; in the decade 1901 to 1910 it was close to twelve million. Of course, most of this movement was transatlantic, part of an exodus from Western Europe to the Americas that had been going on since the 1500s. This now reached its climax. Between 1900 and 1914, a total of 1.5 million people left the United Kingdom for Canada, most of whom settled there permanently. Nearly four million Italians and more than a million Spaniards also left Europe, the majority bound for the United States or Argentina. However, a rising proportion of European emigrants were now heading eastward. Scotsmen and Irishmen in particular were flocking to Australia and New Zealand; by the eve of the First World War, nearly one in five British emigrants was bound for Australasia; by the middle of the century it would be one in two. Settlers from Britain, Holland and France were also busily establishing themselves as planters in Malaya, the East Indies and Indo-China. Meanwhile, a growing number of Central and East European Jews, inspired by Zionist leaders like Theodor Herzl, were moving to Palestine in the hope of establishing a Jewish state there.*

---

* Zionism was, in essence, the Jewish form of nationalism. As the Irish revived Gaelic in the nineteenth century, so Jewish scholars resuscitated Hebrew. Its political expression was made difficult by the lack of an obvious geographical focus; turning the Pale of Settlement (see p. 59) into a Jewish state was never a realistic option. From the 1860s, therefore, organizations like *Hoveve Zion* (Friends of Zion) began to establish colonies in Ottoman-controlled Palestine, a movement that won support

Finally, as we shall see, a very large number of Russians were also heading east, to Central Asia, Siberia and beyond. All this movement was in large measure voluntary, unlike the enforced shipment of millions of Africans to American and Caribbean plantations that had taken place in the seventeenth and eighteenth centuries. However, comparable numbers of indentured labourers from India and China were also on the move in 1900, their condition only marginally better than slavery, to work in plantations and mines owned and managed by Europeans. Asians would have preferred to migrate in larger numbers to America and Australasia, but were prevented from doing so by restrictions imposed on Japanese and Chinese immigration in the late nineteenth century.*

This great *Völkerwanderung* was a response to a combination of pushes and pulls, some economic, some political. Many emigrants who crossed the Atlantic or took the longer journeys to South Africa, Australia and New Zealand did so simply because land was cheaper and labour better rewarded. A minority left Europe to escape racial or religious persecution; this was especially true of the Jews of Tsarist Russia (see below). New World societies were not only less densely populated than those of Europe; they were also, at least in some respects, more tolerant. Yet we should not lose sight of the role played by imperial political structures in making mass migration seem so attractive. Migrants who left Europe around 1900 were largely bound for destinations where colonization had been going on for up to three centuries. From Boston to Buenos Aires, from San Francisco to Sidney, earlier generations of colonists had built replica European cities, the languages and laws of which were fundamentally similar to those in the 'Old Country' and the customs of which were in many respects preferable. Even where European settlement was limited – as in India, which was already densely settled and climatically unappealing to Europeans – empire guaranteed Europeans more or less safe passage. The British-born population of India never accounted for more than

___

from, among others, Baron Edmond de Rothschild. The Budapest-born journalist Herzl's book *Der Judenstaat* was published in 1896, having originally been drafted as a proposal to the Rothschilds to become the royal family of a new Jewish kingdom.
* The US Chinese Exclusion Act was passed in 1882. Among its proponents was the labour leader Samuel Gompers, himself of Jewish origin.

0.05 per cent of the total. But it was extraordinarily powerful, not merely governing the country but also dominating its economy. Many of the great ports of East Asia were, as we have seen, also run by privileged European minorities.

We tend to think of nineteenth-century empires as primarily sea-borne. But they could cross vast expanses of land with equal, if not greater, ease. By the end of the nineteenth century, Tsarist Russia had acquired not only a substantial Western empire in Europe, extending into Finland, Poland and the Ukraine, but also a string of Caucasian colonies stretching to the borders of Persia, and a vast Central Asian empire that reached across Kazakhstan and through Manchuria as far as the border of Korea and the Sea of Japan. One after another, the peoples of Eurasia were subjugated; indeed, by 1900 non-Russians accounted for more than half of the population of the Tsar's domains. In 1858, capitalizing on Britain's victory over China in the Second Opium War and the outbreak of the Taiping Rebellion, Russia had seized Chinese territory north of the Amur River; China was also forced to cede the land between the Ussuri River and the Sea of Japan. It was here that the Russians built their principal Pacific port, Vladivostok – 'ruler of the east'.

Perhaps nothing symbolized Russian power in Asia more strikingly than the vast Trans-Siberian Railway, which runs six thousand miles from Moscow to Vladivostok, passing through Yaroslavl on the Volga, Ekaterinburg in the Urals and Irkutsk on Lake Baikal, before finally reaching the Pacific coast just north of the Korean peninsula. By the turn of the century it was all but complete; work had begun on the final stretch of line, across Manchuria to Vladivostok, in 1897. By dramatically reducing journey times between European and Asiatic Russia – from a matter of years to a matter of days – the railway greatly accelerated the Russian colonization of Central and East Asia. Between 1907 and 1914, no fewer than 2.5 million Russians made new lives for themselves in Siberia, the great northern strip of Asia that stretches from the Ural Mountains to the Pacific. Despite the region's later notoriety as destination for political prisoners, only a small minority of these migrants were forced to go. In any case, many of those who were exiled there were pleasantly surprised by what they found. In 1897 Vladimir Ulyanov, a hereditary nobleman who had embraced socialism in his student days, was sentenced to three years' 'administrative exile' in Siberia for his involvement with the revolutionary Union of Struggle. He found life in Shushenskoe, in the Minusinsk district, remarkably pleasant. 'Everyone's found that I've grown fat over the summer, got a tan and now look completely like a Siberian,' he wrote cheerfully to his mother. 'That's hunting and the life of the countryside for you!' When not hunting, shooting and fishing, Lenin – as he would later prefer to be known – was free to read and write prolifically. He was even able to marry and to bring his wife and mother-in-law to live with him.

Further East, the Russian presence was spread thin. Only 90,000 people settled along the Amur between 1859 and 1900; indeed, the entire Russian population along the Siberian border was barely 50,000. Like so many Asian ports in 1900, Vladivostok was a multi-ethnic city, with its Chinatown on the shores of the Amur Bay, its partly Russified Korean community and its Japanese small businesses and brothels. Nearly two-fifths of the population were, as the Russians put it, yellow. There was, as so often on colonial frontiers, intermarriage; in the words of one visitor, 'The Russian woman does not object to the Chinese as a husband, and the Russian takes a Chinese wife.' There were also mixed marriages between European men and Japanese women. But such mingling took place in the context of an unambiguous racial hierarchy. One Vladivostok newspaper referred to 'beating the Manza [Chinese]' as 'a custom with us. Only the lazy don't indulge in it.' In Khabarovsk, on the Siberian-Chinese border, the typical Russian settler was said to

live in a house built by Chinese labor . . . the stove is made of Chinese bricks . . . In the kitchen the Chinese boy gets the . . . samovar ready. The master of the house drinks his Chinese tea, with bread . . . from a Chinese bakery. The mistress of the house wears a dress made by a Chinese tailor . . . In [the] yard a Korean boy is at work chopping wood.

At the railway station, foreign visitors were reminded of British India:

Instead, however, of British officers walking up and down with the confident stride of superiority while the Hindus . . . gave way . . . there were Russian officers clean and smart promenading the platform while the . . .

cowering Chinese and the cringing . . . Koreans made room for them . . . The Russian . . . is the white, civilized Westerner, whose stride is that of the conqueror.

Chinese workers were indispensable when it came to the bigger jobs too, not least railway construction and shipbuilding. In 1900 nine out of ten workers in the Vladivostok shipyards were Chinese. Yet Russian administrators felt no compunction about expelling surplus Asians in order to maintain Russian dominance. In July 1900, at the time of the intervention against the Boxers, between 3,000 and 5,000 Chinese were drowned at Blagoveshchensk when they were forced by whip-wielding Cossacks and local Russian police to swim across the wide and fast-flowing Amur to the Chinese side. No boats were provided and those who resisted or refused to get in the water were shot or cut down with sabres. This little-known incident, a harbinger of so many twentieth-century massacres, lay bare the utter contempt with which the Russians regarded all Asiatic peoples. As Nikolai Gondatti, the governor of Tomsk, explained in 1911: 'My task is to make sure that there are lots of Russians and few yellows here.'

Vast though their Asian domains had become, the Russians were not content. Influential figures, led by Admiral Evgenii Ivanovich Alekseev, commander of Russian forces in the Far East, and the Minister for War Aleksei Nikolaevich Kuropatkin, argued that at least the northern part of the Chinese province of Manchuria, the ancestral home of the Qing dynasty, should be added to the Tsarist Empire, not least to secure the final Trans-Siberian rail link to Vladivostok. The Russians already leased the Liaodong peninsula from China and had a permanent naval presence at Port Arthur (modern Lüshun). The Boxer Rebellion offered an opportunity to realize the scheme for a partial or total annexation of Manchuria. On July 11, 1900, the Russian government warned the Chinese ambassador in St Petersburg that troops would have to be sent into Manchuria to protect Russian assets in the area. Three days later, hostilities broke out when the Russians ignored a Chinese threat to fire on any troopships that sailed down the River Amur. Within three months, all Manchuria was in the hands of 100,000 Russian troops. 'We cannot stop halfway,' wrote the Tsar. 'Manchuria must be covered with our troops from the North to the South.' Kuropatkin agreed: Manchuria must become 'Russian property'. The only obstacle that seemed to stand in the way of a complete takeover was the resistance of the other European powers. This alone imposed caution on St Petersburg. The Russians promised to withdraw their troops but dragged their feet, pressing the Chinese to concede *de facto* if not *de jure* sovereignty. What the complacent Russians forgot was that their strengths – above all, their technological superiority – were not a permanent monopoly conferred by Providence on people with white skin. There was in fact nothing biological to prevent Asians from adopting Western forms of economic and political organization, nor from replicating Western inventions. The first Asian country to work out how to do so was Japan.

## TSUSHIMA

Since the restoration of imperial authority in 1868, when the fifteen-year-old Emperor Mutsuhito had been plucked from Kyoto to become the figurehead of a new regime in Tokyo, Japan had been engaged in a breakneck modernization of its economic, political and military institutions. The divine emperor had become a Prussian-style monarch. Shinto had been transformed into a state religion, like the nationalistic Protestantism of the North European established churches. The feudal warriors known as *samurai* had been transformed into a European-style officer corps, their retinues replaced by a conscript army. The country had also acquired entirely new political and monetary institutions. In 1889 a constitution had been adopted that was closely modelled on that of Prussia. Japan's fiscal and monetary institutions had also been reformed; she now had a central bank and a currency based on the British gold standard. Moreover, her hitherto agrarian economy had begun to industrialize with the growth of textile production and the emergence of the business conglomerates known as the *zaibatsu*. Even sartorially, Japan's leaders went West, the civilians in sober, black frockcoats, the soldiers in close-fitting blue uniforms. Yet the men who engineered this transformation – men like Itō Hirobumi, Yamagata Aritomo and Matsukata Masayoshi – were far from slavish Westernizers. Rather, they sought to harness Western institutions to Japanese ends, a programme encapsulated in the slogan *fukoku kyōhei* ('rich country, strong army'), in the belief that Japanese 'essence' could only be preserved by embracing 'Western science'. The aim was not to subordinate Japan to the West, but precisely the opposite: to make Japan capable of resisting Western dominance. The new Meiji (literally 'enlightened') constitution might bear the stamp 'made in Prussia', just as the new navy looked British and the new schools looked French. The Emperor and his ministers might dance Western dances and even, in violation of traditional Japanese propriety, smile Western smiles. But their underlying and deadly earnest aim was always to wipe the smiles off European faces. There was only one certain means of doing so, and that was by winning wars.

In 1895 Japan went to war with China. So swift and comprehensive was the Japanese victory that European observers were both impressed and alarmed. The governments of Russia, France and Germany hurriedly pressurized the Japanese to drop their territorial demands, beyond the island of Formosa (now Taiwan),* in exchange for a larger cash indemnity and other economic concessions, though these effectively acknowledged Japan as an equal participant in the system of 'unequal treaties' with China – hence Japan's participation in the international expedition against the Boxers in 1900. No one was more alarmed by this new manifestation of the 'yellow peril' than Kuropatkin, who firmly believed that the twentieth century would witness 'the great struggle in Asia between Christians against non-Christians'. After a visit to Japan in 1903 he reported to the Tsar: 'I was surprised at the high level of development . . . there is no doubt that the population is as culturally advanced as Russians . . . on the whole, Japan's army struck me as an effective fighting force.' What worried Kuropatkin was that this army posed a direct threat to Port Arthur. Port Arthur was a very long way from St Petersburg. It was also very near to Tokyo.

---

* Japan's expansion had in fact begun in the 1870s, when she annexed the Bonin and Kuril Islands (1875) and the Ryūkū Islands, including Okinawa (1879). The original Japanese demands in 1895 had included the Liaodong peninsula. Having reluctantly surrendered it, the Japanese were dismayed when it was leased and occupied by the Russians in 1898.

The Tsar's appointment of Admiral Alekseev as 'Viceroy' of the Far East in 1903 and the deployment of Russian troops along the Yalu River had incensed the Japanese, who saw their own ambitions to colonize Korea directly threatened. Not unreasonably, they proposed a compromise carve-up: Russia could retain its dominance in Manchuria if Japan's interests in Korea were acknowledged. The Russian response was dismissive. As the editor of the Port Arthur newspaper *Novyi Krai* put it: 'Japan is not a country that can give an ultimatum to Russia, and Russia should not receive an ultimatum from a country like Japan.' On February 5, 1904, the Japanese minister in St Petersburg presented just such an ultimatum. Four days later the first shots were exchanged in Inchon (Chemulpo) harbour. That night, the Japanese navy launched a torpedo attack on Port Arthur, hitting the battleship *Tsarevich* and the cruiser *Pallada*. The next day the Japanese inflicted further damage on Russian vessels at Inchon. These raids, which came before any formal declarations of war, were met with incredulity and then anger in Russia. A stirring patriotic song was composed in honour of the crew of the *Varyag*, who had been blockaded in Inchon harbour by fifteen Japanese warships, but who nevertheless refused to surrender:

> We are leaving a safe pier for a battle,
> Heading for threatening death.
> We shall die for our Motherland in the open sea
> Where yellow-faced devils are awaiting us!
>
> . . .
>
> Neither stone nor cross will show where we died
> For the glory of the Russian flag.
> Only sea waves will glorify
> The heroic wreck of the *Varyag*.

The Tsar and his ministers resolved to retaliate with maximum force. Kuropatkin was appointed commander in the Far East and Admiral Stepan Ossipovich Makarov sent to take charge of naval operations at Port Arthur. In June it was also decided to send the pride of the Imperial Russian navy, the Second Fleet, from its base in the Baltic to what was literally the other side of the world. People in

St Petersburg looked forward with confidence to victory and vengeance. As one Russian officer remarked, although 'no longer the rabble of an Asiatic horde', the Japanese army was 'nevertheless no modern European army'. It would be enough for Russian troops simply to 'pelt them with our caps' to throw them into disarray. The press portrayed the Japanese as puny, jaundiced monkeys (*makaki*), fleeing in panic before the giant white fist of Mother Russia; or as Oriental spiders, crushed beneath a giant Cossack hat. According to Prince S. N. Trubetskoi, Professor of Philosophy at Moscow University, Russia was now defending the whole of European civilization against 'the yellow danger, the new hordes of Mongols armed by modern technology'. Academics at the University of Kiev preferred to portray the war as a Christian crusade against 'insolent Mongols', a sentiment echoed by the painter Vasilii Vereshchagin, who actually sailed with the Pacific Fleet.

Not for the last time in the twentieth century, notions of innate racial superiority were to prove deceptive. The Russian naval expedition proceeded with astonishing slowness, not least because its Commander-in-Chief, Admiral Zinovy Petrovitch Rozhestvensky, was privately convinced that he was doomed to fail. Fearful of another surprise attack by the Japanese, the Russians mistakenly opened fire on British trawlers at the Dogger Bank in the North Sea, sinking one and inflicting damage on their own cruiser *Aurora*. They travelled with their holds full of coal and other supplies, as if expecting the Japanese fleet to be lying in wait off the next coaling station. The Japanese had in fact achieved naval dominance off the Manchurian coast by August. Meanwhile their army had occupied Seoul and landed troops at Inchon (February 1904), effectively taking over the Korean peninsula; Japanese troops proceeded to inflict heavy defeats on Russian forces at Yalu (April) and Fengcheng (May). Following the landing of the Japanese 2nd Army at Kwantung, the Russian garrison at Port Arthur found themselves under siege. There was heavy fighting throughout the second half of 1904, culminating in the Japanese capture of the crucial hill overlooking the harbour on December 5. Although they suffered heavy casualties, the Japanese finally secured Port Arthur's surrender on January 2, 1905. Two months later, after wave upon wave of bloody frontal assaults by Japanese soldiers, Kuropatkin was forced to surrender Mukden (Shenyang). By the time the Russian fleet reached the scene, then, the war was effectively over. In due course, Admiral Rozhestvensky's premonitions of doom were amply fulfilled. At Tsushima on May 27–28, 1905, the Japanese fleet under Admiral Tōgō Heihachirō sent two-thirds of the Russian fleet – 147,000 tons of naval hardware and nearly 50,000 sailors – to the bottom of the Korea Strait.

Returning home in disgrace, Kuropatkin could only reflect bitterly on what seemed to him a turning point in world history:

The battle is only just beginning. What happened in Manchuria in 1904–5 was nothing more than a skirmish with the advance guard ... Only with a common recognition that keeping Asia peaceful is a matter of importance to all of Europe ... can we keep the 'yellow peril' at bay.

Yet in many ways the Japanese had won by being more European than the Russians; their ships were more modern, their troops better disciplined, their artillery more effective. To Leo Tolstoy, the titan of Russian letters, Japan's victory looked like a straightforward triumph of Western materialism. By comparison, it was the Tsarist system that suddenly looked 'Asiatic' – and ripe for overthrow. Now, it seemed, the Japanese could concentrate on acquiring the other indispensable accessory of a great power: a colonial empire.

The Western empires most interested in the region were not at all sorry to see Russia humiliated. On the other hand, they were again eager to limit the spoils Japan might claim on the basis of her victory. In the negotiations that led to the signing of a Russo-Japanese peace treaty at Portsmouth naval base in Maine in September 1905, they therefore pressed the Japanese to be content with informal rather than formal power. Russia was to recognize Japan's 'paramount political, military, and economic interests' in Korea, but Korea itself was to remain independent. The Japanese acquired the Liaodong peninsula as a leased territory, including Port Arthur, and – in lieu of a cash indemnity – Russian economic assets in southern Manchuria, notably the South Manchurian Railway Company; but politically Manchuria was to remain a Chinese possession. Not everyone in Japan was satisfied with these gains; radical nationalists formed an Anti-Peace Society and there were riots in Tokyo, Yokohama and Kōbe. The essential point, however, was that the Western powers were now clearly obliged to treat Japan as an equal; there was no serious objection when the Japanese proceeded to annex Korea in 1910. At the same time, from the point of view of Japanese businessmen, equal treatment allowed them to exploit their natural advantages – both geographical and cultural – in developing the potentially enormous Chinese market.

The Russo-Japanese War had more profound geopolitical implications than these, however. First, the intensity of the fighting – especially at Mukden, which was a bigger military engagement than any in the preceding century – was an intimation that a new zone of conflict had come into existence, comparable in its potential instability to Central and Eastern Europe. Here was another great fault line, running through Manchuria and northern Korea, between the Amur and the Yalu, where the over-extended Russian Empire met the new and dynamic Japanese Empire. In the century that lay ahead, the tremors in this region would be comparable in their magnitude with those that shook Eurasia's western conflict zone between the Elbe and the Dnieper. Secondly, the military earthquake at Mukden had been followed by a naval tsunami. If the West had still dominated the East at the dawn of the new century, then the Japanese victory at Tsushima signalled the waning of that dominance.

The revelation that there was, after all, no inherent advantage to being a European swept like an enormous wave not just over Russia, but over the whole of the Western world.

## MARXISM TURNS EASTWARDS

That January, as military disaster was unfolding in the Far East, dissatisfaction erupted into revolution in the Russian capital, St Petersburg, after troops fired on a peaceful demonstration by workers and their families. The leader of the demonstration, a priest named Father Georgi Gapon, was himself no revolutionary, though he was subsequently represented as one. But the wave of strikes, riots and mutinies that swept the country in the aftermath of 'Bloody Sunday' (January 22, 1905) presented Russia's real revolutionaries, most of whom lived in exile, with what seemed a golden opportunity. For a time in 1905 St Petersburg was effectively run by a new kind of institution – a council (*soviet*) of workers' deputies, elected by local factory employees. Among its members was a flamboyant socialist journalist who went by the name of Leon Trotsky.

To Trotsky, the naval defeat at Tsushima was an indictment of all that was wrong with the Tsarist system. 'The Russian fleet is no more,' he declared. '[But] it is not the Japanese who destroyed her. Rather, it is the Tsarist government . . . It is not the people that need this war. Rather, it is the governing clique, which dreams of seizing new lands and wants to extinguish the flame of the people's anger in blood.' When, three days after peace had been concluded, the Tsar's government reluctantly published a constitution creating the first representative parliament, the Duma, Trotsky publicly tore it up. The regime, he wrote, was 'the vicious combination of the Asian knout and the European stock market'. Russia's socialists wanted more than merely the constitutional monarchy that seemed to be on offer. Their vision was of a revolution led by the industrial working class, the proletariat, which would overturn not just the Tsarist regime but the entire system of Western imperialism.

Yet Trotsky's rhetoric did not impress the majority of the Tsar's subjects. The Left itself was deeply divided; as a former member of the Menshevik (minority) Social Democrats, Trotsky was viewed with intense suspicion by Bolshevik (majority) party leaders like Vladimir Ulyanov, who had renamed himself Lenin four years before.* More importantly, whatever its appeal to the workers in the huge factories of St Petersburg, Marx's doctrine of proletarian class struggle had little resonance with the overwhelming majority of Russians, who were peasants. The revolution of 1905 took many forms, few of them anticipated by Marx, who had always assumed that the proletariat would rise up amid the smokestacks and slums of Lancashire or the Ruhr, if not in the traditional revolutionary setting of central Paris. Aboard the battleship *Potemkin*, indignant sailors hoisted the red flag because of maggots in their meat. In Volokolamsk, meanwhile,

* The Bolsheviks, despite their name, were not in fact the majority, but a relatively small splinter group.

peasants formed their own 'Markovo Republic', proclaiming their independence from St Petersburg. Elsewhere, peasants looted and burned down their landlords' residences, or cut down timber from landlords' forests. As one of those who ransacked the Petrov estate in Bobrov county (Voronezh) explained: 'It is necessary to rob and burn them. Then they will not return and the land will pass over to the peasants.' The police chief in Pronsk county (Riazan) reported that peasants were saying: 'Now we are all gentlemen and all are equal.'

There was another difficulty. Born Leib (Lev) Bronshtein, the son of a prosperous Ukrainian landowner, Trotsky, whose family originally hailed from a *shtetl* near Poltova, was a Jew. To many Russians that automatically made him a suspect figure. Indeed, there were those who maintained that Russia's defeat at the hands of the Japanese was itself the result of a Jewish conspiracy. According to S. A. Nilus, a secret Jewish council known as the Sanhedrin had hypnotized the Japanese into believing they were one of the tribes of Israel; it was the Jews' aim, Nilus insisted, 'to set a distraught Russia awash with blood and to inundate it, and then Europe, with the yellow hordes of a resurgent China guided by Japan'. The Minister for the Interior, Vyacheslav Pleve, insisted: 'There is no revolutionary movement in Russia; there are only the Jews who are the enemy of the government.' The chairman of the Council of Ministers, Count Sergei Witte, took the same view, citing Jews as 'one of the evil factors of our accursed revolution'.

As we have seen, no other European country had a larger Jewish population than the Russian Empire. Ashkenazi Jews had moved eastwards from Germany into Poland in the medieval period, in response to discrimination and persecution in the Holy Roman Empire. They had moved further east into the Grand Duchy of Lithuania in the fifteenth and sixteenth centuries and, despite the violence directed against them during the 1648 Ukrainian revolt, had continued this eastward pattern of migration and settlement into the eighteenth century. With the partitions of Poland, the areas of densest Jewish settlement came under Russian rule, though (as we have seen) there were also substantial Jewish populations in Galicia, which had been acquired by Austria, and in Posen, which had been acquired by Prussia. Russia's three million Jews were emphatically second-class subjects of the Tsar. A Pale of Settlement, outside which Jews were not supposed to reside, had been established by Catherine II in 1791, though it was not precisely delineated until 1835. It consisted of Russian-controlled Poland and fifteen *gubernia* (provinces): Kovno, Vilna, Grodno, Minsk, Vitebsk, Mogilev, Volhynia, Podolia, Bessarabia (after its acquisition in 1881), Chernigov, Poltava, Kiev (except for the city of Kiev itself), Kherson (except the town of Nikolaiev), Ekaterinoslav and Tavrida (apart from Yalta and Sevastopol). Jews were not permitted to enter, much less reside in, the Russian interior. In today's terms, then, the Pale extended in a broad strip from Latvia and Lithuania, through eastern Poland and Belarus, down to western Ukraine and Moldova. There were in fact exceptions to this residence restriction. In 1859 Jewish merchants who were members of the first guild, the highest social rank to which a Russian businessman could aspire, were permitted to reside and trade all over Russia, as were Jewish university graduates and (after 1865) artisans. There were thus communities of Jewish merchants in all the principal Russian cities: St Petersburg, Moscow, Kiev and Odessa. Some other Jews chose to live illegally outside the Pale, but they were subject to periodic round-ups by the authorities (a characteristic feature of Jewish life in Kiev).

The restriction on their place of abode was only one among many imposed on Jews by the Tsarist regime. From the 1820s until the 1860s, Jews, like all Russians, became subject to military conscription for a period of twenty-five years, a system that weighed disproportionately heavily on the younger sons of poor families. This was part of a sustained campaign to convert Jews to Christianity; once removed from their homes, young conscripts could be subjected to all kinds of pressures to renounce their faith. Bounties were also offered to Jewish adults who converted, including incentives designed to encourage Jewish men to divorce their wives. If they resisted these pressures, as most did, they had to pay a special tax on meat killed by kosher butchers. They were forbidden to employ Christians as domestic servants. Although permitted to attend high schools (*gymnasia*) and universities, they were subject to quotas; even in the Pale they could not account for more than 10 per cent of students. Nor could they become local councillors, even in towns where they were a majority of the population.

Popular hostility to the Jews had spread eastwards across Europe for centuries; it arrived in Russia relatively late. For example, the libel that Jews ritually murdered Christian children to mix their blood in the unleavened bread baked at Passover appears to have originated in twelfth-century England. By the fifteenth century it had reached German-speaking Central Europe; by the sixteenth, Poland, and by the eighteenth century it was firmly established all over Eastern Europe, from Lithuania to Romania. In 1840 there was an international outcry over a 'blood libel' case in Damascus. But such allegations did not manifest themselves in Russia until the later nineteenth century. Nor was outright violence against Jewish communities a Russian tradition. What became known in Russia as 'pogroms' – literally 'after thunder' – had been a recurrent feature of life in Western and Central Europe from medieval times onwards. The Jewish ghetto in Frankfurt was ransacked in 1819; there was even a pogrom-like outbreak when striking miners ransacked Jewish shops in Tredegar, South Wales, in 1911. The earliest recorded pogroms in Russian territory – in Odessa in 1821, 1849, 1859 and 1871 – were in fact the work of the city's Greek community.

Pogroms occur in all kinds of different settings and can be directed at all kinds of different 'pariah' minorities. There were, nevertheless, four distinctive features of life in the Pale of Settlement *circa* 1900 that help to explain why anti-Jewish violence flared up there, even as it appeared to be dying away elsewhere. The first was the very rapid growth of the Jewish urban population. In Elizavetgrad, for example, their numbers had increased during the nineteenth century from 574 to 23,967 – 39 per cent of the population. In the industrial town of Ekaterinoslav, Jews went from being 10 per cent of the city's population in 1825 to being 35 per cent in 1897. The population of Kiev nearly doubled in the decade between 1864 and 1874, but its Jewish population grew five-fold in the same period. These cases were not untypical. Jews accounted for high proportions of the urban population in many (though not all) of the locations of pogrom activity (see Table 2.1).

It would be quite wrong to think of Jews in the Pale as an ethnic minority within a predominantly Russian population. Rather, the Pale was a patchwork of different ethnic groups, inhabited not only by

Table 2.1: Principal locations of the 1881–2 pogroms

| Gubernia/town | No. of pogroms | Jews as % of population |
| --- | --- | --- |
| Kherson | 52 | |
| Elizavetgrad | | 39 |
| Anan'ev | | 50 |
| Odessa | | 35 |
| Kiev | 63 | |
| Kiev | | 11 |
| Podolia | 5 | |
| Balta | | 78 |
| Ekaterinoslav | 38 | |
| Aleksandrovsk | | 18 |
| Poltava | 22 | |
| Lubna | | 25 |
| Chernigov | 23 | |
| Nyezhin | | 33 |
| Volhynia | 5 | |
| Tavrida | 16 | |
| Berdjansk | | 10 |

Source: Goldberg, 'Die Jahre 1881–1882', pp. 40f.

Jews and Russians but also by Poles, Lithuanians, Ukrainians, Byelo-russians, Germans, Romanians and others. In Elizavetgrad, Jews in fact were the largest single group in an ethnically mixed population, despite accounting for less than two-fifths of the total. Although there were slightly more Russians in Ekaterinoslav, they accounted for just 42 per cent of the population, only slightly more than the Jews. Around 16 per cent of the population were Ukrainians, while a significant proportion of the remainder were Poles or Germans. Indeed, the 1897 census revealed that the city's population included natives of every province of European Russia, as well as people from the ten provinces of the Caucasus, the ten of Central Asia and the seven of Siberia – to say nothing of twenty-six foreign countries. This helps to explain why Jews in the Pale were generally not confined to ghettos. Though there were sometimes distinct Jewish quarters, these were not products of an imposed segregation. On the contrary, there was a high degree of social integration, especially among upper-income groups. Wealthy Jewish families, like the Brodsky family of Kiev, were

respected local notables who did not confine their philanthropic generosity to their own religious community. In Ekaterinoslav, too, the
Jews were an integral part of the local elite.

The second, and not unrelated, point was the extraordinary economic success achieved by some (not all) Jews living under Russian
rule. The late nineteenth century was a time of enormous economic
opportunity as the Tsarist regime, having abolished serfdom, embarked on an ambitious programme of agrarian reform and industrialization. Trade, international and domestic, flourished as never
before. Excluded by law from the ownership of land, schooled to be
more literate and more numerate than their Gentile neighbours, the
Jews of the Pale were well situated to seize the new commercial
opportunities that presented themselves. By 1897 Jews accounted for
73 per cent of all merchants and manufacturers in Russian-controlled
Poland and were establishing comparable positions of dominance
in urban areas further east. At around the same time, they accounted
for around 13 per cent of the population of Kiev, but 44 per cent of
the city's merchants, handling around two-thirds of its commerce.
They accounted for just over a third of the population of Ekaterinoslav
in 1902, but 84 per cent of the merchants of the first guild and 69 per
cent of those of the second guild. That is not to imply that all
Jews in the Pale were wealthy merchants. Many continued to play
their traditional role as 'middle men' between peasants and the
market economy, or as innkeepers and artisans. A considerable
number of Jews were miserably poor. The 'pestilent' cellars of Vilna
(modern Vilnius), renowned as the cultural capital of East European
Jewry, and the 'crammed' slums of industrial Łódź, supposedly the
Manchester of Poland, appalled one British MP who toured the Pale
in 1903. The polarization of fortunes within the Jewish communities
of the Pale was in fact a crucial factor in the violence of the pogroms,
which may have been inspired by the riches of the merchant elite, but
were almost always directed against the property and persons of the
poor.

A third and crucial factor, much exaggerated at the time but nevertheless undeniable, was the disproportionate involvement of Jews in
revolutionary politics. Trotsky was no anomaly. To be sure, the Jewish
woman Hesia Helfman played only a minor role in the assassination

of Alexander II, which was the catalyst for the 1881 pogroms. Yet there is no question that Jews were over-represented in the various left-wing parties and revolutionary organizations that spearheaded the 1905 Revolution, against which the pogroms of that year were directed. For example, Jews accounted for 11 per cent of the Bolshevik delegates and 23 per cent of the Menshevik delegates at the 5th Congress of the Russian Social Democratic Party in 1907. A further fifty-nine delegates, out of a total of 338, were from the socialist Jewish Workers' League, the *Bund*. In all, 29 per cent of the delegates at the Congress were Jewish – as against 4 per cent of the Russian population. The *Bund*'s rhetoric in the wake of the Kishinev pogrom did nothing to allay the suspicion that the revolutionary movement had a Jewish character. One Yiddish flysheet explicitly linked the struggle against capitalism and Tsarism with the struggle against anti-Semitism: 'With hatred, with a threefold curse, we must weave the shroud for the Russian autocratic government, for the entire anti-Semitic criminal gang, for the entire capitalist world.'

Finally, it is important to recognize the shift that occurred in the late nineteenth century from traditional anti-Judaism to a more 'modern' anti-Semitism, linked – though not identical – to the racist ideology that had swept the nineteenth-century West. It was an apostate named Brafman who, in *The Book of the Kahal*, first alleged the existence of a secret Jewish organization with sinister powers. This conspiracy theory greatly appealed to new organizations like the League of the Russian People, which combined reactionary devotion to autocracy with violent anti-Semitism. It was in the League's St Petersburg newspaper *Russkoye Znamya* that the Moldavian anti-Semite Pavolachi Krushevan published the fake 'Protocols of the Elders of Zion' (1903), a series of articles subsequently reprinted with the imprimatur of the Russian army as *The Root of Our Misfortunes*. Though the 'Protocols' would exert a greater malign influence in the inter-war years, they were Tsarist Russia's distinctive contribution to the poisonous brew of pre-war prejudice. Once, Russia's rulers had believed that the 'Jewish question' could be answered by the simple expedient of enforced conversion. The new conspiracy theorists made it clear that this simply would not suffice. In the words of *Russkoye Znamya*:

The government's duty is to consider the Jews as a nation just as dangerous for the life of humanity as wolves, scorpions, snakes, poisonous spiders and other creatures which are doomed to destruction because of their rapaciousness towards human beings and whose annihilation is commended by law . . . The *Zhids* must be put in such conditions that they will gradually die out.

As we have seen, such language was not unknown in German anti-Semitic circles. But it was in the Russian Empire that words first led to deeds.

## POGROM

The pogroms of 1881 are usually seen as a response to the assassination of Tsar Alexander II; there were widespread rumours of an official order to inflict retribution on the Jews. It is no coincidence, however, that the violence began just after Easter, traditionally a time of tension between Christian and Jewish communities. On April 15, three days after Easter Sunday, a drunken Russian got himself thrown out of a Jewish-owned tavern in Elizavetgrad. This was the catalyst. Amid cries of 'The Yids are beating our people', a crowd formed which proceeded to attack Jewish stores in the marketplace and then moved on to Jewish residences. Few people in Elizavetgrad were killed or even injured, though one elderly Jewish man was later found dead in a tavern. Rather, there was an orgy of vandalism and looting, which left 'many houses with broken doors and windows' and 'streets . . . covered with feathers [from looted bedding] and obstructed with broken furniture'. In the succeeding days, there were similar outbreaks in Znamenka, Golta, Aleksandriia, Anan'ev and Berezovka. The worst violence took place between April 26 and 28 in Kiev, where a number of Jews were murdered and twenty cases of rape were reported. Once again, the trouble then spread to nearby districts. In the months that followed, there were attacks on Jews in places all over the southern half of the Pale. In Odessa attacks on Jews began on May 3 and lasted nearly five days. On June 30 a new pogrom broke out in Pereyaslav and continued for three days, despite the arrival on the scene of the Governor of Poltava himself. All told, the authorities counted some

224 pogroms between April and August. Though the total number of fatalities was just sixteen, damage to property was substantial. Nor was that the end. On Christmas Day there was a pogrom in Warsaw. Easter 1882 saw further attacks on Jews in Bessarabia, Kherson and Chernigov; at the end of March there was a particularly violent pogrom in Balta, in which forty Jews were killed or seriously wounded.

What caused this unprecedented spate of attacks on Jews, variously described by past historians as a wave or an epidemic? It used to be argued that the government had instigated them. Some have blamed Nikolai Ignatiev, the Minister of the Interior, others the regime's *éminence grise*, the procurator-general of the Orthodox Synod, Constantine Pobedonostsev, still others the new Tsar himself. Yet Pobedonostsev ordered the clergy to preach against pogroms, while it is clear that the new Tsar, Alexander III, deplored what was happening. The government, to be sure, argued that the *pogromshchiki* had legitimate economic grievances against the Jews, who were said to be 'exploiting . . . the original population', profiting from 'unproductive labour' and monopolizing commerce, which they were said to have 'captured'. The Tsar himself saw 'no end' to anti-Jewish feeling in Russia, because: 'These Yids make themselves too repulsive to Russians, and as long as they continue to exploit Christians, this hatred will not diminish.' But such comments scarcely amount to evidence of official responsibility. The spurious allegations of Jewish exploitation reflected an effort by the authorities to understand more than to excuse popular motives. Other officials pointed nervously to evidence that anarchists had encouraged the pogroms. In the words of the chairman of the Committee of Ministers, Count Reutern:

Today they hunt and rob the Jews, tomorrow they will go after the so-called kulaks, who morally are the same as Jews only of Orthodox Christian faith, then merchants and landowners may be next . . . In the face of . . . inactivity on the part of the authorities, we may expect in a not too distant future the development of the most horrible socialism.

In reality the pogroms seem to have been a largely spontaneous phenomenon, eruptions of violence in economically volatile, multi-ethnic communities. If the pogroms had instigators they were most probably the Jews' economic rivals: Russian artisans and merchants. Often the perpetrators were unemployed; many were drunk; over-whelmingly they were male. Of the 4,052 rioters who were arrested, only 222 were women. But otherwise the perpetrators were remark-able for their social diversity. The official investigation noted: 'Clerks, saloon and hotel waiters, artisans, drivers, flunkeys, day labourers in the employ of the Government, and soldiers on furlough – all these joined in the movement.' One witness of events in Kiev saw 'an immense crowd of young boys, artisans, and labourers . . . [a] "bare-footed brigade"'. The rioters in Elizavetgrad included 181 towns-people, 177 peasants, 130 former soldiers, six 'foreigners' and one honorary nobleman. Detailed occupational data survive for only 363 of those arrested, including 102 unskilled workmen, 87 day-labourers, 77 peasants and 33 domestic servants. Peasants certainly played their part, many in the sincere belief that the new Tsar had issued an *ukaz* to 'beat the Jews'. Some villagers in Chernigov were so convinced of this that they asked the local 'land captain' for a written guarantee that they would not be punished if they *failed* to attack the local Jews. However, the main role of peasants was to loot Jewish property after pogroms had happened; they arrived on the scene with empty carts, not weapons. More likely to be involved in the actual violence were migrant workers, like the many unemployed Russians then seeking work in Ukraine, or the demobilized soldiers returning from the recent war with Turkey.

The key to understanding the way the violence spread lies in the role played by railway workers. It was they who transmitted the idea of attacking Jews along some of the principal railways of the Pale: from Elizavetgrad to Aleksandriia; from Anan'ev to Tiraspol; from Kiev to Brovary, Konotop and Zhmerinka; from Aleksandrovsk to Orekhov, Berdiansk and Mariupol'. Railways had seemed to be the sinews of modern imperial power; that had been the rationale behind the Trans-Siberian. Now it turned out that they could also be trans-mission mechanisms for public disorder. Almost as important in this regard was the role *not* played by local authorities. The official report noted 'the complete indifference displayed by the local non-Jewish inhabitants to the havoc wrought before their eyes'. This indifference allied with a chronic shortage of police manpower to give the rioters free rein. In Elizavetgrad there were just eighty-seven policemen for a total population of 43,229. To make matters worse, the local police chiefs took no action for two days. In short, the 1881 pogroms illustrate the way a local ethnic riot could spread contagiously in the presence of modern communications and in the absence of modern policing.

In the aftermath of the pogroms, the government did take steps to punish those responsible. Altogether 3,675 persons were arrested for participation in pogroms in 1881, of whom 2,359 were tried, giving the lie to the notion that the pogroms were officially instigated. Yet the Tsar and his ministers largely ignored the regional commissions of inquiry it had appointed, many of which recommended a relaxation of the residential and other restrictions imposed on the Jews. Instead, an official Committee on the Jews introduced the supposedly temporary Laws of May 3, 1882 which prohibited new settlement by Jews in rural areas or villages, as well as banning Jews from trading on Sundays and Christian holidays. Plans for wholesale expulsions from the countryside were seriously considered, though not adopted. In short, the situation of the Jews was made worse, not better, in the wake of the attacks against them. Nor did the punishment of those responsible for the pogroms prevent sporadic outbreaks of anti-Jewish violence in the succeeding years. As we have seen, many Russian Jews responded by emigrating westwards, to Austria-Hungary, to Germany, to England, to Palestine and, above all, to the United States.

What happened between 1903 and 1906 was quite different in character. This second outbreak of Russian pogroms had four distinct phases. It began in Kishinev in Bessarabia on April 19, 1903, once again at the time of the Orthodox Easter. The catalyst was a classic 'blood libel', prompted by the discovery of the corpse of a young boy, who, so the anti-Semitic newspaper *Bessarabets* alleged, had been the victim of a ritual murder by local Jews. In the violence that ensued, hundreds of shops and homes were looted or burned. This time, however, many more people were killed. In Kishinev alone, forty-seven Jews lost their lives, and this was merely the first of four phases of violence. The second phase coincided with the beginning of the Russo-Japanese War: these were the so-called mobilization pogroms, which tended to occur in places where troops were preparing to depart for the East; there were forty in 1904, followed by another fifty between January and early October of 1905. The third and worst phase of the violence came in mid-October, the high point of the Revolution. On October 17, the day the Tsar published the liberal October Manifesto, Jews in Odessa once again came under attack; at a minimum, 302 were killed. Kiev erupted into violence a day later; as in 1881, there was extensive destruction of Jewish property – feathers from torn-up bedding once again littered the streets – but this time there was killing too. On October 21 it was the turn of Ekaterinoslav. Between October 31 and November 11 there were pogroms in 660 different places; more than 800 Jews were killed. The final phase happened in Białystok in June 1906 and in Siedlice three months later; in the former, eighty-two Jews were killed. Not only were these pogroms much more violent than those of 1881 (altogether, as many as 3,000 Jews may have died), they were also much more widespread. Violence against Jews happened as far away as Irkutsk and Tomsk in Siberia, though, as in 1881, there was no violence in the northernmost provinces of the Pale.

What was different? There was, no doubt, an element of escalation through repetition – those who remembered 1881 were able to proceed more quickly from violence against property to violence against persons. More important, however, was the fact that this time some Jewish communities fought back with 'self-defence' forces organized by local Bundists and Zionists. This was the case in Kishinev, as well as in Gomel. In Odessa there were pitched battles. Yet it was the fact that they took place in the context of a revolutionary crisis that was really crucial, for this ensured that, unlike in 1881, these pogroms were truly political events. Nicholas II told his mother that the *pogromshchiki* represented 'a whole mass of loyal people', reacting angrily to 'the impertinence of the Socialists and revolutionaries . . . and, because nine tenths of the trouble-makers are Jews, the People's whole anger turned against them.' This analysis was accepted by many foreign observers, notably British diplomats like the ambassador at St Petersburg, Sir Charles Hardinge, his councillor, Cecil Spring Rice, and the Consul-General in Moscow, Alexander Murray. On the other hand, Jewish organizations portrayed the pogroms as officially instigated, a verdict echoed by more than one generation of scholars.

Neither view was wholly correct. The authorities certainly exaggerated the role played in the Revolution by Jews, who accounted for far less than 90 per cent of Russian socialists. On the other hand, the evidence of orchestration by the Minister for the Interior himself has been exposed as bogus. Indeed, Pleve seems to have taken steps to mitigate the situation of the Jews in the Pale in the wake of the Kishinev pogrom, holding meetings with the Zionist leader Theodor Herzl as well as with Lucien Wolf, head of the Joint Foreign Commission for the Aid of the Jews of Eastern Europe.

So who was to blame? The instigators were a mixture of rabid anti-Semites like Pavolachi Krushevan, who, in addition to publishing the 'Protocols of the Elders of Zion', was the editor of the inflammatory *Bessarabets*, and counter-revolutionary militias like the irregular Black Hundreds, who had taken up arms to combat the Revolution. There is some evidence that the perpetrators attacked Jews precisely because they saw them as pro-revolutionary. In Kiev, for example, the leading *pogromshchiki* shouted, 'This is your freedom! Take that for your Constitution and revolution!' Yet there is little evidence that Gentile socialists rallied to the side of the Jews. This can be inferred from the limited evidence we have on the social origins of the *pogromshchiki*. In Kiev, as in 1881, the looting of Jewish homes and stores was carried out mainly by 'urchins, vagabonds and assorted riff-raff', most of them teenagers. Elsewhere, however, the dregs of the *lumpenproletariat* were joined by members of the working class, in whose name the Bolsheviks and Mensheviks claimed to be acting. According to a member of one of the Jewish self-defence organizations, the Odessa rioters included 'nearly all classes of Russian society . . . not only barefoot beggars, but also factory and railroad workers, peasants, chiefs of station . . .'. In Ekaterinoslav the *pogromshchiki* were said to include 'petty bourgeois, peasants, factory workers, day-labourers, off-duty soldiers and school children'. Moreover, these groups were joined in a number of cases by local policemen, who egged on the rioters, fired on Jewish self-defence forces and sometimes even joined in the ransacking of Jewish residences. In the aftermath of the upheaval, three Kiev police officers, including a colonel, were suspended and charged with dereliction of duty, though they never stood trial and the colonel had been reinstated by 1907. If so many different social groups were ready to assault and murder Jews, the old idea that Russia's revolution was a manifestation of 'social polarization' begins to look rather doubtful. Ethnic polarization might be a more accurate description.

Violence against Jews was, after all, not the only sign of the ethnic conflict inherent in the Tsarist system. Poles, Finns and Latvians had been among the minorities most aggressively targeted for 'Russification' by the imperial regime; their reaction to the Revolution, predictably, was to press for political autonomy. They too were over-represented in the Social Democratic parties. By contrast, the minority most closely identified with the old order, the German aristocracy of the Baltic provinces, were the targets for ferocious attacks in 1905; around 140 manor houses in Courland (Latvia) were razed to the ground by marauding peasants. Russian socialists, in short, might talk the language of class. But other Russians – or, to be precise, other subjects of the Tsar who lived on the Russian Empire's multi-ethnic western periphery – answered in the language of race. The pogroms of 1905 proved to be the first of an escalating series of earthquakes that would devastate and ultimately destroy the Pale of Settlement in the first half of the twentieth century. They were an intimation of much that was to follow.

## RUSSIA TURNS WESTWARDS

The division between the socialist and nationalist impulses of the 1905 Revolution helped the Tsarist regime to reassert its control. By the end of December 1905 the Soviet had been shut down. Trotsky languished in jail along with the rest of its leadership.

The Tsar and his ministers might have been expected to learn prudence from the events of 1905. To avoid another defeat and another revolution, they might simply have opted to avoid another war. But their assumption seems to have been that future wars with their imperial rivals were unavoidable. As General A. A. Kireyev had noted in his diary for 1900, 'We, like any powerful nation, strive to expand our territory, our "legitimate" moral, economic and political influence. This is in the order of things.' His greatest fear was that, as he put it nine years later, 'We have become a second-rate power.' The main thing was that next time Russia must be better armed – and fight closer to home. Undaunted by the danger of renewed revolution, the government embarked on a massive programme of rearmament. This time, however, the railways they built ran not eastwards to Asia, but westwards towards Germany and her ally Austria-Hungary. Nobody was in any doubt that a primary function of these railways would be to carry not goods but troops.

The European empires, and none more than Tsarist Russia, had extended and consolidated their power by building tens of thousands of miles of railway track. The ethnic conflicts of 1881 and 1905, however, had revealed that railways could transmit disorder as well as order. The summer of 1914 brought a new revelation, as millions of men were transported by rail to battlefields all over Europe. The empires, it suddenly became clear, would travel to their own destruction by train. Yet there was no predictable railway timetable for war, as A. J. P. Taylor once famously argued. When it came, war took most people by surprise. In that respect, as in others, the end of the era of European mastery resembled nothing more than the most terrific train crash.

# 3

# Fault Lines

*Now comes a war and shows that we still haven't crawled out
on all fours from the barbaric stage of our history. We have
learned to wear suspenders, to write clever editorials, and to
make chocolate milk, but when we have to decide seriously a
question of the coexistence of a few tribes on a rich peninsula
of Europe, we are helpless to find a way other than mutual
mass slaughter.*                Leon Trotsky

## DEATH IN RURITANIA

On June 28, 1914 a tubercular nineteen-year-old Bosnian youth
named Gavrilo Princip carried out one of the most successful terrorist
acts in all history. The shots he fired that day not only severed fatally
the jugular vein of the Archduke Francis Ferdinand, the Habsburg
heir to the thrones of Austria and Hungary. They also precipitated a
war that destroyed the Austro-Hungarian Empire and transformed
Bosnia-Herzegovina from one of its colonies into a part of a new
South Slav state. These were in fact more or less precisely the things
Princip had hoped to achieve, even if he cannot have anticipated such
far-reaching success. Yet these were only the intended consequences
of his action. The war he triggered was not confined to the Balkans;
it also drew broad and hideous scars across northern Europe and the
Near East. Like gargantuan abattoirs, its battlefields sucked in and
slaughtered young men from all the extremities of the globe, claiming
in all nearly ten million lives. It brought forth new and terrible
methods of destruction, hitherto the stuff of Wellsian science-fiction:

cavalry charges by armed and armoured vehicles, lethal clouds of poison gas, invisible fleets of submarines. It rained down bombs from the air and cluttered the Atlantic seabed with sunken ships. It lasted longer than any major war in Europe in living memory, dragging on for four and a quarter years. And, besides the Habsburgs, it toppled three other imperial dynasties: the Romanovs, the Hohenzollerns and the Ottomans. Even when an armistice was proclaimed, the war refused to stop; it swept eastwards after 1918, as if eluding the grasp of the peacemakers.

The First World War changed everything. In the summer of 1914 the world economy was thriving in ways that look distinctly familiar. The mobility of commodities, capital and labour reached levels comparable with those we know today; the sea lanes and telegraphs across the Atlantic were never busier, as capital and migrants went west and raw materials and manufactures went east. The war sank globalization – literally. Nearly thirteen million tons of shipping went to the bottom of the sea as a result of German naval action, most of it by U-boats. International trade, investment and emigration all collapsed. In the war's aftermath, revolutionary regimes arose that were fundamentally hostile to international economic integration. Plans replaced the market; autarky and protection took the place of free trade. Flows of goods diminished; flows of people and capital all but dried up. The European empires' grip on the world – which had been the political undergirding of globalization – was dealt a profound, if not quite fatal, blow. The reverberations of Princip's shots truly shook the world.

Yet political assassinations were far from uncommon in the early twentieth century, as we have already seen in the case of the unfortunate President McKinley. His successor, Theodore Roosevelt, only narrowly escaped assassination too. Between 1900 and 1913 no fewer than forty heads of state, politicians and diplomats were murdered, including four kings, six prime ministers and three presidents. In the Balkans alone there were eight successful assassinations, the victims of which included two kings, one queen, two prime ministers and the commander-in-chief of the Turkish Army. Why did this particular political murder have such vast consequences?

Part of the answer is that when the Archduke was shot he was driving along one of the world's great fault lines – the fateful historical border between the West and the East, the Occident and the Orient. From the fifteenth century until the late nineteenth, Bosnia and neighbouring Herzegovina had been parts of the Ottoman Empire. Many of their inhabitants had converted to Islam, the better to serve their Turkish rulers and to reap the full benefits of Ottoman rule. But Bosnia was never an entirely Muslim country; there were also substantial populations of Orthodox Serbs and Catholic Croats, to say nothing of Vlachs, Germans, Jews and Gypsies. To one Victorian visitor, the River Sava between Bosnia and Habsburg Croatia seemed to be the dividing line between Europe and Asia. Others saw the Miljacka, which runs through Sarajevo itself, as the border; or the Drina, which runs through Višegrad to the east. In truth, with the protracted decline of Ottoman power, the whole of Bosnia became a contested frontier. In 1908 Austria-Hungary had formally annexed Bosnia, over which it had enjoyed *de facto* control since the Congress of Berlin in 1878. When Francis Ferdinand visited Sarajevo just six years later, he was touring a new imperial acquisition, in which considerable sums had been invested on new roads, railways and schools, but where thousands of Austro-Hungarian troops still had to be stationed to maintain order.

The trouble with geological fault lines is that, as the earth's tectonic plates grind uneasily against one another, they are where earthquakes happen. In the years before 1914 the geopolitical tectonic plates known as empires were shifting underneath Sarajevo. Turkey's was giving way; Austria's was pushing forward; so, too, was Russia's. Russian Pan-Slavists were appalled by the Austrian annexation of Bosnia. General A. A. Kireyev reacted with mortification to the news of his government's acquiescence: 'Shame! Shame!' he wrote in his diary. 'It would be better to die!' Yet the principal opponent of the Austrian takeover was not strictly speaking an empire but a nation state, albeit one with imperial ambitions. This was Serbia.

Nation states were a comparative novelty in European history. Much of the continent in 1900 was still dominated by the long-established and ethnically mixed empires of the Habsburgs, Romanovs and Osmanli. The United Kingdom of Great Britain and Ireland was another such entity. Some smaller countries were also ethnically heterogeneous:

Belgium and Switzerland, for example. And there were numerous petty principalities and grand duchies, like Luxembourg or Lichtenstein, that had no distinct national identity of their own, yet resisted absorption into bigger political units. These patchwork political structures made practical sense at a time when mass migration was increasing rather than reducing ethnic intermingling. Yet in the eyes of political nationalists, they deserved to be consigned to the past; the future should belong to homogeneous nation states. France, which had nurtured in the Swiss political philosopher Jean-Jacques Rousseau the prophet of popular sovereignty, also provided a kind of model for nation-building. A republic forged and re-forged in repeated revolutions and wars, France by 1900 seemed to have subsumed all its old regional identities in a single 'idea of France'. Auvergnais, Bretons and Gascons alike all considered themselves to be Frenchmen, having been put through the same standardized schooling and military training.

Nationalism at first had seemed to pose a threat to Europe's monarchies. In the 1860s, however, the kingdoms of Piedmont and Prussia had created new nation states by combining the national principle with their own instincts for self-preservation and self-aggrandizement. The results – the kingdom of Italy and the German Reich – were no doubt very far from being perfect nation states. To Sicilians, the Piedmontese were as foreign as if they had been Frenchmen; the true unification of Italy came after the triumphs of Cavour and Garibaldi, with what were in effect small wars of colonization waged against the peoples of the south. Many Germans, meanwhile, lived outside the borders of Bismarck's new Reich; what historians called his wars of unification had in fact excluded German-speaking Austrians from a Prussian-dominated *Kleindeutschland*. Nevertheless, an imperfect nation state was, in the eyes of most nationalists, preferable to no nation state at all. In the late nineteenth century other peoples sought to follow the Italian and German example. Some – notably the Irish and the Poles, to say nothing of Bengalis and other Indians – saw nationhood as an alternative to subjugation by unsympathetic empires. A few, like the Czechs, were content to pursue greater autonomy within an existing imperial structure, keeping hold of the Habsburg nurse for fear of meeting something worse. The situation of the

Serbs was different. At the Congress of Berlin (1878), along with the Montenegrins, they had recovered their independence from Ottoman rule. By 1900 their ambitions were to follow the Piedmontese and Prussian examples by expanding in the name of South Slav (Yugoslav) national unity. But how were they to achieve this? One obvious possibility was through war, the Italian and German method. But the odds against Serbia were steep. It was one thing to win a war against the crumbling Ottoman Empire (as happened when Serbia joined forces with Montenegro, Bulgaria and Greece in 1912) or against rival Balkan states (when the confederates quarrelled over the spoils of victory the following year). It was an altogether bigger challenge to take on Austria-Hungary, which was not only a more formidable military opponent, but also happened to be the principal market for Serbia's exports.

The Balkan Wars had revealed both the strengths and the limits of Balkan nationalism. Its strength lay in its ferocity. Its weakness was its disunity. The violence of the fighting much impressed the young Trotsky, who witnessed it as a correspondent for the newspaper *Kievskaia mysl*. Even the peace that followed the Balkan Wars was cruel, in a novel manner that would become a recurrent feature of the twentieth century. It no longer sufficed, in the eyes of nationalists, to acquire foreign territory. Now it was peoples as well as borders that had to move. Sometimes these movements were spontaneous. Muslims fled in the direction of Salonika as the Greeks, Serbs and Bulgarians advanced in 1912; Bulgarians fled Macedonia to escape from invading Greek troops in 1913; Greeks chose to leave the Macedonian districts ceded to Bulgaria and Serbia by the Treaty of Bucharest. Sometimes populations were deliberately expelled, as the Greeks were from Western Thrace in 1913 and from parts of Eastern Thrace and Anatolia in 1914. In the wake of the Turkish defeat, there was an agreed population exchange: 48,570 Turks moved one way and 46,764 Bulgarians the other across the new Turkish-Bulgarian border. Such exchanges were designed to transform regions of ethnically mixed settlement into the homogeneous societies that so appealed to the nationalist imagination. The effects on some regions were dramatic. Between 1912 and 1915, the Greek population of (Greek) Macedonia increased by around a third; the Muslim and Bulgarian population declined by 26 and 13 per cent respectively. The Greek population of Western Thrace fell by 80 per cent; the Muslim population of Eastern Thrace rose by a third. The implications were distinctly ominous for the many multi-ethnic communities elsewhere in Europe.

The alternative to outright war was to create a new South Slav state through terrorism. In the wake of the annexation of Bosnia, a rash of new organizations sprang up, pledged to resisting Austrian imperialism in the Balkans and to liberate Bosnia by fair means or foul. In Belgrade there was *Narodna Odbrana* (National Defence); in Sarajevo *Mlada Bosna* (Young Bosnia). In 1911 a more extreme and highly secret group was formed: *Ujedinjenje ili Smrt* (Unification or Death), also known as *Crna Ruka* (The Black Hand). Its declared aim was to make Serbia 'the Piedmont of . . . the Unification of . . . Serbdom'. Its seal depicted:

a powerful arm holding in its hand an unfurled flag on which – as a coat of arms – there is a skull with crossed bones; by the side of the flag, a knife, a bomb and a phial of poison. Around, in a circle, there is the following inscription, reading from left to right: 'Unification or Death'.

The Black Hand's leader was Colonel Dragutin Dimitrijevic, nicknamed 'Apis' (Bee), one of seven officers in the Serbian army who were among its founders. It was Dimitrijevic who trained three young terrorists for what was from the outset intended to be a suicide mission: to murder the heir to the Austro-Hungarian throne when he visited Sarajevo. The assassins – Nedjilko Cabrinovic, Trifko Grabez and Gavrilo Princip – were sent across the border with four Browning M 1910 revolvers, six bombs and cyanide tablets. As if to entice them, the Archduke chose to visit Sarajevo on the anniversary of the fourteenth-century Battle of Kosovo – the holiest day in the calendar of Serbian nationalism, St Vitus' Day (*Vidovdan*).

Born and raised in the impoverished village of Bosansko Grahovo in the Krajina, in north-western Bosnia, Gavrilo Princip was in many ways the archetypal suicide bomber: enough of a student to believe fervently in the cause of Serbian nationalism, enough of a peasant to be shocked by the Austrian occupiers as they quaffed their schnapps and disported themselves in the Sarajevo bordellos. The more he saw of their antics, the more attracted he was by the idea of kicking the

Austrians out of Bosnia and making it part of a new South Slav state, along with neighbouring Serbia. He was, as he later explained at his trial, 'a Yugoslav nationalist, aiming for the unification of all Yugoslavs, and I do not care what form of state, but it must be free from Austria . . . We thought: unification by whatever means . . . by means of terror.' His aim, he said, had been 'to do away with those who obstruct and do evil, who stand in the way of unification.' He might have preferred to achieve that aim by means of conventional warfare; alas, he had been rejected by the Serbian army in 1912 as 'too small and too weak'.

On the fateful morning, he and his fellow conspirators took up their positions on the procession route along the Appel Quay, the city's central riverside avenue. Initially, it seemed that the job had been botched. Cabrinovic threw a bomb at the Archduke's open-top car, but it bounced off the folded roof, injuring two people in the vehicle behind and about twenty bystanders. The archducal chauffeur was understandably ready to speed off to safety, but Francis Ferdinand insisted on turning back to see how the injured were faring, and then proceeded as scheduled to the town hall. After that, he decided he should visit the casualties. When the nervous chauffeur took a wrong turning on the way to the hospital, turning right into Franz-Josef Strasse, Princip, who was in the process of buying himself some lunch, suddenly found himself face to face with his intended targets. His vision blurred and, 'filled with a peculiar feeling' of 'excitement', he aimed his gun and fired. He fatally wounded both the Archduke, whom he shot through the throat, and his pregnant wife, the Duchess Sophie, whom he hit in the stomach by accident (he was in fact aiming for the military governor, General Oskar Potiorek). It was the royal couple's fourteenth wedding anniversary.

Their mission achieved, Princip and Cabrinovic both tried to commit suicide, but the cyanide in the capsules they carried had oxidized and failed to kill them. Princip also tried to shoot himself but was prevented from doing so. At his trial, Princip was asked about the intended consequences of his actions. He replied: 'I never thought that after the assassination there would be a war.' Was this ingenuous or disingenuous? Historians have tended to assume that it was one or the other. It seems scarcely credible that Princip could have acted as he did without some sense of the earthquake that was to follow. Yet we should bear in mind that earthquakes are not easily predictable events. Nor was the First World War. Though the Archduke's assassination proved to be the tipping point – the fatal stimulus that caused the tectonic plates of empire to move convulsively right across Europe – that was not immediately obvious at the time. Over-determined though the war now seems as an event, we cannot truly understand it until we have grasped its apparently low probability in the eyes of contemporaries.

## THE SHOCK OF WAR

Historians have, on the whole, tended to portray the years before the outbreak of the First World War as a time of mounting tension and escalating crises. War, they have claimed, did not burst onto the scene in the summer of 1914; rather, it approached over a period of years, even decades. A not untypical example of the way they have retrospectively ordered events is the structure of the eleven-volume official history, *The British Documents on the Origins of the War, 1898–1914*, published between 1926 and 1938. The titles of the individual volumes offer a clear narrative framework of the war's origins, extending over seventeen years:

   I  The End of British Isolation
  II  The Anglo-Japanese Alliance and the Franco-British Entente
 III  The Testing of the Entente, 1904–6
 IV  The Anglo-Russian Rapprochement, 1903–7
  V  The Near East: The Macedonian Problem and the Annexation of Bosnia, 1903–9
 VI  Anglo-German Tension: Armaments and Negotiation, 1907–12
 VII  The Agadir Crisis
VIII  Arbitration, Neutrality and Security
 IX  Part 1. The Balkan Wars: The Prelude. The Tripoli War; Part 2. The Balkan Wars: The League and Turkey
  X  Part 1. The Near and Middle East on the Eve of War; Part 2. The Last Years of Peace
 XI  The Outbreak of War

Nearly all books about the origins of the war are variations on this narrative. Some authors go back further in time. One recent German history portrayed the outbreak of war as the last of a succession of nine diplomatic crises: the 1875 Franco-German 'War in Sight' crisis, the 1875–8 Eastern crisis, the 1885–8 Bulgarian crisis, the 1886–9 Boulanger crisis, the 1905–6 Moroccan crisis, the 1908 Bosnian crisis, the 1911 Agadir crisis and the 1912–13 Balkan crisis. The first volume of a monumental new British history of the war also traces its origins back to the foundation of the German Reich in 1871, emphasizing in particular Anglo-German naval competition after 1897. Studies of the pre-war arms race on land have tended to concentrate rather more on the immediate pre-war decade. Some writers who centre their accounts on the policy of Austria-Hungary tend to start the countdown to war even later. But few people today would seriously claim that the war was a bolt from the blue in the summer of 1914.

The idea of a gradually approaching conflict accords well with the idea that people had been prophesying war for years before the summer of 1914; in this view, the actual outbreak of hostilities came more as a relief than a surprise. The Left had predicted for decades that militarism and imperialism would eventually produce an almighty crisis; the Right had been almost as consistent in portraying war as a salutary consequence of Darwinian struggle. European societies, it is now widely agreed, were ready for war long before war came. Imperialism, nationalism, Social Darwinism, militarism – the libraries overflow with causes of the First World War. Some emphasize domestic political crises, others the instability of the international system; all are agreed that it had deep roots. The question, however, is how far the many narratives of escalating crisis have been constructed by historians not to capture the past as it actually was in 1914, but to create an explanation of the war's origins commensurate with the vast dimensions of what happened in the succeeding four years. One way of addressing this question is to look more closely at the attitudes of other contemporaries to the diplomatic crises so familiar to historians. Doing so reveals just how far history is distorted by the dubious benefit of hindsight. For the reality is that the First World War was a shock, not a long-anticipated crisis. Only retrospectively did men decide they had seen it coming all along. Precisely for that reason the consequences of the war were so world-shaking. It is the unforeseen that causes the greatest disturbance, not the expected.

If any social group had a strong interest in anticipating the approach of a world war, it was investors and the financiers who served their needs in the City of London, the biggest international financial market in the pre-war world. The reason is obvious: they had a great deal to lose in the event of such a war. In 1899 the Warsaw financier Ivan Bloch estimated that 'the immediate consequence of war would be to send [the price of] securities all round down from 25 to 50 per cent'. The journalist Norman Angell made similar points about the negative financial consequences of great-power conflict in his best-selling tract of 1910, 'The Great Illusion'. Both authors expressed the hope that this consideration might make a major war less likely, if not impossible. But investors, especially investors with holdings of bonds issued by the great powers, could scarcely afford to take this for granted. We would therefore expect any event that made such a war seem more likely to have had a detectable effect on investor sentiment. Yet it would seem that the City, including some of its best-informed financiers, discerned the imminence of world war only at a very late stage indeed.

In 1914 N. M. Rothschild & Sons was still the pre-eminent firm in the City. Closely associated with their cousins in Paris and Vienna, the London Rothschilds had dominated the bond market for very nearly a century, since Nathan Mayer Rothschild had made the family's fortunes before and after the Battle of Waterloo. Between them the Rothschild houses had capital in excess of £35 million on the eve of the First World War, all of it family money; it was the job of the partners to manage this huge portfolio. A large part of it they held in the form of European government bonds, the most secure form of investment and also the kind of security the Rothschilds knew best, since they had long been the principal underwriters for new bond issues on the London market. They, more than anyone, stood to lose in the event of a European war, not least because such a war would almost certainly divide the three houses, pitting Paris and perhaps also London against Vienna. Yet the outbreak of war caught them almost entirely by surprise. On July 22, 1914 Lord Rothschild told his relatives in Paris that he 'rather fanc[ied] the well founded belief in influential quarters that unless Russia backed up Servia the latter will eat humble pie and that the inclination in Russia is to remain quiet, circumstances there not favouring a forward movement'. The following day he wrote that he expected 'that the various matters in dispute will be arranged without appeal to arms'. Before the details of the Austrian ultimatum to Serbia were known, he anticipated that the Serbs would 'give every satisfaction'. On July 27 he expressed 'the universal opinion that Austria was quite justified in the demands she made on Servia and it would ill-become the great Powers if by a hasty and ill-conceived action they did anything which might be viewed as condoning a brutal murder'. He was confident that the British government would leave 'no stone . . . unturned in the attempts which will be made to preserve the peace of Europe'. 'It is very difficult to express any very positive opinion,' he told his French relatives on July 29, 'but I think I may say we believe [French opinion] . . . to be wrong . . . in attributing sinister motives and underhand dealings to the German Emperor[;] he is bound by certain treaties and engagements to come to the assistance of Austria if she is attacked by Russia but that is the last thing he wishes to do.' He and the Tsar were 'corresponding directly over the wires in the interests of peace'; the German government sincerely wished any war to be 'localised'. As late as July 31, Rothschild continued to give credence to 'rumours in the City that the German Emperor [was] using all of his influence at both St Petersburg & Vienna to find a solution which would not be distasteful either to Austria or to Russia'. Only at this, the eleventh hour, did he show signs of grasping the scale of what was happening.

Rothschild was by no means exceptionally slow on the uptake. On July 22 – more than three weeks after the assassination at Sarajevo – *The Times* published what seems to have been the first English-language allusion to the possibility that the crisis in the Balkans might have negative financial consequences. The report appeared on page 19 and read as follows:

STOCK EXCHANGE
DEPRESSED BY FOREIGN POLITICAL NEWS

LATE RALLY IN AMERICANS

Stock markets at the opening were entirely overshadowed by the news that the relations between Austria-Hungary and Servia are daily growing more strained . . . Owing to the increasing gravity of the situation in the Near East the attention of members [of the Stock Exchange] has for the moment appeared to be diverted from the Ulster crisis . . . there being a general disinclination to increase commitments in view of the obscurity of the outlook both at home and abroad.

In its July 24 edition, however, *The Economist* was more concerned about 'the continual suspense over Ulster' than about events in the Balkans. The same magazine's August 1 edition made it clear just how surprised the City was by the events of the intervening week:

The financial world has been staggering under a series of blows such as the delicate system of international credit has never before witnessed, or even imagined . . . Nothing so widespread and so world-wide has ever been known before. Nothing . . . could have testified more clearly to the impossibility of running modern civilisation and war together than this . . . collapse of prices, produced not by the actual outbreak of a small war, but by fear of a war between some of the Great Powers of Europe.

The key phrase here is 'fear of a war'. Although Austria had declared war on Serbia on July 28, even at this late stage it was still far from certain that the other great powers would join in. As late as August 1 – by which time Russia had begun general mobilization – the headline on the front page of the *New York Times* was the wildly optimistic: CZAR, KAISER AND KING MAY YET ARRANGE PEACE.

Financial market data – specifically, movements in the prices of government bonds – strongly reinforce the impression that the war came as a surprise to the people who had the biggest incentive to anticipate it. The five generally acknowledged great powers – Britain, France, Germany, Russia and Austria-Hungary – had all issued very large quantities of interest-bearing bonds to finance wars in the past and all could be relied upon to do so again in the event of a major European conflict. In 1905 bonds issued by the five powers accounted for nearly 60 per cent of all sovereign fixed-income securities quoted in London. Bonds issued by France, Russia, Germany and Austria accounted for 39 per cent of the total, or 49 per cent of all foreign sovereign debt. It is the regularly quoted market interest rates on these bonds – the yields, to use the technical term – that allow us to infer changes in investors' expectations of war in the years up to and including 1914.

Political events were especially important to investors before 1914 because news about them was more readily and regularly available than were detailed economic data. Modern investors tend to look at a wide variety of economic indicators such as budget deficits, short-term interest rates, actual and forecast inflation rates and growth rates of gross domestic product. They are inundated on a daily basis with information about these and a host of other measures of fiscal, monetary and macroeconomic performance. In the past, however, there were fewer economic data on which to base judgements about default risk, future inflation and growth. Prior to the First World War, investors in the major European economies had fairly good and regular information about certain commodity prices, gold reserves, interest rates and exchange rates, but fiscal data apart from annual budgets were scanty, and there were no regular or reliable figures for national output or income. In non-parliamentary monarchies, even annual budgets were not always available or, if they were published, could not be trusted. Instead, investors tended to infer future changes in fiscal and monetary policy from political events, which were regularly reported in private correspondence, in newspapers and by telegraph agencies. Among the most influential bases for their inferences were three assumptions:

1  that any war would disrupt trade and hence lower tax revenues for all governments;
2  that direct involvement in war would increase a state's expenditure as well as reducing its tax revenues, leading to substantial new borrowings; and

3    that the impact of war on the private sector would make it hard
for monetary authorities in combatant countries to maintain the
convertibility of paper banknotes into gold, thereby increasing the
risk of inflation.

On that basis, any event that seemed to increase the probability of
war should have had a discernible impact on the bond market. War
meant new bond issues, in other words an increase in the supply of
bonds, and hence a reduction in the price of existing bonds. War also
meant an increase in the supply of paper money, and hence a decrease
in the purchasing power of the currencies in which most bonds were
denominated. A rational investor who anticipated a major war would
sell bonds in anticipation of these effects. If financial markets saw the
war of 1914–18 coming, we should expect to see declines in bond
prices or rises in bond yields (since the yield is essentially the interest
paid on a bond divided by its market price).

Far from registering the approach of a world war, however, most
financial market indicators in the years leading up to July 1914 implied
a decline in the risks to investors. Political events, which had caused
sizeable movements in bond prices from the 1840s to the 1870s,
seemed to matter less and less in the subsequent two decades. Volatility
in the international bond market also declined quite markedly. Bond
prices did fall sharply once investors realized that a great-power war
was a real possibility, but the striking thing is that this did not happen
until the last week of July 1914 – to be precise, in the week after the
publication of the Austrian ultimatum to Serbia, which demanded
cooperation with an Austrian inquiry into the Sarajevo assassinations.
That ultimatum was delivered on July 23. Between July 22 and July
30 (the last day when quotations were published), consol prices fell
by 7 per cent, French rentes by just under 6 per cent and German bonds
by 4 per cent. The declines were roughly twice as large for Austrian
and Russian bonds. Even so, these were not by any means unprecedented market movements. The explanation is simple: when the
London market closed on July 31 the magnitude of the crisis had still
not yet become fully apparent. Had the market remained open, prices
of all securities would have fallen much further. It was not until July 31

Table 3.1: Bond prices of the European great powers,
July–December 1914

| | July 8 | July 22 | July 27 | July 30 | Aug. 20 | Sept. 18 | Dec. 19 | percentage change July 22–July 30 | July 22–Dec. 19 |
|---|---|---|---|---|---|---|---|---|---|
| Consols 2½% | 75.8 | 75.5 | 72.5 | 70.0 | 70.0 | 68.8 | 68.5 | -7.3% | -9.3% |
| Austrian 4% | 84.5 | 84.5 | 82.0 | 76.5 | | | 65.0 | -9.5% | -23.1% |
| French 3% | 82.5 | 81.0 | 77.5 | 76.5 | | | | -5.6% | |
| French 3%* | 83.0 | 81.3 | | 82.5 | | 73.7 | 70.6 | 1.5% | -13.2% |
| German 3% | 76.0 | 75.0 | 73.5 | 72.0 | | | | -4.0% | |
| Russian 5% | 102.5 | 102.5 | 98.0 | 93.0 | | 90.5 | 93.5 | -9.3% | -8.8% |

* Bordeaux prices.

that Russia, after three days of indecision, began general mobilization and the German government issued its ultimatums to St Petersburg and Paris. The Germans declared war on Russia only on August 1; the declaration of war on France came two days later. Britain did not enter the fray until the 4th – a decision that was opposed by both the Rothschilds and the editors of *The Economist*. In the eyes of these strongly interested parties, then, what happened between July 22 and July 30 was essentially a sharp rise in the perceived probability of a great-power war on the continent; Armageddon was still not seen as a certainty, even when the markets were forced to close.

As the probability of war suddenly rose, the financial crisis long ago foreseen by Bloch, Angell and others unfolded with terrible swiftness. What happened was a classic case of international financial contagion. The Vienna and Budapest markets, which had been sliding for more than a week, were closed on Monday, July 27, St Petersburg followed two days later, and by Thursday *The Economist* regarded the Berlin and Paris bourses as shut in all but name. The closure of the continental stock markets caused a twofold crisis in London. First, foreigners who had drawn commercial bills on London found it much harder to make remittances; those British banks which had accepted foreign bills suddenly faced a general default as the bills fell due. At the same time, there were large withdrawals of continental funds on deposit with London banks and sales of foreign-held securities. As Lord Rothschild nervously reported to his French cousins on July 27, 'All the foreign Banks and particularly the German ones took a very large amount of money out of the Stock Exchange to-day and ... the markets were at one time quite demoralized, a good many weak speculators selling *à nil prix*.' London became, as *The Economist* put it, 'a dumping ground for liquidation for the whole Continent of Europe'. On July 29, with the clearing banks declining to accommodate their hard-pressed Stock Exchange clients, trading effectively ceased and the first firms began to fail. The next day the news broke that the well-known stockbrokers Derenburg & Co. had been 'hammered' (declared bankrupt); this, coupled with the Bank of England's decision to raise its discount rate from 3 to 5 per cent, deepened the gloom. On the morning of the 31st came what *The Economist* called the 'final thunderclap' – the closure of the Stock Exchange, followed by the Bank of England's decision to raise the discount rate again, to 8 per cent. There is no need to detail here the subsequent steps taken by the authorities to avert a complete financial collapse. The crucial point is that by July 31 the crisis had closed down the London stock market, and it stayed closed until January 4, 1915. There could be no better testimony to the size of the financial shock caused by the outbreak of war.

The closure of the Stock Exchange could only disguise the crisis that had been unleashed; it could not prevent it. The isolated bond prices recorded for the period when the market was closed (based on significant transactions conducted outside the usual channels) make this clear. The price quoted for Austrian bonds on December 19 was 23 per cent below the pre-crisis level on July 22. For French rentes the differential was 13 per cent, for British consols and for Russian bonds (surprisingly) just 9 per cent. This was merely the end of the beginning, however. In the course of the war, large new issues of bonds as well as money creation through the discounting of treasury bills led – just as the experts had predicted – to sustained rises in the yields of all the combatants' bonds. These movements would have been significantly larger had it not been for the various controls imposed on the capital markets of the combatant countries, which made it difficult for investors to reduce their exposure to pre-war great-power bonds, as well as by systematic central bank interventions to maintain bond prices. Even so, they were substantial. From peak to trough, consol prices declined 44 per cent between 1914 and 1920. The figures for French rentes were similar (a 40 per cent price drop). Moreover, Britain and France were the two great powers that emerged on the winning side of the war. The other three all suffered defeat and revolution. The Bolshevik government defaulted outright on the Russian debt, while the post-revolutionary governments in Germany and Austria reduced their real debt burdens drastically through hyper-inflation. For all save the holders of consols, who could reasonably hope that their government would restore the value of their invest-ments when the war was over (as had happened after all Britain's wars since the reign of George I), these outcomes were even worse than the most pessimistic pre-war commentators had foreseen. The impact of war on the Rothschilds was devastating. In 1914 alone their losses – close to £1.5 million – were the largest in the firm's history. Between 1913 and 1918 the London partners' capital was reduced by more than half. The fact that the financial markets do not seem to have considered such a scenario until the last days of July 1914 surely tells us something important about the origins of the First World War. It seems as if, in the words of *The Economist*, the City only saw 'the meaning of war' on July 31 – 'in a flash'.

The story on Wall Street was the same – the *New York Times* spoke of a 'conflagration' – though the crisis took a different form. There it was the desire of hard-pressed Europeans to liquidate their holdings of American railroad securities (20 per cent of which were in foreign hands) that threatened to unleash a financial crisis even more severe than the last great 'panic' of 1907. Interestingly, there had in fact been significant outflows of gold from New York throughout the summer of 1914, apparently caused by Russian efforts to build up reserves in St Petersburg. But the withdrawals reached a peak after the news of the Austrian ultimatum to Serbia. Sterling soared against the dollar as investors sought desperately to remit funds back to Europe; those who would normally have engaged in arbitrage to exploit this weaken-ing of the dollar were deterred by the wartime leap in insurance premiums for gold shipments. Naturally, European sales dented US stock prices, which fell by 3.5 per cent on the news of the Austrian declaration of war five days later. As in London – indeed, on the same day – the decision was taken, with the strong encouragement of the

Treasury Secretary William McAdoo, to close the Stock Exchange. It is true that unofficial quotations on the outdoor New Street market indicate that the market might not have collapsed completely (by the end of October they were down a further 9 per cent). But that was only because the unofficial market was too small to allow Europeans to realize all that they wanted to sell and because McAdoo was simultaneously working to inject emergency banknotes into the US banking system to avoid a default by the City of New York on its sizeable foreign debt, and to encourage, through the creation of a Bureau of War Risk Insurance, the shipment of American exports to Europe to get gold flowing back across the Atlantic. In the absence of these emergency measures, Wall Street would surely have witnessed a wave of bank failures even bigger than had been seen seven years before.

Why were the financial markets caught napping? Did investors in the pre-war period simply come to underestimate the potential impact of a war on their bond portfolios, as the memory of the last great-power war faded? One possibility is, of course, that the financiers were the first victims of what has come to be known as short-war illusion. They had read their Ivan Bloch and Norman Angell, both of whom had argued that the unprecedented costs of a major war would render such a war if not impossible, then at least brief. On November 1, 1914, the French Finance Minister Ribot argued that the war would be over by July 1915, a view shared by the English statistician Edgar Crammond. Almost as optimistic, it is worth adding, was the much cleverer John Maynard Keynes, who excitedly explained to Beatrice Webb on August 10, 1914 that,

he was quite certain that the war could not last more than a year ... The world, he explained, was enormously rich, but its wealth was, fortunately, of a kind which could not be rapidly realized for war purposes: it was in the form of capital equipment for making things which were useless for making war. When all the available wealth was used up – which he thought would take about a year – the Powers would have to make peace.

Yet the young don's jejune optimism was not widely shared in the City – which perhaps helps to explain why he clashed so violently with the bankers when he swept down from Cambridge to offer the

Treasury his wartime services. The Rothschilds understood full well the scale of the crisis they were facing. 'The result of a war ... is doubtful,' Lord Rothschild observed on July 31, 'but whatever the result may be, the sacrifices and misery attendant upon it are stupendous & untold. In this case the calamity would be greater than anything ever seen or known before.' On August 1, *The Economist*'s editors foresaw with trepidation 'a great war on a scale of unprecedented magnitude, involving loss of life and a destruction of all that we associate with modern civilisation too vast to be counted or calculated, and portending horrors so appalling that the imagination shrinks from the task'. There is little evidence that the City expected it to be 'all over by Christmas'.

It may be that technical economic factors were behind the pre-war decline in volatility and risk premiums. Perhaps, as more and more countries joined the gold standard, investors ceased to fear international currency crises, though the evidence for this is not compelling. Perhaps global financial integration was reducing financial risk by broadening the international capital market, though the effect may equally well have been to increase the risks of financial contagion. Perhaps the fiscal positions of most countries before the war were genuinely improving, though investors would still have anticipated big deficits in the event of a war. Alternatively, it may have been the liquidity generated by the deepening of national capital markets that reassured investors. Large numbers of new savings institutions had been created all over the developed world in the late nineteenth century, which for the first time allowed smaller savers to have indirect access to the bond market. The 'home bias' of such institutions (often, as in Britain, legally enforced) undoubtedly had the effect of driving down domestic bond yields and reducing market volatility. Yet we cannot rule out the possibility that investors genuinely regarded the outbreak of a major European war as a highly unlikely occurrence for most of the period after 1880 – indeed, until the very last week of July 1914.

Even to the financially sophisticated, then, the First World War appears to have come as a real surprise. Like people who live on a fault line, investors knew that an earthquake was a possibility and understood how dire its consequences would be, but its timing remained impossible to predict and therefore beyond the realm of normal risk assessment. The more time passed since the last great earthquake, the less people thought about the next one. If this view is correct, then much of the traditional historiography on the origins of the war has, quite simply, over-determined the event. Far from a 'long road to catastrophe', there was but a short slip. Such a conclusion does not tend to support those who still think of the war as an inevitable consequence of deep-seated great-power rivalries – a pre-destined cataclysm. But it certainly accords with the notion that the outbreak of war was an avoidable political error.

## THE END OF THE *PAX BRITANNICA*

Why might the war of 1914–18 have been a surprise? One answer is that contemporaries had more confidence than was entirely justified in the post-Victorian *pax Britannica*; in the ability of the world's biggest empire to limit the global ramifications of a continental crisis. We now know, looking back, that the British Empire was in many ways overstretched. Some contemporaries suspected it, too. Yet the persistence of British naval dominance may have encouraged investors to underestimate the Empire's vulnerabilities. The *pax Britannica* looked very real to investors; that was why they were willing to lend to emerging markets under British rule at rates that were only a few basis points higher than those on consols. In any case, peace was more than just a function of British military or financial power. It was also based on the success of great-power diplomacy. Concepts like the balance of power and the concert of Europe were in large measure discredited by the war; indeed it became an article of faith among American internationalists that the war itself had been caused by a defective system of secret diplomacy. Yet the international institutions that failed in July 1914 had in fact done a reasonably good job of avoiding a major great-power war throughout the preceding century.

Writing in 1833, the German historian Leopold von Ranke had taken a sanguine view of the century that was unfolding. Pessimists, he said, might think that 'our age possesses only the tendency, the pressure, towards dissolution. Its significance seems to lie in putting an end to the unifying, binding institutions which have remained since the Middle Ages.' Conservatives might be dismayed by 'the irresistible inclination towards the development of great democratic ideas and institutions, which of necessity causes the great changes which we are witnessing'. Yet Ranke was optimistic:

. . . far from merely satisfying itself with negations, our century has produced the most positive results. It has completed a great liberation, not in the sense of a dissolution, but in a constructive, unifying sense. Not only has it first of all created the great powers; it has renewed the principle of all states, religion and law; and revitalized the principle of each individual state. In just this fact lies the characteristic of our age . . . [With states and nations] the union of all depends on the independence of each . . . A decisive positive dominance of one over the others would lead to the others' ruin. A merging of them all would destroy the essence of each. Out of separate and independent development will emerge true harmony.

Ranke had faith in the capacity of the great powers to strike a balance with one another, and thereby to avoid that dominance of one continental power over all the others which Napoleon had all but achieved. His faith was not misplaced. Between 1814 and 1907 there were seven congresses (of sovereigns or premiers) and nineteen conferences (of foreign ministers) at which the principal diplomatic issues were discussed and, in large measure, settled. Though lacking all the institutional trappings of the international order of our own time, these regular summits in fact performed a role not so very different from that played today by the permanent members of the United Nations Security Council. The treaties they signed and agreements they brokered did not prevent war, but they limited it, so that no European crisis in the hundred years between the Congress of Vienna and the assassination at Sarajevo escalated into a full-scale conflict involving all the great powers. This was no small achievement.

Those years between 1815 and 1914 were not, of course, truly peaceful; the European empires waged a multitude of wars to impose their authority in Asia, America and Africa. Yet Europe itself saw relatively little war. According to one estimate, there were just twenty-one major wars in the entire period between the Napoleonic Wars and the First World War, and they were nearly all remarkable for their limited geographical extent, short duration and low casualties. The nineteenth century compared very favourably indeed with the three centuries before it and the one after it. Defining war more broadly, to include smaller colonial conflicts, it can be shown that most wars happened outside Europe. Out of one sample of 270 wars between 1789 and 1917, fewer than a third happened in Europe. Of these, only twenty-eight were between nation states, as opposed to wars for national independence (twenty-eight) or civil wars (nineteen). Out of a total of 184 wars in another dataset, which counts only conflicts that caused more than 1,000 battle fatalities per year, just fifty-one took place in Europe. The nineteenth century was not quite the golden age of peace that it came to seem in retrospect to the generation of 1914. But there was no recurrence of the kind of war that had turned Europe upside down between 1792 and 1815.

Nor, despite all that has been written on the subject, was militarism especially pronounced in either the sums the great powers spent on their armed forces, or the numbers of men they mobilized in them. Between 1870 and 1913, only Russia spent more than 4 per cent of net national product on defence on average; Britain, Germany and Austria all spent just over 3 per cent. Over the same period, only France and Germany employed on average more than 1 per cent of their population in their armed forces; respectively, 1.5 and 1.1 per cent. It was only with hindsight that Europe appeared an armed camp, eagerly anticipating mobilization.

## THE HOUSE OF SAXE-COBURG

A further reason for complacency in the summer of 1914 was the extraordinary integration of Europe's nominal ruling elite. The Archduke Francis Ferdinand was, of course, a Habsburg. But he was also a member of that genealogically intertwined elite of predominantly German royal dynasties that had provided the majority of European sovereigns since the seventeenth century.

Aside from Switzerland, France (after the advent of the Third Republic) and a smattering of city-states, nearly all the states of Europe between 1815 and 1917 were either empires, kingdoms, principalities or grand duchies. In all of them, the office of head of state was hereditary, not elective. Between the more or less enlightened despotism of Russia and the liberal monarchy of Norway there was a bewildering variety of constitutional forms. Yet none of these entirely deprived the hereditary sovereign of power, nor did away with that crucial institution of government, the royal court. Moreover, quite apart from their domestic political powers – which remained great in terms of patronage even if they were circumscribed in other respects – the emperors, kings, queens, princes and grand dukes had a distinctive role in the sphere of interstate relations. Despite industrialization and all the other associated phenomena of modernization, dynastic politics still mattered. Wars were fought over the successions to the dukedoms of Schleswig and Holstein and the throne of Spain – to give just two examples – not merely because they furnished ingenious statesmen with convenient pretexts for nation-building. When attention is focused on the most important of all the nineteenth-century dynasties, the Saxe-Coburgs, it becomes apparent that there was much about this supposedly modern epoch that was still distinctly early-modern.

The rise of the House of Saxe-Coburg can be dated from the Napoleonic Wars and can be followed in the diary of Augusta, second wife and, from 1806, widow of Francis Frederick, Duke of Coburg. Coburg was one of those petty German states threatened with extinction when Napoleon swept away the Holy Roman Empire and created the Confederation of the Rhine; but Augusta's sons managed to steer a careful course between France and Russia and were duly rewarded when, under Russian pressure, the duchy was restored to her eldest son Ernest in 1807. Augusta's children married well. With the exception of one daughter, all either married royalty, achieved royal status in their own right or secured it for their children. One daughter married the brother of Alexander I of Russia; another, the King of Württemberg; a third married Britain's Duke of Kent, a brother of George IV. But it was Augusta's youngest son, Leopold, who was the real founder of the Saxe-Coburg fortunes. Leopold suffered a setback when his first wife, Princess Charlotte, daughter of George IV of Britain, died in childbirth in November 1817, just eighteen months after their marriage. But his circumstances were transformed when, having previously toyed with the idea of accepting the throne of Greece, he became King of the Belgians in 1831.

As *The Times* noted in 1863, the history of the Saxe-Coburgs showed 'how much one success leads to another in Princely life'. They had

> been able to advance to a position in Europe almost beyond the dreams of German ambition. [They] have spread far and wide, and filled the lands with their race. They have created a new Royal House in England. The Queen is a daughter of Leopold's sister; her children are the children of Leopold's nephew. The Coburgs reign in Portugal; they are connected with the Royal though fallen House of Orleans, and more or less closely related to the principal families of their own country. Prince Leopold has himself for thirty years governed one of the most important of the minor states of Europe, and his eldest son is wedded to an Archduchess of the Imperial House of Austria.

Moreover, all but one of Victoria and Albert's nine children married royally. Queen Victoria's sons-in-law included Frederick of Prussia, briefly Prussian King and German Emperor, Prince Christian of Schleswig-Holstein and Henry of Battenberg, whose brother Alexander became Prince of Bulgaria; her daughters-in-law included Princess Alexandra of Denmark and Princess Marie, daughter of Tsar Alexander II and sister of Tsar Alexander III. Besides George V, Victoria's grandchildren included Sophie, who married Constantine, King of Greece; Kaiser William II of Germany; Prince Henry of Prussia; Elizabeth, who married Sergei, brother of Tsar Alexander III of Russia; Alexandra, who married Tsar Nicholas II of Russia; Marie, who married Ferdinand I of Romania; Margaret, who married Gustav Adolf VI of Sweden; Victoria Eugenie, who married Alfonso XIII of Spain; and Maud, who married Carl of Denmark, later Haakon VII of Norway. By the time the future Nicholas II made his first visit to England in 1893, a family reunion had come to resemble an international summit:

> We drew into Charing Cross. There we were met by: Uncle Bertie [the future Edward VII], Aunt Alix [Alexandra of Denmark], Georgie [the future George V], Louise, Victoria and Maud . . .

Two hours later Apapa [Christian IX of Denmark], Amama and Uncle Valdemar [Prince of Denmark] arrived. It is wonderful to have so many of our family gathered together . . .

At 4.30 I went to see Aunt Marie [wife of Alfred, Duke of Saxe-Coburg] at Clarence House and had tea in the garden with her, Uncle Alfred, and Ducky [their daughter, Victoria Melita].

When this last married Ernst Ludwig, heir to the Grand Duchy of Hesse-Darmstadt, the guests included an emperor and empress, a future emperor and empress, a queen, a future king and queen, seven princes, ten princesses, two dukes, two duchesses and a marquess. They were all related. In 1901, the year of Queen Victoria's death, members of the extended kinship group to which she belonged thus sat on the thrones not only of Great Britain and Ireland, but also of Austria-Hungary, Russia, Denmark, Spain, Portugal, Germany, Belgium, Greece, Romania, Bulgaria, Sweden and Norway.

While more and more commoners fretted about the supposed evil effects of miscegenation, the royal elite of Europe had to worry about the opposite – the dangers of inbreeding. In 1869 Queen Victoria had argued that it might be better to 'infus[e] new and healthy blood into it [the royal family], whereas all the Princes abroad are related to one another; and while I could continue these Foreign Alliances with several members of the family, I feel sure that new blood would strengthen the throne morally as well as physically.' 'If no fresh blood was infused occasionally,' she had written in defence of the projected marriage of another granddaughter – Victoria Moretta – to Alexander of Battenberg in 1885, 'the races would degenerate physically and morally.' This was all too true: systematic inbreeding had genuine medical disadvantages. The blood-clotting disease haemophilia spread through the royal family tree with tragic consequences for the male line (because it is carried in the X chromosome). There were at least nine sufferers among Victoria's descendants: her eighth son Leopold, Duke of Albany, her grandson Frederick William of Hesse, her daughter Beatrice's son Leopold, her granddaughter Irene's sons Waldemar and Henry, her granddaughter Alexandra's son Aleksei, her granddaughter Alice's son Rupert, and her granddaughter Victoria Eugenie's sons Alfonso and Gonzalo. Porphyria too was transmitted through the royal line, from George III to Victoria's eldest daughter Vicky and Kaiser William II's sister Charlotte.

Yet the benefits of royal consanguinity seemed obvious; what better check could be imagined to the fractious tendencies of nineteenth-century nationalism than the systematic intermarriage of the continent's sovereigns? By 1892, Queen Victoria was happy to accept the convenient advice of Sir William Jenner, who assured her that 'there was no danger & no objection as they [Victoria Melita and Ernst Ludwig] are so strong & healthy & Aunt Marie also. He said that if the relations were strong intermarriages with them only led to g[rea]ter strength & health.' Two years later, she was pleased to be addressed as 'Granny' by the future Tsar Nicholas II, after his betrothal to yet another of her granddaughters. When her great-grandson, the future Edward VIII, was born two months later, Victoria urged that he be christened Albert, as if to set the seal on the familial achievement:

This will be the *Coburg line*, like formerly the Plantagenet, the Tudor (for Owen Tudor) the Stewart & the Brunswick for George the 1st – he being the gt. gd. son of James I & this wd. be *the Coburg Dynasty* – retaining the Brunswick & *all* the others preceding it, joining in it.

The key to understanding European royalty is thus that it was genuinely European; conventional national identity was fundamentally incompatible with an essentially multinational monarchy. Queen Victoria, for example, always thought of her family as 'our dear Coburg family' and regarded Saxe-Coburg as the royal family's proper surname. She liked her children to converse in German as well as in English, as her 'heart and sympathies' were, in her own words, 'all German'. It was typical of her to Germanize the name of her daughter Helena to Lenchen, for example. 'The German element', she once declared, 'is one I wish to be cherished and kept up in our beloved home.' 'My heart', she told Leopold of the Belgians in 1863, 'is so German'. Yet she could just as easily speak of herself as the embodiment of England, Scotland – even India. In much the same way, Tsar Nicholas II invariably wrote to his German-born wife in English, as he did in his many affectionate letters to the German Kaiser. The Queen of the Belgians spoke fluent Hungarian because she was an Austrian archduchess; her husband's father was German, his mother

French. Partly as a result of this cosmopolitanism, the European royals were, literally, in a class of their own. Despite being spread across the continent, the various branches of the family were held together by correspondence and by frequent meetings. State visits by one monarch to another were an integral part of nineteenth-century diplomacy. But behind the formalities, these were genuine family gatherings. The members of the extended royal family even knew one another by affectionate nicknames. Prince George of Battenberg was 'Georgie Bat' in Nicholas II's letters to his wife, while she invariably referred to the King of Greece as 'Greek Georgie'. To Queen Victoria, Prince Alexander of Bulgaria was always 'dear Sandro'.

This system could only be preserved if the members of the various dynasties continued to marry one another; to wed even the grandest of non-royal aristocrats would break up the magic royal circle, because aristocratic families were emphatically members of one or other national elite. When Queen Victoria's daughter Louise married a son of the Duke of Argyll, the match seemed so unusual that its constitutional propriety had to be defended by the Queen. But she drew the line when her son-in-law Ludwig of Hesse-Darmstadt contemplated marrying 'a divorced Russian lady' following the death of his first wife, Victoria's daughter Alice. The root of Alexander III's grudge against Alexander of Battenberg – and one reason he forced him off the Bulgarian throne – was that the Battenbergs were the issue of a morganatic (non-royal) marriage. When the Archduke Francis Ferdinand defied his uncle, the Emperor Francis Joseph, by marrying Sophie, Countess Chotek, he was never really forgiven at court. Indeed, the old Emperor regarded the couple's assassination in Savajevo as a kind of divine retribution for this lapse; mourning at the court in Vienna verged on the perfunctory. In 1907, for similar reasons, Kaiser William II effectively forbade what would have been the morganatic marriage of Prince Frederick William of Prussia to Paula, Countess von Lehndorff. Marriage to fellow-royals was the rule, and exceptions were made only *in extremis*, when the sole alternative was spinsterhood.

The result of all this was an extraordinary genealogical tangle. To give just one example, which Queen Victoria noted with evident relish, Queen Maria Christina of Spain was the 'daughter of the late Archduke Frederick and the Archduchess Elisabeth, Marie of Belgium's elder sister. Her Grandfather was the celebrated Archduke Charles, whose wife was a Princess of Nassau, and she is second cousin to Helen, also second cousin to Lily, on her mother's side.' Christopher, Prince of Greece, had an equally convoluted family tree: 'My father was King George I of Greece, born Prince William of Denmark, brother of Queen Alexandra of England ... My mother was the Grand Duchess Olga of Russia, daughter of the Grand Duke Constantine and granddaughter of the Czar Nicholas I.' It was scarcely surprising that this inbred multinational elite aroused enmity in certain quarters. In the wake of the ill-fated Bulgarian adventure of Alexander of Battenberg, Herbert von Bismarck – the son of the Saxe-Coburgs' most formidable adversary – complained half-seriously: 'In the English Royal Family and its nearest collaterals, there is a sort of worship of the undiluted family principle and Queen Victoria is regarded as a kind of absolute Chief of all branches of the Coburg clan. It is associated with codicils, which are shown to the obedient relation from afar.' What really made the Saxe-Coburgs so successful, and what rankled so much with the Bismarcks, was that they were broadly liberal in their social and political inclinations (something that distinguished them from that other German dynasty associated with Britain, one which was to come to grief at Bismarck's hands, the Hanoverians). The French polemicist who compared the Saxe-Coburgs with the Rothschilds in the 1840s was closer to the mark than he knew: for these two South German dynasties had an almost symbiotic relationship with one another. Dismayed by the influence of Queen Victoria's daughter and namesake over her husband, the ill-starred Frederick III, Bismarck did his utmost to drive a wedge between their son and the so-called 'Coburg cabal'.

Yet it would be a mistake to see this rift as presaging the war of 1914–18. To be sure, William II felt a deep ambivalence towards his English relations. For example, he refused to see the Prince of Wales when both men were in Vienna in 1889, having heard that the Prince had called for the return of Alsace and Lorraine to France. When it turned out that he had been misrepresented, the Kaiser refused to apologize. As Prince Christian of Denmark explained, 'The Kaiser is as yet too new in his position to feel quite sure of himself and his ability to do the right thing. He is therefore constantly afraid of compromising his dignity, and he is particularly sensitive lest his older relatives should treat him as the "Nephew" and not as the "Kaiser".' Only with the passage of time, however, did such tiffs take on the aspect of harbingers of war (not least in the Kaiser's own excitable mind). In the years before 1914, he had in fact made sincere efforts to improve relations with Russia, the state most feared by German military planners and diplomats. He had positively encouraged the Tsar to take a hard line over Manchuria, pledging German support if it came to war. In 1904 he was asked to become godfather to the Tsar's son, a request he welcomed with enthusiasm. In 1909, too, when he sent his Easter gift to the Tsar, he was careful to point out that it was 'a token of undiminished love and friendship . . . a symbol for our relation to each other'.

What suddenly became clear in the crisis of that summer was that the Kaiser, like his Saxe-Coburg relatives, lacked the power to override the military and political professionals if they were resolved to go to war. This was the reality of constitutional monarchy: that dynastic family ties could no longer transcend the imperatives of a war between whole peoples in arms. Still, no one could be entirely sure of that until the monarchs had been overruled. Until they were, there remained the possibility of some kind of royal compromise. The British ambassador in St Petersburg wanted to know if it would 'be possible in the last resort for Emperor Nicholas to address [a] personal appeal to Emperor of Austria to restrict Austria's action within limits which Russia could accept'. The Germans sent the Kaiser's brother, Prince Henry, to London, to see if George V could be won over to neutrality. The monarchs themselves acted as if it really was in their power to stop the war. 'I spoke to Nicky', the Tsar's sister Olga recalled, 'and he replied that Willy was a bore and an exhibitionist, but he would never start a war.' 'Willy' and 'Nicky' each endeavoured to localize the war, the Kaiser by urging the Austrians to 'halt in Belgrade', the Tsar by delaying Russian general mobilization. Indeed, the two sovereigns continued to seek a compromise even after hostilities had broken out, as the British ambassador in Berlin, Sir William Goschen, somewhat reluctantly acknowledged:

Of course a good deal of it [the German case] is true; namely, that particularly at the end Germany (incl. the Emperor) did try and persuade them at Vienna to continue discussions and accept Sir E[dward] Grey's proposals . . . That the Emperor and Co. have worked at Vienna is certainly true – and the German case, to put it in a nutshell, is that while the Emperor at the Czar's request, was working at Vienna – Russia mobilised – or rather ordered mobilisation . . . The last thing I hear is that Russia has informed the Imperial Government that the Czar has not been told that the Emperor was working at Vienna – and they have demanded three hours more to consider the German demand. Certainly up to the time of writing this, no mobilisation order has been issued by the Emperor . . . Jagow [the German Foreign Secretary] told me that the Emperor was fearfully depressed and said that his record as a 'Peace Emperor' was finished with.

'Both you and I did everything in our power to prevent war,' George V wrote to Nicholas II on July 31, 'but alas we were frustrated and this terrible war which we have all dreaded for so many years has come upon us.' The 'we' he had in mind was, of course, that pan-European kinship group to which nearly all the monarchs had belonged, which had seemed in itself a bulwark against war. Now, as Marie of Battenberg lamented, the days of cosmopolitanism were at an end. Henceforth

the Tsarina of Russia [though German by birth] was a Russian, just as the Queen of the Belgians, a Bavarian princess by birth, is a Belgian; and the Duchess Marie of Saxe-Coburg-Gotha a German; although she was born a Russian, and became by marriage an English princess. The Duchess of Albany, also, although by birth a princess of Waldeck, is English, and her son, an English prince, by inheriting the Dukedom of Saxe-Coburg, became a German, and remained so during the war. Often did I think during that painful time: It is all very well for you to talk, you fortunate German people, whose blood remains unmixed with that of foreigners!

The Duke of Saxe-Coburg she alluded to was Charles Edward, one of Queen Victoria's legion of great-grandsons. Though educated in England, he had inherited the dukedom in 1900 and spent most of the war in German uniform, albeit (at his request) on the Eastern Front. In deference to wartime sentiment, the Coburg line was renamed the

'Windsor' line in 1917, and Battenbergs became Mountbattens. The European earthquake shook every social class, but none more than the continent's cosmopolitan royal elite. Far from causing it, as is still sometimes claimed, they had been powerless to prevent it.

## THE GENERALS' WAR

Early on the morning of July 30, 1914, the German ambassador in St Petersburg sent a telegram to Berlin relaying a long conversation he had just had with the Russian Foreign Minister S. D. Sazonov. The gist of it was that Russian military mobilization in defence of Serbia 'could no longer possibly be retracted', despite 'the danger of a European conflagration'. According to Sazonov, the Austrian government had made unacceptable demands of the Serbian government in the wake of the assassination. (The Austrians had insisted that their officials be represented in the Serbian investigation of the conspiracy that had led to the Archduke's murder, and declared war after the Serbs refused.) The German ambassador explicitly pointed out 'the automatic effect that the mobilization here would have on us in consequence of the German-Austrian alliance'. But Sazonov was adamant. 'Russia could not leave Serbia in the lurch. No Government could follow such a policy here without seriously endangering the Monarchy.' The Kaiser's comments on this telegram provide a fascinatingly unorthodox interpretation of the origins of the First World War, which deserves to be quoted at length. After a succession of increasingly indignant marginal exclamations ('Nonsense!' 'Aha! As I suspected!'), he exploded:

Frivolity and weakness are to plunge the world into the most frightful war, which eventually aims at the destruction of Germany. For I have no doubt left about it: England, Russia and France have agreed among themselves – after laying the foundation of the *casus foederis* for us through Austria – to take the Austro-Serbian conflict for an *excuse* for waging a *war of extermination* against us. Hence [the British Foreign Secretary Sir Edward] Grey's cynical observation to [the German ambassador in London, Prince] Lichnowsky [that] 'as long as the war is *confined* to Russia and Austria, England would sit quiet, only when we and France *are mixed up in it* would he be compelled to make an active move against us'; i.e., either we are shamefully to betray our allies, sacrifice them to Russia – thereby breaking up the Triple Alliance, or we are to be attacked in common by the Triple Entente for our fidelity to our allies and punished, whereby they will satisfy their jealousy by joining in totally ruining us. That is the real naked situation *in nuce*, which, slowly and cleverly set going, certainly by Edward VII, has been carried on, and systematically built up by disowned conferences between England and France and St Petersburg; finally brought to a conclusion by George V and set to work. And thereby the stupidity and ineptitude of an ally is turned into a snare for us. So the famous 'encirclement' of Germany has finally become a complete fact, despite every effort of our politicians and diplomats to prevent it. The net has been suddenly thrown over our head and England sneeringly reaps the most brilliant success for her persistently prosecuted purely *anti-German world-policy*, against which we have proved ourselves helpless, while she twists the noose of our political and economic destruction out of our fidelity to Austria, as we squirm *isolated* in the net. A great achievement, which arouses the admiration of him who is to be destroyed as its result! Edward VII is stronger after his death than am I who am still alive! And there have been people who believed that England could be won over or pacified, by this or that puny measure!!! Unremittingly, relentlessly she has pursued her object . . . until this point was reached. And we walked into the net . . . !!! All my warnings, all my pleas were voiced for nothing. Now comes England's so-called gratitude for it! From the dilemma raised by our fidelity to the venerable old Emperor of Austria, we are brought into a situation which offers England the desired pretext for annihilating us under the hypocritical cloak of justice, namely, of helping France on account of the reputed 'balance of power' in Europe, i.e., playing the card of all the European nations in England's favour against us!

Was there any substance at all to this at first sight hysterical tirade? Few, if any, historians would accept that there was. The consensus has for many years been that it was the German government that wilfully turned the Balkan crisis of 1914 into a world war. Yet that is surely to understate the shared responsibility of all the European empires. For one thing, the Austrian government could hardly be blamed for demanding redress from Serbia in the wake of the

Archduke's murder. Their ultimatum to Belgrade, delivered after much prevarication on July 23, essentially demanded that the Serbian authorities allow Austrian officials to participate in the inquiry into the assassinations. This was, all things considered, not an unreasonable demand, even if it did imply a violation of Serbia's sovereignty. After all, Serbia was what we today would call a rogue regime. Its ruling monarch had come to power in a bloody coup in 1903 in which the previous king, Aleksandar Obrenović, had been murdered by none other than 'Apis'. Even if the assassins had been sent to Sarajevo by the same 'Apis' without the approval of the Serbian government, the authorities in Belgrade had almost certainly known what was afoot. As *The Economist* put it on August 1:

It is fair ... to ask ... what Great Britain would have done in a like case – if, for example, the Afghan Government had plotted to raise a rebellion in North-West India, and if, finally, Afghan assassins had murdered a Prince and Princess of Wales? Certainly the cry of vengeance would have been raised, and can we be sure that any measure milder than the Note sent from Vienna to Belgrade would have been dispatched from London or Calcutta to Kandahar?

From a modern standpoint, the only European power to side with the victims of terrorism against the sponsors of terrorism was Germany.

It is true that when the Kaiser first informed the Austrian ambassador that Germany would back Austria, he explicitly stated that that support would be forthcoming 'even if it should come to a war between Austria and Russia'. But an offer of support conditional on Russian non-intervention would have been quite worthless. Why, in any case, did the Russians feel so strongly impelled to intervene on the side of the Serbs? They had no real influence over the regime in Belgrade. Their motive was purely a matter of prestige – the belief that if they allowed Serbia to be humiliated, it would be interpreted as yet another defeat for Russia, less than a decade after the calamity of Tsushima, to say nothing of the Austrian annexation of Bosnia. It was on this basis that Sazonov and the chief of the Russian General Staff, General Nikolai Yanushkevich, persuaded the hesitant Tsar to order general mobilization of the huge Russian army. A Russian general mobilization clearly implied more than the defence of Serbia. It also implied an invasion of eastern Germany.

Without doubt, the German generals eagerly seized the opportunity for war and delayed their own mobilization only in order that Russia would appear the aggressor. Yet German anxieties about the pace of Russia's post-1905 rearmament were not wholly unjustified; there were legitimate reasons to fear that their Eastern neighbour was on the way to becoming militarily invincible. That was why Helmuth von Moltke, the Chief of the German General Staff, argued insistently that 'we would never again find a situation as favourable as now, when neither France nor Russia had completed the extension of their army organizations'. As he explained to Jagow just six weeks before the Sarajevo assassination:

Russia will have completed her armaments in two or three years. The military superiority of our enemies would be so great that he did not know how we might cope with them. In his view there was no alternative to waging a preventive war in order to defeat the enemy as long as we could still more or less pass the test.

The Germans were not, as the phrase 'more or less' makes clear, optimistic. Moltke himself had warned the Kaiser as early as 1906 that the next war would be 'a long wearisome struggle' which would 'utterly exhaust our own people, even if we are victorious'. 'We must prepare ourselves', he wrote in 1912, 'for a long campaign, with numerous tough, protracted battles.' He was just as gloomy when he discussed the issue with his Austrian counterpart, Franz Conrad von Hötzendorff, in May 1914: 'I will do what I can. We are not superior to the French.' In any case, 'The sooner the better' was not the watchword of Moltke alone. His Russian counterpart, Yanushkevich, threatened to 'smash his telephone' after the Tsar had finally approved general mobilization, to avoid the risk of being told of a royal change of heart. The Germans, as is well known, had for some years contemplated an invasion of northern France as a way of avoiding the heavy fortifications that lined France's eastern frontier. But the French generals, whose belief in the morale-building benefits of the offensive was second to none, were scarcely less eager for war. They had no intention of standing by while Germany defeated their Russian ally, but planned instead to invade southern Germany through Alsace-Lorraine as soon as hostilities began.

Where the Kaiser erred most egregiously was in believing that the encirclement of Germany had been carefully planned by the Entente powers, above all by Great Britain. In reality, neither Edward VII nor his successor George V had remotely considered this possibility; nor had politicians in either the Liberal or the Conservative Party. On the contrary, the Liberal Foreign Minister Sir Edward Grey had been prevented by his party colleagues from making any kind of binding commitment to France, much less to Russia. Next to no military preparations were made for the eventuality of a continental war in which Britain would be directly involved. Throughout the last week of July 1914, as far as most Britons were concerned, a continental conflict was unfolding which need not involve them. In the words of the editors of *The Economist*, the 'quarrel' in the Balkans was 'no more of our making and no more our concern than would be a quarrel between Argentina and Brazil or between China and Japan'.

Yet the fact that the Germans intended to march across Belgium on their way to France confronted the British government with a dilemma. The neutrality of Belgium was something guaranteed by international law – by a treaty that all the European powers, including Germany, had signed in 1839. Serbia might well be a rogue regime; Belgium, with its Saxe-Coburg monarch and strategically vital location, was a different matter. Its neutral status was an integral part of that web of agreements between the great powers that had more or less preserved the European peace for a century. Was His Majesty's Government – least of all a Liberal Cabinet – going to stand idly by while international law was flouted? And, law or no law, were they prepared to see Germany defeat France, raising the prospect of German naval bases on the Channel coast? On the other hand, could Britain's available ground troops – six divisions plus one of cavalry – really make a difference to a European war? Henry Wilson, the Director of Military Operations from 1910, candidly admitted that six divisions were 'fifty too few'. Indeed, until as late as 1911 the assumption was that in the event of a European war any British Expeditionary Force would be deployed in Central Asia; in other words, it was still taken for granted that the foe in such a war would be Russia. It was patently obvious that a British intervention against German forces in Western Europe would require the mobilization of the entire naval, financial and manpower resources of Britain's global empire to be decisive. That could only happen if the war was prolonged.

As so often in the twentieth century, what was at stake rather eluded British politicians. When the Cabinet met over lunch on Sunday, August 2 (a time when most of its members would much rather have been away in the country) the discussion was strangely recondite. Some of those who favoured neutrality argued speciously (and incorrectly) that the Germans were going to pass through only a part of Belgium. The proponents of intervention – who were in a decided minority, but had the sympathy of the Prime Minister, Herbert Asquith – argued that standing aside would be dishonourable. Perhaps more persuasively, they pointed out that not intervening would bring the government down and let in the Opposition, who would go to war anyway. The real dilemma Asquith and his colleagues had to address was not really articulated: would this be a continental war, one the Germans would probably win, or a world war, the outcome of which no one could foresee? They opted, after much humming and hawing, for the latter.

To the bankers, war was a calamity that came as a bolt from the blue. To the diplomats, it was a last resort when the usual routine of correspondence, confabulations and conferences had failed. To the generals, it suddenly seemed a pressing necessity, since delay could only benefit the other side. The monarchs, who still dreamed that international relations were a family affair, were suddenly as powerless as if revolutions had already broken out. Yet those who overruled their rulers had only a shadowy conception of what they were embarking on.

For the shifting tectonic plates in the Balkans had now triggered a global earthquake that would shake all the great European empires to their foundations. Suddenly, the vast resources of the European industrial economies were diverted from production to destruction. In the space of five days 1,800 special trains ran south to Southampton, one arriving every three minutes for sixteen hours a day. Fourteen French railways each carried fifty-six trains a day. One German train crossed the Rhine at Cologne every ten minutes. Between them, the French and Germans mobilized roughly four million men each. It took just a matter of days to get them to their designated railheads. Yet – contrary to the expectations of those who had hoped that a war would weaken the Left – the revolutionary forces already at work before the war were ultimately strengthened by the mobilization of the masses that was now under way. Even more disturbingly, the new forms of ethnic conflict that had been discernible in the Russian programs of 1905 and the Balkan Wars of 1912–13 now came to be adopted as legitimate methods of warfare by the great powers themselves. The net effect of this geopolitical earthquake was to deal a heavy, if not fatal, blow to that dominance of the West which had seemed so reassuringly secure until the very last week of July 1914.

# 4

## The Contagion of War

*'Für Menschenleben geht's bei uns nicht an.' ('For us, human
life isn't a consideration.')*
A German prisoner of war to Violet Asquith, October 1914

*We are not hurling our grenades against human beings.*
Remarque, *All Quiet on the Western Front*

### WORLD WAR

The war that broke out in the summer of 1914 was always very likely
to become a world war. Even before the conflict began, British experts
like the Chief of the Admiralty War Staff, Sir Frederick Sturdee, saw
clearly that 'our next maritime war will be world-wide, more so even
than former wars.' It was precisely the prospect of British intervention
that prompted Moltke to say to his adjutant on the night of July
30: 'This war will grow into a world war.' *The Times*'s military
correspondent Charles à Court Repington is usually credited with
coining the phrase 'First World War'; his contribution was to recognize that there would very likely be more than one. The globalization
of the conflict was an inevitable consequence of British involvement.
An empire that controlled around a quarter of the planet's land surface and an even higher proportion of its sea lanes, but had only a
'contemptibly' small European army, was bound by its very nature to
wage a global war.

Of course, it would not have become a world war if, as in 1870,
the Germans had vanquished the French in a matter of weeks. But

that was never very likely. The basic problem confronting German strategists was, of course, that they had to fight on (at least) two fronts. It has long been assumed that they had only one answer to this question: the plan for a high-speed envelopment of the French army devised by Moltke's predecessor as Chief of the General Staff, Alfred von Schlieffen. According to the classic account by the German historian Gerhard Ritter, whose source was a private memorandum drafted by Schlieffen after his retirement, the plan was for the right wing of the German army to advance west and then south of Paris, coming at the French from behind and 'annihilating' them. In order to maximize the vulnerability of the enemy's rear, Schlieffen's plan envisaged that the Germans might withdraw from Lorraine, creating a kind of revolving door; as the French advanced to reclaim Lorraine, the Germans would swing into northern France behind them. However, the recently rediscovered records of the regular General Staff 'Rides' (*Generalstabsreisen*) and other pre-war exercises suggest that this was not what Schlieffen planned while he was in office. Given the limitations of German manpower, he aimed instead to 'defeat the French army in battles along the frontier, and then to break the French fortress line'. Indeed, he may even have intended to let the French make the first move, then counterattack. In this scenario, the defeat of France would have come only after a protracted second campaign. Schlieffen's subsequent plan for the envelopment of Paris was thus merely an illustration, drawn up in his retirement, of what Germany might be able to do if she had a bigger army. Nevertheless, the dream of a modern Cannae (the battle at which Hannibal had enveloped and annihilated the more numerous Romans) was an alluring one to Schlieffen's successor precisely because the German army seemed to be too small to wage a prolonged war on two fronts against both France and Russia. The possibility that a small but proficient British Expeditionary Force might join the French seemed merely to strengthen the argument for sending the right wing of the German force through Belgium. The fatal flaw was that the troops concerned were being asked to march too far. General Alexander von Kluck's 1st Army – which included 84,000 horses needing two million pounds of fodder a day – had to cover an average of 14.4 miles every day for three weeks.

In one respect the Germans came remarkably close to their objective of annihilating the enemy. The total number of French dead by the end of December 1914 was 265,000; indeed their casualties of all types had already reached 385,000 by September 10. Not only that, but the French had lost a tenth of their field artillery and half a million rifles. Worst of all, a very substantial part of their heavy industrial capacity was now under enemy control. The puzzle is why these heavy losses did not lead to a complete collapse – as had happened in 1870 and would happen again in 1940. Some credit must certainly go to the imperturbable French Commander-in-Chief Joseph Joffre, and particularly to his ruthless purge of senescent or incompetent French commanders as the crisis unfolded. Fundamentally, however, time was against Moltke for the simple reason that the French could redeploy more swiftly than the Germans could advance once they had left their troop trains. On August 23 the three German armies on Moltke's right wing constituted twenty-four divisions, facing just seventeen and a half Entente divisions; by September 6 they were up against forty-one. The chance of a decisive victory was gone, if it had ever existed. At the Marne, the failure of Moltke's gamble was laid bare. He himself suffered a nervous breakdown.

The Germans' difficulties in the West were compounded by the unforeseen demands made on them in the East by their own ally. There had been a woeful lack of coordination between Berlin and Vienna: 'It is high time', declared the German military attaché in Vienna on August 1, 1914, 'that the two general staffs consult now with absolute frankness with respect to mobilization, jump-off times, areas of assembly and precise troop strength.' By then it was much too late. The Austrians wanted to fight the Serbs, but were forced to turn round and fight the Russians. They were duly smashed in Galicia, losing 350,000 men at a stroke. The Austrians, too, might have been expected to collapse, as they had in 1859 and 1866. But the Russians were unable to press home their advantages. Their railway network lacked lateral links between the two major theatres on the Eastern Front. They were also saddled with some lamentable generals (notably P. I. Postovskii, nicknamed the 'Mad Mullah'). When the Germans confronted Russians at Tannenberg, they inflicted a Cannae-like defeat on them. What had failed in the West succeeded in the East.

With these battles the scene was set for the ensuing stalemate: the Germans unable to break French morale on the Western Front before British reinforcements had arrived, while at the same time forced to prop up the Austrians in the East – unable, in short, to win – yet so much more effective tactically and operationally than their opponents that they could not easily be defeated.

## WHY THE GERMANS LOST

War was waged all over the world after July 1914. All sides, beginning with the Germans, sought to resolve the strategic impasse in Europe by winning victories in extra-European theatres. The Kaiser himself had set the tone as early as July 30, when he called on 'our consuls in Turkey, in India, agents etc., [to] ... fire the whole Mohammedan world to fierce rebellion against this hated, lying, conscienceless nation of shop-keepers; for if we are to be bled to death, England shall at least lose India.' This was more than mere royal ranting. Three and a half months later, in the presence of Germany's new ally the Ottoman Sultan, the Sheikh-ul-Islam issued a *fatwa* that declared an Islamic holy war on Britain and her allies. Swiftly translated into Arabic, Persian, Urdu and Tatar, it was addressed to both Shi'ite and Sunni Muslims. Given that roughly 120 million of the world's 270 Muslims were under British, French or Russian rule, this was a potentially revolutionary call to *jihad*.

However, the Germans laboured under three insuperable disadvantages when it came to global warfare. At sea, they were simply outnumbered. True, they had achieved technical superiority over the Royal Navy in a number of respects. The Germans were ahead in wireless communications, while the British stuck to Nelson-era semaphore – impossible for the enemy to read at a distance, but not much more legible to a dispersed fleet in the fog of battle. On the whole, too, the German battleships fired more accurately and were better armoured than their British opponents. Their officers may also have been better trained; the British had too many incompetents like the disastrous Flag Lieutenant Ralph Seymour, who repeatedly garbled vital signals at Jutland, or Captain Thomas Jackson, Director of the

Operations Division of the Admiralty, who specialized in misreading or ignoring crucial intelligence. At the start of the war, the Germans also made more of the element of surprise. The Russian commander whose ship was torpedoed by SMS *Emden* off Penang on October 28, 1914, was certainly unprepared for the new age of global conflict. Only twelve rounds of ammunition were ready on deck; but there were sixty Chinese prostitutes below.

Yet the odds were overwhelmingly against a German victory at sea. After their defeat at the Falklands, they were forced to concentrate their naval forces in Europe, preparing their surface fleet for the decisive battle they hoped to fight in the North Sea and deploying their submarines in the eastern Atlantic (often around the Irish coast). It remained true that, in Churchill's famous phrase, the First Sea Lord, Admiral John Jellicoe, was 'the only man on either side who could lose the war in an afternoon'. Jellicoe was too good a commander to do that. He was, admittedly, not quite good enough to win it in an afternoon either; the Royal Navy's attempt to bombard and capture the Gallipoli peninsula was a dismal failure. ('No human power could withstand such an array of might and power,' thought the British flotilla's commander as he neared the Black Sea Straits. He was wrong: Turkish guns and mines did so easily.) Fortunately, not losing the war was enough, since time was on the side of Britain, her empire and her allies. They had the greater resources and were therefore better able to withstand that disruption of trade which became the secondary goal of the naval war after the primary goal of a decisive engagement proved unattainable. Significantly, the first Royal Navy action of the war – on August 5, the day after Britain's entry – was the severing of all Germany's international telegraph cables, which ran along the ocean floor to France, Spain, North Africa and the United States. The British understood better than German military planners how a world war could be won. They began by literally cutting the enemy off from the global economy. They also learned more quickly the importance of intelligence. The German navy began the war with three main codes. By the end of 1914 the British had cracked all three and were able to read German radio signals undetected throughout the war. Although MI5 was notably unsuccessful at disrupting its network of agents, the German Naval Intelligence

Service (*Nachrichtenabteilung im Admiralstab*) achieved nothing of comparable value.

Perhaps just as importantly, the British saw more clearly than the Germans the need to win the battle for what we would now call world opinion. Making the maritime blockade of Germany effective was only possible by ignoring international agreements, like the Declaration of London of 1908, which set out clear rules governing the treatment of neutral shipping in wartime but which the House of Lords had refused to ratify. This, and the ruthless way in which the Royal Navy harassed neutral ships believed to be trading with Germany, was not calculated to win friends abroad. Nevertheless, the British were adept at diverting attention to German misdemeanours at sea. For their part, the Germans failed to see that, when they shelled British ports or ordered their submarines to sink merchant vessels without warning, they were doing as much damage to themselves as to their enemies. The British and American press liked nothing better than tales of women and children blown to pieces or drowned by German *Schrecklichkeit* (frightfulness). As the former German Colonial Secretary Bernhard Dernburg put it shortly after the sinking of the liner *Lusitania* by a German submarine: 'The American people cannot visualize the spectacle of a hundred thousand . . . German children starving by slow degrees as a result of the British blockade, but they can visualize the pitiful face of a little child drowning amidst the wreckage caused by a German torpedo.' Quite why 128 Americans should have felt entitled to cross the Atlantic on a British ship during a world war with impunity was never entirely clear. But instead of emphasizing this, the Germans struck commemorative medals to celebrate the *Lusitania*'s fate, medals which were promptly seized upon and replicated in London as examples of German viciousness.

In the absence of a truly colossal blunder by the Royal Navy, then, the war at sea was a foregone conclusion. Equally hopeless were German attempts to foment a world insurrection against Entente imperialism. The great strategist Colmar von der Goltz, who was to die a heroic if futile death in Mesopotamia, maintained that:

The present war is most emphatically only the beginning of a long historical development, at whose end will stand the defeat of England's world position

... [and] the revolution of the coloured races against the colonial imperialism of Europe.

But these events came to pass long after the war had been lost; indeed, they did not happen until Germany had lost a second world war. In the short run, the efforts of the Central Powers to accelerate decolonization were as laughable as they were fruitless. The dissolute ethnographer Leo Frobenius sought in vain to win over Lij Yasu, the Emperor of Abyssinia, to the German side. Even more absurd was the German expedition to the Emir of Afghanistan, the fifteen members of which travelled via Constantinople equipped with copies of W. and A. K. Johnston's general world atlas and disguised as a circus troupe. The British had so much more experience of the imperial Great Game that such ventures were unlikely to succeed. In Africa, it is true, German forces were able to keep fighting for a surprisingly long time and to inflict real casualties. Total British losses in East Africa were over 100,000 men, the vast majority black troops and porters. But what was the point? The German aim was to tie up colonial soldiers who might otherwise have been deployed in Europe, yet few of those engaged in the African campaigns would have been sent to Europe under any circumstances. In any case, most of the fighting took place in Germany's colonies, particularly in German East Africa (Tanganyika). South-West Africa surrendered to the South Africans as early as July 1915. The others – Togoland and the Cameroons – were in Entente hands long before the end of the war.

The third weakness of the German position was financial. Britain could borrow far more money to fund her war effort than Germany and at lower rates of interest, thanks to the breadth and depth of her financial institutions, and the international pre-eminence of London as a financial market. She could borrow at home, from the public and, if need be, from the Bank of England; she could borrow abroad, not only from her imperial dominions and other possessions, but also from the United States; she could also lend generously to her less creditworthy continental allies. Pre-war experts like Ivan Bloch and Norman Angell had assumed that the huge costs of a twentieth-century war would swiftly drive the combatant powers to bankruptcy. Yet the ratio of the British national debt to gross domestic product was not much higher in 1918 than it had been in 1818. 'Success means credit,' declared Lloyd George in 1916: 'Financiers never hesitate to lend to a prosperous concern.' This was true as far as it went, but it overlooked the fact that even when the war went badly for Britain the financiers – led by J. P. Morgan in New York – were unlikely to pull the plug. The Entente by that time really was too big to fail, in the sense of being too big a customer for American exports. By 1916 merchandise exports had risen to 12 per cent of US gross domestic product – double the pre-war figure and, indeed, the highest percentage in any year between 1869 and 2004. Around 70 per cent of those exports were bound for Europe, going overwhelmingly to Britain and her allies. Even if the German campaigns of unrestricted warfare had not brought the United States into the war in April 1917, Britain would surely have been bailed out financially, if not militarily. The alternative – as the American ambassador in London pointed out on March 5, 1917 – would have been to kill off transatlantic trade, which would be 'almost as bad for the United States as for Europe'. Those American Senators like George Norris of Nebraska who accused President Woodrow Wilson of 'putting a dollar sign on the American flag' were not wholly wide of the mark, though it is clear that American intervention in April 1917 was intended mainly to give the United States a seat at the peace conference; like many other people in Washington Wilson erroneously thought the Allies were close to victory and did not anticipate that substantial numbers of American troops would have to fight.

As a world war, then, the war of 1914–18 was not one Germany could ever have won. Yet as a European war its outcome was far less certain – and it was in Europe, despite all that happened on the high seas or on the colonial periphery, that the war was decided. To give just one example, 92 per cent of all British casualties were suffered in France. From that point of view, it was a world war only in the sense that men came to fight in Europe from all around the world. In 1914 Britain's army in India was bigger than its army in Europe, so soldiers from the Punjab soon found themselves knee deep in the mud of Flanders. They were joined by volunteers from all over the British Empire – from Canada, Australia, New Zealand and South Africa. The French too deployed colonial troops, from North and West Africa.

By the end of the war these forces had been joined by more than four million men from the United States. Likewise, the Russian army drew men from all over the Tsarist Empire. Indeed, it was partly the ability of all sides to reach out beyond their national heartlands that allowed the European war to be waged for so long and on such a large scale.

There were in fact multiple European wars: one in Belgium and Northern France; another that raged from the Baltic through Galicia to Bukovina; a third that was fought in the Alps between Austria and Italy; a fourth that was waged in the Balkans and the Black Sea Straits. It might be said that the Central Powers won the second, third and fourth of these wars, defeating Russia, Romania and Serbia, shattering the Italian army at Caporetto (October–November 1917) and repulsing the British invasion of Gallipoli. But they could not win the first; or, rather, it was only when they began to lose in the West that their positions in the other theatres crumbled. The Western Front, then, was the key. From late 1914 until early 1918 the war there looked like a stalemate. In essence it was one vast siege, in which French and British forces sought with minimal success to shift the Germans from the trenches they had dug after their initial offensives were halted. Siege warfare was nothing new. This, however, was the first truly industrialized siege. Trains transported men to and from the front lines as if they were shift-workers. There, they generally spent more of their time building and maintaining trenches, saps and dugouts than fighting; this was construction work, but ultimately for the sake of destruction. For the sappers tunnelling towards enemy positions, trench warfare was a species of mining. But the essence of industrialized warfare was the work of the artillery. Advances in the size, mobility and accuracy of artillery and in the destructive power of explosives meant that vast numbers of men could be killed from afar by other men whose sole activity was to service and fire giant guns. It was the shells they fired that accounted for the overwhelming majority of casualties on the Western Front, yet without conferring decisive advantage on either side. Thus did the war become, as many contemporaries said, like a colossal machine, chewing up men and munitions like so much raw material. The strategy of attrition, of 'wearing down' the other side, seemed the only way of ending this mechanized slaughter, since until 1918 nearly all breakthroughs proved unsustainable beyond a fairly short distance.

## COMRADES

The soldiers who faced one another along the Western Front were drawn from remarkably similar societies. On both sides there were industrial workers and farm labourers. On both sides there were aristocratic senior officers and middle-class junior officers. On both sides there were Catholics, Protestants and Jews. Anyone seeking fundamental differences of national character will look in vain in the records of the trenches. There could be no better illustration of this point than four of the finest novels written about the war by former soldiers – Henri Barbusse's *Under Fire*, Erich Maria Remarque's *All Quiet on the Western Front*, Frederic Manning's *Middle Parts of Fortune* and Emilio Lussu's *Sardinian Brigade* – which depict the experience of service in the ranks in almost interchangeable ways. All the authors, for example, make much more of the differences within their respective armies than the differences between the opposing armies themselves. 'What race are we?' asks Barbusse of his fellow *poilus*. 'All races. We've come from everywhere.' One man in his company is from Calonne, another from Cette, a third from Brittany, a fourth from Normandy, a fifth from Poitou, and so on. Manning (himself an Australian) several times remarks on the unintelligibility of the 'Scotch bastards' who are supposed to be his comrades in arms. In Remarque's novel a key character – the ever-ingenious Kat – is evidently of Polish extraction (his full name is Katczinsky), while Tjaden hails from North Germany.

Likewise, the men on all sides detest 'slackers' at home. 'There's not just one country, it's not true,' declares Barbusse's Volpatte after an unhappy visit to Paris. 'There's two. I'm telling you, we're divided into two foreign countries: the front, over there . . . and the rear, here.' 'They don't care a fuck 'ow us'ns live,' says Manning's Martlow bitterly. 'We're just 'umped an' bumped an' buggered about all over fuckin' France, while them as made the war sit at 'ome waggin' their bloody chins, an' sayin' what they'd 'ave done if they was twenty years younger.' Paul Bäumer in *All Quiet* feels much the same way when he encounters one of his former schoolmasters when home on leave. All concerned share the impatience of Lussu's narrator with romanticized press accounts of life at the Front. 'It appeared . . . that we attacked to the sound of music, and that war was, for us, one long delirium of song and victory . . . We alone knew the truth about the war, for it was there before our eyes.'

Englishmen, Frenchmen, Germans and Italians were equally irreverent about what they were supposedly fighting for. Here are Barbusse's *poilus* on the subject:

'It's a bore,' says Volpatte.

'But we hang on,' Barque grumbles.

'You've got to,' says Paradis.

'And why?' Marthereau asks, without real feeling.

'For no reason, since we've got to.'

'There isn't any reason,' Lamuse agrees.

'Yes, there is,' says Cocon. 'It's that . . . Well, there's lots, in fact.'

'Belt up! It's better to have no reasons, since we've got to hang on.'

'*Even so*,' says Blaire, in a hollow voice . . . 'Even so, they wanna kill us.'

'To begin with,' says Tirette, 'I thought about loads of stuff, turning it over, working it out. Now, I don't think any more.'

'Nor me.'

'Nor me.'

'I've never tried.' . . .

'You only need to know one thing and that one thing is that the Boche are over here, and that they're dug in, and that they mustn't get through and that one day they're even going to have to bugger off – the sooner the better,' says Corporal Bertrand.

Manning's soldiers strike a similar note. The officers may talk about 'liberty, an' fightin' for your country, an' posterity, an' so on; but [one asks] what I want to know is what all us'ns are fightin' for . . .':

'We're fightin' for all we've bloody got,' said Madeley, bluntly.

'An' that's sweet fuck all,' said Weeper Smart . . .

'I'm not fightin' for a lot o' bloody civvies,' said Madeley, reasonably. 'I'm fightin' for myself an' me own folk. 'Twere Germany made the war.'

'A tell thee,' said Weeper, positively, 'there are thousands o' poor buggers, over there in the German lines, as don' know, no more'n we do ourselves, what it's all about.'

'Then what did the silly fuckers come an' fight for?' asked Madeley, indignantly. 'Why didn' they stay 't 'ome? . . .'

'What a say is, that it weren't none o' our business. We'd no call to mix ourselves up wi' other folks' quarrels,' replied Weeper.

One man suggests that it 'would be a bloody good thing for us'ns, if the 'un did land a few troops in England. Show 'em what war's like.' Another adds that he is 'not fightin' for any fuckin' Beljums, see. One o' them buggers wanted to charge me five frong for a loaf o' bread.' The debate on the war's origins in *All Quiet* is not very different. 'It's funny when you think about it,' says Kropp, one of Bäumer's friends. 'We're out defending our homeland. And yet the French are there defending their homeland as well. Which of us is right?' Tjaden asks how wars begin and is told 'Usually when one country insults another one badly.' 'A country?' he replies. 'I don't get it. A German mountain can't insult a French mountain, or a river, or a forest, or a cornfield.'

What most united the combatants was the conditions in which – and against which – they had to fight: the cold of winter; the heat of summer; the damp of dugouts; the stench of corpses; above all, the fear of death. The life of the ordinary soldier was nicely summed up by Manning: 'Out of one bloody misery into another, until we break.' The morale of the ordinary soldier was prevented from breaking by a variety of means, some officially sanctioned, some not. Military training and discipline were, of course, crucial, though the use of the death penalty was a good deal less frequent than is commonly supposed; in all, 269 British soldiers were shot for desertion, while the Germans executed only eighteen. Just as important in sustaining morale was the elementary point that soldiers spent only a small fraction of their time in the front line, and only occasionally were required to attack – an experience represented universally as almost cathartic compared with cowering impotently under an artillery barrage. In between there was transportation, drill, rest, training, fatigues, leave. Such was the reality of 'soldiering': at once tedious and anaesthetically mindless –

'not really worse', as Lussu remarks, 'than the kind of everyday life which, in normal times, is lived by millions of miners'. Men on all sides were kept going by the prospect, if not always the reality, of sleep, warmth, food, nicotine, alcohol and sex. In *The Middle Parts of Fortune*, almost the first thing Manning's hero Bourne does as he stumbles back from the initial Somme offensive – despite being parched with thirst – is to smoke. Later, tormented by his friend Shem's nightmare, he lights 'the inevitable cigarette'. The badly wounded are offered cigarettes; they inhale only to expire. Even more important is alcohol: the second thing the returning combatant does after smoking is to gulp down some whisky. Indeed, Bourne's life is punctuated by drinking bouts and 'skinfuls'. He and his comrades covet whisky. They toss back 'plonk' (*vin blanc*). They despise French beer even as they swig it. They treat themselves to cheap 'champagne'. All these drinks are judged according to their potency. The British soldier's principal desideratum, it becomes clear, is drunkenness. Their French counterparts, by contrast, crave wine more for its taste than its intoxicating effects, but they crave it no less. They smoke pipes more than cigarettes, but they smoke with the same addicted relish. Remarque's soldiers yearn for rum, beer and chewing tobacco. As Lussu's Italian colonel explains, alcohol is 'the moving spirit of this war . . . And that's why the men, in their infinite wisdom, refer to it as "petrol" . . . It is a war of canteen against canteen, cask against cask, bottle against bottle.' Almost as important is the matter of food. From the *poilus*' impatient wait for their lunch (which opens *Under Fire*) to the Germans' puerile delight in their thunderboxes (which opens *All Quiet*), life in the trenches revolved around the digestion. Happiness in the German trenches is four purloined cans of lobster or a stolen goose; indeed, Paul Bäumer and his pals spend more time scrounging for supplementary provisions than fighting the enemy. Tellingly, Remarque signals the demise of the German war effort in the declining quality of the rations his characters are given.

Sex is inevitably the least easily attainable pleasure of the flesh. One of Barbusse's characters is haunted by a pretty peasant girl, but is able to lay hands on her only when he stumbles across her corpse. On the other side the men fantasize with the same vain relish about bedding a 'big bouncy kitchen wench with plenty to get your hands round'.

Yet in all four novels, real emotional fulfilment takes the form of what would now be called male bonding. It has often been argued that this is the real key to military cohesion: not patriotism, not even 'cap-badge' loyalty to regiment ('They can say what they bloody well like . . . but we're a fuckin' fine mob'), but 'mateship' – loyalty to one's friends within the smallest fighting unit. 'Good comradeship takes the place of friendship,' Bourne declares. 'It is different: it has its own loyalties and affections; and I am not so sure that it does not rise on occasion to an intensity of feeling which friendship never touches.' As Manning shows, the reality seldom lived up to this billing. Relationships struck up in front-line units were necessarily vulnerable, not only to sudden death but also to promotion or transfer. 'That's the worst o' the bloody army,' observes Martlow, 'as soon as you get a bit pally with a chap summat 'appens.' Even Bourne's temporary absence doing secretarial work in the orderly room undermines his friendships with Martlow and Shem. Still, mateship almost certainly contributed more to maintaining morale than the hierarchy of command. None of Manning's characters feels sympathy for Miller the deserter, because he has committed the cardinal sin of letting his mates down:

'What will you do if he tries to do a bunk again?' Bourne asked.
'Shoot the bugger,' said Marshall, whitening to the lips.

As their morose mate Weeper puts it: 'We're 'ere, there's no gettin' away from that, Corporal. 'Ere we are, an since we're 'ere, we're just fightin' for ourselves; we're just fightin' for ourselves, an' for each other.' More or less exactly the same sentiments are expressed by Barbusse's *poilus* and Remarque's *Frontschweine*. Hearing his friends' voices, Paul Bäumer feels a 'surprising warmth':

Those voices . . . tear me with a jolt away from the terrible feeling of isolation that goes with the fear of death, to which I nearly succumbed . . . Those voices mean more than my life, more than smothering a fear, they are the strongest and most protective thing that there is: they are the voices of my pals . . . I belong to them and they to me, we all share the same fear and the same life, and we are bound to each other in a strong and simple way. I want to press my face into them, those voices, those few words that saved me, and which will be my support.

That sense of 'brotherhood on a large scale', of comradeship ephemeral in reality but eternal in spirit, was truly universal.

In all these respects, the armies on the Western Front were like mirror images of one another. Indeed, towards the end of *Under Fire*, a wounded French aviator relates a striking vision of the trenches from the air which makes precisely this point:

... I could make out two similar gatherings among the Boche and ourselves, in these parallel lines that seem to touch one another: a crowd, a hub of movement and, around it, what looked like black grains of sand scattered on grey ones. They weren't moving; it didn't seem like an alarm! ... Then I understood. It was Sunday and these were two services being held in front of my eyes: the altars, the priests and the congregations. The nearer I got the more I could see that these two gatherings were similar – so exactly similar that it seemed ridiculous. One of the ceremonies – whichever you liked – was a reflection of the other. I felt as though I was seeing double.

## HATRED IN THE TRENCHES

All the resemblances between the combatants have led many writers before and since to wonder why the opposing armies did not fraternize more with one another. Famously, some British and German soldiers did just that on Christmas Day of 1914 when they played football together in no man's land as part of an unofficial truce. Less well known is the fact that over a longer period a kind of 'live and let live' system evolved in certain relatively quiet sectors of the line. Yet the hopes of socialists that soldiers would ultimately repudiate their national loyalties for the sake of international brotherhood were never realized on the Western Front. Why was this?

The answer is that as the war went on, mutual hatred grew, expunging the common origins and predicament of the combatants. 'The German officers,' reflects Barbusse's Tiroir, 'oh, no, no, no, they're not men, they're monsters. They really are a special, nasty breed of vermin, old man. You could call them the microbes of war. You've got to see them close to, those horrible great stiff things, thin as nails, but with calves' heads on them.' In the harrowing attack that is the climax of *Under Fire*, the enemy become simply 'the bastards':

'You bet, mate, instead of listening to him, I stuck me bayonet in his belly so far I couldn't pull it out.'

'Well, I found four of them at the bottom of the trench, I called to them to come out and each one, as he came, I bumped him off. I was red right up to my elbows. My sleeves are sticky with it.' . . .

'I had three of them to deal with. I hit out like a maniac. Oh, we were all like beasts when we reached here.'

Likewise, when they go over the top, the soldiers in *Middle Parts of Fortune* hate the enemy. 'Fear remained,' Manning writes, 'an implacable and restless fear, but that, too, seemed to have been beaten and forged into a point of exquisite sensibility and to have become indistinguishable from hate.' Almost deranged by Martlow's death, Bourne runs amok in the German lines:

Three men ran towards them, holding their hands up and screaming; and he lifted his rifle to his shoulder and fired; and the ache in him became a consuming hate that filled him with exultant cruelty, and he fired again, and again . . . And Bourne struggled forward again, panting, and muttering in a suffocated voice.

'Kill the buggers! Kill the bloody fucking swine! Kill them!'

As Manning admits, this blood lust has a pleasurable quality: he even talks of 'the ecstasy of battle', by comparison with which even 'the physical ecstasy of love . . . is less poignant'. A certain type of soldier, he notes, 'comes to grips, kills, and grunts with pleasure in killing'. Bourne himself is 'thrust forward' by:

a triumphant frenzy . . . [He] was at once the most abject and the most exalted of God's creatures. The effort and rage in him . . . made him pant and sob, but there was some strange intoxication of joy in it, and again all his mind seemed focused into one hard bright point of action. The extremities of pain and pleasure had met and coincided too.

This is very close to Remarque's account of combat in *All Quiet*, in which Paul Bäumer and his comrades 'turn into dangerous animals':

We are not fighting, we are defending ourselves from annihilation . . . We are maddened with fury . . . we can destroy and we can kill to save ourselves, to save ourselves and to take revenge . . . We have lost all feelings for others, we barely recognize each other when somebody else comes into our line of vision . . . We are dead men with no feelings, who are able by some trick, some dangerous magic, to keep on running and keep on killing.

The Frenchmen whose positions they overrun are killed horribly, their faces split in two by entrenching tools, or smashed with the butt of a rifle. Attackers and attacked are simultaneously reduced to the level of animals.

Nothing illustrates the intensification of front-line animosity more strikingly than the change that occurred during the First World War in attitudes towards enemy prisoners. The laws of war made it clear that men who surrendered had to be properly treated; it was a crime under the Hague Conventions to kill prisoners. Contemporaries also clearly understood the practical benefits of taking prisoners alive, not only for the purposes of gathering intelligence through interrogation but also for the sake of propaganda. A substantial proportion of the British film *The Battle of the Somme* consists of footage of captured Germans. Sergeant York's capture of 132 Germans was one of the highlights of American war propaganda in 1918. The humane treatment of prisoners also came to play an important part in the propaganda directed at the enemy. Towards the end of the war, a sustained effort was made to convey the idea that Germans would be well treated if they surrendered; indeed, would be better off than they were in their own lines. Thousands of leaflets were dropped on German positions, some of them little more than advertisements for conditions in Allied prisoner-of-war camps. Official British photographers were encouraged to snap 'wounded and nerve-shattered German prisoners' being given drink and cigarettes. The Americans even devised cheerful cards for surrendering Germans to sign and send to their relatives: 'Do not worry about me. The war is over for me. I have good food. The American army gives its prisoners the same food it gives its own soldiers: beef, white bread, potatoes, beans, prunes, coffee, butter, tobacco etc.'

Nevertheless, many men on both sides of the Western Front were deterred from surrendering by the growth of a culture of 'take no prisoners', part of the cycle of violence that grew spontaneously out of the war of attrition. The rationales offered by men for killing prisoners shed startling light on the primitive impulses that the war unleashed.

In some cases, prisoners were killed in revenge for attacks on civilians. The Germans had been the first to cross this threshold during the opening weeks of the war, when their troops carried out brutal reprisals for alleged attacks by *francs-tireurs* (snipers in civilian clothes). Entire villages in Belgium, Lorraine and the Vosges were razed and their male populations summarily shot, despite the fact that many of the 'attacks' were in fact friendly fire by other trigger-happy Germans, or legitimate actions by French regular forces. In all, around 5,500 Belgian civilians were killed, victims more of nervousness verging on paranoia on the part of the invaders than of a systematic policy of terrorizing the local populace. These 'atrocities' certainly happened. One soldier, a physician from Stuttgart named Pezold, recorded in his diary the fate of the inhabitants of the Belgian village of Arlon, more than 120 of whom were shot dead for alleged sniping and molestation of German wounded:

They were then dragged by the legs and thrown onto a pile, and the corporals shot with their revolvers all those who had not been killed by the infantry. The whole exceution was witnessed by the pastor, a woman and two young girls, who were the last to be shot . . .

Such incidents were, however, luridly embroidered in Entente propaganda; in addition to shooting civilians, the Germans were accused of rape and infanticide. As early as February 1915, B. C. Myatt, one of the 'Old Contemptibles' of the British Expeditionary Force, noted in his diary:

We know we are suffering these awful hardships to protect our beloved one's [sic] at home from the torture and the rape of these German pigs [who] have done some awful deeds in France and Belgium cutting off childrens hands and cutting off womans breasts awful deeds [sic].

An Australian soldier described in August 1917 how an officer shot two Germans, one wounded, in a shell hole:

The German asked him to give his comrade a drink. 'Yes,' our officer said, 'I'll give the —— a drink, take this,' and he emptied his revolver on the two of them. This is the only way to treat a Hun. What we enlisted for was to kill Huns, those baby-killing ——.'

The Germans were also the first to bomb cities; the Zeppelins over Scarborough and London were harbingers of a new era in which death would rain down from the sky on defenceless town-dwellers. These attacks too incited reprisals. One British soldier recalled how a friend had to be restrained from killing a captured German pilot:

He tried to find out whether he had been over [London] dropping bombs. He said, 'If he's been over there, I'll shoot him! He'll never get away.' He would have done too. Life meant nothing to you. Life was in jeopardy and when you'd got a load of Jerries stinking to high heaven, you hadn't much sympathy with their Kamerad and all this cringing business.

But it was above all the Germans' intermittent use of unrestricted submarine warfare against merchant and passenger ships that embittered men on the other side. 'Some [surrendering Germans] would crawl on their knees,' recalled one British soldier, 'holding a picture of a woman or a child in their hands above their heads but everyone was killed. The excitement was gone. We killed in cold blood because it was our duty to kill as much as we could. I thought many a time of the Lusitania. I had actually prayed for that day [of revenge], and when I got it, I killed just as much as I had hoped fate would allow me to kill.' In May 1915 the avant-garde sculptor Henri Gaudier-Brzeska wrote from the Western Front to Ezra Pound, describing a recent skirmish with the Germans: 'We also had a handful of prisoners – 10 – & as we had just learnt the loss of the "Lusitania" they were executed with the [rifle] butts after a 10 minutes dissertation [sic] among the N.C.[O.] and the men.'

More often, prisoners were killed in retaliation for more proximate enemy action. This pattern of behaviour manifested itself right at the start of the war, with German soldiers killing French prisoners on the ground that French soldiers had previously killed Germans who had surrendered. In his diary for June 16, 1915, A. Ashurt Moris recorded his own experience of killing a surrendering man:

At this point, I saw a Hun, fairly young, running down the trench, hands in air, looking terrified, yelling for mercy. I promptly shot him. It was a heavenly sight to see him fall forward. A Lincoln officer was furious with me, but the scores we owe wash out anything else.

Private Frank Richards of the Royal Welch Fusiliers recalled seeing another man in his regiment walk off down the Menin Road with six prisoners only to return some minutes later having 'done the trick' with 'two bombs'. Richards attributed his action to the fact that 'the loss of his pal had upset him very much'. Though sometimes spontaneous, this kind of behaviour seems to have been encouraged by some commissioned officers, who believed that the order 'Take no prisoners' enhanced the aggression and therefore the combat effectiveness of their men. A verbal order to finish off French prisoners was issued to some German troops as early as September 1914. But there was nothing peculiarly German about this kind of thing. One British brigadier was heard by a soldier in the Suffolks to say on the eve of the Battle of the Somme: 'You may take prisoners, but I don't want to see them.' Another man, in the 17th Highland Light Infantry, recalled the order 'that no quarter was to be shown to the enemy and no prisoners taken'. Private Arthur Hubbard of the London Scottish Regiment also received strict orders not to take prisoners, 'no matter if wounded'. His 'first job', he recalled, 'was when I had finished cutting some of the wire away, to empty my magazine on 3 Germans that came out of their deep dugouts, bleeding badly, and put them out of their misery, they cried for mercy, but I had my orders, they had no feelings whatever for us poor chaps'. In his notes 'from recent fighting' by II Corps, dated August 17, 1916, General Sir Claud Jacob urged that no prisoners should be taken, as they hindered mopping up. According to Arthur Wrench, battalion orders before an attack at Third Ypres included the words: 'NO PRISONERS' which 'with the line scored through meant "do as you please"'.

Sometimes the order was given to kill prisoners simply to avoid the inconvenience of escorting them back to captivity. As Brigadier General F. P. Crozier observed: 'The British soldier is a kindly fellow and it is safe to say, despite the dope [propaganda], seldom oversteps the mark of propriety in France, *save occasionally to kill prisoners he cannot be bothered to escort back to his lines.*' John Eugene Crombie of the Gordon Highlanders was ordered in April 1917 to bayonet surrendering Germans in a captured trench because it was 'expedient from a military point of view'. Other more spuriously practical arguments were also used. Private Frank Bass of the 1st Battalion, Cambridgeshire Regiment, was told by an instructor at Étaples: 'Remember, boys ... every prisoner means a day's rations gone.' Jimmy O'Brien of the 10th Dublin Fusiliers recalled being told by his chaplain (an English clergyman named Thornton):

Well now boys, we're going into action tomorrow morning and if you take any prisoners your rations will be cut by half. So don't take prisoners. Kill them! If you take prisoners they've got to be fed by your rations. So you'll get half rations. The answer is – don't take prisoners.

On June 16, 1915, Charles Tames, a private in the Honourable Artillery Company, described an incident following an attack at Bellewaarde near Ypres:

We were under shell fire for eight hours, it was more like a dream to me, we must have been absolutely mad at the time, some of the chaps looked quite insane after the charge was over, as we entered the German trenches hundreds of Germans were found cut up by our artillery fire, a great number came out and asked for mercy, needless to say they were shot right off which was the best mercy we could give them. The Royal Scots took about 300 prisoners, their officers told them to share their rations with the prisoners and to consider the officers were not with them, the Scots immediately shot the whole lot, and shouted 'Death and Hell to everyone of ye s——' and in five minutes the ground was ankle deep with German blood . . .

In its most extreme form, however, prisoner killing was justified on the basis that the only good German was a dead German. When the 12th Battalion of the Middlesex Regiment attacked Thiepval on September 26, 1916, Colonel Frank Maxwell VC ordered his men not to take any prisoners, on the ground that 'all Germans should be exterminated'. On October 21 Maxwell left his battalion a farewell message. In it he praised his men for having 'begun to learn that the only way to treat the German is to kill him'. In the words of Private Stephen Graham, 'The opinion cultivated in the army regarding the

Germans was that they were a sort of vermin like plague-rats that had to be exterminated.' A Major Campbell allegedly told new recruits: 'If a fat, juicy Hun cries "Mercy" and speaks of his wife and nine children, give him the point – two inches is enough – and finish him. He is the kind of man to have another nine "Hate" children if you let him off. So run no risks.'

The fact that these attitudes could take root on the Western Front, where the ethnic differences between the two sides were in fact quite minimal, was an indication of how easily hatred could flourish in the brutalizing conditions of total war. In other theatres of war, where the differences were deeper, the potential for unconstrained violence was greater still.

Exactly how often such prisoner killings occurred is impossible to establish. Clearly, only a small minority of men who surrendered were killed in this way. Equally clearly, not all of those who received such orders approved of them or felt able to carry them out. Hundreds of thousands of German soldiers were taken prisoner, especially in the final phase of the war, without suffering ill treatment. But the numbers involved mattered less than the perception that surrender was risky. Men magnified these episodes: they passed into trench mythology. The German trench newspaper *Kriegsflugblätter* devoted its front page on January 29, 1915, to a cartoon depicting just such an incident. 'G'meinhuber Michel' advances on a Tommy; the Tommy puts his hands up; the Tommy then shoots at the advancing Michel; Michel then gets the Tommy by the throat; he proceeds to beat him to a pulp with his rifle butt, crying 'I'll turn ye into an English beef steak' (*Doass muass a englisches Boeffsteck wer'n*'); and is duly rewarded with the Iron Cross. In real life, such incidents were more often than not the result of uncoordinated surrendering rather than duplicity; it only needed one man to keep shooting, unaware that his comrades had laid down their arms. But trench lore favoured the notion of trickery. And units that felt they had lost men this way were less likely to take prisoners in future. When Private Jack Ashley was captured at the Somme, his German captor told him that the British shot all their prisoners and that the Germans 'ought to do the same'.

## THE SURRENDER

The First World War confirmed the truth of the nineteenth-century military theorist Carl von Clausewitz's dictum that it is capturing not killing the enemy that is the key to victory in war. Despite the huge death toll inflicted on the Allies by the Germans and their allies, outright victory failed to materialize: demography meant that there were more or less enough new French and British conscripts each year to plug the gaps created by attrition. However, it did prove possible, first on the Eastern Front and then on the Western, to get the enemy to surrender in such large numbers that his ability to fight was fatally weakened. Large-scale surrenders (and desertions) in 1917 were the key to Russia's military defeat. Overall, more than half of all Russian casualties took the form of men who were taken prisoner – nearly 16 per cent of all Russian troops mobilized. Austria and Italy also lost a large proportion of men in this way: respectively a third and quarter of all casualties. One in four Austrians mobilized ended up a prisoner. The large-scale surrender of Italian troops at Caporetto came close to putting Italy out of the war. The low point of British fortunes – from around November 1917 to May 1918 – saw large increases in the numbers of Britons in captivity: in March 1918 alone, around 100,000 were taken, more than in all the previous years of fighting combined. In August 1918, however, it was German soldiers who began to give themselves up in large numbers. Between July 30 and October 21 the total number of Germans in British hands rose by a factor of nearly four. This was the real sign that the war was ending. Significantly, foreign exchange dealers in the unregulated Swiss market took the same view. They bought marks when the Germans bagged large numbers of prisoners in the spring of 1918 and dumped them when the tables were turned in August.

Why did German soldiers, who had hitherto been so reluctant to give themselves up, suddenly begin to surrender in their tens of thousands in August 1918? The best explanation – again following Clausewitz – is that there was a collapse of morale. This was primarily due to the realization among both officers and men that the war could not be won. General Erich Ludendorff's spring offensives had worked tactically but failed strategically, and in the process had cost the Germans dear, whereas the Allied offensive of August 7–8 outside Amiens was, as Ludendorff admitted, 'the greatest defeat the German Army has suffered since the beginning of the war'. Unrestricted submarine warfare had failed to bring Britain to her knees; occupation of Russian territory after Brest-Litovsk was wasting scarce manpower; Germany's allies were beginning to crumble; the Americans were massing in France, inexperienced but well fed and numerous; perhaps most importantly, the British Expeditionary Force had finally learned to combine infantry, artillery, armour and air operations. Simply in terms of numbers of tanks and trucks, the Germans were by now at a hopeless disadvantage in the war of movement they had initiated in the spring. A German victory was now impossible, and it was the rapid spread of this view down through the ranks that turned non-victory into defeat, rather than the draw Ludendorff appears to have had in mind. In this light, the mass surrenders described above were only part of a general crisis of morale, which also manifested itself in sickness, indiscipline and desertion.

Yet no matter how hopeless their situation, German soldiers had to feel they could risk surrendering before the war could end. And that meant that Allied soldiers had to be ready to take prisoners, rather than kill those who surrendered. The testimony of Lt RNR Blaker of the 13th (S) Battalion, Rifle Brigade, illustrates how the process worked. On November 4, 1918, during a heavy barrage of German positions at Louvignies, Blaker went ahead of his men to scout for enemy machine-gun emplacements. Having surprised and shot two German sentries, he was able to persuade 'five pretty scared looking Germans' to emerge from their dugout. 'I motioned them to go back through the barrage towards our lines,' Blaker recalled, 'and after a slight hesitation, they had to do so.' He then repeated this process with a second machine-gun crew. At this point, with dawn breaking, Blaker was startled to see 'all dotted about just round by the orchards and the open grass fields beyond, enemy heads occasionally peeping out'. Deciding that he had 'better to try to get them out of their holes', he went on. 'They didn't like coming out into the barrage and why they didn't fire at me, goodness knows,' but he succeeded in clearing out all he could see, disarming them and sending them back to the

British lines. Knowing that his men were not far behind him, the intrepid Blaker pressed on. A decisive moment was when he came upon a solitary house:

I came from the back of it and went round to the front, where there was no door, and peeped inside a room which opened into the road and saw there a crowd of Germans, some sitting down and some standing. I don't know who was more surprised – they or I. Anyway I managed to pull myself together a bit quicker than they did and advanced just under the doorway holding a Mills bomb in my left hand and my revolver in my right, the only thing I could think of to say was 'Kamerad', and so I said it, at the same time menacing them with my revolver, they didn't seem very willing to surrender, so I repeated 'Kamerad', and to my surprise and delight they 'Kameraded', 2 officers and 28 other ranks. My idea is that they were holding some sort of conference, as the barrage was not then reaching them in full force. Both officers and three of the other ranks had Iron Cross ribbons on!

Having made them all drop their weapons, Blaker induced these men also to march towards the British lines, despite the continuing British barrage. After this point, he was able to round up twenty-five or thirty more Germans, including the crews of two machine-guns and a trench mortar.

Five things about this account stand out. First, what began quite tentatively soon developed a momentum of its own. Clearly, the German units Blaker had stumbled upon had already been close to cracking; his appearance was the catalyst for a collapse, beginning with a few individuals and culminating in a large group. Secondly, at least some of those he captured were not raw recruits but seasoned troops, with five Iron Crosses between them. Thirdly, it is clear that for the Germans there was safety in numbers, because a single English officer simply could not gun down more than a handful. Fourthly, the role of the German officers was vital in legitimizing the decision to surrender and ensuring all complied. Once Blaker had them in the bag, the rest came quietly. Finally, and perhaps most importantly, Blaker only shot Germans who reached for their guns; from the outset he spared those who reached for the sky. (Or perhaps it would be more accurate to say that he delegated prisoner killing to the artillery by forcing his captives to march through the barrage to the British lines. Not all of them survived.) Plainly, after a certain point Blaker lacked the means to kill those who surrendered to him. Had they wished to, the German officers could have ordered their men to kill or capture him; he could have shot only a few of them before being overwhelmed. But the Germans felt sufficiently confident that they would be well treated that they elected instead to surrender.

Blaker's experience was typical of the way the First World War ended on the Western Front. By the last weeks, the German army had reached a point of what natural scientists call 'self-sustaining criticality'. Quite simply, the arguments against surrender outlined above had been overwhelmed by the arguments in favour of it. Defeated, German officers led their men into captivity – further evidence, if it were needed, that Germany was fatally stabbed in the front, not the back.

## THE WAR IN THE EAST

Although the heaviest fighting took place on the Western Front, the First World War ultimately changed remarkably little in Europe west of the Rhine. The biggest territorial change was that Alsace and Lorraine went back to France, but they had been French before 1871. In any case, such were the human and economic losses suffered by France that even this restoration seemed unlikely to endure. Britain and the United States had intervened decisively, but as soon as the German occupation of Belgium and northern France ended, they lost interest and went home. A relatively narrow strip of territory from the Channel to the Alps had suffered varying degrees of destruction, but the more profound consequences of the war in the west – which were demographic, economic and psychological – only slowly became apparent. At first, the balance of power seemed unchanged. By contrast, the much more mobile war that was fought on the Eastern Front seemed to change almost everything east of the River Elbe.

There is an unforgettable passage in Joseph Roth's novel *The Radetzky March* which helps to explain why this was. The scene is a crowded hotel ballroom on the night of June 28, 1914, in a remote garrison town near the Russian border – a place where, as Roth puts it, 'the civilized Austrian was menaced . . . by bears and wolves and even more dreadful monsters, such as lice and bedbugs'. The assembled infantry officers are of virtually every nationality in the Dual Monarchy and each reacts in his own way to the garbled telegram bearing the news of the assassination of the heir to the throne. Major Zoglauer urges that the party be broken up at once; Rittmeister Zschoch disagrees. 'Gentlemen,' declares Reserve Rittmeister von Babenhausen, 'Bosnia is far away. We don't give a damn about rumours. As far as I am concerned, to hell with them!' 'Bravo!' exclaims Baron Nagy Jenö, a Magyar nobleman impelled by the fact of having a Jewish grandfather in Bogumin to take on 'all the defects of the Hungarian gentry': 'Herr von Babenhausen is right, absolutely right! If the heir to the throne has been assassinated, then there are other heirs left!'

Herr von Senny, more Magyar in blood than Herr von Nagy, was filled with a sudden dread that someone of a Jewish background might outdo him in Hungarian nationalism. Rising to his feet he said, 'If the heir to the throne has been assassinated, well, first of all we know nothing for certain, and secondly, it doesn't concern us in the least.' . . .

First Lieutenant Kinsky, who had grown up on the banks of the Moldau, claimed that in any case the heir to the throne had been a highly precarious choice for the monarchy . . . Count Battyanyi, who was drunk, hereupon began speaking Hungarian to his compatriots . . . [Rittmeister] Jelacich, a Slovene, hit the ceiling. He hated the Hungarians as much as he despised the Serbs. He loved the monarchy. He was a patriot . . . And he did feel a wee bit guilty [since] . . . both his teenage sons were already talking about independence for all southern Slavs.

Though he himself understands Magyar, Jelacich insists the Hungarians speak in German, whereupon one of them declares that he and his countrymen are 'glad that the bastard is gone!' Lieutenant Trotta, the grandson of a Slovene knighted at the Battle of Solferino, rises drunkenly in response to this scandalous utterance. Threatening to shoot anyone who says another word against the dead man, he shouts 'Silence!', despite the fact that the Hungarians outrank him. Count Benkyö orders the band to play Chopin's funeral march, but the drunken guests keep dancing and the band involuntarily speeds up. Outside a storm rages. The resulting *danse macabre* ends only when the footmen clear away the musicians' instruments. Trotta resolves to resign his commission; his Ukrainian batman decides to desert and go home to Burdlaki. 'There was no more Fatherland. It was crumbling, splintering.'

In Western Europe the stakes were strategic, not ethnic. The British had concluded that they could not allow Germany to defeat France and Russia, for fear of a threat to Britain's security comparable with that posed a century before by Napoleon. When war came, Bretons did not turn on Gascons, nor did Walloons and Flemings fight one another. Scotsmen, Welshmen, Englishmen and many Irishmen fought alongside one another without serious ill-feeling. Only in Ireland did the First World War usher in a civil war and even that was not as bloody a conflict as is sometimes assumed. In Eastern Europe, by contrast, it was understood early on that war spelt the dissolution of the old order of multi-ethnic empires and ethnically mixed communities. On the Western Front, Belgian and French civilians were only briefly in the firing line, in the opening phase of the war. Once the battle lines hardened, however, the combat zone was effectively militarized; thereafter, as a rule, civilians became casualties only as a result of the enemy's inaccurate artillery fire or their own incaution. The Eastern Front was very different. There, from the Baltic to the Balkans, the great advances and retreats that characterized the fighting repeatedly exposed large civilian populations to both accidental and deliberate violence.

Predictably, it was the Jewish communities of the Russian Pale of Settlement who had the most to fear. In the opening phase of the war, at least a hundred Jews were summarily executed by the Russian army on suspicion of espionage, the assumption being that Jews could not possibly be loyal to the Tsarist regime. There was also a policy of systematic plundering. On October 14, 1914, some 4,000 Jews were driven from their homes in Grozin (Warsaw province); they were denied any means to transport their possessions with them. In response to an enquiry about requisitioning, the Staff of the 4th Army of the South-Western Front issued the order, 'From the kikes take everything.' In the Kovno region fifteen localities witnessed pogroms in July 1915, while in the Vilna region nineteen *shtetls* were demolished in

August and September 1915. There were also attacks on Jews in Minsk, Volhynia and Grodno. In many villages, Jewish women were raped by soldiers.

Jews in Galicia were also systematically mistreated when the Russians marched into Austrian territory in the opening phase of the war. There were pogroms in Brody and in Lemberg immediately after their occupation by Russian forces. Nine Jews were killed in the former; seventeen in the latter. In the words of a Jewish doctor in the Russian army: 'The methods were everywhere the same: after some provocative shot from a never disclosed person, came robbery, fire, and massacre.' In December 1914 one general told the troops of his division:

Remember, brothers, that your first foe is the Germans. They have long sucked our blood, and now want to conquer our land. Don't take them prisoner, bayonet them – I'll answer for it. Your second foe are the kikes [*zhidy*]. They are spies and aid the Germans. If you meet a *zhid* in the field – bayonet him, I'll answer for it.

The behaviour of Cossack units was notoriously bad. A Jewish soldier in the Russian army described one among many incidents:

When our brigade marched through one village, a soldier spotted a house on a hill, and told our commander that it was probably the home of Jews. The officer allowed him to go and have a look. He returned with the cheerful news that Jews *were* indeed living there. The officer ordered the brigade to approach the house. They opened the door and found some twenty Jews half dead with fear. The troops led them out, and the officer gave his order: 'Slice them up! Chop them up!'

Another Russian unit ordered the Jews of a *shtetl* near Wolkowisk to strip naked, dance with one another, and then ride on pigs; they then proceeded to shoot every tenth person. Between April and October 1915, as the Russians retreated from Galicia, there were roughly one hundred separate pogroms or minor anti-Jewish incidents, nearly all instigated by soldiers. To deprive the Austrians of conscripts, the Russians also attempted to take with them all of the male population between the ages of eighteen and fifty; the Jews of the occupied area were also moved as an 'unreliable element' to the small area around Tarnopol that the Russians continued to occupy.

Violence towards Jews, as we have seen, had been a feature of life in Eastern Europe before the war began. Yet it would be a mistake to view pogroms in isolation. Throughout the East European theatre of war there were attacks on ethnic minorities, sometimes but not always perpetrated by occupying armies. Germans in Galicia were forced to flee their homes following the Austrian defeats at Lemberg and Przemyśl in 1914. As the Austrians retreated, numerous German villages – for example Mariahilf – were burned to the ground by Russian regulars and Cossacks. When German reinforcements under General August von Mackensen turned the tide, the Russians took hostages from these villages back with them to Russia. The Austrians, meanwhile, executed numerous Poles and Ukrainians accused of collaborating with the Russians during their occupation. Similar scenes were repeated in Bukovina, which was overrun by the Russians within a few weeks of the outbreak of war, and saw renewed fighting during the Russian Brusilov offensive in the summer of 1916. In the confusion of 1917 and 1918, when it seemed the Germans had won the war in the East, expectations of independence in Poland and the Ukraine precipitated bitter fighting between the various ethnic groups in Galicia. Germans further east also fell victim to the war, even though they lived many miles from the front lines. From the outset, the Russian Commander-in-Chief, the Grand Duke Nikolai Nikolaievich, and the Chief of the General Staff, General Nikolai Yanushkevich, viewed the non-Russian population of Russia's Western frontier with the utmost suspicion. It was not only Jews but also Germans, Gypsies, Hungarians and Turks who were deported from the empire's western provinces during the war; in all, around 250,000 people.

The war had the same disruptive effect in the Balkans, where it had, after all, begun. Serbian losses were among the highest of the entire war in relative terms. Not all violent deaths came about as a result of formal military engagements. In his novel *The Bridge on the Drina*, Ivo Andrić memorably described the impact of the outbreak of war in 1914 on the ethnically mixed Bosnian town of Višegrad:

The people were divided into the persecuted and those who persecuted them. That wild beast, which lives in man and does not dare to show itself until the barriers of law and custom have been removed, was now set free. The signal was given, the barriers were down. As has so often happened in the history of man, permission was tacitly granted for acts of violence and plunder, even for murder, if they were carried out in the name of higher interests, according to established rules, and against a limited number of men of a particular type and belief. A man who saw clearly and with open eyes and was then living could see how this miracle took place and how the whole of a society could, in a single day, be transformed ... It is true that there had always been concealed enmities and jealousies and religious intolerance, coarseness and cruelty, but there had also been courage and fellowship and a feeling for measure and order, which restrained all these instincts within the limits of the supportable and, in the end, calmed them down and submitted them to the general interest of life in common ... Men ... vanished overnight as if they had died suddenly, together with the habits, customs and institutions which they represented.

In this case it was the Serbian minority that was persecuted with the encouragement of the Austrian authorities, but both the Muslim and Jewish communities were, sometimes literally, caught in the crossfire. Andrić's novel is superficially a chronicle of recurrent ethnic conflict, dating back to the sixteenth century, when the Ottoman authorities began to construct the bridge of the book's title. Yet the bridge on the Drina is intended to symbolize the capacity for harmony of a multi-ethnic society like Višegrad's; it is 'the link between East and West', where men and, later, women of the town's different faiths and cultures meet to smoke, sip coffee and gossip. Despite occasional manifestations of violence upon it, the bridge withstands all the stresses and strains of Ottoman decline. It is only in 1914 that the conflict between Serbs, Muslim 'Turks' and German 'Swabians' becomes uncontainable and the bridge is literally blown apart.

Višegrad was only one of many multi-ethnic towns rent asunder by the Great War. In Andrić's words, it merely 'provided a small but eloquent example of the first symptoms of a contagion which would in time become European and then spread to the entire world'. The Western Front had revealed a new level of industrialization in warfare – had seen the introduction of machines of death comparable in their lethal effectiveness with those Wells had imagined in *The War of the Worlds*. But the Eastern Front had seen an equally important transformation in warfare. There the death throes of the old Central and East European empires had dissolved the old boundaries between combatant and civilian. This kind of war proved much easier to start than to stop.

# 5

# Graves of Nations

*On the whole, great multinational empires are an institution*
*of the past, of a time when material force was held high*
*and the principle of nationality had not yet been recognized,*
*because democracy had not been recognized.*

Thomas Masaryk, 1918

*Great was the year and terrible the year of Our Lord 1918,*
*but the year 1919 was even more terrible.*

Mikhail Bulgakov, *The White Guard*

## THE RED PLAGUE

The peace that followed the First World War was the continuation of
war by other means. The Bolsheviks proclaimed an end to hostilities,
only to plunge the Russian Empire into a barbaric civil war. The
Western statesmen drafted peace treaties – one for each of the defeated
Central Powers (Germany, Austria, Hungary, Bulgaria and Turkey) –
each of which was a *casus belli* in its own right. Nor, as Keynes
predicted in *The Economic Consequences of the Peace*, did 'vengeance
. . . limp'. As it turned out, Keynes was only half right. He expected
that the financial burdens imposed under the Treaty of Versailles
would be the principal bone of post-war contention; the European
'civil war' would come, he wrote, 'if we aim deliberately at the im-
poverishment of Central Europe . . . if we take the view that for at
least a generation to come Germany cannot be trusted with even a
modicum of prosperity . . . that year by year Germany must be kept

impoverished and her children starved and crippled'. The causes of the Second World War in Europe were not economic, however; at least, not in the sense Keynes had in mind. They were territorial – or, to be more precise, they arose from the conflict between territorial arrangements based on the principle of 'self-determination' and the realities of ethnically mixed patterns of settlement. Keynes also expected that the first reaction against the peace treaties would come from Germany. In fact it came from Turkey, though what happened there foreshadowed much that the Germans would later do.

The road to civil war began in Petrograd, as the Russian capital had been renamed during the war as a sop to national sentiment ('Sankt Peterburg' had too German a ring to it). Nicholas II, a pious, puritanical man of limited intellectual capacity, came to regard ruling Russia as one long test of inner strength. He worked himself hard, as if determined to prove the veracity of his claim that he was 'the crowned worker'. 'I do the work of three men,' he had declared. 'Let everyone learn to do the work of at least two.' Unfortunately the two other jobs he relished doing – rather more, it would appear, than that of Tsar – were those of secretary and gardener. While conditions at the front deteriorated, he doggedly ploughed through routine correspondence, pausing only to sweep the snow from his own paths. His German-born wife, the Empress Alexandra, did not help, having embraced her own caricature version of Orthodoxy and autocracy. 'Ah my Love,' she wrote to him (in English, as in all their correspondence), 'when *at last* will you thump with your hand upon the table & scream at [your ministers] when they act wrongly[?] – one does not fear you – & one *must* . . . Oh, my Boy, make one tremble before you – to love you is not enough . . . Be Peter the G., John [Ivan] the Terrible, Emp. Paul – crush them all under you – now don't you laugh, naughty one.' It was hopeless. To the last, Nicholas declined to 'bellow at the people left right & centre'. On December 16, 1916, the royal couple's charismatic and corrupt holy man Rasputin was murdered by the Tsar's own cousin, Grand Duke Dmitry, aided and abetted by the effete Prince Felix Yusupov and a right-wing politician named V. M. Purishkevich, in the belief that the monk was exerting a malign influence on the Tsar and on Russian foreign policy. But things did not improve. Deserted by his own generals in what amounted to a mutiny in early March 1917, Nicholas agreed to abdicate, complaining bitterly of 'treachery, cowardice and deceit'. Neither he nor his wife ever understood the revolution that was now unfolding. Indeed, Alexandra's comment on its outbreak deserves wider celebrity as one of the great mis-diagnoses of history: 'It's a *hooligan* movement, young boys & girls running about & screaming that they have no bread, only to excite – . ... if it were cold they wld. probably stay in doors.'

The Provisional Government that took the Tsar's place aimed to establish a republic with a liberal constitution and parliamentary institutions. Its prospects were far from bad. However, the determination of its leaders to keep the war going and to postpone decisions on the burning question of land reform until after a Constituent Assembly had been elected created a window of opportunity for more extreme elements. The Bolsheviks had in fact been taken by surprise by the revolution. 'It's staggering!' exclaimed Lenin when he heard the news in Zurich. 'Such a surprise! Just imagine! We must get home, but how?' The German High Command answered that question, providing him not only with a railway ticket to Petrograd but also, through two shady intermediaries named Parvus and Ganetsky, with funds to subvert the new government. Instead of having him and his associates arrested, as they richly deserved to be, the Provisional Government dithered. On August 27, egged on by conservative critics of the new regime, the Supreme Commander of the Russian Army, General Lavr Kornilov, launched an abortive military coup. The unintended effect was to boost support for the Bolsheviks within the soviets, which had sprung up as a kind of parallel government not only in Petrograd (as in 1905) but in other cities too. Two months later, on October 24, 1917, the Bolsheviks staged a *coup d'état* of their own. At the time, it did not seem like a world-shaking event. Indeed, more people were hurt in Sergei Eisenstein's subsequent reenactment for his film *October*. Hardly anyone expected the new regime to last.

The Bolsheviks promised their supporters 'Peace, Bread and Power to the Soviets'. Peace turned out to mean abject capitulation. At Brest-Litovsk, in the sprawling brick fortress that guards the River Bug, the German High Command demanded sweeping cessions of territory from a motley Bolshevik delegation (to keep up revolutionary appearances, a token peasant named Roman Stashkov had been picked up en route). Trotsky, who was in charge of Bolshevik foreign policy during the negotiations, played for time, defiantly if somewhat opaquely proclaiming 'neither peace nor war'. His hope was that if the negotiations could be spun out for long enough, world revolution might supervene. The Germans simply advanced into the Baltic provinces, Poland and the Ukraine. There was almost no resistance from the demoralized Russian forces. Indeed, for a moment it seemed as if the Germans might even take Petrograd, and the Bolshevik leadership was forced hastily to remove themselves to Moscow, henceforth their capital. When Trotsky finally yielded to Lenin's argument for capitulation – after stormy debates that led the Left Socialist Revolutionaries to quit the revolutionary government – the Bolsheviks had to sign away a third of the pre-war Russian Empire's agricultural land and population, more than half of her industry and nearly 90 per cent of her coalmines. Poland, Finland, Lithuania and the Ukraine became independent, though under German tutelage. The war in the East was the war the Germans won. The money they had used to send Lenin back to Russia had, it seemed, paid a handsome return.

Yet the Russian Revolution proved to be not the end of the war, merely its mutation. After Germany's eastern triumph was rendered null and void by her defeat in the West, the war in the East changed into a terrible civil war, in many ways as costly in human life as the conventional war between empires that preceded it. Two epidemics swept the world in 1918. One was Spanish influenza, the first recorded outbreak of which was at a Kansas army base in March 1918. As if to mock the efforts of men to kill one another, the virus spread rapidly across the United States and then crossed to Europe on the crowded American troopships. By June it had reached India, Australia and New Zealand. Two months later, a second wave struck all but simultaneously in Boston, Massachusetts, Brest in France and Freetown in Sierra Leone. At least 40 million people died as a result of the epidemic, the majority of them suffocated by a lethal accumulation of blood and other fluid in the lungs. Ironically, unlike most flu epidemics, but like the war that preceded and spread it, the influenza of 1918 disproportionately killed young adults. One in every hundred American males between the ages of 25 and 34 fell victim to the 'Spanish

Lady'. Strikingly, the global peak of mortality was in October and November 1918. The Germans had been prepared to combat lice-borne typhus, which was an especially serious threat on the Eastern Front; indeed they devoted considerable resources to eradicating it when they occupied cities like Białystok. They were as surprised as anyone by this unlooked-for menace from the West. There is reason to believe that this was a factor in the collapse of the German army in those months (see Figure 5.1).

The other epidemic was Bolshevism, which for a time seemed almost as contagious and ultimately proved as lethal as the influenza. With the end of the war, Soviet-style governments were proclaimed in Budapest, Munich and Hamburg. The red flag was even raised above Glasgow City Chambers. Lenin dreamed of a 'Union of Soviet Republics of Europe and Asia'. Trotsky declared that 'the road to Paris and London lies via the towns of Afghanistan, the Punjab and Bengal'. Even distant Buenos Aires was rocked by strikes and street fighting.

In Russia itself, however, the Bolsheviks' authority was non-existent outside the big cities. Against them were arrayed three counter-revolutionary or 'White' armies led by experienced Tsarist generals: Anton Denikin's Volunteers, an army of many officers and few men which had started life on the banks of the Don, Admiral Aleksandr Kolchak's force in Siberia and General Nikolai Yudenich's in the north-west. Moreover, the Whites had foreign support. The Czech Legion had been formed by Czech and Slovak nationalists to fight on the Russian side against Austria-Hungary and at the outbreak of the Revolution numbered around 35,000 men. Determined to continue their fight for independence, the Legion's commanders decided to travel eastwards, along the Trans-Siberian Railway, with a view to crossing the Pacific, North America and the Atlantic and rejoining the fray on the Western Front. They took around 15,000 men with them. When the Bolsheviks at Chelyabinsk sought to disarm them the Czechs fought back. They then joined forces with the Socialist Revolutionaries in Samara, helping them to establish a Committee of Members of the Constituent Assembly (known as the *Komuch*) as a rival government to Lenin's. Between May and June, the Czechs swept eastwards, capturing Novo-Nikolaevsk, Penza, Syzran, Tomsk, Omsk, Samara and finally Vladivostok. Meanwhile, Russia's former allies sent

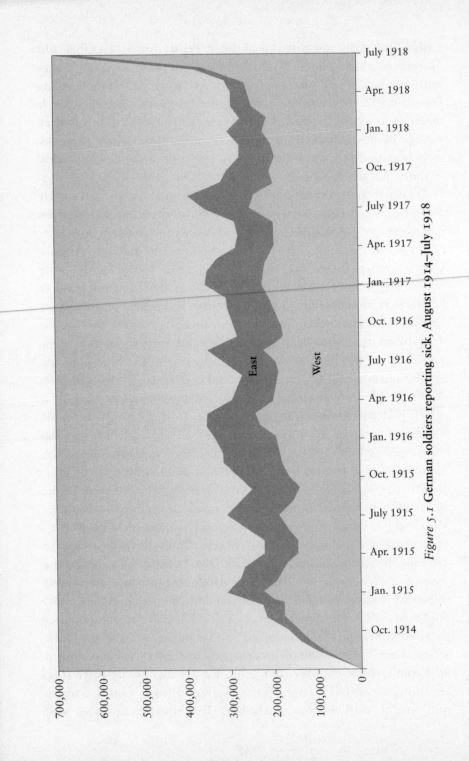

*Figure 5.1* German soldiers reporting sick, August 1914–July 1918

expeditionary forces, whose primary aim was to keep Russia in the war. The British landed troops at Archangel and Murmansk, as well as at Vladivostok; the French sent men to Odessa, the Americans to Vladivostok. The Allies also supplied the White armies with weapons and other supplies. The Japanese seized the opportunity to march across the Amur River from Manchuria. Meanwhile, the cities that were supposed to be the headquarters of the Revolution emptied as factories closed and supplies of food and fuel dried up. When Denikin called on all the White forces to converge on Moscow in July 1918, it seemed more than likely that the Bolshevik regime would be overthrown.

On August 6, 1918, White forces in combination with the renegade Czech Legion captured Kazan. The Bolshevik 5th Army was haemorrhaging deserters. Ufa had fallen; so too had Simbirsk, Lenin's own birthplace. Another step back along the Volga would bring the forces of counter-revolution to the gates of Nizhny-Novgorod, opening the road to Moscow. Having resigned his post as Commissar for Foreign Affairs in favour of Military Affairs, Trotsky now had the daunting task of stiffening the Red Army's resolve. He was, as we have seen, by training a journalist not a general. Yet the goatee-bearded intellectual with his pince-nez had seen enough of war in the Balkans and on the Western Front to know that without discipline an army was doomed. It was Trotsky who insisted on the need for conscription, realizing that volunteers would not suffice. It was Trotsky who brought in the former Tsarist NCOs and officers – many of them hitherto languishing in jail – whose experience was to be vital in taking on the Whites.

Trotsky had two advantages. Firstly, the Bolsheviks controlled the central railway hubs, from which he could deploy forces at speed. Indeed, it was from his own specially designed armoured railway carriage that he himself directed operations, travelling some 100,000 miles in the course of the war. Secondly, though the Bolsheviks lacked experience of war, they did have experience of terrorism; like the Serbian nationalists, they too had employed assassination as a tactic in the pre-war years. It was to terror, in the name of martial law, that Trotsky now turned.

When he arrived at Kazan, the first thing he did was to uncouple the engine from his train; a signal to his troops that he had no intention of retreating. He then brought twenty-seven deserters to nearby Syvashsk, on the banks of the Volga, and had them shot. The only way to ensure that Red Army recruits did not desert or run away, Trotsky had concluded, was to mount machine-guns in their rear and shoot any who failed to advance against the enemy. This was the choice he offered: possible death in the front or certain death in the rear. 'We must put an end once and for all', he sneered with a characteristically caustic turn of phrase, 'to the papist-Quaker babble about the sanctity of human life.' Units that refused to fight were to be decimated. It was a turning point in the Russian civil war – and an ominous sign of how the Bolsheviks would behave if they won it. In the bitter fighting for the bridge over the Volga at Kazan, Trotsky's tactics made that outcome significantly more likely. The bridge was saved, and on September 10 the city itself was retaken. Two days later Simbirsk also fell to the Reds. The White advance faltered as they found themselves challenged not only by a rapidly growing Red Army, but also by recalcitrant Ukrainians and Chechens to their rear. The Czechs were weary of fighting; the Legion disintegrated as it was driven back to Samara and then beyond the Urals. The *Komuch* fell apart, leaving Kolchak to proclaim himself 'Supreme Ruler' – of what was not clear. By the end of November Denikin had lost Voronezh and Kastornoe.

The end of the war on the Western Front was well timed for the Bolsheviks. It undermined the legitimacy of the foreign powers' intervention, especially as they now had left-wing outbreaks of their own to deal with. Only the Japanese showed any inclination to maintain an armed presence on Russian soil, and they were content to stake out new territorial claims in the Far East and leave the rest of Russia to its fate. To be sure, the Bolsheviks controlled only a small part of the former Tsarist Empire. The German withdrawal from the Ukraine had created a vacuum of power to the west, a state of affairs memorably described in Mikhail Bulgakov's novel *The White Guard*. Chaos reigned as rival forces of nationalists, peasant Greens, Whites and Bolsheviks vied for control of the countryside and dwindling stocks of grain. In south-eastern Ukraine, a hard-drinking anarchist peasant named Nestor 'Batko' Makhno led a 15,000-strong peasant army against all comers: Germans, nationalists, Whites, Reds. The Don Cossacks were supportive of the Whites but reluctant to venture far from their homes; their dilemmas are at the core of Mikhail Sholokhov's *Quiet Flows the Don*, the tragic central character of which, Grigory Melekhov, fights successively for the Whites, the Reds and nationalist guerrillas. There was a Siberian separatist army, too, marching under a green and white flag. It was briefly allied to a 'Provisional All-Russian Government', which had its offices in a railway carriage in Omsk. The area east of Lake Baikal was in the hands of a renegade warlord named Grigorii Semenov. Above all, there was recurrent resistance to Bolshevik rule by peasants.* The real civil war was not just between Whites and Reds; it also between Reds and Greens, country-dwellers who rejected the Bolshevik vision of a dictatorship of the urban proletariat and took up arms to fend off arbitrary grain seizures.

Nevertheless, from November 1918 onwards the tide of the civil war ran the Bolsheviks' way. By April 1919 Kolchak's forces had been beaten and by July Perm was back in Bolshevik hands, followed by Omsk itself in November. Denikin enjoyed some success in the Ukraine in the summer of 1919 but had lost Kiev by the end of the year. Yudenich's attempt to capture Petrograd had also failed, thanks in large measure to Trotsky's rallying of the city's defenders, who drove the defeated White army back into Estonia, whence they had come. General Peter Wràngel's Caucasian Army had captured Tsaritsyn that June, but by January 1920 it was clear that the war was effectively over. The Allies cut off their aid to the Whites. One by one the generals fled or, like Kolchak, were captured and executed. By the summer of 1920 Lenin felt confident enough to export the Revolution westwards, ordering the Red Army to march on Warsaw and confidently talking of the need to 'sovietize Hungary and perhaps Czechia and Romania too'. Only their decisive defeat by the Polish army on

---

* Politically conscious peasants tended to identify themselves with the Socialist Revolutionaries. It was peasant support that made the SRs the clear victors of the elections to the Constituent Assembly. But the party was divided between Left and Right, with the former initially willing to join forces with the Bolsheviks, and lacked leaders who could match the ruthlessness of Lenin and Trotsky.

the banks of the River Vistula halted the spread of the Bolshevik epidemic.

Terror by this time had become the keystone of Bolshevik rule. A typical Trotsky order promised that 'shady agitators, counter-revolutionary officers, saboteurs, parasites and speculators will be locked up, except for those who will be shot at the scene of the crime'. The crisis of the summer of 1918 legitimized Lenin's urge to play the part of Robespierre, assuming dictatorial powers in the spirit of 'the Revolution endangered'. The only way to ensure that peasants handed over their grain to feed the Red Army, he insisted, was to order exemplary executions of so-called *kulaks*, the supposedly rapacious capitalist peasants whom it suited the Bolsheviks to demonize. 'How can you make a revolution without firing squads?' Lenin asked. 'If we can't shoot a White Guard saboteur, what sort of great revolution is it? Nothing but talk and a bowl of mush.' Convinced that the Bolsheviks would not 'come out the victors' if they did not employ 'the harshest kind of revolutionary terror', he called explicitly for 'mass terror against the kulaks, priests, and White Guards'. 'Black marketeers' were to be 'shot on the spot'. The whole notion of exemplary violence seemed to fire Lenin's imagination. On August 11, 1918 he wrote a letter to Bolshevik leaders in Penza that speaks volumes:

Comrades! The kulak uprising must be crushed without pity . . . An example must be made. 1) Hang (and I mean hang so that the people can see) not less than 100 known bloodsuckers. 2) Publish their names. 3) Take all their grain away from them . . . Do this so that for hundreds of miles around the people can see, tremble, know and cry: they are killing and will go on killing the bloodsucking kulaks . . . P.S. Find tougher people.

Kulaks were 'foes of the Soviet government . . . blood-suckers . . . spiders . . . [and] leeches'. Egged on by this kind of splenetic language, Bolshevik food brigades felt no compunction about killing anyone who tried to resist their raids.

The very insecurity of the Revolution encouraged terrorist tactics. In the early hours of July 17, just hours after Lenin had wired a Danish paper that the 'exczar' was 'safe', the Bolshevik commissar Yakov Yurovsky and a makeshift firing squad of twelve assembled the royal family and their remaining servants in the basement of the commandeered house in Ekaterinburg where they were being held and, after minimal preliminaries, shot them at point-blank range. Trotsky had wanted a spectacular show trial, but Lenin decided it would be better 'not [to] leave the Whites a live banner'.* Unfortunately, because the women had large amounts of jewellery concealed in the linings of their clothes, they were all but bullet-proof. One of the executioners was very nearly killed by a ricochet. Contrary to legend, Princess Anastasia did not survive but was finished off with a bayonet. Only the royal spaniel, Joy, was spared. Other relatives of the Tsar were also taken hostage, including the Grand Dukes Nikolai, Georgy, Dmitry, Pavel and Gavril, four of whom were subsequently shot. Violence begat violence. A month after the execution of the Tsar, an assassination attempt that nearly killed Lenin was the cue for an intensification of the revolutionary terror.

At the heart of the new tyranny was the 'All-Russian Extraordinary Commission for Combating Counter-Revolution and Sabotage' – the Cheka for short. Under Felix Dzerzhinsky the Bolsheviks created a new kind of political police which had no compunction about simply executing suspects. 'The Cheka', as one of its founders explained, 'is not an investigating commission, a court, or a tribunal. It is a fighting organ on the internal front of the civil war . . . It does not judge, it strikes. It does not pardon, it destroys all who are caught on the other side of the barricade.' The Bolshevik newspaper *Krasnaya Gazeta* declared: 'Without mercy, without sparing, we will kill our enemies in scores of hundreds. Let them be thousands, let them drown themselves in their own blood. For the blood of Lenin . . . let there be floods of blood of the bourgeoisie – more blood, as much as possible.' Dzerzhinsky was happy to oblige. On September 23, 1919, to give just one example, sixty-seven alleged counter-revolutionaries were summarily shot. At the top of the list was Nikolai Shchepkin, a liberal member of the Duma (parliament) that had been set up after 1905. The announcement of their execution was couched in the most vehement language, accusing Shchepkin and his alleged confederates of 'hiding

---

* Despite all the pre-war talk of monarchical solidarity, George V decided against offering his Russian cousins asylum in Britain. They were shunted pathetically from Tobolsk to Ekaterinburg as the Bolsheviks tried to work out what to do with them.

like bloodthirsty spiders [and] put[ting] their webs everywhere from the Red Army to schools and universities'. Between 1918 and 1920, as many as 300,000 such political executions were carried out. These included not just members of rival parties, but also fellow Bolsheviks who were so rash as to challenge the new dictatorship of the party leadership.

Much of the violence of the civil war was hot blooded. On both sides, prisoners were killed, even mutilated; whole villages were put to the sword. Kornilov himself had spoken of 'burn[ing] half of Russia and shed[ding] the blood of three-quarters of the population' in order to 'save Russia'. His Volunteer Army slaughtered hundreds of peasants on its 'Ice March' from the Don to the Kuban and back. But a clear and chilling sign of the true character of the new regime was the construction of the first concentration camps. By 1920 there were already more than a hundred camps for the 'rehabilitation' of 'unreliable elements'. Their locations were carefully chosen to expose prisoners to the harshest possible conditions – places like the former monastery of Kholmogory, in the icy wastes beside the White Sea. The Cheka had unusual ideas about how to rehabilitate prisoners. In Kiev a cage full of starved rats was tied to prisoners' bodies and heated; the rats devoured the victim's innards in their struggles to escape. In Kharkov they boiled the skin off prisoners' hands – the so-called 'glove trick'. With methods like these it is perhaps not surprising that the Reds were able to recruit more soldiers than the Whites. It helped, however, that many White officers seemed intent on restoring the old regime, complete with their own privileges as landowners; given the choice, many peasants preferred the devil they did not know – especially when the diabolical figure of Lenin was transmuted into a pseudo-saint, all but martyred for the sake of revolution. The personality cult that sprang up around him was intentionally designed to provide a surrogate religion for the Revolution, at a time when churches and monasteries were being destroyed, priests and monks murdered.

The Revolution had been made in the name of peace, bread and Soviet power. It turned out to mean civil war, starvation and the dictatorship of the Bolshevik Party's Central Committee and its increasingly potent subcommittee, the Politburo. Workers who had

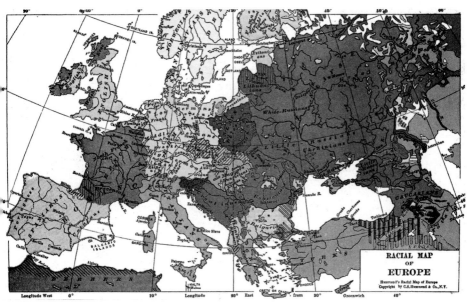

1. The limits of self-determination: this 'Racial Map of Europe' (1923) (strictly speaking, an ethno-linguistic map) shows why it was so hard to construct homogeneous nation states in that zone of heterogeneity stretching from the Baltic to the Balkans and the Black Sea.

2. 'The Yellow Peril': drawing of 1895 by Hermann Knackfuss based on a sketch by the German Emperor William II and sent to Nicholas II and other European sovereigns to alert them to the supposed threat from the East.

3. Europeans in Asian bondage: European soldiers captured at the Battle of Yang-Cun are brought before the Boxer generals Songs, Dong and Li.

4. '*Bon appetit*!': the Japanese David gives the Russian Goliath a bloody nose and bids for the Manchurian cake, from a German cartoon of March 1904.

5. Pogrom victims and survivors, Odessa 1905.

6. West meets East on the Habsburg frontier: the Archduke Francis Ferdinand meets Bosnian dignitaries in Sarajevo, June 28, 1914, just hours before his murder.

7. Gavrilo Princip (*front row, third prisoner from the left*) and the other members of 'Young Bosnia' accused of conspiring to murder the Archduke Francis Ferdinand, in court in Sarajevo.

8. The world comes to make war in Europe: two soldiers from France's West African colonies during the First World War.

9. Scottish prisoners of war are pleasantly surprised to be fed by their German captors.

10. Little 'Red' Riding Hood confronts the imperial German wolf: Russian cartoon of the peace negotiations at Brest-Litovsk, 1917–18.

11. The Bolshevik Revolution in White eyes: Jewish leadership and Asiatic methods. An anti-Semitic caricature of Trotsky from the Civil War era. Note the Chinese executioners. The caption reads 'Peace and Freedom in the Sovdepiya', short for 'Soviet-Deputatov', i.e, the Soviet state.

12. The waterfront at Danzig (Gdánsk): view over the Mottlau showing the tower of the town hall on the left, St Mary's Church in the centre and the Crane Gate to the right.

13. The bodies of Armenian children, Turkey 1915.

14. Rudolf Schlichter, 'Armenian Horrors', watercolour on paper c. 1920. Sexual violence was to be a recurrent feature of genocide throughout the twentieth century, though like the 'lust murders' Schlichter also depicted, the Armenian genocide was something he read about in the newspapers rather than witnessed.

15. Ethnic cleansing in action: Greek refugees throng the docks at Smyrna, fleeing from Turkish troops, September 1922.

supported the Bolsheviks in the expectation of a decentralized soviet regime found themselves being gunned down if they had the temerity to strike at newly nationalized factories. With inflation rampant, their wages in real terms were just a fraction of what they had been before the war. 'War Communism' reduced hungry city dwellers to desperate bartering expeditions to the country and to burning everything from their neighbours' doors to their own books for heat. As the conscription system grew more effective, more and more young men found themselves drafted into the Red Army, which grew in number from less than a million in January 1919 to five million by October 1920, though desertion rates remained high, especially around harvest time. When the previously pro-Bolshevik sailors of Kronstadt mutinied in February 1921, they denounced the regime for crushing freedom of speech, press and assembly and filling prisons and concentration camps with their political rivals. Their formal resolution, setting out their demands, was a coruscating indictment of Bolshevik rule:

In view of the fact that the present soviets do not represent the will of the workers and peasants, [we demand]:

To re-elect the soviets immediately by secret voting, with free canvassing among all workers and peasants before the elections.

Freedom of speech and press for workers, peasants, Anarchists and Left Socialist Parties.

Freedom of meetings, trade unions and peasant associations.

To convene, not later than March 1, 1921, a non-party conference of workers, soldiers and sailors of Petrograd City, Kronstadt and Petrograd Province.

To liberate all political prisoners of Socialist Parties, and also all workers, peasants, soldiers and sailors who have been imprisoned in connection with working-class and peasant movements.

To elect a commission to review the cases of those who are imprisoned in jails and concentration camps.

To abolish all Political Departments, because no single party may enjoy privileges in the propagation of its ideas and receive funds from the state for this purpose. Instead of these Departments, locally elected cultural-educational commissions must be established and supported by the state . . .

To abolish all Communist fighting detachments in all military units, and also the various Communist guards at factories. If such detachments and guards are needed they may be chosen from the companies in military units and in the factories according to the judgement of the workers.

To grant the peasant full right to do what he sees fit with his land and also to possess cattle, which he must maintain and manage with his own strength, but without employing hired labour.

To permit free artisan production with individual labour.

We demand that all resolutions be widely published in the press.

The Bolsheviks crushed the revolt with a force of 50,000 troops. Those sailors who did not manage to flee to Finland were either shot summarily or sent to the camps. Small wonder the veteran revolutionary writer Maxim Gorky came, for a time at least, to despair of the revolution he had earlier hailed.

Nor did the Bolsheviks' betrayal of the Revolution end there, for there was a third epidemic in 1918 – an epidemic of nationalism. The non-Russians within the Tsarist Empire at first had greeted the Revolution as a springtime of the peoples; a second 1848, but extending much further eastwards. In the confusion of the civil war, Finland, Estonia, Latvia, Lithuania, Poland, Byelorussia and the Ukraine all proclaimed their independence – or, rather, sought to make a reality of the fictitious independence granted at Brest-Litovsk. The Cossacks, too, aspired to statehood, electing their own *Krug* (assembly) and *Ataman* (chieftain). There seemed every likelihood that the old Russian Empire would fragment along ethnic lines into a hundred pieces. At first the Bolsheviks simply swam with the tide, proclaiming 'the right of all peoples to self-determination through to complete secession from Russia'. Anxious to learn from the pre-war problems of Austria-Hungary, they offered virtually every ethnic minority a measure of political autonomy. Ukrainians got their own Soviet Socialist Republic; so did Armenians, Byelorussians and Georgians. Tatars and Bashkirs were given autonomous republics within a new Russian federation; there was also a confusingly named Kirghiz (Kazakh) Republic. All told, there were around a hundred different nationalities recognized by the regime and granted, in proportion to their numbers and concentration, their own national republics, regions or townships. Jews were later given their own autonomous region in Birobidzhan, as well as seventeen Jewish townships in

Crimea and South Ukraine. Koreans were allowed a Korean National District around Posyet. The policy of Russification joined the rest of the old regime in Trotsky's rubbish bin of history; henceforth non-Russians would be schooled in their own language and encouraged to identify their ethnic identity with the Bolshevik regime.

Yet the man the Bolsheviks put in charge of implementing this policy, although himself a Georgian by birth, was an unlikely champion of minority rights. His name was Iosif Vissarionovich Dzhugashvili – Stalin ('man of steel'), to his fellow revolutionaries. As People's Commissar for Nationalities' Affairs he revealed from the outset that he understood the difference between outward form and inner content. Stalin saw at once that the nationalities question was spiralling out of control; reports of ethnic conflict were coming in from all over the country. In the Baltic states, fighting was raging between pro-Bolshevik forces – including ferocious Latvian riflewomen – and German landowners, assisted by so-called 'free corps' of bellicose German students and veterans who had not yet had their fill of fighting. This was a vicious conflict, in which both sides seemed 'bent on exterminating each other': 'Hate prevailed. In combat, prisoners were not taken – that was understood; in victory they were taken but then murdered, in a kind of ritual, to make the point about victory clear.' Similar conflicts raged all over the empire. In the Caucasus, Georgians fought Armenians; Armenians fought Azeris; Abkhazians fought Georgians. In May 1920 the entire Japanese population of the Far Eastern town of Nikolaievsk – 700 men, women and children – were massacred by Russian Bolsheviks. In Kazakhstan there was a mass expulsion of Slavic settlers and Cossacks; whole villages of Russians were literally 'driven out into the frost' by Kirghiz tribesmen.

Of all the Russian Empire's peoples, it might be thought, the Jews stood to gain most from a revolution. They could look forward to an end to the restrictions the old regime had placed on their freedom of movement and civil rights. And, indeed, the new regime did turn out to mean not just emancipation but unprecedented opportunities for social advancement for Jews in Russia – conditional upon their abandonment of Judaism and unswerving conformity to the Party line. In their tens of thousands they deserted the *shtetls* for the big cities, increasing the Jewish population of Moscow by a factor of nearly seventeen by 1939 and that of Petrograd (now renamed Leningrad) by a factor of six. Trotsky and Dzerzhinsky were only two of many Bolshevik leaders who were of Jewish origin. In the short term, however, the civil war merely meant an intensification of the violent persecution that had gone on in the Pale of Settlement since the 1880s. Some of the violence came, predictably enough, from the White forces, which included at least some of those ultra-nationalist elements that had been responsible for the programs of 1905. Denikin's forces were involved in brutal attacks on Jews in Ekaterinoslav; anti-Bolshevik Jews there complained that they had expected salvation from the Whites and instead had been subjected to rape and pillage. Non-Russian nationalists were also responsible for attacks on Jews; for example, Ukrainian nationalists also attacked Jews in Bratslav (Podolia), Dmitriev (Kursk) and Kiev itself. Often the perpetrators lumped 'Yids' and Bolsheviks together, echoing the counter-revolutionary rhetoric of 1905 and, of course, anticipating a standard trope of Central and East European anti-Semitism throughout the inter-war period.

Yet Bolshevik forces were also involved in attacks on Jews. Working-class food riots of the sort that occurred in towns and cities all over Europe in the last phase of the war tended to lead to the looting of shops; since these were often Jewish-owned in the provinces of the Pale, protests about prices or shortages could easily take on the character of pogroms. Such incidents occurred in 1917 in Kalush, Kiev, Kharkov, Roslavl (Smolensk) and Starosiniavy (Podolia). After the Bolshevik seizure of power, there were also pogrom-like incidents in Bograd (Bessarabia) and in Mozyr (Minsk). In November 1917, at the time of the elections to the Constituent Assembly, the Jewish journalist Ilya Ehrenburg heard a Bolshevik campaigner tell a queue of Muscovites: 'Those who are against the Yids – vote for list No. 5; those who are for the world revolution – vote for list No. 5', which was the Bolshevik list of candidates. In Cherepovets one Bolshevik leader brandished a revolver and shouted: 'Kill the Yids, save Russia!' A particularly brutal pogrom in Glukhov (Chernigov) in March 1918 was blamed on retreating Soviet forces. Likewise, Red Army instructors at Smolensk were accused of preparing 'a Massacre of St Bartholomew' for the Jews prior to the pogrom of May 1918. As the Red Army withdrew from territory ceded at Brest-Litovsk there was a spate of similar attacks on Jews. In November 1920 the Red Army's First Cavalry Army swept through the Jewish communities of Ukrainian towns like Rogachev, Baranovichi, Romanov and Chudnov, killing and looting as they went. Lenin himself was personally informed about pogroms in Minsk and Gomel the following year. His sole comment scrawled on the reports he received was: 'For the archives.' By the end of the civil war, pogroms in southern Russia and Ukraine had claimed up to 120,000 lives.

In clamping down on such behaviour, Stalin soon revealed that he was more than a match for Trotsky and Lenin when it came to ruthlessness. He approved concentration camps for anti-Bolshevik elements in Estonia, calling them 'excellent'. He ordered exemplary burnings of villages in the northern Caucasus, ordering local Bolsheviks to 'be absolutely merciless'. When the Bashkirian Revolutionary Committee showed signs of disloyalty, Stalin had its leaders arrested and brought to Moscow for interrogation. He forced Azerbaijan, Armenia and Georgia into a more easily controlled 'Transcaucasian Federation'. He yoked Chechens, Ossetians and Kabardians together in an autonomous Mountain Republic in the northern Caucasus. He dismissed the idea out of hand when one of his own staff, himself a young Tartar, proposed an independent Pan-Turkic republic. The aim of Bolshevik policy towards the Jews became 'to re-socialize the Jewish population so that it would become politically Bolshevized and sociologically Sovietized'. National autonomy, in other words, would be firmly within the context of a centralized one-party dictatorship. So hard did Stalin knock heads together in his native land that Lenin was prompted to accuse him of 'Great Russian chauvinism'. But as Lenin's health failed following a stroke in May 1922, Stalin was able to kill off the idea of a truly federal Union of Soviet Republics. If it had been left entirely to him, all the other republics would simply have been absorbed back into Russia. By the mid-1920s, the creation of Autonomous Soviet Republics in Moldavia and Karelia was motivated mainly by a desire to advertise the benefits of Soviet rule to neighbouring countries: such republics were to be to their peoples beyond the Soviet border what Piedmont had once been to Italy, a magnet for their national aspirations.

Between 1918 and 1922, around seven million men had fought in the Russian civil war. Of these, close to 1.5 million had lost their lives as a result of fighting, executions or disease. But that figure probably represents no more than a fifth of the war's victims. The chaos unleashed in the aftermath of the Revolution led to a severe famine in 1920–21. As malnourished refugees travelled in search of food, they succumbed to and spread contagious diseases, of which cholera and typhus claimed the most victims. There were also outbreaks of smallpox and plague, to say nothing of an epidemic of venereal disease, which afflicted 12 per cent of the population of Leningrad. The total number of deaths due to epidemics alone may have exceeded eight million. If this estimate is added to the figures for battlefield casualties, political murders and deaths due to famine, the excess mortality caused by the civil war approaches the global death toll for the First World War. Civilian casualties, including the wounded, outran military casualties nine to one. Between 1917 and 1920, it has been estimated, the population of the Soviet Union fell by around six million. For Western Europe, the war might have ended in November 1918, but for anyone living between Vilnius and Vladivostok the years after the 'end' of the First World War brought anything but peace. And the outcome? By the end of 1922, a new Russian Socialist Federal Republic extended from the Baltic to the Bering Straits. It, along with the far smaller Byelorussian, Ukrainian, Transcaucasian and Far Eastern republics, made up the new Union of Soviet Socialist Republics. Apart from a westward strip running from Helsinki down to Kishinev, remarkably little of the old Tsarist edifice had been lost – an astonishing outcome given the weakness of the Bolshevik position in the initial phase of the Revolution, and a testament to the effectiveness of their ruthless tactics in the civil war. In effect, then, one Russian empire had simply been replaced by another. The 1926 census revealed that slightly less than 53 per cent of the citizens of the Soviet Union regarded themselves as of Russian nationality, though nearly 58 per cent gave Russian as the language they knew best or most often used.

Some cynics added that the political system had not changed much either; for what was Lenin if not a Red Tsar, wielding absolute power through the Politburo of the Russian Communist Party (which, crucially, maintained direct control over the parties in the other republics)?* Yet that was to miss the vast change of ethos that separated the new empire from the old. Though there had been 'terrible' Tsars in Russia's past, the empire established by Lenin and his confederates was the first to be based on terror itself since the short-lived tyranny of the Jacobins in revolutionary France. At the same time, for all the Bolsheviks' obsession with Western revolutionary models, theirs was a revolution that looked east more than it looked west. Asked to characterize the Russian empire as it re-emerged under Lenin, most Western commentators would not have hesitated to use the word 'Asiatic'. That was also Trotsky's view: 'Our Red Army', he argued, 'constitutes an incomparably more powerful force in the Asian terrain of world politics than in European terrain.' Significantly, 'Asiatic' was precisely the word Lenin had used to describe Stalin.

## REDRAWING THE MAP

Was the port at the mouth of the River Vistula called Danzig, its German name? Or was it to be Gdańsk, as the Poles called it? Once a free, self-governing Hanseatic city under the protection of the Teutonic Knights, Danzig had recognized the sovereignty of the Polish crown from the mid-fifteenth century until the end of the eighteenth century. But in 1793 it was annexed by Prussia, then, after a brief period of independence during the Napoleonic era, in 1871 it became part of the German Reich. More than 90 per cent of the town's population were German. Most of the peasants in the surrounding countryside, however, were Polish or Slavonic Kashubes.

Danzig was one of countless questions to confront the Western leaders and their entourages when they gathered at Versailles in 1919. The great optimist and moralist among them, the Virginian-born and Presbyterian-raised US President Woodrow Wilson, believed he had the answers.† Some of these were familiar liberal nostrums, like free

---

* His successor, Stalin, was more self-consciously Tsarist. 'The Russian people are Tsarist,' he once observed. 'The people need a Tsar, whom they can worship.' He explained his position in the 1930s in a letter to his mother: 'Mama, do you remember our tsar? Well, I'm something like the tsar.'

† Having travelled some moral distance from his Welsh Methodist roots, the British

trade and freedom of the seas. Others built on pre-war and wartime proposals for collective security, arms control and an end to 'secret diplomacy'; from these Wilson fashioned his League of Nations, with its biblical 'Covenant'. The most radical of Wilson's schemes, however, envisaged a reordering of the European map on the basis of national 'self-determination'. From December 1914 onwards Wilson had argued that any peace settlement 'should be for the advantage of the European nations regarded as Peoples and not for any nation imposing its governmental will upon alien people'. In May 1915 he went further, asserting unequivocally that 'every people has a right to choose the sovereignty under which they shall live'. He repeated the point in January 1917 and elaborated on its implications in points five to thirteen of his Fourteen Points. According to Wilson's original draft of the Covenant, the League would not merely guarantee the territorial integrity of its member states but would be empowered to accommodate future territorial adjustments 'pursuant to the principle of self-determination'. This was not entirely novel, needless to say. British liberal thinkers since John Stuart Mill had been arguing that the homogeneous nation state was the only proper setting for a liberal polity, and British poets and politicians had spasmodically stuck up for the right to independence of the Greeks and the Italians, whom they tended to romanticize. When trying to imagine an ideal map of Europe in 1857, Giuseppe Mazzini had imagined just eleven nation states ordered on the basis of nationality. But never before had a statesman proposed to make national self-determination the basis for a new European order. In combination with the League, self-determination was to take precedence over the integrity of the sovereign state, the foundation of international relations since the Treaty of Westphalia two and a half centuries before.

Applying the principle of self-determination proved far from easy, however, for two reasons. First, as we have seen, there were more than thirteen million Germans already living east of the borders of the pre-war Reich – perhaps as much as a fifth of the total German-

---

Prime Minister David Lloyd George sneered that Wilson came to Paris 'like a missionary to rescue the heathen Europeans, with his "little sermonettes"'. His French counterpart Clemenceau reacted similarly to Wilson's sanctimony. Of Wilson's Fourteen Points he remarked acidly that God had been content with ten commandments.

speaking population of Europe. If self-determination were applied rigorously Germany might well end up bigger, which was certainly not the intention of Wilson's fellow peacemakers. From the outset, then, there had to be inconsistency, if not hypocrisy, in the way Germany was treated: no *Anschluss* of the rump Austria to the Reich – despite the fact that the post-revolutionary governments in both Berlin and Vienna voted for it – and no vote at all for the 250,000 South Tyroleans, 90 per cent of whom were Germans, on whether they wanted to become Italian, but plebiscites to determine the fate of northern Schleswig (which went to Denmark), eastern Upper Silesia (to Poland) and Eupen-Malmédy (to Belgium). France reclaimed Alsace and Lorraine, lost in 1871, despite the fact that barely one in ten of the population were French-speakers. In all, around 3.5 million German-speakers ceased to be German citizens under the terms of the Versailles Treaty. Equally important, under the terms of the 1919 Treaty of St Germain-en-Laye, more than 3.2 million Germans in Bohemia, southern Moravia and the hastily constituted Austrian province of Sudetenland found themselves reluctant citizens of a new state, Czechoslovakia. There were just under three-quarters of a million Germans in the new Poland, the same number again in the mightily enlarged Romania, half a million in the new South Slav kingdom later known as Yugoslavia and another half million in the rump Hungary left over after the Treaty of Trianon.

The second problem for self-determination was that none of the peacemakers saw it as applying to their own empires – only to the empires they had defeated. Wilson's original draft of Article III of the League Covenant had explicitly stated that:

Territorial adjustments . . . may in the future become necessary by reason of changes in present racial conditions and aspirations or present social and political relationships, pursuant to the principle of self-determination, and . . . may . . . in the judgment of three-fourths of the Delegates be demanded by the welfare and manifest interest of the peoples concerned.

This was too much even for the other Americans at Paris. Did Wilson seriously contemplate, asked General Tasker Bliss, 'the possibility of the League of Nations being called upon to consider such questions as the independence of Ireland, of India, etc., etc.?' His

Table 5.1: Germany's territorial and population losses under the Treaty of Versailles

| Territory | To | Area (km²) | Population in 1910 (000) | Of which, German-speakers | % | Of which, migrated to Reich by 1925 | % |
|---|---|---|---|---|---|---|---|
| Posen | Poland | 26,042 | 1,946 | 670 | 34 | 468 | 43 |
| West Prussia | Poland | 15,865 | 965 | 412 | 43 | | |
| Southern E. Prussia | Poland | 501 | 25 | 9 | 36 | | |
| Pomerania | Poland | 10 | 0.2 | 0.2 | 100 | | |
| Silesia | Poland | 512 | 26 | 9 | 35 | | |
| Danzig | Free city | 1,914 | 331 | 315 | 95 | 44 | 14 |
| Memel | Lithuania | 2,657 | 141 | 72 | 51 | 15 | 21 |
| E. Upper Silesia | Poland | 3,213 | 893 | 264 | 30 | 90 | 34 |
| Hultschin | Czechoslovakia | 316 | 48 | 7 | 15 | 3 | 43 |
| Northern Schleswig | Denmark | 3,992 | 166 | 40 | 24 | 12 | 30 |
| Eupen-Malmédy | Belgium | 1,036 | 60 | 49 | 82 | 5 | 10 |
| Alsace-Lorraine | France | 14,522 | 1,874 | 1,634 | 87 | 132 | 8 |
| TOTAL | | 70,580 | 6,475 | 3,481 | 54 | 769 | 22 |

colleague, the legal expert David Hunter Miller warned that such an Article would create permanent 'dissatisfaction' and 'irredentist agitation'. As a result, Wilson's draft was butchered. What became Article X merely reasserted the old Westphalian verity: 'The Members of the League undertake to respect and preserve as against external aggression the territorial integrity and existing political independence of all Members of the League.' As the British historian turned diplomat James Headlam-Morley sardonically noted: 'Self determination is quite *demodé*.' He and his colleagues 'determine[d] for them [the nationalities] what they ought to wish', though in practice they could not wholly ignore the results of the plebiscites in certain contested areas. There were, it is true, serious attempts to write 'minority rights' into the various peace treaties, beginning with Poland. But here again British cynicism and self-interest played an unconstructive role. Revealingly, Headlam-Morley was as sceptical of minority rights as he was of self-determination. As he noted in his *Memoir of the Paris Peace Conference*:

Some general clause giving the League of Nations the right to protect minorities in all countries which were members ... would give [it] the right to protect the Chinese in Liverpool, the Roman Catholics in France, the French in Canada, quite apart from more serious problems, such as the Irish ... Even if the denial of such a right elsewhere might lead to injustice and oppression, that was better than to allow everything which means the negation of the sovereignty of every state in the world.

The fate of Danzig illustrates the kind of bargains being struck. At the suggestion of the British Prime Minister, David Lloyd George, Danzig and the surrounding area (in all, just over 750 square miles) now reverted to its historic status as a free city, though it was now placed under League of Nations protection; the Poles were awarded their own free port, post office and control of the railways. Danzig had its own currency and stamps, but its foreign policy was determined in Warsaw. This was just part of a larger geographical anomaly. Danzig was roughly equidistant between Berlin, beyond the River Oder, and Warsaw further down the River Vistula. But the territory to the west of Danzig was now Polish since the formerly German provinces of West Prussia and Posen had been ceded to Poland, while the territory to the east, the province of East Prussia, remained German. The creation of the 'Polish Corridor' running from Upper Silesia to Danzig thus left East Prussia as a bleeding chunk of Germany between the Vistula and the Niemen. Was Danzig really a free city? Or was it actually a Polish captive? And was that also the true situation of East Prussia? To assert their claims, the Poles sought to monopolize the Danzig postal service; at the same time, they constructed a rival port, Gdynia, to divert commerce away from the Free City. Danzigers who wished to travel to Germany (including Prussia) required a Polish transit visa. The poisoned atmosphere generated by such petty sources of friction is well preserved in Günter Grass's Danzig trilogy, *The Tin Drum*, *Cat and Mouse* and *Dog Years*. It is no accident that the most memorable fictional personification of the German catastrophe, the stunted drummer Oscar Matzerath, is born in Danzig in 1924.

All over Europe there were similar collisions between the ideal of the nation state and the reality of multi-ethnic societies. Previously diversity had been accommodated by the loose structures of the old dynastic empires. Those days were now gone. The only way to proceed, if the peace was to produce viable political units, was to accept that most of the new nation states would have sizeable ethnic minorities (see Figure 5.2).

In the new Czechoslovakia, for example, 51 per cent of the population were Czechs, 16 per cent Slovaks, 22 per cent Germans, 5 per cent Hungarians and 4 per cent Ukrainians. In Poland around 14 per cent of the population were Ukrainians, 9 per cent Jews, 5 per cent Byelorussians and more than 2 per cent Germans. Roughly a third of the population of all the major cities was Jewish. Romania had reaped a handsome territorial dividend from her wartime sufferings, acquiring Bessarabia (from Russia), Bukovina (from Austria), southern Dobruja (from Bulgaria) and Transylvania (from Hungary). But the effect was that nearly one in three inhabitants of the country was not Romanian at all: 8 per cent were Hungarians, 4 per cent Germans, 3 per cent Ukrainians – in all there were eighteen ethnic minorities recorded in the 1930 census. The preponderance of non-Romanians was especially pronounced in urban areas. Even the Romanians themselves were divided along religious lines, between the Uniate Christians

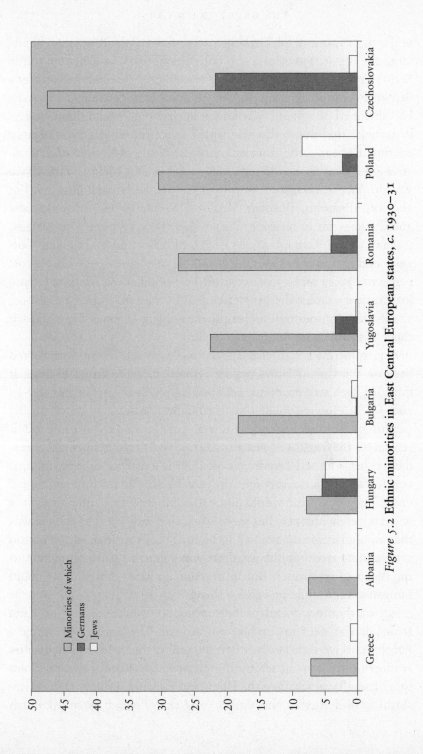

*Figure 5.2* Ethnic minorities in East Central European states, *c.* 1930–31

of Transylvania and the Orthodox Christians of the Romanian heartland, the Regat. Yugoslavia – initially known as 'The Kingdom of the
Serbs, Croats and Slovenes', which named only three of the country's
seventeen or more ethnic groups – was another hodgepodge. The Serbs
had dreamed of a South Slav kingdom that they would dominate; as
if to make that point, the new state's constitution was promulgated
on June 28, 1921, the anniversary of the Battle of Kosovo and of the
Archduke Francis Ferdinand's assassination. In reality, Yugoslavia
was an uneasy amalgam not just of Croats, Serbs and Slovenes, but
also of Albanians, Bosnian Muslims, Montenegrins, Macedonians
and Turks – not to mention Czechs, Germans, Gypsies, Hungarians,
Italians, Jews, Romanians, Russians, Slovaks and Ukrainians. Bulgaria and Hungary both retained sizeable minorities – accounting for,
respectively, 19 and 13 per cent of their populations, despite having
lost territory under the peace treaties. In these five countries alone,
around twenty-four million people were living in states that regarded
them as members of minority groups.

It is sometimes said that the Paris Peace settlement was flawed
because the United States Senate refused to ratify it; or because it
imposed such stiff economic reparations on Germany; or because its
vision of an international system of collective security based on the
League of Nations was not realistic. Yet the single most important
reason for the fragility of peace in Europe was the fundamental contradiction between self-determination and the existence of these minorities. It was, of course, theoretically possible that all the different ethnic
groups in a new state would agree to sublimate their differences in a
new collective identity. But more often than not what happened was
that a majority group claimed to be the sole proprietor of the nation
state and its assets. In theory, there was supposed to be protection of
the rights of minorities. But in practice the new governments could
not resist discriminating against them.

As for the new era of peace supposedly ushered in by the Paris
treaty, it was over in the blink of an eye. The borders of the new
Polish state were themselves determined as much by violence as by
voting or international arbitration. Between 1918 and 1921, the Poles
fought small wars against the Ukraine, Germany, Lithuania, Czechoslovakia and Russia; the upshot was that Poland extended much

further east than the peacemakers had planned. In Eastern Poland, Ukrainians were excluded from government employment; so hostile were they to the new Polish state that Ukrainian terrorist organizations were soon active, in turn provoking brutal pacification expeditions by the Polish authorities into the chronically unquiet *kresy*, the borderlands. Yet it would be too harsh to blame all this on President Wilson. It was not he who had called nationalism into being in Central and Eastern Europe; it had torn the Habsburg Empire apart even before he got to Paris. Moreover, as we have seen, Wilson had envisaged a strong League of Nations with the power to intervene and arbitrate in border disputes. It was hardly his fault that the US Senate refused to endorse this permanent 'entanglement' of the United States in the affairs of strife-torn Europe; hardly his fault that his efforts to sell the League to the American public precipitated a stroke which all but paralysed him for the last sixteen months of his presidency.

Two groups felt especially vulnerable in the new post-war order. The Germans, who had once been the dominant people in so much of Central and Eastern Europe, feared reprisals from the new masters of the successor states. And with good reason. German communities came under attack by Polish mobs in Bydgoszcz (formerly Bromberg) and Ostrowo (formerly Ostrow). In Czechoslovakia the Germans were effectively excluded from the 1919 elections; in clashes with Czech gendarmes and troops – the so-called massacre of Kaaden of March 14, 1919 – fifty-two Germans were killed and eighty-four wounded. Not that the Germans were in every case innocent victims. In many of the territories that were ceded by Germany and Austria they formed belligerent and often armed self-defence groups. The mood of the Germans in Bukovina was not untypical. Gregor von Rezzori had grown up near Czernowitz (now Cernaŭti) as the self-confidently German-speaking son of an Austrian official. He was bewildered by the transformation of his hometown when, along with the rest of Bukovina, it became a part of Romania. As he later recalled,

a thin foil of civilization appeared to have been superimposed on an untidily assorted ethnic conglomerate from which it could be peeled off all too readily ... The Romanians holding important government posts established themselves as the new masters under the aegis of the Romanian military establishment, which flaunted the brassy glitter of its fresh victory, and they remained largely isolated from those who spoke other languages and now were the minorities . . . the Jews in caftans . . . the rabbis and solid ethnic-German burghers in their stiff shirt-collars worn, according to local tradition, with wide knickerbockers and Tyrolean hats.

Rezzori's family withdrew into a kind of inner exile; they had, as he put it, 'ended up in a colony deserted by its colonial masters'. They were 'no longer masters of anything, taken over by another class to which we deemed ourselves superior but which, in fact, treated us as second-rate citizens because of the odium attached to an ethnic minority'. Romania was 'part of the East', whereas the Rezzoris 'felt definitely and consciously that we were "Occidentals"'. Of course, the Germans had never been anything other than a minority in the Bukovina. Around 38 per cent of the population were Ukrainians and 34 per cent were Romanians; a mere 9 per cent were Germans, though that proportion rose to 38 per cent in Czernowitz itself. Yet with its Habsburg bureaucracy and German university, Czernowitz had once seemed to be the gateway from 'Half-Asia' to 'Germandom'. Cernăuti, by contrast, was more of a German ghetto than a gateway – a place where Romanian students could with impunity storm the German Theatre to disrupt a performance of Schiller's *Die Räuber*. From mastery to minority represented a precipitous fall.

As the German case illustrates, it was not always violent persecution that the minorities suffered; it was more that as the economic role of the state expanded in the 1920s – most obviously when 'land reform' (meaning selective expropriation and redistribution) was attempted or industries nationalized – so the opportunities for real and imagined discrimination also grew. German schools were closed down by the Czech authorities, while new Czech schools were built even in towns where only a few Czech families lived. Similar things went on in Poland, though the discrimination against Ukrainian and Byelorussian schools was more severe. Literally not one secondary school existed for ethnic minorities in inter-war Hungary, though there were 467 German primary schools. The Romanian authorities drove German-speaking teachers out of Bukovina if their grasp of Romanian was insufficient; one effect was to cripple the German literature department of Czernowitz's once renowned university. German civil servants in Czechoslovakia were obliged to pass an examination in Czech; the effect was to halve the proportion of Germans in the civil service. The Polish post office refused to deliver letters addressed to the old German place names in West Prussia and Posen. In the same spirit, the Italian authorities forced the Germans of the Tyrol to learn Italian, while at the same time offering incentives to Italians to settle in the province. Political organization by German minorities was also hampered. In 1923, for example, the Polish government banned the Bydgoszcz-based Germandom League (*Deutschtumsbund*). Small wonder so many Germans opted to leave the so-called 'lost territories' and resettle in the reduced Reich. By 1926 some 85 per cent of the Germans in the towns of West Prussia and the formerly Prussian province of Posen had left. Those who remained were mostly isolated farmers or defiant landowners like the family of Oda Goerdeler, whose East Prussian estate became part of Działdowo county. As she recalled, the German community to which she belonged was 'haunted by feelings of superiority, which had previously been taken for granted'. After 1919 they simply 'sealed [themselves] off from the Polish element'.

Yet the most vulnerable minority in Central and Eastern Europe were – as in the Russian civil war – not the Germans but the Jews. The very moment of national independence in many countries was marred by outbreaks of anti-Jewish violence. In the Slovakian town of Holesov, for example, two Jews were killed and virtually the entire Jewish quarter was gutted. In Lwów Polish troops ran amok in Jewish neighbourhoods, incensed by Jewish protestations of neutrality in the contest for the city between Poles and Ukrainians. A program at Chrzanow in November 1918 saw widespread looting and pillaging of Jewish homes and businesses; in Warsaw synagogues were burned. Further east, there were also pogroms in Vilnius and Pińsk – where Polish troops shot thirty-five people for the offence of distributing charitable donations from the United States – while in Hungary there was an anti-Semitic 'White Terror' following the suppression of the Jewish socialist Béla Kun's short-lived soviet regime in Budapest. The revolutionary movement cut through these and other Jewish communities like a double-edged sword. Sometimes they were accused of having sided with the Germans during the war; sometimes they were accused of siding with the Bolsheviks during the Revolution.

Violence gave way to discrimination during the 1920s, despite the fine words of the Minorities Treaties. In Poland Sunday became a compulsory day of rest for all. Jews who could not prove pre-war residence were denied Polish citizenship. It was difficult for a Jew to become a schoolteacher; to become a university professor was next to impossible. State assistance was made available to Polish schools only, not to Jewish schools. The number of Jewish students at Polish universities fell by half between in 1923 and 1937. As one Polish politician put it, the Jewish community was 'a foreign body, dispersed in our organism so that it produces a pathological deformation. In this state of affairs it is impossible to find a way out other than the removal of the alien body, harmful through both its numbers and its uniqueness.' The leader of the Nationalist Party, Roman Dwomski, spoke in similar terms. Not untypical of the post-war mood was the poem that appeared in *Przegląd powszechny* in December 1922:

> Jewry is contaminating Poland thoroughly:
> It scandalizes the young, destroys the unity of the common people.
> By means of the atheistic press it poisons the spirit,
> Incites to evil, provokes, divides . . .
> A terrible gangrene has infiltrated our body
> And we . . . are blind!
> The Jews have gained control of Polish business,
> As though we were imbeciles,
> And they cheat, extort, and steal,
> While we feed on fantasies,
> Our indolence grows in strength and size,
> And we . . . are blind!

Things were not a great deal better in Romania. Jews were not given full citizenship unless they had served in the Romanian army or been born of two parents both of whom had also been born in Romania. Jewish enrolment in universities was restricted. In Bukovina the introduction of a Romanian school-leaving examination in 1926 caused all but two out of ninety-four Jewish candidates to fail. Only through bribery could non-Romanian candidates hope to pass.

There were three possible responses to such discrimination. The first was to leave. Yet despite the importance of Zionism in Polish-Jewish politics, only a small proportion of Polish Jews drew the conclusion that they would be better off trying to find a Jewish state in the new 'home' their people had been granted in what was now the British 'mandate' in Palestine. Even in the 1930s just 82,000 Polish Jews emigrated there, though as we shall see this also reflected British nervousness about the effect of continued Jewish immigration on Palestine's internal stability. In fact, only a minority of Polish Zionists were committed to systematic colonization of the Holy Land; the majority were just as interested in what could be achieved in Poland itself. It was easier in more ways than one for a West Prussian to leave Poland for neighbouring Germany than for a Jew to leave Poland for the more distant Holy Land.

A second possibility was to withdraw into a more or less segregated Jewish society within a society. This came quite naturally to the relatively poor Yiddish-speaking Ashkenazim of the Galician *shtetl*, the majority of whom still cleaved to Orthodox observance and attire and would probably have chosen segregation under any circumstances. But segregation was not unique to them. Itzik Manger, the leading Yiddish poet, spoke no Polish despite having lived in Warsaw for years. In Antoni Słonimski's words, there was an 'ethnic border which ran through the town somewhere around Bielanska Street, separating Srodmiescie from the Jewish district'. 'The ghetto district of Craców', remarked the British author Hugh Seton-Watson, 'is little less different from the Christian quarter than is an Arab town from the west end of London.' Segregation was more than a residential phenomenon. Typically, there was a Polish socialist party and two Jewish socialist parties, the *Bund* and Zionist *Poale Zion*. There was a thriving Yiddish and Hebrew press and a proliferation of Yiddish and Hebrew schools. Rich Jews went to different holiday resorts from rich Poles. They might deal with Poles when it came to business, but their relations went no further. In Poland Judaism was not just a religion; it was also a national identity. Clear majorities of those who described themselves as Jewish by religion – 74 per cent in the census of 1921 – also described themselves as Jewish by nationality.

The third possibility was assimilation. In Brańsk, for example, Jewish and Polish children played together in a band that performed at parties and weddings. In Kołomyja friendships between Poles and Jews were so common that it was said 'every Jew has his Pole'. Even on the edge of Kazimierz, the Jewish quarter of Kraków, it was possible to live 'in a sort of isolation from Polish society' while at the same time 'absorbing Polish culture, Polish poetry, or Polish music and art in the depths of [one's] being'. To the generation of Polish Jews who grew up in the 1920s this was a widely shared experience; a majority of them attended Polish language schools. Yet even those Jews who had long sought assimilation, like the Magyarized Jews of Budapest, the Romanized Jews of Bucharest or the Germanized Jews of Prague, found they were viewed with only slightly less suspicion than the Orthodox Jews of the *shtetls*. Trudi Levi, both of whose parents were atheists, grew up on the Hungarian-Austrian border speaking both Magyar and German with equal fluency; but the Hungarian authorities insisted that all Jews learn Hebrew even if, like the Levis, they had abandoned religious observance. Elizabeth Wiskemann was shocked to find Sudeten Germans boycotting Jewish shops by the early 1930s, not something that would have happened in pre-war Bohemia. Many Prague Jews became conscious of their Jewish origins only when they encountered such anti-Semitism. Abraham Rotfarb, a Jew born and raised in Warsaw, expressed the acute, agonizing vulnerability that so many assimilated Jews came to feel in the inter-war years:

I am a poor assimilated soul. I am a Jew and a Pole, or rather I was a Jew, but gradually under the influence of my environment, under the influence of the place where I lived, and under the influence of the language, the culture, and the literature, I have also become a Pole. I loved Poland. Its language, its culture, and most of all the fact of its liberation and the heroism of its independent struggle, all pluck at my heartstrings and fire my feelings and enthusiasm. But I do not love that Poland which, for no apparent reason, hates me, that Poland which tears at my heart and soul, which drives me into a state of apathy, melancholy, and dark depression. Poland has taken away my happiness, it has turned me into a dog who, not having any ambitions of his own, asks only not to be abandoned in the wasteland of culture but to be drawn along the road of Polish cultural life. Poland has brought me up as a Pole, but brands me a Jew who has to be driven out. I want to be a Pole, you have not let me; I want to be a Jew, but I don't know how, I have become alienated from Jewishness. (I do not like myself as a Jew.) I am already lost.

The two minorities with the most to lose under the new post-war dispensation might conceivably have made common cause. In cities like Prague, after all, the relationship between Germans and Jews had long been characterized by symbiosis more than conflict. Throughout the 1920s Jews in Czechoslovakia were far more likely to send their children to German-speaking than to Czech-speaking schools. When riots broke out in Prague in November 1920, following reports that a Czech school had been forcibly closed down in Cheb, both Germans and Jews were attacked. The Latvian Thunder Cross pledged to 'eradicate with sword and fire every German, Jew, Pole and even Latvian who threatens Latvian independence and welfare'. Indeed, there were Jews, like Yitzhak Gruenbaum, the Polish Zionist leader, who sincerely hoped for a united front of German and Jewish minorities. Yet far from uniting in their common adversity, insecure Germans turned against even more insecure Jews. In 1920 and again in 1923 demonstrations in favour of keeping Upper Silesia German escalated into pogrom-like attacks on Jewish property. As early as 1925, doctors in Breslau founded a medical association that excluded Jews and began campaigning for a boycott of Jewish doctors. Gregor von Rezzori described how Romanians and Germans alike could agree on one thing: their contempt for Jews. An encounter between a Romanian youth 'wearing the well-known costume of short, sleeveless and colourfully embroidered sheepskin jacket, and coarse linen shirt over linen trousers tightly belted in blue-yellow-and-red' and a German student, dressed in the uniform of one of the German duelling fraternities ('stiff collar, kepi worn at a snappy angle, fraternity colours displayed across the chest on a broad ribbon') might have come to blows. But on this occasion

both are distracted by the appearance of a Hasidic rabbi in black caftan, with the pale skin of a bookworm and long corkscrew side-locks under a fox-pelt hat, an apparition that forthwith unites the former opponents in the happy recognition that the newcomer is the natural target of their aggression.

As Rezzori recalled, all the other groups in Cernaŭti 'despised the Jews, notwithstanding that Jews not only played an economically decisive role but, in cultural matters, were the group who nurtured traditional values as well as newly developing ones'. This was not a traditional attitude but something new. As we have seen, prior to Bukovina's incorporation in Romania, Germans and Jews had attended the same schools and been members of the same cultural associations. Between the wars this harmony gradually vanished. Few towns in Eastern Europe had seen a more advanced German-Jewish symbiosis. But here, as elsewhere in East Central Europe, there was to be no solidarity between the minorities; quite the reverse.

## THE DEATH THROES OF EMPIRE

It was not just East Central Europe that posed a challenge for the peacemakers, however. In the erstwhile territory of the Ottoman Empire the fate of other multi-ethnic societies also had to be decided. These were not European societies, so naturally the West European powers assumed that they represented potential additions to their overseas empires. In 1916 the British and French agreed between themselves to carve up large tracts of the Ottoman territory, the former claiming what was to become Palestine, Jordan and the greater part of Iraq (then known as Mesopotamia), the latter Syria and the rest of Iraq. Under the terms of the Treaty of Sèvres these arrangements were confirmed and extended to satisfy the territorial cravings of other victorious powers. The Italians were given the Dodecanese Islands, including Rhodes and the Anatolian port of Kastellorizzo. The Greeks were to have Thrace and Western Anatolia, including the port of Smyrna (today Izmir). Armenia, Assyria and the Hejaz (now part of Saudi Arabia) were to be independent. Plebiscites were to decide the fate of Kurdistan and the area around Smyrna. Sèvres was to do for the Ottoman Empire what St Germain-en-Laye had done for the Habsburg Empire: to sheer it right down to the bone, but on the basis of imperialism rather than nationalism – though the British and French acquisitions were labelled 'mandates' rather than colonies, in deference to American and Arab sensibilities.

Yet all this presupposed that the Middle East could be treated as the passive object of traditional imperial designs. In reality, the same nationalist aspirations and ethnic conflicts that were creating such upheaval in Central and Eastern Europe were also at work on the other side of the Black Sea straits. The difference was that in Europe these forces worked slowly. It took nearly two decades to nullify the terms of the Treaty of St Germain-en-Laye. The Treaty of Sèvres, by contrast, was a dead letter within a matter of months.

Even before the outbreak of the First World War, Turkey had been evolving from an empire into a nation state, inspired by the teachings of Ziya Gökalp, the prophet of a homogeneous Turkey with a uniform national culture (harsı millet). In 1908 the Young Turks – a group of intellectuals like Gökalp and army officers like Ismail Enver – had emerged as the dominant force in Ottoman politics. Their Committee of Union and Progress (CUP) aimed at modernizing the Empire lest it become simply another Asian subsidiary of the West or suffer a lingering death by a thousand territorial cuts. By 1913 they were in control in Constantinople. Like the Japanese before them, the Young Turks had taken the Germans as their role models. Colmar Freiherr von der Goltz acted as a military adviser to the Sultan between 1883 and 1895, though his influence was largely confined to officer training. In January 1914 another German general, Otto Liman von Sanders, was appointed the army's Inspector General; meanwhile German bankers were cajoled by their government into financing the extension of the Berlin–Constantinople railway line as far as Baghdad. The Young Turks' subsequent decision to join in the war on the side of Germany followed more or less logically from these initiatives. Nor was it strategically irrational, given the secret promises the British government had made to hand the Black Sea straits to Russia in the event of a swift Entente victory, and their own designs on the oilfields of Mesopotamia.

For all their modernizing rhetoric, however, the Young Turks had suffered only reverses since coming to power. Bulgaria had declared independence and Austria had annexed Bosnia-Herzegovina. The

Italians had occupied Libya. The Serbs and their confederates had defeated them in the First Balkan War, leaving a small piece of Thrace around Adrianople (Edirne) as the sole remnant of their Balkan empire. These experiences deepened the Young Turks' mistrust of the non-Turkish populations within their borders. The far worse ravages of war* against the combined might of the British, French and Russian empires turned mistrust into murder, with malice aforethought. Nothing illustrates more clearly that the worst time to live under imperial rule is when that rule is crumbling. Not for the last time in the twentieth century, the decline and fall of an empire caused more bloodshed than its rise.

Like the Jews in Central and Eastern Europe, the Armenians were doubly vulnerable: not only a religious minority, but also a relatively wealthy group, disproportionately engaged in commerce. Like the Jews, they were heavily, though by no means exclusively, concentrated in one border region: the six *vilayets* (provinces) of Bitlis, Van, Erzurum, Mamuretülaziz, Diyarbakir and Sivas, on the Ottoman Empire's eastern frontier. Like the Jews, although more credibly, the Armenians could be identified as sympathizing with an external threat, namely Russia, historically the Ottoman Empire's most dangerous foe. Like the Serbs, they had their extremists, who aimed at independence through violence. There had in fact been state-sponsored attacks against them before.† In the mid-1890s irregular Kurdish troops had been unleashed against Armenian villages as the Ottoman authorities tried to reassert the Armenians' subordinate status as infidel *dhimmis*, or non-Muslim citizens. The American ambassador estimated the number of people killed at more than 37,000. There was a fresh outbreak of violence at Adana in 1909, though this was not instigated by the Young Turks. The murderous campaign launched against the Armenians from 1915 to 1918 was qualitatively different, however;

---

* It cannot be without significance that a very high proportion of Ottoman casualties were incurred in the first year of the war, which accounted for 64 per cent of those killed in action, 41 per cent of those missing in action, 33 per cent of those who died as a result of wounds and 58 per cent of those who were permanently incapacitated by wounds. Total wartime losses were in relative terms the highest of the war.
† It was in 1892 that an Ottoman official told the French ambassador at Constantinople: 'The Armenian Question does not exist, but we shall create it.'

so much so that it is now widely acknowledged to have been the first true genocide. With good reason, the American consul in Smyrna declared that it 'surpasse[d] in deliberate and long-protracted horror and in extent anything that has hitherto happened in the history of the world'.

To this day, the Turkish government refuses to acknowledge the Armenian genocide. This is strange, since the historical evidence of what happened is plentiful. Western observers like the US ambassador in Constantinople, Henry Morgenthau, wrote detailed reports about what was being done – including the telling statement of Mehmed Talaat Pasha, the Interior Minister, that all the Armenians had to perish because 'those who were innocent today might be guilty tomorrow'. Western missionaries too wrote harrowing accounts of what they witnessed. Their testimony formed an important part of the wartime report on 'The Treatment of the Armenians' compiled by Viscount Bryce, who had also investigated the German atrocities in Belgium in 1914. It might conceivably be argued that the citizens of Christian powers already – or later to be – hostile to the Turks had an interest in misrepresenting them. The Young Turks themselves insisted that they were merely retaliating against a pro-Russian fifth column. That was also the line taken by the Sultan in his reply to Pope Benedict XV's intercession on behalf of the Armenians.

Yet agents of the Turks' own wartime allies gave the lie to these claims. Rafael de Nogales, a South American mercenary who served as Inspector General of the Turkish forces in Armenia, reported that the Governor-General of the province had ordered the local authorities in Adil Javus 'to exterminate all Armenian males of twelve years of age and over'. A German schoolteacher at Aleppo was appalled by what he saw of the 'extermination of the Armenian nation' and wrote urging his own government to 'put a stop to the brutality'. According to Joseph Pomiankowski, the Austrian Military Plenipotentiary in Constantinople, the Turks had undertaken the 'eradication of the Armenian nation in Asia Minor' (he used the terms *Ausrottung* and *Vernichtung*). Pomiankowski rejected the Turkish government's claim that they were acting in response to a concerted Armenian insurrection. The alleged 'uprisings' at Van and elsewhere were, in his view, 'acts of desperation' by Armenians who 'recognized that the general butchery had begun and would soon come to them'. One of his colleagues in the Austrian embassy referred to the Turkish 'extermination of the Armenian race'. His ambassador called the massacres 'a stain on the Turkish government', for which the Turks would one day be held to account. The German ambassador was, by contrast, reluctant to express disapproval, but German sources nevertheless confirm that mass murder was being perpetrated. There is even contemporary Turkish testimony that corroborates these reports. One Turkish officer ordered to deport the Armenians from Trebizond admitted that he 'knew that deportations meant massacres'.

The measures taken by the Turks were quite systematic. To begin with, Armenian men of military age were called up. Their political and religious leaders were arrested and deported. The violence mostly took place in 1915, though there were isolated incidents at the end of 1914. Armenian villages in the vicinity of Van were burned down, and the men and boys older than ten massacred. The more attractive young women were raped and abducted. Women, children and the elderly were driven towards the Persian frontier, often having been stripped. Usually the perpetrators plundered the homes of their victims. Money and other valuables were stolen. Rape was rampant. At Trebizond in July 1915 hundreds of Armenian men were 'taken out of town in batches of 15 or 20, lined up on the edge of ditches prepared beforehand, shot, and thrown into the ditches'. The bodies of thousands of men, women and children from Bitlis and Zaart were dumped in the river or nearby ravines. Similar atrocities occurred in so many different places during 1915 that the existence of a deliberate plan for a violent 'solution' of the Armenian question cannot seriously be disputed. Equally well organized were the deportations of the Armenian women, children and old people. Trains ran along the Baghdad Railway carrying tens of thousands of them, crammed into carriages eighty or ninety at a time. Beyond the railheads people were made to walk literally until they dropped. For those who were marched half-naked and without water through the Syrian desert, 'deportation' meant death. The Bavarian theologian Josef Engert summed up these horrors in a memorandum to Eugenio Pacelli, the Papal nuncio and future Pope Pius XII:

Around a million Armenians perished ... Even if the Armenians were guilty of revolt (the proof has not yet been furnished because certain German officials assured me at the front that only great need and incessant torture caused the Armenians to take up ... arms ... ) of what are [the] women and children guilty? The destiny of these miserable ones was still more horrible than that of the men: by the thousand they were abandoned in deserts and steppes, where they were left to hunger and thirst and to every sort of suffering ... Thousands of women and girls were sold ... and passed from owner to owner for a sum of twenty lira. They were consigned to harems and made concubines ... The boys were abandoned to Turkish orphanages and compelled to adopt the Islamic religion ... The Turkish affirmation that 'The Armenian question is answered for us' in reality meant the extermination of the Armenians.

As Engert's account makes clear, forced conversions also occurred, especially for young women and children; apostasy and sexual subjugation were alternative solutions to the 'Armenian question'. But death was clearly the Young Turks' first choice.* The number of Armenian men, women and children who were killed or died prematurely may have been even higher than a million, a huge proportion of a pre-war population that numbered, at the very most, 2.4 million, but was probably closer to 1.8 million. These acts, in short, were much more than pogroms in the Russian style.

The Armenian genocide was a horrific illustration of the convulsions that could seize a multi-ethnic polity trying to mutate from empire into nation state. As the Archbishop of Aleppo vainly protested: 'We don't wish to separate ourselves from the Turkish state. A separation would be impossible, since nationalities and religions are so mixed that a pure division by nations is impossible. Additionally, the various groups are economically interdependent, one upon the other, in such a way that, should a division come, they would be destroyed.' The methods used wilfully to destroy the Armenians – the train journeys

---

* The evidence that Talaat expressly ordered massacres in telegrams to provincial officials is controversial. It has been claimed that the telegrams were forgeries, but the originals were cited in the post-war trial of Talaat's assassin and the court did not question their authenticity. Incriminating exchanges between Talaat and other Turkish officials were also intercepted by the British.

to hellish wildernesses, the death marches, the neat rows of emaciated bodies – would be imitated and refined in the decades ahead, though it would be wrong to infer a direct link between Armenia and Auschwitz from the direct complicity of a few German soldiers in the first genocide,* much less from the German military's fondness for the term 'annihilation'.†

Yet this was only the beginning of a wave of ethnic conflict that would fundamentally transform the social structure of the lands between the Aegean and the Black Sea.

The Greek population of western Anatolia and the Black Sea littoral (the Pontus) had numbered around two million on the eve of the First World War. Their communities were very ancient; they had been there for more than two thousand years, a fact to which magnificent edifices like the theatre at Ephesus bore witness. They continued to thrive in the modern world, as any visitor to the busy waterfront of Smyrna could see. Yet as early as October 1915 the German military attaché reported to Berlin that Enver wanted 'to solve the Greek problem during the war . . . in the same way that he believes he solved the Armenian problem'. The process began in Thrace. It was in fact more

---

* The anonymous German author of *Horrors of Aleppo* was deeply worried that his country would be blamed for the fate of the Armenians. *'Ta'alim el aleman* [the teaching of the Germans]', he reported, was 'the simple Turk's explanation to everyone who asks him about the originators of these measures [against the Armenians]'. He also noted the 'ominous silence' on the part of German officers when the subject of the Armenians was raised. This tallies with the case of a German officer who reprimanded a subordinate for putting his signature on a document relating to the Armenian deportations. The American consul in Aleppo certainly regarded the Germans as having 'condoned . . . the extermination of the Armenian race'. Indeed, the Austrian consul in Trebizond believed that the Germans had given the 'first encouragement' for the 'neutralization' (*Unschädlichmachung*) of the Armenians, but added that they had envisaged less drastic means (presumably forced conversion). His counterpart in Adrianople reported that German officers had been present during deportations of Armenians 'and had not lifted a finger to prevent them'. For his part, Morgenthau was shocked by the hostility of the German ambassador and the German naval attaché towards the Armenians when he raised the issue with them. The latter told him: 'Both Armenians and Turks cannot live together in this country. One of these races has got to go.'

† See, for example, 'When . . . we speak of the defeat of the enemy, we mean that, by the annihilation of a portion of his fighting power, we make him despair altogether of any subsequent favourable turn in the hostilities.' (Goltz, *Conduct of War*, p. 8)

plausible for the Turks to portray the Greeks as a fifth column, since the Greek Prime Minister Eleftherios Venizelos strongly favoured Greek intervention on the side of the Entente powers and, although King Constantine resisted until finally driven to abdicate in June 1917, the presence of an Anglo-French force at Salonika from October 1915 cast doubt on the credibility of Greek neutrality. Viewed from Salonika, the First World War was the Third Balkan War, with Bulgaria joining Germany and Austria in the rout of Serbia; indeed, it was to shore up the disintegrating Serbian position that the Entente powers had sent their troops to Salonika. It was too late. The Anglo-French force remained penned in, unable, despite Greece's belated entry into the war, to prevent the German-Bulgarian defeat of Romania in 1917. Yet the final phase of the war saw a collapse as complete as that suffered by the Germans on the Western Front. An offensive on the Salonika Front forced Bulgaria to sue for peace on September 25, 1918; six days later the British marched into Damascus, having defeated the Turkish army in Syria. On October 30 the Turks surrendered.

For Venizelos it was a moment of intoxicating triumph. He had begun his political career by leading the revolt that had driven the Turks out of Crete; he had led Greece to victory in the First and Second Balkan Wars; he had finally got his way over the Third, and won that too. Now he saw an opportunity to extend Greek power further, from the Peloponnese across the Aegean to Anatolia itself. It was in fact the British government that initially encouraged Greek forces to occupy Smyrna. Lloyd George's motive was to forestall Italian moves to annex the city; mutinous Italian troops, led by the flamboyant poet Gabriele D'Annunzio, had already acted unilaterally by occupying Fiume on the Adriatic in defiance of the other members of the Big Four. At first the campaign went the Greeks' way. They advanced deep into Anatolia. In the best traditions of classical Greek drama, however, hubris was soon followed by nemesis. The crisis of defeat had led to revolution in Turkey. In April 1920 a Grand National Assembly was established in Ankara, which repudiated the Treaty of Sèvres and offered the post of President to the fair-haired, blue-eyed, hard-drinking General Mustafa Kemal. Almost simultaneously, Venizelos fell from power in Athens and the

British, French and Italians withdrew their support for the Greek expedition.*

Born in Salonika, Kemal had played a key role in the defence of Gallipoli against British invasion in 1915. He now masterminded the expulsion of the Greeks from Anatolia. After fierce fighting in the area of Eskişehir, 100 miles west of Ankara, the Greeks cracked. Those who did not surrender took to their heels. As they fled towards the Aegean, their ranks were swelled by tens of thousands of civilians, hoping that in Smyrna they would find protection from the reprisals already being taken against Greek communities along the Black Sea littoral, who were being deported and in some cases massacred much as the Armenians had been seven years before. There was in fact still a large Armenian community living in Smyrna, who had been spared during the war, possibly at the insistence of General Liman von Sanders. In September 1922, however, Kemal's army occupied the town. They sealed off the Armenian quarter and began systematically butchering its 25,000 inhabitants. Then they set fire to it, to incinerate any survivors. The American consul, George Horton, described the unfolding horror:

At first, civilian Turks, natives of the town, were the chief offenders. I myself saw such civilians armed with shotguns watching the windows of Christian houses ready to shoot at any head that might appear. These had the air of hunters crouching and stalking their prey ... The hunting and killing of Armenian men, either by hacking or clubbing or driving out in squads into the country and shooting, caused an unimaginable panic ... I saw a young couple wade out into the sea. They were a respectable, attractive pair and the man was carrying in his arms a small child. As they waded deeper and deeper into the water, till it came nearly up to their shoulders, I suddenly realized that they were going to drown themselves.

The London *Daily Mail*'s reporter filed copy that might have been lifted straight from *The War of the Worlds*:

---

* This switch was famously attributed by Churchill, as an example of the role of chance in history, to the death of the Greek King Alexander from a monkey bite in October 1920. The restoration of his Germanophile father Constantine was not calculated to please the Western powers, given his refusal to join their side during the war.

What I see . . . is an unbroken wall of fire, two miles long; against this curtain of fire, which blocks out the sky, are silhouetted the towers of the . . . churches, the domes of the mosques, and the flat square roofs of the houses . . . The sea glows a deep copper-red, and, worst of all, from the densely packed mob of thousands of refugees huddled on the narrow quay, between the advancing fiery death behind and the deep water in front, comes continuously such a frantic screaming of sheer terror as can be heard miles away.

When the desperate refugees arrived at the quayside they saw a flotilla of foreign ships in the harbour – more than twenty British, French and American warships. It must have seemed as if salvation was at hand. Yet the Western forces did next to nothing; not for the last time in twentieth-century history, an international contingent looked on as (in the phrase of one British diplomat) 'a deliberate plan to get rid of minorities' was carried out. What better symbol could be imagined of the decline of the West, than the brutal expulsion of the heirs of Hellenic civilization from Asia Minor – except perhaps the utter failure of the heirs of ancient Greek democracy to do anything to prevent it?

To the appalled George Horton, who desperately tried to buy a few Greeks and Armenians safe passage with his own money, the destruction of Smyrna was 'but the closing act in a consistent programme of exterminating Christianity throughout the length and breadth of the old Byzantine Empire; the expatriation of an ancient Christian civilization'. The idea persists that religion was the principal motivation for what happened. Yet the emergent Turkish republic was not an Islamic state; on the contrary, Kemal would later introduce the separation of religion and state and abort moves towards parliamentary democracy precisely in order to stop a nascent Islamist opposition from reversing this. In reality, what happened between 1915 and 1922 was more ethnic cleansing than holy war. As Horton himself noted bitterly: 'The problem of the minorities is here solved for all time.' The *New York Times* detected the sexual dimension of Turkish policy, reporting that 'the Turks frankly do not understand why they should not get rid of the Greeks and Armenians from their country and take their women into their harems if they are sufficiently good looking.' Kemal saw no need to massacre all the Greeks in Smyrna, though a substantial number of able-bodied men were marched inland, suffering assaults by Turkish villagers along the way. He merely gave the Greek government until October 1 to evacuate them all. By the end of 1923 more than 1.2 million Greeks and 100,000 Armenians had been forced from their ancestral homes. The Greeks responded in kind. In 1915 some 60 per cent of the population of Western Thrace had been Muslims and 29 per cent of the population of Macedonia. By 1924 the figures had plunged to 28 per cent and zero per cent, their places taken by Greeks.

The Armenian genocide, the massacres of the Pontic Greeks and the agreed 'exchanges' of Greek and Turkish populations after the sack of Smyrna illustrated with a terrible clarity the truth of the Archbishop of Aleppo's warning: when a multi-ethnic empire mutated into a nation state, the result could only be carnage. It was as if, for the sake of a spuriously modern uniformity, the basest instincts of ordinary men were unleashed in a kind of tribal bloodletting. There was certainly no meaningful economic rationale for what happened. Along the Anatolian coast it is still possible to find ruined villages whose inhabitants were forced to flee in 1922 but which were never subsequently reoccupied. At least five hundred people must once have lived in the village of Sazak, not far from what is now the holiday resort of Karaburun. With its well-built stone houses and its steep cobbled streets, Sazak has the air of vanished peasant prosperity. Now it is a ghost town, visited only by wandering goats and sea mists – a desolate memorial to the death throes of an empire.

## THE GRAVES OF NATIONS

The old multi-national empires of continental Europe had been the architects of their own destruction. Like train drivers knowingly steaming full tilt towards one another, they themselves had caused the great train crash of 1914. But though it spelt the end of four dynasties and the creation of ten new independent nation states, the end of the war did not mean the end of empire. The British and French empires grew fatter on the remnants of their foes' domains. Meanwhile, two of the defunct empires were able to reconstitute themselves with astonishing speed and violence. A new and more ruthless Russian empire emerged behind the façade of the Union of Soviet Socialist Republics. A new and less tolerant Turkey was born in Ankara, abandoning the ruins of the Sublime Porte, just as the Bolsheviks had moved their capital eastwards to Moscow.

And what of the Germans, who had lost not one but two empires in the débâcle of 1918 and who now found themselves divided up between two rump republics, with a diaspora scattered across more than seven other states? Keynes, who proved to be the most influential of all the critics of the Paris Peace, was quite right to foresee a period of severe economic crisis in Germany, though how far the hyper-inflation of 1922–3 was a direct consequence of the Versailles Treaty, as opposed to German fiscal and monetary mismanagement, remains debatable. Keynes's remedy was clear: reparations should be set at the relatively modest level of £4 billion, to be paid in thirty annual instalments starting in 1923.* Germany should be lent money, allowed to trade freely, encouraged to rebuild her economy. This was not a matter of altruism, but enlightened self-interest. For there could be no stability in Central Europe without a German economic recovery.

'Unless her great neighbours are prosperous and orderly,' Keynes remarked in the final chapter of his *Economic Consequences*, 'Poland is an economic impossibility with no industry but Jew-baiting.' With Russia in chaos, the only salvation could come through 'the agency of German enterprise and organisation'. Hence the Western powers must 'encourage and assist Germany to take up again her place in Europe as a creator and organiser of wealth for her eastern and southern neighbours'. The alternative would be 'a final civil war between the forces of reaction and the despairing convulsions of revolution, before which the horrors of the late . . . war will fade into nothing, and which will destroy, whoever is victor, the civilisation and the progress of our generation'.

Yet what would a German recovery mean for the politics of *Mitteleuropa* – for the new states created by the peacemakers and for the

---

* Instead, after much wrangling, the Allies agreed in May 1921 to demand a total of £6.5 billion with payments to begin immediately.

minorities within them? If the transition from Ottoman Empire to Turkish Republic had been attended by genocide and mass expulsions, what was to prevent similar things happening in the fractious patchwork-quilt of nation states that the peacemakers had made in Central and Eastern Europe? As the German-Jewish physician Alfred Döblin succinctly put it: 'Today's states are the graves of nations.'

# PART II

# Empire-States

# 6

# The Plan

*I know all too well that great plans, great ideas and great interests take precedence over everything, and I know it would be petty of me to place the question of my own person on a par with the universal-historical tasks resting, first and foremost, on your shoulders.*

> Nikolai Bukharin in his last letter to Stalin

*We shake your hand, beloved father,*
*For the happiness you have given us.*
*You are a vital ray of the sun*
*And now the peasant is well fed*
*The warrior is strong in battle.*

> Poem addressed to Stalin by the workers
> of the South Ossetian Autonomous Oblast

*We shall destroy such enemies, be he an old Bolshevik or not, we will destroy his kin, his family.*    Toast proposed by Stalin

## FROM JAZZ TO BLUES

In the immediate aftermath of the First World War, most of the world danced to an American rhythm. A victorious latecomer to the war, the United States was the unquestioned winner of the peace. Despite legal restrictions like the prohibition of alcohol introduced in 1920 and the older system of racial segregation, America stood for new freedoms in economic, social and political life. Nothing captured the ambivalent quality of the new freedom better than jazz, a music born in the black communities of the Mississippi delta, transported by black migration to the industrial cities of the Mid-West and North-East, and transformed on Broadway into mood music for a decade-long global party. As F. Scott Fitzgerald suggested in his novel *The Great Gatsby*, this flight into hedonism suited everyone: not only those who had suffered during the war and wanted to forget it, but also those who only visited the trenches as post-war tourists and invented their own war stories out of guilt or vanity. Cinema and short skirts, cocktails and convertible cars, speakeasies and chain-smoked cigarettes: New York, Chicago and Los Angeles offered all these pleasures and more. But the American mood of post-war hedonism was as contagious as the influenza before it. The once austere Prussian capital, Berlin, was transformed into 'Chicago on the Spree'. In Tokyo, too, the 1920s were the *eroguro* age – *ero* for erotic, *guro* for grotesque; at night the Ginza district seethed with American sounds and styles.

Shanghai, above all, was a garden of earthly delights: 'Nothing more intensely living can be imagined,' enthused the English author Aldous Huxley, who succumbed to nearly every temptation it had to offer. The Viennese-born film director Josef von Sternberg – whose oeuvre in the 1920s included *Underworld*, *Street of Sin* and *The Dragnet*, and who would later make Marlene Dietrich a star with *The Blue Angel* and *Shanghai Express* – was at once fascinated and appalled by the city's Great World Centre, a veritable cornucopia of consumption:

On the first floor were gambling tables, singsong girls, magicians, pick pockets, slot machines, fireworks, birdcages, fans, stick incense, acrobats, and ginger. One flight up were the restaurants, a dozen barbers, and earwax extractors. The third floor had jugglers, herb medicines, ice cream parlors, photographers, a new bevy of girls, their high-collared gowns slit to reveal their hips . . . and, under the heading of novelty, several rows of exposed toilets.

The trumpeter Buck Clayton and his Harlem Gentlemen were among the American bands who played the Canidrome Ballroom, the self-styled 'Rendezvous of Shanghai's elite'. Among that elite's most debauched members was a young man named Chiang Kai-shek, who married his second wife (bigamously) in the Great Eastern Hotel in the Wing On department store building. (On their honeymoon he introduced her to his first wife and to gonorrhoea.) Just a few years later he married again, this time the wealthy, Wellesley-educated heiress Soong Meiling. A thousand people attended the reception in the rose-bedecked Majestic Hotel. The date was December 1, 1927, just a few days after the tenth anniversary of the Russian Revolution, and the party was, regrettably, marred when a crowd of down-at-heel Russian émigrés pelted the Soviet consulate with sticks and stones.

December 1927 was also the month Louis Armstrong and the Hot Five recorded 'Got No Blues' and 'Hotter than That'. The good times were indeed rolling; between 1921 and 1929 the US economy grew at an average annual rate of 6 per cent. Yet they rolled mainly for a wealthy elite. By 1928 nearly 20 per cent of total US income was being earned by the top 1 per cent of taxpayers, and more than 3 per cent by the top 0.01 per cent. A staggering 40 per cent of American wealth was in the hands of the top 1 per cent of households, and more than 10 per cent of it belonged to just 0.01 per cent. This partly reflected the unprecedented rise in stock prices between 1919 and 1929. Between August 1921 and August 1929 the Dow Jones Industrial index increased by a factor of 4.4. Other prices, however, had not risen so far. Some were already falling. For those fortunate enough not to be fighting it, the First World War had been a two-fold boon. The temporary diversion of so much European production into the business of destruction had allowed Asian and American producers to expand mightily, but they could not wholly compensate for the disruption caused by the war. It was a global seller's market. At the same time, the inflationary financing of the war, as governments printed money to pay for their deficits, pushed up world prices. The spot price of wheat in the Chicago market – a reasonably good proxy for traded primary commodity prices – hit roughly treble its pre-war average in 1917 and again in 1920. The twin stimuli of dearth and currency depreciation ended thereafter, and a global recession in 1920–21 saw steep declines in the prices of primary products and manufactures. Thereafter, they barely recovered. The price of wheat peaked in February 1925 at 182 cents a bushel (compared with 294 cents in May 1920) and by May 1929 it was down to 102 cents. Similar forces were driving down the world prices of other key commodities like iron and steel. This deflation was the overture to the Great

Depression. In the 1920s it meant poverty for farmers, but easy living for those who received the profits of industry and finance.

The Depression was an economic catastrophe unmatched before or since. It was signalled by a collapse in American asset prices. On October 29, 1929 – 'Black Tuesday' – the Dow Jones Industrial index fell by nearly 12 per cent, one of the steepest one-day declines in its history. The market had in fact begun to slide after September 3; by November 13 it had fallen by nearly 50 per cent. This signified a slump in the confidence of investors in the future profitability of US corporations, magnified by panic selling on the part of speculators who had been trading on margin (in effect, with borrowed money). The subsequent rally, which lasted until April 1930, proved illusory. From then until July 1932 the market slid inexorably downwards. At its nadir on July 8, 1932 stock prices had fallen to just 11 per cent of their 1929 maximum. With the exception of 1914, the stock market had never seen such volatility, and nothing remotely like it has happened since.

The symptoms of the Depression were much easier to discern than its causes. Between 1929 and 1933 American gross national product fell by nearly half in nominal terms, or 30 per cent when allowance is made for the simultaneous decline in prices. The first sector to be severely affected was construction; by 1930, however, the collapse in activity had spread to agriculture, manufacturing and finance. Investment imploded; so did exports. This crisis of capitalism was not confined to the United States; it was a global phenomenon, as Figure 6.1 makes clear. The combined output of the world's seven biggest economies declined by close to 20 per cent between 1929 and 1932. But there were significant national and, indeed, regional differences in the timing and severity of the Depression. The United States was not the first to suffer, partly because monetary tightening there initially affected other countries by luring short-term capital back to New York, and partly because other central banks were restricting credit for reasons of their own. Argentina, Australia, Brazil, Canada, Germany and Poland all turned down sooner. But only two countries suffered such severe contractions as the United States. One was Germany, where construction had peaked as early as 1927. The other was Austria.

It was the phenomenon of industrial unemployment that shocked contemporaries most. 'Next to war,' remarked *The Times* in an editorial ten years after the nadir of the downturn, 'unemployment has been the most widespread, the most insidious, and the most corroding malady of our generation: it is the specific social disease of Western civilisation in our time.' As a percentage of the civilian labour force, unemployment in the United States rose from 3.2 per cent on the eve of the Depression to a peak of 25 per cent in 1933. It remained above 15 per cent for the remainder of the decade. In Germany, which used a somewhat different definition, unemployment exceeded 50 per cent of trade union members in 1932. Yet just as painful for many people was the collapse in prices, which ruined countless farmers all over the world, or the failure of thousands of banks, which took the savings of depositors down with them. Indeed, it was the disintegration of the American banking system, more than anything else, that deepened and prolonged the crisis. Between 1929 and 1933, around 10,000 of the United States' 25,000 banks closed their doors. There were also major banking crises in Austria and Germany, as well as in France and Switzerland. Figure 6.1 shows that more countries were affected by severe deflation than by severe reductions in output. This tends to confirm the view that the Depression was partly a consequence of a global financial crunch, with banking crises in some countries, currency crises in others and both kinds of crisis in an unlucky few.

Contemporaries struggled to explain what had gone wrong with capitalism. The American President, Herbert Hoover, was no uncritical believer in *laissez-faire* economics. During the 1920s, he had expressed his support for export promotion, collective bargaining, agricultural cooperatives and business 'conferences' as ways of tackling economic problems. In Hoover's eyes, however, there were limits to what government could do. The Depression was a 'worldwide' phenomenon due to 'overproduction of . . . raw materials' and 'overspeculation'; the ensuing 'retribution' was similar in its character to what had happened in 1920 and 1921. The country's 'fundamental assets', he argued, were 'unimpaired'. All that was needed was for the Federal Reserve to continue to supply 'ample . . . credit at low rates of interest', while maintaining the dollar's price in terms of gold; for the government to expand public works, though without unbalancing the budget; and for the necessary 'savings in production costs' to be

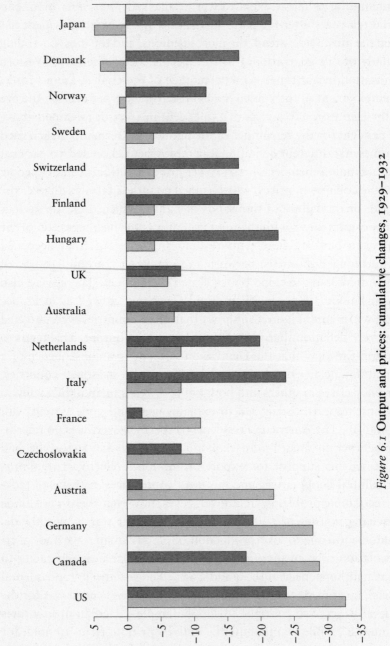

*Figure 6.1* Output and prices: cumulative changes, 1929–1932

shared between 'labor, capital and the consumer'. Hoover also backed an increase in the numerous tariffs that had long protected American producers of food, textiles and other basic products from foreign competition. Unfortunately, none of this sufficed to counter the plunge in economic confidence. On the contrary, the policy made matters worse. By refusing to relax monetary policy, the Federal Reserve failed disastrously to avert waves of bank closures in 1930 and 1931, actually raising its discount rate in October 1931; the attempt to run a balanced budget meanwhile prevented any kind of counter-cyclical fiscal stimulus; and the protectionist Smoot-Hawley trade bill enacted in June 1930, though it did not radically increase tariff rates, nevertheless dealt a blow to financial confidence. The German economy had to swallow an equally lethal policy brew of interest rate hikes, tax increases, spending cuts and protection.

There were without question structural imbalances in the global economy that condemned traditional policy responses to failure. The downward pressure on prices of commodities and manufactures was a matter of international supply and demand more than policy. The war had burdened America's principal trading partners with hard-currency debts – reparations in the case of Germany – which they could only service by exporting to the United States or to one another. The increased power of trade unions had made labour markets more rigid than before the war, so that falls in prices and profits did not translate into lower wages but into factory closures and unemployment.* In his inaugural address on March 4, 1933 Hoover's successor Franklin Roosevelt offered a better diagnosis when he identified 'fear itself – nameless, unreasoning, unjustified terror' – as the root cause of the Depression. Expectations of investors had taken a severe battering; it would be years before their spirits recovered. Yet the measures Roosevelt proposed on becoming president proved little more effectual than Hoover's. Roosevelt wanted to raise agricultural prices and to cut government spending, an unpromising combination at the best of times; the majority of his schemes merely tended to increase the power of the federal government by demanding stricter

---

* In Germany the problem was especially debilitating. Real wages rose by roughly 75 per cent between 1924 and 1931.

supervision on banks, national planning for public utilities and centralized control over relief efforts. The resulting jobs for bureaucrats made only a modest dent in the unemployment numbers. The policy changes that made the most difference were ones generally forced on governments. In 1931 more than forty countries had been on the gold standard; by 1937 virtually none were. Both the United Kingdom and then the United States, the two anchors of the international monetary system, were forced to float their currencies, allowing their central banks to focus on lowering domestic interest rates without worrying about how changes in their gold reserves or capital flows would affect the exchange rate. At the same time, government deficits rose, as a result of increased public spending and collapsing revenues; this happened well in advance of the breakthrough in economic theory represented by Keynes's *General Theory of Employment, Interest and Money* (1936), though only two countries ran deficits sufficiently large to provide an economic stimulus.

Currency devaluations stimulated recovery in two ways: allowing nominal interest rates to fall and, so long as people began to anticipate less deflation and perhaps even inflation, reducing real interest rates and real wages. Employing people began to look as if it might become profitable again – though the rate of recovery was not closely correlated to movements in real wages, suggesting that other inhibitions were at work, especially in the United States. Unfortunately the paroxysm of protectionism that by now had swept the world, persuading even the British to abandon free trade, meant that looser monetary and fiscal policies could do little to stimulate trade. Globalization was over; flows of goods were constrained by import duties, flows of capital by exchange controls and other devices, flows of labour by new restrictions on immigration. Indeed, Keynes came to believe that economic recovery could be sustained only in a more or less closed economy that aimed at autarky. As he remarked casually in the preface to the German edition of his book, 'The theory of output as a whole . . . is much more easily adapted to the conditions of a totalitarian state, than is the theory of the production and distribution of a given output produced under conditions of free competition and a large measure of *laissez-faire*.'

Keynes's choice of word was revealing. Although the term owed its origins to Italian fascism,* the first truly totalitarian regime had been in existence for more than a decade when the Depression struck. By crippling the American colossus for a decade and laying waste to its trading partners and debtors, the economic crisis seemed to vindicate the Soviet model. For, if Marxism-Leninism stood for anything, it was the prediction that capitalism would collapse under the weight of its own contradictions. Now it seemed to be doing precisely that. Understandably, the more the American dream turned to nightmare, the more people were attracted to the Russian alternative of a planned economy – insulated from the vagaries of the market, yet capable of feats of construction every bit as awesome as the skyscrapers of New York or the mass-produced cars of Henry Ford. All the totalitarian state asked in return was complete control of every aspect of life. Only in your dreams were you free from its intrusion, and even there the omnipresent demi-god figure of the Leader was liable to intrude. The justification for this abolition of individual freedom was equality: from each according to his abilities, to each according to his needs, as the slogan put it. The aim was not just rapid industrialization; it was the 'liquidation' of the bourgeoisie and other property-owning classes.

Yet, as George Orwell would later observe, on the Soviet 'Animal Farm' some animals turned out to be more equal than others. It did not take long for a 'new class' (as the dissident Yugoslav Milovan Djilas later called it) to spring up, composed of the elite functionaries of the totalitarian state. Their control over every aspect of economic life and their freedom from any kind of independent scrutiny or popular accountability made it easy to justify and pay for a whole range of Party privileges; the *nomenklatura* were also in position to enrich themselves unofficially through peculation and corruption. There was another catch. The planned economy had an insatiable appetite not only for

* Its earliest appearance, according to Adrian Lyttleton, was as a pejorative term in an article in *Il Mundo* in May 1923; Mussolini subsequently adopted it. In Italy, as we shall see, it remained more an aspiration than a reality, however. Academics have long and tediously debated the meaning and utility of the term. During the Cold War, as Iuri Igritski remarked in 1993, it was 'a tennis ball' that each side tried 'to hit harder into [the] opponent's court'. We can now see more clearly its applicability to both Stalin's Soviet Union and Hitler's Third Reich. Neither regime achieved the complete control over individuals imagined by Orwell in *1984*. But both came closer than any previous polity.

workers but also for raw materials. These the Soviet Union had inherited in copious quantities from the Tsarist Empire. But other countries that adopted the totalitarian model were less well endowed. In Germany and Japan, the planned economy set a very different political tempo from the swinging syncopation of the jazz age. By the mid-1930s people there were no longer dancing; they were marching.

## FELLOW TRAVELLERS

In the summer of 1931, in his seventy-fifth year, the playwright George Bernard Shaw paid a nine-day visit to the Soviet Union. What he saw – or thought he saw – was a workers' paradise under construction. Among the sites he inspected was that of the projected Moscow–Volga Canal. The canal was intended to link the Soviet capital with the Volga River, not only to facilitate river traffic but also to supplement the rapidly expanding city's water supply. In stark contrast to the dole queues of the West, the site would soon be swarming with workers. Here was a symbol of the apparently realizable dream of state socialism, and Western visitors like Shaw reacted ecstatically. They had seen the future, and – compared with an apparently defunct capitalist system – it seemed to work.

One of a motley tour party organized by Nancy and Waldorf Astor (among the other tourists was Philip Kerr, Marquis of Lothian), Shaw set off in his customary ironical mood, but soon succumbed to his Soviet hosts' calculated flattery. Granted an audience with Stalin himself, Shaw was 'disarm[ed] . . . by a smile in which there is no malice but also no credulity . . . [He] would pass . . . for a romantically dark eyed Georgian chieftain'. In an impromptu speech in Leningrad, Shaw declared enthusiastically: 'If this great communistic experiment spreads over the whole world, we shall have a new era in history . . . If the future is the future as Lenin foresaw it, then we may all smile and look forward to the future without fear.' 'Were I only 18 years of age,' he told journalists on his way back to England, 'I would settle in Moscow tomorrow.' In his hastily written book *The Rationalization of Russia* (1931), Shaw went still further: 'Stalin has delivered the goods to an extent that seemed impossible ten years ago,' he rhapsodized. 'Jesus Christ has come down to earth. He is no longer an idol. People are gaining some sort of idea of what would happen if He lived now.' For once, Shaw's irony was unintended.

'Socialism in one country' was Stalin's solution to the problem that had repeatedly divided the leadership of the Bolshevik Party since Lenin's death in 1924. How could the revolutionary regime achieve the industrialization of Russia's backward rural economy without the resources of the more developed West? Trotsky had seen world revolution as the only answer. When that failed to materialize, other Bolshevik leaders, notably Nikolai Bukharin, were inclined to conclude that rapid industrialization was no longer an option. The pace would have to be slow. Stalin, ruthlessly positioning himself to be Lenin's successor – suppressing Lenin's deathbed warning against him – rode roughshod over these rarefied debates. Rapid industrialization, he insisted, *was* possible within the borders of the Soviet Union. All that was needed was a plan, and the iron willpower that had won the civil war. What Stalin meant by 'socialism in one country' was a new revolution – an economic revolution that he, the self-styled 'man of steel', would lead. Under the first Five-Year Plan, Soviet output was to be increased by a fifth. Managers were encouraged to 'over-fulfil their quotas'; workers were exhorted to work superhumanly long shifts in imitation of the heroic miner and shock worker (*udarnik*) Aleksei Stakhanov.

Ostensibly, the aim was to strengthen the Soviet Union, to make it the economic, and hence the military, equal of the 'imperialist' powers still ranged against it. Yet Stalin always saw the strategic benefits of industrialization as secondary to the social transformation it implied. By forcing a huge transfer of manpower and resources from the countryside into the cities, he aimed to enlarge at a stroke the Soviet proletariat on which the Revolution was supposedly based. He succeeded: between 1928 and 1939 the urban labour force trebled in size. How precisely this was achieved was something Stalin's star-struck Western admirers preferred to ignore. Even as the working class was artificially bloated in size, around four million people were 'disfranchised' because they had been 'class enemies' before the Revolution. 'Non-toilers' found themselves ousted from their jobs, from schools and hospitals, from the system of food rationing, even from their homes. In Stalin's eyes, all surviving elements of the pre-revolutionary society – former capitalists, nobles, merchants, officials, priests and kulaks – remained a real threat 'with all their class sympathies, anti-pathies, traditions, habits, opinions, world views and so on'. They had to be unmasked and expelled from the Soviet body politic. Only in late 1935, after years of denunciations, disfranchisements and all the attendant deprivations, did Stalin seem to signal an end to the campaign against the offspring of 'class aliens' – but only to turn public attention to a new category of 'enemies of the people'.

It is sometimes still said that Stalin's crimes were 'necessary' to modernize an antiquated country. That was precisely how he justified the costs of collectivization to Churchill. But the human cost was out of all proportion to the gains in economic efficiency. And this was by no means accidental. The Dnipropetrovsk Party Secretary Mendal M. Khataevich made it clear to his party subordinates that the policy of collectivization of agriculture was only superficially an attempt to improve Soviet agriculture. Its true goal was the destruction of the class enemy – to be precise, 'the liquidation of the kulaks as a class':

Your loyalty to the Party and to Comrade Stalin will be tested and measured by your work in the villages. There is no room for weakness. This is no job for the squeamish. You'll need strong stomachs and an iron will. The Party will accept no excuses for failure.

Predictably, the consequence of the systematic annihilation of any farmer suspected of being a kulak was not economic growth but one of the greatest man-made famines in history. As Party functionaries descended on the countryside with orders to abolish private property and 'liquidate' anyone who had accumulated more than the average amount of capital, there was chaos. Who exactly was a kulak?* Those

---

* Six criteria had been laid down at the instigation of the Finance Ministry in 1927, any one of which qualified someone as a kulak: (1) the hiring of two or more labourers; (2) ownership of three or more draught animals; (3) sown area of more than 10–16 desyatins (the threshold varied by region); (4) ownership of any kind of processing enterprise; (5) ownership of a trading establishment; or (6) ownership of one or more agricultural machines or of a considerable quantity of good-quality implements. However, these were modified in 1929 and were still far from easy to apply in the field when collectivization began.

who had been better-off before the Revolution or those who had done well since? What exactly did it mean to 'exploit' other peasants? Lending them money when they were short of cash? Rather than see their cattle and pigs confiscated, many peasants preferred to slaughter and eat them, so that by 1935 total Soviet livestock was reduced to half of its 1929 level. But the brief orgy of eating was followed by a protracted, agonizing starvation. Without animal fertilizers, crop yields plummeted – grain output in 1932 was down by a fifth compared with 1930. Grain seizures to feed Russia's cities left entire villages with literally nothing to eat. Starving people ate cats, dogs, field mice, birds, tree bark and even horse manure. Some went into the fields and ate half-ripe ears of corn. There were even cases of cannibalism. As in 1920–21, typhus followed hard on the heels of dearth. Perhaps as many as eleven million people died in what was a wholly unnatural and unnecessary disaster. In addition, almost 400,000 households, or close to two million people, were deported as 'special exiles' to Siberia and Central Asia. Many of those who resisted collectivization were shot on the spot; perhaps as many as 3.5 million victims of 'dekulakization' subsequently died in labour camps. It was a crime the regime did its utmost to conceal from the world, confining foreign journalists to Moscow and restoring the Tsarist passport system to prevent famine victims fleeing to the cities for relief.* Even the 1937 census was suppressed because it revealed a total population of just 156 million, when natural increase would have increased it to 186 million. Only a handful of Western reporters – notably Gareth Jones of the *Daily Express*, Malcolm Muggeridge of the *Manchester Guardian*, Pierre Berland of *Le Temps* and William Chamberlin of the *Christian Science Monitor* – had the guts to publish accurate reports about the famine. The bulk of the press corps in Moscow, notably Walter Duranty of the *New York Times*,† knowingly connived

---

* The situation was just the reverse of the famine of 1920–21, when there had been food in the country but none in the cities. This gave rise to the joke: 'What is the difference between Bolshevism and Communism?' 'Bolshevism is when there is no food in the cities, and Communism is when there is no food in the country.'

† It was Duranty who wrote the line 'You can't make an omelet without breaking eggs' in his report of May 14, 1933. Three months later he dismissed 'any report of a famine in Russia ... today' as 'an exaggeration or malignant propaganda' (August 23, 1933).

at the cover-up for fear of jeopardizing their access to the *nomenklatura*.

Meanwhile, behind the bombast of Stalinist propaganda, the Five-Year Plans were turning Russia's cities into congested hellholes, with vast mills both darker and more satanic than anything ever seen in the West. New industrial metropolises like Magnitogorsk in the southern Urals could never have been constructed without massive coercion. With temperatures plunging to –40°C in winter and rising to 40°C in summer, conditions for those who built the city's vast steelworks – which was intended to be the world's largest single milling and shaping factory – were close to unendurable. For years after work began there in March 1929, many of the workers were housed in tents or mud huts. When finally residential buildings were constructed, only the most rudimentary resources were made available. Even when complete, the new apartment blocks had no kitchens or toilets, since workers were supposed to use communal facilities. These, however, did not exist. The 'linear city' model proposed by the German architect Ernst May proved wholly unsuitable to the winds of the steppe, which howled between the long rows of apartment blocks. All over the Soviet Union, the haste with which people were drafted into industry condemned a generation to live in the most cramped conditions imaginable, with only the most basic amenities. Their places of work were even worse, with horrendous rates of industrial injury and mortality, as well as life-shortening quantities of toxins in the air (in Magnitogorsk the snow was black with soot). The American John Scott, who spent five years in Magnitogorsk, guessed that 'Russia's battle of ferrous metallurgy alone involved more casualties than the battle of the Marne'. He was almost certainly right. One who survived was a young man from a village near Kursk named Alexander Luznevoy, who had been sent to Magnitigorsk by his mother to escape the famine at home. Underclad and underfed – he received just 600 grams of bread a day, provided he fulfilled his quota of eight cubic metres of ditch – Luznevoy soon realized that his only hope was to seize the opportunities for social mobility that were inherent in the Stalinist system.* He learned to read, became a lathe

---

* The Soviet Union in the 1930s has been called a 'quicksand society', but people could rise up from the bottom just as others sank. Indeed, what gave the regime its

operator, studied at night and joined the Komsomol youth organization, which entailed voluntary work at weekends. Taking up poetry, he ended his career as a member of the Writers' Union – a self-made member of the *nomenklatura*.

It was all economic lunacy, perfectly symbolized by the palm trees the workers at Magnitogorsk built for themselves out of telegraph poles and sheet steel in lieu of real foliage. Collectivization wrecked Soviet agriculture. Forced industrialization misallocated resources as much as it mobilized them. Cities like Magnitogorsk cost far more to support than the planners acknowledged, since coal had to be transported there from Siberian mines more than a thousand miles away. Just heating the homes of miners in Arctic regions burned a huge proportion of the coal they dug up. For all these reasons the economic achievements of Stalinism were far less than was claimed at the time by the regime and its numerous apologists. Between 1929 and 1937, according to the official Soviet statistics, the gross national product of the USSR increased at an annual rate of between 9.4 and 16.7 per cent and per capita consumption by between 3.2 and 12.5 per cent, figures that bear comparison with the growth achieved by China since the early 1990s. But when allowances are made for idiosyncratic pricing conventions, real GNP growth was closer to 3–4.9 per cent per annum, while per capita consumption rose by no more than 1.9 per cent and perhaps by as little as 0.6 per cent per annum – roughly a fifth or a sixth of the official figure. In any case, what do per capita figures mean when the number of people is being drastically reduced by political violence? If there was any productivity growth under the Five-Year Plans – and the statistics suggest that there was – it was partly because so much labour was being shed for political rather than economic reasons. No serious analysis can regard a policy as economically 'necessary' if it involves anything up to twenty million excess deaths. For every nineteen tons of additional steel produced in the Stalinist period, approximately one Soviet citizen was killed. Yet

---

dynamism was the incentives it created for men like Luznevoy to better themselves through overwork and conformism. Others were encouraged to participate in the cycle of Terror by denouncing their superiors, or even their neighbours if they saw a chance of getting a better apartment.

anyone who questioned the rationality of Stalin's policies risked incurring the wrath of his loyal lieutenants. As Khataevich explained to one waverer:

I'm not sure that you understand what has been happening. A ruthless struggle is going on between the peasantry and our regime. It's a struggle to the death. This year was a test of our strength and their endurance. It took a famine to show them who is master here. It has cost millions of lives, but the collective farm system is here to stay. We've won the war.

Breakneck industrialization, in short, was always intended to break necks.

This was the crucial point that Western dupes like Shaw failed to see: the planned economy was in reality a slave economy, based on levels of coercion beyond the darkest nightmares of Bloomsbury. Like so many of the grandiose Soviet construction projects of the 1930s, the Moscow–Volga Canal was in fact built by thousands of convicts. The workforce that built Magnitogorsk also included around 35,000 deported prisoners. Lurking behind the seeming miracles of the planned economy was the giant network of prisons and camps known simply as the Gulag.*

## THE BIG ZONE

It was in the former monastery on the Solovetsky Islands, a barely habitable archipelago in the White Sea just ninety miles from the Arctic Circle, that the Gulag was born. There had of course been camps since the earliest days of the Revolution. As early as December 1919, there were already more than twenty; within a year that number has quintupled. But it was not at first quite clear what the purpose of incarcerating 'class enemies' was: to reform them, to punish them, or to kill them? The camp established at Solovetsky in 1923 provided the answer. The initial objective was simply to send the opponents of the Bolsheviks as far away as possible from the centre of political decision-making. But as the number of political prisoners grew – so

* Gulag is an acronym for *Glavnoe upravlenie lagerei*, Main Camp Administration.

rapidly that the Cheka's successor organization, the OGPU,* could barely cope – an ingenious possibility suggested itself. The commander of Solovetsky, Naftaly Aronovich Frenkel, was himself a former prisoner.† Instead of merely starving or freezing the inmates, Frenkel came to realize, the camp authorities could make them work. After all, their labour was free. And there was no task the so-called *zeki* could refuse to perform. In 1924 the Solovetsky camp journal called for 're-educat[ing] prisoners through accustoming them to participating in organized productive labour'. However, re-education mattered less to Frenkel than the possibility of profiting from slave labour. The authorities in Moscow merely wanted the camps to be self-supporting sinks that would reduce the country's overcrowded prisons. Frenkel believed he could do better than that. By the end of the 1920s Solovetsky and the other 'northern special significance camps' had become a rapidly growing commercial operation involved in forestry and construction.

In a matter of years, there were camps dotted all over the Soviet Union: camps for mining, camps for road building, camps for aircraft construction, even camps for nuclear physics. Prisoners performed every conceivable kind of work, not only digging canals but also catching fish and manufacturing everything from tanks to toys. At one level, the Gulag was a system of colonization enabling the regime to exploit resources in regions hitherto considered uninhabitable. Precisely because they were expendable, *zeki* could mine coal at Vorkuta in the Komi Republic, an area in the Arctic north-west, benighted half the year, swarming with blood-sucking insects the other half. They could dig up gold and platinum at Dalstroi, located in the equally

---

* *Ob'edinennoe Gosudarstvennoe Politicheskoe Upravlenie*, the All-Union State Political-cal Directorate, formed in 1923. Renamed the GUGB (*Glavnoe Upravlenie Gosudarstvennoi Bezopastnosti*, the Main Directorate of State Security), in 1934 it was subordinated to the NKVD (*Narodnyi Kommissariat Vnutrennikh Del*, the People's Commissariat for Internal Affairs). By 1930 the OGPU wielded control over nearly all the camps and exile settlements in the Soviet Union.
† Frenkel was a small-time Jewish trader born in 1883 in Haifa, in Ottoman Palestine. In 1923 he was sentenced to ten years in the camp for illegal border-crossing. Within a short time he had been promoted from prisoner to guard and was formally released in 1927.

inhospitable east of Siberia.* Yet so convenient did the system of slave labour become to the planners that camps were soon established in the Russian heartland too. The author Aleksandr Solzhenitsyn described the Gulag as 'an amazing country . . . which, though scattered in an Archipelago geographically . . . crisscrossed and patterned that other country within which it was located . . . cutting into its cities, hovering over its streets.' To prisoners within the Gulag, the rest of the Soviet Union was merely *bolshaya zona*, 'the big [prison] zone'.

The key thing in this vast system of slavery was to ensure a sustained flow of new slaves. The alleged spies and saboteurs convicted in show trials like the Shakhty Trial (1928), the Industrial Party Trial (1930) and the Metro-Vickers Trial (1933) were victims of only the most spectacular of innumerable legal and extra-legal procedures. By defining the slightest grumble as treason or counter-revolution, the Stalinist system was in a position to send whole armies of Soviet citizens to the Gulag. Files now available in the Russian State Archives show just how the system worked. Berna Klauda was a little old lady from Leningrad; she could scarcely have looked less like a subversive element. In 1937, however, she was sentenced to ten years in the Perm Gulag for expressing anti-government sentiments. 'Anti-Soviet Agitation' was the least of the political crimes for which one could be convicted. More serious was 'Counter-revolutionary Activity'; worse still, 'Counter-revolutionary Terrorist Activity' and, worst of all, 'Trotskyist Terrorist Activity'. In fact, the overwhelming majority of people convicted for such offences were guilty – if they were guilty of anything at all – of trivial misdemeanours: a word out of turn to a superior, an overheard joke about Stalin, a complaint about some aspect of the all-pervasive system, at worst some petty economic infraction like 'speculation' (buying and re-selling goods). Only a tiny fraction of political prisoners were genuinely opposed to the regime – revealingly, in 1938 little more than 1 per cent of camp inmates had higher education; a third were illiterate. By 1937 there were quotas for arrests just as there were quotas for steel production. Crimes

---

* Extraordinary official photograph albums have been preserved which convey if nothing else the scale of these camps.

were simply made up to fit the punishments. Prisoners became mere outputs, referred to by the NKVD as 'Accounts' (male prisoners) and 'Books' (pregnant female prisoners).

At the height of the Gulag system, there was a total of 476 camp systems scattered all over the Soviet Union, each, like Solovetsky, composed of hundreds of individual camps. All told, around eighteen million men, women and children passed through the system under Stalin's rule. Taking into account the six or seven million Soviet citizens who were sent into exile, the total percentage of the population who experienced some kind of penal servitude under Stalin approached 15 per cent.

Many of the camps were located, like Solovetsky, in the remotest, coldest regions of the Soviet Union; the Gulag was at once colonial and penal. Weaker prisoners died in transit since the locked carriages and cattle trucks used were unheated and insanitary. The camp facilities were primitive in the extreme; *zeki* at new camps had to build their own barracks, which were little more than wooden shacks into which they were packed like sardines. And the practice – also pioneered by Frenkel – of feeding strong prisoners better than weak ones ensured that, literally, only the strong survived. The camps were not primarily intended to kill people (Stalin had firing squads for that) but they were run in such a way that mortality rates were bound to be very high indeed. Food was inadequate, sanitation rudimentary and shelter barely sufficient. In addition, the sadistic punishments meted out by camp guards, often involving exposing naked prisoners to the freezing weather, ensured a high death toll. Punishment was as arbitrary as it was brutal; the guards, whose lot in any case was far from a happy one, were encouraged to treat the prisoners as 'vermin', 'filth' and 'poisonous weeds'. The attitudes of the professional criminals – the clannish 'thieves-in-law' who were the dominant group among inmates – were not very different. On December 14, 1926, three former Solovetsky inmates wrote a desperate letter to the Presidium of the Party's Central Committee, protesting against

the arbitrary use of power and the violence that reign at the Solovetsky concentration camp . . . It is difficult for a human being even to imagine such terror, tyranny, violence, and lawlessness. When we went there, we could not conceive of such a horror, and now we, crippled ourselves, together with several thousands who are still there, appeal to the ruling centre of the Soviet state to curb the terror that reigns there . . . the former tsarist penal servitude system in comparison to Solovetsky had 99 per cent more humanity, fairness, and legality . . . People die like flies, i.e., they die a slow and painful death . . . The entire weight of this scandalous abuse of power, brute violence, and lawlessness that reign at Solovetsky . . . is placed on the shoulders of workers and peasants; others, such as counterrevolutionaries, profiteers and so on, have full wallets and have set themselves up and live in clover in the Soviet State, while next to them, in the literal meaning of the word, the penniless proletariat dies from hunger, cold, and back-breaking 14–16 hour days under the tyranny and lawlessness of inmates who are the agents and collaborators of the State Political Directorate [GPU].

If you complain or write anything ('Heaven forbid'), they will frame you for an attempted escape or for something else, and they will shoot you like a dog. They line us up naked and barefoot at 22 degrees below zero and keep us outside for up to an hour. It is difficult to describe all the chaos and terror that is going on . . . One example is the following fact, one of a thousand . . . THEY FORCED THE INMATES TO EAT THEIR OWN FAECES . . .

[I]t is possible, that you might think that it is our imagination, but we swear to you all, by everything that is sacred to us, that this is only one small part of the nightmarish truth . . .

Of the 100,000 prisoners sent to Solovetsky in the years up to its closure in 1939, roughly half died. Yet when Maxim Gorky visited the camp in June 1929, three years before his return to the Soviet Union from self-imposed exile, he made it sound almost idyllic, with healthy inmates and salubrious cells.

Perhaps nothing illustrates better the diabolical character of the Stalinist regime than the 140-mile Belomor Canal, built at Stalin's instigation to link the Baltic Sea and the White Sea. Between September 1931 and August 1933, somewhere between 128,000 and 180,000 prisoners – most of them from Solovetsky, with Frenkel directing their efforts – hacked out a waterway, equipped only with the most primitive pick-axes, wheelbarrows and hatchets. So harsh were the conditions and so inadequate the tools that tens of thousands of them died in the process. This was hardly unforeseeable; for six months of the year the ground was frozen solid, while in many places the prisoners had to cut through solid granite. And, as so often, the net result was next to worthless economically: far too narrow and shallow to be navigable by substantial vessels. Yet when Shaw's fellow Fabians Sidney and Beatrice Webb were given a tour of the finished canal they were oblivious to all this. As they put it in their book *Soviet Communism: A New Civilization?* (1935), it was 'pleasant to think that the warmest appreciation was officially expressed of the success of the OGPU, not merely in performing a great engineering feat, but in achieving a triumph in human regeneration'. The Webbs explicitly rejected the 'naive belief that . . . penal settlements are now maintained and continuously supplied with thousands of deported manual workers and technicians, deliberately for the purpose of making, out of this forced labour, a net pecuniary profit to add to the State revenue.' Such notions were simply 'incredible' to 'anyone acquainted with the economic results of the chain-gang, or of prison labour, in any country in the world'. Slavery always has its apologists, but seldom are they so ingenuous. The thirty-six Soviet writers who, under Gorky's direction, produced the hyperbolic book *The Belomor–Baltic Canal Named for Stalin* at least had the excuse that the alternative to lying might be dying. The Webbs wrote their rubbish in the safety of Bloomsbury.*

In earlier slave states there had been a clear division between the masters and the enslaved. But that was not the case in the Soviet Union. Those who commanded in the morning might find themselves in chains – or worse – by the afternoon. When the Moscow–Volga Canal was opened by Stalin, the chief contractor made a speech. Immediately afterwards he was taken away and shot. More than two hundred of the project's other managers were also executed because

---

* Margaret Cole recalled a second visit to Moscow with Sidney Webb in 1934: 'As we inspected factories, farms, cooperative stores, schools, hospitals, maternity homes, reformatories, community centres, parks of recreation and rest, visited crowded theatres and opera houses, seated in the state box or side-by-side with rough-handed peasants and workers, attended trade union meetings or industrial courts, or watched, at work or at play, healthy and happy-looking peasants and workers, young mothers and children, Sidney would whisper to me, with the relish of the scientist whose theoretic proposition has stood the test of practical experiment: "See, see, it works, it works."'

of delays in the canal's construction. Indeed, no revolution in history has consumed its own children with such an insatiable appetite as the Russian Revolution. Lenin had first introduced the practice of 'purging' the party periodically, to get rid of 'idlers, hooligans, adventurers, drunkards and thieves'. Stalin, who compulsively mistrusted his fellow Communists, went much further. Few groups were more ruthlessly persecuted in the 1930s than those Old Bolsheviks who had been Stalin's own comrades in the decisive days of revolution and civil war. Senior Party functionaries lived in a state of perpetual insecurity, never knowing when they might fall victim to Stalin's paranoia. Those who had been most loyal to the Party were suddenly as likely to be arrested and imprisoned as the most notorious criminal. Loyal Leninists, passionate believers in the Revolution, were now arrested as 'wreckers' loyal to the imperialist powers or as 'Trotskyites' in league with Stalin's disgraced and exiled arch-rival (whom he finally succeeded in having murdered in 1940). To other pariah groups, Stalin had shown a kind of mercy. They had been sent to dig canals in the tundra. Towards the enemy within the Party he was entirely pitiless. What had begun as a crackdown on corrupt or inefficient officials in 1933 escalated after the murder (almost certainly on Stalin's orders) of the Leningrad Party boss Sergei Kirov in December 1934 into a bloody and self-perpetuating purge. One after another the men and women who had been in the vanguard of the Revolution were arrested, tortured, interrogated until they were induced to confess to some 'crime' and to denounce yet more of their comrades, and then shot. Between January 1935 and June 1941, there were just under twenty million arrests and at least seven million executions in the Soviet Union. In 1937–8 alone the quota for 'enemies of the people' to be executed was set at 356,105, though the actual number who lost their lives was more than twice that. These quotas, too, were over-fulfilled. To visit the gloomy Levashovo Forest outside St Petersburg is to visit a mass grave, where at least 20,000 bodies of those executed were secretly buried.

In Mikhail Bulgakov's novel *The Master and Margarita*, the Devil comes to Moscow. What follows is a fearful spiral of denunciation, disappearance and death, at once arbitrary and spiteful, calculated and yet deranged. No work better captures the loathsome quality of the Terror; no scene gets closer to illuminating the surreal atmosphere of the show trials than Nikanor Bosoy's nightmare of being exposed as a foreign currency dealer while sitting in the audience of a variety show in a Moscow theatre. For not every act in the drama required Stalin's instigation; his role was to create an environment in which ordinary men and women – even members of the same family* – would denounce one another; in which today's torturer could be tomorrow's victim; in which today's camp commandant could spend the night in the punishment cells. Stalin carefully plotted and tracked the destruction of the Party leaders he personally knew. But the tens of thousands of local officials who were denounced by those they had bullied or robbed were the victims of social forces he had merely unleashed. To Western dupes like Shaw and the Webbs, of course, it was all perfectly excusable. Shaw's commentary on the show trials in Moscow was a bizarre mixture of the callous and the facile:

The top of the ladder is a very trying place for old revolutionists who have had no administrative experience, who have had no financial experience, who have been trained as penniless hunted fugitives with Karl Marx on the brain and not as statesmen . . . They often have to be pushed off the ladder with a rope around their necks . . . We cannot afford to give ourselves moral airs when our most enterprising neighbour humanely and judiciously liquidates a handful of exploiters and speculators to make the world safe for honest men.

The defendants at show trials did not attempt to dispute the charges against them, argued the Webbs, because they had never been exposed to the pointlessly adversarial Anglo-Saxon system of justice. The accused were guilty and knew it; that was why they confessed. As for freedom of speech, was that really so important? 'So called "free thought and free expression by word and by writ" mocks human progress, unless the common people are taught to think, and inspired

* Pavlik Morozov, a 14-year-old schoolboy from a village east of Ekaterinburg, became a hero for denouncing his own father. When he was subsequently murdered, four of his relatives – his grandparents, a cousin and an uncle – were arrested and shot. Morozov became a Stalinist martyr, endlessly celebrated in Soviet propaganda. In fact he had denounced his father at his mother's instigation because he had walked out on her.

to use this knowledge, in the interests of their Commonwealth ... It is this widespread knowledge, and devotion to the public welfare, that is the keynote of Soviet Democracy.' In truth, at the height of Stalin's Terror, 'public welfare' meant total private insecurity. Literally no one could feel safe – least of all the men who ran the NKVD.* Those who survived this life 'beneath the gun' – like the poet Anna Akhmatova, whose 'Requiem' best captures the agony of the bereaved, or the composer Dmitry Shostakovich, whose opera *Lady Macbeth of Mtsensk*, was denounced in *Pravda* as 'Muddle Instead of Music' – were not necessarily the conformists. They were merely lucky.

Among those arrested were fifty-three members of the Leningrad Society for the Deaf and Dumb. The charges against this alleged 'fascist organization' was that they had conspired with the German secret service to blow up Stalin and other Politburo members with a home-made bomb during the Revolution Day parade in Red Square. Thirty-four of them were shot; the rest were sent to the camps for ten or more years. One of the victims was Jacob Mendelevich Abter, a thirty-year-old Jewish worker. The idea of a society of deaf mutes trying to assassinate the devil incarnate would almost be comic if the fate of this gentle-looking man had not been so cruel.†

## KILLING PEOPLES

We tend to think of class as a category quite distinct from race, since in Western societies today the former can be more readily changed than the latter. Yet the dividing line is not always so clear-cut. In most medieval and early modern European societies, class was a hereditary

---

* Genrikh Yagoda was shot as a Trotskyite in 1938; Nikolai Yezhov, his successor, was shot as a British spy in 1940; Lavrenti Beria was shot shortly after Stalin's own death.
† What had in fact happened was that the chairman of the Society had informed on some members who had been selling things on local trains to make ends meet. This denunciation led to the NKVD's involvement. The chairman himself was subsequently implicated in the alleged conspiracy and shot. The following year the NKVD decided that the original investigation itself was suspect. The local police were then arrested.

attribute; in India today it remains difficult to shed one's caste origins. In 1930s Russia, too, class was treated as an inheritable trait. If your father was a worker, you were a worker; if your father belonged to one of those groups defined as 'class enemies', then woe betide you – unless you were somehow able to get a forged internal passport or to marry someone from a respectably proletarian family. One local soviet reported that it had expelled thirty-eight secondary school students because:

They are all sons of big hereditary kulaks . . . In the great majority of cases, these kulaks' sons were instigators in stirring up nationalism, spreading various kind of pornography, and disorganizing study . . . All these 38 persons hid their social position while they were in school, registering themselves falsely as poor peasants, middle peasants, and some even as agricultural labourers.

In 1935 a Leningrad newspaper published a series of exposés of class enemies in a local hospital; they give a nice flavour of the atmosphere of the time:

Troitskii, a former White officer and son of a priest, has found a refuge [in the hospital]. The economic manager considers that this lurking enemy is 'an irreplaceable accountant'. Registrar Zabolotskaia, nurse Apishnikova and disinfector Shestiporov are also offspring of priests. Vasileva changed her profession from nun to nurse, and also got a job at that hospital. Another nun, Larkina, followed her example . . . A former monk, Rodin, got himself a job as doctor's assistant and even substitutes for the doctor in making house calls.

No one could expunge their or their parents' pre-revolutionary class origins. Yet it was not only classes that were to be crushed under the wheels of the Stalinist juggernaut. Whole peoples were also marked down for destruction. For Stalin regarded certain ethnic groups within what was still a vast multi-national Russian empire as inherently unreliable – class enemies by dint of their nationality.

Foreigners and all those who had contact with them were by definition suspect, regardless of their ideological credentials. Of the 394 members of the Executive Committee of the Communist International in January 1936, 223 had fallen victim to the Terror by April 1938, as had forty-one of the sixty-eight German Communist leaders who had fled to the Soviet Union after 1933. Those Old Bolsheviks who had spent significant periods in exile before 1917, or who had been involved in fomenting revolution abroad in the 1920s, were among the first to be purged.*

Almost equally suspect were those ethnic groups who inhabited the borders of the Soviet Union, since they were more likely to have contact with foreigners than were people in the Russian heartland. In 1937 the new third secretary in the British embassy in Moscow was a bold young Scotsman named Fitzroy Maclean. Curious to visit the great cities of Central Asia – he was apparently more interested in sight-seeing than in gathering intelligence – Maclean ignored the

---

* The process is unforgettably delineated in the former Party member Arthur Koestler's *Darkness at Noon*, published in 1940. The depths to which the Old Bolsheviks could sink was epitomized by Nikolai Bukharin's letter to Stalin of December 10, 1937:

'I am innocent of those crimes to which I admitted . . . All these past years I have been honestly and sincerely carrying out the Party line and have learned to cherish and love you wisely . . . I have formed . . . the following conception of what is going on in our country: there is something great and bold about the political idea of a general purge.

'It is connected a) with the pre-war situation and b) . . . with the transition to democracy. This purge encompasses 1) the guilty; 2) persons under suspicion and 3) persons potentially under suspicion.

'This business could not have been managed without me . . . It is here that I feel my deepest agony and find myself facing my chief, agonizing paradox . . .

'My heart boils over when I think that you might believe that I am guilty of these crimes and that in your heart of hearts you think that I am really guilty of all these horrors. My head is giddy with confusion, and I feel like yelling at the top of my voice. I feel like pounding my head against the wall. What am I to do? What am I to do?

'I am oppressed by one fact which you have perhaps forgotten: once . . . I was at your place, and you said to me: "Do you know why I consider you my friend? After all, you are not capable of intrigues, are you?" And I said: "No, I am not."

'At that time, I was hanging out with [Lev] Kamenev [already executed in August 1936]. Oh God, what a child I was! What a fool! And now I am paying for this with my honour and with my life. Forgive me, Koba! [Stalin's nickname]

'I weep as I write. But . . . I bear no malice towards anyone . . . I ask your forgiveness . . . Oh Lord, if only there were some device which would have made it possible for you to see my soul flayed and ripped open! If only you could see how I am attached to you, body and soul.'

In vain, Bukharin pleaded to be allowed to go into exile in the United States, or to be sent to a labour camp in Siberia, or at least to be allowed to drink poison rather than be shot. He faced a firing squad on March 14, 1938.

regime's travel restrictions and took a train to Baku, where he caught a steamer to the Caspian port of Lenkoran. The next morning he was amazed to see a convoy of trucks 'driving headlong through the town on the way to the port, each filled with depressed-looking Turko-Tartar peasants under the escort of NKVD frontier troops with fixed bayonets'. Their arrests, a local man explained, 'had been decreed from Moscow and merely formed part of the deliberate policy of the Soviet Government, who believed in transplanting portions of the population from place to place as and when it suited them. The places of those now being deported would probably be taken by other peasants from Central Asia'. Undeterred by his subsequent arrest by NKVD border police and forcible return to Moscow, Maclean resumed his peregrinations a few months later by taking the Trans-Siberian Express to Novisibirsk, where (once again illegally) he caught a train south to Barnaul. At Altaisk station he noticed a number of cattle trucks being hitched onto his train:

These were filled with people who, at first sight, seemed to be Chinese. They turned out to be Koreans, who with their families and their belongings were on their way from the Far East to Central Asia where they were being sent to work on the cotton plantations. They had no idea why they were being deported . . . Later I heard that the Soviet authorities had quite arbitrarily removed some 200,000 Koreans to Central Asia, as likely to prove untrustworthy in the event of a war with Japan.

What Maclean had witnessed was just one episode in a vast programme of ethnic deportation that modern historians have only recently rediscovered. On October 29, 1937, Nikolai Yezhov, the head of the NKVD, wrote to inform Vyacheslav Molotov, Chairman of the Council of People's Commissars, that all Koreans in the Soviet Far East – a total of 171,781 people – had been deported to Central Asia, the consummation of plans first contemplated in the mid-1920s as a way of securing the Soviet Union's eastern frontier.

Koreans were only the first ethnic group to come under suspicion. Balkars, Chechens, Crimean Tatars, Germans, Greeks, Ingushi, Meskhetians, Kalmyks, Karachai, Poles and Ukrainians – all these different nationalities were subjected to persecution by Stalin at various times. The rationales for this policy subtly mixed the languages of class and race. Baltic Germans were 'kulak colonizers to the marrow of their bones'. Poles were informed: 'You are being de-kulakized not because you are a kulak, but because you are a Pole.' One internal OGPU report contained the telling phrase *Raz Poliak, znachit kulak*: 'If it's a Pole, then it must be a kulak.' As early as March 1930 thousands of Polish families were being deported eastwards from Byelorussia and the Ukraine, partly because of their resistance to collectivization and partly because the authorities feared they planned to emigrate westwards. There was a fresh wave of deportations in 1935, which removed more than eight thousand Polish families from the border regions of Kiev and Vinnitsya to eastern Ukraine. Two years later, an investigation into what was alleged to be 'the most powerful and probably the most important diversionist-espionage networks of Polish intelligence in the USSR' led to the arrest of no fewer than 140,000 people, nearly all of them Poles.

Perhaps the most remarkable case of all is that of the Ukrainians. Indeed, it is not too much to say that the man-made famine caused by collectivization in the Ukraine was Stalin's brutal answer to what he regarded as the 'Ukrainian question'. A backlash against the relative autonomy of the Ukraine had begun as early as the spring of 1930. 'Keep in mind', Stalin had warned darkly in 1932, 'that in the Ukrainian Communist Party ... there are not a few ... rotten elements, conscious and subconcious Petlyurites' (supporters of the Ukrainian nationalist leader Simon Petlyura). To be sure, the effects of the 1932–3 famine were not confined to the Ukraine; Kazakhstan, the northern Caucasus and the Volga region were also affected. Careful analysis, however, reveals that the victims of the famine were disproportionately Ukrainian. It is surely no coincidence that fewer than one in ten Ukrainians had voted for the Bolsheviks in the elections to the Constituent Assembly in 1917, whereas more than half had voted for Ukrainian parties. It was in fact one of the stated aims of collectivization to achieve 'the destruction of Ukrainian nationalism's social base – the individual land-holdings'. Collectivization was pushed further and faster there than in Russia. Grain quotas were deliberately stepped up even as production was falling. This explains why about half the victims of the famine were Ukrainians – nearly one in five of the total Ukrainian population. Nor did Stalin regard starvation as a sufficient solution to the problem of Ukrainian disloyalty. The composer Shostakovich recalled how itinerant Ukrainian folksingers were rounded up and shot. All of this was possible because the Ukraine was in effect being run as a Russian colony. Although Russians accounted for just 9 per cent of the republic's population, 79 per cent of the Ukrainian Party and 95 per cent of government officials were Russians or Russified.

The other ethnic group to suffer disproportionately during collectivization were the Kuban Cossacks, whose resistance to the policy led to their wholesale deportation to Siberia. Nor were these the only victims of Stalin's 'ethnic cleansing'. Between the spring of 1935 and the spring of 1936 around 30,000 Finns were sent to Siberia. In January 1936 thousands of Germans were consigned from the western borderlands to Kazakhstan. In 1937 over a thousand Kurdish families were deported from the southern border region; a year later it was the turn of two thousand Iranians. By this time the regime had thrown aside all restraint. In January 1938 the huge sweep that had initially been launched against Poles was extended by the Politburo into an 'operation for the destruction of espionage and sabotage contingents made up of Poles, Latvians, Germans, Estonians, Finns, Greeks, Iranians, Kharbintsy, Chinese, and Romanians, both foreign subjects and Soviet citizens', as well as 'the Bulgarian and Macedonian cadres'.

It is sometimes imagined that the Soviet regime was less bureaucratic in its methods than other totalitarian regimes. Yet the evidence in the Russian archives suggests otherwise. Officials drew up meticulous ledgers, breaking down the inmates of the Gulag by nationality, presumably to allow Stalin and his henchmen to monitor the various persecution campaigns. It is also sometimes suggested that Stalin was less murderous than Hitler in his approach to ethnic cleansing. But the difference is one of quantity not quality. To be sure, Soviet camps were concerned more to extract labour from prisoners than to kill them; prisoners were shot in batches at a punishment *lagpunkt* (labour camp) like Serpantinka, but it was not an extermination camp in the way that, say, Treblinka was. Nevertheless, we should not understate the number of people who lost their lives as a result of Stalin's persecution of non-Russians, which happened (unlike the Holocaust) in

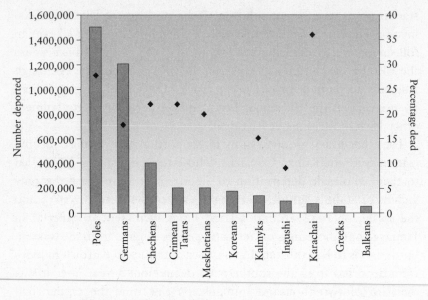

■ Deported ◆ Percentage dead

*Figure 6.2* **Victims of Stalinist 'ethnic cleansing', *c.* 1926–1954**

the context not of a total war but of a largely imaginary civil war. Between 1935 and 1938 around 800,000 individuals were arrested, deported or executed as a result of actions against non-Russian nationalities. At the height of the Terror, between October 1936 and November 1938, members of persecuted nationalities accounted for around a fifth of all political arrests but more than a third of all executions. In fact, nearly three-quarters of those who were arrested in the actions against nationalities ended up being executed. Altogether, throughout Stalin's reign, more than 1.6 million members of non-Russian nationalities died as a result of forcible resettlement (see Figure 6.2).

One ethnic minority, it might be said, stood out in the Soviet Union – for its eagerness not to stand out. The Jews had been pariahs under Tsarist rule. But they had played a disproportionate role in the Bolshevik Party during the revolutionary years. The 1920s were a good time for Soviet Jews, many of whom embraced the new political culture of the dictatorship of the proletariat. By 1926 around 11 per cent of Jewish trade union members were also members of the Party, compared with a national average of 8 per cent. A year later Jews accounted for 4.3 per cent of Party members, as compared with 1.8 per cent of the Soviet population. One indicator of the increased social integration of the period was the sharp rise in mixed marriages. In the Ukraine and Byelorussia – the heartland of the old Pale – the proportion of Jews marrying out of their faith remained low: less than 5 per cent of marriages in the former were mixed and just over 2 per cent in the latter. In Russia, by contrast, the proportion rose from 18.8 per cent in 1925 to 27.2 per cent two years later. This was not part of a general Soviet-wide trend towards ethnic intermingling, it should be stressed; there was virtually no intermarriage between Russians and Muslims in Central Asia. Even the ethnic barrier between Russians and Ukrainians seems to have been slower to fall. An increasingly urbanized Jewish community also showed signs of abandoning its traditional Yiddish language in favour of Russian. Yet because such a high proportion of the original Bolsheviks had been Jews, attracted to Communism as a way out of Tsarist persecution, a high proportion of victims of Stalin's Terror were also Jews. And although his prejudice did not manifest itself before the war, Stalin was sooner or later bound to focus on the Jews as an ethnic group whose loyalty could not be depended upon. Why should they – or anyone else, for that matter – have been exempt indefinitely from his pathological mistrust?

Even before the outbreak of war in 1939, indeed even before 1933, the demonic Georgian had revealed himself, just as Lenin had vainly warned he would, as 'a real and true "nationalist-socialist"', and even a vulgar Great Russian bully'. To the Western Left, of course, there always seemed a profound difference between communism and fascism. Until as late as the 1980s, Jürgen Habermas and others zealously upheld the dogma that the Third Reich could not legitimately be compared with Stalin's Soviet Union. But were not Stalin and his German counterpart in reality just two grim faces of totalitarianism? Was there any real difference between Stalin's 'socialism in one country' and Hitler's National Socialism, except that one was put into practice a few years before the other? We can now see just how many of the things that were done in German concentration camps during the Second World War were anticipated in the Gulag: the transportation in cattle trucks, the selection into different categories of prisoner, the shaving of heads, the dehumanizing living conditions, the humiliating clothing, the interminable roll-calling, the brutal and arbitrary punishments, the differentiation between the determined and the doomed. Yes, the regimes were very far from identical, as we shall see. But it is at least suggestive that when the teenage *zek* Yuri Chirkov arrived at Solovetsky, the slogan that greeted him was 'Through Labour – Freedom!' – a lie identical to the wrought-iron legend *Arbeit Macht Frei* that would later welcome prisoners to Auschwitz.

# 7

# Strange Folk

*We want to protect the eternal foundation of our life: our national identity (*Volkstum*) and its inherent strengths and values ... Farmers, burghers and workers must once again become one German people (*ein deutsches Volk*).*
Hitler, speech at the opening of the Reichstag, March 21, 1933

*I have studied with great interest the laws of several American states concerning prevention of reproduction of people whose progeny would, in all probability, be of no value or injurious to the racial stock.*     Hitler to Otto Wagener, SA Chief of Staff

## THE LEADER SPEAKS

It was March 1933. The national mood was feverish and yet expectant. In the wake of his sweeping election victory, the country's charismatic new leader addressed a people desperate for change. Millions crowded around their radios to hear him. What they heard was a damning indictment of what had gone before and a stirring call for national revival.

In sombre tones, he began with a survey the country's dire economic predicament:

Values have shrunken to fantastic levels; taxes have risen; our ability to pay has fallen; government of all kinds is faced by serious curtailment of income; the means of exchange are frozen in the currents of trade; the withered leaves of industrial enterprise lie on every side; farmers find no markets for their produce; the savings of many years in thousands of families are gone. More important, a host of unemployed citizens face the grim problem of existence, and an equally great number toil with little return.

Who was to blame? He left his audience in no doubt. It was 'the rulers of the exchange of mankind's goods ... through their own stubbornness and their own incompetence'. But the 'practices of the unscrupulous money changers' now stood 'indicted in the court of public opinion'; they had been 'rejected by the hearts and minds of men':

Faced by failure of credit, they have proposed only the lending of more money. Stripped of the lure of profit by which to induce our people to follow their false leadership, they have resorted to exhortations, pleading tearfully for restored confidence. They know only the rules of a generation of self-seekers. They have no vision, and when there is no vision the people perish. The money changers have fled from their high seats in the temple of our civilization. We may now restore that temple to the ancient truths. [Applause] The measure of the restoration lies in the extent to which we apply social values more noble than mere monetary profit.

This was strong language, indeed, but there was more to come. Contrasting 'the falsity of material wealth' with 'the joy and moral stimulation of work', he inveighed against 'the standards of pride of place and personal profit', to say nothing of the 'callous and selfish wrongdoing' that had come to characterize both financial and political life. 'This Nation', he declared to further applause, 'asks for action, and action now.'

The action the new leader had in mind was bold, even revolutionary. Jobs would be created by 'direct recruiting by the Government itself, treating the task as we would treat the emergency of a war'; men would be put to work on 'greatly needed projects to stimulate and reorganize the use of our natural resources'. At the same time, to correct what he called 'the overbalance of population in our industrial centres', there would be a 'redistribution' of the workforce 'to provide a better use of the land for those best fitted for the land'. He would introduce a system of 'national planning for and supervision of all forms of transportation and of communications and other utilities' and 'a strict supervision of all banking and credits and investments' to bring 'an end to speculation with other people's money' – measures that won enthusiastic cheers from his audience. The country's 'international trade relations' would have to take second place to 'the establishment of a sound national economy'. 'We must move,' he declared, his voice now rising to a climax,

as a trained and loyal army willing to sacrifice for the good of a common discipline, because without such discipline no progress is made, no leadership becomes effective. We are, I know, ready and willing to submit our lives and property to such discipline, because it makes possible a leadership which aims at a larger good. This I propose to offer, pledging that the larger purposes will bind upon us all as a sacred obligation with a unity of duty hitherto evoked only in time of armed strife. With this pledge taken, I assume unhesitatingly the leadership of this great army of our people dedicated to a disciplined attack upon our common problems.

Not content with this vision of a militarized nation, he concluded with a stark warning to the nation's newly elected legislature: 'An unprecedented demand and need for undelayed action may call for temporary departure from . . . the normal balance of executive and legislative authority.' If the legislature did not swiftly pass the measures he proposed to deal with the national emergency, he demanded 'the one remaining instrument to meet the crisis – broad Executive power to wage a war against the emergency, as great as the power that would be given to me if we were in fact invaded by a foreign foe'. This line brought forth the loudest applause of all.

Who was this demagogue who so crudely blamed the Depression on corrupt financiers, who so boldly proposed state intervention as the cure for unemployment, who so brazenly threatened to rule by decree if the legislature did not back him, who so cynically used and re-used the words 'people' and 'Nation' to stoke up the patriotic sentiments of his audience? The answer is Franklin D. Roosevelt, and the speech from which all the above quotations are taken was his inaugural address as he assumed the American presidency on March 4, 1933.

Less than three weeks later, another election victor in another country that had been struck equally hard by the Depression gave a remarkably similar speech, beginning with a review of the country's dire economic straits, promising radical reforms, urging legislators to transcend petty party-political thinking and concluding with a stirring call for national unity. The resemblances between Adolf Hitler's speech to the newly elected Reichstag on March 21, 1933, and Roosevelt's inaugural address are indeed a great deal more striking than the differences. Yet it almost goes without saying that the United States and Germany took wholly different political directions from 1933 until 1945, the year when, both still in office, Roosevelt and Hitler died. Despite Roosevelt's threat to override Congress if it stood in his way, and despite his three subsequent re-elections, there were only two minor changes to the US Constitution during his presidency: the time between elections and changes of administration was reduced (Amendment 20) and the prohibition of alcohol was repealed (Amendment 21). The most important political consequence of the New Deal was significantly to strengthen the federal government relative to the individual states; democracy as such was not weakened. Indeed, Congress rejected Roosevelt's Judiciary Reorganization Bill. By contrast, the Weimar Constitution had already begun to decompose two or three years before the 1933 general election, with the increasing reliance of Hitler's predecessors on emergency presidential decrees. By the end of 1934 it had been reduced to a more or less empty shell. While Roosevelt was always in some measure constrained by the legislature, the courts, the federal states and the electorate, Hitler's will became absolute, untrammelled even by the need for consistency or written expression. What Hitler decided was done, even if the decision was communicated verbally; when he made no decision, officials were supposed to work towards whatever they thought his will might be. Roosevelt had to fight – and fight hard – three more presidential elections. Democracy in Germany, by contrast, became a sham, with orchestrated plebiscites in place of meaningful elections and a Reichstag stuffed with Nazi lackeys. The basic political freedoms of speech, of assembly, of the press and even of belief and thought were done away with. So, too, was the rule of law. Whole sections of German society, above all the Jews, lost their civil as well as political rights. Property rights were also selectively violated. To be sure, the United States was no utopia in the 1930s, particularly for African-

Americans. It was the Southern states whose legal prohibitions on interracial sex and marriage provided the Nazis with templates when they sought to ban relationships between 'Aryans' and Jews. Yet, to take the most egregious indicator, the number of lynchings of blacks during the 1930s (119 in all) was just 42 per cent of the number in the 1920s and 21 per cent of the number in the 1910s. Whatever else the Depression did, it did not destroy American democracy, nor worsen American racism.*

The contrast between the American and German responses to the Depression illuminates the central difficulty facing the historian who writes about the 1930s. These were the two industrial economies most severely affected by the economic crisis. Both entered the Depression as democracies; indeed, their constitutions had much in common – both republics, both federations, both with a directly elected presidency, both with universal suffrage, both with a bicameral legislature, both with a supreme court. Yet one navigated the treacherous interwar waters without significant change to its political institutions and its citizens' freedoms; the other produced the most abominable regime ever to emerge from a modern democracy. To attempt to explain why is to address perhaps the hardest question of twentieth-century history.

Recovery from the Depression plainly called for new economic policies in all countries; by 1933, as Roosevelt said, the traditional remedies favoured by his predecessor Herbert Hoover had been discredited. Any country that adhered tenaciously to the combination of sound money (the gold standard) and a more or less balanced budget was doomed to a decade of stagnation. Nor were tariffs the answer. However, there was a variety of different ways to engineer economic recovery. At one extreme were the policies of the Soviet Union, based on state ownership of the means of production, central planning and the ruthless coercion of labour. At the other, there was the British combination of currency devaluation, modest budget deficits and a protectionist imperial customs union. Other measures – such as the system of bank deposit insurance introduced in the United States –

---

* Roosevelt nevertheless opposed the Costigan–Wagner Anti-Lynching Bill for fear that to support it might cost him the Southern states in the 1936 election.

did not constitute a drastic break with the liberal economic order. Most countries adopted policies somewhere in between these two extremes, combining increased state involvement in employment, investment and the relief of poverty with looser fiscal and monetary policies and measures to limit the free flow and/or pricing of goods, capital and labour. The key point is that the political consequences of these new economic policies varied much more between countries than the policies themselves. Only in some countries was the adoption of new economic policies subsequent to, if not actually conditional upon, a political switch to dictatorship. The English-speaking world saw a variety of departures from economic orthodoxy without any erosion of democracy. So too did Scandinavia; it was in the 1930s that the Swedish Social Democrats laid the foundations of the post-1945 European welfare state. Ironically, moves away from democracy in other countries were sometimes justified by the need for more stringently orthodox fiscal policies, on the ground that the parliamentary system, with its special interests represented in the legislature, made it impossible to run balanced budgets. In fact, unbalanced budgets provided a generally beneficial stimulus to demand. It should also be remembered that changes of monetary policy did not require any diminution of democracy since in most countries before the Depression central banks were not democratically accountable. Some had their independence from parliamentary control legally enshrined. Others – notably the Bank of England and the Banque de France – were still considered to be private firms, accountable to their shareholders rather than to voters, even if their role and mode of operation were governed by statute.

Moreover, only in a sub-set of countries did the end of democracy also mean the end of liberty and the rule of law. Although the weakening of parliamentary power was often associated with increased persecution of ethnic minorities, it was in fact logically possible to have the one without the other. Liberal critics of democracy since Madison, de Tocqueville and Mill had warned against the 'tyranny of the majority'. It was already apparent in East Central Europe before the Depression that democracy could indeed lead ethnic majorities to discriminate against minorities (see Chapter 5). To be sure, executives unhampered by parliamentary scrutiny found it easier to violate existing laws or constitutions. But the degree to which inter-war authoritarian regimes persecuted individuals or particular social groups varied widely. In some cases dictators may actually have been better for ethnic minorities than elected governments willing to give full vent to majority prejudice. More than is commonly realized, authoritarian rulers could act as a check on violently intolerant fascist movements, most obviously in Romania, but also in Poland (see below).

Finally, only in a very few countries – a sub-set of the sub-set of dictatorships – did the end of parliamentary power and the rule of law also mean an aggressive foreign policy. The majority of authoritarian regimes were in fact relatively peaceable.

## MUSSOLINI'S MOMENT

In 1918 Roosevelt's predecessor Woodrow Wilson had declared: 'Democracy seems about universally to prevail ... The spread of democratic institutions ... promise[s] to reduce politics to a single form ... by reducing all forms of government to Democracy.' For a time he seemed to be right. Political scientists have attempted to quantify the global spread of democracy since the early nineteenth century. Their calculations point to a marked upsurge in both the number of democracies and the quality of democratization between 1914 and 1922. The proportion of countries with a democracy 'score' of higher than 6 out of 10 rose from 22 per cent to nearly 37 per cent. The mean level of democracy in the world rose from 7.8 to 8.7. This was the 'Wilsonian moment' and its impact was authentically global, not only transforming the landscape that had once been the Habsburg monarchy, but causing the earth to move uneasily under the European empires that had won the war. But it was only a moment. In the two decades after 1922 numerous democracies failed. By 1941 fewer than 14 per cent of countries were democracies; the mean level of democracy plunged to 6.4. The levels attained in 1922 were not seen again for some seventy years.

The story of a democratic wave, flowing then ebbing, is essentially a continental European story. In the English-speaking world (excluding undemocratic and only partly Anglophone South Africa) there was never a serious threat to democracy. Meanwhile, because the West European empires had survived the war intact, and indeed grew slightly in size, there was next to no democracy in Asia and Africa before or after the war. Japan, as we shall see, was the only Asian country to experience the democratic wave. In Latin America a few countries did go from more or less democratic regimes to dictatorships: Argentina, where the army overthrew the Radical president, Hipólito Irigoyen, in 1930, as well as Guatemala, Honduras and Bolivia. But the majority of countries south of the Rio Grande were not democracies to begin with and stayed that way. One, Costa Rica, was a democracy throughout. A few – Colombia, Peru and Paraguay – actually achieved modest progress towards democracy between the wars. Chile suffered a military coup in 1924, but constitutional rule was restored by General Carlos Ibáñez in 1932.

Of twenty-eight European countries – using the broadest credible definition of Europe – nearly all had acquired some form of representative government before, during or after the First World War. Yet eight were dictatorships by 1925, and a further five by 1933. Five years later only ten democracies remained. Russia, as we have seen, was the first to go after the Bolsheviks shut down the Constituent Assembly in 1918. In Hungary the franchise was restricted as early as 1920. Kemal, fresh from his trouncing of the Greeks, established what was effectively a one-party state in Turkey in 1923, rather than see his policies of secularism challenged by an Islamic opposition. However, it was events in Italy the previous year that seemed to set a more general pattern.

Benito Mussolini was the first European leader not only to dispense with multi-party democracy but also to proclaim a new fascist regime. A blacksmith's son, a socialist and the author of two crudely anti-clerical books, *The Cardinal's Mistress* and *John Huss the Veracious*, Mussolini had switched to nationalism even before the Italian Socialists opposed their country's entry into the First World War. The Roman *fasces* – the bundle of rods of chastisement that symbolized the power of the state – had been adopted by various pro-war groups; it was one of these that Mussolini joined. Here was the formula for fascism: socialism plus nationalism plus war. After a brief and undistinguished period of military service, Mussolini reverted to journalism, his true *métier*. But his political moment came with peace.

Like their counterparts all over Europe, Italy's political establishment felt vulnerable as the Bolshevik contagion swept into the factories of Turin and the villages of the Po Valley. With his flashy charisma, Mussolini offered an echo of Francesco Crispi, the hero of the previous generation of Italian nationalists. With his newly formed *Fasci di Combattimento*, he offered muscle in the form of gangs of ex-soldiers, the *squadristi*. Even before his distinctly theatrical March on Rome on October 29, 1922 – which was more photo-opportunity than coup, since the fascists lacked the capability to seize power by force* – Mussolini was invited to form a government by the king, Victor Emmanuel III, who had declined to impose martial law. The old Liberals were confident they could continue business as usual. They underestimated Mussolini's appetite for power; it was entirely in character that at one point he held seven ministerial portfolios as well as the premiership. The press, the only thing he was competent to control, began to promote him as an omnipotent Duce, but behind the surface glamour there was always the threat of violence. Following the murder of the Socialist deputy Giacomo Matteotti in 1924 (almost certainly ordered by Mussolini) political opposition was suppressed. The likes of the Leninist Antonio Gramsci were consigned to prison. Henceforth, the National Fascist Party brooked no competitors. Newspaper editors were required to be fascists, and teachers to swear an oath of loyalty. Parliament and even trade unions continued to exist, but as sham entities, subordinated to Mussolini's dictatorship.

Italy was far from unusual in having dictatorship by royal appointment. Other dictators were themselves monarchs. The Albanian President, Ahmed Bey Zogu, declared himself King Zog I in 1928. In Bulgaria King Alexander seized power in 1929. In Yugoslavia King Alexander staged a coup in 1929, restored parliamentarism in 1931 and was assassinated in 1934; thereafter the Regent Paul re-established royal dictatorship. In Greece the king dissolved parliament and in

---

* It has been argued persuasively that the March on Rome was an 'historical event which never occurred'. The press talked up the effectiveness of fascist moves to seize power in Cremona, Pisa, Florence, Turin and elsewhere, but these were only successful when unopposed. The only thing that actually 'marched' on Rome was the train that took Mussolini from Milan to the capital on the evening of the 29th, after the King had asked him to form a government.

1936 installed General Ioannis Metaxas as dictator. Two years later Romania's King Carol established a royal dictatorship of his own. In Hungary there was no king, but the political elites retained the fiction that the country was a monarchy, with Admiral Miklós Horthy as Regent; power was wielded in his name by two strongmen, first Count Stephen Bethlen and then Gyula Gömbös. Elsewhere it was elected presidents who simply did away with parliaments. Antanas Smetona established a dictatorship in Lithuania in 1926. Konstantin Päts ruled Estonia by decree for four years as *Riigihoidja* (Protector) and then President after 1934, the same year that Prime Minister (later President) Karlis Ulmanis dissolved parliament in Latvia.

In other cases, it was the army that seized power. General Jósef Piłsudski, Poland's Cromwell, marched on Warsaw in 1926 to become *de facto* dictator until his death in 1935, when much, though not all, of his power passed to another soldier, Edward Śmigły-Rydz. In Spain there was a constitutional monarchy from 1917 until 1923, then a military dictatorship under Primo de Rivera until 1930, then a republic that drifted steadily to the Left, culminating in the formation of the Popular Front coalition, which included both Communists and Social-ists. After a bitter three-year civil war initiated in 1936 by a group of army officers and supported by the parties of the National Front, General Francisco Franco established himself as dictator, the ben-eficiary not only of German and Italian intervention but also of the debilitating 'civil war within the civil war' between the various factions of the Left. The transition in Portugal was similar, though smoother. There, the army seized power in 1926; six years later the finance minister António de Oliveira Salazar became premier, promulgating an authoritarian constitution which established him as dictator the following year. Engelbert Dollfuss tried to pull off the same trick in Austria, governing by decree after March 1933. Though assassinated in July 1934, he was able to bequeath a functioning authoritarian system to his successor Kurt Schuschnigg.

Considering the emphasis the new dictatorships laid on their sup-posedly distinctive nationalistic traditions, they all looked remarkably alike: the coloured shirts, the shiny boots, the martial music, the strutting leaders, the gangster violence. At first sight, then, there was little to distinguish the German version of dictatorship from all the rest – except perhaps that Hitler was marginally more absurd than his counterparts. As late as 1939, Adolf Hitler could still be portrayed by Charlie Chaplin in his film *The Great Dictator* as an essentially comic figure, bawling incomprehensible speeches, striking preposterous poses and frolicking with a large inflatable globe. Yet there were in reality profound differences between National Socialism and fascism. Nearly all the dictatorships of the inter-war period were at root conservative, if not downright reactionary. The social foundations of their power were what remained of the pre-industrial *ancien régime*: the monarchy, the aristocracy, the officer corps and the Church, supported to varying degrees by industrialists fearful of socialism and by frivolous intellectuals who were bored of democracy's messy compromises.* The main function the dictators performed was to crush the Left: to break their strikes, prohibit their parties, deny voice to their voters, arrest and, if it was deemed necessary, kill their leaders. One of the few measures they took that went beyond simple social restoration was to introduce new 'corporate' institutions supposed to regiment economic life and protect loyal supporters from the vagaries of the market. In 1924 the French historian Élie Halévy nicely characterized fascist Italy as 'the land of tyranny ... a regime extremely agreeable for travellers, where trains arrive and leave on time, where there is no strike in ports or public transport'. 'The bourgeois', he added, 'are beaming.' It was, as Renzo De Felice said in his vast and apologetic biography of the Duce, 'the old regime in a black shirt'. Even the Catholic Church, which the young Mussolini had despised,

---

* A list of all the treasonous clerics who flirted or did more than flirt with fascism would be a book in its own right. If only to give an illustration of how widespread the phenomenon was, dishonourable mention may be made of the writer Gabriele D'Annunzio, who established his own tinpot tyranny in post-war Fiume; the poet T. S. Eliot, who wrote that 'totalitarianism can retain the terms "freedom" and "democracy" and give them its own meaning'; the philosopher Martin Heidegger, who, as Rector of Freiburg University, lent his enthusiastic support to the Nazi regime; the political theorist Carl Schmitt, who devised pseudo-legal justifications for the illegalities of the Third Reich; the novelist Ignazio Silone, who shopped former Communist comrades to the fascists; and the poet W. B. Yeats, who wrote songs for the Irish Blueshirts. Thomas Mann, who had made his fair share of mistakes during the First World War and only with difficulty broke publicly with the Nazi regime, was not wrong when he spoke of 'the thoroughly guilty stratum of intellectuals'.

was accommodated under the terms of the 1929 Concordat. True, there were fascist leaders and movements in some of these countries whose rhetoric went further, conjuring up visions of national regeneration rather than merely reaffirming the old order. But the fascism of the *Falange Española de las Juntas de Ofensiva Nacional Sindicalista* – to give the Spanish fascist party its full, grandiose title – was only a small component of Franco's fundamentally conservative support; the key word in Franco's merged *Falange Española Tradicionalista* was the last one. In other cases, notably in Austria, Hungary and Romania, the dictatorship acted to suppress or at least restrain fascist parties.

Only in Germany was fascism both revolutionary and totalitarian in deed as well as in word. Only in Germany did dictatorship ultimately lead to industrialized genocide. There were good reasons for this. Fascist movements were optional accessories for most dictators. Not in the German case. As Figure 7.1 shows, no other fascist parties came close to achieving the electoral success of the National Socialists. In terms of votes, fascism was a disproportionately German phenomenon; add together all the individual votes cast in Europe for fascist or other extreme nationalist parties between 1930 and 1935, and a staggering 96 per cent were cast by German-speakers.

Viewed globally, the collapse of democracy cannot easily be blamed on the Depression; as we have seen, too many democracies survived deep economic crises and too many dictatorships were formed before the slump or in the wake of quite modest declines in output. Viewed in strictly European terms, however, it is hard to ignore the correlation between the magnitude of a country's economic difficulties and the magnitude of its fascist vote (see Figure 7.2). By and large, the countries with the deepest Depressions were the ones that produced the most fascist voters. The economic crisis was most severe in Central and Eastern Europe. That was also where the political appeal of fascism was greatest. But the crucial point is that it was Germans – inside and outside the Reich – who were most attracted to fascism; or, to put it differently, the only variant of fascism that was truly a mass movement was German National Socialism.

Two things made the German experience unique. The first was Hitler himself, who was in many ways more bizarre than Chaplin knew. An art-school reject who had once scraped a living by selling

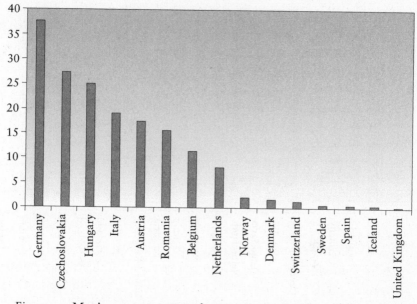

*Figure 7.1* **Maximum percentage of votes won by fascist or 'semi-fascist'
parties in free national elections held during 1930s**

kitschy picture postcards; an Austrian draft-dodger who had ended
up a decorated Bavarian corporal; a lazy mediocrity who rose late
and enjoyed both Wagner's operas and Karl May's cowboy yarns –
here indeed was an unlikely heir to the legacy of Frederick the Great
and Otto von Bismarck. In Munich in the early 1920s he could be
seen attending the soirées of a Romanian princess 'in his gangster hat
and trenchcoat over his dinner jacket, touting a pistol and carrying as
usual his dog-whip'. It is not altogether surprising that President
Hindenburg assumed he was Bohemian. Others thought he looked
more like 'a man trying to seduce the cook', or perhaps a renegade tram
conductor. If it had not been for the advice of his publisher Max Amann,
he would have called his first book *Four and a Half Years of Struggle
against Lies, Stupidity and Cowardice* instead of the distinctly catchier
*My Struggle*. The longer title captures something of Hitler's shrill and
vituperative personality. As for his sexuality, about which there has
long been speculation on the basis of circumstantial or tainted evidence,
he may have had none. Hitler hated. He did not love.

The second crucial difference between the Third Reich and the

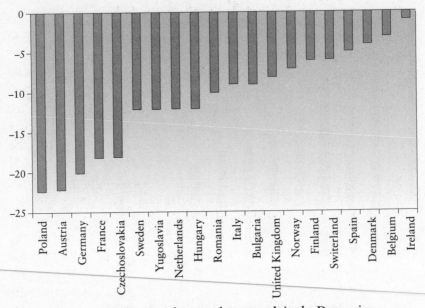

*Figure 7.2* **Real output from peak to trough in the Depression**

other fascist regimes of the 1930s was simply Germany. Most of the countries where democracy failed between the wars were relatively backward, with half or more of the working population engaged in agriculture in around 1930. Indeed, there would have been a relatively close negative correlation between this proportion and the likely duration of democracy, but for two outliers. Those were Germany and Austria, both societies where fewer than one in three people worked on the land. The challenge is to explain how a pathological individual like Hitler was able to gain total control over what seemed to many people, at least prior to 1933, to be the most sophisticated country in Europe, if not the world.

# BROTHER HITLER

To many visitors, Germany in the 1920s was the United States of Europe: big, industrial, ultra-modern. It was home to some of Europe's biggest and best corporations: the electrical engineering giant Siemens, the financial titan Deutsche Bank, the automobile maker Mercedes Benz, the chemical conglomerate IG-Farben. Berlin boasted the biggest film industry in Europe, producing in Fritz Lang's *Metropolis* the science-fiction masterpiece of the twenties and in the same director's *M* the definitive *film noir*. Berlin had newspapers as sensational as William Randolph Hearst's (the *8Uhr-Abendblatt*); department stores as big as Macy's (the Kaufhaus des Westens); sports stars as idolized as 'Babe' Ruth (the boxer Max Schmeling). So pervasive was the transatlantic influence that Franz Kafka felt able to write *Amerika* without even going there. Indeed, in one vital respect Germany went one better than the United States. It had by far the best universities in the world. By comparison with Heidelberg and Tübingen, Harvard and Yale were gentlemen's clubs, where students paid more attention to football than to physics. More than a quarter of all the Nobel prizes awarded in the sciences between 1901 and 1940 were awarded to Germans; only 11 per cent went to Americans. Einstein reached the pinnacle of his profession not in 1932, when he moved to Princeton, but in 1914, when he was appointed Professor at the University of Berlin, Director of the Kaiser Wilhelm Institute for Physics and a member of the Prussian Academy of Sciences. Even the finest scientists produced by Cambridge felt obliged to do a tour of duty in Germany.

There was, however, another Germany – a Germany of provincial hometowns that felt no affection for the frenzied modernism of the *Grossstadt*. This Germany had been traumatized by the upheavals that had begun with the ghastly revelation of military defeat in November 1918.* Nearly all the revolutionary events of the immediate post-war

---

* The German reaction to defeat was brilliantly captured by Sebastian Haffner: 'How shall I describe my feelings – the feelings of an eleven-year-old boy whose entire inner world has collapsed? However much I try, I find it difficult to find an equivalent in ordinary, everyday life. Certain fantastic catastrophes are only possible in dream worlds. Maybe one could imagine someone who year after year has deposited large

period took place in the big cities: Berlin, Hamburg, Munich. Despite the decision to draft the new republic's constitution in the sleepy capital of Thuringia, the Weimar Republic was always a metropolitan affair. Not much changed in the provinces, as the English 'wandering scholar' Patrick Leigh Fermor found when he set off to walk from the Rhine to the Danube in late 1933. His first encounter in the Third Reich was with a troop of brownshirts in a small Westphalian town, who held a perfunctory parade in the main square and then repaired to the nearest inn for beer and a hearty sing-song. From the Krefeld workhouse run by Franciscan monks to the book-lined study of a deceased professor, from the hold of a Rhine barge to a farmhouse near Pforzheim, Fermor passed through a Germany little different from the Germany his father or even his grandfather would have seen had they made the same journey. As the industrialist and philosopher Walther Rathenau complained to the diarist Harry, Count Kessler, 'There was no revolution. The doors only sprang open. The wardens ran away. The captives stood dazzled in the prison courtyard, incapable of moving their limbs.'

The Republic attempted the impossible: simultaneously to create a welfare state and to pay the reparations imposed under the Treaty of Versailles. The strains this imposed on Germany's economy produced not just one but two crises: first hyperinflation in 1923 and then steep deflation after 1929. It is hardly surprising that these twin crises undermined Weimar's already frail legitimacy. The inflation seemed to signal a collapse not just of monetary values but of all the values of the pre-war *bürgerliche Gesellschaft* (bourgeois society). What price the *Rechtsstaat* – the state based on law – if long-standing contracts could be fulfilled only with worthless paper marks? As for *Ruhe und Ordnung*, the peace and order that had been so dear to nineteenth-century Germans, there seemed little left of that. In every year between 1919 and 1923 there were attempted coups by the extreme Left or the extreme Right, to say nothing of a spate of assassinations by sinister secret societies, one of which claimed the life of Rathenau, who as Foreign Minister had become identified with the effort to fulfil

---

sums of money in his bank, and when one day he asks for a statement, discovers a gigantic overdraft instead of a fortune; but that only happens in dreams.'

the Versailles obligations. In the wake of the currency collapse, many voters drifted away from the middle-class parties of the centre-right and centre-left, disillusioned with the horse-trading between business and labour that seemed to dominate Weimar politics. There was a proliferation of splinter parties and special interest groups, a slow process of fission that was the prelude to the political explosion of 1930, when the Nazi share of the vote leapt to seven times what it had been in 1928. The Depression was crucial not because the unemployed voted for the Nazis, but because so many of them swung to the Communists; as in so many other countries, fascism seemed to many a rational political response to the threat of Red revolution. The Depression also exposed the dysfunctional character of the Weimar system, which seemed too democratic – or, rather, too representative of well-organized interests – to deal with so vast and universally perceptible a crisis. But the political disintegration of republican Germany had begun seven years prior to the election breakthrough of 1930, with the wheelbarrows of worthless cash that symbolized Weimar's bankruptcy.

There were, of course, alternatives to Hitler. It was just that none of them was viable. Gustav Stresemann of the People's Party had offered compromise with the Western powers – symbolized by the 1925 Treaty of Locarno – and the hope of revanche in the East. But he had died of a heart attack on October 3, 1929, at the age of just fifty-one. Heinrich Brüning of the Catholic Centre Party offered government by presidential decree and dreamt vaguely of restoring the monarchy. But his deflationary policies only served to deepen the slump. Franz von Papen, another Catholic, betrayed his party for the sake of becoming Chancellor, in the vain belief that he could do better than Brüning. But neither he nor his successor General Kurt von Schleicher – whom Papen had picked as his own Defence Minister – had anything resembling popular support and, while the Reichstag had been temporarily sidelined by Brüning, it proved impossible to rule indefinitely without some kind of parliamentary majority. Elections in July 1932 saw the Nazi vote soar above 37 per cent. True, it fell back to 33 per cent when new elections were held in November, not least because signs of economic recovery were at last manifesting themselves, but the party's entitlement to form a government was by now hard to dispute since it was still easily the biggest grouping in the Reichstag. Ever the schemer, Papen now persuaded Hindenburg to dump Schleicher and, against the President's better judgement, to appoint Hitler to lead a coalition with the conservative German Nationalist Party – the only party except for the Communists to gain significant numbers of new votes in the November election. Hitler duly became Chancellor on January 30, 1933. Thus did German democracy wreak its own destruction. Given the paralysing enmity between the Social Democrats and the Communists, the only way to avoid the Third Reich would have been if Hindenburg himself had shut down the Reichstag and banned the Nazis, an option he does not seem to have contemplated.

Superficially, Hitler's appeal to German voters is easy to understand. He simply offered more radical remedies to the Depression than his political rivals. Others might offer piecemeal solutions to unemployment; Hitler was willing to contemplate a bold programme of public works. Others might worry that financing public works with deficits would trigger a new inflation; Hitler bluntly stated that the hoodlums of his *Sturmabteilung* would deal with any profiteers who charged excessive prices. Others might argue, as Rathenau and Stresemann had, that Germany must try to pay reparations, if only to prove the impossibility of doing so, or must borrow to the hilt in New York so as to drive a rift between the Western creditors; Hitler essentially argued for default. It helped, of course, that the reparations system had itself collapsed by 1932; Germany had already defaulted, albeit with American consent, by the time Hitler came to power. It helped, too, that the Nazis were able to recruit the widely respected former Reichsbank President Hjalmar Schacht, who had resigned his post in 1930 after effectively endorsing Hitler's campaign against the revised reparations schedule known as the Young Plan.* Yet even with his

* The Young Plan, named after the American banker Owen D. Young, replaced the 1924 Dawes Plan, which had also been named after an American, Charles G. Dawes. By rescheduling German payments over 58½ years, the Young Plan reduced Germany's annual payments from around 2.5 billion gold marks – i.e. marks of 1913 – to just over 2 billion. It also removed the Reparations Agent, who had exerted a limited foreign control over German economic policy. But the reduction was much smaller than the Germans had hoped for.

imprimatur on them, it took real political skill to sell such unorthodox economic solutions to a relatively sophisticated and highly variegated electorate. The Nazis' success without doubt owed much to Joseph Goebbels, the evil genius of twentieth-century marketing, who sold Hitler to the German public as if he were the miraculous offspring of the Messiah and Marlene Dietrich. The Nazi election campaigns of 1930, 1932 and 1933 were unprecedented assaults on public opinion, involving standardized mass meetings and eye-catching posters, as well as rousing songs (like the *Horst-Wessel Lied*) and calculated physical intimidation of opponents. Though much of this owed its inspiration to Mussolini – not least the snazzy uniforms for supporters, and the Roman salutes – Goebbels understood the need for finesse as well as bombast. For one thing, he saw more clearly than the star himself the need to adjust Hitler's message according to which of the German electorate's many segments was being addressed.

The most impressive indicator of the success of these tactics was, of course, the dramatic growth of the Nazi vote in the crucial elections of 1930 and 1932. Contrary to the old claims that it was the party of the countryside, or of the north, or of the middle class, the NSDAP attracted votes right across Germany and right across the social spectrum. Analysis at the level of the main electoral districts misses this point and exaggerates the differences between regions. More recent research based on the smallest electoral unit (the *Kreis*) has revealed the extraordinary breadth of the Nazi vote. There is an almost fractal quality to the picture that emerges, with each electoral district somewhat resembling the national map, and hotspots of support (Oldenburg in Lower Saxony, Upper and Middle Franconia in Bavaria, the northern parts of Baden, the eastern region of East Prussia) scattered all over the country. It is true that places with relatively high Nazi votes were more likely to be in central northern and eastern parts, and those with relatively low Nazi votes were more likely to be in the south and west. But the more important point is that the Nazis were able to achieve some electoral success in nearly any kind of local political milieu, covering the German electoral spectrum in a way not seen before or since. The Nazi vote did not vary proportionately with the unemployment rate or the share of workers in the population. As many as two-fifths of Nazi voters in some districts were working class, to the consternation of the Communist leadership. In response, some local Communists openly made common cause with the Nazis. 'Oh yes, we admit that we're in league with the National Socialists,' said one Communist leader in Saxony. 'Bolshevism and Fascism share a common goal: the destruction of capitalism and of the Social Democratic Party. To achieve this aim we are justified in using every means.' It was a mark of Goebbels' skill in making the party seem all things to all men that, simultaneously, dyed-in-the-wool Prussian Conservatives could regard the Nazis as potential partners in an anti-Marxist coalition. Thus were political rivals lured into what proved to be fatal forms of cooperation. The only significant constraint on the growth of the Nazi vote was the comparatively greater resilience of the Catholic Centre party compared with parties hitherto supported by German Protestants.

Other fascist movements, as we have seen, depended heavily on elite sponsorship to gain power. The Nazis did not need to. For all the attention that has been paid to them, the machinations of the coterie around Hindenburg were not the decisive factor, as those of the Italian elites had been in 1922. If anything, they delayed Hitler's appointment as Chancellor, an office that was rightfully his after the July 1932 election. It was not the traditional elite of landed property that was drawn to Hitler; the real Junker types found him horribly coarse. (When Hitler shook hands with Hindenburg, one conservative was reminded 'of a headwaiter closing his hand around the tip'.) Nor was it the business elite, who not unreasonably feared that National Socialism would prove a Trojan horse for socialism proper; nor the military elite, who had every reason to dread subordination to an opinionated Austrian corporal. The key to the strength and dynamism of the Third Reich was Hitler's appeal to the much more numerous intellectual elite; the men with university degrees who are so vital to the smooth running of a modern state and civil society.

For reasons that may be traced back to the foundation of the Bismarckian Reich or perhaps even further into Prussian history, academically educated Germans were unusually ready to prostrate themselves before a charismatic leader. Marianne Weber recalled how, in the wake of the 1918 Revolution, her husband, the great sociologist

Max Weber, had explained his theory of democracy to the architect of Germany's defeat General Erich Ludendorff:

WEBER: Do you think that I regard the *Schweinerei* that we now have as democracy?
LUDENDORFF: What is your idea of a democracy, then?
WEBER: In a democracy, the people choose a leader whom they trust. Then the chosen man says, 'Now shut your mouths and obey me.' The people and the parties are no longer free to interfere in the leader's business.
LUDENDORFF: I should like such a 'democracy'.
WEBER: Later, the people can sit in judgment. If the leader has made mistakes – to the gallows with him!

After a politics lesson like that – from a man who was considered a liberal in the German academy – it was not really surprising that Ludendorff ended up a Nazi member of the Reichstag. Professionals, too, proved exceptionally susceptible to Hitler's appeal. Lawyers and doctors were substantially over-represented within the NSDAP, as were university students (then a far narrower section of society than today). To fat middle-aged lawyers, he was the heir to Bismarck. For their sons, he was the Wagnerian hero Rienzi, the demagogue who unites the people of Rome. 'Right down to the last, deepest fibre in myself, I belong to the Führer and his wonderful movement,' wrote the Nazi lawyer Hans Frank in his diary after a concert he had attended with Hitler on February 10, 1937. 'We are in truth God's tool for the annihilation of the bad forces of the earth. We fight in God's name against Jews and their Bolshevism. God protect us!' Such thoughts helped him and many other lawyers to come to terms with the systematic illegality that characterized the regime from the very outset: the arrests without trial (26,000 people were already in 'protective custody' as early as July 1933), the summary executions (beginning with the Night of the Long Knives in June 1934, when between eighty-five and two hundred people, including the over-mighty leaders of the SA, were murdered in cold blood) and, of course, the escalating discrimination against racial and social minorities.

In similar fashion, artists and art historians turned a blind eye to the fundamental tackiness of Nazi aesthetics. Though Hitler's youthful daubs confirm that the Vienna Academy of Fine Arts had been right to reject him, his extravagant ambitions for German art were simply irresistible to men like Dr Ernest Buchner, the General Director of the Bavarian State Painting Collections, or the sculptor Arno Breker, who had been hailed as the German Rodin in the 1920s. In May 1933, like thousands of other opportunists, Buchner joined the Nazi party. Before long he was busy replacing 'degenerate' (modern) artworks with the kitsch favoured by the Führer. Breker struck the same Faustian pact. By the 1940s his atelier was mass-producing busts of Hitler. Economists were also drawn to Nazism. Statisticians at the German Institute of Business-Cycle Research in Berlin were excited at the prospect of policies that aimed at full employment through state-led investment; its Chilean-born chief Ernest Wagemann understood as well as Keynes, and perhaps before him, the need for a reflationary response to the Depression. Having quarrelled with Brüning, Wagemann joined the Nazis in the (correct) belief that they would do a better job of bringing about an economic recovery. Others found economic rationales for the Nazis' policies of 'racial hygiene'. Karl Binding and Alfred Hoche had published their *Permission for the Destruction of Life Unworthy of Life* in 1920, which sought to extrapolate from the annual cost of maintaining one 'idiot' 'the massive capital ... being subtracted from the national product for entirely unproductive purposes'. There is a clear line of continuity from this kind of analysis to the document found at the Schloss Hartheim asylum in 1945, which calculated that by 1951 the economic benefit of killing 70,273 mental patients – assuming an average daily outlay of 3.50 marks and a life expectancy of ten years – would be 885,439,800 marks. Many historians were little better, churning out tendentious historical justifications for German territorial claims in Eastern Europe.

Later, after it was all over, the historian Friedrich Meinecke tried to explain 'the German catastrophe' by arguing that technical specialization had caused some educated Germans (not him, needless to say) to lose sight of the humanistic values of Goethe and Schiller; thus they were unable to resist Hitler's 'mass Machiavellianism'. Thomas Mann was unusual in being able to recognize even at the time that, in 'Brother Hitler', the entire German *Bildungsbürgertum* possessed a monstrous younger sibling who embodied some of their

deepest-rooted aspirations. An academic education, far from inoculat-
ing people against Nazism, made them more likely to embrace it. So
much for the greatness of the German universities. Their fall from
grace was personified by the readiness of Martin Heidegger, the
greatest German philosopher of his generation, to jump on the Nazi
bandwagon, a swastika pin in his lapel.

Were German intellectuals worse in these respects than their
counterparts elsewhere? Possibly. Yet other intellectuals were never
exposed to Hitler's supernatural magnetism – and that, surely, was
the crucial factor. For, on closer inspection, what Hitler offered Germans was something much more than Roosevelt was offering Americans. Roosevelt spoke of frankness, action and leadership in a national
emergency. But he emphasized in his inaugural address that the nature
of that emergency was purely material; spiritually and morally there
was nothing wrong with American society. Hitler, by contrast, saw
Germany's economic problems as mere symptoms of a more profound
national malaise. Roosevelt made eight references in his speech to the
'people'; Hitler used the word *Volk* no fewer than eighteen times. His
role was not just to restart the economy but to be the nation's saviour,
the redeemer who would end years of national division by forging a
*Volksgemeinschaft* – a folk-community. Tellingly, Hitler's first speech
as Chancellor ended as follows:

I cherish the firm conviction that the hour will come at last in which the
millions who despise us today will stand by us and with us hail the new,
hard-won and painfully acquired German Reich we have created together,
the new German kingdom of greatness and power and glory and justice.
Amen.

The response that this messianic proposition elicited was quasi-
religious in its fervor. As an SA sergeant explained: 'Our opponents
. . . committed a fundamental error when equating us as a party with
the Economic Party, the Democrats or the Marxist parties. All these
parties were only interest groups, they lacked soul, spiritual ties.
Adolf Hitler emerged as bearer of a new political religion.' The Nazis
developed a self-conscious liturgy, with November 9 (the date of the
1918 Revolution and the failed 1923 Beer Hall *putsch*) as a Day of
Mourning, complete with fires, wreaths, altars, blood-stained relics

and even a Nazi book of martyrs. Initiates into the elite *Schutzstaffel* (SS) had to incant a catechism with lines like 'We believe in God, we believe in Germany which He created . . . and in the Führer . . . whom He has sent us.' It was not just that Christ was more or less overtly supplanted by Hitler in the iconography and liturgy of 'the brown cult'. As the SS magazine *Das Schwarze Korps* argued, the very ethical foundation of Christianity had to go too: 'The abstruse doctrine of Original Sin . . . indeed the whole notion of sin as set forth by the Church . . . is something intolerable to Nordic man, since it is incompatible with the "heroic" ideology of our blood.'

The Nazis' opponents also recognized the pseudo-religious character of the movement. As the Catholic exile Eric Voegelin put it, Nazism was 'an ideology akin to Christian heresies of redemption in the here and now . . . fused with post-Enlightenment doctrines of social transformation'. The journalist Konrad Heiden called Hitler 'a pure fragment of the modern mass soul' whose speeches always ended 'in overjoyed redemption'. An anonymous Social Democrat called the Nazi regime a 'counter-church'. Two individuals as different as Eva Klemperer, wife of the Jewish-born philologist Victor, and the East Prussian conservative Friedrich Reck-Malleczewen could agree in likening Hitler to the sixteenth-century Anabaptist Jan of Leyden:

As in our case, a misbegotten failure conceived, so to speak, in the gutter, became the great prophet, and the opposition simply disintegrated, while the rest of the world looked on in astonishment and incomprehension. As with us . . . hysterical females, schoolmasters, renegade priests, the dregs and outsiders from everywhere formed the main supports of the regime . . . A thin sauce of ideology covered lewdness, greed, sadism, and fathomless lust for power . . . and whoever would not completely accept the new teaching was turned over to the executioner.

Still, all this leaves one question unanswered: What had gone wrong with the existing religions in Germany? For if National Socialism was a political religion, the fragmentation of the old political parties cannot satisfactorily be presented as the essential precondition for its success. Evidence of declining religious belief among German Christians is in fact not hard to find: a substantial proportion of Germans exercised the option to be registered as *konfessionslos* in the 1920s. There were marked declines in church attendance, particularly in North German cities. Significantly, unlike the Catholic Church, the Lutheran Church had suffered very heavy financial losses in the hyper-inflation. Morale among the Protestant clergy was low; many were attracted to the Nazi notion of a new 'Positive Christianity'. All this may offer a clue as to why the former were more likely than the latter to vote Nazi in the crucial elections of 1930–33 – as we have seen, the single most striking sociological characteristic of NSDAP support, though here too there was considerable regional variation and it would be quite wrong to infer from this anything stronger than inertia in Catholic voting patterns. After all, Austrians were scarcely less enthusiastic about National Socialism and they were virtually all Catholic. And nearly all the fascist dictators were themselves raised as Catholics: Franco, Hitler, Mussolini, to say nothing of wartime puppets like Ante Pavelić in Croatia and Jozef Tiso in Slovakia, who was himself a priest.

## INSIDE THE 'FOLK-COMMUNITY'

In some superficial respects, it should be emphasized, the Third Reich resembled the more innovative democracies in its responses to the Depression. As in the United States, the government embarked on an ambitious programme of highway construction that would at its peak employ more than 100,000 men. As in the United States, the Nazi 'New Deal' involved a significant expansion of public sector employment; soon around 18,000 people were employed purely to manage the new currency controls introduced by Hjalmar Schacht, appointed Reichsbank President and later Minister of Economics by Hitler. As in the United States, it was rearmament that provided the crucial push for the return to full employment. In Germany, however, rearmament got under way immediately; under Roosevelt it came much later. The scale of the Nazi economic achievement should not be underestimated. As Figure 7.3 shows, it was real and impressive. No other European economy achieved such a rapid recovery – though no other European economy had sunk so low between 1929 and

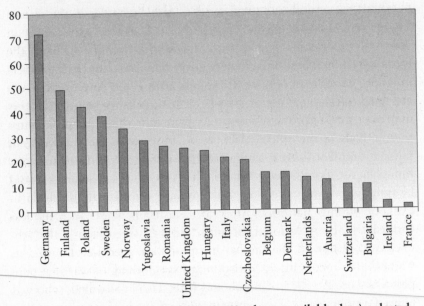

*Figure 7.3* **Real output, trough to 1938 (or latest available date), selected European countries**

1932. More than six million Germans had been unemployed when Hitler became Chancellor. By June 1935 the number had fallen below two million, by April 1937 below one million and by September of the same year below half a million. In August 1939 just 34,000 Germans were registered as unemployed.

How was it done? It was plainly not through the credit-financed job-creation schemes that had been initiated under Hitler's predecessors. Investment had collapsed in the Depression; the government led its recovery with substantial increases in expenditure on armaments and (often defence-related) infrastructure – which accounted for roughly even shares of gross fixed investment between 1933 and 1938 – and the private sector followed, accounting for two-thirds of all fixed investment. The annual growth rate of gross fixed investment, adjusted for inflation, was 29 per cent. The increase in public sector investment, from an average of just over 3 per cent of national income in the Weimar period to more than 10 per cent by 1938, was financed in large measure by running deficits. Total government expenditure had risen steeply between 1925 and 1932 from 30 to 45 per cent of national income and continued its rise under the Nazis, despite a brief decline in 1935 and 1936, to reach 53 per cent by 1938. But taxes did not keep pace after 1933. Weimar deficits after 1924 had averaged just 2.1 per cent of national income. Between 1933 and 1938 the total public sector deficit averaged 5.2 per cent (though it rose steeply from less than 2 per cent in 1933 to more than 10 per cent in 1938). Gross domestic product grew, on average, by a remarkable 11 per cent a year. Private consumption grew more slowly; indeed, as a share of GDP it declined from a peak of 90 per cent in 1932 to just 59 per cent. The Keynesian multiplier, which determines the knock-on effect of deficit spending on aggregate demand, was evidently not high for 1930s Germany. But for most people, the most important thing was the dramatic growth of employment. Given all the warnings that had been uttered during the Weimar years, the mystery was that all this was achieved without a significant increase in inflation. Consumer prices rose at an average annual rate of just 1.2 per cent between 1933 and 1939. This meant that German workers were better off in real as well as nominal terms: between 1933 and 1938, weekly net earnings (after tax) rose by 22 per cent, while the cost of living rose by just 7 per cent. The explanation lies in the complex of controls on trade, capital flows and prices which the Nazis inherited and extended, and the surreptitious ways in which some of the new government borrowing was financed, combined with the destruction of trade union autonomy, which removed the chronic 'wage push' that had afflicted the German economy in the 1920s. Keynes, in other words, was right when he said that a totalitarian regime would be able to achieve full employment with an expansionary fiscal policy, precisely because it would be able to impose the necessary controls.

There were, it is true, limits to what could be achieved by these means, most obviously in the realm of the balance of payments. Germany's position was certainly easier than it had been in the last Weimar years, when the withdrawal of foreign capital and the continued need to pay reparations and interest on foreign loans had imposed a crippling burden, ultimately precipitating a devastating banking crisis in 1931. On the other hand, Schacht's suspension of interest payments on some (though at first not all) of Germany's long-term foreign debt could not entirely solve the underlying problem: the Reich's continued and growing need for imports, despite all talk of autarky, and the limited opportunities she had for increasing her exports, because of foreign tariffs, worsening terms of trade, a pegged and overvalued exchange rate and other impediments such as the bilateral clearing arrangements established with creditor countries. In prices of 1913, Germany was running trade deficits of unprecedented size during the 1930s. This was not a sustainable state of affairs, as Schacht well knew – just as he knew that fiscal deficits in excess of 5 per cent of GDP could not be financed other than by money creation, increasing the potential for future inflation. There was a full-blown currency crisis in mid-1934, which practically emptied the Reichsbank of its reserves, forcing Schacht to extend the German default to all foreign debt.

Yet what did the average German care about the intricacies of Schacht's New Plan, introduced to try to economize on scarce foreign exchange by strictly controlling imports and subsidizing exports? To most people in 1930s Germany it seemed there had been an economic miracle. The *Volksgemeinschaft* was more than mere rhetoric; it meant full employment, higher wages, stable prices, reduced poverty, cheap radios (the *Volksempfänger*) and budget holidays. It is too easily forgotten that there were more holiday camps than concentration camps in Germany between 1935 and 1939. Workers became better trained, farmers saw their incomes rise. Nor were foreigners unimpressed by what was happening. American corporations including Standard Oil, General Motors and IBM all rushed to invest directly in the German economy. Germans in 1938 were not, to be sure, as rich as Americans; US per capita national income was roughly twice as high. But they were unquestionably better off than Germans in 1933.

Hitler's folk-community implied more than national unity, however. It also implied the exclusion of 'folk-alien' (*Volksfremd*) social groups. There was no doubt who was meant by that. From his earliest days as a political agitator, Hitler had repeatedly expressed his hatred of the Jews. He blamed them for Germany's defeat in the First World War. 'If at the beginning of the War and during the War,' he notoriously wrote in *Mein Kampf*, 'twelve or fifteen thousand of these Hebrew corrupters of the people had been held under poison gas, as happened to hundreds of thousands of our very best German workers in the field, the sacrifice of millions at the front would not have been in vain. On the contrary: twelve thousand scoundrels eliminated in time might have saved the lives of a million real Germans, valuable for the future.' That he and his minions ultimately used precisely that method as part of their genocidal campaign against the Jews during the Second World War has led many historians to regard anti-Semitism as the defining characteristic of the Third Reich. There is no question of its importance to Hitler and a substantial number of leading National Socialists. Yet it is far from clear that they were tapping a deeply rooted 'eliminationist anti-Semitism' within the German population as a whole.

There were in fact few European countries in the world where ethnic minorities were less of a problem than Germany after the First World War. There were fewer than 503,000 Jews in Germany in 1933, a tiny 0.76 per cent of population, and the number had been falling steadily since the war as a result of a striking decline in the Jewish birthrate to roughly half that of the rest of the population. The overwhelming majority of members of this dwindling community were almost completely assimilated into the middle class as lawyers, doctors, academics, businessmen and so on. Indeed, Jews were disproportionately represented in Germany's financial, cultural and intellectual elites. Their children attended the same schools as Gentiles, they lived in the same neighbourhoods as Gentiles. Writing in 1921, Jacob Wassermann looked back on his childhood in Fürth in Franconia in terms that most German Jews of his generation would have echoed:

As far as clothing, language and mode of life were concerned, the adaptation was complete. I attended a public State-supported school. We lived among Christians, associated with Christians. The progressive Jews, of whom my father was one, felt that the Jewish community existed only in the sense of religious worship and tradition. Religion, fleeing the powerful seductions of modern life, took refuge in secret and unworldly groups of zealots. Tradition became a legend, a matter of phrases, an empty shell.

Though his family had once kept feast days and fast days, observing the Sabbath and eating only kosher food, 'as the struggle for bread grew keener, as the spirit of the new age became more importunate, these commandments too were neglected, and our domestic life approximated to that of our non-Jewish neighbours':

We still acknowledged membership in the religious community, though hardly any traces remained of either community or religion. Precisely speaking, we were Jews only in name, and through the hostility, aversion or aloofness of the Christians about us, who, for their part, based their attitude only on a word, a phrase, an illustrative state of affairs. Why, then, were we still Jews, and what did our Jewishness mean? For me this question became ever more and more importunate; and no one could answer it.

The insight Wassermann finally arrived at was a profound one, which brilliantly captures the ambivalence of the German-Jewish love-hate relationship in the 1920s:

A non-German cannot possibly imagine the heartbreaking position of the German Jew. German Jew – you must place full emphasis on both words. You must understand him as the final product of a lengthy evolutionary process. His twofold love and his struggle on two fronts drive him close to the brink of despair. The German and the Jew: I once dreamt an allegorical dream, but I am not sure that I can make it clear. I placed the surfaces of two mirrors together; and I felt as though the human images contained and preserved in the two mirrors must needs fight one another tooth and nail ...

I am a German and I am a Jew; one as much and as fully as the other; I am both simultaneously and irrevocably ... It was disturbing ... because on both sides I constantly encountered arms that received or repelled me, voices that cried a welcome or a warning.

To call the German-Jewish relationship a love-hate relationship is by no means as inappropriate as might be thought. A crucial symptom of German-Jewish assimilation was the rise in the rate of intermarriage between Jews and non-Jews. For Germany as a whole the percentage of Jews marrying outside their own faith rose from 7 per cent in 1902 to 28 per cent by 1933. It reached a peak of more than a third in 1915 (see Figure 7.4). Though Hamburg and Munich saw the highest rates of intermarriage, the figures were also well above average in Berlin, Cologne, the Saxon cities of Dresden and Leipzig as well as Breslau in Silesia. When Arthur Ruppin gathered data for other European cities, he found only Trieste had a higher rate of intermarriage. Though also relatively high, the rates for Leningrad, Budapest, Amsterdam and Vienna lagged behind those in the major German cities. Of

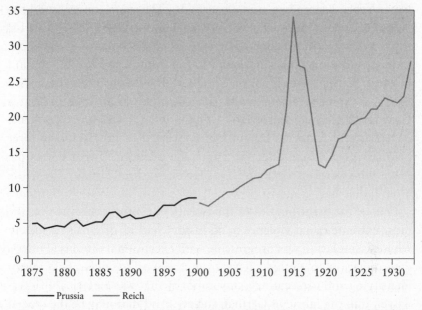

*Figure 7.4* **Percentage of Prussian/German Jews who married outside the faith, 1875–1933**

164,000 Jews who remained in Germany in 1939, 15,000 were part-ners in mixed marriages. When the Nazis came to define the children of mixed marriages as *Mischlinge*, they estimated there were nearly 300,000 of them, though the real figure lay between 60,000 and 125,000. It is hard to speak of deep-rooted collective hatred when there is so much evidence of love between individuals of different ethnic origins. And these figures, needless to say, tell us nothing about sexual relationships outside marriage.

A perfect example of German-Jewish assimilation was Victor Klemperer. Born in 1881, the son of a Brandenburg rabbi, Klemperer – like Hitler – served in the Bavarian army during the First World War. In 1906 he married Eva Schlemmer, a Protestant from that most Protestant of Prussian towns, Königsberg. Like so many German Jews of his generation, and so many members of his family, Klemperer excelled academically. In 1920 he was appointed Professor of Romance Languages and Literature at Dresden Technical University. His attitude towards Judaism was almost wholly negative. When a friend named Isakowitz insisted on making him celebrate the Jewish

New Year, Klemperer was dismayed: 'The man came from the "temple"', he noted in his diary, '(I have not heard that word for thirty years), his head covered he read from the Torah, a hat was put on my head too, candles burned. I found it quite painful. Where do I belong? To the "Jewish nation" decrees Hitler. And *I* feel the Jewish nation recognized by Isakowitz is a comedy and am nothing but a German or German European. – The mood . . . was one of extreme depression.' Klemperer had in fact converted to Protestantism after his marriage. Throughout the 1930s, he maintained that it was the Nazis who were 'un-German': 'I . . . feel shame for Germany,' he wrote after Hitler had come to power. 'I have truly always felt German.'

One of the great puzzles of the twentieth century, then, is that the most extreme racial violence in all history had its origins in a society where assimilation was progressing with exceptional rapidity. Hitler's determination to exclude Jews from the *Volksgemeinschaft* meant identifying and persecuting a tiny minority that was inextricably inter-woven into the fabric of German society. And that may be the crucial point. Perhaps the anti-Semitism of the Nazis is best understood as a reaction to the very success of German-Jewish assimilation. In the words of Peter Drucker, author of *The Jewish Question in Germany* (published in Vienna in 1936): 'The Jewish Question was so especially sensitive in Germany because the assimilation [*Selbstauflösung* – liter-ally 'self-dissolution'] of the Jews had advanced further there than anywhere else.' Can it really be a mere coincidence that Martin Heidegger, who so eagerly embraced Hitler's new order, was also embroiled between 1925 and 1928 in a passionate love affair with his Jewish student, Hannah Arendt?

## THE SIN AGAINST THE BLOOD

Hitler had made his own views on the specific question of racial intermarriage clear as early as February 1922: 'Every Jew who is caught with a blonde girl should be [Interjection: 'Strung up!'] I don't want to say "strung up", but there should be a court to condemn these Jews. [Applause.]'

In *Mein Kampf* he elaborated on the point at considerable and revealing length. 'Race,' he declared, 'does not lie in the language, but exclusively in the blood.' No one understood this better than

the Jew, who attaches very little importance to the preservation of his language, but all importance to keeping his blood pure ... While he seems to overflow with 'enlightenment', 'progress', 'freedom', 'humanity', etc., he himself practises the severest segregation of his race. To be sure, he sometimes palms off his women on influential Christians, but as a matter of principle he always keeps his male line pure. He poisons the blood of others, but preserves his own. The Jew almost never marries a Christian woman; it is the Christian who marries a Jewess. The bastards, however, take after the Jewish side. Especially a part of the higher nobility degenerates completely. The Jew is perfectly aware of this, and, therefore, systematically carries on this mode of 'disarming' the intellectual leader-class of his racial adversaries. How close they see the approaching victory can be seen by the hideous aspect which their relations with the members of other peoples takes on.

In a crucial passage, he proceeded to indulge in one of those perverted sexual fantasies which recur in anti-Semitic propaganda:

With satanic joy in his face, the black-haired Jewish youth lurks in wait for the unsuspecting girl whom he defiles with his blood, thus stealing her from her people. With every means he tries to destroy the racial foundations of the people he has set out to subjugate. Just as he himself systematically ruins women and girls, he does not shrink from pulling down the blood barriers for others, even on a larger scale.

The moral for Hitler was clear: '[A] racially pure people which is conscious of its blood can never be enslaved by the Jew. In the world he will forever be master over bastards and bastards alone.' But that meant that the Jews' efforts 'systematically to lower the racial level by a continuous poisoning of individuals' had to be resisted:

In heedlessly ignoring the question of the preservation of the racial foundations of our nation, the old Reich disregarded the sole right which gives life in this world. Peoples who bastardise themselves, or let themselves be bastardised, sin against the will of eternal Providence, and when their ruin is encompassed by a stronger enemy it is not an injustice done to them, but only the restoration of justice ... The lost purity of the blood alone destroys inner happiness forever, plunges man into the abyss for all time, and the consequences can never more be eliminated from body and spirit ... [T]he question of preserving or not preserving the purity of the blood will endure as long as there are men. All really significant symptoms of decay of the pre-War period can in the last analysis be reduced to racial causes.

Despite this allusion to pre-war decay, Hitler's anti-Semitism seems to have grown markedly during and after the war; it was only retrospectively that he denounced Vienna as 'the incarnation of the desecration of the blood' (*Blutschande*), 'with its repulsive racial mix of Czechs, Poles, Hungarians, Ruthenians, Serbs and Croatians' and 'Jews and more Jews'. Here and in later statements, Hitler struck a pseudo-moralistic tone of revulsion at Jewish sexuality, portraying the individual Aryan 'victim' of *Blutschande* as essentially passive in the absence of an aggressive 'folk-community'. The relatively open Weimar debates on questions such as abortion, homosexuality, prostitution and venereal disease struck Hitler as further proof of the 'total capitulation' of 'those who guide the nation and the state' to the 'Jewification of the spiritual life and mammonization of the mating instinct'. These would 'sooner or later destroy all our descendants' if no remedial action was taken.

The key point is that when Hitler accused the Jews of aiming to 'pollute the blood' of the Aryan race, he had in mind precisely the upsurge in mixed marriages that had characterized the 1920s. Nor was he alone in thinking this way. One of the best-selling books of the decade was Arthur Dinter's *Sin Against the Blood* (1918), which tells the story of a young woman whose 'blood' has been fatally polluted because her father, a press baron with a sinister interest in women's magazines, is a Jew. Her German fiancé Hermann Kämpfer comes to realize the indelible nature of this 'curse' when their unmistakably Jewish sons are born. (The first is described as a 'dark-skinned ... scarcely human something ... [with] deep, dark eyes ... under long dark eyelashes ... [and] a squashed flat nose like an ape's'.) When Hermann later marries a more authentically Nordic Frau, the same thing happens – simply because his new wife had once slept with a Jew! These experiences are Hermann's punishment for 'sinning against the holy blood of his race'. But they awaken him to a shocking truth:

The German *Volk* was being systematically corrupted and poisoned! ... If the German *Volk* does not succeed in shaking off and rendering harmless the Jewish vampire that it is unwittingly allowing to batten on the blood of its heart ... it will come to grief in the foreseeable future.

Within a year of publication, Dinter's book had gone through twenty-eight printings and sold 120,000 copies. By 1929 a quarter of a million copies had been printed.

Dinter was only one of many post-war writers to write in these terms. Otto Kernholt's *From the Ghetto to Power* (1921) warned at length about mixed marriages as a strategy aimed at enfeebling the German race. The same preoccupation manifested itself in the nationalist press. In the hope of incriminating Jewish students, anti-Semitic *agents provocateurs* at Frankfurt University were alleged to have scrawled on the walls such graffiti as: 'Yesterday this horny Jew raped a little blonde girl'. Another frequent accusation, dating back to the 1890s and beyond, was that Jews were involved in the white slave trade. Everything – even the fall of the Hohenzollern monarchy – could be explained in terms of sexual relations between Jews and Gentiles. Debate raged as to the effects of intermarriage. Were such marriages more or less fruitful than endogamous marriages? What would be the effect on the 'racial health' of the German *Volk* if mixed marriages were not banned?

The attacks on mixed marriages need to be seen in the wider context of Weimar sexuality. Because of its identification with the campaign to relax the laws against homosexuality, Magnus Hirschfeld's Institute for Sexual Science presented an obvious target for Nazi attacks on 'Jewish morality'. As the newspaper *Völkische Beobachter* put it, 'Jews are forever trying to propagandize sexual relations between siblings, men and animals, and men and men.' It was also possible to draw tendentious political inferences from the crimes of *Lustmörder* (rapist-murderers) like Fritz Haarmann, Wilhelm Grossmann, Karl Denke and Peter Kürten, 'the Düsseldorf vampire'. (It did not help matters that the serial killer in Fritz Lang's *M* was played by a Jewish actor, Peter Lorre.) Interracial sex was in the news in the 1920s. There were bitter controversies about the role of *Ostjuden* as either pimps or prostitutes in what would now be called the sex industry. Following the deployment in the French-occupied Rhineland of colonial troops from Senegal, Morocco and elsewhere, there was a vehement press campaign against the so-called Black Disgrace (*schwarze Schmach*). Semi-pornographic postcards and cartoons were published showing grotesque Negroes menacing half-dressed white women. 'Shall we silently accept', demanded one Dr Rosenberger in a typical contribution to the campaign, 'that in future instead of the beautiful songs of white, pretty, well-formed, intellectually developed, lively, healthy Germans, we will hear the raucous noise of horrific, broad skulled, flat nosed, ungainly, half-human, syphilitic half-castes on the banks of the Rhine?' The fact that there genuinely were around 500 'Rhineland bastards' confirms that miscegenation was no imaginary construct. That the Bavarian Ministry of the Interior could recommend as early as 1927 that these children be sterilized also illustrates that the desire to circumscribe the rights of 'racial aliens' (*Volksfremde*) predated Hitler's accession to power. Hitler too complained about 'the Negroes [in] the Rhineland' and the 'necessarily resulting bastardization', but characteristically represented this as merely an aspect of a wider Jewish conspiracy to 'poison the blood' of the German *Volk*.

Along with most of his most senior henchmen, Hitler seems genuinely to have believed that Jews posed an insidious biological threat to the German *Volk*. Yet it is impossible to overlook an element of self-repression in much Nazi propaganda on this issue; those most publicly averse to the idea of interracial sex often gave the unintended impression that this was precisely the direction of their own private fantasies. As a young man, Goebbels became engaged to Else Janke, an elementary school teacher who was half-Jewish. She helped him to find a job at the Dresder Bank during the 1923 hyperinflation, but was reluctant to marry him, possibly because of his club foot. Shortly after she told him that her mother was Jewish, Goebbels noted that 'the original magic was gone'. 'The discussion recently about the race question kept ringing in my ears,' she wrote to him after a quarrel. 'I could not get it out of my mind, and almost saw the problem as an obstacle to our further life together. I am firmly convinced, you see, that in this respect your thinking goes decidedly too far.' It was at this time that the future Propaganda Minister first read Oswald Spengler's *Decline of the West*, where he found 'the root of the Jewish question

... laid bare'. Goebbels's first references in his diary to the Jews as 'filthy pigs', 'traitors' and 'vampires' date from the breakdown of his relationship with Janke. Even the young Heinrich Himmler could acknowledge the appeal of a Jewish woman. No one – not even Hitler – was more obsessed with the sexual aspects of race: in 1924, for example, he described in his diary his Nordic archetype's 'shining skin flushed with blood, blond hair, clear conquering eyes [and] the perfect movements of a perfect body'. This was 'the ideal picture' of racially pure womanhood 'which we Germans dream of in youth and as men are prepared to die for'. But when he met a Jewish dancer named Inge Barco in a Munich café in July 1922, Himmler was evidently attracted, insisting she had 'absolutely nothing of the Jew in her manner, at least so far as I can judge'. There are other examples too: for example, Ludwig Clauss, an expert on racial 'psyches' much in demand in the Third Reich, who had an affair with his Jewish assistant Margarethe Landé.

Once in power, the Nazis made miscegenation a recurrent theme of their propaganda. Press attacks on Jewish doctors were based on their allegedly lecherous 'attitude' towards 'German women'. The theme that the Jews sought to 'pollute' Aryan blood through sexual contact recurs time and again in Nazi propaganda. It is there, for example, in Kurt Plischke's *The Jew as Racial Polluter*, which called for the public naming and shaming of German women who 'secretly or openly go with Jews', and in Gerhard Kittel's *Historical Preconditions of Jewish Racial Mixing*, which accused the Jews of having tried to turn Germany into a 'racial mishmash'. The message was spelt out with a crudely pornographic undertone in a story entitled 'What Happened to Inge at the Jewish Doctor's', published in Julius Streicher's *Der Stürmer*:

Inge sits in the Jew doctor's reception room. She has to wait a long time. She looks through the magazines on the table. But she is much too nervous even to read a few sentences. Again and again she remembers her talk with her mother. And again and again her mind dwells on the warnings of her BDM [League of German Girls] leader: 'A German must not consult a Jew doctor! And particularly not a German *girl*! Many a girl who has gone to a Jew doctor to be cured has found disease and disgrace!' ...

The door opens. Inge looks up. There stands the Jew. She screams. She's so frightened she drops the magazines. She jumps up in terror. Her eyes stare into the Jewish doctor's face. His face is the face of a devil. In the middle of this devil's face is a huge crooked nose. Behind the spectacles two criminal eyes. And the thick lips are grinning. A grin that says: 'Now I've got you at last, little German girl!'

There are similar themes in the two historical films made in 1940 to coincide with the release of the anti-Semitic documentary *Der ewige Jude* (The Eternal Jew), a vicious caricature of East European Jews as insalubrious degenerates. In *Jud-Süss*, the 'court Jew' Süss-Oppenheimer rapes Dorothea Sturm (played by Kristine Söderbaum), who then commits suicide. Similarly, in *Die Rothschilds*, the Jewish banker Nathan Rothschild is portrayed as lusting after the heroine, the wife of Rothschild's 'Aryan' rival Turner. In exhibitions, too, the sexual leitmotif was employed. The Frankfurt Anti-Jewish Exhibition of November 1940 illustrated 'the rapacity, the uncontrolled sexuality, and the parasitic nature of the Jews' with a newspaper cutting describing how the 'Jew Klein from Vegesack near Bremen was seen to have sexual intercourse with [his] Aryan maidservant'. Another illuminating example is Friedrich Ekkehard's novel *Sturmgeschlecht* [*Storm Generation*]: *Zweimal 9. November* (1941), which portrays a Freikorps troop falling into a trap laid for them by a 'stunningly beautiful' Jewish-Bolshevik *femme fatale*. Here, as in so much Nazi anti-Semitic propaganda, the erotic if not pornographic undertone is unmistakable.

## PROTECTING THE BLOOD

The first concrete measures against the Jews taken by the Nazis were concerned with economics rather than miscegenation. There was a brief boycott of Jewish businesses and shops – brief because of the domestic disorder and international outrage it threatened to unleash. In April 1933, under the Law for the Restoration of the Professional Civil Service, all Jewish civil servants, including judges, were removed from office, followed a month later by university lecturers. Victor

Klemperer was to be among the victims of this later purge, an experience he pondered in his diary:

March 10, 1933 ... It is astounding how easily everything collapses ... wild prohibitions and acts of violence. And with it, on streets and radio, never-ending propaganda. On Saturday ... I heard a part of Hitler's speech in Königsberg ... I understood only a few words. But the tone! The unctuous bawling, truly bawling, of a priest ... How long will I retain my professorship?

In fact, Klemperer managed to hang on to his chair for another two years. On May 2, 1935, however, the blow fell:

On Tuesday morning, without any previous notification – two sheets delivered by post. 'On the basis of para 6 of the Law for the Restoration of the Professional Civil Service I have ... recommended your dismissal' ... At first I felt alternately dumb and slightly romantic; now there is only bitterness and wretchedness.

Five months later, to add insult to injury, he was barred from the university library reading room 'as a non-Aryan'. What followed was a kind of whittling away of his rights as a citizen. The authorities successively confiscated his sabre – a souvenir of his military service – his typewriter, his driving licence and finally his car. He was banned from public parks. He was banned from smoking. Segregation took myriad forms: Jews were barred from swimming baths and specified park benches. Much more problematic, however, was what to do about Klemperer's marriage to an Aryan woman.

Although Alfred Rosenberg and the lawyer Roland Freisler had expressed support for a legal ban on sexual relations between Jews and Aryans, in July 1934 the Supreme Court had refused to annul the marriage of an Aryan petitioner who had married a Jew in 1930 and who now wanted a divorce on racial grounds. The following year, however, supposedly spontaneous actions by party activists – including the public humiliation of women accused of sleeping with Jews – as well as police reports about Jewish employers molesting their Aryan female employees provided the government with a cue for action. In July 1935 the Interior Minister Wilhelm Frick issued

a circular to registrars informing them that 'the question of marriage between Aryans and Non-Aryans' would soon be 'regulated
... through a general law' and that until then all mixed marriages
between 'full Aryans' and 'full Jews' should be postponed. In the
same month, the head of the SS *Sicherheitsdienst*, Reinhard Heydrich,
demanded 'that in view of the disturbance among the population
by the racial miscegenation of German women ... the prevention
of mixed marriages [should] be legally fixed but also extramarital
sexual relations between Aryans and Jews should be punished'. At a
rally in Berlin in August 1935 a giant banner proclaimed: 'The Jews
are our Misfortune. Women and Girls, the Jews are Your Ruin'. All
this points to an orchestrated campaign instigated from above. The
crucial legislation was duly drafted before or during the September
1935 Nuremberg party rally, following a call by the Reich Doctors'
leader Gerhard Wagner for action to prevent further 'bastardization'
of the German people. In addition to laws stripping Jews of their
citizenship and prohibiting them from raising the Nazi flag, a Law
for the Protection of German Blood and German Honour was drafted
which banned not only 'marriages between Jews and citizens of
German or kindred blood', but also extramarital sexual relations
between them. Jews were also forbidden 'to employ female citizens of
German or kindred blood under 45 years of age as domestic servants'
– the implication being that Jewish masters habitually indulged in
sexual abuse of their maids. The penalties for these new crimes of
*Rassenschande* (racial defilement) included imprisonment and hard
labour.

The new legislation was implemented with some zeal: altogether
between 1935 and 1939 there were 1,670 prosecutions for alleged
racial defilement. Roughly half of all cases arose in three cities:
Berlin, Frankfurt and Hamburg. In Hamburg between 1936 and
1943 a total of 429 men were prosecuted, of whom 270 were Jews;
altogether 391 of those accused were convicted and jailed. Overall, around 90 per cent of those charged were found guilty. At first
(as the Gestapo complained), their sentences were relatively lenient, ranging from six weeks to one and a half years, but that soon
changed. Half of all those sentenced in Hamburg received between
two and four years, and some received six years. A typical case

was that of a Jewish man who was found guilty of continuing a long-standing relationship with an Aryan woman. He was sentenced to two and a half years' penal servitude. Elsewhere, the courts went well beyond the letter of the law. In Frankfurt a fifty-six-year-old Jewish teacher was sentenced to ten months in prison for 'molesting' two Aryan women in a department store; it is not clear from the record whether he so much as laid a finger on them. To encourage such broad interpretations, but also to avoid 'confront[ing] the courts with almost insuperable difficulties of proof and ... necessitat[ing] the discussion of the most embarrassing questions', the Reich Supreme Court ruled that with respect to the Nuremberg Laws 'the concept of sexual intercourse ... includes all natural and unnatural intercourse, i.e., apart from intercourse itself, all sexual activities with a member of the opposite sex which are intended in place of actual intercourse to satisfy the sexual urges of at least one of the partners'.

The significance of the 'racial defilement' trials is twofold. They reveal the way that German lawyers and judges were willing to transform the crude prejudices of the Nazi leadership into a sophisticated system of discrimination and humiliation. But they also reveal how ordinary people instrumentalized anti-Semitic legislation for their own purposes. For the most important point to note about the prosecutions for 'racial defilement' is how most of them originated – not as the result of Gestapo investigations, but as the result of denunciations by members of the public.

Nazi Germany was a police state, increasingly under the control of Himmler and his henchman Heydrich,* but it was an understaffed

---

* Himmler's ascent had an important bearing on the institutional development of the Third Reich. The SS was at first subordinate to Ernst Röhm's SA. Himmler's first official post was as Commissary President of the Munich Police. In 1934, however, he became Inspector of the Prussian Secret State Police ('Gestapo' for short) and after Röhm's murder in the Night of the Long Knives succeeded in merging the Gestapo with the political police in all the other *Länder*. From 1936 he controlled all police activity and was accorded the uniquely grand title of *Reichsführer-SS*. Heydrich's SD was not a state institution, but a party one. Nevertheless, his power grew along with Himmler's and was cemented with the creation of the over-arching Reich Main Security Office (RSHA) in 1939.

one. The twenty-two Gestapo officials in Würzburg, for example, were responsible for the entire population of Lower Franconia, which numbered more than 840,000 in 1939. The town of Krefeld was more closely supervised; around 170,000 people lived there, under the watchful eye of between twelve and fourteen Gestapo officers. In both towns, the Gestapo had to rely heavily on local people for tip-offs about breaches of the law. The surviving police files reveal that these were not in short supply. Of the eighty-four cases of 'racial defilement' investigated in Würzburg between 1933 and 1945, forty-five – more than half – originated with a denunciation from a member of the public. The character of these denunciations sheds vital light on popular attitudes towards the 'Jewish Question'. A Jewish man and an Aryan woman were arrested because the woman's estranged husband alleged they were having a sexual relationship; their accuser's main motive seems to have been to get rid of his wife, but her alleged lover committed suicide in custody. An apparently mixed couple having a drink together were reported to the Gestapo because the man was blond-haired (both parties were in fact Jewish, so no charge could be pressed). In Krefeld the Gestapo were able to be more active: the proportion of cases involving Jews rose sharply from less than 10 per cent before 1936 to around 30 thereafter. Of these cases, some 16 per cent were decided by the courts; in over two-fifths of cases, however, the Gestapo sent the individuals concerned to concentration camps or imposed 'protective custody'. Yet even in Krefeld more than two-fifths of the cases brought against Jews before the war were initiated by denunciations, a much higher proportion than for other cases, suggesting that denunciation was disproportionately directed against Jews.

Does this confirm the thesis that most ordinary Germans were anti-Semites? No. At most, denouncers amounted to just 2 per cent of the population. What it does suggest is that anti-Semitic legislation was a powerful weapon in the hands of a minority of Germans: the morally vacuous lawyers who drafted and implemented it, the Gestapo zealots who enforced it, and the odious sneaks who supplied the Gestapo with incriminating information. There was one major stumbling block for this unholy trinity, however. The legacy of decades of intermarriage between Jews and Gentiles was a substantial group of people who defied clear-cut racial categorization because they had only one Jewish parent, or fewer than four Jewish grandparents. Were they Jews? Characteristically, when he was presented with four alternative drafts of the Law for the Protection of German Blood and German Honour, Hitler chose the least radical, but struck out a crucial sentence – 'This law is only valid for full Jews'. This created the potential for a broad interpretation of the new law and was welcomed by the party rank-and-file at Nuremberg. The result was interminable arguments between the Ministry of the Interior and party representatives about degrees of Jewishness. While Frick was willing to exempt anyone with fewer than three Jewish grandparents from legal discrimination, Wagner wished to include those with just two Jewish grandparents as well, so that only 'quarter Jews' (with one Jewish grandparent) could be given the status of 'Reich citizens'. The First Supplementary Decree of the Reich Citizenship Law, issued in November 1935, represented a victory for Frick, in that it defined a Jew as 'anyone who is descended from at least three grandparents who were racially full Jews' and 'an individual of mixed Jewish blood (*Mischling*)' as anyone 'descended from one or two grandparents who were racially full Jews'. It also marked a retreat for the party's racial theorists, in that the decree explicitly identified 'membership of the Jewish religious community' as the criterion for determining a grandparent's race. However, someone with only two Jewish grandparents could still be categorized as a Jew if he or she belonged to the Jewish religious community, married another Jew or was the issue of a mixed marriage or sexual relationship which post-dated the Nuremberg Laws. And the power to distinguish between so-called '*Mischlinge* of the first degree' (individuals with two Jewish grandparents) and those 'of the second degree' (one Jewish grandparent) was given to 'racial experts', who were empowered to take physical as well as religious factors into account. A further modification of the legal status of *Mischlinge* followed in December 1938, when a distinction was introduced between couples with children in which 'the father is a German and the mother a Jewess', those in which 'the father is a Jew and the mother a German' and those without children. Childless couples with a Jewish male partner were 'to be proceeded against as if they were full-blooded Jews'. There was an explicit incentive for the non-Jewish wives in such cases to divorce their husbands. In the end, however, bureaucratic inertia prevented the majority of German *Mischlinge* from being categorized as Jews. This was a source of considerable frustration to the likes of Richard Schulenburg, *Oberkriminalsekretär* of the Krefeld Gestapo, who thirsted to make his small part of the folk-community 100 per cent 'Jew-free' (*judenrein*).

The Nuremberg Laws, needless to say, were only a part of the Nazis' efforts to preserve and enhance the biological purity of the Aryan race. Jews were not the only 'alien' group to be victims of escalating discrimination. The provisions of the Nuremberg Laws were also extended to Germany's 30,000 Sinti and Roma – so-called gypsies – whose fate became the preoccupation of a Reich Central Office for the Fight against the Gypsy Nuisance, established as part of the Reich Criminal Police Office in 1938. The mentally ill were the first group to be subjected to compulsory sterilization under the terms of the July 1933 Law for the Prevention of Hereditarily Diseased Progeny. Between 1933 and 1945 at least 320,000 people were sterilized on the basis of this law, including sufferers from schizophrenia, manic depression, epilepsy, Huntington's chorea, deafness, deformity and even chronic alcoholism. In 1935 the law was amended to allow abortion up to the end of the second trimester for pregnant mentally ill women. Still Hitler was not content. As early as 1935, he told a senior Nazi medic that 'if war should break out, he would take up the euthanasia question and implement it'. In fact, he did not even wait for the war. In July 1939 he initiated what became known as the *Aktion T-4*. It was, he said, 'right that the worthless lives of seriously ill mental patients should be got rid of'. Here, as with the persecution of the Jews and Gypsies, the regime encountered little popular resistance and some active support. In a poll of 200 parents of mentally retarded children conducted in Saxony, 73 per cent had answered 'yes' to the question: 'Would you agree to the painless curtailment of the life of your child if experts had established that it was suffering from incurable idiocy?' Some parents actually petitioned Hitler to allow their abnormal children to be killed. Apart from the Catholic

Bishop Clemens von Galen, whose sermons against the euthanasia programme in July and August 1941 led to a temporary halt in the killings, only a handful of other individuals openly challenged 'the principle that you can kill "unproductive" human beings'. Others who objected turn out, on closer inspection, merely to have disliked the procedures involved. Some wished for formal legality – a proper decree and public 'sentencing'; others (especially those living near the asylums) simply wanted the killing to be carried out less obtrusively.

Cleansing the *Volk* was a multifaceted undertaking. In 1937 the so-called Rhineland bastards were compulsorily sterilized by Gestapo Special Commission No. 3, after Göring had referred the matter to Dr Wilhelm Abel of the Kaiser Wilhelm Institute for Anthropology, Heredity and Eugenics. Homosexuals were manifestly of no racial value; between 1934 and 1938 the number prosecuted annually under Paragraph 175 of the Reich Criminal Code rose by a factor of ten to 8,000. Since criminality was viewed as hereditary, those who broke the law were also targeted as asocial. The November 1933 Law against Dangerous Habitual Criminals authorized the castration of sexual offenders.

The obverse of all this was the effort to encourage the right sort of Germans to breed in the right sort of way. For racial purification involved not only the exclusion of those deemed to be *Volksfremd* but also the multiplication of racially healthy *Volksgenossen*. The Reich Agriculture Minister, Walther Darré, made the parallel with stud farming explicit when he wrote: 'Just as we breed our Hanoverian horses using a few pure stallions and mares, so we will once again breed pure Nordic Germans.' The Nazi eugenicists had all manner of ingenious ideas to boost Aryan procreation. The Law for the Reduction of Unemployment (June 1933) introduced marriage loans for couples who did not both work; the debts, which were intended to finance the purchase of consumer durables, were cancelled if the wife produced four children. A special handbook was made available to nubile young couples. In among the handy housekeeping tips and recipes, it contained a useful list of 'Ten Commandments for Choosing a Spouse':

1   Remember that you are German.

2   If of sound stock, do not remain unwed.

3   Keep your body pure.

4   Keep spirit and soul pure.

5   As a German, choose someone of German or Nordic blood for your partner.

6   When choosing your spouse, look into their lineage.

7   Health is a precondition of external beauty.

8   Marry only out of love.

9   Seek not a playmate but a partner in marriage.

10  Wish for as many children as possible.

There was also the German Mothers' medal, awarded to any woman who over-fulfilled her quota as a medium for the propagation of Aryan blood. In a kind of childbearing Olympics, mothers were rewarded with gold, silver or bronze medals depending on how many children they had. Jews and other 'ethnic aliens' were, needless to say, ineligible. In order to make sure that only the right sort performed these feats of procreation, couples intending to marry had to secure certificates of suitability. Here was another way in which the professionals extended their competence under the Third Reich. Doctors could determine who was fit to breed. Hereditary Health Courts could order the sterilization of those deemed unfit, a procedure which, quite apart from its intended result, was in itself both painful and dangerous. And officials like Karl Astel of the Thuringian Office for Racial Matters could compile information that would ultimately allow racial profiling of the entire population.

Yet, despite all these inducements, stud farming turned out to be harder with humans than with horses. It greatly worried Himmler that his own SS men were not naturally attracted to the right racial types:

I see in our marriage requests [he complained] that our men frequently marry in a complete misunderstanding of what marriage means. With the requests

I often ask myself, 'My God, must that one of all people marry an SS man' – this chit of misfortune and this twisted, in some cases impossible shape who might marry a small eastern Jew, a small Mongolian – for that such a girl would be good. In by far the greater number of instances, these concern radiant, good-looking men.

In order to rectify this, he began to intervene in SS officers' matrimonial decision-making. Not only did new recruits have to trace their pure German ancestry back five generations; they were allowed to marry only partners approved as racially suitable by Himmler himself. And they were then exhorted to have at least four children, 'the minimum necessary for a good and healthy marriage'. Children of the SS were supposed to undergo an alternative form of baptism with SS standard-bearers instead of clergy officiating, and a portrait of Hitler rather than a font as the focal point of the ceremony. The prize for producing a seventh child was to have the *Reichsführer* himself as its godfather. In a further departure from traditional social conventions, Himmler came to believe that Aryan types should also be encouraged to breed out of wedlock. It was he who inspired the *Lebensborn* (literally 'source of life') programme, which was designed to allow SS officers to sire children with selected concubines located in fifteen delivery suites-cum-kindergartens. Himmler was quite explicit about the objective of all this: 'To establish the Nordic race again in and around Germany and ... from this seed bed [to] produce a race of 200 million.' 'It must be a matter of course that we have children,' he declared in 1943. 'It must be a matter of course that the most copious breeding should be from this racial elite of the German people. In 20 or 30 years we must really be able to provide the whole of Europe with its ruling class.'

Of course, not everyone in the Nazi regime subscribed to such notions. But that did not greatly matter. For there were other, more mercenary reasons for backing racial persecution. The German Jews were few, no doubt, but they were on average relatively well off. What simpler way to raise cash for rearmament – or simply to line the pockets of the Nazi leadership – than to steal it in the name of Aryanization? In the year from April 1938 the number of Jewish-owned businesses in Germany declined from 40,000 to 15,000. The boardrooms of corporate Germany saw surreal meetings at which Jewish directors – who were the founders of a firm or the founder's heirs – stepped down, bequeathing their seats and shares to Aryan colleagues who, if they privately pledged to act as no more than trustees, often found it convenient to forget those pledges. The events of November 1938 illustrated the developing nexus between hatred and cupidity. On November 9, 1938, at Hitler's instigation, Nazi thugs vandalized, ransacked or burned down nearly two hundred synagogues and thousands of Jewish businesses in towns all over Germany. Jewish cemeteries were desecrated and individual Jews beaten up; around ninety were killed. Some 30,000 Jews were arrested and sent to labour camps, though most were released later. The pretext for this massive pogrom was the assassination of Ernst vom Rath, an official at the German embassy in Paris, by a seventeen-year-old Jew named Herschel Grynszpan, whose Polish parents had been deported from Hanover by the Nazis. This was a pogrom worthy of Russia in 1905, though with far more overt state direction. To Göring, however, the violence was also a fiscal opportunity. In the aftermath, a heavy 'collective fine' of a billion marks was levied on the German Jewish community to pay for the damage done, as if the Jews themselves had perpetrated it. The November 9 *Reichskristallnacht* – an allusion to the broken glass that littered the streets afterwards – was a significant moment, revealing not only the violent urge at the root of the regime's policy towards the Jews, but also the complicity of those Germans who did not feel hatred towards the Jews, merely indifference.

Nazi anti-Semitism was 'something new in the history of the world,' wrote the perceptive liberal journalist Sebastian Haffner in 1940, 'an attempt to deny humans the solidarity of every species that enables it to survive; to turn human predatory instincts, that are normally directed against animals, against members of their own species, and to make a whole nation into a pack of hunting hounds':

It shows how ridiculous the attitude is . . . that the anti-Semitism of the Nazis is a small side issue, at worst a minor blemish on the movement, which one can regret or accept, according to one's personal feelings for the Jews, and of 'little significance compared to the great national issues'. In reality these 'great national issues' are unimportant day-to-day matters, the ephemeral business of a transitional period in European history – while the Nazis' anti-Semitism is a fundamental danger and raises the spectre of the downfall of humanity.

With the benefit of hindsight, we are bound to ask ourselves why a man like Victor Klemperer failed to discern the approaching calamity. Why did the Jews of Germany, and indeed of Europe, not flee sooner to avoid the hellish fate that Hitler had in mind for them? In fact, a substantial proportion did precisely that. In 1933 around 38,000 left the country, followed by 22,000 in 1934 and 21,000 in 1935. Over 200 of the country's 800 Jewish professors departed, of whom twenty were Nobel laureates. Albert Einstein had already left in 1932 in disgust at Nazi attacks on his 'Jewish physics'. The exodus quickened after the 'Night of Broken Glass'. In 1938 40,000 Jews left Germany; nearly twice that number left in 1939. By the time voluntary departures ceased to be possible, there were little more than 160,000 Jews left in Germany, less than 30 per cent of the pre-1933 figure. It is often forgotten how successful the Nazi policy of encouraging emigration was, though it would probably have achieved even more had it not been for the high taxes levied by Schacht on those leaving Germany.

As we have seen, Nazism was a political religion and Hitler delighted in playing the part of prophet. 'If the international Jewish financiers in and outside Europe', he declared in a speech to the Reichstag on January 30, 1939, 'should succeed in plunging the nations once more into a world war, then the result will not be the Bolshevizing of Europe, and thus the victory of Jewry, but the annihilation of the Jewish race in Europe!' As its context makes clear, however, this was as much a threat designed to induce further emigration as a prophecy of a coming genocide.

# WHERE TO GO?

Nevertheless, it is not hard to see why a man like Klemperer, who considered himself so emphatically a German, chose to stay. Even as late as 1939, it was by no means clear that the Nazis were the worst anti-Semites in continental Europe. Nor was their racial state at this stage unique in the world.

In neighbouring Poland, for example, there was no shortage of newspaper articles that could equally well have appeared in the Nazi *Völkische Beobachter*. As early as August 1934, an author writing under the pseudonym 'Swastika' in the Catholic newspaper *Pro Christo* argued: 'We should count as a Jew not only the follower of the Talmud . . . but every human being who has Jewish blood in his veins . . . Only a person who can prove that there were no ancestors of Jewish race in his family for at least five generations can be considered to be genuinely Aryan.' 'Jews are so terribly alien to us, alien and unpleasant, that they are a race apart,' a contributor to *Kultura* wrote in September 1936. 'They irritate us and all their traits grate against our sensibilities. Their oriental impetuosity, argumentativeness, specific mode of thought, the set of their eyes, the shape of their ears, the winking of their eyelids, the line of their lips, everything. In families of mixed blood we detect the traces of these features to the third or forth generation and beyond.' Some nationalists like Stefan Kosicki, editor of the *Gazeta Warszawaska*, began calling for the expulsion of the Jews. Others went further. Already in December 1938 the daily *Mały dziennik* was calling for 'war' on the Jews, before 'the Jewish rope' strangled Poland. The National Democrat (Endek) leader Roman Dmowski prophesied an 'international pogrom of the Jews' which would bring an 'end to the Jewish chapter of history'. Nor was anti-Semitic violence purely verbal. There had already been pogroms in Wilno (Vilnius) in 1934, Grodno in 1935, Przytyk and Minsk in 1936 and Brzesc (Brest) in 1937. In 1936 Zygmunt Szymanowski, a professor of bacteriology at the University of Warsaw, was shocked by the conduct of Endek students in Warsaw and Lwów, who assaulted Jewish students between lectures. In the mid-thirties, between one and two thousand Jews suffered injuries in attacks; perhaps as many as thirty were killed.

Neither the Catholic Church nor the Polish government wholly condoned such violence, it is true. Yet Cardinal Hlond's pastoral letter of February 1936 had scarcely been calculated to dampen down Polish anti-Semitism. 'It is a fact', he declared,

that Jews oppose the Catholic Church, are steeped in free-thinking, and represent the avant-garde of the atheist movement, the Bolshevik movement, and subversive action. The Jews have a disastrous effect on morality and their publishing-houses dispense pornography . . . Jews commit fraud, usury, and are involved in trade in human beings.

The temporal authorities were little better, despite the fact that the 1921 Constitution expressly ruled out discrimination on racial or religious grounds. In the 1920s Jews in the formerly Russian parts of the country had merely had to put up with the reluctance of the new regime to abolish what remained of the old Tsarist restrictions – many of which remained in force until as late as 1931 – and the inconvenience of the law banning work on Sundays. Worse was to come. The Camp of National Unity (OZN), founded in 1937 to mobilize popular support for Piłsudski's successors, aimed to achieve the 'Polonization' of industry, commerce and the professions at the expense of Jews, who were declared to be 'alien' to Poland. There is no question that Jews were disproportionately successful, particularly in higher education and the professions. Though by 1931 fewer than 9 per cent of the Polish population were Jewish, the proportion rose above 20 per cent in Polish universities. Jews accounted for 56 per cent of all private doctors in Poland, 43 per cent of all private teachers, 34 per cent of lawyers and 22 per cent of journalists. Official boycotts of Jewish businesses led to dramatic declines in the number of Jewish-owned shops – in the Białystok region from 92 per cent of all shops in 1932 to just 50 per cent six years later. Jews were driven out of the meat trade by bans on ritual slaughter; Jewish students were segregated in university classrooms; they were excluded from the legal profession. By 1937–8 their share of university enrolments had fallen to 7.5 per cent. By the end of 1938 it was the government's official policy to 'solve the Jewish question' by pressurizing Polish Jews into emigration. But that was scarcely an option for the many poor Jews in cities like Łódź, where over 70 per cent of Jewish families lived in a single room, often an attic or a cellar, and around a quarter were in receipt of charitable assistance.

Anti-Semitism was also rife in Romania, thanks to the efforts of Alexandru Cuza and Octavian Goga's National Christian Party and Corneliu Codreanu's Legion of the Archangel Michael, with its green-shirted youth wing known as the Iron Guard. As capable as Hitler of equating Jews simultaneously with communism and capitalism, Codreanu had pledged to 'destroy the Jews before they can destroy us'. He was not alone. In 1936 the president of the Totul pentru Tara Party, General Zizi Cantacuzino-Granicerul, had also called for the extermination of the Jews. To Goga, a poet by vocation, the Jews were like 'leprosy' or 'eczema'. Even before 1937, Jews found themselves driven out of the Romanian legal profession, while Jewish students were subjected to harassment and intimidation. In 1934 Mihail Sebastian – born Iosif Hechter, but an apostate and a wholly assimilated Romanian – had written to Nae Ionescu, Professor of Philosophy at the University of Bucharest, inviting him to write a preface to his new book. Ionescu's preface contained the following dark admonition:

Iosif Hechter, you are sick. You are sick to the core because all you can do is suffer . . . The Messiah has come, Iosif Hechter, and you have had no knowledge of him . . . Iosif Hechter, do you not feel that cold and darkness are enfolding you? . . . It is an assimilationist illusion, it is the illusion of so many Jews who sincerely believe that they are Romanian . . . Remember that you are Jewish! . . . Are you Iosif Hechter, a human being from Braila on the Danube? No, you are a Jew.

With Goga briefly serving as Prime Minister after the far right made sweeping gains in the 1937 elections, Jewish newspapers and libraries were closed and Jews' economic opportunities limited by the introduction of quotas for business and the professions. Although King Carol clamped down on the fascists when he dissolved parliament and established his own dictatorship in February 1938, the arrest and execution of Codreanu and twelve other Iron Guard leaders did not significantly improve the situation of the Romanian Jews. By September 1939 more than a quarter of a million had been deprived of their citizenship on the ground that they were illegal immigrants.

What of other European states? Italian fascism had not at first been notably anti-Semitic. Yet in 1938 Mussolini introduced legislation closely modelled on the Nuremberg Laws. France was still a democracy, but one shot through with anti-Semitic prejudice. '*Plutôt Hitler que Blum*' ('Better Hitler than Blum') was not only a jibe at the Jewish Socialist Léon Blum, the French premier from 1936 until 1937, but also a prophecy of sorts. In Hungary the mood was similar. A Jewish child risked being stoned if left alone in the streets of Szombathely.

If the Jews could not feel safe in Europe, where else could they go? The English-speaking world was scarcely welcoming. The United States had been the first major country of European settlement to introduce immigration quotas in the 1920s, the culmination of a campaign for restriction dating back to the 1890s. As a result of new literacy requirements, quotas and other controls, the annual immigration rate fell from 11.6 per thousand in the 1900s to 0.4 per thousand in the 1940s. Others followed the American example as the Depression bit: South Africa introduced quotas in 1930, while Australia, New Zealand and Canada had all introduced other kinds of restriction by 1932. What the Jews of Europe needed was, of course, political asylum more than economic opportunity. But although large and influential Jewish communities existed in all these countries, there were countervailing tendencies at work. The restriction of immigration was never purely an economic matter, a question of unskilled native-born workers seeking to raise the drawbridge in the face of low-wage competitors. Racial prejudice also played a key role in identifying Jews (along with Southern Italians) as immigrants inferior to previous generations from the British Isles, Germany or Scandinavia. In the Anglophone world, anti-Semitism was a social if not a political phenomenon. Symptomatically, a Bill to admit 20,000 Jewish children to the United States was rejected by the Senate in 1939 and again in 1940.

In any case, the United States could hardly claim to be a model of racial tolerance in the 1930s. As late as 1945, thirty states retained constitutional or legal bans on interracial marriage and many of these had recently extended or tightened their rules. In 1924, for example, the state of Virginia redefined the term 'white person' to mean a 'person who has no trace whatsoever of any blood other than Caucasian' or 'one-sixteenth or less of the blood of the American Indian and . . . no other non-Caucasic blood'. Henceforth even a single 'Negro' great-grandparent made a person black. It was not only African-Americans and American Indians who were affected; some states also discriminated against Chinese, Japanese, Koreans, 'Malays' (Filipinos) and 'Hindus' (Indians). How profound were the differences between a case of 'racial defilement' in 1930s Hamburg and a case of miscegenation in 1930s Montgomery? Not very. Was it so very different to be in a mixed marriage in Dresden and to be in one in Dixie? Not really. Moreover, the influence of eugenics in the United States had added a new tier of discriminatory legislation which was not only similar to that introduced in Germany in the 1930s, but was also the inspiration for some Nazi legislation. No fewer than forty-one states used eugenic categories to restrict marriages of the mentally ill, while twenty-seven states passed laws mandating sterilization for certain categories of people. In 1933 alone California forcibly sterilized 1,278 people. The Third Reich, in short, was very far from the world's only racial state in the 1930s. Hitler openly acknowledged his debt to US eugenicists.

There was, of course, one particular part of the world to which Jews inspired by the ideology of Zionism had been migrating for decades: Palestine, where a Jewish 'national home' had been proclaimed by the British in 1917. Between 1930 and 1936, more than 80,000 Jews left Poland for Palestine, many of them young idealists determined to construct a new society with the communal kibbutz as its building block. As one young emigrant explained: 'At home there were no prospects for the future. Business was bad. I did not see any prospects for a future after I had finished school. And even in this tragic situation, despite no prospects for the future, I wanted to finish school . . . If anyone asked me then what I would do after finishing school, I would not have known how to answer. In this terrible situation I took to Zionism like a drowning person to a board.' Yet in 1936 the British imposed restrictions on Jewish immigration into Palestine, fearing (not unreasonably) an Arab backlash. By 1938 it was taking eleven infantry battalions and a cavalry regiment to maintain anything resembling order as the mandate slid towards full-blown civil war.

To a thoroughly German-minded man like Klemperer, of course, emigration was precisely what the Nazis wanted, since it would by definition acknowledge that he was a Jew and not a German. Klemperer had no desire to start a new life in Palestine. As he put it: 'If specifically Jewish states are now to be set up ... that would be letting the Nazis throw us back thousands of years ... The solution to the Jewish question can be found only in deliverance from those who have invented it. And the world – because now this really does concern the world – will be forced to act accordingly.' The world's response was not edifying. By the late 1930s the principle of resettlement of the Jews was scarcely challenged; the only question was where the Jews should go. Other colonial destinations were considered: British Guiana, for example. In 1937 the Polish government proposed shipping a million Jews either to South Africa (the British demurred) or to French Madagascar, but the Polish Jews who visited the latter concluded that no more than 500 families could realistically be settled there. The nadir of this tawdry process was the 1938 Evian conference, where delegates from thirty-two different countries gathered to offer their excuses for not admitting more Jewish refugees. Many Jews travelled to Bucharest, despite the anti-Semitism that was rife in Romania, in the hope of getting to Turkey or Palestine.

For many – perhaps as many as 18,000 – Shanghai was the last resort, simply because the internationalized city required no visas for entry. There, it seemed to Ernest Heppner, a teenage refugee from Breslau, Jews 'were just another group of *nakonings*, foreigners'. Yet Shanghai was to prove anything but a safe haven, for events in Asia were in advance of events in Europe. There, an authoritarian regime had already gone beyond the pursuit of national regeneration from within, and had turned its mind to territorial aggrandizement. The Western powers had proved incapable of enforcing the protection of minorities that had been written into the Paris peace treaties. That was perhaps not surprising, given that tradition of non-intervention in the internal affairs of states which dated back to the Treaty of

Westphalia and which Woodrow Wilson could not overthrow. But when dictators challenged the borders that had been drawn up after 1918; when they invaded and occupied sovereign states – how then would the erstwhile peacemakers respond?

The answer was by seeking a continuation of peace at almost any price, provided the price was not paid by themselves.

# 8

# An Incidental Empire

*Bushidō ... perhaps, fills the same position in the history of ethics that the English Constitution does in political history.*
                                        Nitobe Inazō, *Bushido*, 1899

*Sixty-five million Japanese of pure blood all stand up as one man ... Do you suppose that they all go mad?*
                        Matsuoka Yōsuke, speech to the League of Nations, 1932

## LIVING SPACE

Camps were springing up everywhere in the 1930s. In Germany there were concentration camps for those whom the regime wished to ostracize and holiday camps for those whose loyalty it sought. In the Soviet Union there were labour camps for anyone whose loyalty Stalin and his henchmen doubted. In the United States the camps of the Depression years, called Hoovervilles, were not labour camps but the opposite: camps for the millions thrown out of work, named after the hapless president, Herbert Hoover, on whose watch the Depression had struck. The camps in Japan were different again. The inmates at a typical Japanese camp of the period were woken every morning at 5.30. They worked relentlessly all day, often enduring intense physical hardship, and scarcely resting until lights out at 10 p.m. They slept in unheated dormitories, their mail was censored, they were not allowed to drink alcohol or to smoke. But they were not prisoners. They were army cadets training to be officers. And the object of the harsh regime was not to punish them but to inculcate them with an almost superhuman military discipline. These military training camps were the camps of the future. By the end of the 1940s an astonishingly high proportion of able-bodied men born between around 1900 and 1930 would have passed through at least one.

As we have seen, the Depression caused radical changes in economic policy in most countries, but radical changes in political and legal arrangements in only some. The sub-set of countries that also radically altered their foreign policies was smaller still. Most responded to the crisis as Britain and the United States did, by seeking as far as possible to avoid external conflicts. In his inaugural address in 1933, Roosevelt promised to base US foreign policy on the 'good neighbor' principle, winding up his predecessors' interventions in Central America and the Caribbean and preparing the ground for the independence of the Philippines. This was as much out of parsimony as altruism; the assumption was that the cost of fighting unemployment at home ruled out further expenditures on small wars abroad. Even the majority of authoritarian regimes were quite content to persecute internal enemies and bicker with their neighbours over borders. Stalin had no strong interest in the acquisition of more territory; he already possessed a vast empire. Military dictators like Franco were more likely to wage civil war than inter-state war; as a conservative he understood that foreign wars ultimately helped domestic revolutionaries. Only three countries aspired to territorial expansion and war as a means to achieve it. They were Italy, Germany and Japan. Their dreams of empire were the proximate cause of the multiple wars we know as the Second World War. As we shall see, however, those dreams were far from being irrational responses to the Depression.

Why did only these three authoritarian regimes adopt and act upon aggressive foreign policies? A conventional answer might be that they were in thrall to anachronistic notions of imperial glory. All certainly harked back to stylized histories of their countries, Mussolini invoking the memory of the Romans to justify his African adventures, Hitler laying claim to the 'lost territories' of the Teutonic knights, the Japanese imagining their 'Yamato race' as if it were more than a mere offshoot of Chinese civilization. Yet there was nothing anachronistic about the idea of empire in the 1930s. In a world without free trade, empires offered all kinds of advantages to those who had them. It was undoubtedly advantageous to Britain to be at the centre of a vast sterling bloc with a common currency and common tariffs. And what would Stalin's Soviet Union have been if it had been confined within the historic frontiers of Muscovy, without the vast territories and resources of the Caucasus, Siberia and Central Asia?

The importance of empire became especially obvious to the self-styled 'have not' powers when they adopted rearmament as a tool of economic recovery. For rearmament in the 1930s, if one wished to possess the most up-to-date weaponry, demanded copious supplies of a variety of crucial raw materials (see below). Neither Italy, Germany nor Japan had these commodities within their own borders other than in trivial quantities. By contrast, the lion's share of the world's accessible supplies lay within the borders of one of four rival powers: the British Empire, the French Empire, the Soviet Union and the United States. Thus, no country could aspire to military parity with these powers without substantial imports of commodities whose supply they all but monopolized. For three reasons, it was not possible for the 'have nots' to rely on free trade to acquire them. First, free trade had been significantly reduced by the mid-1930s, thanks to the imposition of protectionist tariffs. Second, Italy, Germany and Japan lacked adequate international reserves to pay for the imports they required. Third, even if their central banks' reserves had been overflowing with gold, there was a risk that imports might be interdicted by rival powers before rearmament was complete. There was therefore a compelling logic behind territorial expansion, as Hitler made clear in his memorandum of August–September 1936, which outlined a new Four-Year Plan for the German economy.

This important document, drafted by Hitler himself, begins by restating his long-run aim of a confrontation with 'Bolshevism, the essence and goal of which is the elimination and the displacement of the hitherto leading social classes of humanity by Jewry, spread throughout the world'. Strikingly, Hitler singles out as a particular cause for concern the fact that 'Marxism – through its victory in Russia – has established one of the greatest empires as a base of operations for its future moves.' The existence of the Soviet Union, he argues, has enabled a dramatic growth in the military resources available to Bolshevism. Because of the decadence of the Western

democracies and the relative weakness of most European dictatorships, who need all their military resources merely to remain in power,
only three countries 'can be regarded as being firm against Bolshevism': Germany, Italy and Japan. The paramount objective of the
German government must therefore be 'developing the German Army,
within the shortest period, to be the first army in the world in respect
to training, mobilization of units [and] equipment'. Yet Hitler then
goes on to enumerate the difficulties of achieving this within Germany's existing borders. First, an 'overpopulated' Germany cannot
feed itself because 'the yield of our agricultural production can no
longer be substantially increased'. Second, and crucially, 'it is impossible for us to produce artificially certain raw materials which we do
not have in Germany, or to find other substitutes for them'. Hitler
specifically mentions oil, rubber, copper, lead and iron ore. Hence:
'The final solution lies in an extension of our living space, and/or the
sources of the raw materials and food supplies of our nation. It is
the task of the political leadership to solve this question one day in
the future.' Yet Germany is not yet in a military position to win living
space through conquest. Rearmament will therefore only be possible
through a combination of increased production of domestically available materials (for example low-grade German iron ore), further
restriction of non-essential imports such as coffee and tea, and substitution of essential imports with synthetic alternatives (for example
*ersatz* fuel, rubber and fats).

Hitler's memorandum was primarily an emphatic repudiation of
the earlier New Plan favoured by Hjalmar Schacht, which had aimed
at replenishing Germany's depleted hard currency reserves through a
complex system of export subsidies, import restrictions and bilateral
trade agreements. Hitler dismissed brusquely Schacht's arguments for
a slower pace of rearmament and a strategy of stockpiling raw
materials and hard currency. The memorandum was also an explicit
threat to German industry that state control would be stepped up if
the private sector failed to meet the targets set by the government:

It is not the task of the governmental economic institutions to rack their
brains over production methods. This matter does not concern the Ministry
of Economics at all. Either we have a private economy today, and it is its

task to rack its brains about production methods, or we assume that the determination of production is the task of government; in which case we no longer need the private economy at all ... The ministry has only to set the tasks; business has to fulfil them. If business considers itself unable to do so, then the National Socialist state will know how to resolve the problem by itself ... German business must either understand the new economic tasks or else they will prove unfit to exist any longer in this modern age, when the Soviet state builds up a gigantic plan. But in that eventuality, it will not be Germany who will be destroyed, but only some industrialists!

However, the most important point in the entire report was the time-table it established. Hitler's two conclusions could not have been more explicit:

I. The German armed forces must be ready for combat within four years.

II. The German economy must be fit for war within four years.

Historians have long debated whether this should be treated as evidence of a concrete Nazi plan for war. Of course it should. By decisively sanctioning an acceleration in the pace of rearmament and overriding Schacht's warnings of another balance of payments crisis, Hitler's Four-Year Plan memorandum significantly increased the like-lihood that Germany would be at war by 1940. In the words of Major-General Friedrich Fromm of the Army's Central Administrative Office: 'Shortly after completion of the rearmament phase, the Wehr-macht must be employed, otherwise there must be a reduction in demands or in the level of war readiness.' The interesting thing to note is that, by aiming for war in late 1940, Hitler was being relatively realistic about how long his proposed strategy of autarky could be sustained. By 1940 at the latest, in other words, Germany would need to have begun acquiring new living space.

The concept of *Lebensraum*, or living space, had been devised in the late 1890s by Friedrich Ratzel, Professor of Geography at Leipzig, and developed by the Orientalist and geopolitical theorist Karl Haus-hofer, whose pupil Rudolf Hess may have introduced the term to Hitler in the early 1920s. We can now see that the argument was based on an excessively pessimistic view of economic development. Since 1945 gains in both agricultural and industrial productivity have allowed 'haves' and 'have nots' alike to sustain even larger populations than they had in 1939. By the end of the twentieth century, Italy's population density was 17 per cent higher than sixty years before, Britain's 28 per cent, France's 42 per cent, Germany's 64 per cent and Japan's 84 per cent. As a result of decolonization, all these countries had been 'have nots' (in the inter-war sense) for most of the intervening years, yet their economies had grown significantly faster than in the periods when some or all of them had been 'haves'. Clearly, living space was not as indispensable for prosperity as Haushofer and his disciples believed. Yet in the context of the 1930s the argument had a powerful appeal – and particularly in Germany, Italy and Japan. In the late 1930s, as Figure 8.1 shows, Germany had the fourth-highest population density of the world's major economies (363 inhabitants per square mile), after the United Kingdom (487), Japan (469) and Italy (418). Under the Treaty of Versailles, however, Germany had been deprived of her relatively few colonies, whereas Britain had added to her already vast imperium, as had France. If, as Hitler had learned from Haushofer, living space was essential for a densely populated country with limited domestic sources of food and raw materials, then Germany, Japan and Italy all needed it. Another way of looking at the problem was to relate available arable land to the population employed in agriculture. By this measure, Canada was ten times better endowed than Germany and the United States six times better. Even Germany's European neighbours had more 'farming space': the average Danish farmer had 229 per cent more land than the average German; the average British farmer 182 per cent more and the average French farmer 34 per cent more. To be sure, farmers in Poland, Italy, Romania and Bulgaria were worse off; but further east, in the Soviet Union, there was 50 per cent more arable land per agricultural worker.

Living space had a secondary meaning, however, which was less frequently articulated but in practice much more important. This was the need that any serious military power had for access to strategic raw materials. Here changes in military technology had radically altered the global balance of power – arguably even more so than post-1918 border changes. Military power was no longer a matter of

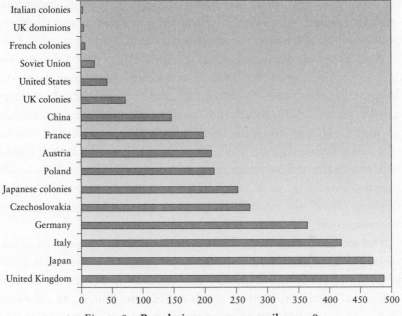

*Figure 8.1* **Population per square mile, 1938**

'blood and iron', or even coal and iron, as it had been in Bismarck's day. Just as important were oil and rubber. The production of these commodities was dominated by the United States, the British Empire and the Soviet Union or countries under their direct or indirect influence. American oilfields alone accounted for just under 70 per cent of global crude petroleum production; the world's next largest producer was Venezuela (12 per cent). The Middle Eastern oilfields did not yet occupy the dominant position they enjoy today: between them, Iran, Iraq, Saudi Arabia and the smaller Gulf states accounted for less than 7 per cent of total world production in 1940. The critical point was that oil production in all these countries was in the hands of British or American firms, principally Anglo-Persian, Royal Dutch/Shell and the successors to Standard Oil. Nor was modern warfare solely a matter of internal combustion engines and rubber tyres. Modern planes, tanks and ships – to say nothing of guns, shells, bullets and the machinery needed to make all these things – required a host of sophisticated forms of steel, which could be manufactured only with the admixture of more or less rare metals like antimony, chromium, cobalt, manganese, mercury, molybdenum, nickel, titanium, tungsten and vanadium. Here too the situation of the Western powers and the Soviet Union was dominant, if not monopolistic. Taken together, the British Empire, the French Empire, the United States and the Soviet Union accounted for virtually all the world's output of cobalt, manganese, molybdenum, nickel and vanadium, around three-quarters of all chromium and titanium, and half of all tungsten. The former German colony of South-West Africa, now securely in British hands, was practically the only source of vanadium. The Soviet Union, followed distantly by India, accounted for nearly all manganese production. Nickel was virtually a Canadian monopoly; molybdenum an American one.

The case that Germany, Italy and Japan lacked living space was therefore far from weak. Germany had abundant domestic supplies of coal and the biggest iron and steel industry in Europe, but before the 1930s needed to import all its rubber and oil. Japan relied on imports for 100 per cent of its rubber, 55 per cent of its steel and 45 per cent of its iron. Around 80 per cent of Japanese oil was imported from the United States in the 1930s and 10 per cent from the Dutch East Indies; the nearest other source was on the Soviet-controlled island of Sakhalin. Italy was not much better off. A crucial consequence of Hitler's Four-Year Plan memorandum was therefore a huge investment in new technologies capable of producing synthetic oil, rubber and fibres using domestic materials such as coal, as well as the creation at Salzgitter of a vast state-owned factory designed to manufacture steel from low-quality German iron ore. Yet by the time Hitler addressed his senior military leaders on November 5, 1937 – a meeting summarized by Colonel Friedrich Hossbach – it had become apparent that this enormously expensive mobilization of internal resources could not possibly deliver the level of rearmament the service chiefs regarded as necessary before 1943–45. It was for this reason that Hitler turned his attention to the possibility that living space and the resources that came with it might be acquired sooner rather than later, and without the need for a full-scale war with the Western powers or the Soviet Union.

He had good reason to think this. Italy had acquired new living space in Abyssinia without having to fight a wider war. Even more impressively, Japan too seemed well on her way out of the ignominious category of 'have nots'. But whereas Hitler and his acolytes looked eastwards for their living space* and the Italians looked southwards, the Japanese looked westwards – to China.

## THE OTHER ISLAND STORY

Japan had much in common with Great Britain, besides high population density. An archipelago of islands located not far from a well-developed continent with a longer-established civilization, Japan had emerged from an era of civil war to embrace constitutional monarchy. Japan was Asia's first industrial nation, just as Britain was Europe's. Both rose to economic power by manufacturing cloth and selling it to foreigners. Victorian Britain was famous for its stuffy social hierarchy; so too was Meiji Japan. The English had their state religion, propounded by the Church of England; the Japanese had theirs, known as Shinto. Both cultures engaged in what looked to outside eyes like emperor- (or empress-) worship. Both cultures venerated and romanticized the chivalric codes of a partly imagined feudal past. The enduring power of Second World War propaganda still makes it hard for Western observers to acknowledge these similarities; we prefer to accentuate the 'otherness' of inter-war Japan. To ignore them, however, is to miss the essential legitimacy of the basic Japanese objective after 1905: to be treated as an equal by the Western powers. To the Japanese this meant more than the share of the Chinese market that was on offer under the system of unequal treaties. The British had acquired a large and lucrative empire, the core of which was their total control of the defunct Asian empire of the Mughals but which also afforded them vast tracts of living space in North America and

* In a speech in early 1936 Walther Darré defined 'the natural area for settlement by the German people' as 'the territory to the East of the Reich's boundaries up to the Urals, bordered in the South by the Caucasus, Caspian Sea, Black Sea and the watershed which divides the Mediterranean basin from the Baltic and the North Sea'.

Australasia. The Japanese saw no reason why they should not build an empire of their own, complete with living space, in the ruins of the no less defunct Qing empire. The biggest difference between Japan and Britain was one of timing. Economically, at least in terms of per capita gross domestic product, Japan was around a century and a half behind, if not more. Strategically, too, Japan was roughly where Britain had been in the first half of the eighteenth century. Her opponents, however, were more numerous and more formidable than Hanoverian Britain's had been.

The First World War presented Japan with an ideal opportunity not only to expand her production of heavy industrial goods like ships, which she did prodigiously, but also to enlarge her living space in Asia. Japan was able to take the side of the Entente powers at minimal cost, seizing the German outpost of Tsingtao, on the Shandong peninsula, as well as the Marshall Islands, the Carolines and the Marianas in the North Pacific. Apart from sending a naval squadron to the Mediterranean, Japan contributed nothing to the war effort that was not directly to her own advantage. This was also true of her intervention in the Russian civil war, which merely gave the Japanese a pretext to seize Russian territory in the Far East. Meanwhile, under cover of war, Japan pressed China to make a whole range of economic and political concessions known as the Twenty-one Demands. These included the transfer to Japan of economic rights over the Shandong peninsula, the expansion and extension of Japanese rights in southern Manchuria and eastern Mongolia, the exclusion of other foreign powers from any future coastal concessions and the granting of various privileges to Japanese-owned railway and mining companies. The most radical, however, were for the appointment of Japanese advisers to the Chinese government, as well as of Japanese representatives to assist with the 'improvement' of the Chinese police. These last demands the Chinese – with British and American support – refused to accept. But the rest were acceded to with minimal modifications; the alternative, as the Japanese had made abundantly clear, was war.

The line the Japanese now took was that China was on the verge of disintegration. 'A civil war or collapse in China may not have any direct effect on other nations,' Special Ambassador Ishii Kikujirō had explained to the American Secretary of State Robert Lansing in 1917, 'but to Japan it will be a matter of life and death. A civil war in China will immediately be reflected in Japan, and the downfall of China means the downfall of Japan.' Privately, however, some Japanese leaders increasingly coveted China as a potential source for the vital raw materials Japan herself lacked. The Western powers were under no illusions as to Japan's intentions. 'Today,' wrote the British ambassador to China, 'we have come to know Japan – the real Japan – as a frankly opportunist, not to say selfish, country, of very moderate importance compared with the Giants of the Great War, but with a very exaggerated opinion of her own role.' This was a very British way of saying that Japan should leave the exploitation of China to Asia's traditional European masters. Other British observers were even more perturbed. Admiral Sir John Jellicoe, who had commanded the expedition to relieve Beijing in the Boxer Rebellion, suspected that the Japanese ultimately aimed at creating a 'greater Japan which will probably comprise parts of China and the Gateway to the East, the Dutch East Indies, Singapore, and the Malay States'.

The Japanese went to the Paris peace conference in 1919 numbering themselves among the victors; they departed as if they had been on the losing side. On territorial matters, they had no cause for complaint; they inherited the former German concessions in Shandong, including Tsingtao, and were granted the islands they had occupied in the Pacific as mandates (the Palaus, Marianas, Carolines and Marshalls). Taking President Wilson at his idealistic word, however, they also called for an amendment to the League of Nations Covenant that would assert the equality of the world's races. Neither Wilson, with Western democratic sensibilities to consider, nor the Australian premier William Hughes, who had committed himself to a 'Whites Only' immigration policy, was minded to oblige.* The defeat of the amendment was a slap in the face, though it suited the Japanese to parade their injury. As Prince Konoe Fumimaro said of Woodrow Wilson's vision

---

* The amendment in fact commanded majority support on the League Commission; eleven of seventeen members voted for it. But Wilson insisted on the need for unanimity.

of the post-war order, 'Democracy and humanitarianism were nice sentiments, but they were simply a cloak for the United States and Britain to maintain their control over most of the world's wealth.' This spat over race heralded a rapid breakdown of the wartime alliance between Japan and the Western powers. In 1923 the Anglo-Japanese alliance was allowed to lapse; both parties agreed that it was superseded by the five-power treaty on naval arms limitation agreed at Washington the year before. Even more than the British, many Americans now regarded Japan's success as a potential threat. As early as 1917, the US Navy identified Japan as America's most likely enemy in a future war. The atmosphere was further soured in 1924 when Congress, egged on by the xenophobic Hearst press, passed the Johnson–Reed Immigration Act, which was explicitly directed against (among others) the Japanese. Western suspicions were merely confirmed when the Japanese ignored the ban on the construction of military facilities in mandated territories, turning Truk in the Carolines into their main South Pacific naval base.

Yet there was no inexorable march to war leading from 1919 to 1941. Japan in the 1920s showed every sign of accepting her place in a world dominated by the Anglo-Saxon powers. Under the Washington Naval Treaty of 1922, the Japanese government agreed to limit the tonnage of their navy to 60 per cent of that of the British and American fleets and to withdraw their military forces from Tsingtao, Vladivostok and the northern half of Sakhalin. Japan also agreed not to build naval bases in southern Sakhalin and Formosa (Taiwan). By 1924 there had been significant cuts in the strength of both the army and the navy. Total military expenditure was reduced from 42 per cent of the national budget in the early 1920s to 28 per cent by 1927. The standing army numbered 250,000 men. The Japanese also subscribed to the so-called Nine-Power Agreement reasserting the American principle of an 'Open Door' in China, which retained the near fiction of Chinese political sovereignty while allowing the advanced economies to carve her up as a shared captive market. The Japanese did not insist on retaining control of Shandong. It seemed as if – in the words of Matsui Iwane, one of the army's rising stars – Japan would, at least for the time being, have to 'substitute economic conquest for military invasion, financial influence for military control, and achieve our goals under the slogan of co-prosperity and coexistence, friendship and co-operation'. Meanwhile, Japanese domestic politics seemed to move in step with those of the Western democracies, particularly after the introduction of universal manhood suffrage in 1925. Civilian politicians were in charge, and behind them the family-run business conglomerates known as *zaibatsu*. The threats to their position – rural food riots, banking panics, ambitious generals – were the normal threats facing democratic leaders in the volatile post-war world. The fact that two successive prime ministers, Hara Kei and Takahashi Korekiyo, contemplated abolishing the post of army chief of staff is a mark of the confidence of the civilians at this time. Japan's economy continued to grow steadily, propelled forward by productivity gains in agriculture and light industry. Although protective tariffs favoured the growth of heavy industry, it was textile exports that were the key to Japan's rising prosperity in the 1920s.

In Britain the inter-war years were marked by a decline in the power of two traditionally important institutions: the monarchy and the military. In December 1936 Edward VIII abdicated, having been bullied into doing so by the Prime Minister, Stanley Baldwin, who disapproved of the American divorcée he wished to marry and who asserted that the British public (and the governments of the Dominions) shared his sentiments.* The armed forces, meanwhile, were starved of cash on the principle that there would not be another major war for at least ten years – a 'Ten-Year Rule' that was introduced in 1919 and reaffirmed annually until 1932. In Japan the opposite happened. Monarch and military both grew more powerful. The Japanese answer to the Depression was not national socialism, as it was in Germany. It was imperial militarism.

In December 1926 the ailing Emperor Yoshihito died, to be suc-

---

* Baldwin ruled out the traditional compromise of a morganatic marriage, the sort that Archduke Francis Ferdinand had made when he married Sophie Countess Chotek von Chotkova, whose family was not of royal blood. As Duff Cooper noted, however, the timing of events was not to the King's advantage. He waited until after his accession to the throne to raise the question of marrying Wallis Simpson. Nor did it help matters that he was stridently supported by both the Rothermere and Beaverbrook papers, to say nothing of Winston Churchill, at that time in the political wilderness.

ceeded by his twenty-five-year-old son, Hirohito, who had been regent since 1921. Hirohito had visited Britain in 1921, where he had enjoyed the comparatively informal lifestyle of his royal counterparts. His accession to the imperial throne was as elaborate a ritual as any British coronation. Having spent the night in the holiest of Shinto shrines at Ise, communing with his progenitor the sun goddess Amaterasu O-mi-kami, Hirohito was formally reborn as a living god on November 14, 1928. Two weeks later, in his capacity as Commander-in-Chief of the Armed Forces, the new god reviewed a spectacular parade by 35,000 imperial troops. A new era, known, in retrospect ironically, as *Shōwa* (shining peace), had begun. Hirohito was, like most monarchs, quite unsuited to executive power. A marine biologist by inclination, he would probably have been happier in a laboratory than at the centre of an imperial court. He had envied the 'freedom' enjoyed by British royalty, who were under no obligation to behave like deities. Yet he never outwardly doubted his divine status. Nor did he ever seriously question the use that was made of his supreme right of command to strengthen the political power of the armed services – 'the teeth and the claws of the Royal House'.

There was a tension at the heart of the Japanese army too. The first lesson young conscripts learned was the Soldier's Code, the seven duties of the soldier: 'Loyalty; unquestioning obedience; courage; controlled use of physical force; frugality; honour and respect of superiors.' They were taught to value obedience above life itself, on the principle that 'Duty is weightier than a mountain, while death is lighter than a feather.' It was glorious to fall like the cherry blossom, in the pristine state of dutiful youth. Those who died this way joined the *kami* or spirits housed at the Yasukuni shrine in Tokyo. This was not quite the samurai code of *bushidō*, as expounded for British and American readers by Nitobe Inazō in 1899, which had also venerated qualities like rectitude, benevolence, politeness, truthfulness and sincerity – making it recognizably, as Nitobe argued, the cousin of Anglo-French chivalry. Rather, the Japanese army took from *bushido* whatever was best calculated to engender a fanatical subservience to imperial authority and the military command structure – including the preference for suicide, preferably by agonizing disembowelment, over any kind of dishonour or failure. Training was intended to push men to the very limits of their physical and mental endurance. Recruits were drilled until they could run 100 metres inside sixteen seconds, run 1,500 metres inside six minutes, jump nearly four metres and throw a grenade over thirty-five metres – all in full marching dress. A regiment was expected to be able to march twenty-five miles a day for fifteen days with just four days' rest. Harsh physical punishments, including routine face-slapping, became the norm even for minor breaches of discipline. As one who fought against it observed, 'It was his [the individual Japanese soldier's] combination of obedience and ferocity that made the Japanese Army . . . so formidable.'

Yet the backward-looking ethos of Japanese military training was in many ways at odds with the reality of mid-twentieth-century warfare. Officers like Nagata Tetsuzan, head of the War Ministry's military affairs bureau, had seen at first hand the pitiless impact of fire against men – no matter how well trained and spiritually uplifted – in the trenches of the Western Front. He urged that Japan learn from Germany's mistakes in the First World War by preparing systematically for a future total war, drawing up meticulous lists of the national resources that would need to be mobilized. The more men like Nagata studied these lists, the more they appreciated Japan's fundamental weakness. But they inferred from this not the need for caution and conciliation, but the need for territorial expansion, and soon.

## 'THE ONLY WAY OUT'

China, the most likely location of new Japanese living space, was a country in turmoil – the remnant of an ancient empire, the kernel of a new republic, the raw material for one or more colonies. Its predicament had much in common with that which had occurred in Turkey in the aftermath of the Ottoman collapse, with the difference that China's Kemal – Chiang Kai-shek – ultimately failed where Kemal succeeded in establishing a stable nationalist regime. A revolution in 1911 had overthrown the last Qing Emperor, but the republic that succeeded him had proved a precarious structure. Although it had led the revolution and went on to win a clear majority in elections to the National Assembly, the Nationalist Party (Guomindang), led by Sun Yatsen, was forced to yield the presidency to the militarily powerful Yuan Shikai. Yuan was able to crush a second revolution instigated by the Guomindang, but his bid to make himself Emperor ended with his death in 1916. Japanese wartime demands had stoked up nationalist sentiment, particularly among educated Chinese. Indeed, when the Paris peacemakers awarded Japan the former German possessions in Shandong there were furious protests by students in Beijing, culminating in the Tiananmen Square demonstration of May 4, 1919. However, the nationalist movement soon split between a revived Guomindang and a new Chinese Communist Party. The rest of China seemed on the verge of disintegration as warlord clans carved out their own fiefdoms, the Anfu controlling the provinces of Anhui and Fujien, the Zhili running Hebei and the area around Beijing, and the Fengtien notionally in charge of Manchuria. Meanwhile, the country's most important economic centres were under one form or another of foreign control as the system of treaty ports and extraterritoriality reached its zenith.

The extent of China's disintegration in the 1920s is hard to overstate. The People's Republic of today projects itself as a homogeneous society, with more than 90 per cent of the population identified in an official census as members of the Han ethnic group. The China of eighty years ago was anything but a unitary state. Quite apart from the fifty or more other ethnic groups and the eleven or more language groups still identifiable today, inhabitants even of neighbouring villages could speak mutually incomprehensible dialects. The dynasty overthrown in 1911 had been Manchu; the empire's political centre of gravity had been in the north, in Beijing. But many of the decisive political events of the revolutionary and civil war periods took place in Shanghai, far to the south. Both the reformed Guomindang and the Chinese Communist Party were established in Shanghai, which was itself dominated by the French Concession, to the west of the Old City, and the larger International Settlement, which extended along the north bank of the Huangpu River. Ironically, even the supposed nationalists looked to foreign powers for assistance. As early as 1923 Sun Yatsen sent his playboy protégé Chiang Kai-shek to Moscow to ask for assistance. Stalin responded by sending Mikhail Grunzeberg to China, with the task of reorganizing the Guomindang along Marxist-

Leninist lines. Without this Soviet support it is doubtful that the Guomindang would have expanded so quickly from its Cantonese power-base. It was Moscow that ordered the Chinese Communists to subordinate themselves to the Nationalists in a 'united front'.

Within the Guomindang, however, Soviet 'democratic centralism' was slow to take root, particularly on the central question of how best to free China. Indeed, in the wake of Sun's death in 1925 the party threatened to fall apart. As Chairman of the Nationalist government in Nanking, Wang Jingwei favoured a conciliatory approach towards the foreign powers, particularly Japan. Indeed, Wang's rhetoric seemed to echo the pacific sentiments emanating from Japan's long-serving Foreign Minister Shidehara Kijūrō. Chiang, by contrast, sought a break with Moscow and a full-scale military effort to unite China. His Northern Expedition of 1926 aimed to crush the warlords as a prelude to defeating the imperialists. The first problem that dogged Chiang's career, however, was that internal enemies always seemed to take priority over foreign ones. No sooner had he concluded his campaign in the North than he unleashed a ruthless attack on the Communists in Shanghai, allying with local gang leaders to massacre thousands of trade unionists and other suspected Communist members. Chiang's second problem was corruption. Though he called on his fellow Chinese to embrace the four Confucian principles of Li (property), Yi (right conduct), Lian (honesty) and Qi (integrity and honour), the reality of Guomindang rule was rampant graft. Among Chiang's most reliable confederates was the Shanghai gangster 'Big-Eared Du', who was appointed – conveniently, from his own point of view – director of the Opium Suppression Bureau in Shanghai.

In the midst of this confusion, there was little to choose between Japanese and British policy. Although British politicians seemed willing to make concessions on the issue of extra-territoriality, the proverbial men on the spot continued to act as if China were merely an eastward extension of the Raj. In 1925 British police in the Shanghai International Settlement killed fifteen Chinese workers who had gone on strike, provoking another wave of public indignation. A year later British sailors were involved in a pitched battle at Wanhsien on the Yangtze River in which more than 200 Chinese sailors and an unknown number of civilians were killed; the number of British fatalities was just seven. At the end of 1926 Britain sent some 20,000 troops to Shanghai, in response to Guomindang pressure on British concessions up the Yangtze. British and American ships shelled Nanking after Chinese soldiers killed a number of foreigners. Japan's conduct was little different, except perhaps that the use of naked force came slightly later. In May 1927 and again in August, troops were sent to Shandong to protect Japanese assets from Chiang's forces. But once it became clear that, having won the internal power struggle, Chiang was in no hurry to confront the foreign powers, the Japanese seemed content with their share of the spoils of the Washington Treaty system. A visitor to Shanghai in around 1930 would have been struck more by the similarities between British and Japanese interests in China than by their differences.

Chiang's regime was not without its strengths. Where the Left saw only foreign exploitation, there was sometimes genuine foreign-financed development. Thousands of miles of new roads and railways were built between 1927 and 1936, the bulk of the construction financed by European investors. Yet the Chinese state remained exceptionally weak both in fiscal and in military terms. The privileges granted to Western investors hampered the development of China's own institutions. Chiang's China was certainly not capable of withstanding a concerted challenge to the 'Open Door' system by a foreign power intent on monopolizing China's resources.

Had it not been for the Depression, the civilian politicians and the *zaibatsu* might conceivably have retained the upper hand in Tokyo. But the collapse of global trade after 1928 dealt Japan's economy a severe blow – a blow only made more painful by the ill-timed decision to return to the gold standard in 1929 (the very moment it would have made sense to float the yen) and Finance Minister Inoue Junnosuke's tight budgets. The terms of trade turned dramatically against Japan as export prices collapsed relative to import prices. In volume terms, exports fell by 6 per cent between 1929 and 1931. At the same time, Japan's deficits in raw materials soared to record heights (see Figure 8.2). Unemployment rose to around one million. Agricultural incomes slumped.

There were alternatives to territorial expansion as a response to this crisis. As Finance Minister from December 1931, Takahashi Korekiyo

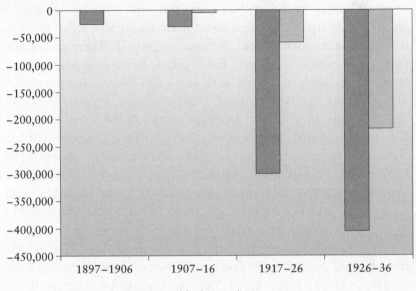

☐ All minerals   ■ Agricultural food commodities

*Figure 8.2* Japan's raw materials deficit, 1897–1936 (thousands of yen)

cut Japan's economy loose from the deadweight of orthodox economics, floating the yen, boosting government spending and monetizing debt by selling bonds to the Bank of Japan. These proto-Keynesian policies worked as well as any tried elsewhere during the Depression. Between 1929 and 1940 gross national product rose at a real rate of 4.7 per cent per annum, significantly faster than the Western economies in the same period. Export volumes doubled. In theory, Japan might have carried on in this vein, reining in the budget deficit as the recovery gathered pace, exploiting her comparative advantage as a textile manufacturer at the heart of an Asian trading bloc. As a percentage of total world trade, intra-Asian trade doubled between 1913 and 1938. By 1936 Japan accounted for 16 per cent of total Chinese imports, a share second only to that of the United States.

Yet the proponents of military expansion forcefully argued against the option of peaceful commercial recovery. As we have seen, the countries best able to withstand the Depression appeared to be those with the biggest empires: not only the Soviet Union, but also Great Britain, which made no bones about restricting Japanese access to imperial markets in the 1930s. Japan's principal export markets were neighbouring Asian countries; could those markets be relied upon to remain open in an increasingly protectionist world? There was, in any case, good reason to suspect the Western powers of preparing to abandon the unequal treaties in response to Guomindang pressure.* Japan was also heavily reliant on imports of Western machinery and raw materials. In 1935 she depended on the British Empire for half her imports of jute, lead, tin, zinc and manganese, nearly half her imports of rubber, aluminium, iron ore and cotton, and one-third of her imports of pig iron. She imported almost as much cotton from the United States as from India and Egypt and large quantities of American scrap metal and oil. At the same time, Japan needed the English-speaking economies as markets for her exports, around a fifth of which went to British imperial markets. In the words of Freda Utley, the left-wing English journalist and author of *Japan's Feet of Clay* (1936), a liberal Japan could 'but oscillate between the Scylla of dependence on the USA and the Charybdis of dependence on British empire markets'. In the short term, the increased military expenditure caused by a shift to formal imperialism would stimulate Japan's domestic economy, filling the order books of companies like Mitsubishi, Kawasaki and Nissan, while in the long term, it was argued, the appropriation of resource-rich territory would ease the country's balance of payments problems, for what use is an empire if it does not guarantee cut-price raw materials? At the same time, Japan would acquire desperately needed living space to which her surplus population could emigrate. In the words of Lieutenant-General Ishiwara Kanji, one of the most influential proponents and practitioners of a policy of territorial expansion:

Our nation seems to be at a deadlock, and there appears to be no solution for the important problems of population and food. The only way out . . . is in the development of Manchuria and Mongolia . . . [The] natural resources will be sufficient to save [Japan] from the imminent crisis and pave the way for a big jump.

* In 1929 the British had restored tariff autonomy to China (as did the Americans and Japanese) and ended their embargo on arms shipments. The following year, they restored the North China naval base of Weihaiwei to Chinese control.

In one respect this argument was not wholly spurious. That Japan faced a Malthusian crisis seemed all too clear when famine struck some rural areas in 1934. Imperialism addressed this problem. Between 1935 and 1940 around 310,000 Japanese emigrated, mostly to the growing Japanese empire in Asia; this certainly eased the downward pressure on domestic wages and consumption. In another respect, however, the case for expansion was deeply suspect. Quite simply, expansion exacerbated precisely the structural problems it was supposed to solve, by requiring increased imports of petroleum, copper, coal, machinery and iron ore to feed the nascent Japanese military-industrial complex. As the Japanese Marxist Nawa Toichi put it, 'the more Japan attempted to expand the productive capacity of her heavy and military-related industries as a preparation for her expansion policy . . . the greater her dependence on the world market and the imports of raw materials' became. The onus of proof was unquestionably on the militarists to demonstrate that Japanese imperialism would not merely exacerbate the condition it was supposed to cure.

## A DISEASE OF THE SKIN

Some empires are acquired by accident, as the British liked to think theirs had been. The Japanese empire in China was acquired by incidents. On September 18, 1931, a Japanese force led by Lieutenant Kawamoto Suemori blew up a short stretch of the South Manchurian Railway five miles north of the town of Mukden. They had been trying to derail the Dairen express, but missed it. Blaming the explosion on Chinese bandits, the Japanese proceeded to occupy the town and take control of the railway. Manchuria, they claimed, was descending into anarchy. It was time, in the words of the Commander-in-Chief of the Kwantung Army – the Japanese force stationed in Manchuria since 1905 – to 'act boldly and assume responsibility for law and order' throughout the province. Within hours of what became known as the Manchurian Incident, the Japanese had also captured Yingkou, Andong and Changchun; by the end of the week they controlled most of the provinces of Liaoning and Jilin.

There would be many such incidents in the course of the next six years.

The transformation of Manchuria into the puppet state of Manchukuo provides a perfect illustration of the tendency of empires to expand spontaneously, as a result of local initiatives rather than central plans. Since the Jinan Incident of May 1928, when General Fukuda Hirosuke had defied orders from Tokyo by clashing with Chinese forces in Shandong, there had been a pattern of military insubordination on the periphery of Japan's Asian empire. A month after the Tsinan Incident, Colonel Kōmoto Daisaku of the Kwantung Army had detonated a bomb underneath the railway carriage of Zhang Zuolin, the leading Chinese politician in Manchuria, in the hope of precipitating a Japanese takeover of Mukden. Zhang's son, Zhang Xueliang, had responded to his father's murder by aligning himself more closely with the Guomindang government in Nanking and endeavouring to reduce Japanese influence in Manchuria. This was bound to cause concern at a time when Nanking was stepping up its pressure for an end to the system of extra-territoriality. The catalyst for the Manchurian Incident was in fact a dispute over the right of Korean farmers, whom the Japanese had encouraged to emigrate across the border, to construct their own irrigation ditches at Wanbaoshan, a small town near Changchun. Clashes between Chinese and Korean villagers set off a chain reaction; there were anti-Chinese riots in both Korea and Japan, which duly elicited anti-Japanese responses in China, including the execution of a Japanese officer accused of spying in Mongolia. The moment seemed propitious to those Kwantung Army officers, such as Ishiwara Kanji and Itagaki Seishirō, who had long argued for a switch from informal to formal empire. They were able to summon reinforcements from Korea, once again without authorization from Tokyo. Time and again lower-ranking officers seized the initiative in China, reflecting the way their training had emphasized strategy over tactics and operations.

The insubordination of Japanese overseas armies raised an obvious question: who ruled in Tokyo? On paper, it was still the civilians, and behind them their patrons in the *zaibatsu*. But the domestic constellation of forces was changing rapidly. It was a sign of the shifting balance of power that the Prime Minister at the time of Zhang

Zuolin's assassination, Tanaka Giichi, had let his murderer off all but
scot-free, merely reprimanding him for failing to provide adequate
security for Zhang's railway carriage. For his part, the Emperor Hirohito viewed the antics of the Kwantung Army and its supporters in
Tokyo with disquiet. His inclination, encouraged by venerable courtiers like the former Prime Minister Prince Saionji Kimmochi, was to
rein in the soldiers. Yet it was in the Emperor's name – or, to be
precise, on the basis of his 'right of supreme command' – that Japan's
military leaders now pressed for still greater latitude. In 1930 a faction
within the Japanese navy challenged the decision by the government
of Hamaguchi Osachi to sign the London Naval Agreement, which
extended the old 5:5:3 ratio for American, British and Japanese capital
ships to cruisers, destroyers and submarines. In November of that
year Hamaguchi was gravely wounded by an assassin. Henceforth
any Japanese politician who stood up to the military was taking his
life in his hands. Nevertheless, it would be misleading to portray what
was happening as a kind of Japanese *pronunciamento* in the Hispanic
style. There is a need to distinguish between the radical young officers
in the Kwantung Army and the top brass of the General Staff, who
in fact shared the Emperor's unease about what was happening in
Manchuria. Indeed, General Kanaya, the Chief of the General Staff,
sought to prevent a complete takeover of Manchuria in the weeks
following the incident. Nor was that the only fissure within the Japanese military. The old clan-like factions like the Satsuma, Saga and
Chōshū were giving way to new societies like Issekikai (the One
Evening Society) as well as more sinister organizations like Sakurakai
(the Cherry Blossom Society) and Ketsumeidan (the Blood Brotherhood),* some of which also recruited members within the civil
service. The civilian politicians were themselves divided. Hamaguchi's
successor as Prime Minister, Wakatsuki Reijirō, pinned his hopes on a
diplomatic compromise with the Chinese, but the opposition Seiyūkai

* A distinctive feature of the radical militarist societies was the influence on them of
the Nichiren Buddhist guru Tanaka Chigaku (1861–1939). Tanaka used the
thirteenth-century mystic Nichiren's teachings as the basis for the claim that Japan's
'heaven-ordained task' was to seek 'a spiritual unity' throughout the world. Among
Tanaka's followers was Ishihara Kanji, mastermind of the Manchurian Incident and
later director of strategy at the General Staff Office.

party backed the Kwantung Army and denounced him as a weakling. In December 1931 he resigned. It was a turning point. Of the fourteen prime ministers who came after him between 1932 and 1945, only four were civilians. Two of those, including Wakatsuki's successor, Inukai Tsuyoshi, were assassinated. Inukai was just one of three prominent civilians murdered in 1932, including the former Finance Minister and the head of the Mitsui *zaibatsu*. Thereafter power was increasingly concentrated in the hands of an inner cabinet, within which the service ministers wielded an unquestioned veto power.

At first sight, it should be noted, there was something to be said for replacing Western imperial dominance in China with Japanese. After all, would not the Japanese understand better than Europeans how to develop a territory like Manchuria? Even before the Manchurian Incident, there were more Japanese than Europeans in China, and there is ample evidence that they were pulling ahead of the British as the principal exponents of 'informal imperialism'. Nor did the Japanese do an altogether bad job of developing their new colony. Between 1932 and 1941, a total of just under 5.9 billion yen was invested there. The conspirators behind the Manchurian Incident had an almost utopian vision of how the region should develop as a 'paradise of benevolent government' based on 'harmonious cooperation among the five races'. The indigenous population would be protected from 'usury, excessive profit and all other unjust economic pressure'. This was not as disingenuous as might be suspected. Not for the last time in the mid-twentieth century, an occupied territory became a laboratory for experiments too radical to be carried out at home.

Why did the Chinese put up so little resistance to the Japanese takeover of Manchuria (a policy of passivity they would continue for a further six years, in the face of repeated Japanese territorial incursions)? As soon as he heard of the Mukden bombing, Chiang Kai-shek advised Zhang Xueliang not to meet force with force, despite the fact that his troops, though inferior in quality, substantially outnumbered the Japanese. The simple explanation is that Chiang was continuing his well-established policy of avoiding confrontation with the Japanese, conserving his resources for the internal war against the Communists. It was not a policy that won him much popularity, particularly with the Communists now calling for resistance against the Japanese. Indeed, the Manchurian Incident precipitated a crisis within the Guomindang regime which forced Chiang temporarily to retire from politics. On the other hand, Chiang's principal rival, Wang Jingwei, was no more eager for war with Japan. His policy was to negotiate in earnest while offering token resistance. The question was with whom to negotiate? One option was to resume talks with the Japanese Foreign Minister Shidehara, in the hope that he would be able to restrain the Japanese military. Alternatively, China could seek the support of the Western powers. It was decided to refer the Manchurian question to the League of Nations and to decline the Japanese government's requests to negotiate on a bilateral basis. Unfortunately for the Chinese, this was probably the wrong decision. A swift deal with the moderates in Tokyo might have limited the damage in Manchuria. Nothing swift, by contrast, was likely to emerge from the League.

Despite its poor historical reputation, the League of Nations should not be dismissed as a complete failure. Of sixty-six international disputes it had to deal with (four of which had led to open hostilities), it successfully resolved thirty-five and quite legitimately passed back twenty to the channels of traditional diplomacy. It failed to resolve just eleven conflicts. Like its successor the United Nations, it was capable of being effective provided some combination of the great powers – including, it should be emphasized, those, like the United States and the Soviet Union, who were not among its members – had a common interest in its being effective. Remarkably, given Manchuria's role as an imperial fault line earlier in the century, this was not the case in 1931. So uninterested was Stalin in the Far East at this point that in 1935 he offered to sell the Soviet-owned Chinese Eastern Railway to Japan and to withdraw all Soviet forces to the Amur River. If the Soviets were not interested in Manchuria, it was hard to see why Britain or the United States should be, especially at a time when both were reeling from severe financial crises.

On September 30, 1931, the Council of the League issued a resolution calling for 'the withdrawal of [Japanese] troops to the railway zone' where they had originally and legitimately been stationed. However, it set no deadline for this withdrawal and added the caveat that any reduction in troop numbers should only be 'in proportion as the safety of the lives and property of Japanese nationals is effectively assured'. Eight days later Japanese planes bombed Jinzhou on Manchuria's south-western frontier with China proper. On October 24 a new resolution was passed setting November 16 as the date by which the Japanese should withdraw. At the end of that month Japanese ground forces advanced towards Jinzhou. In early December, at the Japanese delegate's suggestion, the League Council decided to send a commission of inquiry under the chairmanship of the Earl of Lytton, the former Governor of Bengal (and son of the Victorian Viceroy). Without waiting for its report, the US Secretary of State, Henry L. Stimson, warned Japan that the United States would refuse to recognize any separate agreement that Tokyo might reach with China; in his opinion, Japan was acting in breach not only of the Kellogg–Briand Pact signed in Paris in 1928 (under which the signatories had made 'a frank renunciation of war as an instrument of national policy') but also of the earlier Nine-Power Agreement to maintain the Open Door system in China.

The Japanese were unimpressed by American 'non-recognition'. In March 1932 they proclaimed 'Manchukuo' as an independent state, with the former Chinese Emperor, Puyi, as its puppet ruler – another initiative by the men on the spot which was ratified by Tokyo only after a six-month delay. A week later Lytton submitted his voluminous report, which dismissed the Japanese claim that Manchukuo was a product of Manchurian self-determination and condemned Japan for 'forcibly seiz[ing] and occupy[ing] . . . what was indisputably Chinese territory'. The Japanese pressed on with their policy of conquest. They bombed targets in the province of Rehe in the summer of 1932. In January 1933 there was yet another 'incident' at Shanhaiguan, the strategic pass where the Great Wall reaches the sea. After a few days it too was in Japanese hands. A week's fighting added Rehe to Japan's domain. In February 1933 the League of Nations Assembly accepted Lytton's report and endorsed all but unanimously his proposal to give Manchuria a new autonomous status. Once again Japan was politely asked to withdraw her troops. In March the Japanese finally announced their intention to withdraw – from the League. Two months later they concluded a truce with Chinese military representatives that confirmed Japan's control over Manchuria and Inner Mongolia. It also created a large demilitarized zone running through Hebei province, which the Japanese were soon running on an informal basis.

It is sometimes said that this was a fatal turning point in the history of the 1930s; the beginning of that policy of appeasement which was to culminate in 1939. But that is to misread the Manchurian crisis. It was unquestionably a turning point in Japan's domestic politics. But internationally all that had happened was that the Japanese had achieved their long-standing objective of being treated as an equal by the other imperial powers. They were now entitled to expand their colonial territory, but only in regions where the other powers had no interests. When the Japanese sought to flex their muscles in a quite different part of China – the vital port of Shanghai, through which the lion's share of China's trade flowed – it was a very different matter. The events of January–May 1932, which saw full-scale fighting between Japanese marines and the Chinese 19th Route Army, elicited a much less accommodating response from Britain and the United States (as well as from France, hitherto the neutral arbiter), leading ultimately to a truce on the basis of the *status quo ante*. Indeed, with the British decision to abandon the Ten-Year Rule in 1932, and the resumption of work on the fortification of Singapore, the prospect before the Japanese was of an increasing Western commitment to Asia, even if in the short term the British had good reason to avoid a military showdown with Japan. There was therefore a faint whiff of hubris about the assertion by Amō Eiji, chief of the intelligence section in the Japanese Foreign Ministry, of a Japanese monopoly of power in Asia analogous to the US monopoly of power in the Americas – in effect, an Asian Monroe Doctrine. This was effectual only in as much as Japanese pressure succeeded in disrupting the efforts of the Guomindang Finance Minister Song Ziwen, Chiang's brother-in-law, to secure substantial economic aid from the League of Nations and a loan to purchase American cotton. In other respects it counted for nothing. From 1933 the Chinese were able to rely on military and economic assistance from Nazi Germany. Hitler sent General Hans von Seeckt, who had been in charge of the rump German army after Versailles, as a military adviser to the Nanking government; in 1936 a Chinese–German trade agreement was signed. In 1935 a British delegation led by the Treasury official Sir Frederick Leith-Ross arrived in China with a scheme to reform the Chinese currency by taking it off the silver standard and pegging it to sterling. So much for the Asian Monroe Doctrine. Nor could the Japanese wholly ignore the possibility that American grumbles about Japanese policy would one day be backed up by naval action. The Japanese decision to abrogate the Washington Naval Treaty in December 1934 was predicated on the idea that Japan should settle for nothing less than naval parity; it overlooked the possibility that without any treaty, the United States might conceivably widen the gap between its navy and Japan's. The Japanese also had reason to worry about the Soviet Union's decision to join the League of Nations barely a year after Japan's decision to leave, and to build up its defences in Eastern Siberia. The interlude of Russian indifference to the Far East was at an end.

In that sense 1931–3 was not a turning point at all; rather, it was the continuation of a Japanese policy of colonization dating back as far as the 1890s. The critical *leitmotif* throughout was the limited use the Japanese made of military force to achieve their conquests. Indeed, compared with 1904–5, the 'incidents' of the early 1930s were small-scale affairs, which cost few Japanese lives. In the mid-1930s the Japanese reverted to nineteenth-century British tactics, sending gunboats up the Yangtze to Nanking after their consul temporarily vanished under mysterious circumstances, and to Hankou to protest against anti-Japanese indoctrination by the local Chinese commander. In early 1935 the Kwantung Army staged yet another incident, to oust Chinese troops from Eastern Chahar, to the east of Rehe province. Throughout that year – with a junior officer once again taking the initiative – the whole of Chahar and Hebei provinces were the scenes of repeated incursions by Japanese forces intended to intimidate and undermine the Chinese authorities. Following his appointment as commander of the North China Garrison in the summer of 1935, Lieutenant-General Tada Hayao made no secret of his belief that all of China's northern provinces should become autonomous, in other words be under Japanese rather than Chinese control. A fresh incident erupted in August 1936, this time in Chengdu in Sichuan, prompting still more extreme Japanese demands. The following month it was the turn of Beihai in southern Kwantung. Throughout the period from

1931 to 1937 the Chinese yielded to virtually all such pressure. Chiang Kai-shek remained true to his maxim, 'First internal pacification, then external resistance', concentrating his rhetorical fire on the 'Red bandits' (the Communists) rather than the 'dwarf bandits' (the Japanese) and insisting that until the 'internal disease has . . . been eliminated, the external disorder cannot be cured'. The Japanese, Chiang insisted, represented merely a 'disease of the skin'; the Communists, by contrast, were a 'disease of the heart'. Even as the Japanese tightened their grip on Manchuria, fighting raged between Nationalists and Communists, culminating in the protracted campaign to oust the Communists from their Jiangxi stronghold. Meanwhile, bellicose critics of Chiang's strategy came close to splitting the Guomindang itself. All this seemed merely to vindicate the Japanese claim that China was not an 'organized state' deserving of the protection of the League.

Yet China never became so disorganized that the Japanese could take it over lock, stock and barrel; Chiang's was a policy of appeasement, not capitulation. The fighting in Shanghai in 1932 had revealed that, despite their inferior armaments, the Chinese were capable of holding their own against Japanese forces if they outnumbered them sufficiently; indeed, only the arrival of army reinforcements had averted a Japanese humiliation. The Japanese attack on Suiyuan in November–December 1936 was actually repulsed. Chiang's conviction was that China needed time to build up its strength. And in many ways it did make sense to fight the relatively amateurish Communists first, rather than the highly professional Japanese. With his odd blend of Confucianism and European authoritarianism – which extended to the sponsorship of a fascistic Blue Shirt movement – Chiang had a coherent strategy. It was all a question of timing. Thus, in launching his New Life Movement in the spring of 1934, he made a prediction to a gathering of Guomindang officials. China, he reiterated, was not yet ready for war with Japan; but a second world war would come in 1936 or 1937, and this would be a war for which China would be ready, and from which China would emerge transformed. He did not know how right he was.

## CHINA'S WAR

When did the Second World War begin? The usual answer is September 1, 1939, when the Germans invaded Poland. But that is a European answer. The real answer is July 7, 1937, when full-blown war broke out between Japan and China. And it broke out on the outskirts of Beijing – then called Peiping – at Luokouchiao, known in the West as the Marco Polo Bridge.

At first it seemed like just another 'incident'. Mysterious shots were fired in the night at a company of Japanese troops in the vicinity of the bridge. A Japanese soldier went missing and was wrongly presumed to have been kidnapped (he was actually relieving himself). There were enough Chinese soldiers in the vicinity for the Japanese, as usual, to cry foul, and fighting broke out in the nearby town of Wanp'ing. For a few days it seemed as if the whole thing would blow over with the customary Chinese concession and withdrawal; indeed, an agreement had effectively been reached between the Japanese and Sung Che-yuan, chairman of the local (and more or less autonomous) Hebei-Chahar Political Council. Yet forces on both sides now swept this agreement aside. After much prevarication – the decision was made and cancelled no fewer than four times as rival factions within the army wrangled with one another – the Japanese government ordered three more divisions to northern China and an additional two for Shanghai and Tsingtao. Indeed, the Cabinet went so far as to endorse the idea of autonomy for the whole of North China; in effect, a step in the direction of a Greater Manchukuo. For his part, Chiang had been moving towards a more confrontational stance ever since his break with Wang Jingwei in December 1935, egged on by the militants in the National Salvation Association and other proponents of a united front against the Japanese – not least Zhang Xueliang, the former warlord of Manchuria, who had actually held Chiang captive at Xian until he agreed to a change of policy. Now Chiang mobilized troops on the Honan border. On July 17 he announced that there would be no further diminutions of Chinese sovereignty. Just under a month later the Chinese General Headquarters decreed a general mobilization.

Initially, as the Japanese had expected, the fighting went their way. Within a matter of days, Tongzhou and Peiping had fallen. Given their superiority in machine-guns, mortars and field artillery, the Japanese generally made short work of Chinese riflemen in frontal clashes. The Chinese were further hampered by the mutual distrust between Chiang and his notional subordinates. General Sugiyama Hajime, the Japanese Army Minister, confidently reported to the Emperor that 'the war could be ended within a month'. Yet expansion beyond Manchuria now exposed the limits of Japanese military power. The Japanese had at most 6,000 men in northern China at the time of the Marco Polo Bridge incident. At the start of the war, the most that the General Staff envisaged committing to China was fifteen divisions. By the end of 1937, however, sixteen divisions had already been sent, bringing the total deployment to 700,000 men, more than a hundred times the number in early July. To be sure, the Japanese continued to gain ground. In September Paoting was sacked, a month later it was the turn of Chengting and by the end of the year the capital itself, Nanking, had been literally raped and pillaged (see Chapter 14). In the first year of the war, the Japanese advanced on all fronts, occupying an area of roughly 150,000 square miles, stretching all the way from Inner Mongolia in the north to Hangzhou in the south. Cities as far west as Paotow and Puckow were in Japanese hands, and all China's ports north of Hangzhou. Yet the Chinese simply withdrew further west, moving their capital first to Hankou and then to Chongqing. By the middle of 1940 Japanese forces in China numbered 23 divisions, 28 brigades (the rough equivalent of an additional 14 divisions) and an air division – around 850,000 men in all. Still victory proved elusive.

Hitler began the Second World War with swift victories and then got bogged down in Russia. The Japanese did it the other way round, winning swift victories against the Western powers only after getting thoroughly mired in an equally unmasterable Chinese quagmire. Until it reached the Marco Polo Bridge, Japan's expansion in China had delivered at least some of the benefits that its proponents had promised, at relatively low cost. Henceforth it rapidly worsened precisely those economic problems it had been intended to cure. Japanese visions of a peace based on massive new commercial and mining concessions in northern China proved to be nothing more than the chimerical products of wishful thinking. All this revealed how far the Japanese had deviated from their original intention of being – and being treated as – a normal imperial power, on a par with the European empires in Asia. As we have seen, there had been superficial resemblances between Japan and Britain in 1902, when the two countries had concluded their twenty-year alliance. Yet by 1937 it was clear that the Asian 'island race' had taken a radically different path from the European. The British takeover of India had been based as much on co-optation as coercion, on the winning over of indigenous collaborators as much as on crushing native opposition on the field of battle. Britain's imperial expansion in Asia had also been propelled forward by the men on the spot, but they had generally been businessmen on the spot. There was no real Japanese counterpart to the East India Company (except perhaps the South Manchurian Railway Company). Instead it was the anti-capitalist utopians in the Kwantung Army who made the running.

More crucially, perhaps, there was a drastic difference in the way domestic politics developed as Japan embarked on its bid for imperial grandeur. In Britain, overseas expansion had coincided with the growth in the power of the House of Commons and the Treasury. By comparison, both the monarchy and the armed services were weak. Nothing symbolized that better than Stanley Baldwin, as leader of the Conservative Party and First Lord of the Treasury, insisting on Edward VIII's abdication. It is instructive to compare that crisis with the crisis that happened in Japan in February of the same year, 1936, when a mutinous faction of the army calling themselves the 'Righteous Army of Restoration' murdered the former Prime Minister, Admiral Saitō, the miracle-working Finance Minister, Takahashi Korekiyo, and the Inspector General of Military Education, General Watanabe. Only good luck saved the Prime Minister Okada Keisuke from a similar fate, to say nothing of the Grand Chamberlain Admiral Suzuki, Prince Saionji and Count Makino, who were also on the conspirators' list of targets. According to the assassins, their intended victims had 'trespassed on the prerogatives of the Emperor's rights of supreme command', though the attempted coup is probably best understood as a bid for power by a faction within the army. Despite its being thwarted and the murderers executed, it had the effect of pushing

Japan further down the road towards military rule. With the establishment of the Imperial General Headquarters (*Daihon-ei*) in November 1937, the civilian government, led now by Prince Konoe, faced the real possibility of exclusion from strategic decision-making, since the new body consisted only of the service ministers, the chiefs of staff and the Emperor.* Nothing like this was remotely conceivable in England, where the cartoonist David Low's red-faced Colonel Blimp and P. G. Wodehouse's Roderick Spode – the former usually swathed in a clubhouse towel, the latter resplendent in his black shorts – pretty well summed up the general public's derisive views of both militarism and fascism. That was England's strength. Yet it was also her weakness.

By August 1937 the war in China had spread south to Shanghai, the hub of Western influence in China. In the wake of the usual ritualized 'incidents' by the Japanese, Chiang had decided to open a second front. Aiming to take out the Japanese cruiser *Idzumo*, moored at the Bund itself, he sent his fledgling air force into action. They missed, hitting instead a nearby hotel and department store. The Japanese nevertheless retaliated, doubling the size of their existing garrison within the International Settlement and driving the Chinese to the city's outer perimeter. In the ensuing three-month siege, the Japanese used their superior air power and artillery to inflict heavy casualties on Chiang's much more numerous forces, finally destroying them by landing an amphibious strike force at Chinshanwei, to the Chinese rear. In a radio broadcast at the height of the battle for Shanghai, Chiang's wife Meiling issued an impassioned plea that went to the heart of the matter:

Japan is acting on a preconceived plan to conquer China. Curiously, no other nation seems to care. She seems to have secured their spell-bound silence,

---

* How far Japan should be considered a military dictatorship during the war is controversial. It is true that Tōjō Hideki concentrated considerable power in his own hands, serving for a time simultaneously as Prime Minister, War Minister and Army Chief of Staff. There ceased to be multiple parties or effective opposition in the Diet, which had virtually no influence at all on military decision-making. On the other hand, the essentials of the Meiji constitution remained intact. Although the chiefs of staff and service ministers (also military men) wielded an effective veto power, the institutional structure remained more or less unchanged. Indeed, Tōjō fell from office before the war's end.

uttering the simple magical formula, 'This is not war but merely an incident.' All treaties and structures to outlaw war and to regularize the conduct of war appear to have crumbled, and we have a reversion to the day of savages.

Could Western inaction be interpreted as 'a sign of the triumph of civilization', she asked, or was it 'the death-knell of the supposed moral superiority of the Occident'? This was a rather good question to pose.

The Occidental population of Shanghai itself was doing its best to carry on business and pleasure as usual. As one British survivor of the siege recalled:

Shanghai became a cage, a macabre no-man's land of about 8,000 acres with a perimeter of some 22 miles, where several million people attempted to carry on routine jobs despite showers of badly aimed shrapnel . . . In those feverish summer nights . . . under a sky split by searchlights and tracer shells, one could almost tour the world in the few square miles of the International Settlement and the French Concession. It was possible to spend an ersatz night in Moscow, Paris, Prague, Vienna, Tokyo, Berlin or New York. There were places that could provide the authentic national atmosphere, the cuisine, the music, and, if necessary, even the girls.

But what of the Occidental governments? By this time the Western powers had been watching more or less inertly for over a year as not only Japan but also Italy and Germany rode roughshod over all the international arrangements that had been put in place in the decade after 1918. Why, when faced with the Japanese invasion of northern China after 1931, the Italian invasion of Abyssinia in 1935 and the German reoccupation of the Rhineland in 1936, did the Western democracies do so very little? By November 1936 Germany, Italy and Japan had banded together in the Rome–Berlin Axis and the Anti-Comintern Pact. Yet Britain, France and the United States seemed paralysed. Sir Hughe Knatchbull-Hugessen, the British ambassador to China, was actually wounded by a shot fired from a Japanese plane while being driven from Nanking to Shanghai. The response in London was impotent hand-wringing. The American reaction to the outbreak of the Sino-Japanese War was to mouth platitudes about 'co-operative effort by peaceful and practicable means'. Roosevelt orated obliquely about the need to put someone (he did not say whom) in 'quarantine', since war was 'a contagion'. But the bottom line was the old Washingtonian maxim: 'We avoid entering into alliance or entangling commitments.'

Why, historians have long debated, was it Western foreign policy in the 1930s to appease the aggressors? Were the democracies, like Chiang Kai-shek, quite rationally playing for time? Or is justifying appeasement nothing more than defending the indefensible?

# 9

# Defending the Indefensible

*If only you had ... sought by every means in your power,
by making yourselves fully acquainted with the situation, to
establish feelings of friendliness and cooperation between our
respective nations ... then we could have averted this dire
calamity.*      Lord Londonderry, *Ourselves and Germany*

*How much courage is needed to be a coward! ... We must go
on being cowards up to our limit, but not beyond.*
                    Sir Alexander Cadogan, September 21, 1938


## A CASE FOR PRE-EMPTION?

For obvious reasons, we tend to think of the years from 1933 to 1939
in terms of the origins of the Second World War. The question we
customarily ask is whether or not the Western powers could have
done more to avert the war – whether or not the policy of appeasement
towards Germany and Japan was a disastrous blunder. Yet this may
be to reverse the order of events. Appeasement did not lead to war. It
was war that led to appeasement. For the war did not begin, as we
tend to think, in Poland in 1939. It began in Asia in 1937, if not in
1931, when Japan invaded Manchuria. It began in Africa in 1935,
when Mussolini invaded Abyssinia. It began in Western Europe in
1936, when Germany and Italy began helping Franco win the Spanish
Civil War. It began in Eastern Europe in April 1939, with the Italian
invasion of Albania. Contrary to the myth propagated by the International Military Tribunal at Nuremberg that he and his confederates

were its only begetter, Hitler was a latecomer to the war. He achieved his foreign policy objectives prior to September 1939 without firing a shot. Nor was it his intention to start a world war at that date. The war that broke out then between Germany, France and Britain was nearly as much the fault of the Western powers, and indeed of Poland, as of Hitler, as A. J. P. Taylor contended forty-five years ago in *The Origins of the Second World War*.

Yet Taylor's argument was at best only half-right. He was right about the Western powers: the pusillanimity of the French statesmen, who were defeated in their hearts before a shot had been fired; the hypocrisy of the Americans, with their highfaluting rhetoric and low commercial motives; above all, the muddle-headedness of the British. The British said they wanted to uphold the authority of the League of Nations and the rights of small and weak nations; but when push came to shove in Manchuria, Abyssinia and Czechoslovakia, imperial self-interest trumped collective security. They fretted about arms limitation, as though an equality of military capability would suffice to avoid war; but while a military balance might secure the British Isles, it offered no effective security for either Britain's continental allies or her Asian possessions. With withering irony, Taylor called the Munich agreement a 'triumph for British policy [and] . . . for all that was best and most enlightened in British life'. In reality, war with Germany was averted at the price of an unfulfillable guarantee to the rump Czechoslovakia. If handing the Sudetenland to Hitler in 1938 had been the right decision, why then did the British not hand him Danzig, to which he had in any case a stronger claim, in 1939? The answer was that by then they had given another militarily worthless guarantee, to the Poles. Having done so, they failed to grasp what Churchill saw at once: that without a 'grand alliance' with the Soviet Union, Britain and France might find themselves facing Germany alone. As an indictment of British diplomacy, Taylor's has stood up remarkably well to subsequent scholarship – though it must be said that he offers few clues as to why Britain's statesmen were so incompetent.

Where Taylor erred profoundly was when he sought to liken Hitler's foreign policy to 'that of his predecessors, of the professional diplomats at the foreign ministry, and indeed of virtually all Germans', and when he argued that the Second World War was 'a repeat performance of the First'. Nothing could be more remote from the truth. Bismarck had striven mightily to prevent the creation of a Greater Germany encompassing Austria. Yet this was one of Hitler's stated objectives, albeit one that he had inherited from the Weimar Republic. Bismarck's principal nightmare had been one of coalitions between the other great powers directed against Germany. Hitler quite deliberately created such an encircling coalition when he invaded the Soviet Union before Britain had been defeated. Not even the Kaiser had been so rash; indeed, he had hoped he could avoid war with Britain. Bismarck had used colonial policy as a tool to maintain the balance of power in Europe; the Kaiser had craved colonies. Hitler was uninterested in overseas acquisitions even as bargaining counters. Throughout the 1920s Germany was consistently hostile to Poland and friendly to the Soviet Union. Hitler reversed these positions within little more than a year of coming to power. It is true, as Taylor contended, that Hitler improvised his way through the diplomatic crises of the mid-1930s with a combination of intuition and luck. He admitted that he was a gambler with a low aversion to risk ('All my life I have played *va banque*'). But what was he gambling to win? This is not a difficult question to answer, because he answered it repeatedly. He was not content, like Stresemann or Brüning, merely to dismantle the Versailles Treaty – a task that the Depression had half-done for him even before he became Chancellor. Nor was his ambition to restore Germany to her position in 1914. It is not even correct, as the German historian Fritz Fischer suggested, that Hitler's aims were similar to those of Germany's leaders during the First World War, namely to carve out an East European sphere of influence at the expense of Russia.

Hitler's goal was different. Simply stated, it was to enlarge the German Reich so that it embraced as far as possible the entire German *Volk* and in the process to annihilate what he saw as the principal threats to its existence, namely the Jews and Soviet Communism (which to Hitler were one and the same). Like Japan's proponents of territorial expansion, he sought living space in the belief that Germany required more territory because of her over-endowment with people and her under-endowment with strategic raw materials. The German case was not quite the same, however, because there were already large numbers of Germans living in much of the space that Hitler coveted. When Hitler pressed for self-determination on behalf of ethnic Germans who were not living under German rule – first in the Saarland, then in the Rhineland, Austria, the Sudetenland and Danzig – he was not making a succession of quite reasonable demands, as British statesmen were inclined to assume. He was making a single unreasonable demand which implied territorial claims extending far beyond the River Vistula in Poland. Hitler wanted not merely a Greater Germany; he wanted the Greatest Possible Germany. Given the very wide geographical distribution of Germans in East Central Europe, that implied a German empire stretching from the Rhine to the Volga. Nor was that the limit of Hitler's ambitions, for the creation of this maximal Germany was intended to be the basis for a German world empire that would be, at the very least, a match for the British Empire.

This puts British policy in a rather different light. Throughout the first half of the twentieth century British decision-making was predicated on the assumption of weakness, at first sight a paradoxical stance, since throughout that period Britain's was by far the largest of the world's empires. But it was precisely the extent of their commitments that made the British feel vulnerable. They could not reconcile the need simultaneously to defend the United Kingdom and their possessions in the Middle East and Asia – to say nothing of Africa and Australia – with the imperatives of traditional public finance, to which all but a few heretical thinkers remained in thrall. The peacetime budgets that would have been necessary to make all these territories secure were beyond the imaginings even of Winston Churchill, who had himself evinced as Chancellor of the Exchequer a notable deference to Treasury principles of balanced budgets and sound money. Before 1914 the Foreign Secretary Sir Edward Grey had, with Churchill's support, committed Britain to the side of France and Russia in the event of a continental war, despite the fact that Britain lacked the land forces to honour that commitment other than belatedly and (as the Somme proved) at a painfully high cost. Yet his successors in the 1930s were guilty of still more dangerous miscalculations. Grey had at least committed Britain to a grand coalition that was reasonably likely to defeat Germany and her allies. The worst that can be said of British policy before 1914 was that too little was done to prepare

Britain for the land war against Germany that her diplomacy implied she might have to fight. What was at stake in 1914 was essentially the future of France. What was at stake in 1939 was the future of Britain.

The statesmen of the 1930s were not blind to the danger posed by a Germany dominant on the continent. On the contrary, it became conventional wisdom that the nation's capital would be flattened within twenty-four hours of the outbreak of war by the might of Hermann Göring's Luftwaffe. In 1934 the Royal Air Force estimated that the Germans could drop up to 150 tons a day on England in the event of a war in which they occupied the Low Countries. By 1936 that figure had been raised to 600 tons and by 1939 to 700 tons – with a possible deluge of 3,500 tons on the first day of war. In July 1934 Baldwin declared, 'When you think of the defence of England you no longer think of the chalk cliffs of Dover; you think of the Rhine. That is where our frontier lies.' Yet he and his successor Neville Chamberlain failed altogether to devise a rational response to the German threat. It was one thing to let the Japanese have Manchuria; it meant nothing to British security. The same was true of letting the Italians have parts of Abyssinia; even Albania could be theirs at no cost to Britain. The internal affairs of Spain, too, were frankly irrelevant to the British national interest. But the rise of a Greater Germany was a different matter.

It was of course possible that Hitler was sincere when he protested that German expansion in East Central Europe would pose no threat to the British Empire. There were numerous instances when Hitler expressed his desire for an alliance or understanding with Britain, beginning with *Mein Kampf*. From November 1933, Hitler sought a naval agreement with Britain, and secured one – overriding the wishes of his Foreign Ministry and the German navy – in June 1935. 'An Anglo-German combination', he noted at the time, 'would be stronger than all the other powers.' At times he displayed, as Britain's ambassador in Berlin Sir Eric Phipps put it, 'an almost touching solicitude for the welfare of the British Empire'. Such ideas resurfaced four years later when Hitler started to feel nervous about British intervention on the eve of his invasion of Poland. He had 'always wanted German-British understanding,' he assured the new British ambassador in Berlin, Sir Nevile Henderson, on August 25, 1939. When Britain ignored these blandishments and honoured its pledge to Poland of April, he was dismayed, telling Rosenberg that he 'couldn't grasp' what the English were 'really after': 'Even if England secured a victory, the real victors would be the United States, Japan and Russia.' On October 6, having conquered Poland, he renewed his offer of peace. Time and again after 1939, Hitler expressed regret that he was fighting Britain, because he doubted 'the desirability of demolishing the British Empire'. As he told General Franz Halder, who became his Chief of the General Staff in 1938, he 'did not like' war with Britain: 'The reason is that if we crush England's military power, the British Empire will collapse. That is of no use to Germany . . . [but] would benefit only Japan, America and others.' Hitler often alluded to the racial affinity he believed existed between the Anglo-Saxons and the Germans. As a Propaganda Ministry press briefing put it in 1940: 'Sooner or later the racially valuable germanic element in Britain would have to be brought in to join Germany in the future secular struggles of the white race against the yellow race, or the germanic race against Bolshevism.' Such notions led some at the time, and have led some subsequent historians, to imagine that peaceful coexistence between the British Empire and a Nazi Empire might have been possible, that the great mistake was not appeasement but its abandonment in 1939. Perhaps, it has even been suggested, peace could have been restored in 1940 or 1941, if only someone other than Churchill had been in charge of British policy.

Standing aside had been an option for Britain in 1914. The Kaiser's Germany would not easily have won a war against France and Russia; even in the event of victory, the threat to Britain would have been relatively limited, not least because Wilhelmine Germany was a constitutional monarchy with a powerful organized labour movement. In any case, Britain was not prepared for war with Germany in 1914 and the costs of intervention proved to be very high. Hitler's Germany was a different matter. The Kaiser did not have the Luftwaffe. Hitler did not have to worry about Social Democracy and trade unions. Perhaps Hitler was a sincere Anglophile; the Kaiser had sometimes been one too. But no one could be sure if Hitler was telling the truth or, even if he was, that he might not one day change his mind. We know that he did. Encouraged by a disillusioned Ribbentrop, his ambassador in London, to regard Britain as a declining power, Hitler came to the conclusion as early as late 1936 that 'even an honest [*sic*] German-English rapprochement could offer Germany no concrete, positive advantages', and that Germany therefore had 'no interest in coming to an understanding with England'. As he put it in a meeting with his military chiefs in November 1937 (recorded in the famous Hossbach Memorandum), Britain was a 'hate-inspired antagonist' whose empire 'could not in the long run be maintained by power politics'. It was a view constantly reinforced by Ribbentrop, who saw England as 'our most dangerous opponent' (January 1938). On January 29, 1939 work began on the construction of a new German navy consisting of 13 battleships and battlecruisers, 4 aircraft carriers, 15 *Panzerschiffe*, 23 cruisers and 22 large destroyers known as *Spähkreuzer*. There could be no doubt against whom such a fleet would have been directed, had it ever been built.

In short, Hitler's Germany posed a potentially lethal threat to the security of the United Kingdom. Hitler said he wanted *Lebensraum*. If his theory was right, its acquisition could only make Germany stronger. A bigger Germany would be able to afford a larger air force as well as an Atlantic battle fleet. The likelihood of peaceful coexistence on such a basis was minimal. Yet it is not as easy as it looks to learn lessons from the failure of appeasement, though many have tried. To Neville Chamberlain's defenders, it is important to understand why he and his colleagues took the decision as they did. But *tout comprendre, ce n'est pas tout pardoner*: to understand the appeasers does not mean excusing them. Those who condemn appeasement have a better *prima facie* case. But no case for the prosecution is complete unless it can show that a credible alternative policy existed at the time.

Even a dog has a choice when confronted by a more aggressive dog: to fight or to flee. The British chose to fight in September 1939. By the end of May 1940 they no longer had a choice; they had to flee. This was, despite valiant propaganda about the 'Dunkirk spirit', one of the biggest débâcles in British military history – precisely the defeat they and their allies had spent four and a quarter years avoiding after July 1914. The British had failed to appreciate that their options were better than a dog's. Having identified the potential threat posed by

Hitler, they had four to choose from: acquiescence, retaliation, deterrence or pre-emption.

Acquiescence meant hoping for the best, trusting that Hitler's protestations of goodwill towards the British Empire were sincere, and letting him have his wicked way with Eastern Europe. Until the end of 1938 this was the core of British policy. The second option was retaliation – that is to say, reacting to offensive action by Hitler against Britain or her chosen allies; this was Britain's policy in 1939 and 1940. The defects of those two options are obvious. Since Hitler was not in fact to be trusted, acquiescence gave him several years in which to enlarge Germany and her armaments. Electing to retaliate against him when he attacked Poland was still worse, since this left the timing of the war in the hands of the German and Polish governments. The British also tried deterrence, the third option, but their concept was fatally flawed, as we shall see. Fearful as they were of aerial bombardment, they elected to build bombers of their own, with a range sufficient to reach the biggest German cities. Hitler was undeterred. A far more credible deterrent would have been an alliance with the Soviet Union, but that possibility was effectively rejected in 1939 and had to be thrust upon Britain by Hitler himself in 1941. Thus, the only one of the options that was never seriously contemplated was pre-emption – in other words, an early move to nip in the bud the threat posed by Hitler's Germany. As we shall see, the tragedy of the Second World War is that, had this been tried, it would almost certainly have succeeded.

## THE STRATEGIC CASE FOR APPEASEMENT

Superficially, the arguments for appeasement still seem sensible and pragmatic when one reads them today. The British had the most to lose from a breakdown of peace. Theirs was the world's biggest empire, covering roughly a quarter of the globe. In the words of a 1926 Foreign Office memorandum:

We . . . have no territorial ambitions nor desire for aggrandisement. We have got all that we want – perhaps more. Our sole object is to keep what we want and live in peace . . . The fact is that war and rumours of war, quarrels and frictions, in any corner of the world spell loss and harm to British commercial and financial interests . . . So manifold and ubiquitous are British trade and finance that, whatever else may be the outcome of a disturbance of the peace, we shall be the losers.

Those words were echoed eight years later by Lord Chatterfield, who observed that 'we have got most of the world already or the best parts of it, and we only want to keep what we have got [and] to prevent others from taking it away from us'. Given her vast commitments, Britain certainly seemed in no position to worry about any other country's security. As the Conservative leader Bonar Law remarked in 1922: 'We cannot alone act as the policemen of the world.' The reality was that defending even her own possessions could prove impossible in the face of multiple challenges. In the words of Field Marshal Sir Henry Wilson, Chief of the Imperial General Staff (writing in 1921): 'Our small army is much too scattered . . . in no single theatre are we strong enough – not in Ireland, nor England, nor on the Rhine, nor in Constantinople, nor Batoum, nor Egypt, nor Palestine, nor Mesopotamia, nor Persia, nor India.'

The Royal Navy, too, soon found itself overstretched. The construction of a naval base at Singapore, which began in 1921 but was more or less suspended until 1932, was supposed to create a new hub for imperial security in Asia. But with Britain's naval forces concentrated in European waters, the base itself threatened to become a source of vulnerability, not strength. By the time of the 1921–22 Washington Naval Conference, British policy-makers had abandoned the historical goal of naval preponderance by agreeing to parity with the United States, an advantageous arrangement for the latter given its far fewer overseas commitments. Britannia had ceased to rule the waves, in the Pacific at least. In April 1931 the Admiralty acknowledged that 'in certain circumstances' the Navy's strength was 'definitely below that required to keep our sea communications open in the event of our being drawn into a war'. In the face of a Japanese attack, the Chiefs of Staff admitted in February 1932, 'the whole of our territory in the Far East as well as the coastline of India and the Dominions and our vast trade and shipping, lies open.' Eight months later, the same body admitted that, 'should war break out in Europe, far from having the means to intervene, we should be able to do little more than hold the frontiers and outposts of the Empire during the first few months of the war'. A war in Asia would 'expose to depredation, for an inestimable period, British possessions and dependencies, trade and communications, including those of India, Australia and New Zealand'.

The Dominions – as the principal colonies of white settlement were now known – had played a vital role in the First World War, as suppliers of both materiel and men. Around 16 per cent of all troops mobilized by Britain and her Empire had come from Australia, Canada, New Zealand and South Africa. After the war, their economic importance grew still further, accounting for around a quarter of British trade by 1938. The adoption of 'imperial preference' – empire-wide tariffs – at the Imperial Economic Conference at Ottawa in 1932 was in many ways merely a response to a worldwide swing towards protectionism, but it reinforced the reliance of British business on imperial markets. Including all British possessions, exports to the Empire accounted for more than two-fifths of total exports. Partly encouraged by legislation, and partly by the many inter-war defaults by sovereign borrowers, British investors were also putting more and more of their money into the colonies and Dominions. Between 1924 and 1928 around 59 per cent of the value of overseas capital issues on the London market were for imperial borrowers; ten years later the proportion was 86 per cent. The Empire, as we have seen, was a treasure house of vital raw materials, which grew more important with each new refinement of military technology. In economic as well as in strategic terms, the Empire never seemed so important to Britain as it did in the 1930s. Yet its military (and diplomatic) importance was simultaneously declining. Each of the Dominions in turn made it clear that British policy-makers could not take their support for granted in the event of a second great European conflict. Moreover, as the Chiefs of Staff observed in 1936: 'The greater our commitments to Europe, the less will be our ability to secure our Empire and its communications.' In a review presented to the Chiefs of Staff in July 1936, the Joint Planning Sub-Committee summed up the military case for appeasement exactly:

From a military standpoint, owing to the extreme weakness of France, the possibility of an understanding between Germany and Japan, and even in some circumstances Italy, and because of the immensity of the risks to which a direct attack upon Great Britain would expose the Empire, the present situation dictates a policy directed towards an understanding with Germany and a consequent postponement of the danger of German aggression against any vital interest of ours.

What precisely were Britain's military commitments in Europe? In 1925 the Baldwin government had signed the Treaty of Locarno, guaranteeing the Franco-German and Belgian-German borders as they had been redrawn at Versailles. But Locarno conspicuously made no such international commitment with respect to Germany's eastern frontier. Moreover, just as had been the case before 1914, formal commitments to the security of Western Europe were not followed up by meaningful military contingency planning. As A. J. P. Taylor put it, Locarno seemed to imply that 'Splendid isolation had come again.' As a result, when Britain sought to broker an agreement between France and Germay over disarmament – or, rather, German rearmament, since the British proposals of January 1934 envisaged a trebling of the German army to 300,000 – the French could legitimately ask what kind of practical reassurance London could offer them for the eventuality of another German invasion. The answer was: None. Britain's commitment to the defence of Belgium was arguably less binding than it had been in 1914.

Yet Britain could not pretend that she had no stake in the security of Belgium and France. The May 1934 report of the Defence Requirements Committee reminded the Cabinet of the rather obvious reality that Germany posed a bigger strategic threat to the United Kingdom than Japan and that therefore, as in 1914, Britain might be called on to send troops to the aid of Belgium (and possibly also Holland) in the event of a German invasion. Indeed, the growing importance of air power made it even more imperative than in the past that the Channel coast should not fall into the hands of a hostile continental power. Germany was therefore 'the ultimate potential enemy against whom all our "long-range" defence policy must be directed'. What form should that 'long-range' policy take? If there was one lesson that might have been learned from 1914 it was that a small standing army in Europe was unlikely to deter the Germans. Yet the option of building up a large land force, available for deployment in Western Europe, was rejected in favour of enlarging the 'Metropolitan' (that is, British-based) air force to eighty or more squadrons, leaving the army with little more than five regular divisions available to send across the Channel as a 'Field Force' – almost exactly as few as there had been in 1914. By the end of 1937 its size had actually been reduced. By 1938 it had been turned into an expeditionary force for use only in imperial trouble-spots. The ineffectual Minister for the Co-Ordination of Defence, Sir Thomas Inskip, was not oblivious to the risk that was being run:

If France were again to be in danger of being overrun by land armies, a situation might arise when, as in the last war, we have to improvise our army to assist her. Should this happen, the Government of the day would most certainly be criticized for having neglected to provide against so obvious a contingency.

Nevertheless, the decision was taken, as the Minister for War Leslie Hore-Belisha put it, 'to put the continental commitment last'. General Sir Henry Pownall, the Director of Military Operations and Intelligence, was appalled, but overruled. Incredibly, the army's budget was actually cut in the wake of the Austrian *Anschluss*. Things were no better by the time of the Munich crisis. It was not until February 1939 that the idea of a European expeditionary force was revived, and even at that late juncture it was to be composed of just six regular and four territorial divisions.

The rationale of relying on air power merits further exploration, for it was pregnant with future difficulties. As we have seen, the role envisaged for Britain's enlarged air force was not defensive but offensive; it was to be, in the words of the future Prime Minister Neville Chamberlain, 'an air force of such striking power that no-one will care to run risks with it'. If Britain could credibly threaten to bomb German cities into rubble from the air, so it was argued, the Germans might be deterred from using force against their neighbours. The idea that this might deter Hitler was self-reflexive; because they themselves feared German bombers so much, the British assumed that

Hitler would fear their bombers equally. Though Churchill was right that Germany was out-building Britain as far as numbers of aircraft were concerned, British analysts systematically overestimated the Luftwaffe's capacity to inflict casualties on the population of the capital. That in itself was a grave error, for it caused the government to exaggerate the threat Hitler could pose to Britain in 1938; fantasizing about a flattened London became a substitute for thinking about realistic worst-case scenarios. Also deplorable was the Air Staff's slowness to work out how Britain's own strategic bombing forces would actually be used; when it came to the crunch in September 1939, Bomber Command confined itself to dropping propaganda leaflets, having come to the conclusion that trying to hit German industrial targets would be too costly. Most shocking of all is the comparative neglect, until the eleventh hour, of Britain's air defences, which were to prove the nation's salvation in 1940. True, vital work was being done by the Aeronautical Research Department chaired by Henry Tizard, which adopted the radar technology developed by Robert Watson-Watt at the National Physical Laboratory as early as 1935. But the Air Ministry was much slower to appreciate the need to invest in fighters capable of intercepting incoming bombers. Another side effect of the focus on long-range bombing was that it further diminished the strategic importance of Belgium and France, since it was assumed from the outset that the bombers would fly from British bases.

Thus the British knew they could not defend their Asian empire if the Japanese attacked it; knew they could not defend Belgium and France if Germany struck westwards, much less Poland and Czechoslovakia if Germany struck eastwards; and knew, or thought they knew, that they could not defend London if Hitler sent his Luftwaffe across the Channel. By 1935, incredibly, they were so convinced of their own hopeless vulnerability that they did not even dare fight the Italian navy. In 1938 the Chiefs of Staff ruled out even 'staff conversations' with the French, since the very term 'has a sinister purport and gives an impression ... of mutually assumed military collaboration'. Perish the thought!

# THE ECONOMIC CASE FOR APPEASEMENT

Could not these appalling vulnerabilities have been addressed by increased defence expenditures? No; all that more rapid rearmament would achieve, it was objected by the mandarins of the Treasury, would be to undermine Britain's precarious economic recovery.

Fighting the First World War had increased the British National Debt by a factor of twelve. By 1927 it was equivalent to a crushing 172 per cent of gross domestic product. The interest on the debt accounted for more than two-fifths of public expenditure in the late 1920s. Budget surpluses and an overvalued exchange rate following Churchill's decision, as Chancellor of the Exchequer, to return to the gold standard in 1925 were attained at the expense of jobs in manufacturing. The staple British industries of the late Victorian era – coal, iron, ship-building and textiles – had now been replicated all over the world; export markets for such British products inexorably shrank. Yet 'invisible' earnings from Britain's still immense overseas investments, financial services and shipping were also under pressure. Less obvious but in some ways more profound was the damage that the war had done to the labour force. Under the system of volunteering that had been used to recruit the new divisions needed in the first half of the war, a great many skilled workers had been drawn into the armed forces, of which a substantial proportion were either killed or incapacitated. The official solution to post-war problems was essentially Victorian in conception: budgets should be balanced, the pound should return to gold and free trade should be restored. In the name of 'retrenchment', defence expenditure was reined in, so that as a share of total public spending it fell from nearly 30 per cent in 1913 to just over 10 per cent twenty years later. Baldwin told the International Peace Society: 'I give you my word that there will be no great armaments.' He meant it. The Ten-Year Rule amounted to a spending freeze for the armed services. Even when it was dropped in 1932, the Treasury insisted that 'financial and economic risks' militated against significant increases in the defence budget.

As Chancellor of the Exchequer, Neville Chamberlain had been one of the driving forces behind the creation of the Defence Requirements

Committee, in the belief that a clear ordering of military priorities would make his life easier at the Treasury. He welcomed the identification of Germany as the biggest potential danger. Yet it was also Chamberlain who ruled out as impossible the additional £97 million that would be needed to create and maintain an adequate expeditionary force for use on the continent. His preference for a deterrent strategy based on bombers was motivated in large measure by the fact that it looked cheaper than the alternative. When the DRC proposed in November 1935 that its 'Ideal Scheme' of rearmament be financed by a Defence Loan, there was consternation in the Treasury; again Chamberlain insisted on cutting the spending bids of the navy and the army. But soon the RAF, too, started to look too expensive. As one Treasury official put it after Munich, 'We think that we shall probably not be able to afford it [the Air Ministry's latest proposals] without bringing down the general economy of this country and thus presenting Hitler with precisely that kind of peaceful victory which would be most gratifying to him.' In fact, the RAF was the best treated of the three services (though Chamberlain was ready at any time to curb spending on it in return for an 'Air Pact' with Hitler). The Treasury gave even shorter shrift to the requests of the army and navy for additional funds. As for Churchill's demands for much larger defence expenditures, which he first advanced in 1936, Chamberlain dismissed these out of hand. Only in 1937 was new borrowing undertaken to finance rearmament, to the tune of £400 million, and even then Chamberlain had initially tried to cover the increased costs by raising taxes. His successor at the Treasury, Sir John Simon, insisted that total defence spending from April 1937 to April 1942 should be capped at £1,500 million.

In any case, it was hoped that a policy of economic engagement with Germany might serve to divert the Nazi regime from aggression. On the one hand, officials at the Bank of England and the Treasury wanted to preserve trade with Germany and avoid a total German default on money owed to Britain. On the other, they deprecated the kind of economic controls that would undoubtedly be required if large-scale rearmament was to be undertaken without domestic inflation and a widening current account deficit. When the Secretary of State for Air, Viscount Swinton, pressed for skilled workers to be shifted from the civil to the defence sector in order to speed up aircraft construction, Chamberlain responded that this should be done by means of 'mutual arrangements [between employers and employees], and with a minimum of Government interference' – an echo of the old, failed maxim of 'Business as Usual'. Traditional financial strength was supposed to be the 'fourth arm' of British defence, in Inskip's phrase; hence the Treasury's perennial preoccupation with the balance of payments and the exchange rate. The great fear was that in the event of a prolonged war Britain's credit abroad would prove far weaker than between 1914 and 1918, for the current account deficits of the later 1930s were eating away at Britain's net creditor position, her gold reserves and the strength of sterling. For all these reasons it was not until 1938 that defence expenditure exceeded 4 per cent of gross domestic product and not until 1939 that the same could be said of the government's deficit (see Figure 9.1).

The economic arguments for appeasement reflected British economic strength as much as weakness. Compared with what had happened in Germany and the United States, the Depression in the United Kingdom had been mild. Once Britain had gone off gold in September 1931 and interest rates had been cut to 2 per cent by the Bank of England, recovery came quite swiftly – not, certainly, to the old industrial regions of the North, but to the Midlands and the South-East, where new industries and services were springing up. Cheap money also fuelled a construction boom in England south of the Trent. But for precisely these reasons, it was argued, significantly higher expenditure on rearmament would have created problems of overheating in the British economy, in the absence of matching tax increases or cuts in other government programmes. Keynes himself was to argue in *How to Pay for the War* that, in the event of large-scale defence expenditures, inflation and balance of payments problems could be avoided only if the economy were much more strictly controlled than it had been in the First World War, with severe taxation of consumption. Such an illiberal regime was inconceivable in peacetime. In April 1939 Keynes spelt out the constraints on pre-war rearmament: 'The first is the shortage of labour; the second is the shortage of foreign

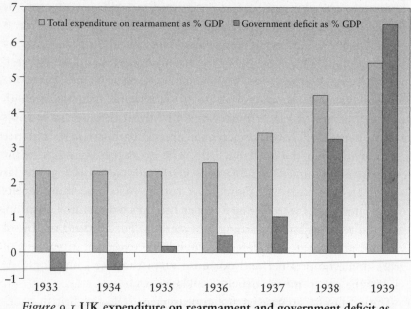

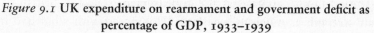

*Figure 9.1* UK expenditure on rearmament and government deficit as
percentage of GDP, 1933–1939

resources.' For once he was articulating the conventional wisdom.
Other eminent authorities – notably Sir Frederick Philips of the
Treasury and Lord Weir, chairman of the engineering firm G. & J.
Weir – said the same. Skill shortages were a potential problem not
only in engineering but in construction. Keynes was only one member
of the Economic Advisory Council, which reported in December 1938
that the balance of payments was 'the key to the whole position'.

Yet these concerns were surely exaggerated. With the annual rate
of growth in consumer prices peaking at just under 7 per cent in
September 1937 and then rapidly declining (see Figure 9.2), and
with long-term interest rates below 4 per cent until the outbreak of
war itself, the Treasury had far more room for manoeuvre than it
admitted. With so much slack in the system – contemporaries with
good reason feared a recession in 1937 – higher levels of borrowing
would not have 'crowded out' private sector investment. On the contrary, they would probably have stimulated growth. As for skilled
labour, that was only an issue because, for originally economic

reasons, Chamberlain had committed Britain to a sophisticated airborne deterrent that turned out not to work; and because the government was almost superstitiously nervous of antagonizing the bloody-minded leadership* of the Amalgamated Engineering Union by 'diluting' the skilled labour force. In practice, the rearmament programme stimulated staple industries as well as the infant aeronautical engineering sector; even on limited budgets the navy needed ships and the army needed guns, tanks and uniforms, so the iron, coal and textile sectors all benefited from rearmament. Wages for skilled labourers did not jump upwards, as the Treasury pessimists had feared; on the contrary, wage differentials narrowed. A more rational policy, both economically and strategically, would have been to build more ships and more tanks and to conscript the unemployed – who still accounted for 14 per cent of insured workers as late as January 1939 (see Figure 9.2) – and prepare a British Expeditionary Force the Germans could not have ignored. Chamberlain was simply wrong to fear that Britain lacked the manpower 'to man the enlarged Navy, the new Air Force, and a million-man Army'.

Finally, fretting about Britain's financial 'fourth arm' of defence presupposed that foreign powers would lend to Britain in a war only if it were financially attractive to do so, whereas both the United States and the Dominions would have powerful strategic and economic incentives to lend to Britain if the alternative was a victory for the dictators and an interruption to Atlantic export shipments. In any case, the current account deficits of the later 1930s were trivial – equivalent to around

---

* See the following rather revealing exchange between Inskip and J. C. Little, President of the AEU, in April 1938: 'Little: Up to now we see very little reason for recommending any kind of relaxation to our members, because frankly we are not satisfied with your policy. Inskip: You mean our foreign policy. Little: Your foreign policy, if you can call it a policy.' This was a sarcastic allusion to the government's policy of 'non-intervention' in the Spanish Civil War, which many trade unionists regarded with good reason as a betrayal of the legitimate republican government, especially given the assistance its enemies were receiving from Italy and Germany. In reality, what probably worried the AEU more was the memory of the First World War, when wartime dilution had been followed by post-war unemployment. Ernest Bevin, general secretary of the Transport and General Workers' Union, feared the AEU would resist dilution 'until the bombs came over'. He was almost right.

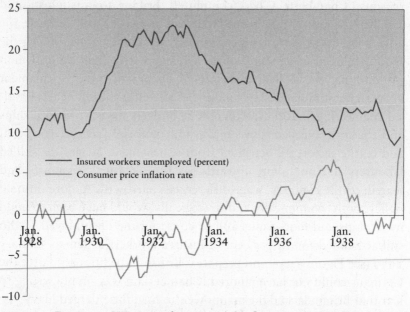

*Figure 9.2* **UK unemployment and inflation, 1928–1939**

1 per cent of GDP a year, compared with net overseas earnings of at least 3.5 per cent on a total stock of overseas assets worth £3.7 billion ($17 billion). Britain was not broke in 1938. The crucial point, as we shall see, was that she might nevertheless be broke by 1939 or 1940 if her hard currency reserves continued to diminish.

Britain, then, might have rearmed with a vengeance. Instead, on the flawed premises of outmoded economics, the British adopted the principle of Dickens's Mr Micawber. Oppressed by the thought of their own debts, they hoped against hope that something would turn up. The Depression inspired the Japanese, the Italians and the Germans to think of foreign conquest. It convinced the British that they could do little to stop them.

## IGNOMINIOUS ISOLATION

It seemed staringly obvious to those who believed the strategic and economic cases for appeasement that Britain needed all the friends she could get. In the words of the Chiefs of Staff in December 1937:

> We cannot foresee the time when our defence forces will be strong enough to safeguard our trade, territory and vital interests against Germany, Italy and Japan at the same time ... We cannot exaggerate the importance from the point of view of Imperial Defence of any political or international action which could be taken to reduce the number of our potential enemies and to gain the support of potential allies.

But who might these potential allies be? Though the French had spent significantly more on armaments than the British since the 1920s, most of their investment had been in defensive fortifications, the psychological effects of which were anything but healthy. The French Foreign Minister, Louis Barthou, sought to create an 'Eastern Locarno' to secure the frontiers of Germany's neighbours to the east and laid the foundation of the Franco-Soviet Mutual Assistance Pact of 1936. However, the British response was lukewarm; the feeling in London was that the French should be willing to make more concessions to the Germans on armament levels. By 1937 France's Prime Minister Léon Blum had embraced the notion that concessions to Germany in both Eastern Europe and overseas were necessary if peace were to be preserved. But Chamberlain had little confidence in the French and did practically nothing to make joint Anglo-French action effective. The Soviet Union was viewed with revulsion by most Conservatives, Chamberlain among them, on ideological grounds. Even Churchill found it hard to contemplate having Moscow in his grand alliance, though that was clearly a logical inference to be drawn from his own analysis of the situation. Much hope was pinned on Mussolini, who in 1934 had appeared to take a firm line against an abortive Nazi *putsch* in Vienna; this was to exaggerate Italy's strength and to underestimate Mussolini's desire to overturn the status quo, which he revealed when he invaded Abyssinia and ignored all inducements to negotiate a settlement. The 1935 'Stresa Front' of Britain, France and Italy proved to be just that: a front. When Italy defected, Britain and France could not agree what to do first: get Mussolini out of Abyssinia or keep Hitler out of the Rhineland. They did neither. This pattern of Anglo-French mal-coordination, not helped by the divergence of domestic politics in the two countries when France briefly had a Popular Front government, was to continue until the outbreak of war. Even after the *Anschluss*, Chamberlain could not bring himself to utter more than the most ambiguous hint of support for France in the event of a continental war. Unfortunately, there was just as much ambiguity in the French position after Édouard Daladier became Prime Minister in April 1938, not least because of the habitual cowardice of Georges Bonnet, his Foreign Minister. In Asia, meanwhile, Britain simply could not choose between her interests in China and the need to avoid war with Japan. The British nightmare was a German-Italian-Japanese combination. Yet the more they sought to avert it by diplomatic expedients rather than military counter-measures, the more likely it became.*

Among the great powers, that left only the United States. Yet the Americans were as eager to appease Germany as anyone in Britain. Franklin Roosevelt proposed the return of the Polish Corridor to Germany almost as soon as he entered the White House, sending Samuel L. Fuller as an unofficial emissary to Berlin in 1935 to sound out Hitler's terms for a general peace settlement. His Secretary of State Cordell Hull repudiated the British model of economic appeasement – based on reaching bilateral economic agreements with Germany – in favour of a more ambitious multilateral approach to trade liberalization. But the net result was not so different. Between 1934 and 1938 American exports of motor fuel and lubricating oil to Germany nearly trebled. American firms supplied Germany with between 31 and 55 per cent of its imported phosphate of lime (for fertilizer), between 20 and 28 per cent of its imported copper and copper alloys, and between 67 and 73 per cent of its imported uranium, vanadium and molybdenum. Half of all German imports of iron and scrap metal came from the United States. US corporations including Standard Oil, General Motors, DuPont and even IBM all expanded their German operations.

---

* In November 1936 Germany and Japan signed the Anti-Comintern Pact, which included a secret protocol committing each to non-intervention in the event that the other should become involved in a war with the Soviet Union. In November 1937 Mussolini removed his opposition to the Austrian *Anschluss*; the quid pro quo, which Hitler had long before envisaged, was the continuation of Italian sovereignty over the Germans of the South Tyrol. In February 1938 Germany recognized Manchukuo.

By 1940 American direct investment in Germany amounted to $206 million, not much less than the $275 million in Britain and far more than the $46 million in France. In Asia, the United States had already established a pattern of calling on others to take stands against aggression, while pursuing its own economic self-interest. When Roosevelt began to do the same in Europe too, Chamberlain concluded that Americans were 'a nation of cads'. 'It is always best and safest', he told his sister Hilda, 'to count on nothing from the Americans except words' – hence his dilatory response to Roosevelt's call for a general great-power conference in 1938. The feeling was mutual. 'The trouble is,' opined Roosevelt, 'when you sit around the table with a Britisher he usually gets 80 per cent of the deal and you get what is left.' American ambassadors like Joseph Kennedy Sr. in London and Hugh Wilson in Berlin saw no objection to giving Hitler a free hand in Central and Eastern Europe. Moreover, American policy-makers, Roosevelt in particular, harboured a thinly veiled ambition to see the British Empire broken up.

Yet merely hoping, in view of Britain's excess of commitments and her insufficiency of funds and friends, to preserve peace by diplomatic concessions was not as sensible and pragmatic a strategy as it seemed. For it failed to contemplate the potential consequences of diplomatic failure. Duff Cooper, as First Lord of the Admiralty, was one of the few members of the Cabinet to grasp this:

The first duty of Government is to ensure adequate defences of the country. What these adequate defences are is certainly more easily ascertainable than the country's financial resources. The danger of underrating the former seems to me greater than the danger of overrating the latter, since one may lead to defeat in war and complete destruction, whereas the other can only lead to severe embarrassment, heavy taxation, lowering of the standard of living and reduction of the social services.

Faster and greater rearmament in the mid-1930s might not look affordable to the Treasury, but how much more expensive would it be in the 1940s if Hitler were to succeed in dominating the continent and if Germany, Italy and Japan chose to make common cause against the British Empire? This hypothetical worst-case scenario was wished away by most decision-makers – an act of negligence, since politicians have an implicit moral obligation to those whom they represent regularly to contemplate the worst case, to attach to it both a probability and an estimated cost and then to insure against it. It was this that both Baldwin and Chamberlain failed to do – an irony, in view of their personal experience of business. An entire 'nation of shopkeepers'* declined to cover itself against a risk that was both large and likely. The supreme irony is that the premium itself might have been quite small. Indeed, the British may even have been paying enough to be covered. But their leaders, captivated by their own wishful thinking, failed to make a claim until it was too late.

## THE SOCIAL CHARACTER OF APPEASEMENT

How are we to explain this grave and, it might be thought, uncharacteristically imprudent misjudgement? To attribute it to popular pacifism will not do; that is not the correct inference to draw from events like the East Fulham by-election of 1933 or the notorious Oxford Union 'King and Country' vote of the same year.† The proponents of

---

* The phrase, often attributed to Napoleon (who called the English *'une nation de boutiquiers'*), in fact originated with Adam Smith in *The Wealth of Nations*: 'To found a great empire for the sole purpose of raising up a people of customers may at first sight appear a project fit only for a nation of shopkeepers. It is, however, a project altogether unfit for a nation of shopkeepers; but extremely fit for a nation whose government is influenced by shopkeepers.'

† The motion on February 9, 1933 was that 'This House will in no circumstances fight for its King and Country'. It was passed by 275 votes to 153. Churchill denounced it as an 'abject, squalid, shameless avowal'; the *Sunday Times* as 'unnecessary and in very poor taste', but 'in no way . . . representative of Oxford thought'. In fact the result reflected the influence of the Left in the Union at that time and is best understood as a vote against the government, not a vote for pacifism. When asked about the vote when he travelled through Germany less than a year later, Patrick Leigh Fermor 'depicted the whole thing as merely another act of defiance against the older generation. The very phrasing of the motion – "Fight for King and Country" – was an obsolete cliché from an old recruiting poster: no one, not even the fiercest patriot, would use it now to describe a deeply-felt sentiment. My interlocutors asked: "Why not?" *"Für König und Vaterland"* sounded different in German ears: it was a bugle-call that had lost none of its resonance. What exactly did I mean? The motion was probably *"pour épater les bourgeois,"* I floundered. Here someone speaking a little French would try

an unqualified renunciation of armed force – men such as George Lansbury and Sir Stafford Cripps – were only a minority, even within the Labour Party. The popular alternative to rearmament was collective security, not pacifism. Thanks to organizations like the Union of Democratic Control, the National Peace Council, the League of Nations Union and the Peace Pledge Union, there was considerable public support for the League, extending across the political spectrum. As Gilbert Murray, the Chairman of the League of Nations Union, remarked in 1928, 'All parties are pledged to the League . . . all Prime Ministers and ex-Prime Ministers support it . . . no candidate for Parliament dares oppose it openly.' Moreover, British voters wanted a League with teeth. In 1935 over 11 million voters returned a questionnaire in the so-called 'Peace Ballot'; over 10 million favoured non-military sanctions against an aggressor, and nearly 7 million accepted the principle of collective military action if these were not effective. The only difficulty was that no one quite knew where the League's military capability was going to come from; it was far easier to talk about disarmament agreements. Few people wanted to face the fact that over Manchuria Japan had defied the League with impunity. The withdrawal of Japan and then Germany from the League ought to have served notice that as an institution it was defunct; Mussolini's invasion of Abyssinia was the *coup de grâce*. For a moment it seemed that the British would use naval power and economic sanctions to enforce the writ of the League; then (with the British general election safely won) it was revealed that the Foreign Secretary Sir Samuel Hoare and the French Premier Pierre Laval had proposed a deal to give a large chunk of Abyssinia to the Italians. It was Manchukuo all over again, with the difference that a Western politician paid a price; the hapless Hoare fell on his sword. The dashing Anthony Eden took his place, pledging 'peace through collective security'; within a few months Abyssinian resistance had collapsed

---

to help. "*Um die Bürger zu erstaunen? Ach, so!*" A pause would follow. "A kind of joke, really," I went on. "*Ein Scherz?*" they would ask. "*Ein Spass? Ein Witz?*" I was surrounded by glaring eyeballs and teeth . . . I could detect a kindling glint of scornful pity and triumph in the surrounding eyes which declared quite plainly their certainty that, were I right, England was too far gone in degeneracy and frivolity to present a problem.'

and the Germans had marched into the Rhineland. Still people clung to the League rather than face the stark realities of the balance of power, which they had been promised was a thing of the past.

It is easy to forget what a lone voice Churchill was in March 1936 when he sought to remind the Conservative Foreign Affairs Committee that 'for four hundred years the foreign policy of England has been to oppose the strongest, most aggressive, most dominating Power on the Continent, and particularly to prevent the Low Countries falling into the hands of such a Power'. Almost no one was as enamoured as Churchill of Britain's bellicose past. Yet, as 1940 demonstrated, that did not mean the British people were incapable of being led back to that past. As early as April 1936 Sir Alfred Zimmern told Harold Nicolson that the task of convincing the public to fight for the sake of Czechoslovakia 'could be done in a month by wireless'. There was dissatisfaction with appeasement among Tory backbenchers almost from the moment Chamberlain became Prime Minister in 1937. And an opinion poll conducted shortly after the Austrian *Anschluss* (1938) revealed a growing popular disillusionment too. Asked 'Should Great Britain promise assistance to Czechoslovakia if Germany acts towards her as she did to Austria?' only a minority of respondents – 43 per cent – said no. A third said yes and a quarter had no opinion. By the time Churchill rose in the Commons on March 14, 1938, to call for 'a grand alliance' on the basis of the League, *The Economist* felt that 'his view represents the view of the majority of the nation'. By September 1938 Britain's ambassador in Berlin Sir Nevile Henderson felt obliged to warn Ribbentrop, now Hitler's Foreign Minister, that:

I had noted in England with amazement and regret the growing strength and unanimity of feeling in regard to Germany. I was struck by the difference even in two months since I was last in London and it was not confined to one but to all classes and to all parties, and I had seen many people.

More important than popular pacifism in underpinning appeasement was the fact that appeasing dictators came naturally to important sections of what a later generation would call the British Establishment. Many firms in the City of London had revived their longstanding pre-1914 links with Germany during the 1920s, only to be caught out by the German banking crisis of 1931. Around £62 million of the £100 million of commercial bills held by the London acceptance houses (the City's principal merchant banks) were covered by the so-called 'Standstill' agreement of 1931, which froze all foreign credits to Germany, but allowed interest payments to continue to flow to the creditors. In all, the credits to Germany of all types had totalled £300 million, of which roughly £110 million was covered by the Standstill agreement. The agreement was renewed on an annual basis, with only around £40 million being liquidated by 1939. Throughout the 1930s, City firms lived in hope that Anglo-German trade would revive and that this would allow a liquidation of outstanding debts. At the same time, the so-called Anglo-German 'Connection', between the Bank of England governor Montagu Norman and his German counterpart Hjalmar Schacht, encouraged the belief that there was a moderate faction within the Nazi regime, whose fortunes would prosper if they were sufficiently rewarded. The hope was expressed by one British diplomat that bilateral economic agreements 'would obviously have great possibilities as a stepping stone to political appeasement'. Such hopes were bolstered by the Payments Agreement of November 1934, whereby in return for a secret credit of £750,000 the Reichsbank committed itself to earmarking 55 per cent of all earnings from German exports to Britain for the use of German firms importing goods from Britain. In short, the City had strong incentives to avoid a breakdown in Anglo-German relations. Fearful of losing altogether the sums they had invested in Germany or lent to Germany before 1933, the bankers surreptitiously propped up German credit. The sums were not large (in January 1939 Sir Frederick Leith-Ross estimated potential losses in the event of a German default at £40 million of short-term bills and a further £80 or £90 million of long-term debts) but the leverage it gave Schacht. That was why it sent a measurable shock through the London bond market – where German bonds issued under the Dawes and Young Plans continued to trade before, during and after the war – when he offered to resign as Economics Minister in August 1937 and was dismissed as Reichsbank President in January 1939.

The bankers had little reason to like Hitler's government. Many of the most important firms with direct or indirect exposure to Germany were owned and managed by Jewish families, and trying to salvage something from the wreckage of the Depression meant holding their noses and dealing with Schacht. The Federation of British Industries sought to negotiate agreements on prices and market shares with its German counterpart; it did so not out of love for Hitler but out of fear of losing the still large German export market or of being driven from Balkan markets by Schacht's bilateral deals; despite the Depression, Germany's trade remained the third largest in the world in the mid-1930s. Other Establishment groups, however, were actuated by something lower than self-interest. Aristocratic grandees, colonial press barons and society hostesses alike found that they genuinely sympathized with aspects of Hitler's policy, including even its anti-Semitism. Lord Londonderry, Secretary of State for Air from 1931 to June 1935, who also happened to be Churchill's cousin, was so keen on Hitler that he wrote an entire book defending the Nazi regime, including its anti-Semitic policies, which were 'justified by the peculiar ideals of racial purity which have been inculcated and in which most Germans firmly believe to-day'. As Londonderry put it, he had 'no great affection for the Jews' since it was 'possible to trace their participation in most of those international disturbances which have created so much havoc in different countries'. Viscount Halifax was another grand figure of the British aristocracy, towering in both stature and snobbery – so much so that when he first met Hitler at Berchtesgaden in November 1937 he mistook him for a footman and very nearly handed him his hat and coat. Fortunately, the gaffe did not prove fatal to the cause of Anglo-German harmony. His friend Henry 'Chips' Channon reported that Halifax had 'liked all the Nazi leaders, even Goebbels, and he was much impressed, interested and amused by the visit. He thinks the regime absolutely fantastic.' Another noble Germanophile was the Duke of Westminster, who, according to Duff Cooper, 'inveighed against the Jews and . . . said that after all Hitler knew that we were his best friends.' Although Hitler's chosen ambassador to London, Joachim von Ribbentrop,* was mocked in

---

* Of all the leading Nazis, Ribbentrop was the one who most resembled a character out of a Heinrich Mann novel. Having tried to make his fortune in Montreal before the First World War, Ribbentrop had married into the Henkell Sekt family; got rich by importing champagne and Scotch; hobnobbed with Catholic politicians and Jewish

some newspapers as 'Herr Brickendrop', he was a social hit in these aristocratic circles. The Marquess of Lothian* took him under his wing, as did the Anglo-German Earl of Athlone (who had renounced the German title of Prince of Teck during the 1914–18 war), to say nothing of the shipping heiress Nancy Cunard and the Mitford sisters, Unity and Diana. Tom Jones, Baldwin's former private secretary, was charmed by Ribbentrop's account of Hitler as 'a being of quite superior attainments and fundamentally an artist, widely read, passionately devoted to music and pictures'.

It was at All Souls College, Oxford, that some of the most influential proponents of appeasement liked to convene: among the Fellows of the period were Halifax, Sir John Simon – his predecessor as Foreign Secretary and Chamberlain's docile Chancellor of the Exchequer – and the editor of *The Times*, Geoffrey Dawson, who had previously been the College's Bursar. At the end of a stressful week, Dawson liked nothing better than to repair to Oxford, to dine and sip claret in the plush parlours of his old college, where he could be sure of finding kindred spirits. In Dawson's eyes, it was the moral duty of every British newspaper to promote harmonious relations between Britain and the new Germany. He had no compunction about toning down or spiking outright the dispatches of his newspaper's experienced Berlin correspondent, Norman Ebbut. Some British foreign correspondents, like Sefton Delmer of the *Daily Express*, were posi-

---

businessmen; and acquired the prefix 'von' by getting himself adopted by a suitably named old lady, who, in true Weimar fashion, had lost her money in the inflation and was grateful for the monthly pension he was offering. (Also in true Weimar fashion, Ribbentrop discontinued the payment some time later.) He met Goebbels in 1928; secured an introduction to Hitler via some old army friends; quietly joined the NSDAP in Bavaria in May 1932; and within months was acting as an intermediary between Hitler and Papen, whom he had known in the war. A number of the decisive meetings which led to Hitler's appointment as Chancellor in January 1933 took place in Ribbentrop's Berlin-Dahlem villa. On October 1936 he was sent as ambassador to England, having convinced Hitler that he knew the 'top people' there. As Göring retorted: 'The trouble is that they also know Ribbentrop.'
* Philip Kerr, 11th Marquess of Lothian, had cut his teeth in Lord Milner's South African 'Kindergarten' of liberal-imperialist administrators. Though a scion of an old Catholic family, his friendship with Nancy Astor, the Conservative MP and wife of Viscount Astor, led him to join the Church of Christ Scientist as well as to visit Russia with George Bernard Shaw.

tively enthusiastic about the new Germany. Not Ebbut. To him, Hitler was nothing more than a 'Sergeant Major with a gift of the gab and a far-away look in his eyes'. Despite warnings from the Nazis to mute his criticism, and frequent raids on his apartment, Ebbut wrote regularly on (among other subjects) the new regime's persecution of dissidents within the Protestant churches. As early as November 1934 he was moved to protest about editorial interference with his copy, giving twelve examples of how his stories had been cut to remove critical references to the Nazi regime. He complained bitterly to his American friend William Shirer that his editors did 'not want to hear too much of the bad side of Nazi Germany'; *The Times* had been 'captured by pro-Nazis in London'. By contrast, articles by Lord Lothian were prominently displayed. In one, published in February 1935, Lothian told readers that Hitler had personally assured him 'that what Germany wants is equality, not war; that she is prepared absolutely to renounce war'. Indeed, Hitler was willing to 'sign pacts of non-aggression with all Germany's neighbours to prove the sincerity of his desire for peace'. All he asked was 'equality' in armaments. 'I have not the slightest doubt', averred Lothian, 'that this attitude is perfectly sincere.' The correct policy for Britain to adopt was 'to turn [Germany] into a "good European" by treating her as one of the European community'. Hitler's concern was not Western Europe, in any case, but the Soviet Union. 'He regards Communism as essentially a militant religion,' explained Lothian. If it were one day to 'try to repeat the military triumphs of Islam', would 'Germany than be regarded as the potential enemy or as the bulwark of Europe, as the menace or the protector of the new nations of Eastern Europe?' *The Times* covered the Night of the Long Knives as if it were a perfectly legitimate political act – a 'genuine' effort 'to transform revolutionary fervour into moderate and constructive effort and to impose a high standard on National-Socialist officials'. In August 1937 Ebbut was expelled from Germany. Seven months later, on March 10, 1938, his editor attended Ribbentrop's farewell reception in London. The next day German troops marched into Austria.

It was the editorials of *The Times* as much as its reporting that made it more influential than its modest circulation might suggest. (As Lord Beaverbrook, the proprietor of the *Daily Express* once remarked,

'The popular Press is nothing, in the way of propaganda, when compared with the unpopular newspapers.') Here Dawson could rely on the misanthropic former diplomat and historian Edward Hallett Carr, of all the proponents of appeasement perhaps the most sophisticated. To Carr, international relations were about power, not morality. As the balance of power in the world shifted, with some powers rising and others declining, the only question was whether adjustments should be violent or peaceful. Carr's view was that the latter were preferable. Appeasement was therefore a matter of adjusting peacefully to the reality of German (and later Soviet) power in the least bloody way, just as the British political system had adjusted to the reality of working-class power without the need for a revolution:

In the latter part of the nineteenth century and the first part of the twentieth the 'have nots' of most countries steadily improved their position through a series of strikes and negotiations, and the 'haves', whether through a sense of justice, or through fear of revolution in the event of refusal, yielded ground rather than put the issue to the test of force. This process eventually produced on both sides a willingness to submit disputes to various forms of conciliation and arbitration, and ended by creating something like a regular system of 'peaceful change' . . . Once the dissatisfied Powers had realized the possibility of remedying grievances by peaceful negotiation (preceded no doubt in the first instance by threats of force), some regular procedure of 'peaceful change' might gradually be established and win the confidence of the dissatisfied; and, once such a system had been recognized, conciliation would come to be regarded as a matter of course, and the threat of force, while never formally abandoned, would recede further into the background.

This was a distinctly fatalistic formula for a world without war – peace on the basis of submission to the might of the dictators. Sneeringly dismissive of 'the vague ideals of altruism and humanitarianism', Carr applauded Hitler's policy, arguing that the Treaty of Versailles was obsolete and that Germany had every right to expand eastwards. Chamberlain's talks with Hitler in Munich in 1938 he hailed as 'a model for negotiating peaceful change'.

*The Times* was far from unique in its soft-soap coverage of Germany. Following his visit in 1937, Halifax lobbied nearly all the leading newspaper proprietors to tone down their coverage of

Germany, even attempting to 'get at' David Low, the *Evening Standard*'s irreverent cartoonist. The government succeeded in pressurizing the BBC into avoiding 'controversy' in its coverage of European affairs – an irony in view of its later wartime reputation for truthful reporting. Lord Reith, the Director-General of the BBC, told Ribbentrop 'to tell Hitler that the BBC was not anti-Nazi'. A programme in the series 'The Way of Peace' was dropped when the Labour MP Josiah Wedgwood refused to delete references in his contribution to Hitler and Mussolini's policies of 'persecution, militancy and inhumanity'. Pressure to toe the line was even stronger in the House of Commons. Conservative MPs who ventured to criticize Chamberlain were swiftly chastised by the whips or their local party associations. In this atmosphere, only a few mavericks in each party ventured to argue the case for rearmament and traditional alliances, and even Churchill – the most eloquent exponent of this view – took a less than consistent line between 1933 and 1939. As his critics pointed out, he was against self-government for India, but for Czech democracy; against the dictators, but for recognition of Franco's regime in Spain; against arms limitation, but for the League of Nations. Chamberlain and his cronies were not above defaming Churchill in the press, and they did the same to Anthony Eden following his resignation as Foreign Secretary in February 1938.

In All Souls, too, a number of the younger Fellows begged to differ from the Dawson line. At around the time of the Abyssinian crisis, the historian A. L. Rowse – who was just thirty-four at the time of Munich – recalled a walk with him along the towpath to Iffley, in the course of which he warned the older man: 'It is the Germans who are so powerful as to threaten all the rest of us together.' Dawson's reply was revealing: 'To take your argument on its own valuation – mind you, I'm not saying that I agree with it – but if the Germans are so powerful as you say, *oughtn't we to go in with them?*' Another youthful critic of appeasement at All Souls was the brilliant explicator of political thought Isaiah Berlin, who strongly disapproved of the attitudes of Dawson and his circle. As Berlin told his biographer many years later:

They didn't talk about appeasement in front of all of us so very much, but they did in the privacy of their own rooms. They brought sympathizers, well-wishers, with them; then they would disappear into one of those big rooms upstairs with one of them, and there they would have practically committee meetings . . . On appeasement, together with everybody else of my age . . . I was strictly against. There were no appeasers except [Quintin] Hogg in our group. In my generation, nobody was, nor people younger than me. No no, certainly not.

Partly because of the appeasement issue, Berlin was drawn to the left-leaning Thursday Lunch Club, among whose members were Richard Crossman, the future Labour minister, and Roy Harrod, Keynes's biographer. Berlin was no socialist. But he had one advantage over other Oxford dons when it came to understanding what was happening on the continent. As a Jew whose family had emigrated from Latvia to escape the chaos of the Russian Revolution, he had every reason to understand what was at stake on the continent. He could see that the older Fellows continued to think of Europe in the old imperialist terms of the 1900s, which was why they were inclined to accept Hitler's overtly racist arguments:

The British Empire Group . . . were fundamentally racist; they weren't anti-Semitic in any overt sense, but they believed in the Aryan ascendancy. They didn't want Italy or France to be part of them, really. They believed in Germany, Scandinavia, the White Empire, you see? And that, fundamentally, had a kind of Cecil Rhodes aspect to it.

There was much truth in this. 'The Teuton and the Slav are irreconcilable – just as are the Briton and the Slav,' observed Henderson in a letter to Halifax. '[The Canadian premier] Mackenzie King told me last year after the Imperial Conference that the Slavs in Canada never assimilated with the people and never became good citizens.'

However, as Berlin had to acknowledge, the appeasers had another and rather stronger argument on their side, and that was their aversion to Stalin's Soviet Union:

The Russians were quite outside [their notion of an extended Commonwealth], quite apart from being communists and terrible that way . . . That was the basis of it, the defence of what might be called white Western values against the horrors of the East. The Germans were a dubious case because they misbehaved. Hitler was rather a misfortune, but still, it was better to be friends with Hitler – I mean protection against Communism, fundamentally, is what stirred them.

Among the many arguments for appeasement perhaps the best was this: that even as late as 1939 Hitler had done nothing to compare with the mass murder that Stalin had unleashed against the people of the Soviet Union. Many a Tory grandee may have knowingly shut one eye to the realities of Nazi rule, but an even larger number of people on the British Left had shut both eyes to the horrors of Stalinism – and they took much longer to open their eyes. Berlin understood that these were two evils between which it was far from easy to choose. As he wrote to his father in November 1938:

All the old conservatives are very nervous . . . They all want to fight for the colonies. But they won't. I feel absolutely certain that one day a Russian-Slavic bloc will form in Europe & sweep away the German penetration. The mood is depressed. Everyone is conscious of defeat.

Such was the Establishment consensus. Fortunately, as we have seen, it was not shared by the British people at large. That was just as well. If it had been, the Second World War might well have been lost.

# 10

# The Pity of Peace

*Of course they want to dominate Eastern Europe; they want as close a union with Austria as they could get without incorporating her in the Reich, and they want much the same things for the Sudetendeutsche as we did for the Uitlanders in the Transvaal.*

Neville Chamberlain to his sister Hilda, November 1937

*If a number of States were assembled around Great Britain and France in a solemn treaty for mutual defence against aggression; if they had their forces marshalled in what you may call a grand alliance; if they had their staff arrangements concerted; if all this rested, as it can honourably rest, upon the Covenant of the League of Nations, agreeable with all the purposes and ideals of the League of Nations; if that were sustained, as it would be, by the moral sense of the world; and if it were done in the year 1938 – and believe me, it may be the last chance there will be for doing it – then I say that you might even now arrest this approaching war.*

Winston Churchill, March 1938

## A FAR-AWAY COUNTRY

Who were the Sudeten Germans? In Neville Chamberlain's notorious phrase they were 'people . . . in a far-away country . . . of whom we know nothing'. Yet Czechoslovakia is not so very far from Britain: London to Prague is just 643 miles, slightly less than the distance between New York and Chicago (711 miles). And the implications of the Sudetenland's annexation by Nazi Germany had a profound bearing on Britain's security. It was therefore unfortunate that Chamberlain took so little trouble to inform himself about the people whose fate he helped to decide in 1938. Had he known more, he might have acted differently.

The term Sudetenland was not much used before the 1930s. At the end of the First World War an attempt had been made to associate the predominantly Germanophone periphery of Bohemia and Moravia with the new post-imperial Austria by constituting Sudetenland as a new Austrian province, but this had come to nothing. The Germans who found themselves under Czechoslovakian rule after the First World War – they accounted for over a fifth of the population, not counting the mainly German-speaking Jews – had at no time been citizens of the Reich of which Hitler was Chancellor. They were first and foremost Bohemians. The role of Bohemia in the evolution of National Socialism had nevertheless been seminal. It had been there that, before the First World War, German workers for the first time defined themselves as both nationalists and socialists in response to mounting competition from Czech migrants from the countryside (see Chapter 1). It had been in Bohemia that some of the most bitter political battles in the history of inter-war Czechoslovakia had been fought, over issues like language and education (see Chapter 5). The industrial regions where German settlement was concentrated were hard hit by the Depression; Germans were over-represented among the unemployed, just as they were under-represented in government employment. On the other hand, Czechoslovakia was unusual in Central and Eastern Europe. It was the only one of the 'successor states' that had arisen from the ruins of the Habsburg Empire that was still a democracy in 1938. It also occupied a strategically vital position as a kind of wedge jutting into Germany, dividing Saxony and Silesia from Austria. Its politics and its location made Czechoslovakia the pivot around which inter-war Europe turned.

The first and greatest weakness of Chamberlain's foreign policy was that by accepting the legitimacy of 'self-determination' for the Sudeten Germans, it implicitly accepted the legitimacy of Hitler's goal of a Greater Germany. Chamberlain's aim was not to prevent the transfer of the Sudeten Germans and their lands to Germany, but merely to prevent Hitler's achieving it by force.* 'I don't see why we shouldn't say to Germany,' so Chamberlain reasoned, 'give us satisfactory assurances that you won't use force to deal with the Austrians and Czecho-Slovakians and we will give you similar assurances that we won't use force to prevent the changes you want if you can get them by peaceful means.' His comparison with the English settlers in the Transvaal on the eve of the Boer War said it all; Chamberlain did not mean to imply that a war was likely, but that the German demands for the Sudetenlanders were as legitimate as his father's had been for the Uitlanders.† To use a different analogy, it had taken generations for British Conservatives to reconcile themselves to the idea of Home Rule for the Irish; they conceded the Sudeten Germans' right to it in a trice. Since Versailles, Germany had been aggrieved. The transfer of the Sudetenland was intended to redress her grievances in what Chamberlain hoped would be a full and final settlement. Nothing better captures the inability of the appeasers to grasp the Nazi mentality than the analysis offered by Edward Hale, a Treasury official, in August 1937. Hale maintained that

the Nazi struggle is primarily one of self-respect, a natural reaction against the ostracism that followed the war; that its military manifestations are no more than an expression of the German military temperament (just as our temperament expresses itself in terms of sport); that Hitler's desire for friendship with England is perfectly genuine and still widely shared; and that the German is appealing to the least unfriendly boy in the school to release him from the Coventry to which he was sent after the war.

But the problems of Central and Eastern Europe could not so easily be translated into the terms of the Victorian Empire, much less into

---

* Hilaire Belloc amused Duff Cooper with a poem that summed up Chamberlain's policy nicely: 'Dear Czechoslovakia / I don't think they'll attack yer / But I'm not going to back yer.'
† The 'Uitlanders' (Afrikaans for 'foreigners') were the British settlers who had been drawn to the Transvaal by the discovery of gold. They were treated by the Boers as aliens, furnishing the British government with a pretext for intervention in the region. Joseph Chamberlain, the arch-enemy of Home Rule for Ireland, demanded 'Home Rule for the Rand', meaning that the Uitlanders should be granted the vote after five years' residence.

the language of the public school playing fields. Hitler was not some kind of Teutonic Cecil Rhodes. Nor was Germany remotely like a character from *Tom Brown's Schooldays*. What Chamberlain and his advisers failed to grasp was the simple fact that Hitler was most unlikely to rest satisfied with the Sudetenland. As others pointed out, there were many more minorities in East Central Europe, each with its own grievances, each with its own desire to redraw Europe's borders. In particular, as we have seen, there were numerous German minority communities, scattered all the way from Danzig, at the end of the Polish Corridor, and Memel, an enclave in Lithuania, down to the picturesque Saxon villages of the Siebenbürgen, now in Romania, and as far east as the banks of the River Volga, in the very heart of Soviet Russia. In all, according to the Nazis' inflated estimates, there were no fewer than thirty million *Volksdeutsche* living outside the Reich – nearly ten times the number of Sudeten Germans. Conceding Hitler's right to the Sudetenland therefore set a very dangerous precedent. The more Hitler was able to cite the trials and tribulations of the *Volksdeutsche* as the basis for border 'rectifications' in one place, the more resources – both economic and demographic – he could stake a claim to in the other states of Central and Eastern Europe. Chamberlain and his advisers were apparently blind to the implications of the rapid spread of National Socialism among not just the Sudeten Germans but nearly all ethnic German minorities after 1933. This ideological conquest was well advanced by 1938. 'From our viewpoint,' recalled Gregor von Rezzori, a young ethnic German in Romania,

the developments in Germany [after 1933] were welcome: a profusion of optimistic images of youth bursting with health and energy, promising to build a sunny new future – this corresponded to our own political mood. We were irked by the disdain with which we as the German-speaking minority were treated, as if the former Austrian dominion in Romania had been one of Teutonic barbarism over the ancient and highly cultured Czechs, Serbs, Slovaks and Wallachians, as if these had freed themselves from their oppressive bondage in the name of civilizing morality.

As early as 1935 the Romanian Germans had found in Fritz Fabritius a confirmed Nazi to act as their leader. To be a National Socialist in

Austria, Neville Laski found in 1934, was to be 'a contingent holder of the job. To be a Nazi was to be an optimist'. By 1938 the Hungarian Germans, too, had formed their own Nazi organization, the *Volksbund*. Before even bidding for living space, Hitler was already winning the 'thinking space' of the *Volksdeutsche*. They became, in effect, his advance guard in the East.

## SEPTEMBER 1938

The failure to appreciate the significance of Hitler's appeal to the ethnic Germans was only the first of five flaws in the policy of appeasement. The second fatal weakness of Chamberlain's policy was that it assumed the existence of 'moderate' elements within the Nazi regime that could be strengthened through conciliation. In reality, the apparently 'polycratic' nature of the regime – the fact that, as the French ambassador to Berlin complained, 'There is not . . . only one foreign office. There are a half-dozen' – was something of an illusion. Hitler was in charge, his broad objectives were no secret and his subordinates 'worked towards the Führer' when he did not specify the means of achieving what he wanted. Talking to Schacht about colonial concessions therefore turned out to be a waste of time, as was talking to Göring about deals on raw materials. Chamberlain's early 'grand design' – which involved such bizarre proposals as the creation of a Central African raw materials consortium and an arms limitation agreement to abolish strategic bombing – was a flop because Hitler had no interest in either. Even more fantastic was the hope, to which the British clung until the war was nearly over, that the German working class would eventually tire of the economic sacrifices demanded by the Nazis and revolt against them.

The third flaw was the assumption, first enunciated by the Permanent Under-Secretary at the Foreign Office, Sir Robert Vansittart, that Britain gained by waiting. As he observed in December 1936, 'Time is the very material commodity which the Foreign Office is expected to provide in the same way as other departments provide *other* war material . . . To the Foreign Office falls therefore the task of holding the situation until at least 1939.' In reality, the 'policy of cunction' (from the Latin *cunctor*, 'I delay') gave Hitler just as much time to build up his military forces and, as we shall see, was positively disadvantageous to Britain from an economic point of view. Fourthly, Chamberlain persisted with the idea – which should have been discredited as early as 1935 – that good relations with Mussolini might be a way of checking Hitler or at least limiting British liability on the continent. Finally, Chamberlain was too arrogant to attach a significant probability to the worst-case scenario that appeasement would fail, so that Britain's position was unnecessarily exposed when, in due course, it did. Although he undeniably presided over substantial if belated increases in defence expenditure, Chamberlain also did a number of things that positively weakened Britain's military position, notably his surrender of the ports still controlled by Britain in Southern Ireland when he recognized the independence of Eire in 1938. He also forced Viscount Swinton to resign as Secretary of State for Air for having quite legitimately accelerated the construction of modern fighters for the purpose of defending Britain from the Luftwaffe. Having earlier committed Britain to build an air force designed to attack Germany, Chamberlain offered to give even that ineffectual deterrent away if Hitler would only agree to a ban on strategic bombing.

Largely as a result of decisions taken during Chamberlain's premiership, by September 1939 the United Kingdom found herself at war in circumstances significantly worse than those of August 1914. By June 1940 she found herself in the most parlous strategic position in her modern history, standing alone – or rather, with only the Dominions and colonies as allies – against a Germany that bestrode the European continent. What, however, if Britain had stood up to Hitler sooner than in 1939? There were numerous moments prior to that year when Hitler had openly flouted the status quo:

in March 1935, when he announced his intention to restore conscription in Germany, in violation of the Versailles Treaty;

in March 1936, when he unilaterally reoccupied the demilitarized Rhineland, in violation of both the Versailles and the Locarno Treaties;

in late 1936 or 1937, when he and Mussolini intervened in the Spanish

Civil War, in contravention of the Non-Intervention Agreement
they had signed in the summer of 1936;

in March 1938, when a campaign of intimidation of the Austrian
government culminated in the replacement of its Chancellor,
Schuschnigg, an 'invitation' to German troops to march into Austria and Hitler's proclamation of the *Anschluss*; or

in September 1938, when he threatened to go to war to separate the
Sudetenland from Czechoslovakia.

Of all of these moments, the most propitious was without doubt
the Sudeten crisis of 1938. Even if Austria's disappearance as an
independent state had not opened Chamberlain's eyes – to him it was
just 'spilt milk' – it opened the eyes of many others in Britain to the
nature of Hitler's ambitions. To be sure, if Hitler had wanted no more
than to stick up for the rights of the Sudeten Germans, it would have
been hard to justify a war. Konrad Henlein, their leader,* struck the
British politicians who met him (Churchill included) as a reasonable
man whose stated programme of autonomy had the backing of the
majority of his people. However, as became apparent in the course of
the crisis, Hitler was merely using the Sudeten Germans to provoke a
war which he intended would wipe Czechoslovakia off the map.

In the opening phase of the crisis, from May until the first week of
September, Sir Nevile Henderson – a quite disastrous choice to rep-
resent Britain in Berlin – was almost completely hoodwinked by the
Germans into thinking the Czechs were the villains of the piece.
Chamberlain's emissary, Lord Runciman, also fell into this trap. Lord
Halifax, now Foreign Secretary, allowed himself to be persuaded by
Henderson that firmness with Hitler would only 'drive him to greater
violence or greater menaces' – a wholly incorrect inference from a war
scare in May when the Czechs had mobilized in the mistaken belief
that Hitler was about to attack. Throughout this period, the Cabinet
did not give serious thought to the option of threatening the use of
force. When First Lord of the Admiralty Duff Cooper proposed 'bringing the crews of our ships up to full complement which would amount
to semi-mobilization', Chamberlain dismissed the idea as 'a policy of

* It is interesting to note that Henlein was himself the product of a mixed marriage;
his mother was Czech.

pin-pricking which ... was only likely to irritate' Hitler. Only four Cabinet members besides Cooper* had serious reservations about Chamberlain's policy at this stage, and all were dispensable. French requests for explicit British warnings to Berlin were politely rebuffed; the Permanent Under-Secretary at the Foreign Office, Sir Alexander Cadogan, was prepared to countenance nothing stronger than a '*private* warning' that 'if Hitler thinks that we shall in *no* circumstances come in, he is labouring under a tragic illusion'. Halifax came very close to sending such a warning – to the effect that Britain 'could not stand aside' if Germany invaded Czechoslovakia and France came to her defence – but despite Churchill's vigorous encouragement (or perhaps because of it) Chamberlain overruled him. Henderson was prepared to go only as far as: 'I begged his Excellency to remind Herr Hitler that if France felt obliged by her honour to intervene on behalf of the Czechs, circumstances *might* be such as to compel us to participate, just as I realized that there were possibly other circumstances which *might* compel Herr Hitler to intervene on behalf of the Sudeten[s].' Unfortunately, he issued this feeble warning to the wrong man. Konstantin von Neurath, of whom he was 'begging', had ceased to be Foreign Minister precisely seven months before. Chamberlain was thus able to use all the political means at his disposal to pressurize the Czech government into making concessions. The Czech President Edvard Beneš at length gave in and accepted Henlein's demands for Sudeten autonomy, but Henlein, under Hitler's instructions, at once broke off the negotiations. Mere autonomy had never been the German objective. It was Hitler who determined the content of Sudeten 'self-determination'.

Reports now reached London that Hitler was planning unilaterally to send in his troops. Now the second act of the drama began. The French premier, Daladier, informed the British ambassador in Paris, Sir Eric Phipps, that if Germany invaded Czechoslovakia, France would declare war. Here was another chance to stand firm. At last, on September 9, Chamberlain was prevailed upon by his inner cabinet

---

* They were Oliver Stanley (President of the Board of Trade), Walter Elliot (Minister for Health), Earl Winterton (Chancellor of the Duchy of Lancaster) and Earl de la Warr (Lord Privy Seal).

to send an explicit warning to Berlin that, if France intervened, 'the sequence of events must result in a general conflict from which Great Britain could not stand aside'. But Chamberlain, with the encouragement of Halifax and Henderson, decided at the last minute that the telegram should not be handed to Ribbentrop, now the German Foreign Minister. Halifax's rationale for this was, as he put it to the Cabinet on September 12, that 'If [Hitler] made his mind up to attack, there was nothing that we could do to stop him ... Any serious prospect of getting Herr Hitler back to a sane outlook would probably be irretrievably destroyed by any action on our part ... involving him in a public humiliation.' Four months earlier, when it had seemed the Germans might send in troops, Halifax had blown hot and cold; many believed (wrongly) that Hitler had drawn back for fear of Anglo-French intervention. Now, however, Halifax warned the French *not* to count on British support 'automatically'. He was unimpressed by Daladier's assurance that, 'if German troops cross the Czechoslovak frontier, the French will march to a man. They realise perfectly well that this will be not for *les beaux yeux* of the Czechs but for their own skins, as, after a given time, Germany would, with enormously increased strength, turn against France.' As far as Halifax was concerned, Czechoslovakia was already as good as finished:

I did not think that British opinion would be prepared, any more than I thought His Majesty's Government would be prepared, to enter upon hostilities with Germany on the account of aggression by Germany on Czechoslovakia. As I had more than once said ... while we naturally had the French obligations clearly in mind, it was none the less true that by no action that anyone could take on behalf of Czechoslovakia could the latter be effectively protected from German attack should such be launched. Nor, if one might imagine European statesmen after another war sitting down to draw the boundaries of Czechoslovakia in the drafting of a new peace treaty, could anyone suppose that the exact boundary as it stood today would be maintained. To fight a European war for something you could not in fact protect, and did not expect to restore, was from this point of view a course which must deserve most serious thought.

This was a circumlocutory way of saying: 'You're on your own.' Small wonder the French wilted. By this time, at last, both Halifax and

Chamberlain had begun to question Hitler's sanity. Yet this insight impelled them to be more rather than less conciliatory.

It is a myth that there was a consensus for appeasement in the months leading up to Munich. As Duff Cooper later recalled:

... we were being advised on all sides to do the same thing – to make plain to Germany that we would fight. This advice came from the press, almost unanimous on Sunday, from the Opposition, from Winston Churchill, from the French Government, from the United States Government, and even from the Vatican: this advice supported by such an overwhelming weight of opinion we were rejecting on the counter-advice of one man, the hysterical Henderson.

Doubts within the Conservative Party were growing rapidly even before Chamberlain began his experiment with shuttle diplomacy. Cadogan, however, snidely dismissed the critics of appeasement as 'war-boys'. Rather than approve naval mobilization, as Cooper urged, Chamberlain's inner circle backed his ill-judged 'Z Plan' – a flight to Germany to make a face-to-face appeal to, of all things, Hitler's vanity (a trait Chamberlain could at least claim to understand). 'The right course', the Prime Minister argued, 'was to open by an appeal to Herr Hitler on the grounds that he had a great chance of obtaining fame for himself by making peace in Europe and thereafter establishing good relations with Great Britain.' In truth, this was a kind of fame Chamberlain coveted for himself. What the Z Plan meant in practice was that Hitler would be offered a plebiscite in the Sudetenland, at which the inhabitants could be expected to vote for another *Anschluss*. The rump Czechoslovakia might then be given some kind of guarantee. The French wilted still further at being thus left out in the cold. The Soviets were even less impressed, though Chamberlain blithely dismissed Vansittart's warning that excluding them would drive Stalin into Hitler's arms.

The first meeting between Chamberlain and Hitler was held on September 15 at the latter's mountain retreat, the Berghof, just outside Berchtesgaden. Extraordinarily, Hitler's interpreter Paul Schmidt was the only other person present when the two leaders conferred in the Führer's study. Chamberlain had set out to flatter Hitler; indeed, the very fact of the British Prime Minister's coming as far as the Bavarian Alps to see the German dictator in his holiday house was a fine piece of flattery in itself. Chamberlain believed he was stooping to conquer; Hitler, whom he erroneously thought of as a former house painter, struck him as 'the commonest looking little dog'. Yet it was Hitler who played on Chamberlain's vanity the more successfully, as the latter's account of the meeting makes clear: 'I have had a conversation with *a man*, he [Hitler] said, and one with whom I can do business and he liked the rapidity with which I had grasped the essentials. In short I had established a certain confidence, which was my aim, and in spite of the hardness and ruthlessness I thought I saw in his face I got the impression that here was a man who could be relied upon when he had given his word.' Hitler made it clear he would settle for nothing less than the immediate cession of the Sudetenland to Germany, without a plebiscite. 'The thing has got to be settled at once,' he declared. 'I am determined to settle it. I do not care whether there is a world war or not. I have determined to settle it and to settle it soon and I am prepared to risk a world war rather than allow this to drag on.' Even if it did not come to war, he threatened to discard the Anglo-German Naval Agreement if he did not get his way. Persuading himself that Hitler's objectives were nevertheless 'strictly limited' to 'self-determination' for the Sudetenland – a leap of faith of no small magnitude – Chamberlain did not dissent and returned to London.

After much deliberation, and objections from Cooper and the other 'war-boys', the Cabinet acquiesced, provided that a plebiscite would be held before the 'transfer'. The next step was to place the blame for the sell-out on the French since, as Halifax put it, 'it was the French and not we ourselves who had treaty obligations with the Czechoslovak Government'. Rather than brief Daladier on what had been said at Berchtesgaden, Chamberlain proposed that 'if the French asked us our opinion, we should reply that it was France which was primarily involved, but that we thought they would take a wise course if they said that they would not fight to prevent the self-determination of the Sudeten Germans.' This was yet more circumlocution to the same effect as before: Britain would not fight. When Daladier came to London he expressed understandable indignation, but to no avail. The most he could achieve was to persuade Chamberlain that Britain and France should guarantee what was left of Czechoslovakia after the transfer of the Sudetenland. All that remained to be done, it seemed, was to bully Beneš into capitulating. This was an exceedingly painful process. Nevertheless, on September 21, deserted by the French, who blamed their desertion on the British, he did so.

Chamberlain set off for Germany again – this time bound for Bad Godesberg on the Rhine – with what he hoped was the solution. He met Hitler on September 22, a day later than the Germans had been led to expect. The meeting was a fiasco. Claiming that he now had to take into account Polish and Hungarian claims with respect to their minorities in Czechoslovakia, Hitler rejected the idea of a plebiscite out of hand ('*Es tut mir fürchtbar Leid, aber das geht nicht mehr*' – 'I am terribly sorry, but that will no longer do'). In desperation, Chamberlain offered to drop the plebiscite if only territory with a population that was over 50 per cent German were handed over at once; the rest could be referred to a commission, as had happened with disputed territory after 1918. Alleging continued violations of the Sudeten Germans' rights, Hitler insisted on immediate cession of the territory, to be followed by German military occupation. Indeed, if no agreement were reached, he threatened to send troops into the Sudetenland on September 28, just six days later. To reinforce this crude ultimatum, more German troops were moved to the Czech border, bringing the total number of divisions there to thirty-one. Chamberlain blustered, saying that British public opinion would not tolerate a military occupation; Hitler replied that German opinion would stand for nothing less. Chamberlain complained that Hitler was presenting him with a *Diktat*; Hitler solemnly replied that, if he read the text of the German demands carefully, he would see that it was in fact a 'memorandum'. Flummoxed, Chamberlain agreed to communicate this 'memorandum' to the Czechs. Hitler responded by agreeing to postpone the date of his threatened occupation by three days, a quite empty 'concession'. The Prime Minister returned to London and put on a brave face, his analysis of the situation mystifyingly unaltered. Hitler had no ambition beyond the Sudetenland. He was a man Chamberlain could do business with:

Herr Hitler had a narrow mind and was violently prejudiced on certain subjects; but he would not deliberately deceive a man whom he respected and with whom he had been in negotiation ... The crucial question was

whether Herr Hitler was speaking the truth when he said that he regarded
the Sudeten question as a racial question which must be settled, and the
object of his policy was racial unity and not the domination of Europe ...
The Prime Minister believed that Herr Hitler was speaking the truth ... He
[Chamberlain] thought that he had now established an influence over Herr
Hitler, and that the latter trusted him and was willing to work with him.

Predictably, Duff Cooper now pressed for 'full mobilization',
echoed by Winterton, Stanley, de la Warr and Elliot. Leslie Hore-
Belisha, the War Minister, also declared himself in favour of mobilizing the army. Halifax too – hitherto so loyal to Chamberlain – jibbed;
Hitler was 'dictating terms, just as though he had won a war'. So did
Lord Hailsham, another erstwhile supporter. With the news that the
French as well as the Czech government had rejected the German
demands, and the appearance of Daladier to confirm France's readiness to fight if necessary, Chamberlain had no alternative but finally to
take a firmer line. Now Chamberlain proposed sending his confidant
Horace Wilson to Germany to present Hitler with a choice: to refer
the dispute to a joint German, Czech and British Commission or face
war with Britain too if France should enter on the side of the Czechs.
This was such a 'complete reversal' that Duff Cooper could 'hardly
believe' his ears and had to ask Chamberlain to repeat what he had
said.

For a fleeting moment it seemed as if Hitler had overplayed his
hand. The Czechs were readying for war. The French sent a telegram
to London asking the British '(a) [to] mobilize simultaneously with
them: (b) [to] introduce conscription: [and] (c) [to] "pool" economic
and financial resources', requests repeated when General Maurice
Gamelin, Chief of the French General Staff, visited London on the
26th. Chamberlain phoned Wilson, now in Germany, and informed
him that the French had 'definitely stated their intention of supporting
Czechoslovakia by offensive measures if [the] latter is attacked. This
would bring us in: and it should be made plain to Chancellor [Hitler]
that this is [the] inevitable alternative to a peaceful solution.' Although
Chamberlain still refused to heed Churchill's advice to link Russia to
the Anglo-French threat, Halifax issued a press statement that, in the
event of a German attack on Czechoslovakia, 'France will be bound

to come to her assistance and Great Britain and Russia will certainly stand by France.' Far from running counter to popular pacifism, this accurately reflected the public mood, which had never been as supine as Chamberlain and his inner circle. A Mass Observation Opinion Poll conducted at around the time of the Bad Godesberg meetings showed only 22 per cent of the public in favour of appeasement, with 40 per cent against. After Munich, despite the defeats suffered by anti-appeasement candidates in Oxford and Kinross, there was a marked drop in government support at by-elections and a surge in support for the Opposition parties – enough to dissuade Chamberlain from holding the general election he had contemplated. The mood in the House of Commons also shifted at this time. In France even Phipps had to admit that there had been a 'complete swing-over of [French] public opinion since Hitler's demands had become known'. On September 27, Chamberlain reluctantly agreed to mobilize the fleet, a decision Duff Cooper was able to make known to the press. In London, gas masks were issued and trenches dug in the parks; the fantasy that war would mean instantaneous German air raids on the capital continued to exert its fascination. Even in the Berlin embassy 'there was general satisfaction that the die had been cast'.

Yet, unbeknown to his colleagues, Chamberlain had diluted his instructions to Wilson by sending a message via the German embassy that Hitler should not consider the rejection of his demands as the last word. Instead of warning Hitler of Britain's intention to support France and Czechoslovakia in the event of a war, Wilson allowed himself to be intimidated by Hitler's fury at Czech intransigence. Within a few days, Hitler declared, 'I shall have Czechoslovakia where I want her.' To Wilson's consternation, 'He got up to walk out and it was only with difficulty he was prepared to listen to any more and then only with insane interruptions.' This was precisely the kind of theatrics at which Hitler excelled.* To increase the pressure on

---

* Ivone Kirkpatrick, from the British embassy, who accompanied Wilson, was mesmerized: 'At intervals he rose from his chair and drifted towards the door as if resolved to leave the room. I gazed at him in fascination. During one of his many tirades I was unable to take my eyes off him and my pencil remained poised above the paper ... At times, particularly when Wilson spoke about the Prime Minister's desire for a peaceful solution, Hitler pushed back his chair and smote his thigh in a gesture of frustrated rage.'

Chamberlain's feeble emissary, Hitler brusquely brought forward the deadline for acceptance of his demands to 2 p.m. on September 28, just two days later. Göring added, for good measure, that Germany could count on Polish support in the event of a war. Wilson went even weaker at the knees after hearing Hitler rant and rave at the Berlin Sportpalast, and recommended not relaying Chamberlain's warning at all. He was overruled and did as he was asked on the 27th, but 'more in sorrow than in anger'. Hitler was unmoved: 'If France and England strike, let them do so,' he retorted. 'It is a matter of complete indifference to me. I am prepared for every eventuality.'

Wilson returned to London, and Chamberlain now argued that the Czechs should be asked to withdraw their troops from the contested area, pending arbitration, though the majority of ministers rejected this course. The British military attaché at Berlin was brought in to testify to the poor state of Czech defences and morale, subjects about which he was less than well informed; his less pusillanimous colleague in Prague was not invited to offer an opinion. The appeasers also expressed scepticism about French intentions. When French ministers visited London, they were 'cross-examined' by the Chancellor of the Exchequer Sir John Simon (by training a lawyer) and their answers found wanting. Gamelin's plans were taken to mean that the French would advance into Germany but flee back to the Maginot Line if they encountered serious resistance. Chamberlain's broadcast to the nation on September 27, in which he expressed his deep reluctance 'to involve the whole of the British Empire in war simply on . . . account [of] a small nation confronted by a big and powerful neighbour', dealt another blow to the 'war-boys':

It was the most depressing utterance [complained Duff Cooper]. There was no mention of France in it or a word of sympathy for Czechoslovakia. The only sympathy expressed was for Hitler, whose feelings about the Sudetens the Prime Minister said that he could well understand, and he never said a word about the mobilization of the Fleet. I was furious. Winston rang me up. He was most indignant and said that the tone of the speech showed plainly that we're preparing to scuttle.

This was prophetic.

Chamberlain took to the air once more. What was agreed at the

Munich conference on September 29 affected only the timing of the dismemberment of Czechoslovakia and the means whereby Hitler would achieve his goal. Instead of the Sudetenland's being forcibly occupied forthwith, as Hitler had demanded, the occupation was spread over the first ten days of October. Plebiscites were supposed to be held under the supervision of an international commission, which would also determine the new boundary between Germany and Czechoslovakia and other matters such as property disputes and currency questions. Individuals were to have the right to opt in or opt out of the territories to be transferred. Of these German concessions, only the first, specifying the timing of the German occupation, was ever implemented. Chamberlain returned home waving a piece of paper that he had persuaded Hitler to sign when the two met privately in Hitler's apartment. It read:

We regard the agreement signed last night and the Anglo-German Naval Agreement as symbolic of the desire of our two peoples never to go to war again. We are resolved that the method of consultation shall be the method adopted to deal with any other questions that may concern our two countries, and we are determined to continue our efforts to remove possible sources of difference and thus contribute to assure the peace of Europe.

It was this that Chamberlain, in a moment of ill-judged euphoria on his return to Downing Street, described as signifying 'peace in our time'. The next day, Duff Cooper resigned, the only member of the Cabinet to do so, on the ground that Munich meant imminent war, not peace, and that the Prime Minister's statement would make it hard to justify the accelerated rearmament that was needed.

Cooper was right. By the end of October the Germans had made it clear where their next territorial claims would be: the Lithuanian city of Memel and the international city of Danzig. By the end of November the *News Chronicle* was reporting that Hitler was preparing to march on Prague. The final boundary settlement between Germany and Czechoslovakia was so far from 'self-determination' that it placed 30,000 Czechs under German rule. Nothing was done in response, because the promised guarantee to the rump Czechoslovakia never took concrete form. Meanwhile, Hitler made a mockery of Chamberlain's hopes for disarmament, openly pledging to achieve parity with the Royal Navy in submarines. Then, less than six months after Munich, on March 15, 1939 German troops marched into Prague, catching the British almost completely by surprise. With German encouragement, Slovakia declared independence and Czechoslovakia ceased to exist – precisely the outcome Churchill had predicted in the Commons just a few days after Chamberlain's return from Munich.

## THE WAR NOT FOUGHT

All of this makes it tempting to follow the conventional line that the events that led to Munich were the greatest failure of diplomacy in modern British history. Yet, as A. J. P. Taylor said, Munich was at least in one respect a triumph – for Chamberlain. Not only did he outwit his opponents in England, he also outwitted Hitler himself. After all, what was agreed at Munich was much closer to what Chamberlain had proposed initially at Berchtesgaden than to what Hitler had demanded at Bad Godesberg. As a result of Chamberlain's diplomacy, Hitler had been obliged to abandon his design to 'smash Czechoslovakia by military action', which he had been harbouring since the end of May. In most British accounts of the crisis, it is Hitler who seems to set the pace. Yet in Goebbels' diary, it is Chamberlain – the 'ice cold . . . English fox' – who 'suddenly goes to get up and leave as if he has done his duty, there is no point continuing and he can wash his hands innocently'. At the beginning of September, according to Goebbels, Hitler had felt confident that London would not intervene, but four weeks later he was driven to ask Chamberlain's aide Horace Wilson 'straight out if England wants world war'. Goebbels himself, who six days earlier had still been confident that London was 'immeasurably frightened of force', was forced to conclude that 'we have no peg for a war . . . One cannot run the risk of a world war over amendments.' Göring took the same view.

The decisive breakthrough had come on the evening of September 27, when Hitler sent a note to Chamberlain effectively dropping his earlier threat to use military force by 2 p.m. the next day. In this note Hitler agreed that German troops would not move beyond the territory the Czechs had already agreed to cede; that there would be a plebiscite; and offered to make Germany a party to any international guarantee of Czechoslovakia's future integrity. Evidently, Wilson's warning ('more in sorrow than in anger') had been more effective than it had appeared at the time. As Hitler said to General Alfred Jodl, Chief of the Army Leadership Staff in the German High Command (OKW), he could not 'attack Czechoslovakia out of a clear sky . . . or else I would get on my neck the whole world. I would have to wage war against England, against France, which I could not wage.' This explains why he so eagerly accepted Mussolini's suggestion of a 24-hour suspension of mobilization. That was why he so hastily sent a message to London inviting Chamberlain to attend a four-power conference in Munich. Had Mussolini not become involved, Hitler would presumably have seized with equal readiness the French proposal for a compromise. Looked at from this point of view, the Munich agreement's short-lived popularity among MPs – only forty Tories abstained when it was put to the vote – becomes more intelligible. Chamberlain really had averted a war.

But was he right to have done so? For all this goes to show how weak Hitler's position had become, and how foolish it was to let him off the hook. It was Chamberlain, after all, who prompted Mussolini to suggest a last-ditch diplomatic solution. But why involve the Italians at all, when they made their sympathy for the German side quite explicit? Why exclude the Czechs at this pivotal moment? Why once again leave the Soviets out of the negotiations? Had Chamberlain pressed home the advantage, rather than rushing off to Munich, the pressure on Berlin would have been intense. For – and this is perhaps the crucial point – Germany was simply not ready for a European war in 1938. Her defences in the West were still incomplete; in the words of Jodl, there were only 'five fighting divisions and seven reserve divisions on the western fortifications, which were nothing but a large construction site to hold out against one hundred French divisions'. No senior German military officer dissented from this view. Nor could Germany count on Stalin's repudiating the Soviet commitment (made in 1935) to defend Czechoslovakia; Red Army units in the military districts of Kiev and Byelorussia were in fact brought to a state of readiness during the Czech crisis. It is not inconceivable that the Romanian government would have granted them passage to the Czech frontier. Moreover, the Soviet Foreign Secretary Maxim Litvinov repeatedly stated that the Soviets would honour their commitments to Czechoslovakia if the French did so too, or would at least refer the matter to the League of Nations. Indeed, on September 24, Litvinov explicitly told the British delegation to the League that, if the Germans invaded Czechoslovakia, the 'Czechoslovak-Soviet Pact would come into force' and proposed a conference between Britain, France and the Soviet Union to 'show the Germans that we mean business'.

For these reasons, only a part of the Wehrmacht's seventy-five divisions – the British military attaché in Paris estimated just twenty-four, though the Czechs were ready for all seventy-five – could have been deployed in an attack on Czechoslovakia. Nor were the Czechs to be dismissed lightly; the British military attaché fully expected their thirty-five well-equipped divisions to 'put up a really protracted resistance' against an attacker who would have enjoyed neither decisive numerical superiority nor the element of surprise. In 1939 German reserve officers confessed to a British journalist that the Czech defences had been 'impressive and impregnable to our arms. We could have gone round them, perhaps, but not reduced them.' Hitler himself later admitted that he had been 'greatly disturbed' when he discovered the 'formidable' levels of Czech military preparedness. 'We had run a serious danger.' Operation Green, the planned pincer movement by the 2nd and 10th Armies, might have ended in disaster had it been launched. As General Sir Henry Pownall put it, even if the Germans had left only nine divisions along the Siegfried Line in the West and five to defend East Prussia against the Red Army, what Hitler was contemplating was 'certainly a bit risky'.

This was vintage understatement. German naval preparations were also woefully behindhand; in all there were just seven destroyers, three 'pocket' battleships and seven ocean-going submarines available. Moreover, the Germans could count on no effective support from abroad. Poland might possibly have come in on the German side for a share of the Czech carcass, though she might equally well have jumped the other way. The same could be said of Hungary. Mussolini might conceivably have sided with Hitler. But none of these countries posed a significant threat to the Western powers. On the contrary, it would have been relatively easy for the British and French to inflict heavy losses on the Italian Mediterranean fleet. As for Japan, it is highly unlikely that her government would have chosen this moment to pick a fight with the Western empires, given the difficulties they were encountering in China and the growing preoccupation of her generals with the Soviet threat from the north.

Finally, Germany's capacity to bomb London was largely a figment of the British imagination, the result of a grave failure of intelligence gathering and interpretation. In fact, the Germans preferred to see bombers in a tactical role, supporting ground forces (hence the small dive-bombers like the Junkers Ju-87 'Stuka' developed in the mid-1930s and 'tested' in the Spanish Civil War). Their investment in bombers capable of cross-Channel operations was far smaller than the British feared, and when they did launch the Battle of Britain they initially targeted airfields and other military targets, not urban centres. There was no plan whatever to bomb Britain in the event of a war in 1938, despite Göring's brazen threat to Henderson that the Luftwaffe would leave 'little of London ... standing'. That was a bluff. As General Helmuth Felmy, commander of the 2nd Air Fleet, admitted in late September 1938, 'given the means at his disposal a war of destruction against England seemed to be excluded'. British preparations for possible German attacks were thus pointless. A more likely target of Luftwaffe attacks would have been Paris, though here too the threat was exaggerated.

German military unreadiness had important political implications within the Third Reich. No one was more aware of Germany's military weaknesses than Ludwig Beck, the Chief of the General Staff since 1935. Beck was convinced from the moment the idea was first bruited that Hitler was playing with fire in contemplating an attack on Czechoslovakia. In his view, Hitler's strategy of building up the diplomatic tension and then presenting the great powers with a *fait accompli* was fraught with danger. Such a move might well lead to a general European war that Germany could not hope to win. Unlike others who had ventured to doubt Hitler's wisdom as a strategist – notably the Minister for War, Field Marshal Werner von Blomberg, and the Commander-in-Chief of the Army Werner von Fritsch – Beck survived the purge of January 1938. Hitler had certainly strengthened his control over the German military by replacing Blomberg with himself as Commander-in-Chief and Keitel as his obedient instrument, and putting the supine Walther von Brauchitsch into Fritsch's former post. Beck's resignation in late August therefore removed what was probably the biggest political threat to Hitler's position. But it did not end the possibility of military opposition to Hitler. Beck urged his successor, General Franz Halder, to involve himself in the coup against Hitler that was now being seriously discussed by Lieutenant-Colonel Hans Oster, director of the Central Department of the *Abwehr* (military intelligence), and Hans Gisevius, an official in the Interior Ministry. Halder later claimed that he, Beck, the retired General Erwin von Witzleben and others had conspired to overthrow Hitler, but that Chamberlain's decision to fly to Germany had deprived them of their opportunity.

To be sure, the anti-Hitler elements within the German military and civilian elites were diverse and disorganized. We have no way of knowing if a coup might have succeeded had Hitler suffered a major diplomatic reverse over Czechoslovakia. Yet the refusal of the British authorities to heed the signals reaching them – even from such impeccable sources as Ernst von Weizsäcker, State Secretary in the German Foreign Office – was, to say the least, strange. After Munich, the chances of a regime change in Berlin faded swiftly. The misnamed 'opposition' did not abandon attempts to establish dialogue with London. Carl Goerdeler, the former Price Commissioner and Mayor of Leipzig, visited England at Christmas 1938. Six months later Adam von Trott zu Solz, a well-connected former Rhodes Scholar, met with both Chamberlain and Halifax. Other visitors included Lieutenant-Colonel Count Gerhard von Schwerin, who urged that Churchill be brought into the government. But the moment had passed.

Nor should we overlook a further dimension to German weakness at that time. As Hitler was disgusted to discover, the German people, the *Volk* whose living space he was striving to enlarge, had little appetite for war. The British were well aware of this. Junior officials at the Berlin embassy reported that public opinion was 'much alarmed at German military measures'; there was 'a general fear that an attack on Czechoslovakia may lead to a European war which Germany would be likely to lose'. Henderson himself noted that 'not a single individual in the streets applauded' when a mechanized division paraded through Berlin on September 27. 'War would rid Germany of Hitler,' Henderson remarked on October 6, in a rare moment of perspicacity. 'As it is by keeping the peace, we have saved Hitler and his regime.'

The tragedy of 1938 is that the British and French governments so completely misread the balance of power at the very moment it tipped most strongly against Germany. Cadogan was convinced: 'We *must* not precipitate a conflict now – we shall be smashed.' The Chiefs of Staff shared this view. 'Chamberlain is of course right,' General Edmund Ironside, head of the Eastern Command, wrote in his diary: 'We have not the means of defending ourselves . . . We cannot expose ourselves now to a German attack. We simply commit suicide if we do.' Gamelin was equally in awe of the Germans. Like the British, the French were convinced that the Germans had the capacity to bomb their cities 'to ruins'. One of his senior staff officers envisaged such rapid mobilization in Germany that fifty divisions would quickly be available for deployment against France. The result – incredibly – was that no Anglo-French military talks were held at any point during the Sudetenland crisis; the most the Chiefs of Staff were willing to contemplate was the dispatch of just two ill-equipped Field Force divisions to France in the event of war. Generals are often criticized for planning to fight the last war instead of the next one. In 1938 British generals did not even plan to fight the last war. If they had, things might have turned out very differently. For it was the Germans, not the British and French, who risked being 'smashed' in 1938. All the British had to do was to commit unequivocally to a joint Anglo-French defence of Czechoslovakia, instead of blowing hot and cold, and to expedite talks between the British and French general staffs, instead of waiting until February 1939. Rather than flying back and forth like a supplicant, Chamberlain should have sat tight in London, declining to take calls from Germany. We cannot, of course, say for sure what would have happened. But the chances of a German humiliation would have been high. Almost any outcome, even war itself, would have been preferable to what in fact happened. For although he himself had wanted to get Czech territory by force, Hitler was actually better off getting it peacefully.

Time, as Vansittart had said, was crucial. The Chiefs of Staff argued, on the basis of the RAF's fears of a German knock-out blow, that 'from the military point of view the balance of advantage is definitely in favour of postponement . . . we are in bad condition to wage even a defensive war at the present time'. Certainly Fighter Command had been woefully neglected up until this point and much more had to be done to get British air defences ready to withstand an assault by the Luftwaffe. The British army too could only become stronger after Munich; it could scarcely have got any weaker. But time is relative. Its passage no doubt did allow the British to bolster their defences. But it simultaneously allowed Hitler to increase his offensive capability too. It is true that German rearmament had to be reined in towards the end of 1938. It is also true that the Germans became convinced that time would be against them if they delayed war much after 1939. But, on balance, time was more on Germany's side than on Britain's in the year after September 1938. As Table 10.1 makes clear, the German army grew significantly more than the British and French armies combined between 1938 and 1939. In naval terms, Germany stood still while the British and French added substantially to their fleets, but in the air, which contemporaries tended to see as crucial, the rivals were at best neck and neck. German additions to first-line Luftwaffe strength were somewhat exceeded by British additions to the Royal Air Force reserves. In combination, the British and French had more first-line aircraft than the Germans in 1939, but the difference had been larger in 1938 (589 compared with 94). Another way of demonstrating this is to compare figures for military aircraft production in 1939. Germany built 8,295, Britain 7,940 and France 3,163. The Soviet Union out-built all three with 10,565 new aircraft. But in 1938 the Western powers could consider the Soviets as potential allies. By 1939 Stalin was Hitler's ally.

What was more, Hitler gained immediately from Munich. With Czechoslovakia emasculated, Germany's eastern frontier was significantly less vulnerable. Moreover, in occupying the Sudetenland, the Germans acquired at a stroke 1.5 million rifles, 750 aircraft, 600 tanks and 2,000 field guns, all of which were to prove useful in the months to come. Indeed, more than one in ten of the tanks used by the Germans in their Western offensive of 1940 were Czech-built. The industrial resources of Western Bohemia further strengthened

Table 10.1: The balance of military forces, 1938 and 1939

| | January 1939 | | | September 1939 | | |
|---|---|---|---|---|---|---|
| | France | Germany | UK | France | Germany | UK |
| Army | 581,000 | 782,000 | 376,000 | 629,000 | 1,366,000 | 394,000 |
| Battleships | 5 | 5 | 12 | 7 | 5 | 15 |
| Battlecruisers | 1 | 2 | 3 | 7 | 1 | 15 |
| Cruisers | 18 | 6 | 62 | 11 | 6 | 49 |
| Aircraft carriers | 1 | | 7 | 1 | | 7 |
| Destroyers | 58 | 17 | 159 | 61 | 21 | 192 |
| Torpedo boats | 13 | 16 | 11 | 12 | 12 | 11 |
| Submarines | 76 | 57 | 54 | 79 | 57 | 96 |
| First-line aircraft | 1,454 | 2,847 | 1,982 | 1,792 | 3,609 | 1,911 |
| Serviceable first-line | n/a | 1,669 | 1,642 | n/a | 2,893 | 1,600 |
| Reserves | 730 | n/a | 412 | 1,600 | 900 | 2,200 |

Notes: Battleships includes German pocket battleships, of which there were three; British estimates for Luftwaffe first-line strength were August 1938, 2,650; September 1939, 4,320.

Germany's war machine, just as the *Anschluss* had significantly added to Germany's supplies of labour, hard currency and steel. As Churchill put it, the belief that 'security can be obtained by throwing a small state to the wolves' was 'a fatal delusion': 'The war potential of Germany will increase in a short time more rapidly than it will be possible for France and Great Britain to complete the measures necessary for their defence.' 'Buying time' at Munich in fact meant widening, not narrowing, the gap that Britain and France desperately needed to close. To put it another way: it would prove much harder to fight Germany in 1939 than it would have proved in 1938.

## THE ECONOMIC CASE FOR WAR

It was not just in military terms that Germany was weak in 1938. Of equal importance was her acute economic vulnerability. Schacht's New Plan had been abandoned two years before because his system of bilateral trade agreements could not deliver the amounts of raw materials needed for the rapid rearmament Hitler wanted. But the

Four-Year Plan could not possibly have improved matters much by 1938. Domestic iron ore production had certainly been boosted, but the increment since 1936 was just over a million tons, little more than a tenth of imports in 1938. No more than 11,000 tons of synthetic rubber had been produced, around 12 per cent of imports. The rationale for annexing Austria and Czechoslovakia – as Hitler had made clear to his military and diplomatic chiefs on November 5, 1937 – was precisely to address the shortages of raw materials that were continuing to hamper German rearmament. Had war come in 1938, the journalist Ian Colvin had it on good authority that Germany had only sufficient stocks of gasoline for three months. In addition, the economy was by now suffering from acute labour shortages. The irony was that German problems were in large measure a consequence of the upsurge in arms spending that had been set in train by the Four-Year Plan. Göring himself had to admit that the German economy was now working at full stretch. By October, German economic experts were in agreement that a war would have been a catastrophe.

As Colvin's testimony suggests, Germany's economic problems were no secret. Indeed, their financial symptoms were highly visible. Schacht's resignation as Economics Minister – which he submitted in August 1937, though it was not accepted until November – was widely seen as a blow to the regime's fiscal credibility, although he stayed on as Reichsbank President. Aside from his objections to the Four-Year Plan, Schacht had two concerns: the mounting inflationary pressure as more and more of the costs of rearmament were met by printing money, and the looming exhaustion of Germany's hard currency reserves. These problems did not go away. In volume terms, German exports were 15 per cent lower in 1938 than in the year before. In July 1938 Germany had to give in when Britain insisted on a revision of the Anglo-German Payments Agreement and the continued payment of interest due on the Dawes and Young bonds. The anti-appeasing commercial attaché in the British embassy in Berlin had a point when he argued for cancelling the Agreement. By further reducing Germany's access to hard currency, that would have struck at the German economy's Achilles' heel. Small wonder the German stock market slumped by 13 per cent between April and August 1938; the

German Finance Minister Schwerin von Krosigk warned that Germany was on the brink of an inflationary crisis. In a devastating Reichsbank memorandum dated October 3, 1938, Schacht said the same. Hitler might brush aside these arguments, urging Göring to step up the already frenetic pace of rearmament, but by now the goals had entered the realm of fantasy: an air force with more than 20,000 planes by 1942; a navy with nearly 800 vessels by 1948. Even if there had been enough steel for such feats of engineering, there would not have been enough fuel for half the bombers to fly or half the ships to sail. The Reichsbank was now manifestly struggling to finance the government's mounting deficits by selling bonds to the public; its hard currency reserves were exhausted. When Schacht and his colleagues repeated their warnings of inflation Hitler fired them, but he could no longer ignore the need to 'export or die'.

As we have seen, British officials worried a great deal about Britain's shortages of labour and hard currency. But in both respects the German position was far worse. Did contemporaries not realize this? One way of seeing the Munich crisis afresh is to view it from the vantage point of investors in the City of London. It is sometimes claimed that the Munich agreement lifted the London stock market. Little evidence can be found to support this. The market was in any case depressed by the recession of 1937. To make matters worse, there were substantial outflows of gold, amounting to £150 million, between the beginning of April and the end of September 1938. It is significant that Munich did nothing to arrest these outflows: another £150 million left the country in the months after the conference. The Chancellor of the Exchequer attributed these outflows to

the view [that] continues to be persistently held abroad that war is coming and that this country may not be ready for it, and lying behind that anxiety is, of course, the further anxiety created by the obvious worsening of our financial position, by the heavy increase in the adverse balance of trade, and by the growth of armament expenditure.

On this basis, the Treasury was able to make its usual argument that rearmament could not be accelerated any further. But it could now equally well be argued that Britain might as well fight sooner rather than later, when her reserves might be still further depleted. By

July 1939, Britain's gold reserves were down to £500 million; in addition the Bank had around £200 million in disposable foreign securities. The drain on British reserves by this stage was running at £20 million a month. In the face of widening current account deficits, the pound could no longer be kept at a rate of $4.68. As Oliver Stanley, President of the Board of Trade, put it: 'The point would ultimately come when we should be unable to carry on a long war.' This is the key. What it means is that *Britain would have been better off financially, as well as militarily, if there had been a war in 1938.* Not only would war have come sooner. It would almost certainly have been shorter, given the weaknesses of the German position described above. This gives the lie to the old claim that appeasement bought Britain precious time. For Britain, time was at a discount.

Under the circumstances, the stock market was hardly likely to be buoyant. It is nevertheless revealing to see the preferences of investors as reflected in the differentials between the various bonds and stocks quoted on the London market. A rational investor who believed appeasement was working would presumably have held on to continental bonds, including those of Central European countries, up until the German occupation of Prague. He would not have sold off his shares in the Cunard shipping line and taken long positions in the Vickers armaments company until the spring of 1939. But in reality the spreads between continental bonds and British bonds – traditionally the most secure financial asset from the point of view of a British investor – widened steadily from the mid-1930s onwards. The effect of the Sudetenland crisis, including the Munich agreement, was fairly minimal. Moreover, investors shifted out of what may be regarded as peace stocks and into war stocks from as early as 1933. The City, which had been so badly caught out in July 1914, was not to be fooled twice. Investors in London evidently anticipated some kind of war in the second half of the 1930s. Their uncertainty seems to have been about how general such a war would be – hence the singular absence of correlations between the bond yields of individual countries.

Historians have long sought the economic foundations of appeasement. They have looked in the wrong place. No doubt it is true that businessmen did not want war. But investors expected it nonetheless. There was thus no economic advantage to appeasement. With the City fundamentally pessimistic about the international outlook, it was Churchill not Chamberlain who had the economically rational foreign policy. What the situation called for was pre-emption, not deterrence, much less détente. Hitler simply had to be stopped before Britain's financial 'fourth arm' of defence got any weaker. The markets were braced for war in 1938; the situation, as *The Economist* pointed out in its post-Munich edition, was the very reverse of 1914, when war had come as a bolt from the blue. For one thing, the City was far less exposed to continental commercial bills, which had shrunk in importance as a financial instrument as a result of the Depression. For another, the financial community was 'prepared to face the blow of an outbreak of war'. And the authorities would not respond, as they had in 1914, by raising the Bank of England's discount rate to punitive heights. 'In the last few weeks,' the magazine's editors noted, 'there can have been few people in the City who did not envisage the strong possibility of an armed conflict in which Great Britain would be heavily involved . . . The outbreak of war would not have taken the financial markets by surprise.' The markets might not have rallied if war had come, but they would not have collapsed either. Even the price of German bonds traded in London – for example, those issued to finance the Young Plan – did not decline significantly during the crisis months of the summer. It was in 1939 that they fell through the floor (see Figure 10.1). This was because investors understood that Britain stood a good chance of beating Hitler, the serial defaulter, in 1938. A year later the tables had been turned, and it was the defaulter who looked like winning.

## TOWARDS THE DÉBÂCLE

The extraordinary thing about the aftermath of Munich is the relatively leisurely pace of British rearmament. As late as August 1939 Britain still had only two divisions ready to be sent to the continent. Far from using the peace he had bought as an opportunity to speed

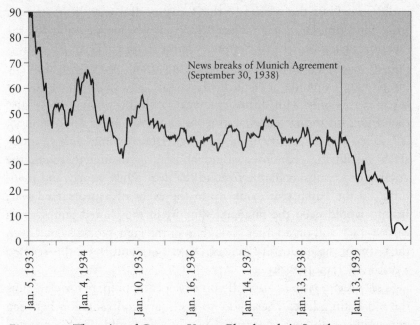

*Figure 10.1* The price of German Young Plan bonds in London, 1935–1939

up preparations for war, Chamberlain was equivocal. 'It was ... clear', he conceded on October 3, 'that it would be madness for the country to stop rearming until we were convinced that the other countries would act in the same way. For the time being, therefore, we should relax no particle of effort until our deficiencies had been made good. That, however, was not the same as to say that as a thanks offering for the present détente, we should at once embark on a great increase in our armaments programme.' Lord Swinton, the former Air Minister, offered Chamberlain his support, 'provided that you are clear that you have been buying time for rearmament'. 'But don't you see?' Chamberlain replied, 'I have brought back peace.' He opposed the Admiralty's request for new convoy escort vessels. He resisted Churchill's demands to create a Ministry of Supply. He clung to the policy of appeasement and the dream of disarmament. 'All the information I get seems to point in the direction of peace,' he declared in February 1939, 'and I repeat once more that we have at last got on top of the dictators.' Rearmament did accelerate, as we have seen, but it did so against the wishes of the Treasury and with little support from the Prime Minister. When Inskip also began pressing for the creation of a Ministry of Supply, Chamberlain sacked him. It was only gradually that the Treasury's resistance was overwhelmed by the burgeoning demands of the armed services, and particularly the air force; it was only with difficulty that it could be persuaded to raise the ceiling for the Defence Loan from £400 million to £800 million; it rejected Keynes's contention that higher borrowing, with so much slack still in the economy, would boost growth and therefore the volume of savings available to fund the debt. Only slowly and painfully did the harsh truth sink in: in the event of a protracted war, Britain would need the financial support of the United States at an earlier stage and on a larger scale than in the First World War. Given the terms of the Neutrality Acts of 1935, 1936 and 1937, this seemed a distinctly remote prospect.

*Si vis pacem, para bellum*: 'If you wish peace, prepare for war' runs the old Latin adage. There was no necessary contradiction between appeasement and rearmament; Chamberlain could have continued trying to accommodate Hitler's demands for *Lebensraum* while rearming at full speed. He chose not to do so. Worse, he simultaneously sought to relieve the pressure on the German economy. From Berlin, Henderson wrote reassuringly to him that Hitler was 'determined democratically to respect' popular anti-war sentiment; 'The Germans are not contemplating any immediate wild adventure,' he reported in February 1939, 'and ... their compass is pointing towards peace.' Nevertheless, fearful that economic difficulties might make Hitler more rather than less ready to gamble on war, Chamberlain suggested a new Anglo-German trade agreement that would have reduced Germany's dependence on bilateral trade agreements with the Balkan states and increased her access to sources of hard currency. The Governor of the Bank of England, Montagu Norman, even travelled to Berlin to discuss a possible British loan to Germany. Business leaders joined with the Bank and the Treasury in arguing that trade with Germany must be maintained and even stimulated, for the earnings from German exports to Britain were being used to pay off some of the outstanding German debts to British lenders. The fact that British exports to Germany were predominantly raw materials for the

German arms industry had to be pointed out by the Foreign Office. To no avail; the government continued to extend export credit guarantees to companies selling to Germany. Total short-term credits under this scheme rose from £13 million in January 1939 to more than £16 million on the eve of the war. If Hitler had been interested in economic concessions from Britain, he could probably have had more. But as Göring's unofficial emissary Helmut Wohltat admitted after he met Horace Wilson and other British officials in July 1939, 'to his sorrow he thought that [economics] played very little part in the Führer's mind.' In Chamberlain's mind, as we have seen, economics loomed larger. It was unfortunate that he so completely misunderstood the significance of Germany's economic weakness. The Americans at least had the wit to impose a punitive tariff on German imports after the fall of Prague.

There may have been no necessary contradiction between appeasement and rearmament, but there was a contradiction between appeasement and deterrence. Britain and France now faced a dilemma. If they gave in to Hitler's next demand so easily, where would it all stop? But if they threatened to fight, why would anyone believe them? It was not just honour that was lost at Munich. It was also credibility. This helps to explain the surprising eagerness with which Chamberlain began to issue guarantees to other European countries as it transpired that he had, after all, been duped over Czechoslovakia. The first step in this direction came even before the fall of Prague, when rumours (if not misinformation) began to circulate of a German plan to strike west against the Netherlands. It was agreed that this would be a *casus belli*. Moreover, the prospect of such a war in the West was enough to force a change of policy towards the army. It was now decided to construct a six-division continental army and to increase the size of the Territorial Army. There followed an unequivocal public commitment to France. So far, this was not much more than a return to the posture of 1914. Within a few short weeks, however, Britain's continental commitments ceased to be confined to the western half of the continent; they became truly pan-European. In response to bogus claims by the Romanian ambassador that the Germans were about to turn his country into an economic vassal, the Cabinet began to contemplate some kind of commitment to Bucharest. Further suspect intelligence – this time of an impending German attack on Poland – led to the fateful guarantee of that country's integrity which Chamberlain announced in the Commons on March 31, a guarantee that was extended to Romania and Greece two weeks later following the Italian invasion of Albania.

None of this did anything to enhance Chamberlain's credibility, however. The Chiefs of Staff pointed out that 'neither Great Britain nor France could afford Poland and Roumania direct support by sea, on land or in the air to help them resist a German invasion', and that therefore 'assistance from the U.S.S.R.' would be indispensable if the guarantees were to be more meaningful than the earlier sham guarantee to the rump Czechoslovakia. The more or less simultaneous doubling of the Territorial Army (March) and introduction of a watered-down form of conscription (April), as well as the belated creation of the Ministry of Supply (May), also made a minimal impact, since the new forces seemed destined to spend the better part of the coming year either in training or manning air defences. In any case, Chamberlain declined to appoint the increasingly popular Churchill to the new department, choosing instead the uninspiring former Minister of Transport, Leslie Burgin. Even Chamberlain's most loyal supporters do not deny the 'fumbling' quality of his policy by this stage. A leader in *The Times*, published the day after the guarantee to Poland was announced, gave the game away: Britain was not guaranteeing 'every inch of the current frontier of Poland' since there were 'problems in which adjustments are necessary'. In other words, this was just appeasement by other means; Chamberlain's hope was that by sprinkling guarantees around Europe he could somehow lure Hitler back to the negotiating table.

There was another crucial difference between 1939 and 1914. By the eve of the First World War, Britain had established ententes with both France and Russia. In 1939, however, the Soviet Union was left to align itself with Germany, despite the fact that 87 per cent of respondents to a UK Gallup poll in April had favoured a 'military alliance between Great Britain, France and Russia'. Why was this? The obvious answer is that, hard though it had been for pre-1914 Liberals to join forces with Tsarist Russia, it was impossible for British Conservatives to do the same with Stalin's Soviet Union. This was

16. *Berlin bei Nacht*: few works of art better anticipated the bright lights and deep shadows of Weimar Germany than Georg Grosz's *Grossstadt* (1917).

17. The American nightmare: poverty in the Depression.

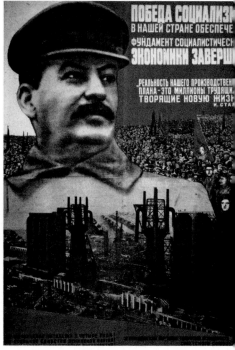

18. 'Look, you boob . . . !':
after a brief junket in the
Worker's Paradise, George
Bernard Shaw points out the
superiority of Soviet
Communism to an
incredulous Yankee capitalist.

19. Stalin, God of Soviet
Industrialization: 'The
Victory of Socialism in Our
Country has been Secured.
The Foundation of Socialist
Economics is Complete. The
Reality of Our Industrial
Plan – Millions of
Labouring Comrades,
Creating a New Life.'

20. The myth of collectivization: the slogan reads, 'Collectivization Will Shock Harvesting Productivity'. Especially for Ukrainians, the reality was mass starvation.

21. The myth of self-determination: fortunately for Georgians, Stalin did not view his own people with that intense mistrust he felt towards so many of the other minority peoples of the Soviet Union.

22. Gulag prisoners build socialism – and redeem themselves – with pre-industrial tools. Thousands perished as canals of questionable economic value were hacked out of the frozen Russian ground by ill-equipped slave labourers.

23. Jacob Abter, one of the members of the Leningrad Society for the Deaf and Dumb, executed during the Great Terror for his alleged complicity in a non-existent plot to assassinate Stalin and other Politburo members.

24. *Lebensraum* imagined: an ethnic German family takes a break from harvest toil for the benefit of magazine readers 'home in the Reich'.

25. Illustration from a children's book published by the Stürmer Verlag in 1935: 'The German is a handsome man / Who knows how to work and knows how to fight / Because he has guts and looks so grand / The Jew detests him with all his might.' 'This is the Jew, you see at once / The biggest rogue in all the land / He thinks himself a very prince / But is in truth an ugly man.'

26. Victor Klemperer, survivor and philologist of the language of the Third Reich , as well as of the Fourth (Soviet) Reich that succeeded it in Dresden.

27. Isaiah Berlin's diplomatic pass, issued on September 15, 1945. It was in Moscow that Berlin had his celebrated encounter with the poet Anna Akhmatova.

28. Hershel Elenberg and his wife Rivka: just two of the victims of Jedwabne pogrom, murdered by their own Polish neighbours in July 1941.

29. Henryka Łappo(*left*) with a friend, before the former's deportation from eastern Poland to the Soviet Union.

ВИННИЦА

30. A Nazi wartime poster blaming atrocities on 'Jewish-Bolshevism'. As at Katyn, these bodies exhumed by the Germans at Vinnitsa in the Ukraine were indeed victims of the NKVD. But the SS lost no time in filling new mass graves with the bodies of the town's Jews.

31. Having been forced to undress, these five Jewish women and girls are about to be shot. They were among 2,700 Jews murdered outside Liebau (Liepaja), in Lativa, by German police and Latvian auxiliaries in December 1941.

32. Victims of the Rape of Nanking, sexually assaulted and brutally murdered by Japanese troops at some point between December 1937 and February 1938.

33. Indiscriminate war: a man tends children wounded in a Japanese raid on Shanghai railway station, 1937.

no doubt a factor for many Tories. Yet Churchill, once the ardent anti-Bolshevik, had no difficulty in praising 'the loyal attitudes of the Soviets to the cause of peace' in pursuit of his Grand Alliance (now euphemistically renamed 'the Peace Bloc'). Chamberlain's lukewarm response to this, as to all Churchill's suggestions, may have owed more to his lingering faith in appeasement than to an especially strong ideological aversion to Communism. More importantly, Britain's new commitments to countries like Poland and Romania made it harder rather than easier to reach agreement with Stalin. The Soviets tended to ask for military access through these countries; how else were they to fight the Germans? With good reason, the East Europeans suspected their motives. The Poles had refused to be co-signatories of the declaration of mutual 'consultation' proposed by Chamberlain in March 1939. Not only did the guarantee to Poland bind Britain's destiny to that of a regime that was every bit as undemocratic and anti-Semitic as that of Germany. It also precluded the kind of alliance with the Soviet Union that might conceivably have deterred or more easily defeated Hitler. When the Soviets proposed a triple alliance between Britain, France and Russia, to defend not only themselves but also Russia's immediate neighbours from German aggression, they were rebuffed. Chamberlain had flown to Germany thrice to confer with Hitler; he never even contemplated taking a plane to Moscow. He declined even to send Eden (much less Churchill) as a special envoy. Only in late May did preliminary talks begin with the Soviets and they proceeded with painful slowness. Not until August were British and French military delegations sent to Moscow, and they travelled by sea not air, with low-ranking officers at their head. Chamberlain, meanwhile, took the train to Scotland, for a holiday. Here was another missed opportunity. Had Chamberlain been replaced by Churchill in the summer of 1939, an alliance with the Russians might still have been achievable.

Still another difference between 1939 and 1914 was the threat posed by Japan, which had been Britain's ally on the eve of the First World War. By April 1939 the Naval Staff made the position clear:

It is not open to question that [in the event of Japanese intervention] a capital ship force would have to be sent [to the Far East] but whether this could be done to the exclusion of our interests in the Mediterranean is a matter which would have to be decided at the time . . . The effect of the evacuation of the Eastern Mediterranean on Greece, Turkey and the Arab and Moslem world . . . are political factors which make it essential that no precipitate action should be taken in this direction . . . It is not possible to state definitively how soon after Japanese intervention a Fleet can be dispatched to the Far East. Neither is it possible to enumerate the size of Fleet we could afford to send.

This was a veiled admission that the order of priorities in a world war would be: the British Isles, the Middle East and, finally, Singapore and Britain's other Asian possessions. As it turned out, the Japanese were not yet ready to join forces with Germany against Britain. But no one in London could count on that.

Under the circumstances, it is not surprising that Hitler expected Chamberlain to keep appeasing him, selling Danzig and perhaps even the Polish Corridor the way he had sold the Sudetenland, in return for yet another reprieve. True, he now regarded war with Britain as all but inevitable. Addressing his army commanders in May 1939, Hitler expressed his 'doubts whether a peaceful settlement with England is possible. It is necessary to prepare for a showdown. England sees in our development the establishment of a hegemony which would weaken England. Therefore England is our enemy and the showdown with England is a matter of life and death.' Yet it was probably not his intention to precipitate that showdown as early as September 1939. He simply did not believe that Chamberlain, a man armed only with his habitual rolled umbrella, had the guts to fight. Thus he did almost nothing in the course of 1939 to encourage Chamberlain's lingering hopes that Europe might soon be out of the danger zone. On March 23, three days after Ribbentrop had threatened the Lithuanian government with war, Hitler sailed into Memel harbour aboard a German warship, even as Chamberlain was trying to cobble together a four-power declaration against such acts of aggression.

Nor was Hitler the sole troublemaker in Europe. Italy invaded Albania in April, in what was supposed to be the prelude to an Italian takeover of the Balkans; the following month Mussolini impulsively concluded a 'Pact of Steel' with Hitler. Undaunted, Chamberlain continued to regard the Italian dictator as a possible partner in his effort to restrain Hitler. To be sure, the Italians proved to be most unreliable allies to the Germans, declining to join in the war until the fall of France was imminent. On the other hand, precisely this unreliability minimized Mussolini's influence in Berlin. Chamberlain persisted in believing that Hitler would not 'start a world war for Danzig'. He failed to see that Hitler did not anticipate a world war; he anticipated another Munich.

If Hitler was confident before the conclusion of the Nazi-Soviet Pact that Chamberlain would not fight over Poland – as German military deployments on the Polish border would seem to indicate – he was all but certain of it thereafter. 'Now Europe is mine!' was his comment when the news from Moscow was relayed to him at Berchtesgaden in the early hours of August 24. That was not strictly true, in that he had to allow Stalin half of Poland, Finland and all three of the Baltic states. Moreover, by doing a deal with Stalin, Hitler made it less likely that either Italy or Japan would immediately join his side. But Hitler's remark illustrates how completely he assumed he had outmanoeuvred the Western powers. He can hardly have been impressed by the reappearance of the spineless Henderson to restate the British guarantee to Poland. 'Our enemies are little worms,' he remarked, two days before the treaty with Russia was signed; 'I saw them at Munich.' And, indeed, Chamberlain probably would have given him another Munich had it not been for his Cabinet colleagues, who insisted that the guarantee to Poland be honoured, and the Poles, who were suicidally determined to fight. Still he clung to the idea of another conference – which once again the Italians proposed – venturing to mention the idea in the Commons even after Poland had been invaded. Though war was now forced upon Chamberlain, he still sought to avoid (as Samuel Hoare put it) 'going all out'.

In one respect, British policy did have credibility, despite Chamberlain's worst efforts. Most members of the Nazi ruling elite continued to regard a war against the Western powers as both likely and dangerous. Göring was far from keen to risk such a war; he knew the true strength of the Luftwaffe. Goebbels, too, remained fearful of British intervention even after he heard the news of Ribbentrop's coup in Moscow. The news that the Italians were not ready to fight and that the British were resolved to stand by Poland convinced Goebbels that, as over Czechoslovakia, a temporary diplomatic 'minimal' agreement would have to be worked out with Britain, giving Germany back Danzig and at least part of the Polish Corridor. The extent to which Hitler himself, suddenly 'cautious', was prepared to contemplate this course is striking. Almost at the last minute, he postponed the invasion of Poland, which was originally scheduled for dawn on August 26, in order to see Henderson again and offer a crude deal: arms limitation and minimal colonial demands in return for a 'free hand' in Poland. Three days later, when that had been turned down, he tried another gambit, requesting that a Polish plenipotentiary be sent forthwith to Berlin. However, this was not sincerely meant and Ribbentrop did his best to make it impossible for the Poles to comply, which they did not in any case wish to do. By August 30, with all preparations complete, Hitler had reverted to his earlier confidence ('The English believe Germany is weak. They will see they are deceiving themselves'). The next day he overruled Göring and Goebbels, despite their 'scepticism' about English non-intervention: 'The Führer does not believe England will intervene.' Apart from Hitler, Ribbentrop alone was keen for war, encouraging Hitler to believe that Munich had been 'a first-class stupidity' and assuring him the British would not act. By the morning of September 3, when the British ultimatum was delivered, they had both been proven wrong.

Hitler the gambler had in fact been doubly wrong: wrong to think that Chamberlain had been earnest about war in September 1938 and wrong to think that he was bluffing in August 1939. Yet Hitler's miscalculations were lucky ones. For if Chamberlain had acted as he expected in 1938 – had actually called Hitler's bluff rather than folding – Germany's position would have been far more exposed than it was in 1939, when Hitler guessed that Chamberlain would fold again. By going to war later rather than sooner, Chamberlain unwittingly saved the Third Reich, vastly improving Hitler's chances of winning the war he had always intended to fight. Hitler presented Britain with a choice. Unfortunately, Britain's Prime Minister chose the wrong year. In that sense, Churchill was half right. The war of 1939 was indeed an 'unnecessary war'. But what was necessary to stop it was a war in 1938.

## THE END OF APPEASEMENT

The policy of appeasement was not quite dead after the war began. The option of reaching some kind of negotiated peace with Germany was not closed off until Churchill replaced Chamberlain as Prime Minister in May 1940. It was in these last months of his premiership, more than a year and a half too late, that Chamberlain finally began to take seriously the idea of some kind of regime change in Germany. On January 17, 1940, Harold Nicolson heard that there was 'still a group in the war Cabinet working for appeasement and at present in negotiation via the former Chancellor Brüning to make peace with the German General Staff on condition that they eliminate Hitler'. But the chance that the German 'opposition' might play the *deus ex machina* was long gone. Roosevelt was even less realistic. He continued to act as if a compromise peace might still be concocted on the basis of Munich-style concessions to the dictators; hence the 1940 trips to Europe by the Under-Secretary of State, Sumner Welles, and the Vice-President of General Motors, James Mooney, the former touting concessions to Germany that even Chamberlain and Halifax thought laughable. Only with the fall of France was appeasement finally buried. Paradoxically, it was at its moment of supreme weakness that the British Empire rediscovered the virtue of defiance. True, a few faint hearts still wondered if somehow the Empire might be salvaged by conceding all Europe to Hitler and Mussolini. But this was not appeasement; it was defeatism. Churchill gave them their answer at the War Cabinet meeting of May 28, 1940: 'The Germans would demand our Fleet ... our naval bases, and much else. We should become a slave state.'

This was surely right. As Hitler had told Keitel and the chiefs of his army, navy and air force on October 9, 1939, his aim was 'to effect the destruction of the strength of the Western Powers and their capability of resisting still further the political consolidation and continued expansion of the German people in Europe.' Even his later decision to attack Russia had an anti-British objective; as he put it on July 31, 1940, twelve days after once again offering to make peace with Britain: 'Russia is the factor on which Britain is relying the most ... With

Russia shattered, Britain's last hope would be shattered.' The idea that a peace could have been struck with 'That Man', as Churchill called him, was always an illusion. The proof that the policy of appeasement had been a disastrous failure lay precisely in the strength of Hitler's position by the summer of 1940 – victorious from the Channel to the River Bug, protected to the East by a non-aggression pact, able to bomb Britain from French airfields, in a position to make disingenuous offers of peace. Though Great Britain herself could not yet be described as being at Hitler's mercy, her few allies were vanquished and large swathes of her Empire would be vulnerable to invasion in the event of a Japanese attack. Henceforth – and with good reason – the term 'appeasement' would be used exclusively as a term of abuse.

# PART III

# Killing Space

# 11

# Blitzkrieg

*A new order of ethnographic relationships, that is to say a resettlement of the nationalities so that, at the end of the process, there are better dividing lines than is the case today.*

Hitler, October 6, 1939

*We are paying very heavily now for failing to face the insurance premiums essential for security of an Empire! This has usually been the main cause for the loss of Empires in the past.*

General Alan Brooke, 1942

## LIGHTNING WAR

At 4.45 a.m. on September 1, 1939, the tranquillity of daybreak in Western Poland was shattered by a deafening military thunderclap. Five German armies comprising more than 1.8 million men swept across the Polish borders, launched from ideally situated bridgeheads in Western Pomerania, East Prussia, Upper Silesia and German-controlled Slovakia. Almost as loud as the barrages of the German artillery were the roars of engines; the German advance was spearheaded by more than three thousand tanks and hundreds of armoured cars and personnel carriers. From the sky, Ju-87 dive-bombers shrieked down on the hastily mobilizing Poles, their precision bombs destroying bridges, roads and supply convoys, their terrifying sirens sowing panic among the defending forces. The aim was to avoid the protracted attrition of the last war by achieving rapid penetration of territory and swift, annihilating encirclements of enemy forces.

With its devastating combination of artillery, infantry, armour and air power, this was precisely what the blitzkrieg made possible.

*Blitzkrieg* is, of course, a German word meaning 'lightning war'. The ironic thing is that it was in many ways a British invention, derived from the lessons of the Western Front in the First World War. Captain Basil Liddell Hart had drawn his own conclusions from the excessively high casualties suffered by both sides. As an infantry subaltern, he himself had been gassed, the long-term effects of which forced him to retire from the army in 1927, after which he turned to journalism, working as defence correspondent for the *Daily Telegraph* and then *The Times* and publishing numerous works of military history. In Liddell Hart's view, the fatal mistake of most offensives on the Western Front had been their ponderous and predictable directness. A more 'indirect approach', he argued, would aim at surprising the enemy, throwing his commanders off balance, and then exploiting the ensuing confusion. The essence was to concentrate armour and air power in a lethal lightning strike. Liddell Hart defined the secret as lying

partly in the tactical combination of tanks and aircraft, partly in the unexpectedness of the stroke in direction and time, *but above all* in the 'follow-through' – the way that a break-through is exploited by a deep strategic penetration; carried out by armoured forces racing on ahead of the main army, and operating *independently*.

The good news for Liddell Hart was that his work was hugely influential. The bad news was that it was hugely influential not in Britain but in Germany. With the notable exception of Major-General J. F. C. Fuller,* senior British commanders like Field Marshal Earl Haig simply refused to accept that 'the aeroplane, the tank [and] the motor car [would] supersede the horse in future wars', dismissing motorized weapons as mere 'accessories to the man and horse'. Haig's brother concurred: the cavalry would 'never be scrapped to make room for the tanks'. By contrast, younger German officers immedi-

---

* Fuller had been the mastermind behind the British tank offensive at Cambrai in 1917. His frustration with the British Establishment led him to support Oswald Mosley's British Union of Fascists.

ately grasped the significance of Liddell Hart's work. Among his most avid fans was Heinz Guderian, commander of the 19th German Army Corps in the invasion of Poland. As Guderian recalled, it was from Liddell Hart and other British pioneers of 'a new type of warfare on the largest scale' that he learned the importance of 'the concentration of armour'. Moreover,

it was Liddell Hart who emphasized the use of armoured forces for long-range strokes, operations against the opposing army's communications, and [who] also proposed a type of armoured division combining panzer and panzer-infantry units. Deeply impressed by these ideas, I tried to develop them in a sense practicable for our own army . . . I owe many suggestions of our further development to Captain Liddell Hart.

Guderian – who was happy to describe himself as Liddell Hart's disciple and pupil and even translated his works into German – had learned his lessons well. In September 1939 his panzers were unstoppable. The Poles did not, as legend has it, attempt cavalry charges against them, though mounted troops were deployed against German infantry, but they lacked adequate motor transport and their tanks were fewer and technically inferior to the Germans'. Moreover, like the Czechs before them, the Poles found Anglo-French guarantees to be militarily worthless. At the Battle of Bzura they mounted a desperate counteroffensive to hold up the German assault on Warsaw, but by September 16 their resistance was crumbling. By the 17th the Germans had reached the fortress at Bresc (Brest) on the River Bug. On September 28 Warsaw itself fell. Eight days later the last Polish troops laid down their arms. The entire campaign had lasted barely five weeks.

The Poles had fought courageously, but they were outnumbered and outgunned. The most striking thing about the war in the West the following year was that the opposite was true. It was perhaps predictable that the Dutch and Belgians would succumb to superior German forces, but the fall of France within a matter of just six weeks was, as the historian Marc Bloch said, a 'strange defeat'. Even without the support of the British Expeditionary Force, the French forces were superior on paper, an advantage that ought to have been magnified by their fighting a defensive campaign. They had twice the number of wheeled vehicles and 4,638 tanks to the German 4,060. Moreover, French tanks had thicker armour and bigger guns. Yet when the German offensive was launched on May 10, 1940, many units put up only token resistance. On May 15 General Erwin Rommel's 7th Panzer Division was able to take 450 prisoners in the course of two small skirmishes; later they captured 10,000 in the space of two days. Rommel* himself was struck by the readiness of the French officers to give themselves up, and by their insouciant 'requests, including, among other things, permission to keep their batmen and to have their kit picked up from Philippeville, where it had been left'. Another German officer saw 'several hundred French officers who had marched 35 kilometres without any guard from a prisoner of war dispatch point to a prisoner of war transit station . . . with apparently none having made their escape'. Karl von Stackelberg, a reporter in one of the new 'propaganda companies', was baffled: '20,000 men . . . were heading backwards as prisoners . . . It was inexplicable . . . How was it possible, these French soldiers with their officers, so completely downcast, so completely demoralized, would allow themselves to go more or less voluntarily into imprisonment?' British soldiers captured in 1940 could not help noticing that 'the French had been prepared for capture and so were laden down with kit, while we were all practically empty-handed.' In all, around 1.8 million French troops were taken prisoner in 1940, of whom nearly a million were kept in Germany as forced labourers until 1945. It is true that perhaps as many as half of those who surrendered did so in the period between June 17, when the new Prime Minister, Marshal Pétain, announced that he was seeking an armistice, and its implementation five days later. But it is still remarkable that more than a third of the French army had already been taken prisoner before Pétain's statement. Indicative of the poor state of morale is the fact that colonial troops from French Africa fought with more determination than their supposed masters; their units certainly took heavier casualties.

---

* Like Guderian, Rommel had also thought deeply about tank warfare. His two pre-war books, *Infantry Attacks* and *Tank Attacks*, brought him to Hitler's attention, leading to his appointment as head of Hitler Youth training and later commander of Hitler's personal security battalion, which accompanied the Führer when he visited occupied Czechoslovakia.

What lay behind the French collapse? To Liddell Hart – who was so appalled by the outbreak of war that he suffered a nervous breakdown – it was essentially a failure of military doctrine:

The panzer forces' thrust could have been stopped long before reaching the Channel by a concentrated counterstroke with similar forces. But the French, though having more and better tanks than the enemy, had strung them out in small packets ... The one British armoured division available was not despatched to France until after the German offensive was launched, and this arrived too late for the first, and decisive, phase ... This *Blitzkrieg* pace was only possible because the Allied leaders had not grasped the new technique, and so did not know how to counter it ... Never was a great disaster more easily preventable.

Marc Bloch agreed that the débâcle was due at least in part to the abysmal quality of French generalship. A decisive factor was the German decision to switch the direction of their main attack from Luxembourg and the Low Countries, as Hitler had originally planned, to the line running between Liège and Namur, through the supposedly impenetrable forests of the Ardennes. The French would have fared better against the original strategy; they were wholly taken by surprise when five panzer divisions thrust their way through the Ardennes and captured the bridges over the River Meuse. Thereafter, their reactions were culpably slow or inept. Yet what happened in 1940 was more than just a military failure. At root, as Bloch argued, it was a collapse of morale.

Even during the 'Phoney War' of late 1939 and early 1940, Lieutenant-General Alan Brooke, who commanded the British Expeditionary Force's 2nd Corps, had been deeply troubled by the mood of the French army, which he was inclined to attribute to the defensive character of French strategy. The heavily fortified Maginot Line's 'most dangerous aspect' as it ran down the border with Germany, Brooke noted in his diary, was 'the psychological one; a sense of false security is engendered, a feeling of sitting behind an impregnable iron fence; and should the fence perchance be broken then French fighting spirit [might well] be brought crumbling with it!' There was more to French defeatism than this, however. To many Frenchmen, the Third Republic simply did not seem worth dying for, when so many of their fathers, brothers and friends had died for it already between 1914 and 1918. This was the mood – the refusal to pursue another Pyrrhic victory – that had been foreshadowed in Louis-Ferdinand Céline's *Voyage au bout de la nuit* (1932), with its stomach-churning evocation of the slaughter of the last war's opening phase. The same mood inspired the Nobel laureate Roger Martin Du Gard's letter to a friend in September 1936: 'Anything rather than war! Anything . . . even Fascism in Spain . . . Even Fascism in France: Nothing, no trial, no servitude can be compared to war: Anything, Hitler rather than war!' In the words of one German officer: 'French spirit and morale had been . . . broken . . . before the battle even began. It was not so much the lack of machinery . . . that had defeated the French, but that they did not know what they were fighting for . . . The Nazi revolution had already won the Battle of France before our first armoured divisions went to work.'

Some Frenchmen on the Right, no doubt, saw distinct advantages to a German victory. Most, however, simply underestimated the costs of defeat. It is unlikely that the French would have surrendered in such large numbers and in such an orderly fashion if they had not expected these costs to be comparatively light. The assumptions clearly were that, with the war seemingly over, they would soon be returned to their native land; and that any German occupation would be short lived. Some senior generals seem to have been more worried about a possible left-wing revolt at home than by the prospects of German occupation. These expectations were rooted in the more distant memories of 1871 rather than 1914. They were to be bitterly confounded. The French Left melted away. The Germans stayed.

It is usually assumed that the mood in Britain was not so defeatist. Certainly, some British soldiers in France in 1940 refused to surrender even when ordered to do so. 'Not fucking likely, you yellow bastard!' was the furious reaction of one member of the 51st (Highland) Division when ordered to lay down his arms by an officer of the Kensington Regiment in June 1940. Yet this bellicose Scot was in a minority. Most of his comrades in the British Expeditionary Force saw little reason to fight to the death for France when the French themselves were manifestly so reluctant to do so. In British folk memory, the evacuation from the beaches at Dunkirk was a triumph. The German newsreels more accurately depicted it as a humiliating defeat. So chaotic was the British retreat – accompanied as it was by rumours of a 'fifth column' supposedly sabotaging the Allied effort behind the lines – that the shattered survivors had to be quarantined on their return for the sake of civilian morale. As Corporal W. R. Littlewood of the Royal Engineers put it: 'We were beginning to think that the Germans were almost superhuman . . . At every turn [they] seemed to have the answers.' Discipline came close to breaking down. One officer was shot in the face by one of his own battle-fatigued men. In Calais an old woman was gunned down by a soldier in the Queen Victoria's Rifles in the belief that she was one of the ubiquitous fifth columnists, since the Germans were reputedly masters of disguise as well as of warfare. Belgian civilians suspected of spying – including farm labourers accused of mowing grass 'in the formation of an arrow' to guide Stuka pilots to British troop formations – were summarily shot, in scenes reminiscent of the German army's conduct in the same region twenty-six years before. In the final frantic scramble for boats at Dunkirk, some French soldiers found themselves being fired on by their own allies. The most that can be said about Dunkirk is that the British were very lucky. Hitler made his first real mistake in stopping Rommel's marauding panzers from finishing them off. The killing or capture of around 338,226 Allied troops – the total number evacuated in Operation Dynamo, of whom 110,000 were in fact French – would have been a devastating blow from which British morale might never have recovered. In the event, only 41,340 British servicemen ended up as prisoners.

Just how vulnerable the morale of British troops was becomes clear when one considers their performance in other settings. Although Churchill was fond of phrases like 'never surrender', British troops as a rule did not fight to the death. In Crete in 1941 they failed to withstand a German parachute invasion, despite initially inflicting heavy casualties. The first campaigns in North Africa were also disappointing. Later, Churchill was especially troubled by the refusal of the garrison at Singapore – whom he had explicitly exhorted to fight to the last man – to hold out against what was in fact an outnumbered and very weary Japanese force (see Chapter 14). Even Alan Brooke, perhaps Churchill's harshest critic, who took over as Chief of the

Imperial General Staff in December 1941, was perturbed. His constant worry was that, as in the First World War, Churchill's appetite for 'subsidiary theatres' of war would lead him to spread British forces too thinly and 'fritter away our strength' instead of concentrating force 'at the vital point'. For this reason he was disinclined to give priority to Asia or any other theatre, having convinced himself that Britain must concentrate on the Mediterranean and North Africa. Nevertheless, he was appalled by the collapse of resistance in the Far East. 'It is hard to see why a better defence is not being put up,' he confided in his diary as the Japanese closed on Singapore. 'I have during the last 10 years had an unpleasant feeling that the British Empire was decaying and that we were on a slippery slope. I wonder if I was right? I certainly never expected that we should fall to pieces as fast as we are.' With the Japanese threatening to overrun Burma too, he became distraught: 'Cannot work out why troops are not fighting better. If the army cannot fight better than it is doing at present we shall deserve to lose our Empire!'

To be sure, unlike their French counterparts in 1940, British soldiers did not lay down their arms out of defeatism. In most cases, they were ordered to surrender because their officers saw no point in fighting on when a position became indefensible. The typical capture narrative in Anglophone war memoirs has the enemy completely surrounding a unit and the officer ordering his men to lay down their arms rather than 'die pointlessly'. Yet despite the consolation of discretion's being the better part of valour, British servicemen taken prisoner were often surprised by their own feelings of guilt; capture was not something they had been prepared for. Many Asian observers interpreted the reluctance of British officers to fight to the last man – and, indeed, the willingness of some officers to run for their lives if they saw a chance of escape – as evidence that the British had lost faith in their own imperial role. If Frenchmen were not ready to 'die for Danzig', their British counterparts were just as reluctant to perish for Penang.

The British at home nevertheless lived to fight another day, even if they had left a large part of their army's weaponry on the beaches between Nieuport and Gravelines. For, whatever the state of their soldiers' morale, they still enjoyed two advantages. The first was maritime. For all the setbacks on land, the Royal Navy still had the upper hand at sea. Their fleet was roughly three and a half times larger than Hitler's.* True, the English Channel is not wide – just twenty-one miles separate Dover from Cape Gris-Nez, the nearest France comes to England. Yet it would have been a colossal gamble, even for such a risk-taker as Hitler, to send a German invasion force across this slender gap. The second British advantage was in the air, though here the advantage was much smaller. Served up to the House of Commons on August 20, 1940, Churchill's tribute to Fighter Command – 'Never in the field of human conflict was so much owed by so many to so few' – remains one his most memorable utterances. At the time, however, pilots joked that it was an allusion to the size of their unpaid mess bills. Churchill's own private secretaries felt the speech 'seemed to drag' because it contained 'less oratory than usual'. His phrase 'the few' implied that the Royal Air Force was outnumbered by the Luftwaffe; and indeed that was what British intelligence believed at the time. In reality, the RAF had a narrow edge. On August 9, just before the Germans launched their crucial offensive against Britain's air defences, the RAF had 1,032 fighters. The German fighters available for the attack numbered 1,011. Moreover, the RAF had 1,400 trained pilots, several hundred more than the Luftwaffe, and they proved more than a match for the Germans in skill and courage. Britain was at last out-producing Germany when it came to aircraft. During the crucial months from June until September, 1,900 new fighters were churned out by British factories, compared with 775 in Germany. Just as they had in the years of appeasement, the British overestimated the Germans – by a factor of around seven in the case of pilot strength. The Germans also overestimated themselves. Göring was sure that half of all British fighters had been destroyed by the end of August; in fact Fighter Command's operational strength at that point was only slightly less than it had been when the battle had commenced. By broadening the scope of their targets to include ports and industrial centres, the Germans threw away their chance of inflicting a decisive blow on RAF command and control capabilities.

* At the outbreak of war, the British had seven aircraft carriers, the Germans none; fifteen battleships to the Germans' five; forty-nine cruisers to the Germans' six; 192 destroyers to the Germans' twenty-one.

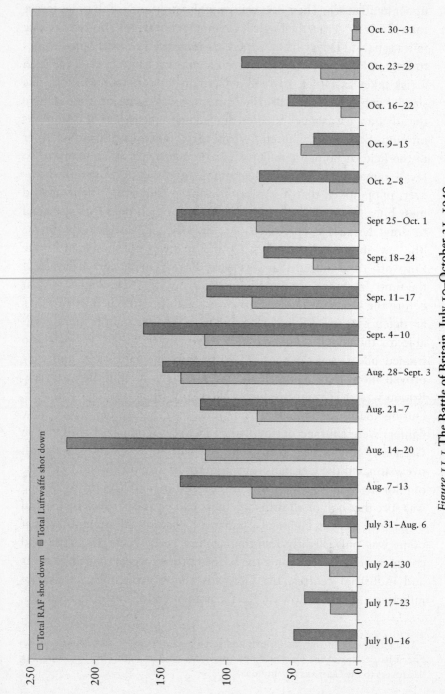

*Figure 11.1* The Battle of Britain, July 10–October 31, 1940

As late as December, Goebbels could still gloat that the war was 'militarily as good as won'. In reality the technical advantage conferred by radar, combined with the judicious leadership of Air Marshal Sir Hugh Dowding, meant that total German losses (including bombers) were nearly twice the British (1,733 to 915). Every week until October 9 the RAF consistently shot down more German planes than they lost in combat (see Figure 11.1).

The British fought on, then, partly because they could. They also fought on because it was becoming more apparent with every passing day that the price of capitulation to Hitler was much higher than many Frenchmen had assumed. The French were in fact comparatively fortunate. Like the inhabitants of the other West European countries the Nazis occupied, the majority of French people were regarded as 'worthy of life'. (Indeed some, notably the Dutch, were judged to be essentially a Germanic people.) What that meant in practice was that they would be economically exploited, but not murdered – unless, that is, they happened to be Jewish. France became the milch cow of the German war economy, to be plundered ruthlessly for materials, manufactures and labour, to say nothing of the countless works of art the Nazi leaders looted from public and private collections. But there was no thought that France should cease to be France. Indeed, occupied Paris became the preferred destination for Wehrmacht and SS officers on leave or in need of a cushy posting. This was not a fate Londoners were eager to share; on the other hand, it was not unendurable. For that reason, relatively few Frenchmen and women opted for active resistance to German rule until the tide of war had turned. 'Collaboration' is a term of abuse, but it covers a host of sins, both venial and cardinal, ranging from the readiness of eminent writers to carry on with their trade under the new dispensation,* to the active involvement of some French officials in the deportation of French Jews to their deaths.

---

* Two striking examples: Louis-Ferdinand Destouches (Céline) and Georges Rémi (Hergé). The former was a confirmed anti-Semite well before the war and was imprisoned after the war for his role in the Vichy period. The latter (who was Belgian rather than French) had somewhat weaker prejudices against Jews and Americans, was strongly anti-Japanese and less than pro-German, but was certainly quite firmly anti-Communist. Some of the best of his Tintin stories were in fact produced during the German occupation: *Le Crabe aux pinces d'or*, *Le Secret de la licorne*, *Le Trésor*

The story to the East was very different. There, the indigenous populations were regarded by Nazi theorists as racially inferior and an obstacle to the expansion of German 'living space'. The blitzkrieg against Poland was accompanied by horrific brutality against prisoners and civilians. This was not spontaneous, but carefully premeditated. It revealed for the first time the true and hideous face of Hitler's empire.

## 'LET CHAOS FLOURISH'

Berchtesgaden was Hitler's mountain retreat in the Bavarian Alps, where he and selected members of the master race could hatch their plans for conquest in a suitably grandiose setting. In 1926, as an obscure political agitator just out of jail, he had retired there to dictate the second half of *Mein Kampf*, with its seminal pledge to lead the German *Volk* 'from its present restricted living space to new land and soil ... tak[ing] up where we broke off six hundred years ago and turn[ing] our gaze towards the land in the East'. Shortly after he became Reich Chancellor in 1933 – by which time the book had become a belated bestseller – he used his royalties to buy a house at Obersalzberg, which became the 'Berghof', literally his 'mountain court'. Over the next few years, locals were forced to sell four square miles of land in the vicinity so that a complex of residences and administrative buildings could be built as a summer playground for the inner circle of the Third Reich. It was a telling illustration of what 'living space' meant in practice.

It was at the Berghof that Hitler had chosen to meet Neville Chamberlain when the latter came to broker the Czech cession of the Sudetenland. A year later, on August 22, 1939, it was the scene of a very different meeting, between Hitler and his military leaders. The notes made by one of those present make it clear what Hitler intended to achieve after the Polish army had been defeated:

---

*de Rackham le rouge* and *Les Sept Boules de crystal*, all published in *Le Soir* between 1940 and 1944. After the war, Hergé was arrested for collaboration, but responded that he had merely answered King Leopold's appeal not to abandon his country.

Destruction of Poland in the foreground. The aim is elimination of living forces, not the arrival at a certain line. Even if the war should break out in the west, the destruction of Poland shall be the primary objective ... Have no pity. Brutal attitude. Eighty million [German] people shall get what is their right. Their existence has to be secured. The strongest has the right. Greatest severity.

As Hitler told senior Nazis in October of that year, it was not Germany's mission to bring order to Poland but rather to let 'chaos flourish'. But this was chaos with a purpose. Ever since *Mein Kampf*, Hitler had conceived of the Nazi empire in terms of both murder and resettlement. Inferior races would be killed or expelled in order to make room for German colonists who would go forth and multiply. The aim was nothing less than to redraw the ethnic map of Europe, turning what had once been the fantasies of racial theorists into a horrific reality. In his diary, Goebbels defined Hitler's aim as 'annihilating' (*vernichtend*). Halder, the Chief of the General Staff, believed that 'it was the intention of the Führer and Göring to destroy and eliminate the Polish people'. There was, Hitler said, to be a 'harsh racial struggle' without 'legal restrictions'. Not all Poles were to be killed, however. In the words of Reinhard Heydrich, head of the Reich Main Security Office: 'The little people we want to spare, but the nobles, priests and Jews must be killed.' The aim was to decapitate Polish society – and to reduce the survivors to the status of a 'helot race', little better than slaves.

Prior to the invasion of Poland, the SS created five special Security Police units known as *Einsatzgruppen* ('Special Task Forces').* Their role was to deal with 'all anti-German elements in hostile country behind the troops in combat'. Even before the Germans marched into Poland, they had drawn up a list of 30,000 people they intended to arrest. Within the brief period of military rule – from the Polish surrender on September 28 until October 25 – between 16,000 and 20,000 Poles were summarily executed, most of them victims of the

---

* Significantly, 15 out of 25 leaders of the *Einsatzgruppen* had doctorates. These were more extraordinary than ordinary men – members of the German academic elite. The number of groups was later increased from five to seven, with an additional *Einsatzkommando* from Danzig.

*Einsatzgruppen.* Members of the aristocracy, the professions, the intelligentsia and the clergy were the principal targets. Following Hitler's call in his Reichstag speech of October 6 for a 'new order of ethnographic relationships', ordinary Poles were to be expelled from Danzig, West Prussia, Posen and eastern Upper Silesia, all of which Hitler now restored to the Reich,* and resettled in the rump 'Government-General for the Occupied Polish Territories'. Families were given as little as twenty minutes to quit their homes; they were allowed to take no more than hand luggage and, as a rule, 20 zlotys in cash. No effort was made to rehouse them; many were simply dumped along the railroad. Such was the fate of roughly one in every ten of the inhabitants of those territories annexed to the Reich. Exceptions were made for around 1.6 million Masurians, Kashubes and so-called *Wasserpolen* of Silesia, all of whom were deemed racially acceptable and allowed to remain. In addition, around five million 'indigestible' Poles were retained temporarily as agricultural workers.

The job of realizing Hitler's vision in the new Government-General fell to a Bavarian named Hans Frank, who had been among the Nazis' earliest recruits from the legal profession. Aged thirty-nine when he installed himself in the historic Wawel Castle in Kraków, Frank was immediately gripped by delusions of grandeur. He told his wife she was to be the 'queen of Poland', though in practice he was in charge of only the four districts of Kraków, Radom, Warsaw and Lublin. The Government-General was to become 'the first colonial territory of the German nation'. Like so many of those who became Hitler's accomplices in mass murder, Frank considered himself to be a man of sophisticated sensibilities. He kept on the Polish curators at the Wawel to maintain what he now regarded as his personal art collection.

---

* It should be remembered that most of these territories had been ceded by Germany only under the terms of the Treaty of Versailles. Technically, they now became two new *Reichsgaue*: Danzig-West Prussia (including Danzig, Bromberg and Marienwerder) and Wartheland (including Posen and Littmannstadt, as Łódź was renamed). These were administratively part of the Reich but with the exception of Danzig treated as foreign territory for the purposes of travel. It was significant that they were defined as *Gaue*, the regional unit of party rather than state organization in Germany. Here the party would be able to act without the constraints of pre-1933 administrative institutions.

When the Italian war correspondent Curzio Malaparte visited Frank's court he found him

sitting on his high stiff-backed chair as if he were ... on the throne of the Jagellons and Sobieskis. He appeared to be fully persuaded that the Great Polish traditions of royalty and chivalry were being revived in him. His black glossy hair was brushed back revealing a high ivory-white forehead. A slight film of sweat covered his face, and by the light of the large Dutch lamps and the silver candlesticks that ranged along the table and were reflected in the Bohemian glass and Saxon china, his face shone as if it were wrapped in a cellophane mask. 'My one ambition', said Frank, thrusting himself back against his chair by propping his hands against the edge of the table, 'is to elevate the Polish people to the honour of European civilization.'

In reality, he was about to plunge them into an abyss of barbarism.

The Jagellonian University in Kraków is one of Central Europe's most ancient seats of learning. Founded in 1364, it had been Nicolaus Copernicus's Alma Mater. On November 6, 1939 the occupying authorities invited the faculty of the university to a lecture by one *Obersturmbannführer* Müller. It was a trap. At gunpoint 183 of them were herded into trucks and deported to Sachsenhausen concentration camp. Though they were subsequently released, this was a harbinger of the fate Frank intended for the Polish intelligentsia. The next summer, under the so-called Extraordinary Pacification Programme (*AB-Aktion*), 3,500 more intellectuals were rounded up and shot in a forest outside Warsaw. By the end of 1940, the total number of victims of this campaign had reached 50,000.

The Polish elites were only one of the 'problems' Frank had to address. In Germany, Jews had made up less than 1 per cent of the population. By contrast, around 9 per cent of the Polish population – an estimated 2.3 million of those living in the Government-General – were Jews. It seemed self-evident that so many Jews could not be tolerated so close to the heartland of the new German empire. Had not Hitler likened them to a kind of malign racial disease, seeking to contaminate the Aryan race? They would clearly have to go, especially from Frank's splendid new capital. But where? In the opening phase of the German invasion, scores of Jews had been shot in places such as Roznan, Blonie and Pultusk. But this was not yet a systematic policy of annihilation; objections by Wehrmacht officers applied a brake to the *Einsatzgruppen*'s activities. Slaughtering civilians was bad – bad, that is, for morale and the maintenance of local order. It was easier to encourage the Jews to flee eastwards across the border. After some deliberation, it was decided to herd those who still remained into ghettos, in effect to restore that enforced segregation which had been commonplace throughout Central Europe up until the end of the eighteenth century. This was a major administrative undertaking in its own right, necessitating the introduction of arm-bands bearing the Star of David to identify Jews and the creation of local Jewish councils, whose role it would be to run the ghettos. Yet from the outset the concentration of the Polish Jews in ghettos was intended to be no more than a prelude to expulsion. Although Friedrich Uebelhoer, the *Regierungspräsident* in charge of Kalisch and Łódź, already spoke of the 'final goal' as being to 'burn out this plague-boil', this was not yet official policy. Indeed, Himmler explicitly ruled out 'the Bolshevik method of physical extermination of a people out of inner conviction' as 'un-German and impossible'.

For a while, Himmler and Frank toyed with the idea of sending the Jews to the Indian Ocean island of Madagascar, which the Polish government had already considered; it was agreed that this could happen only after the war. Then Hitler spoke of concentrating them on the new Poland's eastern frontier, between the Vistula and the Bug. Later, Siberia was mentioned. In the meantime, the Lublin district became a kind of dumping ground for deported Jews, tens of thousands of whom were crowded into hastily constructed camps, while the supposedly transitional ghettos of Łódź, Warsaw, Łowicz and Glowno took on a more permanent quality. Not that they could have endured indefinitely. For one thing, they were intolerably cramped; a third of the population of Warsaw was crammed into 2.4 per cent of the city's residential area. At the same time, food rations for Jews were reduced so that by 1941 their daily calorific content was just over 25 per cent of the standard Polish allocation and a meagre 7 per cent of the German, far less than the subsistence minimum. Over-crowding and underfeeding were themselves intended to be lethal – which indeed they were, with mortality rates soaring to 10 per cent in Warsaw in 1941. 'It's high time that this rabble is driven together in ghettos,' declared Himmler, 'and then plague will creep in and they'll croak.' In the summer of 1942 Frank described sentencing 1.2 million Jews to death by starvation as 'just a marginal issue'.

Yet the more Frank got to know his fiefdom, the more he began to doubt the wisdom of expelling or starving nearly one in ten of the population, to say nothing of the dangers of allowing epidemics to break out in the principal cities. In the early 1930s, Jews had accounted for nearly half of Poland's highest income-earners. A very high proportion of the entrepreneurs, managers and skilled workers of Polish cities were Jewish. One of the first acts of the German occupation had been to authorize the seizure of all Jewish property – the beginning of a campaign of systematic and ruthless plunder. At around the same time Frank had issued an edict imposing a general obligation for forced labour on all male Jews between the ages of twelve and sixty. Whether for their capital or their labour, Jews had an unquestionable economic value; simply stealing the former and eliminating the latter was patently not a profit-maximizing strategy. Unless Frank wanted to return the Polish economy to the Middle Ages, he needed to work out a compromise between the dictates of racist ideology and the economics of empire. He outlined his planned compromise during a visit to Berlin in November 1941:

A problem that occupies us in particular is the Jews. This merry little people [*Volklein*], which wallows in dirt and filth, has been gathered together by us in ghettos and [special] quarters and will probably not remain in the Government-General for very long. [Vigorous applause] But these Jews are not that parasite gang alone, from our point of view, but strangely enough – we only realized it over there [in Poland] – there is another category of Jews, something one would never have thought possible. There are labouring Jews over there who work in transport, in building, in factories, and others are skilled workers such as tailors, shoemakers, etc. We have put together Jewish workshops with the help of these skilled Jewish workers, in which goods will be made which will greatly ease the position of German production, in exchange for the supply of foodstuffs and whatever else the Jews need urgently for their existence.

It was as if the Nazis could not decide which they wanted: to exploit the Jews ('production') or to starve them into extinction ('attrition').

For the time being the 'Jewish question' in Poland was left unresolved, a contradiction at the heart of the Government-General. A half-starved kind of normality descended on the Łódź ghetto, where by the summer of 1941 around 40,000 Jews were employed in producing clothing, textiles and other manufactures, including military supplies.

Killing the Polish elites and cramming the Jews into ghettos were, nevertheless, only preludes to the fundamental transformation of Central Europe to which the Nazis aspired. The 'cleansing' (*Flurbereinigung*) of the occupied territories was merely a means to an end. That end was to re-settle Germany's newly acquired living space with members of the Aryan master race.

## HIMMLERTOWN

In the spring of 1940, in his capacity as the newly created Reich Commissioner for the Strengthening of Ethnic Germandom, Heinrich Himmler took a tour of the Polish countryside with his friend, the Nazi poet and honorary SS officer Hanns Johst.* Himmler's role in the new German empire was twofold. As well as eliminating 'the harmful influence of those alien sections of the population which constitute a danger to the Reich and German national community' (meaning Jews principally), he was charged with the 'forming of new German settlements'. Periodically the two men would stop their car and stride across rolling fields where, according to Johst, Himmler looked 'across the wide, wide space which was full, abundantly full, with this good, fertile earth . . . All of this was now once more German soil! Here [Himmler enthused] the German plough [would] soon change the picture.'

Along the way, Himmler and Johst passed through the town of Zamość. Himmler was so impressed with its Italianate Renaissance

* It was Johst who wrote the famous line, usually misattributed to Göring: '*Wenn ich Kultur höre . . . entsichere ich meinen Browning*' (When I hear the word culture . . . I take the safety catch off my Browning). The line comes from the opening scene of Johst's best-known play, *Schlageter* (1933), a tribute to the Nazi 'martyr' Albert Leo Schlageter. He described his visit to Poland with Himmler in the book *Ruf des Reiches – Echo des Volkes! Eine Ostfahrt* (1940).

architecture – so completely at odds with his stereotyped assumptions about Polish backwardness – that he decided to rename the town. 'Himmlerstadt', as it would henceforth be known, would become the first foothold of the German *Volk* on a new Eastern frontier. The first step towards its Germanization was straightforward. The town's Jews were rounded up and deported, to await their fate in the ghettos. The next step was to get rid of the Poles. As in the annexed territories to the west, the SS carried out a careful classification of the indigenous population. Those in Class I ('Nordic') and Class II ('Phalian') were sent to the Łódź camp for ethnic Germans for screening. Those in Class III ('Mixed') were sent as slave labour to the Reich, apart from the elderly, who were rehoused in former Jewish residences. The fate of Poles in Class IV ('Asocial and Racially Inferior') was to be exterminated. Those who resisted, or were thought capable of resistance, were taken to the old fortification known as the Rotunda on the edge of town. Later in the war, the Rotunda became a bloody slaughterhouse, where prisoners were shot almost indiscriminately. To begin with, however, the Germans selected their victims quite precisely: priests, lawyers, judges, businessmen, teachers – anyone who might conceivably be able to organize Polish national resistance. Even boy scouts and girl guides were regarded as potential threats. Among the earliest victims in Zamość was sixteen-year-old Grażyna Kierszniewska, one of thirty-six guides and scouts executed as potential Resistance leaders.

Now, with the town cleansed of racial impurities, there was one remaining question to be resolved: who would be the new German settlers, the bold Aryan pioneers who would colonize the living space conquered by Hitler's armies? Precious few citizens of the Reich proper seemed interested in making a new life in Poland. In all, no more than 400,000 Germans from the Old Reich took advantage of the opportunity to move eastwards, and most of these were either bureaucrats who had drawn the short straw, or carpet-bagging businessmen. German peasants, the type of people who were supposed to provide the yeoman backbone of the new colonies, were simply not interested. However, there were Germans living elsewhere in Europe who were less reluctant to move. Himmler's new responsibilities also included repatriating 'persons of Germanic race or nationality resident abroad who are considered suitable for permanent return to the Reich'. The idea was to invite ethnic Germans living further east than the new frontier to come and re-settle in the freshly annexed and ethnically cleansed Polish territory. In response, around 57,000 came from eastern Galicia, 67,000 from Volhynia and 11,000 from the area around Białystok. A further 50,000 ethnic Germans came from Latvia and just under 14,000 from Estonia, under agreements reached with the Baltic governments in October 1939. Unlike the expulsions of Poles, these were voluntary moves. Indeed, as Soviet rule was imposed in these areas, there was a rush to accept the Nazi invitation to come *heim ins Reich* – 'home into the Reich'. Around 189,000 ethnic Germans left Bessarabia and Bukovina after these territories were annexed by the Soviet Union in 1940, and around 53,000 came from Lithuania after their country had suffered the same fate. Some came in specially organized trains and ships; others, like the peasants of Galicia, rode westwards with their farm carts piled high with possessions. This seemed a strange, back-to-front procedure for a regime supposedly in search of living space – to persuade German communities, some of which were centuries old, to leave their ancestral homes and move west. The rationale, which was not revealed to the ethnic Germans, was to screen them for their racial purity. Only those with satisfactory 'physical fitness, origin, ethnic-political attitude and vocational training' – which in practice tended to mean the degree of their past association with non-Germans – were fit to be colonists in the Reich's newly conquered or re-conquered territory. By the summer of 1941, Himmler's Commissariat had settled 200,000 *Volksdeutsche* in the Germanized parts of western Poland; a further 275,000 still languished in temporary resettlement centres. By the end of 1943, some 176,000 Romanian *Volksdeutsche* had been settled there. Around 25,000 ethnic Germans found their way to the Himmlerstadt area.

This was a beginning. But it was not a wholly encouraging beginning. The ethnic Germans were in some ways rather a disappointment to the Nazis. Many did not seem quite German enough; they had, it was muttered by the more rigorous racial theorists, gone native, perhaps even allowed their racial purity to be diluted by interbreeding with their former Slav neighbours. By contrast, Himmler could not help noticing how distinctly Aryan many Poles seemed to look. There were in fact rather more blond-haired, blue-eyed specimens here than in his native Bavaria. One possibility he had contemplated as early as 1939 was to '"screen" the incorporated eastern territories and later also the General-Government' for the offspring of mixed marriages 'in order to make this lost German blood available again to our own people'. In a memorandum of May 1940 entitled 'Some Thoughts on the Treatment of the Alien Population in the East', Himmler explained how his intended screening process would 'fish out the racially valuable people from the mishmash, take them to Germany and assimilate them there'. All six- to ten-year-olds were to be 'sifted each year to sort out those with valuable blood' and the 'racially first class children' sent to the Reich. As the head of the SS Race and Settlement Main Office (RuSHA) in Breslau put it in 1942, some Poles had

a significant proportion of Nordic blood which, in contrast to the otherwise fatalistic Slavic strains, has enabled them to take the initiative . . . The racially valuable Polish families ought to be creamed off so that at least the next generation of these former carriers of Germanic blood can be restored to the German nation through a programme of education in the Old [pre-war] Reich.

To be sure of retaining every viable Aryan, German women, who became known as the 'Brown Sisters', were employed to patrol the streets with sweets to lure potentially eligible children. Those who were taken captive were never seen by their parents again. As Himmler explained to SS leaders in Posen in October 1943: 'What the [conquered] nations can offer in the way of good blood of our type we will take, if necessary by kidnapping children and raising them here with us.'

Similar policies were adopted in other annexed or occupied areas. In the new Reich Protectorate of Bohemia and Moravia (formerly the rump Czechoslovakia), the former Foreign Minister and now Reich Protector Konstantin von Neurath argued for:

absorption of about half the Czech nation by the Germans, in so far as this is of significance in view of its value from a racial or other standpoint . . .

The remaining half of the Czech nation must be deprived of its power, removed from its country by all sorts of methods. This is particularly true of the section which is racially Mongolian.

Hitler's view was that some Czechs were capable of Germanization; if racially suitable, they might be admitted to German educational institutions. There is no question that some Czechs opportunistically sought to go down this route. Ota Filip recalled resisting his father's attempts to make him attend the German elementary school in Schlesisch Ostrau (Slezská Ostrava); hearing the son's protests, the local Czech teacher rebuked the father for being an *'ersatz* Teuton'. The question, however, was how exactly to identify German blood in an individual. Neurath's deputy, a Sudeten German named Karl Frank, defined a German national as 'one who himself professes allegiance to the German nation, as long as this conviction is confirmed by certain facts, such as language, education, culture etc.', adding: 'Any more precise elaboration of the term "German national" is not possible given current relationships.' Likewise, in the 'blossoming, pure German' province of West Prussia after 1939, Reich Governor Forster simply 'assume[d] the presence of German blood in a family on the basis of typically German abilities and gifts (e.g., technical skills, a sense of how to look after household and farm appliances properly) . . . personal and domestic hygiene'. Tell-tale 'Slavic racial characteristics', on the other hand, included 'a markedly disorderly and careless family life, demonstrating a complete lack of feeling for order, for personal and domestic cleanliness, or any ambition to advance oneself'. In other words, race in West Prussia was identifiable in behaviour. By contrast, Forster's counterpart in the neighbouring Warthegau, Artur Greiser, insisted on 'a minimum of 50 per cent German ancestry for entry in the German Ethnic Registry', which was supposed to divide the population into four distinct racial categories on the basis of rigorous genealogical criteria.

When the Interior Ministry attempted to rule on the fate of non-Polish minorities, the confusion between cultural and biological definitions of race became painfully apparent:

The mixed population in the areas of Oppeln and Kattowitz, which has been for centuries greatly under German influence, is not to be regarded as Polish

... The same applies to a class of population living in the Reich province of Danzig-West Prussia, which is of predominantly Polish descent, but tends to German nationality owing to mixed marriages and cultural influence. The Kashubes, in spite of their Slavonic dialect, are never to be treated as Poles. This is still more the case with the Masurians. Anybody belonging to these nationalities is, however, to be treated as a Pole if he professes to be one, or has done so before the incorporation.

The journal *Ostland* went so far as to deny that the Polish nationality existed, asserting instead the existence of myriad petty 'tribal types': Mazovians, including Podlasians, Kurpians and Lowiczians, and Malopolanians, including Cracovians, Lachs, Lazowiaks, Sandomierzians and Lubliners. Moreover, as the Nazis looked further east, new dilemmas presented themselves. Alfred Rosenberg, the minister responsible for the occupied territories in Eastern Europe, argued that all the inhabitants of the Baltic States should be regarded as eligible for Germanization, but this position was initially rejected by those who regarded the 'Finno-Ugric' Estonians and the supposedly 'Slavic' Lithuanians as racially alien. Later, Rosenberg's view prevailed; indeed, Hitler contemplated integrating the Baltic States into the Reich, though only after a gradual process of cultural Germanization. Ukrainians were also considered as potentially salvageable. Hitler argued that women aged between fifteen and thirty-five should be deported from the Ukraine to the Reich to work as housemaids. This, he argued, would retrieve German blood that had supposedly been lost when the ancient Gothic realm in the Ukraine had been conquered by the Huns in the fifth century.

Typical of the pseudo-scientific basis of all this was the report drawn up in April 1942 on 'The Solution of the Polish Question' by Dr Erhard Wetzel, lawyer and desk officer for racial matters in the Reich Ministry for Eastern Territories:

From a racial standpoint the Poles contain essentially almost the same racial strains as the Germans, although the proportions of the individual races are different. The nordic-phalian racial type is certainly fairly strongly present ... That is the result of the strong strain of German blood which the Polish population of this area have received through the Polonization (*Verpolung*) of the Germans ... On the other hand, the eastern Balt racial strain is present in the Polish population to a far greater degree than in the German population. Moreover, in addition to dinaric, *westisch* and *ostisch* strains, there are also some fairly primitive *ostisch* types about whom one must have grave doubts as to whether they can be regarded as identical to *homo alpinus* . . . There is in my view some justification . . . to term these groups 'Lapponoids'.

Equipped with such jargon, RuSHA experts known as 'integration assessors' (*Einigungsprüfer*) had to try to distinguish 'pure or predominantly nordic and phalian types, who are first class in terms of their genetic health and social efficiency' (Group I) from 'balanced crosses with a significant proportion of nordic, phalian or dinaric race, with a small addition of other European races who are satisfactory in terms of their genetic health and social efficiency' (Group II); 'crosses in which *westisch*, *ostisch* or east Baltic racial strains are predominant, but in whom elements of the nordic, phalian or dinarian race are still clearly visible and who are therefore considered to be just adequate as a balanced cross' (Group III+); 'crosses in which *westisch*, *ostisch* or east Baltic racial strains are predominant, in which however nordic, phalian or dinarian race are still faintly discernible' (Group III); 'racially pure *ostisch* and east Baltic types, unbalanced crosses of the European races' (Group IV); and finally 'racial crosses with non-European races and alien races'. By the end of 1943 this bizarre but potentially lethal exercise in racial categorization had largely been completed. Of the 9.5 million people in the incorporated territories, 370,000 were already Reich Germans, a further 353,000 were acknowledged as fully fledged ethnic Germans, 1.7 million were Poles who had satisfied the criteria for inclusion in Groups I and II (and hence automatically became Reich citizens) and 1.6 million were Poles in Group III (who could become citizens only on a case-by-case basis and even then remained subject to discrimination). The rest were either in the fourth category or 'asocial'. As 'protected members of the German Reich' they were likely to end up in concentration camps.

What these policies meant in practice can be illustrated once again with the example of Zamość. In all, as many as 30,000 children were removed from the Zamość area, of whom 4,454 were deemed 'racially valuable' enough to be sent to Germany. The majority were sent to concentration camps. On December 13 and December 16, 1942, transports containing 718 Poles from Zamość arrived at Auschwitz. All the children among them were killed by phenol injection as part of the Nazi doctor Josef Mengele's sadistic medical experiments. Two of his victims were the twin sisters Maria and Czeslawa Krajewski. They were just fifteen years old when they were murdered – for the 'crime' of being insufficiently Aryan.

## MORDOR

The war not only created new opportunities for Nazi racial policy abroad. It also permitted a radicalization within Germany. From 1933 until 1939, for example, the Gestapo had harassed the 832 Jews still living in the Rhineland town of Krefeld with increasing zeal. Though they accounted for less than one per cent of the population, they provided the Gestapo with one in ten of their cases before 1936 and one in three thereafter. In over two-fifths of cases, the individuals concerned were taken into 'protective custody' – which put them beyond the reach of what remained of the established legal system – and sent to concentration camps. Nevertheless, it was only after the outbreak of war that Krefeld's Jewish community could systematically be wiped out. By the summer of 1942, nearly all of them had been deported to their deaths, beginning with the first transport to the Łódź ghetto in October 1941. This escalation manifested itself throughout Germany, as anti-Jewish policy was increasingly implemented outside the regular judicial process. In November 1939, for example, a Jew accused of sexual offences against a German girl was simply shot by the police without reference to courts.

For Victor Klemperer, too, despite the partial protection of his mixed marriage, the coming of war meant an acceleration in the pace of his social exclusion. In 1940 he was forced to relinquish the home he had built in the village of Dölzchen and to move into a crowded 'Jews' House' in Dresden. He was banned from public parks. The following year he was imprisoned for a week for failing to observe blackout regulations. He was taxed into penury. He was even banned from smoking. From September 1941 he was obliged to wear the yellow star.* Each successive diminution in his rights as a citizen forced Klemperer to re-examine his attitude towards the country and culture he had once considered his own. As early as 1937 he had come to 'believe ever more strongly that Hitler really does embody the soul of the German people, that he really stands for "Germany" and that he will consequently maintain himself and justifiably maintain himself'. Five years later that feeling of alienation had intensified. Discrimination by now was starting to undermine Klemperer's health. While his wife trudged around in search of potatoes, he was forced despite his age and heart condition to clear snow from the streets and then to toil in a factory. His clothes and shoes were literally disintegrating. His living quarters had shrunk to little more than a cupboard. But these discomforts were as nothing compared with the fear – which constantly grew – of being searched, beaten, arrested, even murdered. 'I can no longer believe in the completely un-German character of National Socialism,' he reflected in June 1942, 'it is home-grown, a malignant growth out of German flesh, a strain of cancer.'

True, not all Germans were afflicted by this disease. In June 1943 Klemperer remarked in his diaries on the 'altogether comradely, easy-going, often really warm behaviour of the male and female workers towards the Jews . . . they are certainly not Jew-haters'. On several occasions he recorded how people (particularly middle-aged workers with Social Democrat or Communist backgrounds) signalled their sympathy, if only by shaking his hand and muttering encouragement. But such incidents were clearly outnumbered by occasions when perfect strangers abused him in the street. For example: 'A group of boys on bicycles, 14 or 15 years of age . . . overtake me: "He'll get shot in the back of the head . . . I'll pull the trigger . . . He'll be hanged on the gallows – stock exchange racketeer."' It is significant that the majority of these incidents involved young Germans – evidence, in Klemperer's

---

* The introduction of the star in Germany reopened the debate about the status of mixed marriages. It was decreed that the star would not be mandatory for '(a) a Jewish husband living in a mixed marriage if there are children born of this marriage who are not considered Jews. This also applies if the marriage is dissolved or if the only son was killed in the present war [and] (b) a Jewish wife in a childless mixed marriage for the duration of the marriage'.

eyes, of the effectiveness of Nazi propaganda in the schools and Hitler Youth. It is also evidence that ordinary Germans were well aware of the violence the regime was perpetrating against Jews, if not its precise nature.

It was not only Jews who fell victim to what has been called the Third Reich's 'cumulative radicalization'. As we have seen, the murder of mentally ill Germans had begun even before the outbreak of war with the *Aktion T-4* (see Chapter 7). The process was accelerated under wartime conditions; significantly, Hitler's personal order authorizing the 'euthanasia' policy was dated September 1, 1939. The case of the asylum in Hadamar, north-west of Frankfurt, makes it clear just how overtly the Nazi state was now capable of committing murder. Between January and August 1941 more than 10,000 people were put to death there in a specially constructed gas chamber in the cellar, most of them mental patients transported from other psychiatric hospitals. Although the policy was supposed to be secret, local people knew perfectly well what was being done. As the president of the higher state court in Frankfurt reported to the Reich Minister of Justice, 'even children call out when such transport cars pass: "There are some more to be gassed."' The smoke from the crematorium chimney was clearly visible hanging over the town. The personnel from the asylum were shunned by the local populace when they came to drink in local pubs after work. The Bishop of Limburg, in whose diocese Hadamar lay, followed Bishop Galen's lead in protesting at what was being done. He too noted the absence of secrecy. Local schoolchildren referred to the buses that brought patients to Hadamar as 'murder-boxes' and taunted one another by shouting: 'You're crazy; you'll be sent to the baking oven in Hadamar.' A particular source of local concern was that elderly people would be next: 'After the feeble-minded have been finished off,' local people were heard to say, 'the next useless eaters whose turn will come are the old people.' These complaints led to a suspension of the killings and the decommissioning of the gas chambers, but this proved to be only a tactical pause. Later in the war Hadamar once again became a slaughterhouse, though this time the victims were around 500 Poles and Russians, allegedly sufferers from tuberculosis. Because the smoke from the crematorium was seen as having precipitated the earlier protest, these victims of

Nazism were given lethal injections, or orally administered drug over-doses, and buried in the asylum grounds.

When it became necessary to suspend the 'euthanasia' campaign, its perpetrators lost little time in applying their techniques elsewhere. Concentration camps like Buchenwald were preferable to mental hospitals because they were located further from centres of population. (Buchenwald, surrounded by trees as the name suggests, was in the Ettersburg forest outside Weimar; it was invisible even from the nearby Ettersburg Castle.) By 1941 doctors like Friedrich Mennecke were routinely selecting prisoners there and in other camps as 'unworthy of life' purely on the grounds of their racial origins or 'asocial' behaviour. One such victim was Charlotte Capell, a forty-seven-year-old nurse from Breslau, who was condemned to death for 'persistent racial defilement' and 'hid[ing] her Jewish origin behind Catholicism [by hanging] a Christian cross around her neck'. Another was Christine Lehmann from Duisburg, who was sent to Auschwitz after being identified as a 'half-gypsy' (*Zigeunermischling*) and found guilty of 'asocial' and 'community endangering' behaviour, namely a 'marriage-like relationship' with a German man. Marlies Müller, an unmarried Jewish servant, was condemned to be gassed for 'continual racial defilement with German soldiers', compounded by her 'insolence and laziness' in the camp where she had been held after her arrest.

Such was the ethos of the new empire that was taking shape in Europe. It was based on an ideology not merely of racial hierarchy and segregation but of sweeping ethnic transformation, to be achieved by the systematic and unrestrained use of violence against civilians in conquered territory and at home. To be sure, all empires – and indeed most states of any size – involve some measure of violence and subjugation. To end the Iraqi insurgency of 1920, to take just one example, the British had relied on a combination of aerial bombardment and punitive village-burning expeditions. Indeed, they had contemplated using mustard gas too, though supplies had proved to be unavailable. Churchill, no faint heart in these matters, was shocked by the actions of some trigger-happy pilots and vengeful ground troops, just as he had been dismayed by the Amritsar Massacre in India the year before. As Churchill freely acknowledged, British rule in the Middle East and India rested ultimately on soldiers, guns and 'the whole apparatus of scientific war'. But he made it clear on numerous occasions that he regarded British power as being fundamentally constrained by the rule of law and the sovereignty of parliament. Mowing down civilians, as he put it, was 'not the British way of doing business'. As Macaulay had put it a century before, 'the most frightful of all spectacles [was] the strength of civilisation without its mercy'. In the face of the Quit India movement of 1942, to be sure, the British did not hesitate to use force, but this was in the face of a wave of riots, strikes, attacks on communications and other acts of sabotage.* The leaders of the nationalist Congress were jailed but they were not murdered, as they surely would have been had the Germans or the Japanese been running India. And it is worth noting that this took place after Sir Stafford Cripps† had explicitly proposed that after the war a self-governing India be set up within the British Commonwealth under an Indianized Executive Council acting as a British-style Cabinet, with an elected constituent assembly renegotiating the terms of the new Anglo-Indian relationship, up to and including the possibility of provincial non-accession to the Commonwealth (leaving the way open to independence for a Muslim Pakistan). The British aim, as Cripps said, was 'to give India full self-government at the earliest possible moment'.

Facile comparisons between British rule in India and Hitler's empire in Europe, or for that matter Stalin's Soviet Union, are sometimes drawn. Indeed, as we shall see, Hitler drew them himself (see Chapter 14). To be sure, the British had no illusions about their position in wartime India. 'For the duration of the war and probably for some time after,' wrote the Military Secretary of the India Office in 1943, 'India must be considered as an occupied and hostile country.' But there is a profound difference between, for example, the famine that struck India in 1943 and the systematic mass murder of civilians that was

---

* The scale of the Quit India revolt, which was condoned by the supposedly non-violent Gandhi ('I will prefer anarchy to the present system of administration'), is often forgotten. In all, more than 60,000 people were arrested. According to official statistics 1,028 people were killed and 3,125 seriously injured, though the total number shot dead may have been as high as 2,500. More than 300 railway stations were destroyed or severely damaged.

† During his pre-war Marxist phase, Cripps had been expelled from the Labour Party for proposing a 'Popular Front' with the British Communists. This recommended him to Churchill as a potentially effective ambassador in Moscow.

undertaken as a deliberate policy by the Nazis in Europe after 1939. It is undeniable that a combination of incompetence, complacency and indifference, tinged with resentment of the previous year's riots, ensured that the official response to the 1943 famine was woefully inadequate. Yet the famine began with a cyclone and the loss of imports from Japanese-occupied Burma, not with an order from Churchill to starve Bengalis. Hitler's imperialism, as we have seen, was quite different in character. As he had already explained to the Foreign Secretary Lord Halifax in 1937, his approach to the problem of Indian nationalism would have been to 'shoot Gandhi, and if that does not suffice to reduce them to submission, shoot a dozen leading members of Congress; and if that does not suffice, shoot 200 and so on until order is established'. Even Mussolini, whose imperialism was in some respects more old-fashioned than Hitler's, not only enthusiastically ordered the use of mustard gas in the conquest of Abyssinia but also bombarded his Viceroy there, Marshal Rodolfo Graziani, with instructions to shoot 'all rebels made prisoner', to 'finish off rebels' with gas and to 'initiate and systematically conduct [a] policy of terror and extermination against rebels and populations in complicity with them'.

Historians have sometimes represented the Nazi empire as if its extreme violence had an ultimately self-defeating character. This is not how it appeared at the time. From a British vantage point, the ruthlessness of German imperialism was at once appalling and deeply impressive. So enfeebled did their own colonial imperium seem by comparison that relatively few Englishmen consciously considered themselves to be fighting to preserve it. Rather, they imagined themselves fighting for an idealized England. On leave, Geoffrey Wellum, an eighteen-year-old Battle of Britain pilot, yearned to go away 'deep into the country and get lost, to the type of place I sometimes dream about, somewhere with sun-drenched water meadows and grazing cattle, hedges, meandering streams and so forth'. As he flew, he looked down on 'the rolling colourful countryside, English countryside, surely a green and pleasant land [with] small cars on small roads passing through small villages'. The difference in scale with the grandiose visions of the Nazis could scarcely have been more complete. J. R. R. Tolkien always denied that his *Lord of the Rings* trilogy, conceived during the First World War and largely written during the Second, was an allegory of contemporary events. Yet, as he conceded, it was certainly applicable to them. 'The Shire', with its thatched cottages, dappled sunlight and babbling brooks, was England precisely as she imagined herself in 1940 – not a mighty world empire, but an innocent rural backwater, albeit one acutely vulnerable to contamination from outside. Mordor was the totalitarian antithesis, a blasted industrial hell, 'bored and tunnelled by teeming broods of evil things', spewing forth monstrous hordes and devilish weaponry; a realm of slaves and of camps. Like Tolkien's hobbits, the English considered themselves the plucky little underdogs pitted against an all-knowing, all-powerful foe. *The Lord of the Rings* is a fairy story, in its author's own phrase, but one that was 'quickened to full life by war' – indeed, Tolkien himself also referred to the work as 'a history of the Great War of the Ring' and a homage 'to England; to my country'. It is a celebration of 'the indomitable courage of quite small people against impossible odds' – and in that respect a quite different kind of Ring saga from the Wagnerian version revered by Hitler.

The odds did indeed look well-nigh impossible. By the spring of 1941 the best encouragement Alan Brooke could give himself was that Hitler might abandon his efforts to defeat Britain and 'thrust into Russia' instead. Strikingly, however, in his diaries Brooke did not expect even this to give Britain much relief: 'Whatever the next thrust may be on the continent it is certain that the process of attempted strangulation will continue full blast with attacks on trade routes, Western Approaches, Western Ports and industry. If these attempts are sufficiently successful eventually invasion will be attempted.' He did not expect the Soviets to hold out against a German invasion for longer than '3 or 4 months'. Others in London put the likely duration of Russian resistance at three or four weeks; the expectation was that the Wehrmacht would go through the Red Army 'like a knife through butter'. Churchill himself expected that the Soviets would 'assuredly be defeated'. Those now seem excessively pessimistic judgements. Given the staggering negligence of the man running the Soviet Union, however, it was far from unreasonable. Empires, it has already been noted, rely on collaboration as much as on coercion. One of the supreme ironies of the Second World War was that in its first two years Hitler's empire found no more loyal collaborator than Josef Stalin.

# 12

# Through the Looking Glass

*[There are] two breeds of Bolshevism ... there is nothing to choose between the philosophies of Moscow and Berlin.*
Duff Cooper, August 23, 1939

*He had opened his morning newspaper on the headlines announcing the Russian-German alliance. News that shook the politicians and young poets of a dozen capital cities brought deep peace to one English heart ... Now, splendidly, everything had become clear. The enemy at last was plain in view, huge and hateful, all disguise cast off. It was the Modern Age in arms.* Evelyn Waugh, *Sword of Honour*

*Historically they are both an attempt to get away from an effete civilization which the countries we represent are trying desperately hard to cling to and to revivify. It is indeed a revolutionary war and we are on the side of the past – at the moment.* Sir Stafford Cripps, September 25, 1940

## PAN AND FIRE

Henryka Łappo was just twelve years old when she, her mother and her elder brother were deported from Ulanowka. It happened in the middle of the bitterly cold night of February 10, 1940:

Suddenly ... came the rapping at our door ... What offences had we committed? Where, what for and why did we have to leave our home and farm at this time and in such weather? . . . But the insistent 'quickly' spurred us into action and onto the sledges with our very sparse possessions which we had packed in just under an hour. Thus we moved off towards the station . . . Similar loads of families and bundles left from every house . . .

In the cattle trucks there huddled together grown-ups and children, men and women, friends and strangers. There was no means of washing or changing for the night, no food but, cold and hungry, we felt like animals caught in a trap, unsure what the next day would bring or when and where this journey would end for no-one knew our destination.

Their uncertainty was understandable. Although Poland had been invaded by Germany the previous year, Henryka and her fellow captives were not being deported on the orders of Hitler. They were being deported on the orders of his ally, Stalin, and they ended up in a one-room hut near the village of Ivaksha, in the benighted Soviet province of Arkhangel'sk.

Central Europe had a mirror-image quality after September 1939. For it had not only been Hitler who had ordered his troops to invade Poland. Under the terms of the Nazi-Soviet Pact signed in Moscow that August, Josef Stalin had done the same, on September 17. To conservatives like Duff Cooper or Evelyn Waugh, it seemed a moment of revelation, laying bare the essential identity of the two totalitarian systems, National Socialism and 'socialism in one country'. The signatories themselves appreciated the irony of their partnership. When he flew to Moscow to sign the pact, Ribbentrop had joked that Stalin would 'yet join the Anti-Comintern Pact', Hitler and Mussolini's anti-Communist alliance. Nevertheless, the partition of Poland did not produce exactly identical totalitarian twins. The Soviet zone of occupation was in many respects a mirror image of the German zone but, as with a true mirror image, right and left were transposed.

On September 18, several days after the Germans had taken the town, the 29th Light Tank Brigade of the Red Army rolled into Brest. They had seen little action since crossing the frontier, for the Poles had concentrated their efforts on resisting the invasion from the West. Indeed, most of the fighting was over by the time the Soviets arrived on the scene. The demarcation line between the two occupation zones was, under the terms of the Boundary and Friendship Treaty signed ten days later, to pass just to the west of the fortress. After an amicable joint parade, the Germans therefore withdrew back across the River Bug and the Russians took over. On the Soviet side of the line, thirteen million Poles – including 250,000 prisoners of war – were about to discover for themselves the distinctive charms of life in the workers' paradise.

The Germans and Soviets had pledged in their latest treaty 'to assure to the peoples living . . . in the former Polish state . . . a peaceful life in keeping with their national character'. Actions on the German side of the new border had already given the lie to those fine words. The Soviet approach was slightly different. At first, attempts were made to woo a sceptical local populace, many of whom remembered all too clearly the last Soviet invasion of 1920, when the Red Army had advanced as far as the Vistula. Soviet soldiers received as much as three months' salary in advance, with orders to spend it liberally in Polish villages. This honeymoon did not last long, however. Soviet officials lost no time in throwing Poles out of choice apartments in Brest and elsewhere, commandeering them without compensation. Meanwhile, Soviet promises of plentiful jobs in the Donbas region proved to be illusory. Worst of all, Poles soon came to know the Stalinist system of organized terror. 'There are three categories of people in the Soviet Union,' people were told: 'Those who have been in jail, those who are in jail, and those who will be in jail.' Soon Poles began to joke bleakly that the initials NKVD stood for *Nie wiadomo Kiedy Wroce do Domu* ('Impossible to tell when I will return home'). Incredibly, a substantial number of Polish Jews who had fled East at the outbreak of war sought to be repatriated to the German zone of occupation, not realizing that it was only *Volksdeutsche* who were wanted. This speaks volumes for their experience of nine months of Russian rule.

From Stalin's point of view, the Nazi vision of a Germanized western Poland, denuded of it social elites, seemed not menacing but completely familiar. Stalin had, after all, been waging war against the ethnic minorities of the Soviet Union for far longer and on a far larger scale than anything thus far attempted by Hitler. And he regarded few minorities with more suspicion than the Poles. Even before the outbreak of war, 10,000 ethnic Polish families living in the western border region of the Soviet Union had been deported. Now the entire

Polish population of the Soviet-occupied zone was at Stalin's mercy. Beginning on the night of February 10, 1940, the NKVD unleashed a campaign of terror against suspected 'anti-Soviet' elements. The targets identified in a set of instructions subsequently issued in November of the same year were 'those frequently travelling abroad, involved in overseas correspondence or coming into contact with representatives of foreign states; Esperantists; philatelists; those working with the Red Cross; refugees; smugglers; those expelled from the Communist Party; priests and active members of religious congregations; the nobility, landowners, wealthy merchants, bankers, industrialists, hotel [owners] and restaurant owners'. Like Hitler, in other words, Stalin wished to decapitate Polish society.

By the spring of 1940, around 14,700 Poles were being held in prisoner of war camps, of whom the majority were officers of the vanquished army. But there were also police officers, prison guards, intelligence personnel, government officials, landowners and priests. In addition, 10,685 Poles were being held in the western region of the Ukraine and Byelorussia, including not only ex-officers but also landowners, factory owners and government officials. At the suggestion of Lavrenty Beria, who had replaced Nikolai Yezhov as head of the NKVD in November 1938, Stalin ordered that these 'sworn enemies of Soviet authority full of hatred for the Soviet system' be tried by special tribunals. Their physical presence would not be required, nor would evidence need to be heard, since the verdicts had already been reached: death. In the forest of Katyn, near Smolensk, more than 4,000 of them were tied up, shot in the back of the head and buried in a mass grave, a crime the Soviets subsequently sought to blame on the Nazis. This was only one of a series of mass executions. All told, more than 20,000 Poles were killed. Further 'liquidations' followed, notably the emptying of the prisons of Lwów, Pińsk and other towns in the summer of 1941. Between September 1939 and June 1941 the Germans killed approximately 100,000 Jewish Poles and 20,889 non-Jewish Poles in their occupation zone; the NKVD came close to matching that body-count in just two operations. Yet these murders were only a part of Stalin's plan for Poland. By February 1940 the Soviet authorities were also ready to undertake the wholesale deportation of Poles they had been preparing since October.

The peace of Polish family life was shattered, without any preliminary announcement or warning, by a knock at the door, usually
just as dawn was breaking. Armed Soviet militiamen burst in, read
out a deportation order and gave those present as little as half an
hour to pack up whatever possessions the militia did not take for
themselves. These incursions were often accompanied by gratuitous
violence and vandalism. Janusz Bardach, a Jewish teenager in the
town of Włodzimierz-Wołyński, watched in amazement as one
NKVD man, evidently the worse for drink, smashed the mahogany
desk of the doctor he was arresting, shouting: 'Capitalist swine!
Motherfucking parasites! We need to find these bourgeois exploiters!'
One peasant woman described her own traumatized reaction:

He tells us to listen what he will read and he read[s] a mortal decree that in
half an hour we must be ready to leave, wagon will come . . . I immediately
went blind and I got to laugh terribly, NKVD man screams get dressed, I run
around the room and laugh . . . children are crying and begging me to pack
or there will be trouble, and I have lost my mind.

Once removed from their homes, the unfortunate captives were
then marched or driven in carts to the nearest railway station and
herded into cattle trucks, with sometimes as many as sixty or seventy
people in each. In the sub-zero winter temperatures many babies and
young children died before the trains had even departed. In four major
operations, between February 1940 and June 1941, around half a
million Polish civilians were rounded up in this fashion. Sometimes
the militiamen lied about where the victims were being sent, claiming
their destination was Germany or another part of Poland. In fact,
most were deported to the camps and collective farms of Siberia and
Kazakhstan, the most remote and least hospitable regions of the Soviet
Union. It seemed like a journey through purgatory to hell. 'We are
being carried through this endless space,' recalled Zofia Ptasnik, 'such
a flat and huge land with only a few scattered human settlements here
and there. Invariably, we see squalid mud huts with thatched roofs
and small windows, dirty and dilapidated, with no fences or trees.'
Many of the younger and older deportees did not survive to disembark
at their destination. For those who did, there was seldom anything
approaching adequate food or shelter. They died in their tens of

thousands of cold, hunger and disease. By 1942, according to some estimates, barely half the deportees were left alive.

Those who did not perish could only listen incredulously to the attempts by Soviet instructors to 're-educate' them. Antoni Ekart recalled how one camp lecturer 'address[ed] the prisoners on the nobility of putting all their effort into work. He would tell them that noble people are patriots, that all patriots love Soviet Russia, the best country in the world for the working man, that Soviet citizens are proud to belong to such a country, etc. etc. for two solid hours – all this to an audience whose very skins bore witness to the absurdity and the hypocrisy of such statements.' Elsewhere the language was harsher. A villager in Pałusza, who had seen his own neighbours carted off eastwards, was told:

This is how we annihilate the enemies of Soviet power. We will use the sieve until we retrieve all bourgeois and kulaks . . . You will never see again those that we have taken from you. They will disappear over there, like a field-mouse.

Not everyone was worse off under Soviet rule. The Jews of Grodno were positively relieved by the arrival of Soviet forces, since they shut-down the pogrom that had broken out when the Polish army capitulated to the Germans. Elsewhere, Jews welcomed Soviet rule as an improvement on the increasingly bigoted Polish regime of the post-Piłsudski era. In the village of Brańsk, which initially had been occupied by the Germans, some Jews welcomed the Red Army with flowers and banners. Many who found themselves on the German side of the demarcation line hastened across to the Soviet side, little realizing that some of their co-religionists were fleeing in the opposite direction. Only a minority were as unlucky as Julius Margolin, a visitor from Palestine, who moved from western Poland to Pińsk, but was arrested by the Soviets for not possessing the correct papers and sentenced to five long years in the Gulag. To many Jews, who had endured mounting persecution during the 1930s, Soviet rule was an opportunity. Many willingly joined the new institutions established to administer the Soviet zone. There was remarkably little resistance to the aggressive policy of secularization adopted by the Soviet authorities, which aimed 'to uproot religious beliefs and customs as well as Jewish nationalism'. Particularly in the eyes of many younger Polish Jews, this seemed a tolerable price to pay for being treated on an equal footing with Gentiles. In some areas, former Polish officials claimed they were told by local Jews: 'Your time has passed, a new epoch begins.'

The apparent affinity between the Soviets and the Jews would not be forgotten by Poles, who were quick to discern proof of the alleged affinity between Judaism and Bolshevism. 'The relations between the Poles and Jews are at present markedly worse than before the war,' noted one Polish observer in Stryj in June 1940. 'The entire Polish population adopted a negative attitude towards the Jews because of their blatant cooperation with the Bolsheviks and their hostility against the non-Jews . . . The people simply hate the Jews.' Memories of symbolic acts of betrayal lingered long after the war was over. One man remembered a Jewish boy whom he knew from school 'reaching for our white and red national flag and . . . ripping it in half, tearing the white part off the red one'. The boy told him, 'Your bloody Poland is finished.' A woman from Wilno recalled 'a Jew, with a red [arm]band, [taking] a sabre out of the sheath and read[ing] out "honour and fatherland"'. He laughed 'like mad', she recalled: 'Ha! Ha! They stood up for their fatherland with honour.' Such recollections were no doubt embellished with the passage of time. Nevertheless, they indicate the divisive effect of the Soviet rule on Poland's already fractured society. In other parts of the country, the Soviets gave preferential treatment to Ukrainians and Byelorussians. They deliberately encouraged Ukrainian violence against Poles with slogans like *Poliakam, panam, sobakam – sobachaia smert'!* ('To Poles, landowners and dogs – a dog's death!'). Ethnic divisions widened in a similar way when the Red Army occupied Lithuania in June 1940. Whereas Jews had played a minimal role in the public life of the country during its independence, two members of the Soviet-installed People's Government were Jews. When Lithuania was annexed by the Soviet Union, five members of the Supreme Soviet and two of the fifteen members of its Presidium were Jews, as were two members of the Council of Commissars and two of the nine Supreme Court justices.

Poland had been partitioned between German and Russian empires before, but never like this. Both Hitler and Stalin subjected the population to a horrific reign of terror. Their shared aim was quite simply to obliterate the political and cultural life of the Polish people for ever, so that Poland would cease to exist not merely as a place, but also as an idea. It would become simply a frying pan and a fire. Looking in the mirror that was occupied Poland, Stalin had good reason to believe he had met his match – a match made in Hell, perhaps, but one that had every reason to endure.

## TWO FACES OF TOTALITARIANISM

Their maltreatment of the Poles was only one of many ways in which the Nazi and Soviet regimes had grown to resemble one another. Not only was German National Socialism looking more and more like Soviet 'socialism in one country'. Hitler increasingly resembled a kind of apprentice Stalin, rather like some sort of junior devil.

When Iosif Dzhugashvili, the son of a Georgian shoemaker, looked at Adolf Schicklgruber, the son of an Austrian customs clerk, he seemed to see in the younger man a kindred spirit. As schoolboys, each had regarded the world with the same clenched-jawed defiance. Hitler was a failed artist, Stalin a dropout seminarian. Both men had been revolutionaries who had gone to jail under the regimes they had later overthrown. Both had come to power as members and then leaders of anti-capitalist workers' parties. Both worked erratically, favouring late nights and summer retreats (Stalin's equivalent of Obersalzberg was his villa at Sochi on the Black Sea). Both had difficulties with women. Hitler's niece Geli Raubal, on whom he had jealously doted, had shot herself in September 1931; Stalin's wife Nadezhda Alliluyeva had done the same thing just fourteen months later, also driven to suicide by the attentions of an obsessive older man – twenty-two years older in each case. Both girls were replaced by more robust types: the wholesome receptionist Eva, the plump housekeeper Vatcheka. Moreover, although ten years his junior, Hitler seemed be learning fast from Stalin's example just what it took to be a dictator. On the Night of the Long Knives he had shown that he too could purge his own party of potential rivals; Stalin was impressed. ('Did you hear what happened in Germany?' he remarked to Anastas Mikoyan. 'Some fellow that Hitler! Splendid! That's a deed of some skill!') In the SS and Gestapo Hitler had created a secret police system that looked and functioned a good deal like Stalin's NKVD. He had openly modelled his Four-Year Plan for the German economy on Stalin's Five-Year Plans, breaking with his Economics Minister Schacht to impose something more like a command system. Now, in Poland, Hitler was demonstrating a promising propensity for mass murder – though at this stage he still seemed unlikely to catch up with Stalin, who had already been responsible for at the very least six million deaths by the end of 1938.

The two regimes even looked the same. This had been obvious since the Paris World Exposition of 1937, when the Nazi and Soviet pavilions had confronted one another like totalitarian obelisks on the right bank of the River Seine. The German pavilion, designed by Hitler's pet architect, Albert Speer, was a 500-foot tower crowned with a giant eagle and swastika, surrounded by nine pillars decorated with gold mosaics and more swastikas. At its foot stood the sculptor Josef Thorak's *Comradeship*, two 22-foot-high nude supermen, hand in hand. The Soviet pavilion, by Boris Iofan, was an equally monolithic tower, supporting Vera Mukhina's stainless steel statue *Worker and Collective Farm Girl*. To be sure, the pavilions were not identical. The Germans sneered at the 'barbaric formalism' of the Soviet pavilion, while the Russians decried the 'sterile and false . . . fascist neoclassicism' of the Nazi pavilion. Nevertheless, as the Italian artist Gino Severini noticed, the exhibits had much in common – particularly 'their obvious intention of making size, making immense pompous size'. This was not accidental. According to Speer, while looking over the site before the Exposition he had 'stumbled into a room containing the secret sketch of the Soviet pavilion':

A sculpted pair of figures thirty-three feet tall, on a high platform, were striding towards the German pavilion. I therefore designed a cubic mass, also elevated on stout pillars, which seemed to be checking the onslaught, while from the cornice of my tower an eagle with a swastika in its claws looked down on the Russian sculptures.

The exhibits at the Exposition revealed to the world what had already been underway for some time – the extraordinary convergence of Nazi and Soviet iconography. The huge domed hall that was to be built in Hitler's transfigured capital, Germania, was in many ways a riposte to Iofan and Vladimir Shchuko's winning design for a Palace of Soviets in Moscow, the style of which, as Anatoly Lunacharsky put it, 'did not avoid classical motifs, but attempted to surpass classical architecture'. Both regimes erected shrines to their own pseudo-religions; both depicted their leaders as deities and national father-figures. In Soviet art, as in Nazi art, the same male archetypes were represented: the party martyr, the shock worker, the hero soldier. Franz Eichhorst's *Streetfighting* was virtually a replica of Aleksandr Deineka's earlier *Defence of Petrograd* (1927), just as Hermann Otto Hoyer's *SA Man Rescuing Wounded Comrade* (1933) owed a debt to Cosima Petrov-Bodkin's *Dying Commissar* (1928) and Arthur Kampf's *In the Steelworks* (1939) was almost indistinguishable from Nikolai Dorimidontov's *Steelworks* (1932). Equally common in both cultures was the figure of the peasant woman as fertility symbol, almost interchangeable in Leopold Schmutzler's *Farm Girls Returning Home* and Yevgeny Katzman's *Kaliazin Lacemakers* (1928). Even the 'enemy images' of Jews and 'Nepmen' (traders who were allowed to operate under the pre-Stalin New Economic Policy) had a suspiciously large amount in common, especially as the Stalinist regime moved in the direction of an official anti-Semitism in the 1940s. Both regimes offered boundless opportunities for a generation of conservatively inclined or merely opportunistic artists working in virtually all media to overthrow the modernists who had made so much of the running in the 1920s. To be sure, Hitler had railed against *Kunstbolschewismus* ('Bolshevik art') in *Mein Kampf*, asserting that 'the morbid excrescences of insane and degenerate men . . . under the collective concepts of Cubism and Dadaism [were] the official and recognised arts of [Bolshevized] states'. Yet the state-sponsored backlash against modernism was even then beginning in the Soviet Union. As early as 1926 Robert Pelshe, the editor of *Sovetskoe iskusstvo*, had railed against 'the mental disease of the "left" radicals . . . Futurism, Cubism, Expressionism, Verism, Dadaism, Suprematism, against foolishness and laziness, against careless indifference and doubt'. The Soviet decree 'On the Restructuring of Literary and Artistic Organizations' was passed in 1932, before Hitler had come to power in Germany. Even the institutions developed by Goebbels to impose central control on every branch of German culture bore a striking resemblance to those that had already been established under Stalin. So similar was Nazi art to Soviet art by the late 1930s that Stalin could legitimately have accused Hitler of plagiarism.

Of course, there were differences between Nazism and Communism, just as there were between Hitler and Stalin. Hitler was a demagogue, a man who could electrify an audience with his messianic rants; Stalin a bureaucrat, obsessively micro-managing everything from screw production to mass executions. Hitler had come to power by more or less democratic means, Stalin by machinations within the Communist *apparat*. Hitler took over one of the world's most advanced industrial societies; in 1938 the per capita GDP of the Soviet Union was less than half that of Germany. Hitler lacked Stalin's murderous paranoia; it was far safer to be a functionary at the court of the former. The aesthetics of the two regimes also diverged in a number of intriguing ways. German representations of the countryside tended to be self-consciously pre-modern, whereas Soviet rural scenes generally involved at least one tractor. There were many more nude women in Nazi art, whereas Soviet female figures were demurely clad in boiler suits or picturesque national costumes. The debts owed by Nazi art were to neo-classicism and romanticism; by contrast, the origins of Socialist Realism have been traced back to the Peredvizhniki (the Wanderers), whose members had seceded from the academic establishment in the 1860s. Apart from an aversion to modernism in nearly all its forms, the two dictators themselves had distinctly different tastes. Hitler was a Wagnerian, Stalin more or less cloth-eared, though he did enjoy Gluck's *Ivan Susanin* (especially the scene when the Poles are lured into a forest by a Russian and left there to freeze). Apart from Ziegler's *Four Elements* and Breker's bust of Wagner, Hitler's private apartments were largely adorned with nineteenth-century works. Stalin, by contrast, had nothing more than a few dog-eared Peredvizhniki prints pinned to the bedroom walls of his dacha.

Perhaps most crucially, one of the dictators showed no sign of being satisfied with the territory he had thus far acquired. If he meant what he had written in *Mein Kampf*, then Hitler's pact with Stalin could only be a temporary expedient. As the astute German diplomat Ulrich von Hassell put it, 'It is still an open question how far the [Nazi-Soviet] Pact is merely a dishonest expedient for both authoritarian regimes or how far it goes toward drawing the two countries close together on the basis of further nationalization of the Soviets and the bolshevisation of the Nazis.' Stalin regarded this question as closed. Far from fearing a future betrayal by Hitler, he exhorted his subordinates to give top priority to maintaining harmonious relations with his new best friend. Trade between the two totalitarian regimes flourished, with Soviet exports to Germany reaching heights not seen since 1930. Sometimes this trade is portrayed as if Stalin were simply giving Hitler raw materials in return for nothing. In reality, as Table 12.1 shows, Germany was also exporting substantial quantities of manufactures to the Soviet Union in 1940, principally machinery, precision instruments and electrical equipment, as well as 3.4 million tons of coal. Indeed, the volume of German exports to the Soviet Union exceeded the volume of imports from there. However, this was largely due to the bulk of the coal that went eastwards. In value terms, it was the Soviet Union that was running the trade surplus. This was unusual. For much of the inter-war period the Soviet Union had run a trade deficit with Germany, particularly in the period of the first Five-Year Plan, when imports of German machinery had surged. Not so in 1940. The Soviet Union supplied Germany with goods that had an aggregate value 76 per cent greater than the goods it was receiving. The lion's share was made up of agricultural raw materials (including timber and cotton), foodstuffs (mainly barley) and more than 600,000 tons of militarily vital oil. In addition, Stalin allowed the German navy to use the White Sea port of Murmansk for refuelling, and no effort was spared to facilitate German attacks on British shipping.

Hitler was happy to reassure him that all was well. According to some Russian sources, Hitler personally wrote to Stalin in December 1940 and May 1941, swearing on his 'honour as a chief of state' that the German troops massing in the German-occupied half of Poland were in fact preparing to invade England; they were in Poland simply to keep them out of range of British bombers. Hitler's only anxiety was that:

Table 12.1: The main components of Soviet–German trade, 1940

| | Exports to Germany | | | Imports from Germany | |
| | tons | 000 roubles | | tons | 000 roubles |
|---|---|---|---|---|---|
| Agricultural raw materials | 1,120,710 | 229,982 | Machines | 29,188 | 147,652 |
| Foodstuffs | 896,118 | 168,115 | Generating and electrical equipment | 4,233 | 8,917 |
| (of which: Barley | 732,536 | 137,622) | Instruments and appliances | 536 | 14,600 |
| Energy sources, minerals, metals | 801,430 | 122,366 | Energy sources, minerals, metals | 3,519,692 | 139,366 |
| (of which: Oil | 657,398 | 102,893) | (of which: Coal | 3,414,318 | 64,014) |
| Chemicals | 168,347 | 11,369 | Chemicals | 1,802 | 9,926 |
| TOTAL | 3,032,830 | 555,862 | TOTAL | 3,555,457 | 316,301 |

one of my generals might deliberately embark on . . . a conflict [with Soviet border forces] in order to save England from its fate . . . I ask you not to give in to any provocations that might emanate from those of my generals who might have forgotten their duty . . . And, it goes without saying, try not to give them any cause.

Stalin deserves his reputation as one of the most paranoid, untrusting individuals in modern history. The supreme irony is, as Aleksandr Solzhenitsyn once observed, the Soviet dictator only ever trusted one man. Unfortunately, that man was the most unscrupulous liar in history.

# PRELUDES

On April 20, 1939, Hitler received an extraordinary fiftieth birthday present from Martin Bormann, the man who would later become his private secretary and one of the most powerful figures in wartime Germany. Perched on top of the Kehlstein mountain, six thousand feet above the Nazi elite's Obersalzberg playground, the Eagle's Nest was a magnificent granite lodge built in the best *völkisch* style. Apart from its fireplace, a gift from Mussolini, and the carpet in the main hall, which had been sent to Hitler by the Emperor Hirohito, every part of it was of impeccably German origin. To get Hitler there, Fritz Todt – the builder of the *Autobahnen* and the Siegfried Line – had constructed a winding four-mile road up the mountainside, a remarkable feat of engineering in its own right, the more remarkable for having been partly built in the depths of the Alpine winter. A torch-lit pedestrian tunnel, more than 300 yards long, led to a sumptuous brass-panelled elevator, the shaft for which had been blasted out of the mountain's core. By these means the Führer was elevated to the literal pinnacle of his power. From here it seemed as if the whole of Europe lay prostrate beneath his famously piercing gaze. If the Nazi empire was Mordor, then this was Sauron's Tower.

Sadly for Bormann, Hitler hated it. The tunnel to the lift made him claustrophobic and the outlook from the top gave him vertigo. But in one respect the Eagle's Nest provided inspiration, in the form of its magnificent view of the mountain known as the Untersberg. Here, according to legend, lay slumbering the twelfth-century Hohenstaufen Emperor Frederick I: Friedrich Barbarossa. It seemed an appropriate name to give to the most ambitious military operation – and the most bloody act of betrayal – of the twentieth century.

Hitler had always intended to attack the Soviet Union. *Mein Kampf* made it clear that only here could the German *Volk* find the living space it needed. Austria, Czechoslovakia and Poland were mere appetizers for the Nazi empire. They could not supply sufficient agricultural land for the anticipated hordes of German settlers – nor, perhaps more importantly, the oil and other minerals essential to the German war machine. But, as Hitler put it in November 1936, he meant to 'get into the paternoster lift [only] at the right time'; invading Russia was never intended to be his first military move. Three years later he explained his priorities to Carl Burckhardt, the Swiss Commissioner to the League of Nations in Danzig: 'Everything that I undertake is directed against Russia. If those in the West are too stupid and too blind to understand this, then I shall be forced to come to an understanding with the Russians to beat the West, and then, after its defeat, turn with all my concerted force against the Soviet Union.'

Hitler also had at least two good military reasons for invading in the summer of 1941. First, the Red Army's poor performance in Poland and subsequently in Finland (which Stalin had invaded in

November 1939) had exposed how enfeebled the Soviet officer corps had been by Stalin's purges. The Red Army, Hitler and his military advisers agreed, would be easy meat for the Wehrmacht's tried and tested blitzkrieg tactics. Secondly, and crucially, Hitler had failed to win the Battle of Britain. However, he persuaded himself that British morale would be dealt a death-blow if the Soviet Union could now be put to the German sword. With Russia smashed, he had reasoned in July 1940, England's last hope would be extinguished.

There was another reason for fighting Stalin. The partition of Poland had been a generous deal from the Soviet point of view. Despite leaving nearly all the fighting to the Germans, the Soviets ended up with a slightly larger share of the Polish population. They also proceeded to acquire the Baltic states, which included territory coveted by proponents of German *Drang nach Osten* ('eastward drive') like the Estonian-born Alfred Rosenberg. In June 1940, following alleged 'acts of provocation', Estonia, Latvia and Lithuania were occupied by Soviet troops. As in eastern Poland, occupation was followed in short order by the arrest and deportation of tens of thousands of alleged 'counter-revolutionaries'. Stalin's attack on Finland was only one of several moves he had made further to extend the Soviet empire. In June 1940, in violation of the secret protocols of the Ribbentrop–Molotov pact, he unilaterally demanded that Romania cede to him Bessarabia and northern Bukovina, which included some of Romania's most productive agricultural land. This was land the Germans had been hoping would provide them with soya beans and other valuable imports; it was also home to substantial ethnic German communities, not least in the town of Cernaŭti (Czernowitz). The Soviet acquisition of this territory brought them to within 120 miles of the Ploeşti oilfields, a crucial source of fuel for the Wehrmacht. When the Soviets made it clear that they intended to extend a 'security guarantee' to Bulgaria, Hitler discerned fresh evidence that Stalin intended to pre-empt him in the Balkans. (In March 1941 Hitler had persuaded Bulgaria to join Romania and Hungary as new recruits to the Axis side.)

In July 1940 Hitler gave the initial order to prepare for an invasion of the Soviet Union; he confirmed that this was his intention at a meeting with his military chiefs held at the Berghof on July 31. On

December 18, 1940, he authorized Directive Number 21, the plan for Operation Barbarossa. Originally intended for the spring of 1941, the attack was postponed until June 22 to allow the Wehrmacht to secure the Balkans. This delay was Mussolini's fault. The Italian invasion of Greece, launched in October 1940, had gone disastrously wrong. By March 1941 the Greeks had successfully expelled the invaders and crossed the border into Albania, which had been occupied by Mussolini in 1939. Hitler had hoped to rectify the situation with a swift attack on the Greek rear, but this was dependent on being given transit rights across not only Bulgaria but also Yugoslavia. On March 25 the Regent Paul had agreed to join the Axis, but two days later he was overthrown in a military coup. This encouraged Hitler to broaden the scope of his planned offensive. On April 6 Yugoslavia was invaded; eight days later the government in Belgrade had to ask for an armistice. By now the Germans were sweeping into Greece, out-manoeuvring the Greeks and forcing another British expeditionary force to take to their heels. On April 30 the British evacuated the Peloponnese, retreating to Crete where British troops had been sent the previous October. Onwards the Germans swept; their airborne invasion of the island (May 20–31) forced yet another desperate British evacuation. This Balkan blitzkrieg cost Hitler precious time, yet it also seemed to furnish fresh proof of the irresistible might of German arms. Small wonder the British expected the Red Army to fold in a matter of weeks. They themselves had now done so not just once but three times: in France, in Greece and in Crete.

Just a few hours before the offensive against the Soviet Union was due to be unleashed, Hitler had invited Albert Speer into his private apartment in the Reich Chancellery in Berlin. Turning on his gramophone, he played Speer the bombastic fanfare from Liszt's *Les Préludes*. 'You'll hear that often in the near future,' Hitler told him, 'because it is going to be our victory fanfare for the Russian campaign ... How do you like it?' As if to reassure the architect that he too would benefit from this new undertaking, he added: 'We'll be getting our granite and marble from there, in any quantities we want.'

## MONKEY'S BET

The bloodiest divorce in history was not hard to foresee. So wide-spread was anticipation of the German attack that it reached even into the most sheltered retreats of British academic life. On June 16, 1941, six days before the Germans invaded the Soviet Union, Claude Hurst, Tutor in Physics at Jesus College, Oxford, made a bet with his geographer colleague J. N. L. 'Monkey' Baker, then a Flight Lieuten-ant in the RAF. The stake was 'one bottle of Port Wine', and the bet was 'that before noon GMT on July 1st 1941 German armed forces will have crossed the Russian frontier'. It was a bet the Physics Tutor won with eight days to spare. It is thus not too much to say that anyone but a monkey could have predicted Operation Barbarossa.

Hurst's bet was not an instance of astonishing clairvoyance, much less a lucky guess. Having cracked the German Enigma code, British intelligence was well informed about German troop movements in the months leading up to June 22. Churchill later made much of his hint to Stalin that Hitler was up to no good, though he left Stalin to draw the right inference from the information that three panzer divisions had been ordered to Poland following the Yugoslav Regent Paul's agreement to join the Axis. But Stalin had no need of a British tip-off. His own intelligence service had received numerous reports of an impending German attack. As early as May 1939 he was sent a six-page document entitled 'The Future Plans of Aggression by Fascist Germany', based on a German briefing obtained by Soviet spies in Warsaw. In December 1940 the Soviet agent Rudolf von Scheliha (codenamed Ariets) reported that Hitler planned to declare war on the Soviet Union 'in March 1941'. On February 28, 1941, the same agent was able to provide a provisional launch date of May 20. This intelligence was corroborated by sources in Bucharest, Budapest, Sofia and Rome, to say nothing of the famous spy Richard Sorge (code-named Ramsay) in Tokyo, who had it on especially good authority since he was the former lover of the German ambassador Eugen Ott's wife. On March 5 Sorge was able to send microfilm copies of German documents indicating that an attack was planned for mid-June. On May 15 he gave the date as June 20. Four days later he reported that

150 divisions were being readied by the Germans for a full-scale invasion. His sources, he assured Moscow, were '95 per cent certain' the attack would come 'in [the] latter part of June'. He reiterated the warning on June 20. The story was confirmed from sources in Germany and its Bohemian protectorate. On April 17, for example, a Prague informant predicted a German invasion 'in the second half of June'. The precise date and time of the invasion were revealed by a source in Berlin fully three days before the Germans attacked. On June 21 the Soviet ambassador in Berlin confirmed that the attack would happen the next morning. One estimate puts the total number of such warnings relayed to Moscow at eighty-four. It is, in short, impossible to fault Soviet intelligence-gathering in 1941. With sources planted in the German Economics Ministry, Air Ministry and Foreign Ministry, they knew all the essentials of Hitler's plan.

All of this Stalin ignored. Typically, he scrawled on the bottom of one Prague report: 'English provocation! Investigate!' On seeing yet more evidence of German intentions from a source inside the German Air Ministry, Stalin exploded: 'The "source" in the Staff of the German Air Force should be sent to his fucking mother! This is no source but a disinformer!' Sorge he dismissed as 'a little shit'. Even Marshal Semyon Timoshenko's warnings of the impending débâcle were crudely brushed aside: 'Timoshenko is a fine man, with a big head, but apparently a small brain ... If you're going to provoke the Germans on the frontier by moving troops there without our permission, then heads will roll, mark my words.' A German soldier who ventured across the frontier on June 21 to warn the Soviets what the next day would bring was shot on Stalin's orders. The problem was compounded by the fact that the entire Soviet intelligence service had, like the senior echelons of the Red Army itself, fallen victim to the purges, and was now largely staffed at the centre by inexperienced stooges whose sole concern was self-preservation. Receiving reports from agents in the field that did not fit in with Stalin's preconceived notions, the analysts doctored their contents before presenting them to him. Warnings of a German invasion plan thus mutated into evidence of Anglo-American efforts 'to worsen the relations between the USSR and Germany'.

The result was that far too little was done to prepare for the German assault. To be sure, some work had been done to modernize Russia's western defences, but the new fortifications were far from complete, while the old Stalin Line had been allowed to decay. Soviet armies in occupied Lithuania and eastern Poland were in highly exposed locations, with the exception of the garrison at Brest. Soviet planes were not camouflaged. Troops were not in defensive positions; indeed, they were ordered *not* to occupy such positions, for fear of provoking the Germans. Worse, Stalin responded to the gathering storm with yet another purge of suspected threats to his own authority. In June 1941 around 300 senior service personnel were arrested, among them no fewer than twenty-two bearers of the highest Soviet military decoration. On the very eve of destruction, Stalin still refused to issue a full-scale invasion warning to his border troops, telling his generals: 'It's too soon for such a directive. Perhaps the questions can still be settled peacefully.' It is hard to think what more he could have done to help Hitler, short of handing him the keys to the Kremlin on a silver salver.

## BARBAROSSA

Neatly bisecting the little town of Przemyśl, the River San marked the border between Nazi-occupied Poland and the Soviet sector. On the Soviet side, it seemed like just another quiet summer night. After all, the work of transporting suspect Poles to Siberia was all but complete. It was the same all along the frontier. The senior Russian officers at the frontier town of Novgorod-Volynsk were attending a concert. The commander of the Western Military District was at the theatre in Kiev. At Siemiatycze a dance was in full swing to which the local German officers had even been invited. They had politely declined, pleading a prior engagement.

The Russian troops in Brest had spent the day drilling to the sound of a military band. That night they got drunk. At midnight the regular Moscow–Berlin train rolled into the station. It was laden down with grain for Germany – part of the continuing boom in Nazi-Soviet trade. As dawn broke, the early morning coal train arrived from the other direction. Suddenly, as it drew to a halt, German machine-gunners leapt out. Immediately the Brest fortress was bombarded with a lethal rain of 5,000 shells per minute. Heinz Guderian – whose panzers had already fought their way to Brest two years before – was soon back at the fortress walls. But this time he had no intention of stopping there.

Operation Barbarossa was in many ways the supreme achievement of the art of blitzkrieg. The vast German invasion force comprised 153 divisions, 600,000 vehicles, 3,580 tanks, 7,184 artillery pieces and 2,740 planes – not forgetting 600,000 horses, since the operation far exceeded the Wehrmacht's motorized capabilities.* In the first phase, the Luftwaffe swept over all the Soviet airfields within flying range, destroying 890 aircraft by the late morning, almost as many aircraft as the British had lost to enemy action in the whole of the Battle of Britain. Most of them never even got off the ground. Along a front stretching for 930 miles, the German forces poured eastwards in three huge army groups led, as always, by their armoured divisions. The first and second groups were to strike through the Baltic states and the Ukraine and to converge on Leningrad and Moscow; the third was to head in the direction of Kiev. In a series of huge encircling manoeuvres, the Germans captured hundreds of thousands of Soviet troops who appeared to the invaders to be ill-prepared, ill-trained, ill-equipped and above all ill-led. By July 9, Army Group Centre, now well past Minsk, had captured 287,704 prisoners. It was a similar story at Białystok and Smolensk, though resistance at the latter was notably stiffer. By the end of August, the total number of Soviet captives stood at 872,000. The fall of Kiev in September added 665,000 more. The pincer movement that encircled Vyazma and Briansk added another 673,000. By the autumn more than three million men were captives. From the Russian point of view, it was the biggest military disaster in all history. German radio sets blared out Liszt's *Préludes* to the point of monotony.

When the first reports of the German invasion reached Stalin, he was at his dacha at Kuntsevo, twelve miles from the centre of Moscow, a building as modest as Hitler's Eagle's Nest was grandiose, even if it

---

* Out of the 153 divisions, there were 19 panzer divisions and just 15 of motorized infantry.

was significantly larger and more luxurious than the typical Muscovite's rural retreat. He was stunned. As his recently appointed Chief of Staff, Marshal Georgi Zhukov, recalled, when he phoned the news through Stalin was 'speechless . . . only his heavy breathing could be heard'. 'Did you understand what I said?' Zhukov asked. More silence. Finally, Stalin responded. 'Where's the Commissar?' he asked, meaning Molotov, the Commissar for Foreign Affairs and architect of the Nazi-Soviet Pact. When Zhukov came to the Kremlin a couple of hours later, Stalin was 'very pale . . . sitting at the table clutching a loaded unlit pipe in both hands'. 'Bewildered', he could only suggest that the attack was 'a provocation of the German officers'. 'Hitler surely does not know about it,' he insisted. When the news of the invasion was confirmed, 'Stalin sank back in his chair and fell into deep thought. A long heavy silence ensued.'

How could it be? How could Hitler, the one man he had trusted, the man with whom he had carved up Poland, have betrayed him? Though, in his usual paranoid way, Stalin had been toying with the idea of a pre-emptive strike against Germany, preparations for such a move had barely got off the drawing board – contrary to the myth that Stalin was himself on the brink of attacking Hitler.* Why had he got it so catastrophically wrong? Was he simply 'the most completely out-witted bungler of the Second World War', as Churchill later put it?

Stalin may, of course, have calculated that Hitler would never risk a two-front war (Germany's undoing in the First World War), particularly without a significant numerical advantage in manpower. He may also have ruled out invasion so late in the year as June 22, given the limited time that would remain before autumn rains turned the Russian roads into impassable bogs. If these were Stalin's rationales for complacency they at least had the merit of being right – in

---

* For this sensationalist hypothesis, see Viktor Suvorov, *Icebreaker* (1990) and Constantine Pleshakov, *Stalin's Folly* (2005). Suvorov's (wholly circumstantial) evidence was the destruction of defensive assets along the Soviet western frontier in 1940 and early 1941. The documents cited by Pleshakov – several drafts 'on the principles of the USSR's armed forces deployment' from 1940 and 1941 – show only that Stalin was contemplating a pre-emptive strike. They are mere sketches, without any of the sort of detailed operational planning the Germans had been working on since July 1940.

the end. Yet other, less intelligible considerations also seem to have influenced him. One possible interpretation is that his sincerely held Marxist beliefs inclined him to regard the British imperialists as his true enemies. Thus Churchill's attempt to warn Stalin of Hitler's intentions simply convinced Stalin that the British wanted to dupe him into war with Hitler, so that they could change sides and resume their anti-Communist policy. In just the same way, Stalin was certain that the Nazi Party Deputy Leader Rudolf Hess's madcap flight to Scotland on May 10, 1941,* was the prelude to an anti-Soviet Anglo-German peace. Evidence that has come to light more recently suggests that it was history rather than ideology that blinded Stalin to the danger he faced. Stalin was a man obsessed with the traditions of Russian diplomacy and strategy, as well as being fatally Machiavellian in his interpretations of other powers' policies. In the months before June 22 he constantly harked back to the Crimean War, convinced that Russia had as much to fear from a British strike against the Black Sea Straits as from Germany. 'Historically the danger has always come from there,' he explained to the Bulgarian General Secretary of the Communist International, Georgi Dimitrov, citing as examples 'the Crimean War [and] the capture of Sebastopol' as well as British support for the Whites during the civil war. Incredibly, when Barbarossa was launched, one of Stalin's first thoughts was to expect a simultaneous attack on Leningrad by the Royal Navy. All of these preconceptions meant that Stalin swallowed whole the *real* disinformation that was fed to him by the Germans. Thus did Hitler's psychopathic mendacity trump Stalin's pathological mistrust.

Stalin's policy of trusting Hitler was a calamitous blunder without equal in the history of the twentieth century. Eight days after the German invasion, on the afternoon of June 30, 1941, Molotov led a deputation from the Politburo to Stalin's dacha, where 'the boss' had

* Hess appears to have acted on his own initiative in the hope of brokering a separate peace with Britain on the eve of Barbarossa. He flew to Scotland apparently in the erroneous belief that the Duke of Hamilton – whom he had met at the 1936 Olympics – might be open to such an initiative. Hess parachuted from his Me 110, landing at Floors Farm near Eaglesham, on the bleak moors south-west of Glasgow. On hearing the news of Hess's capture, Churchill declared: 'Hess or no Hess, I am going to see the Marx Brothers.'

been skulking for nearly two days. Stalin seems to have feared that this was his comeuppance: 'Why have you come?' he muttered, as if expecting to be arrested. Instead, these inveterate underlings – who had survived the Great Terror only by their abject subservience to his will – cravenly invited him to return to the Kremlin to lead the Soviet war effort.

We can only speculate how the war might have turned out if they had dared to give the ultimate Nazi collaborator his just deserts.*

* Russians remain reluctant to acknowledge Stalin's gross negligence in 1941. In a poll conducted on the 50th anniversary of his death, the Russian Centre for Public Opinion found that 53 per cent of Russians still regard him as a 'great' leader. He was, a Russian pensioner told the BBC's Moscow correspondent, 'the father of the family, the person who took care of us'.

# 13

# Killers and Collaborators

*Most of you will know what it means when 100 bodies lie together, when there are 500 or when there are 1000. And to have seen this through, and . . . to have remained decent . . . is a page of glory never mentioned and never to be mentioned.*
Heinrich Himmler to SS Generals, 1943

*I kept thinking, 'You people know who we are – we are not foreigners; not so long ago we were your neighbours . . . I lived my whole life next to you, I went to school here and had the same education you did, and now you look at this as punishment I deserved.'*     Boris Kacel, Holocaust survivor

*It is an odd state of affairs that the 'Beasts' we have been fighting against are now living with us in closest harmony.*
Col. Helmuth Groscurth, Chief of Staff, XI Corps

## GENERAL PLAN EAST

It is a truth almost universally acknowledged that the attack on the Soviet Union was Hitler's fatal mistake. It was, to be sure, a huge military gamble. 'I feel', Hitler himself was heard to say, 'as if I am pushing open the door to a dark room never seen before, without knowing what lies behind the door.' Yet in many respects attacking Stalin strengthened the Third Reich. It had not been easy for Goebbels and his propaganda machine to reconcile the strongly anti-Communist

strain in National Socialism with the realpolitik of the Ribbentrop–
Molotov pact. Now that constraint was gone.

Albert Speer was not the only person Hitler sought to enthuse about
the invasion he had launched. In the middle of the night, Mussolini
was woken to receive a message from his German counterpart. 'Since
I have won through to this decision, I again feel inwardly free,' it read.
'At night I don't even disturb my servants,' grumbled Mussolini,
'but the Germans make me jump out of bed without the slightest
consideration.' Hitler himself did not go to bed until 2.30 a.m., declar-
ing: 'Before three months have passed, we shall witness a collapse in
Russia, the like of which has never been seen in history.' In Germany
itself, as Victor Klemperer noted in his diary, there was popular
enthusiasm for this new war, much more than there had been in 1939.
In a crowded Dresden restaurant, a tipsy commercial traveller told him:
'Now we know where we stand, we'll get it over with more quickly –
we're ready and armed.' Their waiter, a First World War veteran,
agreed: 'The war will come to an end more quickly now.' Returning
home past a ballroom full of 'cheerful faces', Klemperer was forced to
conclude: 'The Russian war is a source of pride for people.'

The occupation of Europe could now be reconfigured. Invasion of
the Soviet Union was represented as a 'crusade for Europe'; the entire
continent could unite in a 'European United Front against Bolshevism'. Just as the invasion of the European empires in Asia would allow
the Japanese to recast their own imperialism in terms of East Asian
'Co-Prosperity', so now the Germans could portray the European
*Grossraumwirtschaft* (literally, 'great space economy') as a German-
led bulwark against Bolshevism. Collaborators in occupied Europe
latched on to this new theme of propaganda with alacrity. On October
30, 1941, Marshal Pétain, the doddering figurehead of the Vichy
regime, vowed that France would flourish 'within the framework of
the constructive activity of a New European order'. Similar sentiments
were expressed in Belgium, Finland and elsewhere. The Nazis' European rhetoric struck a chord with all those conservatives for whom
German dominance seemed a lesser evil than Soviet Communism.
Only as the war in the East turned from blitzkrieg to attrition, and
the need supervened to wring every last penny out of the occupied
West, did the emptiness of this rhetoric gradually manifest itself.

For the peoples of Eastern Europe and the Soviet Union – some sixty million of whose citizens at some time or other came under Nazi occupation – a different but equally resonant note could now be struck. As an Estonian, Alfred Rosenberg well understood the visceral hostility felt by many East European peoples towards Stalin's Soviet Union, which had inflicted immense cruelties on them behind a façade of national self-determination. It was not only the (relatively few) ethnic Germans who welcomed the advancing Wehrmacht. German troops were fêted when they marched into Lwów and Riga. Ukrainian peasants saw the black crosses on the invaders' panzers as the insignia of a holy crusade against the Antichrist of Moscow. At Hrubieszów the people greeted the Germans with bread and salt. Rosenberg now envisaged not only a German protectorate over Lithuania, Latvia, Estonia and Byelorussia ('Baltica'), but also an expanded Ukraine, a Caucasian federation – perhaps even a Crimean Muftiate and a 'Pan-Turanic' bloc in Soviet Central Asia. Appeals were directed at ethnic minorities, notably the Chechens, Karachai and Balkars, in the hope of stripping away all Russia's imperial possessions, to leave nothing more than a rump Muscovy. In truth, neither Hitler nor Goebbels had ever sincerely believed in harnessing the power of East European nationalism.* A far truer indication of Nazi intentions were the various versions of the 'General Plan East' (*Generalplan Ost*) devised to extend German settlement as far as Archangel in the north and Astrakhan in the south (the so-called A-A Line). One draft, by SS *Oberführer* Professor Konrad Meyer, proposed establishing three vast 'marcher settlements' ('Ingermanland', 'Memel-Narew' and 'Gothengau') with around five million German settlers. A rival scheme drawn

---

* Goebbels noted in his diary for March 16, 1942: 'Nationalistic currents are increasingly observable in all former Baltic states. The populations there apparently imagined that the German Wehrmacht would shed its blood to set up new governments in these midget states . . . This is a childish, naïve bit of imagination which makes no impression on us . . . National Socialism is much more cold-blooded and much more realistic in all these questions. It does only what is useful for its own people, and in this instance the interest of our people undoubtedly lies in the rigorous establishment of a German order within this area without paying any attention to the claims . . . of the small nationalities living there.' Hitler, as we have seen, wanted Ukrainians to be like Indians in his imagined British Empire: docile, uneducated consumers of brightly coloured textiles made in Germany.

up by the Reich Main Security Office envisaged twice as many settlers and the expulsion of an estimated forty-five million of the existing inhabitants. In fact, as was punctiliously pointed out by Erhard Wetzel, the racial expert in Rosenberg's Ministry, this estimate included between five and six million Jews and failed to take into account high Slavic birth rates, so that the total unwanted population would be closer to fifty or even fifty-seven million, assuming that 15 per cent of Poles, 25 per cent of Ruthenians and 35 per cent of Ukrainians would need to be retained as agricultural labourers, the rest being deported to Siberia. The Russian population would wither away through the use of contraception, abortion and sterilization. The Jews would be exterminated.

## WAR OF EXTERMINATION

To achieve an ethnographic transformation on this scale, a new kind of war had to be waged. From the outset Hitler had determined that his campaign against the Soviet Union would be fought according to new rules – or rather, without rules at all. It was to be, as he had told his generals on March 30, 'a war of extermination' in which the idea of 'soldierly comradeship' would have no place. This meant the 'destruction of the Bolshevik commissars and the Communist intelligentsia'. The decision systematically to shoot certain Red Army prisoners, foreshadowed by the brutal way the war in Poland had been fought, was taken on the eve of Operation Barbarossa and subsequently elaborated on during the campaign. The 'Guidelines for the Conduct of Troops in Russia' issued on May 19, 1941 called for 'ruthless and vigorous measures against the Bolshevik inciters, guerrillas, saboteurs [and] Jews'. The 'Commissar Order' of June 6 required any captured political commissars to be shot out of hand. The justification for this was that

hate-inspired, cruel, and inhumane treatment of prisoners can be expected on the part of *all grades of political commissars* ... To act in accordance with international rules of war is wrong and endangers both our own security and the rapid pacification of conquered territory ... Political commissars have initiated barbaric, Asiatic methods of warfare. Consequently they will be dealt with *immediately* and with maximum severity. As a matter of principle, they will be shot at once.

The Wehrmacht High Command reiterated this by decreeing that the army was to 'get rid of all those elements among the prisoners of war considered Bolshevik driving forces'; this meant handing them over to the SS *Einsatzgruppen* for execution. 'Politically intolerable and suspicious elements, commissars and agitators' were to be treated in the same way, according to an order issued by the Army Quartermaster-General Eduard Wagner. In September 1941 the High Command issued a further order that any Soviet troops who had been overrun but then reorganized themselves should be regarded as partisans and shot on the spot. Such orders were passed on by front-line commanders in less euphemistic terms. Troops were 'totally to eliminate any active or passive resistance' among prisoners by making '*immediate* use of weapons'. General Erich Hoepner, the commander of Panzer Group 4, took his orders to mean that 'every military action must be guided in planning and execution by an iron will to exterminate the enemy mercilessly and totally . . . no adherents of the present Russian-Bolshevik system are to be spared.' The commander of the 12th Infantry Division told subordinate officers: 'Prisoners behind the front-line . . . Shoot as a general principle! Every soldier shoots any Russian found behind the front-line who has not been taken prisoner in battle.' In the confusion that reigned after the huge German advances into Soviet territory, this could be interpreted as a licence to kill almost anyone.

Nazi propaganda deliberately encouraged lawless violence. In issuing instructions to the Propaganda Ministry in July 1941, for example, Hitler emphasized the need for 'shots of Russian cruelty towards German prisoners to be incorporated in the newsreel so that the Germans know exactly what the enemy is like. He specifically requested that such atrocities should include genitals being cut off and the placing of hand grenades in the trousers of prisoners.' The results were as Hitler had intended: the 'great racial war' became a war to the death. In the first weeks of Barbarossa, the Germans may have summarily executed as many as 600,000 prisoners; by the end of the first winter of the campaign some two million were dead. Some were killed on the spot because German troops refused to accept their surrender. The recollections of one German soldier give a flavour of the attitudes that quickly took hold:

Sometimes one or two prisoners might emerge from their hideout with their hands in the air, and each time the same tragedy repeated itself. Kraus killed four of them on the lieutenant's orders; the Sudeten two; Group 17, nine. Young Lindberg, who had been in a state of panic ever since the beginning of the offensive, and who had been either weeping in terror or laughing in hope, took Kraus's machine gun and shoved two Bolsheviks into a shell hole. The two wretched victims . . . kept imploring his mercy . . . But Lindberg, in a paroxysm of uncontrollable rage, kept firing until they were quiet . . .

We were mad with harassment and exhaustion . . . We were forbidden to take prisoners . . . We knew that the Russians didn't take any . . . [that] it was either them or us, which is why my friend Hals and I threw grenades . . . at some Russians who were trying to wave a white flag.

Elsewhere Soviet prisoners were taken but then lined up and shot. Those who were spared found themselves herded into improvised camps where they were given neither shelter nor sustenance. Many starved or died of disease; others were taken out and shot in batches. Some were transported to concentration camps like Buchenwald, where they were shot in the course of fake medical examinations, or to the death camp at Auschwitz. Altogether in the course of the war over three million Soviet soldiers died in captivity – substantially more than half and perhaps close to two-thirds of the total number taken prisoner, a mortality rate more than ten times higher than that for Russian prisoners in the First World War. Once again, living space turned out to mean killing space.

As in Poland, the killing was directed not only against captured combatants but also against certain civilians. To be precise, anyone identified as a partisan was liable to be killed. The process whereby 'partisan' became a blanket term including Jews, Gypsies and anyone else the Germans felt inclined to kill is not easily traced in written records. We have seen that the war against Communism was always, in Hitler's mind, a war against the Jews. The surprising thing is how many ordinary Germans seem to have understood from the outset that this was an integral part of Operation Barbarossa. On the eve of the invasion, for example, the commander of Order Police Battalion 309 told his men that Jews, regardless of age or sex, were to be destroyed. Within days they were putting his words into effect in Białystok, herding five hundred men, women and children into a synagogue and burning them alive. Just a few weeks after the invasion, it was becoming clear that the Jews were to be totally eradicated.

The Nazis estimated that there were nearly 5.5 million Jews* living in the former Soviet territory they occupied by the end of 1941, as many as in all the rest of occupied Europe. The success of Operation Barbarossa put the Germans in complete control of the entirety of the old Tsarist Pale of Settlement, from the Baltic to the Black Sea. Hitler was never wholly precise about what should be done with the Jews; he spoke merely of taking 'all necessary measures', of 'eradicating whatever puts itself against us' and of 'shooting anyone who even looks sideways at us'. 'If there were no more Jews in Europe,' he explained to the Croatian Commander-in-Chief Slavko Kvaternik on July 22, 1941, 'then the unity of the European states would no longer be destroyed.' But 'if even just one state for whatever reasons tolerates one Jewish family in it, then this will become the bacillus source for a new decomposition'. At this time, Madagascar was still being mentioned as a possible post-war destination. However, Adolf Eichmann, who had devised the Reich Main Security Office's Madagascar Project, now entrusted his subordinate Friedrich Suhr with a new brief: the 'Final solution of the Jewish question'. On July 31 Heydrich obtained Göring's authorization to make 'all necessary preparations' for a 'total solution of the Jewish question in the German sphere of influence in Europe' and to draw up a 'comprehensive' draft plan. It seems unlikely that he would have sought Göring's approval if all this had meant was more deportations and more ghettos. It also seems

---

* Significantly, the guidelines issued by the Reich Security Main Office for the 'treatment of the Jewish question in the occupied territories of the USSR' introduced a new and wider definition than had hitherto been used in the Reich: 'A Jew is anyone who is or has been a member of the Jewish religion or otherwise declares himself to be a Jew or has done so or whose membership of the Jewish race is apparent from other circumstances. Anyone who has one parent who is a Jew within the meaning of the previous sentence is regarded as a Jew.'

significant that not long after this the commander of *Einsatzgruppe* A, Franz Walter Stahlecker, referred to orders relating to the treatment of the Jews 'from a higher authority to the Security Police which cannot be discussed in writing'. Stahlecker was arguing against the creation of new ghettos in former Soviet territory and in favour of 'an almost 100 per cent immediate cleansing of the entire Ostland of Jews'. Such arguments dovetailed neatly with the pressure from other parts of the Nazi empire – France, Serbia and the Reich itself – to deport 'their' Jews eastwards, so that they too might be subsumed in the projected 'final solution', as well as the reluctance of the authorities in Poland to accept a new influx of Jews to their ghettos. Thus the genocidal concept would seem to have crystallized in the last week of September and the first weeks of October 1941, at the very zenith of Hitler's fortunes, with Kiev in his hands, Leningrad besieged and the onslaught on Moscow poised to begin. He unveiled his intentions at a meeting of senior party functionaries in Berlin on December 12. The order – 'liquidate them', in Hans Frank's words – was swiftly relayed down the chain of command.

## PERPETRATORS

Who were the perpetrators of what came to be known as the Holocaust? In the wake of the invasion of the Soviet Union the first phase of systematic killing was carried out by four roving *Einsatzgruppen*, as had happened in Poland.* By the end of July 1941 they had murdered around 63,000 men, woman and children, 90 per cent of whom were Jews. By mid-April 1942, the *Einsatzgruppen* had already killed precisely 518,388 people; again, the vast majority were Jews.

---

* *Einsatzgruppe* A massacred Jews in Kovno, Riga and Vilna, to name just three locations. *Einsatzgruppe* B operated in Byelorussia and the area west of Smolensk, killing Jews in Grodno, Minsk, Brest, Slonim, Gomel and Mogilev. *Einsatzgruppe* C ranged from eastern Poland into the Ukraine, carrying out mass murders in Lwów, Tarnopol, Kharkov and Kiev. *Einsatzgruppe* D was active in the southern Ukraine and the Crimea, especially in Nikolaiev, Kherson, Simferopol and Sebastopol. It will be seen that the role of the *Einsatzgruppe* was essentially to obliterate the historic Pale of Jewish Settlement.

Predominantly this was a war against the Jews, waged behind the lines as a kind of counterpoint to the real war against the Red Army. Other groups were equally at risk, however, notably Gypsies and mental patients, and such was the scale of the diabolical undertaking that it could not possibly be carried out by the *Einsatzgruppen* alone. From an early stage, therefore, other less specialized formations became involved, including not only Wehrmacht units but also regular police battalions.

As dawn broke on July 13, 1942, Reserve Battalion 101 arrived at the Polish village of Józefów, which had been bombed by the Germans and briefly occupied by the Russians two years previously. Their commander, Major Wilhelm Trapp, explained to his men that their orders were to round up the local Jews, of whom there were around 1,800. They were to pick out the able-bodied young men who could be used as forced labourers or 'work Jews'; there were around 300 of these. Using trucks, they would then drive the rest – the sick, the elderly, the women and the children – to a quarry in the nearby forest. There they would shoot them all.

Reserve Battalion 101 was not a hardened group of Nazi fanatics. Most of its 486 men came from working-class and lower middle-class neighbourhoods of Hamburg. On average, they were older than the men in front-line units. Over half were aged between thirty-seven and forty-two. Very few were members of the Nazi Party, though Trapp had joined in 1932. They were, without a doubt, just ordinary Germans. They were also willing executioners. Often, after the war, those accused of war crimes claimed that they were merely following orders. That was not the case at Józefów. Before the killings began, Trapp made an extraordinary offer to his battalion: if anyone did not feel up to the task that lay before them, he could step forward and be assigned to other duties. Only twelve men did so.

Killing people is harder than it looks in the cinema, which is the closest most of these middle-aged policemen had previously come to murder. The standard procedure was to get the victims to kneel down in rows, then to shoot each one individually through the nape of the neck. Despite instructions from the battalion physician on where exactly to point their weapons, the men were soon spattered with blood, bone splinters and brains. As one of them later recalled, 'Through the point-blank range shot that was ... required, the bullet struck the head of the victim at such a trajectory that often the entire skull or at least the entire ... skullcap was torn off.' Once the shooting began, several more soldiers asked to be relieved of their duties. Later, a number of others broke down and could not continue. But the majority pressed on with their dirty work. By midday they were being offered bottles of vodka to 'refresh' them. This evidently helped. The killing continued throughout the afternoon and evening. It took seventeen hours in all. The bodies of the victims were left unburied, a sign of the amateurishness of the operation. (*Einsatzgruppen* knew to get their victims to dig a pit before shooting them on the edge of it so that they fell in neat rows, the dying on top of the dead and half-dead; burial would suffocate any chance survivors.) Finally, at about 9 o'clock that night, the weary battalion returned to the village. The marketplace was deserted except for the piles of luggage belonging to the victims, which the soldiers proceeded to burn. In the grotesquely euphemistic language of the Third Reich, Józefów was now *Judenrein* – 'cleansed of Jews'.

The men of Reserve Battalion 101 were beginners. But practice makes perfect. Between the summer of 1942 and the autumn of 1943 they and other mobile police units were responsible for shooting approximately 38,000 Jews and deporting a further 45,000, most of them to the Treblinka extermination camp. By the end of 1943 the Germans had killed around 2.7 million Soviet Jews, nearly half the pre-Barbarossa population.

Why did they do it? One view is that they, like most Germans, were imbued with a virulent brand of anti-Semitism that needed only the right opportunity to manifest itself in murder. Certainly, some of the letters that soldiers wrote home indicate that they had thoroughly internalized Hitler's message that, to quote one lance-corporal, 'Only a Jew can be a Bolshevik, for this blood-sucker there can be nothing nicer than to be a Bolshevik.' Another described to his parents how he and his comrades had killed a thousand Jews in Tarnopol 'with clubs and spades', having found sixty mutilated German corpses nearby; the Jews could be held responsible, since they had occupied 'all the leadership positions' under the Soviet regime 'and, together with the Soviets, had a regular public festival while executing the Germans and Ukrainians'. How deeply rooted such notions were in

German culture and how far they were mere products of post-1933 indoctrination is debatable. Even Victor Klemperer could not be sure of this, sometimes believing that National Socialism was a 'home-grown ... strain of cancer' and at other times dismissing 'the idea that all Germans, including the workers, are without exception anti-Semites' as a 'nonsensical thesis'. Another interpretation, based in large measure on post-war testimony, is that these 'ordinary men' were well aware that what they were doing was wrong, but suppressed their qualms because of a mixture of deference to authority (shirking might damage chances of promotion or leave) and peer-group pressure.

Nevertheless, we should not forget the obvious impulse of self-preservation. Though far smaller than those they inflicted, the casualties suffered by the German forces in the first phase of Operation Barbarossa were in fact much heavier than in any of Hitler's earlier campaigns. In July 1942, the month of the Józefów massacre, the total number of German soldiers killed or missing in action was just under 40,000 and it rose to more than 60,000 the following month. In the midst of a full-scale war, killing Jews was a soft option compared with front-line duties. Old men, women and children could, after all, be relied on not to shoot back. When the SS Cavalry Brigade swept through the Pripet Marshes in August 1941, slaughtering 14,000 mostly Jewish civilians, their total casualties numbered just two, both killed when they drove over a stray landmine. That same month the 1st SS Brigade shot 44,125 people, mostly Jews, in the vicinity of Kamenets, having been explicitly ordered by Himmler to spare only 'working Jews'. Again, no one fought back. It was not until the Warsaw ghetto uprising of April–May 1943 that the Germans encountered any serious resistance from Jewish populations.

Just how easy the task of mass murder could become is chillingly clear from a German eyewitness account of the mass execution of 500 Jews at Dubno in the Ukraine in 1942:

The people who had got off the lorries – men, women and children of all ages – had to undress on the orders of an SS man who was carrying a riding or dog whip in his hand. They had to place their clothing in separate piles for shoes, clothing and underwear. I saw a pile of shoes containing approximately 800–1,000 pairs, and great heaps of underwear and clothing ...

I can still remember how a girl, slender and dark, pointed at herself as she went past me saying 'twenty-three'.

I walked round the mound and stood in front of the huge grave. The bodies were lying so tightly packed together that only their heads showed, from almost all of which blood ran down over their shoulders. Some were still moving. Others raised their hands and turned their heads to show they were still alive. The ditch was already three quarters full. I estimate that it already held about a thousand bodies. I turned my eyes towards the man doing the shooting. He was an SS man: he sat, legs swinging, on the edge of the ditch. He had an automatic rifle resting in his knees and was smoking a cigarette. The people, completely naked, climbed down steps which had been cut into the clay wall of the ditch, stumbled over the heads of those lying there and stopped at the spot indicated by the SS man. They lay down on top of the dead or wounded: some stroked those still living and spoke quietly to them. Then I heard a series of rifle shots . . . I was surprised not to be ordered away, but I noticed three postmen in uniform standing nearby. Then the next batch came.

By this time stripping the victims had become standard practice. The motivation was as much prurience as parsimony; a desire to degrade and humiliate those who were about to die, as well as to ogle the younger women. Indeed, as this account makes clear, there was something consciously spectacular about these monstrous crimes. There were voyeurs as well as perpetrators; some even took photographs.

Some men – like police secretary Walter Mattner from Vienna – were able to rationalize shooting women and children by the hundred. 'When the first truckload arrived,' he wrote to his wife from Mogilev in Byelorussia in October 1941, 'my hand was slightly trembling when shooting, but one gets used to this. When the tenth load arrived I was already aiming more calmly and shot securely at the many women, children, and infants. Considering that I too have two infants at home, with whom these hordes would do the same, if not ten times worse. The death we gave to them was a nice, quick death compared with the hellish torture of thousands upon thousands in the dungeons of the GPU. Infants were flying in a wide circle through the air and we shot them down still in flight, before they fell into the pit and into the water. Let's get rid of this scum that tossed all of Europe into the war and is still agitating in America ... After our return home, then it will be the turn of our Jews.' Not everyone was so utterly devoid of human feeling. Only gradually did the SS come to realize that steps should be taken to conceal what was being done – and to find a more efficient, and less demoralizing, mode of murder. Himmler himself did not much relish the sight of the one mass execution he witnessed, at Minsk in August 1941. Was there no third way, preferable both to mass shootings and to starvation or epidemics in the ghettos, which were becoming impossibly crowded as the first transports of Jews began to arrive from Western Europe?

As early as July 16, 1941 *Sturmbannführer* Rolf Heinz Hoppner wrote to Eichmann asking whether the use of 'a quick-acting agent' would not be 'the most humane solution to dispose of the Jews, insofar as they are not capable of work'. The answer had, as we have seen, already been pioneered in the mental asylums of Germany. In September 1941, following the example of the T-4 'euthanasia' programme, 500 mental patients were gassed at Mogilev. Three months later, at Chelmno, specially designed vans with exhaust pipes connected to sealed rear compartments were used for the first time to asphyxiate Jewish prisoners. The first and only industrialized genocide had begun.

## NEIGHBOURS

The executioners at Józefów knew few, if any, of their victims personally. They were in a war zone, in an unfamiliar landscape, killing alien people. But 150 miles to the north, the Jews of Jedwabne – who had accounted for over 60 per cent of that town's population of just over 2,000 in 1931 – were killed by their very own neighbours, people they had lived alongside all their lives.

On the morning of July 10, 1941, eight Germans came to Jedwabne and met with the town authorities, including the mayor, Marian Karolak. The Germans argued that at least one Jewish family from each profession should be left alive, but a local Polish carpenter replied: 'We have enough of our own craftsmen, we have to destroy all the Jews, none should stay alive.' The mayor and other Poles present agreed. According to the testimony of Szmul Wasersztajn, one of the few Jewish survivors, what followed was a full-scale pogrom: 'Beards of old Jews were burned, newborn babies were killed at their mothers' breasts, people were beaten murderously and forced to sing and dance. In the end they proceeded to the main action – the burning.' The Jews were herded into the barn of the town baker, Bronislaw Sleszynski, and incinerated. This was not the work of a few local ruffians, but of roughly half the male Polish population, led by respectable notables like Karolak and Sleszynski. Any Jews who tried to escape were hunted down in the surrounding fields – again, by their own neighbours. The few Germans present confined themselves to taking photographs. In the words of historian Jan Gross, 'Everybody who was in town on this day, and in possession of a sense of sight, smell, or hearing, either participated in or witnessed the tormented deaths of the Jews of Jedwabne.' Only a handful of people acted to save their fellow citizens. Stanislaw Ramotowski helped his future wife Rachela Finkelsztejn to hide. Antonina Wyrzykowska kept seven Jews hidden in her house, among them Szmul Wasersztajn, with whom she had an affair. The father of Leszek Dziedzic also helped Wasersztajn to survive the war. It is notable that two out of these three were sexually involved with at least one of the people they saved, underlining the degree of intimacy that had previously existed between Jews and Christians in Jedwabne.

What happened there was by no means unique. In Józefów, too, some local Poles had helped the Germans to round up the town's Jews. The same happened in the village of Radzilow, where the Poles prevented their Jewish neighbours from fleeing, as well as in Oleksin. In Kraków some Poles eagerly joined in the German-led looting of Jewish stores and public beatings of Jews, and readily seized the opportunity to acquire Jewish property at bargain-basement prices. It is simply not credible to attribute all such violence to active German encouragement. Nor was this phenomenon peculiarly Polish. In Lwów in July 1941, Jews were massacred by Ukrainians on the ground that they had collaborated with the NKVD. There were similar though smaller-scale reprisals in Kremets. In other Ukrainian towns like Stanyslaviv, Tarnopol, Skalat and Kosiv, local people initiated pogroms, digging mass graves for their victims without any need for German direction. In the Latvian capital, Riga, there was a ferocious pogrom on the night of July 1, directed not by the Germans but by local Thunder Cross members. Boris Kacel, who had grown up in a 'middle-class neighbourhood' of the city where 'the various ethnic groups . . . were friendly to each other' was astonished by what he witnessed:

The Latvians expressed their hatred of the Jews through physical acts and angry words. They accused the Jews of being Communists and blamed them for all the ills to which they had been subjected during Soviet rule. In my wildest dreams, I could never have imagined the hidden animosity the Latvians had for their Jewish neighbours. Trucks arrived carrying small vigilante groups of ten to fifteen armed Latvians, who wore armbands in their national colours of red, white, and red. These men intended to kidnap Jews off the street and take away their personal belongings. The prisoners were then forcibly loaded onto the trucks, taken to the woods, and killed. It was terrifying to go outside, as one had to be aware of the vigilante groups that drove around the streets. The mobile killing squads . . . were in full command of the city, and nobody challenged their presence or their unconscionable killings. I did not expect such a severe assault; after all, the Jews had lived with the Latvians for many years. The two groups had always tolerated each other and had lived together in a friendly, harmonious atmosphere . . . The greatest tragedy was that these crimes were committed not by strange, invading forces, but by local Latvians, who knew their victims by their first names . . . The Jews soon had to seek German protection from the vicious Latvian hordes.

Similar scenes were played out in Latgale and Daugavpils, where more than a thousand Jews were murdered before a single German had materialized. One German observer described what he saw in Latvia as 'monstrous'. There was little difference to the south in Lithuania, where nationalist underground posters proclaimed 'the fateful and final hour . . . to settle our account with the Jews'. In Kaunas, German soldiers merely stood and watched as locals beat Jews to death in the streets. Between half and two-thirds of the Jews there were killed not by Germans but by other Lithuanians. In Borisov, across the border in Byelorussia, it was drunken policemen who rounded up, stripped and shot the Jews. In parts of Romania, too, the

Jews were killed before the Germans had even arrived. On the night of January 21, 1941, ninety-three Jews were stripped naked and shot in the Jilava forest, near Bucharest; others were slaughtered at the Stralueti abattoir, their bodies hung on meat hooks with labels reading 'Kosher Meat'. Five months later 4,000 Jews were killed in Iasi in a week-long orgy of violence witnessed by Curzio Malaparte, correspondent for the *Corriere della Sera*:

Hordes of Jews pursued by soldiers and maddened civilians armed with knives and crowbars fled along the streets; groups of policemen smashed in house doors with their rifle butts; windows opened suddenly and screaming dishevelled women in nightgowns appeared with their arms raised in the air; some threw themselves from windows and their faces hit the asphalt with a dull thud. Squads of soldiers hurled hand grenades through the little windows level with the street into the cellars where many people had vainly sought safety; some soldiers dropped to their knees to look at the results of the explosions within the cellars and turned laughing faces to their companions. Where the slaughter had been the heaviest the feet slipped in blood; everywhere the hysterical and ferocious toil of the program filled the houses and streets with shot, and weeping, with terrible screams and cruel laughter.

Far from disappearing after Corneliu Codreanu's execution (see Chapter 7), the Iron Guard had grown in power; indeed, after the overthrow of the monarchy, General Ion Antonescu had appointed Codreanu's successor, Horia Sima, as his Vice-Premier and proclaimed a 'National Legionary State'. As loyal allies, Romanian troops were also responsible for some of the worst anti-Semitic violence after the invasion of the Soviet Union, notably in Odessa. Some Hungarians also betrayed their Jewish neighbours, if only by denouncing them once the Germans had occupied their country.

In short, while the 'final solution' was unmistakably German in design, it is impossible to overlook the enthusiasm with which many other European peoples joined in the killing. Nor did the anti-Semitic violence of the early 1940s come as a bolt from the blue. It had been prefigured by the escalating persecutions of the 1930s. It did not take much to move some Poles from prejudice to discrimination to violent exclusion and finally, as in Jedwabne, extermination. Yet the point about Jedwabne is that it is simply an extreme, and now well-documented, case of a Europe-wide phenomenon. Collaborators could be found not only in countries that allied themselves with Germany – Italy, Romania, Hungary and Bulgaria – but also in Norway, Denmark, Holland, Belgium, France, Yugoslavia, Greece and the Soviet Union, countries the Germans invaded and occupied. Some were undoubtedly motivated by a hatred of the Jews as violent as that felt by the Nazi leadership. Others were actuated by envy or base greed, seizing the opportunity afforded by German rule to steal their neighbours' property. Self-preservation also played its part. There were even Jewish collaborators, like the uniformed men of the Office to Combat Usury and Profiteering who policed the Warsaw ghetto, or the leaders of the various Jews' Councils who helped organize the liquidation of the ghettos, or the concentration camp prisoners who accepted a measure of delegated authority in the (usually vain) hope of saving themselves.

The experience of Jedwabne typifies the way German rule also fomented civil war. It was as if even the approach of German troops encouraged conflict to erupt in multi-ethnic communities. Poles were not the only killers, Jews not the only victims. Germans themselves could fall victim to this kind of violence. Between four and five thousand ethnic Germans were murdered in Poland in September 1939 as Poles took revenge for their country's invasion. They then retaliated by forming 'self-protection' groups, which were ultimately subordinated to SS leadership. By the time that had happened, however, these groups had already massacred more than four thousand Poles. As a philologist, Victor Klemperer was struck by the way the Nazis delighted in euphemistic neologisms like *Volkstumskampf* (ethnic conflict) and *Flurbereinigung* (fundamental cleansing). This daily subversion of the German language, he believed, was far more effective than the more overt kinds of propaganda. Sanitized language also made the cycle of ethnic violence easier to live with.

The Ukraine was perhaps the most blood-soaked place of all. In Volhynia and Eastern Galicia, members of the Organization of Ukrainian Nationalists (OUN), egged on by the Germans, massacred between 60,000 and 80,000 Poles. Whole villages were wiped out, men beaten to death, women raped and mutilated, babies bayoneted. In the Polish village of Leonowka, Dominik Tarnawski was shot by

Ukrainians but managed to escape; his family was not so fortunate. His friend Tadeusz Piotrowski describes their fate:

First, they raped his wife. Then, they proceeded to execute her by tying her up to a nearby tree and cutting off her breasts. As she hung there bleeding to death, they began to hurl her two-year-old son against the house wall repeatedly until his spirit left his body. Finally, they shot her two daughters. When their bloody deeds were done and all had perished, they threw the bodies into a deep well in front of the house. Then, they set the house ablaze.

This was not an isolated atrocity. Waldemar Lotnik, a Polish teenager who escaped from a German labour camp and joined a Polish 'Peasant Battalion', was just about to rape a girl when he realized he knew her family and remembered her as a child. As another Pole recalled, 'Stories abounded of Polish mothers being held by the Ukrainian Nationalists and forced to watch as their families were dismembered piece by piece; of pregnant women being eviscerated; of vivisected pregnant women having cats sewn into their bleeding abdomens; of Ukrainian husbands murdering their own Polish wives; of Ukrainian wives murdering their own Polish husbands; of Ukrainian fathers murdering their own sons in order to prevent them from murdering their own Polish mothers; of sons of Polish-Ukrainian heritage being sawn in half because, the Nationalists said, they were half Polish; of children being strung up on household fences; of helpless infants being dashed against buildings or hurled into burning houses.' Here was ethnic conflict not merely between neighbours, but within families. The internecine war in the Ukraine only grew more ferocious as the war progressed, with some Ukrainians fighting for the Axis, some for the Allies and others for an independent Ukraine.

In the Balkans, too, there were multiple civil wars along ethnic, religious and ideological lines. Yugoslavia had fallen apart in the wake of the German invasion of April 1941. Seizing the moment, the Croatian leader Ante Pavelić had pledged to side with Hitler. In the ensuing chaos, his Ustašas waged a brutal campaign of ethnic cleansing against their Serbian neighbours in Croatia and Bosnia-Hercegovina, torturing and killing hundreds of thousands of them. The populations of entire villages were packed into their churches and burned to death, or were transported to be murdered at camps like

Jasenovac. Serbian Četniks and Partisans repaid these crimes in kind. Of the million or so people who died in Yugoslavia during the war, most were killed by other Yugoslavs. This included nearly all of Bosnia's 14,000 Jews. In Greece the German occupation was the cue for bitter conflict. There, as in Yugoslavia, a three-cornered war raged – between the foreign invaders and nationalists, but also between nationalists and indigenous Communists. When Bulgaria annexed southern Dobruja from Romania, tens of thousands of people were expelled from their homes on either side of the new border.

Most empires purport to bring peace and order. They may divide in order to rule, but they generally rule in pursuit of stability. The Nazi empire divided the peoples of Europe as it ruled them – though, ironically, the divisions that opened up in Central and Eastern Europe generally had as much to do with religion as with race (most obviously in the conflicts between Poles and Ukrainians or between Croats and Serbs). But the 'skilful utilization of inter-ethnic rivalry' the Germans consciously practised did not lead (in the words of one German officer) to the 'total political and economic pacification' of occupied territory. On the contrary, in many places their rule soon degenerated into little more than the sponsorship of local feuds; the institutionalization of civil war as a mode of governance.

## HITLER'S MELTING POT

There was, it must be said, an irony in all of this. For the more the Germans relied on foreign allies and collaborators the more multi-ethnic their empire necessarily became.

The first symptom of this unintended transformation was the changing complexion of Hitler's armed forces. The army that invaded the Soviet Union included 600,000 Croats, Finns, Romanians, Hungarians, Italians, Slovaks and Spaniards. In addition to fighting alongside troops from allied countries, German soldiers also increasingly saw foreigners wearing German uniforms. Franco had declined to join Hitler's war in the West, but he permitted the formation of a Spanish 'Blue Division' (named after the blue shirts of its Falangist volunteers) to fight against the Soviet Union; it served with distinction between October 1941 and December 1943, when it was reduced to a rump 'Legion' to maintain the credibility of Spanish neutrality. French volunteers also fought, in the *Légion des Volontaires Français contre le Bolchevisme*, as part of a Wehrmacht infantry division. Other foreigners generally wore the uniform of the Waffen-SS, the combat arm of the SS, a reflection of Himmler's enthusiasm for broadening the available pool of 'Nordic' blood, as well as the Wehrmacht's reluctance to surrender large numbers of Germans of military age to the SS.

Formally, some of these foreigners were not supposed to be foreign at all; they were *Volksdeutsche*, like the 17,000 Croatian Germans recruited or conscripted into the Prinz Eugen division, the 1,300 Danish Germans who volunteered to serve in the Wiking division and the Hungarian Germans who served in the Horst Wessel and Maria Theresa divisions. Residents of Alsace, Lorraine or Luxembourg who could claim two or more German grandparents were also offered Reich citizenship if they joined the Waffen-SS. From an early stage, however, non-Germans were also recruited, beginning with Dutchmen, Belgian Flemings, Danes and Norwegians in the summer of 1940. These nations were supposedly 'Germanic' or 'Nordic' in character, though there were also Waffen-SS recruits from Latin countries, notably Belgian Walloons. In all, these West European countries produced at most 117,000 men, not counting the tiny British Free Corps, made up of around fifty prisoners of war. Recruiting proved easier in Eastern Europe. May 1941 saw the formation of a Finnish legion, which proved to be a highly effective fighting force, followed by Latvian and Estonian divisions. The Waffen-SS also accepted Ukrainians, Slovaks and Croats. With every passing month after Stalingrad, the criteria for Waffen-SS membership grew more elastic, forcing Himmler to cite the multinational structure of the old Habsburg army as a precedent. Ukrainians were recruited; so were Hungarians, Bulgarians and Serbs. In February 1943 the first of three divisions was formed of Bosnian and Albanian Muslims, who wore fezes decorated with SS runes and were led in their prayers by regimental imams notionally under the supervision of the Grand Mufti of Jerusalem. Out of all forty-seven Waffen-SS divisions, twenty were formed wholly or partly out of non-German recruits or conscripts and a further five out of *Volks-*

*deutsche*. Towards the end of the war, in fact, there were more non-Germans than Germans serving in Himmler's army. At a meeting with the Chief of Staff of the Latvian Legion, Himmler himself offered a rationale for this seeming paradox:

Every SS officer, regardless of nationality ... must look to the whole living space of the family of German nations [Himmler specified the German, Dutch, Flemish, Anglo-Saxon, Scandinavian and Baltic nations]. To combine all these nations into one big family is the most important task at present. It is natural in this process that the German nation, as the largest and strongest, must assume the leading role. [But] this unification has to take place on the principle of equality ... [Later] this family ... has to take on the mission to include all Roman nations, and then the Slavic nations, because they, too, are of the white race. It is only through unification of the white race that Western culture can be saved from the danger of the yellow race. At the present time, the Waffen-SS is leading in this respect because its organization is based on equality. The Waffen-SS comprises not only German, Roman and Slavic but even Islamic units ... fighting in close togetherness.

Also fighting on the German side as auxiliaries – usually known as 'Hiwis' (short for *Hilfswillige*, literally 'those willing to help') or *Osttruppen* – were a variety of different groups from the occupied Soviet Union: not only ethnic Germans from 'Transnistria', the Romanian-occupied area between the lower reaches of the rivers Dnestr and Bug, but also Ukrainians. Six months after the launch of Operation Barbarossa, six new national legions were formed from former Soviet peoples identified as racially and politically reliable: Armenians, Azeris, Georgians, North Caucasians, Turkestanis and Volga Tatars. By late 1942 there were fifteen battalions of such troops; by early 1943 an additional six had been created. Don and Kuban Cossack defectors and deserters were also employed, not only on the Eastern Front but also in the Balkans and even in France. At Stalingrad, Paulus's 6th Army had around 50,000 such auxiliaries attached to its front-line divisions, over a quarter of its total strength, rising to around a half in the case of the 71st and 76th infantry divisions. When the 6th Army was encircled, between 11 and 22 per cent of those still fighting were non-German. After Stalingrad as many as 160 battalions of Soviet PoWs fought on the German side, numbering as many as a million men. 'Does this mean you will kill your own people?' one group of these unfortunates was asked. 'What can we do?' they replied. 'If we run back to the Russians, we would be treated as traitors. And if we refuse to fight, we'll be shot by the Germans.' As this suggests, most of those Soviet citizens who fought for the Germans were non-Russians.* But even some ethnic Russians were, after much debate, permitted to bear arms on the German side. Various anti-Soviet forces had in fact sprung into being in the immediate aftermath of Barbarossa, including a Russian National Army of Liberation and the Russian People's National Army, though the Germans had been very reluctant to legitimize such spontaneous organizations. Only in the final stages of the war did they sanction the creation of a Committee for the Liberation of the Peoples of Russia and an anti-Communist Russian Liberation Army under General Andrey Andreyevich Vlasov, who had been taken prisoner by the Germans in July 1942 after an unsuccessful bid to raise the siege of Leningrad. Though sent to the front in March 1945, Vlasov's army saw action only briefly before refusing to follow German orders and joining Czech nationalists in Prague in their revolt against the SS.

Meanwhile, running counter to all the grandiose plans for German colonization of foreign living space, the insatiable demand for labour of the Third Reich's military-industrial complex and the conscription of a rising share of able-bodied Germans into the armed forces meant that Germany itself began to be 'colonized' by foreign workers. The number in the Reich rose from 301,000 in 1939 (less than 1 per cent of all employees) to around two million in the autumn of 1940, to more than seven million by 1944 – nearly a fifth of the workforce. They came from all over Europe, some voluntarily, others under duress: from Belgium, Denmark, France, Holland and Italy; from Hungary and Yugoslavia too. At first, it was skilled workers from Western Europe who were attracted by the rapidly growing German economy; the men who built the road to the Eagle's Nest were in fact Italian stonemasons, willing beneficiaries of Hitler's boom. As the war

---

* One estimate puts the total towards the end of the war at around 647,000, of whom around a third were from the Ukraine, 17 per cent apiece from the Caucasus and Turkestan and 12 per cent from the Baltic states. Some 11 per cent were Cossacks, 5 per cent were Tatars, 2 per cent Kalmyks and 2 per cent Byelorussians.

wore on, however, it was Poles who came to predominate. Few of them came of their own volition. Already in September 1941 there were more than a million Poles working in the Reich, accounting for just under half the total foreign workforce. By July 1943 around 1.3 million workers, not including prisoners of war, had been sent to the Reich from the Government-General. There were soon more Poles in Germany than Germans in Poland. After 1941 they were joined by comparable numbers of Ukrainians and other former Soviet citizens. Many of these were women; in the autumn of 1943, there were 1.7 million female foreign workers employed in the Reich, most of them from occupied Polish or Soviet territory. Here was a headache for a regime that aspired to Germanizing Europe – an ethnographic Euro-peanization of Germany, a process in conflict at once with their own racial theory and with the sentiments of ordinary Germans.

## THE DEFILED EMPIRE

One unintended consequence of all this was that, even as Nazi racial experts engaged in the laborious racial classification of Poles and Czechs, the very tendency they wished to eradicate – miscegenation – was continuing. Indeed, the chaos caused by war and forced resettle-ment positively increased the sexual contact between Germans and non-Germans. On March 8, 1940, new police regulations had to be issued for Polish workers in Germany, the seventh of which specified bluntly that 'anyone who has sexual intercourse with a German man or woman, or approaches them in any other improper manner' would be liable to the death penalty (later specified as death by hanging). If a Polish woman became pregnant by a German, the pregnancy would be compulsorily terminated. The only qualification was that, as in the annexed territories, RuSHA assessors had the option of rec-ommending a convicted Pole for Germanization if he or she fulfilled the requisite racial criteria. Beginning in late 1940, 'prohibited contact with foreigners and prisoners of war' became a criminal offence; this applied not just to sexual relations but to almost any kind of intimacy, including giving foreigners food, drink or tobacco. A special Reich Law of May 1943, 'concerning Protected Membership of the German

Reich', imposed further limits on Polish workers' sexual freedom: in addition to facing execution if they had sexual relations with German women, they were not to marry until they were aged twenty-eight in the case of men or twenty-five in the case of women, and their choice of spouse was confined to Poles not eligible for Germanization. As with the 'racial defilement' legislation, these measures were implemented. As early as August 1940 a seventeen-year-old Polish farm worker was publicly hanged for having sex with a German woman who was actually a prostitute. In the first half of 1942 a total of 530 out of 1,146 death sentences handed out by regular courts were passed against Poles, including ten for sex with German women and forty-seven for 'moral offences'. Under an RSHA decree of August 1940, British and French prisoners of war caught *in flagrante* with German women were also supposed to be sentenced to death, though in practice they were generally given up to three years' imprisonment. German men convicted of sleeping with Polish women faced up to three months in a concentration camp. Steps were also taken against German women who had relations with 'foreign workers'. A Krupp factory girl was sentenced to fifteen months in jail for an illicit liaison with a French PoW. In some cases, transgressors were publicly humiliated (by having their hair shaved off) or even sent to concentration camps like Ravensbrück (where they were known as 'bed politicals').

Such measures evidently enjoyed at least some popular support. Nevertheless, an SD report from January 1942 makes it clear that, in the eyes of the more radical Nazis, they were ineffective as a deterrent:

Reports from every part of the Reich [specific complaints were appended from Potsdam, Bielefeld, Bayreuth, Chemnitz, Halle and Leipzig] reveal that the deployment of millions of foreign workers has resulted in a steady increase in sexual relations with German women. This fact has had a not inconsiderable effect upon the mood of the people. Today influential circles estimate the number of illegitimate children German women have had by foreigners as being at least 20,000. The threat of infiltration of German blood becomes ever greater due to the conscription for military service of many millions of German men, the absence of a general prohibition on sexual intercourse for foreigners, and the increasing number of foreign workers . . . In the case of women of German blood, one is often dealing with the less valuable part of the German population. These are often women with pronounced sexuality, who find foreigners interesting and therefore make it easy for the latter to approach them.

Despite attempts to confine foreign workers to specially created brothels, staffed by strictly non-German prostitutes, the problem persisted. In September 1943 the Propaganda Ministry found it necessary to remind German citizens: 'Every act of sexual intercourse [with a foreigner] is a defilement of the German people and an act of treason against them, and will be harshly punished by law.' The RuSHA was reduced to vetting the hundreds of illegitimate children of Polish and Soviet workers for signs that their fathers were of 'good racial stock'; those who did not make the grade were packed off to special 'nursing' homes, where mortality rates were predictably high. There was grave anxiety that the growing number of 'foreign children' in Germany 'would ultimately lead to a total blurring of the absolutely necessary distinction that must be maintained between Germans and *Fremdvölkische* [racial aliens]'.

The problem was predictably even more serious in the occupied territories of what had once been Poland. As early as October 27, 1939, the German police chief of Thorn (Toruń) in West Prussia had to issue special orders 'to curb the insolent behaviour of a section of the Polish population' which included the following:

7. Anyone molesting or accosting a German woman or girl will receive exemplary punishment . . .
8. Polish women who accost or molest Germans will be confined to brothels.

The idea that the initiative for such 'insolence' came from the Polish side was, of course, a fiction. As one Dr Krieg lamented in the ethnic German journal *Volksdeutsche Heimkehr*:

We must elevate the German people to be a master race . . . You can see that time and time again in the Protectorate the Germans either 'crack the whip' or 'ingratiate themselves with the Czech women'. Let this be changed. Let the German people be taught to keep a certain distance from the Pole. Polish PoWs who are working for German farmers are not to be treated as one of the family and German women are not to fraternize with Poles. Every time German nationals mix with Poles our standards sink.

In the Warthegau, too, Greiser felt obliged to issue orders decreeing that:

Any individuals belonging to the German community who maintain relations with Poles which go beyond those deriving from the performance of services or economic considerations will be placed in protective custody. In serious cases, especially when an individual belonging to the German community has seriously injured the ethnic interests of the Reich through relations with Poles, *he will be transferred to a concentration camp* ... Members of the German community who enter into physical relations with Poles will be placed in protective custody.

Such initiatives had Himmler's backing; as he put it, 'there was no more of a connection [between Germans and Poles] than between us and the negroes'; Polish men who had sexual relations with German women were to be hanged. But here the Nazis were fighting a losing battle. Indeed, Greiser's own suggestion that 'Poles of the female sex who permit physical relations with members of the German community may be sent to a brothel' amounted to an admission that racially illicit sex could not be prevented. Typical of the way social reality forced the ideologues to adapt was the decision by the Chief of the Race Office of the RuSHA in February 1942 to issue SS racial assessors and RuSHA branch officials with specimen forms for determining whether or not any Pole found guilty of 'racial defilement' could be considered 'eligible for Germanization'. Further east, in the occupied Soviet Union, no serious attempt was made to prevent German military personnel from forming sexual relations with racially unsuitable partners. Oskar Dirlewanger, commander of an SS brigade entirely composed of convicted criminals like himself, was one of many transgressors in Lublin, murdering Jews by day and sleeping with one by night. Stories were legion of the debauchery that prevailed there and in Lwów.

The concentration camps were, of course, intended to provide definitive solutions to the problem of racial pollution. Before the 'final solution' was decided on, Himmler encouraged Nazi doctors to look for 'a cheap and rapid method of sterilization which could be used on enemies of the German Reich such as Russians, Poles and Jews'. As his personal secretary Rudolf Brandt later explained: 'The hope was that in this way one could not only conquer the enemy but also destroy him. The labour power of those who were sterilized could be utilized by Germany, while their procreative capabilities would be destroyed.' Professor Carl Clauberg conducted experiments involving blocking the uteruses of Auschwitz prisoners with injections of irritant fluid. Dr Horst Schumann attempted to achieve the same results with large doses of X-rays on both men and women. Yet even in the camps, members of the supposed master race were unable to resist the temptations of interracial sexual relationships. There was a camp brothel at Buchenwald where SS officers sexually exploited female prisoners. Rudolf Höss kept a Jewish mistress while he was commander at Auschwitz, as did Amon Goeth at Płaszów.

Hitler's Empire was thus inherently incapable of becoming the racially hierarchical utopia envisaged in the *Generalplan Ost*. The more the Nazis sought to appeal to Pan-European or anti-Soviet sentiment among the peoples they had conquered, the more they relied on collaborators to help them with the bloody business of genocide and the more they had to wage total war in pursuit of their monstrous Aryan paradise, the more ethnic mingling went on. Nor was this phenomenon unique to Nazi imperialism. Remarkably, given the superficial differences between the Germans and their Far Eastern allies, the Japanese Empire in Asia evinced precisely the same contradictory tendencies. There too the empire-builders conceived of conquering living space and settling it with thoroughbred settlers who would preserve their racial purity as they went forth and multiplied. There too it was possible to exploit local disenchantment with existing – and, as it turned out, much weaker – imperial regimes. Yet there too the need for collaborators and slave workers militated against the original vision of a racially ordered empire. Like the Nazi *Grossraumwirtschaft*, the Japanese 'Co-Prosperity Sphere' began as racist utopia and ended as a cross between an abattoir, a plantation and a brothel.

# 14

# The Gates of Hell

*To view those who are in essence unequal as if they were equal is in itself inequitable. To treat those who are unequal unequally is to realize equality.*

'An Investigation of Global Policy with
the Yamato Race as Nucleus' (1943)

*Over the town the planes broke formation and dive bombed the centre of the town. The din was terrific especially the rat tat tat of machine gun fire. About 10 a.m. casualties began to arrive and were put on to the floor outside the receiving room. Soon casualties began to pour in – literally hundreds of them. Scene was like something particularly gruesome out of one of Well[s]'s novels rather than real life.*

Dr Oscar Elliot Fisher, Malaya, December 11, 1941

## A RACIAL WORLD ORDER

Hitler visualized some aspects of his new world order more clearly than others. He was intentionally vague about how precisely he wished the Jews to disappear from his European empire. Few things, by contrast, were more precisely delineated in his imagination than the future architecture of the imperial capital, Berlin:

One will arrive there along wide avenues containing the Triumphal Arch, the Pantheon of the Army, the Square of the People – things to take your breath away! It's only thus that we shall succeed in eclipsing our sole rival in the world, Rome. Let it be built on such a scale that St Peter's and its Square will seem like toys in comparison . . .

Those who enter the Reich Chancellery should feel that they stand before the lords of the world . . .

Granite will ensure that our monuments will last forever. In ten thousand years they'll be standing, just as they are . . .

Albert Speer drew up detailed plans designed to realize his Führer's grandiose schemes. Berlin was to become 'Germania', a permanent exhibition of classical hypertrophy. At the centre would be a vast new Reich Chancellery. To the north they envisaged a giant rectangular lake and, next to the Reichstag, a vast meeting hall, with a dome 825 feet in diameter – so large that clouds would have formed on the inside of it. From there, visitors would be able to promenade down a breathtaking boulevard, 130 yards wide and three miles long, towards the biggest triumphal arch in history, standing 400 feet high, on which would be engraved the names of all the Germans who had fallen in the First World War. From this megalopolis, so Hitler had prophesied in *Mein Kampf*, a new empire of living space for the Aryan race would radiate eastwards to the Ukraine and beyond. Elevated highways would stretch from Berlin to Warsaw and on to Kiev. Along these, hardy German settlers and their buxom wives would drive in their Volkswagens – 'people's cars' – bound for one or other of the fortified settlements studded between the Baltic and the Crimea. Once established there, they and their broods of bouncing blond babies would rule over a rump, semi-educated populace, purified of all racially dangerous elements by a systematic policy of expulsion and extermination.

Since he had never visited the Soviet Union, Hitler's visions of *Lebensraum* were a strange mélange of *Lives of a Bengal Lancer* and the cowboy yarns of Karl May – part North-West Frontier, part Wild West. Curiously, in view of his commitment to the idea of an empire of colonial settlement in Eastern Europe, he seems to have found the former rather more attractive as a model for his own empire. In *Mein Kampf*, he made much of the ruthlessness of British rule in India, which he contrasted with German naivety on colonial questions. Since the British appeared able to rule India with a tiny elite of expatriate administrators and soldiers, he reasoned, Germany ought to be able to do the same in Eastern Europe. The crucial lesson to be drawn from the British experience was to maintain subject peoples in a state of poverty and illiteracy. 'The vast spaces over which [the English] spread their rule', he asserted in August 1941, a time when the challenge of ruling vast spaces was much on his mind, 'obliged them to govern millions of people – and they kept these multitudes in order by granting [themselves] unlimited power ... What India was for England, the territories of Russia will be for us.' A crucial point for Hitler, to which he often returned during his rambling dinner-table monologues, was the hypocrisy of British imperialism; the fact that, for all their pious talk of a civilizing mission, the British in reality did little to alter the living standards or the cultures of the peoples they governed:

They [the English] are an admirably trained people. They worked for three hundred years to assure themselves the domination of the world for two centuries. The reason why they've kept it so long is that they were not interested in washing the dirty linen of their subject peoples.

It was a theme he reverted to in January 1942:

The wealth of Great Britain is the result less of a perfect commercial organization than of the capitalist exploitation of the three hundred and fifty million Indian slaves. The British are commended for their worldly wisdom in respecting the customs of the countries subject to them. In reality this attitude has no other explanation than the determination not to raise the natives' standard of living ... The climax of this cynical behaviour of the English is that it gives them the prestige of liberalism and tolerance. [But] the prohibition of 'suttee' [ritual suicide] for widows and the suppression of starvation-dungeons were dictated to the English by the desire not to reduce the labour-force, and perhaps also by the desire to economize [on] wood! They so cleverly set about presenting these measures to the world that they provoked a wave of admiration. That's the strength of the English: to allow the natives to live whilst they exploit them to the uttermost.

Here, then, was a model for Nazi rule in Eastern Europe – a model of malign neglect. It was a model Hitler adhered to throughout the fleeting existence of his East European empire. He objected, for example, when measures were proposed to improve public health in the occupied territories. The British, he insisted, knew better than

to exercise their bureaucracy in occupied territory to the advantage of the local inhabitants and the detriment of their own country! They have a genius for keeping others at a distance and in winning and preserving respect. Here, perhaps, we have the worst possible example of our [own] methods – de-lousing infuriates the local inhabitants, as does our fanatical desire to civilize them. The net result is that they say to themselves: 'These people aren't really our superiors.'

By contrast, India had 'educated the British and gave them their feeling of superiority. The lesson begins in the street itself; anyone who wastes even a moment's compassion on a beggar is literally torn to pieces by the beggar hordes; anyone who shows a trace of human sentiment is damned forever.'

Hitler's grotesque fantasies are, unfortunately, better known today than they were before 1939. When the Queen sent a copy of *Mein Kampf* to Lord Halifax in 1939, she advised him not to read it, 'or you might go mad and that would be a great pity. Even a skip through gives one a good idea of his mentality, ignorance and obvious sincerity.' Today, by contrast, extracts of *Mein Kampf* are pored over by students in schools and universities, while numerous works of fiction seek to imagine the world as it might have looked had Hitler's dreams been realized. A few attempts have been made to argue that a Nazi victory over the Soviet Union might not have been wholly disadvantageous to the Western powers, and that therefore a second phase of appeasement after 1941 might have been preferable to continued war. Some British Tories, notably the late Alan Clark, have suggested that the British Empire might have been spared ignominious bankruptcy, decline and fall, had a separate peace been made along the lines Rudolf Hess seems to have envisaged and Hitler repeatedly mused about in his evening monologues; in a similar vein, some American conservatives argue that the Cold War might have been avoided had Roosevelt kept the United States out of the shooting war in Europe. On the whole, however, most writers have tended to take the view that a Nazi victory would have been a worse outcome than that of 1945. Even if a victorious Third Reich had opted for peace with Britain and America – which cannot be regarded as very probable – the price would have been horrendously high for the millions of people left under Nazi rule. All nine million of the Jews of Europe might have been murdered, rather than the nearly six million who actually were,* to say nothing of the vast human suffering that would have been inflicted on other ethnic groups by the implementation of the *Generalplan Ost*, which envisaged deporting around fifty million East Europeans to Siberia.

Less familiar, but no less chilling – and in many respects strikingly similar – are the blueprints for a new order drawn up by some Japanese writers in the early 1940s. Japan, it is true, had no Hitler, no single ideologue adumbrating a utopia which all others could 'work towards'. But it had many little Hitlers. In 'An Investigation of Global Policy with the Yamato Race as Nucleus', a report completed in July 1943, officials in the Population and Race Section of the Japanese Health and Welfare Ministry's Research Bureau took as their premise that the Japanese were the 'leading race' of Asia, whose mission was to 'liberate the billion people of Asia' by planting as much Japanese 'blood' as possible in Asian soil. This would be possible, however, only if the right demographic resources existed at home. 'We should actively improve our physical capacity eugenically by promoting such methods as mental and physical training as well as selective marriages,' the report urged. Japan's population needed to rise 'as rapidly as possible' from around 70 million in 1938 to 100 million by 1960, with each Japanese couple being encouraged to have around five children. This would provide the surplus of Japanese necessary to colonize and run what had been known since 1940 as the Greater East Asia Co-Prosperity Sphere. There were no necessary limits to the extent of that sphere. In 1942 Komaki Tsunekichi, a professor of geography at Tokyo Imperial University, had proposed that both Europe and Africa should henceforth be regarded as part of the Asian continent, while America should be known as 'Eastern Asia' and Australia as 'Southern Asia'. All the world's oceans, since they were

---

* The most precise figures for the destruction of European Jewry during the Second World War are as follows: total population in 1939 – 9,415,840; lowest estimate of losses – 5,596,029; highest estimate – 5,860,129.

interconnected, should simply be renamed the 'Great Sea of Japan'. The authors of the 'Investigation of Global Policy' were no more modest in their ambitions. Stages One and Two of their planned 'Enlargement of the Sphere of the East Asia Co-Operative Body' envisaged the incorporation of the whole of China, as well as nearly all French, British and Dutch possessions in Asia. Stage Three would have added the Philippines, India and all Soviet territory east of Lake Baikal. Finally, in Stage Four, the Co-Prosperity Sphere would have been extended to 'Assyria, Turkey, Iran, Iraq, Afghanistan and other Central Asian countries, West Asia [and] Southwest Asia'.

More than the Germans, the Japanese understood the importance of eliciting collaboration by protesting the emancipatory character of their new order. Thus the aim of the war was to vanquish 'Anglo-American imperialistic democracy'. The new order that would take its place would be based on 'racial harmony' and 'mutual prosperity . . . of all the peoples concerned'. In the Co-Prosperity Sphere, the kindred nations of Asia would be bound together by reciprocal relationships like those between 'parent and child, elder and younger brother'. 'We will obliterate the former European and British superiority complex and American and British world view,' declared the 'Plan for the Leadership of Nationalities in Greater East Asia' issued by the General Staff Headquarters in August 1942. 'Europe and America don't want Asia to awaken,' wrote Ōkawa Shūmei in his book *The Establishment of the Greater East Asian Order* (1943). 'Therefore they prevent [Asia] from remembering a common culture and ideology . . . [But now] the dark night enveloping Asia has begun to break and the light of hope has shone from the East . . . Now Asia is on the verge of overturning European control everywhere and is about to destroy corrupt indigenous social traditions and to shed blood in building independent nations.' Victorious Japanese commanders issued proclamations in the same vein, disavowing any 'intention of conquering any Asiatic people' or any 'thought of establishing [a] regimented sphere of imperialism in East Asia'. The Co-Prosperity Sphere was to be 'a union of neighbouring states, sharing to a greater or lesser degree common racial and cultural origins and geographical propinquity, founded by their voluntary agreement for the purpose of assuring their common safety and promoting their common happiness and prosperity'. The sole aim was to rid Asia of 'the poisonous dung of [Western] material civilization'.

On closer inspection, however, this new order was intended to be a good deal like the old one. The authors of the 'Investigation of Global Policy' envisaged that by 1950 there would be no fewer than twelve million Japanese settlers – mostly farmers – living permanently abroad, including two million in Australia and New Zealand. Another official report, entitled 'Outline of Economic Policies for the Southern Areas', made it clear that Japanese financial institutions would 'assume the financial hegemony hitherto held by the enemy institutions'. The development of manufacturing industries in Japanese-occupied territory was to be 'discouraged'. Other Asians must learn Japanese. They must adopt the Japanese calendar. They must kowtow to the Japanese. In short, Co-Prosperity simply meant a new imperialism, with the Japanese taking the place of the Europeans as the masters. All that remained to be seen was whether they would be more cruel or less – though the example of Japanese rule in Korea, where nationalist stirrings had been crushed with unrestrained violence in the 1920s and where linguistic and cultural Japanization was intensified in the 1930s, was not encouraging. The Korean language was banned from schools. Koreans were to attend Shinto services and, after 1939, to adopt Japanese names. Nor was this process of cultural subjugation mitigated by economic progress. Living standards were miserably low in Korea. Per capita income was roughly a quarter of what it was in Japan, while the mortality rate from contagious diseases was more than twice as high.

Like the Nazis, the more radical theorists of Japanese imperialism saw racial 'pollution' as one of the gravest threats to their own innate superiority. The new generation of Japanese settlers would therefore have to be careful to avoid contaminating their Yamato blood by mingling with the inferior races of the continent, such as the 'Han race' (the Chinese). Living space could be developed only on the basis of their expulsion or segregation. The peoples of Asia might, for the purposes of Japanese propaganda, be represented as one happy family. But Japan was to be the stern *pater familias*, and relationships with 'child countries' would not be tolerated. Like the Nazis, too, the Japanese romanticized the business of settling conquered territory. In stories like 'The New Brides Who Protected the Village' or photographs with captions like 'The Joy of Breeding', colonists in Manchuria were portrayed as both hardy and fecund, tough enough to withstand a bad harvest, fertile enough to bring forth numerous healthy offspring. The obverse of such idylls was a deep contempt for the 'dirty races' that were to come under Japanese rule. It is no coincidence that both the Germans and the Japanese spoke of those they conquered as less than human; the term used for bedbugs in Manchuria – 'Nanking vermin' – tells its own story. 'The Chinese people', wrote General Sakai Ryū, the Chief of Staff of the Japanese forces in North China in 1937, 'are bacteria infesting world civilization.' Somewhat more subtly, the General Staff's 'Plan for Leadership of Nationalities' divided Asians into 'master peoples' (the Japanese), 'friendly peoples' (Koreans) and 'guest peoples' (Han Chinese). The 'anti-Japanese enemy character' of the last of these groups was to be 'extirpated'. Those who did not 'swear loyalty to Japan' would be 'driven out of the Southern Area'.

There was thus more than mere diplomatic convenience underpinning the Tripartite Pact of September 27, 1940, which formalized the German-Italian-Japanese Axis and its members' shared interest in a 'new order of things'. For all the differences between them – and it is worth emphasizing that neither the Italians nor the Japanese shared Hitler's obsessive antipathy to the Jews\* – Nazi Germany, Fascist Italy and Imperial Japan shared certain fundamental assumptions about the character of the world they hoped to forge in the fires of

---

\* In 1938 Mussolini's government passed legislation which forbade marriage between Jews and non-Jews and banned Jewish teachers from schools. However, Italians were generally reluctant to assist the Germans with their wartime policies of deportation and mass murder. Between 1939 and 1943 many thousands of Jews sought refuge in Italy and Italian-occupied territory. This changed radically when the Germans occupied Italy in the autumn of 1943. Nevertheless, despite German efforts to round up and deport the Italian Jews, 40,000 out of a pre-war population of around 50,000 survived the war. Less well known is the story of the approximately 21,000 Jews who found sanctuary under Japanese rule. For example, thousands of refugees who had fled to Lithuania in 1939 were provided with exit visas by the Japanese diplomat Sugihara Chiune. In all, around 4,500 Jews from Nazi-occupied countries fled eastwards by such means, of whom all but a thousand succeeded in proceeding to safe destinations. Those left behind were moved to Shanghai, where there was already a large community of around 18,000 'stateless' Jewish refugees. The Jews were confined to the Hongkew area of Shanghai in February 1943, but survived the war, despite German pressure for their extermination.

war. It was to be a world ruled by three empire-states, imperial in the extent of their power, but state-like in the centralized nature of that power. It was to be a world shared between three master races: the Aryan, the Roman and the Yamato. As one of the Pact's Japanese architects put it: 'World totalitarianism will take the place of Anglo-Saxonism, which is bankrupt and will be wiped out.'

To be sure, those assumptions are easy to ridicule today. So much of what the Axis powers set out to do seems simply deranged; so little of it was in any case achieved or, if it was achieved, endured for more than a year or two. Yet these plans came much closer to being realized than is generally understood. Between 1937 and 1942 no army seemed able to withstand for long the forces of Germany and Japan. If anything, the impact of the Japanese blitzkrieg of 1941–2 was even more spectacular than that of its German forerunner of 1939–41. The effect was radically to reduce the odds against the Axis in terms of potential output and potential manpower. Everything therefore depended on how far Germany and Japan, to say nothing of their less formidable ally Italy, would be able to harness the resources that conquest had put at their disposal. They certainly did not set out to curry favour with the peoples they vanquished. The Axis armies were not content merely to defeat their enemies in the field. They treated prisoners of war with murderous contempt, in violation of the traditional and more recently formalized laws of war. Nor did they hesitate to extend the purview of warfare to menace, molest and murder defenceless civilians. Entire cities were laid waste; whole populations wiped out. Their notoriously violent character is, of course, the principal reason why most writers find it so hard to contemplate Nazi Europe and Japanese Asia with anything other than revulsion. Yet this is not necessarily the reason why the Axis empires failed to endure. On the contrary; the remarkable thing is that their ruthless employment of physical force did not prevent the Japanese – any more than it prevented the Germans – from acquiring in large quantities the one vital ingredient upon which all empires depend: collaborators.

For sixty-six million Germans to aspire to rule over more than three hundred million Europeans in a *Grossraum* stretching from the Channel Islands to the Caucasus was not, in fact, so very preposterous. Nor was it impossible to envisage seventy million Japanese lording it over upwards of four hundred million Asians in a Greater East Asia Co-Prosperity Sphere extending from Manchuria to Mandalay. In 1939, after all, a mere forty-five million Britons could still claim to stand at the apex of an empire that had a total population ten times that size and a territorial extent so great that the sun was literally always shining on some part of it. To be sure, Hitler the flophouse autodidact failed to understand that the foundation of British power was not coercion or contempt but collaboration with indigenous elites. Nevertheless, as they advanced into new territory, the Axis powers, too, found plentiful supplies of local personnel ready and willing to support their new imperial order.

The year 1942, then, was the year the twentieth century teetered on a knife edge. It was the year when the entire map of Eurasia appeared to have been redrawn. Huge tranches of land from the Rhine to the Volga and from Manchuria to the Marshall Islands had changed political hands. Now, in the name of 'living space', they were to change populations as well. The brutal methods the Axis powers used to build their empires swiftly turned living space into killing space. It still remained to be seen how far those methods were fundamentally inimical to the collaborative relationships without which no empire can expect to endure.

## RAPE

The Japanese had in fact waged a kind of prototype blitzkrieg in China in the months after full-scale war broke out at the Marco Polo Bridge. But the fighting was harder and a good deal more costly in lives and treasure than Japan's leaders had anticipated. In December 1937, as Japanese troops neared Chiang Kai-shek's capital, Nanking, a decision appears to have been taken to make an example of it, in the hope of dealing a fatal blow to Chinese resistance and bringing the war to a swift conclusion. It is not entirely clear who took this decision. After the war, the blame was laid on General Matsui Iwane, Commander-in-Chief of the Japanese forces in central China. It seems more likely that the real culprit was the Emperor's uncle, Prince Asaka Yasuhiko, who took over command on December 2. It was under his seal that orders were issued three days later – marked 'Secret, to be destroyed' – to 'Kill all Captives'. As they fought their way along the road from Shanghai, two officers gave their men an indication of what was to come. They engaged in a killing competition, which was covered by the Japanese press like a sporting event. On December 7 the *Tokyo Nichi Nichi Shimbun* published this report:

> SUB-LIEUTENANTS IN RACE TO FELL 100 CHINESE
> RUNNING CLOSE CONTEST
> Sub-Lieutenant Mukai Toshiaki and Sub-Lieutenant Noda Takeshi, both of the Katagiri unit at Kuyang, in a friendly contest to see which of them will first fell 100 Chinese in individual sword combat, are well in the final phase of their race, running almost neck to neck [*sic*].

The score was given as Mukai 89, Noda 78. A week later the paper reported that, as the two men could not agree who had reached the one hundred mark first, they had upped their target to 150. By this time, all battalions had been issued with orders to divide their prisoners into batches of a dozen and shoot them.

As news of the approaching Japanese army reached the city of Nanking, the Chinese authorities decided to shut all but one of the gates in the wall that encircled the city. Vainly attempting to keep the invaders out, they ended up locking the inhabitants in. The Japanese 10th Army arrived on December 8. The 30,000 battle-weary but still bloodthirsty troops immediately surrounded the city. Chiang Kai-shek had fled weeks earlier, leaving behind him only a poorly equipped force to defend the 500,000 or so people who had not followed his example. They held out for just five days. On December 13 the Japanese breached the city wall at three separate points and marched through. Inside, they found a ready-made slaughterhouse. Tens of thousands of young men were murdered in the weeks that followed, regardless of whether they were in uniform or not. Some were simply lined up in rows and machine-gunned. Others were beheaded, bayoneted or buried alive. One group was sprayed with gunfire and then soaked with gasoline and set on fire. A few were hung by their tongues on metal hooks. A horrified journalist working for the *Tokyo Nichi*

*Nichi Shimbun* watched Japanese soldiers line up prisoners on top of the wall near the Chungshan Gate and bayonet them:

One by one the prisoners fell down to the outside of the wall. Blood spattered everywhere. The chilling atmosphere made one's hair stand on end and limbs tremble with fear. I stood there at a total loss and did not know what to do.

Asked by another journalist to justify what was happening, Lieutenant-Colonel Tanaka Ryukichi replied simply:

Frankly speaking, you and I have diametrically different views of the Chinese. You may be dealing with them as human beings, but I regard them as swine. We can do anything to such creatures.

General Matsui entered Nanking on December 17, four days after his troops had begun their rampage. Though he subsequently claimed to be dismayed by what he witnessed, he did (or could do) little to stop it. The murderous orgy continued for a further five and a half weeks. It reached its peak in the week from January 28 to February 3, 1938, after civilians had been ordered to return to their homes from the refugee camps outside the city whence they had fled. For days, thousands of unburied bodies littered the streets. The International Military Tribunal of the Far East later estimated that more than 260,000 non-combatants had died at the hands of Japanese soldiers at Nanking – more than four times the number of British civilians killed during the entire war.

The Japanese did not content themselves with murder, however. There was also a systematic campaign of arson and other destruction. John Rabe, the German Chairman of the International Committee for the Nanking Safety Zone, described the state of the city on January 17:

Taiping Lu, the pride of Nanking, which was the main business street before and whose lights at night were equal to those on Nanking Road in Shanghai, is totally ruined, everything burned down. There is not one building left intact, just fields of rubble, left and right. Fu Tze-Miao, the former amusement district, with its teahouses and big market, is likewise totally destroyed. As far as the eye can see – nothing but rubble!

But the most striking feature of the attack on Nanking were the rapes. Although the International Committee's meticulous investigation did not specify how many of the 'injured females' it recorded had been raped, modern estimates put the total at somewhere between 8,000 and 20,000. The American missionary James McCallum estimated that there had been 'at least 1,000 cases a night'. The diaries of Dr Robert Wilson, a surgeon born and raised in Nanking but educated at Princeton and Harvard Medical School, provide a contemporaneous account of what happened. It was, he wrote on December 18,

the modern Dante's Inferno, written in huge letters with blood and rape. Murder by the wholesale and rape by the thousands of cases. There seems to be no stop to the ferocity, lust and atavism of the brutes . . . Last night the house of one of the Chinese staff members of the university was broken into and two of the women, his relatives, were raped. Two girls about 16 were raped to death in one of the refugee camps. In the University Middle School where there are 8,000 people the Japs came in ten times last night, over the wall, stole food, clothing, and raped until they were satisfied.

On December 17 a gang of Japanese soldiers broke into the grounds of Ginling College, where missionaries had offered shelter to ten thousand women and children. They abducted eleven young women. The nine who returned had all been 'horribly raped and abused'. One young woman, Li Xouying, ended up with no fewer than thirty-seven bayonet wounds when she attempted to resist three Japanese soldiers who found her hiding in the basement of an elementary school. Seven months pregnant at the time, she lost her baby but was saved by doctors at the Nanking Hospital. Many other victims were not so fortunate; post-war depositions indicate that a high proportion of those raped were also killed. Chang Kia Sze saw her own sister-in-law raped and murdered in full view of her husband and two young children, who were also killed. Other victims were mutilated by having sticks, bayonets or other objects stuck into their vaginas. Some survivors later proved to have been infected with venereal disease.

Harrowing testimony like Chang Kia Sze's was subsequently borne out in interviews with surviving Japanese soldiers. One of them, Tadokoro Kozo, confessed to his own involvement:

Women suffered most. No matter how young or old, they all could not escape the fate of being raped. We sent out coal trucks . . . to the city streets and villages to seize a lot of women. And then each of them was allocated to 15 to 20 soldiers for sexual intercourse and abuse.

Azuma Shiro, another former Japanese soldier, described the part he played:

At first we used some kinky words like 'Pikankan' . . . 'Pikankan' means, 'Let's see a woman open up her legs.' Chinese women didn't wear underpants. Instead, they wore trousers tied with a string. There was no belt. As we pulled the string, the buttocks were exposed. We 'pikankan'. We looked. After a while we would say something like, 'It's my day to take a path,' and we took turns raping them. It would [have been] all right if we [had] only raped them. I shouldn't say all right. But we always stabbed them and killed them. Because dead bodies don't talk.

How is what became known as the Rape of Nanking to be understood? As a breakdown of military discipline, fuelled by alcohol and battle-fatigue? As a deliberate imperial policy? As the hideous offspring of what one writer called a 'militarist monster, forged in late Meiji from a mixture of late Edo [pre-Meiji] nativism and borrowed German racial theories'?

Three impulses were consciously unleashed by those in command. The first was the contempt felt for those who surrendered. Japanese troops were trained to regard surrender as dishonourable. It was preferable to commit suicide rather than capitulate. Trainees were also encouraged to believe the corollary: that an enemy who did surrender was essentially worthless. This contempt went hand in hand with a culture of extreme physical brutality. If a Japanese colonel felt displeased with one of his majors, it was not unusual for him to strike the offending officer a blow across the face. The major chastised in this way would then lose no time in striking the first junior officer to incur his displeasure, and so it would continue on down the chain. Right at the bottom came enemy captives, so that any aggrieved Japanese NCO or private had one obvious and defenceless target on which to vent his frustrations.

The second impulse was not peculiar to the Japanese army. As the Turks had treated the Armenians, as Stalin's henchmen were treating the kulaks, Poles and other 'enemies of the people', as the Nazis were soon to start treating Jews, Gypsies and the mentally ill, so the Japanese now thought of and treated the Chinese: as sub-humans. This capacity to treat other human beings as members of an inferior and indeed malignant species – as mere vermin – was one of the crucial reasons why twentieth-century conflict was so violent. Only make this mental leap, and warfare ceases to be a formalized encounter between uniformed armies. It becomes a war of annihilation, in which everyone on the other side – men, women, children, the elderly – can legitimately be killed.

The third impulse, to rape, is the hardest to interpret. Is it possible for men simultaneously to despise people as vermin and yet to feel lust towards them? Were Japanese troops giving in to a primitive urge to impregnate the womenfolk of their enemy? Or was rape just bayoneting by other means? Perhaps the best answer is that all of these impulses were at work, reinforced by some element of peer-group pressure, since many of the assaults reported were gang rapes. As Hino Ashihei put it in his book *War and Soldiers*, 'We would be friendly with Chinese individuals and indeed came to love them. But how could we help despising them as a nation? . . . To us soldiers, they were pitiful, spineless people.' After the war, General Matsui told the International Military Tribunal, which would sentence him to hang for his role at Nanking:

The struggle between Japan and China was always a fight between brothers within the 'Asian family' . . . It has been my belief during all these years that we must regard this struggle as a method of making the Chinese undergo self-reflection. We do not do this because we hate them, but on the contrary because we love them too much.

This seemed then and still seems preposterous. Yet it captures the vile ambivalence that lay behind the phenomenon of mass rape.

The Rape of Nanking has become the most notorious of Japanese atrocities in China. It was, however, not an isolated incident. Other towns experienced similar treatment, not just in China but elsewhere in Asia too. Yet it would be a mistake to assume that such atrocities condemned the Greater East Asia Co-Prosperity Sphere to ultimate failure. On the contrary; what the Japanese were demonstrating was that brutality was by no means incompatible with the creation of a new world order based on racial subjugation – and fear.

## PUPPETS

Japanese atrocities may have played some part in the refusal of Chiang's government to contemplate a negotiated peace after 1937, despite German efforts to broker a truce. Of more importance was probably the manifest inability of the Japanese to inflict a decisive defeat on Guomindang forces, despite the poor leadership, low morale and appalling under-equipment that afflicted the latter.* Although the Japanese armies continued to advance steadily westwards in the course of 1938, capturing Canton, Wuhan and Xuzhou, they suffered increasingly heavy casualties as their lines of communication became over-extended. At Taierhchuang in March 1938, for example, the 10th Division found itself all but surrounded and ended up losing 16,000 men in days of intense house-to-house fighting. Eighteen months later the 11th Army was heavily defeated at Changsha (Hunan). The invasion of Guangxi at the end of 1939 was short-lived; by the end of the following year the Japanese had been forced to abandon Chinhsien, Nanning and Pinyang. By 1940 they had more or less reached their limits in China and the location of the front line did not significantly change again until 1944. The effect of all this was to strengthen the hand of the more extreme elements within the Japanese military, the so-called 'Control Faction', who advocated ignoring the existing Chinese authorities and dealing with puppet regimes, as they had done in Manchuria.

Here, it might be thought, the Japanese had miscalculated. Who in China would want to lend his support to invaders capable of such terrible atrocities? As in other theatres of war, however, the key to securing collaboration turned out to have little, if anything, to do with the cruelty or kindness of the invading forces. The decisive factor was the extent to which the invaded people were divided among themselves. The Japanese invasion did not elicit national unity, as some Chinese Nationalists had hoped it might. It boosted support for

---

* The fighting strength of the Chinese army was around 2.9 million, divided into 246 divisions and 44 independent brigades. However, each division had just 324 machine-guns between nine and a half thousand men. In all, the Chinese army had little more than one million rifles and just 800 pieces of artillery.

the Communist Party, which under Mao Zedong's leadership now committed itself to a campaign of protracted guerrilla warfare. At the same time, Japanese incursions tended to widen divisions within the Guomindang. The more recruits the Communists were able to find among impoverished and disillusioned peasants, the more tempted some Nationalists were to compromise with the Japanese. The further Chiang retreated to the west – and he did not stop until he reached Chongqing in the province of Sichuan, 800 miles from his starting point, Nanking – the greater the incentive for those left behind to make their peace with the Japanese.

Already by 1937 the Japanese had established three puppet regimes in Chinese territory: the 'Empire of Manchukuo', the supposedly autonomous Mongolian regime of Prine Te and the East Hebei Autonomous Anti-Communist Council. By the middle of the following year, two more had been added: the Provisional Government of the Republic of China set up in Peiping by the North China Area Army, and the Reorganized Government of the Republic of China established in Nanking by the Central China Area Army. In March 1940 the Japanese pulled off a major diplomatic coup when they succeeded in persuading the former Nationalist leader Wang Jingwei to become the figurehead in charge of the latter. After renewed attempts to negotiate some kind of peace with Chiang had foundered, Wang's regime was officially recognized as the legitimate government of China. Wang himself had been duped; he had been led to expect concessions like a definite date for Japanese troop withdrawals and a unification of the various puppet regimes under his authority. He ended up having to recognize the independence of Manchukuo, to allow the indefinite stationing of Japanese troops in China and to accept joint control of the maritime customs and other tax agencies. This meant that by 1940 the Japanese and their puppets controlled virtually the entire Chinese coast and a large proportion of the country's eastern provinces. These were by far China's most prosperous regions. Wang alone was nominally in charge of half a million square miles of territory and around 200 million people. Many Chinese agreed with the economist T'ao His-sheng, a leading collaborator in Wang's regime: 'China is a weak nation. In adopting a policy of being "friendly to distant countries and hostile to neighbours" [she] will inevitably bring about a situation which is summed up in the proverb: "Water from afar cannot extinguish a fire nearby."' Collaborationist slogans such as *Tong Sheng Ghong Si* ('Live or Die Together') were not wholly empty of meaning.

The Japanese had sought living space in China. Now they had it. All that remained was to stamp out the Communist guerrillas behind their own lines – ironically, the chief beneficiaries of Japanese victories over the Nationalists – and to finish off the apparently isolated Chiang. This, however, was easier said than done. The Japanese responded to Communist attacks with the brutal 'three all' policy: 'Take all, kill all, burn all.' They reacted to Chiang's retreat into Sichuan with air raids on Chongqing. In one important respect, this strategy bore fruit: in January 1941 the Second United Front between the Guomindang and the Communists fell apart when Nationalist troops attacked Ye Ting's New 4th Army at Maolin in Anhui. Yet still victory seemed to elude the Japanese commanders. And the more bogged down their operations in China became – a metaphor that Chiang's destruction of the Yellow River dykes turned into muddy reality – the more tempting it became to seek some kind of strategic breakthrough elsewhere.

## JAPAN TURNS SOUTHWARDS

Already in 1940 there were those in Tokyo who argued that it was Western aid that was keeping Chinese resistance going, despite the very limited amount of material that was reaching Chiang's forces in Hunnan from British-ruled Burma* and French Hanoi. In the words of General Nishio Toshizō in 1940:

The true cause of the current conflict derives from the forgetfulness of the Japanese and Chinese peoples of the fact they are East Asians. They have succumbed to the maddening influence of the individualistic materialism of Europe and America . . . Britain, the United States, France, and other powers

---

* Because of the poor quality of the roads and rampant theft, it was estimated that 14,000 tons had to leave Lashio in Burma for 5,000 tons to arrive in Chungking. At most 30,000 tons got through each month.

are providing aid to Chongqing in order to perpetuate China's dependent status.

In late 1938, the new Deputy Minister for War, Tōjō Hideki, denounced not only Britain for assisting the Chinese, but also the Soviet Union and the United States. The difficulty with this diagnosis was that it was unclear which of these external threats should be confronted first. The Kwantung Army had a historic predilection for confrontation with Russia. But by mid-1938 forces in the North had been so depleted by the war in China that the odds were heavily in the Red Army's favour. Two 'incidents' in 1938 and 1939 – border clashes at Changkufeng Hill on the eastern Manchurian-Soviet border and at Nomonhan on the border with Outer Mongolia – exposed the limitations of Japanese arms. Although the former clash could be regarded as a minor Japanese victory (though for no territorial gain), the latter was a disaster. The Japanese 6th Army was all but obliterated by the tanks, artillery and aircraft of the First Soviet Mongolian Army Group, under the command of Lieutenant-General (later Marshal) Georgi Zhukov. One reason the Japanese elected not to wage war against the Soviet Union – an option that would have been far superior from the point of view of combined Axis strategy in 1941 – was their realization that they might actually lose out in such a contest, so clear was their inferiority in terms of both tanks and planes. This, combined with the vain hopes of Foreign Minister Matsuoka Yōsuke that the Soviet Union might somehow be brought into the Tripartite Pact, helps to explain the Japanese readiness to sign a non-aggression pact with Stalin in April 1941. The Japanese never quite believed in this arrangement, keeping between thirteen and fifteen divisions along their northern borders throughout the war for fear of a Soviet surprise attack, but it did more or less rule out a Japanese offensive in the North. When Matsuoka argued for such an attack in support of Hitler's invasion just two months later, he was overruled and ousted from office.

The preference of the Navy Staff was to launch assaults on Hong Kong, Singapore and Malaya, while at the same time overrunning Dutch Sumatra, Borneo and Java. Their assumption, which proved entirely correct, was that the European empires in Asia had been dealt a lethal blow at home by the German occupation of the Netherlands and France and the continuing German threat to the British Isles. The Dutch colonies, in particular, looked like easy quarry; they had the added allure of being oil-rich. Malaya, meanwhile, was the world's biggest producer of rubber. Living space for Japanese settlers was all very well, but the Japanese Empire needed strategic raw materials far more urgently. In 1940 army planners had argued for an invasion of Indo-China, to provide new bases from which to attack the Chinese Nationalists in Sichuan. As War Minister in the new Cabinet formed by Prince Konoe in July 1940, Tōjō had insisted that unless Japan struck soon, she risked being too late. By 1941, it is true, some senior generals had become less enthusiastic about this idea. But by now the proponents of the Southern strategy had the upper hand.

So much better known is the war in South-East Asia and the Pacific that it is easy to forget that these theatres were always subordinate to China in terms of the resources committed by the Japanese. China was to Japan what the Soviet Union was to Germany, absorbing the greater part of its military manpower – up to a million men at the peak. In all, 52 per cent of Japanese military personnel deployed overseas served in China, compared with 33 per cent in the Pacific theatre and 14 per cent in South-East Asia. These figures also provide some indication of the relative ease with which the Japanese were able to oust the European empires. By any standards, these were low-hanging fruit. The Dutch colonies were defended by a fleet of 5 cruisers, 8 destroyers and 24 submarines, an air force of 50 obsolescent planes and an army of just 35,000 regulars with 25,000 reservists. Singapore, the supposedly impregnable British fortress, was woefully short of anti-aircraft guns and had virtually no armour. So certain were British planners that the base would face only a naval challenge that its rear was virtually undefended. Even a naval assault might have succeeded, since there was never any serious intention of sending the British fleet east in the event of a war in Asia. Malaya at least had men, altogether around 80,000 Australian, British, Indian and Malay troops. But its air defences were feeble. With good reason the forces of the European empires in Asia have been called 'Forgotten Armies'; in some respects they had been forgotten even before the war began.

The first Japanese move was against French Indo-China. In early

1939 the islands of Hainan and the Spratly Islands in the South China Sea were seized. In June the following year – by which time France had succumbed to the German blitzkrieg – the Japanese demanded that the French authorities admit a forty-man military mission whose role would be to prevent the shipment of war supplies to Chongqing. The French Governor-General acquiesced, but bid for a mutual defence pact in the hope of preserving the colony's integrity. Matsuoka dismissed this, demanding instead rights of transit for Japanese forces through Indo-China and the construction and use of airfields, as well as the stationing of Japanese troops to guard them. Realizing that they stood no chance if it came to a fight, the Vichy authorities agreed to this, leaving it to the Governor-General to handle the practicalities. However, the Japanese government grew impatient and on September 20 delivered an ultimatum to Hanoi, stating that Japanese troops would cross the border in two days' time with or without the consent of the French authorities. Once again the French capitulated. By September 23 northern Indo-China was in Japanese hands. Six months later the Japanese intervened to end clashes that had broken out between French forces and neighbouring Thailand. The effect of the resulting compromise was to bring Thailand too into the Japanese orbit. At the end of July 1941 Japanese troops completed the takeover by occupying southern Indo-China.

After the Netherlands succumbed to German invasion the government of the Dutch East Indies chose to align itself with the Dutch government in exile in London, but from a military standpoint their position was not much better than the French position had been in Indo-China. Once again the initial Japanese moves were diplomatic: demands for a huge increase in oil exports to Japan. Once again the colonial authorities attempted to be accommodating. Former Foreign Minister Yoshizawa Kenkichi's mission presented the Dutch with what amounted to a shopping list: 3,800,000 tons of oil, 1,000,000 tons of tin, 400,000 tons of bauxite, 180,000 tons of nickel, 30,000 tons of coconut oil, 30,000 tons of rubber and 10,000 tons of sugar. The Dutch haggled about quantities, insisting that there be no re-exports to Germany. By May 1941, however, the increasingly assertive Tōjō was once again losing patience. On June 17 Yoshizawa's mission departed for Tokyo. On September 25 the Chiefs of Staff, with Tōjō's support, told Konoe that he had until October 15 to arrive at a diplomatic solution of Japan's problems; this was the deadline for war. Since Konoe resigned on the 16th, allowing Tōjō to form a war government, only one thing can explain its subsequent extension for a further month and a half. This was the realization that any further moves against the European empires in South-East Asia would inevitably entail a confrontation with the United States.

## THE LOGIC OF PEARL HARBOR

The sole obstacle to Japanese hegemony in South-East Asia was America. On the one hand, it was clear that the United States had scant appetite for war, in Asia or anywhere else. On the other, Americans had little desire to see Japan as sole master of China, let alone the whole of East Asia. But those who ran US policy in the Pacific believed they did not need to take up arms to prevent this, because of Japan's dependence on trade with the United States and hence its vulnerability to economic pressure. Around a third of Japan's imports came from the United States, including copious quantities of cotton, scrap iron and oil. Her dependence on American heavy machinery and machine tools was greater still. Even if the Americans did not intervene militarily, they had the option to choke the Japanese war machine to death, especially if they cut off oil exports. This was precisely what made it so hard for American diplomats and politicians to foresee the attack on Pearl Harbor. As normally risk-averse people, they could not imagine the Japanese being so rash as to gamble on a very swift victory when the economic odds were stacked so heavily against them. They assumed that the partial sanctions imposed after the Japanese invasion of Indo-China would send a clear enough signal to deter the Japanese. The effect was precisely the opposite.

The path to war in the Pacific was paved with economic sanctions. The Japanese-American Commercial Treaty of 1911 was abrogated in July 1939. By the end of the year Japan (along with other combatants) was affected by Roosevelt's 'moral embargo' on the export of 'materials essential to airplane manufacture', which meant in practice aluminium, molybdenum, nickel, tungsten and vanadium. At the same time, the State Department applied pressure on American firms to stop exporting technology to Japan that would facilitate the production of aviation fuel. With the National Defense Act of July 1940 the President was empowered to impose real prohibitions on the exports of strategic commodities and manufactures. By the end of the month, after a protracted wrangle between the State Department and the Treasury, it was agreed to ban the export of high-grade scrap iron and steel, aviation fuel, lubricating oil and the fuel blending agent tetraethyl lead. On September 26 the ban was extended to all scrap; two months later the export of iron and steel themselves became subject to licence. No one knew for sure what the effect of these restrictions would be. Some, like the State Department's Advisor on Far Eastern Affairs Stanley Hornbeck, said they would hobble the Japanese military; others, like the US ambassador in Tokyo, Joseph Grew, that they would provoke it. Neither view was correct. The sanctions were too late to deter Japan from contemplating war, since the Japanese had been importing and stockpiling American raw materials since the outbreak of war in China. Only one economic sanction was regarded in Tokyo as a *casus belli* and that was an embargo on oil. That came in July 1941, along with a freeze on all Japanese assets in the United States – a response to the Japanese occupation of southern Indo-China. From this point, war in the Pacific was more or less inevitable.

For a long time the Japanese Foreign Ministry had found it hard to imagine the United States taking up arms against a victorious combination of Germany, Italy and Japan, especially if the Soviet Union were on friendly terms with that combination. A guiding assumption was that the American public was staunchly isolationist, and that the victories of Japan and her allies would reinforce rather than reverse that sentiment. The army was also reluctant to confront the United States, hoping that the conquest of European possessions in Asia could somehow be achieved without precipitating American intervention. Until September 1941 Japan's naval strategists were the only ones prepared to contemplate a war with America. However, they ultimately could see no other way of winning it than to deal a knockout blow to the US Navy at the outset. Conveniently, the main Pacific base of the American fleet had been moved to Hawaii in 1940; had it remained on the Californian coast, a lightning strike would have been out of the question. By April 1941 Admiral Yamamoto Isoroku had convinced himself that the ships stationed at Pearl Harbor could be sunk in one fell swoop. All six Japanese aircraft carriers would be needed, several submarines and around 400 planes equipped with torpedoes or armour-piercing shells. On November 1 Lieutenant-General Suzuki Teiichi assured the participants at a Liaison Conference* that supplies from the territories to be occupied would be sufficient to meet Japan's material needs. 'In 1943,' he declared, 'the material situation will be much better if we go to war.'

This was not the same as saying that Japan's material situation was equal to the challenge of war against the British Empire, the Dutch East Indies and the United States. All Suzuki meant was that Japan's material situation was bound to deteriorate the longer war was postponed. The navy alone was consuming 400 tons of oil an hour, just idly waiting; after eighteen months its stocks of fuel would all be gone. It therefore followed that it was better to strike now than to wait. This rationale was sufficient to commit Japan to war if no diplomatic breakthrough had been achieved by midnight on November 30, 1941.

It is sometimes suggested that the decision-makers in Tokyo were succumbing to some kind of irrational Oriental fatalism, an impression heightened by Tōjō's assertion on October 14 that 'a man sometimes must dare to leap boldly from the towering stage of Kiyomizu Temple.' Links have been drawn between the decision for war against the United States and the samurai code, or a specifically Japanese siege mentality, if not collective hysteria. Yet in many respects this way of thinking was more Western than Eastern in its provenance. Unknowingly, Tōjō was echoing Bethmann Hollweg's arguments for a German war against Russia in 1914 and Hitler's arguments for a German war

---

* Liaison conferences (*Daihon'ei Seifu Renraku Kaigi*) were an innovation dating back to 1937. They brought together representatives of the government and of the High Command. Those present generally included the Prime Minister, the Foreign Minister, the War Minister, the Navy Minister and the two Chiefs of Staff. They were relatively informal, with no individual formally presiding. Decisions had to be ratified at an Imperial Conference (*Gozen Kaigi*), which included members of the Liaison Conference, the President of the Privy Council and the Emperor himself, who sat – usually silently – on a dais in front of a gold screen. His ratification made any decision reached on these occasions binding and all but irrevocable.

against the Western powers in 1939. Even the time frame was similar:

Two years from now [that is, in 1943] we will have no petroleum for military use; ships will stop moving. When I think about the strengthening of American defences in the south-western Pacific, the expansion of the US fleet, the unfinished China Incident, and so on, I see no end of difficulties. We can talk long about suffering and austerity but can our people endure such a life for long? . . . I fear that we would become a third class nation after two or three years if we merely sat tight.

Thus, when Tōjō spoke of 'shutting one's eyes and taking the plunge' he was making a very German argument: to gamble on immediate war rather than submit to relative decline in the near future; to put to use military assets that would certainly bankrupt the country if they continued to sit idle. In the words of a High Command policy paper presented to the Imperial Conference of September 6, 1941, the American aim was 'to dominate the world'; to this end the United States aimed 'to prevent our empire from rising and developing in East Asia'. Japan was in 'a desperate situation, where it must resort to the ultimate step – war – to defend itself and ensure its preservation'. The alternative was to 'lie prostrate at the feet of the United States'.

The Japanese were not fantasists. For Matsuoka, Pearl Harbor was the disastrous culmination of a strategic miscalculation. He had assumed that the combination of the Tripartite Pact with Germany and Italy and the Neutrality Treaty with the Soviet Union would deter the United States from resisting Japanese expansion in Asia. 'The Tripartite Pact was my worst mistake,' he told his adviser Saitō Yoshie on December 7, 1941, the day Japan attacked. 'I hoped to prevent the United States from entering the war. I wanted to adjust our relations with Soviet Russia through the Alliance. I hoped peace would be maintained and Japan would be placed in a secure position. Instead . . . the present calamity . . . indirectly resulted from the Alliance.' Nomura Kichisaburō, the last pre-war ambassador to Washington, had favoured a more moderate policy, seeking a return to the Open Door regime in China, rather than risk war with the United States. Nor were all Japan's senior naval officers persuaded by Yamamoto's plan. Nagano Osami, Chief of the Navy Staff, argued that Japan was 'bound for self-destruction and . . . destined for national extinction' –

though he regarded this, somewhat paradoxically, as true to 'the spirit of defending the nation in a war'. In the summer of 1941 the Economic Mobilization Bureau produced a report which concluded that after two years of hostilities, Japan's economic resources would probably not suffice to sustain air and naval operations. Nagano expected that 'the situation [would] become increasingly worse' as early as the second half of 1942. Tōjō himself admitted that he did not know what Japan would do if war continued after 1943. It was not hubris that led to Pearl Harbor, but a conviction that it was preferable to take the chance of defeat in war than 'to be ground down without doing anything'.

Perhaps the real fantasists were the Americans, who adopted a remarkably confrontational stance in the final pre-war months, given the vulnerability of their own military installations in the Pacific, particularly the Philippines. The British were markedly more conciliatory, even temporarily closing the Burma Road – 700 mostly mountainous miles along which supplies were travelling to China – in response to Japanese pressure. For reasons that are not easy to fathom, Roosevelt consistently exaggerated the actual economic and future strategic importance of China and underestimated the perils of war with Japan. He declined an invitation from Konoe to attend a summit conference in the summer of 1941. Secretary of State Cordell Hull wanted complete withdrawal of Japanese troops from China and Indo-China; he would not hear of any suspension of US aid to Chiang, which the Japanese demanded. In his fateful note of November 26, Hull even proposed a mutual surrender of extraterritorial rights in China – an end, in effect, to the old Open Door system – and recognition of the Guomindang government. With some justification, the policy of the United States towards Japan in this period has been likened to her policy towards the Soviet Union during the Cold War.

Though aware that Japanese troops were heading from Indo-China towards Malaya and Thailand, the American government appears to have been oblivious to the progress of Admiral Nagumo's strike force, which set sail for Pearl Harbor on November 26. How far this was the result of incompetence and how far the result of conspiracy – to be precise, the deliberate withholding by the British government of intelligence about Japanese naval movements – continues to be debated, though it is very hard indeed to see why Churchill would have regarded the destruction of the American Pacific fleet as helpful to the British cause. The prospects of American intervention in Asia were by this time too good to necessitate such a gross betrayal of transatlantic trust, for Roosevelt had already given Halifax (now Britain's ambassador in Washington) a clear commitment of American support in the event of war on December 1 – six days before Pearl Harbor.

## THE CENTRIFUGE

The Japanese knew the odds were at best even and, after 1942, would lengthen against them. Yet victory is victory, and for a time it seemed as if the war really would be over before 1943. At minimal cost to itself, Admiral Nagumo's strike force* wreaked havoc at Pearl Harbor on December 7. True, the American carriers turned out to be away from their base, but the destruction or serious damaging of eight battleships, three destroyers, three light cruisers and three auxiliaries, to say nothing of the 177 planes that were rendered irreparable, was no mean achievement. The Japanese had lost just twenty-nine aircraft in action and fifty-five men, compared with total US military fatalities of 3,297. The vengeful American response is well known; the euphoric Japanese response less so. The literary critic Okuna Takao recalled how

the attitudes of ordinary people, who had felt ambivalent about the war against China, and even of intellectuals who denounced it as an invasion, were transformed as soon as the war against Britain and the US began ... There was a sense of euphoria that we'd done it at last; we'd landed a punch on those arrogant great powers Britain and America, on those white fellows. As the news of one victory after another came in, the worries faded, and fear turned to pride and joy ... All the feelings of inferiority of a coloured people

---

* The Japanese force comprised 58 ships: 4 large and 2 light carriers (each with a complement of around 70 aircraft), 2 battleships, 2 cruisers, 9 destroyers, 8 fuel tankers and 30 submarines, five of which were equipped with midget submersibles and three of which were sent ahead as an advance guard.

from a backward country, towards white people from the developed world, disappeared in that one blow ... Never in our history had we Japanese felt such pride in ourselves as a race as we did then.

And this was merely the opening salvo. Thereafter, Japanese forces fanned out across the Pacific and South-East Asia in a vast centrifugal offensive that achieved breathtaking speed and success. On December 8, the first Japanese troops landed on the eastern side of the Malay peninsula, followed two days later by the rest of General Yamashita Tomoyuki's 25th Army. Naval aircraft based in Saigon smashed the British naval force off Malaya, sinking the battleships *Prince of Wales* and *Repulse*. Lieutenant-General Iida Shōjirō's 15th Army stormed up the Kra isthmus into the heart of Burma, routing better-armed but less mobile British forces. British Borneo was invaded on December 16; a month and three days later it surrendered. Hong Kong's garrison of 12,000 held out for barely a week after Japanese troops landed there on December 18; it surrendered on Christmas Day. Meanwhile the 25th Army was advancing down the Malayan peninsula towards Singapore, using bicycles to speed down the well-tended plantation roads. On February 15 Lieutenant-General Arthur E. Percival and his garrison of 16,000 Britons, 14,000 Australians and 32,000 Indians surrendered, unaware of the exhausted condition of their 30,000 adversaries, who had all but run out of food and ammunition. Here was a humiliation even worse than that of May 1940, and there was more to come. Rangoon fell in March, despite Chinese attempts to assist Burma's beleaguered British-Indian defenders; Mandalay followed on May 1, along with the Andaman Islands in the Bay of Bengal. As General Henry Pownall admitted, the British had been 'out-generalled, outwitted and outfought ... by better soldiers'.

The same went for the Americans. On December 8 the first units of General Honma Masaharu's 14th Army landed on the island of Luzon, after air raids had smashed defences at Manila. Further landings on the 22nd and 24th were followed by the surrender of the Filipino capital on January 2. In the Central Pacific, Guam, Wake and the Bismarck Islands were all in Japanese hands by the end of January 1942. On April 9 American-led forces on the Bataan peninsula surrendered, followed a month later by those still fighting on Corregidor;

this effectively ended resistance in the Philippines. The spring of 1942 also saw Japanese forces take the Admiralty Islands and the Bismarck Archipelago, including the Solomon Islands. The Dutch, too, crumbled in the face of the Japanese onslaught. General Imamura Hitoshi's forces made their first landing in Dutch territory on the northern Celebes. By the end of February all of Sumatra had been taken and a makeshift Allied fleet had been wiped out off Java. On March 8 the Dutch surrendered. That same month their resistance in southern Borneo also collapsed. All this was achieved with a smaller military force than was stationed in either Manchuria or China.

The Germans had already made the concept of 'lightning war' their own. But never in military history has lightning struck in so many places with such devastating results as it did in Asia and the Pacific between the beginning of December 1941 and the end of April 1942. Moreover, the distances involved were vastly greater than those being covered simultaneously by the Germans in Europe. At its maximum extent, the Japanese Empire stretched 6,400 miles from west to east and 5,300 miles from north to south; its circumference was a staggering 14,200 miles. By the beginning of May 1942 the Japanese could plausibly contemplate attacks on Midway, New Caledonia, Fiji, Samoa, New Guinea and even Australia, Ceylon and India.

The European empires had simply caved in, as if the Japanese attack had exposed a fundamental loss of self-belief. An English teacher, hearing the desperate destruction of the causeway between Singapore and the mainland, asked a passing young man what the noise was. Lee Kuan Yew (who would be Singapore's first Prime Minister after independence) replied: 'That is the end of the British Empire.' And so it seemed to be. Stories are legion of British troops taking to their heels in the face of the Japanese advance, their officers in the lead. Practically the first effectual resistance the Japanese encountered was from Australians on the Kokoda Trail in New Guinea. Nor was the initial American response especially impressive. General Douglas MacArthur's exit from the Philippines was precipitate to say the least. The Americans' fighting spirit was not a great deal better than that of their British counterparts. In the words of American Marine Chester Biggs, captured by the Japanese in 1941: 'It is all right to die for a cause if the cause is a good one, but to die just for the sake of saying

"We fought to the last man and didn't surrender" is not a very good cause.' It was the same story at Bataan. As American PoW Andrew Carson recalled:

We had been trained to [re]act instinctively, immediately to commands like 'Attention', 'At ease', 'About face', 'Man your battle stations' and 'Fire when ready', but the word 'Surrender' was foreign. It had not been programmed into our minds and therefore brought no response.

He and his comrades could only weep, swear and try to convince themselves that 'we had done our very best'.

The Americans vainly attempted to achieve swift retaliation by bolstering the Chinese war effort, sending Lieutenant-General Joseph Stilwell to oversee American aid to Chiang. Unfortunately, the two got on badly from the outset. 'The trouble in China is simple,' Stilwell told one journalist. 'We are allied to an ignorant, illiterate, superstitious, peasant son of a bitch.' Stilwell wanted to rationalize and centralize the Chinese command structure; he resented the conspicuous consumption of Chiang's court, referring to him privately as 'Peanut' or 'the rattlesnake'. He himself had earned the soubriquet 'Vinegar Joe' for his acerbic candour. His efforts to take command of the relief operation in Burma were frustrated by the refusal of the commander of the Chinese 5th Army, Du Yuming, to obey his orders. The Japanese riposte was to launch a series of offensives which routed Chinese forces in Zhejiang province, bringing the region's principal railway under Japanese control.

Small wonder, then, that the new authorities in South-East Asia felt entitled to crow. What Japan's military leaders lacked in hubris was amply compensated for by 'educational announcements' like this:

Nippon is the sun: protector of the land and provider of light to all beings on earth. The Nippon Empire will increase in power and importance, like the sun rising higher in the sky – this is eternal and is also the meaning of the name Nippon.

In the creation of the world, land was the first. And the first land was Nippon, Land of the Rising Sun. No one can challenge the sun – to do so is like the snow melting in the heat of the sun. This is the iron-clad law on earth . . . Those opposing Nippon will undergo the same experience as the snow.

## PRISONERS AND COLLABORATORS

Many of the less exalted traits that had already manifested themselves during the China campaign were also features of the Japanese army's conduct in South-East Asia. The difference was that those on the receiving end now included 'those white fellows'. The notorious maltreatment of Allied prisoners of war was partly a consequence of the stigmatizing of surrender *per se* mentioned above. Physical assaults – most commonly slaps in the face and beatings – were a daily occurrence in some camps. Executions without due process were frequent. Official policy encouraged such brutality by applying the Geneva Convention only *'mutatis mutandis'*, which the Japanese chose to translate as 'with any necessary amendments'. Thousands of American prisoners died during the infamous Bataan 'Death March' in 1942.* Elsewhere, PoWs were used as slave labour, most infamously on the Burma–Siam (Thailand) railway line. Some prisoners were made to wear armbands bearing the inscription: 'One who has been captured in battle and is to be beheaded or castrated at the will of the Emperor.' Attempting to escape – which Western powers regarded as a prisoner's duty – was treated by the Japanese as a capital offence, though the majority of Allied prisoners who died (see Table 14.1) were in fact victims of malnutrition and disease exacerbated by physical overwork and abuse.

Yet it is important to emphasize that Japanese maltreatment was not confined to European prisoners. They murdered, enslaved and otherwise abused far larger numbers of the indigenous populations of the territories they occupied, giving the lie to their specious claims to be the liberators of Asia. Between 5,000 and 50,000 Chinese were massacred in Singapore in a series of 'purification-by-elimination' (*sook ching*) operations. The majority of those who died on the Bataan Death March were in fact Filipinos, just as ten or even twenty times as many Asians as Europeans died building the Death Railway. Of

---

* The Japanese forced some 78,000 survivors of the Bataan campaign to walk the 65 miles from Mariveles to San Fernando. The majority died en route as a result of physical violence, malnourishment and disease.

Table 14.1: Prisoners of the Japanese Southern offensive
and their fates, 1941–45

|  | Prisoners | Died | % died |
|---|---|---|---|
| British, Australian & Indian | 130,000 | 8,100 | 6.2 |
| American | 25,600 | 10,650 | 41.6 |
| Dutch | 37,000 | 8,500 | 23.0 |
| Indonesian forced labourers | 300,000 | 230,000 | 77.0 |
| Undocumented Asian prisoners | 300,000 | 60,000 | 20.0 |
| Civilians interned | 130,895 | 14,657 | 11.2 |
| TOTAL | 923,000 | 332,000 | 36.0 |

the 78,204 slave workers sent there from Malaya, for example, no fewer than 29,638 died.

No less enslaved and little more likely to survive were the tens of thousands of Korean girls who were abducted to serve as 'comfort women' – *ianfu*, colloquially known as 'Ps', from the Chinese *p'i* (cunt) – to Japanese troops all over 'Greater East Asia', often to front-line areas. Victims of what amounted to institutionalized gang rape, their recollections make harrowing reading. Kim Busŏn was just fifteen when she was lured away from her village in Gyeongbuk province with the promise of employment in a rubber factory. She was then taken to Taiwan where she was incarcerated in a military brothel:

Weekdays and weekends from 10 in the morning to 11 at night, soldiers came to do it. Sometimes they would come through the night. During the weekdays, less soldiers came, but mostly the place was always crowded with them. Countless soldiers came, grouped in tens and twenties. I can never forget the torturing experience I had during those times ... Officers always came late at night. They would come at 11 pm or even at midnight. They would sometimes go to sleep and leave in the next morning. We would sit on the entrance till it got very late at night. When we were called by an officer, we would go with him into a room to do it ... Nobody would behave well before us. They acted brutally. Even now when I see a soldier, he looks like an animal to me ... We often contracted gonorrhoea. We were not hospitalized, but treated with medication or sometimes given injections. When we had disease, we wrote 'vacation' on the door.

During the war she was moved to the Philippines, where she 'received thirty to forty soldiers every day'. The imperialism of sexual domination is seldom more starkly exposed than in these accounts. Kim Yongsuk, who was just twelve when she was recruited by the Japanese, was brutally abused by a Japanese officer in Mukden:

[He] came in and asked me what my name was. And he called me Okada. He gave me a Japanese suit and told me to get changed. It was a cheep gaudy cloth you could take off easily with flip of a finger. In a couple of days, that guy came in again, and said, 'I am Nakamura! This Korean girl looks quite cute. Let me play with you!' I was only twelve at the time. He showed me his penis. I ran away, but nobody helped me. He held me fast with his rough hands and cut my vagina. In a couple of days, he came in one more time. He said, 'I will eat your liver! You don't even recognize what benevolence you receive from the Heavenly Emperor of the Japanese Empire.' Then he twisted my legs with his foot with boots on, and cut my belly with a knife, and scratched my breast.

Kim Busŏn recalled how she was forced by her pimp and some soldiers to recite the Imperial Citizen's Charter, which began: 'I wish to be a citizen of the Empire' (*kōkoku shimmin nari*). It clearly struck them as funny to hear a sex slave ask for citizenship.

George Orwell, in his capacity as wartime propagandist, was quite right to ask: 'Why . . . do the Japanese constantly make war against other races who are Asiatics no less than themselves?' He might equally well have asked why the 'liberation' of Singapore necessitated the imposition of the Japanese language, calendar and even Tokyo time on its inhabitants. The experience of the renamed 'Syonan' exemplified the Japanese determination to create a culturally homogeneous empire on the basis of *Nippon Seishin*, the Japanese spirit. Similar things were attempted in occupied Java.

Nevertheless, none of this could wholly detract from the powerful symbolism of the Japanese subjugation of their European captives. As one wartime British report put it, there seemed to be 'an official policy of humiliating white prisoners of war in order to diminish their prestige in native eyes'. Lieutenant-Colonel Edward Dunlop, one of the survivors of the Death Railway, early on formed the impression that the Japanese were 'just breaking men on this job'. 'It must be rather amusing', he reflected in his secretly kept diary, 'for a Japanese to see the "white lords" trudging the road with basket and pole while they roll by on their lorries!' Such surmises were correct. As Itagaki Seishiro, Commander-in-Chief of the Japanese Army in Korea told Tōjō, 'It is our purpose by interning American and British prisoners of war ... to make the Koreans realize positively the true might of our Empire as well as to contribute to the psychological propaganda work for stamping out any ideas of worship of Europe and America.'

We should not overlook the extent to which this policy worked, at least initially, in legitimizing the Japanese claim to be liberators of Asia. When Japanese spokesmen referred to 'the shared ideals of all Asian peoples' and declared that 'the Great East Asia project' was 'based entirely on justice, and is opposed to the exploitative, aggressive, exclusionary egotism of Britain and America', they were able to elicit enthusiastic responses. Resentment of European rule ran deep among the educated inhabitants of Asian cities; Orwell, who had served as a sub-divisional police officer in pre-war Burma, was not the only one who had noticed it – and not the only one to have his faith in British rule shaken by the disquieting experience of being hated.* Nationalists from the former Dutch colonies hailed Japan as 'the Leader of Asia, the Protector of Asia and the Light of Asia'. For Sukarno, Indonesia's future president, Japan's war was indeed a war for national independence. Ba Maw, the Burmese nationalist leader whom the British had imprisoned in 1940, told delegates at the Tokyo conference of the Greater East Asiatic Nations in November 1943: 'This is not the time to think with our minds, this is the time to think

---

* Orwell's essay 'Shooting an Elephant' epitomizes the subtle demoralization of the British in Asia in the 1930s. When an elephant runs amok, Orwell is expected to shoot it. He finds the task intensely distasteful and only does so out of a fear of 'looking a fool': 'With the crowd watching me, I was not afraid in the ordinary sense, as I would have been if I had been alone. A white man mustn't be frightened in front of "natives"; and so, in general, he isn't frightened. The sole thought in my mind was that if anything went wrong those two thousand Burmans would see me pursued, caught, trampled on and reduced to a grinning corpse like that Indian up the hill. And if that happened it was quite probable that some of them would laugh. That would never do.'

with our blood.' The pre-war Filipino ministers José Laurel and Jorge Vargas declared that the Japanese victories 'vindicated the prestige of all Asiatic nations'. Nor were Japanese promises of liberation entirely empty. On August 1, 1943, Burma was declared to be independent; for the Philippines independence came on October 14. India and Indonesia were also promised independence.

Even Asians who had never experienced European rule were capable of impressive enthusiasm for the Japanese cause. Between 1939 and 1943 more than 700,000 Koreans volunteered to serve in the Japanese army – many writing their applications in their own blood to prove the depth of their commitment to be 'more Japanese than the Japanese' – though the Japanese accepted fewer than 18,000. In 1942 more than 425,000 Taiwanese, around 14 per cent of the male population, put themselves forward when 1,000 volunteers were sought. In all, more than 200,000 Taiwanese ended up serving as soldiers or as civilians working for the Japanese military.

The Japanese encountered resistance from some indigenous peoples, to be sure, and not only from those ethnic groups and elites that had done relatively well under Western colonial rule. The overwhelming majority of Indians showed no interest in the kind of liberation the Japanese had in mind for them. In the Philippines the peasant *Hukbalahap* movement waged a guerrilla war against them; in Burma the Karen and Kachin hill tribes also resisted Japanese rule. Nevertheless, the Japanese had no difficulty in finding collaborators among both anti-European nationalists and opportunists. Indian nationalists had not forgotten the 1919 Amritsar Massacre; it was in March 1940 that Udham Singh assassinated Sir Michael O'Dwyer, who had been Lieutenant-Governor of the Punjab at that time. Though the majority of Congress leaders eschewed collaboration with the Japanese – in practice, 'Quit India' meant neutrality, albeit with a great deal of circumlocution – Subhas Chandra Bose enthusiastically hailed 'the end of the British Empire' and called on Indians to join the Axis side. Around 3,500 answered the initial call from Berlin of the self-proclaimed *Netaji* ('leader') to form an Indian Army of Liberation, most of them Indians who had been taken prisoner by the Germans in North Africa. When he reached Asia – having travelled by U-boat from Kiel to Sumatra – Bose was able to recruit a further 45,000 men (again mostly prisoners from Singapore and elsewhere) to his Indian National Army and the Axis cause. More than the somewhat ambivalent Hitler, Tōjō seemed sincere in his declarations of support for India's 'desperate struggle for independence'. 'Without the liberation of India,' he told the Japanese Diet in early 1942, 'there can be no real mutual prosperity in Greater East Asia.' Ba Maw and Aung San's Burma Independence Army also enjoyed Japanese backing, though at the price of being reduced in size and renamed the Burma Defence Army until the Japanese had made up their minds to grant Burmese independence. In Java and Bali volunteer armies known as *Peta* (Army Defenders of the Homeland) were also formed. In Malaya, Sumatra, Indo-China and Borneo there were volunteer defence forces too, known as *Giyūgun*.

To be sure, the numbers of these forces were not large – at most 153,000 trained men. However, they could certainly have been much larger. The original Burma Independence Army had mustered 200,000 recruits, but was reduced by the Japanese to just 4,000, rising to 55,000 by the end of the war. Moreover, although the Japanese-trained armies in South-East Asia were small in relation to the total number of men mobilized by Japan during the war, they were quite large compared with the number of Japanese soldiers who actually served in the Southern theatre – around 300,000. In other words, roughly a third of the soldiers available to the Japanese there were members of the supposedly liberated Asian peoples. Only gradually did disillusionment set in with what Ba Maw later called 'the brutality, arrogance, and racial pretensions of the Japanese militarists' – and it was not unrelated to the decline in Japan's military fortunes after 1942 and the deepening crisis of the Co-Prosperity Sphere, which had become something more like a Co-Poverty Sphere by 1944.

Most military histories of the Second World War in Asia take it for granted that Japan was doomed to lose. This may underestimate the strengths of the Japanese position in mid-1942. Further attacks at Pearl Harbor might have significantly slowed down the US recovery at sea. Conceivably, it has been suggested, the Americans might have made the mistake of committing themselves prematurely to a costly reconquest of the Philippines; indeed, prior to 1939 it had been their intention to try to hold the islands in the event of a war. More plausibly, the Japanese navy's proposal to seize Ceylon, if it had been acted upon, could have seriously disrupted British communications to the Persian Gulf and Egypt, with dire implications for the build-up of British strength prior to El Alamein in October 1942. Japan might also have launched attacks on India from Burma, an option that was certainly contemplated (and of course belatedly executed in 1944). The Japanese had 700,000 troops in Manchuria and around one million in China; these could have been redeployed earlier to meet the inevitable Anglo-American counter-offensives. Even without them, there was nothing preordained about the Japanese reverses at the battles of the Coral Sea, Midway and Guadalcanal.

The Axis powers were not bent on their own self-destruction, as historians have sometimes been tempted to assume. On the contrary, they drew real strength from the territory they conquered, from the collaborators they recruited, even from the internecine violence they fomented. So powerful were these evil empires, and so ruthlessly did they impose their ideological visions on vast tracts of Eurasia, that we are forced to consider seriously one of the most deceptively difficult questions of the twentieth century: how on earth did the Axis end up losing a war they seemed, by the middle of 1942, to have all but won?

# PART IV

# A Tainted Triumph

# 15

# The Osmosis of War

*Something quite worthless, a poor parody of civilization, had*
*been driven out; he and his fellows had moved in, bringing the*
*new world with them; the world that was taking firm shape*
*everywhere all about him, bounded by barbed wire and reeking*
*of carbolic . . . He was engaged in a war in which courage and*
*a just cause were quite irrelevant to the issue.*

Evelyn Waugh, *Sword of Honour*

'*When we look one another in the face, we're neither of us*
*looking at a face we hate – no, we're gazing into a mirror . . .*
*You may think you hate us, but what you really hate is your-*
*selves – yourselves in us . . . When we strike a blow against*
*your arms, it's ourselves that we hit. Our tanks didn't only*
*break through your defences – they broke through our own*
*defences at the same time. The tracks of our [own] tanks are*
*crushing German National Socialism . . . But our victory will*
*be your victory . . . And if you should conquer, then we shall*
*perish only to live in your victory. Through losing the war we*
*shall win the war – and continue our development in a different*
*form.*'     The Gestapo interrogator to the Old Bolshevik
prisoner, in Vasily Grossman, *Life and Fate*

'*There's an osmosis in war, call it what you will, but the victors*
*always tend to assume the . . . the, eh, trappings of the loser.*'
Norman Mailer, *The Naked and the Dead*

## AUSCHWITZ AND HIROSHIMA

It is a name that has become synonymous with evil: Auschwitz – the Germanized name for the unprepossessing Polish town of Oświęcim, thirty-seven miles west of Kraków. It was in the nearby brick-walled barracks converted by the Germans into a concentration camp that a pesticide called Zyklon B was first used for the purpose of mass murder. The date was September 1941, and the initial victims were Soviet prisoners of war. But this was always intended as a test-run for genocide. Initially, the SS converted two farmhouses into provisional gas chambers at a new purpose-built camp known as Auschwitz-Birkenau. When these proved insufficient, four large crematoria were erected between March and June 1943, each consisting of an area for undressing, a large gas chamber and ovens for incinerating the asphyxiated victims. The purpose was to murder Jews from all over Europe and dispose of their remains in the most efficient way possible. At the peak of its operations, more than 12,000 people were being killed at the complex each day. Altogether, it has been calculated, 1.1 million people were murdered at Auschwitz, all but 122,000 of them Jews. That means that just under a fifth of all Holocaust victims perished there.

It is its efficiency that makes Auschwitz so uniquely hateful. Among the exhibits visitors can see today are vast piles of human hair shaved from the heads of prisoners which were still awaiting shipment to German textile factories, neatly stuffed into sacks, when the camp was overrun by Soviet forces. In a separate display are examples of the products that were made from earlier consignments: coarse cloth, naval ropes and a peculiarly vile brown netting. Almost as disturbing are the great mounds of dull and dusty shoes; of false limbs; of spectacles; of suitcases with their owners' addresses painted on them in the vain hope of return, addresses from all over Europe. And these are the merest traces, a tiny fraction of the detritus of genocide. Long gone is the gold from the victims' pockets, off their fingers, from their teeth. For the Nazis were not content merely to kill those they defined as subhuman. They were impelled also to exploit them economically. A tiny minority were selected to work as slave labourers, some in the death camp itself, others – like Primo Levi, a trained chemist from

Turin – in the adjoining factory run by IG Farben at Auschwitz III (also known as Buna or Monowice); still others were employed in nearby farms, mines and arms factories. Most, however, were simply gassed and then processed like so much waste product. You feel, after visiting Auschwitz, that the Germans did everything conceivable to those whom they killed except eat them. No other regime has come so close to H. G. Wells's nightmare of a mechanized sucking out of human life by voracious aliens.

Though it was the most efficient, Auschwitz was not necessarily the cruellest of the Nazi death camps. The first people to be gassed by the Third Reich were, as we have seen, German mental patients; they had been asphyxiated with pure carbon monoxide gas. This method was then exported to Eastern Europe, but using exhaust fumes, first in specially converted vans, then in static gas chambers equipped with large diesel engines. This was how people were killed at Sobibor, Treblinka and Bełżec, the camps set up to implement the 'Action Reinhard' in the autumn of 1941. Compared with inhaling Zyklon B, which killed most victims within five to ten minutes, this was a slow way to die. Rudolf Hoess, the commandant of Auschwitz, regarded his own methods as 'humane' compared with those of his counterpart at the last of these camps, the notoriously sadistic Christian Wirth. Shortly before committing suicide in 1945, the SS officer Kurt Gerstein left a harrowing account of what he witnessed at Bełżec:

The train arrives: 200 Ukrainians fling open the doors and chase people out of the wagons with their leather whips. Instructions come from a large loudspeaker: Undress completely, including artificial limbs, spectacles etc. . . . Then the women and girls go to the hairdressers who, with two or three snips of the scissors, cut off their hair and put it into potato sacks. 'That is for some special purpose to do with U Boats, for insulation or something like that,' the SS *Unterscharführer* on duty told me.

Then the procession starts to move. They all go along the path with a very pretty girl in front, all naked, men, women, and children, cripples without their artificial limbs . . . And so they climb the little staircase and then they can see it all: mothers with their children at their breasts, little naked children, adults, men, women, all naked. They hesitate but they enter the death chambers, driven on by the others behind them or by the leather whips of the SS, the majority without saying a word. A Jewess of about forty, eyes blazing, curses the murderers. She receives five or six lashes with his riding whip from Captain Wirth personally and then disappears into the chamber . . .

[After half an hour, all were dead from inhaling diesel fumes.]

The corpses are thrown out wet with sweat and urine, smeared with excrement and menstrual blood on their legs . . . The riding whips of the Ukrainians whistle down on the work details. Two dozen dentists open mouths with hooks and look for gold . . . Some of the workers check genitals and anus for gold, diamonds and valuables.

Between March and December 1942 an estimated 600,000 people, nearly all Jews (among them the members of the Jewish Council of Zamość), were brutalized, murdered and physically plundered in this fashion. From each transport to Bełżec around 500 were selected to remain alive in order to help dispose of the corpses; after a certain point they too were killed and replaced. Only five people are known to have escaped from the camp, of whom only two survived the war. One of them, Rudolf Reder,* was forever haunted by the cries of little children in the gas chamber: 'Mummy! But I've been good! It's dark! It's dark!' At another camp in Poland, Majdanek, around 170,000 prisoners were murdered not only with gas but also with bullets, beatings and hangings, culminating in the shooting of around 18,000 in Operation Harvest Festival (November 3, 1943). Such were the vile realities of the 'final solution' alluded to so elliptically by Reinhard Heydrich at the conference of state secretaries held on the manicured banks of Berlin's Wannsee on January 20, 1942.

Other regimes had perpetrated mass murder, as we have seen. Even more people were murdered for political reasons in Stalin's Soviet Union; and many aspects of life and death in the Nazi concentration camps – especially the vile sadism of the lower ranks – clearly had their analogues in the Gulag. More people would perish as a result of Mao's tyranny in China. Yet there was something qualitatively different about the Nazis' war against the Jews and the other unfortunate

---

* Reder was a trained chemist who was deported from Lwów in August 1942. He worked as a member of the 'death crew', digging graves and dragging bodies out of the gas chambers. After four months he was sent to Lwów to help fetch a consignment of sheet metal for the camp. While his guard slept, he made his escape.

minorities they considered to be 'unworthy of life'. It was the fact that it was carried out by such well-educated people, the products of what had been, at least until 1933, one of the most advanced educational systems in the world. It was the fact that it was perpetrated under the leadership of a man who had come to power by primarily democratic means. The Nazi death machine worked economically, scientifically and euphemistically. In a word, it was very, very modern. A few examples may help to illustrate the point:

The fares charged by the German state railway company, the Reichsbahn, for transporting the Jews of Europe to their deaths: 0.04 reichsmarks per adult-kilometre, with half-price fares for children over four and for groups of 400 or more.

The Breslau University Ph.D. thesis submitted by one Victor Scholz in 1940 and entitled 'On the Possibilities of Recycling Gold from the Mouths of the Dead'.

The careful technical and financial calculations of Kurt Prüfer, an engineer at the Erfurt firm of Topf & Sons, who designed the furnaces for the crematoria at Auschwitz.

The bald account by a Ravensbrück survivor of the experimental operations on female prisoners (known as 'rabbits') by Doctors Fischer and Oberhäuser, which included the injection of streptococci into their bones, the insertion without anaesthetic of toxic chemicals into their uteruses and the amputation of entire limbs 'to replace damaged body parts of wounded German soldiers'.

The signs hung on the path to the Buchenwald crematorium which read: 'There is one path to freedom. Its milestones are called obedience, industry, honesty, order, discipline, cleanliness, sobriety, willingness to sacrifice and love of the fatherland.'

The insistence of the SS-men at Bełżec that their victims were only 'going for a bath, and afterwards would be sent to work', a lie reinforced by the employment of a small camp orchestra to drown out the screams of the dying by playing tunes like 'Highlander, Have You No Regrets?'

The overwhelming impression is of professionals transformed into psychopaths – morally blinded, perhaps, by their narrow specialisms (that, at least, was the historian Friedrich Meinecke's theory). Whether collecting rail fares, conducting experiments, devising slogans, writing theses or designing ovens, it was thousands of people like Scholz, Prüfer, Fischer and Oberhäuser who turned Hitler's deranged dream of genocide into reality. They, just as much as the sadistic SS-men described by Rudolf Reder, were the real perpetrators.

So monstrous were the crimes perpetrated at Auschwitz, Majdanek and Bełżec – to say nothing of the other death camps at Chelmno, Sobibor and Treblinka – that Americans, Britons, Canadians and Russians have come to derive satisfaction from the belief that, when they fought Nazi Germany, their countries were engaged in a just war. We forget all too easily the extent to which the Allies, too, meted out death to innocent men, women and children to achieve their victory, albeit in quite different ways and with quite different motives. This was no simple war of evil against good. It was a war of evil against lesser evil. For the Axis powers did not collapse spontaneously under the weight of their own depravity. They could be vanquished only by the application of immense and contrary force. But this in turn required terrible moral compromises on the part of the Western powers. It seemed as if the Axis could be defeated only by turning their own inhuman methods against them.

For many Japanese today, Hiroshima is Asia's Auschwitz, a supreme symbol of man's inhumanity to man. Yet Hiroshima was only one of many cities that Allied bombers laid to waste in the later stages of the Second World War. The historian cannot evade the question: what is the difference between Auschwitz and Hiroshima? One possible answer is that, for Hitler, gassing Jews was an end in itself and he would have continued gassing Jews until there were none left, even if the war had ended with a Nazi victory in 1942. By contrast, for Churchill and Roosevelt, strategic bombing was designed not to annihilate the German and Japanese peoples, but simply to end the war. Churchill once joked over lunch about sterilizing the defeated Germans, but that was just black humour (like his symbolic urination on the Siegfried Line and in the Rhine); the 'final solution' of the German question would take the old-fashioned, supposedly humane form of partition. Churchill's paramount objective was not to kill all Germans, any more than it was to save all the Jews, or to liberate the French and the Poles. It was quite simply to bring the war to a victorious conclusion at a cost tolerable to the British people. His secondary objective, much less widely shared, was to avoid 'presid[ing] over the liquidation of the British Empire'. And his third, which hardly anyone but he thought seriously about until after the war, was to try to ensure that the German threat to Britain was not simply replaced by a Soviet threat. To attain the first of these ends, Churchill was prepared to use all available means.

Britain emerged on the victorious side of the Second World War at a lower cost in life (though not in treasure) than that imposed by the First World War. This was Churchill's achievement. Her empire, however, was only partly preserved and gravely weakened. And by 1947, the year that India departed the imperial fold, it became obvious to everyone that another world war, still more devastating than the second, was a distinct possibility. Herein lay the greatest flaw of the Allied victory: its principal beneficiary was the totalitarian regime with which the Western democracies had joined forces in the summer of 1941, Stalin's Soviet Union. Churchill had joked that if Hitler invaded Hell he would 'at least make a favourable reference to the Devil in the House of Commons';* in effect, that was precisely what had happened – and Churchill had offered Stalin much more than fond words. The wartime alliance with Stalin, for all its inevitability and strategic rationality, was nevertheless an authentically Faustian pact, though Britain and America were able to settle their debts to the Soviet Satan with the souls of others. That was why, for so many people in both Europe and Asia, the victories of 1945 did little more than to replace one version of totalitarianism with another.

It is sometimes asserted that this outcome was only right and proper, in view of the disproportionate contribution of the Soviets to victory. Yet that may be to underestimate the role of the United Kingdom and the United States in slaying the Axis dragons.

---

* Ironically, Hitler said the same about the Japanese in May 1942: 'The present conflict is one of life or death, and the essential thing is to win – and to that end we are quite ready to make an alliance with the Devil himself.'

## IMAGINED VICTORIES

After the devastating losses inflicted on the Soviet Union by Operation Barbarossa, a second offensive in late 1941 had taken the German army beyond the Moscow–Volga Canal to the very outskirts of the capital itself. So grave did the position look that the Soviet government – though not Stalin, who remained to direct the newly created *Stavka* (Headquarters) – was removed to Kuibyshev (formerly Samara), more than 500 miles to the south-east. A special refrigerated railway carriage transported the embalmed body of Lenin to safety. On November 1, though the front line was barely forty miles away from Red Square, it was decided to proceed with the usual ceremonies to mark the anniversary of the Revolution. Normally, Stalin would have given a speech in the Bolshoi Theatre but, as it had been bombed, the event was held in the ornate but also bomb-proof precincts of the Mayakovskaya Square Metro station, which was decked out to look like the Bolshoi. In his speech, Stalin had a defiant message for his former confederate, Hitler: 'If they want a war of extermination they shall have it . . . Our task now will be to destroy every German to the very last man. Death to the German invaders!' This was the language of desperation as much as defiance.

Fortunately for Stalin, he had received – and this time had the sense to believe – intelligence from Richard Sorge in Tokyo that in December 1941 the Japanese intended 'only an advance into the South Pacific, nothing more'. It was Sorge's assurance that 'the Soviet Far East may be considered guaranteed against Japanese attack at least until the end of winter' that enabled Stalin to divert fifty-eight divisions from Siberia to the West. The weather too was turning against the Germans, freezing fuel and fingers alike, and their casualty rate was soaring as Soviet resistance stiffened. The era of the blitzkrieg was over; what Curzio Malaparte ironically called the 'Thirty-Year Lightning War' had begun. Nevertheless the predicament of the Soviet Union in the months that followed Zhukov's Moscow counteroffensive showed little sign of sustained improvement. German forces overran the Crimea. By the summer of 1942, they had reached the banks of the River Don, the gateway to the Caucasus, and were pressing on towards the Volga. The Soviet oilfields at Maykop were captured; the swastika flew on the peak of Mount Elbruz. Poland, the Baltic states, the Ukraine and Byelorussia: all were in German hands. By this stage in the war, Germany and her allies controlled virtually all of Western and Central Europe too, with the exception of a handful of neutral countries (Eire, Portugal, Sweden, Switzerland and Spain). As one Russian commentator put it, 'Paris, Vienna, Prague and Brussels had become provincial German cities.' The Balkans had yielded to German arms, as had Crete. In North Africa it was very nearly the same story. On June 21, 1942, Rommel's Afrika Korps captured the British stronghold of Tobruk and then thrust into Egypt to within fifty miles of Alexandria. Intoxicated by victory, Hitler contemplated the future German conquest of Brazil, of Central Africa, of New Guinea. The United States, too, would ultimately be 'incorporated . . . into the German World Empire'. Ribbentrop's shopping list for a post-war 'supplementary colonial area' included British and French West Africa, French Equatorial Africa, the Belgian Congo, Uganda, Kenya, Zanzibar and Northern Rhodesia. Japan, meanwhile, had achieved no less astonishing victories in Asia and the Pacific. By 1941, as we have seen, the greater part of eastern China was in Japanese hands. The six-month onslaught that began with Pearl Harbor created a vast Greater East Asia Co-Prosperity Sphere, embracing modern-day Indonesia, Malaysia, Myanmar, Thailand and Vietnam, to say nothing of a huge arc of Pacific islands.

By the summer of 1942, then, only an incurable optimist could be certain that the Allies would win the war. In March of that year, following the Japanese triumphs in Asia, Churchill seriously contemplated resigning. Eden, who might have succeeded him, was fearful that the Soviets would make a separate peace with Hitler. 'We have already lost a large proportion of the British Empire,' lamented Alan Brooke in his diary, 'and are on the high road to lose a great deal more of it.' Britain seemed to be 'a ship . . . heading inevitably for the rocks . . . Would we able to save India and Australia? . . . Egypt was threatened . . . Russia could never hold, [the] Caucasus was bound to be penetrated.' The Germans might even reach the Gulf oilfields ('our Achilles' heel').

Could the Axis powers have consolidated their lightning victories of 1939–42 in such a way as to achieve ultimate victory? Military historians have long debated the strategic options open to Germany and Japan, in search of alternative decisions that might have tipped the war Hitler's and Hirohito's way. Leaving aside unlikely scenarios like a successful German invasion of Britain in 1940, a cancellation of Operation Barbarossa or a Japanese decision to attack the Soviet Union rather than the United States, four more or less plausible possibilities have been suggested:

1. Hitler might have accepted his military leaders' advice (notably that of Admiral Raeder) and focused his attention on winning the war in the Mediterranean in 1941, before invading the Soviet Union. He might, for example, have struck across the Eastern Mediterranean to Cyprus, Lebanon and Syria; or through Turkey (violating her neutrality) towards the Caucasus; or across Egypt to Suez and beyond. Even as it was, the British positions in Malta and Egypt were acutely vulnerable. Rommel might well have been able to drive the British out of Egypt if he had been sent the twenty-nine German divisions that were sitting more or less idle in Western Europe.

2. Alternatively, Hitler might have diverted more resources into winning the Battle of the Atlantic in 1942. Certainly, the German submarines were inflicting severe losses on Allied shipping throughout 1942 and into the spring of 1943.

3. Hitler might have waged his war against the Soviet Union more intelligently. Again, he might have listened to the experts (Halder and Guderian among them), who advised him to concentrate German efforts on capturing Moscow rather than diverting Field Marshal Gerd von Rundstedt's Army Group southwards towards Kiev. In a similar vein, Hitler might not have squandered his 6th Army so profligately at Stalingrad; Alan Brooke's fear was that Paulus might instead conquer the Caucasus, opening the way to the Caspian Sea and Persian Gulf oilfields.

4. The Japanese could have waged a different war against the Western powers, attacking Ceylon rather than Port Moresby and Midway in 1942 in order to challenge British dominance of the Indian Ocean. They might also have diverted troops away from China and Manchuria – where 56 per cent of their overseas forces were still stationed at the end of the war – to reinforce their line of defence in the Pacific.

The difficulty with all these counterfactuals – aside from their post-ulating a Hitler who was not as deaf to expert military advice as the real Hitler was – is that virtually none of them suggests a way in which the Axis powers could have overcome the overwhelming economic odds against them once they had taken on simultaneously the British Empire, the United States and the Soviet Union. To be sure, the blitzkrieg campaigns of 1939–42 narrowed the economic gap between the Axis and the Allies. The Germans very successfully sucked resources out of occupied Western Europe; at their peak in 1943 unrequited transfers from France amounted to 8 per cent of German gross national product, equivalent to a third of pre-war French national income. Germany all but monopolized the exports of the West European countries she occupied. The former Czechoslovakia, too, was a substantial net contributor to the German war effort. So deep did Operation Barbarossa and subsequent offensives penetrate that they captured more than half of Soviet industrial capacity. More-over, the Germans were able to treat their empire as a bottomless reservoir of cheap labour. Foreign workers accounted for a fifth of the active civilian labour force by 1943. After being put in charge of German armaments production, Albert Speer galvanized the Reich's economy, almost trebling weapons output between 1941 and 1944 by imposing standardization on the manufacturers and achieving startling improvements in productivity. The Japanese also performed feats of economic mobilization, increasing aircraft production by a factor of five and a half between 1941 and 1944.

Yet it was nowhere near enough. The Big Three Allies had vastly superior material resources. In 1940, when Germany and Italy had faced Britain and France, the latter combination's total economic output had been roughly two-thirds that of the other side's. The defeat of France and Poland lengthened the odds against Britain, but the German invasion of the Soviet Union restored the economic balance. With the entry of the United States into the war, the scales tipped the other way; indeed, they all but toppled over. Combined Allied GDP was twice that of the principal Axis powers and their dependencies in 1942. It was roughly three times as large in 1943, and the ratio continued to rise as the war went on, largely as a result of the rapid growth of the US economy (see Figure 15.1). Between 1942 and 1944

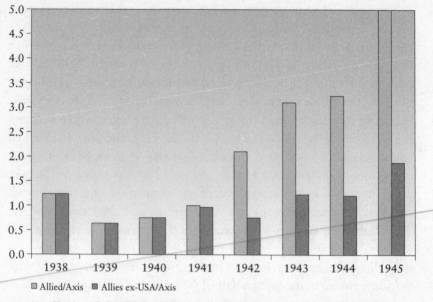

Note: This chart calculates the ratio of Allied to Axis combined gross domestic product. The bars to the right remove not only US GDP from the calculation but also the value of American aid to the UK and Soviet Union.

*Figure 15.1* **Ratio of Allied to Axis GDP, with and without the United States, 1938–1945**

American military spending was nearly twice that of Germany and Japan combined. It is difficult to see how different strategic decisions could have prevented this disastrous lengthening of the economic odds against an Axis victory. So much of the increment in Allied production simply lay beyond the reach of Axis arms, in the United States and beyond the Urals. Moreover, the additional oilfields that might have come within Hitler's reach had he fought the war differently were still far too modest in their output to have narrowed significantly the petroleum gap between the two sides.*

It is important also to bear in mind that the Axis powers were

---

* 'We must at all costs advance into the plains of Mesopotamia and take the Mosul oilfields from the British,' declared Hitler on August 5, 1942. 'If we succeed here, the whole war will come to an end.' But three-quarters of total world oil production in 1944 came from the United States, compared with just 7 per cent from the whole of North Africa, the Middle East and the Gulf.

fighting not only against the British, Russians and Americans; they were fighting against the combined forces of the British, Russian and American empires as well. The total numbers of men fielded by the various parts of the British Empire were immense. All told, the United Kingdom itself mobilized just under six million men and women. But an additional 5.1 million came from India, Canada, Australia, New Zealand and South Africa. Victories like El Alamein and even more so Imphal were victories for imperial forces as much as for British forces; the colonial commitment to the Empire proved every bit as strong as in the First World War. Especially remarkable was the fact that more than two and a half million Indians volunteered to serve in the British Indian Army during the war – more than sixty times the number who fought for the Japanese. The rapid expansion of the Indian officer corps provided a crucial source of loyalty, albeit loyalty that was conditional on post-war independence. The Red Army was also much more than just a Russian army. In January 1944 Russians accounted for 58 per cent of the 200 infantry divisions for which records are available, but Ukrainians accounted for 22 per cent, an order of magnitude more than fought on the German side, and a larger proportion than their share of the pre-war Soviet population. Half the soldiers of the Soviet 62nd Army at Stalingrad were not Russians. The American army, too, was ethnically diverse. Although they were generally kept in segregated units, African-Americans accounted for around 11 per cent of total US forces mobilized and fought in all the major campaigns from Operation Torch onwards. Norman Mailer's reconnaissance platoon in *The Naked and the Dead* includes two Jews, a Pole, an Irishman, a Mexican and an Italian. Two of the six servicemen who raised the Stars and Stripes on Iwo Jima were of foreign origin; one was a Pima Indian. More than 20,000 Japanese-Americans served in the US army during the war. As John Hersey put it in *A Bell for Adano*, the hero of which is 'an Italian-American going to war in Italy':

America is the international country . . . Our Army has Yugoslavs and French-men and Austrians and Czechs and Norwegians in it, and everywhere our Army goes in Europe, a man can turn to the private beside him and say: 'Hey, Mac, what's this furriner saying?' . . . And Mac will be able to translate. This is where we are lucky. No other country has such a fund of men who speak the languages of the lands we must invade ... Just as truly as Europe once invaded us, with wave after wave of immigrants, now we are invading Europe, with wave after wave of sons of immigrants.

Hence the irony of Hersey's insight that the typical GI's sole war aim was to 'go home'.

The Germans, as we have seen, had made some efforts to mobilize other peoples in occupied Europe, as had the Japanese in the Far East, but these were dwarfed by what the Allies achieved. Indeed, the abject failure of the Axis empires to win the loyalty of their new subjects ensured that Allied forces were reinforced by a plethora of exile forces, partisan bands and resistance organizations. Even excluding these auxiliaries, the combined armed forces of the principal Allies were already just under 30 per cent larger than those of the Axis in 1942. A year later the difference was more than 50 per cent. By the end of the war, including also Free French* and Polish forces, Yugoslav partisans and Romanians fighting on the Russian side, the Allies had more than twice as many men under arms. Fifty-two different nationalities were represented in the Jewish Brigade formed by the British in 1944. They followed an earlier wave of 9,000 or so refugees from Spain, Germany, Austria and Czechoslovakia who had joined the so-called Alien Companies, nicely nicknamed the 'King's Own Loyal Enemy Aliens'.

The best measure of the Allied advantage was in terms of military hardware, however, since it was with capital rather than labour – with machinery rather than manpower – that the Germans and the Japanese were ultimately to be defeated. In every major category of weapon, the Axis powers fell steadily further behind with each passing month. Between 1942 and 1944, the Allies out-produced the Axis in terms of machine pistols by a factor of 16 to 1, in naval vessels, tanks and mortars by roughly 5 to 1, and in rifles, machine-guns, artillery and combat aircraft by roughly 3 to 1. Blitzkrieg had been possible when

---

* It is seldom acknowledged that for most of the period from 1940 until D-Day, black Africans constituted the main elements of the rank and file in the Free French Army. Even as late as September 1944, they still accounted for 1 in 5 of de Gaulle's force in North-West Europe.

the odds were just the other way round. Once both sides were motorized – one of the defining characteristics of total war – the key to victory became logistics, not heroics. The fourfold numerical superiority of British armour was one of the deciding factors at El Alamein. The average ratio of Soviet to German armour at the beginning of the offensives of 1944 and 1945 was just under eight. The ratio in terms of combat aircraft on the Eastern Front rose from three in July 1943 to ten by January 1945. Likewise, Allied dominance of the skies ensured the success of D-Day and guaranteed the ultimate defeat of the Germans in Western Europe. One German soldier clearly remembered 'the day that it was all made clear to me, the impossibility of Germany prevailing':

It was July 26, 1944. There had been an air raid by 1,500 American 'Flying Fortresses' and I didn't see one Luftwaffe plane in the sky to challenge them. Of course, superior forces don't always win, but when the superiority is as enormous as that, there's nothing you can do. Close by us was the SS Tank Division *Das Reich* and contingents from the Hitler Youth. They were totally smashed up from the air. They didn't even have the chance to show how brave they were. When that sort of thing happens, you know it must be the end . . . it was hopeless, we couldn't possibly have won the war.

In the Pacific, meanwhile, the United States simply swamped Japan with a tidal wave of mass-produced armaments. American submarines reduced the Japanese merchant marine by three-quarters, cutting off the supply of indispensable imports. American anti-aircraft guns shot down Japanese planes faster than Japanese factories could build them. American shipyards built and repaired battleships while Japan's sat idle for want of materials. By 1944 the United States was producing twenty-six times as much high explosives as Japan. In terms of tanks and trucks the Japanese were in the same second-class league as the Italians. In terms of medical provision, an area where the Allies made major advances during the war, they were in the nineteenth century. Again, it is impossible to imagine any alternative Japanese strategy after Pearl Harbor that could have compensated for this immense economic imbalance. In putting their faith in increasingly suicidal tactics, Japanese commanders revealed themselves as (in Alvin Coox's apt phrase) 'medieval samurai warriors masquerading as practitioners of modern military science'. The Americans, by contrast, were the masters of overkill, whose first principle was: 'always have on hand more of everything than you can ever conceivably need'.

That total war would ultimately be decided by material rather than moral factors was not lost on the Germans. 'The first essential condition for an army to be able to stand the strain of battle', wrote Rommel, 'is an adequate stock of weapons, petrol and ammunition. In fact, the battle is fought and decided by the quartermasters before the shooting begins. The bravest men can do nothing without guns, the guns nothing without plenty of ammunition; and neither guns nor ammunition are of much use in mobile warfare unless there are vehicles with sufficient petrol to haul them around.' By the final year of the war, an active US army division was consuming around 650 tons of supplies a day. Because a single army truck could carry just five tons, this posed a formidable logistical challenge. Indeed, as supply lines were stretched from 200 to 400 miles in the months after D-Day, deliveries to the advancing armies slumped from 19,000 tons a day to 7,000 tons – hence the slackening of the pace of the Allied advance in the second half of 1944 and one defect of Montgomery's grab for Arnhem. The last phase of the war revealed the importance (consistently underrated by both the Germans and the Japanese) of assigning ample numbers of men to the task of supply rather than combat. The ratio of combatants to non-combatants in the German army was two to one; but the equivalent American ratio in the European theatre was one to two. In the Pacific, the Japanese ratio was one to one; the Americans had eighteen non-combatants for every man at the front. As the war came to an end, the United States had nearly as many men under arms as the Soviet Union (around twelve million in each case) but only a minority of Americans were actually engaged in combat. Those who were – the riflemen who landed in Normandy, the pilots in the Flying Fortresses – suffered heavy casualties.* It was in fact

---

* Nearly three-quarters of the men in the four US divisions that took part in the Normandy landings became casualties within seven weeks of going ashore. Mortality rates among American riflemen were between 16 and 19 per cent. More than a quarter of the officers in some British rifle battalions were killed. Nearly half of Bomber Command crews ended up killed or missing in action. Only German submarine crews had a higher fatality rate (82 per cent).

probably just as well that the Western powers put their faith in fire-power over manpower. Significantly less well trained than their opponents, three out of every four American soldiers did not shoot to good effect in combat, and many did not shoot at all. Most American and British casualties admitted to military hospitals were victims of disease and injury, not enemy action. The 'greatest generation' may have been greater than other American generations; they were far from being the greatest warriors of World War II.

Though much more reliant than the Western Allies on pitting men directly against enemy fire, the Soviet Union also out-produced Germany in military hardware. From March 1943 onwards, the Russians had consistently been able to field between twice and three times as many tanks and self-propelled guns as the Germans. This was remarkable, given the relative backwardness of the Russian economy and the enormous challenge of relocating production eastwards after the German invasion. Magnitogorsk, Sverdlovsk and Chelyabinsk became the heartland of a new military-industrial complex, the defining characteristic of which was increased productivity through standardization and economies of scale. The T-34 battle tank was one of the great triumphs of wartime design. Simple to build, easily manoeuvrable, protected with innovative sloped armour and packing a hefty punch, it was the very antithesis of the notoriously inadequate American Sherman M4. The later IS-1 and IS-2 'Josef Stalin' tanks were a match even for the German Panther V and VI and the Tiger I and II, which were also vulnerable to the giant SU-152 anti-tank gun. The volumes produced of these and other weapons were large. Soviet production accounted for one in four Allied combat aircraft, one in three Allied machine-guns, two-fifths of Allied armoured vehicles and two-thirds of Allied mortars.

It is no doubt entertaining to imagine how Hitler might have used a Nazi atomic bomb to negate these disadvantages, but the reality is that Werner Heisenberg and the German scientists came nowhere near devising one. Even had the Germans achieved more rapid improve-ments in their air defences – for example, developing and deploying jet-powered fighters earlier – material constraints would have limited the number of these that could have been built. In the unmanned V1 flying bomb and the V2 rocket the Germans did produce remarkable new weapons that inflicted heavy casualties and dented civilian morale in London; but they were not the war-winning innovations of Hitler's dreams. The Japanese were even further away from a decisive technological breakthrough.

In short, while they might well have been able to defeat the British Empire had it fought unassisted, and while they might even have defeated Britain and the Soviet Union had the United States remained neutral, those were not wars Hitler and his confederates chose to fight. They staked their claim to world power against all three empires: the British, the Russian and the American. If anything was inevitable in the history of the twentieth century, it was the victory of this overwhelming combination. Neutral investors certainly thought so, to judge by the wartime performance of German bonds traded in Switzerland, which plunged 39 per cent on the outbreak of war, rallied during 1940, then declined again in response to the aftermath of Operation Barbarossa, slumping at the time of the Yalta Conference in February 1945 to roughly the same low point they had first touched in September 1939. Different outcomes in particular military engagements – for example, the battles of the Coral Sea, Midway, Guadalcanal or even Leyte Gulf – would have done no more than delay the unavoidable denouement. Even if the Germans had succeeded in repelling the Allied landings in Italy and France – which is not inconceivable, given the inherent riskiness of Operation Overlord – or in checking for longer the Allied advance through the Ardennes, they would still not have been in a position to win the war. Indeed, diverting German forces westwards in 1944 served to hasten the collapse in the East.

## ANATOMY OF AN ALLIANCE

In view of what happened after 1945 – when decolonization and economic decline so swiftly demoted Britain from the elite of great powers – it is tempting to assume that the defeat of the Axis was primarily an American and Russian achievement. Until the concluding months of the war, however, the British were equal partners in the alliance. The British inflicted Hitler's first, crucial defeat in 1940 by winning the battle for the skies over their own country, at a time when the Soviet Union was still on the German side and the United States was still neutral. Despite the disaster of Tobruk, the British were able to hold on and win in North Africa. The British contribution to the Battle of the Atlantic was also vital. And it was British imperial forces led by General William Slim that inflicted perhaps the heaviest of all the Japanese army's defeats, at Imphal and Kohima in Burma. To be sure, Britain lacked the vast economic resources of the United States and the vast manpower reserves of the Soviet Union. Yet quality also counts. British intelligence was second to none. No single source mattered more in the war than Ultra, the deciphered German signals sent using the supposedly uncrackable Enigma machine. Thanks to the team of Oxbridge Egyptologists and other assorted boffins assembled at Bletchley Park, the Allies were consistently one step ahead of the Germans, perhaps most decisively in North Africa. The German submariners' Triton code was also cracked.

Not all that the British did was so obviously clever. To read English memoirs of the war is to be struck by the extraordinary resilience of the public school mentality – the persistence of sang-froid and frivolity, no matter how savagely the other combatants waged their total war; the dogged determination to treat every operation, regardless of its dangers, as either a foxhunt, a cricket match or a dormitory prank. All of these qualities are exhibited in William Stanley Moss's account of the abduction of the German commander from Crete in 1944. Few prisoners in the war can have been shown more gentlemanly consideration. Off-duty fighter pilots conducted themselves like Oxford undergraduates; while based in India, Group Captain Frank Carey founded the Scree-chers' Club, new members of which were 'allowed to drink only as long as [they] remained amusing'; success entailed promotion through the ranks from Hiccough to Roar, then Scream and finally Screech. Musical accompaniment was provided by the 'Prang Concerto', the last movement of which 'demanded the complete demolition of the piano'. Also engaged in fighting the last war but one, if not two, was Lord Lovat, who insisted that his 1st Special Service Brigade be piped ashore on the beaches of Normandy on D-Day. (Miraculously, the bagpiper survived.) After four years of German occupation the Dutch were mystified by the good manners of British officers, who politely asked permission to fire from their bedroom windows. Only at the very end of the war, inside Germany itself, was the mask of sportsmanship let slip: 'This has not been a football match' was the sole comment of Lieutenant-Colonel R. F. S. Gooch of the Coldstream Guards, declining the proffered hand of a German officer following the surrender of the 6th Parachute Regiment. Equally striking is the cynicism, even anti-heroism, of rank-and-file soldiers, well captured in the recollections of Rifleman Alex Bowlby:

'I'm telling you! It was a different sort of war [in the desert]. There were no civvies mixed up in it. It was clean. When we took prisoners we treated them fine and they treated us fine. The fighting was different, too . . . We had a go at them, or they had a go at us. Then one of us fucked off!'

'You fucked off about five hundred miles without stopping, if I remember rightly.'

Yet this strange combination of upper-class puerility and working-class bloody-mindedness was itself part of the secret of ultimate British success. Since they had no very lofty notions of what they were fighting for – Beveridge's welfare state was an altogether more popular war aim than Churchill's reconstituted Empire – the British proved difficult to demoralize.

The quality of British strategic decision-making was also vital. As is his due, Churchill is still remembered on both sides of the Atlantic as the saviour of his nation and the architect of the Allied victory. But if Churchill had enjoyed the same untrammelled power as Hitler, he might well have lost the war, so erratic were his strategic judgements.*

---

* Alan Brooke was contemptuous of Churchill's inability to 'grasp the relation of various theatres of war to each other'. In 1943 he was driven to distraction by the Prime Minister's hobbyhorse, an occupation of northern Sumatra. Churchill was 'temperamental like a film star, and peevish like a spoilt child'. By early 1944 Brooke was convinced that Churchill's age and alcohol consumption were impairing his judgement; he went so far as to wish he would 'disappear out of public life . . . for the good of the nation and . . . his own reputation'. 'The wonderful thing', he wrote on September 10, 1944, 'is that ¾ of the population of the world imagine that Winston Churchill is one of the great Strategists of History . . . and the other ¼ have no conception what a public menace he is.' Brooke was, admittedly, a bitter man. He felt that he, not Eisenhower, should have led the invasion of France, but this was to underestimate the rapidly growing disparity between the US and UK contributions to the war.

It was the limitation of Churchill's power that was Britain's greatest strength – the fact that the other members of the British Chiefs of Staff Committee, notably Brooke, were able not merely to disagree with 'the old man', but frequently to dissuade him. Britain waged war by committee. No individual's will was supreme. The armed services were forced to hammer out their differences and subscribe to a coherent strategy. The result was no doubt sometimes ponderous, but the chances of a catastrophic error were thereby much reduced. The same could also be said of the unwieldy but nevertheless vital Anglo-American Combined Chiefs of Staff meetings. Indeed, it may be that it was Brooke's caution and tenacity in argument that restrained the Americans from a premature attempt to open a Second Front in Western Europe, in the face of intense pressure from Stalin as well as from sections of the British public. Hitler, by contrast, could and did sack any commander whose obedience he so much as doubted. There was nothing to prevent him from issuing counter-productive orders that merely wasted German lives – nothing to prevent him descending eventually into the realm of fantasy, moving non-existent divisions into what were in any case untenable positions. Nor was there any effective co-ordination of strategy between the leaders of the three Axis powers; Plan 21 – the idea of a German-Italian thrust towards Suez combined with a Japanese attack on India – was little more than a pipedream. If even the Japanese army and navy could not agree on how to wage the war, how likely was a rational Axis plan for victory?

It is often said that Hitler's greatest strategic blunder was to declare war on the United States in December 1941 as a sign of solidarity with Japan after Pearl Harbor. This is not entirely fair, since Roosevelt had been stretching the meaning of neutrality to breaking point for some considerable time. Economic ties with Britain had been boosted by the 1938 Anglo-American Trade Agreement. Economic sanctions had been imposed on Germany by the US following the dismemberment of Czechoslovakia. Roosevelt began pressing Congress to repeal the Neutrality Acts as soon as the war in Europe broke out. As early as December 29, 1940, Roosevelt had denounced the Axis powers as an 'unholy alliance of power and pelf' that intended to 'enslave the whole of Europe and then . . . the rest of the world'; the United States, he declared, was the 'great arsenal of democracy' against a 'gang of outlaws'. In fact a *de facto* state of war between Germany and the United States had existed since September 11, 1941, when Roosevelt had authorized American naval commanders who encountered German vessels to fire at them 'on sight'. This was possible because the tide of American public opinion had been running against the Axis powers, despite the best efforts of isolationists like Senator Hiram W. Johnson, neutralists like the lawyer and legal historian Charles Warren and crypto-fascists like the aviator Charles Lindbergh. Ordinary Americans did not want war. Many believed they had been duped into the last war by the machinations of British imperialists and North-Eastern business interests. They were strongly attracted to the neutralists' idea that by prohibiting military supplies or loans to combatant countries Congress could avoid another such entanglement. But they supported American rearmament from as early as 1936. They clearly favoured Britain over Germany from 1938 onwards. Above all, Americans did not want to see an Axis victory – and by September 1939 a majority of voters saw that this was best insured against by supplying arms and material to Britain. The German victories of 1940 caused that view to spread. There was public support, too, for the sanctions imposed on Japan which set the course for Pearl Harbor.

Still, there is no question that Hitler fatally underestimated the United States. 'I don't see much future for the Americans,' declared the *Stammtisch* sage in 1942, in one of his dinner-table monologues:

In my view, it's a decayed country. And they have their racial problem, and the problem of social inequalities. Those were what caused the downfall of Rome, and yet Rome was a solid edifice that stood for something ... The German Reich has 270 opera houses – a standard of cultural existence of which they over there have no conception. They have clothes, food, cars and a badly constructed house – but with a refrigerator! This sort of thing does not impress us.

This was to misunderstand, firstly, the role of race in American politics. No doubt, blacks were second-class citizens, especially in the Southern states, where all kinds of legal discrimination still existed. But the same Southerners who were white supremacists were also among the strongest proponents of American intervention in the war, not least because of the South's high export-dependence. Isolationist, neutralist and Anglophobe sentiments were certainly strong in those regions of the United States with large ethnically German populations descended from nineteenth-century immigrants. But their influence was counterbalanced and perhaps even outweighed by the country's large and articulate Jewish community (which accounted for around 3.4 per cent of the population), afforced by over 300,000 refugees from Nazi-controlled Europe, many of whom were also Jewish. Ironically, many Americans harboured at least some anti-Semitic prejudices. Just under half of Americans polled in 1942 thought that Jews had 'too much power in the United States'. More than two-fifths of those surveyed in 1940 were opposed to mixed marriages. Just under a fifth of Americans considered Jews a 'menace to America' and nearly a third expected 'a widespread campaign against Jews in this country', which more than 10 per cent said they would support. Nevertheless a Gallup Poll showed that the American public overwhelmingly condemned Hitler's persecution of the Jews.

Hitler also missed the point completely about American economic capabilities, for the cars and the refrigerators he sneered at were being produced by corporations that led the world in techniques of mass production and modern management. The Axis leaders deluded themselves into believing that, with the Great Depression, the American economic model had disintegrated. Yet despite the sluggish growth of aggregate demand in the mid to late 1930s, firms like General Motors were taking tremendous strides forward in efficiency, exploiting those economies of scale that were unique to the huge American market. Exports to Britain and the Soviet Union had given GM and its peers a foretaste of what was to come. With the American entry into the war, they were inundated with government orders for military hardware. In the First World War, the result had been a mess: production bottlenecks, chronic waste and inflationary pressure. In 1942 the opposite happened. 'The real news,' as Charles E. Wilson of General Motors put it, 'is that our American methods of production, our know-how about the business, could be applied to mass production of all these war things . . . and that is the one factor that I think our Axis enemies overlooked.' Here, too, a compromise was involved. With astonishing speed the big corporations converted themselves from the champions of a consumer society to the servants of a command economy. As

John Hancock and Bernard Baruch observed: 'With the coming of war a sort of totalitarianism is asserted. The government tells each business what it is to contribute to the war program.'

In macroeconomic terms the results were startling enough. By 1942 US gross national product was more than 60 per cent higher than it had been in 1938. By 1944 it was more than double its pre-war level. Between 1940 and 1943, five million new jobs were created. This was the result of an immense fiscal stimulus, which saw federal deficits rise above 20 per cent of GNP, and an attendant surge in both private investment and personal consumption. Though some raw materials did have to be rationed, the United States was, as Wilson of GM put it, the first country to work out how to have both guns and butter in wartime. Much of the credit for this success must go to the corporate executives – the so-called 'dollar-a-year men' like Philip Reed of General Electric – who gave their services effectively gratis to the government during the war, and facilitated the remarkably smooth cooperation between the War Department and the big manufacturers, hitherto staunch opponents of Roosevelt. Never before or since has the federal government intervened on such a scale in American economic life, building and sometimes also owning a vast number of new industrial facilities. Agencies like the National Defense Advisory Commission, the Office of Production Management, the War Production Board and the Office of War Mobilization transformed the regulatory landscape. It was at the microeconomic level, however, that the output war was really won. For the biggest wartime advances in mass production and management were made in vast factories like Ford's mile-long bomber assembly line at Willow Run, Boeing's B-29 plant at Seattle or General Motors' aero-engine factory at Allison. At peak, Boeing Seattle was churning out sixteen B-17s a day and employing 40,000 men and women on round-the-clock shifts. Never had ships been built so rapidly as the Liberty ships, 2,700 of which slid down the slipways during the war years. It was at wartime General Motors that Peter Drucker saw the birth of the modern 'concept of the corporation', with its decentralized system of management. And it was during the war that the American military-industrial complex was born; over half of all prime government contracts went to just thirty-three corporations. Boeing's net wartime profits for the years

1941 to 1945 amounted to $27.6 million; in the preceding five years the company had lost nearly $3 million. General Motors Corporation employed half a million people and supplied one-tenth of all American war production.* Ford alone produced more military equipment during the war than Italy. Small wonder some more-cerebral soldiers felt they were risking their necks not in a 'real war ... but ... in a regulated business venture', as James Jones put it in *The Thin Red Line*. It was strange indeed that the recovery of the American economy from the Depression should owe so much to the business of flattening other peoples' cities.

Yet the Americans did more than just equip themselves for total war. They also equipped their Allies. It is well known that the system of Lend-Lease provided a vital multi-billion pound economic lifeline to Britain. Net grants from the United States totalled £5.4 billion between 1941 and 1945, on average around 9 per cent of UK gross national product. Less well known are the vast quantities of material that the Americans made available to the Soviets. All told, Stalin received supplies worth 93 billion roubles, between 4 and 8 per cent of Soviet net material product. The volumes of hardware suggest that these official statistics understate the importance of American assistance: 380,000 field telephones, 363,000 trucks, 43,000 jeeps, 6,000 tanks and over 5,000 miles of telephone wire were shipped along the icy Arctic supply routes to Murmansk, from California to Vladivostok, or overland from Persia. Thousands of fighter planes were flown along an 'air bridge' from Alaska to Siberia. Nor was it only hardware that the Americans supplied to Stalin. Around 58 per cent of Soviet aviation fuel came from the United States during the war, 53 per cent of all explosives and very nearly half of all the copper, aluminium and tyres, to say nothing of the tons of tinned Spam – in all, somewhere between 41 and 63 per cent of all Soviet military supplies. American engineers also continued to provide valuable technical assistance, as they had in the early days of Magnitogorsk. The letters 'USA' stencilled on the Studebaker trucks were said to stand

---

* 'For years I thought what was good for the country was good for General Motors and vice versa,' Charles Wilson famously told the Senate Armed Services Committee before his appointment as Secretary of Defense was confirmed.

for *Ubit Sukina sina Adolf* – 'to kill that son-of-a-bitch Adolf'. The Soviets would have struggled to kill half so many Germans without this colossal volume of aid.

It was not an aspect of what the Russians call the Great Patriotic War that Stalin was particularly eager to publicize. But without this vast contribution of American capital – as both Marshal Zhukov and Stalin's successor Nikita Khrushchev privately conceded – the Soviet Union might well have lost the war or would, at least, have taken much longer to win it. If the Red Army the Germans faced in the summer of 1943 was a more formidable foe than the one that had all but collapsed in the summer of 1941, this was in significant measure a result of American assistance. Yet the improvement was also, without question, a consequence of Stalin's near total control over his subjects' lives. The 1930s had taught the Soviets that nearly any material obstacle could be overcome, provided the lives of the workforce were regarded as expendable. So when Stalin gave the order to relocate and reconstruct Soviet industry to the east of the Ural Mountains, it was just another feat of inhuman economics, as mind-boggling in its ambition as the Five-Year Plans – and almost as wasteful of human life.[*]

It might have been hoped that in the crisis of war Stalin would suspend the Terror. On the contrary; the slave state that was the Soviet camp system carried on consuming its victims in their millions. Prisoners were hastily moved eastwards, often on forced marches, as the Germans advanced; guards shot or bayoneted those who fell by the wayside rather than let the Germans liberate them. Hundreds of thousands of the workers who manned Soviet industry during the war were prisoners, toiling up to sixteen hours a day on subsistence rations. The pace of Soviet ethnic cleansing was also accelerated. In 1941 prisoners in Poland and the Baltic states were slaughtered to save

---

[*] Soviet losses during the Second World War are estimated to have been around 25 million. This breaks down as follows: at least 8.7 million military deaths, though the number may have been as high as 10.2 million if German rather than Soviet figures are accepted for prisoners who died in captivity; 13.7 million victims of German occupation, of whom 7.4 million were executed, 2.2 million worked to death in Germany and the remaining 4.1 million succumbed to starvation or disease. Yet at least two million and probably more Soviet citizens died in places beyond the reach of Germans. It would be an error to blame Hitler for all the Soviet war victims.

moving them eastwards. Around 1.2 million ethnic Germans were deported from European Russia to Siberia and Central Asia, including the easternmost of the *Volksdeutsche*, the Volga Germans. More than 66,000 Germans were also expelled from the south-western region briefly run by the Romanians as Transnistria. With the German retreat from the Caucasus in late 1943, the Crimean Tatars and the Chechens were subject to collective deportation on the grounds that they had collaborated with the enemy. Other ethnic groups deemed to be suspect were also exiled: Balkars, Bulgarians, Greeks, Ingush, Iranians, Kalmyks, Karachai, Kurds, Khemsils (Muslim Armenians) and Meskhetian Turks. Jews, too, now began to fall under Stalin's suspicion. Ordinary Russian civilians found themselves living in a 'single war camp', working seven-day weeks on rations roughly a fifth of those enjoyed by their British counterparts.

Soviet military discipline, meanwhile, was draconian. It was Stalin's old enemy Trotsky who had pioneered the rule that if Red Army soldiers advanced they might be shot, but if they fled, they would definitely be shot. Stalin was happy to revive that one vestige of Trotskyism. Order No. 227 ('Not a Step Back') was issued by the People's Commissar of Defence, namely Stalin, on July 28, 1942:

We can no longer tolerate commanders, commissars and political officers whose units leave their positions at will. We can no longer tolerate the fact that commanders, commissars and political officers allow several cowards to run the show at the battlefield, that the panic-mongers carry away other soldiers in their retreat and open the way to the enemy. Panic-mongers and cowards are to be exterminated on the spot.

From now on the iron law of discipline for every officer, soldier [and] political officer should be – not a single step back without order from higher command. Company, battalion, regiment and division commanders, as well as the commissars and political officers of corresponding ranks, who retreat without order from above, are traitors to the Motherland. They should be treated as traitors to the Motherland. This is the call of our Motherland.

Officers who allowed their troops to retreat were to be court-martialled. In imitation of the German example, Stalin ordered the creation of special squads behind the lines 'to execute panic-mongers and cowards' and penal battalions for shirkers, 'thus giving them an opportunity to redeem their crimes against the Motherland by blood'. Punishments for desertion were extended to include the command-ing officers and, under Order No. 270, even the families of deserters and of men taken prisoner. When Stalin's own son Yakov was cap-tured near Vitebsk, his wife was arrested and spent two years in the Lubyanka; her father-in-law ordered her release only when news came of Yakov's death in German custody. Those Soviet prisoners of the Germans lucky enough to survive the war subsequently found them-selves imprisoned once again under equally harsh conditions for 'Betrayal of the Motherland'.

What all this reminds us is that in order to defeat an enemy they routinely denounced as barbaric the Western powers had made common cause with an ally that was morally little better – but ulti-mately more effective at waging total war. 'The choice before human beings,' George Orwell observed in 1941, 'is not . . . between good and evil but between two evils. You can let the Nazis rule the world: that is evil; or you can overthrow them by war, which is also evil . . . Whichever you choose, you will not come out with clean hands.' Orwell's *Animal Farm* is nowadays revered as a critique of the Russian Revolution's descent into Stalinism; people forget that it was written during the Second World War and turned down by no fewer than four publishers (including T. S. Eliot, on behalf of Faber & Faber) for its anti-Soviet sentiments. Nothing better symbolized the blind eye that the Western powers now turned to Stalin's crimes than the American Vice-President Henry Wallace's visit to the Kolyma Gulag in May 1944. 'No other two countries are more alike than the Soviet Union and the United States,' he told his hosts. 'The vast expanses of your country, her virgin forests, wide rivers and large lakes, all kinds of climate – from tropical to polar – her inexhaustible wealth, [all] remind me of my homeland . . . Both the Russians and the Americans, in their different ways, are groping for a way of life that will enable the common man everywhere in the world to get the most good out of modern technology. There is nothing irreconcilable in our aims and purposes.' All were now totalitarians; in the words of Norman Mailer's general in *The Naked and the Dead*:

As kinetic energy, a country is organization, co-ordinated effort . . . fascism . . . The purpose of this war is to translate America's potential into kinetic energy . . . America is going to absorb that [fascist] dream, it's in the business of doing that now. When you've created power, materials, armies, they don't wither away of their own accord . . . Your men of power in America . . . are becoming conscious of their real aims for the first time in our history.

## DEEP WAR

Albert Speer had sensed the turning point as early as April 1942. By the winter of that year, the Germans knew that the days of blitzkrieg were gone, never to return. Their lines of communication were perilously over-extended. Their equipment remained ill-suited to the Russian winter. More importantly, however, the enemy was now for the first time capable of matching them on the battlefield. At Stalingrad, the Germans found themselves bogged down in a war of attrition that resembled the Western Front in the First World War – only far colder and crueller. The surrender of Paulus's 6th Army on January 31–February 1, 1943, is often portrayed as the moment of truth. But it was the Battle of Kursk six months later that was the true beginning of the end for the Axis. For it was here, in what Vasily Grossman called the 'cauldron of totalitarian violence', that the full devastating might of the three-cornered Allied combination was revealed.

At Stalingrad the Germans had been surrounded and succumbed in the end to shortages of supplies. At Kursk the Wehrmacht met the Red Army head to head. The sheer scale of what happened at the Kursk salient, in the stormy days of July 1943, is hard to grasp. The battlefield was the size of Wales; it takes three hours to drive from one end of it to the other. The Germans planned a classic pincer movement from north and south, with the aim of encircling the Soviet force within the salient. The Russian response was defence in depth. The aim was to fortify the salient and then use *maskirovka* – deceptive camouflage – to lure the Germans to their destruction. They dug 3,000 miles of trenches, laid 400,000 mines and assembled 1,336,000 men (two-fifths of the entire Red Army), 3,444 tanks, 2,900 aircraft and

19,000 guns. On the other side there were around 900,000 German soldiers in fifty divisions. The Germans might once have been able to overcome such a numerical disadvantage. But they now faced a Red Army primed with British intelligence and armed with the latest American hardware. Soviet commanders were communicating with one another using American radios. There were squadrons of P-39 Air Cobra tankbusters lined up on Soviet airfields.

The German offensive, codenamed Citadel, was timed for 2.30 on the morning of July 4. At 2.20 precisely, forewarned thanks to the codebreakers of Station X at Bletchley Park,* Zhukov unleashed a ferocious pre-emptive bombardment, so deafening it sounded to him like a 'symphony of hell'. A dozen penal battalions were marched at gunpoint to the front line and left there to blunt the initial German attacks. The Germans were caught by surprise, but pressed on, relying on the superior firepower of their brand-new Panther tanks. General Hermann Hoth drove the crack Death's Head and *Das Reich* divisions of the 4th Panzer Army deep into the Soviet southern flank. It was the job of General Pavel Rotmistrov's 5th Guards Tank Army to stop him. Speeding westwards from the Soviet reserves, Rotmistrov hurled his forces into the battle at the crucial point, Prokhorovka Hill. Eight days after the battle had begun, two massive tank armies literally collided – 850 Soviet T-34s against 600 German panzers. For a time, scarcely anything could be seen in the smoke and dust. Rotmistrov's tank commanders had to steer their tanks with the pressure of their feet on their drivers' shoulders. Then torrential rain all but liquefied the battlefield. When the fighting finally stopped, all that remained was a ghastly morass of burnt-out tanks and charred bodies. For weeks after the battle, the whole region, thirty miles long and wide, remained, as the Soviet journalist Ilya Ehrenburg put it, a 'hideous desert': 'Villages destroyed by fire, shattered towns, stumps of trees, cars bogged down in green slime, field hospitals, hastily dug graves – it all merges into one.'

---

* The Soviets got their intelligence from Bletchley by two routes, one official and one illicit. Among those working at Bletchley was John Cairncross, the 'fifth man' of the Cambridge spy ring, who supplied information about German operations to his NKVD controller in London, Anatoli Gorsky. German deserters confirmed the British prediction about the timing of the planned German offensive.

This was what Ehrenburg called 'Deep War'. There had never been a conflict like it. It was pitiless. It was remorseless. And yet it could not be endless. For although both sides finished more or less where they began, the German losses were far more serious in relative terms: more than half their men and half their vehicles. In the succeeding weeks, they were driven back relentlessly, losing Orel, then Briansk, then Belgorod, then Kharkov. A fortnight after Kursk, near Karachev, Ehrenburg saw a signpost: '1,209 miles to Berlin'. That seemed to symbolize the sudden realization that Germany's defeat was now inevitable.

For it was not only on the Eastern Front that the tide had irrevocably turned. In every theatre, as Brooke put it, the Allies had begun 'to stop losing the war and [were] working towards winning it'. The Germans had been on the retreat in North Africa since the success of Operation Torch (the Allied landings at Casablanca, Oran and Algiers) and Montgomery's victory at El Alamein in early November 1942. The Afrika Korps surrendered on May 12, 1943. The Battle of the Atlantic was effectively over by the summer of 1943, thanks to the improved detection and destruction of German submarines; the following year the Allies lost just thirty-one merchant ships to U-boat attacks, compared with over a thousand in 1942.

In the Pacific, too, the tide had turned – and even more swiftly than in Eastern Europe. At the battles of the Coral Sea and Midway (May and June 1942), Admiral Chester W. Nimitz's carriers first checked and then inflicted heavy casualties on the numerically superior Japanese fleet. As at Kursk, both sides suffered substantial losses, but the relative cost of the battle to the already over-stretched Axis power was far higher; the Japanese would never replace their four sunk carriers, whereas the Americans were still far from the peak of their shipbuilding capacity. The series of battles fought on and around the island of Guadalcanal in the Solomons between August 1942 and February 1943 exposed the vulnerability of Japanese ground forces once the Americans had established naval and air superiority. In May 1943 US forces destroyed the Japanese forces on the Aleutian island of Attu and forced them to abandon Kiska; by September Japanese strategy had degenerated into holding an 8,000-mile last line of defence which they were already losing the means of supplying. Even in China there was progress. Colonel Claire Lee Chennault's 'Flying

Tigers' inflicted severe damage on Japanese targets, notably the Taiwanese airfields. In late 1943 Chennault's arch-rival, General Joseph Stilwell, finally got the Chinese army to make an effective incursion into Burma. Together, all these advances signalled that the Axis powers were doomed, that they could not hope to win a war against the combined might of the British Empire, the Soviet Union and the United States. The Italians saw the writing on the wall and overthrew Mussolini in July 1943, only to be overrun by the Germans.

Two months after the Battle of Kursk, the Joint Intelligence Sub-Committee of the British War Cabinet drew up a fascinating report, noting the 'striking similarities' between Germany's predicament in 1943 and her predicament in 1918. Allied air raids were producing as big 'and perhaps [an] even greater sense of hopelessness and loss of morale' as the naval blockade of the previous war:

Germany's European Allies ... are again only waiting the first opportunity to get out of the war. One [Italy] has already done so ... In these circumstances the German High Command in 1918 recognised the inevitability of eventual defeat and the futility of continuing the struggle. We believe that a similar feeling that Germany has lost all hope of winning the war, and that further fighting can only lead to useless bloodshed and destruction[,] is prevalent in Germany today and that it is shared even by some of the military leaders ... A study of the picture as a whole leads us inevitably to the conclusion that Germany is, if anything, in a worse position today than she was at the same period in 1918.

Despite the much higher level of political repression and the much harsher peace terms the Germans could now expect, the possibility could not be ruled out, the report concluded, that there might be a 'crisis' – perhaps even 'some sudden change of regime' – in Germany before the end of the year, paving the way to an armistice. In December 1943, no such crisis having occurred, Churchill asked a gathering of British and American chiefs of staff when Germany would be defeated; their answers ranged between March and November 1944.

How could such well-informed authorities have been so right about the inevitability of Allied victory but so wrong in their prediction of when it would come? For the Germans and the Japanese fought on for nearly two long years after Kursk – a period, moreover, that saw

34 & 35. Marja and Czeslawa Krajewski from Zamość, murdered in medical experiments at Auschwitz in 1943.

36. The Axis powers as aliens: American wartime poster.

37. Tatars in the Red Army, which was not a Russian but a genuinely multinational Soviet force.

38. A shattered German soldier sits on the remains of a wrecked artillery piece in the wake of the Battle of Kursk in July 1943. The failure of the German Operation Citadel dealt a death blow to German hopes of stemming the Soviet tide on the Eastern Front.

39. The Allies as aliens: Nazi poster for Dutch consumption, depicting the United States as a monstrous synthesis of beauty contests, jazz music, black boxers, gangsters, the Ku-Klux-Klan and, of course, Jewish plutocracy.

40. Counting the dead after the destruction of Dresden in February 1945. Many victims were reduced to mere ash.

41. The enemy as subhuman, I: Japanese megalomania personified in the *Seattle Post-Intelligencer's* caricature 'Mr Moto'.

42. The enemy as subhuman, II: Phoenix war-worker Natalie Nickerson writes to thank her Navy boyfriend for the Japanese soldier's skull he sent her as a souvenir from New Guinea. According to *Life* magazine, she named it 'Tojo'.

43. 'Monstrous beings of metal moving about in the distance' (Wells): two American tanks advance under Japanese fire during the Battle for Okinawa, June 1945.

44. The face of surrender: a Japanese naval lieutenant is persuaded to lay down his arms on Okinawa. Japanese aversion to dishonour and mistrust of Allied intentions meant that a majority of the island's defenders preferred to fight to the death.

45. A Soviet soldier tries to steal a Berlin woman's bike. This was the least of the crimes committed by the Red Army as they advanced through Germany.

46. The Third World's War: soldiers training in Guatemala to fight the Guerrilla Army of the Poor. Although notionally a war between capitalists and Communists, on close inspection the Guatemalan civil war was as much an ethnic conflict between Ladinos and Mayans.

47. The new face of totalitarianism: Chinese children read from Chairman Mao's 'Little Red Book', a manifesto for civil war between the generations.

48. My enemy's enemy: the butcher of Cambodia, Pol Pot (*left*), greets the modernizer of China, Deng Xiaoping (*right*), in Phnom Penh in 1978. The common enemy in question was Vietnam. Deng was not above butchery himself, as he proved eleven years later when pro-democracy demonstrations in Tiananmen Square threatened the Communist monopoly on power in China.

49. Self-esteem through genocide: Milan Lukić, who stands accused of murdering Bosnian Muslims in his home town of Višegrad in 1992.

the highest mortality of the entire war. No doubt it is possible to think of ways in which the Allies might have brought the war to a swifter conclusion. There are those who continue to believe (as the Soviets argued at the time) that a 'Second Front' could have been opened in Western Europe a year earlier than D-Day; that the landings in North Africa and Italy were simply a diversion from the main event, which was France. Many military analysts since Basil Liddell Hart – and, indeed, Siegfried Westphal, Rundstedt's Chief of Staff – have argued that the Anglo-American advance after D-Day could have been faster if it had not been spread over such a broad front. Yet the decisive factor in the war's protracted ending was not Allied over-caution so much as astonishing Axis tenacity. Any counterfactual of an early end to the war falls foul of the fact that between June 1943 and May 1944 the Wehrmacht lost a minimum of 900,000 men. Those who still remained to fight after the Allied landings fought well enough; how much better would the Germans have fought a year earlier? Perhaps it was as well to have dress rehearsals for the decisive amphibious landings, first in North Africa and then in Italy.

## TO THE DEATH

'If we were fighting reasonable people,' an aide to the American General Omar Bradley remarked in December 1944, 'they would have surrendered long ago.' It is true that there were some major German surrenders before 1945: that of Paulus's 6th Army at Stalingrad; the collapse of Army Group Centre in July 1944, when twenty-five divisions gave themselves up; the surrender of more than eighteen divisions at Iasi in August 1944. Yet the vast majority of German prisoners were captured only *after* the official surrender signed by General Jodl at 2.41 a.m. on May 7, 1945. According to one estimate, the Western Allies had captured just 630,000 Germans prior to the capitulation. The post-war Maschke Commission put the total number of Germans held prisoner in the first quarter of 1945 at more than two million, roughly shared between the Eastern and Western theatres of the European war. In all, the number of prisoners on the eve of the German capitulation cannot have exceeded three million.

In other words, at least eight million of the final total of eleven million German soldiers laid down their arms only after the official surrender. Not untypical was the Courland Army, which resisted to the bitter end despite having been surrounded by the Red Army as early as January 1945. What is more, an unknown but surely large proportion of the three million pre-capitulation prisoners clearly gave themselves up only in the very last weeks of the war.

The Japanese fought even more tenaciously than the Germans. In the Pacific war, the Western armies' ratio of captured to dead was around 4:1. The Japanese ratio was 1:40. Only 1,700 Japanese prisoners were taken in Burma, compared with 150,000 who were killed; of the former, only 400 were physically fit, and all tried to commit suicide in their first week of captivity. Despite the fact that their position was patently hopeless, the Japanese defended Okinawa to the death after the Americans landed there in March–April 1945. Desperate hand-to-hand fighting, not least in the warren of caves into which the Japanese retreated, left more than 100,000 Japanese troops dead. Only around 7,000 of the defenders ended up as prisoners. Perhaps as many as 42,000 civilians also lost their lives. American casualties exceeded 49,000 (of whom some 12,000 died), the worst for any of the Pacific battles. Meanwhile, nearly 8,000 pilots in suicidal *tokkōtai* units – the so-called *kamikaze* ('divine wind') – flew their planes directly into American ships, sinking thirty-six and destroying 763 of the aircraft on board. Not until they were on the verge of starvation in the closing weeks of the war did significant numbers of Japanese troops begin to give themselves up. And even in late July 1945 in south Burma 17,000 lost their lives in a futile attempt to break out from the hills and cross the formidable Sittang river. Unlike other nationalities, the Japanese tended to be captured singly and only when incapacitated. One Japanese soldier refused to lay down his arms until 1974. There is little question that the majority of those forces mobilized for the final defence of mainland Japan would have gone down fighting rather than surrender in the absence of an imperial command to do so.*

* The Japanese still had 169 infantry divisions, 4 tank divisions and 15 air divisions – around 5.5 million men – and the air force had 9,000 operational aircraft.

How can we explain the tenacity of the German and Japanese armies in the Second World War? Why did they keep fighting after any rational hope of victory had evaporated? Part of the answer lies in the realm of military discipline. In Britain the death penalty for desertion was abolished in 1930 and never restored. The Americans too were lenient; only one GI was executed for desertion during the entire Second World War. But on the German side, as on the Russian, the penalties for desertion were significantly stiffened as the war went on. The Wehrmacht executed between 15,000 and 20,000 of its own men, mainly in the later stages of the war for the so-called political crimes of desertion or *Wehrkraftzersetzung* (undermining of the war effort), and effectively sentenced many thousands more to death by assigning them to punishment battalions. Such draconian measures became increasingly important on the Eastern Front when very high casualty rates (up to 300 per cent of the original strength of some divisions) prevented the formation of 'primary group' loyalties and desertion rates began to rise. Phrases like 'most severe punishment' and 'ruthless use of all means' became routine euphemisms for summary executions. By the end of the war, German *Landsers* faced a stark choice: 'Death by a bullet from the enemy or by the "thugs" of the SS'. As one German deserter who made it to the Russian lines explained in October 1942, the reason more of his comrades did not surrender was fear 'that if they deserted their families would be punished, that if they were seen trying to cross over they would be shot, and that if they were caught they would be executed'.

A second reason Axis forces refused to surrender was not fear of punishment but fear of dishonour. On the Japanese side, certainly, this played a crucial role. The Japanese military had long sought to stigmatize surrender. Although there was no formal regulation against it in either the army or the navy's pre-war criminal codes and disciplinary regulations, by the beginning of the Pacific war capitulation had become taboo. 'Never live to experience shame as a prisoner' was the stark message of the 1941 Field Service Code, and the Japanese army simply refused to acknowledge the existence of Japanese prisoners of war. In the words of Saitō Mutsuo, who trained as a kamikaze pilot:

You see, the Japanese army had no concept of surrender. Even if there was no hope of beating the enemy you were still supposed to fight to the end. That, we were told, was *Yamato damashii* – the Spirit of Japan. We were made to believe that there was something shameful in the way that American and British troops gave up the fight so easily, as they had done at Singapore and other places.

The American war correspondent Ernie Pyle was told by a group of marines how a Japanese officer had responded to being surrounded on a beach by decapitating six of his own men and then brandishing his bloody sword until he was shot dead. At Attu the Japanese mounted suicidal *banzai* charges rather than capitulate. Those Japanese soldiers whom the Allies did succeed in capturing often committed suicide or attempted suicidal escapes. Even at the end of the war, there was extreme reluctance to make use of 'surrender passes' bearing the word 'surrender' in either Japanese (*kōsan*, *kōfuku*) or English; 'I cease resistance' was the preferred euphemism. Some Japanese soldiers refused to lay down their arms until the Imperial Headquarters issued an order on August 15, 1945, that 'servicemen who come under the control of the enemy forces . . . will not be regarded as PoWs'. Many civilians felt the same reluctance to acquiesce in defeat; on Saipan and the Kerama Islands, men killed their own families and then themselves rather than surrender. The Allied insistence on unconditional surrender – announced by Roosevelt at Casablanca in January 1943 – may have stiffened resistance, since it seemed to imply the deposition of the Emperor.

There was something of the same aversion to surrender in the German army. When the American psychologist Saul Padover interrogated Lieutenant Rudolf Kohlhoff after his capture in December 1944, he elicited a revealing response to his question about the possibility of a German defeat:

But I tell you Germany is not going to be defeated. I don't know how long it will take to achieve victory, but it will be achieved. I am convinced of it, or I would not have fought. I have never entertained thoughts of losing. I could not tell you how victory will come but it will. Our generals must have good reason to fight on. They believe in the *Endsieg* [final victory]. Otherwise they would not sacrifice German blood . . . The Wehrmacht will never give up. It did not give up in the last war either. Only the civilians gave up and betrayed the army. I tell you, the Americans will never reach the Rhine. We will fight to the end. We will fight for every city, town and village. If necessary we will see the whole Reich destroyed and the population killed. As a gunner, I know that it is not a pleasant feeling to have to destroy German homes and kill German civilians, but for the defence of the German Fatherland I consider it necessary.

Another prisoner, a young parachutist, told the same interrogator that he was 'deeply humiliated for having permitted himself to be captured' and felt he 'should have died "on the field of honour"'. Such attitudes were obviously more prevalent among those troops who had been most thoroughly indoctrinated by the regime. As American troops neared Marienbad in the Sudetenland in April 1945 Günter Koschorrek, a disillusioned veteran of the Eastern Front, had no doubt that 'in this endgame, some brain-damaged troop leaders . . . [would] follow Hitler's orders to the letter and fight to the last round of ammunition'. Yet even self-consciously unpolitical professionals were influenced by Hitler's orders to fight to the death. When Martin Pöppel, an experienced paratrooper, found his unit surrounded by the Gordon Highlanders in April 1945, he and his men found the decision to surrender far from easy:

I discussed the situation with the last *Unteroffizier*. The Führer order was very much in my mind: 'If a superior officer no longer appears in a position to lead, he is to hand over command to the nearest rank below.' Personally, I was ready to surrender – me, who had been a paratrooper from the very first day of the war. Yet although the struggle was completely hopeless, men came to me in tears. 'As paratroopers, how will we be able to look our wives in the face, if we surrender voluntarily.' A phenomenon, incredible . . . Then, after long silence, they said that if the 'Old Man' . . . thought we should surrender, then they would follow me. [Pöppel was 24.]

One American corporal noted that 'the Krauts always shot up all their ammo and then surrendered' – unlike (by implication) American soldiers, who would surrender when in a hopeless situation. It was exceedingly hazardous to try to parley with Germans who still had bullets left to fire, even if they were surrounded.

In the final analysis, however, it was not only the fear of disciplinary action or of dishonour that deterred German and Japanese soldiers from surrendering. More important for most soldiers was the perception that prisoners would be killed by the enemy anyway, and so one might as well fight on. The Germans were of course the ones who had started killing prisoners on the Eastern Front. At the time, a number of officers and ordinary men sensed that this was not a wise policy. Guy Sajer recalled how he and his comrades had reacted after they had thrown grenades at surrendering Russians:

[Later] we began to grasp what had happened . . . We suddenly felt gripped by something horrible, which made our skins crawl . . . For me, these memories produced a loss of physical sensation, almost as if my personality had split . . . because I knew that such things don't happen to young men who have led normal lives . . .

'We really were shits to kill those Popovs [Russians] . . .' [Hals said.]

He was clearly desperately troubled by the same things that troubled me.

'[That's] how it is, and all there is,' I answered . . . Something hideous had entered our spirits, to remain and haunt us forever.

Quite apart from its illegality, some Germans saw the folly of prisoner killing, and not just because of the value of prisoners as intelligence sources. Wolfgang Horn, who admitted to shooting 'cowardly' Russians himself if they were too slow to raise their hands, nevertheless deplored the decision of the lieutenant commanding his unit to shoot prisoners. It was not only 'unchivalrous' but also 'stupid' because 'Russians hiding in the forest might have seen the prisoners being shot and so they might fight better the next time.' Alfred Rosenberg foresaw as 'an obvious consequence of [the] politically and militarily unwise treatment [of prisoners] . . . not only the weakening of the will to desert but a truly deadly fear of falling into German captivity'. Officers in the 18th Panzer Division came to the same conclusion: 'Red Army soldiers . . . are more afraid of falling prisoner than of the possibility of dying on the battlefield.' So did the commander of the Grossdeutschland Division, who appealed to his men to 'understand that the ultimate result of the maltreatment or shooting of PoWs after they had given themselves up in battle would be . . . a stiffening of the enemy's resistance, because every Red Army soldier fears German captivity'. Orders against 'senseless shootings' went largely unheeded by soldiers on the ground, however. Indeed, the practice of prisoner killing became routine: 'We take some prisoners, we shoot them, all in a day's work.'

The fear of retaliation helps to explain why many Germans found the prospect of surrender unpalatable even when their position had become patently hopeless. Ordinary soldiers were plagued by fear 'of falling into the hands of the Russians, no doubt thirsty for revenge'. By no means exceptional was the intransigent officer who declared after the capitulation at Stalingrad: 'There'll be no surrender! The war goes on!' and then shot a Russian officer. In July 1944 the lieutenant in charge of Eduard Stelbe's unit shot himself rather than fall into the hands of the Red Army. Gottlob Bidermann's description of the 132nd Infantry Division's surrender provides further evidence of the extreme reluctance of some front-line officers to obey direct orders to capitulate, even as late as the war's end on May 8, 1945. One officer shot himself through the head; another ran back screaming 'No surrender!' to the next German line, where he tried to force the commander of a self-propelled gun to engage the enemy. He had to be knocked out with a rifle butt. 'Why did you continue to fight?' asked the Red Army colonel who accepted Bidermann's surrender. His answer was: 'Because we are soldiers.' But this was not a sufficient explanation. A large part of the reason was that, having committed war crimes themselves, Wehrmacht troops expected no quarter from the Red Army. Günter Koschorrek knew full well that the Soviets did not 'treat their prisoners in accordance with the terms of the Geneva Convention . . . We have fought against the Soviets – we can imagine what awaits us in Siberia.' The dread of defeat was compounded by the involvement of the Wehrmacht in massacres of civilians. 'If we should lose tomorrow,' wrote Guy Sajer, 'those of us still alive . . . will be judged without mercy . . . accused of an infinity of murder . . . spared nothing.' One soldier who had witnessed the slaughter of thousands of Jews in Lithuania could say only: 'May God grant us victory because if they get their revenge, we're in for a hard time.' Those Japanese who were aware of their own side's brutal mistreatment of prisoners – in particular, the medical experiments conducted by Unit 731 in Manchukuo – may have felt similar apprehensions.

Retribution was not slow in coming. 'We have badly mistreated our [own] people,' a Soviet prisoner told his German interrogators, 'in fact so bad that it was almost impossible to treat them worse. [But] you Germans have managed to do that . . . Therefore we will win the war.' 'Do not count days, do not count miles,' thundered Ilya Ehrenburg in the *Red Star* army newspaper. 'Count only the number of Germans you have killed. Kill the German – this is your mother's prayer. Kill the German – this is the cry of your Russian earth. Do not waver. Do not let up. Kill.' The Soviets treated the Germans precisely as the Germans had treated them. Prisoners were frequently shot immediately after interrogation, a practice explicitly justified as retaliation for German treatment of Soviet prisoners. Zinaida Pytkina, a SMERSH interrogator, recalled how she personally despatched a German officer with a shot in the back of the neck:

It was joy for me. The Germans didn't ask us to spare them and I was angry . . . When we were retreating we lost so many 17-, 18-year olds. Do I have to be sorry for the German after that? This was my mood . . . As a member of the Communist Party, I saw in front of me a man who could have killed my relatives . . . I would have cut off his head if I had been asked to. One person less, I thought. Ask him how many people he killed – he did not think about this?

The wounded at Stalingrad were simply finished off after the German surrender. In turn, German troops on the other side were 'told that the Russians have been killing all prisoners'. Ruthenians drafted into the Wehrmacht would have deserted in larger numbers had they not 'believe[d] the officers' stories that the Russians [would] torture and shoot them'. Eduard Stelbe was genuinely surprised when the first words of the Russian officer to whom he surrendered were simply: 'Does anyone have a cigarette?' When some female soldiers pointed their pistols at him and his comrades as they trudged to captivity, he fully expected them to fire; in fact the pistols had been emptied. It was just, he recalled, 'a little show of sadism'.

It was not only on the Eastern Front that a cycle of violence manifested itself. In the Pacific theatre, too, ill treatment and murder of prisoners were commonplace. It is clear from many accounts that American and Australian forces often shot Japanese surrenderers. It happened at Guadalcanal, especially after twenty Marines fell victim to an apparent Japanese surrender that turned out to be an ambush. The Marines' battle cry on Tarawa was 'Kill the Jap bastards! Take no prisoners!' At Peleliu, too, American troops had no compunction about bayoneting Japanese soldiers who had just surrendered. On New Guinea in 1944 Charles Lindbergh heard it 'freely admitted that some of our soldiers tortured Japanese prisoners and were as cruel and barbaric at times as the Japs themselves. Our men think nothing of shooting a Japanese prisoner or soldier attempting to surrender. They treat the Japs with less respect than they would give to an animal, and these acts are condoned by almost everyone.' This behaviour was not merely sanctioned but actively encouraged by Allied officers in the Pacific. An infantry colonel told Lindbergh proudly: 'Our boys just don't take prisoners.' Nor was this a peculiarity of American forces. The testimony of Sergeant Henry Ewen confirms that Australian troops killed prisoners at Bougainville 'in cold blood'. When Indian soldiers serving with the British in Burma killed a group of wounded Japanese prisoners, George MacDonald Fraser, then an officer in the 14th Army, turned a blind eye.

Killing prisoners was sometimes justified as retaliation. The orderly of a popular Marine company commander who had been killed at Okinawa 'snatched up a submachine gun and unforgivably massacred a line of unarmed Japanese soldiers who had just surrendered'. British troops, too, killed Japanese prisoners in revenge for earlier atrocities against Allied wounded. However, there is evidence that 'taking no prisoners' simply became standard practice. 'The [American] rule of thumb,' an American PoW told his Japanese captors, 'was "if it moves, shoot it".' Another GI maxim was 'Kill or be killed.' The war correspondent Edgar L. Jones later recalled: 'We shot prisoners in cold blood, wiped out hospitals, strafed lifeboats . . . finished off the enemy wounded.' War psychologists regarded the killing of prisoners as so commonplace that they devised formulae for assuaging soldiers' subsequent feelings of guilt. Roughly two-fifths of American army chaplains surveyed after the war said that they had regarded orders to kill prisoners as legitimate. This kind of thing went on despite the obvious deterrent effect on other Japanese soldiers who might be contemplating surrender, making it far from easy to distinguish the self-induced aversion to surrender discussed above from the rational fear that the Americans would kill any prisoners. In June 1945 the US Office of War Information reported that 84 per cent of interrogated Japanese prisoners had expected to be killed by their captors. This fear was clearly far from unwarranted. Two years before, a secret intelligence report said that only the promise of free ice cream and three days' leave would induce American troops not to kill surrendering Japanese.

This brings us to one of the most troubling aspects of the Second World War: the fact that Allied troops often regarded the Japanese in the same way that Germans regarded Russians – as *Untermenschen*. General Sir Thomas Blamey, who commanded the Australians in New Guinea, told his troops that their foes were 'a cross between the human being and the ape', 'vermin', 'something primitive' that had to be 'exterminated' to preserve 'civilization'. 'The Japs . . . had renounced the right to be regarded as human,' recalled Major John Winstanley, who fought with the Royal West Kent Regiment at Kohima. 'We thought of them as vermin to be exterminated.' To Lieutenant Lintorn Highlett of the Dorsetshires, they were 'formidable fighting insects' – an echo of General Slim's description of the Japanese soldiers as 'part of an insect horde with all its power and horror'. Wartime cartoonists often portrayed the Japanese as monkeys or apes. 'A searing hate arises in me whenever I see a Nip,' wrote Edward Dunlop in his diary of the Death Railway. 'Disgusting, deplorable, hateful troop of men – apes.' Such sentiments were even more widespread among Americans, where the popular reaction to Pearl Harbor ('Why, the yellow bastards!') built on pre-existing racial prejudices. On May 22, 1944, *Life* magazine published a picture of a winsome blonde gazing at a human skull. A *memento mori* perhaps, in the tradition of the Metaphysical poets? On the contrary:

When he said goodby [sic] two years ago to Natalie Nickerson, 20, a war worker of Phoenix, Ariz., a big, handsome Navy lieutenant promised her a Jap. Last week Natalie received a human skull, autographed by her lieutenant and 13 friends, and inscribed: 'This is a good Jap – a dead one picked up on the New Guinea beach.' Natalie, surprised at the gift, named it Tojo.

Boiling the flesh off enemy skulls to make souvenirs was a not uncommon practice. Ears, bones and teeth were also collected. In April

1943 the *Baltimore Sun* ran a story about a mother who petitioned the authorities to let her son post her a Japanese ear so that she could nail it to her front door – an unusual alternative to tying a yellow ribbon round the old oak tree. The United States had already all but embraced the command economy. Now the war against totalitarianism had forced Americans to adopt another of totalitarianism's defining characteristics: they had dehumanized the enemy in order more easily to annihilate him. The Chairman of the War Manpower Commission, Paul V. McNutt, declared in April 1945 that he was in favour of 'the extermination of the Japanese *in toto*'. Polls revealed that at least 13 per cent of Americans shared his view.

Thus, when American met German in the battlefields of Western Europe after the invasion of Italy, both had experience of lawless racial war, even if the scale of the German experience was vastly greater. Not surprisingly, prisoner killing was carried over into the new European theatres. Perhaps the most notorious example was the murder of seventy-seven American prisoners at Malmédy by the SS Battle Group Peiper on December 17, 1944. That taught Allied troops to fear Waffen-SS units more than regular Wehrmacht units. Yet such atrocities were committed by both sides. On July 14, 1943, for example, troops of the American 45th Infantry Division killed seventy Italian and German PoWs at Biscari in Sicily. Sergeant William C. Bradley recalled how one of his comrades killed a group of German prisoners captured in France. On June 7, 1944, an American officer admitted that US airborne forces did not take prisoners but 'kill them as they hold up their hands coming out. They are apt in going along a road with prisoners and seeing one of their own men killed, to turn around and shoot a prisoner to make up for it. They are tough people.' Stephen Ambrose's study of E Company, 506th Regiment, 101st Airborne Division, suggests this was not wholly without foundation. As one British diplomat noted:

American troops are not showing any great disposition to take prisoners unless the enemy come over in batches of twenty or more. When smaller groups than this appear with their hands up, the American soldiers ... are apt to interpret this as a menacing gesture ... and to take liquidating action accordingly ... There is quite a proportion of 'tough guys', who have experienced the normal peace-time life of Chicago, and other great American cities, and who are applying the lessons they learned there.

As in the Pacific theatre, American troops often rationalized their conduct as retaliation. The tenacity of German troops, their reluctance to surrender and their ability to inflict casualties until their supplies of ammunition were exhausted were intensely frustrating to Americans certain of victory, who saw such resistance as futile. However, prisoner killing continued to be overtly encouraged by some American officers. General George Patton's address to the 45th Infantry Division before the invasion of Sicily could not have been more explicit:

When we land against the enemy ... we will show him no mercy ... If you company officers in leading your men against the enemy find him shooting at you and, when you get within two hundred yards of him, and he wishes to surrender, oh no! That bastard will die! You must kill him. Stick him between the third and fourth ribs. You will tell your men that. They must have the killer instinct. Tell them to stick it in. He can do no good then. Stick them in the liver.

Major-General Raymond Hufft ordered his troops to 'take no prisoners' when he led them across the Rhine. And, as in the Pacific, American troops were encouraged to regard their foes as subhuman. One American interrogator described an eighteen-year-old parachutist captured after the Ardennes counteroffensive as a 'fanatical Hitler youth', a 'totally dehumanized Nazi' and a 'carefully formed killing machine':

I wondered why the M[ilitary] P[olice] had not fulfilled his wish [to die in battle], particularly after he had killed one of their comrades. They had merely knocked him out cold. Hard-eyed and rigid of face, he was arrogant with an inner, unbending arrogance. He aroused in me an urge which I hope never to experience again, an urge to kill. I could have killed him in cold blood, without any doubt or second thought, as I would a cockroach. It was a terrible feeling to have, because it was without passion. I could not think of him as a human being.

Countless memoirs testify to the desperate but lethal quality of the German defence in the final months of the war. Since the Axis powers appeared to fight more doggedly the more their strategic situation worsened, the question became: how on earth could they be defeated at a tolerable human cost? The obvious answer was simply to try to persuade German and Japanese soldiers that, contrary to their own expectation, it was safe to lay down their weapons. Accordingly, the many leaflets fired or dropped onto German positions, as well as radio broadcasts and loudspeaker addresses, emphasized not only the hopelessness of Germany's military position but also the lack of risk involved in surrendering. Key themes of 'Sykewar' were the good treatment of PoWs – in particular, the fact that German PoWs were given the same rations as American GIs, including cigarettes – and Allied observance of the Geneva Convention. Typical was the leaflet which began simply:

> ONE MINUTE, which can save your life.
> TWO WORDS, which have saved 850,000 lives.
> THREE WAYS, to get home.
> SIX WAYS, to get yourself killed.

The words which had saved 850,000 lives were of course 'I surrender' – or rather 'Ei Ssörrender', spelt out phonetically.

Though it is not easy to assess its effectiveness – PoW questionnaires revealed persistent trust in Hitler and belief in the possibility of victory until as late as January 1945 – it seems likely that 'Sykewar' did something to encourage already disaffected individuals to surrender. Once the crucial bonds of group solidarity began to break down in the Wehrmacht in the last months of the war, Allied propaganda began to be effective; indeed, it cannot be ruled out that the line of causation went the other way. Perhaps the best evidence of the effectiveness of such psychological warfare was the evident preference of German troops to surrender to American units. 'God preserve us!' one German soldier wrote in his diary on April 29, 1944. 'If we have to go to prison, then let's hope it's with the Americans.' That was a widespread sentiment. Until the third quarter of 1944 more than half of all German prisoners were held in the East. But thereafter the share captured by the Western powers rose rapidly, as Figure 15.2 shows. This was not just a function of the increased contact with British and American forces after D-Day. It is clear that many German units

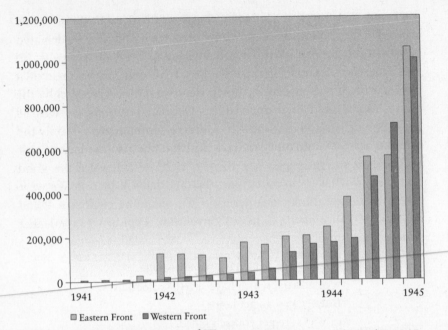

*Figure 15.2* **German Prisoners of War, 1st quarter 1941–1st quarter 1945**

sought to surrender to the Americans in preference to other Allied forces, and particularly the Red Army. With the benefit of hindsight, they might have done better to look for British captors, since the British treated German prisoners better than the Americans and were also less willing to hand them over to the Soviets. But psychological warfare led the Germans to expect the kindest treatment from US forces.

Similar efforts were made to encourage Japanese soldiers to capitulate. 'Surrender passes' and translations of the Geneva Convention were dropped on Japanese positions, and concerted efforts were made to stamp out the practice of taking no prisoners. On May 14, 1944, MacArthur sent a telegram to the commander of the Alamo Force demanding an 'investigation . . . of numerous reports reaching this headquarters that Japanese carrying surrender passes and attempting to surrender in Hollandia area have been killed by our troops'. The Psychological Warfare Branch representative at 10th Corps, Captain William R. Beard, complained that his efforts were being negated 'by the front-line troops shooting [Japanese] when they made an attempt to surrender'. But gradually the message got through, especially to more experienced troops. 'Don't shoot the bastard!' shouted one veteran when a Japanese soldier emerged from a foxhole waving a surrender leaflet. By the time the Americans took Luzon in the Philippines, 70 per cent of all prisoners made use of surrender passes or followed the instructions they contained. The Philippines had been deluged with over 55 million such leaflets, and it seems plausible to attribute to this propaganda effort the fall in the ratio of prisoners to Japanese dead from 1:100 in late 1944 to 1:7 by July 1945. Still, the Japanese soldier who emerged with six surrender leaflets – one in each hand, one in each ear, one in his mouth, and one tucked in a grass band tied around his waist – was wise to take no chances.

As on the Western Front in the First World War, then, the crucial determinant of an army's willingness to fight on or surrender was soldiers' expectations of how they would be treated if they did lay down their arms. In regard to prisoner killing in the heat of battle, information about enemy conduct was relatively easy to obtain; eyewitness accounts of prisoner killings tended to circulate rapidly and widely among front-line troops, often becoming exaggerated in the telling. By contrast, news of the way prisoners were treated away from the battlefield was slower to spread, depending as it did on testimony from escaped PoWs or the letters from PoWs to their families relayed by the International Committee of the Red Cross. (It should be borne in mind that both of the latter channels were effectively closed between Germany and the Soviet Union because of the geographical distances between enemy camps and safe territory, and the refusal of the Germans to acknowledge Stalin's belated subscription to the Geneva Convention.) Such information mattered, because treatment of prisoners varied so enormously between theatres and armies, as we have seen. A British prisoner in German hands had a reasonably good chance of surviving the war, as only one in twenty-nine died in captivity; but a Russian prisoner of the Germans was more likely to die than survive. A substantial proportion of the large number of German troops taken prisoner at the end of the war also died in captivity, though the numbers remain controversial. Barely one in ten of those who surrendered at Stalingrad survived their time in Soviet hands –

indeed, half had died within a few months of laying down their arms – and perhaps as few as two-fifths of all those captured on the Eastern Front. The mortality rate for German PoWs in Soviet hands reached a peak of over 50 per cent in 1943. Germans who surrendered to the Western Allies were far luckier. Although it has been alleged that as many as 726,000 who fell into American hands died of starvation or disease, these calculations almost certainly exaggerate both the number of prisoners the Americans took and their mortality. The most that can be said is that those Germans who preferred to surrender to American rather than to British forces made a miscalculation, since the mortality rate for German PoWs in American hands was more than four times higher than the rate for Germans who surrendered to the British (0.15 per cent to 0.03 per cent).

Yet – and here is the twist in the tale – it was not always the paramount aim of Allied strategy to induce the Axis armies to surrender at the front line. As much if not more importance was attached, from an early stage in the war, to the idea that Germany and Japan could be bombed into submission. That, indeed, was the thrust of the Joint Intelligence Sub-Committee's assessment in 1943. It was not, however, the Axis armies that were to be bombed. It was their civilian populations. The Axis powers had treated the civilians of countries they occupied with an astonishing brutality. In the eyes of the Allied leaders, this was ample justification for 'payback'.

# 16

# *Kaputt*

*. . . The flames immediately crackle and flare up high, so high that the fire fills the whole space in front of the hall and seems to seize on this too. Terrified, the men and women press to the extreme foreground . . . The entire stage appears to be completely filled with flame . . . leaving . . . a cloud of smoke which drifts towards the background and lies on the horizon like a dark pall of cloud . . . Through the cloud bank that lies on the horizon breaks an increasingly bright red glow . . . From the ruins of the palace, which has collapsed, the men and women, in the utmost apprehension, watch the growing fire-light in the sky . . . Bright flames seem to set fire to the hall of the gods. As the gods become completely hidden from view by the flames, the curtain falls.*

Wagner, stage direction for *Götterdämmerung*

*After tea we went back to Berlin . . . to see Hitler's dugout . . . A sordid and unromantic spot. Absolute chaos outside of concrete mixers, iron reinforcing bars, timber, broken furniture, shell holes, clothes etc. etc. Down below even worse chaos . . . We also had a look at the Air Ministry and a drive round Berlin. The more one sees of it the more one realizes how completely destroyed it is.*

General Alan Brooke, Diary, July 19, 1945

## TWILIGHT OF THE DEVILS

In the final climactic scene of Wagner's *Götterdämmerung* – 'Twilight of the Gods' – the heroine Brünnhilde restores the stolen ring of power to the River Rhine and hurls herself onto her dead lover Siegfried's funeral pyre. Her act of sublime self-sacrifice unleashes a fiery conflagration that topples the stronghold of the gods, Valhalla, in an almost un-stageable apocalypse. Hitler's lifelong obsession with Wagner's music had made it something like the official soundtrack of the Third Reich; indeed, Albert Speer was attending a concert performance of the finale of *Götterdämmerung* (the Berlin Philharmonic's last performance under the Third Reich) when the news of Roosevelt's death reached Berlin. 'The war isn't lost, Roosevelt is dead!' exclaimed Hitler. In reality, however, the year 1945 was to see the twilight of the devils. According to one intercepted Axis communication from a Japanese diplomat in Berlin, Hitler was planning 'to embark alone in a plane carrying bombs and blow himself up in the air somewhere over the Baltic'. The intention was that 'the one million fervent admirers of the Führer among the German people . . . would believe that he had become a god and was dwelling in heaven.' It was to be Brünnhilde's immolation, in a Messerschmitt.

In *Mein Kampf*, Hitler had bitterly recalled the trauma of 1918, when political discussions among new conscripts – 'the poison of the hinterland' – had undermined the morale of the army. Twenty years later, when Goebbels concluded a speech at the Sportpalast with the words 'a November 1918 will never be repeated', Hitler 'looked up to him, a wild, eager expression in his eyes . . . leaped to his feet and with a fanatical fire in his eyes . . . brought his right hand, after a great sweep, pounding down on the table and yelled . . . "Ja!" '. 'As long as I am alive,' he told Halder in August 1939, 'there will be no talk of capitulation.' Not surrendering, it appears, mattered more to Hitler than victory. Perhaps from as early as November 1941, as his forces ground to a halt outside Moscow, and certainly after the failure of his second offensive in the East, a drive for the Caucasus oilfields in spring 1942, he began to suspect that it would be impossible to defeat the Soviet Union. Yet honourable defeat, which for Hitler meant nothing less than a Wagnerian finale, was in itself desirable, perhaps even preferable to victory. This was the lesson Hitler took from Clausewitz's *Confessions*, as well as from Siegfried's death in *The Ring*: that a heroic death (*Heldentod*) had a redemptive quality which might sow the seeds of a future regeneration of Germany. Only those races 'who keep their courage to fight to the death even without hope have any prospect of surviving and achieving a new flowering', he declared; 'Out of the sacrifice of our soldiers and out of my own close ties with them unto death, the seed will one day germinate . . . and give rise to a glorious rebirth of the National Socialist movement, and this to the realization of a true *Volksgemeinschaft*.' Hitler's last official proclamation of February 24, 1945, called for a last-ditch war of resistance on German soil, while the so-called 'Nero Orders' of March 1945 envisaged a scorched earth policy that implied the complete destruction of the country's infrastructure. 'No German blade shall feed the enemy,' the *Völkische Beobachter* had declared in September 1944; 'no German mouth shall impart information; no German hand shall offer help. The enemy should find every little bridge destroyed, every road blocked – nothing but death, destruction and hate will await him.' Hitler got his funeral pyre. By the time he put a bullet through his own head the entire German Reich had become one.

'Long live war,' he had told the Sudeten German leader, Henlein, in 1938, 'even if it lasts from two to eight years.' Hitler's war lasted less than six. By the end it had cost the lives of at least 5.2 million German servicemen – three in every ten men mobilized – and more than 2.4 million German civilians. More German soldiers lost their lives in the last twelve months of fighting than in the whole of the rest of the war (see Figure 16.1). The crucial point is that to Hitler this monstrous toll meant nothing whatever – as little as the deaths of the many more people his troops killed.* 'Life is horrible,' he once mused over dinner. 'Coming into being, existing, and passing away, there's always a killing. Everything that is born must later die.' Humanity,

---

* It is not easy to say precisely how many people the Germans killed. Suffice to say that the ratio of Allied to Axis military deaths was 3.0:1 and the ratio of Allied to Axis civilian deaths was 5.8:1.

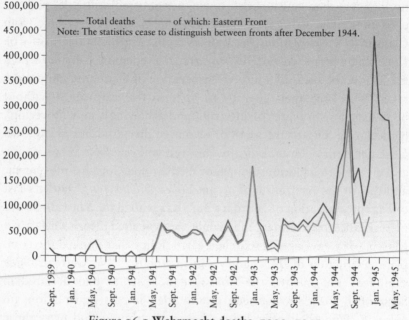

*Figure 16.1* **Wehrmacht deaths, 1939–1945**

he declared on another occasion, was 'a ridiculous cosmic bacterium' (*eine lächerliche Weltraumbakterie*).

If they had been rational, the Axis leaders would have moderated their conduct in anticipation of a future peace, in the hope of somehow diminishing the victors' appetite for retribution and minimizing the loss of life on their own side. It is true that there were attempts by some generals, diplomats and even leading Nazis to extend peace feelers to Britain or to the Soviet Union. At Bełżec the Nazis did seek to cover up at least some of the crimes they had committed. As early as the summer of 1943 they turfed over the site of the death camp, planting trees and even building a fake farmhouse. Yet elsewhere the killing was not merely continued; it was positively stepped up. The worse the war went for them, the more fanatically the Germans pursued their policies of violence towards those unfortunates still in their power, as if willing the final cataclysm. Göring said to Goebbels, 'On the Jewish question we are so committed that there is no escape for us at all.' But to Goebbels that was good: 'Experience shows that a movement and a people that have burned their bridges fight more unconditionally than those who still have the chance of retreat.' The worse the crimes they committed, the less the Nazis could conceive of surrendering themselves to the judgment of the Allies. As Goebbels put it in early 1945: 'If we have to leave, we'll close the door behind us with a slam that all the world will hear.' 'Everyone now has a chance to choose the part which he will play in the film of a hundred years hence,' Goebbels told his staff at the Propaganda Ministry on April 17, inspired by the Third Reich's last cinematic feat, *Kolberg*, an epic depiction of that town's last-ditch defence during the Napoleonic Wars. 'I can assure you that it will be a fine and elevating picture . . . Hold out now, so that . . . the audience does not hoot and whistle when you appear on the screen.' Thus was the Third Reich to go down: in an inglorious blaze.

The implications of this mentality became crystal clear to Victor Klemperer in Dresden as rumours spread of the conduct of German forces being driven back towards the borders of the Reich:

October 24th, 1944. On Sunday evening Konrad was here for a couple of minutes . . . He believes . . . that before the retreats everyone was murdered, that we shall see no one again, that six to seven million Jews (of the 15 million that had existed) have been slaughtered (more exactly: shot and gassed). He also considers that the prospects of the small Jewish remnant, left here in the clutches of the desperate beasts, remaining alive were also very slight.

Across the territory still controlled by the Nazis, the 'final solution' was pursued in a mood of hypertrophic fanaticism. Virtually all the 438,000 Jews of Hungary were deported to Auschwitz between April and July 1944; nearly all of them were murdered. Even as the Red Army neared Auschwitz, the Germans ordered those prisoners still capable of walking to march to the Austrian border – a distance of 90 miles. There would be no liberation for those spared the gas chambers; they must be marched until they dropped. Of 714,000 concentration camp inmates who still remained in January 1945, around 250,000 perished in these death marches, including 15,000 out of the 60,000 evacuated from Auschwitz. Nor were Jews the only victims of the death throes of Nazism. In the last years of the regime there was a dramatic increase in capital punishment, as ordinary Germans who dared to express their disenchantment were summarily strung up for defeatism. Between 1942 and 1944 there were more than 14,000 death sentences passed by the German courts, nearly ten times the number during the first three years of the war. And these figures do not include the numerous extra-judicial executions carried out by the SS.

Yet Hitler was not alone in wanting to turn Germany into one vast charnel house. For their part, the Allied leaders laid their plans for victory in ways that more or less ensured that, as twilight fell on the Third Reich and Imperial Japan, the devils would take the maximum possible number of human souls down with them.

## PAYBACK

The idea that a country could be bombed into submission long pre-dated the Second World War. H. G. Wells's aliens were on the point of unleashing flying machines on London when they succumbed to earth's fatal microbes. Shortly before the First World War, Kipling had imagined (in his short story 'As Easy as ABC') a world brought to heel by a single International Air Force. Air raids on civilian targets by the Germans between 1914 and 1918 had, admittedly, been of negligible military value. As for their impact on civilian morale, they almost certainly aroused more vengefulness than panic. The main role of air forces proved to be reconnaissance rather than bombing. Nevertheless, the idea of flattening cities from the air had captured the public imagination and it remained fashionable throughout the inter-war years. As Secretary of State for War and Air, Churchill used air power without compunction to help quell the Iraqi revolt of 1920. The world was more shocked when the Germans used bombers against Guernica; Mesopotamian villages were seen as fair game, European cities not so. Japanese air strikes against China after 1937 only seemed to confirm the adage that 'the bomber would always get through', and with devastating results.

As we have seen, British strategy in the 1930s was to invest not in defensive but in offensive air power, in the hope of deterring a German attack from the air rather than repulsing it. This was an irrational response to the threat posed by the Luftwaffe. But it did mean that by 1940 Britain had the beginnings of a strategic bombing capability. This early investment was important given the time it took – more than two years – to train pilots and navigators. On the other hand, the 488 bombers that Britain had ready in September 1939 were far from equal to the task of conducting air raids on Germany. Nevertheless, within less than a week of becoming Prime Minister, Churchill – true to form – ordered the RAF to do just that. Indeed, in this regard, Churchill may be said to have pre-empted Hitler, whose Blitz against London was seen in Germany as an act of retaliation following the British raids on Berlin. Hitler later declared: 'It was the British who started air attacks' – though it had scarcely been 'moral scruples' that had dictated German strategy. Yet Churchill could cite the German bombing of Rotterdam, to say nothing of the use of dive bombers against Polish civilians, as a perfectly good precedent.

But what exactly should the targets of British air raids be? Since German fighting forces were quite widely dispersed for much of the war, the obvious targets were economic – the factories that were supplying Hitler's forces with weapons and the infrastructure that allowed these to be transported to the various fronts. However, most of these economic targets were, by their very nature, located in densely populated areas like the Ruhr. Moreover, British bombers were very far from accurate. In October 1940 the British ruled that, in conditions of poor visibility, their airmen could drop their bombs in the vicinity of targets, in so-called 'free fire zones'. This made it more likely that German civilians would be hit – a necessity which Churchill sought to make into a virtue. As he put it on October 30, 'The civilian population around the target areas must be made to feel the weight of war.' Throughout 1941 Churchill repeatedly emphasized the need for Bomber Command to target the morale of ordinary Germans. The strategy of 'area bombing' – the aim of which was in fact to incinerate urban centres – was in place even before Air Marshal Arthur 'Bomber' Harris took over Bomber Command. Nine days before Harris's appointment, on St Valentine's Day, 1942, Air Vice-Marshal N. H. Bottomley, Deputy of the Air Staff, wrote to Bomber Command to convey the decision 'that the primary object of your operations should now be focused on the morale of the enemy civil population and in particular, of the industrial workers', and that these operations should take the form of 'concentrated incendiary attacks'. The letter was accompanied by a list of 'selected area targets', at the top of which was Essen. By attacking it first, 'the maximum benefit should be derived from the element of surprise'. Like the other prime targets, Duisberg, Düsseldorf and Cologne, Essen was without question an industrial city. Yet the criteria listed for calculating the 'estimated weight of attack for decisive damage' were the size and population of the built-up area. Attacks on factories and submarine building yards were to be considered 'diversionary', and were to be undertaken preferably 'without missing good opportunities of bombing your primary targets'.

What this meant was that a rising proportion of first British and then American resources were diverted into the destruction of German and Japanese cities – in other words, the slaughter of civilians. This was precisely the policy the US State Department had denounced as 'unwarranted and contrary to principles of law and humanity' when the Japanese had first bombed Chinese cities. It was precisely the policy that Neville Chamberlain had once dismissed as 'mere terrorism', a policy to which 'His Majesty's government [would] never resort'.

What made the concept of strategic bombing so appealing? Air war was not necessarily cheaper, since the planes themselves were expensive to produce and the crews expensive to train. For the crews themselves, needless to say, it was a harrowing business. Flying at altitudes of up to 28,000 feet in temperatures so cold that naked flesh could stick inseparably to gun metal and icicles could form on oxygen masks, and with virtually no armour around them (to minimize additional weight), Lancaster bomber crews were nothing if not brave men. Mortality rates were among the highest in the war; the life expectancy of a Lancaster was estimated at just twelve missions, while the average odds of survival for bomber crews were worse than 1 in 2. Those who made it through multiple missions were often psychologically if not physically scarred for life. Nor did they have the consolation of the laurels that were heaped upon their comrades who flew fighters. Yet, to civilian politicians, strategic bombing was preferable to relying on ground troops because of the comparatively small numbers of men involved. Air war was in large part about the substitution of capital for labour – of machinery for men. A single crew of trained fliers could hope to kill a very large number of Germans or Japanese even if they flew only twenty successful missions before being killed or captured themselves.

Revealingly, Churchill spoke of 'pay[ing] our way by bombing Germany' when he visited Moscow in 1942; the currency he had in mind was German lives, not British. The more Stalin pressed the Western powers to open a Second Front in Western Europe, the more Churchill extolled the virtues of strategic bombing, promising attacks that would 'shatter the morale of the German people'. He was equally sanguine about the benefits of bombing Italy, arguing that 'the demoralization and panic produced by intensive heavy air bombard-ment' would outweigh 'any increase in anti-British feeling'. In such views he was greatly encouraged by his scientific adviser and head of the wartime Statistical Department, the physicist Frederick Linde-mann. As so often in war, inter-service rivalry played its part, too. In appointing Sir Charles Portal, Commander-in-Chief of Bomber Command, to the post of Chief of the Air Staff in October 1940, Churchill ensured that a dogmatic proponent of area bombing would have a seat at Britain's strategy-making high table. Alan Brooke was sceptical about Portal's insistence that 'success lies in accumulating the largest air force possible in England and that then, and then only, success lies assured through the bombing of Europe.' But he could not prevent the diversion of substantial resources to Portal's squadrons.

Similar calculations persuaded Roosevelt to invest in strategic bombing: first, wild exaggeration of what German bombers could do to America, then a somewhat smaller exaggeration of what American bombers could do to Germany. To be sure, the American approach was in other respects different from the British. While the British favoured night area bombing, the Americans prided themselves on the greater accuracy of their planes. Equipped with the Norden bomb sight, the Flying Fortress was almost certainly a better machine than its British counterpart. But it was still far less precise than had been hoped, even with the benefit (though also the cost, in terms of greater vulnerability) of attacking during the day. By the time of the Casablanca Conference of January 1943, the Americans had come round to the Churchillian notion that their aim should be 'the progressive destruction and undermining of the morale of the German people to a point where their capacity for armed resistance is fatally weakened'. Roosevelt's confidant, Harry Hopkins, was among those who firmly believed this.

The effects of the Allied bombing campaigns against Germany and Japan were, as is well known, horrendous. What the RAF and USAAF did dwarfed what the Luftwaffe had been able to inflict on Britain during the Blitz. Beginning on the night of July 24, 1943 vast swathes of the city of Hamburg were destroyed in a raid codenamed 'Operation Gomorrah'. Sheltered from detection by the new device known as 'Window' (a shower of aluminium strips that smothered German radar), 791 RAF bombers rained down high explosive and incendiary bombs, creating a devastating firestorm* that raged out far beyond the control of the German emergency services. Around three-quarters of the city was laid waste in the succeeding days, as the initial bombardment was followed up by both American and British raids. At the very least, 45,000 people were killed and nearly a million rendered homeless. The flames were visible more than a hundred miles away. The author Hans Nossack, who had left his Hamburg home for a few days in the country, returned to find flies and rats feasting on – and, incongruously, geraniums sprouting from – the charred human remains of his fellow citizens. Inhabitants of the smart suburbs along the Elbe to the west of the city saw their gardens turn grey with ash. All this was achieved at a remarkably low cost to Bomber Command, whose losses amounted to less than 3 per cent of the planes involved. Nor did the Allies relent as the war drew to a close. Around 1.1 million tons of the total 1.6 million tons of explosives dropped by Bomber Command and the 8th US Air Force – some 71 per cent – were dropped during the last year of the war. Once the Allies had developed a long-range fighter escort (in the form of the P-51 Mustang), they were in a position to bomb Germany in daylight with something approaching impunity.

---

* The incendiary bombs were filled with highly combustible substances such as magnesium, phosphorus or petroleum jelly. After the target was burning, the hot air above it began to rise rapidly, sucking in colder air from the surrounding area. The effect was greatly magnified if the wind was in the right direction, as was the case in both Hamburg and Dresden.

On the night of February 13, 1945 a force of 796 British Lancaster bombers set off to bomb Dresden. They were followed over the next two days by waves of American Flying Fortresses. Among the thousands of people in the line of fire was Victor Klemperer, one of Dresden's few surviving Jews. For months he had been expecting to be rounded up by the SS. But what if the other side got him first? On September 15, 1944 he had written in his diary:

I am so accustomed to news of cities destroyed by bombing that it makes no impression on me at all ... Eva [his wife]'s home town [Königsberg] is 75 per cent destroyed, according to official reports 5,000 are dead and 20,000 injured ... That shook me, and in the morning – dark glowing, deep purple dawn – as I washed myself and looked out at the Carola Bridge and the row of houses on the other side, I could not stop imagining that this row of houses was suddenly collapsing before my eyes ... Until now Dresden itself really has been spared.

Klemperer's predicament symbolized the warped morality of the last months of the war. For, on the morning of February 13, 1945 he was ordered to deliver deportation notices to a substantial number of the remaining Jews in Dresden. There was no longer any doubt what deportation meant. And it seemed inevitable that he would be next:

Tuesday afternoon, perfect spring weather ... We sat down for coffee at about a half past nine on Tuesday evening, very weary and depressed because during the day, after all, I had been running around as the bringer of bad tidings, and in the evening Waldemann had assured me with very great certainty that those to be deported on Thursday were being sent to their deaths and that we who were being left behind would be done away with in a week's time.

Yet February 13 was to prove deadly in a very different way – not just for Jews, but for all the city's inhabitants. For it was now Dresden's turn to be on the receiving end of Allied payback:

A full scale warning sounded ... Very soon we heard the ever deeper and louder humming of approaching squadrons, the light went out, an explosion nearby ... in some groups there was whimpering and weeping – approaching aircraft again, deadly danger once again, explosion once again ... Suddenly the cellar window on the back wall opposite the entrance burst open and outside it was bright as day . . . Fires were blazing. The ground was covered with broken glass. A terrible strong wind was blowing.

The firestorm unleashed on Dresden engulfed 95,000 homes. At the very least, 35,000 people died, including those who sought safety in the city's fountains only for them to boil dry and others who were asphyxiated in the bomb shelters underneath the main railway station. A schoolgirl named Karin Busch and her twin brother found themselves wandering the streets in the midst of the firestorm after an unexploded bomb had forced them to flee their family shelter:

Flames were licking all around us and somehow we found ourselves by the River Elbe. I could see phosphorus dancing on the water, so for people throwing themselves into the river to get away from the fire, there was no escape. There were bodies everywhere and the gasmasks that people were wearing were melting into their faces . . . We started looking for a cellar to hide in, but in every cellar we looked into, we saw people sitting dead because the fires had sucked the oxygen out and suffocated them.

Finally, they found their way back to the family shelter.

Inside, I saw a pile of ashes in the shape of a person. You know when you put wood into a furnace and it burns and becomes red hot and it keeps its shape with an inner glow but when you touch it, it disintegrates? That's what this was – the shape of a person but nothing left of the body. I didn't know who it was but then I saw a pair of earrings in the ashes. I knew the earrings. It was my mother.

So intense was the heat that many corpses were reduced to the size of dolls, small enough to be removed in buckets. And yet even in hell, miracles can happen. Clambering out of the bunker designated for Jews, Klemperer ripped the yellow star from his coat and, in the chaos that raged around them, escaped with his wife. They were able to conceal his identity from the authorities until they reached the safety of American-occupied territory. Ironically, had it not been for 'Bomber' Harris, we would almost certainly not now have Klemperer's diary, the most penetrating and insightful account that was ever written of life and death under the swastika.

Was the strategy of area bombing in any sense justifiable? For many years it was fashionable to deny that Bomber Command made any significant contribution to victory. Much continues to be made by critics of the inaccuracy as well as the cruelty of strategic bombing. Even some RAF personnel on occasion expressed concern that they were being asked, in effect, to 'do in . . . children's homes and hospitals'. It has been argued that they would have been better employed bombing the approaches to Auschwitz. It has even been suggested that an offer to stop the bombing could have been used as a bargaining chip to save the Jews destined for the death camps. In the case of Dresden, doubts have been expressed about the official justification for the raid, namely that the Soviets had requested the attacks after a batch of Enigma decrypts revealed German plans to move troops from Dresden to Breslau, where the Red Army was encountering fierce resistance. In fact, the main railway links out of the city survived more or less unscathed; trains were running again within a few days. It is difficult to avoid the conclusion that the aim of the mission was quite simply to devastate one of the few major German cities that had not yet been hit. In denouncing the bombing war, one German writer has consciously applied the language normally associated with the crimes perpetrated by the Nazis: this was *Vernichtung* (extermination) perpetrated by flying *Einsatzgruppen*, who turned air-raid shelters into gas chambers.

To be sure, the effect of such attacks on German morale was far less than the pre-war strategists had predicted. Sir Hugh Trenchard's pre-war assertion that the moral effect of bombing was twenty times greater than the material effect proved to be nonsense. If anything, the indiscriminate character of the air attacks aroused more defiance than defeatism. While it undoubtedly served to undermine the credibility of the Nazi regime in the minds of some Germans, it simultaneously enhanced its credibility in the minds of others. One woman, Irma J., wrote an unsolicited letter to Goebbels, demanding 'on behalf of all German women and mothers and the families of those living here in the Reich' that '20 Jews [be] hanged for every German killed in the place where our defenceless and priceless German people have been murdered in bestial and cowardly fashion by the terror-flyers'. Georg R. wrote from Berlin in a similar vein. 'Having been burned out once and bombed out twice,' he indignantly demanded:

No extermination of the German People
and of Germany
but rather
the complete extermination of the Jews.

There can be no question that a campaign aimed at crippling military and industrial facilities would have been preferable. As early as 1942, in his book *Victory through Air Power*, Alexander Seversky enunciated the principle that 'Destruction of enemy morale from the air can be accomplished only by precision bombing.' Economic assets, not populous conurbations, were 'the heart and vitals of the enemy'. The Allies achieved far more with their focused attack on the German V2 base at Peenemünde on August 17, 1943 than they had achieved the previous month by laying waste to Hamburg. Their attacks on oil-refining facilities were also very successful (see below).

On the other hand, precision attacks could go wrong precisely because the Germans could work out where to expect them – as the Americans discovered to their cost when they attacked Schweinfurt, a centre of ball-bearing production in northern Bavaria, on August 17 and October 14, 1943. In the first raid, thirty-six B-17s were shot down out of an initial strike force of 230; twenty-four were lost the same day in a similar attack on Regensburg. In the October attack – the 8th Air Force's 'Black Thursday' – sixty out of 291 B-17s were shot down and 138 badly damaged. Comparable costs might have been incurred for no military benefit by bombing Auschwitz, significantly further east. The 186 aircraft which flew from Italy (at Churchill's insistence) to drop supplies to the Poles during the 1944 Warsaw Rising suffered losses at a rate of 16.8 per cent, three times the casualty rate over Germany.

For all its indiscriminate character, there is no denying that area bombing inflicted significant damage on the German war effort. It diverted air cover away from the strategically vital Eastern Front. In the spring of 1943, 70 per cent of German fighters were in the western European theatre, leaving German ground forces in the East increasingly vulnerable to Soviet air attacks. Lack of air support was one of the reasons the German tanks were beaten at Kursk. By April 1944 there were only 500 single-engine fighters left on Eastern Front, facing around 13,000 Soviet aircraft. Moreover, as Speer later noted, 'the nearly 20,000 anti-aircraft guns stationed in the homeland could almost have doubled the anti-tank defences on the Eastern Front.' (The German 88 mm AA guns were equally fearsome anti-tank weapons when dug in and firing low.) The situation on the Eastern Front was, indeed, the principal rationale for the bombing of Dresden. 'In the midst of winter,' the RAF crews who flew the mission were told in their briefing notes, 'with refugees pouring westwards and troops to be rested, roofs are at a premium':

Dresden has developed into an industrial city of first-class importance . . . its multiplicity of telephones and rail facilities is of major value for controlling the defence of that part of the front now threatened by [the Soviet] offensive. The intentions of the attack are to hit the enemy where he will feel it most, behind an already partially collapsed front . . . and incidentally to show the Russians when they arrive what Bomber Command can do.

That illustrates how difficult it was to distinguish military from civilian targets by this stage in the war. Although the aim was partly to render German civilians homeless (and dead, though that was not made explicit) as well as to impress the Soviets, bombing Dresden was also designed to weaken German command and control capabilities. The relentless pressure exerted by the bombing raids also helped the British and American armies by eroding German fighter strength on the Western Front; at the time of D-Day, the Germans had barely 300 serviceable planes available to repel the invaders, as against 12,000 on the British and American side.

Furthermore, strategic bombing greatly hampered Speer's considerable efforts to mobilize Germany's economy for total war. In May 1944, for example, the Germans were still producing 156,000 tons of aviation fuel, but bombing of their oil installations, which began in that month, cut production to 17,000 tons in August and just 11,000 tons in January 1945. Not all the available statistics are, it is true, so impressive. As we have seen, the Allies dropped around 1.6 million tons of explosives and incendiaries on Germany and North-West Europe, more than twenty times the amount the Germans dropped on Britain throughout the entire war, including the V1 flying bombs and V2 rockets. The impact on German armaments production was, at first sight, minimal. As Figure 16.2 shows, the major raids of July 1943 merely slowed the growth of arms production, which had resumed its upward trend by March 1944. It was not until after July 1944, as the Allied raids reached their devastating climax, that output from Speer's factories declined. Even then, production in January 1945 was merely reduced to the level of December 1943; it was still more than double what it had been in 1941. A breakdown of the main components of German arms output suggests that bombing hampered only some sectors of the economy (see Table 16.1). The production of vehicles, ships, gunpowder and explosives were all substantially reduced between June 1943 and January 1945. Yet the production of rifles and pistols rose by a fifth and that of tanks by nearly two-thirds. Production of aircraft and ammunition was virtually unchanged.

Nevertheless, the best measure of the impact of strategic bombing is not actual output, but the difference between actual and potential output. In January 1945 Speer and his colleagues sought to calculate the damage done by Allied bombing in the previous year. The figures are impressive: 35 per cent fewer tanks than planned, 31 per cent fewer aircraft and 42 per cent fewer trucks. No fewer than two million men were tied down in air defence; valuable manpower that might have been productively employed. We cannot know exactly what wonders Speer might have worked with the German economy in the absence of sustained bombardment, but what we do know is that Speer himself called the air war 'the greatest lost battle on the German side'.

Moreover, there is at least some evidence that by 1943, especially following the Hamburg firestorm, German civilian morale was showing signs of strain. To be sure, bombing did not encourage Germans

Table 16.1: The impact of allied bombing (percentage change between June 1943 and January 1945)

| German armaments production index | Weapons | Tanks | Vehicles | Aircraft | Ship-building | Ammu-nition | Powder | Explosives | Tonnage dropped by Allies |
|---|---|---|---|---|---|---|---|---|---|
| 0 | +19 | +64 | −63 | −1 | −21 | −2 | −19 | −36 | +116 |

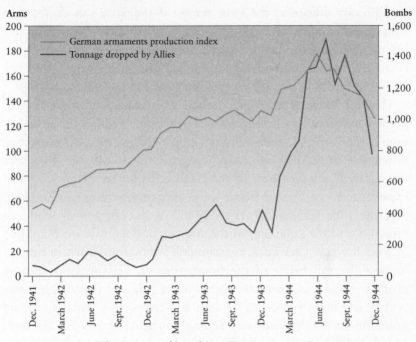

*Figure 16.2* **The impact of bombing, January 1942–January 1945**
(January 1943 = 100)

to overthrow Hitler, as had been hoped in the wake of the Battle of Kursk. But the devastating scale of Allied attacks did much to undermine ordinary Germans' belief in their government's propaganda. One joke doing the rounds in December 1943 was sufficiently close to the bone that SD agents made a note of it:

Dr Goebbels has been bombed out in Berlin. He rescues two suitcases and brings them onto the street and goes back into the house to hunt for other things. When he comes out again, both suitcases have been stolen. Dr Goebbels is very upset, weeps and rails: when asked what was so valuable in the suitcases, he replies: 'In the one was Retaliation (*Vergeltung*) and in the other Final Victory (*Endsieg*).'

Demoralization was not a political phenomenon; rather it led to apathy and cynicism, one symptom of which was rising absenteeism in the workplace. No one who reads Gerd Ledig's harrowing post-war novel *Payback* (*Vergeltung*), based on his own experiences as an anti-aircraft officer in the later stages of the war, can doubt that Churchill did achieve his object of demoralizing the German population. In the inferno Ledig depicts, ordinary Germans are reduced to bestiality, murdering and raping one another in a struggle that has ceased to be about anything as rational as survival.

The moral cost of strategic bombing was nevertheless high. As was pointed out in 1943 by the Bishop of Chichester, George Bell, 'To bomb cities as cities, deliberately to attack civilians, quite irrespective of whether or not they are actively contributing to the war effort, is a wrong deed, whether done by the Nazis or by ourselves.' Few airmen experienced – or lived to relate – the bizarre role reversal that befell Sergeant John Charnock, a 23-year-old Australian gunner who was blown out of his Lancaster at the start of an RAF raid on Frankfurt in March 1944. Charnock parachuted to the ground just in time to witness the full brunt of the bombardment. Having landed, by a grotesque irony, in a freshly dug grave, he survived the raid, but was very nearly beaten to death by an angry crowd of Germans who set upon him in Bruchfeldstrasse. Yelling '*Luftgangster*! Terror bomber! Murderer! *Schwein*!', they spat on him and beat him with bricks, iron bars and even an unexploded incendiary bomb. Other airmen shot down over Germany were hanged from lampposts. In Ledig's *Payback*, the American airman who stumbles half-naked through the mayhem he himself has helped to create is manifestly just as demoralized as his German victims.

For those who completed their missions, none of this was apparent. 'Flying is such a clinical business,' one RAF officer explained after the war. 'You took off and, unless you were hit or anything happened to you, you just came back to a relatively civilized world. You were obviously in some danger when you were flying, but you were not as emotionally involved in what goes on to the extent that you would be in a tank.' Even the deaths of comrades could be subsumed into the less painful 'death' of their plane. Typical was the way the bomber's target looked to one pilot, who flew numerous missions over Germany:

It was an awesome sight. Below, a carpet of red where thousands of incendiaries had fallen, with big yellow bubbles of light as bombs hit the deck, especially the 4,000lb Cookies. It was like looking at a pile of red hot ashes, with violent eruptions of sudden light from the explosions. Drifting down in the sky would be the Pathfinders' red and green flares, dripping clusters of light, whilst all around was the crack, red flashes and puffs of black smoke from the flak. Searchlights in their hundreds sometimes illuminated the target, fingers of light waving backwards and forwards, occasionally trapping an aircraft in their beam. It looked like some sort of hellish inferno. On one trip, to Nuremburg, I recall the light from the fires below illuminating the sky so much it was like daylight and I was able to read my log at 18,000ft.

Reading the log by the light of an inferno 18,000 feet below; it is a vivid summation of the bomber's disconnection from the indiscriminate death and destruction he is causing. This was precisely the attitude that allowed 'civilized' men to engage in the mass slaughter of civilians. The higher the Allied planes could fly, and the more their routes were fixed by technologies like 'Pathfinder', the more the bomber crews' sense of detachment grew. Herein lay the practical difference between incinerating women and children from thousands of feet in the air and herding them into gas chambers. It was possible to pulverize a city without looking into the eyes of those civilians being invisibly consigned to hell below. Allied bombing was as indiscriminate as Nazi racial policy was meticulously discriminating. The moral difference – which has lately been forgotten by some German writers – is that the crews of Bomber Command were flying their missions in order to defeat Nazi Germany and end the war. Whether or not this was the best means of achieving that end was not for them to decide; their intent was not dishonourable. For the Nazis, let it be reiterated, the murder of Jews and other 'alien' civilians was always an end in itself. Hatred filled the minds of the SS men at Bełżec; it was absent from the thoughts of Allied airmen.

## 'LITTLE BOY'

It may remain debatable how far bombing served to end the war against Germany. There can be little doubt that it hastened the end against Japan. At no point prior to the attack on Hiroshima did Japan's leaders evince readiness to end hostilities other than on terms designed to preserve the untrammelled power not merely of the Emperor but also of the military. Some members of the government, including the Prime Minister Admiral Suzuki Kantarō, as well as senior courtiers and even the Emperor himself, were willing to contemplate a negotiated peace through either Switzerland or, preferably, the Soviet Union, but the War Minister, Anami Korechika, and the Chiefs of Staff, General Umeza Yoshijirō and Admiral Toyoda Soemu, insisted on 'prosecuting the war to the bitter end in order to uphold our national essence (*kokutai*), protect the imperial land and achieve our goals of conquest'. Suzuki himself publicly spoke of 'fighting to the end, the entire population uniting as one body'. Given the fanatical mood of resistance that the Americans had already encountered on Okinawa and other outlying islands, there was every reason to expect an amphibious invasion of Japan itself to be exceedingly bloody. As in Europe, it was the last year of the war that was the most lethal. In the year after July 1944, US forces had suffered more than 185,000 casualties and more than 53,000 deaths – more than half of all the fatalities in the entire Pacific war. The Japanese had lost many more men, perhaps as many as half a million, in the same period but were still very far from having exhausted their reserves of manpower and will. Indeed, the Supreme Command had already prepared 'Operation Decision' (*Ketsu-gō*), which envisaged the deployment of 2.35 million troops along the Japanese coast to repel any Allied landings; these would be reinforced by four million civilian employees of the armed services and a civilian militia numbering twenty-eight million. It is easy to forget that the Japanese armed forces had suffered significantly fewer fatalities than the German – the total death toll for the entire period between 1937 and 1945 has been put at 1.74 million. A conventional invasion of Japan would have been no D-Day; it might have been more like Stalingrad by the sea.

The bombing campaign against Japan may be said to have begun with the Doolittle Raid of April 1942, when a small force of thirteen B-25 bombers from the carrier USS *Hornet* successfully raided the Japanese capital. However, it was not until the final phase of the war that the Americans were able to overcome the obstacle of distance

that had forced them to rely on relatively insecure Chinese airbases.*
Armed with the new B-29 Super-Fortress, and securely based on the
Marianas, General Curtis LeMay's XX Bomber Command waged a
merciless war of destruction against Japanese cities, exploiting the
extreme flammability of their wood, bamboo and paper houses. A
survivor of the disastrous Regensburg raid of August 1943, LeMay
lost no time in abandoning the strategy of high-altitude daylight precision bombing in favour of low-altitude nocturnal carpet bombing.
The B-29s flew in vast aerial armadas numbering three hundred or
more, leaving death and devastation in their wake. On March 9, 1945,
Tokyo suffered the first of a succession of raids that claimed the lives
of between 80,000 and 100,000 people, 'scorched and boiled and
baked to death' as LeMay frankly put it. Within five months, roughly
two-fifths of the built-up areas of nearly every major city had been
laid waste, killing nearly a quarter of a million people, injuring more
than 300,000 and turning eight million into refugees. Besides Tokyo,
sixty-three cities were incinerated. Japan's economy was almost entirely
crippled, with steel production down to 100,000 tons a month and aviation fuel having to be manufactured from pine trees. All this was
achieved with significantly less effort than was expended against Germany. In all, the Americans dropped under 200,000 tons of high explosives and incendiaries on Japan, less than 12 per cent of what fell on
Germany and occupied North-West Europe. Because of the feebleness
of Japanese air defences, casualties were also lower than in Europe.

Why, then, was it necessary to go further – to drop two atomic
bombs on Hiroshima and Nagasaki? LeMay could quite easily have
hit both these targets with conventional bombs. As if to make that
point, Tokyo was scourged with incendiaries one last time on August
14 by a horde of more than a thousand aircraft; it was the following

---

* A number of the Doolittle airmen were captured and executed, inspiring the film
*Purple Heart*. Shortly before his execution one of the pilots tells his captors: 'You can
kill us – all of us ... But if you think that's going to put the fear of God into the
United States of America and stop them from sending other fliers to bomb you, you're
wrong – dead wrong. They'll blacken your skies and burn your cities to the ground
and make you get down on your knees and beg for mercy. This is your war – you
wanted it – you asked for it. And now you're going to get it – and it won't be finished
until your dirty little empire is wiped from the face of the earth!'

day that the Emperor's decision to capitulate was broadcast, not the day after Hiroshima. In all probability, it was the Soviet decision to dash Japanese hopes of mediation and to attack Japan that convinced all but the most incorrigible diehards that the war was over. Defeat in the Pacific mattered less to the Japanese generals than the collapse of their much longer-held position in Manchuria and Korea. Indeed, it was the Soviet landing on Shikotan, not far from Japan's main northern island of Hokkaido, that forced the military finally to sign the instrument of surrender. Historians have sometimes interpreted Harry Truman's decision to use the Bomb against Japan as a kind of warning shot intended to intimidate the Soviet Union; an explosive overture to the Cold War. Others have argued that, having seen $2 billion spent on the Manhattan Project, Truman felt compelled to get a large bang for so many bucks. Yet if one leaves aside the technology that distinguished the bombs dropped on August 6 and August 9 – and the radiation they left in their wakes – the destruction of Hiroshima and Nagasaki was simply the culmination of five years of Allied strategic bombing. Roughly as many people were killed immediately when the bomb nicknamed 'Little Boy' exploded 1,189 feet above central Hiroshima on the morning of August 6 as had been killed in Dresden six months before, though by the end of 1945 the Japanese death toll had risen much higher, to as many as 140,000 in Hiroshima and 70,000 in Nagasaki.

Part of the appeal of the atomic bomb was that it allowed one plane (or, to be precise, seven, since the Enola Gay did not fly alone) to achieve what had previously required hundreds. In more than 30,000 sorties between June 1944 and August 1945, only seventy-four B-29s were lost, a casualty rate of 0.24 per cent. That sounds small enough, and it was certainly better than the losses suffered by the Americans in Europe. Yet seventy-four B-29s translates into nearly nine hundred highly trained men. There was therefore an inexorable logic that led from area bombing with a lethal rain of high explosives to the obliteration of an entire city by a single super-bomb. Since 1940 the Allies had been applying the principle of maximum enemy casualties for minimum Allied casualties. The creation of the atomic bomb certainly required a revolution in physics. But it did not require a revolution in the political economy of total war. Rather, it was the logical culmination of the Allied way of war. When Truman spoke of 'a new era in the history of civilization' he was looking to the future and the harnessing of nuclear power for peaceful purposes; Hiroshima, by contrast, was just another devastated city; just another step away from civilization.

As in the realm of intelligence, the Anglo-American victory in the scientific race to design and build an atomic bomb revealed the limitations of the totalitarian regimes. The Nazis' anti-Semitism had more than decimated German science, driving many of the best brains in the pre-1933 German academic profession out of their laboratories and into exile. (Stalin too had his ways of interfering with scientific research, though he was more pragmatic than Hitler when he belatedly grasped just how high the stakes were.) The Bomb was poetic justice of a sort, in the sense that it was in substantial measure the achievement of Jewish scientists, among them a number of refugees from Nazi-occupied Europe. They were not to know that it would be used on the Germans' allies rather than the Germans themselves.

So the atomic bomb was a triumph for the West's openness to scientific inquiry and freedom from anti-Semitism. Yet it also represented the extent to which the Western Allies had thrown moral restraint aside in order to bring the war to an end. Certainly, it was not a sense of their own moral superiority that led Roosevelt and Churchill to keep the Bomb secret from Stalin. Both men understood all too well the power the new weapon would confer on the West once their alliance with the Soviet Union had served its purpose. Indeed, the remarkable thing is that mutual suspicion between the two Anglophone powers did not do more damage to their alliance during the war, a testament to the confidence Roosevelt had in Churchill. Stalin, too, immediately grasped that it would represent almost as serious a setback for the Soviet Union if the Western powers were able to monopolize the atomic bomb as it would have been if Nazi Germany had been first to split the atom. As early as June 1942 the NKVD instructed its agents in New York and London to 'take whatever measures you think fit to obtain information on the theoretical and practical aspects of the atomic bomb projects, on the design of the atomic bomb, nuclear fuel components, and on the trigger mechanism'. In short order, Soviet agents succeeded in penetrating the Manhattan Project. By the spring of 1945 there were three Soviet agents inside the Los Alamos complex in New Mexico where the first bomb was built, each unaware that the others were spies. (It only heightened the subsequent security panic that the scientist in charge of the Manhattan Project, J. Robert Oppenheimer, was a fellow-travelling Communist, if not actually a Party member.) In February 1943 Stalin authorized work to begin on a Soviet bomb. But in the end the first Soviet bomb was a carbon copy of the US bomb tested at Alamogordo on July 16, 1945; an achievement of espionage as much as of science. It came as no surprise to Stalin when Truman obliquely forewarned him of the attacks on Japan at the Potsdam Conference (July 17–August 2, 1945). Stalin knew already what the Americans had achieved; knew, too, that it was an achievement that the Soviet Union must match. Stalin disingenuously told the American ambassador in Moscow that the Bomb 'would mean the end of war and aggressors'. Harriman concurred that 'it could have great importance for peaceful purposes'; to which, with a stony face, Stalin replied: 'Unquestionably.'

# SLAUGHTERHOUSE '45

On January 27, 1945 – three and a half months after an abortive revolt by the Jewish *Sonderkommandos* at Crematoriums II and VI – the first Soviet troops reached the gates of Auschwitz. Among the 7,000 or so prisoners who had been not been sent to Wodzisław or Blechhammer for transportation to camps in Germany was Primo Levi, the Italian chemist whose scientific skills had saved him from the gas chambers. In unforgettable prose, he described the moment:

They did not greet us, nor did they smile; they seemed oppressed not only by compassion but by a confused restraint, which sealed their lips and bound their eyes to the funereal scene. It was that shame we knew so well: the shame the Germans did not know; the feeling of guilt that such a crime should exist . . . So for us even the hour of liberty rang out grave and muffled . . . so that we should have liked to wash our consciences and our memories clean from the foulness that lay upon them. We felt that now nothing could ever happen good and pure enough to rub out the past, and that the scars of the outrage would remain with us forever. No one has ever been able to grasp better than us the incurable nature of the offence.

Similar scenes were repeated at concentration camps all over the disintegrating Nazi empire: skeletal survivors staggering amid the corpses; incredulous soldiers like beings from another planet.

Yet there was something deeply paradoxical about the idea of 'liberation' by Stalin's Soviet Union.* For the regime that had produced the Gulag had no serious interest in liberation in any meaningful sense. Returning to what little remained of Dresden, Victor Klemperer was too well attuned to the language of totalitarianism not to detect the uncanny resemblances between the liberators and those from whom he had just been liberated. He could not help but notice that the 'monotonous' radio broadcasts and 'politicized' newssheets produced by the Soviet occupying authorities had much in common with those of the previous regime. 'I must slowly begin to pay systematic attention', he wrote in his diary, 'to the language of the *fourth Reich*. It sometimes seems to me, that it is less different from that of the *third* than, say, the Saxon [dialect] of Dresden from that of Leipzig. When, for example, Marshal Stalin is the greatest living man, the most brilliant strategist etc. . . . I want to study our news sheet . . . very carefully with respect to LQI [*lingua quartii imperii* – Language of the Fourth Reich].' He soon began to spot numerous 'analogies between Nazistic and Bolshevistic language':

The LTI [*lingua tertii imperii* – Language of the Third Reich] lives on . . . In Stalin's speeches, extracts of which regularly appear, Hitler and Ribbentrop are cannibals and monsters. In the articles about Stalin, the supreme commander of the Soviet Union is the most brilliant general of all times and the most brilliant of all men living . . . It is impossible to say just how often I hear 'orientation', 'action', 'militant'. All that's missing now is 'fanatical' . . . the same, the very same words – LTI = LQI!!! 'align', 'militant', 'true democracy' etc. etc.

---

* That was not lost on the Moscow cinema-goers in whose company I watched the film *Schindler's List* in 1993. At the moment towards the film's denouement when a Red Army soldier on horseback shouts to the surviving prisoners: 'You are being liberated by the forces of the Soviet Union,' the audience erupted into derisive laughter. A Russian audience understood only too well that this was a contradiction in terms.

Even on the streets there were similarities: 'On Albertplatz the picture of "Marshal Stalin" . . . could just as well be Hermann Goering.' As far as Klemperer could see, Communist rule – and he saw at once that this would be the upshot of Soviet-style 'true democracy' – would merely 'replace the old lack of freedom with a new one'. These were indeed 'merciless victors . . . And because I have observed all this in the Third Reich, and because I must now, whether I like it or not, regard everything with respect to its effect on the Jews, I do not feel very happy about it.' 'I see a new Hitlerism coming,' he wrote as early as September 1945. 'I do not feel at all safe.' Given the anti-Semitism that characterized post-war Stalinism, this was prescient.

Nothing illustrated more starkly what was really happening in the summer of 1945 than the fact that, within weeks of taking possession of the Buchenwald concentration camp, the Soviets were using it to incarcerate political prisoners of their own. To be sure, the Holocaust was over; Stalin's suspicion of the Soviet and East European Jews – denounced in the official press as 'cosmopolitans' or 'passportless vagabonds' – never portended a return to the gas chambers. At any event, Stalin died before the alleged 'Doctors' Plot' could be worked up into a full-scale wave of persecution. In other ways, however, all that had changed were the criteria whereby certain groups and individuals were deprived of their freedom. The concentration camps of Eastern Europe were merely under new management.

At Potsdam and in the subsequent Nuremberg trials, the victors struck splendidly sanctimonious attitudes. 'Stern justice', they promised, would be 'meted out to all war criminals, including those who have visited cruelties upon our prisoners'. Despite the absence of an appropriate body of international law, the Americans insisted on full criminal prosecutions of a substantial number of Germans and Japanese who had occupied positions of power before and during the war. 'The wrongs we seek to condemn and punish,' declared the US Attorney-General Robert H. Jackson, 'have been so calculated, so malignant and devastating, that civilization cannot tolerate their being ignored.' The crux of the case at Nuremberg, as agreed by the victorious powers in London in the summer of 1945, was that the leaders of Germany and Japan had premeditated and unleashed 'aggressive war' and 'set in motion evils which [had left] no home in the world untouched'. They were accused, firstly, of the 'planning, preparation, initiation, or waging of a war of aggression, or war in violation of international treaties, agreements and assurances, or participation in a common plan or conspiracy for the accomplishment of any of the foregoing'. Yet whose side had the Soviet Union been on in 1939? By the same token, the charges against the Japanese leaders who stood trial in Tokyo included 'the wholesale destruction of human lives, not alone on the field of battle ... but in the homes, hospitals, and orphanages, in factories and fields'. But what else had the Allies perpetrated in Germany and Japan in the last months of the war?

Death came not only from the sky. As the Soviets advanced inexorably, around five million Germans fled their homes, trudging westwards with carts piled high with their possessions. German ports along the Baltic were jammed with refugees. By January 1945 the scenes in Gdynia – renamed Gotenhafen by the Nazis – were next to apocalyptic. Tens of thousands of people thronged the waterfront, desperate to secure evacuation by sea to Western Germany. This was their only hope of escaping from the marauding Red Army, whose artillery could be heard drawing ever nearer. The 4,400 refugees who managed to scramble aboard the former pleasure cruiser *Wilhelm Gustloff* must have thought themselves fortunate. In all, including soldiers, marines, wounded and crew, there were more than 6,000 people crowded on board when she set off on January 30 – four times the number she was designed to carry. With only a minimal escort (a single aged torpedo boat), the captain was relying on the blizzard conditions for protection. As they ploughed westwards through heavy seas, Hitler's last broadcast was relayed to the exhausted passengers over the public address system. Reassured by their progress and the warmth emanating from the ship's straining engines, many of them settled down to sleep in the crowded cabins. Shortly before 8 p.m. the ship was sighted by the Soviet submarine S-13, commanded by Captain Aleksandr Marinesko. Under the cloud of a disciplinary investigation after going AWOL on a drinking binge in Finland, Marinesko was eager to make amends. The *Wilhelm Gustloff* seemed a heaven-sent opportunity. 'I was sure,' Marinesko later said, 'that it was packed with men who had trampled on Mother Russia and were now fleeing for their lives.' He ordered all four torpedoes to be fired at it. Each of the three that hit the ship bore a painted inscription: 'For Leningrad', 'For the Motherland' and 'For the Soviet People'. The first torpedo struck its target at 9.16 precisely. Only 964 of those on board were picked up by German rescuers; at least some of them later died of exposure. It was one of the worst shipping disasters in history, with a death toll five times that of the *Titanic*.

Marinesko's torpedoes encapsulated the vengeful frame of mind in which the Soviet forces closed on Germany for the kill. When they reached Berlin, sections of the Red Army – generally not the front-line troops – ran amok in scenes reminiscent of the Rape of Nanking. German women were treated not merely as the sexual spoils of war, but as targets for brutal retribution. In the Haus Dahlem orphanage and maternity hospital in the leafy suburb of Dahlem, Mother Superior Cunegundes and the other sisters could only cower in the cellar and pray as the fighting raged around them between front-line Red Army units and the last desperate remnants of the German *Volkssturm*. Shells landed within feet of the orphanage. For days the nuns and their wards lived 'like the first Christians in the catacombs'. On April 26, ten Russians burst into the house and demanded their crosses, rings and watches. It was the first of many intrusions and very far from the worst. On the night of the 29th, Soviet officers and their men ransacked the wine cellar of a nearby villa (it had belonged to Ribbentrop) and then proceeded to hunt down women to rape. The nuns tried their best to conceal the pregnant women and new mothers in the orphanage, as well as the younger lay sisters. But it was far from clear that the inebriated Soviet troops would respect even the nuns themselves. The Mother Superior herself was shot at when she tried to protect the Ukrainian cook. Late on the 30th a group of drunk officers broke into the maternity ward. They raped even the women who were in labour or who had just given birth. To the nuns it was all too clear: 'Our people have sinned greatly. The time for atonement is upon us.' 'That's what the Germans did in Russia,' Ilse Antz was told after a Russian had raped her. As at Nanking, sexual desire was mingled with bloodlust. Hannelore von Cmuda was shot three times by the drunk Russians who gang raped her. Others had their heads battered in. The two main Berlin hospitals estimated the number of victims in the capital at between 95,000 and 130,000. Such behaviour had already been experienced by Germans further east, in Posen, Danzig and Breslau. According to one British prisoner of war in Pomerania, 'Red soldiers . . . raped every woman and girl between the ages of twelve and sixty.' Altogether it seems likely that Soviet soldiers raped over two million German women. This should be compared with the 925 sentences for rape passed by US Army courts martial in all theatres of war between 1942 and 1946.

In this atmosphere, with Goebbels's blood-curdling propaganda prophecies being fulfilled almost to the letter, it is not entirely surprising that a wave of suicides swept Berlin and other parts of Germany. Hitler was not the only Nazi to follow Brünnhilde's example. Goebbels, Bormann and Himmler all committed suicide, as did the Minister of Justice Otto-Georg Thierack and the Minister for Culture Bernhard Rust, as well as eight out of 41 regional party leaders, seven out of 47 senior SS and police chiefs, fifty-three out of 553 army generals, fourteen out of 98 Luftwaffe generals and eleven out of 53 admirals. (To escape the hangman's rope, Göring would follow them when the Nuremberg judges denied him the firing squad he requested.) This suicidal impulse was not confined to the Nazi elite, however. Ordinary Germans in untold numbers responded to the prospect of defeat in the same way. Many of those who equipped themselves with potassium cyanide capsules – or were given them, like the audience at the Berlin Philharmonic's last concert – opted to swallow them rather than face the retribution that was bearing down upon them. In April 1945 there were 3,881 recorded suicides in Berlin, nearly twenty times the figure for March. The most common motivation was 'fear of the Russian invasion'. In villages like Schönlanke and Schivelbein in Pomerania, 'whole, good churchgoing families took their lives – drowned themselves, hanged themselves, slit their wrists or allowed themselves to be burned up along with their homes.' On March 12 the advancing Russians opened the doors of a shed just outside Danzig to find sixteen bodies with their throats and wrists slashed – all that remained of three families murdered by Irwin Schwartz, who believed it was 'better to die than live with Russians'. Untold numbers of rape victims also committed suicide. In her diary, Ruth-Andreas Friedrich, a Berlin schoolgirl, recorded how her teacher had told the class: 'If a Russian soldier violates you, there remains nothing but death.' In the days that followed, her classmates 'kill[ed] themselves by the hundreds. The phrase "honour lost, everything lost" had been the words of a distraught father who press[ed] a rope into the hand of his daughter who had been violated twelve times. Obediently she goes and hangs herself.' Critics of National Socialism had sometimes referred to it as 'the brown cult'. Like other more recent cults, the Hitler cult ended with mass suicide.

The Red Army was not alone in meting out collective punishment to the entire German people. All over Eastern Europe there were brutal reprisals against both Reich German and ethnic German populations. As early as February 5, 1945, a Polish radio broadcast made it clear that there could be no reconciliation now: 'Through their bestiality and the enormity of their crimes, the Germans have created between themselves and the Poles an abyss which cannot be bridged . . . It is our wish that there should not be any German minority in Poland.' Demonstrators in Katowice declared that 'the Poles should treat the Germans in the same way as the German invaders treated the Poles.' The position of Polish Communist leader Władysław Gomułka was that 'countries are built on national lines and not multinational ones.' This had profound implications, given Stalin's decision, more or less sanctioned at the Tehran Conference (November 27–December 1, 1943), to move the Polish border westwards as far as the Rivers Oder and Neisse, so that East Prussia, West Prussia, Pomerania, Posen and Silesia all ceased to be German territory. The tables were turned as Germans in Silesian towns like Bad Salzbrunn were confronted with proclamations ordering their enforced 'resettlement' westwards. Now it was Germans, not Poles, who were given just hours to leave their homes; who were restricted to just 20 kilograms of baggage; whose remaining property was seized without compensation; who were marched at gunpoint in wretched columns. Western journalists in Prague encountered the same uncompromising antipathy. As Dorothy Thompson reported in the Washington *Evening Star* on June 22, 1945: 'The people's hatred of all Germans, including those native to Prague, is 100 per cent and, indiscriminately, they wish to expel from the country everyone whose native tongue is German.' There was a wave of murderous violence directed against the German occupiers and Sudeten Germans.

The story was similar all over Central and Eastern Europe: retributive ethnic cleansing, which the Allied leaders formally sanctioned at the Potsdam Conference. In Hungary the villages of the Danube Swabians became ghost towns, though the expulsions from Hungary were suspended in February 1946 at the request of the American and Soviet occupation authorities in Germany, who could no longer cope with the flow of refugees. Those who stayed had good reason to abandon their German identity. By the time of the Hungarian census of January 1949, only 22,453 people still gave German as their mother tongue, though the actual number of ethnic Germans remaining there was probably much larger. 'Law Number 1' in Yugoslavia expropriated all Germans and removed their civil rights; in the immediate post-war period, tens of thousands of Germans were murdered or interned in concentration camps. Around 100,000 Romanian Germans had retreated with the Wehrmacht. Many of those who remained behind came to regret it. Beginning in January 1945, around 73,000 ethnic Germans – women as well as men, Communists as well as Nazis – were transported from Romania to perform 'reparations labour' in the mines of the Donets Basin and the Urals. In all, around 400,000 Germans from all over Soviet-occupied Europe suffered the same fate. Around 200,000 formerly Soviet Germans who had attempted to reach Germany from what had briefly been 'Transnistria' never completed their trek; the Red Army overtook them and sent them back and beyond the Urals in sealed freight cars. They were joined there later by tens of thousands more former Soviet Germans whom the Western Allies handed over for repatriation from their zones of occupation in Germany. The *Volksdeutsche* had staked everything on Hitler's *Volksgemeinschaft*. It had brought them scant reward even in the halcyon days of Greater Germany, when around three-quarters of a million of them had been resettled in one way or another. Now the problem that had once been posed by their minority status in the post-1918 nation states was solved once and for all. Romania was the only East European state that did not aim at a complete obliteration of its ethnic German communities; even so, its population of ethnic Germans was reduced by nearly half. In all, then, around seven million ethnic Germans were expelled or deported from their homes in Czechoslovakia, Poland (including the former Eastern provinces of the Reich),

Hungary, Romania and Yugoslavia, following on the heels of the 5.6 million who had already fled westwards to elude the Red Army. Add the Germans thus removed to the number of *Volksdeutsche* the Nazis themselves had resettled prior to 1944, and the total figure for Germans removed either westwards or eastwards from Central and Eastern Europe comes to around 13 million (Table 16.2). The number of people who died in this great upheaval may have been as high as two million.

The German exodus was only part of a vast displacement of peoples that followed in the wake of the war, though it was the most important part. In all, between 1944 and 1948, an estimated 31 million people all over Central and Eastern were uprooted from their homes, in one of the largest and most brutal mass movements of population in all history. In the Balkans there was yet more ethnic cleansing, as Bulgarians left eastern Macedonia and western Thrace, and Serbs settled wartime scores with Croats. With the westward shift of Poland's boundaries agreed at Tehran, Poles and the country's few remaining Jews went west, while Ukrainians, Byelorussians and Lithuanians went east. Czechs and Slovaks quit Subcarpathian Rus' and Volhynia rather than endure Soviet rule. Magyars were expelled from southern Slovakia and were exchanged for Serbs and Croats living in Hungary.

Did the British and the Americans feel no unease as the crimes of the Nazi regime were repaid with new crimes by their Soviet allies? If so, they did not say so very loudly. The mood in London was anything

Table 16.2: The involuntary exodus of the Germans

| | 1939–1944 | 1944–1946 | | | 1939–1946 |
|---|---|---|---|---|---|
| | Resettlement | Flight | Deportation | Expulsion | TOTAL |
| Soviet Union | 588,000 | | | | 588,000 |
| Poland | 30,000 | 500,000 | | | 530,000 |
| Romania | 69,000 | 100,000 | 73,000 | | 242,000 |
| Czechoslovakia | | | | 3,000,000 | 3,000,000 |
| Hungary | | n/a | n/a | 250,000 | 250,000 |
| Lithuania | 66,000 | | | | 66,000 |
| Yugoslavia | 21,000 | | | | 21,000 |
| Bulgaria | 2,000 | | | | 2,000 |
| Eastern Germany | | 5,000,000 | 215,000 | 3,325,000 | 8,540,000 |
| TOTAL | 776,000 | 5,600,000 | 288,000 | 6,575,000 | 13,239,000 |

but magnanimous towards the vanquished foe. In the House of Lords, the former Foreign Secretary Lord Simon spoke for many when he attributed the rise of Hitler to a deep-rooted deformity of the German national character. A. J. P. Taylor's *The Course of German History*, published in 1945, remains a monument to the post-war cast of mind. Long before West German historians themselves began to ponder the German *Sonderweg* – a peculiarly German route to perdition, stretching back into the nineteenth century and beyond – the idea was a commonplace in Britain. Churchill himself viewed the deportation of 'the Austrians, Saxons and other German or quasi-German elements' from Romania to Russia with equanimity:

Considering all that Russia has suffered, and the wanton attacks made upon her by Roumania, and the vast armies the Russians are using at the front at the present time, and the terrible condition of the people in many parts of Europe, I cannot see that the Russians are wrong in making 100 or 150 thousand of these people work their passage.

The *de facto* partition of Germany had already begun as early as November 1943, when Roosevelt and Churchill agreed to hand over the Prussian port of Königsberg to the Soviet Union and to move the Polish border westwards. At the Yalta Conference in February 1945 the Big Three agreed vaguely to divide the rest of Germany up into zones of occupation and this duly happened. From the new Polish frontier on the Oder-Neisse line to the River Elbe – what had once been Central Germany – became the Soviet zone of occupation. Western Germany was divided up between Britain, the United States and France; Berlin became a four-power island in the Soviet zone. Austria too was divided into zones of occupation. The expulsion of the Germans from territory east of the Oder-Neisse line was ratified – largely *ex post facto* – at Potsdam. After the First World War, slices had been removed from the periphery of the German Reich. After the Second, the Reich itself was rent asunder. Germany did not cease to exist, since the Americans in particular made it clear from the outset that they intended a swift transition to German self-government. But the German Reich was finished, as was Prussia, its begetter.

It was not only the Germans who bore the brunt of the Red Army's westward advance, however. By the end of 1944 most of Eastern and much of Central Europe – including Austria, Czechoslovakia, Hungary, Poland, Romania and Yugoslavia – was in the hands of the Red Army. All this had been envisaged by the Big Three at Tehran. It was also a reflection of military reality; the American Chief of Staff, George C. Marshall, and the Allied Supreme Commander, Dwight D. Eisenhower, simply had no interest in racing the Russians to Berlin, much less to Prague, nor in competing with them for control of the Balkans. 'Personally,' declared Marshall, 'and aside from all logistic, tactical or strategical implications, I would be loath to hazard American lives for purely political purposes.' No such inhibitions held Stalin and Zhukov back from throwing yet more Soviet soldiers' lives away in over-hasty offensives. But no one could pretend that Russian occupation was the outcome hoped for by the subject peoples of the Nazi empire. While Tito's Communist Partisans were only too happy to welcome the Russians to Belgrade, the mood elsewhere – where the numbers of committed Communists were pitifully small – was hostile and resentful. Few Poles, aside from those who fought on the Soviet side under the command of Lieutenant-Colonel Zygmunt Berling, welcomed 'liberation' at Russian hands. Stalin had shed no tears when the Polish resistance forces, known as the Home Army, were annihilated after staging a doomed rising in Warsaw against the Germans between August 1 and October 2, 1944. (How far the Red Army had been in a position to intervene decisively on the Home Army's side is debatable. But Stalin would not have acted even if it had been; it was too convenient to have the Germans get rid of the most committed nationalists in the Polish capital.) Only the most half-hearted efforts were made by the Western powers to press the claims of the non-Communist Polish government-in-exile. 'Not only are the Russians very powerful,' explained Churchill to Harold Nicolson in February 1945, 'but they are on the spot; even the massed majesty of the British Empire would not avail to turn them off that spot.' In his diary Nicolson added that 'it seemed to him [Churchill] a mistake to assume that the Russians are going to behave badly. Ever since he had been in close relations with Stalin, the latter had kept his word with the utmost loyalty.' But the commitment Churchill probably had in mind – the notorious 'percentages agreement' he and Stalin had jotted down to carve up the Balkans in 1944 – was little better than a blueprint for the partition of Europe. 'Do you intend', Churchill had asked Fitzroy Maclean, who had been sent to Bosnia to assist Tito, 'to make Yugoslavia your home after the war?' 'No, Sir,' replied Maclean. 'Neither do I,' returned the Prime Minister. 'And, that being so, the less you and I worry about the form of Government they set up, the better. That is for them to decide.' But was it for the Yugoslavs to decide? At Yalta, Roosevelt and Churchill had secured a commitment from Stalin that the liberated peoples would be free to choose their form of government. Not even Roosevelt expected Stalin to abide by it; the Russians, he told the economist Leon Henderson, would 'suit themselves'. 'Do not worry,' Stalin reassured his Foreign Minister Molotov. 'We can implement it in our own way later.' All across the Eastern half of Europe Stalin lost no time in erecting a new network of camps, numbering very nearly 500 by the time of his death. Stalag gave way to Gulag.

The irony was not lost on Churchill that it was now his policy to appease Stalin; whereas many of the anti-Communist Tories who had once been the staunchest appeasers of Hitler were now violently hawkish in their denunciations of Soviet conduct. Only *The Times* was consistent. Jesuitically, the newspaper pointed out that the 1939 guarantee to Poland had only pledged its defence in the event of a *German* invasion; it did not commit Britain to restore Poland to her pre-war borders against Stalin's wishes. In keeping with the power-worshipping realism of E. H. Carr, *The Times* counselled that Stalin, like Hitler before him, had legitimate claims to 'security' which it was the job of British diplomacy to divine and to fulfil. Nicolson, meanwhile, tried to justify himself as best he could:

People say to me, 'But why, when you cursed us for wishing to appease Hitler, do you advocate the appeasement of Stalin?' I reply, 'For several reasons. First, because the Nazi system was more evil than the Soviet system. Secondly, because whereas Hitler used every surrender on our part as a stepping-off place for further aggression, there does exist a line beyond which Stalin will not go.'

In May 1945 such confidence in the self-restraint of Stalin was no more than a pious hope.

Nothing revealed more clearly the nature of the pact the Allies had struck with Stalin than the way Soviet prisoners of war were treated. At Yalta, it had been agreed that all Soviet citizens in Axis hands should be returned to the Soviet authorities, including not only prisoners of war and slave labourers but also those Russians who had fought on the Axis side, like the 150,000 troops who had trained under the leadership of the turncoat General Andrei Vlasov or the 20,000 Cossacks who had joined the Germans to fight against their Soviet oppressors. In 1945 alone 1.7 million Soviet prisoners and slave labourers were returned, but this was only the beginning of a vast process of repatriation which by 1953 had sent nearly five and a half million people back to the Soviet Union. Of these around a fifth were either executed or sentenced to the maximum of twenty-five years in labour camps. Shamefully, British troops used deception and brute force to implement this agreement, despite glaring evidence of the fate that awaited those handed back to Stalin. Even those who were not shot or exiled after their interrogation by the NKVD lived the rest of their lives under a cloud, excluded from respectable employment.

Of course, not all the murder, the rape and the pillage that devastated Central and Eastern Europe in 1944 and 1945 should be blamed on Stalin. The dance of death that played itself out in the ruins of the Third Reich was only partly choreographed in Moscow. Much of the violence against ethnic Germans was local and spontaneous. Poles and Ukrainians continued their savage border war for several years after 1945, even as the border itself moved beneath them. On Palm Sunday 1945 a band of Ukrainians dressed in NKVD uniforms drew up outside a Polish church in Hrubieszów and threw grenades at the congregation. Meanwhile, the civil war that the Axis powers had sponsored in the Balkans raged on, to the advantage of the Communists in Yugoslavia, to their disadvantage in Greece. As a cruel reminder that the Holocaust had not been an exclusively German undertaking, violence continued to be directed against the surviving Jews in Poland. There was a fully fledged pogrom in Kielce in July 1946, aimed at Jews who were attempting to return to their old homes.

Nevertheless, by the end of 1947, if not earlier, the net effect of the war in Europe was clear. In 1939 Britain had gone to war with Germany ostensibly to prevent Poland being overrun by Germany, as

Czechoslovakia had been the year before. By the end of 1945 neither country was any nearer freedom and with each passing month that prospect grew more distant. Central and Eastern Europe as far as the banks of the River Elbe was in Stalin's iron fist. If the war had been about the fate of that region, then he had won it.

## WAR WITHOUT END?

Who, moreover, had really won the war in Asia? It is true, the West European empires were not wholly broken up. Although the price of India's loyalty turned out to be its independence (and partition) Britain regained control of Hong Kong, Singapore and Malaya. French power was restored in Indo-China. The experience of Japanese occupation had no doubt weakened the notions of European superiority on which colonial rule in some measure rested. On the other hand, local elites in Malaya and elsewhere had good reasons to welcome back European forces, if the alternative was to surrender power to more popular political forces within their own societies.

Yet the main beneficiary of victory in Asia, as in Europe, was once again the Soviet Union. At Tehran, Stalin had pledged to enter the war against Japan after the defeat of Germany, and at Yalta he had been promised an ample remuneration: the Kuril Islands, South Sakhalin, Outer Mongolia, Dairen, Port Arthur and the Manchurian railways. He had kept his word. On August 9, 1945, he had sent a vast force of 1.7 million troops into Japanese controlled Manchuria, Korea, Sakhalin and the Kurils. Fighting in this forgotten campaign had been heavy; the Japanese suffered very heavy casualties as they fought tenaciously against Soviet amphibious landings along the Korean coast. This, perhaps, was the war the Japanese should have fought; one which, had it broken out in 1941, might have dealt the Soviet Union a fatal blow from behind. But by 1945 their forces lacked the material means to prevail. The logical next step for Stalin was to make the Russian presence in Manchuria and Korea permanent – the pre-revolutionary Russian strategy that had been thwarted by the Japanese forty years before. The hasty American response was to divide the country into two provisional zones of occupation, leaving

Stalin all the territory north of the somewhat arbitrarily selected 38th parallel. Thus, as in Europe, the end of the war in Asia meant an improvised partition of contested territory. It also represented a triumph of Russian foreign policy beyond the fondest imaginings of the Tsars.

It was not so much that Stalin had a premeditated plan for Asian empire; rather, the Americans underestimated the extent to which nationalist movements in East Asia would run out of their control. The notion that Korea could be placed in some kind of international trusteeship proved completely unrealistic as indigenous politics burst into life after the Japanese defeat. Both Kim Il Sung and Syngman Rhee were, first and foremost, nationalists, and it was their ambitions more than the superpowers' that set Korea on course for partition. At the same time, the Americans overestimated the stability of the Chinese Nationalist regime of Chiang Kai-shek, whose value both to the war effort and to the future stability of East Asia was always much less than Roosevelt had hoped. Chiang, the President had said, was an 'unconquerable man . . . of great vision [and] . . . great courage'. He had been given the red-carpet treatment at the Cairo Conference of November 1943. Post-war China, Roosevelt insisted, would be one of the Big Four, along with the United States, the Soviet Union and Great Britain. It turned out that Stilwell's low opinion of 'Peanut' had been the right one. With the Japanese gone, the miseries suffered by the Chinese peasantry since the 1930s could no longer be blamed on a foreign invader. Increasingly, the Communists' criticisms of Chiang's regime as corrupt and incompetent won converts in the countryside. Even with American support, Chiang's position began to crumble as the Communist forces – even without Russian support – advanced southwards and the civil war resumed. The Truman administration relaxed when Stalin recognized Chiang's government and withdrew Soviet troops from Manchuria in March 1946. So low was Truman's estimation of Chiang's regime that he seemed indifferent to the possibility that Chiang might be ousted altogether by an indigenous (but Soviet backed) Communist revolution. This relaxation was unwarranted.

In one of his last political musings, dictated to Martin Bormann on April 2, 1945, none other than Hitler, in a rare moment of percipience, had foretold the coming Cold War:

Between the defeat of the Reich and the rise of nationalist movements in Asia, Africa and perhaps also South America there will be only two powers in the world that can face each other on the basis of equal strength: the USA and Soviet Russia. The laws of history dictate that these two colossuses will test their strength, whether militarily, or just economically and ideologically.

In this he was surely right. The Second World War had undoubtedly ended in the summer of 1945 – on May 7 in Western Europe, on May 8 in Eastern Europe and on August 15 in Asia (or perhaps on September 2, when the Japanese belatedly signed the document confirming their surrender). Yet the War of the World was very far from over. For what had begun in the European borderlands of Poland and in the Asian borderlands of Manchuria continued more or less unabated in the years after 1945.

Churchillian appeasement of Stalin was short-lived. It was on May 13, 1945 – less than a week after VE Day – that Churchill alarmed Brooke with the vehemence of his views on the future of Yugoslavia; so 'delighted' was the Prime Minister by 'a telegram from Truman, full of bellicose views and ready to be rough with Tito', that he gave Brooke the feeling he was 'already longing for another war! Even if it entailed fighting Russia!' The Chiefs of Staff had actually considered the possibility of a future confrontation with the Soviets as early as October 1944, though Brooke regarded the idea as 'fantastic and the chances of success quite impossible'. Churchill, however, countered that the atomic bomb 'would redress the balance with the Soviets', as an appalled Brooke recorded in his diary:

The secret of this explosive, and the power to use it, would completely alter the diplomatic equilibrium which was adrift since the defeat of Germany! Now we had a new value which redressed our position (pushing his chin out and scowling), now we could say if you insist on doing this or that, well we can just blot out Moscow, then Stalingrad, Sebastapol etc. etc. And now where are the Russians!!!

This was prophetic indeed, before the Bomb had even been dropped on Hiroshima. In July 1945 Churchill asked the defence chiefs to work out the viability of a surprise attack on the Soviet Union – using, if necessary, German troops. With good reason this notion was given the name 'Operation Unthinkable'.

Yet the most puzzling thing about the origins of the Cold War is that Churchill proved to be wrong. The Bomb did not redress the balance – or, rather, did not tip the balance decidedly in favour of the Western powers – as it should have. Stalin was without question impressed by it. 'War is barbaric,' he had declared on hearing details of the destruction of Hiroshima, 'but using the A-bomb is a superbarbarity.' It was 'a powerful thing, pow-er-ful!' If he were to act in such a way that a Third World War broke out, he told a Chinese delegation to Moscow, 'the Russian people would not understand us. Moreover, they would chase us away. For underestimating all the wartime and post-war efforts and suffering. For taking it too lightly.' Yet Stalin was careful to conceal his anxiety, insisting in an interview that 'atomic bombs are meant to frighten those with weak nerves'. He refused to appear intimidated, despite the fact that the first successful Soviet test did not take place until August 1949; despite the fact that throughout the 1950s the balance of nuclear advantage was overwhelmingly in favour of the United States. Moreover – and perhaps Stalin divined this – Truman was deeply reluctant to use atomic weapons again after Hiroshima and Nagasaki. The Bomb might be 'powerful', but not if its owners were bluffing.

In the Middle East, to be sure, the Soviet tide was decisively turned back. The Western powers rejected Stalin's demands for Turkish territory and control of the Black Sea Straits – another traditional Russian imperial objective – and insisted on his withdrawal from Iran, referring the matter to the new United Nations Security Council and deploying the American 6th Fleet in the Eastern Mediterranean. Here was proof that the 'strategy of containment' recommended by the diplomat George Kennan could work; it was not proof, however, that the atomic monopoly would make it work. The period up until 1956 saw a reassertion of British and French influence and a new assertion of American power through Saudi Arabia and Israel. Likewise in Turkey and Greece the American assistance that counted was conventional (and financial) more than nuclear.

In Central Europe and Asia, on the other hand, the Soviet flood continued in full spate. True, Stalin did not succeed in getting his hands on all of Germany, as he had hoped. The generosity of the 1947 European Recovery Plan, named the Marshall Plan after Truman's Secretary of State General George C. Marshall, was sufficient to begin the transformation of the post-war occupation zones into enduring political blocs. The 1948–9 Berlin blockade was a failure too, but again it was aid that the American planes transported eastwards, not atomic bombs (though Truman himself believed that only the Bomb had deterred the Russians from 'taking over Europe'). In Czechoslovakia, however, hopes for democracy were dashed by a Soviet-backed coup in February 1948. This was the beginning of a series of coups in Central and Eastern Europe, the effect of which was to confer monopolies of power on ruthlessly Stalinized Communist Parties. Moreover, there seemed every reason to fear a Communist takeover in some West European countries. In December 1945 the Italian Communists had 1.8 million members and gained 19 per cent of the popular vote in free elections. The French Communist party had nearly a million members. In November 1947, at the instigation of Stalin's Cominform, two million workers struck throughout France. Similar strikes paralysed Italy. In Asia, meanwhile, the Soviet triumph was very nearly complete. As early as July 1946, Truman declared that Korea was 'an ideological battleground upon which our entire success in Asia may depend', but for a time in 1947 it seemed as if the United States was about to withdraw from the peninsula altogether. In January 1950 Secretary of State Dean Acheson indicated that he did not regard South Korea as vital to American security.

Yet the American mood began to change after the Russians refused to allow free, UN-supervised elections to go ahead in their zone of occupation. When, with Stalin's blessing, North Korea invaded South Korea on June 25, 1950, the United States went to war, with the authority of a United Nations Security Council resolution. Armed conflict had resumed, with the potential to escalate once again into world war. Why?

The answer lay in China, where more than twenty years of intermittent civil war had finally ended with Communist victory. Shanghai had fallen to Mao Zedong's Communist forces in May 1949; on October 1 Mao had proclaimed the People's Republic of China (PRC); on December 10 Chiang Kai-shek fled mainland China for the island of Formosa (now Taiwan). Mao had already made it abundantly clear that he intended to align China with the Soviet Union and in December 1949 set off for Moscow to pledge his allegiance to Stalin – in return, it should be added, for the Manchurian ports, which Stalin felt unable to deny his fellow revolutionary. After no less than two months in the Soviet capital, Mao returned with a treaty of mutual defence. Indeed, it is not too much to describe the PRC as Moscow's biggest satellite throughout the first decade of its existence. Characteristically insouciant even in the face of catastrophe, Chiang repaired to the Taiwanese resort of Sun Moon Lake and went fishing. Retreat was not defeat to Chiang; it was a way of life, a strategy in a very, very long game. His confident assumption was that within a matter of years there would be a Third World War between the United States and Communism, after which he would be able to return to his rightful place. He was very nearly right. Having lost the Manchurian ports, Stalin had been inclined to give the green light to the North Korean invasion. Resolved to avoid an 'Eastern Munich', Truman's first action in response to the invasion was to send the US 7th Fleet to the Taiwan Strait and to put the glory-hungry General MacArthur in charge of defending South Korea. He did more than this, outflanking the North Koreans at Inchon and sweeping across the 38th parallel with reckless indifference to the international consequences. On November 26, 1950, the Chinese launched a brilliantly executed though hardly unforeseeable offensive across the Yalu River (the Korean-Manchurian border), driving MacArthur's forces back in the utmost disorder. At this point, many people in the West felt justified in asking: Who had *really* won the Second World War? Four days after the Chinese intervention, Truman pointedly refused to rule out the use of atomic weapons 'to meet the military situation'. Was this the beginning of a Third World War?

To win the Second World War, the Western powers had allied themselves with a despot who was every bit as brutal a tyrant as Hitler. They had adopted tactics that they themselves had said were depraved, killing prisoners and bombing civilians. This is not, let it be repeated, to suggest a simple moral equivalence between Auschwitz and Hiroshima. The Axis cities would never have been bombed if the Axis powers had not launched their war of aggression. And the Axis powers might have killed even more innocent people than they did, had it not been for the determination of the Allied powers to prevail by any means, fair or foul. Yet it is to acknowledge that the victory of 1945 was a tainted victory – if indeed it was a victory at all. It is also to advance the hypothesis that the underlying war between West and East no more ended in 1945 than it had begun in 1939. For the Korean War was more than a mere Asian aftershock; it was waged at its outset with the same destructive intensity that had characterized the final phase of the previous war. In the space of three years it claimed up to three million lives. Eighteen countries sent troops to fight in it. But, as in the Second World War, the majority of casualties were civilians; as in the Second World War, air raids – which levelled both Pyongyang and Seoul – were the principal cause of death. The challenge is to understand what stopped this war from escalating, as previous regional conflicts had, into yet another world war.

# Epilogue

# The Descent of the West

*The time has gone forever when the Western powers were able to conquer a country in the East merely by mounting several cannons along the coast.*

Peng Dehuai, Chinese supreme commander
in the Korean War, September 1953

*We have condoned counter-terror; we may even in effect have encouraged or blessed it. We have been so obsessed with the fear of insurgency that we have rationalized away our qualms and uneasiness. This is not only because we have concluded we cannot do anything about it, for we never really tried. Rather we suspected that maybe it is a good tactic, and that as long as Communists are being killed it is alright. Murder, torture and mutilation are alright if our side is doing it and the victims are Communists. After all hasn't man been a savage from the beginning of time [?] so let us not be too queasy about terror. I have literally heard these arguments from our people.*

Viron Vaky, US diplomat in Guatemala, March 1968

## CHICKENS

When did the War of the World end? Perhaps the best answer is July 27, 1953, when the armistice was signed that ended the Korean War. Why did that conflict peter out, rather than escalate into a global conflict between the superpowers? One tempting explanation is that the exponential increase in destructive power that began with the first atomic test raised the stakes too high to permit a full-scale conflict. Truman had already revealed himself to be deeply reluctant to use atomic weapons again after Hiroshima and Nagasaki. 'The human animal . . . must change now,' he had written in 1946, 'or he faces absolute and complete destruction and maybe the insect age or an atmosphere-less planet will succeed him.' On this point, he and Stalin were at one. 'Atomic weapons', the latter remarked in 1949, 'can hardly be used without spelling the end of the world.'

Despite the huge advantage enjoyed by the United States over the Soviet Union at the time of the Korean War – the Americans had 369 operational bombs, the Soviets no more than five – Truman declined to drop the Bomb on Chinese targets. With the American decision to develop a thermonuclear super-bomb, the likelihood of a nuclear exchange diminished still further, for the move from fission to fusion raised the stakes by several orders of magnitude. One H-bomb tested on March 1, 1954, had a yield of 15 megatons, 750 times the size of Little Boy, the Hiroshima A-bomb. A single weapon could now devastate three or four hundred square miles and generate lethal quantities of radioactive fallout. Both sides understood that a full-scale thermonuclear exchange could 'create on the whole globe conditions impossible for life'. In a Soviet first strike, the Pentagon estimated in 1953, around three million Americans would die. By 1956 they had raised the projected number of casualties to 65 per cent of the entire US population. The paradox was that only by embracing this reality could both sides be deterred from launching such a first strike. Missiles should be targeted at cities; there should be no option for a limited nuclear war. This was the logic of 'Mutually Assured Destruction'.

Yet the world came so desperately close to nuclear war on at least one occasion that this technological-strategic explanation, for all its elegance, is ultimately unconvincing. Moreover, it is clear that senior political and military figures in the United States regarded the use of both A-bombs and H-bombs as far from unimaginable. Among those who argued for a 'preventive war' against the Soviet Union in the late 1940s were the Democratic Senator Brien McMahon, and the architect of 'containment', George Kennan. Also eager to 'break up Russia's five A-bomb nests' were – among others – General Orvil Anderson, commanding officer of the US Air War College, General George

Kenney, first commander of the Strategic Air Command and his successor, the incinerator of Tokyo, Curtis LeMay. Even after the ending of the American monopoly, many people thirsted to use the Bomb again. MacArthur was eager to drop A-bombs on Chinese forces in Korea in early 1951; in this he had the sympathy of the Secretary of the Navy and the Secretary of Defense. Their views were overruled mainly because the American position in Europe looked too vulnerable to a Soviet attack and because the Labour government in Britain, still Washington's most important ally, was vehemently opposed; that did not preclude atomic strikes in, say, 1952 or 1953, when Europe was less militarily and politically precarious. Truman himself seriously contemplated using a nuclear ultimatum to break the Korean deadlock. Eisenhower also considered using atomic weapons 'on a sufficiently large scale' to bring the conflict to an end. Doing so would not have been unpopular. Asked if they favoured 'using atomic artillery shells against communist forces ... if truce talks break down', 56 per cent of Americans polled said yes. Nuclear strikes were also considered when China attacked the Quemoy-Matsu islands in the Taiwan Strait. Eisenhower took extremely seriously the argument for an American first strike; that was the basis for the exercise known as Project Solarium. In his view, the strain of maintaining nuclear forces sufficiently massive* to deter a Soviet first strike might prove intolerable: 'In such circumstances, we would be forced to consider whether or not our duty to future generations did not require us to *initiate* war at the most propitious moment.' As Chairman of the Joint Chiefs of Staff, Admiral Arthur Radford approved the Air Force's strategy for such a preventive war. Henry Kissinger made his reputation as a public intellectual by arguing, in *Nuclear Weapons and Foreign Policy* (1957), that a limited nuclear war was conceivable. As late as 1959 Eisenhower was still asking himself whether the United States should 'start fighting now' rather than 'waiting to go quietly down the drain'.

In the view of the British philosopher Bertrand Russell, both superpowers were attracted to the idea of breaking the nuclear stalemate in a way that was almost adolescent in its recklessness:

---

* The 'Single Integrated Operations Plan' would have retaliated to a Soviet attack by unleashing all 3,267 American nuclear weapons against the entire Eastern bloc.

'Brinkmanship' is a policy adapted from a sport which, I am told, is practised by some youthful degenerates. This sport ... is played by choosing a long straight road ... and starting two very fast cars towards each other from opposite ends ... As they approach each other, mutual destruction becomes more and more imminent.

The analogy of a teenage game was highly appropriate. Strategists like John von Neumann and Hermann Kahn were helping to develop a new academic discipline – 'game theory' – which they believed held the key to superpower relations in the nuclear age. Mathematical models like the 'prisoner's dilemma' were developed to illustrate why brinkmanship made sense. But the game Russell was reminded of was the simple and lethal game played by James Dean in *Rebel Without a Cause* – 'Chicken':

If one of them swerves from the white line before the other, the other, as he passes, shouts 'Chicken!' and the one who has swerved becomes an object of contempt ... The game may be played [by eminent statesmen] without misfortune a few times, but sooner or later ... the moment will come when neither side can face the derisive cry of 'Chicken!' from the other side. When that moment is come, the statesmen of both sides will plunge the world into destruction.

The eve of destruction very nearly came on Saturday, October 27, 1962. The American Defense Secretary Robert McNamara remembered stepping outside the White House to savour the livid sunset: 'To look and to smell it,' he recalled, 'because I thought it was the last Saturday I would ever see.' In Moscow at precisely that moment, Fyodor Burlatsky, a senior Kremlin adviser, telephoned his wife. He told her to 'drop everything and get out of Moscow'.

The cause of the crisis was the island of Cuba. At the beginning of 1959 Fidel Castro's guerrillas had seized power in Cuba, informally an American dependency since the time of Theodore Roosevelt. A charismatic nationalist, Castro had been fêted by the American media when he had visited the United States that spring, not least at Harvard University. But the rapid penetration of the new Cuban regime by the Soviet Union had precipitated a quite different reaction in Washington. In March 1961, less than two months after his inauguration,

President John F. Kennedy had authorized an invasion of Cuba by anti-Castro exiles, armed and organized by the CIA. Inadequately supported from the air, its failure at the Bay of Pigs had been abject and a smarting Kennedy had reverted to a policy of dirty tricks aimed at destabilizing and perhaps even assassinating Castro. Castro had seized the moment to take Cuba into the Soviet bloc in return for copious quantities of arms.

Nikita Khrushchev, the coal miner's son who had emerged as First Secretary of the Soviet Communist Party after Stalin's death in 1953, saw the Cuban Revolution as Christmas for world Communism. Repeatedly during the subsequent crisis, he insisted that his motivation was simply to defend Cuba and its experiment with Marxism. In reality, he had seized on the idea of using the island as a kind of missile launching-pad, which would, at a stroke, narrow the gap in nuclear capability between the United States and the Soviet Union. That gap was still wide. The ratio of American to Soviet deliverable nuclear warheads was between eight and seventeen to one in favour of the United States. The Americans had six times as many long-range missiles as the Soviets; few if any of the Soviet missiles were in bomb-proof silos. The United States also had three times as many long-range bombers. The Soviets knew that their intercontinental ballistic missiles were anything but reliable, but from Cuba – just ninety miles from the coast of Florida – even intermediate range missiles could strike at the United States. Khrushchev's military advisers recommended sending forty missiles: twenty-four R-12s (with a range of 1,050 miles) and sixteen R-14s, which had double that range. Both carried one-megaton warheads. At a stroke, Khrushchev would double the number of missiles capable of reaching the United States. Now Washington would be a potential target, to say nothing of the Americans' own long-range missile silos in the Mid-West and air bases in the South – the key objectives of any Soviet first strike. To justify this action, Khrushchev only had to look out from his Black Sea holiday house at Pitsunda towards Turkey. There the Americans had recently stationed fifteen Jupiter missiles. 'What do you see?' he would ask visitors, handing them binoculars. 'I see US missiles in Turkey, aimed at my dacha.' The Cuban missiles would give the Americans 'a little of their own medicine'. 'It's been a long time since you could spank us like a little boy,' he had gleefully told Secretary of the Interior Stewart Udall, who happened to be visiting the Soviet Union that September. 'Now we can swat your ass.'

To ship so many missiles and over 50,000 men some 7,000 miles at the height of the hurricane season was a bold gambit. Even more astonishing was how long it took the Americans to cotton on to 'Operation Anadyr'. Because US aerial surveillance of Soviet naval activities and of Cuba itself had been stepped down, Kennedy did not hear that a U-2 spy plane had spotted missiles near Havana until the morning of Tuesday, October 16. Even two days later, the Soviets were still denying it. On being quizzed by Secretary of State Dean Rusk, Foreign Minister Andrei Gromyko acted, in Khrushchev's gleeful words, 'like a gypsy who's been caught stealing a horse: It's not me, and it's not my horse'. According to the myth perpetuated by Kennedy's acolytes, what followed was a triumph of hardball diplomacy. In the phrase of Dean Rusk which has adorned a thousand textbooks, Kennedy and Khrushchev were 'eyeball to eyeball' over Cuba and 'the other fellow . . . blinked'. This was far from the truth. On the contrary, Kennedy and his key advisers (assembled on what became known as the Executive Committee of the National Security Council, or 'ExComm') were thrown into confusion by the audacity of the Soviet move. Already, the CIA reported, up to eight medium-range missiles could be fired from Cuba. Within six to eight weeks, the two longer-range missile sites would be ready too. Once all the missiles were installed, it was estimated, only 15 per cent of US strategic forces would survive Soviet attack. '[It's] just as if we suddenly began to put a major number of medium range ballistic missiles in Turkey,' fumed Kennedy. 'Well, we did, Mr President,' someone reminded him. Kennedy's next thought was to order air strikes against the missile sites. But the Joint Chiefs of Staff could not guarantee that all the missiles would be destroyed in such a raid, leaving the possibility open of Soviet retaliation. Instead, Kennedy adopted a twin-track approach. He decided to impose a naval blockade to halt further Soviet shipments of military hardware to Cuba. At the same time, he issued an ultimatum demanding that the Soviets withdraw their missiles; this was broadcast on television. In case this ultimatum was rejected, he ordered the preparation of an invasion force of 90,000 ground troops.

At 10 o'clock in the evening of October 24, the Russian barman at the National Press Club in Washington overheard two seasoned hacks discussing an impending 'operation to capture Cuba'. The news reached Khrushchev – dishevelled by a night on his office sofa – the next day. OPLAN 316, which envisaged an air strike followed by an amphibious invasion, was indeed ready to get underway. And repeatedly during the following days key figures like McNamara urged invasion, even if it meant the Soviet Union 'doing something' in Europe in response. As Kennedy himself admitted, an invasion would have been 'one hell of a gamble'. He did not know how big a gamble. For the two Red Army regiments Khrushchev had sent to accompany the missiles were equipped with eighty short-range missiles carrying nuclear warheads. Each had an explosive power of between five and twelve kilotons. On September 7, as tension first began to mount, Khrushchev had dispatched a further six atomic bombs for the Ilyushin Il-28 bombers on Cuba, along with twelve nuclear Luna rockets. Each of these could blow a hole 130 feet wide and deep and kill everything within a radius of a thousand yards. Khrushchev had also sent four submarines with nuclear-tipped torpedoes. Although he had expressly forbidden his commanding officer in Cuba to use these weapons without his permission, a full-scale American invasion would have presented him with little alternative – other than abject surrender.

Yet even this would not have worried some senior military figures – and not only the chronically bellicose LeMay. The new head of Strategic Air Command, General Tommy Powers, was known to be undaunted by the prospect of a nuclear war. (It was he who once said: 'At the end of the war, if there are two Americans and one Russian, we win.') Former Secretary of State Dean Acheson (also an ExComm member) argued that an American strike on Cuba would lead to a Soviet strike on Turkey, which would require the US 'to respond by knocking out a missile base inside the Soviet Union'. 'Then what do we do?' he was asked. The politicians had no illusions about what war would mean. Kennedy spoke of 200 million dead; Khrushchev of 500 million. 'If the United States insists on war,' he told a visiting American businessman (one of many informal channels used during the crisis), 'we'll all meet in hell.' This did not mean that war was impossible. It meant that the two sides were now playing the game of chicken in earnest.

There is, of course, a 'cooperative' outcome in the game of chicken. If both players swerve, nobody wins, but both come out alive, and no one can call the other a chicken. That was indeed what happened in the Cuban game. Khrushchev offered Kennedy two possible deals, one delivered through the usual, rather slow channel of the diplomatic telegraph, the other broadcast on Radio Moscow. The first simply envisaged a withdrawal of the missiles in return for an American guarantee not to invade Cuba; it reached the State Department at 9 p.m. on Friday, September 26. The second, which reached the White House as the ExComm convened thirteen hours later, offered a withdrawal of the Cuban missiles in return for the withdrawal of the Jupiter missiles in Turkey. According to the legend spread by Kennedy's hagiographers, the second of these proposals was spurned. In fact, it had already been suggested by the Americans themselves to the Soviet agent Georgi Bolshakov, probably at the instigation of Kennedy's brother Robert, the Attorney-General and the President's closest confidant. Nevertheless, a war could still have broken out that weekend, despite the search for a compromise. Castro certainly thought so. In the early hours of Saturday 27th, fuelled by sausages and beer, he drafted a letter to Khrushchev which essentially urged him to go nuclear if the Americans invaded, 'however harsh and terrible the solution would be'. The 'Maximum Leader' was enjoying the effect of the crisis on the popular mood. 'We did not even arrest anyone,' he later remarked, in a revealing moment of candour, 'because the unity of the people was so staggering.' Later that morning, at 10.22 a.m., an American U-2 spy plane was shot down over Cuba by a Soviet SA-2 rocket. The pilot, Rudolf Anderson, was killed. Cuban anti-aircraft batteries subsequently fired at other low-flying American reconnaissance planes. Meanwhile, another U-2 had unintentionally strayed into Soviet airspace near the Bering Straits. When Soviet MiGs took off to intercept it, Alaskan-based F-102As were scrambled. Elsewhere, mere accidents came close to triggering the apocalypse. A bear at Duluth airbase led to the mobilizing of nuclear-armed F-106s in Minnesota. A routine test at Cape Canaveral was mistaken for a Soviet missile by a radar unit in New Jersey.

By the afternoon of the 27th, the members of ExComm were in a state of high anxiety. The day had begun with a warning from

J. Edgar Hoover that the Soviet officials in New York were shredding documents, apparently in the expectation of war. Then came Khrushchev's second, very public proposal, apparently contradicting his first. Of all those present, only the President himself seemed to take seriously the idea of trading Turkish missiles for Cuban; the majority of his advisers saw it as a bid to weaken NATO, the transatlantic military alliance of which Turkey was a member. At 4 p.m. came the news of the downed U-2. We know from the tape recordings Kennedy secretly made of this meeting how he reacted to this bombshell: 'How do we explain the effect?' he asked, barely coherent. 'This Khrushchev message of last night and their decision . . . How do we – I mean that's a . . .' The phrase on the tip of his tongue was presumably something like 'a provocation we can't ignore'. But if that was what Kennedy nearly said, he stopped himself. Instead, he sent his brother Robert to discuss the Cuban–Turkish missile swap with the Soviet ambassador, lining up the UN Secretary-General to raise the issue the next day if he drew a blank. The key point, as Robert Kennedy explained to the Russians, was to avoid 'public discussion of the issue of Turkey'. He did not have to spell out his brother's and the Democratic Party's vulnerability on the issue. There had been repeated Republican accusations that the administration was backsliding over Cuba; and Congressional elections were due the following month. It must also be remembered that the Cuban crisis came just a year after the building of the Berlin Wall, the latest in a succession of Soviet challenges to the four-power control of the former German capital.

Khrushchev was asleep on his Kremlin sofa while all this was happening. The ambassador's report did not reach the Soviet Foreign Ministry until the following morning. As soon as he was briefed about what Robert Kennedy had said, Khrushchev drafted another public letter, which was duly broadcast at 5 p.m. Moscow time, 9 a.m. Eastern Standard Time. (It should have been earlier, but the courier got stuck in rush-hour traffic.) This time Khrushchev merely said that the missiles in Cuba would be dismantled, crated and returned home. It was over. 'I felt like laughing or yelling or dancing,' recalled one intensely relieved member of ExComm. The British journalist Alistair Cooke watched a seagull soar in the sky above him and wondered why it was not a dove. Yet a gull was perhaps the right bird. For at the same time Khrushchev sent two private messages to Kennedy. The second said that the missiles were being withdrawn only 'on account of your having agreed to the Turkish issue'. Later, the American ambassador to the UN, Adlai Stevenson, would be accused of having raised the Turkish issue. This was a smear; it was the Kennedy brothers who had done it. Nor was the crisis quite at an end. The Pentagon continued to prepare its invasion of Cuba, still unaware (or ignoring the fact) that there were ten times as many Soviet troops on the island as they had estimated and that they were armed with battlefield nuclear missiles. It was not until November 20, when Khrushchev agreed also to withdraw the Il-28 bombers, that the game of chicken was really at an end.

When both drivers swerve, as we have seen, there is no winner. True, having concealed from the American public his readiness to abandon either toppling Castro or the Turkish missiles, Kennedy could strike a tough-guy pose as the Soviets dismantled their missiles. But his military chiefs were disgusted; to the President's face, LeMay called it 'the greatest defeat in our history'. On the other hand, so convincing was Kennedy's claim to have made Khrushchev blink over Cuba that, just over a year later, a Castro sympathizer named Lee Harvey Oswald shot him dead.* Khrushchev also emerged from the crisis weaker. At a meeting of the Central Committee on November 23, he sought to make the best of it, with characteristic peasant humour: 'It was not necessary to act like the Tsarist officer who farted at the ball and then shot himself.' A Soviet missile had downed an American plane. 'What a shot! And in return we received a pledge not to invade Cuba. Not bad!' But the men with the medal-bedecked chests felt that he had acted recklessly for little net benefit. In October 1964, two years after trading Cuban missiles for Turkish, Khrushchev himself was traded in for Leonid Brezhnev. In truth, Castro was the sole beneficiary of the crisis – and he was the only one of the three leaders who was disappointed by the peaceful outcome. According to Ernesto 'Che' Guevara, when Castro heard of the compromise, 'he

---

* Attempts to uncover a conspiracy involving Pentagon hawks, to say nothing of the Mafia, have been unsuccessful, though the Kremlin was certain such a plot existed. Other theories point the finger of blame at the KGB itself.

swore, kicked the wall and smashed a looking glass'. Yet Castro's position was enormously strengthened by the crisis. Kennedy was soon dead, Khrushchev ousted. The Cuban leader, however, would enjoy more than four more decades in power.

## THE THIRD WORLD'S WAR

The Cuban missile crisis showed just how close to a Third World War it was possible for the United States and the Soviet Union to come, despite their vastly increased destructive capabilities. Yet it also revealed that even if they both chose to swerve in the great game of nuclear chicken, war could still be waged in other ways. It is sometimes claimed that the advent of 'Mutually Assured Destruction' ushered in an era of world peace. But this is to misunderstand the character of the Cold War. The real and bloody Third World War was in fact fought by the likes of Castro – in the Third World itself. The War of the World had been a succession of head-to-head collisions between the world's empires, played out in the crucial conflict zones at either end of the Eurasian land mass. The Third World's War, by contrast, was fought indirectly in new and more remote theatres, where the strategic stakes (though not the human costs) were lower.

There were three reasons for this relocation of conflict. First, the possibility of ethnic conflict in the western and eastern borderlands of Eurasia, the principal battlefields of the first half of the century, had been dramatically diminished. Not only had ethnic cleansing during and after the Second World War decimated minority populations, homogenizing societies as never before; at the same time, the most contested frontiers of all were hermetically sealed. After 1953 the border between North and South Korea was transformed into a heavily fortified zone across which no human being dared venture. In 1961, as we have seen, a wall was built across Berlin and through the heart of Germany, with the intention of stemming the flow of East Germans absconding to the western Federal Republic; its effect, however, was to formalize not only the partition of Germany but also the division of Europe. Central Europe disappeared. Henceforth there would be only Western and Eastern Europe. Churchill had earlier warned of the dangers of an Iron Curtain stretching between 'Stettin in the Baltic and Trieste in the Adriatic'. Yet once it was drawn, this geopolitical drape turned out to have unexpected benefits. Political segregation turned out to stop what had once been one of the principal sources of conflict in Central and Eastern Europe – friction between the peoples of the imperial borderlands. As Kennedy rightly observed, 'a wall is a hell of a lot better than a war'.

The second reason conflict moved was economic. The War of the World had been propelled forward by economic volatility. It had been the great interruption to globalization caused by the First World War that had plunged the world economy into three decades of upheaval. Inflation, deflation, boom, bust and depression; these had been the forces that had intensified the instability of both Europe and East Asia. They had weakened the existing empires. They had undermined the new democracies. They had heightened racial antipathies. They had paved the way for the empire-states that arose in Turkey, Russia, Japan and Germany, each with its own pathological yearning for ethnic homogeneity and hierarchy. It had been economic volatility that had justified Stalin's creation of the planned economy, a new kind of slave state based on state ownership of capital and unfree labour. Above all, it had been economic volatility that had inspired a new and ruthless imperialism, based on the seductive notion of 'living space' – of economic recovery through territorial expansion.

The 1950s and 1960s were quite different. In both the West and the East, economic growth rates rose to unprecedented heights. Average per capita growth rates for the period 1950–73 were higher than those for 1913–50 in almost every major economy except India's. In Spain growth was 34 times higher; in Germany and Austria just under 30 times higher; in Japan 9 times higher; in Italy 6 times higher. The Eastern Bloc economies also fared well; Stalinist planning proved a remarkably effective way of reconstructing economies ruined by war. Hungarian growth was eight times higher in the 1950s and 1960s than it had been in the era of world wars and depression; Eastern Europe as a whole enjoyed per capita growth of nearly 3.8 per cent, more than four times the pre-1950 figure. The Soviet Union achieved annual growth of just under 3.4 per cent, nearly a full percentage point higher than the United States (2.4 per cent). Ironically, the highest growth rates of all were achieved in the vanquished Axis countries. Moreover, the vulnerability of the major economies to cyclical slumps declined markedly. Between 1945 and 1971 the volatility of growth in the world's seven biggest economies was less than half what it had been between 1919 and 1939.

Economic rivalry began to take over from strategic conflict, a change vividly illustrated by Vice-President Richard Nixon's visit to Moscow in July 1959. His host loved to taunt the West. 'Whether you like it or not, history is on our side,' Khrushchev famously warned: 'We will bury you.' Nixon's inauguration of the American Exhibition at the Sokolniky Park in Moscow was the American reply. The highlight of the exhibition was an all-mod-cons kitchen, complete with dishwasher, electric cooker and – the American domestic goddess's most cherished possession – a huge refrigerator. It was, Nixon declared expansively, 'like those of our houses in California'. 'We have such things,' replied Khrushchev. Nixon seemed not to hear him: 'This is our newest model. This is the kind which is built in thousands of units for direct installation in the houses. In America, we like to make life easier for women.' Khrushchev shot back: 'Your capitalistic attitude toward women does not occur under Communism.' No matter what Nixon showed him, Khrushchev flatly refused to be impressed. If the American kitchen was ahead of the Soviet kitchen, it was merely a matter of historical happenstance:

KHRUSHCHEV: How long has America existed? Three hundred years?
NIXON: One hundred and fifty years.
KHRUSHCHEV: One hundred and fifty years? Well then, we will say America has been in existence for 150 years and this is the level she has reached. We have existed not quite forty-two years and in another seven years we will be on the same level as America. When we catch you up, in passing you by, we will wave to you.

It was all bluster. For ordinary Russians, accustomed to the primitive facilities of cramped communal housing, the exhibit was a glimpse of a parallel universe. Around 50,000 visitors came to see it every day; in all, it was visited by 2.7 million Soviet citizens. Richard Nixon's domestic critics used to ask: 'Would you buy a used car from this man?' Most people in Eastern Europe would gladly have bought a used fridge from him.

Nixon's icebox looked like a Cold War-winning weapon. As Khrushchev rightly said: 'What we were really debating was not a question of kitchen appliances but a question of two opposing systems: capitalism and socialism.' The Americans understood this too. Another attraction at the American exhibition was the latest IBM RAMAC 305 computer, which enabled visitors to have their questions answered about American culture and material achievements. It responded to some 10,000 enquiries during the first ten days:

VISITOR: What is meant by the American dream?
IBM: That all men shall be free to seek a better life, with free worship, thought, assembly, expression of belief and universal suffrage and education.

The Soviet Union might not be able to offer its citizens those freedoms. Yet its leaders always insisted that it could more than match the West when it came to economics. Stalin himself had built a Park of Soviet Economic Achievement in Moscow as a showcase for Communist consumer durables to come. One Russian propaganda film even featured a flying car, a kind of Soviet Chitty Chitty Bang Bang. The American Exhibition made it painfully clear how far the Soviets were from realizing such visions.

Yet it would be to misunderstand the Cold War to dismiss it as a one-horse race, which the United States was always bound to win. For all its economic limitations, the Soviet Union had other formidable weapons at its disposal. It was not only in the realms of culture and sport that the Soviets could hold their own, though it did no harm to Russian self-esteem that they were nearly always the favourites in chess matches, piano competitions and ice hockey matches.* Not

---

* Admittedly, the Americans liked nothing better than to think of themselves as the plucky underdogs. They exulted when Van Cliburn, a Texan boy, won the 1958 International Tchaikovsky Piano Competition in Moscow. They went into ecstasies when Bobby Fischer beat the Russian chess grandmaster Boris Spassky in 1972. And nine years later they could scarcely contain themselves when their ice hockey team narrowly beat the Soviet world champions. The Soviets, for their part, showed no sign of wishing to challenge American dominance in the realms of country music, surfing or baseball.

many Americans made high-profile defections to the other side of the Iron Curtain, as did some Russian ballet stars, notably Rudolf Nureyev and Mikhail Baryshnikov. But the Soviets undoubtedly had greater success in penetrating the other side's intelligence agencies through the undetected recruitment of equally mercurial characters, notably Kim Philby and Guy Burgess. In the realm of global strategy, too, the Soviet Union was a match – and sometimes more than a match – for the United States. That was why, for more than forty years, the outcome of the Cold War was anything but certain. And that was also why there were many parts of the world where the Cold War was not cold at all. For the third determinant of global conflict – imperial decline – continued to operate in the 1950s and 1960s. Now, however, it was different empires that were declining in different parts of the world. The decline and fall of the British Empire was attended by bitter intercommunal violence between Hindus and Muslims in India; between Israelis and Arabs in Palestine; between Sunnis and Shi'ites in Iraq; between Protestants and Catholics in Ireland. It was never entirely clear, and remains hard to say even today, which was the better option: to cut and run (as in India) or to hang on and fight (as in Kenya). Suffice to say that there were comparatively few happy endings as the European empires expired, and even where the transition to independence went smoothly, a descent into violence was not long in coming. That was the pattern throughout most of sub-Saharan Africa.

Among the waning empires that spawned this host of conflicts was the more or less informal American empire in Central America and the Caribbean. In 1952 Guatemala's left-wing government, led by President Jacobo Arbenz, enacted Decree 900, a reform that took idle land away from some of the country's biggest estate owners and redistributed it to poor peasants. Among the landowners dismayed by this development was the American United Fruit Company, which owned around 10 per cent of Guatemala's prime agricultural land. In February 1953 the Arbenz government confiscated a quarter of a million acres of company land, offering in return government bonds worth just over $1 million, a twentieth of what United Fruit said the land was worth. When the Guatemalan Supreme Court struck down the reform as unconstitutional, the government fired the judges. 'One can live without tribunals,' one trade union leader declared, 'but one can't live without land.' United Fruit had friends in high places (the future Secretary of State John Foster Dulles was one of its lawyers, his brother Allen was Deputy Director of the CIA) but it did not need United Fruit's lobbyists to convince American politicians that Arbenz's government was a Soviet Trojan horse in America's back yard. The US ambassador to Guatemala, James Puerifoy, summed up the official line when he said: 'Communism is directed by the Kremlin all over the world, and anyone who thinks differently doesn't know what he's talking about.' In the words of a National Security Council staff member, Guatemala was to be 'a prototype area for testing means and methods of combating Communism'. Something similar seemed to be afoot in Iran. The answer in both cases was a CIA-sponsored coup. First in Iran in 1953, then in Guatemala the following year, Eisenhower gave the green light for regime change.

In fact, the anti-Communist invasion launched in June 1954 was almost a fiasco. But the crisis gave the Guatemalan army its cue to seize power from Arbenz. The new military government received Washington's official blessing from none other than Vice-President Richard Nixon. On a visit to Guatemala, Nixon alleged that the Soviet Union had sent 'mountains and mountains of literature . . . attempting to change the minds of the people and warp them over to supporting international communism'. There was, he alleged, clear evidence that Arbenz's government had been under 'direct control from the international Communist conspiracy'. The message to Moscow was unambiguous. In the words of the American ambassador to the United Nations: 'Stay out of this hemisphere and don't try to start your plans and your conspiracies over here.' Yet the reality was that the Soviets did not really need to intervene directly in Latin America, for there were Marxists in Latin America who felt they could overthrow capitalism without any need for Soviet assistance – which had, in any case, been non-existent in Guatemala. Not for the last time, a CIA covert operation had unforeseen consequences. Shortly before the military takeover, an impressionable young Argentine doctor had arrived in Guatemala. In the wake of the coup, he fled to Mexico where he met another political refugee, a flamboyant Cuban lawyer. Five years later, the doctor, Ernesto Guevara, helped the lawyer, Fidel Castro, to take over Cuba.

The Cuban Revolution was a grave setback for the American anti-Communist strategy, undoing at a stroke the success of the Guatemalan coup. Despite repeated attempts, the CIA could not pull off the same trick in Havana. Yet the American assumption that Cuba had now become a kind of Caribbean branch office of the Soviet Communist Party was in many ways mistaken. As the Soviets later admitted, they had only limited influence over Castro. For Castro was Pinocchio, a puppet who had no strings. With scarcely any prompting from Moscow, he pursued a strategy of his own to spark off revolution right across what was coming to be called the Third World. He and Guevara sought to foment copy-cat revolutions in the Dominican Republic, Nicaragua and Haiti. Later, Castro sent Cuban weapons to Algeria and Cuban troops to Congo, Guinea-Bissau and Ethiopia. In 1975 Castro ordered his biggest intervention yet, sending a Cuban army to repel a South African invasion of newly independent Angola. Unbeknown to the Americans, he did so in defiance of orders from Moscow to stay out.

Angola was typical of the kind of place where the Cold War was distinctly hot. On one side, there was the Popular Movement for the Liberation of Angola (MPLA), which seized power in Luanda after independence from Portugal was finally granted in 1975; on the other, two rival guerrilla organizations, UNITA and the FNLA. And just as the majority of the troops sent to support the MPLA were Cuban rather than Russian, so UNITA derived the bulk of its military support from South Africa rather than the United States. In September 1987, when the war in Angola came to a head at Cuito Cuanavale, a remote military base in the south-east of the country not far from the Namibian border, the Angolan government forces were equipped with Soviet-made T-55 tanks and MiG fighters, but the tank crews and pilots were mainly Cuban. On the other side, the 8,000 UNITA troops were supported by around 3,000 South Africans – an infantry company from the 32nd 'Buffalo' battalion, a heavy artillery battery equipped with sixteen huge G-5 guns and the 61st Mechanized Battalion Group with their Ratel-90 armoured cars – assisted by the South African Air Force, which flew sorties against MPLA positions along the Lomba River.

Faraway battles like these make it absurd for us to remember the

Cold War fondly as a time of peace and stability. The reality is that the second half of the twentieth century was not much less violent than the first. Altogether between 1945 and 1983 around 19 or 20 million people were killed in around 100 major military conflicts. It was just the venues of violence that had changed. Instead of fighting head on, as they came so close to doing in Cuba in 1962, the superpowers now fought one another through intermediaries in what they regarded as peripheral theatres. But to those caught up in them there was nothing peripheral about these numerous hot wars. The degree of superpower sponsorship varied from case to case. Sometimes, as in Vietnam or Afghanistan, American and Soviet troops were in the front line. More often, they were behind the lines, training or supplying local armies. Sometimes, as in Africa and the Middle East, the support itself was subcontracted to other countries. Yet here, as in so many other respects during the Cold War, the United States found that it was at a fundamental disadvantage.

When Trotsky had called for world revolution after 1917, the results had been disappointing. But when Khrushchev spoke buoyantly of 'an era when socialism, communism and global revolution will triumph', it was a different story. All over the Third World there were popular nationalist movements which aimed to overthrow the last vestiges of West European colonial rule and establish some form of popularly based self-government. The Soviets proved remarkably good at persuading many such movements to adopt their own political and economic model. Decolonization was the wave the Soviets rode; 'popular liberation' was a phrase they knew well how to use. Of course, the American political system had also been the product of a revolt against imperial rule. Yet somehow Lenin, Stalin and Mao had more appeal in the 1960s and 1970s than Washington, Jefferson and Madison. The American model of democracy plus capitalism had far fewer takers than the Soviet alternative of one-party rule plus socialism. This was partly because poor former colonies like Guatemala, Cuba and Angola had a large, impoverished peasantry, of the sort that had been decisive in backing the Russian and Chinese revolutions, but only a small middle class, of the sort that had made the American one. Partly it was because ambitious Third World 'freedom fighters' liked the opportunities the distinctly unfree Soviet system had to offer them. In a one-party system, the first winner takes all; there is no danger of his being asked to hand over power to some rival within just a few years. And with a planned economy, the new political rulers can acquire any economic asset they like in the name of 'nationalization'.

The Soviets had a further advantage. They knew better than anyone how to arm illiterate peasants with cheap, reliable and user-friendly weapons. Mikhail Kalashnikov made his first rifle in 1947 – hence the abbreviated name AK-(*Automat Kalashnikov*)47 – just as the pace of decolonization was quickening and superpower relations were worsening. Such weapons were shipped in crate-loads to Third World countries, part of a low-profile small arms race running parallel to the headline-grabbing nuclear arms race. It was not long before the AK-47 became the Marxist guerrilla's weapon of choice. What could the Americans do in response? Aside from simply yielding the southern hemisphere to Khrushchev and his successors, there were three possibilities. They could prop up or resuscitate the old colonial regimes that the Third World Lenins were aiming to destroy. That did not come easily to US leaders, with their deep-rooted anti-imperial assumptions, but there were places where they were willing to try it. No one complained in Washington, for example, when the British defeated the Communists in Malaya. The Americans also encouraged the British to prolong their informal sphere of influence in the smaller states of the Persian Gulf. A more appealing response was to find pro-American freedom fighters – in other words, to back democratic political parties that favoured multi-party elections, not to mention free markets. But experience in Eastern Europe and Asia immediately after the Second World War tended to suggest that true liberals were perilously weak in relatively backward societies. Fresh in the memories of all American policy-makers were the examples of Poland, Czecho-slovakia, Hungary and the rest, where all the non-Communist political parties had effectively been snuffed out or emasculated. And, lest these memories fade, the Soviets did not hesitate to crush outbreaks of popular dissent in their European satellites – in East Berlin in 1953, Budapest in 1956, Prague in 1968 and Gdańsk in 1981.

The third option for American foreign policy was to fight dirty – as dirty, in fact, as the Soviets. In practice, Soviet victories always meant dictatorship and the repression that comes with it. For the Americans, it was therefore tempting to back anyone who showed signs of being able to beat the Soviet-backed revolutionaries, even if it meant imposing a capitalist dictatorship instead. The problem with this was that very quickly the United States found itself tainted by association with and support for regimes that were every bit as vicious as the worst Communist tyrannies of Eastern Europe or Asia. Worse, it was seldom clear beyond all reasonable doubt that the dictators backed by Washington were always the lesser evil, since the popular movements they crushed generally did not have the chance to show their true colours in power. Those left-wing leaders who were overthrown or murdered by CIA-backed regimes swiftly became martyrs not only in Soviet propaganda but also in the liberal press of the West. While experience strongly suggested that Marxists showed scant respect for human rights once in power, those who never made it to power or who held it only briefly could always be given the benefit of the doubt. Like Jekyll and Hyde, then, American foreign policy in the Cold War seemed to come in two guises: by day talking the language of freedom, democracy and the shining city on a hill; by night using dirty tricks to stymie suspected Soviet clients and to promote local 'strongmen' – a polite term for dictators. Nowhere was this more obvious than in what the United States regarded as its own geopolitical backyard: Central America, the birthplace of the dictum: 'It doesn't matter if he's a sonofabitch, so long as he's our sonofabitch.' This was the hard essence of what some commentators called realism.

In their last days in power in Guatemala, the Communists had resorted to mass arrests, torture and executions. Now the tables were turned. With American encouragement, a list was compiled of 72,000 suspected Communist sympathizers. Yet, just as the Soviets had found in Cuba, the Americans were soon reminded that Central (and South) American puppets came with few strings attached. By the mid-1960s, paramilitary death squads like the *Mano Blanca* (White Hand) were roaming the Guatemalan streets and countryside, engaging in what the US State Department admitted were kidnappings, torture and summary executions. Soon the Americans had to admit that, in the words of Thomas L. Hughes, the 'counter-insurgency' was 'running wild'. CIA agent John Longan was sent in to bring the situation under control. But his Operation Cleanup was anything but clean. Between

March 2 and 5, 1966, more than thirty leftist leaders, among them the former trade union leader Victor Manuel Gutiérrez, were arrested and taken to the Guatemalan military's headquarters at Matamaros. There they were tortured and killed. The Guatemalan military then put their bodies in sacks and dropped them out of a plane into the Pacific. The CIA memo outlining the operation stated simply: 'The execution of these persons will not be announced and the Guatemalan government will deny that they were ever taken into custody.' That was what the CIA meant by a cleanup: a dirty war that left no incriminating fingerprints. Operation Cleanup introduced what was to become the signature tactic of proxy Cold War violence in Latin America, the 'disappearance' of opponents. Over the next thirty years more than 40,000 people would disappear in Guatemala. It was the same story in other military regimes in the region – in Argentina, Uruguay, Brazil and Chile. *Los Desaparacidos* became a euphemism for those murdered by the military. With good reason, Viron Vaky, second-in-command of the US embassy in Guatemala, lamented the 'tarnishing' of America's image in the region.

Yet who exactly was being made to disappear? As far as the CIA was concerned, the answer was simply Communist sympathizers, potential revolutionaries whom Moscow might already have recruited to its side in the Cold War. In reality, however, the social conflicts that bedevilled the Third World throughout the Cold War were often as much ethnic conflicts as they were ideological. In this respect, the Third World's War had much in common with the War of the World; it was the old violence in new premises. Just as the Cold War in Angola was essentially a tribal battle for power between the primarily Kimbundo MPLA and the mainly Ovimbundu UNITA, so too in Guatemala the struggle between government and 'subversion' had a distinctly ethnic character. Guatemalan society was hierarchically ordered, with the relatively well-off Ladino descendants of conquistadors and their native concubines at the top, and the land-hungry indigenous peoples at the bottom. The proxy war that the CIA was underwriting in Guatemala was therefore not so much a war between capitalists and communists as a war between Ladino *latifundista* and Mayan peasants. Accused of sympathizing with the communist Guerrilla Army of the Poor, Mayan tribes like the Ixil and Kekchí were subjected not only to wholesale massacres but also to forced relocation and incarceration in 'strategic hamlets'. Hundreds of villages identified as 'red' were literally obliterated; their inhabitants tortured, raped and murdered; their homes destroyed and the surrounding forests burned. When the civil war was finally brought to an end in the 1990s, the total death toll had reached around 200,000. Because so many of the victims were Mayan, the Guatemalan military was deemed by the UN-sponsored truth commission to have committed an act of genocide.

The truth about the Cold War, then, is that in most of the southern hemisphere the United States did almost as little for freedom as the Soviet Union did for liberation. American policy involved not only the defence of West European democracies like Italy, France and West Germany, which there is no doubt the Soviets tried their level best to subvert; it also meant the maintenance of dictatorships in countries like Guatemala where Communism – sometimes real, sometimes imagined – was fought by means of the mass slaughter of civilians. This meant that the supposed 'long peace' of the Cold War was on offer only to American and Soviet citizens and those in immediate proximity to them in the northern hemisphere. For a large proportion of the world's citizens, there was no such peace. There was only the reality of a Third World War, a war that involved almost as much ethnic conflict as the First and Second World Wars before it. It was a war that by the late 1960s the United States showed every sign of losing.

## NIXON IN CHINA

When Richard Nixon was inaugurated as President on January 20, 1969, it was becoming hard for Americans to feel optimistic about the Cold War. Their much vaunted capitalist system, which Nixon himself had proudly showcased in Moscow ten years earlier, was faltering. Inflation was rising but, contrary to the Keynesian economic rules of the 1960s, unemployment was refusing to come down. Imports were growing faster than exports; meanwhile, foreigners were rapidly losing their fondness for the dollar, making it harder to finance the resulting deficits. American society itself seemed to be fragmenting. There were race riots in the inner cities and demonstrations in the universities; young fought old, black fought white, redneck fought hippy, student fought cop. Race was one of the main bones of contention. During the 1960s, an alliance of educated African-Americans and white liberals had waged a successful campaign to overthrow the system of racial segregation still operating in the states of the South. As late as 1967, for example, sixteen states still had laws prohibiting racial intermarriage. It was only with a Supreme Court judgment, in *Loving v. Virginia*, that legal prohibitions on interracial marriage were ruled unconstitutional throughout the United States, though Tennessee did not formally repeal the relevant article of its constitution until March 1978 and Mississippi only in December 1987. The political effects of these struggles were in fact more profound than their social effects, for racial integration advanced relatively slowly even when permitted. Nixon won the 1968 election mainly because the Democratic vote was split over the civil rights issue, with nearly ten million voters (13.5 per cent of the total) backing the racist Governor of Alabama, George Wallace, and his American Independent Party.

The biggest source of domestic conflict, however, was not race but Vietnam, the location of one of those many civil wars that were blown out of all proportion by the Cold War. From a military point of view, the war was not unwinnable, but from a political point of view it was already lost before Nixon took office, because of waning popular support. Nixon knew he had to end the war; from an early stage, it was the key to his strategy for re-election in 1972. But he did not want to end it on North Vietnamese terms. He therefore adopted an elaborate strategy of carrots and sticks. The carrots were American troop reductions. The sticks were strategic bombing raids on a scale that ultimately matched the combined efforts of all the air forces in the Second World War. Unfortunately, the more carrots Nixon offered, the more the North Vietnamese became convinced it was worth holding out, no matter how many explosive sticks he threw at them. It was time to change Cold War tactics; to abandon the strategy of war by proxy in favour of great-power diplomacy.

During the spring and summer of 1969, US government officials had watched the ideological and political split between the Soviet Union and the People's Republic of China escalate into fighting on the border in Manchuria – proof that this region remained as prone to strategic earthquakes as ever. There was a real possibility that the Soviet Union might launch attacks on Chinese nuclear weapons facilities. But to Nixon and his National Security Adviser, the Harvard historian Henry Kissinger, this was not a crisis, but an opportunity. Kissinger had never wholly accepted the idea that the world since 1945 had been divided into two mutually antagonistic blocs. In reality, he believed, the twentieth century was, for all its polarized political rhetoric, not all that different from the nineteenth. Others might see the Cold War as a crude game of chicken. To Kissinger, it was more like classical diplomatic chess. Just as Bismarck had sought to enhance German power by playing the other powers off against one another, Kissinger now sought to improve America's position by exploiting the Sino-Soviet antagonism. 'The deepest rivalry which may exist in the world today', he declared in September 1970, 'is that between the Soviet Union and China.' It had been one thing for Yugoslavia, Romania or Albania to break away from the embrace of Moscow. None counted as a great power and, as long as their dictators stuck to the principles of one-party rule and the planned economy, the Soviets could afford to shrug their shoulders. China, with its vast population, was a different matter. It was not so much that Kissinger expected the Chinese to bale the Americans out in Vietnam; rather, he believed an opening to Beijing would force the Soviets to listen to American proposals for a Strategic Arms Limitation agreement. *Détente* was Kissinger's watchword: a reduction in superpower tension aimed at halting the increasingly burdensome nuclear arms race. Both sides now had enough warheads to obliterate each other's populations several times over. First strikes were out because both sides were clearly capable of retaliatory second strikes. What was the point in building ever more numerous, ever more lethal missiles?

The problem was that this plan meant doing business with China, where no American official had set foot since 1949. Nor did this seem an especially opportune moment to re-establish diplomatic ties. In the late 1960s China was in the grip of a second wave of Maoist radicalism, the Cultural Revolution. Officially, this was an attempt by Chairman Mao to resist bureaucratic tendencies and revive revolutionary fervour. In reality it was a lethal power struggle at the top of the

Communist Party which unleashed a ghastly generational conflict. Formed into Red Guards and later Revolution Committees, young militants were encouraged by Mao to subject their teachers and other figures of authority to beatings, torture and ritualized humiliation. In the summer of 1966, more than 1,700 people were beaten to death in Beijing alone. Some victims were killed by having boiling water poured over them; others were forced to swallow nails. More than 85,000 people were exiled to the countryside, where they were forced to work in 'reform-through-labour' camps. At Beijing University during the 'Cleansing the Class Ranks' campaign of 1968, suspect teachers were forced publicly to confess their 'problems' and to denounce each other. Those identified as counter-revolutionaries were subjected to investigation by so-called *zhuan an* groups, which often involved torture. Teachers were held in an improvised jail called the *niupeng* (ox shack). The teachers themselves were referred to as *niuguisheshen* ('ox ghosts and snake demons'). Many were driven to suicide. Pan Guangdan, a professor of anthropology and translator of Darwin's works, told a friend: 'I used to follow a three S's strategy: surrender, submit and survive. Now I added a fourth S: succumb.' At least twenty-three faculty members at Beijing University were 'persecuted to death' in this way. (The Red Guards referred to suicide as 'alienating oneself from the Party and people'.) In 1970, during the campaign against the 'Four Olds' (old ideals, culture, customs and habits), around 280,000 people were labelled as 'counter-revolutionaries' or 'capitalist-roaders' and arrested. All this was done in the name of and at the instigation of Mao, who was revered as a god. In the morning and evening, people had to line up in front of his portrait and chant: 'May the great leader Chairman Mao live ten thousand years'. They sang songs like 'Chairman Mao is the Sun That Never Falls'. In all, between 400,000 and a million people are believed to have died in the mayhem of the Cultural Revolution. In the words of William Buckley, a Republican journalist close to Kissinger, rapprochement with Beijing meant dealing with murderers who put South American dictators in the shade. Indeed, Mao's totalitarian regime was now clearly on a par with Stalin's Soviet Union when it came to persecuting its own citizens.

To Kissinger, such considerations had to be secondary; in the great chess game of diplomacy, the imperative was to check the red king, not to worry about the pawns he sacrificed. In February 1972, the ground having been painstakingly prepared by his National Security Adviser, Nixon set off for China. This time he did not come to boast about the superiority of the American way of life, as he had done in Moscow in 1959. On the contrary, he was perfectly ready to conceal his deep-seated distaste for Communism. 'You don't know me,' Nixon opened, inadvertently sounding once again like a salesman, 'but anything I say I deliver.' Those in Washington who still lamented the 'loss' of China to the Communists could only gape in amazement as Nixon cheerfully swapped toasts with Premier Zhou Enlai. The handshake with Mao, the photo opportunity on the Great Wall, the sound of a Chinese military band playing 'America the Beautiful' at a banquet in the Great Hall of the People – even in his wildest imaginings, Nixon could not have wished for more. What was more, the rapprochement between China and America succeeded in bringing the Soviets to the negotiating table, just as Kissinger had hoped. Within three months, Nixon and Brezhnev had signed two arms control agreements. It was a resounding triumph for diplomacy – and for Nixon's campaign for re-election. Kissinger, the grandmaster of great-power chess, was duly promoted to Secretary of State.

But were he and Nixon in some sense chess pieces on someone else's board? They had assumed that Mao wanted three things: to boost China's international standing, to move closer to annexing Taiwan and to get the United States out of Asia. This was to underestimate the other side. The farewell banquet was awash with liquor and American goodwill – goodwill that the Chinese used to secure all kinds of concessions. Yes, Taiwan could now be marginalized, its seat in the United Nations handed to Beijing. But that was not all; with the United States now so wedded to the idea of good relations with the People's Republic, China could bully its neighbours into satellite status with impunity. Tibet, which had been annexed by the People's Republic in 1951, could now be forcibly colonized by ethnic Chinese. And not just the United States but also the Soviet Union could be kicked out of Indo-China. That had implications for Vietnam that were very different from the ones Nixon and Kissinger had in mind.

It turned out that nothing, not even the Machiavellian genius of

Henry Kissinger, could salvage American honour from the wreckage of Vietnam. Yet it was not failure overseas that destroyed Nixon's presidency. Rather, it was that enthusiasm for domestic gadgets which had so irked Khrushchev back in 1959. Nixon was not the first American president to tap phones and tape-record conversations, but none of his predecessors had done so quite as compulsively. By a rich irony, it was tapes of his own conversations, recordings he himself had requested, that revealed the extent of Nixon's complicity in the Watergate scandal, and forced his resignation. Still, even as he announced his fall from grace on August 9, 1974, Nixon clung to the idea that the opening to China had secured his place in history. As he reminded viewers:

We have unlocked the doors that for a quarter of a century stood between the United States and the People's Republic of China. We must now ensure that the one quarter of the world's people who live in the People's Republic of China will be and remain not our enemies but our friends.

But what kind of friends had Nixon actually made in Beijing? As far as the Chinese were concerned, American weakness presented China with an opportunity to settle two historical scores: one with the Soviet Union, whose leadership of the Communist world Mao wished to challenge; the other with North Vietnam, which had dared to turn to Moscow rather than Beijing for support in its war with the United States. The brunt of this score-settling would be borne by the small state of Cambodia.

Used by the North Vietnamese as a sanctuary and supply route for Vietcong guerrillas, Cambodia had been the target of a supposedly secret bombing campaign ordered by Nixon. The country's ruler, Prince Sihanouk, had tried vainly to play both sides off against one another. On March 18, 1970, Sihanouk was overthrown in a coup led by the pro-American Lon Nol; determined to win back power, Sihanouk joined forces with the Cambodian Communists, the Khmer Rouge. The early 1970s offered the perfect opportunity to the Khmer Rouge. The North Vietnamese forces were able not only to elude American incursions, but also to get the better of Lon Nol's inferior army. The Americans stepped up their bombing, but the resulting civilian casualties merely helped the Khmer Rouge to win new recruits.

When the North Vietnamese withdrew, the days of Lon Nol's regime were numbered. The man who would oust him was Saloth Sar, a failed electronics student who had become a Communist while studying in Paris and went by the *nom de guerre* of Pol Pot. Struck by his leader's cold demeanour and his utter ruthlessness towards their enemies, one of his comrades once compared Pol Pot with a Buddhist monk who had attained the 'third level' of consciousness: 'You are completely neutral. Nothing moves you. This is the highest level.' Just what Pol Pot was capable of doing in this transcendental state became apparent immediately after the capital, Phnom Penh, fell to the Khmer Rouge on April 17, 1975. He and his stony-faced army ordered the immediate and total evacuation of the entire city.

Pol Pot's regime repudiated the very idea of economic progress, seeking to transport Cambodia back into a pre-industrial, pre-commercial, pre-capitalist utopia. 'Year Zero' was proclaimed. The towns were to be emptied. All markets were to be abolished. There would be no money. Everyone would now work in agricultural cooperatives, where there would no private property. They would dress only in black. They would eat communally. The aim was to produce 'Kampuchea': a pure communist agrarian state. Every form of Western contamination was to be eradicated, even modern medicine. And as far as the Khmer Rouge were concerned, it did not much matter how many people died in the process. As they told the bewildered city-dwellers, the so-called 'New People' who had not been on the right side during the civil war: 'To preserve you is no gain, to destroy you is no loss.' Destruction was indeed Pol Pot's only forte, since his sole venture into construction – a complex of new canals and dams intended to rival the temples of Angkor Wat – ended in abject failure. The main supporters of the previous regime were executed in short order, along with their families. Anyone who questioned *Angkar* – 'the Organization' – was treated in the same way. Even to be ill was to betray a 'lack of revolutionary consciousness'. As in China's Cultural Revolution, teachers were viewed with suspicion, but so too were students and university graduates. The Khmer Rouge were short of bullets, so they used axes, knives and bamboo sticks. Children selected for execution had their heads smashed against banyan trees. Executions were often carried out with a pickaxe in the rice paddies – the so-called killing fields. The Toul Sleng prison became an 'extermination centre', where some 14,000 people were tortured to death, many of them Khmer Rouge cadres who had fallen under suspicion. Some victims were publicly disembowelled, their livers cooked and eaten by their executioners. It was not unusual for a revolution to devour its own children; only in Cambodia were they sometimes literally devoured. In all, between 1.5 and 2 million people died as a result of execution, maltreatment or starvation, out of a total population of only seven million.

The fate of Cambodia exemplifies how very far from cold the Cold War was in those parts of the world where crumbling empires and proxy wars created opportunities for fanatics. Yet Pol Pot's was not simply a class war. As in Guatemala and other Cold War sideshows, it also had an ethnic dimension. The Khmer Rouge were as committed to the notion of racial purity as to Communist fundamentalism. 'In Kampuchea there is one nation and one language ... From now on the various nationalities ... do not exist any longer in Kampuchea.' Hostility to the Vietnamese minority within the country had already manifested itself before Pol Pot came to power. Under the Khmer Rouge, however, the violence was systematized and extended to all the country's ethnic minorities. Around 100,000 ethnic Vietnamese were executed. Perhaps as many as 225,000 ethnic Chinese and 100,000 Muslim Chams – roughly half of each minority community – are also thought to have died as a result of disease, starvation or execution. Also vulnerable were the numerous Cambodians in ethnically mixed marriages, for here too the lines between the different groups were far from impermeable. Nor were even 'pure' ethnic Cambodians safe. The regime also targeted Buddhist monks for persecution as well as the inhabitants of the country's Eastern Zone, who found themselves on the wrong side of infighting within the Organization and were accused of having 'Vietnamese minds'. It was as if all the hatreds of the twentieth century – class, religious and ethnic – had been distilled into one toxic movement that was incapable of anything other than savage cruelty.

What ultimately destroyed this maniacal regime was the war it launched against Vietnam in 1977. This was a war with an explicitly genocidal intent. 'So far we have attained our target,' government radio announced on May 10, 1978: 'Thirty Vietnamese killed for every fallen Kampuchean ... So we could sacrifice two million Kampucheans in order to exterminate the fifty million Vietnamese – and we shall still be six million.' Here was a bizarre fulfilment of the American aspiration to exploit discord within the Communist bloc. Two Communist regimes, and two peoples, at war with one another, one backed by the Soviet Union, the other – Pol Pot's – backed by China. Yet precisely the Sino-American rapprochement that Nixon had negotiated led Cold War realpolitik into the realm of the absurd. After the Vietnamese invaded Cambodia, the United States sided with the Khmer Rouge, which had now retreated to the hills to wage another guerrilla war.

The Cold War, then, was only partly a struggle between two rival economic systems. It was only partly a game of chicken between the American and Soviet strategic forces. It was only partly Kissinger's game of chess between the great powers. On the ground, the Cold War was a host of civil wars, many of them sponsored by the superpowers, few of them entirely under their control. Some of the most egregious episodes of genocide were scarcely related to the superpower conflict at all. That was certainly the case in Pakistan in 1971, when the military regime of Mohammad Ayub Khan waged an authentically genocidal campaign against the people of East Pakistan in a vain attempt to prevent their secession by 'reducing this majority into a minority'. And it was true in Iraq in 1988, when Saddam Hussein launched the so-called Anfal (Spoils) campaign against the Kurds, using (among other weapons) poison gas to wipe out whole villages. Realpolitik meant dealing with repugnant leaders like Ayub Khan and Saddam Hussein; turning a blind eye to their violations of human rights, for the sake of some small advantage over the other superpower.

In the end, there could be only one winner in the economic rivalry between the United States and the Soviet Union, even if it seemed far from certain throughout the 1970s that the winner would be the former. The game of chicken could end with no winner at all. But the losers in the Third World's War – which raged out of sight while the grandmasters of Washington, Moscow and Beijing played their chess – could be counted in millions.

# THE WORLD REORIENTATED

We like to think of the revolutions of 1989 as the twentieth century's grand finale – the moment that marked the triumph of the West and an ideological happy ending. With the collapse of Communism in Eastern Europe and then, two years later, the break-up of the Soviet Union itself, many people concluded that the Western model of capitalist democracy had won the day. Some people looked forward to a new world order; others spoke of the end of history. It seemed as if all the problems of the century were at last being solved. The process of international economic integration seemed unstoppable; free trade and free capital movements were the order of the day. The warfare states and welfare states of the mid twentieth century were weakened by a surge of international economic liberalization, pioneered by Margaret Thatcher's government in Britain. Western Europe had shown since the war that economic integration would bring peoples together and terminate old military rivalries. Now that seemed to be happening on a global scale. The extreme ideologies of communism and fascism were also defunct. Meanwhile, the science of genetics was revealing that race was a meaningless concept, while some societies – notably that of the United States, but also the United Kingdom – did seem to be moving towards genuine racial and ethnic integration. The great-power conflicts that had rent the world apart were over too. The Soviet empire was suddenly gone. The United States had won the Cold War, all the while protesting that it had no imperial pretensions of its own. With a little encouragement, optimists hoped, the world would spontaneously adopt the Western model of capitalism and democracy. It seemed, in short, as if the War of the World was finally over.

Yet events in the Balkans soon made a mockery of this historical happy ending. For the peoples of Yugoslavia appeared to turn their backs on the brave new world of liberal capitalism. Within months of the collapse of Communism elsewhere in Eastern Europe, they began to tear their country apart in a war of secession characterized by atrocities against civilians and systematic 'cleansing of the ground' (*ciscenje terena*). History, it seemed, did not want to end. It wanted to go right back to the century's beginning.

On June 28, 1914, Gavrilo Princip had set the Balkans ablaze by murdering the heir to the Austrian throne Francis Ferdinand. His aim had been to create a united Yugoslavia. Seventy-five years later, the Communist President of Serbia, Slobodan Milošević, lit the fuse that would reignite the region with a rabble-rousing speech to mark the 600th anniversary of the Battle of Kosovo. His aim was to undo Princip's achievement. Milošević had made his political reputation in Serbia by taking a hard line against the efforts of ethnic minorities, in particular the Muslims of Kosovo, to increase their autonomy from Belgrade. But it was in Bosnia that the harvest of ethnic hatred was first reaped.

Across the road from the Sarajevo sepulchre where Princip's remains are preserved, in the shadow of the stadium where the Winter Olympics were held in 1984, is a second monument to Serbian nationalism – thousands of white crosses, each one marking the grave of a victim of the Bosnian civil war. The plan to partition Bosnia, hatched in March 1991 by the Serbian leader Milošević and the Croatian leader Franjo Tudjman, was always genocidal in its intent. As Tudjman himself later remarked, there would be 'no Muslim part' after the carve-up, despite the fact that Muslims accounted for nearly two-fifths of the Bosnian population. On October 2, 1992, some 100,000 people marched through the streets of Sarajevo to demonstrate for peace. The next day, the first mortars were fired by the Serb-dominated Yugoslav National Army from the hills that surround the city. For nearly four years, UN planes flew aid into Sarajevo airport, while Serbian guns rained down shells and bullets on the city centre. As the world looked on, 12,000 people perished in a siege that lasted 1,200 days. They had to dig up football pitches to find room to bury the dead. At the time, British diplomats and politicians strongly opposed any kind of intervention to halt the bloodshed, or even to arm the Bosnian Muslims so that they could defend themselves. They claimed that 'ancient hatreds' had been unleashed by the end of the Cold War. Tito had merely kept these hatreds in suspended animation; now it was back to Balkan butchery as usual.

At first sight the Bosnian civil war seems to stand in marked contrast to previous twentieth-century genocides. Yugoslavia was not poor; it was one of the most prosperous of the Eastern Bloc states, not least because economic reform had begun earlier there than anywhere else. Yugoslavia had ceased to be a strategic fault line between empires. After Tito's defection from Stalin's empire, it had become better known in Western Europe as a holiday destination and a source of migrant workers. As for ancient hatreds, there was little sign of these before 1989. In towns like Višegrad churches stood next to mosques in what was a relatively secular culture. Around 12 per cent of marriages in Bosnia were mixed, a proportion that had changed little since the 1960s and was more or less in line with the Yugoslavian average. Among men who married in 1989, for example, 16 per cent of Bosnian Croats, 13 per cent of Bosnian Serbs and 6 per cent of Bosnian Muslims took women from one of the republic's other ethnic groups as their wives. In towns like Sarajevo and Mostar the proportions of mixed marriages were even higher. By comparison with Muslims in other parts of Yugoslavia (especially Kosovo), Bosnian Muslims were significantly more likely to marry out. So intermingled were the people of Bosnia that their separation could only be achieved by the most horrific violence.

One clue as to Milošević's motivation, however, lies in Yugoslavia's demographic trends. These were not going the Serbs' way. In Serbia the population was scarcely growing; whereas in predominantly Muslim Bosnia and Kosovo it rose by, respectively, 15 and 20 per cent in the 1980s. Between 1961 and 1981 the Muslim proportion of the Bosnian population rose from 26 per cent to 40 per cent; the Albanian proportion of Kosovo from 67 to 77 per cent. Another source of friction was economic. The 1980s had seen a slowdown in Yugoslavia as a whole, but some parts of Yugoslavia were doing much better than others. Slovenia and Croatia were growing far more rapidly, while Bosnia and Kosovo were doing markedly worse. By 1988 per capita gross social product in the latter pair was, respectively, 65 and 24 per cent of the Yugoslavian average, compared with 80 per cent and 40 per cent in 1955. The watchword of Milošević's campaign was that the Serbs in Bosnia and Kosovo were 'endangered'. This was true in so far as they were, in each case, a shrinking minority within a stagnating economy. It was upon the Serbian minorities' resulting insecurities that Milošević and his acolytes played.

In the spring of 1992 Serbian paramilitary death squads with names like the Tigers and the White Eagles swept through Eastern Bosnia. At the end of April they reached Višegrad, a town where more than three-fifths of the population were Muslim. Among the White Eagles was a twenty-five-year-old former Višegrad resident named Milan Lukić. What happened under Lukić's reign of terror was like a re-enactment of some of the most gruesome scenes from the Second World War. In two incidents in June, 135 Muslims were burned to death after Lukić and his men locked them in their homes and set off incendiary bombs. On July 11 a car Lukić had stolen – a red Volkswagen Passat – was driven onto the bridge immortalized in Ivo Andrić's *Bridge over the River Drina*, where for centuries the towns-people had met and talked. The car was crammed with six Muslims and at least one armed Serb. Another group of Serbs was already waiting for them in the middle of the bridge. Their leader announced over a megaphone to 'Muslims hiding in the surrounding woods' that they would have a 'bloody holiday, Balkan style'. He also announced that 'every Serb who protects a Muslim will be killed immediately', and that for every Serb killed by a Muslim, a thousand Muslims would be sacrificed. The group then cut off the heads of the six prisoners and threw their bodies into the Drina. About half an hour later, a van arrived with another eight Muslims. They were killed in the same manner. Women and children were included in a third group that was brought to the bridge at about 7 p.m. The killing went on through much of the night. It was the river that brought the first signs of the massacre to neighbouring villages, when a corpse was found floating in the water a couple of miles downstream. Over the next few months the bodies of eighty-two men, women and children were dragged from the river. In all, 860 of the town's Muslims were killed; a further 738 were still listed as missing in August 2005. Only around 100 Muslims remained, out of a total pre-war population of more than 13,000. This pattern was repeated in towns and villages all over Bosnia. The aim of the massacres was not to kill all Muslims, but to kill enough to ensure that the survivors would leave and never return. The most exhaustive database that has been compiled of all those killed and missing – including members of all ethnic groups – contains more than 92,000 names.

On August 5, 2001, survivors of the massacre returned to Višegrad for the burial of 180 bodies that had been exhumed from mass graves and painstakingly identified using DNA tests. The irony is that the tests used there and at other burial sites in Bosnia have confirmed the absence of any genetic difference between Muslims, Serbs and Croats. Whatever the war in Bosnia was about, then, it was not about expelling or murdering members of a different race, because racial differences literally did not exist. Indeed, one Serbian tactic had the effect of confusing the genetic record even further. As we have seen, a recurrent feature of twentieth-century violence – from Armenia in 1915 to China in 1937 to Germany in 1945 – was the accompaniment of mass murder by mass rape. The UN Commission on Human Rights called the incidence of rape in Bosnia 'massive, organized and systematic', carried out to 'humiliate, shame, degrade and terrify the entire ethnic group'. Two hundred women, some of them mere girls, were snatched from their homes in Višegrad by members of the White Eagles and taken to the nearby Vilina Vlas sanitorium. There, they were repeatedly raped. Similar crimes were committed at the fire station, the Bikavac Hotel, the high school and the sports centre.

Nor was Višegrad by any means unique. The European Union estimated that altogether 20,000 women were raped during the Bosnian war; Bosnian sources put the total at 50,000. No one really knows. Some of the victims were murdered. Others – again we cannot be sure how many – became pregnant. It was as if the perpetrators had reverted to the crudest kind of tribal behaviour. Not content simply to kill male Muslims, they also wanted to impregnate their womenfolk with 'little Četniks', as if to increase the Serbian share not only of Bosnian land but also of the Bosnian gene pool. Yet such primitive conduct coincided with subtle political calculations. For it is clear that Milošević's principal motive in playing the Serbian nationalist card was to avoid the fate of Communist leaders in other East European countries. While they had been swept away by the post-1989 wave of nationalism, Milošević was able to ride it; indeed, to whip it up. And for ten years his strategy worked.

What happened in Bosnia was only part of what came routinely to be called a New World Disorder after 1989. In the 1990s wars between states became less common, but the number of civil wars within states soared. The break-up of Yugoslavia was by no means the bloodiest of these conflicts. In Rwanda, following the shooting down of a plane carrying the country's president (and the new president of Burundi), extremists from the Hutu majority attempted to exterminate the country's million or so Tutsis. In 1994, in the space of a hundred days, 800,000 people – mostly Tutsis, but also Hutus who refused to cooperate – were murdered. An army of Tutsi exiles (the Rwandan Patriotic Front) then invaded from Uganda and drove the Hutu killers, and many other Hutus fearful of reprisals, across the border into Congo and Tanzania. Soon nearly all Congo's neighbours had become embroiled in a monstrous orgy of violence. Altogether between 2.5 and 3 million people are estimated to have lost their lives in Central Africa's Great War, the majority from starvation or disease, the pre-modern retinue of war. Again, as in Bosnia, sexual violence was rampant, with the twist that rape in Rwanda accelerated the spread of the African AIDS epidemic. Again there were those who gained from the mayhem: politicians, who could resist pressure for truly representative democracy, and racketeers, who could turn their gangs into full-scale private armies. Again the 'international community' found it convenient to blame the violence on ancient (and by implication incurable) tribal hatreds.

It has been suggested that the bloodshed in Rwanda should be understood as the result of population pressure and ecological crisis. Like neighbouring Burundi, Rwanda had an extraordinarily high population density by 1990, yet primitive agricultural methods were leading to soil exhaustion and erosion, causing average land holdings to shrink to unviable sizes. After the violence had abated, some Rwandans were even heard to say that it had been 'necessary to wipe out an excess of population and to bring numbers into line with the available land resources'. Yet Thomas Malthus in his 1798 seminal *Essay on the Principle of Population* never predicted that a crisis of subsistence agriculture would lead men to hack one another to death with machetes; it was 'misery' or 'vice' that he foresaw, not genocide. The motivation for mass murder owed much more to the now familiar collision between the ideology of race and the reality of an ethnically mixed society. The notion that the societies of the Great Lakes had a dichotomous structure – on one side, the light-skinned Tutsi elite (pastoral/educated/aristocratic), on the other, the dark-skinned Hutu masses (farmers/illiterate/servile) – originated in the usual anthropological simplifications of colonial powers. Such notions were perpetuated and further distorted by the post-independence regimes in both countries; to legitimize continuing minority rule in Burundi ('Hamitism'), to legitimize the Hutu social revolution in Rwanda ('anti-Hamitism'). Social realities, however, were quite at variance with this two-tier racial order. Feudal clans had a much longer history than these supposed races. There were in any case other ethnic groups in Rwanda and Burundi, like the Ganwa and the Twa or pygmies. Most importantly, as in Bosnia, Hutus and Tutsis were very far from socially segregated. They spoke the same language and lived in the same villages. Above all – a point often overlooked at the time – they had long intermarried. Indeed, the first Hutu president of Rwanda, Gregoire Kayibanda, was said to have a Tutsi wife. Although the offspring of a Hutu father and a Tutsi mother were classed as Hutus on their identity cards, intolerance of mixed marriages and their children rose sharply in the period prior to the outbreak of civil war in 1994. The genocide was thus not inflicted on a long-ostracized pariah group, but on neighbours, and sometimes even on relatives. Indeed, in the commune of Kanama there was no clear distinction between Hutu murderers and Tutsi victims; Hutus killed Hutus; fathers killed sons. Europeans shook their heads at African 'tribalism', but what happened in Rwanda – the labelling of the ethnic minority as 'cockroaches', the savage butchering of whole families, the use of rape as a weapon – distinctly echoed events in Europe's own 'Dark Continent' just fifty years before. To believe that Rwandans killed each other for the sake of a few extra acres of farmland is like believing the Germans invaded the Soviet Union simply because they, too, were chronically short of living space.

The distinguishing feature of the genocides in Bosnia and Rwanda, the thing that sets them apart from similar bouts of carnage between

1904 and 1953, is their geopolitical irrelevance. Compared with, say, the Middle East, where ethnic conflict tended to take the form of terrorism rather than genocide, the Balkans and Central Africa were strategically of negligible value. It was that which delayed international intervention in Bosnia and prevented it altogether in Rwanda.* At the same time, the absence of an imperial rival to the United States throughout the 1990s – a condition of 'unipolarity' unknown in the earlier part of the century – lowered the stakes even when a local conflict did break out in the strategically crucial Persian Gulf (as happened when Iraq invaded Kuwait). For these reasons, the New World Disorder never threatened to become a New World War. When the Russian government impulsively sent troops to Pristina airport in June 1999, seemingly to check the American-led NATO advance into Kosovo, the effect was farcical, not tragic. A final question therefore arises: can this state of affairs be relied upon to persist? In other words, may we look forward in the twenty-first century to nothing more than localized disorders as opposed to a new War of the World? As I write, there are some grounds for cautious optimism. According to one recent estimate, global warfare has decreased by over 60 per cent since the mid-1980s and is now at its lowest level since the late 1950s. Since 2003 no fewer than eleven wars have ended, in countries ranging from Indonesia and Sri Lanka in Asia to Rwanda, Sierra Leone, Angola and Liberia in sub-Saharan Africa.

In 1931 Albert Einstein invited Sigmund Freud to join him in establishing 'an association of intellectuals – men of real stature' the purpose of which would be to 'make an energetic effort to enlist religious groups in the fight against war'. Freud replied sceptically, asserting the existence of a perennial human 'instinct to destroy and kill' – the antithesis of the 'erotic' instinct 'to conserve and unify':

---

* Jacques Poos, the Foreign Minister of Luxembourg, declared that 'the hour of Europe' had dawned, as if Brussels could somehow halt the killing. In fact, European diplomatic initiatives did nothing to stop ethnic cleansing and European troops acting under the auspices of the United Nations all but aided and abetted the massacre of 8,000 unarmed Muslim men at Srebrenica in July 1995. It took American firepower and the defection of the Croats to halt the killing in Bosnia – just as it was American firepower that stopped and then reversed the ethnic cleansing Milošević also attempted in the province of Kosovo.

These are, as you perceive, the well known opposites, Love and Hate, transformed into theoretical entities; they are, perhaps, another aspect of those
eternal polarities, attraction and repulsion, which fall within your province
. . . Each of these instincts is every whit as indispensable as its opposite, and
all the phenomena of life derive from their activity, whether they work in
concert or in opposition . . . With the least of speculative efforts we are led
to conclude that [the destructive] instinct functions in every living being,
striving to work its ruin and reduce life to its primal state of inert matter.
Indeed, it might well be called the 'death instinct'; whereas the erotic instincts
vouch for the struggle to live on. The death instinct becomes an impulse to
destruction when, with the aid of certain organs, it directs its action outward,
against external objects. The living being, that is to say, defends its own
existence by destroying foreign bodies . . . The upshot of these observations
. . . is that there is no likelihood of our being able to suppress humanity's
aggressive tendencies . . . Why do we, you and I and many another, protest
so vehemently against war, instead of just accepting it as another of life's
odious importunities? For it seems a natural enough thing, biologically sound
and practically unavoidable.

Freud had already advanced this argument in his reflections on
the First World War, though without the grimly Social Darwinistic
conclusion he now offered Einstein. Whatever one makes of Freud's
theories, it is difficult to dismiss altogether this insight into the human
condition, since it so perfectly captures that destructive urge that
was to annihilate, within little more than a dozen years, the Central
European German-Jewish milieu from which both he and Einstein had
sprung. For all its unscientific and confessedly speculative character,
Freud's analysis went to the elusive heart of hatred itself, by capturing
its essential ambivalence – its combination of *Eros* and *Thanatos*,
of the sexual and the morbid. We have by now encountered that
combination often enough in these pages, in the eruption of genocidal
acts from sexually conjoined communities; in the combination of lust
and bloodlust in mass rapes; in the relationship of master (race) and
slave (race) as personified by Milan Lukić and Igbala Raferović, the
widow of one of his Muslim victims, whom Lukić allegedly kept as a
captive sexual partner.

Yet the twin urge to rape and murder remains repressed in a civilized society. It is only when civilization breaks down or is broken down, as happened in both Bosnia and Rwanda, that the urge is unleashed. And only under certain circumstances does it escalate from pogrom to genocide. To repeat: economic volatility very often provides the trigger for the politicization of ethnic difference. Proximity to a strategic borderland, usually an imperial border, determines the extent to which the violence will metastasize.

Two quite unrelated phenomena, each dating from around 1979, suggest that the era of New World Disorder is now coming to an end. In many ways, the collapse of the Soviet Union late in 1991 and its subsequent aftershocks tended to distract attention from far more profound changes that were happening on the other side of the world. For there, another Communist regime – and another long-established empire – was working out how to have economic reform without making political concessions. How was it that the Chinese Communists were able to achieve reform – and soaring economic growth – without sacrificing their monopoly on power? The simple answer is that when a potentially revolutionary situation developed in 1989, the regime did what Communist regimes had routinely done throughout the Cold War when confronted with internal dissent. It sent in the tanks. On June 4, 1989, the Democracy Wall movement was ruthlessly suppressed. Unknown numbers of the students who had gathered in Tiananmen Square were arrested. Leading dissidents were jailed after show trials. What happened in China was in stark contrast to events in Eastern Europe at the same time, where the Soviet leadership were trying to have both economic reconstruction and political reform – but ended up with political revolution and economic collapse. The Chinese wanted and got economic reconstruction *without* political reform. Since 1979 the Chinese economy has grown at an average rate of just under 10 per cent per annum, contributing to a rapid closing of the gap between Western and Asian incomes (see Figure E.1). This has been achieved not by right-wing Thatcherites, but by card-carrying Communists. Indeed, the man responsible for China's economic miracle was the same man who ordered the tanks into Tiananmen Square.

When Deng Xiaoping arrived in Washington on January 28, 1979, it was the first time that a leader of Communist China had visited the

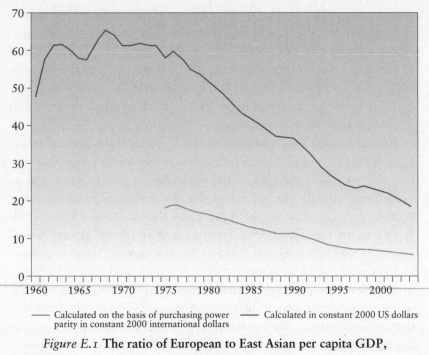

*Figure E.1* **The ratio of European to East Asian per capita GDP,**
**1960–2004**

Calculated on the basis of purchasing power parity in constant 2000 international dollars

Calculated in constant 2000 US dollars

United States. At seventy-four, Deng was the arch-survivor of the Chinese Revolution. He had accompanied Mao on the Long March and had survived the dark days of the Cultural Revolution, when he had been labelled the 'Number 2 capitalist-roader' by the Red Guards. Twice after his rehabilitation, the Gang of Four, led by Mao's toxic wife Jiang Qing, had tried to get rid of him. But Deng had come out on top. His American trip was prompted by a momentous internal upheaval within the Chinese Communist Party. In December 1978, at the Third Plenum of the 11th Congress of the Chinese Communist Party, the decision had been taken, at Deng's instigation, to reorientate China's economy towards the market. Mao's Great Leap Forward by means of state-led industrialization had been a Great Leap Backward that had as many as thirty million lives. Deng's strategy for a real leap forward was to break up communal control of agriculture and encourage the development of Township and Village Enterprises. Within a few years such rural businesses accounted for nearly a third of total industrial production. The other vital ingredient was a Chinese diaspora that had continued to operate within the capitalist system even as the mainland languished under Mao's tyranny. From Hong Kong to Kuala Lumpur, from Singapore to San Francisco, an experienced and wealthy capitalist elite was ready to be wooed.

The crucial thing about Deng's US trip was that it ensured that, as China industrialized, its exports would have access to the vast American market. It also ensured that, when Deng created free-trading Special Economic Zones along the Chinese coast, American firms would be first in line to invest directly there, bringing with them vital technological know-how. For their part, American companies saw Chinese liberalization as a perfect opportunity to 'out-source' production of goods for American consumers. Some analysts even predicted that the Special Economic Zones would become like American colonies in East Asia, while others thought wishfully that exposure to the free market would be bound to weaken the Communist Party's aversion to political freedom. What better conclusion to the American century could be imagined? But it did not quite work out that way.

Like other Asian economic miracles, China's was propelled by trade. Between 1978 and 1988, Chinese exports rose four-fold in dollar terms, and since then they have grown more than ten-fold. The principal destination for Chinese goods was and remains the United States. More than 11 per cent of US imports today come from China, and that number is rising. Though American companies hoped to be beneficiaries of the Chinese export boom by investing in Chinese subsidiaries, barely a tenth of foreign direct investment in China has come from the United States. Instead, the roles have been reversed. As the United States trade deficit has soared to a peak of more than 6 per cent of gross domestic product, it is the Chinese who have been lending to the United States. Meanwhile, more and more American manufacturers are coming under intense pressure from Chinese competition because not only are Chinese wages a fraction of American wages; the Chinese have also restrained the appreciation of their currency against the dollar. And it is no longer just cheap shoes and clothes they are exporting to the US. More than two-fifths of the US–China trade deficit is accounted for by electrical machinery and power generation equipment. Americans had thought China would become a giant economic subsidiary of the United States, in an approximate re-enactment of the 'Open Door' era of the early twentieth century. Instead, they now found themselves facing a new economic rival. Some forecasts suggested that China's gross domestic product would overtake that of the US as early as 2041. Anxious observers began to wonder if this economic competition could ultimately lead to conflict. There was nervous talk of future trade wars – and not only trade wars.

Thus was the supposed triumph of the West in 1989 revealed to be an illusion. The revolution that Deng had launched with his visit to the United States in 1979 had much further-reaching implications than anything that had happened in Britain under Margaret Thatcher. And Deng's ruthless suppression of political opposition in 1989 had been a far more important event than Mikhail Gorbachev's capitulation in the face of it. Yet despite all this, Deng's was still not the most important of the revolutions of 1979. The Chinese, after all, were embracing at least part of what we think of as Western culture – the free market, albeit a Far Eastern version, planned and overseen by a one-party state. What was happening in the *Near* East involved a complete repudiation of Western values. There, the revolution was not about profits; it was about the Prophet. And whereas the Far East exported products, the Near East exported people.

In 1979, the same year that Margaret Thatcher came to power and Deng Xiaoping went to Washington, the *madrassa* or religious school in the grey city of Qom in Iran was the epicentre of another, very different, revolution – a revolution that would transform the world as profoundly as the globalization of free market economics. The year 1979 had brought a woman to power in England, a woman wholly committed to the idea that salvation lay in the free market. But 1979 also brought the Ayatollah Rouhollah Mousavi Khomeini to power in Iran, a man just as committed to the idea that salvation lay in the teachings of the Prophet Mohammed. One leader read Hayek's *Road to Serfdom*, the other the Koran. One revolution pointed to a world based on free trade, the other to a world based on holy writ. There were, of course, many reasons why Iranians rallied to a leader who routinely denounced the United States as 'the Great Satan'. In 1953 it had been the CIA (along with MI6) that had overthrown the popular Prime Minister Mohammad Mossadeq and installed Shah Mohammed Reza Pahlavi as a dictator. The Shah's regime was by no means the most vicious the United States bankrolled during the 1960s and 1970s; nevertheless, his combination of private hedonism and public repression sufficed to put a powder keg under the Peacock Throne. The Iranian revolution of 1979 was partly a matter of settling scores against the Shah's military and secret police. But under Khomeini's leadership its main goal became to turn back the clock; to purify Iranian society of every trace of Western corruption. At the same time, it aimed to challenge American pretensions not only in the Middle East but throughout the Islamic world.

This was much more than just a revival of Islam. As a religion, Islam is of course far from monolithic. There are deep divisions, not least between the Shi'ites who predominate in Iran (and Iraq) and the Sunnis who predominate in the Arab countries. But 'Islamism' was a militantly political movement with an anti-Western political ideology that had the potential to spread throughout the Islamic world, and even beyond it. Ironically, the United States had a hand in its spread. After all, the Soviets found their occupation of Afghanistan so very difficult to sustain because they found themselves fighting a new and highly motivated foe, the mujahidin, armed and trained by the CIA on the old principle that my enemy's enemy is my friend. And which regime has done more than any other to spread the teaching of Islamic fundamentalism since 1979? The answer is Saudi Arabia, the United States' most important ally in the Arab world. For it was not the poor of the Middle East who rushed to join the jihad; often, it was those who had received a Western education.

The greatest of all the strengths of radical Islam, however, is that it has demography on its side. The Western culture against which it has declared holy war cannot possibly match the capacity of traditional Muslim societies when it comes to reproduction. The Islamic revolution ended at a stroke the Westernization of female life in Iran. As dictated by a strict interpretation of shariah law, women were now forced to veil themselves with the *hijab* in all public places. Strict segregation of the sexes was introduced in schools and public transport. Female presenters, actresses and singers were banned from radio and television. Women were prevented from studying engineering, agriculture and finance. They were systematically purged from all high-level government positions as well as the judiciary. In December 1979 the former minister of education Farrokhru Parsa was executed, having been convicted of promoting prostitution, 'corrupting the earth' and 'warring against God'. Contraception and abortion were banned and the age of consent for marriage lowered to just thirteen. The constitution of the Islamic Republic spelt out unambiguously the proper role of women in the new theocracy:

The family unit is the basis of society, and the true focus for the growth and elevation of mankind . . . Women were drawn away from the family unit and [put into] the condition of 'being a mere thing', or 'being a mere tool for work' in the service of consumerism and exploitation. Re-assumption of the task of bringing up religiously minded men and women, ready to work and fight together in life's fields of activity, is a serious and precious duty of motherhood.

Such attitudes help to explain why, although the average fertility rate in Muslim countries did decline from the 1970s onwards, it remained consistently more than twice the European average.

Though very far from being a feminist, Margaret Thatcher herself embodied a profoundly different social change that went hand in hand with the liberalization of the Western economies in the late twentieth century. With the decline of traditional trade unions and the introduction of new flexible working practices, it became easier than ever before for British women to enter the workforce. Legislation against sex discrimination opened all kinds of careers to them that had previously been dominated by men. Market forces encouraged women to work. At the same time, the ready availability of contraception and abortion in the West gave women an unprecedented control over their own fertility. The two things went together. Women wanted to work, or maybe economic pressures obliged them to work. It was much harder to work with three or four children to look after as well; so women opted to have just two, or one, or – in the case of many of the most professionally ambitious – none at all. From the late 1970s, the average West European couple had fewer than two children. By 1999 the figure was just over 1.3, whereas, for a population to remain constant, it needs to be slightly over two. Europeans, quite simply, had ceased to reproduce themselves. The United Nations Population Division forecast that if fertility persisted at such low levels, within fifty years Spain's population would decline by 3.4 million, Italy's by a fifth. The overall reduction in 'indigenous' European numbers would be of the order of fourteen million. Not even two world wars had inflicted such an absolute decline in population.

The consequences of these two diametrically opposite trends were dramatic. In 1950 there had been three times as many people in Britain as in Iran. By 1995 the population of Iran had overtaken that of Britain. By 2050, the population of Iran could be more than 50 per cent larger. At the time of writing, the annual rate of population growth is more than seven times higher in Iran than in Britain. A hundred years ago – when Europe's surplus population was still flocking across the oceans to populate America and Australasia – the countries that went on to form the European Union accounted for around 14 per cent of the world's population. By the end of the twentieth century that figure was down to around 6 per cent, and according to the UN by 2050 it could have fallen to just 4 per cent. That raised at least one awkward question: who was going to pay the taxes necessary to pay for Old Europe's generous state pensions? With the median age of Greeks, Italians and Spaniards projected to exceed fifty by 2050 – one in three people in each of these countries would be sixty-five or over – the welfare states created in the wake of the Second World War looked obsolescent. Either new-born Europeans would spend their working lives paying 75 per cent tax rates, or retirement and subsidized health care would simply have to be scrapped. Alternatively (or additionally), Europeans would have to tolerate substantially more legal immigration. The UN estimated that to keep the ratio of working to non-working population constant at the 1995 level, Europe would need to take in 1.4 million migrants a year from now until 2050. The annual figure for net migration in the 1990s was 850,000.

But where would the new immigrants come from? Obviously, a high proportion would have to come from neighbouring countries. Yet Eastern Europe could not supply anything like the numbers needed. Indeed, the UN expected the population of Eastern Europe to have declined by a quarter by 2050. Those who feared waves of migrants from Eastern Europe were facing the wrong way – east instead of south. The reality was that Europe's fastest growing neighbours by the end of the 1990s were, for the reasons discussed above, countries that were predominantly if not wholly Muslim. Consider the case of Morocco, where the population growth rate is seven times higher than in neighbouring Spain. At the very northernmost tip of Morocco, directly opposite Gibraltar, lies the tiny Spanish enclave of Ceuta, one of the few surviving remnants of Spain's imperial past. Today, however, it is no longer an outpost of an aggressively expansionist European empire, but a defensive bulwark maintained by a continent under siege. Camped outside Ceuta are thousands of people from the Maghreb and beyond, some fleeing zones of conflict, others simply seeking better economic opportunities. Here they sit for days, waiting for a chance to sneak past the Spanish border patrols. The European Union has responded by subsidizing the construction of a five-mile border fence, equipped with razor wire, watchtowers and infra-red cameras.

European officials admit that they have no idea how many people are making their way illegally into Europe. About 50,000 illegal immigrants are seized at Europe's ports or at sea every year, but it is impossible to say how many get through or die in the attempt. Every week Spanish police patrolling the waters between Africa and Europe catch dozens of people, most of them Moroccans, trying to sneak into southern Spain and the Canary Islands in small smuggling boats known as *pateras*. For those who survive the journey, El Ejido is the point of entry into Europe. In the asphyxiating heat of the greenhouses there, 20,000 immigrants work in conditions that few Spaniards are willing to endure. And El Ejido is just one manifestation of what some call 'Eurabia'. A youthful society to the south and east of the Mediterranean is quietly colonizing, in the original Roman sense of the word, a senescent and secularized continent to the north and west of it. Today, at least fifteen million Muslims have their home in the European Union, a number that seems certain to rise. Bernard Lewis's prophecy that Muslims would be a majority in Europe by the end of the twenty-first century may go too far, but they may well outnumber believing Christians, given the collapse of church attendance and religious faith in Europe.

Predictably, the growth of Muslim communities has generated some resentment on the part of what we might as well call the old Europeans. There is clear evidence that whatever the economic benefits of immigration there are also real costs for unskilled indigenous workers. Periodically, violence flares up. There are attacks on the immigrants; sometimes on their mosques. In the eastern outskirts of Paris in 2005 disaffected youths from predominantly Muslim immigrant communities ran amok after two of their number died while hiding from the police. The fact that a minority of European Muslims – not all of them first-generation immigrants – have become involved with extreme Islamist organizations adds fuel to the smouldering fire of mutual antagonism. Once, Spaniards and Britons alike had to worry about terrorism by nationalist minorities. The attacks in Madrid in March 2004 and in London in July 2005 have made it clear that there is a new enemy within.

Such tensions are familiar to the historian. Today's economic optimists celebrate the fact that 'the earth is flat', a level playing field where all countries can compete for world market share on equal terms. A hundred years ago, globalization was celebrated in not dissimilar ways as goods, capital and labour flowed freely from England to the ends of the earth. Yet mass migration in around 1900 was accompanied by increases in ethnic tension from Vladivostok to Višegrad, with ultimately explosive consequences. In 1914 the first age of globalization ended with a spectacular bang because of an act of terrorism by a radicalized Serb in a predominantly Muslim province of the Austro-Hungarian Empire. War escalated because of the German violation of the neutrality of another multi-ethnic country, Belgium. In the mayhem of world war, an extreme anti-capitalist sect gained control of Russia and her empire, proceeding to betray its early promises of self-determination for that empire's minorities. And in the succeeding decades, three diabolical dictators, Stalin, Hitler and Mao, rose to control vast tracts of the great Eurasian landmass that stretches from the English Channel to the China Sea. Their totalitarian regimes and pseudo-religious cults caused unquantifiable suffering and tens of millions of violent deaths, with the peoples who lived on the strategic borderlands between the empire-states suffering the most in relative terms. Could a similar fate befall the second age of globalization in which we live?

Today it is China not Japan that is the rising power in Asia. But it is not difficult to imagine a clash between East and West that would dwarf the Russo-Japanese War of a century ago. What if there were a setback to economic growth in China? Rather than risk popular protests against their monopoly on power (and the rampant corruption that goes with it) might the Chinese Communists be tempted to take refuge in patriotism? Just as Belgium was for Britain and Germany in 1914, so Taiwan could be the *casus belli* that sparks a conflict between China and the United States. The People's Republic has always treated Taiwan as a renegade province and has repeatedly stated that any attempt by it to declare formal independence would warrant military intervention. Meanwhile, as I write, the possibility grows of renewed conflict in the Persian Gulf as Iran is referred to the UN Security Council on account of its suspected nuclear weapons programme. Israel struggles to extricate itself from the territory it occupied in 1967 and to establish a Palestinian state with which it can coexist; yet the Palestinians vote for Hamas, an organization committed to the destruction of Israel *tout court*. The hegemonic role of the United States in the Middle East seems precarious, as Iraq stubbornly refuses to follow the neo-conservative script by becoming a peaceful and prosperous democracy; a descent into civil war still seems the more likely outcome. Galloping economic growth in Asia exerts increasing pressure on global energy supplies, increasing the leverage of the undemocratic regimes that sit on so much of the world's oil and gas reserves and increasing the likelihood of a new era of imperial scrambles for scarce raw materials. A scenario-builder who entirely dismissed the danger of a new War of the World – a new era of ethnic strife, economic volatility and imperial struggle – would be a Pangloss indeed.

In the fifty-second chapter of his *Decline and Fall of the Roman Empire*, Edward Gibbon posed one of the great counterfactual questions of history. If the French had failed to defeat an invading Muslim army at the Battle of Poitiers in 732, would all of Western Europe have succumbed to Islam? 'Perhaps', speculated Gibbon with his inimitable irony, 'the interpretation of the Koran would now be taught in the schools of Oxford, and her pulpits might demonstrate to a circumcised people the sanctity and truth of the revelation of Mohammed.' The idea was to amuse his readers, and perhaps to make fun of his old university. Yet today work is all but complete on the new Centre for Islamic Studies at Oxford, which features, in addition to the traditional Oxford quadrangle, a prayer hall with a dome and minaret tower. That fulfilment of Gibbon's unintended prophecy symbolizes perfectly the fundamental reorientation of the world which was the underlying trend of the twentieth century. The decline of the West has not taken the form that Oswald Spengler had in mind when he wrote *Der Untergang des Abendlandes* soon after the First World War. Rather it was precisely that reawakening of 'the powers of the blood' by the 'new Caesars' whom Spengler anticipated – and the assault they launched on 'the rationalism of the Megalopolis' – which accelerated the material, but perhaps more importantly the moral descent of the West.*

A hundred years ago, the West ruled the world. After a century of recurrent internecine conflict between the European empires, that is no longer the case. A hundred years ago, the frontier between West and East was located somewhere in the neighbourhood of Bosnia-Herzegovina. Now it seems to run through every European city. That is not to say that conflict is inevitable along these new fault lines. But it is to say that, if the history of the twentieth century is any guide, then the fragile edifice of civilization can very quickly collapse even where different ethnic groups seem quite well integrated, sharing the same language, if not the same faith or the same genes. The twentieth century also demonstrated that economic volatility increases the likelihood of such a backlash – especially in the context of the new kind of welfare state that emerged in the first half of the century, with its

---

* Spengler is now seldom read; his prose is too turgid, his debt to Nietzsche and Wagner too large, his influence on the National Socialists too obvious. Yet with his idiosyncratic seasonal theory of cultural rise and fall, he expressed better than almost anyone that inter-war revulsion against all that had been achieved by the West before 1914. 'The last century', he wrote, 'was the winter of the West, the victory of materialism and scepticism, of socialism, parliamentarianism, and money. But in this century blood and instinct will regain their rights against the power of money and intellect. The era of individualism, liberalism and democracy, of humanitarianism and freedom, is nearing its end. The masses will accept with resignation the victory of the Caesars, the strong men, and will obey them.' This was not a bad prediction. In particular, Spengler saw that the backlash he foresaw would manifest itself partly as a war on big cities, the embodiments of a decadent civilization.

high levels of redistributive give and take. For ethnic minorities are more likely to be viewed with greater hostility when times are hard or when income differentials are widening. Finally, it was not by chance that the worst killing fields of the mid-twentieth century were in places like Poland, the Ukraine, the Balkans and Manchuria; while extreme violence in the later twentieth century shifted to more widely dispersed locations, from Guatemala to Cambodia, from Angola to Bangladesh, from Bosnia to Rwanda and, most recently, the Darfur region of Sudan. Time and again it has been in the wake of the decline of empires, in contested borderlands or in power vacuums, that the opportunities have arisen for genocidal regimes and policies. Ethnic confluence, economic volatility and empires on the wane; such was and remains the fatal formula.

On the eve of the twentieth century, H. G. Wells had imagined a 'War of the Worlds' – a Martian invasion that devastated the earth. In the hundred years that followed, men proved that it was quite possible to wreak comparable havoc without the need for alien intervention. All they had to do was to identify this or that group of their fellow men as the aliens, and then kill them. They did so with varying degrees of ferocity in different places, at different times. But the common factors that link together the bloodiest events of the twentieth century should now be clearly apparent.

The War of the Worlds remains science fiction. The War of the World is, however, historical fact. Perhaps, like Wells's story, ours will be ended abruptly by the intervention of microscopic organisms like the avian influenza virus, which could yet produce a worse mutation and pandemic than that of 1918. Until that happens, however, we remain our own worst enemies. We shall avoid another century of conflict only if we understand the forces that caused the last one – the dark forces that conjure up ethnic conflict and imperial rivalry out of economic crisis, and in doing so negate our common humanity. They are forces that stir within us still.

# Appendix

# The War of the World in Historical Perspective

In the introduction, I make the claim that 'The hundred years after 1900 were without question the bloodiest century in history, far more violent in relative as well as absolute terms than any previous era.' It seems worth substantiating that assertion, which is by no means beyond dispute. To attempt to do so is to enter a realm of great statistical confusion. Estimates for death tolls in twentieth-century conflicts are unreliable enough. Those for earlier wars are worse. Dividing such figures by estimates for population only tends to widen the range of possible error.

There are conceptual as well as empirical problems. The notion of violent death – as opposed to natural death – may seem straightforward to a modern reader. Yet many of the millions of victims of war, genocide and other acts of organized violence were not directly killed by a weapon operated by another human being. They died in famines or epidemics that (it seems probable) would not otherwise have happened had it not been for antecedent acts of 'direct' violence. Many of the death tolls calculated by historians are therefore the products of subtraction sums: the population before a war or other violent event minus the population after it, where census figures or credible estimates are available. Clearly, however, figures obtained in this manner are bound to include some deaths by natural causes. Moreover, it is debatable how far even those deaths authentically due to war-induced starvation or disease should be regarded as equivalent to deaths due to weaponry. It is not always possible to say for sure whether or not such indirectly caused mortality was an intended consequence of the original acts of aggression. And what of the unborn? Sometimes historians calculate the net demographic impact of a particular event by estimating a counterfactual population, that is the population as it would have been if there had been no war. Yet here too there is a tendency to inflate the death toll, by counting among the victims 'people' who were never in fact born. It is clearly a dubious procedure to juxtapose figures calculated in this way with figures based on, say, the number of soldiers recorded by military authorities as killed in action. Matters are further confused when aggregate casualty figures – including men missing (but not dead), captured or wounded – are confused with figures for battlefield mortality. In some wars, being taken prisoner or wounded amounted to a death sentence; in others it was a reprieve from the much more dangerous business of combat. As medical science has advanced, so soldiers' chances of surviving battlefield injury have improved. But there has been no such progressive trend in the way prisoners have been treated. Finally, there is the problem of disorganized violence. In times of war and revolution, opportunities are more plentiful for individual acts of murder than in times of peace and political order. Yet this kind of violence is generally treated as a separate phenomenon from organized violence, rather than just another form of 'deadly quarrel', in the phrase of L. F. Richardson, perhaps the most methodologically careful statistician of modern violence.

When expressing non-natural mortality in percentage terms in order to allow for variations in population size, the choice of denominator is also problematic. Is it a worthwhile exercise to express the estimated death tolls of eighteenth- and nineteenth-century great-power wars as percentages of estimates for *world* population, when none of these conflicts was strictly speaking a world war (with the possible exception of the Seven Years War)? Would it not be more worthwhile to have country populations as denominators, so that we may compare, say, the proportion of Germans killed by the Thirty Years War with the proportion killed by the Second World War? Here, too, there are difficulties, not the least of which is the changing character of the entity called Germany. The Holy Roman Empire was a very different thing from the Third Reich. A large proportion – perhaps as many as one in thirteen – of the men killed while fighting on the side of the Third Reich were not German citizens, but members of other nationalities that had been recruited or drafted into the Wehrmacht, the SS and other auxiliary formations. Should we therefore narrow the political or geographical unit down still further, and compare mortality rates in regions or cities? Perhaps, but to do so is to risk concluding that, say, the massacre of the population of a village in German South-West Africa during the Herero Uprising was a more violent act than the destruction of Warsaw during the Second World War, since the dead in the former accounted for a larger percentage of the population than the dead in the latter. Small denominators can produce large percentages, because it is on the whole easier to kill a hundred villagers than to kill a hundred thousand city-dwellers.

This, in turn, raises the question of destructive technology. Should we somehow adjust for the greater 'bangs per buck' of twentieth-century weaponry? Does it require a greater quantity of violence (though I remain unsure in which unit violence should be measured) to kill a hundred people with a machete than with a bomb? Finally, does intention matter? Is it worse to kill people out of racial or religious prejudice than to kill them in pursuit of a strategic objective? Should we allow for the fact that in some cases organized violence is asymmetrically perpetrated against defenceless civilians, while in others it is reciprocally inflicted by well-matched armies? To put it differently, is 'genocide' merely a term for a civil war in which only one side is armed? None of these questions is easily answered, as *The War of the World* makes clear.

There is no question that the twentieth century witnessed a mind-bogglingly large number of deaths by organized violence. Estimates for the total number, which can rest only on some heroic if not downright reckless assumptions, range from 167 million to 188 million. One survey of the available published death tolls concludes that one in every twenty-two deaths during the century was caused by the action of other human beings. But – as I seek to show in this book – lethal organized violence was highly concentrated in both space and time. Indeed, a distinctive feature of twentieth-century warfare noted in the introduction is precisely that it was much more intense (in terms of battle deaths per nation year) than warfare in previous centuries. So the interesting question is not really, 'Why was the twentieth century more violent than the eighteenth or the nineteenth?' but, 'Why did extreme violence happen in Poland, Serbia and Cambodia more than in England, Ghana and Costa Rica?'; and 'Why did so much more extreme violence happen between 1936 and 1945 than between 1976 and 1985?' Altogether, the best available estimates suggest, somewhere in the region of 58 or 59 million people lost their lives as a result of the Second World War. That can be expressed as a percentage of the pre-war world population (2.6 per cent), though it should be borne in mind that many of those people who were living in 1938 died of natural causes by 1945 and some of the babies born after 1938 were killed in the war. Military and civilian death tolls varied widely from country to country in absolute and in relative terms, however. In absolute terms, as is well known, many more Soviet citizens died violently between 1939 and 1945 than people of other nationalities – perhaps as many as 25 million, if not more. This suggests that more than one in ten Soviet citizens was a victim of the war, though it might be more accurate to say that one in ten was a victim of totalitarianism between 1939 and 1945, given the number of lives lost to Stalin's domestic policies.* In percentage terms Poland was the country hardest hit by the war. The Polish mortality rate (total military and civilian fatalities as a percentage of the pre-war population) amounted to just under 19 per cent, of whom a large proportion were Polish Jews killed in the Holocaust. Among other combatants, only Germany (including Austria) and Yugoslavia suffered mortality rates close to 10 per cent.† The next highest rates were for Hungary (8 per cent) and Romania (6 per cent). In no other country for which figures have been published did mortality rise above 3 per cent of the pre-war population, including a number of Central and East European countries, Czechoslovakia (3 per cent), Finland (2 per cent) and Bulgaria (0.3 per cent). For four of the principal combatants, France, Italy, the United Kingdom and the United States, total wartime mortality was less than 1 per cent of the pre-war population.‡ For the three West European countries, the First World War was, at least by this measure, a more costly conflict. Turkey was of course far worse affected by the First World War (some put the total mortality rate at 15 per cent, including the Armenian genocide), since it remained neutral during the Second. Note, too, that Japan's mortality rate during the Second World War (2.9 per cent) was significantly lower than Germany's, as was China's (at most, 5 per cent). These differentials reflect two important features of the war. War itself was waged at a much

---

* The Soviet figures are famously problematic. Total Soviet demographic losses have been put as high as 43–47 million by some recent scholars (i.e. including thwarted normal reproduction). The *Times Atlas of World History*'s total of 21.5 million includes around 7 million deaths of Soviet citizens deported to the gulag and 1 million Soviet citizens deported as members of 'suspect' nationalities. The official Soviet figure for total excess mortality was 26.6 million, but this may include 2.7 million wartime and post-war emigrants as well as normal natural mortality. On the other hand, it may underestimate the number of Soviet prisoners who died in Germany captivity.

† Rüdiger Overmans has substantially revised upwards the estimates for German military losses. His total figure for losses of 5.3 million includes just under 400,000 men who did not have German citizenship in 1939 but nevertheless were recruited or conscripted into the Wehrmacht or SS.

‡ France and Italy – both 0.9 per cent; United Kingdom – 0.7 per cent; United States – 0.2 per cent.

higher human cost in Central and Eastern Europe than anywhere else. The Germans fought to kill. Soviet commanders were also wasteful of the lives of their men. This region also witnessed exceptionally systematic violence against civilians.

The incidence of violent death in Central and Eastern Europe between 1939 and 1945 was high, but other conflicts came close. Between 9 and 10 million men were killed in the First World War, with Serbia and Scotland suffering the highest mortality rates, though the mortality rate was also high in the campaigns between the Entente and the Ottoman Empire, where disease was worse and reserves fewer. Estimates vary widely for the number of deaths in China attributable to Mao's policies, but they must certainly have run to several tens of millions. The total victims of Stalinism within the Soviet Union may have exceeded 20 million. Mortality rates in excess of 10 per cent have also been estimated for Pol Pot's reign of terror in Cambodia, as well as for the civil wars in Mexico (1910–20) and Equatorial Guinea (1972–79), and the Afghan War that followed the Soviet invasion of 1979. By one estimate, sixteen twentieth-century conflicts – wars, civil wars, genocides and sundry mass murders – cost more than one million lives each; a further six claimed between half a million and a million victims; and fourteen killed between a quarter and half a million people. In all, according to the Correlates of War Project, there were at least two hundred inter-state or civil wars between 1900 and 1990. Using slightly different criteria, the Stockholm International Peace Research Institute estimated that there were over a hundred armed conflicts in the last decade of the century, of which more than twenty were still in progress in 1999.

It might be argued that there are precedents in human history for such high rates of lethal organized violence. First, it is clear from archaeological and anthropological studies that pre-historic and pre-modern tribal societies were very violent indeed. The percentage of male deaths due to warfare among the Amazonian Jivaro Indians is known to have been as high as 60 per cent within the recent past. Rates in excess of 20 per cent have been recorded for at least five other tribes.

Secondly, there is reason to believe that two or three Asian tyrants perpetrated mass murder on a scale comparable with that inflicted by their twentieth-century counterparts. The exemplary violence meted out by the thirteenth-century Mongol leader Chingis (Genghis) Khan is said to have resulted in a decline in the populations of Central Asia and China of more than 37 million – a figure which, if correct, is equivalent to nearly 10 per cent of the world's population at that time.* Timur (Tamburlaine)'s late fourteenth-century conquests in Central Asia and Northern India were also notably bloody, with a death toll said to be in excess of 10 million. The Manchu conquest of China in the seventeenth century may have cost the lives of as many as 25 million people. It is important to emphasize, however, that the majority of victims of these conquerors almost certainly died from famines and epidemics arising from their disruptive incursions. The populations of the regions affected lived perilously close to subsistence, so that vandalism of irrigation systems or destruction of harvests could have devastating effects, particularly for urban centres. Nevertheless, these figures help to set the death toll inflicted by the Japanese during their conquest of north-eastern China (which is said to have exceeded 11 million) in some kind of long-term perspective. It seems likely that the hundred years after 1900 were the bloodiest century in European history, in relative as well as absolute terms. It is less certain that the same can be said for Asia, especially if wilfully causing a famine is counted as a form of bloodshed.

Thirdly, moreover, several pre-1900 Chinese rebellions and their suppression caused human suffering on a scale that may have matched or exceeded that inflicted on the people of China by twentieth-century civil wars. The eighth-century An Lushan Revolt is believed to have cost the lives of more than 30 million people. The mid-nineteenth-century Taiping Rebellion (1851–1864) – a peasant revolt led by the self-proclaimed younger brother of Christ against the Qing dynasty, which the rebels accused of capitulation to Western commercial penetration – was estimated by Western contemporaries to have claimed between 20 and 40 million lives. Also devastating to the provinces affected were the roughly contemporaneous Nien and Miao Rebellions and the Muslim rebellions in Yunnan and north-western China. Here, once again, death tolls have to be inferred from provincial and local censuses taken before and after the rebellions. In some cases the declines seem to imply mortality rates ranging from 40 to 90 per cent. At least some part of these declines in population must surely have been due to emigration from, and reduced fertility in, ravaged areas. Still, there clearly was very large-scale

---

* The Mongols habitually and systematically slaughtered the entire populations of cities in the path of their advance. According to Muslim historians, more than one and a half million people were butchered at Nishapur in 1221. Almost as many were put to the sword at Herat and Merv.

organized violence, not least in the way the rebels were systematically exterminated by Qing commanders. Famine was a direct consequence of the scorched earth policy used against the Taiping rebels' 'Celestial Kingdom of Great Peace' centred in Nanking. One hypothesis in *The War of the World* is that the worst time for an empire – in terms of the loss of human life – is when it begins to decline. This is the period when rebellions are most likely, but also when the authorities are most likely to resort to exemplary brutality. The evidence suggests that this was already painfully obvious in China a century before it became apparent in the rest of the world. Another way of thinking about the twentieth century, then, may be to see it as a Western version of Qing China's nineteenth-century death throes.

Finally, there is reason to think that the mortality rates arising from some episodes of West European conquest and colonization of the Americas and Africa were as high as those of the twentieth century. Needless to say, the overwhelming majority of victims of the European conquest of the Americas succumbed to disease, not to violence, so those who speak of 'genocide' debase the coinage of historical terminology just as much as those who call nineteenth-century famines in India 'Victorian holocausts'. However, the forcible enslavement of the Congolese people by the Belgian crown after 1886 and the suppression of the Herero Uprising by the German colonial authorities in 1904 do bear comparison with other twentieth-century acts of organized violence. The proportion of the population estimated to have been killed in the Congo under Belgian rule may have been as high as a fifth. The estimated mortality rate in the Herero War was higher still – more than one in three, making it by that measure the most bloody conflict of the entire twentieth century. (The absolute number of dead was, however, 76,000, compared with an estimated 7 million in the Congo between 1886 and 1908.) Historians have not been slow to find lines of continuity leading from this act of 'annihilation' to the Holocaust, though a more direct line of continuity might be to the earlier wars waged by the British against other southern African tribes such as the Matabele.

Perhaps, then, the twentieth century was not so uniquely bloody, when allowance is made for the century's demographic explosion and for the regional and chronological concentration of the lethal organized violence it witnessed. Yet it was undeniably unique in two respects. The first was that it witnessed a transformation in the kind of war waged by developed Western societies against one another. Throughout European history there had been social and institutional as well as technological limitations on war, which had limited the mortality rates inflicted by organized conflict. Occasional massacres occurred, it is true, but massacre did not become a routinized military method. Even the Thirty Years War and the Napoleonic Wars, though they struck contemporaries as markedly increasing, respectively, the brutality and the scale of war, did not give rise to death rates like those of the mid twentieth century. What happened after 1914 was especially remarkable because of the 'long peace' Europe had enjoyed in the century that had followed Bonaparte's defeat at Waterloo. Like the misnamed 'long peace' of the Cold War, this was not a time without war, but a time when most war took place outside Europe. The wars that were fought within Europe were generally waged in a quite limited way, most obviously in the case of the short, sharp wars fought by Prussia to create the German Reich.

In the twentieth century, it might be said, the sins of nineteenth-century imperialism were visited on Europeans, though retribution was sometimes sent to the wrong address (the Poles could scarcely be held accountable for the miseries of subjugated Africans). Many of the key actors of the First World War had learned the art of annihilation in colonial conflicts; the example of Lord Kitchener – the butcher of Omdurman, appointed Secretary of State for War in 1914 – springs to mind. At the same time, the twentieth century saw Central and Eastern Europe go through what China had experienced in the previous century: a crisis of imperial order spawning cataclysmic civil wars. Perhaps there was also fulfilment of those early twentieth-century fears of a new Mongol horde, except that this time the hordes were European. Hitler and Stalin proved to be worthy heirs to Chingis and Timur.

The second feature that makes the twentieth century beyond question unique – and which remains the paradox at its heart – is the way that the leaders of apparently civilized societies were able to unleash the most primitive murderous instincts of their fellow citizens. The Germans were not Amazonian Indians. And yet, under a democratically elected leader and armed with industrial weaponry, they waged war in Eastern Europe as if actuated by authentically prehistoric motives. It was this development that Wells dimly but intuitively foresaw in *The War of the Worlds*. For what makes Wells's Martians so abhorrent, so terrifying and yet so fascinating is precisely their combination of murderousness and technological sophistication – like the selfish gene with a death ray. These were the very characteristics evinced by twentieth-century men when they waged their own internecine war of the world.

# Notes

## INTRODUCTION

*Page*

xxxiii **Did they dream they might exterminate us?:** Wells, *War of the Worlds,* from Book I, chs. XII, XV, XVI.

xxxiv **and concentration (battle deaths per nation-year):** Levy, *War,* p. 139.

xxxiv **Pol Pot in Cambodia:** In all cases numerous estimates and guesses have been published. For a thorough compilation, see http://users.erols.com/mwhite28/warstat2.htm.

xxxv **1870 and 1998 than it was between 1500 and 1870:** Maddison, *World Economy,* p. 264, table B-21; 1.48 per cent compared with just 0.12 per cent.

xxxv **technological advances and improvements in knowledge:** Mokyr, *Gifts of Athena.*

xxxvi **1990 was 76 years, compared with 48 in 1900:** Fogel, *Escape from Hunger,* table 1.1.

xxxvi **not only lived longer; they grew bigger and taller:** ibid., table 1.2, table 2.6.

xxxvi **third of what it had been at the start of the century:** ibid., table 4.5.

xxxvi **living in large cities more than doubled:** Bairoch, *Cities and Economic Development,* p. 495.

xxxvi **than treble the amount of time available for leisure:** Fogel, *Escape from Hunger,* table 4.1.

xxxvi **In the 1990s the proportion rose above half:** See the Polity IV database at http://www.cidcm.umd .edu/inscr/polity/.

xxxvi **'Want . . . Disease, Ignorance, Squalor and Idleness':** Beveridge, Report 8. Cf. Lindert, *Growing Public.*

xxxvi **closer together, or more destructive weapons:** North, *Process of Economic Change,* p. 94.

xxxvi **armed conflict in the last decade of the century:** Marshall and Gurr, *Peace and Conflict,* 2005.

xxxvi **during and immediately after the world wars:** See the Correlates of War database at www.umich.edu/~cowproj. The increase in the number of wars in progress may partly reflect the more accurate recording of civil wars, which account for all of the increases during and after the Cold War.

xxxvii **as earlier evil 'isms', notably imperialism:** For a recent argument in this vein, see Kershaw, 'War and Political Violence', pp. 111–3.

xxxviii **integration with relatively high growth and low inflation:** See Ferguson, 'Sinking Globalization'.

xxxviii **'secular ideologies of nineteenth-century vintage':** Hobsbawm, *Age of Extremes,* p. 563.

xxxviii **'[and] the repudiation of Judaeo-Christian values':** Johnson, *History of the Modern World,* p. 784.

xxxviii **understand the intellectual origins of totalitarianism:** On the nineteenth-century origins of totalitarianism, see most recently Burleigh, *Earthly Powers.*

xxxix **able-bodied adult male citizen, they could:** See Mann, *Sources of Social Power;* Bobbitt, *Shield of Achilles.*

xxxix **warfare that had transformed the early modern state:** Bean, 'War and the Birth of the Nation State'.

xxxix **It was surely not the welfare state that made total war:** Ferguson, *Cash Nexus.*

xxxix **democracies tend not to go to war with one another:** See e.g., Doyle, 'Liberalism and World Politics'; Russett, 'Counterfactuals about War'.

xxxix **number of civil wars and wars of secession:** Ward and Gleditsch, 'Democratizing for Peace'. Cf. Mansfield and Snyder, *Electing to Fight.*

xl **died as a result of the hardships inflicted on them:** Conquest, *Great Terror,* pp. 484–9; idem, *Nation Killers,* pp. 64, 111; Martin, 'Origins of Soviet Ethnic Cleansing', p. 851.

xl **Soviet Union between 1928 and 1953 is 21 million:** Rummel, *Lethal Politics,* tables 1.3 and 1.B.

xli **World War — the apogee of its unspoken empire:** Ferguson, *Colossus.*

xlii **Second World War 'the great racial war':** Burleigh, *Third Reich,* p. 573.

xlii **have time to sub-divide the species *Homo sapiens*:** Coyne and Allen Orr, *Speciation,* esp. pp. 213–23.

xlii **mingling of the in-comers with indigenous nomads:** Cavalli-Sforza et al., *History and Geography.* See also Cavalli-Sforza, *Genes, People and Languages.*

xliii Biologists today call the process 'demic diffusion': Jones, *In the Blood*.

xliii are genetically not so very different: Olson, *Mapping Human History*, pp. 55, 109, 133, 225. Even among the Lemba people, who historically inhabited the land immediately south of the Limpopo River, traces have been found of the so-called 'Cohen Model Haplotype', the 'marker chromosome' associated with Jewish rabbinical families: ibid., p. 113.

xliii strictly speaking, 'human races do not exist': ibid, pp. 63, 69.

xliii important measure of assimilation in American life: Gordon, *Assimilation in American Life*. For the idea that assimilation went on within several religious sub-melting pots, see Kennedy, 'Single or Triple Melting Pot?', esp. pp. 56f.; Herberg, *Protestant, Catholic, Jew*. Cf. Peach, 'Ethnic Segregation and Ethnic Intermarriage'; Alba and Golden, 'Patterns of Ethnic Marriage'.

xliii 'of the acceptability of different groups and of social integration': Blau and Schwartz, *Crosscutting Social Circles*, p. 13. Blau and Schwartz relate intermarriage and other indicators of social integration to economic stratification. See also Rytina et al., 'Inequality and Intermarriage'.

xliv quadrupled between 1990 and 2000, to roughly 1.5 million: Olson, *Mapping Human History*, pp. 225ff.

xliv unrelated strangers to get rid of potential sexual rivals: Seabright, *Company of Strangers*, pp. 28, 49, 53.

xlv the risk that a genetic abnormality may manifest itself in offspring: According to the 'Westermarck hypothesis', there is in fact a biological mechanism designed to produce an aversion to sexual intercourse between children who are raised together. For a critical discussion, see Leavitt, 'Sociobiological Explanations of Incest Avoidance', p. 972. See also Ekblom, 'Inbreeding Avoidance'.

xlv search for a partner more difficult in prehistoric times: Durham, *Coevolution*, p. 333.

xlv actually be preferable as a mate to a wholly unrelated stranger: Bateson, 'Optimal Outbreeding', esp. p. 262. See also idem, 'Sexual Imprinting and Optimal Outbreeding'.

xlv resulted in remarkably few genetic abnormalities: Olson, *Mapping Human History*, pp. 115ff.

xlv also indirectly through our cousins and other relatives: van den Berghe, *Ethnic Phenomenon*, p. 19.

xlvi of inculcated prejudice is clearly open to question: Olsson et al., 'Role of Social Groups'.

xlvi are in some respects genetically distinguishable: Tang, 'Genetic Structure'.

xlvi nutritional and reproductive resources: Sapolsky, 'Natural History of Peace'.

xlvii 'Herskovits once wrote, 'but they mingle their blood': Mencke, *Mulattoes and Race Mixture*, p. 1.

xlvii respects (language, religious belief, dress, lifestyle): On 'inclusion' see Alexander, 'Core Solidarity'.

xlviii provide valuable networks of trust in nascent markets: See Olzak, *Dynamics of Ethnic Competition*; Nagel, 'Political Competition and Ethnicity'.

xlviii are economically strong but politically weak: Chua, *World on Fire*.

xlviii which have weapons, civil war is more likely than genocide: Collier and Hoeffler, 'On Economic Causes of Civil War'.

xlix high rates of inter-ethnic marriage in previous decades: See epilogue for details.

li blamed for ethnic conflict is not a straightforward emotion: See e.g., Naimark, *Fires of Hatred*.

li relations between white Americans and African-Americans: See e.g., Bastide, 'Dusky Venus, Black Apollo'; Hernton, *Sex and Racism*; Mehlinger, 'Black Man-White Woman'; Smith, *Killers of the Dream*. See also Washington, *Marriage in Black and White*; Stember, *Sexual Racism*; Albert, 'Sexual Basis of White Resistance'; Henriques, *Children of Caliban*, pp. 84–8; Schulman, 'Race, Sex and Violence'; Camper (ed.), *Miscegenation Blues*.

li of ideas the way genes behave in the natural world: Dawkins, *Selfish Gene*, pp. 189–201. Cf. Richerson and Boyd, *Not by Genes Alone*.

li indistinguishable but irreconcilably hostile clans: Though, once again, attraction between members of rival families was perfectly possible—and inflammatory: see *Romeo and Juliet*.

li Jewishness according to 'blood' rather than belief: Kershaw, 'Reply', p. 133.

li through the payment of standard fee to the crown: King, 'Case of Jose Ponciano de Ayarza'.

lii as polygenists insisted, the lack of such a common origin: Gould, *Mismeasure*, p. 66.

lii Athenians at the top and the Australian aborigines at the bottom: Galton, *Hereditary Genius*.

liii early anthropological theories about 'exogamy': Kang, *Marry-out or Die-out*, pp. 1ff. This was a preoccupation of Claude Lévi-Strauss, among many others.

liii 'is sought for, by whom a tawney [sic] breed is produced': ibid., p. 150.

liii 'people is merely an awful example of racial anarchy': Gobineau, *Essai sur l'inégalité des races humaines*, quoted in Young, *Colonial Desire*, p. 114.

liv 'holocaust', without precedent or parallel: For the best survey of the highly politicized German debate see Maier, *Unmasterable Past*.

liv peer-group pressure or systematic military brutalization: See e.g., Browning, *Ordinary Men*.

liv youths in the grip of an immoral 'secular religion': Burleigh, *Third Reich*.

liv world view was fundamental to the Third Reich: Burleigh and Wippermann, *Racial State*.

lv [elsewhere] under the name of anti-Semitism: quoted in Mirelman, *Jewish Buenos Aires*, p. 55.

lvii and Ma'min, who were converts from Judaism): Mazower, *Salonica*.

lvii Ottoman periphery: the Jews and the Armenians: Magocsi, *Historical Atlas of East Central Europe*, p. 97.

lviii eastern frontier of the German Reich of 1871: Mann, 'Perpetrators of Genocide'.

lviii was born in Reval/Tallinn, Estonia: Germann, *Alfred Rosenberg*.
lviii racial theory while breeding horses in East Prussia: Werner, 'Richard Walther Darré'.
lviii family had settled in the nineteenth century: Tooze, *Wages of War*, ch. 6.
lviii from the borderlands to attain high rank in the SS: Whiteside, 'Nationaler Sozialismus', p. 343.
lviii overtly for legislation against miscegenation in 1935: Kulka, 'Nürnberger Rassengesetze', p. 594.
lviii number of anti-Semitic contributions to *Der Stürmer*: Müller, 'Stürmer-Archiv', p. 328.
lviii Germans' from the Baltic and Bohemia: Reder, *Belzec*.
lix incomes can be just as de-stabilizing as a rapid contraction: Here I take respectful issue with Friedman, *Moral Consequences*.
lx and has only recently and partially been equalled: Crafts, 'Globalization and Growth'. See also the essays in Bordo et al. (eds.), *Globalization in Historical Perspective*.
lxi system of fixed exchange rates known as the gold standard: Eichengreen, *Golden Fetters*.
lxi or in altering the distribution of income and wealth: James, *End of Globalization*.
lxi conjuncture between Western profligacy and Asian parsimony: Ferguson, 'Paradox of Diminishing Risk'.
lxiii it remains true of today's Russian Federation: Lieven, *Empire*.
lxiii republic'; some would say it always has been: The phrase is Raymond Aron's: see his *Imperial Republic*. For a recent argument along the same lines, see my *Colossus*. For different perspectives in Lundestad, *American 'Empire'*; Vidal, *Decline and Fall*; Johnson, *Blowback*; Bacevich, *Empire*; Ignatieff, *Empire Lite*; Todd, *Après L'Empire*; Mann, *Incoherent Empire*.
lxiii more violence than the imperial heartlands: Maier, *Among Empires*.
lxiv closely associated with their rise and fall: Lal, *Praise of Empires*; James, *Roman Predicament*. See also O'Brien and Clesse (eds.), *Two Hegemonies*, and on the British case, my own *Empire*.
lxiv existence, and the nature of post-colonial development: See Grossman and Mendoza, 'Annexation or Conquest'; Acemoglu et al., 'Reversal of Fortune'. On the duration of power, see the classic work of synthesis by Kennedy, *Rise and Fall of the Great Powers*.
lxvi sense of the word it lasted barely half that time: For a detailed definition of the term 'empire', see Ferguson, 'Unconscious Colossus'.
lxvii victory of the 'Greatest Generation': Brokaw, *Greatest Generation*.
lxvii model of liberal democratic capitalism: Fukuyama, *End of History*. See also his 'Capitalism and Democracy' and *Great Disruption*, esp. p. 282.
lxviii ruled than used to be acknowledged: See the brilliant account in Bayly, *Birth of the Modern World*.
lxviii scientific breakthroughs from Newton to Einstein: Pace Hobson, *Eastern Origins*.
lxviii that made European domination possible: See for a somewhat different interpretation, Pomeranz, *Great Divergence*.
lxviii had been lost in the four centuries after 1500: Cf. Frank, *ReOrient*.
lxx to my earlier book about the First World War: Ferguson, *Pity of War*.

## CHAPTER ONE: EMPIRES AND RACES

3 an end in August 1914!: Keynes, *Economic Consequences*, ch. 1.
3 a last fling in the old one: Musil, *Man without Qualities*, vol. I, p. 59.
4 nearly complete in practice: Keynes, *Economic Consequences*, ch. 1.
6 'help the working people': Rauchway, *Murdering McKinley*, pp. 18, 27.
7 utmost rapidity and completeness: *The Times*, September 11, 1901, p. 7.
7 doubt our inherited ability to rule: ibid., p. 6.
7 'assist in the defence of his country'?: ibid., p. 7.
8 meditations before making a decision: ibid., p. 3.
8 both the French and the British empires: ibid., p. 4.
8 maintained their old positions: ibid., p. 3.
9 'bit of greed which history recorded': ibid., p. 4.
9 VALUES and BUYS ORIENTAL ART-SPECIALITIES: ibid., p. 1.
9 'into the middle and upper classes': Keynes, *Economic Consequences*, loc. cit.
9 'past made some provision for the future': *The Times*, September 11, 1901, p. 7.
10 complete immunity from Chinese law: Wood, *No Dogs and Not Many Chinese*.
12 second weakest among the great powers: Musil, *Man Without Qualities*, vol. I, p. 32.
12 though nothing had been the matter: ibid., p. 33.
13 writer Jaroslav Hašek in *The Good Soldier Švejk*: Hašek, *Good Soldier Švejk*.
13 for the benefits of ethnic cross-fertilization: Schorske, *Fin-de-Siècle Vienna*.
13 and a multi-ethnic society: See Timms, *Apocalyptic Satirist*.
13 'attempts to get on . . . [had] crystallized earlier': Musil, *Man Without Qualities*, vol. I, p. 33.
13 'together by this thread . . . with its invisible power': Gorky, *My Universities*, p. 69.
14 total population of the empire: See also Service, *Twentieth-Century Russia*, pp. 9–11.
14 only a little behind the German (2.8 per cent): Maddison, *World Economy*, table B-18.
14 network grew by more than 50 per cent: Figures from Mitchell, *International Historical Statistics: Europe*.

14  **European empires on their armies and navies:** See Gatrell, *Government, Industry and Rearmament.*
14  **four fifths of whom lived in the countryside:** Per capita GDP growth has been estimated at just 1.1 per cent, below the world average for the period.
16  **output not seen again until the 1990s:** See the essays in Bordo, Taylor and Williamson (eds.), *Globalization in Historical Perspective.*
16  **giving rise to a kind of 'fractal geometry of empire':** Maier, *Among Empires.*
18  **inherited status and royally conferred rank:** Cannadine, *Ornamentalism.*
18  **flowed to a relatively few wealthy investors:** On the British case, see the contrasting views of Davis and Huttenback, *Mammon;* Edelstein, 'Imperialism' and Offer, 'Costs and Benefits'.
19  **'It's only at seventy-two':** Maupassant, *Bel-Ami,* p. 324.
19  **last half-century of its existence:** See Porter, *Absent-Minded Imperialists.*
19  **problem is not to be propounded off-hand':** *The Times,* September 11, 1901, p. 7.
20  **to a soldier and his (invariably) Indian wife:** Hyam, *Empire and Sexuality,* p. 116.
20  **made no objection to mixed marriages:** Henriques, *Children of Caliban,* pp. 117ff.
20  **North America by the end of the colonial period:** Johnston, *Race Relations in Virginia,* p. 190.
20  **even if largely confined to concubinage:** Henriques, *Children of Caliban,* p. 15.
20  **(common among the Boers in South Africa):** See Conlen, 'Historical Genesis and Material Basis of Racial Endogamy'.
20  **by-product of French colonial settlement:** Henriques, *Children of Caliban,* pp. 123–6.
20  **Domingue, published in 1797:** Sollors, *Neither Black nor White yet Both,* p. 120ff.
20  **influence of white women in India:** Hyam, *Empire,* pp. 117–21. Cf. Stoler, 'Making Empire Respectable', pp. 44–9.
21  **were viewed with undisguised disdain:** See in general Mirsky, 'Mixed Marriages'.
21  **Empire from taking native mistresses:** Hyam, *Empire,* pp. 106, 125, 160–4.
21  **generally accepted in expatriate circles:** Stoler, 'Making Empire Respectable', pp. 50ff.
21  **hearing cases involving white women:** See Ferguson, *Empire,* ch. 4.
21  **as well as in neighbouring Rhodesia:** See for a Marxist account Conlen, 'Historical Genesis'. The 1927 'Immorality Act' banned extra-marital sexual relations between Europeans and Africans throughout South Africa, though it was not until the advent of Afrikaner rule that laws were passed against interracial marriage (1949) and 'immoral or indecent acts' (1950).
21  **circumscribe the rights of mulattoes:** Williamson, *New People,* pp. 7–13. See also Johnston, *Race Relations in Virginia;* Jordan, *White over Black.*
22  **passed similar legislation a year earlier:** Morgan, *American Slavery, American Freedom,* pp. 333–6, makes the point that this early legislation may have been religious rather than racial in character, that is concerned to prevent unions between Christians and 'heathens'.
22  **less lurid literature on the subject:** See Sollors, *Neither Black nor White,* pp. 167–218, 221–34, 286–311.
22  **the 'mullato' was 'a monstrosity of nature':** Knox, *Races of Men,* pp. 51, 66.
22  **'effaced by the white race':** Menand, *Metaphysical Club,* p. 114.
23  **freely into that of our children:** Gould, *Mismeasure of Man,* pp. 80ff. See also Menand, *Metaphysical Club,* pp. 104–16. Agassiz assumed that segregation would occur naturally after emancipation; negroes would tend to cluster in the South, whites in the North.
23  **was the key to the success of Southern arms:** Young, *Colonial Desire,* pp. 144–6. Writing in 1890, Cope argued the return of all American blacks to Africa.
23  **'qualities that accompany vigorous physique':** ibid., p. 117.
23  **themselves or would produce sterile progeny:** Stanton, *Leopard's Spots.*
23  **for 'the acute phases of the so-called race problem':** Reuter, *Mulatto in the United States,* p. 103. But see also his more measured conclusions in idem, *Race Mixture.*
24  **who gives birth to a dark-skinned child:** Sollors, *Neither Black nor White,* p. 64.
24  **intercourse played a central role:** Cell, *Highest Stage of White Supremacy.*
24  **toleration of interracial relationships:** Mumford, *Interzones.*
24  **as a way of reducing racial tensions:** Washington, *Marriage in Black and White,* p. 5.
24  **formal barriers between the races were removed:** See Myrdal, *American Dilemma.*
24  **generally ostracized by white society:** Golden, 'Patterns of Negro-White Intermarriage'.
24  **couples remained a very small minority:** Kalmijn, 'Trends in Black/White Intermarriage'. See also Monahan, 'Occupational Class of Couples'; idem, 'Are Interracial Marriages Really Less Stable?'.
24  **immigrants practiced quite strict endogamy:** Pagnini and Morgan, 'Intermarriage and Social Distance', pp. 429ff.
25  **daughter shalt thou take unto they son:** Deuteronomy, ch. 7, verses 2–3. The prohibition was reinforced in the 2nd century A.D. by Simon ben Jochai. In the 6th century the Council of Orleans imposed a ban from the Christian side.
25  **Henry Fitzroy caused intense family distress:** Ferguson, *House of Rothschild,* vol. II, pp. 319–27.
25  **relatively small size of the Jewish community:** Lipman, *History of the Jews in Britain,* p. 221ff.
25  **whom he wishes to raise as a Jew:** Farquhar, 'Twin Rivals'. See also Rubin, *Images in Transition,* p. 52; Glassman, *Anti-Semitic Stereotypes Without Jews;* Trilling, 'Changing Myth of the Jew'.
25  **develops the theme of Jewish lasciviousness:** Felsenstein, *Anti-Semitic Stereotypes,* pp. 54ff. See also Van der veen, *Jewish Characters in Eighteenth-Century English Fiction,* pp. 109ff.

25 Smollett's *Roderick Random* and *Peregrine Pickle*: Battestin, *Henry Fielding*, p. 347; Rubin, *Images in Transition*, pp. 65ff.
25 George Elliot's relatively benign *Daniel Deronda*: Anderson, *Legend of the Wandering Jew*, pp. 171–90; Roberts, *Gothic Immortals*. See also Modder, *Jew in the Literature of England*; Edgar Rosenberg, *From Shylock to Svengali*, esp. pp. 34, 276ff; Fisch, *Dual Image*; Naman, *Jew in the Victorian Novel*.
25 'white slavery', a euphemism for prostitution: Gilman, *Jew's Body*, pp. 104–20.
25 Gobineau's *Essay on the Inequality of Races* until 1898: Graml, *Reichskristallnacht*, p. 76.
26 apply imported theories of Social Darwinism: On German Social Darwinists such as Wilhelm Schallmeyer and Ludwig Woltmann, see Kelly, *Descent of Darwin*.
26 and 'racial hygiene': Weindling, *Health, Race and German Politics*, ch. 1.
26 'blood is much more corrosive than Roman': Katz, *Wagner*, p. 188.
26 mixed marriages to preserve the purity of German blood: Graml, *Reichskristallnacht*, p. 71. Cf. Schleunes, *Twisted Road to Auschwitz*, p. 27.
26 certain that all his ancestors had resisted Jewish contamination: Weiss, *Lange Weg*, p. 157.
26 as playing a malign role in German society: Frymann, *Wenn ich der Kaiser wär'*, p. 76.
27 'plagues that they thereby facilitate': Weihus, *Bordell-Juden*, p. 29.
27 Jewish girls from Eastern Europe: See Kaplan, *Jüdische Frauenbewegung*, pp. 181–248.
27 in German caricatures at around this time: Fuchs, *Juden in der Karikatur*, pp. 157, 214, 233, 249.
27 now partly or wholly Jewish through marriage: Massing, *Rehearsal for Destruction*, p. 107.
27 by means of 'surgical intervention and medication': Graml, *Reichskristallnacht*, p. 68.
27 them as the British had exterminated the 'Thugs' in India: ibid., p. 79. Unlike other racial concepts, the image of the Jews as a parasite—and the German *Volk* as a host—was in fact an old one, dating back to Martin Luther. Bein, 'Der jüdische Parasit', p. 128n.
27 'ultimately the annihilation of the Jewish people': Weiss, *Lange Weg*, p. 151.
27 'extermination of less valuable elements from the population': ibid., p. 153.
28 and that proportion had been declining for two decades: To be precise, from 1.09 per cent in 1880 to 0.92 per cent in 1910: Statistisches Reichsamt (ed.), *Statistisches Jahrbuch für das Deutsche Reich* (1921/22), p. 31. See also Bennathan, 'Demographische und wirtschaftliche Struktur', p. 94.
28 account for more than 5 per cent of the population: Magocsi, *Historical Atlas*, p. 10. On the decline of the Jewish community of Posen, see Herzberg, *Geschichte der Juden in Bromberg*, p. 106 and Heppner and Herzberg, *Aus Vergangenheit und Gegenwart der Juden*. See also Hagen, *Germans, Poles, and Jews*, pp. 28, 314ff.
28 Jews and non-Jews were removed in 1875: Hetzel, *Anfechtung der Rassenmischehe*, p. 25; Ruppin, *Jews of To-day*, p. 159.
28 (Russian Empire it remained illegal): Brüll, *Mischehe im Judentum*, p. 17; Ruppin, *Jews of To-day*, p. 166.
28 7.8 per cent in 1901 to 20.4 per cent in 1914: Meiring, *Christlich-jüdische Mischehe*, table 1.
28 Jewish communities are relatively small: Tachauer, 'Statistische Untersuchungen'.
28 Munich (15 per cent) and Frankfurt (11 per cent): Ruppin, *Jews of To-day*, p. 163.
28 rise in intermarriage in Breslau: See Rahden, 'Mingling, Marrying and Distancing'.
28 Bukovina there were virtually no mixed marriages: Ruppin, *Jews of To-day*, pp. 167ff. On Prague, see Cohen, *Politics of Ethnic Survival*, pp. 80, 136.
29 German Jews had done in the 1900s: Rosenthal, 'Recent Studies about the Extent of Jewish Out-Marriage in the USA'.
29 communities evinced comparable intermarriage rates: Baar and Cahnman, 'Interfaith Marriage in Switzerland'; Neustatter, 'Demographic and Other Statistical Aspects of Anglo-Jewry'.
29 'to whether there exists any physical antipathy!': Ruppin, *Jews of To-day*, p. 170ff.
29 produced by 'pure' Jewish or Christian marriages: Meiring, *Christlich-jüdische Mischehe*, table 4. Max Marcuse attributed this not to any biological factor but to the greater use of contraception by couples in mixed marriages: Marcuse, *Fruchtbarkeit der christlich-jüdischen Mischehe*. The divorce rate was also higher than average for couples with one Jewish partner: see e.g., May, *Mischehen und Ehescheidungen*.
29 between 30,000 and 40,000: Ruppin, *Jews of To-day*, p. 165.
29 century range from 60,000 to 125,000: Rigg, *Hitler's Jewish Soldiers*, tables 2, 3. For evidence that the figure was at the lower end of that range, see Lowenstein, 'Was Urbanization Harmful?', pp. 100ff.
29 such couples were raised as Jews: Meiring, *Christlich-jüdische Mischehe*, table 5.
29 'for example an officer, would be treated as a Jew': Frymann, *Wenn ich der Kaiser wär'*, p. 75.
30 similar legislation for the German colonies: Sollors, *Niether Black nor White*, p. 405.
30 traditional Jewish practices, most obviously endogamy: See in general Vital, *People Apart*, esp. pp. 314ff.
30 low fertility and physical or mental degeneracy: Ruppin, *Soziologie der Juden*, vol. II, esp. pp. 174ff. See also Theilhaber, *Untergang der deutschen Juden;* Hanauer, 'Jüdische-christliche Mischehe'; Lowenstein, 'Was Urbanization Harmful?'; Rahden, 'Mingling, Marrying and Distancing', pp. 214ff.
30 Judaism that converted him to Zionism: Krolik (ed.), *Arthur Ruppin*, pp. 561–4.
30 assimilation and an antidote to superstition and prejudice: Beller, *Vienna and the Jews*, p. 130.

30 'young men's inclinations and young women's choice in love': Wistrich, *Socialism and the Jews*, p. 379.
31 strengthen the character of East European Jews: Brüll, *Mischehe*, pp, 20ff.
31 'is the breaker down of such limits': Wistrich, *Jews of Vienna*, p. 529.
31 'to Jewry; to Germandom, the past and death': Weiss, *Lange Weg*, p. 142. On Nietzsche's ambivalent view of the Jews, see Maccaby, 'Nietzsche's Love-Hate Affair'.
31 a 'half Jewess' and the third a 'full Jewess': Zimmermann, *Wilhelm Marr*, p. 36.
31 'motivations underlying anti-Semitism': Loewenstein, *Christians and Jews*, quoted in Edwardes, *Erotica Judaica*, p. 222.
32 Toussenel called a new 'financial feudalism': Toussenel, *Les Juifs*.
32 regardless of his religion, as 'the real Jew': Marx, 'On the Jewish Question'.
32 and the Russian anarchist Mikhail Bakunin: Bein, 'Der jüdische Parasit', pp. 128ff.
32 'God makes the thunder . . . the king of gold': Zola, *L'Argent*, pp. 21ff., 91ff., 202.
32 Drumont and others sought to blame on the Rothschilds: Drumont, *France juive*, esp. vol. II, p. 98, 106ff. See also his *Testament d'un anti-Semite* (1891) and *Les juifs contre la France* (1899). Drumont's work inspired numerous imitators. The novel *La Bolsa* by Julián Martel (real name José Maria Miró) was inspired to the point of plagiarism by Drumont. Only the setting had changed to Buenos Aires at the time of the 1889–90 financial crisis: Mirelman, *Jewish Buenos Aires*, pp. 50ff.
32 the Third Republic was wholly in the grip of 'Jewish finance': See Chirac, *Rois de la République* (1883) and idem, *L'Agiotage* (1887).
32 who were the principal constituents for his Anti-Semitic People's Party: Weiss, *Lange Weg*, pp. 143–9; Graml, *Reichskristallnacht*, p. 192.
32 seventeen self-styled Anti-Semites sitting in the Reichstag: Massing, *Rehearsal for Destruction*.
32 and 22 per cent of all Prussian millionaires: Rubinstein, 'Jewish Participation', tables 1, 6.
32 journalists, theatre directors and academics: Bennathan, 'Demographische und wirtschaftliche Struktur', p. 112.
33 and that was the officer corps of the army: Ruppin, *Juden der Gegenwart*, p. 113.
33 late nineteenth and early twentieth century: See Anon., *Ostjuden*, pp. 9ff.
33 among German Gentiles: disquiet, bordering on revulsion: Maurer, *Ostjuden*, pp. 109ff.
33 accounted for a larger share of the urban population: Beller, *Vienna and the Jews*. See also John, 'Jüdische Bevölkerung'.
33 political success in pre-war Austria Hungary: Whiteside, *Socialism of Fools*.
33 'avoided any anti-Semitism against a useful Jew': Hagen, 'Before the "Final Solution"', pp. 353ff.
33 German Catholic magazine *Germania* as early as 1876: Weiss, *Lange Weg*, p. 126.
33 excluded from the teaching profession and the judiciary: Graml, *Reichskristallnacht*, p. 57.
34 collected were from university students: ibid., p. 58.
34 the phrase: 'The Jews Are Our Misfortune!': ibid., p. 66.
35 'protection they enjoy as ethnic aliens (*Volksfremde*)': Frymann, *Wenn ich der Kaiser wär'*, pp. 74–6.
35 now they could make the most of their abilities: ibid., p. 31.
36 in the 1930s and 1940s by Nazi propagandists: Burleigh, *Germany Turns Eastwards*.
37 (Kaliningrad) were all founded by the Order: Kosiek, *Jenseits der Grenzen*, pp. 22–36.
37 fourteenth centuries on the basis of German legal models: See the map in Dralle, *Die Deutschen*, pp. 98ff.
37 Transylvania and worked the mines of Resita and Anina: See Castellan, 'Germans of Rumania', pp. 52ff.
37 2,000 people a year in the twelfth and thirteenth centuries: Dralle, *Die Deutschen*, p. 95.
37 fatherland as if they had crossed the Atlantic: Kosiek, *Jenseits der Grenzen*, pp. 65–8, 73–8.
37 German towns created an acute sense of 'population pressure': Zeman, *Pursued by a Bear*, pp. 28ff.
37 1900 as a result of an influx of Czechs: Cohen, *Politics of Ethnic Survival*, table 3/1.
38 89 per cent German to being 73 per cent German: Zeman, *Pursued by a Bear*, p. 30.
38 the creation of Czech National Socialist Party in 1898: ibid., pp. 34–7.
38 the easternmost parts of Austria-Hungary: On Breslau, see Davies and Moorhouse, *Microcosm*, esp. pp. 302–5.
39 Christianity, ceasing to regard themselves as Jews: ibid., pp. 308, 363; Rahden, 'Mingling, Marrying and Distancing', pp. 201ff.
39 just under half of all the Germans in Prague: Cohen, *Politics of Ethnic Survival*, pp. 76, 80ff, 221. See also ibid., table 3/3. Cf. Spector, 'Auf der Suche nach der Prager deutschen Kultur'.
39 'have said to us that we were not German': Cohen, *Politics of Ethnic Survival*, p. 83.
39 tiny fraction (0.5 per cent) of the population: Rosenfeld, *Polen und Juden*, p. 25.
39 to embrace Hassidic Orthodoxy and Zionism: Röskau-Rydel, *Galicien*, pp. 145–52. Cf. Beller, *Vienna and the Jews*, p. 146.
39 to Vienna, Graz, Strasbourg and finally Berlin: Kłwańska, 'Literatur', pp. 408–18; Turczynski, 'Bukowina', pp. 214, 273.
39 assimilated German-speaking Jews viewed with mistrust: Cohen, *Politics of Ethnic Survival*, p. 137.
39 of Judas during their Holy Week parades: Belova, 'Anti-Jewish Violence in Folk Narratives of the Slavs'.

39 Cossack beat the skinflint Jew in the puppet theatre: Le Foll, 'Byelorussian Case'.
39 associations like gymnastics clubs and student fraternities: Cohen, *Politics of Ethnic Survival*, p. 196.
39 salacious anti-Semites with plentiful raw material: Weihus, *Bordell-Juden*, p. 31.
39 garner applause in Königsberg than in Cologne: On early calls for restriction of immigration see Graml, *Reichskristallnacht*, p. 57.
40 as the simplest solution to the Jewish 'question': Graml, *Reichskristallnacht*, p. 79.
40 Jews and Gentiles seemed to make most sense: These stories formed part of his *Die Juden von Barnow*: Kłwańska, 'Literatur', pp. 414ff. Cf. Turczynski, 'Bukowina', p. 275.
42 their own individual and collective predicament: Beller, *Vienna and the Jews*, chs. 5, 6.

## CHAPTER TWO: ORIENT EXPRESS

43 resistance of all European powers: Röhl, *Wilhelm II*, p. 756. Cf. Schimmelpenninck, *Toward the Rising Sun*, p. 96.
44 'the Great Yellow race': Röhl, *Wilhelm II*, p. 753.
44 imperial capital, Beijing, killing the German Minister: See Cohen, *History in Three Keys*.
44 falls into your hands falls to your sword!: Schimmelpenninck, *Toward the Rising Sun*, p. 96; Röhl, 'Emperor's New Clothes', p. 31.
45 city wall were symbolically blown up: Hevia, 'Leaving a Brand on China'. There are striking parallels with the British response to the Indian Mutiny of 1857.
46 'yellow-faced barbarians . . . surging over the continent': Quoted in Schimmelpenninck, *Toward the Rising Sun*, pp. 83ff–6, 93, 208ff.
46 'as that the sun will shine tomorrow': ibid., pp. 95, 103.
46 This now reached its climax: Chiswick and Hatton, 'International Migration'.
46 middle of the century it would be one in two: Constantine, 'Migrants and Settlers', p. 167. European migration to Asia almost certainly exceeded migration to Africa, despite the success of colonies in Algeria, Kenya, Rhodesia and South Africa.
47 mines owned and managed by Europeans: See e.g., Tinker, *New System of Slavery*.
47 labour better rewarded than in Europe: See Williamson and O'Rourke, *Globalization and History and Williamson*, 'Land, Labor and Globalization'.
48 more than 0.05 per cent of the population: Maddison, *World Economy*, p. 109.
48 44 per cent of the population of the Tsar's domains: Service, *Twentieth-Century Russia*, p. 12.
48 Vladivostok—'ruler of the east': Schimmelpenninck, *Toward the Rising Sun*, p. 113.
49 'the life of the countryside for you!': Quoted in Service, *Lenin*, p. 113.
49 vast Siberian border was barely 50,000: Paine, *Imperial Rivals*, p. 255.
49 Japanese small businesses and brothels: Stephan, *Russian Far East*, pp. 72–9.
49 between European men and Japanese women: ibid., pp. 74, 78.
49 context of an unambiguous racial hierarchy: Forsyth, *Peoples of Siberia*, pp. 220ff.
49 'the lazy don't indulge in it': Stephan, *Russian Far East*, p. 74.
49 is at work chopping wood: Forsyth, *Peoples of Siberia*, p. 221.
50 whose stride is that of the conqueror: ibid., p. 222.
50 Vladivostok shipyards were Chinese: Stephan, *Russian Far East*, p. 73.
50 which the Russians regarded all Asiatic peoples: Paine, *Imperial Rivals*, pp. 213ff.
50 'Russians and few yellows here': Stephan, *Russian Far East*, p. 80.
50 was in the hands of 100,000 Russian troops: Paine, *Imperial Rivals*, pp. 212, 215.
51 'from the North to the South': ibid., p. 216.
51 must become 'Russian property': ibid., p. 223.
51 imposed caution on St Petersburg: ibid., pp. 218ff.
51 closely modelled on that of Prussia: Buruma, *Inventing Japan*, pp. 12–40; Harries, *Soldiers of the Sun*, pp. 7–19.
52 expedition against the Boxers in 1900: Schimmelpenninck, *Toward the Rising Sun*, pp. 130ff. Cf. Duus, 'Japan's Informal Empire in China', pp. xx–xxi.
52 'struck me as an effective fighting force': Schimmelpenninck, *Toward the Rising Sun*, pp. 98–102.
53 'ultimatum from a country like Japan': Paine, *Imperial Rivals*, p. 240.
53 heroic wreck of the Varyag: I am grateful to Maria Razumovskaya for her translation.
54 to throw them into disarray: Schimmelpenninck, *Toward the Rising Sun*, p. 199.
54 actually sailed with the Second Fleet: Figes, *People's Tragedy*, pp. 168ff.
55 we keep the 'yellow peril' at bay: Quoted in Schimmelpenninck, *Toward the Rising Sun*, p. 102.
55 disciplined, their artillery more effective: See Connaughton, *Rising Sun and Tumbling Bear*; Warner and Warner, *Tide at Sunrise*.
55 Manchuria was to remain a Chinese possession: Hata, 'Continental Expansion', pp. 290ff. See also Duus, 'Japan's Informal Empire in China', pp. xxii–xxiii.
58 their independence from St Petersburg: Figes, *People's Tragedy*, p. 184.
58 'all gentlemen and all are equal': Quoted in Manning, *Crisis of the Old Order*, pp. 142, 147.
58 'resurgent China guided by Japan': Forsyth, *Peoples of Siberia*, p. 221.
58 'Jews who are the enemy of the government': Quoted in Lambroza, 'Pogrom Movement', p. 66.

58 'evil factors of our accursed revolution': Quoted in Feldman, 'British Diplomats', p. 590.
59 much less reside in, the Russian interior: Dubnow, *History of the Jews*, vol. II, pp. 39ff.
59 graduates and (after 1865) artisans: Greenberg, *Jews in Russia*, vol. I, pp. 75ff.
59 on the young sons of poor families: Details in Dubnow, *History of the Jews*, vol. II, pp. 15–29.
59 of pressures to renounce their faith: Stanlislawski, *Nicholas I and the Jews*, pp. 17–34.
59 Jewish men to divorce their wives: Errera, *Russian Jews*, p. 75.
59 they were a majority of the population: Feldman (ed.), *Yehude Rusyah*, p. 201.
60 Eastern Europe, from Lithuania to Romania: Klier, 'Blood Libel'. Cf. Goldberg, 'Jahre 1881–1882', p. 17.
60 over a 'blood libel' case in Damascus: For an excellent overview see Green, 'Anti-Jewish Violence'.
60 work of the city's Greek community: Herlihy, *Odessa*, p. 299.
60 different 'pariah' minorities: See Brass (ed.), *Riots and Pogroms*.
61 from 574 to 23,967—39 per cent of the population: Pritsak, 'Pogroms of 1881', p. 16.
62 say nothing of 26 foreign countries: Surh, 'Jews of Ekaterinoslav', p. 219.
62 were an integral part of the local elite: ibid., p. 222.
62 of dominance in urban areas further east: Pritsak, 'Pogroms of 1881', p. 29.
62 handling around two thirds of its commerce: Khiterer, 'October 1905 Pogrom', p. 23.
62 69 per cent of those of the second guild: Surh, 'Jews of Ekaterinoslav', p. 220.
62 economy, or as inn-keepers and artisans: See Zenner, 'Middleman Minorities and Genocide'.
63 against 4 per cent of the Russian population: Feldman, 'British Diplomats', p. 594n.
63 'for the entire capitalist world': Marten-Finnis, 'Outrage', p. 60.
63 organization with sinister powers: Goldberg, 'Jahre 1881–1882', p. 16.
63 Russian Army as The Root of our Misfortunes: Vishniak, 'Antisemitism in Tsarist Russia', p. 138n.
64 conditions that they will gradually die out: Quoted in Vishniak, 'Antisemitism in Tsarist Russia', p. 142.
64 between Christian and Jewish communities: Pritsak, 'Pogroms of 1881', p. 18.
64 trouble then spread to nearby districts: ibid., pp. 23ff. On the role of rape in pogroms, see Brownmiller, *Against Our Will*, p. 121.
64 all over the southern half of the Pale: Aronson, *Troubled Waters*, p. 31.
64 Governor of Poltava himself: There were also assaults on Jews in Borispol and Nyezhin, and arson attacks in Mohilev, Vitebsk, Slonim, Pinsk and Minsk: Dubnow, *History of the Jews*, vol. II, pp. 249–79; Goldberg, 'Jahre 1881–1882', pp. 23–33.
65 damage to property was substantial: Goldberg, 'Jahre 1881–1882', p. 40. See Aronson, *Troubled Waters*, pp. 50–6 for a complete list of all recorded outbreaks. Cf. Pritsak, 'Pogroms of 1881', pp. 33–41.
65 40 Jews were killed or seriously wounded: Praisman, 'Jewish Self-Defence', p. 68.
65 government had instigated them: This was the view of the well-organized Anglo-Jewish community: see Russo-Jewish Committee, *Russian Atrocities*, 1881.
65 still others the new Tsar himself: Dubnow, *History of the Jews*, vol. II, pp. 245, 259–65.
65 clergy to preach against pogroms: Klier, 'Blood Libel'.
65 deplored what was happening: Aronson, 'Prospects', p. 352.
65 which they were said to have 'captured': Dubnow, *History of the Jews*, vol. II, pp. 270ff.
65 'Christians, this hatred will not diminish': Quoted in Aronson, 'Prospects', p. 352.
65 more than to excuse popular motives: Chmerkine, *L'Antisémitisme*. True, some of those who carried out the pogroms shouted slogans like 'The Jews drink our blood' and 'The Jews are sucking out our vital juices.' But these may have been allusions to the old blood libel rather than complaints about economic exploitation. As Chmerkine demonstrated, the presence of Jewish businesses in an area actually drove down rates of profit through competition. There was much more 'exploitation' by non-Jewish traders in areas from which Jews were excluded. Even in mixed areas, Jewish businesses apparently had a lower rate of profit than their non-Jewish competitors. The pogroms, Chmerkine persuasively argued, were more a cause than a consequence of economic disruption.
65 anarchists had encouraged the pogroms: Goldberg, 'Jahre 1881–1882', p. 42n. A flysheet was found in Kiev that urged people to 'attack the Jew not because he is a Jew, but because he sucks the blood of the worker. . . . So attack this kulak-oppressor and attack the government which protects these robbers'.
65 development of the most horrible socialism: Quoted in Vishniak, 'Antisemitism in Tsarist Russia', p. 134. There is in fact some evidence that anti-Jewish circulars grouped together Jews and officials, landowners and other privileged classes: see Aronson, *Troubled Waters*, table 5.
66 economic rivals: Russian artisans: Aronson, '1881 Anti-Jewish Pogroms', p. 23.
66 and merchants: Pritsak, 'Pogroms of 1881', pp. 25–9.
66 Often the perpetrators were unemployed: Goldberg, 'Jahre 1881–1882', p. 14.
66 were arrested, only 222 were women: Klier, 'Pogroms of 1881–2'.
66 'labourers . . . [a] "bare-footed brigade"': Quoted in Dubnow, *History of the Jews*, vol. II, pp. 250, 253. Cf. Goldberg, 'Jahre 1881–1882', p. 17.
66 87 day-labourers, 77 peasants and 33 domestic servants: Pritsak, 'Pogroms of 1881', pp. 18, 20.
66 if they failed to attack the local Jews: Dubnow, *History of the Jews*, vol. II, p. 257. To be on the safe side, they destroyed six Jewish residences anyway.

66 **Great Russians then seeking work in Ukraine:** Aronson, '1881 Anti-Jewish Pogroms', p. 21.

66 **'Orekhov, Berdiansk and Mariupol':** ibid., pp. 19, 24; Pritsak, 'Pogroms of 1881', pp. 22–5.

66 **'havoc wrought before their eyes':** Quoted in Dubnow, *History of the Jews*, vol. II, p. 250.

67 **manpower to give the rioters free rein:** Weissman, 'Regular Police', p. 47. At around this time, the Russian Department of Police had just under 50,000 personnel to police a population of nearly 127 million. In the countryside, an individual constable might be responsible for areas as large as 1,800 square miles.

67 **policemen for a total population of 43,229:** Aronson, *Troubled Waters*, p. 132.

67 **chiefs took no action for two days:** Pritsak, 'Pogroms of 1881', p. 21.

67 **notion that the pogroms were officially instigated:** Klier, 'Pogoroms of 1881–2'.

67 **seriously considered, though not adopted:** Vishniak, 'Antisemitism in Tsarist Russia', p. 133; Goldberg, 'Jahre 1881–1882', pp. 48ff.; Aronson, "Prospects', pp. 350ff.

67 **anti-Jewish violence in the succeeding years:** Pogroms were recorded in Shpola (Kiev province) in February 1897, in Kantakuzenka the following April, in Nikolaiev over Easter 1899 and in Czestochowa in 1902: Vishniak, 'Antisemitism in Tsarist Russia', p. 135; Praisman, 'Jewish Self-Defence', p. 69.

67 **merely the first of four phases of violence:** Lambroza, 'Pogrom Movement', pp. 66–70. According to one account 'people had nails hammered into their heads and eyes were gouged out. Women had their stomachs cut open and breasts cut off, little children . . . had their heads smashed in with stones': Praisman, 'Jewish Self-Defence', p. 69.

68 **troops were preparing to depart for the East:** Lambroza, 'Pogrom Movement', pp. 90ff.

68 **January and early October of 1905:** Praisman, 'Jewish Self-Defence', p. 75.

68 **at a minimum, 302 were killed:** Herlihy, *Odessa*, p. 307.

68 **but this time there was killing too:** Khiterer, 'October 1905 Pogrom', p. 21.

68 **more than 800 Jews were killed:** Zionistische Hilfsfond, *Judenpogrome*, p. 213.

68 **Odessa there were pitched battles:** Praisman, 'Jewish Self-Defence', pp. 78ff.

68 **'whole anger turned against them':** Tsar Nicholas II to Dowager Empress Marie Feodorovna, October 27, 1905, in Bing (ed.), *Letters of Tsar Nicholas and Empress Marie*, p. 187.

68 **Consul General in Moscow, Alexander Murray:** See for example Hardinge to the Marquess of Lansdowne, July 18, 1905, in Feldman (ed.), *Yehude Rusyah*, p. 199. Cf. Feldman, 'British Diplomats'. However, other British diplomats took a different view, emphasizing official orchestration of the pogroms: see e.g., Consul-General Smith to Sir Edward Grey, April 20, 1906, in Lieven (ed.), *British Documents*, pp. 57ff.; Sir Arthur Nicolson to Sir Edward Grey, June 20, 1906, in ibid., pp. 102ff.

69 **himself has been exposed as bogus:** Klier, 'Solzhenitsyn and the Kishinev Pogrom'.

69 **the Jews of Eastern Europe:** Lambroza, 'Pogrom Movement', pp. 74ff.

69 **editor of the inflammatory Bessarabets:** Zionistische Hilfsfond, *Judenpogrome*, p. 192; Almog, *Nationalism and Antisemitism*, p. 56.

69 **arms to combat the revolution:** Manning, *Crisis of the Old Order*, p. 139.

69 **'riff-raff, most of them teenagers':** Khiterer, 'October 1905 Pogrom', pp. 25, 31.

69 **'railroad workers, peasants, chiefs of station':** Herlihy, *Odessa*, pp. 307ff.

69 **even joined in the ransacking of Jewish residences:** See the revealing manuscript account, 'La Situation à Odessa', by a former Duma member, dated November 1907 in the Bibliothèque de l'Alliance Israélite Universelle, Paris. See also Lambroza, 'Pogrom Movement', p. 70; Zionistische Hilfsfond, *Judenpogrome*, pp. 193ff.; Praisman, 'Jewish Self-Defence', p. 79; Khiterer, 'October 1905 Pogrom', pp. 27ff.

69 **the colonel had been reinstated by 1907:** Khiterer, 'October 1905 Pogrom', p. 37.

70 **begins to look rather doubtful:** Haimson, 'Problem of Social Stability'.

70 **ground by marauding Latvian peasants:** Eksteins, *Walking Since Daybreak*, pp. 42–4.

71 **'We have become a second-rate power':** Lieven, *Russia and the Origins of the First World War*, p. 22.

71 **on a massive program of rearmament:** Gatrell, *Government, Industry and Rearmament*.

## CHAPTER THREE: FAULT LINES

72 **other than mutual mass slaughter:** Heyman, 'Trotsky's Military Education', p. 80.

73 **commander-in-chief of the Turkish Army:** Glenny, *Balkans*, p. 303.

74 **Vlachs, Germans, Jews and Gypsies:** Malcolm, *Bosnia*, passim.

74 **dividing line between Europe and Asia:** Mazower, *Balkans*, p. 10.

74 **since the Congress of Berlin in 1878:** The Congress was the decisive event in the modern history of the Balkans, striking as it did a balance between the European great powers in the wake of Russia's victory over the Turks in the war of 1877–8. Serbia and Montenegro became independent. Austria-Hungary was also awarded the Sanjak/Sandzk of Novi Pazar. Macedonia remained an Ottoman possession; Bulgaria secured autonomy under Ottoman suzerainty. Greece had secured its independence in 1830–2: see Glenny, *Balkans*, esp. pp. 146–57.

74 **had to be stationed to maintain order:** Malcolm, *Bosnia*, p. 136. The purpose of his visit was indeed to watch military maneuvers.

74 **'It would be better to die!':** Lieven, *Russia and the Origins of the First World War*, p. 22.

75 **standardized schooling and military training:** Weber, *Peasants into Frenchmen*.

# NOTES

76  Turkish-Bulgarian border: Martin, 'Origins of Soviet Ethnic Cleansing', p. 818.

76  population of Eastern Thrace rose by a third: Pallis, 'Racial Migrations'.

77  left to right: 'Unification or Death': The constitution of the Ujedinjenje ili Smrt, at http://www.lib.byu.edu/~rdh/wwi/1914m/blk-cons.html.

77  M 1910 revolvers, six bombs and cyanide tablets: Glenny, *Balkans*, p. 298. They were joined in Sarajevo by six other conspirators: Muhamed Mehmedbasic, Veljko Cubrilovic, Cvijetko Popovic, Danilo Llic, Misko Jovanovic and Vaso Cubrilovic.

78  'state, but it must be free from Austria': Malcolm, *Bosnia*, p. 150.

78  Serbian army in 1912 as 'too small and too weak': Glenny, *Balkans*, p. 250.

78  Appel Quay, the city's central riverside avenue: Malcolm, *Bosnia*, p. 154. Their itinerary had been conveniently published in the previous day's newspaper.

78  himself but was prevented from doing so: Glenny, *Balkans*, pp. 304–6.

80  the 1911 Agadir crisis and the 1912–13 Balkan crisis: Geiss, *Lange Weg in die Katastrophe*.

80  Anglo-German naval competition after 1897: Strachan, *First World War*, vol. I, pp. 4–35. The same author shifts his focus to the Balkans after 1908 in his *First World War: A New Illustrated History*, pp. 4–8. For another recent account that emphasizes the alleged blunders of German policy, see Sheffield, *Forgotten Victory*, pp. 22–40.

80  on the immediate pre-war decade: See e.g., Herrmann, *Arming of Europe*. David Stevenson identifies the period after 1907 as having witnessed the 'breakdown of equilibrium' in the European military balance: see his *Armaments and the Coming of War*. In his most recent book, however, he dates the 'crumbling' of the 'bases of deterrence' from 1905: idem, *Cataclysm*, p. 8.

80  to start the 'countdown' to war even later: See for a recent example, Williamson, 'Origins of the War', p. 14.

80  in the summer of 1914: Though it begins by evoking an idyllic summer abruptly shattered by an unexpected war, David Fromkin's *Europe's Last Summer* quickly retraces its steps to restate the now familiar case that the war was the culmination of a calculated German policy dating back to the 1890s.

80  hostilities came more as a relief than a surprise: Clarke, *Voices Prophesying War*.

80  'ready for war' long before war came: See Ferguson, *Pity of War*, 'Introduction' for a full discussion.

81  'all round down from 25 to 50 per cent': Bloch, *Is War Now Impossible?*, p. xlv.

81  best-selling tract of 1910, *The Great Illusion*: Angell, *Great Illusion*, p. 209.

82  'circumstances there not favouring a forward movement': Rothschild Archive, London [RAL], XI/130A/8, Lord Rothschild, London, to his cousins, Paris, July 22, 1914.

82  'dispute will be arranged without appeal to arms': ibid., July 23, 1914.

82  Serbs would 'give every satisfaction': ibid., July 24, 1914.

82  'made to preserve the peace of Europe': ibid., July 27, 1914.

82  sincerely wished any war to be 'localised': ibid., July 28 and July 29, 1914.

83  of the outlook both at home and abroad: *The Times*, July 22, 1914.

83  'Ulster' than about events in the Balkans: *Economist*, July 24, 1914.

83  some of the Great Powers of Europe: ibid., August 1, 1914.

83  'CZAR, KAISER AND KING MAY YET ARRANGE PEACE': I am grateful to Professor William Silber for drawing this point to my attention.

84  or half (49 per cent) of all foreign sovereign debt: Mauro, Sussman and Yafeh, 'Emerging Market Spreads', table 1.

85  less and less in the subsequent two decades: Ferguson, 'Political Risk'.

86  bourses as shut in all but name: According to another source, Montreal, Toronto and Madrid closed on July 28, followed by Vienna, Budapest, Brussels, Antwerp, Berlin and Rome on the 29th, and the St Petersburg, Paris and the South American markets on the 30th.

87  'weak speculators selling à nil prix': RAL, XI/130A/8, Lord Rothschild, London, to his cousins, Paris, July 27, 1914.

87  'liquidation for the whole Continent of Europe': *Economist*, August 1, 1914.

87  Bank of England's decision to raise the discount rate to 8 per cent: ibid.

87  authorities to avert a complete financial collapse: The scheduled bank holiday was extended until August 6, a one-month (later three-month) moratorium on commercial bills was proclaimed on August 2 and emergency £1 and 10 shilling notes were also issued. See Keynes, 'War and the Financial System'. Cf. Moggridge, *Keynes*, pp. 236–41.

87  in the yields of all the combatants' bonds: Balderston, 'War Finance', pp. 222–44.

87  central bank interventions to maintain bond prices: Kooi, 'War Finance'.

87  Even so, they were substantial: Morgan, *Studies in British Financial Policy*, p. 152.

88  saw 'the meaning of war' on July 31—'in a flash': *Economist*, August 1, 1914.

88  the *New York Times* spoke of a 'conflagration': *New York Times*, August 4, 1914.

89  bigger than had been seen seven years before: See Silber, 'Birth of the Federal Reserve'; and Silber, *Summer of 1914*. The crisis hit New York before the newly-created Federal Reserve System had begun its operations.

89  shared by the English statistician Edgar Crammond: Strachan, *First World War*, vol. I, p. 816.

89  Powers would have to make peace: Harvey, *Collision of Empires*, p. 279.

90  'greater than anything ever seen or known before': RAL, XI/130A/8, Lord Rothschild to his cousins, July 31, 1914.

90 'horrors so appalling that the imagination shrinks from the task': ibid., August 1, 1914.

90 big deficits in the event of a war: For a review of these possibilities, see Flandreau and Zumer, *Making of Global Finance*.

90 down domestic bond yields and reducing market volatility: Ferguson, 'Political Risk'.

91 consequence of deep-seated great power rivalries—a predestined cataclysm: See for example Schroeder, 'Embedded Counterfactuals'.

91 outbreak of war was an avoidable political error: Ferguson, *Pity of War*, chs. 1 to 5.

91 were only a few basis points higher than those on consols: Ferguson and Schularick, 'Empire Effect'.

92 independent development will emerge the true harmony: Ranke, 'Great Powers', pp. 151, 155.

92 nineteenth century were discussed and, in large measure, settled: Hinsley, *Power and the Pursuit of Peace*, p. 214n.

92 This was no small achievement: The best account remains Taylor's *Struggle for Mastery in Europe*.

93 centuries before it and the one after it: Levy, *War in the Modern Great Power System*, table 4.1.

93 national independence (28) or civil wars (19): Luard, *War in International Society*, appendices.

93 per year, just 51 took place in Europe: Singer and Small, *Correlates of War* database, www.umich.edu/~cowproj.

93 Austria all spent just over 3 per cent: Hobson, 'Wary Titan', p. 479. The Russian and Japanese figures are for the period 1885–1913.

93 armed forces; respectively, 1.5 and 1.1 per cent: Singer and Small, *Correlates of War* database, www.umich.edu/~cowproj.

93 institution of government, the royal court: See Röhl, *Kaiser and His Court*.

94 widow of Francis Frederick, Duke of Coburg: Princess Beatrice (ed.), *In Napoleonic Days*.

95 toyed with the idea of accepting the throne of Greece: See Stockmar, *Memoirs of Baron Stockmar*, vol. I, p. 84.

95 Archduchess of the Imperial House of Austria: *The Times*, March 26, 1863. Leopold I married one of Louis Philippe's daughters, Leopold II married Marie Henriette, Archduchess of Austria, and his sister Charlotte married the ill-starred Archduke Maximilian, briefly Emperor of Mexico.

96 and Ducky [their daughter, Victoria Melita]: Nicholas II Diary, June 18, 1893, in Maylunas and Mironenko, *Lifelong Passion*.

96 two Dukes, two Duchesses and a Marquess. They were all related: See the famous photograph by Professor Uhlenhuth, reproduced in Bachmann, 'Coburg between England and Russia'.

96 'strengthen the throne morally as well as physically': Victoria to 'Bertie', November 24 and 29, 1869, in Longford (ed.), *Darling Loosy*.

96 'the races would degenerate physically and morally': Queen Victoria to Princess Victoria, January 19, 1885, in Corti, *English Empress*, p. 226.

97 eldest daughter Vicky and Kaiser William II's sister Charlotte: Röhl, *Wilhelm II*, pp. 105–15.

97 'them only led to g[rea]ter strength & health': Victoria to Princess Victoria of Hesse, May 18, 1892, in Hough (ed.), *Advice to a Granddaughter*, p.116.

97 betrothal to yet another of her granddaughters: Nicholas Diary, April 12, 1894, in Maylunas and Mironenko, *Lifelong Passion*.

97 Brunswick & all the others preceding it, joining in it: Royal Archives Geo. V., AA. 11, 2, Queen Victoria to George [future George V], June 26, 1894. See also RA Geo. V., AA. 11, 3, Queen Victoria to George Duke of York, July 2, 1894.

97 'cherished and kept up in our beloved home': Queen Victoria to Princess Victoria, November 6, 1862, in Corti, *English Empress*, p. 97.

97 of the Belgians in 1863, 'is so German': Queen Victoria Papers 0330, Queen Victoria to Leopold I, November 19, 1863.

99 'on her mother's side': Queen Victoria's journal, March 27, 1889, in Buckle (ed.), *Letters of Queen Victoria*, p. 481.

99 'granddaughter of Czar Nicholas I': Christopher, Prince of Greece, *Memoirs*, p. 15.

99 Bulgarian adventure of Alexander von Battenberg: See Corti, *Alexander of Battenberg*.

99 'shown to the obedient relation from afar': Herbert von Bismarck memorandum, July 25, 1888, in Dugdale (ed.), *German Diplomatic Documents*, vol. I, p. 365.

99 Saxe-Coburgs with the Rothschilds in the 1840s: Dairnvaell, *Histoire édifiante et curieuse de Rothschild Ier*, p. 8.

99 almost symbiotic relationship with one another: For details see Ferguson, *House of Rothschild*, vol. I.

100 'as the "Nephew" and not as the "Kaiser"': Buckle (ed.), *Letters of Queen Victoria, Third Series*, vol. I, pp. 492–3n.

100 Manchuria, pledging German support if it came to war: Röhl, *Wilhelm II*, pp. 753ff.

100 Tsar's son, a request he welcomed with enthusiasm: Levine (ed.), *Kaiser's Letters to the Tsar*, pp. 123–7.

100 'a symbol for our relation to each other': ibid., pp. 246–8.

100 'action within limits which Russia could accept': Buchanan to Grey, July 28, 1914, in Gooch and Temperley (eds.), *British Documents on the Origins of War*, vol. XI, p. 162.

100 'exhibitionist, but he would never start a war': Maylunas and Mironenko, *Lifelong Passion*.

101 his record as a 'Peace Emperor' was finished with: Goschen to Nicolson, August 1, 1914, in Gooch and Temperley (eds.), *British Documents on the Origins of War*, vol. XI, p. 283

101 'dreaded for so many years has come upon us': George V to Nicholas II, July 31, 1914, in Maylunas and Mironenko, *Lifelong Passion*.
101 blood remains unmixed with that of foreigners!: Marie of Battenberg, *Reminiscences*, p. 270.
101 albeit (at his request) on the Eastern Front: Alice, *For My Grandchildren*.
102 the 'Coburg line' was renamed the Windsor line in 1917: Pogge von Strandmann, 'Nationalisierungs-druck und königliche Namensänderung'.
103 nations in England's favour against us!: Geiss, *July 1914*, no. 135.
103 Balkan crisis of 1914 into a world war: For a more detailed account, see Ferguson, *Pity of War*.
104 been murdered by none other than 'Apis': Glenny, *Balkans*, p. 298.
104 dispatched from London or Calcutta to Kandahar?: *Economist*, August 1, 1914.
104 'should come to a war between Austria and Russia': The Austrian ambassador, Count Szögyény-Marich, quoted in Taylor, *Struggle for Mastery*, p. 521.
104 implied an invasion of eastern Germany: See in general Lieven, *Russia and the Origins of the First World War*.
105 'completed the extension of their army organizations': See Mombauer, *Helmuth von Moltke*.
105 'we could still more or less pass the test': Geiss, *July 1914*, pp. 65–8.
105 'for a long campaign, with numerous tough, protracted battles': Strachan, *First World War*, vol. I, p. 1005.
105 'do what I can. We are not superior to the French': ibid., p. 173.
106 'or between China and Japan': *Economist*, August 1, 1914.
106 that six divisions were 'fifty too few': Strachan, *First World War*, vol. I, p. 200.
107 much humming and hawing, for the latter: For a more detailed account of these events, see Ferguson, *Pity of War*, ch. 6.

## CHAPTER FOUR: THE CONTAGION OF WAR

109 ('For us, human life isn't a consideration'): Pottle (ed.), *Champion Redoubtable*.
109 our grenades against human beings: Remarque, *All Quiet on the Western First*, p. 81.
109 'more so even than former wars': Strachan, *First World War*, vol. I, p. 441.
109 'This war will grow into a world war': ibid., p. 695.
110 Chief of the General Staff, Alfred von Schlieffen: Ritter, *Schlieffen Plan*.
110 'frontier, and then to break the French fortress line': Zuber, 'Schlieffen Plan Reconsidered', p. 280.
111 failure of Moltke's gamble was laid bare: See Mosier, *Myth of the Great War*.
112 'bled to death, England shall at least lose India': Geiss, *July 1914*, doc. 135.
113 'side who could lose the war in an afternoon': Massie, *Castles of Steel*, p. 58.
114 achieved nothing of comparable value: Boghardt, *Spies of the Kaiser*.
114 'amidst the wreckage caused by a German torpedo': Massie, *Castles of Steel*, p. 530.
115 races against the colonial imperialism of Europe: Strachan, *First World War*, vol. I, p. 814.
115 the vast majority black troops and porters: ibid., p. 571.
115 her less creditworthy continental allies: Balderston, 'War Finance'.
116 'never hesitate to lend to a prosperous concern': Strachan, *First World War*, vol. I, p. 818.
116 New York—were unlikely to pull the plug: See in general Burk, *Britain, America and the Sinews of War*.
116 Europe, going overwhelmingly to Britain and her allies: Fordham, ' "Revisionism" Reconsidered'. Fordham shows that congressional support or opposition to U.S. intervention was a function of both economic interests and ethnic allegiance. Legislators from states who had benefited disproportionately from the wartime export boom and had large proportions of immigrants from Great Britain or allied countries were significantly more likely to favour intervention on the Entente side.
116 as bad for the United States as for Europe': Strachan, *First World War*, vol. I, p. 991.
116 numbers of American troops would have to fight: Fleming, 'Illusions and Realities'.
120 were shot for desertion, while the Germans executed only 18: A further 92 British soldiers were executed by firing squad for other offences: Oram, *Military Executions*; Jahr, *Gewöhnliche Soldaten*.
123 system evolved in certain 'quiet' sectors of the line: Ashworth, *Trench Warfare*.
125 Germans was one of the highlights of American war propaganda in 1918: Fooks, *Prisoners of War*, pp. 97ff.
125 nerve-shattered German prisoners' being given drink and cigarettes: See Ferguson, *Pity of War*, p. 368 and plates 25 to 28.
125 'potatoes, beans, prunes, coffee, butter, tobacco etc.': Bruntz, *Allied Propaganda*, p. 112. For evidence that these devices worked, see Watson, 'Chances of Survival', p. 269.
126 spontaneously out of the war of attrition: Stories about such incidents abounded on both sides and can be found not only in post-war memoirs but also in contemporary letters and dairies. The examples given here are additional to those cited in Ferguson, *Pity of War*, ch. 13.
126 two young girls, who were the last to be shot: Horne and Kramer, 'German Atrocities', p. 27.
126 and cutting off womans breasts awful deeds [sic]: Watson, 'Chances of Survival', p. 60.
127 'kill Huns, those baby-killing ____': Keegan and Holmes, *Soldiers*, p. 267.
127 Kamerad and all this cringing business: Macdonald, *Somme*, p. 290.
127 'hoped fate would allow me to kill': Winter, *Death's Men*, p. 210.

127 'dissertation [sic] among the N.C.[O.] and the men': Yale University, Beinecke Rare Book and Manuscript Library, Henri Gaudier-Brzeska to Ezra Pound, May 22, 1915.
127 had previously killed Germans who had surrendered: Horne and Kramer, 'German Atrocities', p. 27.
128 but the scores we owe wash out anything else: Bourke, *Intimate History*, p. 183.
128 'loss of his pal had upset him very much': Holmes, *The Western Front*, p. 179.
128 some German troops as early as September 1914: Horne and Kramer, 'German Atrocities', p. 28.
128 'shown to the enemy and no prisoners taken': Hussey, 'Kiggell and the Prisoners', p. 47.
128 'they had no feelings whatever for us poor chaps': Brown, *Tommy Goes to War*, p. 116.
128 be taken as they hindered mopping up: Griffith, *Battle Tactics of the Western Front*, p. 72.
128 'scored through meant "do as you please"': Watson, 'Chances of Survival', p. 81.
129 'cannot be bothered to escort back to his lines': Brown, *Tommy Goes to War*, p. 73.
129 'expedient from a military point of view': Bourke, *Intimate History*, p. 189.
129 'every prisoner means a day's rations gone': Brown, *Tommy Goes to War*, p. 28.
129 The answer is—don't take prisoners: Dungan, *They Shall Not Grow Old*, p. 136.
129 ground was ankle deep with German blood: Brown, Imperial War Museum book of the Western Front, p. 17.
129 'the only way to treat the German is to kill him off': Loc. cit.
130 'another nine "Hate" children if you let him off. So run no risks': Bourke, *Intimate History*, p. 182.
130 of them or felt able to carry them out: Brown, *Tommy Goes to War*, pp. 117, 183.
130 and is duly rewarded with the Iron Cross: Imperial War Museum, *Kriegsflugblätter*, January 29, 1915.
130 prisoners and that the Germans 'ought to do the same': Watson, 'Chances of Survival', p. 82.
131 killing the enemy that is the key to victory in war: See Ferguson, 'Prisoner Taking and Prisoner Killing'.
131 at Caporetto came close to putting Italy out of the war: On Caporetto, see Seth, *Caporetto*, esp. pp. 80–3, 156–9; Falls, *Caporetto 1917*, pp. 64–9.
131 in all the previous years of fighting combined: Garrett, *P.O.W.*, pp. 100ff.
131 the real sign that the war was ending: War Office, *Statistics of the Military Effort*, p. 632.
131 them when the tables were turned in August: See Hall, 'Exchange Rates'.
132 movement they themselves had initiated in the spring: Ferguson, *Pity of War*, ch. 10.
132 sickness, indiscipline, shirking and desertion: Deist, 'Military Collapse of the German Empire'. See also Bruntz, *Allied Propaganda*, pp. 207–21.
134 be well treated that they elected instead to surrender: Donovan (ed.), *Hazy Red Hell*, pp. 207–13. For a similar account dating from early September 1918, see Watson, 'Chances of Survival', pp. 275–8. Captain G. B. McKean of the 14 Canadian Infantry was able to capture more than a hundred Germans with only a handful of men near the Canal du Nord. An obliging German officer played a key role in ensuring that the capitulation was orderly.
134 what natural scientists call 'self-sustaining criticality': For a somewhat popularized introduction see Buchanan, *Ubiquity*.
136 'no more Fatherland. It was crumbling, splintering': Roth, *Radetsky March*, ch. 19.
137 Jewish women were raped by soldiers: Budnitskii, 'Cause of a Pogrom'.
137 'never disclosed person, came robbery, fire, and massacre': Holquist, 'Role of Personality'.
137 bayonet him, I'll answer for it: ibid.
137 'Slice them up! Chop them up!': ibid.
137 the Russians continued to occupy: Lohr, *Nationalizing the Russian Empire*.
138 collaborating with the Russians during their occupation: Röskau-Rydel, 'Galizien', pp. 154ff.
138 Russian Brusilov offensive in the summer of 1916: Turczynski, 'Bukowina', pp. 284ff.
138 bitter fighting between the various ethnic groups in Galicia: Röskau-Rydel, 'Galizien', pp. 160–8.
138 provinces during the war—in all, around 250,000 people: Martin, 'Origins of Soviet Ethnic Cleansing', pp. 818ff.
139 customs and institutions which they represented: Andrie, *Bridge on the Drina*, pp. 384ff.
139 become European and then spread to the entire world': ibid., p. 361.

## CHAPTER FIVE: GRAVES OF NATIONS

141 recognized, because democracy had not been recognized: Zahra, 'Reclaiming Children', p. 516.
141 Lord 1918, but the year 1919 was even more terrible: Bulgakov, *White Guard*, ch. 20.
142 'children starved and crippled': Keynes, *Economic Consequences*, ch. 7.
142 'you—now dont you laugh, naughty one': Steinberg and Khrustalev, *Fall of the Romanovs*, p. 26.
143 complaining bitterly of 'treachery, cowardice and deceit': ibid., p. 107.
143 'they wld. probably stay in doors': ibid., p. 49.
143 'Just imagine! We must get home, but how?': Volkogonov, *Lenin*, p. 106.
144 enough, world revolution might supervene: See Thatcher, *Trotsky*, p. 96ff.
145 25 and 34 fell victim to the 'Spanish Lady': Brainerd and Siegler, '1918 Influenza Epidemic'.
145 when they occupied cities like Białystok: Weindlng, *Epidemics and Genocide*.
145 'Afghanistan, the Punjab and Bengal': Figes, *People's Tragedy*, p. 703.
145 rocked by strikes and street fighting: Mirelman, *Jewish Buenos Aires*, pp. 61ff.

147 was to be vital in taking on the Whites: Figes, 'Red Army', pp. 176–9.

148 death in the front or certain death in the rear: Volkogonov, *Trotsky*, pp. 178ff.

148 'papist-Quaker babble about the sanctity of human life': Figes, *People's Tragedy*, p. 641.

148 claims in the Far East and leave the rest of Russia to its fate: Forsyth, *History of the Peoples of Siberia*, pp. 268ff. By 1922 they had withdrawn from all save the northern half of the island of Sakhalin.

149 took up arms to fend off arbitrary grain seizures: See Figes, *Peasant Russia, Civil War*; Swain, *Russia's Civil War*.

149 'sovietize Hungary and perhaps Czechia and Romania too': Service, *Twentieth-Century Russia*, p. 120.

150 become the keystone of Bolshevik rule: See Trotsky's celebration of the relationship in Terrorism and Communism (1920).

150 'those who will be shot at the scene of the crime': Volkogonov, *Trotsky*, p. 136.

150 'revolution without firing squads?' Lenin asked: Figes, *People's Tragedy*, p. 630.

150 P.S. Find tougher people: Volkogonov, *Lenin*, p. 70. Cf. Service, *Twentieth-Century Russia*, p. 108.

150 'blood-suckers . . . spiders . . . [and] leeches': Figes, *People's Tragedy*, p. 618.

151 'who are caught in the other side of the barricade': ibid., p. 631.

151 'blood of the bourgeoisie—more blood, as much as possible': Leggett, *Cheka*, p. 108.

152 the Red Army to schools and universities': St Petersburg, Gorokhovaya 2: Museum of the History of Political Police of Russia.

152 such political executions were carried out: Service, *Twentieth-Century Russia*, p. 108.

152 'three-quarters of the population' in order to 'save Russia': Figes, *People's Tragedy*, p. 561.

152 camps for the 'rehabilitation' of 'unreliable elements': Applebaum, *Gulag*, p. 32.

152 in the icy wastes beside the White Sea: ibid., p. 37.

152 hands—the so-called 'glove trick': Figes, *People's Tragedy*, p. 646. Incredibly, the American journalist Louise Bryant (romanticized in the film *Reds*) praised how 'quickly and humanely' Dzerzhinsky 'disposed of' political prisoners: see Pipes, *Russia under the Bolsheviks*, p. 214.

152 being destroyed, priests and monks murdered: 28 bishops and thousands of priests were killed: see Service, *Twentieth-Century Russia*, pp. 115ff.

153 though desertion rates remained high, especially around harvest time: Figes, 'Red Army', p. 187.

154 artisan production with individual labour: Chamberlin, *Russian Revolution*, vol. II, p. 495.

154 ethnic minority a measure of political autonomy: Zeman, *Pursued by a Bear*, pp. 74ff.

155 Korean National District around Posyet: Forsyth, *History of the Peoples of Siberia*, pp. 269ff.

155 their ethnic identity with the Bolshevik regime: Martin, 'Soviet Ethnic Cleansing', p. 825.

155 'to make the point about victory clear': Eksteins, *Walking Since Daybreak*, pp. 72ff.

155 were massacred by Bolshevik forces: Harries, *Soldiers of the Sun*, p. 103.

155 out into the frost' by Kirghiz tribesmen: Russian State Archives, 1235/140/127 1926–28, p. 39.

156 many Bolshevik leaders who were of Jewish origin: The role of the Jews in the Revolution remains controversial. Simply because a number of leading Bolsheviks were Jewish and because Jews on the whole benefited from the Revolution it was always an error to infer that therefore the Revolution itself was 'Jewish', as claimed by Hitler and innumerable other opponents of Communism. See Solzhenitsyn, *Deux siècles ensemble*, vol. II; Slezkine, *Jewish Century*, ch. 3.

156 instead had been subjected to rape and pillage: Brownmiller, *Against Our Will*, p. 123.

156 anti-Semitism throughout the interwar period: Buldakov, 'Freedom, Shortages, Violence'.

156 forces were also involved in attacks on Jews: Budnitskii, 'The Cause of a Pogrom'.

156 for the Jews prior to the pogrom of May 1918: Buldakov, 'Freedom, Shortages, Violence'.

157 reports he received was: 'For the archives': Volkogonov, *Lenin*, p. 204.

157 Ukraine had claimed up to 120,000 lives: Levene, 'Frontiers of Genocide', p .105.

157 Bolshevized and sociologically Sovietized': Gitelman, *Jewish Nationality and Soviet Politics*, p. 13.

157 a magnet for their national aspirations: Martin, 'Origins of Soviet Ethnic Cleansing', pp. 830ff.

158 as a result of fighting, executions or disease: Swain, *Russia's Civil War*, p. 20.

158 epidemics alone may have exceeded 8 million: Gantt, *Russian Medicine*, pp. 138–49.

158 the Soviet Union fell by around 6 million: Timasheff, *Great Retreat*, pp. 286ff.

158 Russian as the language they knew best or most often used: Zeman, *Pursued by a Bear*, p. 75n.

159 'politics than in European terrain': Figes, *People's Tragedy*, p. 703.

159 90 per cent of the town's population were German: Komjathy and Stockwell, *German Minorities*, p. 65.

160 'its governmental will upon alien people': Knock, *To End All Wars*, p. 35.

160 'sovereignty under which they shall live': ibid., p. 77.

160 five to thirteen of his Fourteen Points: ibid., pp. 143ff.

160 'to the principle of self-determination': ibid., p. 152.

161 barely one in ten of the population were French-speakers: Keylor, 'Versailles and International Diplomacy', p. 492.

161 Hungary left over after the Treaty of Trianon: The Treaty of Trianon reduced the proportion of minorities in the population of Hungary from over 45 per cent to just under 8 per cent: Paikert, 'Hungary's National Minority Policies', p. 202.

NOTES

161  manifest interest of the peoples concerned: Manela, 'Ahead of His Time?', p. 1119.
163  permanent 'dissatisfaction' and 'irredentist agitation': ibid., p. 1120.
163  of the plebiscites in certain contested areas: Goldstein, 'Great Britain: The Home Front', p. 151.
163  sovereignty of every state in the world: Fink, 'Minorities Question', p. 258.
163  but its foreign policy was determined in Warsaw: Lloyd George felt the corridor should be kept as narrow as possible, for fear of creating a permanent German grievance. It was at his instigation that a plebiscite was held in the district of Marienwerder, which voted to remain part of Germany: see Macmillan, *Peacemakers*, pp. 217–39.
164  Oscar Matzerath, is born in Danzig in 1924: For a good introduction, see Schmidt et al., *In Gdansk unterwegs mit Günter Grass*.
164  Byelorussians and more than 2 per cent Germans: For these and the following demographic statistics based on 1930 or 1931 census data, see Magocsi, *Historical Atlas*, pp. 131, 135, 137, 141, 148, 171.
164  population of all the major cities was Jewish: Vital, *People Apart*, p. 763.
166  Archduke Francis Ferdinand's assassination: Glenny, *Balkans*, p. 368. Cf. Rothschild, *East Central Europe*, pp. 202–6, 210–3.
167  much further east than the peacemakers had planned: Davies, *God's Playground*, p. 394.
167  into the chronically unquiet *kresy*—the borderlands: Motyl, 'Ukrainian Nationalist Political Violence', pp. 47–51; Seton-Watson, *Eastern Europe*, pp. 334ff. See also Lotnik, *Nine Lives*, pp. 12–15.
167  (formerly Bromberg) and Ostrowo (formerly Ostrow): Blanke, *Orphans*, p. 41.
167  52 Germans were killed and 84 wounded: Rothschild, *East Central Europe*, pp. 78–81; Smelser, 'Castles on the Landscape', p. 91.
168  'and consciously that we were "Occidentals"': Rezzori, *Snows of Yesteryear*, pp. 49, 65, 98, 200.
168  proportion rose to 38 per cent in Czernowitz itself: Livezeanu, *Cultural Politics in Greater Romania*, p. 49; Castellan, 'Germans of Rumania', pp. 52–5.
168  disrupt a performance of Schiller's *Die Räuber*: Turczynski, 'Bukowina', p. 293.
168  for real and imagined discrimination also grew: See e.g., Smelser, 'Castles on the Landscape', pp. 92ff.
168  towns where only a few Czech families lived: Wiskemann, *Czechs and Germans*, pp. 208ff. This was a tactic adopted by most of the successor states too. The Romanian government sought systematically to reverse what it termed 'Ruthenization' by reducing the number of Ukrainian schools in Bukovina: Livezeanu, *Cultural Politics in Greater Romania*, p. 65.
168  discrimination against Ukranian and Byelorussian schools was more severe: Blanke, *Orphans*, pp. 77ff.; Subtelny, *Ukraine*, p. 429; Davies, *God's Playground*, p. 409.
168  though there were 467 German primary schools: Paikert, 'Hungary's National Minority Policies', p. 211.
168  department of Czernowitz's once-renowned university: Turczynski, 'Bukowina', pp. 290, 292.
169  Germans in the civil service: Komjathy and Stockwell, *German Minorities*, p. 21.
169  names in West Prussia and Posen: Blanke, *Orphans*, p. 67.
169  Germandom League (Deutschtumsbund): ibid., p. 73.
169  'sealed [themselves] off from the Polish element': ibid., pp. 33ff., 49ff., 84–8. By the same token, many Poles left those parts of Silesia, like the city of Breslau, that had remained German: see Davies and Moorhouse, *Microcosm*, p. 361.
169  killed and virtually the entire Jewish quarter was gutted: Polonsky and Riff, 'Poles, Czechoslovaks and the Jewish Question', p. 88.
169  businesses; in Warsaw synagogues were burned: Cohen, 'My Mission to Poland', pp. 157ff., 163ff.
169  Béla Kun's short-lived soviet regime in Budapest: Mendelsohn, *Jews of East Central Europe*, pp. 39–42; Polonsky and Riff, 'Poles, Czechoslovaks and the Jewish Question', pp. 75ff. But see Lukas, *Forgotten Holocaust*, pp. 124–6 for a different view.
170  pre-war residence were denied Polish citizenship: Polonsky and Riff, 'Poles, Czechoslovaks and the Jewish Question', p. 78.
170  to become a university professor was next to impossible: Mendelsohn, *Jews of East Central Europe*, p. 43.
170  universities fell by half between in 1923 and 1937: Zeman, *Pursued by a Bear*, p. 99; Rothschild, *East Central Europe*, p. 41.
170  'both its numbers and its uniqueness': Wynot, '"Necessary Cruelty"', p. 1050. See Vital, *People Apart*, p. 766.
170  Dwomski, spoke in similar terms: Wynot, '"Necessary Cruelty"', p. 1036.
170  And we . . . are blind!: Landau-Czajka, 'Image of the Jew', p. 169. For other examples of Polish anti-Semitism in the 1920s, see Segel, *Stranger in Our Midst*, pp. 278–92.
170  Jewish enrollment in universities was restricted: Mendelsohn, *Jews of East Central Europe*, pp. 183–6.
171  only through bribery could non-Romanian candidates hope to pass: Turczynski, 'Bukowina', pp. 296, 298.
171  immigration on Palestine's internal stability: Mendelsohn, *Jews of East Central Europe*, p. 79. See also ibid., pp. 46ff.
171  'from the Jewish district': Bronsztejn, *Polish-Jewish Relations*, p. 71.

669

NOTES

171 'town from the west end of London': Seton-Watson, *Eastern Europe*, p. 290. 'The fact remains', he went on, 'that the majority of Eastern European Jews are an alien element, bound by no tie of sympathy or understanding of the peoples among whom they live': ibid., p. 295.
171 parties, the Bund and Zionist Poale Zion: Mendelsohn, *Jews of East Central Europe*, pp. 46ff.
171 and a proliferation of Yiddish and Hebrew schools: ibid., pp. 63–6.
171 to different holiday resorts from rich Poles: Bronsztejn, 'Polish-Jewish Relations', p. 72.
172 also described themselves as Jewish by nationality: Castellan, 'Social Structure', p. 188. Cf. Vital, *A People Apart*, p. 777; Bronsztejn, 'Polish-Jewish Relations', p. 74.
172 The third possibility was assimilation: See in general Mendelsohn, 'Problem of Jewish Acculturation'.
172 band that performed at parties and weddings: Hoffman, *Shtetl*, pp. 169–84.
172 that it was said 'every Jew has his Pole': Cala, 'Social Consciousness', p. 48.
172 'art in the depths of [one's] being': Gross, *Who Are You, Mr Gymek?*, p. 24.
172 they had abandoned religious observance: Levi, *Cat Called Adolf*, pp. 33–42.
172 would have happened in pre-war Bohemia: Wiskemann, *Czechs and Germans*, pp. 227ff.
172 when they encountered such anti-Semitism: Biglová et al., *Remembering*, pp. 61ff.
173 (I do not like myself as a Jew.) I am already lost: Cala, 'Social Consciousness', p. 52.
173 German-speaking than to Czech-speaking schools: Polonsky and Riff, 'Poles, Czechoslovaks and the Jewish Question', p. 94.
173 both Germans and Jews were attacked: ibid., p. 93.
173 'threatens Latvian independence and welfare': Ekstiens, *Walking Since Daybreak*, p. 107.
173 front of German and Jewish minorities: Mendelsohn, *Jews of East Central Europe*, p. 53.
173 campaigning for a boycott of Jewish doctors: Van Rahden, 'Mingling, Marrying and Distancing', pp. 208ff, 213.
174 'traditional values as well as newly developing ones': Rezzori, *Snows of Yesteryear*, pp. 66, 282ff.
174 members of the same cultural associations: Livezeanu, *Cultural Politics in Greater Romania*, p. 59.
174 wars this harmony gradually vanished: Turczynski, 'Bukowina', pp. 288–308.
174 to decide the fate of Kurdistan and the area around Smyrna: Housepian, *Smyrna 1922*, p. 63.
175 Turkey with a uniform national culture (*harsî millet*): Heyd, *Foundations of Turkish Nationalism*, pp. 57–63; Melson, *Revolution and Genocide*, pp. 159–70. See also Reid, 'Total War', pp. 27ff. Talaat spoke tautologically of 'ottomanizing the Empire': Geary to Lowther, August 28, 1910, in Gooch and Temperley (eds.), *British Documents on the Origins of the War*, vol. IX, No. 181, pp. 208ff.
175 their own designs on the oilfields of Mesopotamia: Strachan, *First World War*, vol. I, pp. 674ff; idem, *Illustrated History*, pp. 102–5.
176 historically the Ottoman Empire's most dangerous foe: See e.g., Talaat, 'Posthumous Memoirs', pp. 294ff.
176 subordinate status as infidel *dhimmis*: See e.g., Cambon to Hanotaux, October 31, 1895, in *Documents Diplomatiques: Affaires Arméniennes*, No. 116, pp. 162ff; Memorandum on the Joint Report of the Consular Delegates to the Sasun Commission of July 20, 1895, in Foreign Office, *Correspondence Relating to the Asiatic Provinces of Turkey*, No. 267, pp. 203–8. Cf. Reid, 'Total War', p. 37.
176 people killed at more than 37,000: National Archives, Washington, RG 59, American ambassador in Constantinople to Secretary of State, February 4, 1896.
176 anti-Armenian rhetoric into practice: In November 1906 the Paris branch of the CUP had issued an open letter, 'To Our Muslim Brothers in [Russian] Caucasia', which described the Armenians as 'the primary obstacles to freedom from the Russian yoke'. 'Therefore . . . their wealth, which is their greatest power, should be attacked' (*tecavüzlerinden*): Bayur, *Türk Inkilâbi Tarihi*, p. 86. On the events of 1909, see Dadrian, *Armenian Genocide*, pp. 155, 182, 225, 233n.
177 'has hitherto happened in the history of the world': George Horton to Secretary of State, November 8, 1915, in Sarafian (ed.), *United States Official Documents*, No. 69, p. 118.
177 to acknowledge the Armenian genocide: Dadrian, *Key Elements in the Turkish Denial*.
177 'innocent today might be guilty tomorrow': Melson, *Revolution and Genocide*, p. 169.
177 wrote harrowing accounts of what they witnessed: See e.g., Knapp, *Mission at Van*. Cf. Horton, *Blight of Asia*, p. 24.
177 German atrocities in Belgium in 1914: Bryce, *Treatment of the Armenians*.
177 active pro-Russian fifth column: See e.g., Anon., *Verité sur le mouvement révolutionnaire*, pp. 13ff; Anon. (ed.), *Documents sur les Atrocités*. See also Talaat, 'Posthumous Memoirs', pp. 294ff.
177 Pope Benedict XV's intercession on behalf of the Armenians: Vatican Secret Archives, Holy Congregation for Special Ecclesiastical Affairs, Austria-Hungary 1915–1916, Pos. 1069, Fasc. 463, The Sultan to Benedict XV, November 19, 1331.
177 'exterminate all Armenian males of twelve years of age and over': Nogales, *Four Years*, p. 60. Emphasis in original.
177 own government to 'put a stop to the brutality': Anon., *Horrors of Aleppo*, p. 3.
178 'begun and would soon come to them': Pomiankowski, *Zusammenbruch des Ottomanischen Reiches*, pp. 160, 165. See also Knapp, *Mission at Van*, p. 14; M. G., *Défense héroïque de Van*, pp. 24, 27.
178 'extermination of the Armenian race': Trauttmansdorff to Burián, September 30, 1915, in Anon. (ed.), *Armenian Genocide*, Vol. II, p. 244.

178 **Turks would one day be held to account:** Pallavicini to Burián, August 13, 1915, and March 10, 1916, in Anon. (ed.), *Armenian Genocide*, Vol. II, pp. 209, 324.

178 **confirm that mass murder was being perpetrated:** Lepsius (ed.), *Deutschland und Armenien*, p. xxiv. See also Trumpener, *Germany and the Ottoman Empire*, pp. 205, 217, 225. For the allegation that the Germans actively supported the Armenian genocide, see Ohandjanian, *Verschwiegene Völkermord*, pp. 208–21; Dadrian, *German Responsibility*.

178 **that he 'knew that deportations meant massacres':** Anon., *Germany, Turkey, and Armenia*, p. 123. See also Dadrian, 'Armenian Question', p. 77; Dadrian, 'Signal Facts', p. 275.

178 **religious leaders were arrested and deported:** Tehlirean (ed.), *Völkermord an den Armeniern*, p. 63.

178 **Persian frontier, often having been stripped of clothing:** M. G., *Défense héroïque de Van*, pp. 13–24.

178 **other valuables were stolen. Rape was rampant:** See e.g., Anon., *Horrors of Aleppo*, pp. 5, 13; M. G., *Défense héroïque de Van*, pp. 16–20; Anon., *Germany, Turkey and Armenia*, p. 126; Sarafian (ed.), *United States Official Documents*, vol. I, No. 55, pp. 106ff (also pp. 49, 145).

178 **'beforehand, shot, and thrown into the ditches':** Anon., *Germany, Turkey and Armenia*, p. 124.

178 **in the river or nearby ravines:** ibid., p. 127.

178 **carriages eighty or ninety at a time:** J. B. Jackson to Morgenthau, August 19, 1915, in Sarafian (ed.), *United States Official Documents*, vol. I, No. 32, pp. 53ff.

178 **walk literally until they dropped:** Gibbons, *Derniers Massacres*, p. 18; Sarafian (ed.), *United States Official Documents*, vol. I, pp. 26, 49; vol. II, p. 123, 127.

179 **in reality meant the extermination of the Armenians:** Vatican Secret Archives, Holy Congregation for Special Ecclesiastical Affairs, Africa/Asia/Oceania, 1918–1922, Pos. 57, Facs. 44, pp. 62–7, Memorandum to His Excellency Monsignor Pacelli at Munich on the Circumstances of Christians in the Orient, 1917.

179 **alternative solutions to the 'Armenian question':** See e.g., Sarafian (ed.), *United States Official Documents*, vol. I, p. 56; vol. II, p. 60. The American consular agent in Adrianople believed the Germans were urging the Turks to adopt conversion as a preferable 'method of securing the disappearance of the Armenian race'. See also Anon. (ed.), *Armenian Genocide*, pp. 315ff.

179 **but was probably closer to 1.8 million:** The statistics are a minefield because of the wide differences in the Ottoman and ecclesiastical estimates for the pre-war population. See Marashlian, *Politics and Demography*, pp. 30ff, 42, 52, 58; Gürün, *Armenian File*, pp. 79–96.

179 **'should a division come, they would be destroyed':** Vatican Secret Archives, Holy Congregation for Special Ecclesiastical Affairs, Africa/Asia/Oceania, 1918–1922, Pos. 57, Facs. 44, pp. 62–7, Memorandum to His Excellency Monsignor Pacelli at Munich on the Circumstances of Christians in the Orient, 1917.

180 **'in the same way that he believes he solved the Armenian problem':** Leon, *Greece and the Great Powers*, p. 275.

181 **defiance of the other members of the Big Four:** Macmillan, *Peacemakers*, p. 438. See Woodhouse, *D'Annunzio*.

182 **Armenians had been seven years before:** See the documents in Fotiadis (ed.), *Genocide of the Pontus Greeks*, pp. 283–99, 309–17.

182 **war at the insistence of Liman von Sanders:** Dobkin, *Smyrna*, p. 47.

182 **realized that they were going to drown themselves:** Horton, *Blight of Asia*, ch. 16.

183 **terror as can be heard miles away:** Glenny, *Balkans*, p. 391.

183 **'deliberate plan to get rid of minorities' was carried out:** Fotiadis (ed.), *Genocide of the Pontus Greeks*, p. 297.

183 **'expatriation of an ancient Christian civilization':** Horton, *Blight of Asia*, "Introduction."

183 **'harems if they are sufficiently good looking':** *New York Times*, June 7, 1922.

184 **zero per cent, their places taken by Greeks:** Pallis, 'Racial Migrations in the Balkans', p. 330.

185 **'wealth for her eastern and southern neighbours':** Keynes, *Economic Consequences*, ch. 7, IV.

185 **'civilisation and the progress of our generation':** Keynes, *Economic Consequences*, ch. 7, I.

186 **'Today's states are the graves of nations':** Hagen, 'Before the "Final Solution"', p. 351.

## CHAPTER SIX: THE PLAN

189 **resting, first and foremost, on your shoulders:** Getty and Naumov, *Road to Terror*, p. 553.

189 **The warrior is strong in battle:** Russian State Archives, 9401c/3/92 1939.

190 **music for a decade-long global party:** On the links between jazz, prohibition and the evolution of interracial relations in the United States, see Mumford, *Interzones*, esp. pp. 19–70.

190 **several rows of exposed toilets:** Fenby, *Generalissimo*, p. 133.

191 **(introduced her to his first wife and to gonorrhoea):** ibid., p. 42.

191 **reception in the rose-bedecked Majestic Hotel:** ibid., pp. 160–7.

191 **pelted the Soviet consulate with sticks and stones:** Davidson-Houston, *Yellow Creek*, pp. 133ff.

191 **10 per cent of it belonged to just 0.01 per cent:** Piketty and Saez, 'Income Inequality'; Kopczuk and Saez, 'Top Wealth Shares'.

192 **restricting credit for reasons of their own:** Eichengreen, 'Still Fettered After All These Years'.

193 'social disease of Western civilisation in our time': *The Times*, January 23, 1943.

193 both kinds of crisis in an unlucky few: Eichengreen, 'Still Fettered After All These Years'.

193 actually raising its discount rate in October 1931: The classic account remains Friedman and Schwartz, *Monetary History*. Recent counterfactual evaluations tend to confirm their hypothesis that a different behaviour by the Fed would have significantly reduced the severity of the Depression. See Bordo, Choudhri and Anna Schwartz, 'Was Expansionary Monetary Policy Feasible'; Christiano, Motto and Rostagno, 'The Great Depression and the Friedman-Schwartz Hypothesis'.

195 nevertheless dealt a blow to financial confidence: James, *End of Globalization*. Cf. 'Herbert Hoover', Harvard Business School Case 9–798–041. The bill was named after Senator Reed Smoot, a Republican from Utah, and Congressman Willis C. Hawley, a Republican from Oregon.

196 capital flows would affect the exchange rate: Eichengreen, *Golden Fetters*.

196 were at work, especially in the United States: Cole, Ohanian and Leung, 'Deflation and the International Great Depression'.

196 'free competition and a large measure of laissez-faire': Keynes, *General Theory*, preface to the German edition of 1936.

199 'sort of idea of what would happen if He lived now': Holroyd, *Shaw*, vol. III, pp. 244–8. Cf. Shaw, *Rationalization of Russia, passim*.

200 food rationing, even from their homes: Fitzpatrick, *Everyday Stalinism*, p. 118.

200 'habits, opinions, world views and so on': ibid., p. 137.

200 public attention to a new category of 'enemies of the people': ibid., p. 130.

200 costs of collectivization to Churchill: Churchill, *Hinge of Fate*, pp. 498ff.

200 The Party will accept no excuses for failure: Kravchenko, *I Chose Freedom*, pp. 111ff.

200 Soviet livestock was down to half of its 1929 level: Gantt, *Russian Medicine*, p. 151.

201 in 1932 was down by a fifth compared with 1930: Jasny, *Socialized Agriculture*, pp. 792, 794.

201 into the fields and ate half-ripe ears of corn: Belov, *Soviet Collective Farm*, p. 13.

201 unnatural and unnecessary disaster: Conquest, *Harvest of Sorrow*, p. 300.

201 as 'special exiles' to Siberia and Central Asia: Fitzpatrick, *Everyday Stalinism*, p. 122.

201 as 3.5 million victims of 'dekulakization' subsequently died in labour camps: Conquest, *Harvest of Sorrow*, p. 301.

201 increase would have increased it to 186 million: Antonov-Ovseyenk, *Time of Stalin*, pp. 207ff.

202 jeopardizing their access to the nomenklatura: See e.g., William Chamberlin, 'Famine Proves Potent Weapon in Soviet Policy', *Christian Science Monitor*, May 29, 1934; idem, 'Soviet Taboos', pp. 432–5. Cf. Markoff, *Famine in Russia*, pp. 3ff; Lyons, *Assignment*, pp. 572–80.

202 He was almost certainly right: Scott, *Behind the Urals*, p. 5. See Kotkin, *Magnetic Mountain*.

203 a self-made member of the nomenklatura: Transcript of interview with Alexander Lutznevoy for PBS documentary *Yanks for Stalin*.

203 fifth or a sixth of the official figure: Rosefielde, 'Excess Deaths and Industrialization', pp. 279ff.

203 shed for political rather than economic reasons: See Rosefielde, 'Excess Deaths and Industrialization', p. 277 and table 1 on p. 285.

203 'necessary' if it involves anything up to 20 million excess deaths: ibid., p. 280.

204 than twenty; within a year that number has quintupled: Applebaum, *Gulag*, pp. 32ff.

205 the camp authorities could make them work: ibid., pp. 51ff.

205 'them to participating in organized productive labour': ibid., p. 220.

205 manufacturing everything from tanks to toys: Applebaum, 'Gulag: Understanding the Magnitude of What Happened'.

206 'cutting into its cities, hovering over its streets': Solzhenitsyn, *Gulag Archipelago*, p. xxii.

206 'the big [prison] zone': Applebaum, *Gulag*, p. 15.

206 little more than 1 per cent of camp inmates had higher education in 1938; a third were illiterate: ibid., p. 270.

207 women and children passed through the system under Stalin's rule: ibid., p. 4.

207 penal servitude under Stalin approached 15 per cent: Applebaum, 'Gulag: Understanding the Magnitude of What Happened'.

207 prisoners to the freezing weather—ensured a high death toll: Applebaum, *Gulag*, p. 45.

208 only one small part of the nightmarish truth: G. Zheleznov, Vinogradov and F. Belinskii to the Presidium of the Central Executive Committee of the All-Union Communist Party (Bolshevik), December 14, 1926: http://www.loc.gov/exhibits/archives/d2presid.html.

208 idyllic, with healthy inmates and salubrious cells: Applebaum, *Gulag*, pp. 59ff.

209 places the prisoners had to cut through solid granite: ibid., pp. 77–80.

209 'or of prison labour, in any country in the world': Conquest, *Great Terror*, p. 331. On their four-month visit in 1932, see Cole, *The Webbs and Their Work*, pp. 224ff. The question mark was dropped from the title of the book in the second 1937 edition.

209 excuse that the alternative to lying might be dying: One of the writers, Victor Shklovsky, may have co-operated because his own brother was imprisoned in one of the canal camps. His brother was subsequently freed but was once again arrested in 1937.

210 'hooligans, adventurers, drunkards and thieves': Service, *History of the Soviet Union*, pp. 117ff.

210 denounce yet more of their comrades and then shot: Conquest, *The Great Terror*, p. 130.
211 audience of a variety show in a Moscow theatre: Bulgakov, *Master and Margarita*, ch. 15.
211 were the victims of social forces he had merely unleashed: See Fitzpatrick, 'How the Mice Buried the Cat'.
211 speculators to make the world safe for honest men: Shaw's responses to questions posed by the journalist Dorothy Royal, quoted in the *Daily Telegraph*, June 18, 2003.
212 'public welfare, that is the keynote of Soviet Democracy': Cole, *The Webbs and Their Work*, p. 229.
212 Jacob Mendelevich Abter, a 30-year-old Jewish worker: Their story has been pieced together at the Memorial Research Centre, Moscow.
213 passport or to marry someone from a respectably proletarian family: Fitzpatrick, *Everyday Stalinism*, pp. 132ff, 136.
213 middle peasants, and some even as agricultural labourers: ibid., pp. 119ff.
213 even substitutes for the doctor in making house calls: ibid., pp. 134ff.
215 'probably be taken by other peasants from Central Asia': Maclean, *Eastern Approaches*, pp. 40ff.
215 Central Asia, as likely to prove untrustworthy in the event of a war with Japan: ibid., p. 60.
215 mid-1920s as a way of securing the Soviet Union's eastern frontier: Russian State Archives, 5446/22a/48 1938.
216 'being de-kulakized not because you are a kulak, but because you are a Pole': Martin, 'Origins of Soviet Ethnic Cleansing', pp. 837ff.
216 'If it's a Pole, then it must be a kulak': Russian State Archives, 3316/64/760 1930, p. 79.
216 authorities feared they planned to emigrate westwards: Martin, 'Origins of Soviet Ethnic Cleansing', pp. 839ff.
216 border regions of Kiev and Vinnitsya to eastern Ukraine: ibid., p. 848.
216 of no fewer than 140,000 people, nearly all of them Poles: Applebaum, *Gulag*, pp. 141ff.
216 answer to what he regarded as the 'Ukrainian Question': Maksudov, 'Geography of the Soviet Famine'.
216 (of the Ukrainian nationalist leader Simon Petlyura): Martin, 'Origins of Soviet Ethnic Cleansing', pp. 844ff.
216 the victims of the famine were disproportionately Ukrainian: ibid., pp. 842–6.
216 more than half had voted for Ukrainian parties: Borys, *Sovietization of Ukraine*, p. 170.
216 nearly one in five of the total Ukrainian population: Conquest, *Harvest of Sorrow*, pp. 219–24, 303, 306.
217 folksingers were rounded up and shot: Volkov (ed.), *Testimony*, p. 215.
217 Russified and 95 per cent of government officials: Liber, *Soviet Nationality Policy*, p. 40.
217 led to their wholesale deportation to Siberia: Martin, 'Origins of Soviet Ethnic Cleansing', p. 846. Cf. Khrushchev, *Khrushchev Remembers*, p. 73.
217 around 30,000 Finns were sent to Siberia: Martin, 'Origins of Soviet Ethnic Cleansing', pp. 849ff.
217 a year later it was the turn of two thousand Iranians: ibid., p. 852.
217 as well as 'the Bulgarian and Macedonian cadres': ibid., p. 854.
218 in the actions against nationalities ended up being executed: ibid., pp. 855–8.
219 members, as compared with 1.8 per cent of the Soviet population: Gitelman, *Jewish Nationality and Soviet Politics*, p. 321.
219 from 18.8 per cent in 1925 to 27.2 per cent two years later: Natsional'naia politika VKP (b) (1930), table 4. Figures for Jewish men. The figures for Jewish women were lower in Russia but slightly higher in Ukraine and Byelorussia.
219 between Russians and Muslims in Central Asia: Pipes, 'Assimilation and the Muslims', pp. 601ff.
219 Russians and Ukrainians seems to have been slower to fall: Inkeles and Bauer, *Soviet Citizen*, pp. 196ff; Bilinsky, 'Assimilation and Ethnic Assertiveness', pp. 156ff.
219 traditional Yiddish language in favour of Russian: Gitelman, *Jewish Nationality and Soviet Politics*, pp. 489–90, 498–500. See also Pinchuk, *Shtetl Jews*, pp. 28ff; Nove and Newth, 'Jewish Population', pp. 136, 141ff.
220 *Arbeit Macht Frei* that would later welcome prisoners to Auschwitz: Applebaum, *Gulag*, p. 173.

## CHAPTER SEVEN: STRANGE FOLK

221 German people [ein deutsches Volk]: http://www.zum.de/psm/ns/hit5_ns_macht.php.
221 in all probability, be of no value or injurious to the racial stock: Burleigh, 'Racial State Revisited', p. 158.
223 quotations are taken was his inaugural address, delivered on March 4, 1933: The address is better heard than read: ftp://webstorage2.mcpa.virginia.edu/library/nara/fdr/audiovisual/speeches/fdr_1933_0304.mp3. I am grateful to Professor David Moss for drawing my attention to the fascistic undertone of Roosevelt's address.
224 thinking and concluding with a stirring call for national unity: Hitler's speech at the opening of the Reichstag, March 21, 1933: http://www.zum.de/psm/ns/hit5_ns_macht.php.
224 whatever they thought his will might be: This is the essential argument of Kershaw, *Hitler: Hubris* and *Hitler: Nemesis*.

NOTES

225 **1920s and 21 per cent of the number in the 1910s:** Figures from the Archives at Tuskegee Institute: http://www.law.umkc.edu/faculty/projects/ftrials/shipp/lynchingyear.html.
227 **'by reducing all forms of government to Democracy':** Modelski and Perry, 'Democratization in Long-Term Perspective', p. 25n.
227 **move uneasily under the European empires that had won the war:** Manela, *Wilsonian Moment*.
227 **were not seen again for some seventy years:** Data kindly supplied by Kristian S. Gleditsch and Michael D. Ward. See Jaggers and Gurr, *Polity III*.
231 **'the bourgeois', he added, 'are beaming':** Halévy, *Correspondance*, p. 666, letter to E. Chartier, January 1, 1924.
233 **or perhaps a renegade tram conductor:** Reck-Malleczewen, *Diary*, p. 36.
236 **grandfather would have seen had they made the same journey:** Fermor, *Time of Gifts*, pp. 31–118.
236 **'dazzled in the prison courtyard, incapable of moving their limbs':** See Easton, *Red Count*.
236 **contracts could be fulfilled with worthless paper marks?:** The definitive study is Feldman, *Great Disorder*. See also Ferguson, *Paper and Iron*. For vivid recollections, see Haffner, *Defying Hitler*, pp. 41ff.
237 **Nazi share of the vote leapt to seven times what it had been in 1928:** Jones, *German Liberalism*.
237 **to deal with so vast and universally perceptible a crisis:** James, *German Slump*. This was the critique advanced by Carl Schmitt in his influential essay 'The Crisis of Parliamentary Democracy' (1923).
237 **worthless cash that symbolized Weimar's bankruptcy:** Feldman, 'Weimar from Inflation to Deflation'.
237 **heart attack on October 3, 1929, at the age of just 51:** See Wright, *Stresemann*.
238 **election. Hitler duly became Chancellor on January 30, 1933:** For an excellent account of the crucial events, see Turner, *Hitler's Thirty Days*.
238 **New York so as to drive a rift between the Western creditors:** See Ritschl, *Deutschlands Krise und Konjunktur*.
239 **calculated physical intimidation of opponents:** Burleigh, *Third Reich*, p. 109.
239 **countryside, or of the North, or of the middle class:** For some early and by no means bad analysis, see Pollock, 'Areal Study'; Loomis and Beegle, 'Spread of German Nazism'.
239 **revealed the extraordinary breadth of the Nazi vote:** The definitive work is Falter, *Hitlers Wähler*.
239 **(region of East Prussia) scattered all over the country:** Noakes, *Nazi Party in Lower Saxony*; Pridham, *Hitler's Rise to Power*; Grill, *Nazi Movement in Baden*.
239 **Nazi votes were more likely to be in the south and west:** John O'Loughlin, Colin Flint and Luc Anselin, 'Geography of the Nazi Vote'.
239 **German electoral spectrum in a way not seen before or since:** O'Loughlin, 'Electoral Geography of Weimar Germany'.
240 **'To achieve this aim we are justified in using every means':** Fischer, *German Communists and the Rise of Nazism*, p. 107.
240 **'of a headwaiter closing his hand around the tip':** Reck-Malleczewen, *Diary*, p. 30.
240 **to dread subordination to an opinionated Austrian corporal:** Turner, *Big Business*.
241 **has made mistakes—to the gallows with him!:** Weber, *Max Weber*, p. 42.
241 **'Jews and their Bolshevism. God protect us!':** Housden, *Frank*, p. 34.
242 **By the 1940s his atelier was mass-producing busts of Hitler:** Petropoulos, *Faustian Bargain*.
242 **do a better job of bringing about an economic recovery:** Tooze, *Statistics and the German State*.
242 **expectancy of ten years—would be 885,439,800 marks:** Burleigh, *Death and Deliverance*, p. ix.
242 **justifications for German territorial claims in Eastern Europe:** Burleigh, *Germany Turns Eastwards*.
242 **unable to resist Hitler's 'Mass Machiavellianism':** Meinecke, *Deutsche Katastrophe*, ch. 5.
243 **greatness and power and glory and justice. Amen:** Burleigh, *Third Reich*, p. 153.
243 **'Adolf Hitler emerged as bearer of a new political religion':** ibid., p. 116.
244 **'He created . . . and in the Führer . . . whom He has sent us':** ibid., p. 194.
244 **'incompatible with the "heroic" ideology of our blood':** ibid., p. 259.
244 **new teaching was turned over to the executioner:** Reck-Malleczewen, *Diary*, p. 31.
245 **many were attracted to the Nazi notion of a new 'Positive Christianity':** Steigmann-Gall, *Holy Reich*.
245 **European economy had sunk so low between 1929 and 1932:** The recovery may have been even more impressive (as high as 90 per cent) or rather less (as low as 60 per cent), depending on which estimates are used. At any event, German growth was still the highest in Europe between 1932 and 1938: see Ritschl, 'Spurious Growth', table 7.
246 **schemes that had been initiated under Hitler's predecessors:** Tooze, *Wages of War*, chs. 1, 2. The role of rearmament has been controversial because a substantial part of the expenditure for military ends did not appear in the official Reich defence budget. According to Tooze's calculations, military spending accounted for 50 per cent of central government spending on goods and services in 1934, rising to 73 per cent the following year. I am grateful to the author for letting me read his book in manuscript.
246 **gross fixed investment, adjusted for inflation, was 29 per cent:** Ritschl, *Deutchlands Krise und Konjunktur*, table B.6. Cf. table B.7.
246 **(2 per cent in 1933 to more than 10 per cent in 1938):** ibid., tables A.12 and B.1.
247 **dramatic growth of employment that was achieved:** Having fallen by 37 per cent during the Depression, employment increased by 73 per cent between the first quarter of 1933 and the third quarter of 1938. Ibid., table C.1.
247 **average annual rate of just 1.2 per cent between 1933 and 1939:** ibid., table B.8.

247 22 per cent; the cost of living rose by just 7 per cent: Figures for wages from Bry, *Wages*.
248 clearing arrangements established with creditor countries: Tooze, *Wages of War*, ch. 3.
248 Germany was running trade deficits of unprecedented size during the 1930s: Ritschl, *Deutchlands Krise und Konjunktur*, tables B.4 and B.7.
248 per capita national income was roughly twice as high: Tooze, *Wages of War*, ch. 5. The best illustration of the difference is the Third Reich's failure to create a mass market for automobiles, despite Hitler's strong personal interest in the Volkswagen, the beetle-shaped design of which originated in a sketch by the Führer himself.
248 were unquestionably better off than Germans in 1933: For a more negative verdict on the Nazi economic recovery, see Evans, *Third Reich in Power*, pp. 322–413.
249 'Germans, valuable for the future': Hitler, *Mein Kampf*, Vol. II, ch. 15.
249 'eliminationist anti-Semitism' within the German population as a whole: Goldhagen, *Hitler's Willing Executioners*, esp. pp. 53ff.
249 striking decline in the Jewish birthrate to roughly half that of the rest of the population: Bachi, *Population Trends*, table 2. Had these trends continued, there would eventually have been no 'Jewish Question' in Germany, a point much discussed by Jewish leaders and commentators of the 1920s.
249 lawyers, doctors, academics, businessmen and so on: Noakes and Pridham (eds.), *Nazism*, vol. II, p. 522.
250 importunate; and no one could answer it: Wassermann, *My Life*, pp. 10ff, 18.
250 voices that cried a welcome or a warning: ibid., pp. 170, 180.
250 It reached a peak of more than a third in 1915: Meiring, *Christlich-jüdische Mischehe*, table 1.
250 and Leipzig as well as Breslau in Silesia: Ruppin, *Soziologie der Juden*, pp. 211ff.; Hanauer, 'Jüdische-christliche Mischehe', table 2 ; Della Pergola, *Jewish and Mixed Marriages*, pp. 122–7. Cf. Gay, *Jews of Germany*, pp. 182, 198, 254. By way of comparison, the comparable percentages for the US were roughly 20 per cent in 1950s and 52 per cent in 1990: Jones, *In the Blood*, pp. 158ff.
250 Amsterdam and Vienna lagged behind those in the major German cities: Ruppin, *Soziologie der Juden*, pp. 211ff. The statistics for Vienna are problematic: see Rozenblit, *Jews of Vienna*, pp. 127–31. As Oxaal has pointed out, counting only marriages between a Jew and a 'confessionless' non-Jew overlooks marriages between Gentiles and Jews who converted to Christianity in order to marry: Oxaal, 'Jews of Young Hitler's Vienna', p. 32. On Prague, see Cohen, *Politics of Ethnic Survival*, p. 135.
251 15,000 were partners in mixed marriages: Burleigh and Wippermann, *Racial State*, p. 110.
251 though the real figure lay between 60,000 and 125,000: Burgdörfer, 'Juden in Deutschland', p. 177. Cf. Rigg, *Hitler's Jewish Soldiers*, tables 2 and 3.
252 The mood . . . was one of extreme depression': Klemperer, *Diaries*, October 6, 1935.
252 'I have truly always felt German': ibid., March 17, 1933.
252 'Jews had advanced further there than anywhere else': Drucker, *Judenfrage in Deutschland*, p. 13.
252 in a passionate love affair with his Jewish student, Hannah Arendt?: Arendt and Heidegger, *Briefe*.
252 should be a court to condemn these Jews. [Applause.]: Evans, *Rituals of Retribution*, p. 626.
254 pre-War period can in the last analysis be reduced to racial causes: Hitler, *Mein Kampf*, vol. I, ch. 11: 'Nation and Race', pp. 283–99.
254 'Serbs and Croatians' and 'Jews and more Jews': Hitler, *Mein Kampf*, Vol. I, ch. 3. Cf. Hamann, *Hitlers Wien*.
254 ('under long dark eyelashes . . . [and] a squashed flat nose like an ape's'): Dinter, *Sünde wider das Blut*, p. 238.
255 it will come to grief in the foreseeable future: ibid., pp. 294, 303, 366.
255 Dinter's book had gone through 28 printings and sold 120,000 copies: Strack, *Jüdische Geheimgesetze*, p. 24.
255 strategy aimed at enfeebling the German race: Kernholt, *Vom Ghetto zur Macht*, esp. pp. 233ff.
255 preoccupation manifested itself in the nationalist press: See e.g., Hermann, *Doppelte Spiegel*, p. 28.
255 'Yesterday this horny Jew raped a little blonde girl': Michel, *Verrat*, p. 5.
255 1890s and beyond, was that Jews were involved in the white slave trade: Leers, *14 Jahre Judenrepublik*, vol. I, p. 34; Pappritz, *Mädchenhandel*; Berg, *Juden-Bordelle*.
255 even the fall of the Hohenzollern monarchy: Anon., *Semi-Imperator*, esp. pp. 13ff, 26, 62ff, 168.
255 marriages more or less fruitful than endogamous marriages?: See e.g., Marcuse, *Fruchtbarkeit der christlich-jüdischen Mischehe*. Cf. Rahden, 'Mingling, Marrying, and Distancing', p. 214.
255 of the German Volk if mixed marriages were not banned?: Leers, *14 Jahre Judenrepublik*, vol. II, p. 121.
255 target for Nazi attacks on 'Jewish morality': Burleigh and Wippermann, *Racial State*, pp. 182ff.
255 'between siblings, men and animals, and men and men': Tatar, *Lustmord*, pp. 56ff.
255 Karl Denke and Peter Kürten, 'the Düsseldorf vampire': ibid., pp. 41–64.
255 prostitutes in what would now be called the sex industry: Maurer, *Ostjuden*, pp. 109–19, 162–7. See also Kaplan, *Jüdische Frauenbewegung*.
256 'Black Disgrace' (schwarze Schmach): Lebzelter, ' "Schwarze Schmach" '.
256 racial aliens (*Volksfremde*) predated Hitler's accession to power: There was a parallel campaign against the Roma and Sinti peoples—known colloquially as 'gypsies' (Zigeuner). As early as 1930,

Frankfurt citizens were complaining about the 'sexual conduct' of gypsies living nearby: Burleigh and Wippermann, *Racial State,* p. 117.

256 to 'poison the blood' of the German Volk: 'It was and is Jews who bring the Negroes into the Rhineland, always with the same secret thought and clear aim of ruining the hated white race by the necessarily resulting bastardisation, throwing it down from its cultural and political height, and himself rising to be its master': Hitler, *Mein Kampf,* Vol. I, ch. 11.

256 date from the breakdown of his relationship with Janke: Reuth, *Goebbels,* pp. 39–53.

257 'youth and as men are prepared to die for': Padfield, *Himmler,* pp. 69, 81.

257 'of the Jew in her manner, at least so far as I can judge': ibid., p. 53.

257 his Jewish assistant Margarethe Landé: Weingart, *Doppel-Leben.*

257 allegedly lecherous 'attitude' towards 'German women': Burleigh and Wippermann, *Racial State,* p. 78.

257 German women who 'secretly or openly go with Jews': Plischke, *Jude als Rasseschänder.*

257 having tried to turn Germany into a 'racial mishmash': Kittel, *Historische Voraussetzung,* p. 44: 'Rassenmischmasch'.

258 A grin that says: 'Now I've got you at last, little German girl!': Noakes and Pridham (eds.), *Nazism,* vol. II, pp. 543ff. Streicher remained wedded to this kind of thinking until the bitter end: see Gilbert, *Nuremberg Diary,* pp. 43, 376. On Streicher's background, see Froschauer and Geyer, *Quellen des Hasses,* pp. 20–2. See also Ogan and Weiss, *Faszination und Gewalt,* p. 53. Jewish doctors were in fact prohibited from practicing as gynaecologists, specifically because of their allegedly lecherous 'attitude': Burleigh and Wippermann, *Racial State,* p. 78.

258 the heroine, the Irish wife of Rothschild's 'Aryan' rival Turner: Welch, *Propaganda,* p. 285. Cf. Kugelmann and Backhaus (eds.), *Jüdische Figure.*

258 'seen to have sexual intercourse with [his] Aryan maidservant': Sington and Weidenfeld, *Goebbels Experiment,* p. 86.

258 by a 'stunningly beautiful' Jewish-Bolshevik femme fatale: Theweleit, *Male Fantasies,* vol. I, pp. 76ff.

258 from office, followed a month later by university lecturers: At the insistence of Hindenburg, exceptions were made for all former Jewish front-line soldiers and any Jew holding government office when war was declared in 1914.

259 How long will I be able to retain my professorship?: Klemperer, *Diaries,* March 10, 1933.

259 romantic; now there is only bitterness and wretchedness: ibid., May 2, 1935.

260 public humiliation of women accused of sleeping with Jews: See e.g., Kulka, 'Nürnberger Rassengesetze', p. 594.

260 employers molesting their 'Aryan' female employees: Angress, ' "Judenfrage" im Spiegel amtlicher Berichte', p. 33.

260 'relations between Aryans and Jews should be punished': Noakes and Pridham (eds.), *Nazism,* vol. II, pp. 532ff.

260 'Women and Girls, the Jews Are Your Ruin': Goldhagen, *Hitler's Willing Excecutioners,* p. 96.

260 included imprisonment and hard labour: Noakes and Pridham (eds.), *Nazism,* vol. II, p. 534. Cf. Schleunes, *Twisted Road to Auschwitz,* pp. 121–5.

261 1,670 prosecutions for alleged 'racial defilement': Przyrembel, *Rassenschande,* table 3.

261 altogether 391 of those accused were convicted and jailed: Johe, 'Beteiligung der Justiz'. See also Gordon, *Hitler, Germans and the Jewish Question,* pp. 211–21.

261 90 per cent of those charged were found guilty: Robinsohn, *Justiz als politische Verfolgung,* p. 78, table 11.

261 sentenced to two and a half years' penal servitude: Noakes and Pridham (eds.), *Nazism,* vol. II, p. 540.

261 'the sexual urges of at least one of the partners': Noakes and Pridham (eds.), *Nazism,* vol. II, p. 541.

261 sophisticated system of discrimination and humiliation: See Robinsohn, *Justiz als politische Verfolgung.*

262 which numbered more than 840,000 in 1939: Gellately, 'Gestapo and German Society', p. 665.

262 watchful eye of between 12 and 14 Gestapo officers: Johnson, *Nazi Terror.*

262 (were in fact Jewish, so no charge could be pressed): Gellately, 'Gestapo and German Society', pp. 670–3.

263 was disproportionately directed against Jews: Johnson, *Nazi Terror.*

263 new law and was welcomed by the party rank-and-file at Nuremberg: Schleunes, *Twisted Road to Auschwitz,* p. 124; Noakes and Pridham (eds.), *Nazism,* vol. II, pp. 534ff.

264 physical as well as religious factors into account: Noakes and Pridham (eds.), *Nazism,* vol. II, pp. 537ff; Rubinstein et al., *Jews in the Modern World,* p. 213. Only one in ten Mischlinge belonged to the Jewish religious community: Burleigh, *Third Reich,* p. 295.

264 incentive for the non-Jewish wives in such cases to divorce their husbands: Noakes and Pridham (eds.), *Nazism,* vol. II, pp. 564ff.

264 German *Mischlinge* from being categorized as Jews: ibid., vol. IV, pp. 1127ff esp. 1132ff.

264 trimester for mentally ill women who became pregnant: Burleigh, 'Racial State Revisited', pp. 160ff.

265 simply wanted the killing to be carried out less obtrusively: Burleigh, *Death and Deliverance.*

265 of the Kaiser Wilhelm Institute for Anthropology, Heredity and Eugenics: Burleigh and Wippermann, *Racial State*, pp. 128ff.

265 Dangerous Habitual Criminals authorized the castration of sexual offenders: Burleigh, 'Racial State Revisited', pp. 161ff.

265 'so we will once again breed pure Nordic Germans': Cf. Werner, 'Darré', p. 57.

266 were cancelled if the wife produced four children: Burleigh, 'Racial State Revisited', p. 163.

267 number of instances, these concern radiant, good-looking men: Padfield, *Himmler*, p. 169.

267 located in around 15 delivery suites-cum-kindergartens: However, like other procreative aspects of the Nazi eugenic programme, it was a practical failure. No more than 7,500 children were produced. SS officers persistently had below the average number of children.

267 'be able to provide the whole of Europe with its ruling class': Noakes and Pridham (eds.), *Nazism*, vol. III, pp. 919ff.

268 Jewish-owned businesses in Germany declined from 40,000 to 15,000: Rubinstein et al., *Jews in the Modern World*, p. 215.

268 On November 9, 1938, at Hitler's instigation: See Goebbels's Diary: 'The Führer . . . decides: let the demonstrations keep going. . . . The Jews should be made to feel the wrath of the people. That is right. . . . The Führer has ordered 20–30,000 Jews to be arrested immediately. . . . The Führer is in accord with everything. His views are very radical and aggressive [and he] . . . wants to go ahead with very severe steps against the Jews.' Goebbels, *Tagebücher*, vol VI, pp. 180ff.

269 raises the spectre of the downfall of humanity: Haffner, *Defying Hitler*, pp. 116ff.

269 departed, of whom 20 were Nobel laureates: Rubinstein et al., *Jews in the Modern World*, pp. 211ff; Burleigh, *Third Reich*, p. 281.

269 less than 30 per cent of the pre-1933 figure: Rubinstein et al., *Jews in the Modern World*, pp. 215ff.

269 'the annihilation of the Jewish race in Europe!': ibid., p. 220.

270 'generations can be considered to be genuinely Aryan': Landau-Czajka, 'Image of Jew in Catholic Press', p. 165.

270 'features to the third or forth generation and beyond': ibid., pp. 165ff.

270 'war' on the Jews, before 'the Jewish rope' strangled Poland: Landau-Czajka, 'Image of Jew in Catholic Press', p. 174.

270 which would bring an 'end to the Jewish chapter of history': Hagen, 'Before the "Final Solution"', p. 368. On the similarities and differences between Germany and Poland, see Vital, *People Apart*, pp. 803ff.

270 in attacks; perhaps as many as thirty were killed: Mendelsohn, *Jews of East Central Europe*, p. 74; Rubinstein et al., *Jews in the Modern World*, p. 141; Wynot, '"Necessary Cruelty"', pp. 1037ff. For an example of how a boycott of Jewish businesses escalated into a pogrom, see Hoffman, *Shtetl*, pp. 197ff. See also Segel (ed.), *Stranger in Our Midst*, pp. 323, 331ff, on the events in Wilno (occasioned by a dispute over the religion of cadavers for dissection at the university's medical school), *Warsaw and Lwów*, and Blumstein, *Little House*, pp. 6ff., on the events in Grodno. Cf. Sieradzki, *Twist of History*, p.10; Bronsztejn, 'Polish-Jewish Relations'.

271 Jews commit fraud, usury, and are involved in trade in human beings: Vital, *People Apart*, p. 767.

271 inconvenience of the law banning work on Sundays: Rudnicki, 'Anti-Jewish Legislation', pp. 149–58.

271 who were declared to be 'alien' to Poland: Wynot, '"Necessary Cruelty"', pp. 1035ff; Rudnicki, 'Anti-Jewish Legislation', p. 160.

271 34 per cent of lawyers and 22 per cent of journalists: Rubinstein et al., *Jews in the Modern World*, pp. 142ff.

271 Białystok region in 1932 to just 50 per cent six years later: Mendelsohn, *Jews of East Central Europe*, pp. 74ff.

271 By 1937–8 their share of university enrolments had fallen to 7.5 per cent: Rudnicki, 'Anti-Jewish Legislation', p. 166.

271 to 'solve the Jewish question' by pressurizing Polish Jews into emigration: ibid., p. 167; Hagen, 'Before the "Final Solution"', p. 374.

272 and around a quarter were in receipt of charitable assistance: Vital, *People Apart*, pp. 775ff.

272 had pledged to 'destroy the Jews before they can destroy us': Vago, *Shadow of the Swastika*, p. 56; Glenny, *Balkans*, p. 448. Cf. Mendelsohn, *Jews of East Central Europe*, pp. 186ff, 204.

272 had also called for the extermination of the Jews: Vago, *Shadow of the Swastika*, p. 59.

272 the Jews were like 'leprosy' or 'eczema': ibid., p. 55.

272 No, you are a Jew: Sebastian, *Journal*.

272 introduction of quotas for business and the professions: Mendelsohn, *Jews of East Central Europe*, pp. 206ff.

272 not significantly improve the situation of the Romanian Jews: Vago, *Shadow of the Swastika*, pp. 43, 49ff.

272 citizenship on the ground that they were illegal immigrants: Mendelsohn, *Jews of East Central Europe*, p. 207.

273 stoned if left alone in the streets of Szombathely: Levi, *Cat Called Adolf*, p. 47.

273 all introduced other kinds of restriction by 1932: Hatton and Williamson, 'International Migration'.

274 a single 'negro' great-grandparent made a person black: Pascoe, 'Miscegenation Law', p. 59. The literature is very extensive: see most recently Moran, *Interracial Intimacy*; Robinson, *Dangerous Liaisons*; Kennedy, *Interracial Intimacies*; Wallenstein, *'Tell the Court I Love My Wife'*.
274 a case of miscegenation in 1930s Montgomery?: Novkov, 'Racial Constructions' shows that the amount of appellate litigation reached its historic peak in the years 1935–44 (see figure 1).
274 mixed marriage in Dresden and to be in one in Dixie?: Bynum, ' "White Negroes" '.
274 new society with the communal kibbutz as its building brick: Figures from Mendelsohn, *Jews of Eastern Europe*, p. 79; Vital, *People Apart*, p. 780
274 'took to Zionism like a drowning person to a board': Mendelsohn, *Jews of East Central Europe*, p. 78.
275 resembling order as the mandate slid towards full-blown civil war: Colville, *Man of Valour*, p. 107. See in general Sherman, *Mandate Days*, pp. 83–126.
275 'concern the world—will be forced to act accordingly': Klemperer, *Diary*, quoted in Burleigh, *Third Reich*, p. 340.
275 no more than 500 families could realistically be settled there: Burleigh, *Third Reich*, pp. 586–96.
275 in Romania, in the hope of getting to Turkey or Palestine: Rosen, *My Lost World*, p. 238.
275 Jews 'were just another group of nakonings, foreigners': Heppner, *Shanghai Refuge*, p. 42.

## CHAPTER EIGHT: AN INCIDENTAL EMPIRE

277 ethics that the English Constitution does in political history: Nitobe, *Bushido*, p. 35
277 Do you suppose that they all go mad?: King, *China and the League of Nations*, p. 53.
279 The German economy must be fit for war within four years: Treue, 'Hitlers Denkschrift'.
281 'demands or in the level of war readiness': Tooze, *Wages of War*, ch. 7.
282 50 per cent more arable land per agricultural worker: ibid., table 4.
283 Royal Dutch/Shell and the successors to Standard Oil: See Yergin, *The Prize*.
284 a Canadian monopoly; molybdenum an American one: *Economist*, October 1, 1938, pp. 25ff.
284 but before the 1930s needed to import all its rubber and oil: Tooze, *Wages of War*, appendix 2.
284 55 per cent of its steel and 45 per cent of its iron: Boyd, 'Japanese Military Effectiveness', p. 143.
284 the Soviet-controlled island of Sakhalin: Coox, 'Effectiveness of the Japanese Military Establishment', p. 19.
286 around a century and a half behind, if not more: Yasuba, 'Shortage of Natural Resources', p. 545. Cf. Maddison, *World Economy*, table B-21.
286 'and the downfall of China means the downfall of Japan': Duus, 'Japan's Informal Empire', p. xxvi.
287 'but with a very exaggerated opinion of her own role': Harries, *Soldiers of the Sun*, pp. 108ff.
287 'the Dutch East Indies, Singapore, and the Malay States': Saxon, 'Anglo-Japanese Naval Cooperation', n.p.
287 'their control over most of the world's wealth': Macmillan, *Peacemakers*, p. 320. On the reasons for the post-war convergence of British and American policy in Asia, see Kennedy, *Realities Behind Diplomacy*, pp. 260–3.
288 naval arms limitation agreed at Washington the year before: Nish, 'Historical Significance of the Anglo-Japanese Alliance'.
288 U.S. Navy identified Japan as America's 'most likely enemy' in a future war: Saxon, 'Anglo-Japanese Naval Cooperation', n.p.
288 explicitly directed against (among others) the Japanese: Kimitada, 'Japanese Images of War with the United States', pp. 115ff.
288 Truk in the Carolines into their main South Pacific naval base: Macmillan, *Peacemakers*, p. 325.
288 inexorable march to war leading from 1919 to 1941: As is sometimes implied: see e.g., Hata, 'Continental Expansion'. The definitive work is Iriye, *Origins of the Second World War in Asia*.
288 Naval bases in southern Sakhalin and Formosa: Boyd, 'Japanese Military Effectiveness', p. 142.
288 The standing army numbered 250,000 men: ibid., p. 134.
288 'existence, friendship and co-operation': Harries, *Soldiers of the Sun*, p. 112.
289 army chief of staff is a mark of the confidence of the civilians at this time: Hata, 'Continental Expansion', p. 284.
289 exports that were the key to Japan's rising prosperity in the 1920s: Yasuba, 'Shortage of Natural Resources', pp. 551ff.
289 happened. Both monarch and military grew more powerful: Details in Lu, *From the Marco Polo Bridge*, pp. 8–13.
290 reborn as a living god on November 14, 1928: Buruma, *Inventing Japan*, p. 64.
290 teeth and the claws of the Royal House': Coox, 'Effectiveness of the Japanese Military Establishment', p. 35.
290 or spirits housed at the Yasukuni shrine in Tokyo: Harries, *Soldiers of the Sun*, p. 18; Shillony, *Politics and Culture*, pp. 135ff.
290 argued, the cousin of Anglo-French chivalry: Nitobe, *Bushido*. I am grateful to my student Yusuke Watanabe for encouraging me to read this important book. Cf. Edgerton, *Warriors of the Rising Sun*, pp. 322ff.

NOTES

290 to march 25 miles a day for 15 days with just 4 days' rest: Harries, *Soldiers of the Sun*, pp. 140–4.
291 norm even for minor breaches of discipline: ibid., pp. 411ff.
291 that made the Japanese Army ... so formidable': Coox, 'Effectiveness of the Japanese Military Establishment', p. 36. The words are General William Slim's.
291 lists of the national resources that would need to be mobilized: Harries, *Soldiers of the Sun*, pp. 112ff.
292 the Guomindang along Marxist-Leninist lines: Fenby, *Generalissimo*, p. 61.
293 Japan's long-serving Foreign Minister Shidehara Kijūrō: Lin, 'Chinese Nationalist Appeasers', pp. 212ff.
293 enemies always seemed to take priority over foreign ones: Coble, *Facing Japan*, pp. 3ff.
293 trade unionists and other suspected Communist members: Fenby, *Generalissimo*, pp. 146–50.
293 the reality of Guomindang rule was rampant graft: ibid., p. 246.
293 director of the Opium Suppression Bureau in Shanghai: ibid., p. 231.
293 Guomindang pressure on British concessions up the Yangtze: Bickers, *Empire Made Me*, p. 177.
293 Shandong to protect Japanese assets from Chiang's forces: Hata, 'Continental Expansion', pp. 287ff; Lin, 'Chinese Nationalist Appeasers', pp. 217ff; Coble, *Facing Japan*, p. 18.
294 Japanese interests in China than by their differences: Iriye, *Origins of the Second World War in Asia*, p. 4. In 1933 Japan's share of total Chinese imports stood at 9.7 per cent, compared with 8 per cent for Germany, 11.4 per cent for Britain and 22 per cent for the United States: Endicott, *Diplomacy and Enterprise*, p. 186. Significantly, however, the Japanese had by now overtaken the British as the most numerous group of foreigners in Shanghai: Davidson Houston, *Yellow Creek*, p. 122. Moreover, Japan's share of Chinese imports grew rapidly, overtaking Britain's in 1934.
294 hampered the development of China's own institutions: See Goetzmann, 'China and the World Financial Markets'.
295 intra-Asian trade doubled between 1913 and 1938: Sugihara, 'Economic Motivations', p. 260.
295 Chinese imports, a share second only to that of the United States: Endicott, *Diplomacy and Enterprise*, p. 186.
295 about restricting Japanese access to imperial markets in the 1930s: ibid., p. 179.
296 iron ore and cotton, and one-third of her imports of pig iron: Neidpath, *Singapore Naval Base*, p. 136.
296 the USA and the Charybdis of dependence on British empire markets': Sugihara, 'Economic Motivations', p. 267. See also ibid., tables 2, 3.
296 imminent crisis and pave the way for a big jump: Yasuba, 'Shortage of Natural Resources', p. 553n. Cf. Hata, 'Continental Expansion', p. 292.
296 pressure on domestic wages and consumption: Yasuba, 'Shortage of Natural Resources', p. 555 and table 5.
297 ore to feed the nascent Japanese military-industrial complex: ibid., p. 555.
297 market and the imports of raw materials' became: Sugihara, 'Economic Motivations', p. 275.
297 responsibility for law and order' throughout the province: Iriye, *Origins of the Second World War in Asia*, p. 8.
298 in the hope of precipitating a Japanese takeover of Mukden: Hata, 'Continental Expansion', pp. 288ff.
298 of a Japanese officer accused of spying in Mongolia: Coble, *Facing Japan*, pp. 22–7.
298 had emphasized strategy over tactics and operations: Fujiwara, 'Role of the Japanese Army', p. 193.
298 Prince Saionji Kimmochi, was to rein in the soldiers: Harries, *Soldiers of the Sun*, pp. 123ff.
299 Japanese capital ships to cruisers, destroyers and submarines: Iriye, *Origins of the Second World War in Asia*, pp. 5–7; Crowley, *Japan's Quest for Autonomy*, pp. 385ff; Boyd, 'Japanese Military Effectiveness', p. 145.
299 new societies like Issekikai (the One Evening Society): See Humphreys, *Way of the Heavenly Sword*.
299 Army and denounced Wakatsuki as a weakling: Crowley, *Japan's Quest for Autonomy*, pp. 379ff, 387ff. Cf. Ogata, *Defiance in Manchuria*, pp. xiii–xvi; Iriye, *Origins of the Second World War in Asia*, pp. 8–10.
299 him between 1932 and 1945, only four were civilians: Buruma, *Inventing Japan*, p. 70.
300 service ministers wielded an unquestioned veto power: Crowley, *Japan's Quest for Autonomy*, pp. 381ff, 389ff.
300 the principal exponents of 'informal imperialism': Duus, 'Japan's Informal Empire in China', p. xxiv.
300 a total of just under 5.9 billion yen was invested there: Sugihara, 'Economic Motivations', table 4.
300 'excessive profit and all other unjust economic pressure': Hata, 'Continental Expansion', p. 297; Ogata, *Defiance in Manchuria*, pp. 180–5.
300 a laboratory for experiments too radical to be carried out at home: On the ethos of those responsible for the takeover of Manchuria, see Feuerwerker, 'Japanese Imperialism in China', p. 432ff.
300 though inferior in quality, substantially outnumbered the Japanese: Coble, *Facing Japan*, pp. 11–17.
301 that he would be able to restrain the Japanese military: Lin, 'Chinese Nationalist Appeasers', p. 225.
301 It failed to resolve just eleven conflicts: Hinsley, *Power and the Pursuit of Peace*, p. 315.
301 and to withdraw all Soviet forces to the Amur River: Hata, 'Continental Expansion', pp. 296ff.

NOTES

301 **at a time when both were reeling from severe financial crises:** See for the U.S. side of the story Graebner, 'Introduction', p. x. Cf. Iriye, *Origins of the Second World War in Asia*, pp. 18–20.
301 **'of Japanese nationals is effectively assured':** King, *China and the League of Nations*, p. 14.
301 **Manchuria's south-western frontier with China proper:** Iriye, *Origins of the Second World War in Asia*, p. 14.
302 **to maintain the Open Door system in China:** King, *China and the League of Nations*, p. 27.
302 **was only ratified by Tokyo after a six-month delay:** Ogata, *Defiance in Manchuria*, pp. 177ff.
302 **'and occupy[ing] . . . what was indisputably Chinese territory':** King, *China and the League of Nations*, pp. 42–6, 50–4.
302 **A week's fighting added Rehe to Japan's domain:** Coble, *Facing Japan*, pp. 90–5.
302 **finally announced their intention to withdraw—from the League:** King, *China and the League of Nations*, pp. 55–61. The announcement in March 1933 gave notice of Japan's intention to withdraw two years later. In March 1935 she did so.
302 **which the Japanese were soon running on an informal basis:** Coble, *Facing Japan*, pp. 111ff.
303 **leading ultimately to a truce on the basis of the status quo ante:** Dilks, ' "Unnecessary War" ', pp. 105ff.; King, *China and the League of Nations*, pp. 30–4; Coble, *Facing Japan*, pp. 39–50. See also Davidson Houston, *Yellow Creek*, p. 139.
303 **had good reason to avoid a military showdown with Japan:** In the words of Sir Francis Lindley, the British ambassador in Tokyo, Japan was 'the only nation in the Far East whose future is, as far as we can judge, reasonably assured and whose power to injure us is almost unbounded'. In his view, Britain should 'examine critically the advantages likely to be gained by following a line laid down by America which, like England in the days of Palmerston, is so invulnerable that she can with perfect impunity indulge the loftiest sentiments of humanity where her own interests are not involved': Parker, *Chamberlain*, p. 39. See also Lowe, *Great Britain and the Origins of the Pacific War*, p. 6ff.
303 **of power in the Americas—in effect, an Asian Monroe Doctrine:** Iriye, *Origins of the Second World War in Asia*, pp. 22ff; Coble, *Facing Japan*, pp. 153–60. Cf. Kimitada, 'Japanese Images of War', p. 129.
393 **in 1936 a Chinese-German trade agreement was signed:** Iriye, *Origins of the Second World War in Asia*, pp. 24ff; Coble, *Facing Japan*, p. 161. Cf. Barber and Hensall, *Last War of Empires*, pp. 183–6.
303 **taking it off the silver standard and pegging it to sterling:** Iriye, *Origins of the Second World War in Asia*, pp. 31–4.
304 **and to build up its defences in Eastern Siberia:** ibid., pp. 29ff. Cf. Barnhart, 'Japanese Intelligence', pp. 430ff.
304 **anti-Japanese indoctrination by the local Chinese commander:** Coble, *Facing Japan*, pp. 175ff, 245ff.
304 **in other words under Japanese rather than Chinese control:** ibid., pp. 195ff, 199–212, 241–52.
304 **was the turn of Beihai in southern Kwantung:** ibid., pp. 317ff, 320ff.
304 **Communists from their Kiangsi stronghold:** ibid., pp. 57, 101ff, 179.
305 **strategy came close to splitting the Guomindang itself:** Lin, 'Chinese Nationalist Appeasers', pp. 228ff.
305 **army reinforcements had averted a Japanese humiliation:** The Chinese suffered disproportionate losses because of their inferior firepower. The Chinese lost 4,086 soldiers, with a further 10,000 wounded. Civilian losses may have been as high as 20,000. The Japanese lost 769 men and around 2,300 wounded: Coble, *Facing Japan*, pp. 47ff.
305 **Suiyuan in November-December 1936 was actually repulsed:** Coble, *Facing Japan*, pp. 327ff.
305 **and from which China would emerge transformed:** ibid., p. 153. Cf. ibid., pp. 182ff.
306 **fighting broke out in the nearby town of Wanp'ing:** Hata, 'Continental Expansion', p. 303; Coble, *Facing Japan*, p. 370; Buruma, *Inventing Japan*, p. 82.
306 **northern China and an additional two for Shanghai and Tsingtao:** Hata, 'Continental Expansion', p. 305. Cf. Li, *Japanese Army*, pp. 4, 15n; Barnhart, 'Japanese Intelligence', pp. 433ff.
306 **a step in the direction of a Greater Manchukuo:** Dreyer, *China at War*, pp. 210ff.
306 **be no further diminutions of Chinese sovereignty:** Coble, *Facing Japan*, p. 373ff.
306 **General Headquarters decreed a general mobilization:** Hata, 'Continental Expansion', pp. 305ff.
307 **reported to the Emperor that 'the war could be ended within a month':** Katsumi, 'Politics of War', p. 290.
307 **Japanese hands, and all China's ports north of Hangzhou:** Dreyer, *China at War*, pp. 215–24.
307 **and an air division—around 850,000 men in all:** Coox, *Pacific War*, p. 319ff.
307 **nothing more than the chimerical products of wishful thinking:** Katsumi, 'Politics of War', pp. 291ff.
308 **probably best understood as a bid for power by a faction within the army:** For differing interpretations see Iriye, *Origins of the Second World War in Asia*, pp. 32ff; Crowley, *Japan's Quest for Autonomy*, pp. 384ff; Jansen, *Japan and China*, pp. 390ff.
309 **landing an amphibious strike force at Chinshanwei, to the Chinese rear:** Dreyer, *China at War*, pp. 216–9. Cf. Farmer, *Shanghai Harvest*, pp. 34, 37, 48, 84; Davidson Houston, *Yellow Creek*, p. 154.
310 **'the death-knell of the supposed moral superiority of the Occident'?:** Fenby, *Generalissimo*, p. 304.
310 **the cuisine, the music, and, if necessary, even the girls:** Farmer, *Shanghai Harvest*, pp. 57ff.
310 **response in London was impotent hand-wringing:** Lu, *From the Marco Polo Bridge*, p. 19.
310 **'We avoid entering into alliance or entangling commitments':** ibid., pp. 18–21.

## CHAPTER NINE: DEFENDING THE INDEFENSIBLE

312 then we could have averted this dire calamity: Londonderry, *Ourselves and Germany*, p. 140.

312 We must go on being cowards up to our limit, but not beyond: Dilks (ed.), *Cadogan Diaries*, p. 102.

313 forty-five years ago in *The Origins of the Second World War*: 'The cause of the war was . . . as much the blunders of others as the wickedness of the dictators. . . . Far from being premeditated, [it] was a mistake': Taylor, *Origins*, pp. 136, 269.

313 'for all that was best and most enlightened in British life': Taylor, *Origins*, p. 235.

313 'ministry, and indeed of virtually all Germans': ibid., p. 97.

313 World War was 'a repeat performance of the First': ibid., p. 41.

314 positions within little more than a year of coming to power: Kershaw, 'Nazi Foreign Policy', pp. 129–32.

315 belatedly and (as the Somme proved) at a painfully high cost: Ferguson, *Pity of War*, passim.

316 outbreak of war by the might of Hermann Göring's Luftwaffe: Wark, 'British Intelligence', p. 627.

316 possible deluge of 3,500 tons on the first day of war: Howard, *Continental Commitment*, p. 111. Cf. Overy, 'Air Power and the Origins of Deterrence Theory'.

316 'you think of the Rhine. That is where our frontier lies': Parker, *Chamberlain and Appeasement*, p. 20.

316 his Foreign Ministry and the German navy—in June 1935: ibid., pp. 30–3; Kershaw, 'Nazi Foreign Policy', p. 132. The agreement entitled Germany to build a navy a third the size of the Royal Navy (to be precise, with tonnage up to 35 per cent of the British total). Here again Hitler broke with past German foreign policy. Both the Foreign Ministry and the Navy opposed the low ratio of German tonnage Hitler was prepared to concede.

316 'an almost touching solicitude for the welfare of the British Empire': Parker, *Chamberlain and Appeasement*, p. 25.

317 'desirability of demolishing the British Empire': See Charmley, *Churchill*.

317 other than Churchill had been in charge of British policy: The argument was perhaps most famously made by the historian and politician Alan Clark in a newspaper article in *The Times*, January 2, 1993. It also underlies John Charmley's critique of Churchill (*The End of Glory*), which Clark's article purported to review.

317 costs of intervention proved to be very high: Ferguson, *Pity of War*.

318 why he and his colleagues took the decision as they did: See e.g., Dilks, ' "Unnecessary War" '; Aster, ' "Guilty Men"?'; Carlton, 'Against the Grain'; Charmley, *Chamberlain and the Lost Peace*.

318 appeasement have a better prima facie case: See e.g., Gilbert and Gott, *Appeasers*.

319 potential threat posed by Hitler, they had four to choose from: For some different analytical frameworks, see Walker, 'Appeasement Puzzle'; Parker, *Chamberlain and Appeasement*, pp. 22ff.

319 of a disturbance of the peace, we shall be the losers: Woodward and Butler (eds.), *Documents on British Foreign Policy*, series 1A, vol. I, pp. 846ff.

320 'prevent others from taking it away from us': Quoted in Endicott, *Diplomacy and Enterprise*, p. 176.

320 'cannot alone act as the policemen of the world': Haigh and Morris, *Munich*, p. 21.

320 'nor Mesopotamia, nor Persia, nor India': Kennedy, *Realities Behind Diplomacy*, p. 250.

320 'communications open in the event of our being drawn into a war': ibid., p. 278.

320 'Dominions and our vast trade and shipping, lies open': Howard, *Continental Commitment*, p. 97. See also Dunbabin, 'British Rearmament', p. 587.

321 'Empire during the first few months of the war': Howard, *Continental Commitment*, p. 104.

321 'including those of India, Australia and New Zealand': Parker, *Chamberlain and Appeasement*, p. 37.

321 from Australia, Canada, New Zealand and South Africa: Ellis and Cox, *World War I Databook*, pp. 245ff.

321 accounted for more than two-fifths of total exports: Mitchell and Jones, *Second Abstract of British Historical Statistics*, pp. 130, 136–140.

321 borrowers; ten years later the proportion was 86 per cent: Cain and Hopkins, *British Imperialism*, p. 439.

321 Empire never seemed so important to Britain as it did in the 1930s: See Meyers, 'British Imperial Interests', pp. 344–7.

321 in the event of a second great European conflict: Kennedy, *Realities Behind Diplomacy*, pp. 248ff. In the words of Malcolm MacDonald, the Dominions Secretary, South Africa and Canada would not fight to 'prevent certain Germans rejoining the Fatherland': Howard, *Continental Commitment*, p. 100. Cf. Ovendale, '*Appeasement*' and the English Speaking World.

321 'ability to secure our Empire and its communications': Howard, *Continental Commitment*, p. 102.

322 danger of German aggression against any vital interest of ours: Bond, *British Military Policy*, p. 235.

322 Belgian-German borders as they had been redrawn at Versailles: There were in fact three treaties and two conventions signed under the heading of the First Protocol of the Locarno Conference. The most important was the Treaty of Mutual Guaranty Between Germany, Belgium, France, Great Britain and Italy. Article 4, clause 3, clearly bound the United Kingdom to 'come to the help' of France in the event of German aggression, including the remilitarization of the Rhineland.

322 not followed up by meaningful military contingency planning: See Dilks, '"Unnecessary War"', p. 103.

322 Locarno seemed to imply that 'Splendid isolation had come again': Taylor, *English History*, p. 222.

322 The answer was: None: See Parker, *Chamberlain and Appeasement*, pp. 16–19. See also Parker, 'Economics, Rearmament, and Foreign Policy', p. 639.

322 Belgium was arguably less binding than it had been in 1914: Belgium reverted to her pre-1914 neutrality in October 1936: Haigh and Morris, *Munich: Peace of Delusion*, p. 7.

322 'our "long range" defence policy must be directed': Howard, *Continental Commitment*, pp. 105ff; Dilks, '"Unnecessary War"', pp. 109–12.

323 almost exactly as few as there had been in 1914: Howard, *Continental Commitment*, pp. 106–10, 113ff.

323 expeditionary force for use only in imperial trouble-spots: Dunbabin, 'British Rearmament', p. 602.

323 'to put the continental commitment last': Howard, *Continental Commitment*, pp. 116ff.

323 Military Operations and Intelligence, was appalled, but overruled: Bond (ed.), *Chief of Staff*, pp. 121ff.

323 budget was actually cut in the wake of the Austrian Anschluss: Shay, *British Rearmament*, pp. 199ff.

323 no better by the time of the Munich Crisis: Bond (ed.), *Chief of Staff*, pp. 156ff.

323 composed of just six regular and four territorial divisions: Dunbabin, 'British Rearmament', p. 603.

323 'striking power that no-one will care to run risks with it': Charmley, *Chamberlain and the Lost Peace*, p. 23. See also Aster, ' "Guilty Men"?', pp. 67ff; Dunbabin, 'British Rearmament', p. 590.

324 assumed that Hitler would fear their bombers equally: Howard, *Continental Commitment*, pp. 107–10. See in general, Lee, ' "I See Dead People" '.

324 inflict casualties on the population of the capital: See Watt, 'British Intelligence', pp. 255–8; Wark, 'British Intelligence', pp. 627–9, 642ff. Cf. Parker, *Churchill and Appeasement*, p. 134.

324 that trying to hit German industrial targets would be too costly: Howard, *Continental Commitment*, pp. 111ff.

324 Watson-Watt at the National Physical Laboratory as early as 1935: Coghlan, 'Armaments, Economic Policy and Appeasement', pp. 205ff. Watson-Watt did not himself invent radar, the credit for which should probably go to Nikola Tesla. But it was Watson-Watt who made radar into an effective tool for air defence.

324 vulnerability that they did not even dare fight the Italian navy: Howard, *Continental Commitment*, pp. 102ff; Kennedy, *Realities Behind Diplomacy*, pp. 283ff.

324 'of mutually assumed military collaboration': Howard, *Continental Commitment*, p. 118; Colville, *Gort*, p. 108.

325 more than two fifths of public expenditure in the late 1920s: Figures for the national debt kindly supplied by Professor Charles Goodhart. Figures for gross domestic product are taken from Feinstein, *National Income, Statistical Tables*, table 3. Debt service is from Flora et al., *State, Economy and Society*, pp. 381ff.

325 services and shipping were also under pressure: Kennedy, *Realities Behind Diplomacy*, pp. 226–30.

325 proportion were either killed or incapacitated: Greasley and Oxley, 'Discontinuities in Competitiveness'.

325 1913 to just over 10 per cent twenty years later: Kennedy, *Realities behind Diplomacy*, pp. 239ff.

325 'I give you my word that there will be no great armaments': Mowat, *Britain Between the Wars*, p. 553.

325 against significant increases in the defence budget: Howard, *Continental Commitment*, p. 98.

326 identification of Germany as the biggest potential danger: Dilks, ' "Unnecessary War" ', pp. 109–12.

326 by the fact that it looked cheaper than the alternative: Howard, *Continental Commitment*, pp. 108ff.

326 on cutting the spending bids for the navy and the army: Newton, *Profits of Peace*, pp. 67ff.

326 'of peaceful victory which would be most gratifying to him': Kennedy, 'Tradition of British Appeasement', p. 233. See in general Peden, *British Rearmament and the Treasury*.

326 requests of the Army and Navy for additional funds: Shay, *British Rearmament*, pp. 282ff.

326 tried to cover the increased costs by raising taxes: Coghlan, 'Armaments, Economic Policy and Appeasement', p. 213; Newton, ' "Anglo-German" Connection', p. 304; Thomas, 'Rearmament', p. 560. See also Dilks, ' "Unnecessary War" ', p. 117.

326 April 1942 should be capped at £1,500 million: Parker, 'Treasury, Trade Unions and Skilled Labour', p. 312.

326 domestic inflation and a widening current account deficit: See in general Newton, *Profits of Peace*, and Wendt, *Economic Appeasement*; Shay, *British Rearmament*.

327 an echo of the old, failed maxim of 'Business as Usual': Shay, *British Rearmament*, pp. 207, 211–6. See also Dunbabin, 'British Rearmament', p. 600.

327 position, her gold reserves and the strength of sterling: Peden, 'Question of Timing'. Cf. Parker, 'Economics, Rearmament, and Foreign Policy', pp. 637ff.

327 matching tax increases or cuts in other government programs: Coghlan, 'Armaments, Economic Policy and Appeasement', pp. 205–9.

327 First World War, with severe taxation of consumption: Keynes, *How to Pay for the War*.

327 'the second is the shortage of foreign resources': Parker, 'Treasury, Trade Unions and Skilled Labour', p. 317.

328  problem not only in engineering but in construction: Thomas, 'Rearmament', p. 562.
328  balance of payments was 'the key to the whole position': Peden, 'Sir Warren Fisher', p. 34.
328  they would probably have stimulated growth: Thomas, 'Rearmament', p. 571.
329  Engineering Union by 'diluting' the skilled labour force: Parker, 'Treasury, Trade Unions and Skilled Labour', pp. 328–43.
329  on the contrary, wage differentials narrowed: Thomas, 'Rearmament', pp. 564ff, 567, 570.
329  'to man the enlarged Navy, the new Air Force, and a million-man Army': Howard, *Continental Commitment*, p. 135; Dunbabin, 'British Rearmament', p. 598.
329  stock of overseas assets worth £3.7 billion ($17 billion): Calculated from Mitchell, *Abstract of British Historical Statistics*, pp. 333ff.
331  potential enemies and to gain the support of potential allies: Kennedy, 'Tradition of British Appeasement', p. 205; Shay, *British Rearmament*, p. 175; Dunbabin, 'British Rearmament', p. 596.
331  psychological effects of which were anything but healthy: Adamthwaite, 'France and the Coming of War', pp. 79ff.
331  more concessions to the Germans on armament levels: Parker, *Chamberlain and Appeasement*, pp. 21–5. Arms limitation agreements in the context of 1935 were inherently asymmetrical, despite endless references to 'equality'. They always implied some worsening of the French position relative to the post-Versailles arrangements. See also Jordan, 'Cut Price War'.
331  overseas were necessary if peace were to be preserved: Adamthwaite, 'France and the Coming of War', pp. 81ff.
331  Chamberlain among them, on ideological grounds: Lammers, *Explaining Munich*, pp. 8–24.
331  to be drawn from his own analysis of the situation: Thompson, *Anti-Appeasers*, p. 39.
331  ignored all inducements to negotiate a settlement: Parker, *Chamberlain and Appeasement*, pp. 22, 29ff; Walker, 'Appeasement Puzzle', p. 226. See also Charmley, *Chamberlain and the Lost Peace*, p. 22; Dunbabin, 'British Rearmament', pp. 594ff.
331  Hitler out of the Rhineland. They did neither: Parker, *Chamberlain and Appeasement*, pp. 60–8; Walker, 'Appeasement Puzzle', pp. 230–4.
332  continue until the outbreak of war: Goldstein, 'Chamberlain', p. 279.
332  support for France in the event of a continental war: Parker, *Churchill and Appeasement*, p. 156; Weinberg, 'French Role', pp. 24ff.
332  cowardice of Georges Bonnet his Foreign Minister: Weinberg, 'French Role', p. 24.
332  out Hitler's terms for a general peace settlement: Marks, 'Six between Roosevelt and Hitler', pp. 970ff; Offner, 'United States and National Socialist Germany', pp. 247ff.
332  ambitious multilateral approach to trade liberalization: Schröder, 'Ambiguities of Appeasement', p. 392. See also Offner, 'Appeasement Revisited', p. 375.
333  Britain and far more than the $46 million in France: Offner, 'Appeasement Revisited', pp. 374ff.
333  Chamberlain concluded that Americans were 'a nation of cads': Parker, *Chamberlain and Appeasement*, p. 44.
333  'nothing from the Americans except words': Dilks, ' "Unnecessary War" ', p. 120.
333  for a general great-power conference in 1938: See Marks, 'Six between Roosevelt and Hitler', pp. 973ff; Offner, 'United States and National Socialist Germany', pp. 251ff.
333  'gets 80 per cent of the deal and you get what is left': Offner, 'United States and National Socialist Germany', p. 246.
333  Hitler a free hand in Central and Eastern Europe: Offner, 'Appeasement Revisited', pp. 376ff; Marks, 'Six between Roosevelt and Hitler', pp. 974ff.
333  ambition to see the British Empire broken up: See Ferguson, *Empire*, ch. 6.
333  the standard of living and reduction of the social services: Shay, *British Rearmament*, p. 201.
335  were only a minority, even within the Labour Party: At its conference in October 1934, the Labour Party had been more divided. The notion supporting the possibility of enforcing collective security by force was supported by 1,500,000 votes, but opposed by 673,000. But by the following year, the Italian invasion of Abyssinia had stiffened the trade union vote; only 100,000 votes were now cast against. In Parliament the party took the line that it was in favour of armaments for the purpose of collective security, but not for national defence. The Liberal position was similar: Parker, *Chamberlain and Appeasement*, pp. 308–15.
335  'no candidate for Parliament dares oppose it openly': Kennedy, *Realities Behind Diplomacy*, p. 244.
335  collective military action if these were not effective: Parker, *Chamberlain and Appeasement*, pp. 45ff, 307ff.
335  deal to give a large chunk of Abyssinia to the Italians: Haigh and Morris, *Munich: Peace of Delusion*, p. 24; Parker, *Chamberlain and Appeasement*, pp. 50–5; Howard, *Continental Commitment*, pp. 102ff.
336  and the Germans had marched into the Rhineland: Parker, *Chamberlain and Appeasement*, pp. 55ff.
336  'Countries falling into the hands of such a Power': Thompson, *Anti-Appeasers*, p. 47.
336  Czechoslovakia 'could be done in a month by wireless': Adamthwaite, 'British Government and the Media', p. 293.
336  the moment Chamberlain became Prime Minister: Crowson, *Facing Fascism*, p. 83.
336  A third said yes and a quarter had no opinion: Adamthwaite, 'British Government and the Media', pp. 291ff.

336 'his view represents the view of the majority of the nation': Parker, *Churchill and Appeasement*, p. 144.

336 to all parties, and I had seen many people: Henderson to Halifax, September 1, 1938, in Woodward and Butler (eds.), *Documents on British Foreign Policy*, Series 3, vol. II, p. 203.

337 only around £40 million being liquidated by 1939: Forbes, 'London Banks', pp. 574ff, 583ff.

337 would prosper if they were sufficiently rewarded: Newton, ' "Anglo-German" Connection', pp. 296–300; MacDonald, 'Economic Appeasement and the German "Moderates" '.

337 'possibilities as a stepping stone to political appeasement': Quoted in Schröder, 'Ambiguities of Appeasement', p. 391.

337 German firms importing goods from Britain: Wendt, ' "Economic Appeasement" ', p. 168; Forbes, 'London Banks', pp. 581ff.

337 bills and a further £80 or £90 million of long-term debts: Newton, ' "Anglo-German" Connection', p. 298.

337 1937 and was dismissed as Reichsbank President in January 1939: Brown and Burdekin, 'German Debt'.

338 trade remained the third-largest in the world in the mid-1930s: Newton, ' "Anglo-German" Connection', pp. 301ff, Wendt, ' "Economic Appeasement" ', pp. 161–5.

338 'have created so much havoc in different countries': Kershaw, *Making Friends*, p. 228; Londonderry, *Ourselves and Germany*, pp. 143ff.

338 footman and very nearly handed him his hat and coat: Roberts, *Halifax*, p. 70. Halifax had been invited to Germany by Göring in his capacity as Master of Foxhounds, on the occasion of a hunting exhibition.

338 'all Hitler knew that we were his best friends': Cooper, *Diaries*, p. 274.

339 Nancy Cunard and the Mitford sisters, Unity and Diana: Bloch, *Ribbentrop*.

339 'widely read, passionately devoted to music and pictures': Rowse, *All Souls and Appeasement*, p. 42.

339 who had previously been the College's Bursar: ibid., pp. 1ff, 5–11.

340 'Sergeant Major with a gift of the gab and a far-away look in his eyes': McDonough, 'Ebbut and the Nazis', p. 413.

340 *The Times* had been 'captured by pro-Nazis in London': ibid., p. 418. Shirer considered Ebbut, who had been based in Berlin since 1925, 'by far the best-informed foreign correspondent in Germany during the 1930s': ibid., p. 408.

340 'the protector of the new nations of Eastern Europe?': Lord Lothian, 'Germany and France: The British Task, II: Basis of Ten Years' Peace', *The Times*, February 1, 1935. For Lothian's proposals to accommodate Hitler's ambitions, including acceptance of German-Austrian Anschluss, see Newton, *Profits of Peace*, pp. 74ff.

340 'a high standard on National-Socialist officials': Rowse, *All Souls and Appeasement*, p. 30.

340 In August 1937 Ebbut was expelled from Germany: McDonough, 'Ebbut and the Nazis', pp. 419ff.

340 The next day German troops marched into Austria: Rowse, *All Souls and Appeasement*, p. 71.

341 'when compared with the unpopular newspapers': ibid., p. 85.

341 would recede further into the background: Carr, *Twenty Years Crisis*, p. 272.

341 'a model for negotiating peaceful change': See Haslam, *Vices of Integrity*.

342 the *Evening Standard*'s irreverent cartoonist: Adamthwaite, 'British Government and the Media', p. 284.

342 later wartime reputation for truthful reporting: ibid., pp. 282ff.

342 and Mussolini's policies of 'persecution, militancy and inhumanity': ibid., p. 285.

342 chastised by the whips or their local party associations: Crowson, *Facing Fascism*, pp. 84–7.

342 against arms limitation, but for the League of Nations: For some striking examples see Parker, *Churchill and Appeasement*, pp. 31, 117–24, 126, 129–32, 143, 148ff, 165. See also Dilks, ' "Unnecessary War" '; Thompson, *Anti-Appeasers*, pp. 45–50; Haigh and Morris, *Munich: Peace of Delusion*, pp. 29ff.

342 'Germans are so powerful as you say, oughtn't we to go in with them?': Rowse, *All Souls and Appeasement*, pp. 27ff.

343 No no, certainly not: Isaiah Berlin, interview with Michael Ignatieff, MI Tape 8, p. 1. I am grateful to Mr Henry Hardy of the Isaiah Berlin Literary Trust, Wolfson College, Oxford, for permission to quote from this transcript. Berlin's account is notably different from that in Rowse, *All Souls and Appeasement*.

343 and Roy Harrod, Keynes's biographer: Margalit, 'On Compromise', p. 1.

343 had a kind of Cecil Rhodes aspect to it: ibid.

343 'people and never became good citizens': Goldstein, 'Chamberlain', p. 282.

344 Communism, fundamentally, is what stirred them: Isaiah Berlin, interview with Michael Ignatieff, MI Tape 8, p. 1.

344 mood is depressed. Everyone is conscious of defeat: Berlin to his father, October/November 1938, in Hardy (ed.), *Berlin Letters*, p. 290.

## CHAPTER TEN: THE PITY OF PEACE

345 as we did for the Uitlanders in the Transvaal: Stewart, *Burying Caesar*, p. 281.

345 then I say that you might even now arrest this approaching war: Parker, *Chamberlain and Appeasement*, pp. 319ff.

345 'of whom we know nothing': Stewart, *Burying Caesar*, p. 306.

346 were under-represented in government employment: Komjathy and Stockwell, *German Minorities*, pp. 17–31.

347 'you want if you can get them by peaceful means': Parker, *Churchill and Appeasement*, p. 128. Cf. idem, *Chamberlain and Appeasement*, p. 28; Thompson, *Anti-Appeasers*, pp. 33–36; Bell, *Origins*, pp. 264ff.

347 him from the Coventry to which he was sent after the war: Shay, *British Rearmament*, p. 177.

347 nearly ten times the number of Sudeten Germans: Bergen, 'Nazi Concept of "Volksdeutsche"', p. 569.

348 but nearly all ethnic German minorities after 1933: On Poland see Polish Ministry of Information, German Fifth Column, pp. 15–50. On Romania see Castellan, 'Germans of Romania', pp. 56–9. On Hungary, see Paikert, *Danubian Swabians*, and idem, 'Hungary's National Minority Policies'.

348 themselves from their oppressive bondage in the name of civilizing morality: Rezzori, *Snows of Yesteryear*, pp. 129ff.

349 'To be a Nazi was to be an optimist': Hagen, 'Before the "Final Solution"', p. 353.

349 had formed their own Nazi organization, the Volksbund: Seton-Watson, *Eastern Europe*, pp. 283ff.

349 They became, in effect, his advance guard in the East: See in general Lumans, *Himmler's Auxiliaries*.

349 when he did not specify the means of achieving what he wanted: Smelser, 'Nazi Dynamics', p. 36.

349 was a flop because Hitler had no interest in either: MacDonald, 'Economic Appeasement and the German "Moderates"', pp. 106–15. Cf. Watt, 'British Intelligence', p. 249; Newton, *Profits of Peace*, pp. 76ff.

349 Sir Robert Vansittart—that Britain gained by waiting: Parker, *Chamberlain and Appeasement*, p. 68; Schmidt, 'Domestic Background', pp. 103–8.

350 'therefore the task of holding the situation until at least 1939': Dunbabin, 'British Rearmament', p. 597.

350 or at least 'limiting' British liability on the continent: Parker, *Chamberlain and Appeasement*, pp. 138–40; Charmley, *Chamberlain and the Lost Peace*, pp. 24–7. Cf. Cooper, *Old Men Forget*, pp. 211ff; Stewart, *Burying Caesar*, p. 283; Shay, *British Rearmament*, pp. 179–82.

350 exposed when, in due course, it did: On Chamberlain's over-confidence, see Parker, *Chamberlain and Appeasement*, pp. 1–11.

350 he recognized the independence of Eire in 1938: Parker, *Churchill and Appeasement*, p. 161.

350 purpose of defending Britain from the Luftwaffe: Shay, *British Rearmament in the Thirties*, pp. 219ff.

350 would only agree to a ban on strategic bombing: Parker, 'Economics, Rearmament, and Foreign Policy', p. 642.

350 violation of both the Versailles and the Locarno Treaties: Halifax, *Fulness of Days*, pp. 197ff; Kirkpatrick, *Inner Circle*, p. 131. Cf. Kissinger, *Diplomacy*, p. 302.

351 eyes of many others in Britain to the nature of Hitler's ambitions: See e.g., Bond (ed.), *Chief of Staff*, p. 138.

351 autonomy had the backing of the majority of his people: Weinberg, 'Reflections on Munich', p. 7; Parker, *Churchill and Appeasement*, pp. 163ff.

351 he intended would wipe Czechoslovakia off the map: Overy, 'Germany and the Munich Crisis', p. 194.

351 the Czechs were the villains of the piece: See e.g., Henderson to Halifax, May 21, 1938; Henderson to Halifax, May 22, 1938, in Woodward and Butler (eds.), *Documents on British Foreign Policy*, Series 3 [henceforth DBFP], vol. I, pp. 329ff, 344ff. Cf. Henderson, *Failure of a Mission*, p. 139; Bond (ed.), *Chief of Staff*, p. 153.

351 emissary, Lord Runciman, also fell into this trap: Runciman to Halifax, August 30, 1938, in DBFP, pp. 192ff; also Newton to Halifax, September 3, 1938, p. 221. Cf. Lamb, *Drift to War*, pp. 239ff.

351 in the mistaken belief that Hitler was about to attack: ibid., p. 195ff. Cf. Henderson, *Failure of a Mission*, pp. 146ff.

351 thought to the option of threatening the use of force: Parker, *Chamberlain and Appeasement*, pp. 156–9.

352 'was only likely to irritate' Hitler: Cooper, *Diaries*, p. 256.

352 policy at this stage, and all were dispensable: Stewart, *Burying Caesar*, pp. 296ff.

352 'circumstances come in, he is labouring under a tragic illusion': Dilks (ed.), *Cadogan Diary*, pp. 94ff. Cf. Halifax to Campbell, August 31, 1938, in DBFP, vol. I, pp. 196–8.

352 (or perhaps because of it) Chamberlain overruled him: Parker, *Churchill and Appeasement*, pp. 172ff.

352 'Herr Hitler to intervene on behalf of the Sudeten[s]': Henderson to Halifax, September 3, 1938, in Woodward and Butler (eds.), DBFP, vol. II, pp. 224ff.

352 **Mere autonomy had never been the German objective:** Runciman to Halifax, September 5, 1938, in *DBFP,* vol. II, pp. 248ff. Cf. Lamb, *Drift to War,* pp. 241ff.; Parker, *Chamberlain and Appeasement,* p. 160.

353 **'conflict from which Great Britain could not stand aside':** Halifax to Kirkpatrick, September 9, 1939, in *DBFP,* vol. II, pp. 277ff. As Cooper noted in his dairy, 'By the Government now is meant the P.M., [Sir John] Simon, Halifax and Sam Hoare': Cooper, *Diaries,* p. 258.

353 **'involving him in a public humiliation':** Colvin, *Chamberlain Cabinet,* pp. 147–51.

353 **drawn back for fear of Anglo-French intervention:** Phipps to Halifax, May 22, 1938; Halifax to Henderson, May 22, 1938; Halifax to Phipps, May 22, 1938 in Woodward and Butler (eds.), *DBFP,* vol. I, pp. 340ff., 356.

353 **with enormously increased strength, turn against France:** Halifax to Phipps, September 7, 1938, Phipps to Halifax, September 8, 1939, in *DBFP,* vol. II, pp. 262ff., 269ff.

353 **which must deserve most serious thought:** Halifax to Phipps, September 9, 1938, in *DBFP,* vol. II, pp. 275ff. Cf. Weinberg, 'French Role', p. 25.

353 **'You're on your own.' Small wonder the French wilted:** See Dilks (ed.), *Cadogan Diaries,* pp. 97ff. Cf. Colvin, *Chamberlain Cabinet,* pp. 152ff; Haigh and Morris, *Munich: Peace of Delusion,* p. 55.

354 **consensus for appeasement in the months leading up to Munich:** See e.g., Dilks, ' "Unnecessary War" ', p. 124.

354 **counter-advice of one man, the hysterical Henderson:** Cooper, *Old Men Forget,* pp. 226ff.

354 **began his experiment with shuttle diplomacy:** Crowson, *Facing Fascism,* pp. 95ff.

354 **dismissed the critics of appeasement as 'war-boys':** Dilks (ed.), *Cadogan Diaries,* p. 97.

354 **Rather than approve naval mobilization, as Cooper urged:** Cooper, *Diaries,* p. 259.

354 **'establishing good relations with Great Britain':** Colvin, *Chamberlain Cabinet,* p. 153.

354 **The French wilted still further at being thus left out in the cold:** Bonnet told Phipps: 'France would accept any solution of Czechoslovak question to avoid war. He said to me "we cannot sacrifice ten million men in order to prevent three and a half million Sudetens joining the Reich".' However, this was after Halifax had made it clear France would receive minimal support from Britain, if any: Phipps to Halifax, September 14, 1938, in *DBFP,* vol. II, pp. 323, 329. Cf. Parker, *Chamberlain and Appeasement,* pp. 160ff.; Weinberg, 'French Role', pp. 25ff.

354 **excluding them would drive Stalin into Hitler's arms:** Dilks (ed.), *Cadogan Diaries,* p. 93.

354 **present when the two leaders conferred in the Führer's study:** Henderson, *Failure of a Mission,* p. 150.

355 **struck him as 'the commonest looking little dog':** Cooper, *Diaries,* p. 260.

355 **'could be relied upon when he had given his word':** Parker, *Chamberlain and Appeasement,* p. 162.

355 **'risk a world war rather than allow this to drag on':** ibid., p. 163.

355 **plebiscite would be held before the 'transfer':** Colvin, *Chamberlain Cabinet,* pp. 156ff; Lamb, *Drift to War,* p. 245; Cooper, *Diaries,* p. 261; idem, *Old Men Forget,* p. 230.

355 **'self-determination of the Sudeten Germans':** Weinberg, 'French Role', p. 27.

355 **left of Czechoslovakia after the transfer of the Sudetenland:** Colvin, *Chamberlain Cabinet,* pp. 159ff.; Dilks (ed.), *Cadogan Diaries,* pp. 100ff; Weinberg, 'French Role', pp. 27ff; Lamb, *Drift to War,* p. 246ff.

356 **blamed their desertion on the British, he did so:** Masaryk to Halifax, September 18, 1938, in *BDFP,* vol. II, p. 400; Newton to Halifax, September 19, 1939, in ibid., pp. 406ff, 411ff, 414ff, 416ff; Phipps to Halifax, September 20, 1939, in ibid., p. 422; Halifax to Newton, September 21, 1938, in ibid., pp. 437ff; Newton to Halifax, September 21, 1938, in ibid., pp. 447, 449ff.

356 **('I am terribly sorry, but that will no longer do'):** Kirkpatrick, *Inner Circle,* p. 115; Henderson, *Failure of a Mission,* p. 153.

356 **bringing the total number of divisions there to 31:** Phipps to Halifax, September 21, 1938; September 22, 1938; Halifax to Newton, September 22, 1938, in *DBFP,* vol. II, pp. 451, 456, 461.

356 **occupation by three days, a quite empty 'concession':** Kirkpatrick, *Inner Circle,* pp. 120ff; Lamb, *Drift to War,* p. 248ff.

357 **latter trusted him and was willing to work with him:** Parker, *Chamberlain and Appeasement,* p. 169.

357 **also declared himself in favour of mobilizing the army:** Cooper, *Diaries,* p. 264; idem, *Old Men Forget,* pp. 234ff.

357 **So did Lord Hailsham, another erstwhile supporter:** Colvin, Chamberlain Cabinet, p. 164; Lamb, *Drift to War,* pp. 151ff; Parker, *Chamberlain and Appeasement,* pp. 170ff. Cf. Halifax to Chamberlain, September 23, 1938, in *DBFP,* vol. II, pp. 483ff., 490.

357 **had no alternative but finally to take a firmer line:** Weinberg, 'French Role', pp. 30ff.

357 **France should enter on the side of the Czechs:** Parker, *Chamberlain and Appeasement,* pp. 173ff. Lamb, *Drift to War,* p. 254.

357 **ask Chamberlain to repeat what he had said:** Cooper, *Diaries,* p. 267.

357 **French General Staff, visited London on the 26th:** Bond (ed.), *Chief of Staff,* p. 163; Weinberg, 'French Role', p. 35.

357 **'[the] inevitable alternative to a peaceful solution':** Halifax to Henderson, September 26, 1938, *DBFP,* vol. II, p. 550. Cf. Dilks (ed.), *Cadogan Diaries,* p. 106.

358 **'Great Britain and Russia will certainly stand by France':** Parker, *Churchill and Appeasement,* pp. 180ff. Chamberlain was 'much put out' by this.

358 public in favour of appeasement; 40 per cent were against: Lamb, *Drift to War*, p. 250.
358 from holding the general election he had contemplated: Parker, *Churchill and Appeasement*, pp. 196–201, 208; idem, *Chamberlain and Appeasement*, p. 190; Crowson, *Facing Fascism*, pp. 106ff.
358 House of Commons also shifted at this time: Stewart, *Burying Caesar*, p. 303.
358 'public opinion since Hitler's demands had become known': Phipps to Halifax, September 26, 1938, in *BDFP*, vol. II, pp. 546ff. See also ibid., p. 558. But see Phipps to Halifax, September 27, 1938, in *BDFP*, vol. II, pp. 579ff; Phipps to Halifax, September 28, 1938, in ibid., p. 588; Dilks (ed.), *Cadogan Diary*, pp. 104ff.
358 Duff Cooper was able to make known to the press: Cooper, *Diaries*, p. 269.
358 air raids on the capital continued to exert its fascination: Parker, *Chamberlain and Appeasement*, p. 178.
358 'general satisfaction that the die had been cast': Kirkpatrick, *Inner Circle*, p. 126.
358 Hitler should not consider the rejection of his demands as the last word: Lamb, *Drift to War*, p. 253.
358 'any more and then only with insane interruptions': Henderson to Halifax, September 26, 1938, in *DBFP*, vol. II, pp. 552ff. See also Kirkpatrick, *Inner Circle*, p. 123.
359 acceptance of his demands to 2 pm on September 28, just two days later: ibid., September 27, 1938, in *DBFP*, vol. II, pp. 574ff. Weinberg, 'French Role', p. 32.
359 could count on Polish support in the event of a war: ibid., September 26, 1938, in *DBFP*, vol. II, p. 543.
359 was asked on the 27th, but 'more in sorrow than in anger': Parker, *Chamberlain and Appeasement*, p. 176; Cooper, *Diaries*, p. 268.
359 'I am prepared for every eventuality': Henderson, *Failure of a Mission*, p. 160; Kirkpatrick, *Inner Circle*, p. 125; Lamb, *Drift to War*, p. 256.
359 though the majority of ministers rejected this course: Lamb, *Drift to War*, p. 257.
359 colleague in Prague was not invited to offer an opinion: Newton to Halifax, September 27, 1938, in *DBFP*, vol. II, p. 581; Lamb, *Drift to War*, p. 257.
359 'cross-examined' by Simon and their answers found wanting: Cooper, *Old Men Forget*, p. 237.
359 Maginot Line if they encountered serious resistance: Dilks (ed.), *Cadogan Diaries*, p. 107; Lamb, *Drift to War*, p. 262.
359 'small nation confronted by a big and powerful neighbour': Haigh and Morris, *Munich: Peace of Delusion*, p. 64. This was the occasion when he referred to 'a quarrel in a far-away country between people of whom we know nothing'.
359 tone of the speech showed plainly that we're preparing to scuttle: Cooper, *Diaries*, p. 268; idem, *Old Men Forget*, pp. 238ff.
360 specifying the timing of the German occupation, was ever implemented: Parker, *Chamberlain and Appeasement*, pp. 179ff.
360 sources of difference and thus contribute to assure the peace of Europe: ibid.
360 euphoria at Heston airfield, described as signifying 'Peace in Our Time': Stewart, *Burying Caesar*, p. 310. Cf. Parker, *Chamberlain*, p. 184.
360 make it hard to justify the accelerated rearmament that was needed: Cooper, *Diaries*, p. 271; *Old Men Forget*, pp. 243ff.
360 the Lithuanian city of Memel and the international city of Danzig: Colvin, *Vansittart in Office*, pp. 277–84.
360 *News Chronicle* was reporting that Hitler was preparing to march on Prague: ibid., p. 281.
360 'self-determination' that it placed 30,000 Czechs under German rule: Colvin, *Chamberlain Cabinet*, pp. 175ff.
360 rump Czechoslovakia never took on concrete form: Adamthwaite, 'France and the Coming of War', p. 84; Parker, *Chamberlain and Appeasement*, pp. 200ff.
360 openly pledging to achieve parity with the Royal Navy in submarines: Colvin, *Chamberlain Cabinet*, p. 176.
361 just a few days after Chamberlain's return from Munich: Parker, *Churchill and Appeasement*, p. 189.
361 Berchtesgaden than to what Hitler had demanded at Bad Godesberg: Stewart, *Burying Caesar*, pp. 308ff, 311.
361 which he had been planning since the end of May: Kershaw, 'Nazi Foreign Policy', pp. 133ff; Overy, 'Germany and the Munich Crisis', pp. 195–7.
361 had been more effective than it had appeared at the time: Dilks (ed.), *Cadogan Diaries*, pp. 106–9.
362 'against France, which I could not wage': Overy, 'Germany and the Munich Crisis', pp. 204, 207–10.
362 of a twenty-four-hour suspension of mobilization: Henderson, *Failure of a Mission*, pp. 163ff.
362 Chamberlain to attend a four-power conference in Munich: Dilks (ed.), *Cadogan Diaries*, p. 109.
362 readiness the French ambassador's proposal for a compromise: Weinberg, 'French Role', pp. 32ff.
362 when it was put to the vote—becomes more intelligible: Crowson, *Facing Fascism*, pp. 96–103; Thompson, *Anti-Appeasers*, p. 42ff.
362 who prompted Mussolini to suggest a last-ditch diplomatic solution: Halifax to Perth, September 28, 1938, in *DBFP*, vol. II, pp. 587ff. Cf. Lamb, *Drift to War*, p. 257; Parker, *Chamberlain and Appeasement*, pp. 178ff.
362 when they made their sympathy for the German side quite explicit?: Perth to Halifax, September 28, 1938, in *DBFP*, vol. II, p. 600.

362  Why exclude the Czechs at this pivotal moment?: Newton to Halifax, September 28, 1938, in *DBFP*, vol. II, p. 604; Halifax to Newton, September 29, 1938, in ibid., pp. 614ff. Cf. Lamb, *Drift to War*, pp. 259–61.

362  Why once again leave the Soviets out of the negotiations?: Lammers, *Explaining Munich*, pp. 3–5.

362  No senior German military officer dissented from this view: Lamb, *Drift to War*, p. 239. Cf. Bell, *Origins*, pp. 262–4; Haigh and Morris, *Munich: Peace of Delusion*, p. 79.

362  in fact brought to a state of readiness during the Czech crisis: Bell, *Origins*, p. 266.

363  government would have granted them passage to the Czech frontier: De la Warr to Halifax, September 15, 1938, in *DBFP*, vol. II, pp. 354ff. Lamb, *Drift to War*, pp. 263ff.

363  least refer the matter to the League of Nations: See e.g., Chilston to Halifax, September 4, 1938; Newton to Halifax, September 6, 1938, in *DBFP*, vol. II, pp. 229ff, 255ff. Cf. Newton, *Profits of Peace*, pp. 81ff.

363  'show the Germans that we mean business': Phipps to Halifax, September 23, 1939; Geneva delegation to Halifax, September 24, 1938, in *DBFP*, vol. II, pp. 489, 497ff.

363  have been deployed in an attack on Czechoslovakia: Watt, 'British Intelligence', p. 253; Lamb, *Drift to War*, p. 251; Newton to Halifax, September 27, 1938, in *DBFP*, vol. II, p. 567. See also Murray, 'War of 1938', pp. 261ff.

363  decisive numerical superiority nor the element of surprise: Newton to Halifax, September 6, 1938 in *DBFP*, vol. II, pp. 257ff; Phipps to Halifax, September 28, 1938 in *DPFP*, vol. II, pp. 609ff.

363  'We had run a serious danger': Colvin, *Vansittart in Office*, p. 274; Wheeler-Bennett, *Nemesis of Power*, p. 419.

363  might have ended in disaster had it been launched: Murray, 'War of 1938', pp. 263ff.

363  what Hitler was contemplating was 'certainly a bit risky': Bond (ed.), *Chief of Staff*, p. 160.

363  3 'pocket' battleships and seven submarines available: Murray, 'War of 1938', p. 265.

364  French to inflict heavy losses on the Italian Mediterranean fleet: ibid., pp. 268ff.

364  grave failure of intelligence gathering and interpretation: Watt, 'British Intelligence', p. 258ff.

364  and other military targets, not urban centres: ibid., pp. 259ff.

364  'of London left standing' in the event of a war: Henderson, *Failure of a Mission*, p. 152. Cf. Wark, 'British Intelligence', pp. 642ff; Haigh and Morris, *Munich: Peace of Delusion*, pp. 76–9.

364  'disposal a war of destruction against England seemed to be excluded': Murray, 'War of 1938', p. 267.

364  preparations for possible German attacks were thus pointless: Colville, *Gort*, p. 112; Lamb, *Drift to War*, p. 253.

364  Paris, though here too the threat was exaggerated: Weinberg, 'French Role', p. 37.

364  with a *fait accompli* was fraught with danger: Reynolds, *Treason Was No Crime*, pp. 148, 151; Weinberg, 'German Generals', pp. 34ff.

364  Werner von Fritsch—Beck survived the purge of January 1938: Hoffman, 'Beck', p. 339; Weinberg, 'German Generals', pp. 29–31.

365  Germany had deprived them of their opportunity: Lamb, *Drift to War*, pp. 266ff.

365  German military and civilian elites were diverse and disorganized: Hoffman, *German Resistance*, p. 63. See also Ritter, *German Resistance*, p. 93.

365  Foreign Office—was, to say the least, strange: See e.g., Warner to Halifax, September 5, 1938, in *DBFP*, vol. II, pp. 242ff. Cf. Hoffman, *German Resistance*, pp. 63–7; idem, 'Question of Western Allied Co-operation'; Astor, 'Revolt against Hitler', p. 7. For a different view see Wheeler-Bennett, *Nemesis of Power*, pp. 414ff; Ben-Israel, 'Cross-Purposes', p. 425. See also Dilks, *Cadogan Diaries*, pp, 94ff. Beck himself sent Ewald von Kleist-Schmenzin to London as his emissary.

365  Rhodes Scholar, met with both Chamberlain and Halifax: Hoffman, 'Question of Western Allied Co-operation', pp. 443ff.

365  urged that Churchill be brought into the government: Parker, *Churchill and Appeasement*, p. 231.

365  'European war which Germany would be likely to lose': Ogilvie-Forbes to Halifax, September 11, 1938, in *DBFP*, vol. II, p. 289. See also Kirkpatrick, *Inner Circle*, pp. 111ff.

366  division paraded through Berlin on September 27: Henderson, *Failure of a Mission*, p. 161.

366  'the peace, we have saved Hitler and his regime': Colvin, *Vansittart in Office*, p. 273.

366  'smashed.' The Chiefs of Staff shared this view: Dilks, '"Unnecessary War"', pp. 103, 123; Lamb, *Drift to War*, p. 265; Shay, *British Rearmament*, pp. 226ff.

366  to a German attack. We simply commit suicide if we do': Howard, *Continental Commitment*, p. 122; Colvin, *Vansittart in Office*, p. 270.

366  Germans had the capacity to bomb to reduce their cities 'to ruins': Phipps to Halifax, September 22, 1938, in *DBFP*, vol. II, pp. 473ff.

366  quickly be available for deployment against France: ibid., pp. 609ff.

366  ill-equipped Field Force divisions to France in the event of war: Bond, *British Military Policy*, pp. 280ff; Colville, *Gort*, p. 112; Weinberg, 'French Role'.

366  We cannot, of course, say for sure what would have happened: For some speculations, see Murray, 'War of 1938'; Haigh and Morris, *Munich: Peace of Delusion*, pp. 51ff.

367  'we are in bad condition to wage even a defensive war at the present time': Howard, *Continental Commitment*, p. 123.

367 air defences ready to withstand an assault by the Luftwaffe: Haigh and Morris, *Munich: Peace of Delusion*, pp. 49ff.

367 it could scarcely have got any weaker: Colville, *Gort*, pp. 115ff; Bond (ed.), *Pownall Diaries*, p. 122. Though the state of the army's equipment was not as dire as is sometimes assumed, see Haigh and Morris, *Munich: Peace of Delusion*, pp. 46–9.

367 against them if they delayed war much after 1939: Tooze, *Wages of War*, ch. 9.

367 The Soviet Union out-built all three with 10,565 new aircraft: Overy, *Air War*, p. 21.

367 Germany's eastern frontier was significantly less vulnerable: Howard, *Continental Commitment*, pp. 124ff. Cf. Bond (ed.), *Pownall Diaries*, p. 164.

367 all of which were to prove useful in the years to come: Lamb, *Drift to War*, pp. 262ff.

367 used by the Germans in their western offensive of 1940 were Czech-built: Haigh and Morris, *Munich: Peace of Delusion*, pp. 80ff.

368 'to complete the measures necessary for their defence': ibid., p. 60.

368 the gap that Britain and France desperately needed to close: Aster, ' "Guilty Men" ', pp. 69ff; Newton, *Profits of Peace*, pp. 83–7; Parker, *Chamberlain and Appeasement*, pp. 183ff.

368 amounts of raw materials needed for the rapid rearmament Hitler wanted: Newton, *Profits of Peace*, pp. 55–7.

369 synthetic rubber had been produced, around 12 per cent of imports: Tooze, *Wages of War*, table 6.

369 materials that were continuing to hamper German rearmament: Overy, 'Germany and the Munich Crisis', pp. 194–200.

369 Germany had only sufficient stocks of gasoline for three months: Colvin, *Vansittart in Office*, p. 273.

369 spending that had been set in train by the Four Year Plan: Tooze, *Wages of War*, ch. 8.

369 although he stayed on as Reichsbank President: Smelser, 'Nazi Dynamics', pp. 38ff. Cf. Brown and Burdekin, 'German Debt', p. 665.

369 Dawes and Young bonds, issued to help finance reparations: MacDonald, 'Economic Appeasement and the German "Moderates" ', pp. 115ff.

369 that would have struck at the German economy's Achilles heel: ibid., p. 121.

370 Hitler fired them, but he could no longer ignore the need to 'export or die': Tooze, *Wages of War*, ch. 9.

370 adverse balance of trade, and by the growth of armament expenditure: Parker, 'Economics, Rearmament, and Foreign Policy', p. 643.

371 The drain on British reserves by this stage was running at £20 million a month: Newton, *Profits of Peace*, pp. 114–8.

371 'ultimately come when we should be unable to carry on a long war': Parker, 'Economics, Rearmament, and Foreign Policy', p. 644.

371 the old claim that appeasement bought Britain precious time: See e.g., Peden, 'A Matter of Timing', pp. 25ff.

371 Historians have long sought the economic foundations of appeasement: See most recently Newton, *Profits of Peace*.

372 by raising the Bank of England's discount rate to punitive heights: 'The City—Then and Now', *Economist*, October 1, 1938.

372 'would not have taken the financial markets by surprise': ibid., October 1, 1938.

372 tables had been turned, and it was the defaulter who looked like winning: My interpretation in this respect differs from that of Brown and Burdekin, 'German Debt'. I am grateful to the authors for making available their weekly price series for the Dawes and Young bonds.

372 divisions ready to be sent to the continent in the event of war: To the amazement of the Soviet Commissar of Defence, Marshal Kliment Voroshilov: Overy, *Russia's War*, p. 46.

373 'at once embark on a great increase in our armaments program': Shay, *British Rearmament*, p. 233.

373 Chamberlain replied, 'I have brought back peace': Colvin, *Chamberlain Cabinet*, p. 168.

373 He opposed the Admiralty's request for new convoy escort vessels: Parker, *Chamberlain and Appeasement*, p. 188.

373 He resisted Churchill's demands to create a new Ministry of Supply: ibid., pp. 201–5.

373 He clung to the policy of appeasement and the dream of disarmament: Colvin, *Chamberlain Cabinet*, pp. 172ff.

373 'once more that we have at last got on top of the dictators': Aster, ' "Guilty men" ', pp. 71ff.

374 Treasury and with little support from the Prime Minister: Shay, *British Rearmament*, pp. 238–42; Colvin, *Chamberlain Cabinet*, pp. 172–5. Cf. Peden, 'A Matter of Timing', pp. 21–4.

374 of a new Ministry of Supply, Chamberlain sacked him: Shay, *British Rearmament*, pp. 263–71.

374 volume of savings available to fund the debt: ibid., pp. 242–5, 277ff; Parker, 'Economics, Rearmament, and Foreign Policy', pp. 645ff; Peden, 'A Matter of Timing', pp. 18–21.

374 1936 and 1937, this seemed a distinctly remote prospect: Peden, 'A Matter of Timing', p. 17; Newton, *Profits of Peace*, pp. 119ff.

374 'and . . . their compass is pointing towards peace': Dilks (ed.), *Cadogan Diaries*, p. 151.

374 and increased her access to sources of hard currency: MacDonald, 'Economic Appeasement and the German "Moderates" ', pp. 118–26. See also Parker, *Chamberlain and Appeasement*, pp. 196ff.

374 off some of the outstanding German debts to British lenders: The debts covered by the Standstill agreements still amounted to £34 million on the eve of the war: Forbes, 'London Banks', p. 585.

375 to more than £16 million on the eve of the war: Newton, *Profits of Peace*, pp. 91ff, 112ff. See also MacDonald, 'Economic Appeasement and the German "Moderates" ', pp. 127ff.

375 Britain, he could probably have had more: Newton, ' "Anglo-German" Connection', pp. 305ff; Wendt, 'Economic Appeasement', pp. 157ff.

375 played very little part in the Führer's mind': MacDonald, 'Economic Appeasement and the German "Moderates" ', pp. 128–31. See also Parker, 'Economics, Rearmament, and Foreign Policy', p. 642.

375 continental army and to increase the size of the Territorial Army: Parker, *Chamberlain and Appeasement*, pp. 191ff; Watt, 'British Intelligence', pp. 247ff; Dilks, ' "Unnecessary War" ', pp. 125ff.

375 unequivocal public commitment to France: Parker, *Churchill and Appeasement*, pp. 206ff; Howard, *Continental Commitment*, pp. 126ff.

375 contemplate some kind of commitment to Bucharest: Newton, *Profits of Peace*, pp. 103ff.

376 which Chamberlain announced in the Commons on March 31: Bond, *British Military Policy*, p. 377; Aster, ' "Guilty Men" ', pp. 72ff; Parker, *Chamberlain and Appeasement*, pp. 212–5.

376 earlier sham guarantee to the rump Czechoslovakia: Bond, *British Military Policy*, p. 378.

376 instead the uninspiring former Minister of Transport, Leslie Burgin: ibid., pp. 304–6, 310; Howard, *Continental Commitment*, pp. 129ff; Shay, *British Rearmament*, pp. 272ff, 289–4; Parker, *Churchill and Appeasement*, p. 221.

376 deny the 'fumbling' quality of his policy by this stage: See e.g., Dilks (ed.), *Cadogan Diary*, pp. 166ff.

376 were 'problems in which adjustments are necessary': Parker, *Chamberlain and Appeasement*, p. 217. Cf. Foster, 'Times and Appeasement', pp. 444ff.

376 had favoured a 'military alliance between Great Britain, France and Russia': Parker, *Churchill and Appeasement*, p. 223.

377 Stalin's Soviet Union. This was no doubt a factor for many Tories: Crowson, *Facing Fascism*, pp. 116–8.

377 to an especially strong ideological aversion to Communism: Parker, *Churchill and Appeasement*, pp. 212ff. Cf. Howard, *Continental Commitment*, p. 132.

377 of mutual 'consultation' proposed by Chamberlain in March 1939: Parker, *Chamberlain and Appeasement*, pp. 207, 209–12.

377 from German aggression, they were rebuffed: ibid., pp. 223–9. Cf. Newton, *Profits of Peace*, pp. 108ff.

377 travelled by sea not air, with low-ranking officers at their head: Overy, *Russia's War*, pp. 45ff.

377 with the Russians might still have been achievable: Parker, *Churchill and Appeasement*, p. ix. For the Russian assessment of the two men, see ibid., p. 245.

378 to enumerate the size of Fleet we could afford to send: Howard, *Continental Commitment*, pp. 138ff.

378 four-power declaration against such acts of aggression: Parker, *Chamberlain and Appeasement*, p. 208.

379 as a possible partner in his effort to restrain Hitler: ibid., pp 246ff; Bond, *British Military Policy*, p. 307.

379 Hitler would not 'start a world war for Danzig': Aster, ' "Guilty men" ', pp. 73ff.

379 Berchtesgaden in the early hours of August 24: Overy, *Russia's War*, p. 49.

379 Henderson to restate the British guarantee to Poland: Parker, *Chamberlain and Appeasement*, p. 330.

379 'I saw them at Munich': Overy, 'Germany and the Munich Crisis', p. 191.

379 idea in the Commons even after Poland had been invaded: Parker, *Churchill and Appeasement*, p. 256.

379 avoid (as Samuel Hoare put it) 'going all out': Newton, ' "Anglo-German" Connection', p. 68.

380 requesting that Polish plenipotentiary be sent forthwith to Berlin: Parker, *Chamberlain and Appeasement*, pp. 331–6.

380 was delivered, they had both been proven wrong: ibid., pp. 338–42.

381 replaced Chamberlain as prime minister in May 1940: Had Halifax rather than Churchill become Prime Minister, of course, he might conceivably have sought to make peace, though it is debatable whether Hitler would have offered terms he would have been able to stomach: Roberts, 'Prime Minister Halifax'.

381 seriously the idea of some kind of regime change in Germany: Details in Hoffman, 'Question of Western Allied Co-operation', pp. 445–51; Ben-Israel, 'Cross-Purposes', pp. 426ff; Newton, ' "Anglo-German" Connection', pp. 309–12.

381 'German General Staff on condition that they eliminate Hitler': Nicolson, *Diaries*, p. 58.

381 that even Chamberlain and Halifax thought laughable: Marks, 'Six between Roosevelt and Hitler', pp. 969, 976–82; Offner, 'Appeasement Revisited', pp. 384–92; idem, 'United States and National Socialist Germany', pp. 254–7.

381 But this was not appeasement; it was defeatism: For some examples, see Nicolson, *Diaries*, p. 72.

381 'We should become a slave state': For a contrary view, see Charmley, *End of Glory*.

381 'continued expansion of the German people in Europe': Jacobsen (ed.), *Dokumente zur Vorgeschichte*, p. 6.

## CHAPTER ELEVEN: BLITZKRIEG

385 there are better dividing lines than is the case today: Kosiek, *Jenseits der Grenzen*, p. 184.

385 been the main cause for the loss of Empires in the past: Alanbrooke, *War Diaries*, p. 229.

386 on ahead of the main army, and operating independently: Liddell Hart, *Memoirs*, p. 164. On Liddell Hart, see Danchev, *Alchemist of War*.

386 weapons as mere 'accessories to the man and horse': Haigh and Morris, *Munich: Peace of Delusion*, p. 36.

386 'be scrapped to make room for the tanks': ibid., p. 39.

387 further development to Captain Liddell Hart: Guderian, *Panzer Leader*, p. 20. See idem, *Achtung-Panzer!*

388 tanks had thicker armour and bigger guns: Weber, *Hollow Years*, p. 275n.

388 'picked up from Philippeville, where it had been left': Horne, *To Lose a Battle*, pp. 411, 479.

388 'with apparently none having made their escape': Weber, *Hollow Years*, p. 282.

388 themselves to go more or less voluntarily into imprisonment?': Horne, *To Lose a Battle*, p. 416.

388 'while we were all practically empty-handed': Gayler, *Private Prisoner*, p. 23; Rolf, *Prisoners of the Reich*, p. 30. For a good example of the mood of the ordinary French soldier, see Folcher, *Marching to Captivity*, pp. 122–31 ('My bed at home, how much I thought of it at that time!').

388 were kept in Germany as forced labourers until 1945: See in general Durand, *Prisonniers de Guerre*.

388 masters; their units certainly took heavier casualties: Echenberg, *Colonial Conscripts*, pp. 92–6; Horne, *To Lose a Battle*, p. 377n.

389 Never was a great disaster more easily preventable: Liddell Hart, *Memoirs*, pp. 280ff.

389 at least in part to the abysmal quality of French generalship: Bloch, *Étrange Défaite*.

389 Thereafter, their reactions were culpably slow or inept: May, *Strange Victory*.

389 'fighting spirit [might well] be brought crumbling with it!': Alanbrooke, *War Diaries*, p. 37. As Brooke noted, 'The French would have done better to invest the money in the shape of mobile defences such as more and better aircraft and more heavy armoured formations than to sink all this money into the ground': ibid., p. 26. Cf. Horne, *To Lose a Battle*, p. 155; Shirer, *Collapse of the Third Republic*, pp. 739–55; Forty and Duncan, *Fall of France*.

390 'compared to war: Anything, Hitler rather than war!': Weber, *Hollow Years*, p. 19.

390 'before our first armoured divisions went to work': Waldeck, *Athene Palace*, pp. 196ff.

390 arms by an officer of the Kensington Regiment in June 1940: Gayler, *Private Prisoner*, p. 13.

391 soldiers found themselves being fired on by their own allies: Prysor, 'British Experience of Retreat'.

391 British morale might never have recovered: Manstein, *Lost Victories*, p. 124. Manstein blamed Göring, who was said to have assured Hitler that the Luftwaffe would take care of the retreating British. See also Durschmied, *Hinge Factor*, ch. 12; Badsey, 'Disaster at Dunkirk'.

392 instead of concentrating force 'at the vital point': See e.g., Alanbrooke, *War Diaries*, pp. 38, 121, 165, 187–91, 207ff.

392 'expected that we should fall to pieces as fast as we are': ibid., pp. 208ff.

392 'at present we shall deserve to lose our Empire!': ibid., p. 231.

392 lay down their arms rather than die 'pointlessly': See e.g., Stedman, *Life of a British POW*, p. 8; Kydd, *For YOU the War Is Over*, pp. 50ff; Kindersley, *For You the War Is Over*, p. 11; Walker, *Price of Surrender*, pp. 31–5.

392 consolation that 'discretion is the better part of valour': Broadbent, *Behind Enemy Lines*, p. 6.

392 which was not something they had been prepared for: See e.g., Rolf, *Prisoners of the Reich*, p. 22; Edgar, *Stalag Men*, pp. 1–13; Garrett, *P.O.W.*, pp. 10–15; Cf. Hunter, 'Prisoners of War: Readjustment and Rehabilitation', pp. 743ff.

392 British counterparts were just as reluctant to perish for Penang: Thorne, *Far Eastern War*, p. 171n.

393 Royal Navy still had the upper hand at sea: See Ellis, *World War II Handbook*, table 47.

393 to send a German invasion force across this slender gap: Manstein, *Lost Victories*, pp. 164ff; Macksey, 'Operation Sea Lion'.

393 more than a match for the Germans in skill and courage: For a good insight into the morale of British fighter pilots in the Battle of Britain, see Wellum, *First Light*.

393 Inflicting a decisive blow on RAF command and control capabilities: See on this point Messenger, 'Battle of Britain'.

395 (including bombers) were nearly double British (1,733 to 915): Overy, *Battle*.

395 Dutch—were judged to be essentially a Germanic people: Warmbrunn, *Dutch under German Occupation*, p. 25.

397 The strongest has the right. Greatest severity: Browning, *Origins*, p. 15.

397 bring order to Poland but rather to let 'chaos flourish': ibid., p. 24.

397 defined Hitler's aim as 'annihilating' (vernichtend): Housden, *Frank*, p. 113.

397 'to destroy and eliminate the Polish people': Browning, *Origins*, p. 17.

397 'harsh racial struggle' without 'legal restrictions': ibid., p. 24.

397 'but the nobles, priests and Jews must be killed': ibid., p. 17.

397 up a list of 30,000 people they intended to arrest: ibid., pp. 15ff.

398 executed, most of them victims of the Einsatzgruppen: ibid., pp. 17ff, 28; Housden, *Frank*, pp. 79ff.
398 retained temporarily as agricultural workers: Kamenetsky, *Secret Nazi Plans*, pp. 52, 55. Cf. Winiewicz, *Aims and Failures*, p. 72.
398 'the first colonial territory of the German nation': Housden, *Frank*, pp. 79–90.
399 'is to elevate the Polish people to the honour of European civilization': Burleigh, *Third Reich*, p. 434.
399 harbinger of the fate Frank intended for the Polish intelligentsia: Housden, *Frank*, p. 113.
399 number of victims of this campaign had reached 50,000: Browning, *Origins*, pp. 34ff.
399 2.3 million of the population of the Government-General: Aly, 'Final Solution', table 2.
400 applied a brake to the Einsatzgruppen's activities: Browning, *Origins*, pp. 19ff.
400 the Jews to flee eastwards across the border: ibid., pp. 29ff.
400 intended to be no more than a prelude to expulsion: ibid., pp. 18ff, 25ff, 111, 116, 122ff.
400 'final goal' as being to 'burn out this plague-boil': ibid., p. 116.
400 'inner conviction' as 'un-German and impossible': Mazower, *Dark Continent*, pp. 170ff.
400 Poland's eastern frontier, between the Vistula and the Bug: Browning, *Origins*, p. 27.
400 were crowded into hastily constructed camps: Burleigh, *Third Reich*, p. 580.
400 Lowicz and Glowno took on a more permanent quality: Browning, *Origins*, pp. 120ff, 124ff, 153.
400 with mortality rates soaring to 10 per cent in Warsaw in 1941: Rubinstein et al., *Jews in the Modern World*, p. 217.
401 'plague will creep in and they'll croak': Burleigh, *Third Reich*, pp. 586–96.
401 'starvation' as 'just a marginal issue': Housden, *Frank*, pp. 139–53.
401 of a campaign of systematic and ruthless plunder: Browning, *Origins*, p. 139.
401 labour on all male Jews between the ages of 12 and 60: ibid., p. 138.
401 dictates of racist ideology and the economics of empire: Housden, *Frank*, pp. 91–102.
401 whatever else the Jews need urgently for their existence: Speech at Berlin University, November 18, 1941, in the Work Diary of Hans Frank, Yad Vashem Archives, JM/21: http://www.jewishvirtual library.org/jsource/Holocaust/Frank.html.
401 ('production') or to starve them into extinction ('attrition'): Browning, *Origins*, pp. 113, 117, 126ff.
402 and other manufactures, including military supplies: ibid., p. 154. See the illuminating photographs in Weber, *Łódź Ghetto Album*.
402 he was charged with the 'forming of new German settlements': Noakes and Pridham (eds.), *Nazism*, vol. III, pp. 930ff.
403 Class IV ('Asocial and Racially Inferior') was to be exterminated: Kamenetsky, *Secret Nazi Plans*, pp. 64ff.
403 Germany colonies—were simply not interested: ibid., p. 60.
404 abroad who are considered suitable for permanent return to the Reich': ibid., pp. 55ff.
404 Volhynia and 11,000 from the area around Białystok: For details on Galicia, see Röskau-Rydel, *Galizien*, pp. 192ff.
404 Lithuania after their country had suffered the same fate: Dralle, *Die Deutschen in Ostmitteleuropa*, pp. 231ff. Dralle also provides the following figures: from the rest of Romania (mainly northern Dobruja) 166,000; from Yugoslavia 35,900 and from Bulgaria 2,000. See also Kosiek, *Jenseits der Grenzen*, pp. 180–5.
404 Germans, was to screen them for their racial purity: For details of the system of classification, see Kamenetsky, *Secret Nazi Plans*, pp. 84–7.
404 still languished in temporary resettlement centers: See also Burleigh, *Third Reich*, pp. 447–50, 580.
404 Romanian Volksdeutsche had been settled there: Castellan, *Germans*, p. 64.
404 Germans found their way to the 'Himmlerstadt' area: Kamenetsky, *Secret Nazi Plans*, p. 65; Aly, 'Final Solution', p. 248.
404 inter-breeding with their former Slav neighbours: Bergen, 'Nazi Concept of "Volksdeutsche"', pp. 572ff.
405 'make this lost German blood available again to our own people': Noakes and Pridham (eds.), *Nazism*, vol. III, pp. 930ff.
405 'racially first class children' sent to the Reich: ibid., p. 932. Cf. Bergen, 'Nazi Concept of "Volksdeutsche"', p. 574.
405 through a program of education in the Old [pre-war] Reich: Noakes and Pridham (eds.), *Nazism*, vol. III, p. 946.
406 true of the section which is racially Mongolian: ibid., p. 877.
406 they might be admitted to German educational institutions: Kamenetsky, *Secret Nazi Plans*, pp. 91ff.
406 teacher rebuked the father for being an 'ersatz Teuton': Zahra, 'Reclaiming Children', p. 501.
406 "German national" is not possible given current relationships: ibid., p. 529.
406 'or any ambition to advance oneself': Zeman, *Pursued by a Bear*, p. 146.
406 distinct racial categories on the basis of rigorous genealogical criteria: Noakes and Pridham (eds.), *Nazism*, vol. III, pp. 946ff.
407 professes to be one, or has done so before the incorporation: Winiewicz, *Aims and Failures*, p. 72.
407 Cracovians, Lachs, Lazowiaks, Sandomierzians and Lubliners: ibid., p. 90.
407 though only after a gradual process of cultural Germanization: Kamenetsky, *Secret Nazi Plans*, pp. 89ff.

407 Ukraine had been conquered by the Huns in the fifth century: ibid., pp. 97, 100.

408 view some justification . . . to term these groups 'Lapponoids': Noakes and Pridham (eds.), *Nazism*, vol. III, pp. 977ff.

408 'racial crosses with non-European races and alien races': ibid., p. 942.

408 they were likely to end up in concentration camps: ibid., p. 950. See also Kamenetsky, *Secret Nazi Plans*, p. 95.

409 Josef Mengele's sadistic medical experiments: Hrabar, Tokarz and Wilczur, *Fate of Polish Children*, esp. pp. 52, 63.

409 were murdered—for the 'crime' of being insufficiently Aryan: Kubica, *Zaglada w KL Auschwitz*, p. 196.

409 first transport to the Łódź ghetto in October 1941: Johnson, *Nazi Terror*.

409 simply shot by the police without reference to courts: Evans, *Rituals*, p. 698.

409 an acceleration in the pace of his social exclusion: The following is based on Klemperer, *To the Bitter End*. On the introduction of the yellow star and the renewed debate over mixed marriages, see Noakes and Pridham (eds.), *Nazism*, vol. III, pp. 1107ff.

410 'maintain himself and justifiably maintain himself': Klemperer, *Diaries*, August 17, 1937.

410 'growth out of German flesh, a strain of cancer': ibid., June 23, 1942.

410 they are certainly not Jew-haters': ibid., June 4, 1943.

411 populace when they came to drink in local inns after work: National Archives Washington, Office of the Chief Counsel for War Crimes, Document No. NO-844, Oberlandesgerichtspräsident to Minister for Justice, May 16, 1941.

411 'eaters whose turn will come are the old people': ibid., Document No. 615-PS, Bishop of Limburg to the Minister for Justice, August 13, 1941.

412 drug overdoses and buried in the cemetery grounds: ibid., Document No. NO-729, Examination of Frederick Dickmann, April 6, 1945. See also, United Nations War Crimes Commission, Law Reports, vol. I, pp. 47–54.

412 Catholicism [by hanging] a Christian cross around her neck': Noakes and Pridham (eds.), *Nazism*, vol. III, p. 1045.

412 'marriage-like relationship' with a 'German' man: Wippermann, 'Christine Lehmann and Mazurka Rose, pp. 112ff.

412 in the camp where she had been held after her arrest: Burleigh, *Death and Deliverance* p. 226.

412 too, though supplies had proved to be unavailable: Barnard, 'Great Iraqi Revolt'.

413 the strength of civilisation without its mercy': Hansard, July 8, 1920.

413 1942, to be sure, the British did not hesitate to use force: Bayly and Harper, *Forgotten Armies*, pp. 247ff.

413 'self-government at the earliest possible moment': Clark, *Cripps Version*, pp. 292–322. Gandhi dimissed as a 'post-dated cheque' ('on a failing bank', added a witty journalist). The sticking point proved to be the wartime arrangements for the defence of India, the responsibility for which Cripps intended to divide between the British Commander-in-Chief and an Indian member of the Executive Council, who would be responsible for 'organizing to the full the military, moral and material resources of India'.

413 Stalin's Soviet Union are sometimes drawn: See the egregious Davis, *Late Victorian Holocausts*, and Elkins, *Britain's Gulag*.

413 'be considered as an occupied and hostile country': Thorne, *Far Eastern War*, p. 168.

414 official response to the 1943 famine was woefully inadequate: Bayly and Harper, *Forgotten Armies*, pp. 282–91.

414 'rebels and populations in complicity with them': Knox, *Mussolini Unleashed*, p. 4.

414 did their own colonial imperium seem by comparison: See Ferguson, *Empire*, ch. 6.

414 'small cars on small roads passing through small villages': Wellum, *First Light*, pp. 23, 186.

415 Second, was an allegory of contemporary events: Tolkien, 'Foreword to the Second Edition', *Lord of the Rings*, pp. xv–xviii. Cf. Shippey, *Tolkien*, p. 163; Friedman, 'Tolkien and David Jones'. Tolkien said he wrote *The Lord of the Rings* between 1936 and 1949, but it is clear from his own account that most of the six books into which the work is divided were written during the war years.

415 Ring saga than the Wagnerian version revered by Hitler: Grotta, *Tolkien*, p. 59; Carpenter, *Tolkien*, pp. 90, 176.

415 German invasion for longer than '3 or 4 months': Alanbrooke, *War Diaries*, pp. 144ff., 166.

415 expected that the Soviets would 'assuredly be defeated': Colville, *Fringes of Power*, vol. I, p. 480.

## CHAPTER TWELVE: THROUGH THE LOOKING GLASS

416 to choose between the philosophies of Moscow and Berlin: Cooper, *Dairies*, p. 273.

416 all disguise cast off. It was the Modern Age in arms: Waugh, *Sword of Honour*, pp. 3ff.

416 are on the side of the past—at the moment: Clarke, *Cripps Version*, p. 196.

417 where this journey would end for no-one knew our destination: Jesmanowa, *Stalin's Ethnic Cleansing*, p. 504ff.

417 Hitler and Mussolini's anti-Communist alliance: Bloch, *Ribbentrop*, p. 98.

418 **in advance, with orders to spend it liberally in Polish villages:** Gross, *Revolution from Abroad*, pp. 28ff.

418 **promises of plentiful jobs in the Donbas region proved to be illusory:** ibid., pp. 188–92.

418 **'jail, those who are in jail, and those who will be in jail':** ibid., p. 230.

418 **their experience of nine months of Russian rule:** ibid., pp. 203–5.

419 **'industrialists, hotel [owners] and restaurant owners':** Applebaum, *Gulag*, p. 382.

419 **since the verdicts had already been reached: death:** Beria to Stalin, March 5, 1940: http://www.geocities.com/Athens/Troy/1791/beria.html.

419 **All told, more than 20,000 Poles were killed:** 21,857 in all: 4,421 in the Katyn Forest, 3,820 in the Starobelsk camp (near Kharkov), 6,311 in the Ostashkovo camp (Kalinin region) and 7,305 in other camps and prisons in western Ukraine and Byelorussia.

419 **matching that body-count in just two operations:** Gross, *Revolution from Abroad*, p. 228; Applebaum, *Gulag*, pp. 377ff.

420 **the militia men did not take for themselves:** Gross, *Revolution from Abroad*, pp. 207ff.

420 **'We need to find these bourgeois exploiters!':** Applebaum, *Gulag*, pp. 133ff.

420 **pack or there will be trouble, and I have lost my mind:** Gross, *Revolution from Abroad*, p. 209.

420 **February 1940 and June 1941, around half a million:** Gross, *Revolution from Abroad*, p. 194; Applebaum, *Gulag*, p. 383; http://www.electronicmuseum.ca/Poland-WW2/soviet_deportations/deportations_2.html.

420 **destination was Germany or another part of Poland:** Gross, *Revolution from Abroad*, p. 210.

420 **'windows, dirty and dilapidated, with no fences or trees':** Applebaum, *Gulag*, p. 384.

421 **tens of thousands of cold, hunger and disease:** For some harrowing narratives, see Gross, *Revolution from Abroad*, pp. 218–21; Applebaum, *Gulag*, p. 385.

421 **'to the absurdity and the hypocrisy of such statements':** Applebaum, *Gulag*, p. 226.

421 **They will disappear over there, like a field mouse:** Gross, *Revolution from Abroad*, p. 222.

421 **the Polish army capitulated to the Germans:** Blumstein, *Little House*, p. 10.

421 **the Red Army with flowers and banners:** Hoffman, *Shtetl*, pp. 201–10. For a similar account from Latvia, see Addison, *Letters*, p. 37.

421 **co-religionists were fleeing in the opposite direction:** Browning, *Origins*, p. 30.

422 **on an equal footing with Gentiles:** Pinchuk, *Shtetl Jews under Soviet Rule*, pp. 21–6, 65–101.

422 **'The people simply hate the Jews':** ibid., p. 98.

422 **'Ha! Ha! They stood up for their fatherland with honour':** Bokszanski, 'Representations of the Jews', pp. 253ff.

422 **('To Poles, landowners, and dogs—a dog's death!'):** Gross, *Revolution from Abroad*, p. 35. See also ibid., pp. 201ff.

422 **Commissars and two of the nine Supreme Court justices:** Shochat, 'Jews, Lithuanians and Russians', esp. pp. 306, 308.

423 **world with the same clenched-jawed defiance:** Witness the photographs reproduced in Bullock, *Hitler and Stalin*.

424 **(Hitler! Splendid! That's a deed of some skill!'):** Sebag-Montefiore, *Stalin*, p. 116.

424 **obelisks on the right bank of the River Seine:** Golomstock, *Totalitarian Art*, pp. 132ff.

424 **two 22-foot-high nude supermen, hand in hand:** Adam, *Art of the Third Reich*, pp. 244ff.

424 **claws looked down on the Russian sculptures:** Speer, *Inside the Third Reich*, p. 130.

425 **leaders as deities and national father-figures:** Compare, for example, Conrad Hommel's *The Führer and Commander in Chief of the Army* (1940) with Aleksandr Gerasimov's *Stalin at the 18th Party Congress* (1939/40).

425 **made so much of the running in the 1920s:** See the revealing examples in *Petropoulos, Faustian Bargain*.

426 **Communism, just as there were between Hitler and Stalin:** See Overy, *Dictators*, for a detailed comparative study.

426 **also diverged in a number of intriguing ways:** Hinz, *Art in the Third Reich*.

426 **members had seceded from the academic establishment in the 1860s:** Taylor, *Art and Literature under the Bolsheviks*, pp. 51ff.

427 **'the Soviets and the bolshevisation of the Nazis':** Hassell, *Diaries*, p. 62: August 27, 1939.

427 **simply giving Hitler raw materials in return for nothing:** See for somewhat different figures Overy, *Russia's War*, p. 53.

428 **saying, try not to give them any cause:** Murphy, *What Stalin Knew*, p. 185 and Appendix 2.

429 **literally been blasted out of the mountain's core:** Anon., *Eagle's Nest*.

429 **'my concerted force against the Soviet Union':** Kershaw, 'Nazi Foreign Policy', pp. 138ff.

430 **Soviet officer corps had been by Stalin's purges:** Overy, *Russia's War*, p. 56.

430 **Britain's last hope would be extinguished:** ibid., pp. 61ff.

430 **of tens of thousands of supposed 'counter-revolutionaries':** One estimate suggests that 96,000 people were arrested in the Baltic States and 160,000 deported: Applebaum, *Gulag*, p. 383.

430 **not least in the town of Cernauţi (Czernowitz):** Glenny, *Balkans*, p. 459; Castellan, *Germans*, pp. 62ff; Waldeck, *Athene Palace*, pp. 51ff. The 1939 Pact had envisaged nothing more than that Bessarabia should come within the Soviet 'sphere of influence'. No mention had been made of the Bukovina.

430 Ploeşti oilfields, crucial sources of fuel for the Wehrmacht: Overy, *Russia's War*, p. 60.
431 'marble from there, in any quantities we want': Speer, *Inside the Third Reich*, p. 116.
432 Physics Tutor won with eight days to spare: I am grateful to the Principal and Fellows of Jesus College, Oxford, for permission to quote from the Betting Book.
432 Yugoslav Regent Paul's agreement to a Pact with Hitler: Clarke, *Cripps Version*, pp. 214ff.
432 briefing obtained by Soviet spies in Warsaw: Murphy, *What Stalin Knew*, p. 15.
432 planned to declare war on the Soviet Union 'in March 1941': ibid., p. 65.
432 lover of the German ambassador Eugen Ott's wife: See Whymant, *Stalin's Spy*, pp. 62, 71–87, 99–109, 122–44.
433 total number of such warnings relayed to Moscow at 84: Overy, *Russia's War*, pp. 70ff; Burleigh, *Third Reich*, pp. 485ff.
433 of one Prague report: 'English provocation! Investigate!': Murphy, *What Stalin Knew*, p. 81.
433 'disinformer!' Sorge he dismissed as 'a little shit': ibid., p. 87. Cf. Whymant, *Stalin's Spy*, pp. 164–84.
433 'permission, then heads will roll, mark my words': See Gorodetsky, *Grand Delusion*.
433 next day would bring was shot on Stalin's orders: Overy, *Russia's War*, p. 71.
434 'Stalin Line' had been allowed to decay: ibid., pp. 64ff.
435 well past Minsk, had captured 287,704 prisoners: Erickson, *Road to Stalingrad*, vol. I, p. 159. See also Overy, *Russia's War*, pp. 85–9.
435 of Kiev in September added 665,000 more: Beevor, *Stalingrad*, p. 29.
435 encircled Vyazma and Briansk added another 673,000: Browning, *Origins of the Final Solution*, p. 328.
436 'A long heavy silence ensued': Gorodetsky, *Grand Delusion*.
436 particularly without a significant numerical advantage in manpower: Overy, *Russia's War*, pp. 71ff.
436 turned the Russian roads into impassable bogs: Service, *Stalin*, p. 42.
437 expect a simultaneous attack on Leningrad by the Royal Navy: Gorodetsky, *Grand Delusion*.
438 he muttered, as if expecting to be arrested: Service, *Stalin*, p. 415. See also Overy, *Russia's War*, pp. 78ff.

## CHAPTER THIRTEEN: KILLERS AND COLLABORATORS

439 a page of glory never mentioned and never to be mentioned: Eksteins, *Walking Since Daybreak*, p. 149.
439 'or show some sympathy for my unfortunate life': Kacel, *From Hell to Redemption*, pp. 85ff.
439 against are now living with us in closest harmony: Beevor, *Stalingrad*, p. 184.
439 the Soviet Union was Hitler's fatal mistake: See for example Kershaw, *Nemesis*.
440 'The Russian war is a source of pride for people': Klemperer, *Diary*, June 1941.
440 'European United Front against Bolshevism': Lukacs, *Last European War*, pp. 492ff.
440 *Grossraumwirtschaft* as a German-led bulwark against Bolshevism: Mazower, *Dark Continent*, p. 152.
440 expressed in Belgium, Finland and elsewhere: Lukacs, *Last European War*, p. 493.
440 emptiness of this rhetoric gradually manifest itself: Geyl, *Encounters in History*, pp. 331ff; Waldeck, *Athene Palace*, pp. 233–40, 243–47.
441 ethnic Germans who welcomed the advancing Wehrmacht: See Lumans, *Himmler's Auxiliaries*, pp. 243–45; Fleischhauer and Pinkus, *Soviet Germans*, pp. 94–100.
441 feted when they marched into Lwow: Gerstenfeld-Maltiel, *My Private War*, p. 53.
441 and Riga: Addison, *Letters*, p. 48.
441 crusade against the Antichrist of Moscow: Beevor, *Stalingrad*, p. 26.
441 greeted the Germans with bread and salt: Lotnik, *Nine Lives*, p. 16.
441 to leave nothing more than a rump Muscovy: Burleigh, 'Nazi Europe', pp. 327ff; idem, *Third Reich*, p. 530.
441 north and Astrakhan in the south (the so-called A-A Line): Overy, *Russia's War*, p. 62.
442 The Jews would be exterminated: Burleigh, 'Nazi Europe', pp. 336ff; Burleigh, *Third Reich*, pp. 546ff.
442 'commissars and the Communist intelligentsia': Burleigh, *Third Reich*, p. 518.
442 'against the Bolshevik inciters, guerrillas, saboteurs [and] Jews': Förster, *German Army*, p. 20.
443 As a matter of principle, they will be shot at once: Kershaw, *Nemesis*, p. 358.
443 them over to the SS Einsatzgruppen for execution: Förster, *German Army*, p. 20.
443 Army Quartermaster General Wagner: ibid., p. 21.
443 regarded as 'partisans' and shot on the spot: Bartov, *Hitler's Army*, p. 84.
443 prisoners by making 'immediate use of weapons': ibid., p. 83.
443 'the present Russian-Bolshevik system are to be spared': Burleigh, *Third Reich*, p. 521.
443 'who has not been taken prisoner in battle': Bartov, *Hitler's Army*, p. 84.
443 this could be interpreted as a license to kill anyone: See Browning, *Origins*, pp. 248ff.
443 'of hand grenades in the trousers of prisoners': Welch, *Propaganda*, p. 249.
444 Russians who were trying to wave a white flag: Fritz, *Frontsoldaten*, pp. 53ff.
444 Elsewhere Soviet prisoners were taken but then lined up and shot: Beevor, *Stalingrad*, pp. 58, 60.

444 others were taken out and shot in batches: Browning, *Origins of the Final Solution*, pp. 259ff.

444 examinations, or to the death camp at Auschwitz: Burleigh, *Third Reich*, p. 521.

444 that for Russian prisoners in the First World War: Calvocoressi et al., *Total War*, pp. 278ff; Bartov, *Hitler's Army*, p. 83; Burleigh, *Third Reich*, pp. 512ff.

444 to kill is not easily traced in written records: Though for a telling example see National Archives Washington. Heeresfeldpolizeichef im Oberkommando des Heeres, 'Entwicklung der Partisanenbewegung in der Zeit vom. 1.1.-30.6.1942'.

445 women and children into a synagogue and burning them alive: Browning, *Origins of the Final Solution*, pp. 255ff.

445 officer that the Jews were to be 'totally eradicated': ibid., p. 261.

445 as in all the rest of occupied Europe: Aly, 'Final Solution', table 2.

445 'shooting anyone who even looks sideways at us': Browning, *Origins of the Final Solution*, pp. 264, 309ff.

445 'bacillus source for a new decomposition': ibid., p. 315.

445 meant was more deportations and more ghettos: ibid., pp. 277, 315ff. But see Burleigh, *Third Reich*, p. 630.

446 'immediate cleansing of the entire Ostland of Jews': Browning, *Origins of the Final Solution*, p. 311.

446 too might be subsumed in the projected 'final solution': ibid., pp. 323–30.

446 a new influx of Jews to the ghettos: Frank had made this more or less clear in his speech at Berlin University on November 18, 1941. 'Work-Jews' could remain in the ghetto, 'but for the other Jews we must provide suitable arrangements. It is always dangerous, after all, to leave one's native land. Since the Jews moved away from Jerusalem there has been nothing for them except an existence as parasites: that has now come to an end.' See the Work Diary of Hans Frank, Yad Vashem Archives, JM/21: http://www.jewishvirtuallibrary.org/jsource/Holocaust/Frank.html.

446 party functionaries in Berlin on December 12: Burleigh, *Third Reich*, p. 648.

446 was swiftly relayed down the chain of command: See e.g., Work Diary of Hans Frank, December 16, 1941: http://fcit.coedu.usf.edu/holocaust/resource/document/DocFrank.htm.

447 They were also willing executioners: For two quite different interpretations of these events, see Browning, *Ordinary Men*, and Goldhagen, *Hitler's Willing Executioners*.

448 the right opportunity to manifest itself in murder: Goldhagen, *Hitler's Willing Executioners*.

448 'can be nothing nicer than to be a Bolshevik': Burleigh, *Third Reich*, p. 529.

448 'festival while executing the Germans and Ukrainians': Browning, *Origins of the Final Solution*, p. 265.

449 '(of promotion or leave) and peer-group pressure: Browning, *Ordinary Men*.

449 both killed when they drove over a stray landmine: Browning, *Origins of the Final Solution*, p. 279. See also ibid., p. 281ff.

449 ordered to spare only 'working Jews' by Himmler: Browning, *Origins of the Final Solution*, pp. 311ff.

450 Then the next batch came: Noakes and Pridham (eds.), *Nazism*, vol. III, p. 1100.

450 well as perpetrators; some even took photographs: Browning, *Origins of the Final Solution*, p. 261.

451 'home, then it will be the turn of our Jews': Browning, *Origins of the Final Solution*, p. 298.

451 efficient, and less demoralizing, mode of murder: ibid., pp. 257ff.

451 Jews began to arrive from western Europe?: ibid., pp. 160ff, 328ff, 350.

451 'dispose of the Jews, insofar as they are not capable of work': ibid., p. 321.

451 500 mental patients were gassed at Mogilev: ibid., p. 283.

451 people they had lived alongside all their lives: Gross, *Neighbours*, pp. 35–53.

452 'we have to destroy all the Jews, none should stay alive': ibid., pp. 16–18.

452 'In the end they proceeded to the main action—the burning': ibid., p. 20.

452 'tormented deaths of the Jews of Jedwabne': ibid., p. 89.

452 also helped Wasersztajn to survive the war: Bikont, *My z Jedwabnego*. Lacking Polish, I have relied on an abridged translation by Lukasz Sommer. I am grateful to Anna Popiel for her assistance.

452 helped the Germans to round up the town's Jews: Browning, *Ordinary Men*, pp. 155–8.

452 prevented their Jewish neighbours from fleeing: Gross, *Neighbours*, pp. 57–69.

452 as well as in Oleksin: Hoffman, *Shtetl*, p. 224.

452 Jewish property at bargain-basement prices: Rosen, *My Lost World*, pp. 88–93, 114ff, 170.

452 violence to active German encouragement: Lukas, *Forgotten Holocaust*, pp. 129, 140–5.

452 There were similar though smaller-scale reprisals in Kremets: Levene, 'Frontiers of Genocide', p. 109; Gerstenfeld-Maltiel, *My Private War*, pp. 60ff., 162.

453 victims without any need for German direction: Weiss, 'Jewish-Ukrainian Relations', pp. 413ff. But see Bilinsky, 'Methodological Problems', pp. 375ff.

453 seek German protection from the vicious Latvian hordes: Kacel, *From Hell to Redemption*, pp. 1–8. See also p. 65.

453 described what he saw in Latvia as 'monstrous': Ecksteins, *Walking Since Daybreak*, p. 149.

453 'to settle our account with the Jews': Shochat, 'Jews, Lithuanians and Russians', p. 310.

453 watched as locals beat Jews to death in the streets: Browning, *Origins of the Final Solution*, pp. 270ff.

453 Jews there were killed not by Germans but by other Lithuanians: Burleigh, *Third Reich*, p. 605. Details of these and other massacres of Soviet Jews can be found in Ehrenburg and Grossman, *Black Book of Russian Jewry*.

453 who rounded up, stripped and shot the Jews: Noakes and Pridham (eds.), *Nazism*, vol. III, pp. 1099ff.

454 meat hooks with labels reading 'Kosher Meat': Sebastian, *Journal*, February, 1941.

454 weeping, with terrible screams and cruel laughter: Burleigh, *Third Reich*, pp. 621ff.

454 Vice-Premier and proclaimed a 'National Legionary State': Vago, *Shadow of the Swastika*, p. 52.

454 invasion of the Soviet Union, notably in Odessa: Burleigh, *Third Reich*, p. 627.

454 once the Germans had occupied their country: Levi, *Cat Called Adolf*, p. 22.

455 case of a European-wide phenomenon: See Gross, 'Themes for a Social History'.

455 as Poles took revenge for their country's invasion: Blanke, *Orphans*, pp. 232–6.

455 already had massacred more than four thousand Poles: Browning, *Origins of the Final Solution*, p. 31.

455 effective than the more overt kinds of propaganda: Klemperer, *LTI*.

455 Germans, massacred between 60,000 and 80,000 Poles: Gross, *Polish Society*, pp. 193ff. Cf. Armstrong, 'Collaborationism', p. 409.

455 women raped and mutilated, babies bayoneted: Lotnik, *Nine Lives*, pp. 59–67.

456 Then they set the house ablaze: Piotrowski, *Vengeance of the Swallows*, p. 86.

456 he knew her family and remembered her as a child: Lotnik, *Nine Lives*, pp. 68ff.

456 'being dashed against buildings or hurled into burning houses': Piotrowski, *Vengeance of the Swallows*, p. 95. See also ibid., pp. 63, 66.

456 some for the Allies and others for an independent Ukraine: Sodol, *UPA*, esp. pp. 16–28.

456 and killing hundreds of thousands of them: Djilas, *Contested Country*, pp. 109–21, 125ff, 140.

457 Serbian Četniks and Partisans repaid these crimes in kind: Mazower, *Balkans*, pp. 111ff; Glenny, *Balkans*, pp. 474–7, 485, 495.

457 expelled from their homes on either side of the new border: Martin, 'Soviet Ethnic Cleansing', p. 820.

457 This included nearly all of Bosnia's 14,000 Jews: Malcolm, *Bosnia*, p. 174.

457 (between Poles and Ukrainians or between Croats and Serbs): Armstrong, 'Collaborationism', p. 406.

457 'and economic pacification' of occupied territory: Browning *Origins of the Final Solution*, p. 278.

458 'Legion' to maintain the credibility of Spanish neutrality: Scurr, *Germany's Spanish Volunteers*, pp. 4–31.

458 to surrender large numbers of Germans of military age to the SS: Keegan, *Waffen SS*, pp. 93ff.

458 served in the Horst Wessel and Maria Theresa divisions: Lumans, *Himmler's Auxiliaries*, pp. 237–41.

458 offered Reich citizenship if they joined the Waffen-SS: Bergen, 'Nazi Concept of "Volksdeutsche"', p. 575.

458 Danes and Norwegians in the summer of 1940: See Landwehr, *Lions of Flanders*, pp. 7–15; Ardenaes, *Norway and the Second World War*, pp. 72ff, 80ff.

458 Corps, made up of around 50 prisoners of war: Keegan, *Waffen SS*, p. 99.

458 fighting force, followed by Latvian and Estonian divisions: Lundin, *Finland in the Second World War*, pp. 112, 168ff.

458 accepted West Ukrainians, Slovaks and Croats as recruits: Armstrong, 'Collaborationism', p. 403.

458 under the supervision of the Grand Mufti of Jerusalem: Keegan, *Waffen SS*, p. 104.

458 non-German recruits or conscripts and a further five out of *Volksdeutsche*: Davies, *Europe*, pp. 1326ff.

459 fighting in close togetherness: ibid., p. 1017.

459 Eastern Front but also in the Balkans and even in France: Newland, *Cossacks in the German Army*, pp. 57–164.

459 in the case of the 71st and 76th infantry divisions: Beevor, *Stalingrad*, p. 184.

459 11 and 22 per cent of those still fighting were non-German: ibid., p. 439.

460 German side, numbering as many as a million men: Andreyev, *Vlasov*, p. 7.

460 'And if we refuse to fight, we'll be shot by the Germans': Beevor, *Stalingrad*, p. 186.

460 very reluctant to legitimize such spontaneous organizations: Andreyev, *Vlasov*, p. 36.

460 unsuccessful bid to raise the siege of Leningrad: ibid., pp. 62–5. See also Strik-Strikfeldt, *Against Stalin and Hitler*.

460 joining Czech nationalists in Prague in their revolt against the SS: Andreyev, *Vlasov*, pp. 72–5.

461 accounting for just under half the total foreign workforce: Herbert, *Hitler's Foreign Workers*, p. 98.

461 had been sent to the Reich from the Government-General: Housden, *Frank*, pp. 102ff.

461 most of them from occupied Polish or Soviet territory: Noakes and Pridham (eds.), *Nazism*, vol. III, pp. 908ff.

461 theory and with the sentiments of ordinary Germans: Herbert, *Hitler's Foreign Workers*, pp. 99–103.

461 if he or she fulfilled the requisite racial criteria: Noakes and Pridham (eds.), *Nazism*, vol. III, p. 985; Herbert, *Hitler's Foreign Workers*, p. 131.

461 including giving foreigners food, drink or tobacco: Herbert, *Hitler's Foreign Workers*, pp. 125ff.

462 was confined to Poles not eligible for Germanization: Noakes and Pridham (eds.), *Nazism*, vol. III, p. 950.

462 with a German woman who was actually a prostitute: Herbert, *Hitler's Foreign Workers*, p. 132.

462 sex with German women and 47 for 'moral offences': Evans, *Rituals*, p. 729.

462  were generally sentenced to three years' imprisonment: Herbert, *Hitler's Foreign Workers*, p. 129.
462  women were faced up to three months in a concentration camp: ibid., p. 132.
462  15 months in jail for an illicit liaison with a French POW: ibid., p. 128.
463  interesting and therefore make it easy for the latter to approach them: Burleigh and Wippermann, *Racial State*, p. 262. See also Herbert, *Hitler's Foreign Workers*, p. 269.
463  'act of treason against them, and each will be harshly punished by law': Gordon, *Hitler, Germans and the Jewish Question*, p. 103.
463  'distinction that must be maintained between Germans and *Fremdvölkische*': Herbert, *Hitler's Foreign Workers*, pp. 270ff.
463  or molest Germans will be confined to brothels: Noakes and Pridham (eds.), *Nazism*, vol. III, p. 951.
463  Every time German nationals mix with Poles our standards sink: Welch, *Propaganda*, p. 137.
464  physical relations with Poles will be placed in protective custody: Noakes and Pridham (eds.), *Nazism*, vol. III, p. 954.
464  'us and the negroes': Burleigh, 'Nazi Europe', p. 334.
464  sexual relations with German women were to be hanged: Burleigh, *Third Reich*, p. 334.
464  could be considered 'eligible for Germanization': Noakes and Pridham (eds.), *Nazism*, vol. III, p. 985ff. Cf. Aly, 'Final Solution', p. 247.
464  Jews by day and sleeping with one by night: Burleigh, *Third Reich*, p. 585.
465  with large doses of X-rays on both men and women: Noakes and Pridham (eds.), *Nazism*, vol. III, pp. 1187ff.
465  SS officers sexually exploited female prisoners: Hackett, Buchenwald Report, pp. 73ff, 235ff.
465  mistress while he was commander at Auschwitz: Todorov, *Facing the Extreme*, p. 170.

## CHAPTER FOURTEEN: THE GATES OF HELL

466  who are unequal unequally is to realize equality: Dower, *War Without Mercy*, p. 264.
466  gruesome out of one of Well[s]'s novels rather than real life: Dr Oscar Elliot Fisher, *Diary of Japanese Invasion of Malaya*, December 11, 1941: http://freespace.virgin.net/sam.campbell/grandpa1a.html.
467  In ten thousand years they'll be standing, just as they are: Burleigh, 'Nazi Europe', pp. 344ff.
467  engraved the names of all the Germans who had fallen in the First World War: Speer, *Inside the Third Reich*, pp. 119–24.
467  which he contrasted with German naivety on colonial questions: See Hitler, *Mein Kampf*, pp. 132ff, 601.
468  maintain subject peoples in a state of poverty and illiteracy: Kershaw, *Hitler*, vol. II, p. 401.
468  'What India was for England, the territories of Russia will be for us': Trevor-Roper (ed.), *Hitler's Table Talk*, pp. 23ff.
468  were not interested in washing the dirty linen of their subject peoples: ibid., pp. 46ff.
468  the natives to live whilst they exploit them to the uttermost: ibid., pp. 198ff.
469  'These people aren't really our superiors': ibid., p. 615.
469  'anyone who shows a trace of human sentiment is damned forever': ibid., p. 654.
469  'idea of his mentality, ignorance and obvious sincerity': Roberts, 'House of Windsor and Appeasement'.
469  to imagine the world as it might have looked had Hitler's dreams been realized: Rosenfeld, *World Hitler Never Made*.
469  envisaged and Hitler repeatedly mused about in his evening monologues: See Trevor-Roper (ed.), *Hitler's Table Talk*, pp. 93, 185, 186–8, 198ff, 236ff.
470  which envisaged deporting around 50 million East Europeans to Siberia: For a historically informed account of what might have been, see Burleigh, 'Nazi Europe'.
470  with each Japanese couple being encouraged to have around five children: Dower, *War without Mercy*, pp 262–8.
471  were interconnected, should simply be renamed the 'Great Sea of Japan': ibid., p. 273.
471  'Afghanistan and other central Asian countries, West Asia [and] Southwest Asia': ibid.
471  'based on 'racial harmony' and 'mutual prosperity . . . of all the peoples concerned': ibid., p. 281.
471  'Greater East Asia' issued by the General Staff Headquarters in August 1942: Lebra (ed.), *Japan's Greater East Asia Co-Prosperity Sphere*, p. 119.
471  'indigenous social traditions and to shed blood in building independent nations': ibid., p. 39.
472  'the poisonous dung of [Western] material civilization': Thorne, *Far Eastern War*, pp. 144ff.
472  including 2 million in Australia and New Zealand: Dower, *War Without Mercy*, p. 275.
472  Japanese-occupied territory was to be 'discouraged': ibid., p. 287.
472  attend Shinto services and, after 1939, to adopt Japanese names: Wan-yao, 'Kōminka Movement', pp. 60ff.
472  mortality rate from contagious diseases was more than twice as high: Ienaga, *Japan's Last War*, pp. 156ff. Cf. Rhee, *Doomed Empire*.
472  only on the basis of the expulsion or segregation of inferior peoples: Dower, *War Without Mercy*, p. 277.
472  and relationships with 'child countries' would not be tolerated: ibid., p. 283.

473 enough to bring forth numerous 'plump and healthy' offspring: Young, *Japan's Total Empire*, pp. 368ff.

473 Manchuria—'Nanking vermin'—tells its own story: ibid., p. 372.

473 'are bacteria infesting world civilization': Doyle, *China and Japan at War*, p. 341.

473 would be 'driven out of the Southern Area': Lebra (ed.), *Japan's Greater East Asia Co-Prosperity Sphere*, pp. 120ff.

473 shared interest in a 'new order of things': Lu, *From the Marco Polo Bridge*, p. 111. But see Minear, *Victors' Justice*, pp. 140ff.

474 'Anglo-Saxonism, which is bankrupt and will be wiped out': Coox, 'Pacific War', pp. 323ff.

475 that the sun was literally always shining on some part of it: Cell, 'Colonial Rule', pp. 232ff.

475 and bringing the war to a swift conclusion: Dreyer, *China at War*, pp. 219ff. Hata, 'Continental Expansion', p. 307.

475 command of the Japanese forces on December 2: Bagish and Conroy, 'Japanese Aggression', pp. 328–31. This is the argument of Bergamini, *Japan's Imperial Conspiracy*.

476 'secret, to be destroyed'—to 'Kill all Captives': Chang, *Rape of Nanking*, p. 38.

476 The score was reported as Mukai 89, Noda 78: ibid., pp. 56ff.

476 prisoners into batches of a dozen each and shoot them: ibid., p. 39.

476 gunfire and then soaked with gasoline and set on fire: Brook (ed.), *Documents*, pp. 224ff.

477 I stood there at a total loss and did not know what to do: Chang, *Rape of Nanking*, p. 47.

477 We can do anything to such creatures: Kibata, 'Japanese Treatment', p. 141.

477 by what he witnessed, he did (or could do) little to stop it: Chang, *Rape of Nanking*, pp. 50ff.

477 camps outside the city whence they had fled: Brook (ed), *Documents*, pp. 7ff.

477 of unburied bodies littered the streets: Rabe, *Good Man of Nanking*, pp. 115, 212.

477 British civilians killed during the entire war: Chang, *Rape of Nanking*, pp. 4ff. Cf. Bagish and Conroy, 'Japanese Aggression', p. 329.

477 As far as the eye can see—nothing but rubble!: Rabe, *Good Man of Nanking*, pp. 134ff.

478 the 'injured females' it recorded had been raped: Brownmiller, *Against Our Will*, p. 58.

478 there had been 'at least 1,000 cases a night': ibid., p. 58.

478 clothing, and raped until they were satisfied: Brook (ed), *Documents*, p. 212.

478 been 'horribly raped and abused': Brownmiller, *Against Our Will*, p. 58.

478 was saved by doctors at the Nanking Hospital: Details of her experience can be found in the permanent exhibit at the Nanjing Massacre Museum.

478 bayonets or other objects stuck into their vaginas: Brownmiller, *Against Our Will*, p. 59ff.

478 later proved to have been infected with venereal disease: Brook (ed.), *Documents*, p. 251.

479 15 to 20 soldiers for sexual intercourse and abuse: Chang, *Rape of Nanking*, p. 49.

479 Because dead bodies don't talk: ibid., pp. 49ff.

479 'nativism and borrowed German racial theories'?: See Buruma, *Inventing Japan*, p. 83.

479 and defenceless target on which to vent his frustrations: Boyle, *China and Japan at War*, p. 343

480 'To us soldiers, they were pitiful, spineless people': ibid., p. 343.

481 but on the contrary because we love them too much: ibid., p. 341.

481 16,000 men in days of intense house-to-house fighting: Dreyer, *China at War*, pp. 226ff.

481 forced to abandon Chinhsien, Nanning and Pinyang: ibid., pp. 237ff.

481 did not significantly change again until 1944: ibid., p. 207.

481 with puppet regimes, as they had done in Manchuria: Lu, *From the Marco Polo Bridge*, pp. 25–8. See also Katsumi, 'Politics of War', pp. 294ff.

482 itself to a campaign of 'protracted' guerrilla warfare: Dreyer, *China at War*, pp. 249–54; Li, *Japanese Army*, pp. 225–33.

482 established in Nanking by the Central China Area Army: Dreyer, *China at War*, pp. 245ff.

482 unification of the various puppet regimes under his authority: Boyle, *China and Japan at War*, pp. 336ff; Lu, *From the Marco Polo Bridge*, pp. 127ff. Cf. Dreyer, *China at War*, pp. 247–9; Katsumi, 'Politics of War', pp. 295ff; Hata, 'Continental Expansion', pp. 307ff.

482 control of the maritime customs and other tax agencies: Lu, *From the Marco Polo Bridge*, pp. 128ff.

482 square miles of territory and around 200 million people: ibid., pp. 238ff.

483 ('sharing each other's fate') were not wholly empty of meaning: Boyle, *China and Japan at War*, p. 353.

483 Communist attacks with the brutal 'three all' policy: 'Take all, kill all, burn all': Li, *Japanese Army*, pp. 12ff; Dreyer, *China at War*, pp. 253ff.

483 Ye Ting's New 4th Army at Maolin in Anhui: Dreyer, *China at War*, p. 255.

483 seek some kind of strategic breakthrough elsewhere: ibid., pp. 227ff.

483 in Hunnan from British-ruled Burma and French Hanoi: Hata, 'Continental Expansion', pp. 308ff.

484 in order to perpetuate China's dependent status: Katsumi, 'Politics of War', pp. 303ff.

484 but also the Soviet Union and the United States: Coox, 'Pacific War', p. 323.

484 that the odds were heavily in the Red Army's favour: ibid., p. 321.

484 victory (though for no territorial gain), the latter was a disaster: ibid., pp. 120–41. Cf. Coox, 'Pacific War', pp. 321ff; Hata, 'Continental Expansion', p. 308.

484  command of Lieutenant-General (later Marshal) Zhukov: Coox, *Nomonhan*, vol. II, pp. 911–1032. See also Hosoya, 'Northern Defense'. Cf. Hata, 'Continental Expansion', p. 313.

484  readiness to sign a Non-Aggression Pact with Stalin in April 1941: Jansen, *Japan and China*, pp. 402ff. Cf. Coox, 'Pacific War', pp. 325ff.

484  throughout the war, for fear of a Soviet surprise attack: Hosoya, 'Northern Defense', p. 13; Lu, *From the Marco Polo Bridge*, pp. 132–40.

484  two months later, he was overruled and ousted from office: Kennedy, 'Japanese Strategy', p. 183; Hosoya, 'Northern Defense', pp. 7–10; Coox, 'Pacific War', p. 327ff.

484  time overrunning Dutch Sumatra, Borneo and Java: Kiyoshi, 'Japanese Strategy', p. 128.

485  from which to attack the Chinese Nationalists in Sichuan: Barnhart, 'Japanese Intelligence', p. 442.

485  insisted that unless Japan struck soon, she risked 'missing the bus': Coox, 'Pacific War', p. 324.

485  proponents of the Southern strategy had the upper hand: Barnhart, 'Japanese Intelligence', pp. 443ff.

485  per cent in the Pacific theatre and 14 per cent in South-East Asia: Ellis and Cox, *World War II Handbook*, p. 228.

485  But its air defences were feeble: Barber and Henshall, *Last War of Empires*, pp. 78–81.

485  they had been forgotten even before the war began: Bayly and Harper, *Forgotten Armies*.

486  By September 23 northern Indo-China was in Japanese hands: Lu, *From the Marco Polo Bridge*, pp. 141–4.

486  compromise was to bring Thailand too into the Japanese orbit: ibid., pp. 145ff.

486  colonial authorities attempted to be accommodating: ibid., pp. 151ff.

486  On June 17 Yoshizawa's mission departed for Tokyo: ibid., pp. 152ff.

487  diplomatic solution of Japan's problems; this was the deadline for war: Coox, 'Pacific War', pp. 332ff.

487  The sole obstacle to Japanese hegemony in South-East Asia was America: See Kinhide, 'Structure of Japanese-American Relations'.

487  United States and hence its vulnerability to economic pressure: Barnhart, *Japan Prepares for Total War*, pp. 178ff.

487  including copious quantities of cotton, scrap iron and oil: Jansen, *Japan and China*, p. 397.

487  to death, especially if they cut off oil exports to Japan: Scalapino, 'Southern Advance', p. 117.

487  economic odds were stacked so heavily against them: Graebner, 'Introduction', pp. xvi–xvii.

487  aluminium, molybdenum, nickel, tungsten and vanadium: Barnhart, *Japan Prepares for Total War*, pp. 179ff.

488  that would facilitate the production of aviation fuel: ibid., pp. 180ff. Cf. Lu, *From the Marco Polo Bridge*, p. 150.

488  of iron and steel themselves became subject to license: Barnhart, *Japan Prepares for Total War*, pp. 182–97. Cf. Lu, *From the Marco Polo Bridge*, p. 144; Cox, 'Pacific War', p. 326.

488  raw materials since the outbreak of war in China: Lu, *From the Marco Polo Bridge*, pp. 244ff.

488  to the Japanese occupation of southern Indo-China: Barnhart, *Japan Prepares for Total War*, pp. 263ff. Barnhart argues that Washington was misreading its intelligence about decision-making in Tokyo, mistaking the move into southern Indo-China as the start of a full-scale South Asian campaign, rather than a holding operation. The Americans consistently underestimated the importance of inter-service rivalries in Japan. Cf. Barnhart, 'Japanese Intelligence', p. 445.

488  the Soviet Union were on friendly terms with that combination: Lu, *From the Marco Polo Bridge*, pp. 109–13.

488  her allies would reinforce rather than reverse that sentiment: Barnhart, 'Japanese Intelligence', pp. 440, 446ff.

488  achieved without precipitating American intervention: Coox, 'Pacific War', p. 325; Fujiwara, 'Role of the Japanese Army', p. 191.

488  deal a knockout blow to the U.S. Navy at the outset: Kiyoshi, 'Japanese Strategy', pp. 129ff.

489  400 planes equipped with torpedoes or armour-piercing shells: Coox, 'Pacific War', pp. 330ff; idem, 'Effectiveness of the Japanese Military Establishment', p. 17.

489  'the material situation will be much better if we go to war': Barnhart, 'Japanese Intelligence', p. 449; Kiyoshi, 'Japanese Strategy', p. 132.

489  British Empire, the Dutch East Indies and the United States: For more realistic assessments of Japan's economic position, see Coox, 'Pacific War', pp. 333ff.

489  just idly waiting; after eighteen months it would all be gone: Jansen, *Japan and China*, pp. 404ff.

489  'dare to leap boldly from the towering stage of Kiyomizu Temple': Coox, 'Effectiveness of the Japanese Military Establishment', p. 14.

490  class nation after two or three years if we merely sat tight: Coox, 'Pacific War', p. 336.

490  would certainly bankrupt the country if they continued to sit idle: Buruma, *Inventing Japan*, p. 96. See also Jansen, *Japan and China*, pp. 405–8.

490  was to 'lie prostrate at the feet of the United States': Coox, 'Pacific War', p. 329.

490  'Instead . . . the present calamity . . . indirectly resulted from the Alliance': Lu, *From the Marco Polo Bridge*, p. 119.

490  regime in China, rather than risk war with the United States: Graebner, 'Introduction', p. xii.

491 **paradoxically, as true to 'the spirit of defending the nation in a war'**: Kimitada, 'Japanese Images', p. 119.
491 **'increasingly worse' as early as the second half of 1942**: Coox, 'Effectiveness of the Japanese Military Establishment', p. 13.
491 **know what Japan would do if war continued after 1943**: Coox, 'Pacific War', pp. 333ff.
491 **in war than 'to be ground down without doing anything'**: Coox, 'Effectiveness of the Japanese Military Establishment', p. 14.
491 **July and October 1940 in response to Japanese pressure**: Lowe, *Great Britain and the Origins of the Pacific War*, pp. 284–7. Cf. Lowe, 'Great Britain and the Coming of the Pacific War', pp. 44ff.
491 **of China and underestimated the perils of war with Japan**: Clayton, 'American and Japanese Strategies', p. 709ff.
491 **system—and recognition of the Kuomintang government**: Coox, 'Pacific War', p. 337.
491 **to her policy towards the Soviet Union during the Cold War**: Iriye, *Power and Culture*, p. 1.
492 **too good to necessitate such a gross betrayal of transatlantic trust**: For a good summary of the literature, see Rasor, 'Japanese Attack', pp. 47–50. The key texts are Wohlstetter, *Pearl Harbor*; Melosi, *Shadow of Pearl Harbor*; Costello, *Days of Infamy*; and Rusbridger and Nave, *Betrayal at Pearl Harbor*.
492 **event of war on December 1—six days before Pearl Harbor**: Lowe, 'Great Britain and the Coming of the Pacific War', pp. 57–61.
492 **compared with total U.S. military fatalities of 3,297**: Coox, 'Pacific War', pp. 341–5; idem, 'Effectiveness of the Japanese Military Establishment', p. 18. A further 20 aircraft were destroyed when they crashed on returning to the carriers.
493 **Japanese felt such pride in ourselves as a race as we did then**: Buruma, *Inventing Japan*, p. 89.
493 **who had all but run out of food and ammunition**: The definitive account of the debacle remains Neidpath, *Singapore Naval Base*.
493 **'been out-generalled, outwitted and outfought . . . by better soldiers'**: Bond (ed.), *Pownall Diaries*, vol. II, p. 85.
494 **Corregidor; this effectively ended resistance in the Philippines**: Kennedy, 'Japanese Strategy', pp. 184ff; Coox, 'Pacific War', pp. 345–79.
494 **to south; its circumference was a staggering 14,200 miles**: Clayton, 'American and Japanese Strategies', p. 717.
494 **Fiji, Samoa, New Guinea, and even Australia, Ceylon and India**: Kennedy, 'Japanese Strategy', pp. 185ff.
494 **Yew replied: 'That is the end of the British Empire'**: Bayly and Harper, *Forgotten Armies*, p. 130.
494 **Australians on the Kokoda Trail in New Guinea**: Bradley, 'The Boys Who Saved Australia'. For examples of very reluctant Antipodean surrender in the Pacific theatre see Bertram, *Shadow of a War*, p. 135; Harrison, *Brave Japanese*, p. 90; Baxter, *Not Much of Picnic*, p. 37.
495 **'"and didn't surrender" is not a very good cause'**: Biggs, *Behind the Barbed Wire*, p. 10.
495 **It was the same story at Bataan**: FitzPatrick and Sweetser, *Hike into the Sun*, pp. 54ff; Bilyeu, *Lost in Action*, pp. 64ff, 73ff.
495 **themselves that 'we had done our very best'**: Carson, *My Time in Hell*, pp. 8–15.
495 **referring to him privately as 'Peanut' or 'the rattlesnake'**: Fenby, *Generalissimo*, pp. 369–81.
495 **soubriquet 'Vinegar Joe' for his acerbic candour**: Dreyer, *China at War*, pp. 268ff.
495 **to obey his orders**: ibid., pp. 269ff.
495 **principal railway under Japanese control**: Coox, 'Pacific War', pp. 354ff.
495 **Nippon will undergo the same experience as the snow**: Waterford, *Prisoners of the Japanese*, p. 26.
496 **stigmatizing of surrender per se mentioned above**: Garrett, *P.O.W.*, pp. 182ff. See also Gilbert, *Second World War*, p. 745.
496 **face and beatings—were a daily occurrence in some camps**: Begg and Liddle (eds.), *For Five Shillings a Day*, pp. 404ff.
496 **most famously on the Burma–Thailand railway line**: Towle, 'Introduction', p. xv; Kinvig, 'Allied POWs'. For some powerful memoirs, see Symons, *Hell in Five*.
496 **'and is to be beheaded or castrated at the will of the Emperor'**: Hynes, *Soldier's Tale*, p. 246.
496 **disease exacerbated by physical overwork and abuse**: For mortality rates of prisoners in Japanese hands, see Waterford, *Prisoners of the Japanese*, pp. 141–6; Kinvig, 'Allied POWs', p. 47n.
496 **their specious claims to be the liberators of Asia**: Towle, 'Japanese Army'.
496 **'purification-by-elimination' (sook ching) operations**: Murfett et al., *Between Two Oceans*, pp. 249ff; Harries, *Soldiers of the Sun*, p. 412ff.
497 **Malaya, for example, no fewer than 29,638 died**: Bayly and Harper, *Forgotten Armies*, p. 405. Cf. Dower, *War Without Mercy*, p. 48; Tinker, *New System of Slavery*, pp. 382ff.
497 **over the 'Greater East Asia', often to front-line areas**: For details of their destinations, based on an admittedly small sample of women who came forward in recent years, see Hicks, *Comfort Women*, pp. xvii.
498 **When we had disease, we wrote 'vacation' on the door'**: Korean Society for Solving the Problems of 'Japanese Comfort Women', *Enforced Sex Slaves*. I am grateful to Jaeyoon Song for his translation.

498  cut my belly with a knife, and scratched my breast: ibid. Estimates for the total numbers of 'comfort women' range from 80,000 to 200,000. Chang argues that the system was a response to the Rape of Nanking; 'comfort houses' were designed to regularize the army's appetite for rape and to conceal it from view: Chang, *Rape of Nanking*, pp. 52ff.

498  'other races who are Asiatics no less themselves?': Dower, *War Without Mercy*, p. 46.

498  on the basis of Nippon Seishin—the Japanese spirit: See Thio, 'Syonan Years'.

498  Similar things were attempted in occupied Java: Thorne, *Experience of War*, p. 159.

499  'in order to diminish their prestige in native eyes': Kibata, 'Japanese Treatment', p. 143.

499  'road with basket and pole while they roll by on their lorries!': Dunlop, *War Diaries*, pp. 191, 209.

499  'any ideas of worship of Europe and America': ibid.

499  they were able to elicit enthusiastic responses: Buruma, *Inventing Japan*, p. 97.

499  'the Protector of Asia and the Light of Asia': Dower, *War Without Mercy*, pp. 3–8.

499  Japan's war was indeed a war for national independence: Thorne, *Far Eastern War*, p. 146.

500  'with our minds, this is the time to think with our blood': Dower, *War Without Mercy*, p. 6.

500  victories 'vindicated the prestige of all Asiatic nations': Thorne, *Far Eastern War*, p. 146.

500  serving as soldiers or civilians working for the Japanese military: Wan-yao, 'Kōminka Movement', pp. 63–6.

500  and Kachin hill tribes also resisted Japanese rule: Fay, *Forgotten Army*, pp. 243ff.

500  among both anti-European nationalists and opportunists: Silverstein, 'Importance of the Japanese Occupation', pp. 5ff.

500  who had been Lieutenant-Governor of the Punjab at that time: Draper, *Amritsar Massacre*, pp. 269–86.

500  'British Empire' and called on Indians to join the Axis side: Jeffery, 'Second World War', p. 319.

501  'there can be no real mutual prosperity in Greater East Asia': Lebra, *Japanese-Trained Armies*, p. 22.

501  had made up their minds to grant Burmese independence: ibid., pp. 61ff.

501  known as Peta (Army Defenders of the Homeland) were also formed: Thorne, *Far Eastern War*, p. 148.

501  volunteer defence forces too, known as Giyūgun: Lebra, *Japanese-Trained Armies*, p. 117. In Malaya there was also an armed police force.

501  forces were not large—at most 153,000 trained men: ibid., p. 190.

501  soldiers who actually served in the Southern theatre—around 300,000: See the figures in Ellis, *World War II Handbook*, pp. 227ff.

501  'arrogance, and racial pretensions of the Japanese militarists': Dower, *War Without Mercy*, p. 46.

501  have significantly slowed down the U.S. recovery at sea: Kennedy, 'Japanese Strategy', pp. 185–8; Shirer, 'Pearl Harbor'. See also Rose, 'Missing Carriers'.

501  intention to try to hold the islands in the event of a war: Dudley, 'Plan Orange'. Cf. Clayton, 'American and Japanese Strategies', p. 710ff.

502  from Burma, an option that was certainly contemplated: Isby, 'Japanese Raj'. See also Lebra, *Japanese-Trained Armies*, p. 22.

502  meet the inevitable Anglo-American counter-offensives: Kennedy, 'Japanese Strategy', p. 191ff.

502  at the battles of Coral Sea, Midway and Guadalcanal: Arnold, 'Coral and Purple'; Cook, 'Midway Disaster'; Burtt, 'Guadalcanal'.

## CHAPTER FIFTEEN: THE OSMOSIS OF WAR

505  courage and a just cause were quite irrelevant to the issue: Waugh, *Sword of Honour*, pp. 123.

505  'and continue our development in a different form': Grossman, *Life and Fate*, p. 216.

505  'always tend to assume the . . . the, eh, trappings of the loser': Mailer, *Naked and the Dead*, p. 320.

506  The initial victims were in fact Soviet prisoners of war: Gutman and Berenbaum (eds.), *Anatomy of the Auschwitz Death Camp*, pp. 159ff.

508  workers check genitals and anus for gold, diamonds and valuables: Noakes and Pridham (eds.), *Nazism*, vol. III, pp. 1149ff.

508  'Mummy! But I've been good! It's dark! It's dark!': Reder, *Belzech*, p. 141.

508  held on the manicured banks of Berlin's Wannsee on January 20, 1942: Noakes and Pridham (eds.), *Nazism*, vol. III, pp. 1127ff. Cf. Aly, 'Final Solution', p. 233.

509  'to replace damaged body parts of wounded German soldiers': National Archives, Washington, RG 238, Office of the Chief Counsel for War Crimes, Deposition of Dr Zdenka Nedvedova-Nejedla, document No. NO-875, December 13, 1946.

509  (that, at least, was the historian Friedrich Meinecke's theory): Meinecke, *Deutsche Katastrophe*.

510  the old-fashioned, supposedly humane form of partition: Charles Eade diary, July 24, 1941, *Sunday Telegraph*, February 15, 1998. Cf. Grigg, *1943*, p. 184, for Churchill's repudiation of Stalin's proposal to shoot fifty thousand German officers and technicians after the war. For Churchill's endearingly puerile urination on crossing into Germany, see Alanbrooke, *War Diaries*, pp. 667, 678.

512  carriage transported the embalmed body of Lenin to safety: Overy, *Russia's War*, pp. 95ff.

512  'German to the very last man. Death to the German invaders!': ibid., pp. 114ff.

512 Stalin to divert 58 divisions from Siberia to the Western Front: ibid., pp. 118ff. Cf. Durschmied, *Hinge Factor*, ch. 14. Sorge's reward never came. He was arrested by the Japanese, whose offer to exchange him for a Japanese prisoner the Soviets spurned: Whymant, *Stalin's Spy*, p. 299.

512 casualty rate was soaring as Soviet resistance stiffened: Hofmann, 'Battle for Moscow', p. 178.

512 'Thirty-Year Lightning War' had begun: Malaparte, *Kaputt*, p. 214.

513 'Prague and Brussels had become provincial German cities': Grossman, *Life and Fate*, p. 195.

513 Uganda, Kenya, Zanzibar and Northern Rhodesia: Burleigh, 'Nazi Europe', pp. 341ff.

513 optimist could be certain that the Allies would win the war: Overy, *Why the Allies Won*, p. 15.

513 Soviets would make a separate peace with Hitler: Alanbrooke, *War Diaries*, p. 236.

513 Britain seemed to be 'a ship . . . heading inevitably for the rocks': ibid., pp. 243ff.

513 might even reach the Gulf oilfields ('our Achilles heel'): ibid., pp. 249, 280–3, 355.

514 towards the Caucasus; or across Egypt to Suez and beyond: Keegan, 'How Hitler Could Have Won the War'. On the (remote) possibility of Turkey's joining the Axis, see Gill, 'Into the Caucasus'.

514 divisions that were sitting more or less idle in Western Europe: Perrett, 'Operation SPHINX'; Griffith, 'The Hinge'. See also Tsouras, 'Operation ORIENT'.

514 into winning the Battle of the Atlantic in 1942: Howarth, 'Germany and the Atlantic Sea-War'. See also Dudley, 'Little Admiral'.

514 Gerd von Rundstedt's Army Group southwards towards Kiev: Lucas, 'Operation WOTAN'. Cf. Downing, *Moscow Option*.

514 conquer the Caucasus, opening the way to the Gulf oil fields: Alanbrooke, *War Diaries*, p. 305.

514 to reinforce their line of defence in the Pacific: This is the implication of Kennedy, 'Japanese Strategic Decisions'. See also Clayton, 'American and Japanese Strategies', p. 715.

515 equivalent to a third of pre-war French national income: Milward, *War, Economy and Society*, p. 140, tables 21, 22.

515 was a substantial net contributor to the German war effort: Trade figures for Central and Eastern Europe in Kaser and Radice (eds.), *Economic History of Eastern Europe*, pp. 523–9.

515 —more than half—of Soviet industrial capacity: To be precise, 71 per cent of the Soviet Union's iron ore mines, two thirds of its aluminium, manganese and copper, 63 per cent of its coal mines, 57 per cent of its rolled steel production, 40 per cent of its electricity generating capacity and a third of its rail network: Overy, *Why the Allies Won*, p. 82; Burleigh, *Third Reich*, p. 498.

515 accounted for a fifth of the active civilian labour force by 1943: Noakes and Pridham (eds.), *Nazism*, vol. III, pp. 908ff.

515 manufacturers and achieving startling improvements in productivity: Overy, *Why the Allies Won*, pp. 198ff, 201–4, 242ff. Though see Budrass, Scherner and Streb, 'Demystifying the German "Armament Miracle" ', which seeks to diminish Speer's contribution.

515 production by a factor of five and a half between 1941 and 1944: Coox, 'Effectiveness', p. 6.

516 spending was nearly twice that of Germany and Japan combined: Goldsmith, 'Power of Victory'.

517 came from India, Canada, Australia, New Zealand and South Africa: Statistics in Ellis, *World War II Data Handbook*, pp. 227ff.

517 Empire proved every bit as strong as in the First World War: See e.g., McKernan, *All In!*, pp. 37–48. 70 per cent of Slim's 14th Army were Gurkha, African or Burmese.

517 albeit loyalty that was conditional on post-war independence: Details in Prasad and Char, *Expansion of the Armed Forces*, appendix 13–16. See also Chenevix-Trench, *Indian Army*; Barkawi, 'Combat Motivation in the Colonies'.

517 larger proportion than their share of the pre-war Soviet population: Alexiev and Wimbush, 'Non-Russians in the Red Army', pp. 432ff, 441. Cf. Rakowska-Harmstone, 'Brotherhood in Arms'; Gorter-Gronvik and Suprun, 'Ethnic Minorities'. Central Asians and Caucasians were, however, under-represented. Indeed, more of them fought for the Germans.

517 Half the soldiers of the Soviet 62nd Army at Stalingrad were not Russians: Beevor, *Stalingrad*, p. 170.

517 and fought in all the major campaigns from Operation Torch onwards: Buckley, *American Patriots*, pp. 262–318; Hargrove, *Buffalo Soldiers*, pp. 3–5.

517 Stars and Stripes on Iwo Jima were of foreign origin; one was a Pima Indian: Davie, *Refugees*, p. 195. The total number of aliens in the Army and Navy was 125,880. Other racial and national minorities identified in the Army's records were 51,438 Puerto Ricans, 20,080 Japanese, 19,567 American Indians, 13,311 Chinese, 11,506 Filipinos, 1,320 Hawaiians: http://www.army.mil/cmh-pg/documents/wwii/minst.htm.

517 Japanese-Americans served in the U.S. Army during the war: Myer, *Uprooted Americans*, pp. 146–53.

518 invading Europe, with wave after wave of sons of immigrants: Hersey, *Bell for Adano*, Foreword.

518 Hersey's insight that the typical GI's sole war aim was 'to go home': ibid., p. 215. See also idem, *Into the Valley*, pp. 74ff; and Cozzens, *Guard of Honor*, pp. 275ff.

518 the Allies had more than twice as many men under arms: Based on the various figures in Harrison (ed.), *Economics of World War II*. For the end of the war, see Ellis, *World War II Data Handbook*, pp. 227ff.

518 nicknamed 'the King's Own Loyal Enemy Aliens': Beckman, *Jewish Brigade*, p. 72; Casper, *With the Jewish Brigade*, p. 21. On the 'KOLEA', see Bentwich, 'I Understand the Risks'.

518 artillery and combat aircraft by roughly 3 to 1: Harrison, 'Overview', p. 17.

519 was one of the keys to victory at El Alamein: Ellis, *World War II Data Handbook*, pp. 228, 230.

519 of the offensives of 1944 and 1945 was just under 8: ibid., pp. 14, 230.

519 Eastern Front rose from 3 in July 1943 to 10 by January 1945: ibid., p. 233.

519 it was hopeless, we couldn't possibly have won the war: Carruthers (ed.), *Servants of Evil*, p. 257.

519 repaired battleships while Japan's sat idle for want of materials: Nalty, 'Sources of Victory'; Willmott, *Barrier and the Javelin*, pp. 521ff; Coox, 'Pacific War', pp. 377ff.

519 26 times as much high explosives as Japan: Coox, 'Effectiveness of the Japanese Military Establishment', p. 21.

519 during the war—they were in the nineteenth century: Clayton, 'American and Japanese Strategies', p. 717. See in general Harrison, *Medicine and Victory*.

519 have compensated for this immense economic imbalance: For a survey of the literature see Peattie, 'Japanese Strategy'.

519 'warriors masquerading as practitioners of modern military science': Coox, 'Effectiveness of the Japanese Military Establishment', p. 39.

520 'have on hand more of everything than you can ever conceivably need': Cozzens, *Guard of Honor*, p. 12. See also ibid., p. 161.

520 'there are vehicles with sufficient petrol to haul them around': Creveld, *Supplying War*, p. 200.

520 the advancing armies slumped from 19,000 tons a day to 7,000 tons: ibid., pp. 216–30 and n23.

520 the Americans had eighteen non-combatants for every man at the front: Overy, *Why the Allies Won*, p. 319.

521 did not shoot to good effect in combat, and many did not shoot at all: Marshall, *Men Against Fire*, p. 70. See also Strachan, 'Training'; Wessely, 'Twentieth-Century Theories'.

521 military hospitals were victims of disease and injury, not enemy action: Ellis, *World War II Data Handbook*, p. 558.

521 relocating production eastwards after the German invasion: Harrison, 'Resource Mobilization', pp. 182–91; Overy, *Why the Allies Won*, p. 181.

521 productivity through standardization and economies of scale: Overy, *Why the Allies Won*, pp. 182, 185ff.

521 of the notoriously inadequate American Sherman M4: Nye, 'Killing Private Ryan'.

521 vulnerable to the giant SU-152 anti-tank gun: Overy, *Russia's War*, pp. 190–3.

521 Allied armoured vehicles and two thirds of Allied mortars: Barber and Harrison, 'Patriotic War'.

521 used a Nazi atomic bomb to negate these disadvantages: Lindsey, 'Hitler's Bomb'; Gill, 'Operation GREENBRIER'.

521 have limited the number of these that could have been built: Price, 'Jet Fighter Menace'; Isby, 'Luftwaffe Triumphant'.

522 were not the war-winning innovations of Hitler's dreams: On increasingly desperate German hopes that new weapons could avert defeat, see Speer, *Inside the Third Reich*, p. 412.

522 further away from a decisive technological breakthrough: Coox, 'Effectiveness of the Japanese Military Establishment', p. 26.

522 it was the victory of this overwhelming combination: Levine, 'Was World War II a Near-Run Thing?'

522 low point they had first touched in September 1939: Frey and Kucher, 'History as Reflected in Capital Markets'.

522 do no more than delay the unavoidable collapse: See Arnold, 'Coral and Purple'; Cook, 'Midway Disaster'; Lindsey, 'Nagumo's Luck'; Burtt, 'Guadalcanal'; Anderson, 'There Are Such Things as Miracles'.

522 still not have been in a position to win the war: Tsouras, *Disaster at D-Day*; Klivert-Jones, 'Bloody Normandy'; Ambrose, 'Secrets of Overlord'; idem, 'D-Day Fails'; Ruge, 'Invasion of Normandy'. See also Anderson, 'Race to Bastogne'; Tsouras, 'Ardennes Disaster'; Prados, 'Operation Herbstnebel'; Campbell, 'Holding Patton'.

522 in 1944 served to hasten the collapse in the East: Manteuffel, 'Battle of the Ardennes'.

523 ahead of the Germans, perhaps most decisively in North Africa: Kahn, 'Enigma Uncracked'.

523 The German submariners' 'Triton' code was also cracked: The Americans were also successful in decrypting Japanese diplomatic signals sent with the Purple machine ('Magic') as well as cracking the Japanese army and navy codes: Clayton, 'American and Japanese Strategies', p. 729.

523 war can have been shown more gentlemanly consideration: 'When they ask their captive if he speaks French, he replies: "Un petit peu." To which we could not resist the Cowardesque reply, "I never think that's quite enough" ': Moss, *Ill Met by Moonlight*, p. 99.

523 of which 'demanded the complete demolition of the piano': Arthur, *Forgotten Voices*, p. 260.

523 on D-Day. (Miraculously, the bagpiper survived.): ibid., pp. 316, 321.

524 asked permission to fire from their bedroom windows: ibid., p. 351.

524 following the surrender of the 6th Parachute Regiment: ibid., p. 428.

524 'without stopping, if I remember rightly': Bowlby, *Recollections*, p. 67.

525 pressure from Stalin as well as from sections of the British public: See Alanbrooke, *War Diaries*, pp. 281ff, 284ff, 307, 346–8, 401, 407ff, 437. Cf. Ehrenburg, *Men, Years—Life*, vol. V, p. 77.

525 Japanese attack on India was little more than a pipedream: Barber and Henshall, *Last War of Empires*, pp. 187ff; Kennedy, 'Japanese Strategic Decisions', pp. 185ff.

526 'arsenal of democracy' against a 'gang of outlaws': Offner, 'United States and National Socialist Germany', pp. 256ff.

526 who encountered German vessels to fire at them 'on sight': Levine, 'Was World War II a Near-Run Thing?', p. 42.

526 crypto-fascists like the aviator Charles Lindbergh: Kennedy, *Freedom from Fear*, pp. 427, 472; Divine, *Illusion of Neutrality*, pp. 288–333. For Warren's views, see his 'Troubles of a Neutral'. On Lindbergh, see Berg, *Lindbergh*, esp. pp. 361, 382, 386–93, 425, 435 and Lindbergh's article 'Aviation, Geography and Race'. On Johnson, see Lower, *Bloc of One*.

526 countries, Congress could avoid another such entanglement: See by way of illustration the cartoon 'As Borah Sees It', *Newsweek*, October 2, 1939.

526 imposed on Japan which set the course for Pearl Harbor: The shift in American public opinion can be traced in Gallup, *Gallup Poll*. See also the regular surveys published in the *Princeton Public Opinion Quarterly* published from January 1937, esp. Cantril, 'America Faces the War'.

526 but with a refrigerator! This sort of thing does not impress us: Trevor-Roper (ed.), *Hitler's Table Talk*, January 7, 1942, August 1, 1942.

526 not least because of the South's high export-dependence: Cole, 'American First and the South'; Dabney, 'South Looks Abroad'; Ratchford, 'South's Stake'. Cf. Trubowitz, *Defining the National Interest*, esp. pp. 131ff.

527 German populations descended from nineteenth-century immigrants: Lubell, 'Who Votes Isolationist?'

527 from Nazi-controlled Europe, many of whom were also Jewish: Davie, *Refugees in America*. See also Fermi, *Illustrious Immigrants*, and the essays in Fleming and Bailyn (eds.), *Intellectual Migration*.

527 which more than 10 per cent said they would support: Stember, *Jews in the Mind of America*, tables 8, 12, 23, 39, 53, 56, 57, 59.

527 public overwhelmingly condemned Hitler's persecution of the Jews: Gallup, Gallup Poll, p. 128. Cf. Fortune, *Jews in America*; Settle, 'Model-T Anti-Semitism'; Alston, *Menace of Anti-Semitism*.

527 'and that is the one factor that I think our Axis enemies overlooked': 'Looking Ahead', Testimony of C. E. Wilson, President of General Motors Corporation, before the Special Committee of the United States Senate to Investigate the National Defense Program (Truman Committee), November 24, 1943, pp. 28ff.

528 'each business what it is to contribute to the war program': Nelson, *Arsenal of Democracy*, p. 393.

528 Between 1940 and 1943, 5 million new jobs were created: Vetter, *U.S. Economy*, p. 16.

528 surge in both private investment and personal consumption: Vernon, 'World War II Fiscal Policies'. See also Rockoff, 'United States'.

528 country to work out how to have both guns and butter in wartime: General Motors Corporation, press conference by C. E. Wilson, President of General Motors, October 19, 1945 (New York, 1945), p. 3.

528 and the big manufacturers, hitherto staunch opponents of Roosevelt: See in general Nelson, *Arsenal of Democracy*. Cf. McQuaid, *Uneasy Partners*, pp. 13ff. On business opposition to the New Deal see Stromberg, 'American Business and the Approach of War'.

528 sometimes also owning a vast number of new industrial facilities: Smith, *Army and Economic Mobilization*, pp. 477ff.

528 War Mobilization transformed the regulatory landscape: Koistinen, *Arsenal of World War II*.

528 day and employing 40,000 men and women on round-the-clock shifts: Rodgers, *Story of Boeing*, p. 65. Cf. Redding and Yenne, *Boeing*.

528 'concept of the corporation', with its decentralized system of management: On General Motors see Drucker, *Concept of the Corporation*, pp. 31–81. It should nevertheless be noted that total factor productivity growth slackened during the war, an inevitable consequence of the conversion from peacetime to wartime products: see Field, 'Impact of World War II'.

528 all prime government contracts went to just 33 corporations: Vetter, *U.S. Economy*, p. 60.

529 five years the company had lost nearly $3 million: Calculated from figures in Boeing Airplane Co. and Subsidiary Companies, Reports to Stockholders (Washington, 1936–1950). Note, however, that the war was less profitable for the chemical conglomerate DuPont, which had fared better in the Thirties, because of the costs of switching production to explosives and steep wartime taxation: see Carpenter, *DuPont Company's Part in the National Security Program*.

529 produced more military equipment during the war than Italy: Overy, *Why the Allies Won*, pp. 193–7

529 'real war . . . but . . . in a regulated business venture': Jones, *Thin Red Line*, p. 35; Heller, *Catch-22*, pp. 292, 298.

529 1945, on average around 9 per cent of UK gross national product: Broadberry and Howlett, 'United Kingdom', p. 51.

529 between 4 and nearly 8 per cent of Soviet net material product: Harrison, 'Soviet Union'.

529 planes were flown along an 'air bridge' from Alaska to Siberia: Forsyth, *Peoples of Siberia*, p. 354.

529 41 and 63 per cent of all Soviet military supplies: Overy, *Russia's War*, pp. 195ff. See also Burleigh, *Third Reich*, p. 734.

530 *Ubit Sukina syna Adolf* — 'to kill that son-of-a-bitch Adolf': Overy, *Russia's War*, p. 197.

530 or would, at least, have taken much longer to win it: ibid., p. 195.

530 **toiling up to sixteen hours a day on subsistence rations:** Applebaum, *Gulag*, pp. 187ff, 376–9, 398–401; Overy, *Russia's War*, pp. 82ff.

531 **region briefly run by the Romanians as 'Transnistria':** Lumans, *Himmler's Auxiliaries*, pp. 243ff; Fleischhauer and Pinkus, *Soviet Germans*, pp. 99ff. Cf. Applebaum, *Gulag*, pp. 386ff.

531 **Khemsils (Muslim Armenians) and Meskhetian Turks:** Martin, 'Origins of Soviet Ethnic Cleansing', p. 820. Cf. Applebaum, *Gulag*, pp. 387ff.

531 **a fifth of those enjoyed by their British counterparts:** Overy, *How the Allies Won*, p. 187.

531 **traitors to the Motherland. This is the call of our Motherland.** Full text at http://www.mishalov .com/Stalin_28July42.html. The order was, however, rescinded after four months; in many ways it was a panic measure in response to a breakdown in discipline at Rostov-on-Don.

532 **under Order No. 270, even the families of deserters:** For the implementation of these orders at Stalingrad, see Beevor, *Stalingrad*, pp. 167, 169.

532 **was arrested and spent two years in a labour camp:** Volkoganov, *Stalin*, p. 450.

532 **harsh conditions for 'Betrayal of the Motherland':** Rees, *War of the Century*, p. 223.

532 **(of Faber & Faber) for its anti-Soviet sentiments:** Shelden, *Orwell*, pp. 327, 400ff.

532 **'There is nothing irreconcilable in our aims and purposes':** Applebaum, *Gulag*, pp. 399, 401.

533 **of their real aims for the first time in our history:** Mailer, *Naked and the Dead*, p. 321. See also Jones, *From Here to Eternity*, p. 316.

533 **'the decisive turning point' as early as April 1942:** Speer, *Inside the Third Reich*, p. 215.

533 **. . . January 30, 1943, is often portrayed as the moment of truth:** Beevor, *Stalingrad*, p. 398.

533 **the three-cornered Allied combination was revealed:** The phrase is Vasily Grossman's: *Life and Fate*, p. 216. See Görlitz, 'Stalingrad'.

533 **camouflage — to lure the Germans to their destruction:** Erickson, 'New Thinking', p. 286; Overy, *Russia's War*, pp. 198–201.

534 **were communicating with one another using American radios:** Overy, *Russia's War*, p. 193.

534 **so deafening it sounded to him like a 'symphony of hell':** ibid., p. 203.

534 **with the pressure of their feet on their drivers' shoulders:** Burleigh, *Third Reich*, p. 504. Cf. Overy, *Russia's War*, pp. 204–10.

534 **'hastily dug graves — it all merges into one':** Ehrenburg, *Men, Years — Life*, vol. V, p. 107.

535 **losing Orel, then Briansk, then Belgorod, then Kharkov:** Overy, *Russia's War*, p. 211.

535 **Karachev, Ehrenburg saw a signpost: '1209 miles to Berlin':** Ehrenburg, *Men, Years — Life*, vol. V, p. 107.

535 **'to stop losing the war and [were] working towards winning it':** Alanbrooke, *War Diaries*, p. 338.

535 **ships to U-boat attacks, compared with over a thousand in 1942:** Overy, *Why the Allies Won*, p. 62. Cf. Rohwer, 'U-Boat War', pp. 307–11.

535 **still far from the peak of their shipbuilding capacity:** Coox, 'Effectiveness of the Japanese Military Establishment', p. 29.

535 **once the Americans had established naval and air superiority:** Willmott, *Barrier and the Javelin*, pp. 513–9; Coox, 'Pacific War', pp. 350–8.

535 **. which they were already losing the means of supplying:** Kiyoshi, 'Japanese Strategy', p. 137.

536 **the Chinese army to make an effective incursion into Burma:** On in the war in China after 1941, see Dreyer, *China at War*, pp. 272–311. Cf. Nalty, 'Sources of Victory', p. 261; Sainsbury, *Churchill and Roosevelt*, pp. 167–75; Clayton, 'American and Japanese Strategies', p. 721.

536 **before the end of the year, paving the way to an armistice:** National Archives, RG 165, Entry 421, Box 340, Office of the Director of Plans and Operations, War Cabinet Joint Intelligence Sub-Committee Report, 'Probabilities of a German Collapse', September 9, 1943. Cf. Wegner, 'Ideology of Self-Destruction'.

536 **their answers ranged between March and November 1944:** Alanbrooke, *War Diaries*, p. 492.

537 **a diversion from the main event, which was France:** See e.g., Grigg, *1943*, esp. pp. x–xi, 212ff. See also Jackson, 'Through the Soft Underbelly'. The most effective counter-argument is provided by Alanbrooke, *War Diaries*. His preferred strategy for ending the war in 1943 was 'to force the Dardanelles by the capture of Crete and Rhodes' and 'set the whole Balkans ablaze', 'getting Rumania and Bulgaria out of the war': ibid., pp. 465, 475. This certainly over-estimated the interest of the Turks in becoming combatants and under-estimated the difficulties of operating in the Balkans.

537 **if it had not been spread over such a broad front:** Arnold, 'Patton and the Narrow Thrust'; Carr, 'VE Day — November 11, 1944'. See also Isby, 'Monty's D-Day'; Tsouras, ' "By the Throat" ' Uffindell, 'Backdoor Into Germany'.

537 **more than eighteen divisions at Iasi in August 1944:** Overmans, 'German Historiography', p. 153. Cf. Gackenholz, 'Collapse of Army Group Centre'.

537 **captured just 630,000 Germans prior to the capitulation:** Zabecki, *World War II*, p. 1249.

537 **between the Eastern and Western theatres of the European war:** Maschke et al., *Deutsche Kriegsgefangenen*, pp. 194ff, 200ff.

537 **eve of the German capitulation cannot have exceeded 3 million:** Overmans, 'German Historiography', p. 141.

538 **dead was around 4:1. The Japanese ratio was 1:40:** Hata, 'Consideration to Contempt', p. 269.

538 **fit and in the first week of captivity all tried to commit suicide:** Kinvig, 'Allied POWs', p. 48.

538 sinking 36 of them and destroying 763 of the aircraft on board: Coox, 'Pacific War', pp. 366ff. See also Gudmundsson, 'Okinawa', pp. 637ff; Weinberg, World at Arms, pp. 848, 877.

538 of Japanese troops begin to give themselves up: Gilmore, You Can't Fight Tanks with Bayonets, pp. 77ff.

538 in a futile attempt to break out of Sittang in Burma: Allen and Steeds, 'Burma: The Longest War', pp. 116ff.

538 One Japanese soldier refused to lay down his arms until 1974: Onoda, No Surrender.

539 answer lies in the realm of military discipline: On combat motivation see in general Hauser, 'Will to Fight'.

539 penalty for desertion was abolished in 1930 and never restored: Sellers, For God's Sake Shoot Straight!, p. 125.

539 desertion during the entire Second World War: Pallud, 'Crime in WWII'.

539 to death by assigning them to punishment battalions: Bidermann, In Deadly Combat, p. 9. See also Bartov, Hitler's Army, pp. 71ff; Fritz, Frontsoldaten, p. 90.

539 loyalties and desertion rates began to rise: See for details Bartov, Eastern Front, pp. 29–36; idem, Hitler's Army, pp. 98–101. Cf. Burleigh, Third Reich, pp. 524ff.

539 'Death by a bullet from the enemy or by the "thugs" of the SS': Fritz, Frontsoldaten, p. 95.

539 'shot, and that if they were caught they would be executed': Bartov, Hitler's Army, p. 99.

539 Japanese military had long sought to stigmatize surrender: The phrase 'shame culture' was coined by the anthropologist Ruth Benedict during the war: Hata, 'From Consideration to Contempt, p. 269. Cf. Gilmore, You Can't Fight Tanks with Bayonets, p. 97.

539 beginning of the Pacific war capitulation had become taboo: Hata, 'Consideration to Contempt', pp. 260ff.

539 acknowledge the existence of Japanese prisoners of war: MacKenzie, 'Treatment of Prisoners of War', pp. 513–7. Cf. Asada, Night of a Thousand Suicides, pp. 2, 7. The Americans swiftly came to appreciate what this meant; see Hill, 'Lessons of Bataan', p. 111.

540 mounted suicidal banzai charges rather than capitulate: Dower, War Without Mercy, pp. 52ff.

540 often committed suicide or attempted suicidal escapes: See e.g., Barber and Henshall, Last War of Empires, p. 150.

540 'I Cease Resistance' was the preferred euphemism: Gilmore, You Can't Fight the Tanks with Bayonets, pp. 139ff.

540 'enemy forces . . . will not be regarded as POWs': Hata, 'Consideration to Contempt', p. 263. Cf. Aida, Prisoner, p. 6: 'If there was a surrender on all fronts, we too would surrender . . . without bearing the stigma of being called "prisoner".' See also op. cit., p. 50, for the distinction between 'prisoners of war' and 'disarmed military personnel'.

540 their own families and then themselves rather than surrender: Dower, War Without Mercy, p. 45; Barber and Henshall, Last War of Empires, pp. 198ff. Cf. Kimitada, 'Japanese Images', p. 136.

540 since it seemed to imply the deposition of the Emperor: But see Lerner, Psychological Warfare Against Nazi Germany, pp. xvi.

541 'defence of the German Fatherland I consider it necessary': Padover, Psychologist, p. 169.

541 'should have died "on the field of honour"': ibid., p. 166.

541 'letter and fight to the last round of ammunition': Koschorrek, Blood Red Snow, p. 309.

541 'then they would follow me. [Pöppel was 24.]': Pöppel, Heaven and Hell, p. 237.

541 had bullets left to fire, even if they were surrounded: Ambrose, 'Last Barrier', p. 548.

542 entered our spirits, to remain and haunt us forever: Fritz, Frontsoldaten, pp. 53ff.

542 because of the value of prisoners as intelligence sources: Beevor, Stalingrad, p. 60.

542 'shot and so they might fight better the next time': Rees, War of the Century, p. 67.

542 'but a truly deadly fear of falling into German captivity': Forster, 'German Army', p. 21.

542 'prisoner than of the possibility of dying on the battlefield': Bartov, Hitler's Army, p. 87.

543 'because every Red Army soldier fears German captivity': ibid., p. 88.

543 unheeded by soldiers on the ground, however: ibid., pp. 85ff.

543 'We take some prisoners, we shoot them, all in a day's work': Fritz, Frontsoldaten, p. 55.

543 'of the Russians, no doubt thirsty for revenge': Beevor, Stalingrad, p. 59.

543 'The war goes on!' and then shot a Russian officer: Dibold, Doctor at Stalingrad, pp. 24, 31. See also Beevor, Stalingrad, p. 369.

543 rather than fall into the hands of the Red Army: Carruthers and Trew (eds.), Servants of Evil, pp. 231ff.

543 His answer was: 'Because we are soldiers': Bidermann, In Deadly Combat, pp. 282–93.

543 'Soviets—we can imagine what awaits us in Siberia': Koschorrek, Blood Red Snow, pp. 309ff.

543 'accused of an infinity of murder . . . spared nothing': Bartov, Eastern Front, p. 38.

543 'because if they get their revenge, we're in for a hard time': Bartov, Mirrors of Destruction, p. 236n.

543 Unit 731 in Manchukuo—may have felt similar apprehensions: Williams and Wallace, Unite 731.

544 have managed to do that. . . . Therefore we will win the war: Alexiev and Wimbush, 'Non-Russians in the Red Army', p. 440.

544 'Russian earth. Do not waver. Do not let up. Kill': Beevor, Stalingrad, p. 125.

544 Germans precisely as the Germans had treated them: Applebaum, Gulag, p. 390.

544 how many people he killed—he did not think about this?: Rees, *War of the Century*, p. 167.

544 Stalingrad were simply finished off after the German surrender: Beevor, *Stalingrad*, p. 384.

544 'told that the Russians have been killing all prisoners': op. cit., p. 369.

544 'stories that the Russians [would] torture and shoot them': Beevor, *Stalingrad*, p. 182.

544 he recalled, 'a little show of sadism': Carruthers and Trew (eds.), *Servants of Evil*, p. 232. The experience of surrender on the Eastern Front is vividly captured in Ledig, *Stalin Organ*, pp. 101, 105–9.

544 Australian forces often shot Japanese surrenderers during the Pacific War: Mackenzie, 'Treatment of Prisoners of War', p. 488.

545 apparent Japanese surrender that turned out to be an ambush: Dower, *War Without Mercy*, pp. 63ff.

545 was 'Kill the Jap bastards! Take no prisoners!': ibid., p. 68.

545 Lindbergh proudly: 'Our boys just don't take prisoners': ibid., p. 70.

545 troops killed prisoners at Bougainville 'in cold blood': Bourke, *Intimate History*, p. 184.

545 then serving in the 14th Army, turned a blind eye: ibid., pp. 185ff.

545 'unarmed Japanese soldiers who had just surrendered': Dower, *War Without Mercy*, p. 63.

545 in revenge for earlier Japanese atrocities against Allied wounded: Arthur, *Forgotten Voices*, pp. 210, 256, 386, 390.

545 told his Japanese captors, 'was "if it moves, shoot it"': Carson, *My Time in Hell*, p. 231.

545 Another GI maxim was 'Kill or be killed': See Hersey, *Into the Valley*, p. 55.

545 'out hospitals, strafed lifeboats . . . finished off the enemy wounded': Dower, *War Without Mercy*, p. 64.

545 assuaging soldiers' subsequent feelings of guilt: Bourke, *Intimate History*, p. 255.

545 war said that they had regarded orders to kill prisoners as legitimate: ibid., p. 293.

545 Japanese soldiers who might be contemplating surrender: Dower, *War Without Mercy*, pp. 63, 70.

546 Japanese prisoners had expected to be killed by their captors: ibid., p. 68.

546 induce American troops not to kill surrendering Japanese: Bourke, *Intimate History*, p. 184.

546 'something primitive' that had to be 'exterminated' to preserve 'civilization': Dower, *War Without Mercy*, p. 71.

546 as 'part of an insect horde with all its power and horror': Arthur, *Forgotten Voices*, p. 386.

546 portrayed the Japanese as monkeys or apes: Dower, *War Without Mercy*, pp. 182–90.

546 'deplorable, hateful troop of men-apes': Dunlop, *Diaries*, p. 231.

546 ('bastards!') built on pre-existing racial prejudices: Dower, *War Without Mercy*, pp. x, 33–7, 48–52.

546 Natalie, surprised at the gift, named it Tojo: *Life*, May 22, 1944, p. 34.

546 sweethearts' was a not uncommon practice: Dower, *War Without Mercy*, pp. 64ff. Ears, bones and teeth were also collected.

547 at least 13 per cent of Americans shared his view: ibid., pp. 53ff.

547 SS Battle Group Peiper on December 17, 1944: Hart, Hart and Hughes, *German Soldier in World War II*, p. 186.

547 units more than regular Wehrmacht units: Spiller (ed.), *Prisoners of Nazis*, pp. 87, 149; Rolf, *Prisoners of the Reich*, p. 21. For incidents of massacres of British and American troops by SS units see Garrett, *P.O.W.*, p. 142.

547 seventy Italian and German POWs at Biscari in Sicily: Bourke, *Intimate History*, p. 183.

547 of German prisoners captured in France: Spiller (ed.), *Prisoners of Nazis*, p. 11.

547 'prisoner to make up for it. They are tough people': Moore, 'Unruly Allies', p. 190.

547 suggests this was not wholly without foundation: Ambrose, *Band of Brothers*, pp. 150, 206, 277.

548 and who are applying the lessons they learned there: Moore, 'Unruly Allies', p. 191.

548 He can do no good then. Stick them in the liver: Bourke, *Intimate History*, p. 183.

548 'take no prisoners' when he led them across the Rhine: ibid., p. 184.

548 'I could not think of him as a human being': Padover, *Psychologist in Germany*, p. 166.

548 quality of the German defence in the final months of the war: See e.g., W. F. Deeds, 'It's the Saddest Spring I Ever Remember', *Daily Telegraph*, July 7, 2005.

549 military position but also the lack of risk involved in surrendering: Lerner, *Psychological Warfare against Nazi Germany*, pp. 23, 43, 101, 133, 136, 184, 208, 216.

549 and Allied observance of the Geneva Convention: op. cit., pp. 174, 279, 358. As one 'Sykewar' veteran commented, 'Much casuistical effort was expended to make surrender compatible with soldierly honour'. Note the case of Major General Botho Elster, who was reluctant to surrender to the American 39th Infantry without a token exchange of fire: Ramsey, 'Germany Surrenders', p. 4. See also Jordan (ed.), *Conditions of Surrender*, p. 130.

549 SIX WAYS, to get yourself killed: Lerner, *Psychological Warfare*, p. 216.

549 encourage already disaffected individuals to surrender: ibid., p. 311. On the questionnaires' results, see op. cit., chart V. Cf. Weinberg, *World at Arms*, p. 584.

549 be ruled out that the line of causation went the other way: Janowitz and Shils, 'Cohesion and Disintegration', esp. pp. 202, 211ff.

549 'If we have to go to prison, then let's hope it's with the Americans': Koshorrek, *Blood Red Snow*, pp. 309ff.

550 and were also less willing to hand them over to the Soviets: In contravention of the Geneva Conventions, a substantial number of German prisoners were transferred to other powers by those to whom

they had surrendered. The Americans handed over 765,000 to France, 76,000 to the Benelux countries and 200,000 to Russia. They also refused to accept the surrender of German troops in Saxony and Bohemia, who were handed over to the Russians: Nawratil, *Die deutschen Nachkriegsverluste*, pp. 36ff.

550 'to surrender in Hollandia area have been killed by our troops': Gilmore, *You Can't Fight Tanks with Bayonets*, p. 60.

551 'shooting [Japanese] when they made an attempt to surrender': ibid., p. 61.

551 emerged from a foxhole waving a surrender leaflet: ibid., p. 66.

551 tied around his waist—was wise to take no chances: Gilmore, *You Can't Fight Tanks with Bayonets*, p. 137. See also Coox, 'Pacific War', p. 365.

551 within a few months of laying down their arms: Beevor, *Stalingrad*, p. 408.

552 hands reached a peak of over 50 per cent in 1943: Details in Ferguson, 'Prisoner Taking and Prisoner Killing'.

552 Americans captured and their mortality: Bacque, *Other Losses*, esp. pp. 173–203. For problems with Bacque's statistics of the mortality of Germans in Allied hands, see Mackenzie, 'On the Other Losses Debate'; Overmans, 'German Historiography', passim. Cf. the figures in Jordan (ed.), *Conditions of Surrender*, p. 151.

552 surrendered to the British (0.15 per cent to 0.03 per cent): This was largely due to the high mortality in the notoriously primitive Rheinwiesenlager. See Overmans, 'German Historiography', pp. 163ff.

## CHAPTER SIXTEEN: *KAPUTT*

553 the more one realizes how completely destroyed it is: Alanbrooke, *War Diaries*, p. 707.

554 when he heard the news of Roosevelt's death: Speer, *Inside the Third Reich*, p. 463.

554 'would believe that he had become a god and was dwelling in heaven': Niall Ferguson, 'Twilight of the Devils', *Sunday Telegraph*, May 22, 1994.

554 'of the hinterland'—had undermined the morale of the army: Hitler, *Mein Kampf*, p. 183. See also pp. 172ff.

554 'pounding down on the table and yelled . . . "Ja"': Kershaw, *Hitler*, vol. II, p. 117.

554 August 1939, 'there will be no talk of capitulation': ibid., p. 217.

554 that it would be impossible to defeat the Soviet Union: Wenger, 'Ideology of Self-Destruction', p. 26.

555 'and this to the realization of a true Volksgemeinschaft': ibid., pp. 32ff.

555 last-ditch war of resistance on German soil: Mommsen, 'Dissolution of the Third Reich', p. 17.

555 'nothing but death, destruction and hate will await him': Wenger, 'Ideology of Self-Destruction', p. 28.

556 'a ridiculous cosmic bacterium' (*eine lächerliche Weltraumbakterie*): Kershaw, *Hitler*, vol. II, pp. 500.

556 peace feelers to Britain or to the Soviet Union: Peace initiatives were made by, among others, Ribbentrop, Speer and even Goebbels and Himmler. Also exploring the possibility of some kind of negotiated end to the war were senior military figures including Canaris, Fellgiebel, Fromm, Heusinger, Milch, Rommel and Rundstedt: Wegner, 'Ideology of Self-Destruction', p. 21.

557 'fight more unconditionally than those who still have the chance of retreat': Wegner, 'Ideology of Self-Destruction', p. 27.

557 'behind us with a slam that all the world will hear': ibid., p. 28.

557 'audience does not hoot and whistle when you appear on the screen': Hastings, *Armageddon*, p. 531.

557 desperate beasts, remaining alive were also very slight: Klemperer, *Diary*, October 24, 1944.

557 April and July 1944; nearly all of them were murdered: Burleigh, *Third Reich*, p. 767.

557 including 15,000 out of the 60,000 evacuated from Auschwitz: Mazower, *Dark Continent*, p. 178.

558 do not include the numerous extra-judicial executions carried out by the SS: Evans, *Rituals of Retribution*, appendix.

558 a world brought to heel by a single International Air Force: Linqvist, *History of Bombing*, n.p. (paragraph 183).

588 from equal to the task of conducting air raids on Germany: Overy, *Why the Allies Won*, p. 107.

559 Churchill—true to form—ordered the RAF to do just that: ibid., p. 103.

559 'moral scruples' that had dictated German strategy: Trevor-Roper (ed.), *Hitler's Table Talk*, September 6, 1942, p. 697.

559 'the target areas must be made to feel the weight of war': Linqvist, *History of Bombing*, n.p. (paragraph 181).

559 Arthur 'Bomber' Harris took over Bomber Command: Overy, *Why the Allies Won*, pp. 112ff.

560 'without missing good opportunities of bombing your primary targets': National Archives, London, S.46368/D.C.A.S, Air Vice-Marshal Bottomley to Air Officer Commanding-in-Chief, Bomber Command, February 14, 1942.

560 of German and Japanese cities—in other words, the slaughter of civilians: According to Overy, 7 per cent of Britain's total war effort in terms of production and combat-man hours went into strategic bombing, rising to 12 per cent in the last two years of war: *Why the Allies Won*, p. 129.

560 when the Japanese had first bombed Chinese cities: Dower, *War Without Mercy*, p. 38.

NOTES

560  to which 'His Majesty's government [would] never resort': Linqvist, *History of Bombing*, n.p. (paragraph 177).
560  Lancaster bomber crews were nothing if not brave men: See Nichol and Rennell, *Tail-end Charlies*.
560  expectancy of a Lancaster was estimated at just 12 missions: There were exceptions, as to every rule. The Lancaster codenamed B-Baker (nicknamed 'B-Bastard'), of 467 (Royal Australian Air Force) based at Waddington (Lincs.), logged over 400 hours flying time before being shot down over Düsseldorf: Rolfe, *Looking into Hell*, p. 7.
561  the currency he had in mind was German not British lives: Harriman, *Special Envoy*, p. 153.
561  that would 'shatter the morale of the German people': Overy, *Why the Allies Won*, pp. 102ff.
561  would outweigh 'any increase in anti-British feeling': Grigg, *1943*, p. 152.
561  Department, the physicist Frederick Lindemann: See Fort, 'Prof'.
561  prevent the diversion of substantial resources to Portal's squadrons: Alanbrooke, *War Diaries*, October 23, 1942 (p. 332); May 24, 1943 (p. 409); May 25, 1943 (p. 411).
561  exaggeration of what American bombers could do to Germany: Overy, *Why the Allies Won*, p. 110.
562  'where their capacity for armed resistance is fatally weakened': ibid., p. 116.
562  The flames were visible more than a hundred miles away: ibid., pp. 118ff.
562  the charred human remains of his fellow citizens: Nossack, *The End*.
562  some 71 per cent—were dropped during the last year of the war: Calculated from figures in Ellis, *World War II Data Handbook*, pp. 22ff.
562  bomb Germany with something approaching impunity: Overy, *Why the Allies Won*, pp. 122ff.
562  Until now Dresden itself really has been spared: Klemperer, *Diary*, September 15, 1944.
564  I knew the earrings. It was my mother: Arthur (ed.), *Forgotten Voices*, pp. 403ff.
565  the inaccuracy as well as the cruelty of strategic bombing: Linqvist, *History of Bombing*, n.p. (paragraph 207).
565  'do in . . . children's homes and hospitals': Rolfe, *Looking into Hell*, p. 53.
565  have been better employed bombing the approaches to Auschwitz: Breitman, *Official Secrets*; Wyman, *Abandonment of the Jews*. But see Rubenstein, *Myth of Rescue*.
565  chip to save the Jews destined for the death camps: Linqvist, *History of Bombing*, n.p. (paragraphs 192, 193).
565  Red Army was encountering fierce resistance: Compare Lindqvist, *History of Bombing*, n.p. (paragraphs 214, 216, 217) with Arthur (ed.), *Forgotten Voices*, p. 403. The literature is very extensive and the controversy bitter. See e.g., McKee, *Dresden 1945*; Garrett, *Ethics and Airpower*. For a vivid evocation of the aftermath of the raid, see Vonnegut, *Slaughterhouse-five*.
565  trains were running again within a few days: Hastings, *Armageddon*, p. 386.
565  who turned air raid shelters into gas chambers: Friedrich, *Der Brand*. See the discussion in Stargardt, 'Victims of Bombing'.
565  times greater than material effect proved to be nonsense: Overy, *Why the Allies Won*, p. 105.
565  the complete extermination of the Jews: Stargardt, 'Victims of Bombing', p. 67.
566  conurbations, were 'the heart and vitals of the enemy': Seversky, *Victory Through Air Power*, p. 16.
566  had achieved the previous month by laying waste to Hamburg: Rolfe, *Looking into Hell*, p. 16.
566  60 out of 291 B-17s were shot down and 138 badly damaged: Overy, *Why the Allies Won*, p. 122. Cf. Bendiner, *Fall of Fortresses*, pp. 172ff; Arthur (ed.), *Forgotten Voices*, p. 277.
566  three times the casualty rate over Germany: Rolfe, *Looking into Hell*, pp. 114, 123.
567  on Eastern Front, facing around 13,000 Soviet aircraft: Overy, *Why the Allies Won*, p. 124.
567  'doubled the anti-tank defences on the Eastern Front': Grigg, *1943*, p. 154.
567  Russians when they arrive what Bomber Command can do: Hastings, *Armageddon*, p. 387.
567  invaders, as against 12,000 on the British and American side: Overy, *Why the Allies Won*, pp. 118, 124. For detailed figures, see Ellis, *World War II Data Handbook*, p. 238.
567  17,000 tons in August and just 11,000 tons in January 1945: Grigg, *1943*, p. 155.
567  throughout the entire war, including the V-1 and V-2 rockets: Ellis, *World War II Data Handbook*, p. 236.
568  per cent fewer aircraft and 42 per cent fewer trucks: Overy, *Why the Allies Won*, pp. 128–33, 204ff.
568  himself called the air war 'the greatest lost battle on the German side': Hastings, *Bomber Command*, p. 241.
569  Germans' belief in their government's propaganda: Kirwin, 'Allied Bombing and Nazi Domestic Propaganda'.
569  '(*Vergeltung*) and in the other Final Victory (*Endsieg*)': Stargardt, 'Victims of Bombing', p. 64.
570  ceased to be about anything as rational as survival: Ledig, *Payback*, esp. pp. 119ff.
570  'is a wrong deed, whether done by the Nazis or by ourselves': Grigg, *1943*, p. 152ff.
570  iron bars and even an unexploded incendiary bomb: Rolfe, *Looking into Hell*, pp. 56–9.
570  'on to the extent that you would be in a tank': ibid., p. 47.
570  subsumed into the less painful 'death' of their plane: Hynes, *Soldier's Tale*, p. 134. Cf. Bendiner, *Fall of Fortresses*, p. 101.
571  daylight and I was able to read my log at 18,000 ft: Rolfe, *Looking into Hell*, pp. 31ff.
571  the more the bomber crews' sense of detachment grew: See e.g., Begg and Liddle (eds.), *For Five Shillings a Day*, pp. 273ff.

572 untrammelled power not merely of the Emperor but also of the military: Hasegawa, *Racing the Enemy.*

572 'protect the imperial land and achieve our goals of conquest': Toland, *Rising Sun*, p. 749.

572 'fighting to the end, the entire population uniting as one body': ibid., p. 752.

572 more than half of all the fatalities in the entire Pacific war: Dower, *War Without Mercy*, p. 300.

572 the armed services and a civilian militia numbering 28 million: Toland, *Rising Sun*, p. 757.

572 entire period between 1937 and 1945 has been put at 1.74 million: Dower, *War Without Mercy*, p. 297.

572 Hornet successfully raided the Japanese capital: Coox, 'Pacific War', p. 350.

573 'scorched and boiled and baked to death' as LeMay frankly put it: Dower, *War Without Mercy*, p. 41.

573 injuring more than 300,000 and turning eight million into refugees: Coox, 'Pacific War', pp. 368–70.

573 what fell on Germany and occupied North West Europe: Ellis, *World War II Data Handbook*, p. 235.

574 of their much longer-held position in Manchuria and Korea: Coox, 'Pacific War', p. 375; Katsumi, 'Politics of War', p. 289.

574 forced the military finally to sign the instrument of surrender: Hasegawa, *Racing the Enemy.*

574 Soviet Union; an explosive overture to the Cold War: Sherwin, 'Atomic Bomb and the Origins of the Cold War', pp. 87–91. Cf. Alperovitz, *Atomic Diplomacy.*

574 compelled to get a large bang for so many bucks: See Broscious, 'Longing for International Control', p. 17.

574 to as many as 140,000 in Hiroshima and 70,000 in Nagasaki: Dower, *War Without Mercy*, p. 298.

575 When Truman spoke of 'a new era in the history of civilization': Broscious, 'Longing for International Control', p. 20.

575 among them a number of refugees from Nazi-occupied Europe: J. Robert Oppenheimer was the son of German Jews and had studied at Göttingen, though he was himself born in New York. Edward Teller, the pioneer of the hydrogen bomb, was a Hungarian Jew who had been based at Göttingen's Institute for Physical Chemistry when the Nazis came to power: Rhodes, *Making of the Atomic Bomb.* In all around 100 physicists moved to the United States between 1933 and 1941. See also Fermi, *Illustrious Immigrants*, pp. 174ff; Wiener, 'A New Site'.

575 West once their alliance with the Soviet Union had served its purpose: Sherwin, 'Atomic Bomb and the Origins of the Cold War', pp. 78ff.

575 a testament to the confidence Roosevelt had in Churchill: ibid., pp. 81–6.

576 was built, each unaware that the others were spies: Andrew and Mitrokhin, *Mitrokhin Archive*, p. 173.

576 In February 1943 Stalin authorized work to begin on a Soviet bomb: Zubok, 'Stalin and the Nuclear Age'.

576 attacks on Japan at the Potsdam conference (July 17–August 2, 1945): Broscious, 'Longing for International Control', p. 24.

576 to which, with a stony face, Stalin replied: 'Unquestionably': Zubok, 'Stalin and the Nuclear Age', p. 44.

577 able to grasp better than us the incurable nature of the offence: Levi, *Reawakening*, p. 6.

577 '[lingua quartii imperii—language of the Fourth Reich]': Klemperer, *Diaries*, June 25, 1945.

577 LTI = LQI!!! 'align', 'militant', 'true democracy' etc. etc.: ibid., July 4, 1945, September 18, 1945, October 26.

578 'could just as well be Hermann Goering': ibid., October 22, 1945.

578 would merely 'replace the old lack of freedom with a new one': ibid., November 20, 1945.

578 'respect to its effect on the Jews, I do not feel very happy about it': ibid., June 1945.

578 as early as September 1945. 'I do not feel at all safe': ibid., September 18, 1945.

579 'conspiracy for the accomplishment of any of the foregoing': Minear, *Victors' Justice*, pp. 6–7, 10–11. See Bagish and Conroy, 'Japanese Aggression'.

579 'hospitals, and orphanages, in factories and fields': Dower, *War Without Mercy*, p. 37.

579 'trampled on Mother Russia and were now fleeing for their lives': Dobson et al., *Cruellest Night.*

580 'Our people have sinned greatly. The time for atonement is upon us': 'Schreckenstage voll Angst und Bangen und schwerer seelischer Not, Gnadenstage voll Vetrauen auf Gottes Schutz und Kraft', manuscript in private possession, Berlin.

580 Others had their heads battered in: Brownmiller, *Against Our Will*, p. 67. For further examples, see Hastings, *Armageddon,* pp. 524, 552ff, 567, 569. It is a fiction inspired by Goebbels's propaganda that the perpetrators were often 'Mongols'. As we have seen, the Red Army in 1945 was overwhelmingly a Russian and Ukrainian force.

581 'raped every woman and girl between the ages of twelve and sixty': Hastings, *Armageddon*, p. 552.

581 soldiers raped over 2 million German women: Naimark, *Russians in Germany*, p. 107; Grossman, 'A Question of Silence'.

581 in all theatres of war between 1942 and 1946: Brownmiller, *Against Our Will*, p. 77.

581 of 98 Luftwaffe generals and 11 out of 53 admirals: Goeschel, 'Suicide at the End of the Third Reich', p. 155.

581 Berlin, nearly twenty times the figure for March: ibid., pp. 162ff.

581 'allowed themselves to be burned up along with their homes': ibid., p. 166.

581 believed it was 'better to die than live with Russians': Hastings, *Armageddon*, p. 520.

582 'Obediently she goes and hangs herself': ibid., p. 567.

582 reprisals against both Reich German and ethnic German populations: Zayas, *Nemesis at Potsdam*.

582 'in the same way as the German invaders treated the Poles': Schechtman, *Postwar Population Transfers*, p. 183.

582 'are built on national lines and not multinational ones': Burleigh, *Third Reich*, p. 794.

582 compensation; who were marched at gunpoint in wretched columns: See the proclamation reproduced in Dralle, *Die Deutschen in Ostmittel- und Osteuropa*, p. 243.

582 'expel from the country everyone whose native tongue is German': Schechtman, *Postwar Population Transfers*, p. 66.

583 leaders formally sanctioned at the Potsdam Conference: ibid., pp. 36ff.

583 Germans remaining there was probably much larger: Zeman, *Pursued by a Bear*, pp. 206ff.

583 of Germans were murdered or interned in concentration camps: Dralle, *Die Deutschen in Ostmittel- und Osteuropa*, p. 242; Koseik, *Jenseits der Grenzen*, p. 192.

583 in the mines of the Donets Basin and the Urals: Castellan, 'Germans of Rumania', pp. 67ff.

583 over Soviet-occupied Europe suffered the same fate: Magocsi, *Historical Atlas of East Central Europe*, p. 165.

583 repatriation from their zones of occupation in Germany: Fleischhauer and Pinkus, *Soviet Germans*, p. 101ff; Dralle, *Die Deutschen in Ostmittel- und Osteuropa*, p. 238.

583 population of ethnic Germans was reduced by nearly half: Castellan, 'Germans of Rumania', pp. 70–3. Cf. Koseik, *Jenseits der Grenzen*, p. 191.

584 died in this great upheaval may have been as high as two million: Mazower, *Dark Continent*, p. 218.

584 while Ukrainians, Byelorussians and Lithuanians went East: Martin, 'Origins of Soviet Ethnic Cleansing', p. 821.

584 and were exchanged for Serbs and Croats living in Hungary: Magocsi, *Historical Atlas of East Central Europe*, p. 164.

585 in 1945, remains a monument to the post-war cast of mind: Taylor, *Course of Germany History*.

585 beyond — the idea was a commonplace in Britain: Ben-Israel, 'Cross-Purposes', p. 430.

585 100 or 150 thousand of these people work their passage: Carlton, 'Against the Grain', pp. 137ff.

586 'to hazard American lives for purely political purposes': Hastings, *Armageddon*, p. 561.

586 Partisans were only too happy to welcome the Russians to Belgrade: See Maclean, *Eastern Approaches*, pp. 504–30.

586 'British Empire would not avail to turn them off that spot': Nicolson, *Letters and Diaries*, February 1945, p. 437.

586 'the latter had kept his word with the utmost loyalty': ibid., February 1945, p. 437.

587 'Government they set up, the better. That is for them to decide': Maclean, *Eastern Approaches*, pp. 402ff.

587 he told the economist Leon Henderson, would 'suit themselves': Schlesinger, 'Hopeful Cynic', p. 13.

587 Stalin reassured Molotov, 'We can implement it in our own way later': Gaddis, *Cold War*, p. 21.

587 numbering very nearly 500 in all by the time of his death: http://www.osa.ceu.hu/gulag/txt1.htm.

587 restore Poland to her pre-war borders against Stalin's wishes: Foster, 'Times and Appeasement', pp. 448ff.

587 'exist a line beyond which Stalin will not go': Nicolson, *Letters and Diaries*, May 1945, p. 464.

588 evidence of the fate that awaited those handed back to Stalin: Applebaum, *Gulag*, pp. 248, 394ff.

588 Polish church in Hrubieszów and threw grenades at the congregation: See e.g., Lotnik, *Nine Lives*, pp. 158–60, 172.

588 continued to be directed against the surviving Jews in Poland: See e.g., Hoffman, *Shtetl*, pp. 239ff.

588 against Jews who were attempting to return to their old homes: Rosen, *My Lost World*, p. 288; Rubinstein et al., *Jews in the Modern World*, pp. 167ff.

589 more popular political forces within their own societies: McCoy, 'Introduction', pp. 1–3. Cf. Silverstein, 'Importance of the Japanese Occupation'.

589 Dairen, Port Arthur and the Manchurian railways: Clayton, 'American and Japanese Strategies', p. 724; Dryer, *China at War*, p. 303ff.

589 tenaciously against Soviet amphibious landings along the Korean coast: Slusser, 'Soviet Far Eastern Policy', pp. 136ff. Cf. Forsyth, *History of the Peoples of Siberia*, p. 354.

590 war in Asia meant an improvised partition of contested territory: Lowe, *Origins of the War in Korea*, pp. 12–20.

590 much that Stalin had a premeditated plan for Asian empire: Simmons, 'Korean Civil War', pp. 143–9, 150–9, 172ff.

590 'superpowers' that set Korea on course for partition: Lowe, *Origins of the War in Korea*, pp. 22ff, 27–37, 42–7, 52–63, 68–74.

590 along with the United States, the Soviet Union and Great Britain: Fenby, *Generalissimo*, pp. 408–19.

590 corrupt and incompetent won converts in the countryside: ibid., pp. 450–66.

590 support—advanced southwards and the civil war resumed: Dreyer, *China at War*, pp. 303–6.

590 altogether by an indigenous (but Soviet backed) Communist revolution: Fenby, *Generalissimo*, pp. 466–82.

591 whether militarily, or just economically and ideologically: Wenger, 'Ideology of Self-Destruction', p. 24.

591 'already longing for another war! Even if it entailed fighting Russia!': Alanbrooke, *War Diaries*, May 13, 1945, p. 690.

591 'fantastic and the chances of success quite impossible': ibid., May 24, 1945, p. 693.

591 Sebastopol etc. etc. And now where are the Russians!!!: ibid., July 23, 1945, p. 709.

592 'atomic bombs are meant to frighten those with weak nerves': Gaddis, *Cold War*, p. 57.

592 and deploying the American 6th Fleet in the Mediterranean: Gaddis, *We Now Know*, pp. 164ff.

592 American power through Saudi Arabia and Israel: See Ferguson, *Colossus*, ch. 3.

592 United States was about to withdraw from the peninsula altogether: Gaddis, 'Korea in American Politics', pp. 278–86.

593 indicated that he did not regard South Korea as vital to American security: Malkasian, *Korean War*, p. 15.

593 supervised elections to go ahead in their zone of occupation: Stueck, *Korean War*, p. 26.

593 with the authority of a United Nations Security Council resolution: Lowe, *Origins of the War in Korea*, pp. 172–9, 183–90.

594 inclined to give the green light to the North Korean invasion: Slusser, 'Soviet Far Eastern Policy', p. 141.

594 glory-hungry MacArthur in charge of defending South Korea: ibid., p. 195ff. See also Gaddis, 'Korea in American Politics', pp. 288–92; Gaddis, *We Now Know*, pp. 78ff.

594 MacArthur's forces back in the utmost disorder: Malkasian, *Korean War*, p. 9; Lowe, *Origins of the War in Korea*, pp. 195–217, 232–5. Cf. Farrar-Hockley, 'China Factor'.

594 out the use of atomic weapons 'to meet the military situation': Gaddis, *Cold War*, p. 48.

595 Pyongyang and Seoul—were the principal cause of death: Simmons, 'Korean Civil War', pp. 168ff. For a compilation of the available statistics, see http://users.erols.com/mwhite28/warstat2.htm.

## EPILOGUE: THE DESCENT OF THE WEST

596 merely by mounting several cannons along the coast: Stueck, *Korean War*, p. 362.

596 I have literally heard these arguments from our people: National Security Archive, NSAEBB32, Viron Vaky to Mr Oliver, State Department, March 29, 1968.

596 full-scale conflict between the superpowers: See e.g., Schell, *Unconquerable World*, pp. 51ff.

597 Truman declined to drop the Bomb on Chinese targets: See Ferguson, *Colossus*, pp. 89–93. Cf. Foot, *Wrong War*.

597 both sides be deterred from launching such a first strike: Gaddis, *We Know Now*, pp. 233, 258–61.

597 This was the logic of 'Mutually Assured Destruction': This paragraph draws heavily on Gaddis, *Cold War*.

598 and his successor, the incinerator of Tokyo, Curtis LeMay: Trachtenberg, ' "Wasting Asset" ', pp. 8ff.

598 less militarily and politically precarious: ibid., pp. 27–32, 46.

598 using a nuclear ultimatum to break the Korean deadlock: Foot, *Wrong War*, pp. 176ff.

598 'sufficiently large scale' to bring the conflict to an end: ibid., p. 25.

598 'down' 56 per cent of Americans polled said yes: Mueller, *War, Presidents and Public Opinion*, p. 105.

598 'did not require us to initiate war at the most propitious moment': Trachtenberg, ' "Wasting Asset" ', p. 39.

598 strategy for such a pre-emptive war ('Project Control'): ibid,. p. 42n.

598 rather than 'waiting to go quietly down the drain': ibid., p. 44.

599 mutual destruction becomes more and more imminent: Poundstone, *Prisoner's Dilemma*, pp. 197ff.

599 statesmen of both sides will plunge the world into destruction: ibid., p. 198.

599 He told her to 'drop everything and get out of Moscow': Fursenko and Naftali, *One Hell of a Gamble*.

600 between eight and seventeen to one in favour of the United States: Gaddis, *We Know Now*, p. 103.

600 'I see U.S. missiles in Turkey, aimed at my dacha': ibid., p. 264.

601 Soviet Union that September. 'Now we can swat your ass': What follows draws heavily on Fursenko and Naftali, *One Hell of a Gamble*.

601 'Well, we did, Mr President,' someone reminded him: Gaddis, *We Know Now*, p. 264.

602 'if there are two Americans and one Russian, we win': See Walker, *Cold War*.

603 out alive, and no one can call the other a chicken: Poundstone, *Prisoner's Dilemma*, p. 201.

607 'a wall is a hell of a lot better than a war': Gaddis, *Cold War*, p. 115.

608 were achieved in the vanquished Axis countries: Maddison, *World Economy*, table A1-d. Growth in Japan averaged more than 8 per cent; in Germany more than 5 per cent; in Italy just under 5 per cent.

608 was less than half what it had been between 1919 and 1939: Crafts, 'Is the World a Riskier Place?', chart 2.

608 catch you up, in passing you by, we will wave to you: Transcript at http://edition.cnn.com/SPECIALS/cold.war/episodes/14/documents/debate/. See also Khrushchev, *Khrushchev Remembers,* pp. 364ff.

608 in all, it was visited by 2.7 million Soviet citizens: Caute, *Dancer Defects,* p. 47.

609 expression of belief and universal suffrage and education: ibid., pp. 48ff.

610 notably Rudolf Nureyev and Mikhail Baryshnikov: See Caute, *Dancer Defects,* passim.

610 characters, notably Kim Philby and Guy Burgess: See Andrew and Mitrokhin, *Mitrokhin Archive;* Dorril, *MI6.*

610 trade union leader declared, 'but one can't live without land': Cullather, *Secret History,* pp. 22ff. Cf. Handy, *Revolution in the Countryside.*

611 His brother Allen was Deputy Director of the CIA: See e.g., CIA FOIA, Memo to the Deputy Director, Plans, from Assistant to the Director, November 5, 1951.

611 Soviet Trojan horse in America's back yard: Gaddis, *We Know Now,* pp. 178–80.

611 'thinks differently doesn't know what he's talking about': Cullather, *Secret History,* p. 26.

611 'testing means and methods of combating Communism': ibid., p. 35.

611 The answer in both cases was a CIA-sponsored coup: CIA FOIA, Memorandum for the Director, 'Guatemalan Situation', July 9, 1952.

611 Guatemalan army its cue to seize power from Arbenz: Cullather, *Secret History,* pp. 84–99, 103; Grandin, *Last Colonial Massacre,* pp. 85ff.

612 revolutions in the Dominican Republic, Nicaragua and Haiti: Gott, *Rural Guerillas,* pp. 31ff.

612 against MPLA positions along the Lomba River: The Cubans claimed to have defended Cuito Cuanavale against South African attack. The South Africans claimed that they had successfully checked an MPLA offensive. See Campbell, 'Cuito Cuanavale'; Allport, 'Cuito Cuanavale'.

613 'and global revolution will triumph', it was a different story: Gaddis, *We Know Now,* p. 183.

615 'if he's a sonofabitch, so long as he's our sonofabitch': Black, *Good Neighbor,* p. 71.

615 the Communists had resorted to mass arrests, torture and executions: Cullather, *Secret History,* pp. 83ff.

615 compiled of 72,000 suspected Communist sympathizers: Cf. Cullather, *Secret History,* pp. 137–41.

615 admit that the 'counter-insurgency' was 'running wild': National Security Archive, NSAEBB32, Thomas L. Hughes to the Secretary of State, October 23, 1967. Cf. Grandin, *Last Colonial Massacre,* pp. 73ff, 88ff.

616 in sacks and dropped them out of a plane into the Pacific: ibid., pp. 96–8.

616 the 'tarnishing' of America's image in the region: Grandin, *Last Colonial Massacre,* p. 190. On the role of the U.S. School of the Americas at Fort Benning in training members of the Guatemalan security forces, see Gill, *School of the Americas.*

616 and 'subversion' had a distinctly ethnic character: Heywood, 'Unita and Ethnic Nationalism'.

616 the land-hungry indigenous peoples at the bottom: See esp. Handy, *Revolution in the Countryside,* pp. 13, 127–30; Handy, 'Sea of Indians'; Jonas, *Battle for Guatemala,* p. 16.

616 communists as a war between Ladino latifundista and Mayan peasants: Schirmer, *Guatemalan Military Project;* esp. p. 40.

617 . . . murdered; their homes destroyed and the surrounding forests burned: ibid., p. 55, 61. See also Jonas, *Battle for Guatemala,* pp. 145ff, 149.

617 commission to have committed an act of genocide: Comisión para el Esclarecimiento Histórico, *Guatemala Memoria del Silencio,* vol. V, pp. 42, 48.

618 16 states still had laws prohibiting racial intermarriage: They were: Alabama, Arkansas, Delaware, Florida, Georgia, Kentucky, Louisiana, Mississippi, Missouri, North Carolina, Oklahoma, South Carolina, Tennessee, Texas, Virginia and West Virginia.

618 until March 1978 and Mississippi only in December 1987: Sollors, *Neither Black nor White,* pp. 395–410.

618 integration advanced relatively slowly even when permitted: See among many studies, Washington, *Marriage in Black and White;* Golden, 'Patterns of Negro-White Intermarriage'; Gordon, *Assimilation in American Life;* Monahan, 'Are Interracial Marriages Really Less Stable?'; idem, 'Occupational Class'; Albert, 'Sexual Basis of White Resistance'; Schulman, 'Race, Sex and Violence'; Bontemps, 'Startling New Attitudes'; Stember, *Sexual Racism.*

619 with its vast population, was a different matter: See Mann, *About Face,* pp. 16–37; Brands, *Devil We Knew,* pp. 121–35; Buckley, *United States in the Asia-Pacific,* pp. 154–63.

619 building ever more numerous, ever more lethal missiles?: See Kissinger, *White House Years.* For one of the more nuanced of many critiques, see Hanhimäki, *Flawed Architect.*

620 They sang songs like 'Chairman Mao Is the Sun That Never Falls': Wang, 'Student Attacks'; idem, 'Second Wave'.

621 ready to conceal his deep-seated distaste for Communism: For Nixon's handwritten notes in preparation for his trip and his meeting with Mao, see National Archives at College Park, Nixon Presidential Materials, Folder China Notes, Box 7; White House Special Files: Staff Member and Office Files: President's Personal Files.

621 again like a salesman, 'but anything I say I deliver': See Mann, *About Face,* pp. 13–16.

621 This was to underestimate the other side: See the argument recently advanced in Chang and Halliday, *Mao.*

624 'nationalities . . . do not exist any longer in Kampuchea': Becker, *When the War Was Over*, p. 253.

624 a result of disease, starvation, or execution: Kiernan, 'Genocidal Targeting', p. 218; Kiernan, 'Kampuchea's Ethnic Chinese'. Cf. Ponchaud, *Cambodia Year Zero*, p. 153; Becker, *When the War Was Over*, p. 239; Anon. (ed.), *Dossier Kampuchéa*, pp. 28ff.

624 within the Organization and were accused of having 'Vietnamese minds': Boua, 'Genocide of a Religious Group'; Kiernan, *Cambodia: The Eastern Zone Massacres*.

625 '50 million Vietnamese—and we shall still be 6 million': Kiernan, 'Genocidal Targeting', p. 212.

625 prevent their secession by 'reducing this majority into a minority': Sethi, *Decisive War*, p. 28. See also Sisson and Rose, *War and Secession*, esp. pp. 154–60; Mascarenhas, *Rape of Bangla Desh*, pp. 111–20; Payne, *Massacre*, pp. 16–29; Malik, *Year of the Vulture*, pp. 79–136; Loshak, *Pakistan Crisis*, pp. 95—107. For details of the policy of systematic rape, see Brownmiller, *Against Our Will*, pp. 79–86.

625 (weapons) poison gas to wipe out whole villages: Human Rights Watch, *Iraq's Crime of Genocide*.

626 the triumph of the West, if not 'the end of history': Fukuyama, *End of History*.

626 towards genuine racial and ethnic integration: See e.g., Alba and Golden, 'Patterns of Ethnic Marriage'; Lieberson and Waters, *From Many Strands*; Moran, *Interracial Intimacy*; Kalmijn, 'Shifting Boundaries'; idem, 'Trends in Black/White Intermarriage'. On Britain, see Bagley, 'Interracial Marriage in England'.

627 mark the 600th anniversary of the Battle of Kosovo: Malcolm, *Bosnia*, p. 213.

627 now it was back to Balkan butchery as usual: Simms, *Unfinest Hour*.

628 or less in line with the Yugoslavian average: Botev, 'Where East Meets West', p. 469.

628 republic's other ethnic groups as their wives: See *Demografska Statistika* 1990.

628 the proportions of mixed marriages were even higher: Malcolm, *Bosnia*, p. 221.

628 respectively, 15 and 20 per cent in the 1980s: Economist Intelligence Unit, 'Yugoslavia Country Profile', August 27, 1990.

628 Albanian proportion of Kosovo from 67 to 77 per cent: Botev, 'Where East Meets West', p. 466.

628 compared with 80 per cent and 40 per cent in 1955: ibid., p. 463.

628 that the Serbs outside Serbia were 'endangered': Glenny, *Balkans*, p. 570.

629 than three fifths of the populations were Muslim: International Criminal Tribunal for the Former Yugoslavia, Case No. IT-98-32-I, The Prosecutor of the Tribunal against Milan Lukić, Sredoje Lukić and Mitar Vasiljević. Lukić, who is charged with eleven counts of crimes against humanity, was arrested in Argentina in August 2005.

629 82 men, women and children were dragged from the river: Ed Vulliamy, 'Bloody Trail of Butchery at the Bridge', *Guardian*, March 11, 1996. See also idem, 'The Warlord of Visegrad', *Guardian*, August 11, 2005.

630 of all ethnic groups—contains more than 92,000 names: I am grateful to Mirsad Tokača of the Research and Documentation Centre, Sarajevo, for allowing me to see the latest figures from his researches.

630 graves and painstakingly identified using DNA tests: See the International Commission on Missing Persons, 'System-Wide Tracking Chart', August 19, 2005.

630 Hotel, the High School and the Sports Centre: Tokača, 'Violation of Norms'.

630 Bosnian sources put the total at 50,000. No one really knows: These figures are highly controversial. The journalist Robert Fox, who covered the war for the *Daily Telegraph*, believes the numbers were much lower.

631 violence on ancient (and by implication incurable) tribal hatreds: See Shawcross, *Deliver Us from Evil*, esp. pp. 106, 118ff, 207ff. Cf. Power, 'Problem from Hell'.

631 'numbers into line with the available land resources': Diamond, *Collapse*, pp. 326. See in general ibid., pp. 319ff. Cf. Miguel and Satyanath, 'Economic Shocks'.

632 the Hutu social revolution in Rwanda ('anti-Hamitism'): Feltz, 'Ethnicité'; Chrétien et al., *Rwanda*, pp. 85ff; Erny, *Rwanda 1994*, pp. 58ff.

632 Burundi, like the Ganwa and the Twa or pygmies: Gahama, *Burundi sous Administration Belge*, p. 275; Chrétien, *Burundi*, p. 316.

632 overlooked at the time—they had long intermarried: Van den Berghe, *Ethnic Phenomenon*, pp. 72ff.

632 their unions rose sharply in the period prior to 1994: Taylor, *Sacrifice as Terror*, pp. 155ff, 167ff.

632 Europe's own 'Dark Continent' just fifty years before: The point is well made in Mazower, *Dark Continent*.

633 Sierra Leone, Angola and Liberia in sub-Saharan Africa: Marshall and Gurr, *Peace and Conflict 2005*.

634 thing, biologically sound and practically unavoidable: Einstein and Freud, 'Einstein-Freud Correspondence'.

634 grimly Social Darwinistic conclusion he now offered Einstein: Freud, *Thoughts for the Time on War and Death*.

637 businesses accounted for nearly a third of total industrial production: Yergin and Stanislaw, *Commanding Heights*, pp. 195–200.

637 wealthy capitalist elite was ready to be wooed: ibid., pp. 206–13. Cf. Buckley, *United States in the Asia-Pacific*, p. 163ff.

637 there, bringing with them vital technological know-how: Yergin and Stanislaw, *Commanding Heights*, pp. 200–3.

638 gross domestic product would overtake that of the U.S. as early as 2041: Wilson and Purusho-thaman, 'Dreaming with the BRICs'.

639 Mossadeq and installed Shah Mohammed Reza Pahlavi as a dictator: Gasiorowski, '1953 Coup d'État'. Cf. Kinzer, *All the Shah's Men*.

639 often, it was those who had received a Western education: Buruma and Margalit, *Occidentalism*, p. 15.

640 activity, is a serious and precious duty of motherhood: http://www.iranchamber.com/government/laws/constitution.php.

640 it remained consistently more than twice the European average: These and other demographic data that follow are from United Nations Population Division, World Population Prospects.

642 El Ejido is the point of entry into Europe: For a shrilly Marxist account, see Nair, 'Fire under Plastic'.

642 just one manifestation of what some call 'Eurabia': Ye'or, *Eurabia*.

642 of church attendance and religious faith in Europe: 'Europa wird am Ende des Jahrhunderts islamisch sein', *Die Welt*, October 20, 2004. On the decline of Christianity in Europe, see Brown, *Death of Christian Britain*.

643 there are also real costs for unskilled indigenous workers: See e.g., Organization for Economic Cooperation and Development, 'Trends in Immigration and Economic Consequences', *OECD Economic Outlook*, 68 (2000), pp. 186–203.

643 befall the second age of globalization in which we live?: Ferguson, 'Sinking Globalization'.

644 independence would warrant military intervention: See e.g., Robert D. Kaplan, 'How We Would Fight China', *Atlantic Monthly*, June 2005.

645 and the assault they launched on 'the rationalism of the Megalopolis': Spengler, *Decline of the West*, p. 396.

# Sources and Bibliography

## ARCHIVES

Archivio Segreto Vaticano
Auswärtiges Amt, Berlin
Beinecke Rare Book and Manuscript Library, Yale University, New Haven
Bibliothèque de l'Alliance Israélite Universelle, Paris
Landeshauptarchiv, Koblenz
The Library of Congress, Washington DC
Memorial Research Centre, Moscow
National Archives, Washington DC
National Archives, Kew, London
National Archives at College Park, Maryland
Research and Documentation Centre, Sarajevo
Rothschild Archive, London
Russian State Archives, Moscow
Royal Archives, Windsor Castle
United States Holocaust Museum Library and Archives

## PUBLISHED WORKS

Acemoglu, Daron, Simon Johnson and James A. Robinson, 'Reversal of Fortune: Geography and Institutions in the Making of the Modern World Income Distribution', *Quarterly Journal of Economics*, 117 (November 2002), 1231–94
Adam, Peter, *The Art of the Third Reich* (London, 1992)
Adamthwaite, Anthony, 'France and the Coming of War', in Patrick Finney (ed.), *The Origins of the Second World War* (London, 1997), 78–90
—— 'The British Government and the Media, 1937–1938', *Journal of Contemporary History*, 18, 2 (April 1983), 281–97
Addison, Lucy, *Letters from Latvia* (London, 1986)
Aida, Yuji, transl. Hide Ishiguro and Louis Allen, *Prisoner of the British: A Japanese Soldier's Experience in Burma* (London, 1966)

Akira, Fujiwara, 'The Role of the Japanese Military', in Dorothy Borg and Shumpei Okamoto (eds.), *Pearl Harbor as History: Japanese–American Relations, 1931–1941* (New York, 1973), 189–96

Alanbrooke, Field Marshal Lord, ed. Alex Danchev and Daniel Todman, *War Diaries, 1939–1945* (London, 2001)

Alba, R. D. and R. M. Golden, 'Patterns of Ethnic Marriage in the United States', *Social Forces*, 65 (September 1986), 202–23

Albert, June True, 'The Sexual Basis of White Resistance to Racial Integration', unpublished PhD thesis (Rutgers University, 1972)

Alexander, Jeffrey C., 'Core Solidarity, Ethnic Outgroup and Social Differentiation: A Multidimensional Model of Inclusion in Modern Societies', in Jacques Dufny and Akinsola Akiwowo (eds.), *National and Ethnic Movements* (London, 1980), 5–28

Alexiev, Aleksander and S. Enders Wimbush, 'Non-Russians in the Red Army, 1941–1945', *Journal of Slavic Military Studies*, 6, 3 (1993)

Alice, Countess of Athlone, *For My Grandchildren: Some Reminiscences of Her Royal Highness Princess Alice* (London, 1966)

Allen, Louis and David Steeds, 'Burma: The Longest War, 1941–45', in Saki Dockrill (ed.), *From Pearl Harbour to Hiroshima: The Second World War in Asia and the Pacific, 1941–45* (Basingstoke, 1994)

Allport, Richard, 'The Battle of Cuito Cuanavale: Cuba's Mythical Victory', http://www.rhodesia.nl/cuito.htm (n.d.)

Almog, Shmuel, *Nationalism and Antisemitism in Modern Europe, 1815–1945* (Oxford / New York, 1990)

Aly, Gotz, *'Final Solution': Nazi Population Policy and the Murder of the European Jews* (London, 1999)

Ambrose, Stephen E., *Band of Brothers: E Company, 506th Regiment, 101st Airborne from Normandy to Hitler's Eagle's Nest* (London, 2001[1992])

—— 'The Last Barrier', in Robert Cowley (ed.), *No End Save Victory: New Second World War Writing* (London, 2002), 527–51

—— 'D-Day Fails', in Robert Cowley (ed.), *More What If? Eminent Historians Imagine What Might Have Been* (London, 2002), 341–8

—— 'The Secrets of Overlord', in Robert Cowley (ed.), *The Experience of War* (New York / London, 1992), 472–80

Ames, Jessie Daniel, *The Changing Character of Lynching, 1931–1941* (Atlanta, 1942)

Andenaes, Johs, O. Riste and M. Skodvin, *Norway and the Second World War* (Oslo, 1966)

Anderson, George K., *The Legend of the Wandering Jew* (Providence, 1965)

Andrew, Christopher and Vasili Mitrokhin, *The Mitrokhin Archive: The KGB in Europe and the West* (London, 1999)

Andreyev, Catherine, *Vlasov and the Russian Liberation Movement: Soviet Reality and Emigré Theories* (London / New York / New Rochelle / Melbourne / Sydney, 1987)

Andrić, Ivo, transl. Lovett F. Edwards, *The Bridge on the Drina* (New York, 1959 [1945])

Angell, Norman, *The Great Illusion: A Study of the Relation of Military Power to National Advantage* (London, 1913 [1910])

Angress, Werner T., 'Die "Judenfrage" im Spiegel amtlicher Berichte 1935', in Ursula Büttner (ed.), *Das Unrechtsregime: Internationale Forschung über den Nationalsozialismus* (Hamburg, 1986), 19–44

Anon., *The Horrors of Aleppo, seen by a German Eyewitness* (London, 1916)

—— *Verité sur le mouvement revolutionnaire Arménien et les mesures gouverne-mentales* (Constantinople, 1916)

—— *Semi-Imperator 1888–1918* (Munich, 1919)

—— *Eagle's Nest, Obersalzburg, in a Historical View* (Bayreuth, n.d.)

—— *Ostjuden in Deutschland* (Berlin, 1921)

—— (ed.), *Germany, Turkey and Armenia: A Selection of Documentary Evidence Relating to the Armenian Atrocities from German and other Sources* (London, 1917)

—— (ed.), *Dossier Kampuchea I* (Hanoi, 1978)

—— (ed.), *Documents sur les atrocités Arméno-Russes* (Constantinople, 1917)

Antonov-Ovseyenko, Anton, *The Time of Stalin: Portrait of a Tyranny* (New York, 1981)

Applebaum, Anne, 'Gulag: Understanding the Magnitude of What Happened', *Heritage Lecture* (October 16, 2003)

Arendt, Hannah and Martin Heidegger, ed. Ursula Ludz, *Briefe 1925–1975* (Frankfurt, 1998)

Armstrong, John A., 'Collaborationism in World War II: The Integral Nationalist Variant in Eastern Europe', *Journal of Modern History*, 40 (1968), 396–410

Arnold, James R., 'Coral and Purple: The Lost Advantage', in Peter G. Tsouras (ed.), *Rising Sun Victorious: The Alternate History of How the Japanese Won the Pacific War* (London, 2001), 83–119

Aron, Raymond, *The Imperial Republic: The United States and the World, 1945–1973* (London, 1975)

Aronson, I. M., 'The Prospects for the Emancipation of Russian Jewry during the 1880s', *Slavonic and East European Review*, 55, 1 (January 1977), 348–69

—— *Troubled Waters: The Origins of the 1881 Anti-Jewish Pogroms in Russia* (Pittsburg, 1990)

—— 'Geographical and Socioeconomic Factors in the 1881 Anti-Jewish Pogroms in Russia', *Russian Review*, 55, 1 (Jan. 1980), 18–31

Arthur, Max, in association with the Imperial War Museum (ed.), *Forgotten Voices of the Second World War: A New History of World War Two in the Words of the Men and Women Who Were There* (London, 2004)

Asada, Teruhiko, transl. Ray Cowan, *The Night of a Thousand Suicides: The Japanese Outbreak at Cowra* (Sydney / London / Melbourne / Singapore, 1970)

Ashworth, T., *Trench Warfare 1914–18: The Live and Let Live System* (London, 1980)

Aster, Sidney, ' "Guilty Men": The Case for Neville Chamberlain', in Patrick Finney (ed.), *The Origins of the Second World War* (London, 1997), 62–78

Aston, Frederick Alfred, *The Menace of Anti-Semitism in America Today* (New York, 1938)

Astor, David, 'Why the Revolt against Hitler was Ignored: On the British Reluctance to Deal with German Anti-Nazis', *Encounter*, 32, 6 (June 1969), 3–13

Baar, Jacob and Werner J. Cahnman, 'Interfaith Marriage in Switzerland', in Werner J. Cahnman (ed.), *Intermarriage and Jewish Life: A Symposium* (New York, 1963), 51–6

Bacevich, Andrew, *American Empire: The Realities and Consequences of U.S. Diplomacy* (Cambridge, Mass. / London, 2002)

Bachi, Roberto, *Population Trends of World Jewry* (Jerusalem, 1976)

Bachmann, Gertraude, 'Coburg between England and Russia', in paper presented at Russian Academy of Sciences conference, European Monarchies in Past and Present (Moscow, May 26–28, 1998)

Bacque, James, *Other Losses: An Investigation into the Mass Deaths of German*

*Prisoners at the Hands of the French and Americans after World War II* (Toronto, 1989)

Bagish, Martin and Hilary Conroy, 'Japanese Aggression against China: The Question of Responsibility', in Alvin D. Coox and Hilary Conroy (eds.), *China and Japan: The Search for Balance Since World War I* (Oxford, 1978), 323–35

Bagley, Christopher, 'Interracial Marriage in England: Some Statistics', *New Community*, 1 (June 1972), 318–26

Bairoch, Paul, transl. Christopher Braider, *Cities and Economic Development* (Chicago, 1988)

Balderston, Theo, 'War Finance and Inflation in Britain and Germany, 1914–1918', *Economic History Review*, 42 (1989), 222–44

Barber, John and Mark Harrison, 'Patriotic War, 1941 to 1945', in Ronald Grigor Suny (ed.), *The Cambridge History of Russia*, vol. III: *The Twentieth Century* (Cambridge, forthcoming)

Barber, Laurie and Ken Henshall, *The Last War of Empires: Japan and the Pacific War* (Auckland, 1999)

Barbusse, Henri, transl. Robin Buss, *Under Fire* (London, 2003 [1916])

Barkawi, Tarak, 'Combat Motivation in the Colonies: The Indian Army in the Second World War', *Journal of Contemporary History* (forthcoming)

Barnard, Daniel, 'The Great Iraqi Revolt: The 1919–20 Insurrections against the British in Mesopotamia', paper presented at the Harvard Graduate Student Conference in International History (April 23, 2004)

Barnhart, Michael A., 'Japanese Intelligence before the Second World War: "Best Case" Analysis', in Ernest R. May (ed.), *Knowing One's Enemies: Intelligence Assessment Before the Two World Wars* (Princeton, 1984), 424–56

—— *Japan Prepares for Total War: The Search for Economic Security, 1919–1941* (Ithaca, 1987)

Bartov, Omer, *Hitler's Army: Soldiers, Nazis, and War in the Third Reich* (New York / Oxford, 1992)

—— *Mirrors of Destruction: War, Genocide and Modern Identity* (Oxford / New York, 2000)

—— *The Eastern Front, 1941–45: German Troops and the Barbarisation of Warfare* (Basingstoke, 1985)

Bastide, R., 'Dusky Venus, Black Apollo', *Race*, 3 (1961), 10–18.

Bateson, Patrick, 'Optimal Outbreeding', in Patrick Bateson (ed.), *Mate Choice* (Cambridge, 1982), 257–77.

—— 'Sexual Imprinting and Optimal Outbreeding', *Nature*, 273, 5664 (June 22, 1978), 659–60

Battestin, Martin, *Henry Fielding: A Life* (London, 1989)

Baxter, John, *Not Much of a Picnic: Memoirs of a Conscript and Japanese Prisoner of War, 1941–1945* (Trowbridge, 1995)

Bayly, C. A., *The Birth of the Modern World, 1780–1914: Global Connections and Comparisons* (Oxford, 2003)

—— and Tim Harper, *Forgotten Armies: The Fall of British Asia, 1941–1945* (London, 2004)

Bayur, Yusuf Hikmet, *Türk Inkilabi Tarihi* (Ankara, 1952)

Bean, Richard, 'War and the Birth of the Nation State', *Journal of Economic History*, 33, 1 (March 1973), 203–21

Beatrice, Princess (ed.), *In Napoleonic Days: Extracts from the Private Diary of Augusta, Duchess of Saxe-Coburg-Saalfeld, Queen Victoria's Maternal Grandmother, 1806–1821* (London, 1941)

Becker, Elizabeth, *When the War Was Over: The Voice of Cambodia's Revolution and Its People* (New York, 1986)

Beckman, Morris, *The Jewish Brigade: An Army with Two Masters, 1944–1945* (Staplehurst, 1998)

Beevor, Antony, *Berlin: The Downfall, 1945* (London, 2002)

Begg, R. C. and Liddle, P. H. (eds.), *For Five Shillings a Day: Experiencing War, 1939–45* (London, 2000)

Bein, Alexander, 'Der jüdische Parasit', *Vierteljahreshefte für Zeitgeschichte*, 13 (1965), 121–49

Bell, P. M. H., *The Origins of the Second World War in Europe*, 2nd edn. (London, 1997 [1986])

Beller, Steven, *Vienna and the Jews 1867–1938: A Cultural History* (Cambridge / New York / Melbourne, 1997 [1989])

Belov, Fedor, *The History of the Soviet Collective Farm* (New York, 1955)

Belova, Olga, 'Anti-Jewish Violence in Folk Narratives of the Slavs', unpublished paper, Stockholm Conference on Pogroms (2005)

Ben-Israel, Hevda, 'Cross-Purposes: British Reactions to the German Anti-Nazi Opposition', *Journal of Contemporary History* 20, 3 (1985), 423–38.

Bendiner, Elmer, *The Fall of Fortresses* (London, 1981)

Bennathan, Esra, 'Die demographische und wirtschaftliche Struktur der Juden', in Werner Mosse (ed.), *Entscheidungsjahre 1932: Zur Judenfrage in der Endphase der Weimarer Republik* (Tübingen, 1966), 87–134

Bentwich, Norman, *I Understand the Risks: The Story of the Refugees from Nazi Oppression who Fought in the British Forces in the World War* (London, 1950)

Berg, A. Scott, *Lindbergh* (New York, 1998)

Berg, Alexander, *Juden-Bordelle: Enthüllungen aus dunklen Häusern* (Berlin, 1892)

Bergamini, David, *Japan's Imperial Conspiracy* (New York, 1972)

Bergen, Doris L., 'The Nazi Concept of "Volksdeutsche" and the Exacerbation of Anti-Semitism in Eastern Europe, 1939–45', *Journal of Contemporary History*, 29, 4 (October 1994), 569–82

Berghe, Pierre L. van den, *The Ethnic Phenomenon* (New York, 1981)

Bernstein, Herman (ed.), *The Willy–Nicky Correspondence, Being the Secret and Intimate Telegrams exchanged between the Kaiser and the Tsar* (New York, 1918)

Bertram, James, *The Shadow of a War: A New Zealander in the Far East 1939–1946* (London, 1947)

Beveridge, Sir William, *Social Insurance and Allied Services: Report . . . Presented to Parliament by Command of His Majesty*, CMND 6404 (London, 1942)

Bickers, Robert, *Empire Made Me: An Englishman Adrift in Shanghai* (London, 2004)

Bidermann, Gottlob Herbert, transl. and ed. Derek S. Zumbro, *In Deadly Combat: A German Soldier's Memoir of the Eastern Front* (Lawrence, Kansas, 2000)

Biggs, Chester M. Jr., *Behind the Barbed Wire: Memoir of a World War II U.S. Marine Captured in North China in 1941 and Imprisoned by the Japanese until 1945* (Jefferson, NC / London, 1995)

Biglova, Katerina, Zdenek Matejcek and Zdenek Dytrych, *Remembering: Voices of Prague Jewish Women* (n.p., 1994)

Bikont, Anna, *My z Jedwabnego* (Warsaw, 2005)

Bilinsky, Yaroslav, 'Methodological Problems and Philosophical Issues in the Study of Jewish-Ukrainian Relations during the Second World War', in Howard Aster and Peter J. Potichnyj (eds.), *Ukrainian-Jewish Relations in Historical Perspective* (Edmonton, 1990), 373–407

—— 'Assimilation and Ethnic Assertiveness among Ukrainians of the Soviet Union', in Erich Goldhagen (ed.), *Ethnic Minorities in the Soviet Union* (New York / Washington / London, 1968), 147–84

Bilyeu, Dick, *Lost in Action: A World War II Soldier's Account of Capture on Bataan and Imprisonment by the Japanese* (Jefferson, NC, 1991)

Bing, Edward J. (ed.), *The Letters of Tsar Nicholas and Empress Marie, Being the Confidential Correspondence between Nicholas II, last of the Tsars, and his Mother, Dowager Empress Marie Feodorovna* (London, 1937)

Black, Conrad, *Franklin Delano Roosevelt* (London, 2004)

Black, George, *The Good Neighbor: How the United States Wrote the History of Central America and the Caribbean* (New York, 1988)

Blanke, Richard, *Orphans of Versailles: The Germans in Western Poland, 1918–1939* (Lexington, Kentucky, 1993)

Blau, Peter M. and Joseph E. Schwartz, *Crosscutting Social Circles: Testing a Macroeconomic Theory of Intergroup Relations* (New York, 1984)

Bloch, Ivan S., *Is War Now Impossible? Being an Abridgment of 'The War of the Future in its Technical, Economic and Political Relations'* (London, 1899)

Bloch, Marc, *Étrange Défaite: Témoignage écrit en 1940* (Paris, 1946)

Bloch, Michael, *Ribbentrop* (London / New York / Toronto / Sydney / Auckland, 1992)

Blumstein, Alexandre, *A Little House on Mount Carmel* (London, 2002)

Bobbitt, Philip, *The Shield of Achilles: War, Peace, and the Course of History* (New York, 2002)

Bokszanski, Zbigniew, 'The Representations of the Jews in Selected Polish Autobiographical Materials from the Period of the Second World War', in Marek S. Szczepanski (ed.), *Ethnic Minorities and Ethnic Majority: Sociological Studies of Ethnic Relations in Poland* (Katowice, 1997), 247–56

Bond, Brian, *British Military Policy between the Two World Wars* (Oxford, 1980)

—— (ed.), *Chief of Staff: The Diaries of Lieutenant-General Sir Henry Pownall*, vol. I: *1933–1940* (London, 1972)

Bontemps, Alex, 'Startling New Attitudes on Interracial Marriage', *Ebony*, (July–December 1975), 144–51

Borchardt, Knut, 'Constraints and Room for Manoeuvre in the Great Depression of the Early Thirties: Towards a Revision of the Received Historical Picture', in *idem*, *Perspectives in Modern German Economic History and Policy* (Cambridge, 1991), 143–60

Bordo, Michael, Alan Taylor and Jeffrey Williamson (eds.), *Globalization in Historical Perspective* (Chicago, 2003)

Bordo, Michael, Ehsan Choudhri and Anna Schwartz, 'Was Expansionary Monetary Policy Feasible During the Great Contraction? An Examination of the Gold Standard Constraint', NBER Working Paper, 1725 (May 1999)

Borys, Jurij, *The Sovietization of Ukraine 1917–1923: The Communist Doctrine and Practice of National Self-Determination* (Edmonton, 1980)

Botev, Nikolai, 'Where East Meets West: Ethnic Intermarriage in the Former Yugoslavia, 1962 to 1989', *American Sociological Review*, 59 (June 1994), 461–80

Boua, Chanthou, 'Genocide of a Religious Group: Pol Pot and Cambodia's Buddhist Monks', in P. Timothy Bushnell, Vladimir Shlapentokh, Christopher K. Vanderpool and Jeyaratnam Sundram (eds.), *State Organized Terror: The Case of Violent Internal Repression* (Boulder, 1991), 227–40

Bourke, Joanna, *An Intimate History of Killing: Face-to-face Killing in Twentieth-Century Warfare* (London, 1999)

Bowlby, Alex, *The Recollections of Rifleman Bowlby* (London, 1999)

Boyd, Carl, 'Japanese Military Effectiveness: The Interwar Period', in Allan R. Millett and Williamson Murray (eds.), *Military Effectiveness*, vol. II: *The Interwar Period* (Boston, 1988), 131–68

Boyle, John Hunter, *China and Japan at War, 1937–1945: The Politics of Collaboration* (Stanford, 1972)

Bradley, James, 'The Boys Who Saved Australia, 1942', in Robert Cowley (ed.), *More What If? Eminent Historians Imagine What Might Have Been* (Macmillan, 2002), 291–304

Brainerd, Elizabeth and Mark V. Siegler, 'The Economic Effects of the 1918 Influenza Epidemic', Centre for Economic Policy Research Discussion Paper, 3791 (February 2003)

Brands, H. W., *The Devil We Knew: Americans and the Cold War* (Oxford, 1993)

Brass, Paul R. (ed.), *Riots and Pogroms* (New York, 1996)

Breitman, Richard, *Official Secrets: What the Nazis Planned, What the British and Americans Knew* (London, 1999)

Broadbent, Gilbert, *Behind Enemy Lines* (Bognor Regis, 1985)

Broadberry, Stephen and Peter Howlett, 'The United Kingdom: "Victory at All Costs"', in Mark Harrison (ed.), *The Economics of World War II: Six Great Powers in International Comparison* (Cambridge, 1998), 43–80

Brokaw, Tom, *The Greatest Generation* (London, 2002)

Bronsztejn, Szyja, 'Polish-Jewish Relations as Reflected in Memoirs of the Interwar Period', in Antony Polonsky, Ezra Mendelsohn and Jerzy Tomaszewski (eds.), *Jews in Independent Poland: 1918–1939* (London / Washington, 1994), 66–88

Brook, Timothy (ed.), *Documents on the Rape of Nanking* (Ann Arbor, 1999)

Broscious, S. David, 'Longing for International Control, Banking on American Superiority: Harry S. Truman's Approach to Nuclear Weapons', in John Lewis Gaddis, Philip H. Gordon, Ernest R. May and Jonathan Rosenberg (eds.), *Cold War Statesmen Confront the Bomb: Nuclear Diplomacy Since 1945* (Oxford, 1999), 15–39

Brown, Callum, *The Death of Christian Britain: Understanding Secularization, 1800–2000* (London / New York, 2001)

Brown, Malcolm, in association with the Imperial War Museum, *The Imperial War Museum Book of the Western Front* (London, 1993)

—— *Tommy Goes to War* (London, 1999)

Brown, William O. Jr. and Richard C. K. Burdekin, 'German Debt Traded in London During the Second World War: A British Perspective on Hitler', *Economica*, 69 (2002), 655–69

Browning, Christopher, *Ordinary Men: Reserve Police Battalion 101 and the Final Solution* (London, 2001)

—— *The Origins of the Final Solution: The Evolution of Nazi Jewish Policy, September 1939–March 1942* (London, 2004)

Brownmiller, Susan, *Against Our Will: Men, Women, and Rape* (Harmondsworth, 1976)

Brüll, Adolf, *Die Mischehe im Judentum im Lichte der Geschichte* (Frankfurt, 1905)

Bruntz, George G., *Allied Propaganda and the Collapse of the German Empire in 1918* (Stanford, 1938)

Bry, Gerhard, *Wages in Germany, 1871–1945* (Princeton, 1960)

Bryce, Viscount (ed.), *The Treatment of the Armenians in the Ottoman Empire, 1915–1916: Documents Presented to Viscount Grey of Falloden* (Beirut, 2nd edn. 1972).

Buchanan, Mark, *Ubiquity: The Science of History . . . Or Why the World is Simpler than We Think* (London, 2000)

Buckle, George Earle (ed.), *The Letters of Queen Victoria: A Selection from Her Majesty's Correspondence and Journal between the Years 1886 and 1901*, 3rd Series (London, 1930, 1931, 1932)

Buckley, Gail, *American Patriots: The Story of Blacks in the Military from the Revolution to Desert Storm* (New York, 2001)

Buckley, Roger, *The United States in the Asia-Pacific since 1945* (Cambridge, 2002)

Budnitskii, Oleg, 'What the Cause of a Pogrom Is, or of Gunshots from Behind', unpublished paper, Stockholm Conference on Pogroms (2005)

Budrass, Lutz, Jonas Scherner and Jochen Streb, 'Demystifying the German "Armament Miracle" during World War II: New Insights from the Annual Audits of German Aircraft Producers', Yale University Economic Growth Center Discussion Paper, 905 (January 2005)

Buldakov, V. P., 'Freedom, Shortages, Violence: The Origins of the "Revolutionary" Anti-Jewish Pogrom in Russia in 1917–1918', unpublished paper, Stockholm Conference on Pogroms (2005)

Bulgakov, Mikhail, transl. Richard Pevear and Larissa Volokhonsky, *The Master and Margarita* (London, 1997 [1966])

—— transl. Michael Glenny, *The White Guard* (London, 1971)

Bull, Eric, *Go Right, Young Man* (Hornby, 2nd edn. 1997)

Bullock, Alan, *Hitler and Stalin: Parallel Lives* (London, 1991)

Burgdörfer, Friedrich, 'Die Juden in Deutschland und in der Welt: Ein statistischer Beitrag zur biologischen, beruflichen und sozialen Struktur des Judentums in Deutschland', *Forschungen zur Judenfrage*, 3 (1938), 152–98

Burk, Kathleen, *Britain, America and the Sinews of War, 1914–1918* (London, 1985)

Burleigh, Michael, *Death and Deliverance: 'Euthanasia' in Germany 1900–1945* (Cambridge, 1994)

—— *Earthly Powers: Religion and Politics in Europe from the Enlightenment to the Great War* (London, 2005)

—— *Germany Turns Eastwards: A Study of Ostforschung in the Third Reich* (Cambridge, 2000)

—— 'Nazi Europe: What If Nazi Germany Had Defeated the Soviet Union?', in Niall Ferguson (ed.), *Virtual History: Alternatives and Counterfactuals* (New York, 1999), 321–47

—— 'The Racial State Revisited', in *idem, Ethics and Extermination: Reflections on Nazi Genocide* (Cambridge, 1997), 155–68

—— *The Third Reich: A New History* (London, 2001)

—— and Wolfgang Wippermann, *The Racial State: Germany 1933–1945* (Cambridge, 1991)

Burtt, John D., 'Known Enemies and Forced Allies: The Battles of Sicily and Kursk', in Peter G. Tsouras (ed.), *Third Reich Victorious: The Alternate History of How the Germans Won the War* (London, 2002), 169–96

Buruma, Ian, *Inventing Japan: From Empire to Economic Miracle, 1853–1964* (London, 2003)

Buruma, Ian and Avishai Margalit, *Occidentalism: The West in the Eyes of Its Enemies* (New York, 2004)

Bynum, Victoria E., '"White Negroes" in Segregated Mississippi: Miscegenation, Racial Identity and the Law', *Journal of Southern History*, 64, 2 (May 1998), 247–76

Cain, P. J. and A. G. Hopkins, *British Imperialism, 1688–2000*, 2nd edn. (Harlow, 2001)

Cala, Alina, 'The Social Consciousness of Young Jews in Interwar Poland', *Polin*, 8 (1994), 42–66

Calvocoressi, Peter, Guy Wint and John Pritchard, *Total War: The Causes and Courses of the Second World War*, 2nd edn. (Harmondsworth, 1989)

Campbell, Horace, 'Cuito Cuanavale', in *The Oxford Companion to Politics of the World*, 2nd edn. (Oxford, 2001), 187

Campbell, Kim H., 'Holding Patton: Seventh Panzer Army and the Battle of Luxembourg', in Peter G. Tsouras (ed.), *Battle of the Bulge: Hitler's Alternate Scenarios* (London, 2004), 205–31

Camper, Carol (ed.), *Miscegenation Blues: Voices of Mixed Race Women* (Toronto, 1994)

Cannadine, David, *Ornamentalism: How the British Saw Their Empire* (London, 2001)

Cantril, Hadley, 'America Faces the War: A Study in Public Opinion', *Public Opinion Quarterly*, 4, 4 (September 1940), 387–407

Carlton, David, 'Against the Grain: In Defence of Appeasement', *Policy Review*, 13 (Summer 1980), 134–50

Carpenter, Humphrey, *Tolkien: A Biography* (Boston, 1977)

Carpenter, W. S., *The Du Pont Company's Part in the National Security Program, 1940–1945: Stockholder's Bulletin* (Wilmington, Del., 1946)

Carr, Caleb, 'VE Day – November 11, 1944', in Robert Cowley (ed.), *More What If? Eminent Historians Imagine What Might Have Been* (Macmillan, 2002), 333–45

Carr., E. H., *The Twenty Years' Crisis, 1919–1939: An Introduction to the Study of International Relations*, reissued with a new introduction and additional material by Michael Cox (Basingstoke, 2001)

Carruthers, Bob and Simon Trew (eds.), *Servants of Evil: New First-hand Accounts of the Second World War from Survivors of Hitler's Armed Forces* (London, 2001)

Carson, Andrew D., *My Time in Hell: Memoir of an American Soldier Imprisoned by the Japanese in World War II* (Jefferson, NC / London, 1997)

Casper, Bernard M., *With the Jewish Brigade* (London, 1947)

Castellan, Georges, 'Remarks on the Social Structure of the Jewish Community in Poland between the Two World Wars', in Bela Vago and George L. Mosse (eds.), *Jews and non-Jews in Eastern Europe, 1918–1945* (New York, 1974), 187–201

—— 'The Germans of Rumania', *Journal of Contemporary History*, 6, 1 (1971), 52–75

Caute, David, *The Dancer Defects: The Struggle for Cultural Supremacy during the Cold War* (Oxford, 2003)

Cavalli-Sforza, Luigi Luca, transl. Mark Seielstad, *Genes, People, and Languages* (New York, 1999)

Cavalli-Sforza, Luigi Luca, Paolo Menozzi and Alberto Piazza, *The History and Geography of Human Genes* (Princeton, 1994)

Cell, John W., *The Highest Stage of White Supremacy: The Origins of Segregation in South Africa and the American South* (Cambridge, 1982)

—— 'Colonial Rule', in Judith M. Brown and Wm. Roger Louis (eds.), *Oxford History of the British Empire*, vol. IV: *The Twentieth Century* (Oxford / New York, 1999), 232–254

Céline, Louis-Ferdinand, *Voyage au bout de la nuit* (Paris, 1956 [1932])

Chalker, Jack Bridger, *Burma Railway Artist: The War Drawings of Jack Chalker* (London, 1994)

Chamberlin, W. H., *The Russian Revolution*, 2 vols. (New York, 1965)

—— 'Soviet Taboos', *Foreign Affairs*, 13 (1935), 431–40

Chang, Iris, *The Rape of Nanking: The Forgotten Holocaust of World War II* (New York, 1997)

Chang, Jung and Jon Halliday, *Mao: The Unknown Story* (London, 2005)

Charmley, John, *Churchill: The End of Glory* (London, 1993)

—— *Chamberlain and the Lost Peace* (London, 1989)

Chenevix-Trench, Charles, *The Indian Army and the King's Enemies, 1900–1947* (London, 1988)

Chirac, Auguste, *Les rois de la République: Histoire des juiveries* (Paris, 1883)

—— *L'agiotage de 1870 à 1884* (Paris, 1887)

Chiswick, Barry R. and Timothy J. Hatton, 'International Migration and the Integration of Labor Markets', in Michael D. Bordo, Alan M. Taylor and Jeffrey G. Williamson (eds.), *Globalization in Historical Perspective* (Chicago / London, 2003), 65–120

Chmerkine, N., *Les Consequences de l'Antisémitisme en Russie* (Paris, 1897)

Chrétien, Jean-Pierre, *Burundi: L'histoire retrouvée: 25 ans de métier d'historian en Afrique* (Paris, 1993)

—— Jean-François Dupaquier, Marcel Kabanda and Joseph Ngarambe, *Rwanda: Les médias du genocide* (Paris, 1995)

Christiano, Lawrence J., Roberto Motto and Massimo Rostagno, 'The Great Depression and the Friedman-Schwartz Hypothesis', NBER Working Paper, 10255 (January 2004)

Chua, Amy, *World on Fire: How Exporting Free Market Democracy Breeds Ethnic Hatred and Global Instability* (New York, 2003)

Churchill, Winston S., *The Hinge of Fate: The Second World War* (Boston, 1950)

Clarke, I. F. (ed.), *Voices Prophesying War, 1763–1984* (London / New York, 1992)

Clarke, Peter F., *The Cripps Version: The Life of Sir Stafford Cripps, 1889–1952* (London, 2002)

Clayton, James D., 'American and Japanese Strategies in the Pacific War', in Peter Paret (ed.), *Makers of Modern Strategy from Machiavelli to the Nuclear Age* (Princeton, 1986), 703–32

Coble, Parks M., *Facing Japan: Chinese Politics and Japanese Imperialism* (Cambridge, Mass., 1991)

Coetzee, M. S., *The German Army League: Popular Nationalism in Wilhelmine Germany* (Oxford / New York, 1990)

Coghlan, F., 'Armaments, Economic Policy and Appeasement: The Background to British Foreign Policy, 1931–7', *History*, 57, 190 (June 1972), 205–16

Cohen, Gary B., *The Politics of Ethnic Survival: Germans in Prague, 1861–1914* (Princeton, 1981)

Cohen, Israel, 'My Mission to Poland (1918–1919)', *Jewish Social Studies*, 13, 2 (April 1951), 149–72

Cohen, Paul, *History in Three Keys: The Boxers as Event, Experience and Myth* (New York, 1998)

Cole, Harold L., Lee O. Ohanian and Ron Leung, 'Deflation and the International Great Depression: A Productivity Puzzle', Federal Reserve Bank of Minneapolis Research Department Staff Report, 356 (February 2005)

Cole, Margaret, *The Webbs and their Work* (New York, 1974)

Cole, Wayne S., 'America First and the South, 1940–1941', *Journal of Southern History*, 22, 1 (February 1956), 36–47

Collier, Paul and Anke Hoeffler, 'On Economic Causes of Civil War', Oxford Economic Papers, 50 (1998), 563–73

Colville, J. R., *Man of Valour: The Life of Field-Marshal the Viscount Gort* (London, 1972)

Colville, John, *The Fringes of Power: Downing Street Diaries, 1939–1955* (Dunton Green, 1986)

Colvin, Ian, *Vansittart in Office: An Historical Survey of the Origins of the Second World War Based on the Papers of Sir Robert Vansittart* (London, 1965)
—— *The Chamberlain Cabinet: How the Meetings in 10 Downing Street, 1937–1939 Led to the Second World War, Told for the First Time from the Cabinet Papers* (London, 1971)
Comision para el Esclarecimiento Historico, *Guatemala Memoria del Silencio: Las Violaciones de los Derechos Humanos y los Hechos de Violencia*, vol. II (Guatemala, 1999)
—— *Guatemala Memoria del Silencio: Conclusiones y Recomendaciones*, vol. V (Guatemala, 1999)
Conlen, Paul, 'The Historical Genesis and Material Basis of Racial Endogamy in Racist Societies', unpublished thesis (University of Lund, 1974)
Connaughton, R. M., *The War of the Rising Sun and Tumbling Bear: A Military History of the Russo-Japanese War, 1904–5* (London, 1988)
Conquest, Robert, *The Great Terror: A Reassessment* (London, 1992)
—— *The Harvest of Sorrow: Soviet Collectivization and the Terror-Famine* (London / Melbourne / Auckland / Johannesburg, 1986)
—— *The Nation Killers* (London, 1970)
Constantine, Stephen, 'Migrants and Settlers', in Judith M. Brown and Wm. Roger Louis (eds.), *The Oxford History of the British Empire*, vol. IV: *The Twentieth Century* (Oxford, 1999), 163–87.
Cook, Theodore F. Jr., 'Our Midway Disaster', in Robert Cowley (ed.), *What If?: The World's Foremost Military Historians Imagine What Might Have Been* (London, 2001), 311–339
Cooper, Duff, ed. John Julius Norwich, *The Duff Cooper Diaries, 1915–1951* (London, 2005)
—— *Old Men Forget* (London, 1953)
Coox, Alvin, 'The Effectiveness of the Japanese Military Establishment in the Second World War', in Allan R. Millett and Williamson Murray (eds.), *Military Effectiveness*, vol. III: *The Second World War* (Boston, 1988), 1–44
—— 'The Pacific War', in Peter Duus (ed.), *The Cambridge History of Japan*, vol. VI: *The Twentieth Century* (Cambridge, 1988), 315–385.
—— *Nomonhan: Japan Against Russia, 1939*, 2 vols. (Stanford, 1985)
Corti, Egon Caeser Conte, *The English Empress: A Study in the Relations between Queen Victoria and her Eldest Daughter, Empress Frederick of Germany* (London, 1957)
—— *Alexander of Battenberg* (London, 1954)
Costello, John, *Days of Infamy: MacArthur, Roosevelt, Churchill* (New York, 1994)
Coyne, Jerry A. and H. Allen Orr, *Speciation* (Sunderland, MA, 2004)
Cozzens, James Gould, *Guard of Honor* (New York, 1948)
Crafts, Nicholas, 'Is the World a Riskier Place?', Merrill Lynch Global Securities Research and Economics Group (May 16, 2005)
—— 'Globalisation and Growth in the Twentieth Century', International Monetary Fund Working Paper, 00/44 (March 2000)
Cray, Ed, *Chrome Colossus: General Motors and its Times* (Boston, 1980)
Creveld, Martin van, *Supplying War: Logistics from Wallenstein to Patton* (Cambridge, 1977)
Crowley, James B., *Japan's Quest for Autonomy: National Security and Foreign Policy, 1930–1938* (Princeton, 1966)
Crowson, N. J., *Facing Fascism: The Conservative Party and the European Dictators, 1935–1940* (London, 1997)

Cullather, Nick, *Secret History: The CIA's Classified Account of Its Operations in Guatemala, 1952–1954* (Stanford, 1999)

Dabney, Virginius, 'The South Looks Abroad', *Foreign Affairs*, 19, 1 (October 1940), 171–8

Dadrian, Vahakn N., *German Responsibility in the Armenian Genocide: A Review of the Historical Evidence of German Complicity* (Watertown, Mass., c1996)

—— 'The Armenian Question and the Wartime Fate of the Armenians as Documented by the Officials of the Ottoman Empire's World War I Allies: Germany and Austria-Hungary', *International Journal of Middle Eastern Studies*, 32 (2002), 59–85

—— *The History of the Armenian Genocide* (Providence, 1997)

—— *The Key Elements in the Turkish Denial of the Armenian Genocide: A Case Study of Distortion and Falsification* (Cambridge, MA, 1999)

—— 'The Signal Facts Surrounding the Armenian Genocide and the Turkish Denial Syndrome', *Journal of Genocide Research*, 5 (2003)

Dairnvaell, Georges ['Satan' (pseud.)], *Histoire édifiante et curieuse de Rothschild Ier, roi des Juifs* (Paris, 1846)

Danchev, Alex, *Alchemist of War: The Life of Basil Liddell Hart* (London, 1998)

Davidson-Houston, J. V., *Yellow Creek: The Story of Shanghai* (London, 1962)

Davie, Maurice R., *Refugees in America: Report of the Committee for the Study of Recent Immigration from Europe* (New York, 1947)

Davies, Norman, *Europe: A History* (Oxford / New York, 1996)

—— *God's Playground: A History of Poland in Two volumes*, vol. II: *1795 to the Present* (New York, 1982)

—— *Rising '44: The Battle for Warsaw* (New York, 2004)

—— and Roger Moorhouse, *Microcosm: Portrait of a Central European City* (London, 2003)

Davis, Lance E. and R. A. Huttenback, *Mammon and the Pursuit of Empire: The Political Economy of British Imperialism, 1860–1912* (Cambridge, 1986)

Davis, Mike, *Late Victorian Holocausts: El Niño Famines and the Making of the Third World* (London, 2001)

Dawkins, Richard, *The Selfish Gene*, 2nd edn. (Oxford / New York, 1989)

Deist, Wilhelm, 'The Military Collapse of the German Empire: The Reality behind the Stab-in-the-Back Myth', *War in History*, 3, 2 (1996), 186–207

Della Pergola, Sergio, *Jewish Mixed Marriages in Milan 1901–1968, with an Appendix: Frequency of Mixed Marriage Among Diaspora Jews* (Jerusalem, 1972)

Diamond, Jared, *Collapse: How Societies Choose to Fail or Succeed* (New York, 2005)

Dibold, Hans, transl. by H. C. Stevens, *Doctor at Stalingrad: The Passion of a Captivity* (London, 1958)

Dilks, David, ' "The Unnecessary War"? Military Advice and Foreign Policy in Great Britain, 1931–1939', in Adrian Preston (ed.), *General Staffs and Diplomacy before the Second World War* (London, 1978), 98–132

—— (ed.), *The Diaries of Sir Alexander Cadogan, 1938–1945* (London, 1971)

Dinter, Artur, *Die Sünde wider das Blut: Ein Zeitroman* (Leipzig, 1920)

Divine, Robert A., *The Illusion of Neutrality* (Chicago, 1962)

Djilas, Aleksa, *Contested Country: Yugoslav Unity and Communist Revolution, 1919–1953* (Cambridge, Mass. / London, 1991)

Dobkin, Marjorie Housepian, *Smyrna 1922: The Destruction of a City* (Kent, Ohio / London, 1988)

Dobson, Christopher, John Miller and Ronald Payne, *The Cruellest Night: Germany's Dunkirk and the Sinking of the Wilhelm Gustloff* (London, 1979)

Donovan, Tom (ed.), *The Hazy Red Hell: Fighting Experiences on the Western Front, 1914–1918* (Staplehurst, 1999)

Dorril, Stephen, *MI6: Fifty Years of Special Operations* (London, 2000)

Dower, John W., *War without Mercy: Race and Power in the Pacific War* (London / Boston, 1986)

Doyle, Michael W., 'Liberalism and World Politics', *American Political Science Review*, 80, 4 (1986), 1151–1167

Dralle, Lothar, *Die Deutschen in Ostmittel- und Osteuropa: ein Jahrtausend europäischer Geschichte* (Darmstadt, 1991)

Draper, Alfred, *The Amritsar Massacre: Twilight of the Raj* (London, 1985)

Dreyer, Edward L., *China at War, 1901–1949* (London, 1995)

Drucker, Peter, *Die Judenfrage in Deutschland* (Vienna, 1936)

Drucker, Peter F., *The Concept of the Corporation* (New York, 1946)

Drumont, Edouard, *La France juive: Essai d'histoire contemporaine*, 2 vols. (Paris, 1885)

—— *Les Juifs contre la France* (Paris, 1899)

—— *Le Testament d'un antisémite* (Paris, 1894)

Dubnow, S. M., transl. I. Friedlaender, *History of the Jews in Russia and Poland from the Earliest Times until the Present Day*, vol. II: *From the Death of Alexander I until the Death of Alexander III (1825–1894)* (New York, 1975)

Dudley, Wade G., 'Be Careful What You Wish For: The Plan Orange Disaster', in Peter G. Tsouras (ed.), *Rising Sun Victorious: The Alternate History of How the Japanese Won the Pacific War* (London, 2001), 39–61

Dugdale, E. T. S. (ed.), *German Diplomatic Documents, 1871–1914*, 4 vols. (London, 1928)

Dunbabin, J. P. D., 'British Rearmament in the 1930s: A Chronology and Review', *Historical Journal*, 18, 3 (September, 1975), 587–609

Dungan, Myles, *They Shall Not Grow Old: Irish Soldiers and the Great War* (Dublin, 1997)

Dunlop, E. E., *The War Diaries of Weary Dunlop: Java and the Burma-Thailand Railway, 1942–1945* (London, 1987)

Durand, Yves, *La vie quotidienne des Prisonniers de Guerre dans les Stalags, les Oflags et les Kommandos, 1939–1945* (Paris, 1987)

Durham, W. H., *Coevolution: Genes, Culture, and Human Diversity* (Stanford, 1991)

Durschmied, Erik, *The Hinge Factor: How Chance and Stupidity Have Changed History* (London, 1999)

Duus, Peter, 'Japan's Informal Empire in China, 1895–1937: An Overview', in Peter Duus, Ramlon H. Myers and Mark R. Peattie (eds.), *The Japanese Informal Empire in China, 1895–1937* (Princeton, 1989), xi–xxix

Easton, Laird M., *The Red Count: The Life of Harry Kessler* (Berkeley, 2002)

Echenberg, Myron, *Colonial Conscripts: The 'Tirailleurs Senegalais' in French West Africa, 1857–1960* (London, 1991)

Edelstein, Michael, 'Imperialism: Cost and Benefit', in Roderick Floud and Donald McCloskey (eds.), *The Economic History of Britain since 1700*, 2nd edn., vol. II (Cambridge, 1994), 173–216

Edgar, Donald, *The Stalag Men: The Story of One of the 110,000 Other Ranks who were POWs of the Germans in the 1939–45 War* (London, 1982)

Edgerton, Robert B., *Warriors of the Rising Sun: A History of the Japanese Military* (London, 1997)

Edwardes, Allen, *Erotica Judaica* (New York, 1967)

Ehrenburg, Ilya, *Men, Years – Life*, vol. V: *The War, 1941–45* (London, 1964)

Ehrenburg, Ilya and Vasily Grossman, transl. David Patterson, *The Complete Black Book of Russian Jewry* (New Brunswick, NJ, 2002)

Eichengreen, Barry, *Golden Fetters: The Gold Standard and the Great Depression, 1919–1939* (New York / Oxford, 1992)
—— 'Still Fettered After All These Years', NBER Working Paper, 9726 (October 2002)
Einstein, Albert and Sigmund Freud, 'The Einstein–Freud Correspondence (1931–1932)', in Otto Nathan and Heinz Norden (eds.), *Einstein on Peace* (New York, 1960), 186–203
Ekblom, Robert, 'Inbreeding Avoidance through Mate Choice', unpublished paper, Evolutionary Biology Centre, Department of Population Biology, Uppsala University, Sweden (n.d.)
Eksteins, Modris, *Walking Since Daybreak: A Story of Eastern Europe, World War II, and the Heart of our Century* (Boston, 1999)
Elkins, Caroline, *Britain's Gulag: The Brutal End of Empire in Kenya* (London, 2005)
Ellis, John, *The World War I Databook: The Essential Facts and Figures for all the Combatants* (London, 1993)
Endicott, Stephen Lyon, *Diplomacy and Enterprise: British China Policy, 1933–1937* (Manchester, 1975)
Erickson, John, *The Road to Stalingrad: Stalin's War with Germany*, vol. I (London, 1975)
—— 'New Thinking about the Eastern Front in World War II', *Journal of Military History*, 56, 2 (April 1992), 283–92
Erny, Pierre, *Rwanda 1994: Clés pour comprendre le calvaire d'un peuple* (Paris, 1994)
Errera, Leo, *The Russian Jews: Extermination or Emancipation?* (New York / London, 1894)
Evans, Richard, *Rituals of Retribution: Capital Punishment in Germany 1600–1987* (Oxford, 1996)
—— *The Third Reich in Power* (New York, 2005)
—— *The Coming of the Third Reich* (London, 2003)
Falls, Cyril, *Caporetto 1917* (London, 1965)
Falter, Jurgen W., *Hitlers Wähler* (Munich, 1991)
Fanon, Frantz, *Black Skin, White Masks* (London, 1952)
Farmer, Rhodes, *Shanghai Harvest: A Diary of Three Years in the China War* (London, 1945)
Farquhar, George, 'The Twin Rivals', in William Myers (ed.), *The Recruiting Officer and Other Plays* (New York, 1995), 79–159
Farrar-Hockley, Sir Anthony, 'The China Factor in the Korean War', in James Cotton and Ian Neary (eds.), *The Korean War in History* (Manchester, 1989), 4–11
Fay, Peter Ward, *The Forgotten Army: India's Armed Struggle for Independence, 1942–1945* (Ann Arbor, 1993)
Feinstein, C. H., *National Income, Expenditure and Output of the United Kingdom, 1855–1965* (Cambridge, 1972)
Feldman, Eliyahu, 'British Diplomats and British Diplomacy and the 1905 Pogroms in Russia', *Slavonic and East European Review*, 65, 4 (October 1987), 579–608
Feldman, Gerald D., *The Great Disorder: Politics, Economics and Society in the German Inflation* (New York / Oxford, 1993)
Felsenstein, Frank, *Anti-Semitic Stereotypes: A Paradigm of Otherness in English Popular Culture, 1660–1830* (Baltimore, 1995)
Feltz, Gaetan, 'Ethnicité, état-nation et démocratisation au Rwanda et au Burundi', in Manassé Esoavelomandroso and Gaetan Feltz (eds.), *Démocratie et développement: Mirage ou espoir raisonnable?* (Paris / Antananarivo, 1995), 277–97
Fenby, Jonathan, *Generalissimo: Chiang Kai-shek and the China He Lost* (London, 2003)
Ferguson, Niall, *Empire: How Britain Made the Modern World* (London, 2003)

—— *Paper and Iron: Hamburg Business and German Politics in the Era of Inflation, 1897–1927* (Cambridge, 1995)

—— 'Political Risk and the International Bond Market between the 1848 Revolution and the Outbreak of the First World War', *Economic History Review* 59, 1 (2006), 70–112

—— 'Prisoner Taking and Prisoner Killing in the Age of Total War: Towards a Political Economy of Military Defeat', *War in History*, 11, 1 (2004), 34–78

—— 'Sinking Globalization', *Foreign Affairs* 84, 2 (March / April 2005), 64–77

—— *The Cash Nexus: Money and Power in the Modern World, 1700–2000* (London, 2001)

—— *The House of Rothschild*, vol. I: *Money's Prophets*; vol. II: *The World's Banker* (New York, 1999)

—— 'The Paradox of Diminishing Risk Perception in a Dangerous World', Drobny Associates Research Paper (July 2005)

—— *The Pity of War* (London, 1998)

—— 'The Unconscious Colossus: Limits of (and Alternatives to) American Empire', *Daedalus*, 134, 2 (2005), 18–33

—— and Moritz Schularick, 'The Empire Effect: The Determinants of Country Risk in the First Age of Globalization, 1880–1913', *Journal of Economic History* 66, 2 (2006), 283–312

Fermi, Laura, *Illustrious Immigrants: The Intellectual Migration from Europe, 1930–1941* (Chicago / London, 1968)

Fermor, Patrick Leigh, *A Time of Gifts: On Foot to Constantinople from the Hook of Holland to the Middle Danube* (London, 2005)

Feuerwerker, Albert, 'Japanese Imperialism in China: A Commentary', in Peter Duus, Ramlon H. Myers and Mark R. Peattie (eds.), *The Japanese Informal Empire in China, 1895–1937* (Princeton, 1989), 431–8

Field, Alexander J., 'The Impact of World War II on US Productivity Growth', unpublished paper, Santa Clara University (September 2005)

Figes, Orlando, *Peasant Russia, Civil War: The Volga Countryside in Revolution (1917–1921)* (New York, 1989)

—— 'The Red Army and Mass Mobilization during the Russian Civil War, 1918–1920', *Past and Present*, 129 (November 1990), 168–211

—— *A People's Tragedy: The Russian Revolution, 1891–1924* (London, 1996)

Fink, Carol, 'The Minorities Question at the Paris Peace Conference: The Polish Minority Treaty, June 28, 1919', in Manfred F. Boemeke, Gerald D. Feldman and Elisabeth Glaser (eds.), *The Treaty of Versailles: A Reassessment after 75 Years* (Cambridge, 1998), 249–74

Fisch, Harold, *The Dual Image: The Figure of the Jew in English and American Literature* (New York, 1971)

Fischer, Conan, *The German Communists and the Rise of Nazism* (London, 1991)

FitzPatrick, Bernard T. and John A. Sweetser III, *The Hike into the Sun: Memoir of an American Soldier Captured on Bataan in 1942 and Imprisoned by the Japanese until 1945* (Jefferson, NC / London, 1993)

Fitzpatrick, Sheila, *Everyday Stalinism: Ordinary Life in Extraordinary Times – Soviet Russia in the 1930s* (Oxford, 1999)

Flandreau, Marc and Frédéric Zumer, *The Making of Global Finance, 1880–1913* (Paris, 2004)

Fleischhauer, Ingeborg and Benjamin Pinkus, ed. Edith Rogovin Frankel, *The Soviet Germans: Past and Present* (New York, 1986)

Fleming, Donald and Bernard Bailyn (eds.), *The Intellectual Migration: Europe and America, 1930–1960* (Cambridge, Mass., 1969)

Fleming, Thomas, 'Illusions and Realities in World War I', *Historically Speaking* (September / October 2004), 7–9

Flora, Peter *et al.* (eds.), *State, Economy and Society in Western Europe, 1815–1975: A Data Handbook*, 2 vols. (Frankfurt, 1983)

Fogel, Robert W., *The Escape from Hunger and Premature Death, 1700–2100: Europe, America, and the Third World* (Cambridge, 2003)

Folcher, Gustave, *Marching to Captivity: The War Diaries of a French Peasant, 1939–45* (London / Washington DC, 1996)

Fooks, Herbert C., *Prisoners of War* (Federalsburg, Md, 1924)

Foot, Rosemary, *The Wrong War: American Policy and the Dimensions of the Korean Conflict, 1950–1953* (Ithaca, 1985)

Forbes, Neil, 'London Banks, the German Standstill Agreements, and "Economic Appeasement" in the 1930s', *Economic History Review*, 2nd Series, 40, 4 (November 1987), 571–87

Fordham, Benjamin O., ' "Revisionism" Reconsidered: Exports and American Intervention in the First World War', unpublished paper, Department of Political Science, Binghamton University (SUNY) (2004)

Foreign Office, *Correspondence Relating to the Asiatic Provinces of Turkey: Part I: Events at Sassoon, and Commission of Inquiry at Moush* (London, 1895)

Förster, Jürgen, 'The German Army and the Ideological War against the Soviet Union', in Gerhard Hirschfeld (ed.), *The Policies of Genocide: Jews and Soviet Prisoners of War in Nazi Germany* (London / Boston / Sydney, 1986), 15–29

Forsyth, James, *A History of the Peoples of Siberia: Russia's North Asian Colony, 1581–1990* (Cambridge / New York / Port Chester / Melbourne / Sydney, 1992)

Fort, Adrian, *'Prof': The Life and Times of Frederick Lindemann* (London, 2004)

Foster, Alan, 'The Times and Appeasement: The Second Phase', *Journal of Contemporary History*, 16, 3 (July 1981), 441–65

Fotiadis, Constantinos E. (ed.), *The Genocide of the Pontus Greeks* (Thessaloniki, 2002)

Frank, Andre Gunder, *ReOrient: Global Economy in the Asian Age* (Berkeley / London, 1998)

Freud, Sigmund, 'Thoughts for the Time on War and Death', reprinted in John Rickman (ed.), *Civilization, War and Death* (London, 1939)

Friedman, Barton, 'Tolkien and David Jones: The Great War and the War of the Ring', *Clio*, 11, 2 (1982), 117–35

Friedman, Benjamin M., *The Moral Consequences of Economic Growth* (New York, 2005)

Friedman, Milton and Anna J. Schwartz, *A Monetary History of the United States, 1867–1960* (Princeton, 1963)

Friedrich, Jörg, *Der Brand: Deutschland im Bombenkrieg, 1940–1945* (Berlin, 2003)

Fritz, Stephen G., *Frontsoldaten: The German Soldier in World War II* (Lexington, 1995)

Fromkin, David, *Europe's Last Summer: Why the World Went to War in 1914* (London, 2004)

Froschauer, Hermann and Renate Geyer, *Quellen des Hasses: Aus dem Archiv des 'Stürmer' 1933–1945. Eine Ausstellung des Stadtarchivs Nürnberg Okt. 1988–Feb. 1989* (Nuremberg, 1988)

Frymann, Daniel [Heinrich Class], *Wenn ich der Kaiser wär' – Politische Wahrheiten und Notwendigkeiten* (Leipzig, 1912)

Fuchs, Edouard, *Die Juden in der Karikatur: Ein Beitrag zur Kulturgeschichte* (Berlin, 1985)

Fukuyama, Francis, 'Capitalism and Democracy: The Missing Link', *Journal of Democracy*, 3 (1992), 100–110

—— *The End of History and the Last Man* (New York, 1992)

—— *The Great Disruption: Human Nature and the Reconstitution of Social Order* (London, 1999)

Fursenko, Aleksandr and Timothy Naftali, *One Hell of a Gamble: Khrushchev, Castro, Kennedy and the Cuban Missile Crisis, 1958–1964* (London, 1997)

Gabrielan, M. C., *Armenia: A Martyr Nation: A Historical Sketch of the Armenian People from Traditional Times to the Present Tragic Days* (New York / Chicago, 1918)

Gackenholz, Hermann, 'The Collapse of Army Group Centre in 1944', in Hans-Adolf Jacobsen and Jurgen Rohwer (eds.), transl. Edward Fitzgerald, *Decisive Battles of World War II: The German View* (London, 1965), 355–83

Gaddis, John Lewis, *The Cold War: A New History* (London, 2006)

—— 'Korea in American Politics, Strategy, and Diplomacy, 1945–1950', in Yōnōsuke Nagai and Akira Iriye (eds.), *The Origins of the Cold War in Asia* (Tokyo, 1977), 277–99.

—— *We Know Now: Rethinking Cold War History* (Oxford, 1997)

Gahama, Joseph, *Le Burundi sous administration Belge: La période du mandat, 1919–1939* (Paris, 1983)

Gallup, George H., *The Gallup Poll: Public Opinion, 1935–1971* (New York, 1972)

Galton, Francis, *Hereditary Genius* (London, 1978 [1869])

Gantt, William Horsley, *Russian Medicine* (New York, 1937)

Garrett, Richard, *P.O.W.* (Newton Abbot / London, 1981)

Garrett, Stephen A., *Ethics and Airpower in World War II: The British Bombing of German Cities* (New York, 1993)

Gasiorowski, Mark J., 'The 1953 Coup d'État Against Mosaddeq', in Mark J. Gasiorowski and Malcolm Byrne (eds.), *Mohammad Mosaddeq and the 1953 Coup in Iran* (Syracuse, 2004)

Gatrell, Peter, *Government, Industry and Rearmament in Russia, 1900–1914: The Last Argument of Tsarism* (Cambridge, 1994)

Gay, Ruth, *The Jews of Germany: A Historical Portrait* (New Haven / London, 1992)

Gayler, Robert, *Private Prisoner: An Astonishing Story of Survival under the Nazis* (Wellingborough, 1984)

Geiger, Jeffrey E., *German Prisoners of War at Camp Cooke, California: Personal Accounts of 14 Soldiers, 1944–1946* (Jefferson, NC / London, 1996)

Geiss, Immanuel, *Der lange Weg in die Katastrophe: Die Vorgeschichte des Ersten Weltkrieges, 1815–1914* (Munich, 1990)

—— *July 1914: The Outbreak of the First World War – Selected Documents* (London, 1967)

Gellately, Robert, 'The Gestapo and German Society: Political Denunciation in the Gestapo Case Files', *Journal of Modern History*, 60, 4 (December 1988), 654–94

Germann, Holger, *Alfred Rosenberg: Sein politischer Weg bis zur Neu- (Wieder-) Gründung der NSDAP im Jahre 1925* (London, 1988)

Gerstenfeld-Maltiel, Jacob, *My Private War: One Man's Struggle to Survive the Soviets and the Nazis* (London, 1993)

Getty, J. Arch and Oleg V. Naumov, *The Road to Terror: Stalin and the Self-Destruction of the Bolsheviks, 1932–1939* (New Haven, 1999)

Geyl, Pieter, *Encounters in History* (London / Glasgow, 1963)

Gibbons, Herbert Adams, *Les Derniers Massacres d'Arménie: Les Responsabilités* (Paris / Nancy, 1916)

Gilbert, Martin, *The First World War: A Complete History* (London, 1989)
—— *Second World War: A Complete History* (London, 1989)
—— and Richard Gott, *The Appeasers* (London, 1963)
Gill, John H., 'Into the Caucasus: The Turkish Attack on Russia, 1942', in Peter G. Tsouras (ed.), *Third Reich Victorious: The Alternate History of How the Germans Won the War* (London, 2002), 146–68
Gill, Lesley, *The School of the Americas: Military Training and Political Violence in the Americas* (Durham, 2004)
Gilman, Sander, *The Jew's Body* (New York / London, 1991)
Gilmore, Allison B., *You Can't Fight Tanks with Bayonets: Psychological Warfare against the Japanese Army in the Southwest Pacific* (Lincoln / London, 1998)
Gitelman, Zvi Y., *Jewish Nationality and Soviet Politics: The Jewish Sections of the CPSU, 1917–1930* (Princeton, 1972)
Glenny, Misha, *The Balkans, 1804–1999: Nationalism, War and the Great Powers* (London, 2000)
Gobineau, Joseph Arthur, comte de, *Essai sur l'inégalité des races humaines* (Paris, 1967 [1853–5])
Goeschel, Christian, 'Suicide at the End of the Third Reich', *Journal of Contemporary History*, 41, 1 (2006), 153–73
Goetzmann, William N., Andrey D. Ukhov and Ning Zhu, 'China and the World Financial Markets', *Economic History Review* (forthcoming)
Goldberg, Mina, 'Die Jahre 1881–1882 in der Geschichte der russischen Juden', unpublished PhD thesis, Friedrich-Wilhelms-Universität zu Berlin (1934)
Golden, Joseph, 'Patterns of Negro-White Intermarriage', *American Sociological Review*, 19 (1954), 144–7
Goldhagen, Daniel Jonah, *Hitler's Willing Executioners* (London, 1997)
Goldsmith, Raymond, 'The Power of Victory', *Military Cultures*, 19 (Spring 1946), 69–81
Goldstein, Erik, 'Great Britain: The Home Front', in Manfred F. Boemeke, Gerald D. Feldman and Elisabeth Glaser (eds.), *The Treaty of Versailles: A Reassessment after 75 Years* (Cambridge, 1998), 147–66
—— 'Neville Chamberlain, the British Official Mind and the Munich Crisis', in Igor Lukes and Erik Goldstein (eds.), *The Munich Crisis, 1938: Prelude to World War II* (London, 1999), 276–93
Golomstock, Igor, transl. Robert Chandler, *Totalitarian Art in the Soviet Union, the Third Reich, Fascist Italy and the People's Republic of China* (London, 1990)
Goltz, Colmar Freiherr von der, transl. G. F. Leverson, *The Conduct of War: A Short Treatise on its Most Important Branches and Guiding Rules* (London, 1899)
Gooch, G. P. and Harold Temperley (eds.), *British Documents on the Origins of the War, 1898–1914*, 11 vols. (London, 1927)
Gordon, Milton M., *Assimilation in American Life: The Role of Race, Religion, and National Origins* (New York, 1964)
Gordon, Sarah, *Hitler, Germans and the Jewish Question* (Princeton, 1984)
Gorky, Maxim, transl. Ronald Wilks, *My Universities* (London, 1979 [1922])
Görlitz, Walter, 'The Battle for Stalingrad, 1942–3', in Hans-Adolf Jacobsen and Jürgen Rohwer (eds.), transl. Edward Fitzgerald, *Decisive Battles of World War II: The German View* (London, 1965), 219–53
Gorodetsky, Gabriel, *Grand Delusion: Stalin and the German Invasion of Russia* (New Haven, 1999)
Gorter-Gronvik, Waling T. and Mikhail N. Suprun, 'Ethnic Minorities and Warfare at the Arctic Front, 1939–1945', *Journal of Slavic Military Studies*, 13, 1 (March 2000), 127–42

Gott, Richard, *Rural Guerrillas in Latin America* (Harmondsworth, 1973 [1970])

Gould, Stephen Jay, *The Mismeasure of Man* (New York, 1996)

Graebner, Norman A., 'Introduction', in Richard Dean Burns and Edward M. Bennett (eds.), *Diplomats in Crisis: United States-Chinese-Japanese Relations, 1919–1941* (Oxford, 1974), ix–xvii

Graml, Hermann, *Reichskristallnacht: Antisemitismus und Judenverfolgung im Dritten Reich* (Munich, 1988)

Grandin, Greg, *The Last Colonial Massacre: Latin America in the Cold War* (Chicago, 2004)

Greasley, D. and L. Oxley, 'Discontinuities in Competitiveness: The Impact of the First World War on British Industry', *Economic History Review*, 99 (1996), 83–101

Green, Abigail, 'Anti-Jewish Violence and the Philanthropic Response', unpublished paper, Stockholm Conference on Pogroms (2005)

Greenberg, Louis, *The Jews in Russia*, vol. I: *The Struggle for Emancipation* (New Haven, 1944)

Griffith, Paddy, *Battle Tactics of the Western Front: The British Army's Art of Attack, 1916–18* (New Haven / London, 1994)

—— 'The Hinge: Alamein to Basra, 1942', in Peter G. Tsouras (ed.), *Third Reich Victorious: The Alternate History of How the Germans Won the War* (London, 2002), 126–45

Grigg, John, *1943: The Victory that Never Was* (London, 1999 [1980])

Grill, Johnpeter Horst, *The Nazi Movement in Baden, 1920–1945* (Chapel Hill, 1983)

Gross, Jan, *Revolution from Abroad: The Soviet Conquest of Poland's Western Ukraine and Western Belorussia* (Princeton, 2002)

—— *Neighbours: The Destruction of the Jewish Community in Jedwabne, Poland, 1941* (London, 2003)

—— 'Themes for a Social History of War Experience and Collaboration', in István Deák, Jan Gross and Tony Judt (eds.), *The Politics of Retribution in Europe: World War II and its Aftermath* (Princeton, 2000), 15–35

—— *Polish Society under German Occupation: The Generalgouvernement, 1939–1944* (Princeton, 1979)

Gross, Natan, *Who are you, Mr Grymek?* (London / Portland, Oreg., 2001)

Grossman, Anita, 'A Question of Silence: the Rape of German Women by Occupation Soldiers', *October*, 72 (1995), 43–63

Grossman, Herschel I. and Juan Mendoza, 'Annexation or Conquest? The Economics of Empire Building', NBER Working Paper, 8109 (February 2001)

Grossman, Vasily, transl. Robert Chandler, *Life and Fate: A Novel* (London, 1985)

Grotta, Daniel, *The Biography of J. R. R. Tolkien* (Philadelphia, 1976)

Guderian, Heinz, *Panzer Leader* (London, 2000)

—— transl. Christopher Duffy, *Achtung – Panzer! The Development of Armoured Forces, their Tactics and Operational Potential* (London, 1992)

Gudmundsson, Bruce I., 'Okinawa', in Robert Cowley (ed.), *No End Save Victory: New Second World War Writing* (London, 2002), 625–38

Gürün, Kamuran, *The Armenian File: The Myth of Innocence Exposed* (London / Nicosia / Istanbul, 1985)

Gutman, Yisrael and Michael Berenbaum (eds.), *Anatomy of the Auschwitz Death Camp* (Bloomington, Ind., 1994)

Hackett, David (ed.), *The Buchenwald Report* (Boulder / San Francisco / Oxford, 1995)

Haffner, Sebastian, *Defying Hitler* (London, 2002)

Hagen, William W., *Germans, Poles, and Jews: The Nationality Conflict in the Prussian East, 1772–1914* (Chicago / London, 1980)

—— 'Before the "Final Solution": Toward a Comparative Analysis of Political Anti-Semitism in Interwar Germany and Poland', *Journal of Modern History*, 68, 2 (June 1996), 351–81

Haigh, R. H. and D. S. Morris, *Munich: Peace of Delusion* (Sheffield, 1998)

Haimson, Leopold, 'The Problem of Social Stability in Urban Russia, 1905–1914', *Slavic Review*, 23 (1964), 619–42 and 24 (1965), 1–22

Halévy, Elie, ed. Henriette Guy-Lo *et al.*, *Correspondance, 1891–1937* (Paris, 1996)

Halifax, The Earl of, *Fullness of Days* (London, 1957)

Hamann, Brigitte, *Hitlers Wien: Lehrjahre eines Diktators* (Munich, 1997)

Hanauer, W., 'Die jüdisch-christliche Mischehe', *Allgemeines Statistisches Archiv*, 17 (1928), 513–37

Handy, Jim, *Revolution in the Countryside: Rural Conflict and Agrarian Reform in Guatemala, 1944–1954* (Chapel Hill, 1994)

—— 'A Sea of Indians: Ethnic Conflict and the Guatemalan Revolution, 1944–1952', *The Americas*, 46, 2 (October 1989), 189–204

Hanhimäki, Jussi M., *The Flawed Architect: Henry Kissinger and American Foreign Policy* (Oxford / New York, 2004)

Hardy, Henry, *Isaiah Berlin: Letters, 1928–1946* (Cambridge, 2005)

Hargrove, Hondon B., *Buffalo Soldiers in Italy: Black Americans in World War II* (Jefferson, NC / London, 1985)

Harries, Meirion and Susie Harries, *Soldiers of the Sun: The Rise and Fall of the Imperial Japanese Army, 1868–1945* (London, 1991)

Harrison, Kenneth, *The Brave Japanese* (Adelaide, 1967)

Harrison, Mark, *Medicine and Victory: British Military Medicine in the Second World War* (Oxford, 2004)

—— 'The Economics of World War II: An Overview', in Mark Harrison (ed.), *The Economics of World War II: Six Great Powers in International Comparison* (Cambridge, 1998), 1–42.

—— 'Resource Mobilization for World War II: The USA, UK, USSR and Germany, 1938–1945', *Economic History Review*, 2nd Series, 41, 2 (1981), 171–92

—— (ed.), *The Economics of World War II: Six Great Powers in International Comparison* (Cambridge, 1998)

Hart, S., R. Hart and M. Hughes, *The German Soldier in World War II* (Staplehurst, 2000)

Harvey, A. D., *Collision of Empires: Britain in Three World Wars, 1792–1945* (London, 1992)

Hasegawa, Tsuyoshi, *Racing the Enemy: Stalin, Truman and the Surrender of Japan* (Cambridge, Mass., 2005)

Hašek, Jaroslav, transl. Cecil Parrott, *The Good Soldier Švejk and his Fortunes in the Great War* (Harmondsworth, 1974)

Hassell, Ulrich von, *The von Hassell Diaries, 1938–1944: The Story of the Forces against Hitler inside Germany, as recorded by Ambassador Ulrich von Hassell, a Leader of the Movement* (London, 1948)

Hastings, Max, *Armageddon: The Battle for Germany, 1944–45* (London, 2004)

—— *Bomber Command* (London, 1979)

Hata, Ikuhiko, 'Continental Expansion, 1905–1941', in Peter Duus (ed.), *The Cambridge History of Japan*, vol. VI (Cambridge, 1988), 271–314

—— 'From Consideration to Contempt: The Changing Nature of Japanese Military and Popular Perceptions of Prisoners of War Through the Ages', in Bob Moore and Kent Fedorowich (eds.), *Prisoners of War and their Captors in World War II* (Oxford / Washington DC, 1996)

Hatton, Timothy J. and Jeffrey G. Williamson, 'International Migration in the Long-

Run: Positive Selection, Negative Selection and Policy', NBER Working Paper, 10529 (May 2004)

Hauser, William L., 'The Will to Fight', in Sam C. Sarkesian (ed.), *Combat Effectiveness: Cohesion, Stress, and the Volunteer Military* (Beverly Hills / London, 1980), 186–211

Heller, Joseph, *Catch-22* (London, 1962)

Henderson, Sir Nevile, *Failure of a Mission, Berlin 1937–1939* (London, 1940)

Henriques, Fernando, *Children of Caliban* (London, 1974)

Heppner, Rabbi Dr A. and J. Herzberg, *Aus Vergangenheit und Gegenwart der Juden und der jüdischen Gemeinden in den Posener Landen*, vol. II (Breslau, 1929)

Heppner, Ernest G., *Shanghai Refuge: A Memoir of the World War II Ghetto* (Lincoln, 1993)

Herberg, Will, *Protestant, Catholic, Jew* (New York, 1960)

Herbert, Ulrich, transl. William Templer, *Hitler's Foreign Workers: Enforced Foreign Labor in Germany under the Third Reich* (Cambridge / New York / Melbourne, 1997)

Herlihy, Patricia, *Odessa: A History, 1794–1914* (Cambridge, Mass., 1986)

Hermann, Georg, *Der doppelte Spiegel* (Berlin, 1926)

Hernton, Calvin C., *Sex and Racism* (New York, 1970 [1965])

Herrmann, David G., *The Arming of Europe and the Making of the First World War* (Princeton, 1996)

Hersey, John, *Into the Valley: A Skirmish of the Marines* (New York, 1943)

—— *A Bell for Adano* (New York, 1944)

Herzberg, Isaak, *Geschichte der Juden in Bromberg, zugleich ein Beitrag zur Geschichte der Juden des Landes Posen* (Frankfurt am Main, 1903)

Hetzel, Marius, *Die Anfechtung der Rassenmischehe in den Jahren 1933–1939* (Tübingen, 1997)

Hevia, James L., 'Leaving a Brand on China: Missionary Discourse in the Wake of the Boxer Movement', *Modern China*, 18, 3 (July 1992), 304–32

Hewitt, Nicholas, *The Life of Céline: A Critical Biography* (Oxford, 1999)

Heyd, Uriel, *Foundations of Turkish Nationalism: The Life and Teachings of Ziya Gökalp* (London, 1950)

Heyman, Neil M., 'Leon Trotsky's Military Education: From the Russo-Japanese War to 1917', *The Journal of Modern History* 48, 2 (June 1976), 71–98

Heywood, Linda M., 'Unita and Ethnic Nationalism in Angola', *Journal of Modern African Studies*, 27, 1 (March 1989), 47–66

Hicks, George, *The Comfort Women: Sex Slaves of the Japanese Imperial Forces* (London, 1995)

Hiemer, Ernst, *Der Giftpilz: Ein Stürmerbuch für Jung und Alt. Erzählungen. Bilder von Fips* (Nuremberg, 1938)

Hinz, Berthold, transl. Robert and Rita Kimber, *Art in the Third Reich* (Oxford, 1980)

Hitler, Adolf, *Mein Kampf*, transl. Ralph Manheim (London, 1992)

Ho, Ping-ti, *Studies on the Population of China, 1368–1953* (Cambridge, Mass., 1959)

Hobsbawm, Eric, *The Age of Extremes: The Short Twentieth Century, 1914–1991* (London, 1994)

Hobson, J. M., 'The Military-Extraction Gap and the Wary Titan: The Fiscal Sociology of British Defence Policy, 1870–1913', *Journal of European Economic History*, 22 (1993), 461–506

Hobson, John, *The Eastern Origins of Western Civilization* (Cambridge, 2004)

Hoffman, Eva, *Shtetl: The Life and Death of a Small Town and the World of Polish Jews* (London, 1998)

Hoffman, Peter, *The History of the German Resistance, 1933–1945*, 3rd edn. (London, 1977 [1969])

—— 'The Question of Western Allied Co-operation with German Anti-Nazi Conspiracy, 1938–1944', *The Historical Journal*, 34, 2 (1991), 437–64

Hofmann, Tessa, *Der Völkermord an den Armeniern vor Gericht: Der Prozess Talaat Pascha* (Göttingen, 1980)

Holmes, Richard, *The Western Front: Ordinary soldies and the defining battles of World War I* (London, 1999)

Holquist, Peter, 'The Role of Personality in the First (1914–1915) Russian Occupation of Galicia and Bukovina', unpublished paper, Stockholm Conference on Pogroms (2005)

Holroyd, Michael, *Bernard Shaw*, vol. III: *1918–1950, The Lure of Fantasy* (London, 1993)

Horne, Alistair, *To Lose a Battle: France 1940* (London / Basingstoke / Oxford, 1990 [1969])

Horne, Charles F. (ed.), *Source Records of the Great War*, vol. III (New York, 1923)

Horne, John and Alan Kramer, 'German Atrocities and Franco-German Opinion, 1914: The Evidence of German Soldiers' Diaries', *Journal of Modern History*, 66, 1 (March 1994), 1–33

Horton, George, *The Blight of Asia: An Account of the Systematic Extermination of Christian Populations by Mohammedans and of the Culpability of Certain Powers; with the True Story of the Burning of Smyrna* (Indianapolis, 1926)

Hosoya, Chihiro, with an introduction by Peter A. Berton, 'Northern Defense: The Japanese-Soviet Neutrality Pact', in James William Morley (ed.), *The Fateful Choice: Japan's Advance into Southeast Asia, 1939–1941* (New York, 1980), 3–115

Hough, R. A. (ed.), *Advice to a Granddaughter: Letters to Princess Victoria of Hesse* (London, 1975)

Housden, Martyn, *Hans Frank, Lebensraum and the Holocaust* (New York, 2003)

Hovannisian, Richard G., 'Intervention and Shades of Altruism during the Armenian Genocide', in *idem* (ed.), *The Armenian Genocide: History, Politics, Ethics* (Basingstoke, 1992)

Howard, Michael, *The Continental Commitment: The Dilemma of British Defence Policy in the Era of Two World Wars* (London, 1972)

Howarth, Stephen, 'Germany and the Atlantic Sea-War: 1939–1943', in Kenneth Macksey (ed.), *The Hitler Options: Alternate Decisions of World War II* (London, 1995), 102–19

Hrabar, Roman, Zofia Tokarz and Jacek E. Wilczur, *The Fate of Polish Children During the Last War* (Warsaw, 1981)

Human Rights Watch / Middle East Watch, *Iraq's Crime of Genocide: The Anfal Campaign Against the Kurds* (New Haven, 1995)

Humphreys, Leonard A., *The Way of the Heavenly Sword: The Japanese Army in the 1920s* (Stanford, 1995)

Hunter, Edna J., 'Prisoners of War: Readjustment and Rehabilitation', in Reuven Gal and David A. Mangelsdorff (eds.), *Handbook of Military Psychology* (Chichester, 1991), 741–58

Hussey, John, 'Kiggell and the Prisoners: Was He Guilty of a War Crime?', *British Army Review* (1993)

Hyam, Ronald, *Empire and Sexuality* (Manchester, 1990)

Hynes, Samuel, *The Soldiers' Tale: Bearing Witness to Modern War* (London, 1998)

Ienaga, Saburo, transl. Frank Baldwin, *Japan's Last War: World War II and the Japanese, 1931–1945* (Oxford, 1979)

Ignatieff, Michael, *Empire Lite: Nation-building in Bosnia, Kosovo and Afghanistan* (London, 2003)

Ike, Nobutaka, *Japan's Decision for War: Records of the 1941 Policy Conferences* (Stanford, 1967)

Inkeles, Alex and Raymond A. Bauer, with the assistance of David Gleicher and Irving Ross, *The Soviet Citizen: Daily Life in a Totalitarian Society* (Cambridge, Mass., 1959)

Institut für Armenische Fragen (ed.), *The Armenian Genocide: Documentation* (Munich, 1987)

Iriye, Akira, *Power and Culture: The Japanese-American War, 1941–1945* (Cambridge, 1981)

—— *The Origins of the Second World War in Asia and the Pacific* (London, 1987)

Isby, David C., 'Luftwaffe Triumphant: The Defeat of the Bomber Offensive, 1944–45', in Peter G. Tsouras (ed.), *Third Reich Victorious: The Alternate History of How the Germans Won the War* (London, 2002), 197–215

—— 'The Japanese Raj: The Conquest of India', in Peter G. Tsouras (ed.), *Rising Sun Victorious: The Alternate History of How the Japanese Won the Pacific War* (London, 2001), 166–85

Jackson, William, 'Through the Soft Underbelly: January 1942–December 1945', in Kenneth Macksey (ed.), *The Hitler Options: Alternate Decisions of World War II* (London, 1995), 120–43

Jacobsen, Hans-Adolf (ed.), *Dokumente zur Vorgeschichte des Westfeldzuges, 1939–1940* (Göttingen, 1956)

Jaggers, Keith and Ted Robert Gurr, *Polity III: Regime Type and Political Authority, 1800–1994* [Computer file], 2nd ICPSR version, Ann Arbor, MI: Inter-university Consortium for Political and Social Research [distributor] (Boulder, 1996)

Jahr, Christoph, *Gewöhnliche Soldaten: Desertion und Deserteure im deutschen und britischen Heer 1914–1918* (Göttingen, 1998)

James, Harold, *The German Slump: Politics and Economics, 1924–1936* (Oxford, 1986)

—— 'Economic Reasons for the Collapse of Weimar', in Ian Kershaw (ed.), *Weimar: Why Did German Democracy Fail?* (London, 1990), 30–57

—— *The End of Globalization: Lessons from the Great Depression* (Cambridge, Mass., 2001)

—— *The Roman Predicament* (forthcoming)

Janowitz, M. and E. A. Shils, 'Cohesion and Disintegration in the Wehrmacht in World War II', in M. Janowitz (ed.), *Military Conflict: Essays in the Institutional Analysis of War and Peace* (Beverly Hills / London, 1975), 177–220

Jansen, Marius B., *Japan and China: From War to Peace 1894–1972* (Chicago, 1975)

Jasny, Naum, *The Socialized Agriculture of the USSR: Plans and Performance* (Stanford, 1949)

Jeffery, Keith, 'The Second World War', in Judith M. Brown and Wm. Roger Louis (eds.), *The Oxford History of the British Empire*, vol. IV: *The Twentieth Century* (Oxford / New York, 1999), 306–28

Jesmanowa, Teresa *et al.* (eds.), *Stalin's Ethnic Cleansing in Eastern Poland: Tales of the Deported, 1940–1946* (London, 2000)

Johe, Werner, 'Die Beteiligung der Justiz an der nationalsozialistischen Judenverfolgung', in Ursula Büttner (ed.), *Die Deutschen und die Judenverfolgung im Dritten Reich* (Hamburg, 1992), 179–90

John, Michael, 'Die jüdische Bevölkerung in Wirtschaft und Gesellschaft Altösterreichs (1867–1918): Bestandsaufnahme, Überblick und Thesen', in Rudolf Kropf (ed.), *Juden im Grenzraum: Geschichte, Kultur und Lebenswelt der Juden im Bürgenlandisch-Westungarischen Raum und in den angrenzenden Regionen vom Mittelalter bis zur Gegenwart* (Eisenstadt, 1993), 198–244

Johnson, Eric, *The Nazi Terror: Gestapo, Jews and Ordinary Germans* (London, 1999)

Johnson, Paul, *A History of the Modern World, from 1917 to the 1990s* (London, revised edn. 1991)

Johnston, James Hugo, *Race Relations in Virginia and Miscegenation in the South* (Amherst, 1970)

Jonas, Susanne, *The Battle for Guatemala: Rebels, Death Squads, and U.S. Power* (Boulder, 1991)

Jones, James, *From Here to Eternity* (New York, 1951)

—— *The Thin Red Line* (New York, 1962)

Jones, Larry E., *German Liberalism and the Dissolution of the Weimar Party System, 1918–1933* (Chapel Hill, 1988)

Jones, Steve, *In the Blood: God, Genes and Destiny* (London, 1996)

Jordan, Nicole, 'The Cut Price War on the Peripheries: The French General Staff, the Rhineland and Czechoslovakia', in Robert Boyce and Esmonde M. Robertson (eds.), *Paths to War: New Essays on the Origins of the Second World War* (London, 1989), 128–66

Jordan, Ulrike (ed.), *Conditions of Surrender: Britons and Germans Witness the End of the War* (London / New York, 1997)

Jordan, Winthrop D., *White over Black: American Attitudes toward the Negro, 1550–1812* (Baltimore, 1969)

Kacel, Boris, *From Hell to Redemption: A Memoir of the Holocaust* (Colorado, 1998)

Kahn, David, 'Enigma Uncracked', in Robert Cowley (ed.), *More What If? Eminent Historians Imagine What Might Have Been* (London, 2002), 305–16

Kalmijn, Matthijs, 'Trends in Black/White Intermarriage', *Social Forces*, 72 (Sept. 1993), 119–46

—— 'Shifting Boundaries: Trends in Religious and Educational Homogamy', *American Sociological Review*, 56 (1991), 786–800

Kamenetsky, Ihor, *Secret Nazi Plans for Eastern Europe: A Study of Lebensraum Policies* (New York, 1961)

Kang, Gay Elizabeth, *Marry-out or Die-out: A Cross Cultural Examination of Exogamy and Survival Value* (Buffalo, 1982)

Kaplan, Marion A., *Die jüdische Frauenbewegung in Deutschland: Organisation und Ziele des Jüdischen Frauenbundes, 1904–1938* (Hamburg, 1981)

Kaser, M. C. and E. A. Radice (eds.), *The Economic History of Eastern Europe, 1919–1975*, 2 vols. (Oxford, 1986)

Katsumi, Usui, with an introduction by David Lu, 'The Politics of War, 1937–1941', in James William Morley (ed.), *The China Quagmire: Japan's Expansion on the Asian Continent, 1933–1941* (New York, 1983), 289–435

Katz, Jacob, *Richard Wagner: Vorbote des Antisemitismus* (Königstein am Taunus, 1985)

Keegan, John, 'How Hitler Could Have Won the War: The Drive for the Middle East, 1941', in Robert Cowley (ed.), *What If?: The World's Foremost Military Historians Imagine What Might Have Been* (London, 2001), 295–305

—— (ed.), *The Times Atlas of the Second World War* (London, 1989)

—— *Waffen SS: The Asphalt Soldiers*, Purnell's History of the Second World War, Weapons Book No. 16 (London, 1970)

—— and Richard Holmes, *Soldiers: A History of Men in Battle* (London, 1985)

Keeley, Lawrence H., *War Before Civilization: The Myth of the Peaceful Savage* (Oxford, 1996)

Kelly, Alfred, *The Descent of Darwin: The Popularization of Darwinism in Germany, 1860–1914* (Chapel Hill, 1981)

Keltie, J. Scott (ed.), *The Statesman's Yearbook: Statistical and Historical Annual of the States of the World for the Year 1913* (London, 1913)

Kennedy, David M., *Freedom from Fear: The American People in Depression and War, 1929–1945* (New York / Oxford, 1999)

Kennedy, Paul, 'Japanese Strategic Decisions, 1939–1945', in Paul Kennedy (ed.), *Strategy and Diplomacy, 1870–1945* (London, 1983), 179–95

—— *The Realities Behind Diplomacy: Background Influences on British External Policy, 1865–1980* (Glasgow, 1981)

—— *The Rise and Fall of the Great Powers: Economic Change and Military Conflict from 1500 to 2000* (New York, 1989)

—— 'The Tradition of British Appeasement', *British Journal of International Studies*, 2, 3 (1976), 195–215

Kennedy, Randall, *Interracial Intimacies: Sex, Marriage, Identity, and Adoption* (New York, 2003)

Kennedy, Ruby Jo Reeves, 'Single or Triple Melting Pot?', *American Journal of Sociology*, 58 (1950), 331–9

Kernholt, Otto, *Vom Ghetto zur Macht: Die Geschichte des Aufstiegs der Juden auf deutschem Boden* (Leipzig / Berlin, 1921)

Kershaw, Ian, *Hitler, 1889–1936: Hubris* (London, 1998)

—— *Hitler, 1936–45: Nemesis* (London, 2000)

—— *Making Friends with Hitler: Lord Londonderry, the Nazis and the Road to War* (London, 2004)

—— 'Nazi Foreign Policy: Hitler's "Programme" or "Expansion without Object"?', in Patrick Finney (ed.), *The Origins of the Second World War* (London, 1997), 121–48

—— 'Reply to Smith', *Contemporary European History*, 14, 1 (2005), 131–4

—— 'War and Political Violence in Twentieth-Century Europe', *Contemporary European History*, 14, 1 (2005), 107–23

Kessler, Harry, Count, transl. Charles Kessler, *Berlin in Lights: The Diaries of Count Harry Kessler* (New York, 1999)

Keylor, W. R., 'Versailles and International Diplomacy', in Manfred F. Boemeke, Gerald D. Feldman and Elisabeth Glaser (eds.), *The Treaty of Versailles: A Reassessment after 75 Years* (Cambridge, 1998), 469–505

Keynes, John Maynard, 'War and the Financial System, August 1914', *Economic Journal*, 24 (September 1914), 460–86

—— *How to Pay for the War: A Radical Plan for the Chancellor of the Exchequer* (London, 1940)

—— *The Economic Consequences of the Peace* (London, 1919)

—— *The General Theory of Employment, Interest and Money* (London, 1936)

Khiterer, Viktoriya, 'The October 1905 Pogrom in Kiev', *East European Jewish Affairs*, 22, 2 (Winter 1992), 21–37

Khrushchev, Nikita, transl. and ed. Strobe Talbott, *Khrushchev Remembers: The Last Testament* (Boston, 1974)

Kibata, Yoichi, 'Japanese Treatment of British Prisoners: The Historical Context', in Philip Towle, Margaret Kosuge and Yoichi Kibata (eds.), *Japanese Prisoners of War* (London / New York, 2000), 135–48

Kiernan, Ben, 'Genocidal Targeting: Two Groups of Victims in Pol Pot's Cambodia', in P. Timothy Bushnell, Vladimir Shlapentokh, Christopher K. Vanderpool and Jeyaratnam Sundram (eds.), *State Organized Terror: The Case of Violent Internal Repression* (Boulder, 1991), 207–26

—— 'Kampuchea's Ethnic Chinese Under Pol Pot: A Case of Systematic Social Discrimination', *Journal of Contemporary Asia*, 16, 1 (1986), 18–29

—— *Cambodia, the Eastern Zone Massacres: A Report on Social Conditions and Human Rights Violations in the Eastern Zone of Democratic Kampuchea Under the Rule of Pol Pot's (Khmer Rouge) Communist Party of Kampuchea* (New York, 1980)

Killingray, David, 'Africans and African Americans in Enemy Hands', in Bob Moore and Kent Fedorowich (eds.), *Prisoners of War and their Captors in World War II* (Oxford / Washington DC, 1996), 181–204

Kimitada, Miwa, 'Japanese Images of War with the United States', in Akira Iriye (ed.), *Mutual Images: Essays in American-Japanese Relations* (Cambridge, Mass., 1975), 115–38

Kindersley, Philip, *For You the War is Over* (Tunbridge Wells, 1983)

King, James F., 'The Case of José Ponciano de Ayarza: A Document on Gracias al Sacar', *The Hispanic American Historical Review*, 31, 4 (November 1951), 640–47

King, Wunsz, *China and the League of Nations: The Sino-Japanese Controversy* (New York, 1965)

Kinhide, Mushakoji, 'The Structure of Japanese-American Relations in the 1930s', in Dorothy Borg and Shumpei Okamoto (eds.), *Pearl Harbor as History: Japanese–American Relations, 1931–1941* (New York, 1973), 595–607

Kinvig, Clifford, 'Allied POWs and the Burma-Thailand Railway', in Philip Towle, Margaret Kosuge and Yoichi Kibata (eds.), *Japanese Prisoners of War* (London / New York, 2000), 17–57

Kinzer, Stephen, *All the Shah's Men: An American Coup and the Roots of Middle East Terror* (New York, 2003)

Kirkpatrick, Ivone, *The Inner Circle: The Memoirs of Ivone Kirkpatrick* (London, 1959)

Kirwin, Gerald, 'Allied Bombing and Nazi Domestic Propaganda', *European History Quarterly*, 15, 3 (1985)

Kissinger, Henry, *Diplomacy* (New York / London / Toronto / Sydney / Tokyo / Singapore, 1994)

—— *The White House Years* (London, 1979)

Kittel, Gerhard, *Die historische Voraussetzung der jüdischen Rassenmischung* (Hamburg, 1939)

Kiyoshi, Ikeda, 'Japanese Strategy and the Pacific War, 1941–1945', in Ian Nish (ed.), *Anglo-Japanese Alienation, 1919–1952: Papers of the Anglo-Japanese Conference on the History of the Second World War* (Bristol, 1982), 125–45

Klanska, Maria, 'Die deutschsprächige Literatur Galiziens und der Bukowina von 1772 bis 1945', in Isabel Röskau-Rydel (ed.), *Deutsche Geschichte im Osten Europas: Galizien* (Berlin, 1999), 379–482

Klemperer, Victor, transl. Martin Chalmers, *I Shall Bear Witness: The Diaries of Victor Klemperer 1933–41* (London, 1998)

—— transl. Martin Chalmers, *To the Bitter End: The Diaries of Victor Klemperer, 1942–45* (London, 1999)

—— transl. Martin Chalmers, *The Lesser Evil: The Diaries of Victor Klemperer, 1945–1959* (London, 2003)

Klier, John D., 'Solzhenitsyn and the Kishinev Pogrom: A Slander against Russia?', *East European Jewish Affairs*, 33, 1 (2003), 50–59

—— 'The Blood Libel in the Russian Orthodox Tradition', unpublished paper (2005)

—— 'Were the Pogroms of 1881–2 a "Deadly Ethnic Riot"?', unpublished paper, Stockholm Conference on Pogroms (2005)

Klivert-Jones, Tim, 'Bloody Normandy: The German Controversy', in Kenneth Macksey (ed.), *The Hitler Options: Alternate Decisions of World War II* (London, 1995), 203–19

Knapp, Grace H., *The Mission at Van: In Turkey in War Time* (n.p., 1916)

Knock, Thomas J., *To End All Wars: Woodrow Wilson and the Quest for a New World Order* (New York / Oxford, 1992)

Knox, MacGregor, *Mussolini Unleashed 1939–1941: Politics and Strategy in Fascist Italy's Last War* (Cambridge / London / New York / New Rochelle / Melbourne / Sydney, 1982)

Knox, Robert, *The Races of Men: A Fragment* (Philadelphia, 1850)

Koestler, Arthur, transl. Daphne Hardy, *Darkness at Noon* (London, 1964)

Koistinen, Paul A. C., *Arsenal of World War II: The Political Economy of American Warfare* (Lawrence, Kan., 2004)

Komjathy, Anthony Tihamer and Rebecca Stockwell, *German Minorities and the Third Reich: Ethnic Germans of East Central Europe Between the Wars* (New York, 1980)

Kopczuk, Wojciech and Emmanuel Saez, 'Top Wealth Shares in the United States, 1916–2000: Evidence from the Estate Tax Returns', NBER Working Paper, 10399 (2004)

Korean Society for Solving the Problems of 'Japanese Comfort Women' (Hanguk Chongsindae Munje Taechaek Hyobuihoe, Chongsindae Yonguhoe pyon), *Enforced Sex Slaves in the Japanese Army (Kangje ro Kkullyogan Chosunin kun wianbudul)* (Seoul, 1993)

Korey, William, 'The Legal Position of Soviet Jewry: A Historical Enquiry', in Lionel Kochan (ed.), *The Jews in Soviet Russia since 1917* (Oxford / London / New York, 1978), 78–105

Koschorrek, Günter K., transl. Olav R. Crone-Aamot, *Blood Red Snow: The Memoirs of a German Soldier on the Eastern Front* (London, 2002)

Kosiek, Rolf, *Jenseits der Grenzen: 1000 Jahre Volks- und Auslandsdeutsche* (Tübingen, 1987)

Kotkin, Stephen, *Magnetic Mountain: Stalinism as a Civilization* (Berkeley, 1995)

Kravchenko, Victor, *I Chose Freedom: The Personal and Political Life of a Soviet Official* (New York, 1946)

Krolik, Schlomo (ed.), *Arthur Ruppin: Briefe, Tagebücher, Erinnerungen* (Königstein am Taunus, 1985)

Kubica, Helena, *Zaglada w KL Auschwitz Polaków wysiedlonych z Zamojszczyzny w latach 1942–1943* (Oświęcim / Warsaw, 2004)

Kugelmann, Cilly and Fritz Backhaus (eds.), *Jüdische Figuren in Film und Karikatur: Die Rothschilds und Joseph Süß Oppenheimer* (Sigmaringen, 1996)

Kulka, Otto Dov, 'Die Nürnberger Rassengesetze und die deutsche Bevölkerung im Lichte geheimer NS Lage- und Stimmungsberichte', *Vierteljahrshefte für Zeitgeschichte*, 32 (1984), 582–624

Kydd, Samuel J., *For YOU the War is Over* (London, 1973)

Lal, Deepak, *In Praise of Empires: Globalization and Order* (New York, 2004)

Lamb, Richard, *The Drift to War, 1922–1939* (London, 1989)

Lammers, Donald N., *Explaining Munich: The Search for Motive in British Policy* (Stanford, 1966)

Landau-Czajka, Anna, 'The Images of the Jew in the Catholic Press during the Second Republic', in Antony Polonsky, Ezra Mendelsohn and Jerzy Tomaszewski (eds.), *Jews in Independent Poland: 1918–1939* (London, Washington, 1994), 146–75

Landwehr, Richard, *Lions of Flanders: Flemish Volunteers of the Waffen-SS, Eastern Front 1941–1945* (Bradford, 1996)

Laqueur, Walter (ed.), *Fascism: A Reader's Guide, Analyses, Interpretations, Bibliography* (Aldershot, 1991)

Larsen, Stein Ugelvik, Bernt Hagtvet and Jan Peter Myklebust, *Who Were the Fascists? Social Roots of European Fascism* (Bergen / Oslo / Tromsö, 1980)

Le Foll, C., 'The Byelorussian Case in the 1881–1882 Wave of Pogroms: Conditions and Motives of an Absence of Violence', unpublished paper, Stockholm Conference on Pogroms (2005)

Leavitt, G. C., 'Sociobiological Explanations of Incest Avoidance: A Critical Review of Evidential Claims', *American Anthropologist*, 92 (1990), 971–93

Lebra-Chapman, Joyce, *Japanese-Trained Armies in Southeast Asia* (Hong Kong / Singapore / Kuala Lumpur, 1977)

—— (ed.), *Japan's Greater East Asia Co-Prosperity Sphere in World War II: Selected Readings and Documents* (Kuala Lumpur, 1975)

Lebzelter, Gisela, 'Die "Schwarze Schmach": Vorurteile – Propaganda – Mythos', *Geschichte und Gesellschaft*, 11 (1985), 37–58

Ledig, Gert, transl. Michael Hofmann, *The Stalin Organ* (London, 2004 [1955])

—— transl. Shaun Whiteside, *Payback* (London, 2003 [1956])

Lee, Gerald Geunwook, ' "I See Dead People": Air-raid Phobia and Britain's Behavior in the Munich Crisis', *Security Studies*, 13, 2 (2003), 230–72

Leers, Johann von, *14 Jahre Judenrepublik: Die Geschichte eines Rassenkampfes* (Berlin-Schöneberg, 1933)

Leggett, George, *The Cheka: Lenin's Political Police* (Oxford, 1981)

Leon, George P., *Greece and the Great Powers, 1914–1917* (Thessaloniki, 1974)

Lepsius, Johannes (ed.), *Deutschland und Armenien 1914–1918: Sammlung diplomatischer Aktenstücke* (Bremen, 1986 [1919])

Lerner, Daniel, *Psychological Warfare against Nazi Germany: The Sykewar Campaign, D-Day to VE-Day* (Cambridge, Mass., 1971 [1949])

Levene, Mark, 'Frontiers of Genocide: Jews in the Eastern War Zones, 1914–1920 and 1941', in Panikos Panayi (ed.), *Minorities in Wartime: National and Racial Groupings in Europe, North America and Australia during the Two World Wars* (Oxford / Providence, 1993), 83–117.

—— *Genocide in the Age of the Nation State*, vol. I: *The Meaning of Genocide*; vol. II: *The Rise of the West and the Coming of Genocide* (London, 2005)

Levi, Primo, transl. Stuart Woolf, *If This is a Man* (London, 1959)

—— transl. Stuart Woolf, *The Reawakening* (New York, 1995 [1965])

Levi, Trude, *A Cat Called Adolf* (Ilford, 1995)

Levine, Alan J., 'Was World War II a Near-run Thing?', *Journal of Strategic Studies*, 8, 1 (1985), 38–63

Levine, Isaac Don (ed.), *The Kaiser's Letters to the Tsar* (London, 1920)

Levy, Jack S., *War in the Modern Great Power System* (Lexington, 1983)

Lewin, Moshe, 'Who Was the Soviet Kulak?', in *idem*, *The Making of the Soviet System: Essays in the Social History of Interwar Russia* (New York, 1985), 121–41

Li, Lincoln, *The Japanese Army in North China, 1937–1941: Problems of Political and Economic Control* (Tokyo, 1975)

Lieberson, Stanley and Mary C. Waters, *From Many Strands: Ethnic and Racial Groups in Contemporary America: The Population of the United States in the 1980s* (New York, 1988)

Lieven, Dominic C. B. (ed.), *British Documents on Foreign Affairs: Reports and Papers from the Foreign Office Confidential Print, Part I: From the Mid-Nineteenth Century to the First World War, Series A: Russia, 1859–1914*, vol. IV: *Russia, 1906–1907* (Frederick, Md, 1983)

—— *Empire: The Russian Empire and Its Rivals* (London, 2000)

—— *Russia and the Origins of the First World War* (New York, 1983)

Lin, Han-sheng, 'A New Look at Chinese Nationalist Appeasers', in Alvin D. Coox and Hilary Conroy (eds.), *China and Japan: A Search for Balance Since World War I* (Oxford, 1978), 211–43

Lindbergh, Charles A., 'Aviation, Geography and Race', *The Reader's Digest*, 35, 211 (November 1939), 64–7

Lindert, Peter H., *Growing Public: Social Spending and Economic Growth since the Eighteenth Century*, 2 vols. (Cambridge, 2004)

Lindqvist, Sven, *A History of Bombing* (London, 2002 [2001])

Lindsey, Forrest R., 'Hitler's Bomb, Target: London and Moscow', in Peter G. Tsouras (ed.), *Third Reich Victorious: The Alternate History of How the Germans Won the War* (London, 2002), 216–30

—— 'Nagumo's Luck: The Battles of Midway and California', in Peter G. Tsouras (ed.), *Rising Sun Victorious: The Alternate History of How the Japanese Won the Pacific War* (London, 2001), 120–43

Lipman, V. D., *A History of the Jews in Britain since 1858* (Leicester, 1990)

Livezeanu, Irina, *Cultural Politics in Greater Romania: Regionalism, Nation Building and Ethnic Struggle* (Ithaca, 1995)

Loewenstein, Rudolph M., *Christians and Jews, a Psychoanalytic Study* (New York, 1951)

Lohr, Eric, *Nationalizing the Russian Empire: The Campaign against Enemy Aliens during World War I* (Cambridge, Mass., 2003)

Londonderry, Marquess of, *Ourselves and Germany* (London, 1938)

Longford, E. (ed.), *Darling Loosy: Letters to Princess Louise, 1856–1939* (London, 1991)

Loomis, Charles P. and Allan Beegle, 'The Spread of German Nazism in Rural Areas', *American Sociological Review*, 11, 6 (December 1946), 724–34

Loshak, David, *Pakistan Crisis* (London, 1971)

Lotnik, Waldemar, *Nine Lives: Ethnic Conflict in the Polish Ukrainian Borderlands* (London, 1999)

Louis, Wm. Roger and Ronald Robinson, 'The Imperialism of Decolonization', *Journal of Imperial and Commonwealth History*, 22, 3 (1994), 463–511

Lowe, Peter, 'Great Britain and the Coming of the Pacific War, 1939–1941', *Transactions of the Royal Historical Society*, 5th Series, 24 (1974), 43–62

—— *Great Britain and the Origins of the Pacific War: A Study of British Policy in East Asia, 1937–1941* (Oxford, 1977)

Lower, Robert Coke, *A Bloc of One: The Political Career of Hiram W. Johnson* (Stanford, 1993)

Lu, David J., *From the Marco Polo Bridge to Pearl Harbor: Japan's Entry into World War II* (Washington DC, 1961)

Luard, Evan, *War in International Society: A Study in International Sociology* (New Haven / London, 1987)

Lubell, Samuel, 'Who Votes Isolationist and Why?', *Harper's Magazine*, 202, 1211 (April 1951)

Lucas, James, 'Operation WOTAN: The Panzer Thrust to Capture Moscow, October–November 1941', in Kenneth Macksey (ed.), *The Hitler Options: Alternate Decisions of World War II* (London, 1995), 54–81

Lukacs, John, *The Last European War, September 1939–December 1941* (London / Henley, 1976)

Lukas, Richard C., *The Forgotten Holocaust: The Poles under German Occupation 1939–1944* (New York, 1997)

Lumans, Valdis O., *Himmler's Auxiliaries: The Volksdeutsche Mittelstelle and the German National Minorities of Europe, 1933–1945* (Chapel Hill /London, 1993)

Lundin, Charles Leonard, *Finland in the Second World War* (Bloomington, 1957)

Lussu, Emilio, transl. Mark Rawson, *Sardinian Brigade* (London, 2000)

Lyons, Eugene, *Assignment in Utopia* (London, 1938)

Lyttelton, Adrian, *The Seizure of Power* (1987)

M. G., *La défense héroïque de Van (Arménie)* (Geneva, 1916)

MacCoby, Hyam, 'Nietzsche's Love-Hate Affair', *Times Literary Supplement* (June 25, 1999)

MacDonald, C. A., 'Economic Appeasement and the German "Moderates", 1937–1939: An Introductory Essay', *Past and Present*, 56 (August 1972), 105–35

MacDonald, Lyn, *Somme* (London, 1983)

Mackenzie, S. P., 'On the Other Losses Debate', *International History Review*, 14, 4 (1992), 661–731

—— 'The Treatment of Prisoners of War in World War II', *Journal of Modern History*, 66, 3 (September 1994), 487–520

Macksey, Kenneth, 'Operation Sea Lion: Germany Invades Britain, 1940', in Kenneth Macksey (ed.), *The Hitler Options: Alternate Decisions of World War II* (London, 1995), 13–34

Maclean, Fitzroy, *Eastern Approaches* (London, 1991 [1949])

MacLeish, Archibald, *Jews in America* (New York, 1936)

MacMillan, Margaret, *Peacemakers: The Paris Conference of 1919 and its Attempt to End War* (London, 2001)

Maddison, Angus, *The World Economy: A Millennial Perspective* (Paris, 2001)

Magocsi, Paul Robert, *Historical Atlas of East Central Europe* (Seattle and London, 1993)

Maier, Charles S., *The Unmasterable Past: History, Holocaust, and German National Identity* (Cambridge, Mass., 1997)

—— *Among Empires* (Cambridge, Mass., 2006)

Mailer, Norman, *The Naked and the Dead* (New York / Toronto, 1998 [1949])

Maksudov, S., 'The Geography of the Soviet Famine of 1933', *Journal of Ukrainian Studies*, 15 (1983), 52–8

Malaparte, Curzio, transl. Cesare Foligno, *Kaputt* (New York, 2005)

Malcolm, Noel, *Bosnia: A Short History* (London, 2001 [1994])

Malik, Amita, *The Year of the Vulture* (New Delhi, 1972)

Malkasian, Carter, *The Korean War, 1950–1953* (Chicago, 2001)

Manela, Erez, *The Wilsonian Moment: Self-Determination and the International Origins of Anticolonial Nationalism* (New York / Oxford, 2006)

—— 'A Man Ahead of His Time? Wilsonian Globalism and the Doctrine of Pre-emption', *International Journal* (Autumn 2005), 1115–24

Mann, James, *About Face: A History of America's Curious Relationship with China from Nixon to Clinton* (New York, 1999)

Mann, Michael, *Incoherent Empire* (London / New York, 2003)

—— *The Sources of Social Power*, vol. II: *The Rise of Classes and Nation-States, 1760–1914* (Cambridge, 1993)

Manning, Frederic, *Middle Parts of Fortune: Somme and Ancre, 1916* (London, 2003 [1929])

Manning, Roberta Thompson, *The Crisis of the Old Order in Russia: Gentry and Government* (Princeton, 1982)

Mansfield, Edward D. and Jack Snyder, *Electing to Fight: Why Emerging Democracies Go to War* (Cambridge, Mass., 2005)

Manstein, Erich von, transl. Anthony G. Powell, *Lost Victories* (London, 1958)

Marashlian, Levon, *Politics and Demography: Armenians, Turks, and Kurds in the Ottoman Empire* (Cambridge, Mass. / Paris / Toronto, 1991)

Marcuse, Max, *Über die Fruchtbarkeit der christlich-jüdischen Mischehe* (Bonn, 1920)

Margalit, Avishai, 'On Compromise and Rotten Compromise', unpublished essay (n.d.)

Marie of Battenberg, *Reminiscences* (London, 1925)

Markoff, A., *Famine in Russia* (New York, 1934)

Marks, Frederick W. III, 'Six between Roosevelt and Hitler: America's Role in the Appeasement of Nazi Germany', *Historical Journal*, 28, 4 (1985), 969–82.

Marshall, Monty G. and Ted Robert Gurr, *Peace and Conflict 2005: A Global Survey of Armed Conflicts, Self-Determination Movements, and Democracy* (College Park, Md, 2005)

Marshall, S. L. A., *Men against Fire: The Problem of Battle Command in Future War* (New York, 1966 [1947])

Martin, Terry, 'The Origins of Soviet Ethnic Cleansing', *The Journal of Modern History*, 70, 4 (December 1998), 813–61.

—— *The Affirmative Action Empire: Nations and Nationalism in the Soviet Union, 1923–1939* (Ithaca / London, 2001)

Marx, Karl, 'On the Jewish Question', in *idem* and Friedrich Engels, *Collected Works*, vol. III: *1843–1844* (London, 1975), 146–74

Mascarenhas, Anthony, *The Rape of Bangla Desh* (Delhi, 1971)

Maschke, Erich, with Kurt W. Böhme, Diether Cartellieri, Werner Ratza, Hergard Robel, Emil Schieche and Helmut Wolff, *Die deutschen Kriegsgefangenen des Zweiten Weltkrieges: Eine Zusammenfassung* (Munich, 1974)

Massie, Robert K., *Castles of Steel: Britain, Germany and the Winning of the Great War at Sea* (New York, 2003)

Massing, Paul W., *Rehearsal for Destruction: A Study of Political Anti-Semitism in Imperial Germany* (New York, 1949)

Maupassant, Guy de, transl. Douglas Parmée, *Bel-Ami* (London, 1975 [1885])

Mauro, Paolo, Nathan Sussman and Yishay Yafeh, 'Emerging Market Spreads: Then Versus Now', Hebrew University of Jerusalem Working Paper (September 2000)

May, Ernest R., *Strange Victory: Hitler's Conquest of France* (New York, 2000)

May, R. E., *Mischehen und Ehescheidungen* (Munich / Leipzig, 1929)

Maylunas, A. and S. Mironenko, *A Lifelong Passion* (London, 1996)

Mazower, Mark, *The Balkans* (London, 2000)

—— *Salonica, City of Ghosts: Christians, Muslims and Jews, 1430–1950* (London, 2004)

McCoy, Alfred W., 'Introduction', in Alfred W. McCoy, *Southeast Asia under the Japanese Occupation* (New Haven, 1980), 1–12

McDonough, Frank, '*The Times*, Norman Ebbut and the Nazis, 1927–37', *Journal of Contemporary History*, 27, 3 (1992), 407–24

McKee, A., *Dresden 1945: The Devil's Tinderbox* (London, 1982)

McKernan, Michael, *All In! Fighting the War at Home* (St Leonards, 1995 [1983])

McQuaid, Kim, *Uneasy Partners: Big Business in American Politics, 1945–1990* (Baltimore / London, 1994)

Mehlinger, Kermit, 'That Black Man–White Woman Thing', *Ebony* (July–December 1970), 130–33

Meinecke, Friedrich, *Die deutsche Katastrophe* (Wiesbaden, 1946)

Meiring, Kerstin, *Die christlich-jüdische Mischehe in Deutschland 1840–1933* (Hamburg, 1998)

Melosi, Martin V., *The Shadow of Pearl Harbor: Political Controversy over the Surprise Attack, 1941–1946* (College Station, 1977)

Melson, Robert, *Revolution and Genocide: On the Origins of the Armenian Genocide and Holocaust* (Chicago, 1992)

Menand, Louis, *The Metaphysical Club* (New York, 2001)

Mencke, John G., *Mulattoes and Race Mixture: American Attitudes and Images, 1865–1918* (Ann Arbor, 1979)

Mendelsohn, Ezra, *The Jews of East Central Europe Between the World Wars* (Bloomington, 1983)

Messenger, Charles, 'The Battle of Britain: Triumph of the Luftwaffe', in Peter G. Tsouras (ed.), *Third Reich Victorious: The Alternate History of How the Germans Won the War* (London, 2002), 65–96

Meyers, Reinhard, 'British Imperial Interests and the Policy of Appeasement', in Wolfgang J. Mommsen and Lothar Kettenacker (eds.), *The Fascist Challenge and the Policy of Appeasement* (London, 1983), 339–52

Michel, Wilhelm, *Verrat am Deutschtum: Eine Streitschrift zur Judenfrage* (Hanover / Leipzig, 1922)

Miguel, Edward and Shanker Satyanath, 'Economic Shocks and Civil Conflict: An Instrumental Variables Approach', New York University Working Paper (October 2003)

Milward, Alan S., *War, Economy and Society 1939–1945* (London, 1987 [1977])

Minear, Richard H., *Victors' Justice: The Tokyo War Crimes Trial* (Princeton, 1971)

Ministère des Affaires Étrangères, *Documents diplomatiques: Affaires Arméniennes: Projets de réformes dans l'Empire Ottoman, 1893–1897* (Paris, 1897)

—— *Commission de publication des documents relatifs aux origines de la guerre de 1914, documents diplomatiques français (1871–1914)*, 1st Series *(1871–1900)*, vol. XI (Paris, 1947)

Mirelman, Victor A., *Jewish Buenos Aires, 1890–1930: In Search of an Identity* (Detroit, 1990)

Mirsky, N. D., 'Mixed Marriages in Anglo-Indian and Indo-Anglian Fiction', unpublished M. Litt. thesis (Oxford, 1985)

Mitchell, B. R., *Abstract of British Historical Statistics* (Cambridge, 1976)

—— *International Historical Statistics: Europe, 1750–1993* (London, 1998)

—— *International Historical Statistics: Africa, Asia, Oceania, 1750–1993* (London, 1998)

—— *International Historical Statistics: The Americas, 1750–1993* (London, 1998)

—— and H. G. Jones, *Second Abstract of British Historical Statistics* (Cambridge, 1971)

Modder, Montague Frank, *The Jew in the Literature of England to the End of the Nineteenth Century* (New York, 1939)

Modelski, George and Gardner Perry III, 'Democratization in Long Perspective', *Technological Forecasting and Social Change*, 39 (1991), 23–34

Moggridge, D. E., *Keynes: An Economist's Biography* (London, 1992)

Mokyr, Joel, *The Gifts of Athena: Historical Origins of the Knowledge Economy* (Princeton, 2002)

Mombauer, Annika, *Helmuth von Moltke and the Origins of the First World War* (Cambridge, 2001)

Mommsen, Hans, 'The Dissolution of the Third Reich: Crisis Management and Collapse, 1943–1945', *German Historical Institute Bulletin*, 27 (2000), 9–24

Monahan, Thomas, 'Are Interracial Marriages Really Less Stable?', *Social Forces*, 37 (1970), 461–73

—— 'The Occupational Class of Couples Entering into Interracial Marriages', *Journal of Contemporary Family Studies*, 7 (1976), 175–92

Moore, Bob, 'Unruly Allies: British Problems with the French Treatment of Axis Prisoners of War, 1943–1945', *War in History*, 7, 2 (2000), 180–98

Moran, Rachel F., *Interracial Intimacy: The Regulation of Race and Romance* (Chicago, 2001)

Morgan, E. V., *Studies in British Financial Policy, 1914–1925* (London, 1952)

Mosier, John, *The Myth of the Great War: A New Military History of World War*

*One. How the Germans Won the Battles and How the Americans Saved the Allies* (London, 2001)

Moss, W. Stanley, *Ill Met by Moonlight* (London, 1950)

Motyl, Alexander J., 'Ukrainian Nationalist Political Violence in Inter-war Poland, 1921–1939', *East European Quarterly*, 19, 1 (March 1985), 45–55

Mowat, C. L., *Britain between the Wars, 1918–1940* (London, 1969)

Mueller, John E., *War, Presidents and Public Opinion* (New York, 1973)

Müller, Arnd, 'Das Stürmer-Archiv im Stadtarchiv Nürnberg', *Vierteljahrshefte für Zeitgeschichte*, 32 (1984), 326–9

Murdoch, J., *The Other Side: The Story of Leo Dalderup as told to John Murdoch* (London, 1954)

Murfett, Malcolm H., John N. Miksic, Brian P. Farrell and Chiang Ming Shun, *Between Two Oceans: A Military History of Singapore from First Settlement to Final British Withdrawal* (Oxford / New York, 1999)

Murphy, David E., *What Stalin Knew: The Enigma of Barbarossa* (New Haven, 2005)

Murray, Williamson, 'The War of 1938: Chamberlain Fails to Sway Hitler at Munich', in Robert Crowley (ed.), *More What If? Eminent Historians Imagine What Might Have Been* (London, 2002), 255–78

Musil, Robert, transl. Eithne Wilkins and Ernst Kaiser, *The Man Without Qualities*, 3 vols. (London, 1979 [1930])

Myer, Dillon S., *Uprooted Americans: The Japanese Americans and the War Relocation Authority during World War II* (Tucson, 1971)

Myrdal, Gunnar, *An American Dilemma: The Negro Problem and Modern Democracy* (New York / London, 1944)

Nagel, Joane, 'Political Competition and Ethnicity', in Susan Olzak and Joane Nagel (eds.), *Competitive Ethnic Relations* (Orlando, 1986), 17–44

Naimark, Norman, *Fires of Hatred: Ethnic Cleansing in Twentieth-century Europe* (Cambridge, Mass. / London, 2001)

—— *The Russians in Germany: A History of the Soviet Zone of Occupation, 1945–1949* (Cambridge, Mass., 1995)

Nair, Parvati, 'Fire under Plastic: Immigration, or the Open Wounds of Late Capitalism', unpublished MS, Queen Mary College, University of London (n.d.)

Nalty, Bernard C., 'Sources of Victory', in Bernard C. Nalty, *The Pacific War: The Story of the Bitter Struggle in the Pacific Theater of World War II* (London, 1999), 252–65

Naman, Ann Aresty, *The Jew in the Victorian Novel: Some Relationships between Prejudice and Art* (New York, 1980)

Nassibian, Akaby, *Britain and the Armenian Question, 1915–1923* (London / Sydney / New York, 1984)

Nawratil, Heinz, *Die deutschen Nachkriegsverluste unter Vertriebenen, Gefangenen und Verschleppten. Mit einer Übersicht über die europäischen Nachkriegsverluste* (Munich / Berlin, 1988)

Neidpath, James, *The Singapore Naval Base and the Defence of Britain's Eastern Empire, 1919–1941* (Oxford, 1981)

Nelson, Donald M., *Arsenal of Democracy: The Story of American War Production* (New York, 1946)

Neustatter, Hannah, 'Demographic and Other Statistical Aspects of Anglo-Jewry', in Maurice Freedman (ed.), *A Minority in Britain: Social Studies of the Anglo-Jewish Community* (London, 1955), 55–133

Newland, Samuel J., *Cossacks in the German Army, 1941–1945* (London, 1991)

Newton, Scott, *Profits of Peace: The Political Economy of Anglo-German Appeasement* (Oxford, 1996)

—— 'The "Anglo-German" Connection and the Political Economy of Appeasement', in Patrick Finney (ed.), *The Origins of the Second World War* (London, 1997), 293–316

Nichol, John and Tony Rennell, *Tail-end Charlies: The Last Battles of the Bomber War, 1944–1945* (London, 2004)

Nicolson, Harold, ed. Nigel Nicolson, *Diaries and Letters*, vol. II: *1939–1945* (London, 1967)

Nish, Ian, 'The Historical Significance of the Anglo-Japanese Alliance', Santory Centre, London School of Economics, Discussion Paper, IS/03/443 (January 2003), 40–47

Nitobe, Inazo, transl. Tokuhei Suchi, *Bushidō: The Soul of Japan – An Exposition of Japanese Thought* (Tokyo, n.d. [1900])

Noakes, Jeremy, *The Nazi Party in Lower Saxony, 1921–1933* (London, 1971)

Noakes, Jeremy and Geoffrey Pridham (eds.), *Nazism, 1919–1945*, vol. II: *State, Economy and Society, 1933–1939* (Exeter, 1984)

—— (eds.), *Nazism, 1919–1945*, vol. III: *Foreign Policy, War and Racial Extermination* (Exeter, 1988)

Nogales, Rafael de, *Four Years beneath the Crescent* (London, 1926)

Nossack, Hans Erich, *The End: Hamburg 1943* (Chicago, 2005)

Nove, Alec and J. A. Newth, 'The Jewish Population: Demographic Trends and Occupational Patterns', in Lionel Kochan (ed.), *The Jews in Soviet Russia since 1917* (Oxford / London / New York, 1978), 132–67

Novkov, Julie, 'Racial Constructions: The Legal Regulation of Miscegenation in Alabama, 1890–1934', *Law and History Review*, 20, 2 (Summer 2002)

Nye, John V. C., 'Killing Private Ryan: An Institutional Analysis of Military Decision Making in World War II', Washington University in St Louis, draft prepared for the ISNIE conference in Boston (2002)

O'Brien, Patrick Karl and Armand Clesse (eds.), *Two Hegemonies: Britain 1846–1914 and the United States 1941–2001* (Aldershot / Burlington, Vt, 2002)

Offer, Avner, 'Costs and Benefits, Prosperity and Security, 1870–1914', in Andrew Porter (ed.), *The Oxford History of the British Empire*, vol. III: *The Nineteenth Century* (Oxford / New York, 1999), 690–711

Offner, Arnold A., 'The United States and National Socialist Germany', in Patrick Finney (ed.), *The Origins of the Second World War* (London, 1997), 245–261

—— 'Appeasement Revisited: The United States, Great Britain and Germany, 1933–1940', *Journal of American History*, 64, 2 (September 1977), 373–93

Ogan, Bernd and Wolfgang W. Weiss, *Faszination und Gewalt: Zur Politischen Ästhetik des Nationalsozialismus* (Nuremberg, 1992)

Ogata, Sadako N., *Defiance in Manchuria: The Making of Japanese Foreign Policy, 1931–1932* (Berkeley, 1964)

Ohandjanian, Artem, *Armenien: Der verschwiegene Völkermord* (Vienna / Cologne / Graz, 1989)

O'Loughlin, John, 'The Electoral Geography of Weimar Germany: Exploratory Spatial Data Analyses (ESDA) of Protestant Support for the Nazi Party', *Political Analysis* 10, 3 (2002), 217–43

—— Colin Flint and Luc Anselin, 'The Geography of the Nazi Vote: Context, Confession, and Class in the Reichstag Election of 1930', *Annals, Association of American Geographers*, 84 (1994), 351–80

Olson, Steve, *Mapping Human History: Discovering the Past through Our Genes* (London, 2002)

Olsson, Andreas, Jeffrey P. Ebert, Mahzarin R. Banaji and Elizabeth A. Phelps, 'The Role of Social Groups in the Persistence of Learned Fear', *Science*, 309 (July 29, 2005), 785–87

Olzak, Susan, *The Dynamics of Ethnic Competition and Conflict* (Stanford, 1992)

Onoda, Hiroo, *No Surrender: My Thirty Year War* (London, 1975)

Oram, Gerard Christopher, *Military Executions during World War One* (London, 2003)

O'Rourke, Kevin H. and Jeffrey G. Williamson, *Globalization and History: The Evolution of a Nineteenth-Century Atlantic Economy* (Cambridge, Mass. / London, 1999)

Ovendale, Ritchie, *'Appeasement' and the English Speaking World: Britain, the United States, the Dominions, and the Policy of Appeasement, 1937–1939* (Cardiff, 1975)

Overmans, Rüdiger, 'German Historiography, the War Losses and the Prisoners of War', in G. Bischof and S. Ambrose (eds.), *Eisenhower and the German POWs: Facts against Falsehood* (Baton Rouge / London, 1992), 127–69

—— *Deutsche militärische Verluste im Zweiten Weltkrieg* (Munich, 1999)

Overy, Richard, 'Air Power and the Origins of Deterrence Theory before 1939', *Journal of Strategic Studies*, 14 (1992)

—— 'Germany and the Munich Crisis: A Mutilated Victory?', in Igor Lukes and Erik Goldstein (eds.), *The Munich Crisis, 1938: Prelude to World War II* (London, 1999), 191–216

—— *Russia's War* (London, 1997)

—— *The Air War, 1939–1945* (London, 1980)

—— *The Dictators: Hitler's Germany and Stalin's Russia* (London, 2004)

—— *Why the Allies Won* (London, 1996)

Oxaal, Ivar, 'The Jews of Young Hitler's Vienna: Historical and Sociological Aspects', in Ivar Oxaal, Michael Pollak and Gerhard Botz (eds.), *Jews, Antisemitism and Culture in Vienna* (London and New York, 1987), 11–39

Padfield, Peter, *Himmler: Reichsführer SS* (London, 1990)

Padover, Saul K., *Psychologist in Germany: The Story of an American Intelligence Officer* (London, 1946)

Pagnini, Deanna L. and S. Philip Morgan, 'Intermarriage and Social Distance among U.S. Immigrants at the Turn of the Century', *American Journal of Sociology*, 96 (1990), 405–32

Paikert, G. C., 'Hungary's National Minority Policies, 1920–1945', *American Slavic and East European Review*, 12, 2 (April 1953), 201–18

—— *The Danube Swabians: German Populations in Hungary, Rumania and Yugoslavia and Hitler's Impact on their Patterns* (The Hague, 1967)

Paine, Sarah C. M., *Imperial Rivals: China, Russia and Their Disputed Frontier* (Armonk, NY / London, 1996)

Pallis, A. A., 'Racial Migrations in the Balkans during the Years 1912–1914', *Geographical Journal*, 66 (October 1925), 315–31

Pallud, Jean Paul, 'Crime in WWII: The Execution of Eddie Slovik', *After the Battle*, 32 (1981), 28–42

Pappritz, Anna, *Der Mädchenhandel und seine Bekämpfung* (Schwelm, 1924)

Parker, R. A. C., 'British Rearmament 1936–9: Treasury, Trade Unions and Skilled Labour', *English Historical Review*, 96, 379 (April 1981), 306–43

—— *Chamberlain and Appeasement: British Policy and the Coming of the Second World War* (London, 1993)

—— *Churchill and Appeasement* (London, 2000)

—— 'Economics, Rearmament, and Foreign Policy: The UK before 1939 – A Preliminary Study', *Journal of Contemporary History*, 10, 4 (1975), 637–47

Pascoe, Peggy, 'Miscegenation Law, Court Cases, and Ideologies of "Race" in Twentieth-Century America', *Journal of American History*, 83, 1 (June 1996), 44–69

Payne, Robert, *Massacre* (New York, 1973)

Peach, Ceri, 'Ethnic Segregation and Ethnic Intermarriage: A Re-examination of Kennedy's Triple Melting Pot in New Haven, 1900–1950', in Ceri Peach, Vaughan Robinson and Susan Smith (eds.), *Ethnic Segregation in Cities* (London, 1981), 193–217

Peattie, Mark R., 'Japanese Strategy and Campaigns in the Pacific War, 1941–1945', in Loyd E. Lee (ed.), *World War II in Asia and the Pacific and the War's Aftermath, with General Themes: A Handbook of Literature and Research* (Westport, 1998), 56–72

Peden, G. C., 'A Matter of Timing: The Economic Background to British Foreign Policy, 1938–1939', *History*, 69, 225 (February, 1984), 15–28

—— 'Sir Warren Fisher and British Rearmament against Germany', *English Historical Review*, 94, 370 (January 1979), 29–47

—— *The Treasury and British Public Policy, 1906–1959* (Oxford, 2000)

Peeters, Benoît, *Hergé: Fils de Tintin* (Paris, 2002)

Perrett, Bryan, 'Operation SPHINX: Raeder's Mediterranean Strategy', in Kenneth Macksey (ed.), *The Hitler Options: Alternate Decisions of World War II* (London, 1995), 35–53

Petropoulos, Jonathan, *The Faustian Bargain: The Art World in Nazi Germany* (London, 2000)

Petzina, Dietmar, Werner Abelshauser und Anselm Faust, *Sozialgeschichtliches Arbeitsbuch*, vol. III: *Materialien zur Statistik des Deutschen Reiches, 1914–1945* (Munich, 1978)

Piketty, Thomas and Emmanuel Saez, 'Income Inequality in the United States, 1913–1998', NBER Working Paper, 8467 (Sept. 2001)

Pinchuk, Ben-Cion, *Shtetl Jews under Soviet Rule: Eastern Poland on the Eve of the Holocaust* (Oxford / Cambridge, Mass., 1990)

Piotrowski, Tadeusz, *Vengeance of the Swallows: Memoir of a Polish Family's Ordeal under Soviet Aggression, Ukrainian Ethnic Cleansing and Nazi Enslavement, and their Emigration to America* (Jefferson, NC / London, 1995)

Pipes, Richard, 'Assimilation and the Muslims: A Case Study', in Alex Inkeles and Kent Geiger (eds.), *Soviet Society: A Book of Readings* (London, 1961), 588–607

—— *Russia under the Bolshevik Regime, 1919–1924* (New York / London, 1995)

Pleshakov, Constantine, *Stalin's Folly: The Tragic First Ten Days of World War II on the Eastern Front* (Boston, 2005)

Pogge von Strandmann, Hartmut, 'Nationalisierungsdruck und königliche Namensänderung in England', in Gerhard A. Ritter and Peter Wende (eds.), *Rivalität und Partnerschaft: Studien zu den deutsch-britischen Beziehungen im 19. und 20. Jahrhundert. Festschrift für Anthony J. Nicholls* (Paderborn / Munich / Vienna / Zurich, 1999), 69–91

Polish Ministry of Information, *The German Fifth Column in Poland* (London / Melbourne, 1941)

Pollock, James K., 'An Areal Study of the German Electorate, 1930–1933', *American Political Science Review*, 38, 1 (February 1944), 89–95

Polonsky, Antony and Michael Riff, 'Poles, Czechoslovaks and the "Jewish Question", 1914–1921: A Comparative Study', in Volker R. Berghahn and Martin Kitchen (eds.), *Germany in the Age of Total War* (London, 1981), 63–101

Pomeranz, Kenneth, *The Great Divergence: China, Europe and the Making of the Modern World Economy* (Princeton / Oxford, 2000)

Pomiankowski, Joseph, *Der Zusammenbruch des Ottomanischen Reiches: Erinnerungen an die Türkei aus der Zeit des Weltkrieges* (Zurich / Leipzig / Vienna, 1928)

Ponchaud, François, transl. Nancy Amphoux, *Cambodia Year Zero* (New York, 1978)

Pöppel, Martin, transl. Louise Willmot, *Heaven and Hell: The War Diary of a German Paratrooper* (Staplehurst, 2000 [1988])

Porter, Bernard, *The Absent-minded Imperialists: What the British Really Thought about Empire* (Oxford, 2004)

Pottle, Mark (ed.), *Champion Redoubtable: The Diaries and Letters of Violet Bonham Carter, 1914–45* (London, 1998)

Poundstone, William, *Prisoner's Dilemma* (Oxford, 1993)

Power, Samantha, *'A Problem from Hell': America and the Age of Genocide* (London, 2003)

Prados, John, 'Operation Herbstnebel: Smoke over the Ardennes', in Peter G. Tsouras (ed.), *Battle of the Bulge: Hitler's Alternate Scenarios* (London, 2004), 181–205

Praisman, Leonid, 'Pogroms and Jewish Self-Defence', *Journal of the Academic Proceedings of Soviet Jewry*, 1, 1 (1986), 65–82

Prasad, Sri Nandan and S. V. Desika Char, ed. Bisheshwar Prasad, *Expansion of the Armed Forces and Defence Organization, 1939–1945* (Calcutta, 1956)

Price, Alfred, 'The Jet Fighter Menace, 1943', in Kenneth Macksey (ed.), *The Hitler Options: Alternate Decisions of World War II* (London, 1995), 172–85

Pridham, Geoffrey, *Hitler's Rise to Power: The Nazi Movement in Bavaria, 1923–1933* (London, 1973)

Pritsak, Omeljan, 'The Pogroms of 1881', *Harvard Ukrainian Studies*, 11, 1/2 (June 1987), 8–41

Prosterman, Roy L., *Surviving to 3000: An Introduction to the Study of Lethal Conflict* (Belmont, Calif. 1972)

Prysor, Glyn, 'The "Fifth Column" and the British Experience of Retreat, 1940', *War in History*, 12 (November 2005), 418–47

Przyrembel, Alexandra, *'Rassenschande': Reinheitsmythos und Vernichtungslegitimation in Nationalsozialismus* (Göttingen, 2003)

Rabe, John, transl. John E. Woods, *The Good Man of Nanking: The Diaries of John Rabe* (New York, 1998)

Rahden, Till van, 'Mingling, Marrying and Distancing: Jewish Integration in Wilhelminian Breslau and its Erosion in Early Weimar Germany', in Wolfgang Benz, Arnold Paucker and Peter Pulzer (eds.), *Jüdisches Leben in der Weimarer Republik / Jews in the Weimar Republic* (Tübingen, 1998), 197–221

Rainey, Lawrence, 'Making History', *London Review of Books* (January 1, 1998), 18–20

Rakowska-Harmstone, Teresa, '"Brotherhood in Arms": The Ethnic Factor in the Soviet Armed Forces', in N. F. Dreisziger (ed.), *Ethnic Armies: Polyethnic Armed Forces from the Time of the Habsburgs to the Age of the Superpowers* (Waterloo, Ontario, 1990), 123–57

Ranke, Leopold von, 'The Great Powers', in R. Wines (ed.), *The Secret of World History: Selected Writings on the Art and Science of History* (New York, 1981 [1833]), 122–55

Rasor, Eugene L., 'The Japanese Attack on Pearl Harbor', in Loyd E. Lee (ed.), *World War II in Asia and the Pacific and the War's Aftermath, with General Themes: A Handbook of Literature and Research* (Westport, Conn., 1998), 45–56

Rauchway, Eric, *Murdering McKinley: The Making of Theodore Roosevelt's America* (New York, 2003)

Reck-Malleczewen, Friedrich Percyval, *Diary of a Man in Despair* (New York, 1970)

Redding, Robert and Bill Yenne, *Boeing: Planemaker to the World* (Hong Kong, 1983)

Reder, Rudolf, *Bełżec* (Kraków, 1999)

Rees, Laurence, *War of the Century: When Hitler Fought Stalin* (London, 1999)

Reichswehrministerium, *Sanitätsbericht über das Deutsche Heer (deutsches Feld- und Besatzungsheer) im Weltkriege 1914–1918*, 3 vols. (Berlin, 1934–5)

Reid, James J., 'Total War, the Annihilation Ethic and the Armenian Genocide, 1870–1918', in Richard Hovannisian (ed.), *The Armenian Genocide: History, Politics, Ethics* (Basingstoke, 1992), 21–349

Remarque, Erich Maria, *All Quiet on the Western Front* (London, [1929])

Reuter, Edward Byron, *Race Mixture: Studies in Intermarriage and Miscegenation* (New York, 1931)

—— *The Mulatto in the United States: Including a Study of the Role of Mixed-blood Races Throughout the World* (Boston, 1918)

Reuth, Ralf Georg, *Goebbels* (London, 1993)

Reynolds, Nicholas, *Treason was No Crime: Ludwig Beck, Chief of the German General Staff* (London, 1976)

Rezzori, Gregor von, *The Snows of Yesteryear: Portraits for an Autobiography* (London, 1989)

Rhee, M. J., *The Doomed Empire: Japan in Colonial Korea* (Aldershot / Brookfield / Singapore / Sydney, 1997)

Rhodes, Richard, *The Making of the Atomic Bomb* (New York, 1986)

Richardson, L. F., *Statistics of Deadly Quarrels* (Pittsburgh, 1960)

Richerson, Peter J. and Robert Boyd, *Not By Genes Alone: How Culture Transformed Human Evolution* (Chicago, 2005)

Rigg, Bryan Mark, *Hitler's Jewish Soldiers: The Untold Story of Nazi Racial Laws and Men of Jewish Descent in the German Military* (Lawrence, Kan., 2002)

Ritschl, Albrecht, *Deutschlands Krise und Konjunktur: Binnenkonjunktur, Auslandsverschuldung und Reparationsproblem zwischen Dawes-Plan und Transfersperre 1924–1934* (Berlin, 2002)

—— 'Spurious Growth in German Output Data, 1913–1938', Centre for Economic Policy Research discussion paper, 4429 (June 2004)

Ritter, Gerhard, *Der Schlieffen Plan: Kritik eines Mythos* (Munich, 1956)

—— transl. R. T. Clark, *The German Resistance: Carl Goerdeler's Struggle Against Tyranny* (London, 1958)

Roberts, Andrew, 'The House of Windsor and Appeasement', in idem, *Eminent Churchillians* (London, 1994)

—— 'Prime Minister Halifax', in Robert Cowley (ed.), *More What If? Eminent Historians Imagine What Might Have Been* (London, 2002), 279–90

—— *The Holy Fox: A Biography of Lord Halifax* (London, 1991)

Roberts, Marie, *Gothic Immortals: The Fiction of the Brotherhood of the Rosy Cross* (London, 1990)

Robinsohn, Hans, *Justiz als politische Verfolgung: Die Rechtsprechung in 'Rassenschandefällen' beim Landgericht Hamburg 1936–1943* (Stuttgart, 1977)

Robinson, Charles F. II, *Dangerous Liaisons: Sex and Love in the Segregated South* (Fayetteville, 2003)

Rockoff, Hugh, 'The United States: From Ploughshares to Swords', in Mark Harrison (ed.), *The Economics of World War II: Six Great Powers in International Comparison* (Cambridge, 1998), 81–121

Rodgers, Eugene, *Flying High: The Story of Boeing and the Rise of the Jetliner Industry* (New York, 1996)

Röhl, John C. G., 'The Emperor's New Clothes', in idem (ed.), *The Corfu Papers* (Cambridge, 1992)

—— *The Kaiser and His Court: Wilhelm II and the Government of Germany* (Cambridge, 1994)

—— transl. Sheila de Bellaigue, *Wilhelm II: The Kaiser's Personal Monarchy, 1888–1900* (Cambridge, 2004)

Rohwer, Jürgen, 'The U-Boat War Against the Allied Supply Lines', in Hans-Adolf Jacobsen and Jürgen Rohwer (eds.), transl. Edward Fitzgerald, *Decisive Battles of World War II: The German View* (London, 1965), 259–313

Rolf, David, *Prisoners of the Reich: Germany's Captives, 1939–1945* (Dunton Green, 1989)

Rolfe, M., *Looking into Hell: Experiences of the Bomber Command War* (London, 2000)

Rose, Elihu, 'The Case of the Missing Carriers', in Robert Cowley (ed.), *What If? The World's Foremost Military Historians Imagine What Might Have Been* (London, 2001), 340–50

Rosefielde, Steven, 'Excess Deaths and Industrialization: A Realist Theory of Stalinist Economic Development in the 1930s', *Journal of Contemporary History*, 23, 2 (April 1988), 277–89

Rosen, Sara, *My Lost World: A Survivor's Tale* (London, 1993)

Rosenberg, Edgar, *From Shylock to Svengali: Jewish Stereotypes in English Fiction* (London, 1960)

Rosenfeld, Gavriel, *The World Hitler Never Made: Alternate History and the Memory of Nazism* (Cambridge, 2005)

Rosenthal, Erich, 'Some Recent Studies about the Extent of Jewish Out-Marriage in the USA', in Werner J. Cahnman (ed.), *Intermarriage and Jewish Life: A Symposium* (New York, 1963), 82–91

Röskau-Rydel, Isabel, 'Galizien', in *idem* (ed.), *Deutsche Geschichte im Osten Europas: Galizien* (Berlin, 1999), 16–212

Roth, Joseph, transl. Joachim Neugroschel, *The Radetsky March* (Woodstock / New York, 1995 [1932])

Rothschild, Joseph, *East Central Europe Between the Two World Wars* (Seattle / London, 1974)

Rozenblit, Marsha L., *The Jews of Vienna, 1867–1914: Assimilation and Identity* (Albany, 1983)

Rubin, Abba, *Images in Transition: The English Jew in English Literature, 1660–1830* (Westport, Conn., 1984)

Rubinstein, Hilary L., Dan Cohn-Sherbok, Abraham J. Edelheit and William D. Rubinstein, *The Jews in the Modern World: A History Since 1750* (London, 2002)

—— 'Jewish Participation in National Economic Elites, 1860–1939, and Anti-Semitism: An International Comparison', paper presented at the Australian Association for Jewish Studies Conference, Sydney (1997)

Rubinstein, William D., *The Myth of Rescue* (London, 1997)

Rudnicki, Szymon, 'Anti-Jewish Legislation in Interwar Poland', in Robert Blobaum (ed.), *Antisemitism and its Opponents in Modern Poland* (Ithaca, 2005), 148–70

Rummel, Rudolph J., *Democide: Nazi Genocide and Mass Murder* (New Jersey, 1992)

—— *Lethal Politics: Soviet Genocide and Mass Murder Since 1917* (New Brunswick, NJ, 1990)

Ruppin, Arthur, *Die Juden der Gegenwart: Eine sozialwissenschaftliche Studie* (Berlin, 1904)

—— *Soziologie der Juden*, vol. I: *Die soziale Struktur der Juden* (Berlin, 1930)

Rusbridger, James and Eric Nave, *Betrayal at Pearl Harbor* (New York, 1991)

Russett, Bruce, 'Counterfactuals about War and Its Absence', in Philip E. Tetlock and Aaron Belkin (eds.), *Counterfactual Thought Experiments in World Politics: Logical, Methodological and Psychological Perspectives* (Princeton, 1996), 171–86

Russo-Jewish Committee, *Russian Atrocities, 1881: Supplementary Statement issued by the Russo-Jewish Committee in Confirmation of 'The Times' Narrative* (London, 1882)

Rutchford, B. U., 'The South's Stake in International Trade', *The Southern Economic Journal*, 14, 4 (April 1948), 361–75

Rytina, Steven, Peter Blau, Terry Blum and Joseph Schwartz, 'Inequality and Intermarriage: A Paradox of Motive and Constraint', *Social Forces*, 66 (1988), 645–75

Sainsbury, Keith, *Churchill and Roosevelt at War: The War They Fought and the Peace They Hoped to Make* (London, 1994)

Sakamoto, Pamela Rotner, *Japanese Diplomats and Jewish Refugees: A World War II Dilemma* (Westport, Conn. / London, 1998)

Sapolsky, Robert M., 'A Natural History of Peace', *Foreign Affairs*, 85 (January / February 2006), 104–20

Sarafian, Ara (ed.), *United States Official Documents on the Armenian Genocide*, vol. II: *The Peripheries* (Watertown, Mass., 1993)

—— (ed.), *United States Official Documents on the Armenian Genocide*, vol. I: *The Lower Euphrates* (Watertown, Mass., 1993)

Saxon, Timothy D., 'Anglo-Japanese Naval Cooperation, 1914–1918', *Naval War College Review*, 53, 1 (Winter 2000); http://www.nwc.navy.mil/press/review/2000/winter/art3-w00.htm

Scalapino, Robert A., 'Southern Advance: Introduction', in James William Morley (ed.), *The Fateful Choice: Japan's Advance into Southeast Asia, 1939–1941* (New York, 1980), 117–25

Schechtman, Joseph B., *Postwar Population Transfers in Europe, 1945–1955* (Philadelphia, 1962)

Schell, Jonathan, *The Unconquerable World: Power, Nonviolence, and the Will of the People* (London, 2004)

Schiel, Juliane, 'Pillars of Democracy: A Study of the Democratisation Process in Europe after the First World War', unpublished BA thesis (Oxford University, 2000)

Schimmelpenninck van der Oye, David, *Toward the Rising Sun: Russian Ideologies of Empire and the Path to War with Japan* (DeKalb, Ill., 2001)

Schirmer, Jennifer G., *The Guatemalan Military Project: A Violence Called Democracy* (Philadelphia, 1998)

Schlesinger, Arthur, Jr., 'Hopeful Cynic', *Times Literary Supplement* (May 27, 2005), 12–13

Schleunes, Karl A., *The Twisted Road to Auschwitz: Nazi Policy toward the Jews, 1933–39* (London, 1972)

Schmidt, Gustav, 'The Domestic Background to British Appeasement Policy', in Wolfgang J. Mommsen and Lothar Kettenacker (eds.), *The Fascist Challenge and the Policy of Appeasement* (London, 1983), 101–24

Schmidt, Sabine, Jan Blaszkowski, Izabela Darecka, Franz Dwertmann, Bogdan Krzykowski, Marcin Milancej, Hanna Olejnik and Danuta Schmidt, *In Gdansk unterwegs mit Günter Grass* (Gdańsk, 1993)

Schorske, Carl E., *Fin-de-siècle Vienna: Politics and Culture* (London, 1980)

Schroeder, Paul W., 'Embedded Counterfactuals and World War I as an Unavoidable War', in Philip Tetlock, Richard Ned Lebow and Geoffrey Parker (eds.), *Unmaking the West: Counterfactual Thought Experiments in History* (forthcoming)

Schulman, Gary I., 'Race, Sex and Violence: A Laboratory Test of the Sexual Threat of the Black Male Hypothesis', *American Journal of Sociology*, 79 (March 1974), 1260–77

Scott, John, *Behind the Urals* (Bloomington / Indianapolis, 1989 [1942])

Scurr, John, *Germany's Spanish Volunteers 1941–45: The Blue Division in Russia* (London, 1980)

Seabright, Paul, *The Company of Strangers: A Natural History of Economic Life* (Princeton, 2004)

Sebag Montefiore, Simon, *Stalin: The Court of the Red Tsar* (New York, 2004)

Sebastian, Mihail, ed. Radu Ioanid and transl. Patrick Camiller, *Journal, 1935–1944* (Chicago, 2001)

Segel, Harold B. (ed.), *Stranger in Our Midst: Respresentations of the Jew in Polish Literature* (Ithaca / London, 1996)

Sellers, Leonard, *For God's Sake Shoot Straight! The Story of the Court Martial and Execution of Temporary Sub-Lieutenant Edwin Leopold Arthur Dyett, Nelson Battalion, 63rd (RN) Division during the First World War* (London, 1995)

Service, Robert, *Stalin: A Biography* (Cambridge, Mass., 2005)

—— *A History of Twentieth-Century Russia* (London, 1997)

—— *Lenin: A Biography* (London, 2000)

Seth, Ronald, *Caporetto: The Scapegoat Battle* (London, 1965)

Sethi, S. S., *The Decisive War: Emergence of a New Nation* (New Delhi, 1972)

Seton-Watson, Hugh, *Eastern Europe Between the Wars, 1918–1941* (Cambridge, 1945)

Settle, Arthur, 'Model-T Anti-Semitism', *Protestant Digest* (August–September 1940), 21–7

Shawcross, William, *Deliver Us From Evil: Warlords and Peacekeepers in a World of Endless Conflict* (London, 2000)

Shay, Robert Paul Jr., *British Rearmament in the Thirties: Politics and Profits* (Princeton, 1977)

Sheffield, Gary, *Forgotten Victory: The First World War, Myths and Realities* (London, 2001)

Shelden, Michael, *Orwell: The Authorized Biography* (London, 1991)

Sherman, A. J., *Mandate Days: British Lives in Palestine, 1918–1948* (New York, 1997)

Sherwin, Martin J., 'The Atomic Bomb and the Origins of the Cold War', in David S. Painter and Melvyn P. Leffler (eds.), *Origins of the Cold War: An International History* (London, 1994), 77–95

Shillony, Ben-Ami, *Politics and Culture in Wartime Japan* (Oxford, 1981)

Shippey, T. A., *J. R. R. Tolkien: Author of the Century* (London, 2000)

Shirer, Frank R., 'Pearl Harbor: Irredeemable Defeat', in Peter G. Tsouras (ed.), *Rising Sun Victorious: The Alternate History of How the Japanese Won the Pacific War* (London, 2001), 62–82

Shirer, William L., *The Collapse of the Third Republic: An Inquiry into the Fall of France in 1940* (London, 1972)

Shochat, Azriel, 'Jews, Lithuanians and Russians, 1939–1941', in Bela Vago and George L. Mosse (eds.), *Jews and Non-Jews in Eastern Europe* (New York, 1974), 301–14

Sieradzki, Mietek, *By a Twist of History: The Three Lives of a Polish Jew* (London, 2002)

Silber, William, 'Birth of the Federal Reserve: Crisis in the Womb', *Journal of Monetary Economics* (forthcoming)

—— *The Summer of 1914: Birth of a Financial Superpower* (forthcoming)

Silverstein, Josef, 'The Importance of the Japanese Occupation of Southeast Asia to the Political Scientist', in *idem*, *Southeast Asia in World War II: Four Essays* (New Haven, Conn., 1966), 1–13

Simmons, Robert R., 'The Korean Civil War', in Frank Baldwin (ed.), *Without Parallel: The American–Korean Relationship since 1945* (New York, 1973), 143–79

Simms, Brendan, *Unfinest Hour: Britain and the Destruction of Bosnia* (London, 2001)

Singer, J. David and Melvin Small, *Correlates of War Database*, University of Michigan, www.umich.edu/~cowproj

Sington, Derrick and Arthur Weidenfeld, *The Goebbels Experiment: A Study of the Nazi Propaganda Machine* (London, 1942)

Sisson, Richard and Leo E. Rose, *War and Secession: Pakistan, India, and the Creation of Bangladesh* (Berkeley, 1990)

Slezkine, Yuri, *The Jewish Century* (Princeton, 2004)

Slusser, Robert M., 'Soviet Far Eastern Policy, 1945–1950: Stalin's Goals in Korea', in Yōnōsuke Nagai and Akira Iriye (eds.), *The Origins of the Cold War in Asia* (Tokyo, 1977), 123–47

Smal-Stocki, Roman, *The Captive Nations: Nationalism of the Non-Russian Nations in the Soviet Union* (New York, 1960)

Smelser, Ronald M., 'Nazi Dynamics, German Foreign Policy and Appeasement', in Wolfgang J. Mommsen and Lothar Kettenacker (eds.), *The Fascist Challenge and the Policy of Appeasement* (London, 1983), 31–48

Smith, Elberton R., *The Army and Economic Mobilization* (Washington DC, 1991)

Smith, Lillian, *Killers of the Dream* (London, 1950)

Sodol, Petro R., *UPA: They fought Hitler and Stalin: A Brief Overview of Military Aspects from the History of the Ukrainian Insurgent Army, 1942–1949* (New York, 1987)

Sollors, Werner, *Neither Black nor White yet Both* (New York, 1997)

Solzhenitsyn, Aleksandr I., transl. Thomas P. Whitney, *The Gulag Archipelago 1918–1956* (London, 1974)

—— transl. Anne Kichilov, Georges Philippenko and Nikita Struve, *Deux siècles ensemble (1917–1972)*, vol. II: *Juifs et Russes pendant la période soviétique* (Paris, 2003)

Spector, Ronald H., *Eagle against the Sun: The American War with Japan* (London, 1987)

Spector, Scott, 'Auf der Suche nach der Prager deutschen Kultur: Deutsch-jüdische Dichter in Prag von der Jahrhundertwende bis 1918', in Deutsches Historisches Museum (ed.), *Deutsche im Osten* (Berlin, 1995), 83–91

Speer, Albert, transl. Richard and Clara Winston, *Inside the Third Reich* (London, 1970)

Spengler, Oswald, ed. Helmut Werner, transl. Charles Francis Atkinson, *The Decline of the West: An Abridged Edition* (London, 1961)

Spiller, Harry (ed.), *Prisoners of Nazis: Accounts by American POWs in World War II* (Jefferson, NC / London, 1998)

Stanlislawski, Michael, *Tsar Nicholas I and the Jews: The Transformation of Jewish Society in Russia, 1825–1855* (Philadelphia, 1983)

Stanton, William, *The Leopard's Spots: Scientific Attitudes toward Race in America, 1815–59* (Chicago / London, 1960)

Stargardt, Nicholas, 'Victims of Bombing and Retaliation', *German Historical Institute, London, Bulletin*, 26, 2 (2004), 57–70

Stedman, James, *Life of a British PoW in Poland. 31 May 1940 to 30 April 1945* (Braunton, Devon, 1992)

Steigmann-Gall, Richard, *The Holy Reich: Nazi Conceptions of Christianity, 1919–1945* (Cambridge, 2003)

Steinberg, Mark D. and Vladimir M. Khrustalev, *The Fall of the Romanovs: Political Dreams and Personal Struggles in a Time of Revolution* (New Haven, 1995)

Stember, Charles Herbert, *Sexual Racism: The Emotional Barrier to an Integrated Society* (New York, 1976)

—— Marshall Sklare and George Salomon, *Jews in the Mind of America* (New York, 1966)

Stephan, John J., *The Russian Far East: A History* (Stanford, 1994)

Stevenson, David, *Armaments and the Coming of War: Europe 1904–1914* (Oxford, 1996)

—— *Cataclysm: The First World War as Political Tragedy* (New York, 2004)

Stewart, Graham, *Burying Caesar: Churchill, Chamberlain and the Battle for the Tory Party* (London, 1999)

Stockmar, Baron E. von, *Memoirs of Baron Stockmar*, 2 vols. (London, 1872)

Stoler, Ann, 'Making Empire Respectable: The Politics of Race and Sexual Morality in 20th Century Colonial Cultures', in Jan Breman (ed.), *Imperial Monkey Business: Racial Supremacy in Social Darwinist Theory and Colonial Practice* (Amsterdam, 1990), 35–71

Stoltzfus, Nathan, *Resistance of the Heart: Intermarriage and the Rosenstrasse Protest in Nazi Germany* (New York, 1996)

Strachan, Hew, *The First World War*, vol. I: *To Arms* (Oxford, 2001)

—— *The First World War: A New Illustrated History* (London / New York / Sydney / Tokyo / Singapore / Toronto / Dublin, 2003)

—— 'Training, Morale and Modern War', *Journal of Contemporary History* (forthcoming)

Strack, Hermann L., *Jüdische Geheimgesetze* (Berlin, 1920)

Strik-Strikfeldt, Wilfried, *Against Stalin and Hitler: Memoir of the Russian Liberation Movement 1941–5* (London and Basingstoke, 1970)

Stromberg, Roland N., 'American Business and the Approach of War, 1935–1941', *Journal of Economic History*, 13, 1 (1953), 58–78

Stueck, William, *The Korean War: An International History* (Princeton, 1995)

Sugihara, Kaoru, 'The Economic Motivations behind Japanese Aggression in the Late 1930s: Perspectives of Freda Utley and Nawa Toichi', *Journal of Contemporary History*, 32, 2 (April 1997), 259–80

Surh, Gerald, 'The Jews of Ekaterinoslav in 1905 as Seen from the Town Hall: Ethnic Relations on an Imperial Frontier', *Ab Imperio: Theory and History of Nationalism and Empire in the Post-Soviet Space*, 4 (2003)

Suvorov, Victor [Vladimir Rezun], *Icebreaker: Who Started the Second World War?* (London, 1990)

Swain, Geoffrey, *Russia's Civil War* (Stroud, 2000)

Symon, Jack, *Hell in Five* (London, 1997)

Tachauer, D., 'Statistische Untersuchungen über die Neigung zu Mischehen', *Zeitschrift für die gesamte Staatswissenschaft*, 71, 1 (1915), 36–40

Talaat Pasha, 'Posthumous Memoirs of Talaat Pasha', *New York Times Current History*, 15, 1 (October, 1921), 287–93

Tang, Hua, *et al.*, 'Genetic Structure, Self-Identified Race/Ethnicity, and Confounding in Case-Control Association Studies', *American Journal of Human Genetics*, 76 (2005), 268–75

Tatar, Maria, *Lustmord: Sexual Murder in Weimar Germany* (Princeton, 1995)

Taylor, A. J. P., *English History, 1914–1945* (Oxford, 1965)

—— *The Course of German History: A Survey of the Development of Germany since 1815* (London, 1945)

—— *The Origins of the Second World War* (London, 1964 [1961])

—— *The Struggle for Mastery in Europe: 1848–1918* (Oxford, 1954)

Taylor, Brandon, *Art and Literature under the Bolsheviks* (London, 1991)

Taylor, Christopher C., *Sacrifice as Terror: The Rwandan Genocide of 1994* (Oxford / New York, 1999)

Thatcher, Ian D., *Trotsky* (London, 2003)

Theilhaber, Felix A., *Der Untergang der deutschen Juden: Eine volkswirtschaftliche Studie* (Munich, 1911)

Theweleit, Klaus, *Male Fantasies*, vol. I: *Women, Floods, Bodies, History* (Minneapolis, 1987)

Thio, Eunice, 'The Syonan Years, 1942–1945', in Ernest C. T. Chew and Edwin Lee (eds.), *A History of Singapore* (Singapore, 1991)

Thomas, Mark, 'Rearmament and Economic Recovery in the Late 1930s', *Economic History Review*, New Series, 36, 4 (November 1983), 552–79

Thompson, Neville, *The Anti-Appeasers: Conservative Opposition to Appeasement in the 1930s* (Oxford, 1971)

Thorne, Christopher, *The Far Eastern War: States and Societies, 1941–1945* (London, 1986)

Timasheff, Nicholas S., *The Great Retreat: The Growth and Decline of Communism in Russia* (New York, 1946)

Timms, Edward, *Karl Kraus, Apocalyptic Satirist: Culture and Catastrophe in Habsburg Vienna* (New Haven, 1986)

Tinker, Hugh, *A New System of Slavery: The Export of Indian Labour Overseas, 1830–1920* (London / New York / Bombay, 1974)

Todd, Emmanuel, *Après L'Empire: Essai sur la décomposition du système américain* (Paris, 2002)

Todorov, Tzvetan, *Facing the Extreme: Moral Life in the Concentration Camps* (London, 1999)

Tokaca, Mirsad, 'Violation of Norms of International Humanitarian Law during the War in Bosnia and Herzegovina', unpublished manuscript, Sarajevo (February 2005)

Tokayer, Marvin and Mary Swartz, *The Fugu Plan: The Untold Story of the Japanese and the Jews during World War II* (New York / London, 1979)

Toland, John, *The Rising Sun: The Decline and Fall of the Japanese Empire, 1936–1945* (London, 2001)

Tolkien, J. R. R., *The Lord of the Rings* (London, 1994 [1954, 1955])

Tooze, Adam J., *The Wages of Destruction: The Making and Breaking of the Nazi Economy* (London, 2006)

—— *Statistics and the German State, 1900–1945: The Making of Modern Economic Knowledge* (New York, 2001)

Toussenel, Alphonse, *Les Juifs, rois de l'époque: Histoire de la féodalité financière* (Paris, 1847)

Towle, Philip, 'Introduction', in *idem*, Margaret Kosuge and Yoichi Kibata (eds.), *Japanese Prisoners of War* (London / New York, 2000), xi–xx

—— 'The Japanese Army and Prisoners of War', in *idem*, Margaret Kosuge and Yoichi Kibata (eds.), *Japanese Prisoners of War* (London / New York, 2000), 1–16

Trachtenberg, Marc, 'A "Wasting Asset": American Strategy and the Shifting Nuclear Balance', *International Security*, 13, 3 (Winter 1988/89), 5–49

Treue, Wilhelm, 'Hitlers Denkschrift zum Vierjahresplan 1936', *Vierteljahreshefte für Zeitgeschichte*, 3 (1955), 184–210

Trevor Roper, H. R. (ed.), *Hitler's Table Talk, 1941–44: His Private Conversations*, transl. Norman Cameron and R. H. Stevens (London, 1973 (2nd edn.) [1953])

Trexler, Richard C., *Sex and Conquest: Gendered Violence, Political Order and the European Conquest of the Americas* (Cambridge, 1995)

Trilling, Lionel, 'The Changing Myth of the Jew', in Diana Trilling (ed.), *Speaking of Literature and Society* (Oxford, 1982), 50–76

Trubowitz, Peter, *Defining the National Interest: Conflict and Change in American Foreign Policy* (Chicago / London, 1998)

Trumpener, Ulrich, *Germany and the Ottoman Empire: 1914–1918* (Princeton, 1968)

Tsouras, Peter, *Disaster at D-Day: The Germans Defeat the Allies, June 1944* (London, 2nd edn. 2004 [1994])

—— 'Operation ORIENT: Joint Axis Strategy', in Kenneth Macksey (ed.), *The Hitler Options: Alternate Decisions of World War II* (London, 1995), 82–101

—— 'Rommel versus Zhukov: Decision in the East, 1944–45', in Peter G. Tsouras (ed.), *Third Reich Victorious: The Alternate History of How the Germans Won the War* (London, 2002), 231–56

Turczynski, Emanuel, 'Die Bukowina', in Isabel Röskau-Rydel (ed.), *Deutsche Geschichte im Osten Europas: Galizien, Bukowina, Molday* (Berlin, 1999), 218–328

Turner, Henry Ashby, *German Big Business and the Rise of Hitler* (Oxford, 1985)

—— *Hitler's Thirty Days to Power: January 1933* (Reading, Mass., 1996)

United Nations Population Division of the Department of Economic and Social Affairs of the United Nations Secretariat, *World Population Prospects: The 2004 Revision and World Urbanization Prospects: The 2003 Revision* (http://esa.un.org/unpp, 14 July 2005)

United Nations War Crimes Commission, *Law-Reports of Trials of War Criminals*, vol. I (London, 1947)

Vago, Bela, *The Shadow of the Swastika: The Rise of Fascism and Anti-Semitism in the Danube Basin, 1936–1939* (London, 1975)

Vatter, Harold G., *The US Economy in World War II* (New York, 1985)

Veen, Harm R. van der, *Jewish Characters in Eighteenth-Century English Fiction and Drama* (Groningen, Batavia, 1935)

Verney, John, *Going to the Wars* (London, 1955)

Vernon, J. R., 'World War II Fiscal Policies and the End of the Great Depression', *Journal of Economic History*, 54, 4 (December 1994), 850–68

Vidal, Gore, *The Decline and Fall of the American Empire* (Berkeley, 1992)

Vishniak, Mark, 'Antisemitism in Tsarist Russia: A Study in Government-Fostered Antisemitism', in Koppel S. Pinson (ed.), *Essays on Antisemitism* (New York, 1946), 121–44.

Vital, David, *A People Apart: The Jews in Europe 1789–1930* (Oxford / New York, 1999)

Volkogonov, Dmitri, *Lenin: Life and Legacy* (London, 1994)

—— *Trotsky: The Eternal Revolutionary* (London, 1996)

Volkov, Solomon (ed.), *Testimony: The Memoirs of Dmitri Shostakovich* (New York, 1979)

Vonnegut, Kurt, *Slaughterhouse-five: or the Children's Crusade: A Duty-Dance with Death* (St Albans, 1992 [1970])

Waldeck, R. G., *Athene Palace, Bucharest: Hitler's 'New Order' comes to Rumania* (London, 1943)

Walker, Ernest, *The Price of Surrender: 1941 – The War in Crete* (London, 1992)

Walker, Martin, *The Cold War and the Making of the Modern World* (London, 1990)

Walker, S., 'Solving the Appeasement Puzzle: Contending Historical Interpretations of British Diplomacy during the 1930s', *British Journal of International Studies*, 6 (April 1980)

Wallenstein, Peter, *'Tell the Court I Love My Wife': Race, Marriage, and Law – An American History* (New York, 2004)

Wan-yao, Chou, 'The Kominka Movement', in Peter Duus, Ramon H. Myers and Mark R. Peattie (eds.), *The Japanese Wartime Empire, 1931–1945* (Princeton, 1996)

Wang, Youqin, 'The Second Wave of Violent Persecution of Teachers: The Revolution of 1968', http://www.chinese-memorial.org/ (n.d.)

—— 'Student Attacks Against Teachers: The Revolution of 1966', http://www.chinese-memorial.org/ (n.d.)

War Office, *Statistics of the Military Effort of the British Empire during the Great War, 1914–20* (London, 1922)

Ward, Michael D. and Kristian Gleditsch, 'Democratizing for Peace', *American Political Science Review*, 92, 1 (1998), 51–61

Wark, Wesley K., 'British Intelligence on the German Air Force and Aircraft Industry, 1933–1939', *Historical Journal*, 25, 3 (1982), 627–48

Warmbrunn, Werner, *The Dutch under German Occupation, 1940–1945* (Stanford / London, 1993)

Warner, Denis and Peggy Warner, *The Tide at Sunrise: A History of the Russo-Japanese War, 1904–1905* (London, 1975)

Warren, Charles, 'Troubles of a Neutral', *Foreign Affairs*, 12, 3 (April 1934), 377–94

Washington, Joseph R. Jr., *Marriage in Black and White* (Boston, 1970)

Wassermann, Jacob, *My Life as German and Jew* (London, 1934)

Waterford, Van, *Prisoners of the Japanese in World War II: Statistical History, Personal Narratives and Memorials Concerning Prisoners of War in Camps and on Hellships, Civilian Internees, Asian Slave Laborers, and Others Captured in the Pacific Theater* (Jefferson, NC, 1994)

Watt, D. C., 'British Intelligence and the Coming of the Second World War in Europe', in Ernest R. May (ed.), *Knowing One's Enemies: Intelligence Assessment before the Two World Wars* (Princeton, 1984), 237–70

Waugh, Evelyn, *Sword of Honour* (London, 1999 [1965])

Weber, Eugen, *The Hollow Years: France in the 1930s* (London, 1995)

—— *Peasants into Frenchmen: The Modernization of Rural France, 1870–1914* (Stanford, 1976)

Weber, Frank, *Eagles on the Crescent: Germany, Austria, and the Diplomacy of the Turkish Alliance, 1914–1918* (Ithaca / London, 1970)

Weber, Marianne, *Max Weber: A Biography* (New York, 1975)

Weber, Thomas, *Łodz Ghetto Album: Photographs by Henryk Ross*, selected by Martin Parr and Timothy Prus (London, 2004)

Wegner, Bernd, 'The Ideology of Self-Destruction: Hitler and the Choreography of Defeat', *German Historical Institute, London, Bulletin*, 26, 2 (November 2004), 18–33

Weihns, W., *Bordell-Juden und Mädchenhandel* (Berlin, 1899)

Weinberg, Gerhard, *A World at Arms: A Global History of World War II* (Cambridge, 1994)

—— 'Reflections on Munich after 60 Years', in Igor Lukes and Erik Goldstein (eds.), *The Munich Crisis, 1938: Prelude to World War II* (London, 1999), 1–13

—— 'The French Role in the Least Unpleasant Solution', in Maya Latynski (ed.), *Reappraising the Munich Pact: Continental Perspectives* (Washington DC, 1992), 21–47

—— 'The German Generals and the Outbreak of War, 1938–1939', in Adrian Preston (ed.), *General Staffs and Diplomacy before the Second World War* (London, 1978), 24–40

Weindling, Paul, *Health, Race and German Politics between National Unification and Nazism, 1870–1945* (Cambridge, 1989)

—— *Epidemics and Genocide in Eastern Europe, 1890–1945* (Oxford, 2000)

Weiner, Amir, *Making Sense of War: The Second World War and the Fate of the Bolshevik Revolution* (Princeton, 2001)

Weingart, Peter, *Doppel-Leben: Ludwig Clauss: Zwischen Rassenforschung und Widerstand* (Frankfurt / New York, 1995)

Weiss, Aharon, 'Jewish-Ukrainian Relations in Western Ukraine during the Holocaust', in Howard Aster and Peter J. Potichnyj (eds.), *Ukrainian-Jewish Relations in Historical Perspective* (Edmonton, 1990), 409–20

Weiss, John, transl. Helmut Dierlamm and Norbert Juraschitz, *Der lange Weg zum Holocaust* (Berlin, 1998)

Weissman, Neil, 'Regular Police in Tsarist Russia, 1900–1914', *Russian Review*, 44, 1 (January 1985), 45–68

Welch, David, *Propaganda and the German Cinema, 1933–1945* (Oxford, 1983)

Wells, H. G., *The War of the Worlds* (London, 2005 [1898])

Wellum, Geoffrey, *First Light* (London, 2004)

Wendt, Bernd-Jürgen, *Economic Appeasement: Handel und Finanz in der britischen Deutschlandpolitik, 1933–1939* (Düsseldorf, 1971)

—— '"Economic Appeasement": A Crisis Strategy', in Wolfgang J. Mommsen and Lothar Kettenacker (eds.), *The Fascist Challenge and the Policy of Appeasement* (London, 1983), 157–72

Werner, Lothar Heinrich, 'Richard Walther Darré und der Hegehofgedanke', unpublished PhD thesis (University of Mainz, 1980)

Wessely, Simon, 'Twentieth-century Theories on Combat Motivation and Demotivation', *Journal of Contemporary History* (forthcoming)

Wheeler-Bennett, John W., *The Nemesis of Power: The German Army in Politics, 1918–1945* (London, 1953)

White, Matthew, *Historical Atlas of the Twentieth Century*, http://users.erols.com/mwhite28/20centry.htm (n.d.)

Whiteside, Andrew G., 'Nationaler Sozialismus in Österreich vor 1918', *Vierteljahrshefte für Zeitgeschichte*, 9 (1961), 333–59

—— *The Socialism of Fools: George Ritter von Schönerer and Austrian Pan-Germanism* (Berkeley, 1975)

Whymant, Robert, *Stalin's Spy: Richard Sorge and the Tokyo Espionage Ring* (London, 1996)

Wiener, Charles, 'A New Site for the Seminar: The Refugees and American Physics in the Thirties', in Donald Fleming and Bernard Bailyn (eds.), *The Intellectual Migration: Europe and America, 1930–1960* (Cambridge, Mass., 1969), 190–322

Williamson, Jeffrey G., 'Land, Labor and Globalization in the Pre-Industrial Third World', *Journal of Economic History*, 62 (2002), 55–85

Williamson, Joel, *New People: Miscegenation and Mulattoes in the United States* (New York, 1980), 190–324

Williamson, Samuel R. Jr., 'The Origins of the War', in Hew Strachan (ed.), *The Oxford Illustrated History of the First World War* (Oxford / New York, 1998), 9–25

Willmott, H. P., *The Barrier and the Javelin: Japanese and Allied Pacific Strategies, February to June 1942* (Annapolis, Md, 1983)

Wilson, Dominic and Roopa Purushothaman, 'Dreaming with the BRICs: The Path to 2050', Goldman Sachs Global Economics Paper, 99 (October 1, 2003)

Winiewicz, Józef Marja, *Aims and Failures of the German New Order* (London, 1943)

Winter, Dennis, *Death's Men: Soldiers of the Great War* (London, 1978)

Wippermann, Wolfgang, 'Christine Lehmann and Mazurka Rose: Two "Gypsies" in the Grip of German Bureaucracy, 1933–60', in Michael Burleigh (ed.), *Confronting the Nazi Past: New Debates on Modern German History* (London, 1996)

Wiskemann, Elizabeth, *Czechs and Germans: A Study of the Struggle in the Historic Provinces of Bohemia and Moravia* (London / Melbourne / Toronto, 1967 [1938])

Wistrich, Robert S., *Socialism and the Jews: The Dilemmas of Assimilation in Germany and Austria-Hungary* (London / Toronto / East Brunswick, NJ 1982)

—— *The Jews of Vienna in the Age of Franz Joseph* (Oxford, 1989)

Wohlstetter, Roberta, *Pearl Harbor: Warning and Decision* (Stanford, 1962)

Wood, Frances, *No Dogs and Not Many Chinese: Treaty Port Life in China, 1843–1943* (London, 1998)

Woodhouse, John, *Gabriele D'Annunzio: Defiant Archangel* (Oxford, 1998)

Woodward, E. L. and Rohan Butler (eds.), *Documents on British Foreign Policy, 1919–1939*, 3rd Series, vol. I (London, 1949)

—— (eds.), with assistance from Margaret Lambert, *Documents on British Foreign Policy, 1919–1939*, 3rd Series, vol. II (London, 1949)

Wright, Jonathan, *Gustav Stresemann: Weimar's Greatest Statesman* (Oxford, 2003)

Wyman, David S., *The Abandonment of the Jews: America and the Holocaust, 1941–1945* (New York, 1984)

Wynot, Edward D. Jnr., ' "A Necessary Cruelty": The Emergence of Official Anti-Semitism in Poland, 1936–39', *American Historical Review*, 76, 4 (October 1971), 1035–58

Yalman, Emin Ahmed, *Turkey in the World War* (New Haven, 1930)

Yasuba, Yasukichi, 'Did Japan Ever Suffer from a Shortage of Natural Resources before World War II?', *Journal of Economic History*, 56, 3 (September 1996), 543–60

Yeghiayan, Vartkes (ed.), *British Foreign Office Dossiers on Turkish War Criminals* (La Verne, 1991)

Ye'or, Bat, *Eurabia: The Euro-Arab Axis* (Madison, NJ, 2005)

Yergin, Daniel, *The Prize: The Epic Quest for Oil, Money and Power* (New York / London, 1991)

—— and Joseph Stanislaw, *The Commanding Heights: The Battle between Government and the Marketplace That is Remaking the Modern World* (New York, 1998)

Young, Louise, *Japan's Total Empire: Manchuria and the Culture of Wartime Imperialism* (Berkeley / Los Angeles / London, 1998)

Young, Robert C., *Colonial Desire: Hybridity in Theory, Culture and Race* (London / New York, 1995)

Zabecki, David T., *World War II in Europe: An Encyclopedia* (New York / London, 1999)

Zahra, Tara, 'Reclaiming Children for the Nation: Germanization, National Ascription, and Democracy in the Bohemian Lands, 1900–1945', *Central European History*, 37, 4 (2004), 501–43

Zayas, Alfred M. de, *Nemesis at Potsdam: The Anglo-Americans and the Expulsion of the Germans: Background, Execution, Consequences* (London, 1979)

Zeman, Z. A. B., *Pursued by a Bear: The Making of Eastern Europe* (London, 1989)

Zenner, Walter P., 'Middleman Minorities and Genocide', in Isidor Wallimann and Michael N. Dobkowski (eds.), *Genocide and the Modern Age* (New York, 1987), 253–81

Zhuravleva, Victoria, 'Anti-Jewish Violence in Russia and American Missionary Activity (1881–1917)', unpublished paper, Stockholm Conference on Pogroms (2005)

Zimmermann, Moshe, *Wilhelm Marr: The Patriarch of Anti-Semitism* (New York / Oxford, 1986)

Zionistische Hilfsfonds in London, *Die Judenpogrome in Russland* (Cologne / Leipzig, 1910)

Zola, Émile, *Les Rougon-Macquart*, vol. V: *Histoire naturelle et sociale d'une famille sous le Second Empire: L'Argent* (Paris, 1967)

Zuber, Terence, 'The Schlieffen Plan Reconsidered', *War in History*, 6, 3 (1999)

Zubok, Vladislav M., 'Stalin and the Nuclear Age', in John Lewis Gaddis, Philip H. Gordon, Ernest R. May and Jonathan Rosenberg (eds.), *Cold War Statesmen Confront the Bomb: Nuclear Diplomacy Since 1945* (Oxford, 1999), 39–62

# Acknowledgements

Although this book is based largely on secondary sources, I was determined to pursue certain issues into the primary sources. In doing so, I and my researchers were fortunate to have assistance from numerous public and private archives. Documents from the Royal Archives at Windsor Castle are quoted with the gracious permission of Her Majesty the Queen. Documents from the Rothschild Archive are quoted with the permission of the Trustees of the Archive. I am also grateful to the staff at the following archives: the Archivio Segreto Vaticano; the Auswärtiges Amt in Berlin; the Beinecke Rare Book and Manuscript Library at Yale University; the Bibliothèque de l'Alliance Israélite Universelle in Paris; the Imperial War Museum, London; the Landeshauptarchiv, Koblenz; the Library of Congress, Washington DC; the Memorial Research Centre, Moscow; the National Archives, Washington DC; the National Archives, Kew; the National Archives at College Park, Maryland; the National Security Archive at the George Washington University, Washington DC; the Research and Documentation Centre, Sarajevo; the Rothschild Archive, London; the Russian State Archives, Moscow; the Royal Archives, Windsor Castle, and the United States Holocaust Museum Library and Archives, Washington DC.

This book has been at least ten years in the making and many hands have contributed to the work. At least a dozen students have helped with the research during vacations, namely Sam Choe, Lizzy Emerson, Tom Fleuriot, Bernhard Fulda, Ian Klaus, Naomi Ling, Charles Smith, Andrew Vereker, Kathryn Ward and Alex Watson. Ameet Gill started off on this part-time basis and then went on to become a full-time researcher at Blakeway Productions, while Jason Rockett became my research assistant when I moved to Harvard. They have done their jobs superbly. But to all my researchers I am indebted; they not only helped to dig, but also to build.

Not all the relevant documents and texts were in languages I could read. I would therefore like to thank the following translators for their work: Brian Patrick Quinn (Italian); Himmet Taskomur (Turkish); Kyoko Sato (Japanese); Jaeyoon Song (Korean); Juan Piantino and Laura Ferreira Provenzano (Spanish).

Many scholars generously responded to my or my researchers' requests for assistance. In particular, I would like to thank Anatoly Belik, senior researcher at the Central Naval Museum, St Petersburg; Michael Burleigh, who generously read draft scripts and offered advice from the very earliest stages of the project; Jerry Coyne of the University of Chicago; Bruce A. Elleman at the Naval War College, Newport, RI; Henry Hardy of Wolfson College, Oxford; Jean-Claude Kuperminc of the Bibliothèque de l'Alliance Israélite Universelle, Paris; Sergio Della Pergola of the Hebrew University of Jerusalem; Patricia Polansky of the University of Hawaii; David Raichlen in the Harvard Department of Anthropology; Bradley Schaffner of the Slavic Division of the Widener Library at Harvard; and Mirsad Tokača and Lara J. Nettelfield at the Research and Documentation Centre, Sarajevo.

This is, I am happy to say, a Penguin book on both sides of the Atlantic. Teams of talented people in both London and New York have worked under extremely pressing deadlines to turn my raw manuscript into a finished book. In London first mention must go to Simon Winder, my editor. He and his opposite number in New York, Scott Moyers, strove with might and main to improve the text; I could not have wished for better editorial advice. Michael Page did a superb job as copy-editor. Thanks are also due (in London) to Samantha Borland, Sarah Christie, Richard Duguid, Rosie Glaisher, Helen Fraser and Stefan McGrath. In New York Ann Godoff played an invaluable role in honing the book's shape and direction.

Like my last two books, *The War of the World* was written concurrently with the making of a television series. One could not have existed independently of the other. It would be impossible here to thank all those responsible for the six-part series made by Blakeway Productions for Channel 4 – that is what the credits at the end of each film are for – but it would be wrong not to acknowledge those members of the television team who in one way or another contributed to the book as well as the series: Janice Hadlow, who was present at the creation, and her successor at Channel 4, Hamish Mykura; Denys Blakeway, the executive producer; Melanie Fall, the series producer; Adrian Pennink and Simon Chu, the directors; Dewald Aukema, the director of photography; Joanna Potts, the assistant producer; and Rosalind Bentley, the archive researcher. I would also like to express my gratitude to Guy Crossman, Joby Gee, Susie Gordon and, last but not least, Kate Macky. Among the many people who helped us film the series, a number of 'fixers' went out of their way to help me with my research for the book. My thanks go to Faris Dobracha, Carlos Duarte, Nikoleta Milasevic, Maria Razumovskaya and Kulikar Sotho, as well as to Marina Erastova, Agnieszka Kik, Tatsiana Melnichuk, Funda Odemis, Levent Oztekin, Liudmila Shastak, Christian Storms and George Zhou.

I am extremely fortunate to have in Andrew Wylie the best literary agent in the world and in Sue Ayton his counterpart in the realm of British television. My thanks also go to Katherine Marino, Amelia Lester and all the other staff in the London and New York offices of the Wylie Agency.

A number of historians generously read chapters in draft. I would like to thank Robert Blobaum, John Coatsworth, David Dilks, Orlando Figes, Akira Iriye, Dominic Lieven, Charles Maier, Erez Manela, Ernest May, Mark Mazower, Greg Mitrovich, Emer O'Dwyer, Steven Pinker and Jacques Rupnik. Needless to say, all errors of fact and interpretation that remain are my fault alone.

Because the book has been the work of a wandering scholar, I have more than the usual number of debts of gratitude to academic institutions. Its origins lay in Jesus College, Oxford, and I must therefore thank my former colleagues there, especially the then Principal, Sir Peter North, and the senior history tutor, Felicity Heal, as well as those present and former Fellows – notably David Acheson, Colin Clarke, John Gray, Nicholas Jacobs and David Womersley – who helped me clarify my thoughts on everything from ethnicity to empire. The Estates Bursar, Peter Mirfield, and Home Bursar, Peter Beer, know the ways in which the College helped me financially as well as intellectually and I am grateful to them too. Vital secretarial support came from Vivien Bowyer and her successor Sonia Thuery. A special debt of gratitude is also due to the Master and Fellows of Oriel College who, thanks to Jeremy Catto, generously provided me with shelter from the Oxford elements after I resigned my tutorship at Jesus.

At New York University I was fortunate to spend two very productive years sharing ideas with (among others) David Backus, Adam Brandenburger, Bill Easterly, Tony

Judt, Tom Sargent, Bill Silber, George Smith, Richard Sylla, Bernard Yeung and Larry White. I also remain deeply in the debt of John and Diana Herzog, as well as John Sexton and William Berkeley, who persuaded me to try my hand at teaching history to business-school students.

Each year my one-month retreat to the Hoover Institution at Stanford gives me a chance to do nothing but read, think and write. Without it I should never have got the manuscript finished. I therefore thank John Raisian, the Director, and his excellent staff, particularly Jeff Bliss, William Bonnett, Noel Kolak, Celeste Szeto, Deborah Ventura and Dan Wilhelmi. Hoover Fellows who have wittingly or unwittingly helped me include Martin Anderson, Robert Barro, Robert Conquest, Larry Diamond, Gerald Dorfman, Timothy Garton Ash, Stephen Haber, Kenneth Jowitt, Norman Naimark, Alvin Rabushka, Peter Robinson, Richard Sousa and Barry Weingast.

It has been at Harvard, however, that the book has finally been born and it is to Harvard that I owe the greatest debt. I am especially grateful to Larry Summers, Bill Kirby and Laura Fisher who took the lead in persuading me to make the move to Cambridge. The Harvard History Department is a wonderful scholarly community to be a part of; my thanks to all its members for their welcome and support, particularly past Chair David Blackbourn and present Chair Andrew Gordon. New colleagues who have contributed to the completion of this book with suggestions and advice are too numerous to list. The Department is very well served by its administrative staff; I am grateful in particular to Janet Hatch, as well as to Cory Paulsen and Wes Chin, all of whom have been forgiving of my many sins of bureaucratic omission and commission. The Center for European Studies is proving to be an ideal home; I cannot praise too highly Peter Hall, its Director, and his excellent staff, especially Executive Director Patricia Craig, as well as Filomena Cabral, George Cumming, Anna Popiel, Sandy Seletsky and Sarah Shoemaker. On the other side of the River Charles I have found another hugely stimulating milieu at Harvard Business School. Former Dean Kim Clark and Acting Dean Jay Light were bold enough to give the idea of a joint appointment a chance, for which I thank them. I am grateful to all the members of the 'Business and Government in the International Economy' unit for initiating me into the case method, in particular Rawi Abdelal, Regina Abrami, Laura Alfaro, Jeff Fear, Lakshmi Iyer, Noel Maurer, David Moss, Aldo Musacchio, Forest Reinhardt, Debora Spar, Gunnar Trumbull, Richard Vietor and Louis Wells. Finally, I thank all my students in Section H, who went up the learning curve with me – at times ahead of me – and, of course, the Tisch family for their generosity in endowing my chair.

What makes Harvard addictive (I realize as I write this) is that the stimulus comes from all sides. Quite apart from the institutions to which I am formally affiliated, there are numerous other settings in which I have been able to refine and improve the arguments advanced here: Graham Allison's Belfer Center for Science and International Affairs; Martin Feldstein's Seminar in Economics and Security; Harvey Mansfield's Seminar in Politics; Stephen Rosen's Seminar in International Security at the Olin Institute for Strategic Studies; Jorge Domínguez's Weatherhead Center for International Affairs; Jeffrey Williamson's Workshop in Economic History – not forgetting the dining hall at Lowell House and, last but by no means least, Marty Peretz's incomparable Cambridge salon.

Yet the transatlantic existence has its penalties, besides jetlag. To my wife Susan and our children, Felix, Freya and Lachlan, this book has been a disagreeable rival, dragging me away to distant shores, or merely confining me in my study during too many weekends and holidays. I beg their forgiveness. In dedicating *The War of the World* to them, I hope I do a little to preserve *The Peace of the Home*.

Cambridge, Massachusetts, February 2006

# Index

and pogroms, 157
purges, 210
as Red Tsar, 158–9
returns to Russia (1917), 143, 144
and royal family, 151
rule of terror, 150–52
in Siberia, 48–9
and Stalin, 157, 199, 219
succession, 199
Leningrad, *see* St Petersburg
Lenkoran, peasant arrests, 215
Leopold, King of the Belgians, 94–5
Levashovo Forest, Russia, 210
Levi, Primo, 576–7
Levi, Trudi, 172
Lewis, Bernard, 642–3
Lewontin, Richard, xliii
Liaodong peninsula, 50
    Japanese annexation (1870s), 52
    Japanese control (1905), 55
    Russian occupation (1898), 52
Libya, Italian occupation, 176
Lichtenstein, 75
Liddell Hart, Captain Basil, 386–7, 389
*Life* magazine, 546
Lij Yasu, Emperor of Abyssinia, 115
Lincoln, President Abraham, 22
Lindbergh, Charles, 526, 545
Lindemann, Frederick, 561
Linnaeus, Carolus, li–lii
Lithuania
    anti-Jewish violence (1941), 453
    dictatorship (1926), 230
    and German invasion of Russia, 441
    Germany threatens (1939), 378
    independence (1917), 144, 154
    Jews, 58, 422
    Soviet occupation (1940), 404, 422, 430
    territorial gains (1919), 162
    war with Poland (1918–21), 167
Little, J. C., 329n
Litvinov, Maxim, 363
Llanbradach colliery explosion (1901), 9
Lloyd George, David, 116, 160n, 163, 181
Locarno, Treaty (1925), 237, 238, 322, 350
Łódź
    ghetto, 400, 402, 409
    Jews, poverty, 271–2
    poverty, 62
Loewenstein, Rudolph, 31

London
    Blitz, 559, 562
    deaths (1901), 9
    Declaration (1908), 114
    distribution networks, 15
    and First World War, 83, 87
    life (1901), 4–5
    Naval Agreement (1930), 299
    and recession (1937), 370, 371
    social conditions (1901), 9–10
    Stock Exchange
    terrorist attack (2005), 643
    Zeppelin raids, 127
Long, Edward, liii
Longan, John, 615
Lon Nol, 623
Lorraine, First World War, 126
Lorre, Peter, 255
Lothian, Philip Kerr, 11th Marquess, 339, 340
Lotnik, Wladimir, 456
Louvignies, captured (1918), 132–4
Lovat, Lord, 523
Low, David, 309, 342
Łowicz, ghetto, 400
Lublin, German communities, 37
Ludendorff, Erich von, 131–2, 241
Luftwaffe
    enlargement, 324
    London Blitz, 562
    pilots, 393
    as threat, 316, 323–4, 364, 559
Lugard, Frederick, 18
Lukić, Milan, 629, 634
Lüshun, *see* Port Arthur
*Lusitania,* sinking, 114, 127
Lussu, Emilio, 118, 121
Lwów
    anti-Jewish violence, 169, 270, 452
    prison, 419
Lyttleton, Adrian, 197n
Lytton, Lord, 302

*M* (film) 235, 255
McAdoo, William, 89
MacArthur, General Douglas, 484, 550, 594
Macaulay, Lord, 413
Macedonia, ethnic population, 76–7
McKinley, President William, assassination, 5–6, 40, 73